HANDBOOKS IN OPERATIONS RESEARCH
AND MANAGEMENT SCIENCE
VOLUME 5

Handbooks in Operations Research and Management Science

Editors

G.L. Nemhauser
Georgia Institute of Technology

A.H.G. Rinnooy Kan
Erasmus University Rotterdam

Volume 5

NORTH-HOLLAND
AMSTERDAM · LONDON · NEW YORK · TOKYO

Marketing

Edited by

J. Eliashberg
University of Pennsylvania

G.L. Lilien
Pennsylvania State University

1993

NORTH-HOLLAND
AMSTERDAM · LONDON · NEW YORK · TOKYO

Elsevier
Radarweg 29, PO Box 211, 1000 AE Amsterdam, The Netherlands
The Boulevard, Langford Lane, Kidlington, Oxford OX5 1GB, UK

Library of Congress Cataloging-in-Publication Data

Marketing / edited by J. Eliashberg, G.L. Lilien.
p. cm.—(Handbooks in operations research and management science ; v. 5)
Includes bibliographical references and index.
ISBN 0-444-88957-4
1. Marketing—Mathematical models. 2. Marketing—Management—Mathematical models.
3. Marketing research—Mathematical models.
I. Eliashberg, Jehoshua. II. Lilien, Gary L., 1946 –.
III. Series.
HF5415.122.M38 1993
658.8—dc20 93-10556
CIP

Transferred to digital printing 2007

For information on all Elsevier publications
visit our website at books.elsevier.com

ISBN: 9780444889577

Printed and bound by CPI Antony Rowe, Eastbourne

For our ladies:
Tova and Keren Eliashberg
and
Dorothy and Amy Lilien

Preface

The battle for markets is intensifying in these days of increasing competition. Where it was once sufficient to produce a superior product and price it attractively, developing a 'competitive advantage', finding a 'market niche', and harvesting the rewards for those advantages are increasingly problematic for marketing management.

In much the same way that the OR/MS approach developed and was brought to bear on the operational problems that demanded improved solutions during and after World War II, the past several decades of marketing warfare have spawned an exciting crop of OR/MS approaches to marketing problems.

In this book we have brought together an outstanding set of marketing scholars, each of whom has provided a state-of-the-art review of his or her area of expertise. The book is intended for the OR/MS audience, that is, a mathematically literate group, but without significant knowledge of the domain of marketing.

The first chapter of the book provides a more comprehensive overview of the field and the motivation for using the OR/MS approach to marketing problems. There are four other parts to the book, organized as follows:

Part II, Models of Market Phenomena, deals with three key building blocks of marketing models: models of individual consumer behavior, models of the behavior of groups (as in family decision-making, negotiations and organizational buying) and models of competition (interactions between competitors in a marketplace). An understanding of the phenomena introduced in this part provides an essential foundation for many marketing decisions.

Part III, Tools and Methods for Market Analysis, supplements the standard OR/MS toolkit with key pieces of technology and methodology that have been developed to address key marketing problems. The chapters in this section cover methods to understand and analyze the structure of markets, market-share models, models to forecast the ultimate sales of new products (packaged goods, primarily) prior to launch, diffusion models (focusing on the dynamics and control of new-product sales) and econometric/time-series market response models.

Part IV, Elements of the Marketing Mix, addresses the individual controls that the marketer has, and deals with them one element at a time. Chapters in this section cover product design, pricing, sales promotion, salesforce compensation and salesforce management.

Part V, Interaction, Strategy and Synergy, links earlier developments. The chapters in this section deal with marketing-mix models, systems to support marketing decisions (reviewing expert systems in the same vein as Marketing

Decision Support Systems), models of marketing strategy and, finally, models of joint marketing and production decision-making.

Each of the chapters was submitted to at least two referees. Many of the authors here provided referee reports for other chapters; the referees not among the list of authors include:

Gregory S. Carpenter, Northwestern University
Kalyan Chatterjee, Penn State University
David P. Christy, Penn State University
Morris A. Cohen, University of Pennsylvania
Timothy Devinney, Vanderbilt University
Stéphane Gauvin, Université Laval, Québec
Donna L. Hoffman, University of Texas at Dallas
Dipak Jain, Northwestern University
Shlomo Kalish, Tel Aviv University
Uday S. Karmarkar, University of Rochester
Rajiv Lal, Stanford University
John D.C. Little, Massachusetts Institute of Technology
Leonard M. Lodish, University of Pennsylvania
John M. McCann, Duke University
Robert J. Meyer, University Of Pennsylvania
Chakravarthi Narasimhan, Washington University at St. Louis
Jagmohan S. Raju, University of Pennsylvania
David C. Schmittlein, University of Pennsylvania
Subrata K. Sen, Yale School of Management
Alan D. Shocker, University of Minnesota
Joe Urbany, University of South Carolina
Piet Vanden Abeele, Catholic University of Leuven, Belgium
Wilfried R. Vanhonacker, INSEAD, France
Berend Wierenga, Erasmus University, Rotterdam

We join with the authors in offering our thanks to all the referees; the material here is both better and richer following their comments and recommendations.

There are a number of topics not covered here. Some did not satisfy the referees. Others were promised, and, sadly, did not appear in written form in time for us to go to press. What is here, while not exhaustive, does cover the majority of major OR/MS work in marketing.

We would like to thank the authors for their contributions and for humoring us when we told each of them that *their* manuscript of the 'one missing and holding up production'. We offer special thanks to Mary Wyckoff who, in addition to helping assemble and coordinate the production of this book, acted as the 'bad cop' (to our 'good cop') when trying to extract material from our more tardy contributors. Without her efforts we would still be waiting for that last manuscript that was 'in typing'.

Jehoshua Eliashberg
Gary L. Lilien

Contents

Preface vii

PART I: INTRODUCTION

CHAPTER 1
Mathematical Marketing Models: Some Historical Perspectives and Future Projections
Jehoshua Eliashberg and Gary L. Lilien 3

1. Reflections on the past 4
2. The 1970s: Early growth period 8
3. The 1980s, to the present 9
4. Some marketing models comparisons 10
5. OR/MS in marketing today 15
6. Marketing models in the future 17
7. Organization and content of the Handbook 20

References 22

PART II: MODELS OF MARKET PHENOMENA

CHAPTER 2
Explanatory and Predictive Models of Consumer Behavior
John H. Roberts and Gary L. Lilien 27

1. An organizing framework for consumer behavior models 27
2. A taxonomy of consumer behavior models 29
3. Need arousal 32
4. Information search 37
5. Evaluation 43
6. Purchase 55
7. Post-purchase attitudes and behavior 61
8. Integration: Combining models to solve management problems 65
9. Future directions for consumer behavior models 72
10. Conclusions 76

References 76

CHAPTER 3
Mathematical Models of Group Choice and Negotiations
Kim P. Corfman and Sunil Gupta 83
1. Introduction 83
2. Focus and definitions 84
3. Models of group choice 85
4. Dimensions of choice situations 117
5. Applications 129
6. Conclusions 136
References 136

CHAPTER 4
Competitive Marketing Strategies: Game-Theoretic Models
K. Sridhar Moorthy 143
1. Introduction 143
2. Preliminaries 144
3. Price competition 148
4. Product competition 162
5. Advertising competition 176
6. Competition in distribution channels 182
7. Conclusion 185
References 187

PART III: TOOLS AND METHODS FOR MARKET ANALYSIS

CHAPTER 5
Non-Spatial Tree Models for the Assessment of Competitive Market Structure: An Integrated Review of the Marketing and Psychometric Literature
Wayne S. DeSarbo, Ajay K. Manrai and Lalita A. Manrai 193
1. Introduction 193
2. Non-spatial tree models for the assessment of competitive market structure 197
3. Discussion, related literature, and directions for future research 248
References 252

CHAPTER 6
Market-Share Models
Lee G. Cooper 259
1. Introduction 259
2. Market share and marketing effort 261

3. Market shares and choice probabilities 273
4. Asymmetries in markets and competition 282
5. A numerical illustration from single-source data 299
6. Issues facing attraction models 309
References 311

CHAPTER 7
Pretest Market Forecasting
Glen L. Urban 315
1. Criteria for pretest market analysis 315
2. Alternative approaches – packaged goods 317
3. Accuracy of pretest market forecasting 331
4. Durable consumer products 336
5. Industrial and services products 345
6. Summary 346
References 347

CHAPTER 8
New-Product Diffusion Models
Vijay Mahajan, Eitan Muller and Frank M. Bass 349
1. Introduction 349
2. The basic first-purchase diffusion models 350
3. Refinements and extensions of the Bass diffusion model 360
4. Uses of diffusion models 369
5. Conclusions and discussion 385
Appendix 391
References 402

CHAPTER 9
Econometric and Time-Series Market Response Models
Dominique M. Hanssens and Leonard J. Parsons 409
1. Introduction 409
2. Market mechanisms 411
3. Static models 413
4. Dynamic models 422
5. Empirical findings and marketing generalizations 437
6. Research issues 444
7. Discussion 453
References 455

PART IV: ELEMENTS OF THE MARKETING MIX

CHAPTER 10
Conjoint Analysis with Product-Positioning Applications
Paul E. Green and Abba M. Krieger 467
1. Introduction 467
2. Compositional versus decompositional preference models 469
3. Basic ideas of conjoint analysis 472
4. Trends in conjoint analysis 480
5. Conjoint simulators and sensitivity analysis 482
6. Applications of conjoint analysis 486
7. From simulator to product optimizer 492
8. The SIMOPT model 494
9. SIMOPT's features 497
10. An empirical application 498
11. Conclusions 507
Appendix 508
References 511

CHAPTER 11
Pricing Models in Marketing
Vithala R. Rao 517
1. Introduction 517
2. A general framework for pricing 522
3. Static models for pricing single products 523
4. Dynamic pricing models for single products 527
5. Multiple-product pricing models 534
6. Behavioral pricing models 538
7. Measurement of price effects 543
8. Directions for future research 545
References 549

CHAPTER 12
Sales Promotion Models
Robert C. Blattberg and Scott A. Neslin 553
1. Introduction 553
2. Descriptive models 556
3. Prescriptive models 587
4. Summary and future research 596
References 606

CHAPTER 13
Salesforce Compensation: A Review of MS/OR Advances
Anne T. Coughlan 611
1. Introduction 611
2. Model structure/techniques: Microeconomic approach 613
3. Model structure/techniques: Agency-theoretic approach 623
4. Empirical evidence on salesforce-compensation models 638
5. Decision support systems for salesforce compensation 641
6. Conclusions and future research directions 648
References 649

CHAPTER 14
Salesforce Operations
Mark B. Vandenbosch and Charles B. Weinberg 653
1. Introduction 653
2. Decision areas in sales management 654
3. Literature review 656
4. Research opportunities 687
5. Summary 691
References 692

PART V: INTERACTION, STRATEGY AND SYNERGY

CHAPTER 15
Marketing-Mix Models
Hubert Gatignon 697
1. Introduction 697
2. The impact of marketing-mix variables and their interactions 698
3. Normative marketing-mix models 712
4. Research needs 726
5. Conclusion 728
References 728

CHAPTER 16
Marketing Decision Models:
From Linear Programs to Knowledge-based Systems
Arvind Rangaswamy 733
1. Introduction 733
2. Key concepts of marketing decision models 734
3. Artificial intelligence 749
4. AI and decision modeling 753
5. Conclusions 765
References 768

CHAPTER 17
Marketing Strategy Models
Yoram (Jerry) Wind and Gary L. Lilien 773
1. Introduction 773
2. Strategy models: Progress to date 776
3. Traditional strategy model examples 789
4. Non-traditional models for marketing and business strategy 804
5. Examples of effective use of non-traditional marketing strategy models 817
6. Strategy in the 21st century and implications for marketing strategy models 820
7. Conclusions 822
References 824

CHAPTER 18
Marketing–Production Joint Decision-Making
Jehoshua Eliashberg and Richard Steinberg 827
1. Introduction 827
2. Decentralized vs. coordinated marketing–production decision-making 833
3. Smoothing unstable demand: Convex-cost models 851
4. Choosing production-run quantities and order quantities: Concave-cost models 862
5. Conclusions 873
References 877

Subject Index 881

Contents of Previous Volumes 893

Part I
Introduction

J. Eliashberg and G.L. Lilien, Eds., *Handbooks in OR & MS, Vol. 5*

Chapter 1

Mathematical Marketing Models: Some Historical Perspectives and Future Projections

Jehoshua Eliashberg

Marketing Department, The Wharton School, University of Pennsylvania, Philadelphia, PA 19104, USA

Gary L. Lilien

Pennsylvania State University, 113 BAB II, University Park, PA 16802, USA

There is an old cartoon, first published in the *New Yorker* magazine, showing two executives at a cocktail party. One says to the other, 'So you're in marketing. That's funny, in my family, my wife does the marketing'.

The image of the field of marketing has, to this day, retained some of the vague, intuitive flavor that the above cartoon suggests. When the term 'marketing' comes to mind, many people think of 'pet rocks', cans of 'New York City air', and the cyclical movement of hemlines in women's fashions; the analysis of the demand for such items seems well removed from the reliance on mathematical models that characterizes much of the work in operations research and management science (OR/MS).

Indeed, many company executives despair of putting marketing on a more scientific basis. Many see marketing processes as lacking the neat quantitative properties found in production and finance. In marketing, human factors play a large role, marketing expenditures affect demand and cost simultaneously and information to support truly systematic decisions is rarely available. Further, the effects of most marketing actions are typically delayed, nonlinear, stochastic and difficult to measure.

Yet, the OR/MS developments in marketing have been profound and substantial: the chapters of this book describe a significant literature, sketching a broad range of applications of OR/MS in marketing. A major force behind these developments is the battle for markets that has been dictating organizational success and failure in recent years. Sales in many markets are flat or declining while competitors have been growing in number and becoming more desperate. Products are exhibiting shorter life-cycles, and leaner staff organizations have become buried in oceans of new types of data (from bar-code scanners and other sources), demanding rapid comprehension and sound decision making in dynamic and risky environments.

This book represents the state of the art in the OR/MS approach applied to marketing problems. Each of the chapters develops the concepts and describes key mathematical models in specific areas of marketing, leading the reader up to the current state of affairs and projecting future developments. Before proceeding, however, it is appropriate to reflect a bit on the history of this field.

1. Reflections on the past

The OR/MS field emerged during and after World War II, focusing primarily on problems in production, operations, and logistics. Early successes in those areas encouraged analysts to engage in a broader set of problems. The OR/MS literature in marketing began to emerge in a significant way in the 1960s.

At that time, several authors provided classification schemes that were useful in trying to organize the growing literature on marketing models. Several of those schemes were:

–iconic vs analog vs symbolic models [King, 1967],
–descriptive vs predictive vs normative models [Montgomery & Urban, 1969],
–macromarketing vs micromarketing models [Kotler, 1971].

For the purpose of this paper, we will use a classification scheme that focuses purely on the purpose of the model.

There are essentially three purposes for modeling in marketing: measurement, decision-making, and theory-building. We will call the corresponding models measurement models, decision-making models, and stylized theoretical models, respectively (although it may be equally helpful to interpret these 'categories' as classification dimensions for interpreting the multiple purposes of models).

1.1. Measurement models

The purpose of measurement models is to measure the 'demand' for a product as a function of various independent variables. The word 'demand' here should be interpreted broadly. It is not necessarily units demanded but could be some other related variable. For example, in conjoint measurement models, the most crucial variable in determining demand is the individual's preference for a choice alternative. In models of diffusion of new durables, the demand variable is captured mainly through 'sales to first adopters'. In some choice models, the dependent variable is whether or not an individual made a purchase of a given brand on a given purchase occasion.

The independent variables in measurement models are usually marketing mix variables – again interpreted broadly to mean any variables the firm controls – but they could include variables to account for seasonality in employment, GNP, consumer characteristics, and competitors' actions. In conjoint measurement models, for example, the independent variables are usually the attributes of the choice alternatives. Diffusion models typically have 'cumulative sales since introduction' as one of the independent variables. Other choice models have several independent variables including whether or not the brand was on deal at a given purchase occasion, regular price of the brand, deal price (if any), brand loyalty of the individual, etc. These examples suggest that measurement models can deal with individual (disaggregate) demand or aggregate (market-level) demand.

Once the demand functions have been specified, they are then 'calibrated' to measure the parameters of the function. Calibration reveals the role of various independent variables in determining demand for this product: which variables are more important and which are less. Also, once the demand function has been calibrated, it can be used to predict demand as well as other relevant performance measures in a given situation. A variety of methods have been used to calibrate demand functions: judgment, econometric techniques, experimentation, simulation, etc.

Note that advances in measurement models can be due to better data (scanner data, for example) or better calibration methods and procedures (maximum likelihood methods for generalized logit models, for example).

1.2. Decision-making models

Models are designed to help marketing managers make better decisions. They incorporate measurement models as building blocks, but go beyond measurement models in recommending marketing-mix decision for the manager. The methods used to drive the optimal policies vary across applications. Typical techniques are dynamic programming, optimal control and calculus of variations techniques, static nonlinear optimization techniques, as well as linear and integer programming, and simulation.

Figure 1.1 shows a general framework for a marketing decision-making system. Note the dashed arrow leading from 'marketer actions' to 'competitive reactions'. This is to recognize that, unlike other environmental variables, competitors' actions could be affected by 'our actions' (and even by announcements concerning our *intended* actions).

1.3. Stylized theoretical models

The purpose of stylized theoretical models is to explain and provide insights into marketing phenomena; a stylized theoretical model typically begins with a set of assumptions that describes a particular marketing environment. Some of these assumptions are purely mathematical, at best intuitively logical, designed to make the analysis tractable. Others are substantive assumptions with real empirical grounding. They can describe such things as who the actors are, how many of them there are, what they care about, the external conditions under which they make decisions, how they have behaved in the past, etc. It is these latter assumptions that will participate in the explanation being offered. Note that the concept of a model in a stylized theoretical fashion is different from the concept of a decision-making model. A decision-making model is defined as a 'mathematical description of how something works' and it often takes the point of view of one particularly

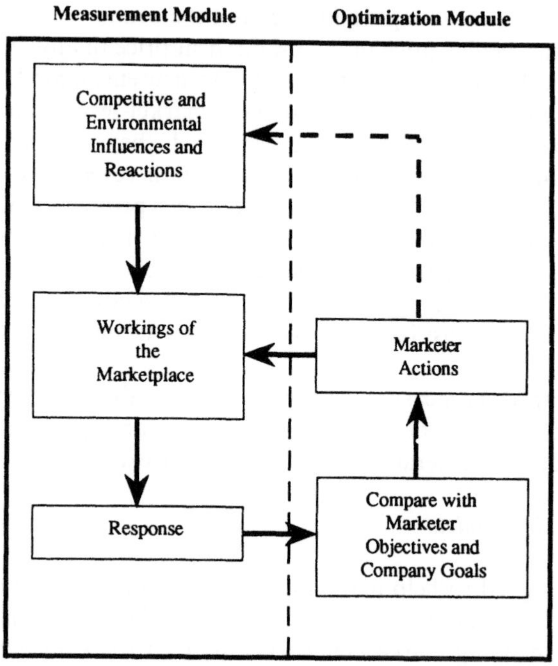

Fig. 1.1. A decision-making system, showing measurement and optimization modules.

interested party. A stylized theoretical model is simply a setting – a subset of the real world – in which 'the action takes place'. It often takes the viewpoint of an outside (objective) third party.

Once a theoretical model has been built, the model builder analyzes its *logical* implications for the phenomenon being explored. Then another model, substantively different from the first, is built – very likely by another model-builder – and its implications are analyzed. The process may continue with a third and a fourth model, if necessary, until all the ramifications of the explanation being proposed have been examined. By comparing the implications of one model with those of another, and by tracing the differences to the different assumptions in the various models, we can develop a theory about the phenomena in question (see Figure 1.2). This is as if a logical experiment were being run, with the various models as the 'treatments'. The key difference from empirical experiments is that, whereas in empirical experiments the subject produces the effects, here the researcher produces the effects by logical argument and (often) mathematical analysis.

The main purpose of theoretical modeling is pedagogy – teaching us how the real world operates – and that purpose is well served by internally valid theoretical experiments. But what about the practical use of such work for marketing managers? Such models are of direct value to managers when they uncover robust results that are *independent* of the unobservable features of the decision-making environment. Under these circumstances the models have two uses:

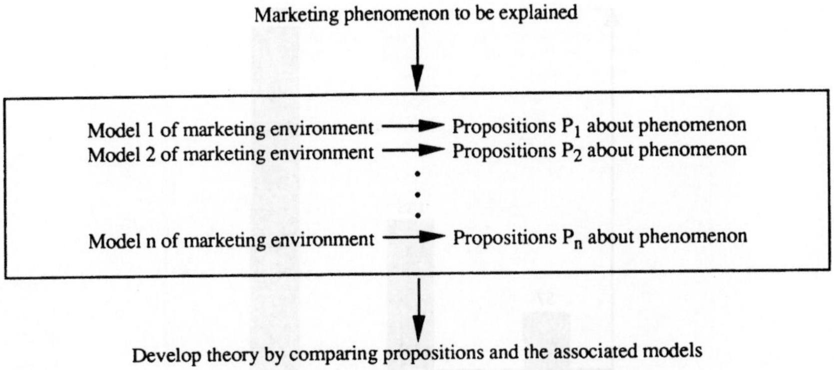

Fig. 1.2. Overview of the theoretical modeling process.

(1) as direct *qualitative* guidance for policy (in our situation, we need low (high) proportions of salesforce compensation in commissions) and
(2) as the basis for specifying operational models and associated decision-making systems that can adapt the theory to a particular environment and generate *quantitative* prescriptions [Moorthy, 1993].

1.4. Methods and applications

Table 1.1 synthesizes a range of OR/MS techniques and the typical problems that they were applied to in the 1960s. Those problems [Kotler, 1971] include product decisions, pricing decisions, distribution system decisions, salesforce management decisions, advertising and mass communication decisions, and promotion decisions. The OR/MS tools that seemed most prevalent in the 1960s and earlier include mathematical programming, computer simulations, stochastic models of consumer choice behavior, response function analysis, and various forms of dynamic modeling (difference and differential equations, usually of first order). Some uses of game theory were reported for competitive situations, but most

Table 1.1
A sample of OR/MS methodology applied to marketing problems prior to 1970

Technique	Typical area(s) of application
• Poisson processes	• Effect of promotional effort on sales
• Differential equations	• Effect of advertising on sales
• Stochastic processes	• Consumer's brand choice
• Decision theory/analysis	• Evaluation of marketing research expenditures
• Mathematical programming	• Advertising decision-making • Advertising media selection • Warehouse location
• Computer simulation	• Microsimulation of market processes and behavior
• Game theory	• Competitive advertising expenditures

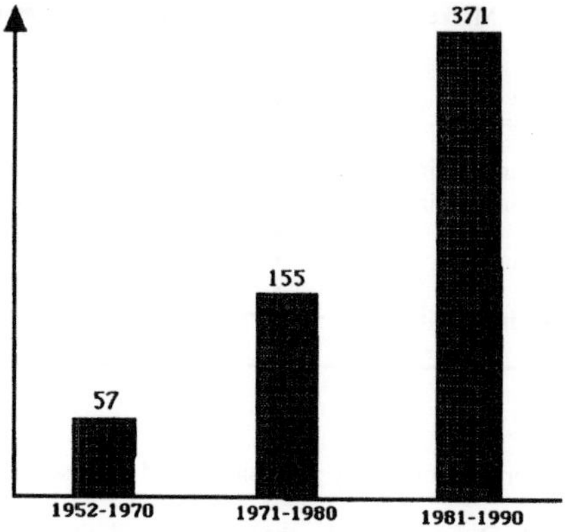

Fig. 1.3. Number of articles on marketing topics published in *Management Science, Operations Research, Interfaces* and *Marketing Science* for 1952–1990 as reported in the *OR/MS Index*, Volumes 1, 2 and 3.

studies involving competition used decision analysis, risk analysis or marketing simulation games.

Note that most of the models being published in the 1960s era were of the 'measurement model' and 'decision-making model' variety introduced earlier, and that the volume of research was more modest than in recent years (Figure 1.3).

Our impression is that the OR/MS work in marketing in the 1960s and before was largely produced by individuals trained as engineers, scientists or applied mathematicians, applying the OR/MS approach to the field of marketing rather than by individuals from business schools trained in marketing, the more dominant trend in recent years.

2. The 1970s: Early growth period

As Figure 1.3 indicates, nearly three times the number of marketing articles appeared in the 1970s as appeared in the period from 1952 through 1969.

In addition to the increase in numbers of articles, reviews by Schultz & Zoltners [1981] and Lilien & Kotler [1983] reveal that a number of new areas had begun to attract attention in the literature. These included descriptive models of marketing decisions, the impact and interaction of marketing models and organizational design, subjective decision models, strategic planning models, models for public and non-profit oganizations, organizational buying models, and the emergence of the concept of the Marketing Decision Support System (MDSS). In addition, while the number of published articles rose dramatically, the impact on organizational performance did not appear to be equally significant, and issues of implementation began to be stressed. Much of the literature in the 1970s pointed to the need for expanding the domain of application in the next decade and beyond. The limitations sections of some of the literature in the 1970s pointed out that many important phenomena that were being overlooked (such as competition, dynamics and interactions amongst marketing decision variables) were both important and inherently more complex to model. Hence, the level of model-complexity and the insightfulness of the analyses in marketing seemed destined to escalate in the 1980s and beyond.

The 1970s saw growth in the areas of measurement models and decision-making models built on the foundation of earlier work. However, stylized theoretical models were beginning to emerge, foreshadowing their growth in the 1980s.

3. The 1980s, to the present

Figure 1.3 demonstrates the explosive growth seen in the marketing models publications in the 1980s in the OR/MS journals that formed the basis for the analysis. Some of that growth was due to the emergence of the journal *Marketing Science*. However, the journal emerged in response to a need to accommodate the volume of OR/MS papers that were being produced in any case, and its appearance coincided with *Operations Research* closing its publication doors to marketing papers. (We leave the analysis of a feedback effect between the emergence of a new journal and the new papers that that journal may encourage to eager, younger researchers.)

Compared to the earlier decades, the area of OR/MS in marketing saw its greatest growth in the emergence of stylized theoretical models. While it is often difficult to derive direct decision-making guidance from stylized theoretical models, many of those models are well grounded in the thirty-plus years of empirical evidence concerning marketing phenomena.

Hence, we have reason to feel that many of the theoretical marketing models are based on well-founded primitives and axioms. In addition, qualitative guidance for policy decisions that can be derived from theoretical models are often of the contingency variety, and can be used as rules in expert systems, as follows. Many expert systems require decision rules with the structure: if (Condition (Event) A or Condition (Event) B), then (Conclusion (Recommendation) C). Stylized theoretical models (confirmed by empirical observation whenever possible) often provide such contingent guidance.

Stylized theoretical modeling of marketing processes represents an important trend in the area of OR/MS in marketing. Such modeling demands greater mathematical sophistication from both researchers and readers of that research.

Another trend in the 1980s has been a shift from outcome modeling to more process-oriented modeling. The shortening of product life-cycles and the impact of competitive reactions in the marketplace preclude most markets from reaching steady state or equilibrium. Hence such areas as consumer behavior modeling (where the temporal nature of the stimuli that affect consumers' reactions has been the focus of some emerging research), the new-product area (where the moves and counter-moves of competitors keep the marketplace in a constant state of flux), and negotiations (where the offers/counter-offers of one party provide much information to the other party and can determine the future flow of the negotiation) have seen new modeling approaches.

4. Some marketing models comparisons

The following examples illustrate the evolution in complexity and sophistication of marketing models. The first example compares two measurement models; the second, two stylized theoretical models.

4.1. Comparison 1: Parfitt & Collins [1968] vs Blattberg & Golanty [1978]

The Parfitt–Collins [1968] model provides a simple method for obtaining an early prediction of ultimate market share with panel data.

Parfitt & Collins see ultimate brand-share as the product of three factors:

$$s = prb \tag{1}$$

where

s = ultimate brand share,
p = ultimate penetration rate of brand (percentage of new buyers of this product class who *try* this brand),
r = ultimate *repeat*-purchase rate of brand (percentage of repurchases of this brand to all purchases by persons who once purchased this brand),
b = buying-rate index of repeat purchase of this brand (average buyer = 1.00).

The model was designed to be used as follows. Assume that a company launches a new brand in an established product field. Its share of new buyers in this product field will rise from zero to some ultimate percentage (*trial*) as weeks pass. The penetration rate generally increases at a decreasing rate beginning at time zero. A curve can be fitted to these data after a few weeks; the authors recommend

$$p(t) = p(1 - \mathrm{e}^{-at}) \tag{2}$$

where

$p(t)$ = cumulative trial by t,
p = ultimate (long-run) trial i (from Equation (1)),
a = growth-rate parameter.

The *repeat rate* for this brand will also be monitored as data come in. This rate shows the percentage of repurchases of this brand relative to purchases of all brands by those who have tried the brand. This rate generally falls with the passage of time toward an asymptote (r) and the earlier triers of a new product tend to like it more than later triers.

If purchasers of the new brand buy at the average volume of purchasers of all brands in this product class, then $b = 1.00$; otherwise it should be adjusted.

The key use of this model is to make an ultimate-share prediction as soon as the penetration rate and the repeat-purchase rate curve tend toward clear asymptotic values, which usually occurs before a stable brand share is achieved.

Blattberg and Golanty's [1978] Tracker model extends Parfitt & Collins's work, by developing explicit models for awareness (ignored by Parfitt & Collins), trial and repeat. The method requires three waves of questionnaires of 500–1000 respondents, launched once every 4 weeks, to support estimation of parameters in the awareness, trial and repeat submodels.

Total brand *awareness* is developed as

$$A_t = \frac{\mathrm{UR}_t + \mathrm{AR}_t}{N} \tag{3}$$

where

A_t = awareness at t,
UR_t = unaided recall of new brand,
AR_t = aided recall of new brand given lack of unaided recall,
N = sample size.

The model also relates the change of awareness at time t to advertising spending as

$$\ln\left[\frac{1 - A_t}{1 - A_{t-1}}\right] = a - b(\mathrm{GRP}_t) \tag{4}$$

where

GRP_t = gross-rating points of advertising at t,
a, b = parameters.

In this model, *trial* rates are estimated with two separate populations: the newly aware and those aware for more than one period. In particular, the authors specify trial rates as

$$T_t - T_{t-1} = c\underbrace{(A_t - A_{t-1})}_{\text{newly aware}} + d\underbrace{(A_{t-1} - T_{t-1})}_{\text{past aware but not yet trying}} \quad \text{for } 0 < d < c < 1 \tag{5}$$

where

T_t = cumulative percentage of triers by period t,
A_t = percentage aware in period t,
c = probability of trial by consumers who become aware this period,
d = probability of trial by consumers aware last period or earlier but who have not yet tried.

Here the model postulates a greater conversion rate among the newly aware. The trial rate in Equation (5) is adjusted for relative price:

$$(T_t - T_{t-1})^* = (T_t - T_{t-1})\mathrm{RP}_t^{\gamma} \tag{6}$$

where

$$\mathrm{RP}_t = \text{relative price at } t,$$
$$\gamma = \text{price-elasticity parameter.}$$

Similarly, an error term is added to Equation (5) for estimation; it is both autocorrelated and heteroscedastic (where the heteroscedasticity is related to relative price). Parameters of the model are assumed constant in a product class and are estimated by a nonlinear procedure, pooling data for a number of products in the class.

The projection model for market share or sales is based on tracing the percentage of triers who become first-time users, second-time users, and so on. Triers or repeat users who discontinue use are classified as non-users. Triers are assumed to have a constant, average purchase rate TU, and repeaters are assumed to have a different use rate RU. Total sales per potential trier is then given as

$$\mathrm{TS}_t = (T_t - T_{t-1})\mathrm{TU} + \sum_{i=1}^{t-1} \mathrm{UC}_{it}\mathrm{RU} \tag{7}$$

where

TS_t = total sales per potential trier during period t,
T_t = new triers during period t,
TU = trial-use rate,
RU = repeat-use rate,
UC_{it} = percentage of new triers in period i who are still users during period t.

To model UC_{it}, the authors use a depth-of-repeat model. For simplicity they assume that

$$\mathrm{UC}_{t-1,t} = r(T_t - T_{t-1}), \tag{8}$$

that is, that the percentage (r) of triers who repeat at least once is independent of time. The rest of the structure of $\mathrm{UC}_{t,t+i+1}$ is developed as $k_i(\mathrm{UC}_{t,t+1})$, where k_i is the percentage of triers in period t who continue to purchase after period $t+i$. Note that the $\{k_i\}$ are also assumed independent of time.

According to the authors, r and RU can be estimated with telephone surveys, while the $\{k_i\}$ are estimated subjectively with product-satisfaction data from the questionnaires; the trial-use rate TU is set equal to one by definition. The reason for the subjective estimates of the $\{k_i\}$ is that no quantitative long-term, depth-of-repeat information is available; this problem exists in all cases where a short purchase history is used to project future sales.

As this comparison shows, Blattberg & Golanty [1978] build on the rather spare structure of the Parfitt & Collins model by (i) adding an awareness model (tying in advertising), (ii) relating (change in) trial to conversion of the newly aware group and to aware-but-not-trying group separately, and (iii) modeling the repeat rate among triers in each period separately. That structure also ties in with a measurement procedure, providing a complete decision-modeling system, with projections and policy diagnostics on advertising, pricing, and other marketing variables.

4.2. Comparison 2: Farley [1964] vs. Basu, Lal, Srinivasan & Staelin [1985]

The two papers we compare here are of the stylized-theoretical-model variety. The papers deal with salesforce compensation: how can the firm develop a compensation plan for its salesforce so that while the salesperson is operating in his or her best interest, he or she is maximizing profit for the firm?

The first paper we deal with [Farley, 1964], addresses the problem in a deterministic environment where the salesperson tries to maximize his or her commission and the firm wants to maximize its revenue.

We use the following notation here:

π = company's gross profit in dollars,
S = salesperson's commission income in dollars,
B_i = commission rate (in percent) paid on product i,
t_i = time devoted to selling product i,
Q_i = quantity of product i sold in units,
P_i = selling price per unit of product i,
K_i = variable non-selling cost per unit of product i,
M_i = gross margin (contribution to overhead and profit) of product i in dollars per unit (equals $P_i - K_i$),
C = total time the salesperson devotes to selling in some appropriately defined time period (month, quarter, etc.).

Farley assumes

$$Q_i = f_i(t_i) \quad \text{and} \quad \frac{\mathrm{d}f_i(t_i)}{\mathrm{d}t_i} > 0, \tag{9}$$

i.e., sales response, Q_i, is an increasing function of t_i (selling effort *only*), and is deterministic.

The firm's problem is:
find $\{B_i\}$ to

$$\text{maximize} \quad \pi = \sum_{i=1}^{n} Q_i[(P_i - K_i)(1 - B_i)] \quad \text{(the firm's gross profit)}, \tag{10}$$

$$\text{subject to} \quad C \geqslant \sum_{i=1}^{n} t_i \quad \text{(the constraint on the salesperson's time)}. \tag{11}$$

Inserting constraint Equation (10) into Equation (9) via Lagrange multipliers, yields an expression that can be maximized by calculus.

The salesperson's problem is to
find $\{t_i)$ to

$$\text{maximize} \quad S = \sum_{i=1}^{n} m_i Q_i B_i \quad \text{(the commission)}, \tag{12}$$

subject to constraint Equation (11) again.

Equations (11) and (12) can again be combined via a Lagrangian operation, and the resulting pair of equations are solved simultaneously to yield the general result that each optimal $B_i = B =$ constant will maximize both the firm's and the salesperson's objective functions. In other words, a compensation scheme based on a constant percentage of gross margin across products is optimal for the problem formulated by Farley.

Farley's result does not specify, however, what level B should be, although it seems evident that if B doesn't compensate the salesperson more than his or her opportunity cost of time, the salesperson would leave the firm.

There have been many key developments expanding upon and qualifying Farley's results. Most of the more recent work has employed the agency theory framework, where three basic assumptions hold: (a) response to salesperson's effort (sales) is only known stochastically, (b) the firm can only observe salesperson's effort imperfectly (if at all), and (c) the firm and the salesperson are assumed to be expected-utility maximizers, with the salesperson typically risk-averse and the firm risk-neutral.

The paper by Basu, Lal, Srinivasan & Staelin (BLSS) [1985] uses this framework with the following assumptions: one salesperson selling one product, and selling time is related to sales volume x via $f(x|t)$ which is a density function of sales, conditional on effort. Specifically, BLSS consider $f(x|t)$ as either gamma or binomial.

The salesperson's objective is to maximize expected utility, which is specified as:

$$W(s, t) = U(s) - V(t) \tag{13}$$

where

W = total utility,
s = total income,
t = selling time,
$U(s), V(t)$ = utility of income and (dis)utility of effort (selling time) respectively.

The salesperson requires some minimum level of utility, m, to be willing to work for the firm.

Other assumptions include:

- c, marginal cost, is a constant fraction of price,
- the firm knows $f(x|t)$ but cannot observe t.

The firm's problem is to find $s(x)$ to

$$\text{maximize} \quad \pi = \int_0^\infty [(1-c)x - s(x)] f(x|t)\mathrm{d}x \tag{14}$$

$$\text{subject to} \quad \int_0^\infty [U(s(x))] f(x|t)\mathrm{d}x - V(t) \geqslant m, \tag{15}$$

$$\int_0^\infty [U(s(x))] \frac{\partial f(x|t)}{\partial t}\mathrm{d}x - \frac{\mathrm{d}V(t)}{\mathrm{d}t} = 0. \tag{16}$$

Equation (14) has the firm looking for a compensation package, $s(x)$, to maximize its expected profits. (Recall the firm is risk-neutral.) Constraint (15) requires the compensation package, $s(x)$, to be at least as attractive as the salesperson's outside alternative, m. Constraint (16) has the salesperson choosing a level of sales effort, t, to maximize his/her expected utility.

The optimization problem characterized by Equation (14) with constraints, Equations (15) and (16), can be solved using calculus of variations or optimal control methods [Holmstrom, 1979]. To obtain specific insights, BLSS study the case of a constant relative risk-aversion salesperson having a utility function

$$U(s(x)) = \frac{s(x)^\delta}{\delta}, \quad \delta < 1 \tag{17}$$

and show that for $f(x|t)$ either gamma or binomial, the optimal compensation scheme is

$$S^*(x) = [A + Bx]^{1/(1-\delta)}, \quad A \geqslant 0, B > 0. \tag{18}$$

Note that Equation (18) has a salary component, A, and a commission component, B. BLSS go on to show how changes in risk-aversion, uncertainty, marginal cost, or minimum expected utility can lead to a range of possible compensation plans, including straight salary, straight commission, progressive sliding commission, salary plus commission, and salary plus commission beyond a sales target. (See Coughlan, Chapter 13, for a complete discussion of this area.)

The comparison of these two papers reflects an evolution in model sophistication. Farley posits a simple model and obtains a simple, but non-intuitive result. The world is more complex, however; BLSS deal with a richer, more realistic set of assumptions and provide some more satisfactory explanations for the more complex set of compensation arrangements we normally observe in practice.

5. OR/MS in marketing today

Everyone has different impressions about what issues are topical and where the frontiers are or should be in any field. We do not claim that what follows is any more than personal impressions, but we will summarize some reasoning before making any prognostic projections and statements.

(1) Marketing models are having an important impact both on academic developments in marketing and on marketing practice. During the 1980s two new and important journals started: *Marketing Science* and the *International Journal of Research in Marketing* (*IJRM*). Both are healthy, popular, and extremely influential, especially among academics. And both reflect the developments of marketing models. In addition, on the practice side from 1980 to 1990, the Edelman Prize Competition (held annually to select the best example of the practice of management science) selected seven finalists in the field of marketing and two winners.

(2) New data sources are having a major impact on marketing modeling developments. One of the single, most influential developments of the 1980s has been the impact of scanner data on the field of marketing models. There are typically two or more special sessions at national meetings on the use of scanner data, a special-interest conference on the topic was held recently, and a special issue of *IJRM* was devoted to the topic. Scanner data and the closely related single-source data (where communication consumption data are tied into diary panel data collected by means of scanners) have enabled marketing scientists to develop and test models with much more precision than ever before. Relatedly, the Marketing Department in *Management Science* and *Marketing Science* have initiated editorial actions to encourage behaviorally oriented submissions. Such papers provide substantive evidence based on which new marketing theories can be developed and new marketing decision-making models can be further improved.

(3) Stylized theoretical modeling has become a mainstream research tradition in marketing. While the field of microeconomics has always had a major influence on quantitative model developments in marketing, that influence became most profound in the 1980s. The July 1980 issue of the *Journal of Business* reported on the proceedings of a conference on the interface between marketing and economics. In January 1987, the European Institute for Advanced Studies in Management held a conference on the same topic and reported that "the links between the two disciplines were indeed strengthening" [Bultez, 1988]. Key papers from that conference were published in issue 4 of the 1988 volume of *IJRM*. Issues 2 and 3 of the 1990 volume of *IJRM* on salesforce management provide several examples of how agency theory (a microeconomic development) is being used to study salesforce compensation. Other major theoretical modeling developments, primarily in areas of pricing, consumer behavior, product policy, promotions, and channel decisions are covered in detail in Lilien et al. [1992]; the impact on the field has been dramatic.

(4) New tools and methods are changing the content of marketing models. The November 1982 issue of the *Journal of Marketing Research* (*JMR*) was devoted to causal modeling. A relatively new methodology at the time, causal modeling has become a mainstream approach for developing explanatory models of behavioral phenomena in marketing. New developments have also occurred in psychometric modeling. As the August 1985 special issue of *JMR* on competition

in marketing pointed out, techniques like game theory, optimal control theory, and market share/response models are essential elements of the marketing modeler's toolkit. And finally, the explosion of interest in and the potential of artificial intelligence and expert systems approaches to complement traditional marketing modeling approaches has the potential to change the norms and paradigms in the field. (See the April 1991 special issue of *IJRM* on expert systems in marketing.)

(5) Competition and interaction is the key marketing models game today. The saturation of markets and the economic fights for survival in a world of relatively fixed potential and resources has changed the focus of interest in marketing models, probably forever. A key word search of the 1989 and 1990 volumes of *Marketing Science*, *JMR* and *Management Science* (marketing articles only) reveals multiple entries for 'competition', 'competitive strategy', 'noncooperative games', competitive entry', 'late entry' and 'market structure'. These terms are largely missing in a comparable analysis of the 1969 and 1970 issues of *JMR*, *Management Science* and *Operations Research* (which dropped its marketing section when *Marketing Science* was introduced, but was a key vehicle for marketing papers at that time).

6. Marketing models in the future

As we have tried to show above, the marketing models area has had important impact on the practice of marketing as well as on the development of an understanding of the nature of marketing phenomena. That trend will continue – the area is healthy and growing. Let us take a crack at a few extrapolations that we think (and hope) will have a dramatic impact on developments in the marketing models area in the next decade.

6.1. Interface modeling

Marketing is a boundary-spanning function, linking the selling organization with buyers and channel intermediaries in some way. To operate most effectively, its activities must be coordinated with other functional areas of the firm. An area that has begun to see research is the marketing–manufacturing interface. In this case, the firm is suboptimizing by looking at the marketing function, given a manufacturing decision; the coordination of efforts allows for significant savings in many situations. We expect this area to be explored both theoretically and empirically in the next decade.

6.2. Process modeling

Models of competition and models of bargaining and negotiations have generally focused on identifying equilibrium (steady-state) outcomes. Yet markets rarely reach such equilibria; indeed, even the equilibria that are obtainable are often determined by the 'transient' part of the analysis. We expect that such models will be built and tested. Those tests will become more doable given the ability of interactive computer networks to capture the dynamics of moves and counter-moves in negotiation contexts, for example.

6.3. *Models of competition and coordination*

The markets of the 1990s will be characterized by strategic competition. This means that our models will focus on those situations (like the tit-for-tat solutions to repeated prisoner's dilemma games that induce cooperation; see, for example, Axelrod [1984]) that induce price coordination in low-margin markets, that allow for mutual 'understandings' about permitting monopolies or near monopolies in small market niches and the like. Competitive signaling represents one major paradigm in this direction. This is in contrast to most of the current models of competition that focus on the 'warfare' aspects of competition.

6.4. *Marketing generalizations*

Meta-analysis must become the norm for the development of operational market response models in the 1990s. It is absurd to analyze data on sales response to price fluctuations, for example, and ignore the hundreds of studies that have previously reported price elasticities. The 1990s will see such 'generalizations' become formal Bayesian priors in estimating response elasticities in marketing models. The grouping of our knowledge in this way will allow the discipline to make direct use of the information that it has been accumulating.

6.5. *New measurement technologies*

Single-source data will boost our ability to tie advertising and communications variables into consumer choice models. The increasing and expanded use of electronic forms of communications, data entry, order entry, expanded bar-coding, and the like will provide explosions of data that will stimulate the development of marketing models parallel to those that resulted from the introduction of scanner data. For example, it is feasible to capture the complete set of computer screen protocols facing a travel agent when making a client's booking. The implications of such technology for model development, experimentation and testing are enormous.

With more emphasis on incorporating the voice of the customer in designing new products, we also expect to see more measurement work related to yet unexplored aspects of consumer behavior processes such as consumption/usage experiences as well as post-purchase attitudes and feelings. This would entail, among other things, close examination and understanding of moods and emotions in addition to the more traditional examinations of judgment and decision-making. Given the inherent complexities of constructs such as consumer emotions, we expect to see explicit recognition of measurement errors in such contexts.

6.6. *New methodologies*

The impact of logit and related choice models had tremendous impact on both marketing model development and applications in the 1980s. (For a striking example of the effect such modeling had at one firm, resulting in an application that won the 1989 Edelman Prize, see Gensch, Arersa & Moore [1990].) We see a similar impact of Bayesian procedures in calibrating marketing models in the 1990s. For example, advances in elicitation of subjective judgments as well as in computation will increasingly allow analysis to exploit coefficient similarity across equations relying on similar data (perhaps from different regions or different market segments) to produce more robust estimates.

6.7. *Intelligent marketing systems*

The 1970s and early 1980s saw the explosion of decision support systems (DSS) in marketing. A DSS can be very powerful but, used inappropriately, can provide results that are either worthless or, possibly, foolish. The 1990s will see the development of a generation of intelligent marketing systems (IMS) that will have the 'autopilots' on board the marketing aircraft (the DSS) to take care of the routine activities and focus the analyst's attention on outliers.

6.8. *More impact on practice*

Even several decades after the earliest operational marketing models were first introduced, their impact on practice remains far below its potential. Shorter life-cycles, more competitive (and risky) decisions, better theory, faster computers, new technologies, and the convergence of the developments outlined above will permit marketing models to impact marketing practices in a way that approaches their impact in the academic realm.

6.9. *New areas of application*

Most reported applications of marketing models have been to consumer products, both for frequently purchased packaged goods and for consumer durables. Yet the business-to-business and services marketplaces have seen only limited modeling activity in spite of the fact that more than twice the dollar volume of transactions takes place between businesses than in the consumer marketplace; and service industries including telecommunications, food, lodging, education, health care, entertainment and the like, account for about 70% of US national income. To take one under-modeled area, the film industry generated revenues of over US $13 billion in 1990 and has seen almost no attention from the marketing modeling community. These observations suggest that there are many under-researched and under-modeled domains available for development of new marketing models and for adaptation of existing models.

7. Organization and content of the Handbook

This book brings together leading marketing scientists with an OR/MS orientation, each of whom has developed a state-of-the-art review of his or her area of expertise. The material spans the marketing discipline and represents excellent coverage of what is known and what problem areas present themselves as ripe for further development.

Each chapter was written with a mathematically sophisticated reader in mind. But that reader is not expected to be an expert on marketing. In each chapter, the authors discuss the motivation – the behavioral foundations or key assumptions – leading to the development of the important models and methods that they review.

We have organized the book around four main areas following this Introduction: Models of Market Phenomena, Tools and Methods for Market Analysis, Elements of the Marketing Mix and, finally, Interactions, Strategy and Synergy.

7.1. Part II. Models of market phenomena

Market phenomena can be addressed at different levels of aggregation: the individual consumer, the dyad (family or bargaining pair), the group (or organizational decision-making unit), or the market as a unit. In this part, Roberts & Lilien (Chapter 2) provide a taxonomy of individual-consumer behavior phenomena that have received modeling attention. They then show how these models can be used and combined to solve managerial problems. Corfman & Gupta (Chapter 3) focus on choice and decision-making models when the decision must be made by a group, defined as a collection of people united by bonds of common interest. Their definition of a group encompasses market phenomena that include: group choice (based on normative models as well as models derived from the literature in social psychology), family decision-making, organizational decision-making, buyer–seller negotiations and interdependent decisions in marketing channels. Finally, Moorthy (Chapter 4) reviews key developments when the actors under analysis are organizations involved in price, product, advertising and distribution decisions in a competitive framework. His review indicates the type of factors that one must consider when analyzing competitive market situations.

7.2. Part III. Tools and methods for market analysis

The marketing scientist's toolkit includes methods developed in OR/MS, psychometrics, econometrics and statistics. These methods have often been adapted to the particular circumstances of marketing problems.

In this part, DeSarbo, Manrai & Manrai (Chapter 5) show how competing products or brands can be represented so that substitution patterns among them can be better understood. They review primarily deterministic and stochastic non-spatial tree models that originated in the psychometric area. Cooper (Chapter 6) also addresses competitive and market structures, but focuses on the relationship between the aggregate concept of market share and disaggregate choice models, relying on methods derived primarily from mathematical psychology and econometrics. Urban (Chapter 7) describes methods designed to develop pre-test market assessments for new products, primarily consumer packaged goods and durables. These methods provide useful diagnostics as well as market penetration forecasts and provide tools for management to assess the likely market response to various marketing plans. Mahajan, Muller & Bass (Chapter 8) focus on diffusion models, dealing with the rate of penetration of new products into the market. In addition to describing and predicting the dynamic patterns of penetration for such products, these models provide normative guidance for pricing policies, advertising strategies, entry timing decision and the like. Hanssens & Parsons (Chapter 9) conclude this part with an econometrics-based review of aggregate (both static and dynamic) sales response functions, i.e. functional relationships between marketing actions and the resulting sales seen by the firms in the marketplace.

7.3. Part IV. Elements of the marketing mix

Marketing management controls a wide range of decisions that affect market response. While many of these decisions interact (as we see in Part V) much research has addressed the impact of these elements in isolation.

The part begins with a review by Green & Krieger (Chapter 10) of the impact of product design on market response. The authors emphasize the role of conjoint analysis, a widely adopted method to assess the relationship between product attributes and consumer preferences and choices. Pricing is perhaps the most frequently mentioned variable under the control of the marketing manager. Rao (Chapter 11) deals with the many complexities of pricing behavior, including the role of competition, the dynamics of price, pricing a line of products and the like. He also examines such behavioral phenomena as the price–quality relationship, as well as measurement issues such as willingness-to-pay and elasticity. Sales promotion is another key marketing-mix element. Blattberg & Neslin (Chapter 12) address that role that consumer promotions such as coupons and deals, as well as trade promotions such as dealer allowances, have on demand and profitability. They discuss both descriptive and normative models of promotional phenomena.

The salesforce consumes the largest share of the marketing budget for most firms and we have two chapters dealing with important issues of salesforce management. Coughlan (Chapter 13) examines models of salesforce compensation, reflecting indirect control of the salesforce. The types of models she reviews are deterministic relationships between salesforce effort and sales, agency-theoretic models of salesforce management, and decision support systems for salesforce compensation. Vandenbosch & Weinberg (Chapter 14) address the direct control of the salesforce through territory design models, call-planning models, and salesforce sizing models.

7.4. Part V. Interactions, strategy and synergy

The models in this part take a broader view of marketing problems, looking at the effect of multiple marketing-mix elements, at using other types of models (like expert systems) to aid decisions, and at larger issues such as marketing strategy and decisions that cross functional boundaries.

Gatignon (Chapter 15) reviews models of the marketing mix. He discusses estimation issues as well as models that permit an optimal allocation of resources across marketing-mix elements. Rangaswamy's focus (Chapter 16) is on marketing decision models more generally, with a particular emphasis on approaches using expert systems and artificial intelligence. Such systems rely on a specific synthesis and representation of knowledge rather than the more concise summarization that more traditional, explicit mathematical models afford. Wind & Lilien (Chapter 17) begin by providing an overview of the accomplishments and limitations of marketing models, moving from models of individual elements of the mix to more general models of marketing strategy. They discuss portfolio models and resource allocation models as well as some more non-traditional approaches (morphological analysis, benchmarking) and assesses their potential to aid marketing practitioners. The part and the book conclude with Eliashberg & Steinberg's discussion (Chapter 18) of cross-functional coordination between marketing and production. Marketing actions affect production and inventory costs, and such costs in turn affect the relative profitability of marketing actions. This final chapter shows the benefit of coordinating efforts in the firm and opens a window onto the type of cross-functional modeling that must take place in the fully integrated firm of the 21st century.

The careful reader will note that we do not have coverage of advertising models, channel models, models dealing specifically with scanner-data environments, product line models or models of the R&D–marketing interface. Our original plans *did* include chapters in these areas. Sadly, such plans did not result in completed chapters that we could include here. Happily, we have an excellent set of papers, written by a stellar group of authors. We hope that our readers will agree that in, at least, a significant domain of the space of OR/MS in marketing, these chapters will define the state of the art for at least a few years to come.

References

Axelrod, R. (1984). *The Evolution of Cooperation*, Basic Books, New York.

Basu, A., R. Lal, V. Srinivasan and R. Staelin (1985). Salesforce compensation plans: An agency theoretic perspective. *Marketing Sci.* 4 (Fall), 267–291.

Blattberg, R.C. and J. Golanty (1978). Tracker: An early test market forecasting and diagnostic model for new product planning. *J. Marketing Res.* 15 (May), 192–202.

Bultez, Alain (1988). Editorial for Special Issue on Marketing and Microeconomics, *Inter. J. Res. Marketing* 5(4), 221–224.

Farley, J.U. (1964). An optimal plan for salesmen's compensation. *J. Marketing Res.* 1 (May), 39–43.

Gensch, D., N. Arersa and S.P. Moore (1990). A choice modelling market information system that enabled ABB Electric to expand its market share. *Interfaces* 20(1) (January/February), 6–25.

Holmstrom, B. (1979). Moral hazard and observability, *Bell J. Econom.* 10, 74–91.

King, W.R. (1967). *Quantitative Analysis for Marketing Management*, McGraw-Hill, New York.

Kotler, P. (1971). *Marketing Decision Making: A Model Building Approach*, Holt, Rinehart and Winston, New York.

Lilien, Gary L. and Philip Kotler (1983). *Marketing Decision Making: A Model Building Approach*, Harper and Row, New York.
Lilien, Gray L., Philip Kotler and K. Sridhar Moorthy (1992). *Marketing Models*, Prentice-Hall, Englewood Cliffs, NJ.
Montgomery, D.B. and G.L. Urban (1969). *Management Science in Marketing*, Prentice-Hall, Englewood Cliffs, NJ.
Moorthy, K.S. (1993). Theoretical modeling in marketing, *J. Marketing* 57 (April), 92–106.
Parfitt, J.H. and B.J.K. Collins (1968). Use of consumer panels for brand share prediction, *J. Marketing Res.* 5 (May), 131–146.
Schultz, R.L. and A.A. Zoltners (1981). *Marketing Decision Models*, North-Holland, New York.

Part II
Models of Market Phenomena

J. Eliashberg and G.L. Lilien, Eds., *Handbooks in OR & MS, Vol. 5*

Chapter 2

Explanatory and Predictive Models of Consumer Behavior*

John H. Roberts
Australian Graduate School of Management, University of New South Wales, Kensington, NSW, Australia 2033

Gary L. Lilien
Pennsylvania State University, 113 BAB II, University Park, PA 16802, USA

The engineer builds on well-established laws of physics that have been derived by theoretical analysis and tested by empirical investigation. Similarly, marketing managers rely on consumer behavior models – models of how individual purchasing agents act in the marketplace – which are based on consumer behavior theory [e.g. Zaltman and Wallendorf, 1979] and then tested in the marketplace. Our objectives for this chapter are (a) to outline the elements of some basic consumer behavior models; (b) to indicate some of the ways those models have been extended; and (c) to illustrate how marketing models have been and can be applied to solve real management problems. We proceed within a framework that decomposes and categorizes consumer decision processes into a number of stages.

The chapter is designed to give quantitative modelers and management scientists unfamiliar with marketing an appreciation of the way in which models of consumer behavior are developed and used. It is also designed to provide a reference and teaching resource for marketing specialists. We assume the reader has a reasonable knowledge of and interest in the mathematics of the models, but has only modest understanding of the marketing models field.

1. An organizing framework for consumer behavior models

The consumer behavior model that we use in a given situation and the consumer behavior theory on which it is based depend on the objectives of the model-builder,

*Some of the material in this paper, prepared by the same authors, also appears in Chapter 2 of Lilien, Kotler & Moorthy [1992], *Marketing Models* (Prentice-Hall, Englewood Cliffs).

the important market phenomena, and the availability of relevant theories and data to support the analysis. The range of consumer behavior models is very broad for several reasons:

Consumers are different. Consumers vary according to their personalities, values, preferences, and a range of other characteristics. These differences mean that a model that is appropriate for describing the behavior of one particular consumer may be inadequate in explaining the behavior of another, even in similar purchase situations.

Choice decisions differ. Not only do consumers differ from one another, but even for one specific consumer, a model that might describe that consumer's behavior for one specific purchase decision may not work for another product, for several reasons. For example, the level of involvement that the consumer has in the decision will determine the amount of cognitive effort and search that he or she is prepared to invest in it. Phenomena associated with low involvement decisions (often called routinized response behavior) include habit, indifference to risk, and lack of search. As the level of involvement grows through limited problem solving to extended problem solving, other phenomena such as brand perceptions and evaluation rules become important.

The context of purchases differs. Consumers vary in their decision-making rules because of the usage situation, the user of the good or service (for family, for gift, for self), and purchase situation (catalogue sale, in-store shelf selection, salesperson-aided purchase). Each such context may invoke a different decision-making strategy. For example, a consumer buying a watch for herself may value consistency with her other jewelry, image, and aesthetics, but when buying one as a gift for a friend, may treat price and manufacturer reputation as the most important attributes.

Managerial needs differ. Models are also important managerial tools and differences in managerial problems may also make some models more appropriate than others. For example, if management is interested in a pricing strategy, then a model that emphasizes the consumer's evaluation process and the role of price in that process may be most appropriate; if management is interested in making consumers aware of a new product launch, then a model that focuses on information search and perception formation may be best. A model that deals with all aspects of consumer behavior in complete detail may be theoretically sound but hopelessly complex in terms of its data requirements and potential for calibration.

Before proceeding to our review, we would like to indicate several categories of consumer behavior models that we explicitly exclude.

First, note that the models that we review generally assume that a single individual is acting as his or her own agent or, at most, as an agent for a household. Thus we exclude *organizational buying* models from consideration. Organizational buying is characterized by derived demand (products purchased by organizations as inputs to satisfy the needs of those organizations' customers), multiple individuals involved in the purchase process (the *buying center*), and extensive use of bargaining, negotiations and long-term relationships to effect an exchange [Lilien, Kotler & Moorthy, 1992, Chapter 3].

Second, we exclude so-called *stochastic models* from consideration. Traditionally, stochastic models have been suggested as modeling frameworks primarily for low-involvement products where little conscious decision-making was assumed to take place. Those models have generally focused most of their attention on the mechanics of an underlying probabilistic process [Massy, Montgomery & Morrison, 1970; Lilien, Kotler & Moorthy, 1992, Chapter 2]. In contrast, the models that we focus on here devote most of their attention to the determinants of choice, with uncertainty arising because of missing variables, simplified specification, incompleteness of consumer information, measurement error and the like. These latter models are generally associated with high-involvement purchase situations, i.e. those that consumers find personally significant. We recognize that there is an imperfect correspondence between stochastic models and low-involvement choice situations, as well as between explanatory/predictive models and high-involvement buying.

Finally, consumer behavior models can either deal with consumers as individuals or as an aggregate group. We deal here with models of the individual, although often with a view toward aggregating those models to make statements about the behavior of the total market. Other chapters in this volume deal with market response as a whole, looking at the relationship between market share and sales to marketing activities (promotion and price, for example) relying solely on aggregate, market-level data. An area of continuing research is the relationship between individual response models and aggregate market models [see, for example, Ehrenberg, Goodhardt & Barwise, 1990, and Chatterjee & Eliashberg, 1990].

2. A taxonomy of consumer behavior models

To achieve parsimony and to help structure our review, we classify consumer behavior models in the framework of a staged or phased process. That is, we visualize consumers going through a number of steps from the time that they recognize a need that they would like to satisfy, through the choice of a product to satisfy that need, through the actual purchase and consumption experience and, finally, through the updating of preferences and perceptions that follow consumption and guide future purchase behavior. Table 2.1 outlines the five organizing phases we use here.

We also use Table 2.1 to demonstrate the applications different marketing models have seen. The applications of these models will often cross over the boundaries of this framework. Although we realize that this classification is not definitive, it has helped us organize the literature and we hope it will help the reader understand the literature better.

The next five sections correspond to the basic elements in Table 2.1. In each of those sections we first review some basic concepts and models of that consumer behavior stage. Then we outline some important extensions and applications. These applications illustrate the types of extensions researchers have undertaken; they are not meant to be comprehensive. Where possible, we cite more complete reviews.

Table 2.1
A framework for classifying consumer behavior models

Stage	Dependent variables of interest	Typical models used for this stage
Need arousal	Purchase (category choice) Purchase timing (Table 2.2)	Binary choice models
Information search	Awareness (aided/unaided) Consideration/evoked set Choice set Belief dynamics (Table 2.3)	Individual awareness models Consideration models Information integration models
Evaluation	Product perceptions (Table 2.4) Product preferences (Table 2.5)	Perceptual mapping/ multidimensional scaling models Attitude models: Compensatory Non-compensatory
Purchase	Brand choice Store choice Quantity choice (Table 2.6)	Discrete choice models Hierarchical models
Post-purchase	Brand satisfaction/satiation Word-of-mouth (Table 2.7)	Satisfaction models Variety-seeking models Communications/network models

Some models span several stages of the taxonomy; we deal with a sample of such models in Section 8, illustrating how models of several of these stages can be combined to address more complex managerial problems. We conclude with a discussion of what we see as key future directions for consumer behavior models.

The elements of Table 2.1 correspond to the following basic consumer processes:

(1) *Need arousal.* A need can be activated (or aroused) through internal or external stimuli. In the first case, one of the person's normal drives – hunger, thirst, sex – rises to a threshold level and becomes a drive. In the second case, need is caused by an external stimulus or triggering cue (an advertisement, sight of an acquaintance's product, etc.). Consumers then determine the type of product that could possibly satisfy the need.

(2) *Information search.* Consumers often do not satisfy an aroused need immediately. Depending on the intensity of the stored need, consumers either undertake *active information search*, or enter a state of *heightened attention* in which they are open to the reception of information passively.

Following the search process, consumers are aware of a group of products or brands that they see as being possibly suitable to satisfy the identified need. This group of products is called the *evoked set*, or *consideration set*. The consideration set comprises the alternatives that enter the next stage, the evaluation phase. As evaluation progresses, further brands may be eliminated: the consideration set is dynamic. When consumers are about to make a purchase, the remaining set of brands is the *choice set*.

(3) *Evaluation*. Evaluation has two components. Consumers establish their beliefs about the features of the alternative products that they consider (*perceptions*) and they determine, based on those perceptions, their attitudes towards the products (*preferences*). In practice, consumers update perceptions continually during the search process.

Perception formation. The fields of psychology [Fishbein, 1967] and economics [Lancaster, 1966] both suggest that consumers see a product as having several attributes. Consumers perceive a particular product in terms of where it lies in the space spanned by the set of attributes relevant to its product class. For example, in the aspirin category, important attributes might be speed of relief, reliability, side effects and price. Individual consumers vary as to which attributes they consider most relevant.

Consumers are likely to develop opinions about where different brands stand on each attribute. The set of beliefs that consumers hold about a particular brand is known as its *brand image*. Consumers' beliefs or perceptions may differ from the 'true' attributes because of consumers' particular experiences and the way consumers gather and process information. It is consumers' perceptions of a product's characteristics that influence their behavior, not the 'true' characteristics.

Preference formation. Consumers use their perceptions in forming brand preferences. Most models assume consumers have a utility function for attributes that describes how the consumer's valuation of the product varies with alternative levels and combinations of attributes. Consumers arrive at an attitude (judgment or preference) toward the brand through some evaluation procedure. Starting with their consideration set, consumers compare products and end up with an ordering of preferences (although not all evaluations follow this process).

(4) *Purchase decision*. When evaluating products, consumers may form a ranked set of preferences for the alternative products in their consideration sets and develop an intention to purchase the product they like best. But a number of additional factors often intervene before a purchase can be made [Sheth, 1974]. One factor is the attitude of others, including the intensity of others' attitudes, and the consumers' motivation to comply with others' wishes [Fishbein, 1967]. Consumers' purchase intentions are also influenced by changes in anticipated situational factors, such as expected family income, the expected total cost of the product, and the expected benefits of the product. Furthermore, when consumers are about to act, unanticipated situational factors may intervene to prevent them from doing so (such as the lack of availability of a preferred product). Finally, measurement error may arise when we try to estimate preferences. Thus, estimated preferences and purchase intentions are not completely reliable predictors of actual buying behavior: while they indicate likely purchase behavior, they fail to include a number of additional factors that may intervene.

(5) *Post-purchase feelings.* After buying and trying the product, consumers will experience some level of satisfaction or dissatisfaction. Swan & Combs [1976] posit that consumers' satisfaction is a function both of expectations and the product's perceived performance. If the seller makes exaggerated claims for the product, consumers experience disconfirmed expectations, which lead to dissatisfaction. The level of satisfaction or dissatisfaction depends on the size of the difference between expectations and performance. Satisfaction with a product will influence consumer choice on subsequent purchase occasions. In addition, consumers are likely to communicate their feelings about the product to other potential consumers who are seeking information. Satisfaction is a more powerful influence in frequently purchased goods where the purchaser's own experience is critical for repurchase and repurchase rates are high, while the opinion of others is a more important consideration for durable products.

We now deal with these elements in our taxonomy in more detail.

3. Need arousal

Need arousal is the trigger that starts the consumer decision process. The modeling of whether and when that need will be satisfied, in our view, corresponds to a category purchase decision. Later we will review *which* specific product or brand the consumer chooses. The models at both stages are similar: the choice of whether to buy or not and the choice of what to buy. Models of these processes draw on discrete choice theory.

When there are exactly two choices (buy in category/don't buy in category, as here) discrete choice models are called *binary choice models*, and have been applied to a wide variety of classification problems within marketing and in other areas [Ben-Akiva & Lerman, 1985].

3.1. Need arousal basics

Assume that the utility that consumer i expects to get from the category at the time of the purchase decision is U_{Bi}, while the utility of not buying within the category is U_{Ni}. Furthermore, assume that we can divide these utilities into two components; a systematic part, V_i and a random component ε_i.

Thus,

$$U_{Bi} = V_{Bi} + \varepsilon_{Bi}, \quad \text{and} \quad U_{Ni} = V_{Ni} + \varepsilon_{Ni}, \tag{1a, b}$$

or, i.e.,

Buy/Not Buy Utility = True Value + Assessment Error.

(In what follows, we drop the subscript i for simplicity.)

There are two components in Equation (1): the true utility value (V) and the assessment error component (ε). One way of structuring V is to compare the utility (net of price) that the category gives to the utility of other alternative uses of that amount of money (the budget constraint). Hauser & Urban [1986] derive and test such a rule, described below. Thus, binary choice models vary in the benchmark used for not buying in the category (V_N). They also vary in their assumptions about the distribution of the disturbance term, ε.

Assuming the following:

(1) $\{\varepsilon_B\}$ and $\{\varepsilon_N\}$ are independent and identically distributed; and

(2) the distribution of $\{\varepsilon_B, \varepsilon_N\}$ is double-exponential (extreme-value):

$$\Pr(\varepsilon \leqslant x) = \exp\{-\mathrm{e}^{-bx}\}.$$

Then we get:

$$\Pr(\varepsilon_N < X_N) = \exp\{-\mathrm{e}^{-bX_N}\}. \tag{2}$$

To buy in the category requires that

$$U_B > U_N$$

which occurs with probability:

$$\Pr(\varepsilon_N < V_B + \varepsilon_B - V_N). \tag{3}$$

To evaluate (3), then, we substitute $V_B + \varepsilon_B - V_N$ for X_N in (2):

$$\Pr(\varepsilon_N < V_B + \varepsilon_B - V_N) = \exp\{-\mathrm{e}^{-b(V_B + \varepsilon_B - V_N)}\} \tag{4}$$

We must now integrate ε_B (the remaining random variable) out of (4):

$$\Pr(\text{Buy}) = \int_{-\infty}^{\infty} \exp\{-\mathrm{e}^{-b(V_B + \varepsilon_B - V_N)}\} f_{\varepsilon_B}(\varepsilon_B)\,\mathrm{d}\varepsilon_B \tag{5}$$

where

$$f_{\varepsilon_B}(\varepsilon_B) = b\exp\{-b\varepsilon_B\}\exp\{-\mathrm{e}^{-b\varepsilon_B}\}. \tag{6}$$

After some algebra, the logit model evolves:

$$\Pr(U_B > U_N) = \frac{1}{1 + \mathrm{e}^{-b(V_B - V_N)}} \tag{7a}$$

or, if the benchmark for not buying is $V_N = 0$, then

$$\Pr(U_B > U_N) = \frac{1}{1 + \mathrm{e}^{-bV_B}}. \tag{7b}$$

3.2. *Need arousal extensions and applications*

Two issues that distinguish need arousal models are their specifications of the systematic component and the specifications of the error term (Table 2.2).

3.2.1. *Specification of the systematic components: V_B and V_N*

A key question that arises in specifying the systematic component in Equation (1b) is how to determine the utility of not buying within the category V_{Ni}. Various authors have suggested different benchmarks against which the utility of buying within the category can be compared. For example, budget constraints compare the utility (net of price) that the category in question gives to that of other durables and a composite good of non-durables. This will result in an ordering that consumers can use to purchase durable products.

Example. Hauser & Urban [1986] derive and test a decision rule where they posit that consumers undertake this budgeting process, called the value priority algorithm. Under the value priority algorithm, consumers select the durables of highest utility per dollar, or highest utility net of price, first and proceed down the list ordered on that basis until they meet their budget constraint. That problem may be expressed as the following linear program (assuming linear, additive utilities of durables):

$$\begin{aligned} \text{maximize} \quad & u_1 g_1 + u_2 g_2 + \cdots + u_n g_n + u_y(y) \\ \text{subject to} \quad & p_1 g_1 + p_2 g_2 + \cdots + p_n g_n + y \leqslant B, \\ & g_j \geqslant 0 \quad \text{for all durables } j \end{aligned}$$

where

u_j = expected utility of durable j,
p_j = price of durable j,
$$g_j = \begin{cases} 1 & \text{if durable } j \text{ is purchased and} \\ 0 & \text{otherwise,} \end{cases}$$
B = budget that the consumer has to spend, of which...
y = money spent on products other than durables, giving a utility of $u_y(y)$.

An equivalent problem for the consumer is to minimize the dual linear program, that is to solve the following problem:

$$\begin{aligned} \text{minimize} \quad & B\lambda + \gamma_1 + \gamma_2 + \cdots + \gamma_n \\ \text{subject to} \quad & \gamma_j \geqslant u_j - \lambda p_j \quad \text{for all } j, \\ & \lambda = \partial u_y(y)/\partial y. \end{aligned}$$

The behavioral interpretation of this problem is that γ_j is the shadow price of the constraint $g_j \leqslant 1$. That is, γ_j is the forgone value of not having durable j or the value of relaxing the constraint that durables are discrete. By the rule of

Table 2.2
Need arousal models: extensions and applications

Issues addressed	Model	Data	Illustrative literature	Comments/application
Alternative benchmarks of deterministic term:				
Other durables	Value priority (math. programming)	Category purchase intent plus other durables; Utility and prices of category and other durables	Hauser & Urban [1986]	Durable good benchmark
Current holdings	Existing stock model	Category purchase intent; Utility of new purchase plus utility of existing stock	Hauser, Roberts & Urban [1983]	Currently held durable benchmark
Time-varying utility	Hazard rate models	Purchase intent or purchase; Level, dynamics and determinants of hazard	Jain & Vilcassim [1991]	Emphasis on dynamics of probability
Alternative specification of error term	Binary logit	Category purchase or intent; Utility of category; Utility of alternative	Domencich & McFadden [1975]; Bodnar, Dilworth & Iacono [1988]; Robinson [1986]; Nooteboom [1989]	Urban travel
	Binary probit	As for binary logit	Lisco [1967]	Transport choice
Overview articles	Review of discrete choice models		Amemiya [1981]	
	Diagnostics and comparison		Gessner, Kamakura, Malhotra & Zmijewski [1988]	

complementary slackness, net utility or consumer surplus, $u_j - \lambda p_j$, is greater than zero if and only if durable j is purchased.

Hauser & Urban fit the model by combining four measures of purchase intent: the reservation price of the durable, the stated probability of purchase, and two different orders of preference for the durable in a lottery. Both value per dollar and net value (assuming the consumer maximizes net utility) predict individual budget plans adequately for the majority of consumers: 60% have a correlation between predicted and actual plans of greater than 0.5 with the former and 84% for the latter.

In addition to other durable goods, benchmarks against which the new purchase might be compared include the utility of existing stock in consumer marketing [Hauser, Roberts & Urban, 1983] and the utility that purchase of the product will provide in business to business marketing (the present value of future income streams [Mansfield, 1961]). Alternatively, the utility of the category after adjusting for price may be compared to the utility of not having purchased, i.e. zero. If the net category utility exceeds zero, the product will be purchased and is said to offer a consumer surplus to the purchaser equal to its net utility. Other, related recent work has been emerging using hazard functions to model the purchase timing decision [Jain & Vilcassim, 1991].

Having specified the expected utility of not buying within the category, V_N, let us consider the determinants of the expected utility of buying within the category, V_B. This can be done in two ways. First, buying within the category can be characterized by the utility that a *typical* product would offer in terms of its anticipated attribute levels. Alternatively, consumers might estimate their expected utilities of all the brands that they would consider. From the utilities of the individual brands, they can gain an estimate of the utility of the category as a whole. For example, if a logit model were used to describe brand choice, then the expected utility of the category would be

$$V_B = E(\max(U_j)) = \ln\left(\sum_{j \in C} \exp V_j\right) \tag{8}$$

where V_j is their expected utility for the jth brand considered (in set C) [Ben-Akiva & Lerman, 1985, p. 105].

3.2.2. Specification of the error component

We considered an extreme value distribution for the error earlier. The most common alternative is to treat the error term as the sum of a large number of unobserved influences. If we can assume independence of those influences then the sum of all of these factors will tend to be normal by the central limit theorem. If we assume that $(\varepsilon_N - \varepsilon_B)$ is distributed as $N(0, \sigma^2)$ (with the corresponding assumed normality but not necessarily independence of ε_N and ε_B), then we can derive the probability of consumer i buying within the category, P_B as a function of the expected utility components, V_B and V_N:

$$P_B = \Pr((\varepsilon_N - \varepsilon_B) > V_B - V_N) \tag{9a}$$

$$= \int_{-\infty}^{V_B - V_N} 1/(\sigma\sqrt{2\pi}) \exp(-(x/\sigma)^2/2) dx. \tag{9b}$$

Equation (9b) is called the binary probit model.

3.2.3. *Other issues in binary choice*

There are a number of other binary choice models available, including the linear probability model (assuming a uniform distribution of ε) and arctan (assuming an arctan distribution) [see Ben-Akiva & Lerman, 1985]. Gessner, Kamakura, Malhotra & Zmijewski [1988] reviewed the relative performance of these and other binary choice models and suggest that in the absence of major violations to their assumptions, all of the choice models they examined (probit, logit, linear probability and two types of discriminant function) fit and predict reasonably well, giving qualitatively similar results. However, this is not the case if there are major violations to the assumptions. Gessner et al. conclude that the choice of model should be data-dependent, that there is little difference between the binary logit and probit models, and that users of these models should test for data inadequacies and transform their data where necessary to avoid them.

4. Information search

Once a consumer recognizes a need, he enters a state of heightened awareness in which he seeks more information about brands or products that could satisfy that need. Evaluation and brand choice take place based on the information resulting from this search.

Information search has two parts. The first is understanding the status of each brand during the search: Will the consumer be aware of it? Will he consider it worth searching further? The second part is how information discovered during search is incorporated into the consumer's belief structure – that is, the dynamics of evaluation beliefs as a result of new information. In practice, the consumer is likely to have prior beliefs about the alternatives that could satisfy his need. The structure of those beliefs and how they are combined to form preferences are discussed in the next section.

Thus, the basic tools for understanding information search are:

- Will awareness be obtained?
- Will aware brands be considered?
- How does the information gained during search affect beliefs?
- When does the consumer stop searching?

4.1. *Information search basics*

4.1.1. *Models of awareness*

Rossiter & Percy [1987] define awareness as 'the buyer's ability to identify (recognize or recall) the brand within the category in sufficient detail to make a purchase'. Most of the related literature links aggregate levels of awareness to levels of advertising and most models have no individual-level interpretation [see Mahajan, Muller & Sharma, 1984]. An exception is work by Blattberg & Jeuland [1981].

There are two elements of individual-level awareness models: advertising exposure and forgetting. Blattberg & Jeuland [1981] use a Bernoulli advertising exposure process and an exponential forgetting process to model awareness. The Bernoulli assumption implies that if there are n advertisements during a period, then the probability that a consumer will be exposed x times is

$$\Pr(x\,\text{exposures}) = [n!/(x!(n-x)!)]q^{x}(1-q)^{n-x} \tag{10}$$

where q is a parameter. Exponential forgetting suggests that if the last advertisement was seen by the consumer at time t_1, the probability of him remembering it (still being aware) at time t, p_t, is given by:

$$\text{p}_t = \exp\{-\alpha(t-t_1)\} \tag{11}$$

where α is a parameter (the forgetting rate).

The probability of a consumer being aware at time t, $f(t)$, may be calculated in terms of the probability of the consumer having seen the most recent advertisement (at time t_1) times the probability of not having forgotten it, plus the probability of having seen the previous advertisement (at time t_2) and not forgetting that (given that he did not see the most recent advertisement), etc. Mathematically we may write:

$$\begin{aligned} f(t) &= q\exp\{-\alpha(t-t_1)\} + q(1-q)\exp\{-\alpha(t-t_2)\} \\ &\quad + q(1-q)^2\exp\{-\alpha(t-t_3)\} + \cdots \\ &= \sum_n q(1-q)^{n-1}\exp\{-\alpha(t-t_n)\}. \end{aligned} \tag{12}$$

At the aggregate level, the interpretation of $f(t)$ is the expected proportion of the target population that is aware.

4.1.2. *Models of consideration-set formation*

Many empirical studies show that consumers do not search and evaluate (consider) all the brands of which they are aware. A key question that arises in modeling consideration is whether the process should be compensatory (in which shortcomings in one attribute may be traded off against benefits on another) or non-compensatory (in which certain thresholds exist for different attributes and the brand must meet some combination of those thresholds, irrespective of its levels of other attributes). While evidence exists for both depending on the situation, in this section we outline a basic compensatory model. Models of non-compensatory processes are described in Section 5.

If we assume that the consumer will choose from the consideration set according to the logit choice model at the purchase stage, as described in Section 6, then (using Equation (8)), we can estimate the expected utility that he or she will derive from buying within the category, given a consideration set of C, $\mathrm{E}_{B|C}$ [see, for example, Roberts & Lattin, 1991]:

$$\mathrm{E}_{B|C} = \ln\left(\sum_{j\in C} \exp(U_j)\right). \tag{13}$$

If the consumer now becomes aware of a new brand, N, with search costs c_N and utility U_N we can use Equation (13) to estimate whether or not it will be considered. It should be considered if the incremental expected benefit from the new consideration set $\mathrm{E}_{B|C\cup N}$ more than offsets the cost of search, c_N; that is, if

$$\mathrm{E}_{B|C\cup N} - \mathrm{E}_{B|C} > c_N. \tag{14}$$

Substituting the expression for expected category utility from Equation (13), and rearranging terms, we can derive the minimum utility that the brand needs to justify entry into the set, or alternatively, the maximum search costs that it can sustain to be included:

$$\mathrm{E}_{B|C\cup N} - \mathrm{E}_{B|C} > c_N \quad \text{if} \quad \ln\left(\sum_{j\in C\cup N} \exp(U_j)\right) - \ln\left(\sum_{j\in C} \exp(U_j)\right) > c_N,$$

i.e.

$$U_N > \ln\left\{\left[\sum_{k\in C} \exp(U_k)\right][\exp(c_N) - 1]\right\} \tag{15a}$$

or

$$c_N < \ln\left\{1 + \exp(U_N)\Big/\left[\sum_{k\in C} \exp(U_k)\right]\right\}. \tag{15b}$$

Equation (15b) shows that even if all brands are of equal utility ($U_k = U$), as the number of brands already considered increases, the maximum search costs that an additional brand can justify decreases.

4.1.3. Information integration

The consumer searches those brands he is aware of and which merit consideration. Basic models address how information discovered during search should be integrated into consumers' perceptions and whether more search should be conducted. The most commonly used updating procedure follows Bayes's rule. If prior beliefs about attribute k are normally distributed with mean $y_{k'}$ and variance $\sigma_{k'}^2$ and new information that is received is also distributed normally (mean $\bar{y}_k$ and variance σ_y^2) then beliefs after updating will be normally distributed with mean $y_{k''}$ and variance $\sigma_{k''}^2$ [DeGroot, 1970] where

$$y_{k''} = (\sigma_y^2 y_{k'} + \sigma_{k'}^2 \bar{y}_k)/(\sigma_y^2 + \sigma_{k'}^2) \quad \text{and} \tag{16a}$$

$$\sigma_{k''}^2 = \{\sigma_y^2/(\sigma_y^2 + \sigma_{k'}^2)\}^2 \sigma_{k'}^2 + \{\sigma_{k'}^2/(\sigma_y^2 + \sigma_{k'}^2)\}^2 \sigma_y^2$$
$$= \sigma_{k'}^2 \sigma_y^2 / \{\sigma_y^2 + \sigma_{k'}^2\}. \tag{16b}$$

The prior and sampling distributions are called a normal–normal conjugate pair [e.g. see Roberts & Urban, 1988].

4.1.4. Optimal stopping rules

Hagerty & Aaker [1984] have developed a model for information search strategies based on the sequential sampling literature that looks at the expected value of sample information (EVSI). They assume a utility-maximizing consumer who will choose the piece of information with the greatest difference between the expected value of the information to search next and the information processing cost. This approach builds on the economics of information literature developed by Stigler [1961] and applied in marketing by Shugan [1980].

To illustrate how the expected value of the sample information (EVSI) is calculated, assume that the consumer is currently considering three brands, 1, 2 and 3, ordered in terms of decreasing expected utility, $E(U_j)$. There is some uncertainty associated with each brand j, σ_j^2. If the distribution of beliefs about the utility of each brand is distributed normally, and if the consumer does not gather any more information, he will choose brand 1, since it has the highest expected utility. To estimate the value of additional search of brand 1 consider the expected utility of brand 1, after the new information has been gathered.

Search will only change the consumer's choice and thus alter the utility that he realizes if, based on the new information, brand 1 has an updated expected utility, m, of less than $E(U_2)$. In that case the expected utility that would be forgone by not undertaking the search is $E(U_2) - m$. What search enables the consumer to do is to reduce the chances of incurring that loss by giving him a better fix on the true value of $E(U_1)$. The expected value of search (EVSI) is $E(U_2) - m$ integrated over the probability distribution of different values of m, $p(m)$, from $-\infty$ to $E(U_2)$:

$$\text{EVSI} = \int_{-\infty}^{E(U_2)} (E(U_2) - m) p(m) \mathrm{d}m. \tag{17}$$

Since prior beliefs are normally distributed, if we assume that new information is normally distributed, the posterior mean (the utility of brand 1 after updating,

m) will also be normally distributed, with variance σ_m^2. From this, Hagerty & Aaker show that in the multibrand case the expected value of sample information from *searching brand* j may be rewritten:

$$\mathrm{EVSI} = \sigma_m \Phi(\delta_y/\sigma_m) \tag{18}$$

where

$$\delta_y = \begin{cases} \mathrm{E}(U_1) - \mathrm{E}(U_j) & \text{for } j \neq 1, \\ \mathrm{E}(U_1) - \mathrm{E}(U_2) & \text{for } j = 1, \end{cases}$$

Φ = the integral of the standard normal distribution.

The extension of this formula to searching all brands is analogous to Equation (18). The problem the consumer faces in deciding which piece of information, y, to process at time t then becomes:

$$\begin{array}{ll} \text{maximum} & \mathrm{EVSI}_t^y - c^y \\ \text{subject to} & \mathrm{EVSI}_t^y - c^y > D \geqslant 0. \end{array} \tag{19}$$

That is, the consumer must maximize the value of the next piece of information minus processing costs as long as the search has a value of greater than D, a threshold below which it is not worth the effort of searching.

4.2. Information search models: extensions and applications

Table 2.3 outlines some key extensions and applications of information search models.

4.2.1. Awareness

Leckenby & Kishi [1984] derive the Dirichlet multinomial distribution (DMD) to model the proportion of the population that will be exposed to $1, 2, 3, \ldots, mn$ of the n insertions in each of m media vehicles. Their model comes from the assumption that exposure to the mn advertisements for any individual consumer is multinomial, while individuals' parameters are distributed Dirichlet across the population. Leckenby & Kishi find superior performance of this model (estimated using a variety of algorithms) over other similar models.

4.2.2. Consideration-set formation

In an alternative approach to modeling consideration-set composition, Hauser & Wernerfelt [1990] assume a probit model at the choice stage rather than logit. They distinguish between the cost of search and the cost of evaluating and deciding between brands. They show that low-search-cost brands are more likely to be considered.

Large consideration sets for individual consumers are associated with lower search and evaluation costs and a higher variance of brands' utilities across

Table 2.3
Information search models: extensions and applications.

Issues addressed	Model	Data	Illustrative literature	Comments/application
Awareness creation:				
Dynamics of awareness	Bernoulli exposure and exponential forgetting	Advertising levels Awareness or sales at an individual or aggregate level	Blattberg & Jeuland [1981]	Fitted at aggregate level
Variety of advertising media	Dirichlet exposure	Advertising schedule	Leckenby & Kishi [1984]	Fitted at aggregate level
Consideration-set formation:				
Consideration-set membership	Cost-benefit inclusion: probit choice	Consideration, utility	Hauser & Wernerfelt [1990]	Aggregate testing
Consideration-set formation and size	Cost-benefit inclusion: logit choice	Consideration, utility, perceptions	Roberts & Lattin [1991]	Existing brands and new concepts
Fuzzy consideration sets	Probabilistic consideration	Probability of consideration, choice	Fotheringham [1988]	No empirical testing
Information integration:				
Information search	Hedonic pricing	Market attributes and prices	Ratchford [1982]	Benefits of search
	Expected value of sample information	Attribute importances and search behavior	Hagerty & Aaker [1984]	Optimal search patterns
Information integration	Linear updating Bayesian updating	Prior beliefs and uncertainties Posterior beliefs and uncertainties Strength and value of word-of-mouth	Meyer & Sathi [1985] Roberts & Urban [1988] Oren & Schwartz [1988]	Linear updating Normal conjugate pairs Beta binomial pairs
Overview	Review of awareness models		Mahajan, Muller & Sharma [1984]	Emphasis on aggregate models

consumption occasions. To establish the market-level implications of consideration, Hauser & Wernerfelt concentrate on testing their model at the aggregate level. They show that observed distributions of consideration-set sizes, order-of-entry effects, asymmetric advertising effects, and level of promotional activity in a number of packaged goods markets are consistent with their model.

In addition to industrial and consumer products, the concept of consideration has also been applied to the selection of retail outlets. Fotheringham [1988] suggests that consideration sets are not dichotomous, but rather are fuzzy sets (whether because consideration is not a discrete process to consumers or because as researchers we are not capable of measuring it). Thus he suggests that brands will be taken into the evaluation and choice phase only with some probability. For the problem of retail choice he makes that probability a function of the closeness of other stores in the awareness set. If closeness leads to a positive effect on the probability, he terms this an agglomeration effect. If it decreases the probability, he calls that a competitive effect.

Application of consideration models has increased in recent years, both for durables and packaged goods. It is important to note that the consideration set is dynamic and if consideration sets are calibrated well before the consumer enters the need-arousal stage, then the results may not be good indicators of later behavior [Day & Deutscher, 1982].

4.2.3. Information search and integration

Updated perceptions are generally a weighted average of consumers' beliefs and the sample information discovered [e.g. Meyer & Sathi, 1985]. Bayes rule, outlined in Equations (16a) and (16b) is the most common form of weighting. In addition to the normal–normal conjugate pairs illustrated there, other conjugate pairs of distributions include the beta–Bernoulli [e.g. see Oren & Schwartz, 1988], gamma–Poisson and exponential. Studies testing the predictive performance of Bayesian updating in consumer decision processes have had mixed findings [see Roberts & Urban, 1988, for a review]. However, in the absence of an obvious alternative contender, Bayes's rule has had considerable popularity in dynamic beliefs updating models.

5. Evaluation

Our taxonomy considers product evaluations as involving two processes: product perceptions and the relationship of those perceptions to preferences.

5.1. Perceptual measurement basics

Beliefs about products (perceptions) can be measured directly by asking consumers how much of a feature they perceive a certain product to contain, or they can be inferred, by asking consumers how similar certain products are and then inferring what discriminates between different products.

The two analytical approaches most frequently used to derive evaluation criteria and build perceptual maps are decompositional methods, based on multidimensional scaling (MDS), and compositional methods, based on factor analysis (FA). MDS procedures infer dimensions that discriminate between consumers' evaluations of different products based on brand interrelationships, while FA methods take explicit attribute data and distill them into underlying dimensions or factors.

5.1.1. Multidimensional scaling (MDS)

MDS is a set of procedures in which a reduced space depicting product alternatives reflects perceived similarities and dissimilarities between products by the interproduct distances. Different types of multidimensional scaling may be distinguished on the basis of the type of data input to the model, the number of dimensions on which the data are collected (modes), and the geometric model used to analyze the data (see DeSarbo, Manrai & Manrai (Chapter 5) and Lilien, Kotler & Moorthy [1992]). Nonmetric multidimensional scaling techniques are applied where similarities have ordinal scaling while metric methods are used with interval-scaled data.

The idea behind MDS is to create a map representing the product stimuli or consumer preferences. The objective is to have the interproduct distances in the map have the same rank order as the direct similarity judgments of products or preferences.

Let δ_{ij} denote the perceived dissimilarity between product alternatives i and j, which can either be obtained directly or be derived from distances using attribute rating scales. Then, with MDS, we find a configuration of points (the product alternatives) in a space of lowest dimensionality such that the ranking of interpoint distances d_{ij} is as close as possible to the ranking of the original dissimilarities δ_{ij}. This result is a monotonic relationship between the d_{ij}'s and the δ_{ij}'s. To reach this objective, MDS algorithms minimize a quantity called stress:

$$\text{Stress} = \left[\sum_{i<j} (\hat{d}_{ij} - d_{ij})^2 \Big/ \sum_{i<j} d_{ij}^2 \right]^{1/2} \tag{20}$$

where $\hat{d}_{ij}$ is a distance as close as possible to the d_{ij} but is monotonic with the original dissimilarities δ_{ij}.

For a given dimensionality the configuration retained is the one that minimizes the stress function. The resultant map shows the relationship between the various products in the market. It may be arbitrarily reflected or rotated to aid interpretability.

This concept may be extended to incorporate both products and preferences on the same map, called a joint space. The process of deriving these two joint spaces is called *unfolding*.

There are also a number of other ways in which joint spaces can be presented. Brands can be represented as points, while respondents' preferences may be represented as vectors. This is called a *projection model* and is more appropriate when the dimensions are monotonically increasing in preference ('more is better' for each dimension). An individual's preference for brands can be obtained by projecting the brand onto the individual's ideal vector. (For a typical application see Moore & Winer [1987].)

Issues that must be considered with multidimensional scaling include the number of products needed, the determination of the dimensions, and the validity of the process. Green & Wind [1973] suggest that the number of dimensions should be less than one-third of the number of products. In practice, the consideration-set size provides an upper bound on the number of brands that can be evaluated. The stress measure can help determine the number of dimensions while the naming of the dimensions can be aided by examining their correlation with brand attribute ratings (if available). Tests of the reliability and validity of MDS have produced encouraging results and the methods are reasonably robust with respect to measurement error.

5.1.2. Factor analysis

Factor analysis was originally developed in connection with efforts to identify the major factors making up human intelligence. Since then, it has been applied to many other problems and is a frequently used technique in performing product-evaluation analyses in marketing.

The basic factor analysis model assumes that original perceptual ratings about a product are generated by a small number of latent variables, or factors, and that the variance observed in each original perceptual variable is accounted for partly by a set of common factors and partly by a factor specific to that variable. The common factors account for the correlations observed among the original variables. This model can be written as

$$x_{ijk} = a_{k1}F_{ij1} + \cdots + a_{kR}F_{ijR} + d_k y_{ijk} + \varepsilon_{ijk} \tag{21}$$

where

R = number of factors common to all items,
x_{ijk} = person i's rating of product j on attribute k,
a_{k1} = effect of common factor 1 on attribute k (called a loading),
F_{ij1} = person i's score of product j on factor 1,
d_k = weight of unique factor y,
y_{ijk} = unique factor of product j on item k for person i,
ε_{ijk} = error term.

Thus, in common-factor analysis, the perceptual model has each observed variable being described in terms of a set of R ($R < k$) common factors plus a factor unique to the original observed variable. Generally, the original items are standardized so that certain relationships hold:

The *loadings* $\{a_{kr}\}$ represent the correlation, ρ, between (hypothetical) factor r and the variable k, and a_{kr}^2 represents the fraction of variance in variable k accounted for by factor r:

$$\rho(F_r, x_k) = a_{kr}. \tag{22}$$

Table 2.4
Perceptual mapping models: extensions and applications

Issues addressed	Model	Data	Illustrative literature	Comments/application
Attribute perceptions:	**Factor analysis:**			
Summarizing perceptions	Principal components	Attribute perceptions	Hauser & Shugan [1980]	Telecommunications services
Modeling error in perceptual measurement	Probabilistic interpretation of model	Attribute perceptions and preference probability	Bechtel [1985]	Soft drinks
Testing hypothesized relations between variables	Confirmatory factor analysis	Multiple measures of factors	Bagozzi [1977]	
Dissimilarities:	**Multidimensional scaling:**			
Product comparisons	Single-mode MDS	Similarity judgments	Lehmann [1971]	Soft drinks
Product and preference comparisons	Two-mode MDS	Preference judgments	Green & Rao [1972]	Breakfast choices
Uncertain judgments	Probabilistic interpretation	Preference, degree of preference of concepts	MacKay & Zinnes [1986]	Housing market
Asymmetric brand effects	Asymmetric MDS	Switching data	Harshman, Green, Wind & Lundy [1982]	Car purchase
Alternative data sources:	Logit choice	Choice data	Elrod [1988] DeSarbo & Hoffman [1987] Katahira [1990]	Coffee panel data Telecommunication equipment Car market

Understanding positioning and its effect on share	Regression sales response MDS in time series analysis	Sales panel data and marketing mix	Moore & Winer [1987]	
Other attribute-based perceptual mapping methods:				
Analyzing the categories in terms of positioning	Correspondence analysis	Categorical data	Hoffman & Franke [1986]	Soft drinks
			Carroll & Green [1988]	Car purchase
Understanding the class products belong to	Multiple discriminant analysis	Attribute data and categorical classification	Albaum & Hawkins [1983]	Geographic mobility
Overview and comparison:				
Comparison of MDS approaches			Cooper [1983]	
Comparison of factor analysis approaches			Mukherjee [1973]	
Comparison of factor analysis and MDS			Hauser & Koppelman [1979]	
			Huber & Holbrook [1979]	

The *communality* h_k^2 expresses the percentage of the variance in variable k accounted for by the R common factors:

$$h_k^2 = \sum_r a_{kr}^2. \tag{23}$$

The *eigenvalue* λ_r represents the contribution of each factor to the total variance in the original variables:

$$\lambda_r = \sum_k a_{kr}^2. \tag{24}$$

In a specific application it is not uncommon to extract a small number of factors that account for the major part of the total variance.

Another useful aspect of factor analysis is the construction of a perceptual map – the matrix of factor scores – that describes the factor scores as a linear function of the original ratings:

$$F_{ijr} = b_{r1}x_{ij1} + \cdots + b_{rK}x_{ijK} + \text{error}, \quad r = 1, \ldots, R \text{ for each individual } i. \tag{25}$$

The perceived position of product j is usually constructed by averaging the F_{ijr} over the respondents, i.

An alternative form to common-factor analysis is principal-components factor analysis. Principal-components factor analysis is the same as that expressed in Equation (21) with the exception that the unique factors, y_{ijk}, are omitted. All the variation between the ratings of stimuli are attributed to the underlying factors (F_{ijr}). Studies comparing principal-components and common-factor analysis generally find similar results. For an example of the application of factor analysis in marketing see Hauser & Shugan [1980].

Both the number and the names of factors are important issues in performing a factor analysis. The number of factors used is often chosen based on the magnitude of the eigenvalue of the last factor chosen and the interpretability of the solution. An examination of factor loadings, supplemented by market knowledge, generally leads to reasonable names or interpretations for factors.

5.2. Perceptual mapping: extensions and applications

Table 2.4 outlines some key extensions and applications of perceptual mapping.

The form of common-factor analysis we discussed above is called exploratory factor analysis. It places no constraints on which variables load on the various factors and assumes that all unique factors are independent. In *confirmatory factor analysis* the researcher imposes constraints motivated by theory as to which common factors are correlated, which observed variables affect which factors, and which pairs of unique factors are correlated.

Thus, if we represent the relationship between the variables that we observe (x's) and the underlying common factors (ξ's) and unique factors (δ's) in Figure 2.1, then the relationship between ξ_1 and ξ_2 would not have been permitted in exploratory factor analysis and all the relationships between the factors (ξ) and observed variables (x) would have had to be included.

In confirmatory factor analysis we can constrain some of the a_{kr}'s in Equation (21) to zero or some other value and test that assumption; we can also allow the unique factors $\{y_{li}\}$ to be correlated. If we assume that the common and unique factors are normally distributed, then we can test hypotheses concerning the appropriateness of alternative structures. Confirmatory factor analysis provides a unique maximum-likelihood estimate of a predetermined structure and also provides a chi-square statistic to test the number of factors necessary to account for the correlation matrix. The seminal work in this area was developed by Jöreskog & Sörbom [1979]. An excellent source for the fundamentals of the approach is Long [1983].

A number of studies have compared the application and performance of multidimensional scaling and factor-analytic methods of building perceptual maps. Shocker & Srinivasan [1979] provide a detailed review of the use of these techniques in new product development and concept evaluation. In comparing the performance of factor analysis with multidimensional scaling, Hauser & Koppelman [1979] conclude that factor analysis is superior from the standpoints of predictive ability, interpretability, and ease of use. However, the difference in nature between the two techniques will lead to differences in the prevalence of their application. In markets that are relatively new and in which the cognitive structure of consumers is not well understood or well developed, multidimensional scaling on dissimilarity data might be preferred because it makes fewer assumptions about the criteria on

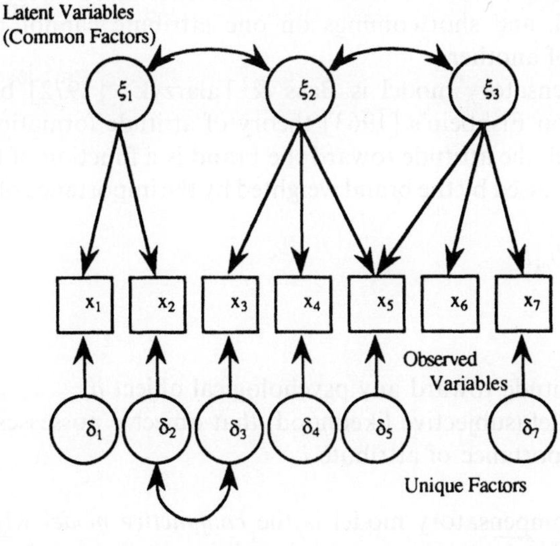

Fig. 2.1. Example of a confirmatory factor analysis model. (Source: Long [1983, p. 14].)

which consumers will evaluate products. Where there is a solid, historical structure for the product category, factor analysis may be preferred since it will add diagnostic richness on which attributes are causing the positioning of products on the perceptual map. In the absence of a well-developed theory of the formation of evaluation criteria, the researcher might well be advised to perform both analyses in search of a convergent picture of the market.

Several other methods have been applied to modeling perceptual spaces, particularly multiple discriminant analysis and correspondence analysis. Multiple discriminant analysis (MDA) is a method of determining which variables explain the groups to which different stimuli belong [Albaum & Hawkins, 1983]. Correspondence analysis is a method that summarizes both the rows and columns of categorical data in a lower-dimensional space (e.g. what are the underlying types of brands in the category and what are the factor dimensions underlying product attributes?). The flexibility of data format is achieved at a cost of not being able to interpret interpoint distances [see Hoffman & Franke, 1986].

5.3. *Preference-formation basics*

The previous section dealt with *perceptions* – what we believe about products. Here we deal with attitudes and preferences – how favorably disposed we feel toward those same products.

Most models of preference formation transform or map consumer judgments on product attributes to a scalar attitude or preference measure.

Basic models of attitude formation are either *compensatory* or *non-compensatory*. In a compensatory model, the weakness of a brand or product on one dimension can be compensated for by strength on another, and those strengths or weaknesses are combined to determine an attitude toward the brand. In non-compensatory models, usually only a small number of attributes (two or three, say) are used to evaluate a brand, and shortcomings on one attribute cannot be overcome by favorable levels of another.

A basic compensatory model is Bass & Talarzyk's [1972] belief-importance model, building on Fishbein's [1963] theory of attitude formation. In the belief-importance model, the attitude toward the brand is a function of the beliefs about the attributes possessed by the brand weighted by the importance of each attribute:

$$A_o = \sum_i b_{oi} I_i \tag{26}$$

where

A_o = attitude toward any psychological object o,
b_{oi} = belief (subjective likelihood) that object o possesses attribute i,
I_i = importance of attribute i.

A basic non-compensatory model is the *conjunctive model* where a consumer considers a brand only if it meets certain minimum, acceptable standards on all of a number of key dimensions. If any one attribute is deficient, the product is eliminated from consideration.

Let

y_{jk} = perceived level of (key) attribute k in brand j,
T_{jk} = minimum threshold level that is acceptable (negatively valued attributes such as price that have a maximum level can be multiplied by -1),

$$\delta_{jk} = \begin{cases} 1 & \text{if brand } j \text{ is acceptable on attribute } k, \\ 0 & \text{otherwise,} \end{cases}$$

$$A_j = \begin{cases} 1 & \text{if it is a preferred brand overall,} \\ 0 & \text{otherwise.} \end{cases}$$

Under the conjunctive model we have:

$$\delta_{jk} = \begin{cases} 1 & \text{if } y_{jk} \geqslant T_{jk}, \\ 0 & \text{if } y_{jk} < T_{jk}, \end{cases} \quad \text{and} \quad A_j = \prod_k \delta_{jk}. \tag{27}$$

Thus, A_j will be non-zero if and only if $y_{jk} \geqslant T_{jk}$ for all (key) attributes.

5.4. *Product preference models: extensions and applications*

Extensions of preference models include compensatory models, structural equation models, utility-theory-based models and non-compensatory models (Table 2.5).

5.4.1. *Compensatory models*

A variety of methods have been advanced for imputing the relative importances of attributes by relating brand preferences to the amount of each attribute that these preferred brands contained. These methods include multiple regression, linear programming, and monotonic analysis of variance. For a review of data-collection techniques and associated estimation methods see Shocker & Srinivasan [1979], Green & Srinivasan [1978], or Horsky & Rao [1984].

Fishbein and others reassessed his original 1963 model to make it more relevant to marketing [Fishbein & Ajzen, 1975], as the extended Fishbein model. The most widely known extension has others, apart from the person making the purchase, influencing the decision in some decision circumstances. In particular,

$$\mathrm{BI} = \sum_i a_i b_i + \sum_j \mathrm{SNB}_j \mathrm{MC}_j \tag{28}$$

where

BI = behavioral intent,
SNB_j = social normative belief, which relates what an individual considers is expected of him or her by an external social group on scale j,

Table 2.5
Preference models: extensions and applications

Issues addressed	Model	Data	Illustrative literature	Comments/application
Preference as a compensatory function of perceptions:	**Compensatory models:**			
Preference in terms of expected outcomes	Behavioral intention	Intention, outcome values Likelihood of outcomes	Burnkrant & Page [1982]	Blood donations
Incorporating the effect of others' beliefs	Extended Fishbein	As above plus social normative beliefs	Bearden & Etzel [1982]	Various products
Decreasing utility returns to scale	Ideal-point model	Preference and attribute perceptions	Lehmann [1971]	TV viewing
Theoretical relationships between constructs	Structural equation modeling	Attributes, attitude, behavior	Bagozzi [1982]	Blood donations
Non-additive utilities and risk-aversion	Non-linear utility models: Utility theory and decision analysis	Utility of attribute mixes	Keeney & Raiffa [1976] Farquhar [1984] Hauser & Urban [1979]	 Health Plans
Non-compensatory preference functions:				
Series of necessary criteria	Conjunctive	Attribute data	Gensch [1987a]	Fertilizer for farmers
Hierarchy of importance of attributes	Lexicographic	Acceptability or preference	Gensch [1987b]	Industrial insulators
Multiphase processing	Phased decision rules		Wright & Barbour [1977]	
Overview/comparison:				
Comparison of compensatory and non-compensatory rules			Johnson & Meyer [1984] Johnson, Meyer & Ghosh [1989]	 Apartment choice

MC_j = motivation to comply with these expectations,
a_i = evaluation (goodness or badness) of attribute i,
b_i = belief that object possesses attribute i.

The extended Fishbein model has generally been shown to perform better than the original model, particularly for goods that were publicly consumed rather than privately, and for goods that were more luxuries than necessities [Bearden & Etzel, 1982]. In addition, Wilson, Matthews & Harvey [1975] and others found that attitudes toward the purchase of a brand and behavioral intention were more closely related to behavior than were attitudes toward the brand itself. (Thus, it may be more relevant to ask consumers whether their teeth will get white if they use Ultra Brite than to ask whether they think Ultra Brite whitens teeth.)

An offshoot of the belief/importance model, the ideal-point model, requires a consumer's rating of an ideal brand along with his or her ratings of the actual brands being analyzed (although ideal levels of attributes can be imputed in the same way that importance weights are estimated).

Example: Lehmann [1971] models television-show choice as follows:

$$A_o = \sum_i V_i |B_{io} - I_i|^k \tag{29}$$

where

A_o = overall attitude (preference for a TV show),
V_i = weight attached to TV-show characteristic i (action, suspense, humor, etc.),
B_{io} = belief about show on dimension i,
I_i = ideal position on dimension i,
k = distance metric.

This model is substantially better at predicting behavior than models based on demographic variables. Attributes should be included in an ideal-point form if, beyond some level (the ideal point), there are negative utility returns for further increases in the attribute. With the width of a car, for example, any rational consumer will find some widths too wide and others not wide enough, implying an ideal level between those extremes. With miles per gallon, however, for most consumers it is likely to be the more the better if all other attributes stay the same, so a belief-importance (or vector) formulation would be more appropriate.

5.4.2. Structural modeling of preferences

Factor analysis can be used in a confirmatory way, as well as to explore the relationship between different measures of a number of variables and their underlying constructs. This framework can be extended to test the relationships between the resultant structures. In the models we have seen in this section so far, there is one measure of attitude or preference and we have attempted to understand it in terms of underlying product attributes. In structural equation modeling there are several physical and/or psychological states and we test the relationship between them and a number of external factors [Bagozzi, 1980].

Thus, a structural equation model may be:

$$y_{ij} = \alpha_i + \sum_l \beta_{il} y_{lj} + \sum_k \gamma_{ik} x_{kj} \tag{30}$$

where

y_{ij} = consumer's response on construct i for product j,
x_{kj} = level of attribute k for product j,
α_i, β_{il} and γ_{ik} = parameters.

5.4.3. *Incorporating uncertainty*

The models of this section have assumed that we have multiple criteria of varying importance and that we wish to combine them into an overall value or preference function. In the literature on decision theory all these functions would be called 'value functions'. They map a set of attributes, known with certainty, into a function called 'value'. But there are dangers with this simplified approach. What about a new product? Is it reasonable to use the same model to predict choice when the attributes of some products are known with more certainty than those of others?

The specific form of the value function in Equation (26) assumes constant variations in value for each given level of change in the level of a specific attribute. It also assumes that the value of a change in the level of an attribute is independent of the levels of the other attributes. We may require more general value functions if these assumptions are violated. Utility theory and the direct assessment of a utility function across attributes are useful both for testing these assumptions and for developing appropriate models when the assumptions are violated. Utility theory is also useful for understanding how consumers adjust their valuation of alternatives in the presence of uncertainty [see Keeney & Raiffa, 1976].

Hauser & Urban [1979] report an application of utility theory in marketing. They present potential customers for health plans with choices between a moderately attractive plan in which the level of the attributes is known with certainty and an alternative plan in which one of the attributes could be very good or very poor. They estimate consumers' attitudes toward uncertainty by asking consumers how high the probability of the attribute being 'very good' would have to be for the consumers to choose the uncertain plan. For other applications of utility theory see Currim & Sarin [1984] and Eliashberg [1980]. Eliashberg & Hauser [1985] provide an error theory that allows hypothesis testing for utility models under certain distributional assumptions.

5.4.4. *Other non-compensatory models*

In a *disjunctive model*, instead of preferred brands having to satisfy *all* of a number of criteria (as in a conjunctive model), they have to satisfy any one of a number of criteria. Under the conjunctive model, the consumer may insist on a computer that has lots of memory *and* software. Under the disjunctive model the consumer may settle for a computer with either a lot of memory *or* a lot of software [Choffray & Lilien, 1980].

Mathematically we can express this as:

$$A_j = \min\left(\sum_k \delta_{jk}, 1\right) \tag{31}$$

where A_j and δ_{jk} are defined as in Equation (27).

It may well be that neither the conjunctive nor the disjunctive rules will give a single preferred brand; either may yield zero or more than one brand, leading to a need for further rules. A *lexicographic model* assumes that all attributes are used, but in a stepwise manner. Brands are evaluated on the most important attribute first; then a second attribute is used only if there are ties; and so forth. Mathematically, if we assume that the attributes are arranged in order from most important to least important, then brand j is preferred to brand m if:

$$y_{1j} > y_{1m} \tag{32}$$

or

$$y_{ij} = y_{im} \quad \text{for } i = 1, \ldots, I \quad \text{and} \quad y_{I+1,j} > y_{I+1,m}$$

for $I <$ number of attributes.

A number of other non-compensatory models have been used: see Bettman [1979] for a more detailed discussion of these and other models.

In general, non-compensatory models require individuals to process information by attribute across brands, while compensatory models require consumers to process information within brand across attributes. Since evaluations are simpler and faster in non-compensatory models, it is likely that they are better representations of decision processes for low-involvement goods or for the screening phase when there are many brands, while compensatory models more accurately describe brand evaluations for high-involvement products in more complex decision-making settings (see Bettman [1979] for a review of the supporting empirical literature). A third alternative is where both types of rules are used in sequence, called a *phased-decision rule* [Wright & Barbour, 1977].

6. Purchase

We do not assume that the consumer will always purchase his or her most preferred brand because of measurement error as well as because of variables such as coupons and deals that intervene between the time of measurement of preferences and purchase. Thus, models of purchase have been developed to relate product preferences to purchase probabilities.

6.1. Purchase model basics

In Section 3 on need arousal, we reviewed binary choice models. When there are three or more possibilities, an additional complexity emerges: how does the choice set affect the probability of choice? A seemingly reasonable assumption, referred to as *Luce's axiom* or the *independence of irrelevant alternatives* (IIA) states that the ratio of choice probabilities of any two products does not change when the consideration set changes as long as both of those products are in that set.

Formally, let

$\Pr(a|C)$ = probability of choosing product a when the choice set is C,
C' = some set of products that includes C as a subset.

Further, let both a and b be products in consideration set C (and, hence, C'). Then the IIA assumption states:

$$\frac{\Pr(a|C)}{\Pr(b|C)} = \frac{\Pr(a|C')}{\Pr(b|C')} \tag{33}$$

(assuming all denominators are non-zero and that the probability measures are all developed similarly).

Luce [1959] proves that if the above choice axiom holds and if a utility measure, X, exists that is strictly proportional to the choice probabilities (i.e. $X(a,b) = \Pr(a|C)/\Pr(b|C) = X(a)/X(b)$), then

$$\Pr(a|C) = \frac{X(a)}{\sum_{j \in C} X(j)}. \tag{34}$$

If $X(j) = \exp(bV_j)$, then Equation (34) reduces to the multinomial logit model, the multivariate extension of Equation (7a). Alternatively, the multinomial logit model can be derived directly from a set of assumptions analogous to those for the binary logit model, with the key assumption being that the error terms have mutually independent, identical extreme-value distributions.

The IIA assumption is violated when some products being considered are more similar than others. For example, if a consumer is thirsty, he may choose to have a beer or a soft drink. Considering an additional soft drink is likely to have little impact on the 'beer vs soft drink' decision, but will have a major impact on which soft drink, conditional on a soft drink being selected. We will see that violations of the IIA assumption have been handled by grouping products into similar categories (hierarchical models), grouping consumers into homogeneous clusters (segmentation), and modeling departures from IIA explicitly.

Hierarchical models of choice have been developed to address a sequential type of choice process. To illustrate, consider a consumer's choice process for deodorants, using the decision hierarchy illustrated in Figure 2.2. The consumer

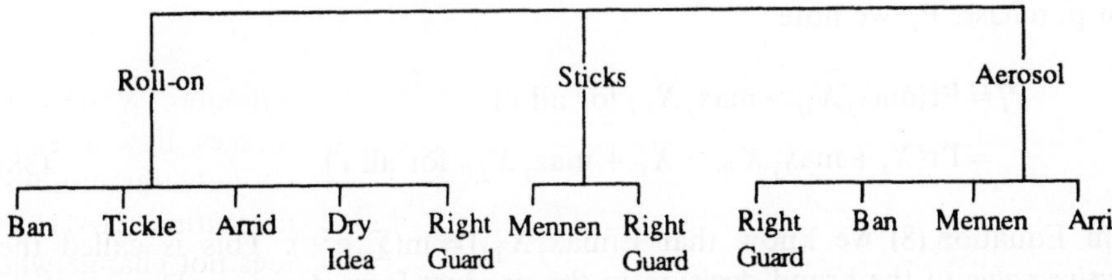

Fig. 2.2. Consumer decision hierarchy for deodorant purchase. (Source: Urban & Hauser [1980, p. 92].)

chooses the form of deodorant and then, conditional on that choice, selects a specific brand. We model the choice of product form and the choice of brand within form separately.

A commonly applied hierarchical model is the *nested logit model*. Algebraically we may write:

$$P_{ij} = P_{j|i} P_i \tag{35}$$

where

P_{ij} = probability of choosing brand j and product form i,
P_i = unconditional probability of choosing product form i,
$P_{j|i}$ = probability of choosing brand j, given product form i.

We assume that utility is separable, as follows:

$$X_{ij} = X_i + X_{j|i} \tag{36}$$

where

X_{ij} = utility from choosing product form i and brand j,
X_i = utility associated with product form i,
$X_{j|i}$ = unique utility of brand j (in product form i).

Brand choice, the bottom level of the hierarchy in Figure 2.2, can be estimated with a multinomial logit model, as before, because it is assumed to satisfy the IIA axiom:

$$P_{j|i} = e^{X_{j|i}} \Big/ \left\{ \sum_k e^{X_{k|i}} \right\} \tag{37}$$

The product-form decision may also be modeled using a logit model as long as the error is double exponential and independent of the error at the brand-choice stage. To gain some intuition about the equation for the probability of product-form purchase, P_i, we note:

$$P_i = \Pr(\max_j X_{ij} > \max_j X_{i'j} \text{ for all } i') = \Pr(X_i + \max_j X_{j|i} > X_{i'} + \max_j X_{j|i'} \text{ for all } i'). \quad (38)$$

From Equation (8) we know that $E(\max_j X_{j|i}) = \ln(\sum_j e^{X_{j|i}})$. This is called the *inclusive value* of the brand decision in the product-form decision. The equation for the product-form probabilities is given by:

$$P_i = \exp\left\{\mu\left\{X_i + \ln\left(\sum_j \exp X_{j|i}\right)\right\}\right\} \bigg/ \sum_{i'} \exp\left\{\mu\left\{X_{i'} + \ln\left(\sum_j \exp X_{j|i'}\right)\right\}\right\} \quad (39)$$

where μ is normalizing constant.

Note that the individual brand utilities also affect the decision at the product-form level through the inclusive value. Substituting (37) and (39) in (35) yields the nested logit model.

6.2. *Purchase models: extensions and applications*

Most extensions to these choice-modeling basics have addressed the issues of estimation, of solving the IIA problem and have considered other alternatives for the error term (Figure 2.6).

The important weights in logit models can be derived using a variety of different estimation algorithms. In a review of estimation techniques, Bunch & Batsell [1989] advocate the use of maximum-likelihood procedures. The weights are often called revealed importances because they are revealed by an analysis of choice behavior rather than from direct measurement. They are interpreted in much the same way as regression coefficients. In most computer packages the statistical significance of each importance weight is determined through a t-test based on asymptotic values of the standard errors of the estimates. Chapman & Staelin [1982] suggest a procedure that exploits the information content of the complete rank-order choice set.

For marketing applications of the logit model, see Gensch & Recker [1979], Punj & Staelin [1978] and Guadagni & Little [1983]. For more detailed discussion, see McFadden [1976, 1980, 1991].

Louviere & Hensher [1983] and Louviere & Woodworth [1983] provide examples of how the logit model can be combined with experimental design to evaluate hypothetical new product concepts and establish the importance weights of product attributes.

Most applications of the logit model pool data from respondents rather than estimating the model separately for each, in order to obtain sufficient degrees of freedom for the estimation process. Any heterogeneity of consumer tastes can add to the IIA problem because individual customers will have similar brands in their

Table 2.6
Purchase models: extensions and applications

Issues addressed	Model	Data	Illustrative literature	Comments/application
Choice probability in terms of brand utility:	Luce choice model	Utilities and probability of choice	Green, Goldberg & Montemayor [1981]	Career choice
A choice transformation based on specific error theories	Logit choice model	Attribute perceptions and probability of choice	Gensch & Recker [1979]	Store choice
			Guadagni & Little [1983]	Coffee brands
Evaluating new product concepts using experimental designs	Logit choice model	Choice from sets of concept descriptions	Louviere & Woodworth [1983]	Various product categories
Solutions to the independence of irrelevant alternatives problem:				
(a) Creating homogeneous product sets (hierarchical choice models)	Nested logit	Attribute perceptions	Dubin [1986]	Heating
		Choice, product class structure		
(b) Creating homogeneous consumer sets	Segmentation models	Attribute perceptions	Gensch [1987a]	Fertilizers
		Choice, knowledge levels		
(c) Explicitly modeling product interdependence:				
Multiplicative competitive interaction	Luce model of product interactions	Attributes and product choice	Cooper & Nakanishi [1983]	Various products
Logit modeling of product interactions	Generalized logit	Choice from constrained sets	Batsell & Polking [1985]	Snacks
		Attribute perceptions choice, product-class structure	Dalal & Klein [1988]	
Normal error theory	Probit	Attributes, choice, perceptual similarity	Currim [1982]	Commuter transport
		Preference ranking	Kamakura & Srivastava [1986]	Distribution of ideal points
Overview and reviews			Corstjens & Gautschi [1983]	
			McFadden [1986]	

consideration sets. One way to overcome this source of violation of IIA is to segment the population into homogeneous groups and then estimate a separate model for each segment. Gensch [1984, 1985, 1987a] calls these models estimated at the segment level *disaggregate choice models.* He shows that a priori segmentation, in one case on the basis of knowledgeability and in another on the basis of strength of preferences, improved forecasts and yielded a much richer set of management implications.

Bechtel [1990] shows how the nested multinomial logit model can be estimated when individual-level choice data are not available, but only market-share data in each period. For a more comprehensive development of the nested logit see Ben-Akiva & Lerman [1985]. For applications in marketing, see Dubin [1986] or the Guadagni & Little [1987] example later in this chapter.

In the nested logit model, the decision of whether to buy a specific alternative is made once, at the bottom of the decision hierarchy. In contrast, there are a number of other hierarchical decision models in which the brand is evaluated a number of times on different criteria. Brands in the consideration or choice set are successively discarded until a final choice is made. Models of this type include Tversky's [1972] elimination by aspects model, Hauser's [1986] agenda theory, and Manrai & Sinha's [1989] elimination by cutoffs. These models, while hierarchical choice models, concentrate more on the attribute processing method by which choice occurs than on the structure of the market.

Ensuring that populations are homogeneous and ensuring that products are relatively homogeneous can alleviate problems that the IIA property of the logit model introduces. A further method of addressing those problems is to explicitly model brand interactions. For example, Batsell & Polking [1985] empirically estimate these interactions. Starting with doubles of products $\{i, j\}$ they move on to examine choice probabilities of triples $\{i, j, k\}$, quadruples $\{i, j, k, l\}$, etc. If the ratio of the probability of choosing brand i to brand j is not the same in the triple $\{i, j, k\}$ as it is in the double $\{i, j\}$ then IIA is violated for this triple and a first-order interaction term is included in the model. Similarly, if the ratio of the probability of choosing brand i to brand j is not the same in the quadruple $\{i, j, k, l\}$ as it is in the double $\{i, j\}$, after allowing for the first-order interaction, then a second-order interaction is included. This process continues until including further interactions does not significantly improve fit. Batsell & Polking suggest that this will usually be achieved reasonably parsimoniously (with only first- or second-order interactions being required).

Ben-Akiva & Lerman [1985, p. 127] warn that arbitrarily adding interactions can lead to counter-intuitive elasticities. A more axiomatic approach to modeling brand interactions is the generalized extreme-value model developed by McFadden [1978]. For an application of the generalized extreme-value to overcome the IIA problem see Dalal & Klein [1988].

An alternative model to incorporate departures from IIA is the multinomial probit model. This model is an extension of the binary probit developed earlier. It uses a normally distributed error structure and allows the covariance between error terms to be non-zero. But it is not possible to write a general analytical expression for the choice probabilities, and estimation and evaluation are quite complex. However, recent developments have led to practical computer programs for this model [Daganzo, 1979] and its consequent application in marketing [Currim, 1982; Kamakura & Srivastava, 1984, 1986; and Papatla & Krishnamurthi, 1991].

7. Post-purchase attitudes and behavior

Consumer behavior is an ongoing process: how a brand performed relative to the consumer's needs and expectations triggers what that consumer is likely to do on future purchase occasions. In addition, especially for durable goods, a consumer is likely to communicate his or her level of satisfaction to others, influencing the behavior of future consumers.

7.1. Post-purchase analysis basics

The modeling of consumer satisfaction is based on the confirmation/disconfirmation paradigm. Confirmation occurs when the consumer's perception of how the product performs after purchase matches the expectation the consumer had prior to purchase. Positive disconfirmation occurs when product performance exceeds expectations; negative expectations occur when the product falls below expectations. Satisfaction goes down as the level of negative disconfirmation goes up. Thus,

$$S_t = f(D_t) = g(\mathrm{E}_{t-1}, P_t) \tag{40}$$

where

S_t = satisfaction at time t,
D_t = disconfirmation at time t,
E_{t-1} = expectation prior to experience at $t-1$,
P_t = perceived performance (post-experience) at time t.

Swan & Combs [1976] and Oliver [1980] pioneered the disconfirmation idea. Swan & Combs suggested that disconfirmation could be of two types: instrumental (based on how the product performs functionally) and expressive (related to the feelings associated with the consumption experience).

Howard & Sheth [1969] suggested that the effect of disconfirmation of post-purchase attitudes can be written as:

$$A_{t+1} = h(P_t - A_t) + A_t$$

where A_t is the attitude of the consumer toward the brand. Oliver points out that if A_t is defined in expectational terms such as in a Fishbein model, the equation above provides a mechanism for updating attitudes on the basis of experience. He notes that two processes are going on here: (1) the formation of expectations and (2) the disconfirmation of those expectations through performance comparisons. Much of the recent literature on customer satisfaction [see Zeithaml, Parasuraman & Berry, 1990, for example] has addressed these two issues in addition to measuring the effect of satisfaction on subsequent behavior.

7.2. Post-purchase attitudes and behavior: extensions and applications

The specification and formalization of Equation (40) has led to models of satisfaction, of variety seeking and purchase feedback as well as network/communication models (Table 2.7).

7.2.1. Satisfaction

Researchers have primarily related satisfaction to perceived product performance through linear models. For example, Bearden & Teel [1983] used structural equation models (LISREL) to explain how expectations, attitudes, intentions and product experience (disconfirmation) determine satisfaction, along with future attitudes and behavior. They only collected data on perceptions relative to expectations to measure degree of disconfirmation; Churchill & Suprenant [1982] develop similar results with separate measures of perceptions and expectations.

Oliver & DeSarbo [1988] test the effect of attribution, expectation, performance, disconfirmation and equity on satisfaction, using an analysis of variance model. They report interactions between constructs in their analysis and are able to segment their sample on the basis of the decision rules the consumers follow. Tse & Wilton [1988] review the customer satisfaction literature and test different decision rules (stated disconfirmation versus perceived performance minus expected performance) as well as difference benchmarks for comparison (expected performance versus ideal level of performance versus equitable performance).

This area is seeing much attention currently, with researchers focusing on the linearity of the relationships (Woodruff, Cadotte & Jenkins [1983] suggest that a zone of indifference exists), the dynamics of customer satisfaction, and the relationship of customer satisfaction to the purchase experience (via the concept of transaction utility, Thaler [1985]). The literature on service quality is evolving rapidly as well [Parasuraman, Zeithaml & Berry, 1985] and clearly relates closely to the satisfaction construct [Bolton & Drew, 1991].

Word-of-mouth has been studied extensively in sociology [Rogers, 1983] and marketing [Westbrook, 1987]. Biehal [1983] also tests the impact of product experience on search. In the extreme, dissatisfaction leads to complaints to the supplier or to other consumers [Singh, 1988].

7.2.2. Models of variety seeking

Stochastic learning models provide one way to relate past purchase patterns to future behavior [see Lilien, Kotler & Moorthy, 1992, Chapter 2]. Stochastic models concentrate on the random element of consumer behavior. In contrast, the

Table 2.7
Post-purchase attitudes and behavior: extensions and applications

Issues addressed	Model	Data	Illustrative literature	Comments/application
Satisfaction/dissatisfaction:				
Effect of usage on satisfaction and attitude	Structural equation modeling	Expectations Perceived performance Satisfaction	Churchill & Surprenant [1982]	Video disk players
			Bearden & Teel [1983]	Auto repair
			Woodruff, Cadotte & Jenkins [1983]	No empirical testing
	Analysis of variance	Satisfaction with concepts of varying expectations and performance	Oliver & DeSarbo [1988]	Stock investments
Negative word-of-mouth	Discriminant analysis	As above plus post-purchase behavior	Richins [1983]	Clothing/appliances
Effect of usage on behavior	Regression analysis	As above	Westbrook [1987]	Auto/CATV
			Biehal [1983]	Auto repair
			Singh [1988]	Various categories
Variety seeking and purchase-event feedback:				
Variety seeking	Luce model	Purchase over time	McAlister [1982]	Soft drinks
		Attributes and preferences	Lattin & McAlister [1985]	Soft drinks
	Logit model	As above	Lattin [1987]	Soft drinks
Social networks/communication patterns:				
	Analysis of network structures	Communication links	Coleman, Katz & Menzel [1957]	Effect of network structure on diffusion of innovations
			Czepiel [1974]	
	Individual-level diffusion models	Adoption of others plus communication links	Burt [1987]	
			Midgley, Morrison & Roberts [1992]	
Overview	Review of variety seeking		McAlister & Pessemier [1982]	
			Kahn, Kalwani & Morrison [1986]	

variety-seeking literature models the effect of current choice on future behavior by understanding the deterministic influences of choice. McAlister & Pessemier [1982] distinguish between several types of behavior by individuals that relate to multiple needs, the acquisition of information, and the alternating purchase of familiar products (variety seeking). They hypothesize that consumers have an ideal point or satiation level for the product's attributes that leads to its decreasing utility after a period of sustained consumption. Thus, if a man drinks six colas there is a good chance that on his next consumption occasion he might wish for a lemon soda 'just for a change', i.e. perform variety seeking.

Let us consider the study by Lattin & McAlister [1985], who used a Luce model to understand the effect of brand similarities on purchase-event feedback. They model a consumer's utility for a brand on a given consumption occasion as diminishing proportionally to the value of the features it shares with the brand the consumer chose on the previous consumption occasion via a first-order Markov scheme.

Thus,

$$V_{i|j} = V_i - \lambda S_{ij} \tag{41}$$

where

$V_{i|j}$ = utility of i given that j was chosen previously,
V_i = unconditional utility of i,
λ = discount factor indicating consumer's variety-seeking intensity,
S_{ij} = value to the customer of all want-satisfying features shared by i and j.

Applying the Luce model to this formulation gives the probability of purchase of i given a previous purchase of j, $\mathrm{P}_{i|j}$ as:

$$\mathrm{P}_{i|j} = (V_i - \lambda S_{ij}) / \sum_k (V_k - \lambda S_{kj}) \tag{42}$$

Lattin & McAlister scale the V_i so that $\sum_k V_k = 1$. Then V_i can be interpreted as the probability of choosing brand i in the absence of variety seeking.

The authors analyze how much previous consumption alters the unconditional brand-choice probability, V_i; that is, $\mathrm{P}_{i|j} - V_i$. Now $\mathrm{P}_{i|j} - V_i < 0$ indicates that product j is a substitute for product i (the consumption of brand j lowers the probability of choosing brand i), while $\mathrm{P}_{i|j} - V_i > 0$ suggests that brand j is a complement to brand i (the consumption of brand j increases the probability of choosing brand i). An examination of Equation (42) shows that brand j will be a substitute for brand i ($\mathrm{P}_{i|j} - V_i < 0$) if $V_i < S_{ij}/\sum_k S_{kj}$, that is, if product i shares more than a proportional amount of its want-satisfying value with product j.

The asymmetry of the effect of product i on product j, and product j on brand i, may be seen by expanding the expression for the effect of product j on i ($\mathrm{P}_{i|j} - V_i$) using Equation (42). Now $\mathrm{P}_{i|j} - V_i$ may be rewritten:

$$\mathrm{P}_{i|j} - V_i = \lambda\left(V_i \sum_k S_{kj} - S_{ij} \right) \Big/ \left(1 - \lambda \sum_k S_{kj} \right). \tag{43}$$

Since $S_{ij} = S_{ji}$, $\mathrm{P}_{j|i} - V_j$ is (by symmetry)

$$\mathrm{P}_{j|i} - V_j = \lambda\left(V_j \sum_k S_{ki} - S_{ij} \right) \bigg/ \left(1 - \lambda \sum_k S_{ki} \right). \tag{44}$$

The intensity of variety seeking λ, will magnify the degree of substitution or complementarity. Lattin & McAlister report the results of analyzing the soft-drink consumption behavior of 27 students over a period of 81 days. They obtain a least squares fit to Equation (43) using constrained non-linear programming, estimating their model at the individual level and averaging across individuals to obtain segment-level estimates. The variety-seeking segment consists of 9 of the 27 respondents with λ's ranging from 0.43 to 0.96. For the other 18 respondents a simple Markov model was sufficient.

In other models of variety seeking, McAlister [1982] considers multiperiod depletion of inventories of attributes, Lattin [1987] explicitly models different levels of variety seeking for different attributes using a logit framework, and Simonson [1990] examines the contextual determinants of variety seeking.

7.2.3. Models of social communication networks

Most aggregate levels of the diffusion process either implicitly or explicitly assume perfect (or at least random) mixing between the members of the population. With models at the individual level we can investigate this assumption. The pioneering work examining the structure of interpersonal networks through which word-of-mouth about innovations diffuse was the study of the diffusion of prescriptions of the drug tetracycline in four Illinois towns by Coleman, Katz & Menzel [1957]. Cziepel [1974] shows that for innovations in steel production not only did specific incomplete networks exist but there were cliques with good communications within them but weak communications between them. Burt [1987] goes further in suggesting that for many innovations the diffusion effect is not directly from adopter to potential adopter but indirectly through some third party who is not part of the network. Midgley, Morrison & Roberts [1992] develop a model of the effect of network structure on the internal diffusion process of firms and test the degree to which departures from the perfect mixing model occur. In addition, they test the degree to which these departures from traditional assumptions at the individual level affect the diffusion process at the aggregate level. They find evidence of cliqueing and determine that it could cause anomalous aggregate-level diffusion patterns. While all of these studies were conducted in industrial markets because of the difficulty in specifying networks for consumer products, the theory is also likely to be valid for consumer markets.

8. Integration: Combining models to solve management problems

We have now examined some of the major tools to understand and predict consumer behavior using process-oriented models. In developing our framework we emphasized the need for parsimony and ease of implementation. Thus, we looked at different stages of the decision process separately to concentrate on only those phenomena that are keys to understanding behavior and product management. However, there are many situations in which more than one stage and more than one type of model are appropriate.

In this section we give three illustrations of how the building blocks that we have developed can be joined and applied to address particular real-world consumer purchase situations. Our illustrations include: (1) the combination of purchase incidence (need arousal) and brand choice (purchase) models, (2) joint consideration and purchase models, and (3) models of information integration and evaluation.

8.1. Application 1: A model of brand choice and purchase incidence

Guadagni & Little [1987] examine how a retail store should price, display and discount products to maximize sales and contribution. To achieve that end, the management needs to understand the source of additional product sales: do those sales come from increases in brand share or from additional sales of the category as a whole? The areas of our process model that correspond to these issues deal with the purchase stage (the brand that will be chosen) and the need-arousal stage (when a category purchase will occur).

Both phenomena can be modeled using logit models: earlier we developed the nested logit model which provides an integrated framework to understand related logit decision processes. Guadagni & Little use this technique to study purchase incidence and brand choice. They examine the purchase of coffee in Kansas City over a 74-week period using scanner panel data on a sample of 200 households.

Their model of brand choice follows their earlier work [Guadagni & Little, 1983]. First, they identify the determinants of *brand choice* for the eight major brand-size combinations of coffee (products) on the market:

X_{1ijt} = brand loyalty in period t of customer i to the brand-size of product j,
X_{2ijt} = size loyalty in period t of customer i to the size of brand-size j,
X_{3jt} = the presence of a promotion (display) on brand-size j in time t,
X_{4jt} = the discount of bránd-size j at time t as a proportion of the average category price,
X_{5jt} = the regular (undiscounted) price of brand-size j at time t relative to the average category price.

They also develop seven product-specific dummy variables to capture the brand equity of each of the products.

The logit brand-choice model estimated across respondents, products and time periods, is:

$$P_{ijt|B} = \exp\left\{\sum_n \beta_n X_{nijt} + \sum_m \gamma_m \delta_{imt}\right\} \Bigg/ \sum_k \exp\left\{\sum_n \beta_n X_{nikt} + \sum_m \gamma_m \delta_{imt}\right\} \quad (45)$$

where

$P_{ijt|B}$ = the probability of individual i purchasing product j in time period t given a purchase in category B,

β_n, γ_m = coefficients of the independent variables and product-specific dummies respectively ($n = 1$ to 5 and $m = 1$ to 7).

Their model of purchase incidence is a binary logit, with the dependent variable being whether a purchase took place or not. Their explanatory variables are:

Z_{1Bi} = a dummy variable for the utility that consumer i gets from buying (B) in the category,

Z_{2Bit} = a variable to denote whether consumer i made multiple purchases when buying on shopping trip t,

Z_{3Bit} = household inventory of coffee,

Z_{4Bit} = the category attractiveness,

Z_{5Bit} = the average category price,

Z_{6Bit} = a dummy variable to account for an announcement of impending price rises due to a crop failure in Brazil.

Household inventory, Z_{3Bit}, can be estimated from purchase history and average seasonal consumption rates. Category attractiveness, Z_{4Bit}, is the inclusive value from the nested logit:

$$Z_{4Bit} = \ln\left\{\sum_k \exp\left\{\sum_n \beta_n X_{nikt} + \sum_m \gamma_m \delta_{imt}\right\}\right\} \tag{46}$$

To calculate the expected category attractiveness of buying later (of *not* buying in this time period), Z_{4Nit}, and the expected price that consumer i would face if he or she bought later (and *not* this period), Z_{5Nit}, Guadagni & Little take an average of the attractiveness and category prices over the previous eight purchase occasions, respectively. For all other variables, ($Z_{1Nit}, Z_{2Nit}, Z_{3Nit}, Z_{6Nit}$), they set the utility of not buying in period t to zero.

Their final binary logit model of whether category purchase will occur on shopping occasion t or not is:

$$P_{Bit} = \exp\left\{\sum_n \alpha_n Z_{nBit}\right\} \Big/ \left\{\exp\left\{\sum_n \alpha_n Z_{nBit}\right\} + \exp\left\{\sum_n \alpha_n Z_{nNit}\right\}\right\} \tag{47}$$

where P_{Bit} is the probability of buying (B) within the category on shopping occasion t and α_n ($n = 1, 2, \ldots, 6$) are parameters.

Guadagni & Little estimate the model by first calibrating Equation (45), the brand-choice equation, using maximum-likelihood techniques. The 'inclusive value' can then be calculated from Equation (46). This enables the purchase-incidence binary logit model, Equation (47), to be calibrated.

At the product level (brand choice), both brand-name loyalty and product-size loyalty are strongly statistically significant. The brand-choice decision also responds to store promotions and price cuts, as well as being sensitive to the usual price of the brand relative to the market. At the purchase-incidence level, all variables except the price of the category are statistically significant, suggesting that coffee purchase does not depend on the price of the category as a whole, but that brand choice is sensitive to price.

Their combined brand-choice/purchase-incidence nested logit model allows forecasts both of brand share and of total brand sales. The effects of individual products' marketing activity are traced through to category effects using the 'inclusive value' from the nested logit. Additionally, their purchase-incidence model enables them to evaluate the effect of external factors, such as multiple purchases, household inventory, and crop failure in Brazil.

By approaching the same problem from a stochastic modeling perspective and incorporating explanatory variables into their model, Hauser & Wisniewski [1982] and Wagner & Taudes [1986] jointly model purchase-incidence and brand-choice decisions and their determinants. Hybrid approaches combining discrete choice and stochastic models include those of Jones & Zufryden [1981] (with a negative binomial distribution purchase-incidence model and logit brand choice) and Gupta [1988] (with an Erlang interpurchase time distribution and logit brand choice). Gupta also models purchase quantities in his framework using a cumulative logit model.

8.2. Application 2: Integrating consideration and choice

Gensch [1987b] studies the management problem of influencing the choice process of electric utilities for an industrial durable in order to better design and position the product. He cites considerable work applying compensatory evaluation rules to examine the relation between product positioning, perceptions and purchase. But evidence in the consumer behavior literature suggests that consumers often use a two-stage procedure [e.g. see Wright and Barbour, 1977]. In our framework this concept corresponds to a screening phase in the information search stage to determine the consideration set, followed by an evaluation and/or purchase stage. Gensch proposes a non-compensatory screening phase, followed by a compensatory evaluation of, and choice between, the surviving alternatives.

8.2.1. Attribute-based screening model

In Gensch's models, consumers screen products sequentially by attribute on a conjunctive basis. That is, consumer i ensures that his or her perception of product j on attribute k, y_{ijk}, suitably scaled, does not fall too far short of the best brand's level on that attribute. Starting with the most important attribute, the consumer screens all brands on this basis to come up with an acceptable consideration set. These brands then enter the purchase phase. Mathematically the model may be written as follows.

First the attribute levels, y_{ijk}, are rescaled by

$$x_{ijk} = [\max_n y_{ink} - y_{ijk}]/\max_n y_{ink} \tag{48}$$

where x_{ijk} is the rescaled perception that consumer i has of attribute k for product j. Gensch then postulates that there are maximum levels of x_{ijk} that the consumer will find acceptable; he calls these thresholds T_k. He assumes the utility that attribute k offers is

$$v_{ijk} = \max(0, T_k - x_{ijk}).$$

Gensch then uses a multiplicative utility function to determine brand j's overall utility to consumer i, V_{ij}:

$$V_{ij} = \prod_k v_{ijk}. \tag{49}$$

Equation (49) implies that if a brand fails to meet the threshold on any one criterion, then it has zero utility, i.e., $V_{ij} = 0$. (A conjunctive decision rule.) He estimates the T_k from the data to maximize:

$$\prod_i \left(V_{ij^*} / \sum_j V_{ij} \right)^{X_i} \cdot \left(1 - V_{ij^*} / \sum_j V_{ij} \right)^{1 - X_i} \tag{50}$$

where

j^* = the chosen alternative,

$$X_i = \begin{cases} 1 & \text{if } j^* \text{ is not screened out in the consideration phase,} \\ 0 & \text{otherwise.} \end{cases}$$

Given estimates of thresholds, T_k, the consideration set consists of brands such that $V_{ij} > 0$, i.e. brands that do not fail any of the threshold criteria. If no brands fulfill this criterion, the consumer chooses the brand(s) eliminated last (i.e. that failed the least important conjunctive criterion) [see Gensch and Svestka, 1984].

8.2.2. Logit discrete-choice model

Given a consideration set from the previous stage, choice data, and respondent perceptions of suppliers on the salient attributes, Gensch fits a standard logit choice model. The probability of purchase of brand j by consumer i, P_{ij}, is given by:

$$\mathrm{P}_{ij} = \exp\left\{ \sum_k b_k y_{ijk} \right\} \Big/ \sum_{n \in C} \exp\left\{ \sum_k b_k y_{ink} \right\} \tag{51}$$

where C is the set of brands surviving the screening process.

8.2.3 Model testing

Gensch tests the model by examining the ratings of four suppliers by 182 buyers of electrical generation equipment on eight attributes, combined with choice data.

The two-stage model gives superior predictions to several a one-stage models. In addition, two attributes dominate the screening process. Of all eliminations 70% occur on the basis of manufacturer quality, while 26% occur on the basis of manufacturer problem-solving ability. The one-stage logit model has both of these variables statistically significant. After incorporating a screening phase, both variables are insignificant. This suggests that these variables are important in gaining consideration, but once consideration is gained, they do not play a significant role in evaluation and choice. The use of this and related models had a major impact on the successful performance of ABB Electric in the 1970s and 1980s [Gensch, Aversa & Moore, 1990].

One of the strengths of Gensch's approach is that it only requires attribute perceptions, perceived importance and choice data, making the data-collection task easier than that for the consideration models described earlier. It also means that care has to be taken in interpreting the screening results: we cannot be sure that non-compensatory screening was in fact the process that took place. Rather, we can only conclude that a non-compensatory screening model combined with a compensatory choice model gives a better fit than does either a single-stage compensatory model or a discrete-choice model.

8.3. Application 3: The dynamics of perceptions, preference and purchase

Roberts & Urban [1988] develop a dynamic brand-choice model to address the problem of forecasting sales of a new consumer durable. With the launch of a new automobile, appeal (perceptions, preference and choice) is important, but so are the dynamics of how that appeal will change as the product diffuses through the adopting population. GM's Buick Division was interested in how word-of-mouth and information from other sources would affect sales. The modeling task combines static choice modeling with a model of information integration to help understand the dynamics of choice.

8.3.1. Probability of purchase model at any point in time

Roberts & Urban use decision analysis theory to show that a (rational) risk-averse consumer with uncertain beliefs will attempt to maximize the expected utility that he or she will get from the brand minus a constant times the uncertainty involved [Keeney & Raiffa, 1976]. They term this quantity the risk-adjusted preference, x. Thus, the risk-adjusted preference for brand j, x_j, is given by:

$$x_j = V_j - (r/2)\sigma_j^2 \tag{52}$$

where

V_j = the expected utility from brand j,
σ_j^2 = the variance of beliefs about V_j,
r = the consumer's risk-aversion.

V_j may be further modeled in terms of its constituent attributes to incorporate product positioning.

If x_j is measured with error following the extreme-value distribution, we can model the probability of choosing brand j in logit terms:

$$\mathrm{P}_j = \mathrm{e}^{x_j} / \sum_{k \in C} \mathrm{e}^{x_k} \tag{53}$$

By substituting Equation (52) into (53) we can see how perceptions, expected preference and the level of uncertainty affect the probability of purchase.

8.3.2. Dynamics of preference uncertainty and choice probability

The literature on diffusion of innovations suggests that information fills two roles: it reduces uncertainty and it can lead to changes in attribute perceptions and thus preference. To model the effect of new product information on an individual's perceptions and uncertainty, Roberts & Urban use Bayesian updating theory. Beliefs about expected preference for the brand after search are a weighted average of the prior beliefs and the level of preference that the new information suggests. Uncertainty is reduced by an amount that depends on the faith that is placed in new information. Mathematically,

$$V''_j = (\sigma^2_{wj} V'_j + \sigma'^2_j V_{wj}) / (\sigma^2_{wj} + \sigma'^2_j) \tag{54}$$

and

$$\sigma''^2_j = \sigma'^2_j \sigma^2_{wj} / \{\sigma^2_{wj} + \sigma'^2_j\} \tag{55}$$

where

V''_j and σ''^2_j = expected preference and uncertainty associated with product j after updating,
V'_j and σ'^2_j = prior expected preference and uncertainty,
V_{wj} and σ^2_{wj} = average preference and uncertainty of the incoming word-of-mouth about product j.

By substituting the dynamics of expected preference and uncertainty (Equations (54) and (55)) into the equation for risk-adjusted preference (Equation (52)) and the probability of purchase (Equation (55)), Roberts & Urban derive a dynamic brand-choice equation that provides a model of the individual-level changes that are driving the aggregate-level diffusion process. They assume that the rate at which new information about product j will become available is proportional to the number of cumulative adopters at time t, Y_{jt}. The variance of word-of-mouth information will be inversely proportional to this rate and thus the cumulative sales of product j:

$$\sigma''^2_{wj} = k_j / Y_{jt} \tag{56}$$

where k_j is a constant reflecting the salience of the new product, j.

8.3.3. *Application*

In an empirical application, Roberts & Urban calibrated their model using 326 respondents' evaluations of the existing US automobile market and a new product concept. After measuring perceptions, uncertainty, and purchase probabilities with respect to the existing market, respondents were exposed to increasing amounts of information about the new car. First, they saw a description, then they took a prototype for a test drive followed by a videotape of owners' reactions to the new car, and finally they were given a consumer report written by an independent testing service. Measures of perceptions, preference, uncertainty, and probability of choice were taken after every information exposure to calibrate the model dynamics.

Respondents were exposed to either positive- or negative-information videotapes. Roberts & Urban traced the effect of these changes through the risk-adjusted preference to calculate the effect of word-of-mouth on individuals' probability of purchase and thus the diffusion of the new product, using Equations (52) and (53).

The results of the perceptual evaluation stage of the model helped shape the advertising copy for the car, stressing that the perceived durability did not come at the expense of comfort and style. An understanding of the dynamics of expected sales of the car under conditions of negative word-of-mouth persuaded management to delay the launch for over six months until a transmission fault was fixed. Finally, although it is difficult to validate durable forecasting models, preliminary indications are that this methodology predicted actual market performance well [Urban, Hauser & Roberts, 1990].

Meyer & Sathi [1985] propose a similar model with exponential-smoothing updating for beliefs and uncertainty. Recent work is addressing the problem of making these dynamic brand-choice models more parsimonious in parameters to allow the aggregate effects of individual-level changes to be examined more readily [Oren & Schwartz, 1988; Chatterjee & Eliashberg, 1990; Lattin & Roberts, 1988].

9. Future directions for consumer behavior models

The field of modeling consumer behavior is evolving rapidly. Changes are being driven by advances in our theoretical understanding of consumer decision processes (e.g. developments in the use of discrete choice models to overcome the independence of irrelevant alternatives), the availability of new data sources (e.g. the new mapping techniques that take advantage of the existence of longitudinal supermarket scanner data at the individual level), and new or more focused concerns of managers (e.g. models of market structure that address problems of market coverage and portfolio management).

Our study of the consumer decision process above also highlights a number of under-researched areas, particularly in terms of need arousal, information integration and post-purchase influences. As the external environment changes at an increasing rate and product life-cycles become shorter, equilibrium models of the five stages of our process are likely to become less popular than those incorporating dynamics.

We expect advances in consumer behavior models in a number of key areas, and we highlight four.

9.1. Accuracy and applicability

Currently most of our models still take a reasonably narrow view of the utility-maximizing consumer, though this understanding has broadened over the last few years. Our models must handle better the phenomena of simplifying heuristics, biases in decision-making, and the effects of framing and context as we broaden our modeling perspective beyond that of a strictly rational consumer.

Simplifying heuristics have been well recognized in the consumer behavior literature for some time [e.g. Lindblom, 1959]. To some extent, the non-compensatory models that we discussed here represent a beginning in this area. However, there is no satisfactory error theory associated with those rules and also there are many simplifying heuristics that consumers employ that are not covered by those models. The situations that trigger different heuristics have attracted attention in consumer behavior [e.g. Payne, Bettman & Johnson, 1988]. In order to quantify these effects, marketing scientists must formalize them in mathematical terms.

Recent research in the area of psychology into the *biases* that consumers exhibit are likely to modify the strict utility-maximizing models that we often apply. Tversky & Kahneman [1974] observe these biases in decision-makers (including consumers): representativeness (in which perceived ideas and stereotypes obstruct learning of new information), availability (in which respondents select events or outcomes that are familiar to them, even in defiance of the true probabilities), and anchoring (in which respondents are reluctant to adjust adequately from their preconceived ideas). Subsequently, Kahneman & Tversky [1979] have also studied asymmetric risk-aversion to gains and losses from the consumer's current position and the over-weighting of low-probability events. Currim & Sarin [1989] develop a method of calibrating and testing these prospect theory models. They show that for paradoxical choices, prospect theory [Kahneman & Tversky, 1979] outperforms utility theory, while for non-paradoxical choices there is little difference. Winer [1986] and Lattin & Bucklin [1989] include reference levels in their models of brand choice to account for anchoring, but little work has been done to model and develop an error theory for the simplifying heuristics that consumers appear to use to make decisions.

Stemming from the work of Kahneman & Tversky above, there is a wide variety of other contextual effects that influence choice, most of which are currently omitted from our models. Meyer & Eagle [1982] show that contextual factors influence the importance weight that is given to attributes. The range of alternatives available, for example, is important in choice [e.g. Alba & Chattopadhyay, 1985, 1986]. The variety-seeking literature also studies one particular form of context. Other interesting work in context includes Thaler's [1985] mental accounting model. Thaler suggests that there are two forms of utility associated with every consumer decision: acquisition utility and transaction utility. The former is the utility modeled in this chapter. Transaction utility reflects the approval or pleasure that consumers gain from the transaction itself. Transaction utility is particularly tied to the concept of fairness and appropriateness. While Urbany, Madden & Dickson [1989] find little evidence of fairness affecting behavioral intentions, there are clearly situations in which transaction utility will be a key determinant of choice.

9.2. Modeling the mental process

The field of consumer behavior is advancing our understanding of the mental processes that consumers undertake. We must begin to incorporate the role of memory into our models, together with the effects of categorization on consumer choice. Also we must determine the influence of too much or too little information (information overload and inferencing, respectively).

We predict that formal modeling of mental processes, *memory* in particular, will see some important advances. Lynch & Srull [1982], for example, have demonstrated the importance of the role of memory in consumer behavior experiments. Information once remembered will not necessarily be recalled and recent work looks at the salience of brands and stimuli [e.g. Nedungadi, 1990].

The study of how a product is perceived and how consumers form personal product classes is called *categorization* [e.g. Sujan, 1985]. The product class then becomes the benchmark against which the product is evaluated, either by use of a prototypical product from the category for comparison, or with an exemplar. The implications of how products are categorized extend to the probability of consideration [Urban, Hulland & Weinberg, 1990], managing cannibalization (competition with the firm's other brands), brand draw (competition with competitors' brands), and product-line extensions [Bridges, 1991].

A considerable body of literature exists on how consumers react when there is incomplete information, or when there is too much information: *information overload and inferencing*. Huber & McCann [1982] show that consumer inferences affect choice, and a number of researchers have developed models to explain this [e.g. Malhotra, 1986]. Dick, Chakravati & Biehal [1990] demonstrate that consumers infer from memory-based knowledge when faced by incomplete external information. Malhotra [1982] and Keller & Staelin [1989] show that information overload also affects choice, though less work has been undertaken to model the simplifying heuristics that the consumer uses to overcome the problem.

9.3. Coping with consumer heterogeneity

Many of our individual models are estimated across all respondents and assume perfect homogeneity to obtain sufficient degrees of freedom. Both by grouping similar people together and estimating at the segment level, and also by estimating some parameters within respondents and others across respondents, we can cope with consumer heterogeneity via richer models.

Much of the consumer behavior work to date has postulated a single model of consumer response and tested its fit in a given sitution against some competiting, single model. We expect to see more work on methods for testing for this assumed customer homogeneity, applying models to homogeneous segments, i.e. *matching models to market segments.* For example, Gensch [1985] shows that prior segmentation of a population into segments homogeneous in perceptions and preferences gave much higher predictive accuracy than when a single model was fitted to the entire population. Such segmentation is particularly powerful when it can be done a priori, as Gensch [1987a] shows on a population of industrial buyers. In this latter application, more knowledgeable buyers are modeled well within a logit model while less knowledgeable buyers closely approximate the assumptions of a hierarchical choice model. We expect that further research will generate a better understanding of what types of models are most likely to be effective a priori, leading to the better application of appropriate, situation-specific consumer behavior models.

9.4. Markets and consumers in flux

Market dynamics need to be incorporated in a number of ways. We have already spoken of the move from modeling demand using comparative statics to using dynamic models. That move will continue. Additionally, the supply side of market dynamics will attract greater attention, as will decisions involving unfamiliar products.

Supply-side feedback, in the form of the game-theoretic implications of a competitor's actions on an organization's optimal strategy are discussed by Moorthy in Chapter 4. However, in many markets, product design evolves over time, reflecting the interplay between customers' needs and the company's manufacturing capability. While Hauser & Simmie [1981] made a start on modeling this process, there is still much that needs to be done.

The problems of decisions involving *unfamiliar alternatives* (e.g. new, technologically sophisticated products) is not well modeled or measured in marketing at present. There is some evidence that novices do not use as rich a mental model as experts [e.g. Alba & Hutchinson, 1987]. Management needs in high-technology areas will continue to push for the development of better methods to assess how consumer decision processes evolve in such markets.

A modeling challenge when studying unfamiliar products is that the benchmarks that consumers use in these areas are generally not comparable to the unfamiliar product. For example, consumers might compare a compact disk player to a stereo cassette player. Johnson [1984, 1986, 1988] has suggested that the more consumers are faced with non-comparable alternatives, the more they resort to hierarchically based processing. That is, he asserts that with non-comparable alternatives, consumers evaluate brands by a very general comparison, rather than a specific attribute-based one. As markets evolve more rapidly and product life-cycles shorten, the need for models to understand the adoption of truly new products will become more evident.

While there will undoubtedly be many other phenomena that will be studied, leading to a more complete understanding of consumer behavior, we have attempted to sketch what we see as some of the major areas. These advances will occur in conjunction with a study of the context in which purchase and consumption take place. Thus, dyadic and family behavior will develop as an example of sociological influences on decision-making. Hedonic behavior and the consumption of services will provide an example of product context influencing behavior. And distribution channel and salesforce influences will shape research on physical context affecting behavior. There will be other advances addressing specific marketing problems (such as the marketing of groups of products as a portfolio in the financial services industry), but we feel that improving the accuracy and validity of our models, ensuring their fit to different customers and the stability of that fit over time will bring the greatest rewards to researchers and managers over the next five years.

10. Conclusions

In a field as vast and diffuse as that of consumer behavior and consumer markets, it is difficult to develop a single best synthesis. We have drawn from developments in the literature of the behavioral sciences, economics, marketing, statistics, and the like and have categorized according to the stage or stages in the decision process to which those developments appear most applicable. Our models overlap these processes and stages but this integrating framework provides a useful way of organizing this large, diverse literature.

We followed our framework from need identification to information search to perception and evaluation and preference formation. From there we went on to purchase and post-purchase feedback models. Finally, we demonstrated the power of developing models that combined several of the above stages in a single framework.

The future of consumer behavior modeling is bright; newer models are richer, more flexible, and more closely attuned to modern data sources. Yet many phenomena are poorly modeled at the moment. We highlighted the areas of modeling consumer purchase heuristics (and information-processing biases), modeling consumers' mental processes, matching models to market segments, and modeling choice for truly new or non-comparable alternatives as fruitful areas that deserve concerted attention in the future. Much has been accomplished; much remains to be done.

References

Alba, J.W., and A. Chattopadhyay (1985). Effects of context and part-category cues on recall of competing brands. *J. Marketing Res.* 22 (August), 340–349.

Alba, J.W., and A. Chattopadhyay (1986). Salience effects in brand recall. *J. Marketing Res.* 23 (November), 363–369.

Alba, J.W., and J.W. Hutchinson (1987). Dimensions of consumer expertise. *J. Consumer Res.* 13, 411–454.

Albaum, G., and D.I. Hawkins (1983). Geographic mobility and demographic and socioeconomic market segmentation. *J. Acad. Marketing Sci.* 11 (Spring), 110.

Amemiya, T. (1981). Qualitative response models: A survey. *J. Econometric Literature* 19 (December), 1483–1583.

Bagozzi, R.P. (1977). Structural equation models in experimental research. *J. Marketing Res.* 14 (May), 209–226.

Bagozzi, R.P. (1980). Performance and satisfaction in an industrial salesforce: An examination of their antecedents and simultaneity. *J. Marketing* 44 (Spring), 65–77.

Bagozzi, R.P. (1982). A field investigation of causal relations among cognitions, affect, intentions and behavior. *J. Marketing Res.* 19 (November), 562–584.

Bass, F.M., and W.W. Talarzyk (1972). An attitude model for the study of brand preference. *J. Marketing Res.* 9 (February), 93–96.

Batsell, R.R., and J.C. Polking (1985). A new class of market share models. *Marketing Sci.* 4(3), 177–198.

Bearden, W.O., and M.J. Etzel (1982). Reference group influence on product and brand purchase decisions. *J. Consumer Res.* 9 (September), 183–194.

Bearden, W.O., and J.E. Teel (1983). Selected determinants of consumer satisfaction and complaint reports. *J. Marketing Res.* 20 (February), 21–28.

Bechtel, G.G. (1985). Generalizing the Rasch model for consumer rating scales. *Marketing Sci.* 4(1), 62–73.

Bechtel, G.G. (1990). Share-ratio estimation of the nested multinomial logit model. *J. Marketing Res.* 27 (May), 232–237.

Ben-Akiva, M., and S.R. Lerman (1985). *Discrete Choice Analysis: Theory and Application to Travel Demand*, Massachusetts Institute of Technology Press, Cambridge.

Bettman, J.R. (1979). *An Information Processing Theory of Consumer Choice*, Addison-Wesley, Reading, MA.

Biehal, G.J. (1983). Consumers' prior experiences and perceptions in auto repair choice. *J. Marketing* 47 (Summer), 82–91.

Blattberg, R.C., and A.P. Jeuland (1981). A micro-modeling approach to investigate the advertising sales relationship. *Management Sci.* 27(9), 988–1004.

Bodnar, J., P. Dilworth and S. Iacono (1988). Cross-sectional analysis of residential telephone subscription in Canada. *Inform. Econom. Policy* 3, 359–378.

Bolton, R.N., and J.H. Drew (1991). A multistage model of customers' assessments of service quality and value. *J. Consumer Res.* 17 (March), 375–384.

Bridges, S. (1991). A schema unification model of brand extensions, Babcock GSM Working Paper, Wake Forest University, Winston-Salem, NC.

Bunch, D.S., and R.R. Batsell (1989). A Monte Carlo comparison of estimators for the multinomial logit model. *J. Marketing Res.* 26 (February), 56–68.

Burnkrant, R.E., and T.J. Page, Jr. (1982). An examination of the convergent, discriminant, and predictive validity of Fishbein's behavioral intention model. *J. Marketing Res.* 19 (November), 550–561.

Burt, R.S. (1987). Social contagion and innovation: Cohesion versus structural equivalence: *Amer. J. Sociology* 92 (May), 1287–1335.

Carroll, D.J., and P.E. Green (1988). An INDSCAL-based approach to multiple correspondence analysis. *J. Marketing Res.* 25 (May), 193–203.

Chapman, R.G., and R. Staelin (1982). Exploiting rank ordered choice set data within the stochastic utility model. *J. Marketing Res.* 19 (August), 288–301.

Chatterjee, R., and J. Eliashberg (1990). The innovation diffusion process in a heterogeneous population: A micromodeling approach. *Management Sci.* 36(9), 1057–1074.

Choffray, J.-M., and G.L. Lilien (1980). *Market Planning for New Industrial Products*, Wiley, New York.

Churchill, G.A. Jr., and C. Suprenant (1982). An investigation into the determinants of customer satisfaction. *J. Marketing Res.* 19 (Novermber), 491–504.

Coleman, J.S., E. Katz and H. Menzel (1957). The diffusion of an innovation among physicians. *Sociometry* 20 (December), 253–270.

Cooper, L.G. (1983). A review of multidimensional scaling in marketing research. *Appl. Psychol. Measurement* 7 (Fall), 427–450.

Cooper, L.G., and M. Nakanishi (1983). Standardizing variables in multiplicative choice models. *J. Consumer Res.* 10 (June), 96–108.

Corstjens, M.L., and D.A. Gautschi (1983). Formal choice models in marketing. *Marketing Sci.* 2(1), 19–56.
Currim, I.S. (1982). Predictive testing of consumer choice models not subject to independence of irrelevant alternatives. *J. Marketing Res.* 19 (May), 208–222.
Currim, I.S., and R.K. Sarin (1984). A comparative evaluation of multiattribute consumer preference models. *Management Sci.* 30(5), 543–561.
Currim, I.S., and R.K. Sarin (1989). Prospect versus utility. *Management Science* 35(1), 22–41.
Czepiel, J.A. (1974). Word of mouth processes in the diffusion of a major technological innovation. *J. Marketing Res.* 11 (May), 172–180.
Daganzo, C. (1979). *Multinomial Probit*, Academic Press, New York.
Dalal, S.R., and R.W. Klein (1988). A flexible class of discrete choice models. *Marketing Sci.* 7(3), 232–251.
Day, G.S., and T. Deutscher (1982). Attitudinal predictions of choices of major appliance brands. *J. Marketing Res.* 19 (May), 192–198.
DeGroot, M.H. (1970). *Optimal Statistical Decisions*, McGraw-Hill, New York.
DeSarbo, W.S., and D.L. Hoffman (1987). Constructing MDS joint spaces from binary choice data: A multidimensional unfolding threshold model for marketing research. *J. Marketing Res.* 24 (February), 40–54.
DeSarbo, W.S., A.K. Manrai and L.A. Manrai (1993). Non-spatial tree models for the assessment of competitive market structure: An integrated review of the marketing and psychometric literature, in: J. Eliashberg and G.L. Lilien (eds.), *Handbooks in Operations Research and Management Science, Vol. 5: Marketing*, North-Holland, Amsterdam, ch. 5.
Dick, A., D. Chakravarti and G. Biehal (1990). Memory-based inferences during consumer choice. *J. Consumer Res.* 17 (June), 82–93.
Domencich, T.A., and D. McFadden (1975). *Urban Travel Demand: A Behavioral Analysis*, North-Holland, Amsterdam.
Dubin, J.A. (1986). A nested logit model of space and water heat system choice. *Marketing Sci.* 5(2), 112–124.
Ehrenberg, A.S.C., G.J. Goodhardt and T.P. Barwise (1990). Double jeopardy revisited. *J. Marketing* 54(3), 82–91.
Eliashberg, J. (1980). Consumer preference judgements: An exposition with empirical applications. *Management Sci.* 26(1), 60–77.
Eliashberg, J., and J.R. Hauser (1985). A measurement error approach for modelling consumer risk preferences. *Management Sci.* 31(1), 1–25.
Elrod, T. (1988). Choice map: Inferring a product-market map from panel data. *Marketing Sci.* 7(1), 21–40.
Farquhar, P.H. (1984). Utility assessment methods. *Management Sci.* 30(11), 1283–1300.
Fishbein, M. (1963). An investigation of relationship between beliefs about an object and the attitude toward the object. *Human Relations* 16, 233–240.
Fishbein, M. (1967). Attitude and prediction of behavior, in M. Fishbein (ed.), *Readings in Attitude Theory and Measurement*, Wiley, New York, pp. 477–492.
Fishbein, M., and I. Ajzen (1975). *Beliefs, Attitude, Intention and Behavior*, Addison-Wesley, Reading, MA.
Fishburn, P.C. (1984). Multiattribute nonlinear utility theory. *Management Sci.* 30(11), 1301–1310.
Fotheringham, A.S. (1988). Consumer store choice and choice set definition. *Marketing Sci.* 7(3), 299–310.
Gensch, D.H. (1984). Targeting the switchable industrial customer. *Marketing Sci.* 3(1), 41–54.
Gensch, D.H. (1985). Empirically testing a disaggregate choice model for segments. *J. Marketing Res.* 22 (November), 462–467.
Gensch, D.H. (1987a), Empirical evidence supporting the use of multiple choice models in analyzing a population. *J. Marketing Res.* 24 (May), 197–207.
Gensch, D.H. (1987b). A two-stage disaggregate attribute choice model. *Marketing Sci.* 6(3), 223–239.
Gensch, D.H., N. Aversa and S.P. Moore (1990). A choice modeling market information system that enabled ABB Electric to expand its market share. *Interfaces* 20(1), 6–25.
Gensch, D.H., and W.W. Recker (1979). The multinomial, multiattribute logit choice model. *J. Marketing Res.* 16 (February), 124–132.

Gensch, D.H., and J.A. Svestka (1984). A maximum likelihood hierarchical disaggregate model for predicting choice of individuals. *J. Math. Psychol.* 28, 160–178.

Gessner, G., W.A. Kamakura, N.K. Malhotra and M.E. Zmijewski (1988). Estimating models with binary dependent variables: Some theoretical and empirical observations. *J. Business Res.* 16(1), 49–65.

Green, P.E., S.M. Goldberg and M. Montemayor (1981). A hybrid utility estimation model for conjoint analysis. *J. of Marketing* 45 (Winter), 33–41.

Green, P.E., and V.R. Rao (1972). *Applied Multidimensional Scaling*, Holt, Rinehart and Winston, New York.

Green, P.E., and V. Srinivasan (1978). Conjoint analysis in consumer research: Issues and outlook. *J. Consumer Res.* 5 (September), 103–123.

Green, P.E., and Y. Wind (1973). *Multi-Attribute Decisions in Marketing*, Dryden Press, Hinsdale, IL.

Guadagni, P.M., and J.D.C. Little (1983). A logit model of brand choice calibrated on scanner data. *Marketing Sci.* 2(3), 203–238.

Guadagni, P.M., and J.D.C. Little (1987). When and what to buy; A nested logit model of coffee purchase, Working Paper #1919-87, Sloan School of Management, Massachusetts Institute of Technology, Cambridge, MA (August).

Gupta, S. (1988). Impact of sales promotion on when, what, and how much to buy. *J. Marketing Res.* 25 (November), 342–355.

Hagerty, M.R., and D.A. Aaker (1984). A normative model of consumer information processing. *Marketing Sci.* 3(3), 227–246.

Harshman, R.A., P.E. Green, Y. Wind and M.E. Lundy (1982). A model for the analysis of asymmetric data in marketing research. *Marketing Sci.* 1(2), 205–242.

Hauser, J.R. (1986). Agendas and consumer choice. *J. Marketing Res.* 23 (August), 199–212.

Hauser, J.R., and F.S. Koppelman (1979). The relative accuracy and usefulness of alternative perceptual mapping techniques. *J. Marketing Res.* 14(3), 495–507.

Hauser, J.R., J.H. Roberts and G.L. Urban (1983). Forecasting sales of a new durable, in F.S. Zufryden (ed.), *Advances and Practices of Marketing Science Management*, The Institute of Management Science, Providence, RI, pp. 115–128.

Hauser, J.R., and S.M. Shugan (1980). Intensity measures of consumer preference. *Oper. Res.* 28(2), 278–320.

Hauser, J.R., and P.D. Simmie (1981). Profit maximizing product positioning. *Management Sci.* 27(1), 33–56.

Hauser, J.R., and G.L. Urban (1979). Assessment of attribute importance and consumer utility functions: Von Neumann–Morgenstern theory applied to consumer behavior. *J. Consumer Res.* 5 (March), 251–262.

Hauser, J.R., and G.L. Urban (1986). The value priority hypotheses for consumer budget plans. *J. Consumer Res.* 12 (March), 449–462.

Hauser, J.R., and B. Wernerfelt (1990). An evaluation cost model of consideration sets. *J. Consumer Res.* 16 (March), 393–408.

Hauser, J.R., and K.J. Wiesniewski (1982). Dynamic analysis of consumer response to marketing strategy. *Management Sci.* 28(5), 455–486.

Hoffman, D.L., and G.R. Franke (1986). Correspondence analysis: Graphical representation of categorical data in marketing research. *J. Marketing Res.* 23 (August), 213–227.

Horsky, D., and M.R. Rao (1984). Estimation of attribute weights from preference comparisons. *Management Sci.* 30(7), 801–822.

Howard, J.A., and J.N. Sheth (1969). *The Theory of Buyer Behavior*, Wiley, New York.

Huber, J. and M.B. Holbrook (1979). Using attribute ratings for product positioning: Some distinctions among compositional approaches. *J. Marketing Res.* 16 (November), 507–516.

Huber, J., and J. McCann (1982). The impact of inferential beliefs on product evaluations. *J. Marketing Res.* 19 (August), 324–333.

Jain, D.C., and N.J. Vilcassim (1991). Investigating household purchase timing decisions: A conditional hazard function approach. *Marketing Sci.* 10(1), 1–23.

Johnson, E.J., and R.J. Meyer (1984). Compensatory choice models of noncompensatory processes: The effect of varying context. *J. Consumer Res.* (June), 528–541.

Johnson, E.J., R.J. Meyer and S. Ghose (1989). When choice models fail: Compensatory models in negatively correlated environments. *J. Marketing Res.* 26 (August), 255–270.
Johnson, M.D. (1984). Consumer choice strategies for comparing noncomparable alternatives. *J. Consumer Res.* 11 (December), 741–753.
Johnson, M.D (1986). Modeling choice strategies for noncomparable alternatives. *Marketing Sci.* 5(1), 37–54.
Johnson, M.D. (1988). Comparability and hierarchical processing in multialternative choice. *J. Consumer Res.* 15 (December), 303–314.
Jones, J.M., and F.S. Zufryden (1981). Relating deal purchases and consumer characteristics to repeat purchase probability. *J. Marketing Res. Soc.* 23, 84–99.
Jöreskog, K., and D. Sörbom (1979). *Advances in Factor Analysis and Structural Equation Models*, Abt Books, Cambridge, MA.
Kahn, B.E., M.U. Kalwani and D.G. Morrison (1986). Measuring variety-seeking and reinforcement behaviors using panel data. *J. Marketing Res.* 23 (May), 89–100.
Kahneman, D., and A. Tversky (1979). Prospect theory: An analysis of decision under risk. *Econometrica* 47 (March), 263–291.
Kamakura, W.A., and R.K. Srivastava (1984). Predicting choice shares under conditions of brand interdependence. *J. Marketing Res.* 21 (Novemeber), 420–434.
Kamakura, W.A., and R.K. Srivastava (1986). An ideal-point probabilistic choice model for heterogeneous preferences. *Marketing Sci.* 5(3), 199–218.
Katahira, H. (1990). Perceptual mapping using ordered logit analysis. *Marketing Sci.* 9(1), 1–17.
Keeney, R.L., and H. Raiffa (1976). *Decisions with Multiple Objectives: Preferences and Value Tradeoffs*, Wiley, New York.
Keller, K.L., and R. Staelin (1989). Assessing biases in measuring decision effectiveness and information overload. *J. Consumer Res.* 15 (March), 504–508.
Lancaster, K. (1966). A new approach to consumer theory. *J. Political Economy* 74(2), 132–157.
Lattin, J.M. (1987). A model of balanced choice behavior. *Marketing Sci.* 6(1), 48–65.
Lattin, J.M., and R.E. Bucklin (1989). Reference effects of price and promotion on brand choice behavior. *J. Marketing Res.* 26 (August), 299–310.
Lattin, J.M., and L. McAlister (1985). Using a variety-seeking model to identify substitute and complementary relationships among competing products. *J. Marketing Res.* 22 (August), 330–339.
Lattin, J.M., and J.H. Roberts (1988). Modeling the role of risk-adjusted utility in the diffusion of innovation, Research paper 1019, Graduate School of Business, Stanford University, Stanford, CA (October).
Leckenby, J.D., and S. Kishi (1984). The Dirichlet multinomial distribution as a magazine exposure model. *J. Marketing Res.* 21 (February), 100–106.
Lehmann, D.R. (1971). Television show preference: Application of a choice model. *J. Marketing Res.* 8 (February), 47–55.
Lilien, G.L., P. Kotler and K.S. Moorthy (1992). *Marketing Models*, Prentice-Hall, Englewood Cliffs, NJ.
Lindblom, C.E. (1959). The science of muddling through. *Public Admin. Rev.* 19, 79–88.
Lisco, T. (1967). The value of commuter's travel time: A study of urban transportation, Ph.D. dissertation, Department of Economics, University of Chicago.
Long, J.S. (1983). *Confirmatory Factor Analysis*. Quantitative Applications in the Social Sciences, Series No. 33, Sage Publications, Beverly Hills, CA.
Louviere, J.J., and D.A. Hensher (1983). Using discrete choice models with experimental design data to forecast consumer demand for a unique cultural event. *J. Consumer Res* 10 (December), 348–361.
Louviere, J.J., and G. Woodworth (1983). Design and analysis of simulated consumer choice or allocated experiments: An approach based on aggregate data. *J. Marketing Res.* 20 (November), 350–367.
Luce, R.D. (1959). *Individual Choice Behavior*, Wiley, New York.
Lynch, J.G., Jr., and T. Srull (1982). Memory and attentional factors in consumer choice: Concepts and research methods. *J. Consumer Res.* 9 (June), 18–37.
MacKay, D.B., and J.L. Zinnes (1986). A probabilistic model for the multidimensional scaling of proximity and preference data. *Marketing Sci.* 5(4), 325–344.
Mahajan, V., E. Muller and S. Sharma (1984). An empirical comparison of awareness forecasting models of new product acceptance. *Marketing Sci.* 3 (Summer), 179–197.

Malhotra, N.K. (1982). Information load and consumer decision making. *J. Consumer Res.* 8 (March), 419–430.

Malhotra, N.K. (1986). An approach to the measurement of consumer preferences using limited information. *J. Marketing Res.* 23 (February), 33–40.

Manrai, A.K., and P. Sinha (1989). Elimination-by-cutoffs. *Marketing Sci.* 8(2), 133–152.

Mansfield, E. (1961). Technical change and the rate of imitation. *Econometrica* 29(4), 741–765.

Massy, W.F., D.B. Montgomery and D.G. Morrison (1970). *Stochastic Models of Buying Behavior*, Massachusetts Institute of Technology Press, Cambridge.

McAlister, L. (1982). A dynamic attribute satiation model of variety-seeking behavior. *J. Consumer Res.* 9 (September), 141–150.

McAlister, L., and E. Pessemier (1982). Variety-seeking behavior: An interdisciplinary review. *J. Consumer Res.* 9 (December), 311–322.

McFadden, D. (1976). Quantal choice analysis: A survey. *Ann. Econom. Social Measurement* 5 (May), 363–369.

McFadden, D. (1978). Modeling to choice of residential location, in A. Karlquist et al. (eds.), *Spatial Interaction Theory and Residential Location*, North-Holland, Amsterdam.

McFadden, D. (1980). Econometric models for probabilistic choice among products. *J. Business*, 53(3), pt. 2 (July), 513–530.

McFadden, D. (1986). The choice theory approach to market research. *Marketing Sci.* 5(4), 275–297.

McFadden, D. (1991). Advances in computation, statistical methods and testing of discrete choice models. *Marketing Lett.* 2(3), 215–230.

Meyer, R.J., and T.C. Eagle (1982). Context-induced parameter instability in a disaggregate-stochastic model of store choice. *J. Marketing Res.* 19 (February), 62–71.

Meyer, R.J., and A. Sathi (1985). A multiattribute model of consumer choice during product learning. *Marketing Sci.* 4(1), 41–61.

Midgley, D.F., P.D. Morrison and J.H. Roberts (1992). The effect of network structure in industrial diffusion processes. *Res. Policy* 21(6) 533–552.

Moore, W.L., and R.S. Winer (1987). A panel-data based method for merging joint space and market response function estimation. *Marketing Sci.* 6(1), 25–42.

Mukherjee, B.N. (1973). Analysis of covariance structures and exploratory factor analysis. *Brit. J. of Math. Statist. Psychol.* 26 (November), 125–154.

Nedungadi, P. (1990). Recall and consumer consideration sets: Influencing choice without changing brand evaluations. *J. Consumer Res.* 17(3), 263–276.

Nooteboom, B. (1989). Diffusion, uncertainty and firm size. *Intern. J. Res. Marketing* 6, 109–128.

Oliver, R.L. (1980). A cognitive model of the antecedents and consequences of satisfaction decisions. *J. Marketing Res.* 17 (November), 460–469.

Oliver, R.L., and W.S. DeSarbo (1988). Response determinants in satisfaction judgments. *J. Consumer Res.* 14 (March), 495–507.

Oren, S.S. and R.G. Schwartz (1988). Diffusion of new products in risk-sensitive markets. *J. Forecasting* 7 (October/December), 273–287.

Papatla, P., and L. Krishnamurthi (1992). A probit model of choice dynamics. *Marketing Sci.* 11(2) 189–206.

Parasuraman, A., V.A. Zeithaml and L.L. Berry (1985). A conceptual model of service quality and its implications for future research. *J. Marketing* 49(4), 41–50.

Payne, J.W., J.R. Bettman and E.J. Johnson (1988). Adaptive strategy selection in decision making. *J. Experimental Psychol.* 14, 534–552.

Punj, G.N., and R. Staelin (1978). The choice for graduate business schools. *J. Marketing Res.* 15 (November), 588–598.

Ratchford, B.T. (1982). Cost-benefit models for explaining consumer choice and information seeking behavior. *Management Sci.* 28(2), 197–212.

Richins, M.L. (1983). Negative word-of-mouth by dissatisfied consumers: A pilot study. *J. Marketing* 47 (Winter), 68–78.

Roberts, J.H., and J.M. Lattin (1991). Development and testing of a model of consideration set composition. *J. Marketing Res.* 28 (November), 429–440.

Roberts, J.H., and G.L. Urban (1988). Modeling multiattribute utility, risk, and belief dynamics for new consumer durable brand choice. *Management Sci.* 34(2), 167–185.

Robinson, M. (1985). A logit model of the all electric residence decision. *Rev. Regional Econom. Business* 11(2), 17–20.

Rogers, E.M. (1983). *Diffusion of Innovations, 3rd edition*, The Free Press, New York.

Rossiter, J.R., and L. Percy (1987). *Advertising and Promotion Management*, McGraw-Hill, New York.

Sheth, J.N. (1974). *Models of Buyer Behavior: Conceptual, Quantitative, and Empirical*, Harper and Row, New York.

Shocker, A.D., and V. Srinivasan (1979). Multi-attribute approaches for product concept evaluation and generation: A critical review. *J. Marketing Res.* 16 (May), 159–180.

Shugan, S.M. (1980). The cost of thinking. *J. Consumer Res.* 7 (September), 99–111.

Simonson, I. (1990). The effect of purchase quantity and timing on variety-seeking behavior. *J. Marketing Res.* 27 (May), 150–162.

Singh, J. (1988). Consumer complaint intentions and behavior: Definitional and taxonomical issues. *J. Marketing* 52 (January), 93–107.

Stigler, G. (1961). The economics of information. *J. Political Economy* 69(3), 213–225.

Sujan, M. (1985). Consumer knowledge: Effects on evaluation strategies mediating consumer judgments. *J. Consumer Res.* 12, 31–46.

Swan, J.E., and L.J. Combs (1976). Product performance and consumer satisfaction: A new concept. *J. Marketing* 40 (April), 25–33.

Thaler, R. (1985). Mental accounting and consumer choice. *Marketing Sci.* 4(3), 199–214.

Tse, D.K., and P.C. Wilton (1988). Models of consumer satisfaction formation: An extension. *J. Marketing Res.* 25 (May), 204–212.

Tversky, A. (1972). Elimination by aspects: A theory of choice. *Psychol. Rev.* 79, 281–299.

Tversky, A., and D. Kahneman (1974). Judgment under uncertainty: Heuristics and biases. *Science* 185, 1124–1131.

Urban, G.L., and J.R. Hauser (1980). *Design and Marketing of New Products*, Prentice-Hall, Englewood Cliffs, NJ.

Urban, G.L., J.R. Hauser and J.H. Roberts (1990). Prelaunch forecasting of new automobiles. *Management Sci.* 36(4), 401–421.

Urban, G.L., J.S. Hulland and B.D. Weinberg (1990). Modeling categorization, elimination, and consideration for new product forecasting of consumer durables, Working Paper No. 3206–90, Sloan School of Management, Massachusetts Institute of Technology, Cambridge, MA.

Urbany, J.E., T.J. Madden and P.R. Dickson (1989). All's not fair in pricing: An initial look at the dual entitlement principle. *Marketing Lett.* 1(1), 17–25.

Wagner, U., and A. Taudes (1986). A multivariate Polya model of brand choice and purchase incidence. *Marketing Sci.* 5(3), 219–244.

Westbrook, R.A. (1987). Product/consumption-based affective responses and postpurchase processes. *J. Marketing Res.* 24 (August), 258–270.

Wilson, D.T., H.L. Matthews and J.W. Harvey (1975). An empirical test of the Fishbein behavioral intention model. *J. Consumer Res.* 1, 39–48.

Winer, R.S. (1986). A reference price model of brand choice for frequently purchased products. *J. Consumer Res.* 13 (September), 250–256.

Woodruff, R.B., E.R. Cadotte and R.L. Jenkins (1983). Modeling consumer satisfaction processes using experience-based norms. *J. Marketing Res.* 20 (August), 296–304.

Wright, P.L., and F. Barbour (1977). Phased decision strategies: Sequels to an initial screening, in M. Starr and M. Zeleny (eds.), *Multiple Criteria Decision Making, North-Holland TIMS Studies in the Management Sciences,* Vol. 6, North-Holland, Amsterdam, pp. 91–109.

Zaltman, G., and M. Wallendorf (1979). *Consumer Behavior: Basic Findings and Management Implications*, Wiley, New York.

Zeithaml, V.A., A. Parasuraman and L.L. Berry (1990). *Delivering Quality Service: Balancing Customer Perceptions*, The Free Press, New York.

J. Eliashberg and G.L. Lilien, Eds., *Handbooks in OR & MS, Vol. 5*

Chapter 3

Mathematical Models of Group Choice and Negotiations

Kim P. Corfman

Leonard N. Stern School of Business, New York University, 40 W. 4th Street, New York, NY 10003, USA

Sunil Gupta

School of Business Administration, University of Michigan, Ann Arbor, MI 48109-1234, USA

1. Introduction

In the last decade increasing numbers of researchers in marketing have recognized the importance of group choice and negotiations in many kinds of consumer behavior, organizational purchasing, management decision-making, and marketing-channel relationships. Families purchasing durables, buying committees selecting suppliers, and salespeople negotiating terms are the examples that come first to mind. However, intra- and inter-firm management teams are increasing in importance and broaden the relevance of group choice and negotiations to a wider variety of management tasks. For example, CalCom Inc. now uses integrated product-development teams that include all of the key disciplines to cut development time (*Sales and Marketing Management*, March 1991). Procter & Gamble, Kraft General Foods, Quaker Oats, and Johnson & Johnson are just a few of the manufacturers who now assign sales teams to work closely with retailer teams on merchandising (*New York Times*, 14 July, 1991). Digital Equipment Corp. and Ramtek have recently begun to engage in team selling to prospects who indicate an interest in the products of both manufacturers (*Sales and Marketing Management*, May 1990). The functioning of these groups requires joint decision-making and negotiations on issues important to all parties.

Despite the prevalence and importance of group decision-making and negotiations in marketing, relatively few researchers are actively exploring this subject and even fewer concentrate on modeling group choice and negotiations. In this chapter, our focus is on models that attempt to describe the outcomes of actual group decisions, including negotiations. (We also review normative models as important background and foundation for descriptive modeling.) Descriptive modeling provides insight into the group decision-making process and the ability to predict the outcomes of those processes, which can be used to guide the actions of decision-makers and help them anticipate each other's actions.

The work that has appeared in marketing has drawn on research from a large number of areas outside marketing including social welfare theory, decision theory, game theory, labor economics, small group processes, social decision schemes, and work on power and influence in a variety of contexts. Few, however, make use of more than one or two research streams in other disciplines. The underlying similarity of the problems being addressed in the many approaches to the study of group choice leads us to suspect that more advantage could be taken of work that has been done in other disciplines, in the development of group choice and bargaining models in marketing. Greater awareness of this work could begin this process and is the goal of the first major section of this paper. One important way in which this body of research can be used is to develop model-classification schemes or typologies to organize our knowledge and serve as guides to the modeling of group choice and negotiations in various contexts. In this paper we also begin this task.

The paper is organized as follows. In Section 2 we establish the scope of the paper. The goal of the first major section, Section 3, is to review the development and testing of mathematical models of group choice and bargaining in marketing and several other relevant disciplines. This review is designed to indicate the progress that has been made in the mathematical modeling of group choice and bargaining and to highlight convergence and inconsistencies in findings across studies. Specifically, Section 3.1 reviews normative models, Section 3.2 reviews models from social psychology with emphasis on social decision schemes, and Section 3.3 reviews modeling in marketing applied to families, organizations, other groups of consumers, and buyers and sellers. In Section 4 we suggest some dimensions that should prove useful in developing model-classification schemes or typologies. The goal of the final section, Section 5, is to demonstrate how specific situations can be described in terms of these classifying dimensions and how classification can serve as a guide to modeling. We provide three examples of areas in which modeling decisions as group choices is important for the accurate representation of the decisions involved and suggest how this modeling might proceed in light of how each problem is positioned on important dimensions.

2. Focus and definitions

The focus of this chapter is on descriptive mathematical models of choice or decision-making in groups. (We treat choice and decision-making as synonyms.) Although many conceptual models of group decision-making have been proposed and many hypotheses concerning group processes have been tested which have implications for the development of mathematical models, we concentrate on the mathematical models themselves.

We define a group as a collection of people who are united by bonds among members' interests and goals that are sufficiently strong to overcome disunifying influences [Deutsch, 1973, p. 49]. These bonds may be complex and enduring, as they are in families, or they may be simpler and more transient, as in many business relationships. Note that our view of groups and group decisions encompasses negotiators and bargaining tasks. Although the contexts from which bargaining models have grown and those to which they are applied tend to differ from the origins and uses of group-choice models, the similarities between the underlying problems are greater than the differences. We view negotiations as a subset of group decision-making, typically involving two parties and an allocation of resources.

Finally, we focus on decision-making as opposed to problem-solving. Laughlin [1980] refers to these as judgmental and intellective tasks, respectively, and suggests that a particular task may be thought of as lying on a continuum anchored by these extremes. Because this is a continuum, the distinction between decision-making and problem-solving is not always clear, but generally problem-solving emphasizes the construction of response alternatives that are demonstrably correct, while decision-making is performed when there is no objectively correct answer and emphasizes the selection of an alternative based on member preferences or opinions.

3. Models of group choice

We begin by reviewing normative models of group choice and negotiations. Then we discuss modeling in social psychology, primarily that motivated by social decision scheme theory. Finally, we review work in marketing that has used group-choice models in the contexts of family consumption, organizational purchasing, various other groups, and buyer–seller negotiations. Table 3.1 lists the models that will be reviewed in this section.

3.1. Normative theories of group choice

In this section we review models of group choice based primarily on social welfare theory, decision theory and game theory.[1] Although our primary interest is in models that explain or describe behavior, normative theories of group choice form an important foundation on which many descriptive models have been and could be built. Also, by making explicit the assumptions needed to support various functional forms, the normative models provide directions regarding the appropriate formulation and the information requirements for a given situation.

The normative approach to group choice deals with the specification of decision rules that map the preferences of individual group members into a collective choice, preference order, or utility function. There are, of course, many possible mappings. Normative research in group decision theory examines how *reasonable* these

[1] Due to space considerations we do not review coalition theory. See Murnighan [1978] and Shubik [1982] for reviews of the social-psychological, political science and game theory approaches.

Table 3.1
Models introduced

Normative models
Condorcet [Arrow, 1950; Guillbaud, 1966]
Group consensus ranking [Kemeny & Snell, 1962]
Decision-theoretic aggregation rules:
  Group utilities under risk [Harsanyi, 1955; Keeney & Kirkwood, 1975]
  Group values under certainty [Dyer & Sarin, 1979; Eliashberg & Winkler, 1981]
Cooperative game theory:
  Nash solution [1950]
  Kalai–Smorodinsky [1975]
  Lexical maximin [Roth, 1979]
  Gupta–Livne [1988]
  Van Damme [1986]
Noncooperative game theory:
  Complete information models [Rubinstein, 1982; Binmore, Shaked & Sutton, 1989]
  Incomplete information models (See Table 3.2)

Models from social psychology
Social decision schemes [Davis, 1973]
  Proportionality
  Equiprobability
  Majority
  Plurality
  Compromise/arithmetic mean/averaging
  Truth wins
  Highest expected value
  Extreme member/most (least) risky wins
  Neutral member
  Risk-supported (conservative-supported or caution-supported) wins
Level of aspiration [Harnett, 1967]
Modified majority rule [Luce & Raiffa, 1957]
Binomial model of jury decisions [Penrod & Hastie, 1979]

Models from marketing
Families:
  Weighted linear/weighted probability model [Kriewall, 1980; Krishnamurthi, 1981]
  Equal weight model [Curry & Menasco, 1979]
  WLM with instrumental variables [Corfman & Lehmann, 1987; Steckel, Lehmann & Corfman, 1988]
  Multiattribute dyadic choice model [Curry, Menasco & Van Ark, 1991]
Organizations:
  Industrial market response model [Choffray & Lilien, 1978, 1980]
    Weighted probability
    Voting
    Minimum endorsement
    Preference perturbation
  WLM with polarization [Rao & Steckel, 1989]
  WLM with constructive vs. destructive power [Steckel & O'Shaughnessy, 1989]
Buyer–seller negotiations (no new models introduced)

decision rules are. Some of the concerns in making a normative evaluation are how *equitable* a decision rule is in its distribution of the benefits or losses resulting from the group's actions, and the *efficiency* of the group's choice. For example, suppose option A provides equal expected benefits to all members, and option B does not. Also, suppose option B is preferred to option A by each individual in the group. How does the decision rule resolve the tradeoff between *efficiency* and *equity*? Further, how are the interests of the various group members weighed one against each other? Are the preferences of all members equally important in determining the group's choice? If not, is there a normative basis for determining the relative weights given to the various individuals? As can be seen even from this brief discussion, the choice of an appropriate group-decision rule is non-trivial. Consequently, much of the normative research in group decision-making is aimed at (i) specifying some primitives that ought to be satisfied by any group-decision rule, and (ii) examining the efficiency and equity characteristics of rules derived on the basis of these primitives.

The foundation for much of this research was laid by the fundamental results of Condorcet, reported in Arrow [1950] and Guillbaud [1966]. Condorcet argued that the only reasonable way to choose one from among several feasible alternatives is to pick the item that is at least as preferred as any other by at least half of the group members. In a democratic society, basing collective decisions on the will of the majority has obvious efficiency and equity appeal. Attractive as this decision rule is, Condorcet also showed that in some situations a majority winner need not exist. For example, consider the following preference orders for a group of three individuals:

$$a \succ b \succ c$$

$$b \succ c \succ a$$

$$c \succ a \succ b$$

Applying Condorcet's principle, the group should prefer a to b, b to c, and c to a, leading to an intransitivity. There is no Condorcet winner. Arrow [1951] showed that this paradox of collective choice is impossible to eliminate.[2] His 'general possibility theorem' showed that there is no procedure for obtaining a group ordering (ranking) of the various alternatives, based on individual members' rankings, that satisfies five reasonable and seemingly innocuous assumptions. Yet, groups must make defensible choices. The focus of much subsequent research has centered on specifying and examining various rules by which groups can make collective choices based on the wishes of their members.

[2]Subsequently, Gibbard [1973, 1977] and Satterthwaite [1975] have shown that any decision rule which satisfies Arrow's axioms is *manipulable* in the sense that it can be to the advantage of some group members to behave strategically (by controlling the agenda, or misrepresenting preferences). Manipulability is generally considered undesirable because it implies that some group members (those who can control the agenda) can exert unacceptable influence on the collective choice.

Much of the work in social welfare theory has been aimed at examining ways in which one or more of Arrow's assumptions can be changed to avoid the impossibility result. For example, Sen [1982] examined the possibility of arriving at a group choice (the single best outcome) rather than an entire ordering. Black [1958] suggested a restriction on the individual preferences (single-peakedness) which, if satisfied, would lead to a group ordering. Others have examined the ways in which commonly used choice procedures (e.g. plurality, Borda sum-of-ranks, and approval voting) satisfy and violate Arrow's requirements. [See Fishburn, 1986; Gupta & Kohli, 1990; Plott, 1976; Sen, 1977 for reviews.] Beginning with Kemeny & Snell [1962], several authors have proposed computational methods for deriving a *group consensus ranking* based on the individual preference orders. Recognizing that a transitive majority order may often not exist, these models attempt to find that ranking of the alternatives which minimizes the sum of its 'distance' from the individual rank orders. [See Ali, Cook & Kress, 1986; Cook & Kress, 1985; Cook & Seiford, 1978; Blin & Whinston, 1974; Bowman & Colantoni, 1973.] Finally, the decision theoretic approach, discussed next, shows that the impossibility can indeed be avoided, but the information requirements on individual preferences must be increased. These models start with cardinal utility functions (instead of Arrow's rank orders), and require interpersonal comparability.

3.1.1. Decision-theoretic aggregation rules.[3]

The decision-theoretic approach is distinguished by its reliance on cardinal measures of individual preferences and the specification of rationality postulates for the group's behavior to derive preference aggregation rules. Individual preferences are assumed to be either risky utility functions (usually assessed through lottery procedures), or measurable value functions (usually assessed through conjoint measurement). We shall use $u_i(x)$ ($v_i(x)$) to denote the ith individual's utility (value) for alternative x (for the need to distinguish between utility and value functions, see Dyer & Sarin [1982], Sarin [1982]), and $G_u(x)$ ($G_v(x)$) to denote the corresponding group preference rules.

Group utilities under risk. Beginning with Harsanyi [1955], the basic concern of this stream of research has been to examine the implications of requiring the group's actions to be governed by postulates of rationality similar to those of expected utility theory for individuals. For example, starting with risky individual utility functions, Harsanyi [1955] showed that if the group is to behave in a Bayesian rational manner then G_u, the group utility function, must be additive:

$$G_u(x) = \sum_{i=1}^{n} k_i u_i(x) \tag{1}$$

where $u_i(x)$ is the ith individual's utility for the consequence, x, of some alternative

[3]This discussion is based largely on Dyer & Sarin [1979], Keeney & Kirkwood [1975] and Keeney & Raiffa [1976].

(u_i's scaled from 0 to 1), and the k_i's are constants which reflect the relative weight accorded to the *i*th individual's preferences.

We can now introduce two important issues regarding group utility functions. First, use of group utility functions requires not only cardinal individual utilities, but also the exogenous specification of k_i's. This implies the need to make interpersonal comparisons among the members. More specifically, the individual utilities must be *cardinally comparable*. That is, if we apply any permissible affine transformation to the *i*th individual's utility function, we must also apply the *same* transformation to every other individual utility function, or adjust the values of k_i's. Thus, the price paid for satisfying Arrow's assumptions has been an increase in the information requirements of individual utilities (interpersonal comparisons are not required in Arrow's formulation). Further, making such comparisons is especially difficult for risky utilities because such functions do not reveal strength of preference [Dyer & Sarin, 1982; Sarin, 1982]. Scaling and weighting individual utility functions can be particularly troublesome in the absence of norms or clear power structures within the group.

The second issue is that of the distribution of benefits among group members. It is best illustrated with the following two-person example from Keeney & Raiffa [1976]. Consider the following three alternatives:

Alternative *A*: $u_1 = 1$ and $u_2 = 0$ for certain,
Alternative *B*: There is a 50–50 chance of either $u_1 = 0$ and $u_2 = 1$, or $u_1 = 1$ and $u_2 = 0$,
Alternative *C*: There is a 50–50 chance of either $u_1 = 1$ and $u_2 = 1$, or $u_1 = 0$ and $u_2 = 0$.

Using the additive function (1), the group must be indifferent among the three alternatives, although this may not be considered equitable. With alternative *B* one of the two will be envious of the other. With alternative *C*, either both get their best outcome or both get the worst outcome, and it may, therefore, be considered more equitable. The additive function only considers the sum of utilities, not its distribution.

An alternative to the additive function, relying on a weaker set of assumptions than Harsanyi's [see Keeney, 1976; Keeney & Kirkwood, 1975; Keeney & Raiffa, 1976, Chapter 10], is given by:

$$G_u(x) = \sum_{i=1}^{n} k_i u_i(x) + k \sum_{\substack{i=1; \\ j>i}}^{n} k_i k_j u_i(x) u_j(x) + \cdots + k^{n-1} k_1 k_2 \cdots k_n u_1(x) u_2(x) \cdots u_n(x) \qquad (2)$$

where $0 < k_i < 1$, $k > -1$, and $\sum k_i \neq 1$. In this formulation, k provides information about the group's attitude toward risk, and k_i denotes the importance assigned to the preferences of the *i*th individual. To see the effect of k, let us return to the three-alternative example. Suppose $k_1 = k_2 = 0.4$, $k = 1.25$. Then, $G_u(x) = 0.4u_1(x) + 0.4u_2(x) + 0.2u_1(x)u_2(x)$. As the group's utilities are specified for consequences of alternatives, the group's expected utility for some *alternative*, say B, is calculated as follows. $G_u(B) = 0.5[(0.4)(1) + (0.4)(0) + (0.2)(1)(0)] + 0.5[0.4(0) + 0.4(1) + 0.2(0)(1)] = 0.4$. This should be contrasted with $0.4(\mathrm{E}u_1(B) = 0.5) + 0.4(\mathrm{E}u_2(B) = 0.5) + 0.2(\mathrm{E}u_1(B) \cdot \mathrm{E}u_2(B) = 0.25) = 0.45$, where $\mathrm{E}u_i(B)$ is the ith individual's expected utility from B. In the latter calculation individuals (not the group) assess the expected utility. Thus, it fails to model the group's behavior under uncertainty. This distinction will be important in dicusssing the cooperative game-theoretic models of bargaining.

So, the group's utilities for alternatives A, B and C are 0.4, 0.4 and 0.5, respectively. The group prefers to take the chance that both people will get the worst outcome (alternative C) rather than assuring the best outcome to one of its members (alternative B). This preference for alternative C has often been interpreted as reflecting the group's concern for posterior equity, represented by the multiplicative term in (2). But there is a problem with this interpretation [Dyer & Sarin, 1979]. Because risky utility functions do not reflect strength of preferences, it is difficult to say whether the preference for alternative C reflects equity proneness or risk proneness. Dyer & Sarin [1979] suggest that the value of k in (2) is better interpreted as a representation of the group's attitude towards risk. When $k = 0$, (2) reduces to the simple additive form proposed by Harsanyi [1955], (1), and the group's risk attitude is completely determined by the risk attitudes of its members. When $k < 0$ ($k > 0$), the group will be more (less) risk-averse than its members. A substantial body of experimental literature has noted 'shifts' in the group's risk preferences. That is, the group's preferences are often observed to be more, or less, risk-averse than those of the average member. Thus, the normative model (2) has considerable descriptive validity.

The ability to reflect 'shifts' in a group's risk attitude comes at a price. It is no longer possible to guarantee that the chosen outcome is Pareto-optimal (i.e., there is no other alternative that is preferred to the chosen one by all group members). To see this, suppose there is a fourth alternative, D, with $u_1 = u_2 = 0.48$ for certain. Note that both individuals prefer $B(\mathrm{E}u_1 = \mathrm{E}u_2 = 0.5)$ to D. Using (2), the group's expected utility for alternative D is 0.43, which is greater than the group's 0.4 expected utility for alternative B. Thus, the group's choice is not Pareto-optimal. Kirkwood [1979] has shown that if $k > 0$, this possibility is inescapable.

Group values under certainty. In the preceding section we saw that the multiplicative part of (2) could not properly be interpreted as a reflection of the group's concern for equity. Yet, the ability to model such concerns is both theoretically and empirically important. Dyer & Sarin [1979] have postulated several assumptions, based on measurable value functions, to obtain the following result:

$$G_v(x) = \sum_{i=1}^{n} \lambda_i v_i(x) + \lambda \sum_{\substack{i=1;\\ j>i}}^{n} \lambda_i \lambda_j v_i(x) v_j(x) + \cdots + \lambda^{n-1} \lambda_1 \lambda_2 \cdots \lambda_n v_1(x) v_2(x) \cdots v_n(x) \qquad (3)$$

where $0 < \lambda_i < 1$, $\lambda > -1$ and $\sum \lambda_i \neq 1$. Note the similarity in the basic forms of Equations (2) and (3). In both cases, individual preferences are measured on a cardinal scale, and the group preference function requires cardinal comparability. But because the preferences are expressed for riskless alternatives, the value functions in (3) reflect strength of preference. Consequently, the important difference lies in the interpretation of λ. When $\lambda = 0$, (3) reduces to a simple additive form and the group is inequity-neutral. Any distribution of v_i's that results in the same sum of values is equally preferred. When $\lambda > 0$ the group is inequity-averse, preferring a balanced distribution of individual values. Finally, when $\lambda < 0$, the group is inequity-prone, preferring variations in individual values. To see this consider the following two-alternative, two-person example:

Alternative *A*: $v_1 = 0.5$ and $v_2 = 0.5$,
Alternative *B*: $v_1 = 1$ and $v_2 = 0$.

If $\lambda = 0$, $\lambda_1 = \lambda_2 = 0.5$, then $G_v(x) = 0.5\,v_1(x) + 0.5\,v_2(x)$, and the group is indifferent between the two alternatives. If $\lambda = 1.25$ and $\lambda_1 = \lambda_2 = 0.4$, then the equal distribution of alternative *A* is preferred. Finally, if λ is negative, the unequal distribution of alternative *B* would be most preferred. Thus, this formulation permits us to model the group's attitude towards equity. But, we are restricted to riskless alternatives.

Together, Equations (2) and (3) provide different preference-based approaches to modeling the experimentally observed phenomena of group polarization and concern for equity. However, neither formulation alone can deal adequately with both. Clearly, shifts in risk attitudes and concerns for equity can arise in the same decision-making situation. One obvious possibility would be to separately assess individual values and utilities, and to calibrate both of these models. Then, by comparing the values of λ and k, shifts in a group's preferences from a simple average could be attributed to the appropriate phenomenon. For example, if $\lambda > k = 0$, shifts in the group's preferences could be attributed to concerns for equity alone. Of course, the cost of this added ability to separate the phenomena is the need for added information about individual preferences.

Eliashberg & Winkler [1981] have proposed an alternative model that can simultaneously incorporate individual and group attitudes toward risk and concern for equity. In their model, each individual's preferences are expressed as cardinal utilities for entire vectors of payoffs to every group member. (By contrast, in Equations (2) and (3), the individual utility functions express only that person's own preference for a consequence.) Thus, the utility functions represent 'an individual's preferences concerning equitable and inequitable distributions' as well as attitudes toward risk. The individual utility functions are then combined (using linear or multilinear aggregation functions) to yield a group utility function. The analysis shows that large groups of risk-averse members might be expected to be approximately risk-neutral (a risky shift).

3.1.2 Bargaining[4]: Game-theory

Two principal traditions characterize the game-theoretic analysis of bargaining. Nash's [1950] bargaining problem is the basic framework adopted by cooperative

[4]Closely related to bargaining is the topic of arbitration, where a third party resolves the conflict between two principals. For a model of arbitration that reflects both the game-theoretic and the decision-theoretic approaches, see Eliashberg [1986].

game theorists for the study of two-person bargaining situations. The approach adopted in this literature is to codify as axioms certain basic negotiation principles and to derive a unique final outcome. The process by which the final outcome is negotiated is not modeled. The noncooperative game-theoretic tradition [Osborne & Rubinstein, 1990; Rubinstein, 1982; Sutton, 1986], by contrast, attempts to model the bargaining process with detailed rules of play and then determine the optimal behavior of the bargainers, as well as the final outcome. The principal models and results of each tradition are discussed next.

Cooperative game theory. In the framework of Nash's bargaining problem, payoffs from each feasible outcome are represented in a two-dimensional space where each axis represents the cardinal utility to one of the parties. Each point (b_1, b_2) in the feasible region (B) represents the utilities that would accrue simultaneously to the two bargainers from some resolution of the conflict. The feasible region is bounded by the *Pareto boundary*, i.e. the set of outcomes that is not dominated by any other feasible outcome. An important assumption made in this approach is that there is a *threat* or *conflict* point, $c = (c_1, c_2)$, that explicates the utilities for each bargainer in the event of no agreement. Given the bargaining problem (B, c), and without regard to the actual physical outcomes involved, cooperative game theorists specify axioms that lead to one of the points on the Pareto boundary as the unique, logical solution concept, $f(B, c)$.

Before proceeding with descriptions of the various solution concepts it is useful to point out the differences between the decision-theoretic models of the previous section and the bargaining problem discussed here. Clearly, in both cases individual cardinal utilities determine the outcome of a group process. However, there are important distinctions. First, the primary emphasis of the decision-theoretic models is to specify how a group should behave so that its actions are consistent with some postulates of rationality. The axiomatic models of bargaining, by contrast, are more concerned with the allocation of payoffs among the individuals and the rationality postulates are imposed on the individuals, not the dyad. Consequently, the decision-theoretic approach for risky alternatives seeks to determine the expected value of the group utility function. The bargaining approach, by contrast, seeks a solution *after* each individual's expected utility has been determined for each possible alternative. Second, the conflict point plays a prominent role in bargaining models. Either negotiator has the opportunity to break off negotiations and receive the conflict payoff. Further, the focus of the models, typically, is on the gains of each individual (relative to the conflict payoff). Such threat points are not of immediate relevance to a theory which seeks to model how a group should behave as a single entity in a rational manner. Consequently, no such outcome is singled out in the group decision models. An important consequence of modeling conflict points, together with a transformation-invariance assumption (see A1 below), is that the game-theoretic models typically do not have to rely on interpersonally comparable utility functions. In fact, as discussed below, we can examine directly the impact of different degrees of interpersonal comparability on the resulting solution concept. A final distinction is that some of the game-theoretic solutions are limited to two-person groups. Extensions to n-person games can lead to indeterminacy in the final outcome.

The most prominent of the solution concepts in cooperative game theory is the *Nash solution* [Nash 1950, 1953]. Nash postulated four properties (axioms) that it would be reasonable for a bargaining solution to satisfy:

A1: *Invariance under affine transformations.* If a bargaining problem (B', c') is obtained from (B, c) by the transformation $b_i \rightarrow \alpha_i b_i + \beta_i$, where $\alpha_i > 0$, for $i = 1, 2$, then, $f_i(B', c') = \alpha_i f_i(B, c) + \beta_i$ for $i = 1, 2$.

Because cardinal utility functions are unique only up to affine transformations, this axiom requires that the particular (arbitrary) scaling chosen ought not to change the outcome of the game (only the utility numbers associated with the outcomes may be different). Because separate transformations may be applied to the utilities of the two negotiators, this condition implies that interpersonal comparisons are neither required, nor even permitted.

A2: *Symmetry.* If the bargaining game (B, c) is symmetric, *i.e.* $c_1 = c_2$, and (b_1, b_2) in B implies (b_2, b_1) in B, then $f_1(B, c) = f_2(B, c)$.

The axiom states that only the utilities associated with the feasible outcomes and the conflict point determine the relative payoffs to the negotiators. No other information in needed or permitted to determine the outcome.

A3: *Independence of irrelevant alternatives.* If (B, c) and (D, c) are bargaining problems with $B \subseteq D$ and $f(D, c) \epsilon B$, then $f(B, c) = f(D, c)$.

That is, suppose that the outcome agreed upon by the two negotiators, with all the alternatives of T available to choose from, also belongs to the smaller set B. Then, if the same negotiators (endowed with the same utility functions, and having the same conflict payoffs) were to negotiate over the smaller set B, they ought still to agree on the same outcome as before, T. The unavailable alternatives of D should be regarded as irrelevant. This has proven to be one of the most problematic of the axioms.

A4: *Pareto optimality.* Suppose (B, c) is a bargaining problem, $b \epsilon B$, $d \epsilon B$, and $d_i > b_i$ for $i = 1, 2$. Then $f(B, c) \neq b$.

This implies that the negotiators never agree on an outcome b whenever another outcome d, which is better for both, is available. It also implies that some agreement should always be reached, because c is not Pareto optimal. It is worth noting that Pareto optimality is required in bargaining models, whereas it can not be guaranteed in any group utility function that is not additive. The difference, once again, arises from Nash's requirement of a weaker form of collective rationality than that demanded by the decision theoretic models of group choice. In fact,

Roth [1979] showed that if A4 is replaced with individual rationality ($f(B,c) \geqslant c$) only the Nash solution, or the conflict point itself can satisfy the axioms. Further, Roth [1977] showed that replacing this axiom with *strong* individual rationality, ($f(B,c) > c$), results uniquely in the Nash solution.

Nash [1950] showed that the four axioms A1–A4 are *uniquely* satisfied by the point on the Pareto boundary that maximizes the product of the gains, over the conflict point, to each of the parties, i.e. $n(B,c) = x$ such that $x \geqslant c$ and $(x_1 - c_1)(x_2 - c_2) \geqslant (b_1 - c_1)(b_2 - c_2)$ for all b in $B, y \geqslant c$ and $b \neq x$. (See Figure 3.1.)

The multiplicative form of the Nash solution is particularly noteworthy. When the individual utilities are assessed on riskless alternatives (value functions), the Nash solution may be seen as emphasizing the concern for equity we noted in the multiplicative group-value function (3). For any given sum of gains over conflict payoffs, the product of value gains will be maximized for more equal individual gains. Thus, one interpretation of the Nash solution is that if each negotiator agrees that the axioms are reasonable, then in the terminology of MacCrimmon & Messick [1976], each is socially motivated by *proportionate cooperation.* That is, each negotiator wants to increase the joint gain, but only to the extent that

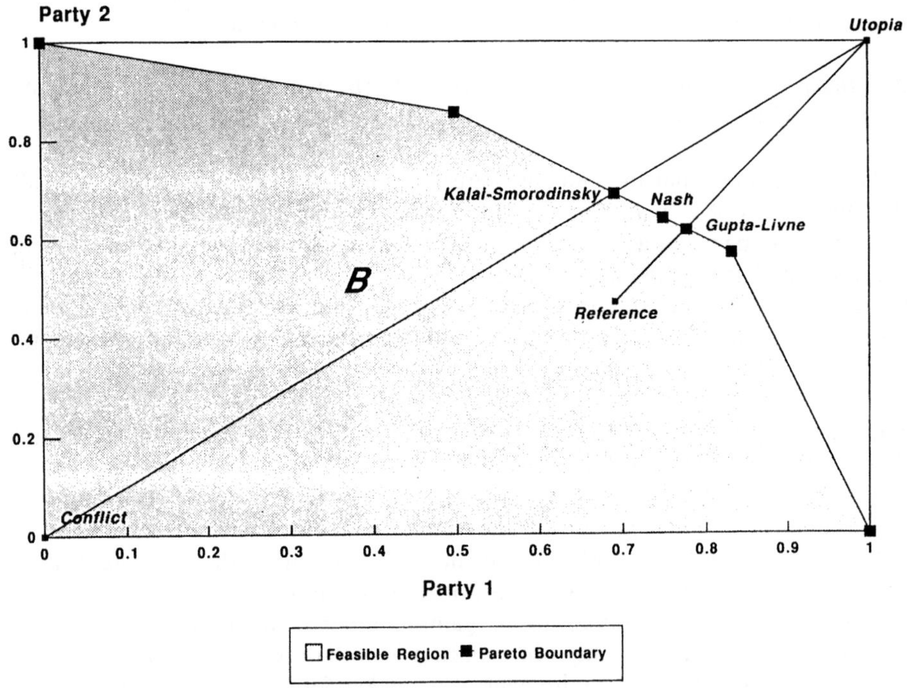

Fig. 3.1. Some solution concepts.

their own share in it also increases. Consequently, if two negotiators, endowed with their personal preferences and the social motive of proportionate cooperation were faced with the bargaining problem (B, c), they would be expected to agree upon the Nash solution $n(B, c)$. Finally, we note that the Nash solution can be extended to n-person groups [Kaneko & Nakamura, 1979]. Note, however, that even if only one individual prefers his or her status quo to an alternative that is everyone else's first choice, the latter alternative will not be the group's choice. Effectively, each individual has the power to veto the desires of all others (there is no such veto power in the decision-theoretic models).

Perhaps the most significant impact of Nash's seminal work has been in demonstrating that the seemingly indeterminate bargaining problem could indeed be structured and unique outcomes could be determined on the basis of simple, reasonable assumptions. Consequently, much of the subsequent game-theoretic research in bargaining has dealt with examining the effects of changing the axioms. In addition to a desire for fuller understanding of the problem, some of this research has also been motivated by a wish to represent the results of actual negotiations more accurately.

Kalai & Smorodinsky [1975] motivated their solution concept with the example shown in Figure 3.2. In the figure, note that compared to the payoffs in the smaller game (B, c) (defined by the convex hull of $(0,0)$, $(0,1)$, $(3/4, 3/4)$ and $(1,0)$), player 2 always gets a larger payoff in the game (D, c) (defined by the convex hull of $(0,0)$, $(1,0.7)$ and $(1,1)$). Yet the Nash solution payoff $n_2(D, c) = 0.7$ is smaller than $n_2(B, c) = 3/4$. That is, player 2's payoff actually decreases even though the possibilities have improved. To resolve this, Kalai & Smorodinsky suggested replacing the independence-to-irrelevant-alternatives axiom (A3) with:

A5: *Individual monotonicity.* If the set B of feasible outcomes is enlarged to the set D in such a way that, for every payoff to player 1, the range of feasible payoffs to player 2 is increased, then player 2's final payoff in the enlarged game, $f_2(D, c)$, should be at least as large as the payoff $f_2(B, c)$ in the smaller game.

They then proved that this monotonicity requirement, along with Nash's other axioms, provides a unique solution $KS(B, c) = x$ such that $x \in B$, $(x_1 - c_1)/(x_2 - c_2) = (U_1 - c_1)/(U_2 - c_2)$ and $x \geqslant b$ for all b in B such that $(b_1 - c_1)/(b_2 - c_2) = (U_1 - c_1)/(U_2 - c_2)$. Here, U_i is the highest utility provided by any feasible outcome to the ith player. The KS solution lies at the intersection of the Pareto boundary with the line joining the conflict point to the 'utopia point' (U_1, U_2). In Figure 3.2, the KS solution is $(10/3, 10/3)$.

The KS solution can also be expressed in the following manner:

$$\text{maximize} \quad k_1 b_1 + k_2 b_2$$

$$\text{subject to} \quad \frac{k_1}{k_2} = \frac{U_1 - c_1}{U_2 - c_2}.$$

We can now examine the relation between the KS solution and the decision-

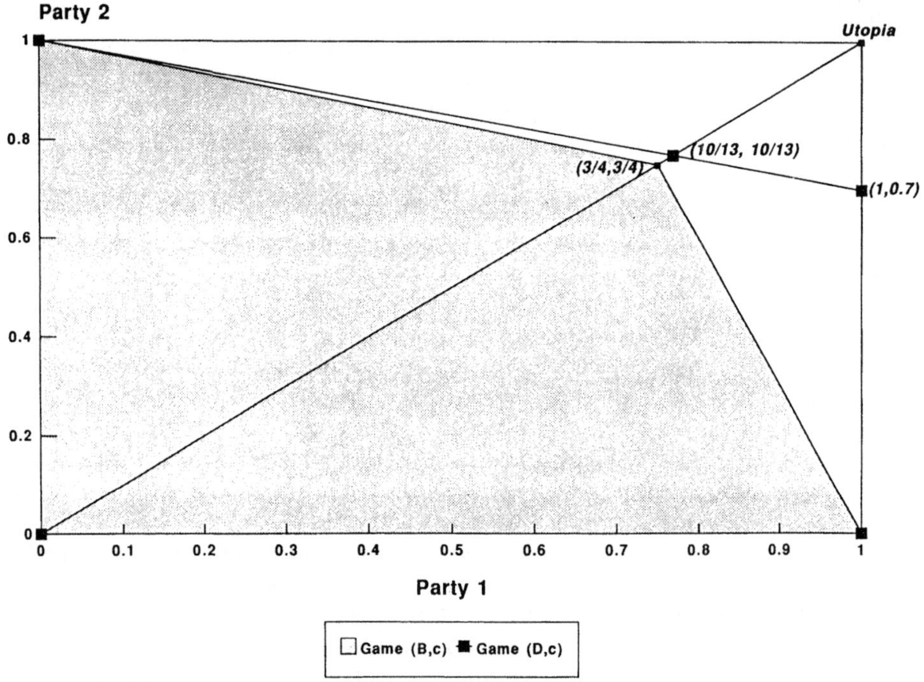

Fig. 3.2. Individual monotonicity.

theoretic models. As in (3) with $\lambda = 0$, the KS solution attempts to maximize the joint payoffs. But, instead of expressing the concern for equity with a multiplicative term, the desirability of an outcome is determined by the ratios in the constraint. If $U_i - c_i$ is interpreted as the ith player's 'need' [Brock, 1980], then the scaling constants k_i can be interpreted as providing more weight to the needier player. Notice that here the weights are determined endogenously as a ratio of differences in cardinal utilities, rather than exogenously as they are in the decision-theoretic models. Because ratios of differences are invariant under affine transformations, interpersonal comparisons of utilities are not needed. Finally, the constraint shows that the KS solution corresponds with MacCrimmon & Messick's [1976] social motive of proportionate equalitarianism; in a symmetric game, choices which decrease the ratio between the larger payoff and the smaller payoff are preferred.

In the bargaining solutions considered so far interpersonal comparisons have not been permitted. We now consider a solution, due to Roth [1979], which relies on ordinal interpersonal comparisons. That is, statements such as, 'You gain more than me if A is chosen', are permissible. Specifically, Roth proposed the following axiom:

A6: *Independence of ordinal transformations preserving interpersonal comparisons.* If B' is derived from B via a transformation $t = (t_1, t_2)$ (of feasible payoff vectors in B to feasible payoff vectors in B') which: (i) preserves each player's ordinal preferences, and (ii) preserves information about which player makes the larger gain at any given outcome, then $f_i(B', c') = t_i(f(B, c))$.

Note that a transformation t which preserves interpersonal comparisons divides the payoff space into the three regions $\{b \mid b_1 - c_1 = b_2 - c_2\}$, $\{b \mid b_1 - c_1 > b_2 - c_2\}$, and $\{b \mid b_1 - c_1 < b_2 - c_2\}$ (see Figure 3.3), and it ensures that each point (after transformation) stays in its original region. Roth showed that $r(B, c) = x$ such that $\min\{x_1 - c_1, x_2 - c_2\} > \min\{b_1 - c_1, b_2 - c_2\}$ for all y in the strong Pareto set of B and $y \neq x$, is the unique solution which satisfies strong individual rationality, strong Pareto optimality, independence of irrelevant alternatives, and independence of ordinal transformations preserving interpersonal comparisons. That is, the solution r picks the strongly Pareto-optimal point which comes closest to giving the players equal gains. And this is true even in a game with an asymmetric payoff space. (See Figure 3.3.) The function r can also be described as a lexical maximin function which seeks to maximize the minimum gains available to either player.

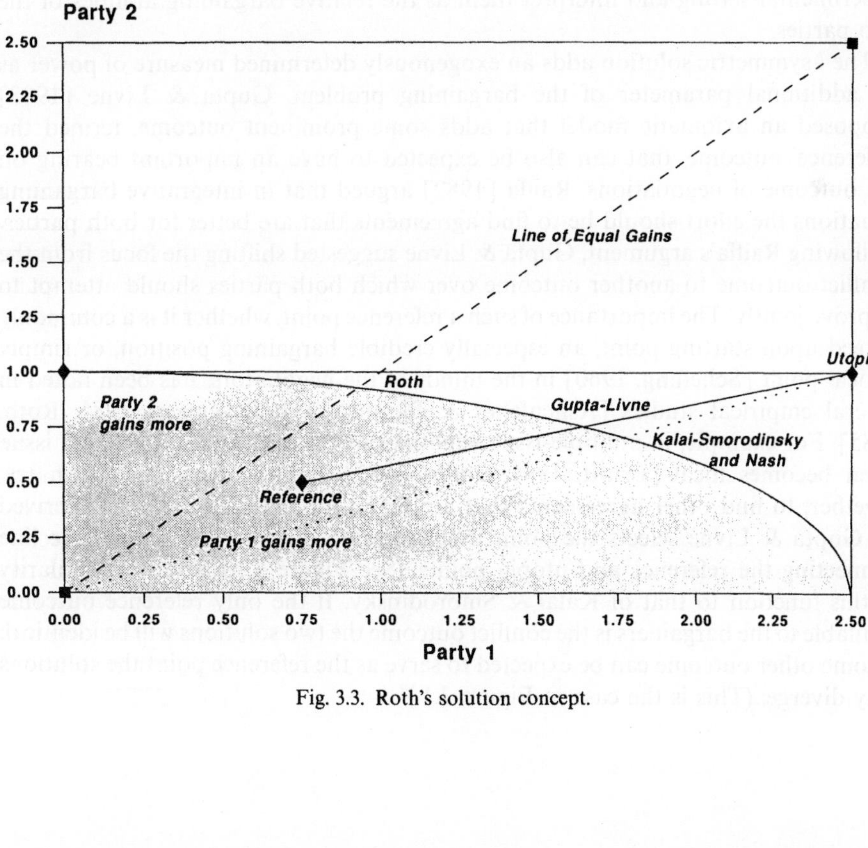

Fig. 3.3. Roth's solution concept.

This interpretation provides a useful link to Rawls's theory of justice. Rawls [1971] argued that such a function is fair because of its concern for the least advantaged person. Although in being solicitous of the disadvantaged, the preferences of a majority can be overridden by those of a small minority. MacCrimmon & Messick [1976] suggest that lexical maximin is a conditional social motive such that one is altruistic when ahead and self-interested when behind. It involves a desire to improve the position of the person who is behind but does not necessarily force the person who is ahead to make a sacrifice. Finally, this solution concept corresponds well with experimental findings that suggest that bargainers do make interpersonal comparisons and outcomes tend toward equality.

The solution concepts described above have the following property in common. When the payoff space is symmetric and the conflict points equal, the final outcome will also be equal. We now discuss two additional solution concepts which need not satisfy this property. Roth [1979] introduced the *asymmetric Nash solution*. He showed that if the symmetry requirement is replaced by the requirement that bargainers receive positive (but not necessarily equal) increments of utility in a symmetric game, the unique resulting solution maximizes $\prod_{i=1}^{n} U_i^{\gamma_i}$, where U_i is the ith person's utility normalized so that the conflict outcome yields zero utility and the γ_i's are some measure of the asymmetry in the negotiations. Svejnar [1986], derived the same result for a bargaining game in which the asymmetry results from exogenously measured differences in the bargaining power of a union compared to that of management. Neslin & Greenhalgh [1983] estimated the γ_i's in an experimental setting and interpret them as the relative bargaining abilities of the two parties.

The asymmetric solution adds an exogenously determined measure of power as an additional parameter of the bargaining problem. Gupta & Livne [1988] proposed an axiomatic model that adds some prominent outcome, termed the 'reference' outcome, that can also be expected to have an important bearing on the outcome of negotiations. Raiffa [1982] argued that in integrative bargaining situations the effort should be to find agreements that are better for both parties. Following Raiffa's argument, Gupta & Livne suggested shifting the focus from the conflict outcome to another outcome over which both parties should attempt to improve jointly. The importance of such a reference point, whether it is a commonly agreed upon starting-point, an especially credible bargaining position, or simply a focal point [Schelling, 1960] in the minds of the negotiators, has been noted in several empirical studies [Ashenfelter & Bloom, 1984; Bazerman, 1985; Roth, 1985]. For example, in multiple-issue negotiations the middle point on each issue often becomes focal [Pruitt, 1981; Raiffa, 1982] and the bargainers then try, together, to find other agreements that are better for both. The solution derived by Gupta & Livne selects the point that is Pareto optimal and lies on the line connecting the reference and utopia points. (See Figure 3.1.) Note the similarity of this function to that of Kalai & Smorodinsky. If the only reference outcome available to the bargainers is the conflict outcome the two solutions will be identical. If some other outcome can be expected to serve as the reference point the solutions may diverge. (This is the case in Figure 3.1.)

Building on Coleman's [1973] and Wilson's (1969) models of logrolling, Gupta [1989] has shown that the reference outcome model is especially appropriate for integrative, multiple-issue negotiations where the two parties do not have equal power. Gupta also shows that any solution which is independent of irrelevant alternatives is particularly inappropriate for multiple-issue negotiations.

Our discussion so far raises an important problem in the cooperative theory of bargaining. There is a multiplicity of solution concepts and each is supported by a set of reasonable axioms. (For more complete reviews of this literature, see Kalai [1985] and Roth [1979].) How, then, is one to choose from among them? What would happen if each party favored a *different* solution concept (had a different social motive)? Is it possible that negotiators may fail to reach an agreement because each of them insists that his or her favored solution concept is the appropriate one to use?

Van Damme's [1986] analysis addresses some of these issues and rests on two postulates: (i) if a player advocates a particular solution concept in one bargaining situation, then the player should adhere to this solution concept in any other bargaining situation; (ii) if the demands of the players are not jointly feasible, the players should continue bargaining over the set of payoffs not exceeding their previous demands. He then showed that if the concession-making process follows these two postulates then the equilibrium strategy for either bargainer is to demand the payoff implied by the Nash solution. Thus, Van Damme provides useful insights into an important indeterminacy. However, as Van Damme has noted, the optimality of the Nash solution is crucially dependent on the specific concession-making process modeled (postulate (ii)). Further, the social psychology literature suggests that the same individual can favor different social motives (solution concepts) in different bargaining situations, violating postulate (i).

Noncooperative game theory. The bargaining problem paradigm and the associated axiomatic approach have been criticized for ignoring some important details of the negotiation process. (See, for example, Svejnar [1986].) In addition to being unable to provide any insight into the negotiation process, inability to predict the time of agreement and Pareto-inefficient breakdowns has been identified as an important shortcoming of the static axiomatic approach. Starting with Harsanyi [1956] and especially since Rubinstein [1982], the new approach in the economics literature is to model bargaining as a *noncooperative game* with detailed rules of play.[5] The typical game has multiple Nash equilibria (pairs of strategies that are best responses to each other). But in many cases, the strategies involve making empty threats off the equilibrium path. Consequently, the objective of the analysis is to identify subgame-perfect or sequential equilibrium strategies for the players.

[5]Bartos [1974], Bishop [1964], Coddington [1968] and Cross [1965] have proposed models of the concession-making process. However, the objective of these models is not to identify equilibria. Rather, the effort is aimed at specifying constructs, processes, and parameter values that can reproduce commonly observed concession-making patterns.

Within this tradition, a principal distinction lies between models that assume bargainers have complete information and those that allow incomplete information.

The *complete information* game analyzed by Rubinstein [1982] has the following characteristics. Two players seek to divide a cake of size 1. If they agree, each receives her share. If they fail to agree, both receive zero. The bargaining process involves the players alternating offers: player 1 makes the initial proposal to receive some share x at stage 0. Player 2 immediately accepts or rejects the offer. In the event of a rejection player 2 makes a counteroffer at stage 1. Player 1 immediately responds and so on. The payoff to player 1 (player 2) equals her share of the cake agreed to at stage t, multiplied by δ_t^1 (respectively δ_t^2), where $\delta_1, \delta_2 < 1$ represent the discount factors which provide incentive to reach an early agreement. A strategy for either player specifies her proposal/reply at each stage, as a function of the history to that point. Clearly, any division of the cake is a Nash equilibrium (not to be confused with the Nash solution concept). So, a *subgame-perfect* equilibrium is sought. That is, neither bargainer may commit to a contingent course of action that it would not be in her best interest to take if the contingency actually arose, even if the contingency lies off the equilibrium path. For example, a threat by player 1 to walk away if she does not receive 80% of the cake is not credible. This is because, if player 2 does offer only 10%, it is not in player 1's best interest to enforce the threat. Subgame-perfect equilibria rule out such empty threats. Remarkably, Rubinstein showed that the subgame-perfect equilibrium is unique and agreement is immediate with player 1 receiving share $(1-\delta_2)/(1-\delta_1\delta_2)$ while player 2 receives share $[\delta_2(1-\delta_1)]/(1-\delta_1\delta_2)$. This outcome is intuitively appealing because the more impatient one is (i.e. the greater the discount factor), the smaller the final payoff is. It has also been shown [Binmore, Rubinstein & Wolinsky, 1986] that this game is equivalent to one in which there is an exogenous risk that the bargaining process will end without an agreement (e.g. the possibility that a third party will exploit the opportunity before the two negotiators can come to terms). Further, when the length of a single bargaining period or the risk of exogenous breakdown is sufficiently small, or the discount factors approach one, the noncooperative equilibrium approaches the corresponding axiomatic Nash solution. Rubinstein [1982] also showed that if there is fixed, per-stage cost of bargaining, c_i, (the ith player's payoff in the tth stage is $1-tc_i$), agreement is immediate but very sensitive to the relative costs of the two players. If c_1 is even slightly smaller than c_2, player 1 receives the entire cake. But, if $c_2 > c_1$, player 1 will receive only c_2.

Binmore, Shaked & Sutton [1989] have applied Rubinstein's formulation to examine the precise role of the conflict outcome in the cooperative framework. Suppose initially that the conflict outcome is $(0,0)$ and the resulting cooperative solution is $(n_1(B,0), n_2(B,0))$. Now, suppose each bargainer has some *outside option* (x_1 for party 1 and x_2 for party 2): an option that the party can achieve if negotiations are not completed. How should the availability of such options affect the final outcome? The typical response in the cooperative framework suggests that the availability of such options potentially changes the relative *power* of the two parties and this should be reflected by changing the conflict outcome (originally at 0,0) to $x = (x_1, x_2)$. A new solution $b = (b_1, b_2)$ should then be computed such that $b \in B$, $b \geqslant x$, and $(b_1 - x_1)(b_2 - x_2) \geqslant (y_1 - x_1)(y_2 - x_2)$ for all $y \in B$, $y \geqslant x$. The noncooperative result, assuming a discount factor approximately equal to 1, suggests tha each party should continue to get its payoff according to the original game (n_1, n_2), unless the party's outside option provides a higher payoff. In the latter contingency, the party with the more favorable outside option (say $x_2 > n_2$) should receive the value of the outside option, (x_2), while the other party gets the rest $(1 - x_2)$. The basic argument supporting this result is that as long as the outside option is inferior to the solution of the original game $(x_i < n_i)$, the threat to leave the negotiations in favor of the outside option is not credible and should therefore not affect *power* at all. If the outside option of one of the parties is superior, the other party need only offer some epsilon in addition to keep the negotiations going. Thus, the noncooperative analysis helps provide useful insight into the cooperative formulation.

The principal drawbacks of this approach are that there is a first-mover advantage even when the game is perfectly symmetric in all other ways and that agreement is immediate. Ochs & Roth [1989] have reported experimental data inconsistent with first-mover advantage and Roth, Murnighan & Schoumaker [1988] have reported experimental results showing that many agreements are reached only at the 'eleventh hour' (labeled the deadline effect). Further, results on the ability of these models to predict the final outcome are inconclusive. Whereas several studies report results largely in agreement with the equilibrium prediction [Binmore, Shaked & Sutton, 1985, 1989; Weg & Zwick, 1991], others report systematic deviations in the direction of equal division of payoffs [Güth, Schmittberger & Schwarz, 1982; Güth & Tietz, 1987; Neelin, Sonnenschein & Spiegel, 1988; Ochs & Roth, 1989; Zwick, Rapport & Howard, 1992].

In contrast to the complete information models which suggest that all agreements will be efficient and immediate, models of *incomplete-information* bargaining suggest the possibilities of inefficient delays and impasse. The typical imperfect information model posits a seller who owns a single indivisible unit of an object and a potential buyer. The seller's (buyer's) valuation $s(b)$ represents the lowest (highest) price for which the seller (buyer) is willing to sell (buy). Typically, each player knows her own valuation, but may be uncertain about the other's valuation. In games of *one-sided uncertainty* one of the valuations, say s, is common knowledge. The seller, however, is uncertain about b. In games of *two-sided uncertainty* both players are uncertain about the other's valuation. The uncertainty is typically represented by either a continuous distribution (e.g. uniform) or by discrete probabilities on the other's type (e.g. a buyer with a high or low valuation). These distributions or probabilities are common knowledge.

Because games with imperfect information do not have proper subgames, subgame-perfect equilibria are inapplicable. Instead, the attempt is to identify *sequential equilibria*. For a sequential equilibrium, in addition to specifying the offer strategy, each uncertain player's beliefs given every possible history must also be specified. A sequential equilibrium is a set of strategies and beliefs such that for every possible history each player's strategy is optimal given the other's strategy

Table 3.2

Features of some bargaining models with incomplete information (adapted from Srinivasan and Wen [1991]

Features	Authors	Fudenberg & Tirole		Sobel & Takahashi	Cramton	Rubinstein	Grossman & Perry	Perry	Admati & Perry	Chatterjee & Samuelson	Cramton
	Year	1983		1983	1984	1985	1986	1986	1987	1988	1991
Incomplete information[1]		2	1	1	2	1*	1	2	1	2	1
Distribution of uncertainty[2]		D	D	C	C	C	C	D	D	D	C
Offer pattern[3]		U	U	U	U	A	A	A	A	A	A
Time horizon of bargaining[4]		2	2	∞	∞	∞	∞	∞	∞	∞	∞
Bargaining cost[5]		δ	δ	δ	δ	δ	δ	c	δ	δ	δ & C
Strategic delay		N	N	N	N	N	N	N	Y	N	Y
Unique equilibrium		N	Y	Y	N	Y	Y	Y	Y	N	N
Delays		2	2	Y	Y	2	Y	N	Y	Y	Y
Pareto-inefficient breakdown		Y	Y	N	N	N	N	Y	N	N	Y

Notes:

1. 1: One-sided uncertainty
   2: Two-sided uncertainty
2. D: Discrete
   C: Continuous
3. U: Uninformed player makes all offers
   A: Alternating offers
4. 2: Two-period game
   ∞: Infinite-horizon game
5. δ: Discount factor
   c: Fixed cost per stage

and her current beliefs about the other's valuation, and the beliefs are consistent with Bayes rules. Typically, weaker players (e.g. buyers with high valuations) attempt to conceal their types by making non-revealing offers and strong players attempt to take actions (such as rejecting offers) aimed at convincing the other player of their strength. Because information can be transmitted credibly only through offers and counteroffers, the process of learning typically requires multiple stages, leading to delays in reaching agreements.

The precise results differ depending on the particular assumptions made about the negotiations (see Table 3.2, adapted from Srinivasan & Wen [1991]). We summarize the principal results:

(i) *Length of delay in reaching an agreement.* In games where the two players alternate offers at fixed times (Rubinstein's game), negotiations are expected to require more stages when information is imperfect. However, if the time delay between successive offers is sufficiently short, agreements could be reached almost immediately and the uninformed party loses all her bargaining power [Gul & Sonnenschein, 1988; Gul, Sonnenschein & Wilson, 1986]. Thus, delays would merely occur due to the mechanics of the time required to make offers, not because they serve some strategic purpose. To better account for the significant delays often observed in negotiations, some authors have considered the effects of allowing *strategic delays* in making offers and responses [Admati & Perry, 1987; Cramton, 1991]. That is, players are permitted to respond or make counteroffers *at any time* after some minimum time between offers has passed. This leads to a signaling equilibrium in which the informed bargainer chooses to signal her position with strategic delays in responding. The minimum time between offers is now shown not to be critical in determining the equilibrium.

Sharp differences in the length of delay also result from assumptions about bargaining costs. In fixed-stage cost models agreements or failures to reach agreement occur immediately [Perry, 1986]. By contrast, in discounting models bargaining continues until the players are convinced that gains are not possible. Cramton [1991] models both types of costs and finds that if one of the players has a significant cost advantage or if the informed party's valuation is sufficiently low, negotiations end immediately (sometimes at an impasse). Otherwise, the delays resemble those in discounting models.

(ii) *Pareto-inefficient breakdowns.* If only discounting costs apply, Pareto-inefficient breakdowns can occur only if the bargaining horizon is finite or there is an exogenous risk of breakdown. In fixed-cost models, breakdown can occur even in infinite horizon models [Perry, 1986; Cramton, 1991]. For example, in Cramton's model, if the buyer's valuation is sufficiently low the buyer terminates negotiations immediately because the gross profits from negotiations are smaller than the transaction costs. Bargaining impasse is also possible in Vincent's [1989] common value model where the buyer, in addition to being uncertain about the seller's valuation, is also uncertain about her own. Finally, in each of these models, breakdowns either occur right at the start of negotiations, or not at all.

(iii) *Uniqueness of equilibrium.* Without uniqueness some coordination among the players would be required. And coordination is not a part of the types of models being considered here. (See Crawford (1990) for a discussion of the coordination issues raised by multiplicity of equilibria.) Recall that in sequential equilibria uninformed players update their beliefs using Bayes's rule. But, if the other's behavior is off the equilibrium path (an event assigned zero likelihood) Bayesian updating is not possible. This may provide incentives to the players to deviate from the equilibrium path, increasing the number of possible outcomes. Two approaches have been adopted to deal with this problem. First, in games of one-sided uncertainty, if the informed player is permitted merely to accept or reject offers, uniqueness is possible [e.g. Fudenberg & Tirole, 1983; Vincent, 1989]. For example, if the buyer makes all the offers and the buyer's valuation is known, the offers reveal no information. Along the equilibrium path there is always a positive probability that the buyer will either accept or reject. Thus, there is no out-of-equilibrium behavior for the informed player or updating complications. But once both players can make offers or both are uncertain, out-of-equilibrium behavior cannot be ruled out. In such cases the approach is to prespecify conjectures regarding off-equilibrium actions such that it is no longer in the best interests of the deviating player to do so. For example, under optimistic conjectures, if an off-equilibrium offer is made by player 1, then player 2 updates her beliefs to assume that player 1 is of the weakest type [Rubinstein, 1985]. Thus, with optimistic conjectures, only pairs of strategies that are sequentially rational along the equilibrium path have to be identified. However, even with conjectures (optimistic or otherwise), multiple equilibria can be supported in games of two-sided uncertainty [Chatterjee & Samuelson, 1988; Fudenberg, Levine & Tirole, 1985]. Further, because the choice of conjectures is arbitrary, there is some difficulty in singling out a particular equilibrium.

(iv) *The final outcomes.* There is general agreement that impatient players, (i.e. buyers (sellers) with high (low) valuations or higher costs) obtain less favorable outcomes. However, in the models of Cramton [1991, 1984], Fudenberg & Tirole [1983] and Perry [1986], a very impatient (high-cost) player can benefit because her threat to walk away if her offer is rejected is credible. Finally, the less uncertain player stands to gain more from the negotiations [see, for example, Grossman & Perry, 1986].

The preceding summary of results and Table 3.2 show that the noncooperative approach adds much to our understanding of the bargaining process. Many of the implications listed above are intuitively plausible, but the precise results are also very sensitive to the particular assumptions made about the bargaining process, as Sutton [1986] points out. Because details of the bargaining process can differ so widely from one case to another, it becomes imperative for future research to examine other scenarios. We suggest two of particular interest to marketers: multiple-issue negotiations and negotiations in which the players are permitted communication in addition to just offers and responses.

In multiple-issue negotiations one player's gain is not necessarily the other player's loss. Especially, in imperfect information situations it may be the case that passage of time does not necessarily reduce the payoffs, but actually increases them as the bargainers 'discover' opportunities for joint gains. This could provide an explanation not yet considered in the noncooperative models for delays in reaching agreements.

Many of the groups of interest to marketers have long histories of joint decisions (e.g. families and manufacturer–retailer dyads). Two characteristics of these groups are particularly noteworthy. First, negotiations among the individuals are often strongly influenced by past agreements [Corfman & Lehmann, 1987; Corfman, Lehmann & Steckel, 1990]. (See the earlier discussion of reference and focal points.) Second, because they can often communicate freely, it is possible for them to reach agreements that are not necessarily self-enforcing. Rather, their agreements may be rendered stable through external factors such as the force of law or pressure from public opinion, internal factors such as prestige and credibility considerations, or because the individuals are simply unwilling to renege on moral grounds. Harsanyi & Selten [1988] and Harsanyi [1977] suggest that cooperative models are more appropriate under these circumstances. While the use of cooperative models may be reasonable, they still do not provide insight into the process itself. Issues such as why or when the individuals may feel obliged to be socially motivated or accede to the external or internal factors mentioned above are not examined.

Examining these and other scenarios in a noncooperative framework should help distill some principles which will hold over a wide range of possible processes and identify the critical factors that render one bargaining situation different from another. Such insights could help in reformulating or creating new sets of axioms within the largely context-free framework of cooperative models and guide us in their application.

3.1.3. Conclusion

The motivation of normative models is to determine the best group decision given certain explicit and 'reasonable' assumptions about the characteristics the decision or the decision process should have. Given that these assumptions hold or are adopted by the decision-makers, normative theories 'predict' outcomes. The literature on empirical tests (primarily experimental) of the predictive ability of these models is very large and we will not attempt to review it here (though the marketing literature is examined in some detail in the next section). Here we shall discuss an important regularity in deviations of actual outcomes from those predicted by these models and its consequences for future research in model development.

A common finding is that subjects tend to choose outcomes with payoffs to group members that are closer to equal than is predicted by the models (see, especially, Ochs & Roth [1989] for an insightful analysis of several bargaining experiments). In fact, examining the results of several experiments designed to test noncooperative game-theoretic models, Güth & Tietz [1987] concluded that even those results that did correspond to model predictions did so 'solely due to the moderate predictions of equilibrium payoffs which makes the game theoretic solutions more acceptable'. Because the noncooperative models make their predictions solely on the basis of maximizing individual utilities, one may hypothesize that if the objectives of the decision-makers explicitly include some preference for equity, as suggested in work by Corfman & Lehmann [1991], such deviations from model predictions may be eliminated.

In most of the models discussed above individual utilities are idiosyncratic. (With the exception of Eliashberg & Winkler [1981], others' utilities are not a part of one's own utility.) These individual utilities are then combined and the combination function attempts to reflect the relevant concerns for equity and fairness. Yet, when these models make predictions of unequal payoffs a common result is that the mean tends to be closer to equal division than predicted. It should, however, be noted that in many of these same instances simple equal division is also a poor predictor of the final outcome [e.g. Gupta & Livne, 1990; Miller & Komorita, 1986; Ochs & Roth, 1989; Selten, 1972]. Some have suggested that it might be appropriate to develop models in which distributional concerns are incorporated in the individual utility functions themselves [e.g. Camerer, 1990; Ochs & Roth, 1989]. The suggestion is supported by results from behavioral decision theory that imply that people have clear notions about what is fair [Kahneman, Knetsch & Thaler, 1986a, 1986b]. Eliashberg & Winkler's [1981] approach explicitly incorporates each individual's equity concerns in the utility functions and could prove to be particularly useful in future research. However, there are some important modeling difficulties with this suggestion. Suppose individual preference functions were adjusted for distributional concerns. Once these adjusted preferences were known to the other decision-makers, would there be a need to readjust for the 'new' preferences? If individuals continued to make such adjustments to individual utility functions in what cases would conflict remain to be resolved by the group decision rule or the bargaining function? And, is it not the express purpose of these models to suggest how *conflicting individual* preferences ought to be resolved? Gupta & Livne's [1988] approach to escaping these questions is to leave the individual utility functions unadjusted and add a reference outcome as an additional parameter of the model, to reflect the equity concerns. The modeling effort is to specify how conflicting preferences can be reconciled in the presence of a prominent, perhaps equity-induced, candidate outcome. Alternatively an approach similar to that of Van Damme's [1986] could be adopted. First, each individual's favored notion of fairness could be determined. Then the procss of resolving conflicts in both the notions of fairness and individual preferences for outcomes could be modeled.

The literature of behavioral decision theory suggests that people's notions of fairness are quite context-specific. This may mean that small differences in group or task characteristics can have significant impacts on the favored notions of fairness and on the final outcomes. This would render the task of developing useful models especially difficult. Yet, the success of the approaches that have already been proposed, and the advances made in modeling situation-specific effects in other areas of marketing suggest that this is a fruitful direction for both theoretical and empirical research. To this end, a model classification scheme that can serve as a guide to context-specific modeling of group choice and negotiations is suggested in Section 4.

3.2. Social psychology

Most mathematical modeling of group choice in social psychology has been motivated by Davis's [1973] theory of social decision schemes. This is a very useful general theory into which a wide variety of group choice models can be incorporated. A social decision scheme is a model that dictates how individual preferences will be combined to create a group choice. A well-defined social decision scheme for n alternatives can be represented as an $m \times n$ stochastic matrix, $\boldsymbol{D}$, which operates on Π, a vector of probabilities that each of m possible distributions of member preferences will occur (where m is determined by the numbers of members and alternatives). Together Π and $\boldsymbol{D}$ determine the probabilities that various alternatives will be chosen by a group, $(P_1, P_2, \ldots, P_n)$:

$$(P_1, P_2, \ldots, P_n) = \boldsymbol{\Pi D} = (\pi_1, \pi_2, \pi_3, \ldots, \pi_m) \times \begin{bmatrix} d_{11} & d_{12} & \cdots & d_{1n} \\ d_{21} & d_{22} & \cdots & d_{2n} \\ \vdots & \vdots & & \vdots \\ d_{m1} & d_{m2} & \cdots & d_{mn} \end{bmatrix}. \quad (4)$$

Given the ith distribution of member preferences, d_{ij} is the probability that the group will choose alternative j. As observed by Davis [1973, p. 102], the d_{ij}'s reflect 'tradition, norms, task features, interpersonal tendencies, local conditions, or some combination of these within which the group is embedded'.

For the most part, social-decision-scheme theory has been used by researchers in one of two ways: model-fitting and model-testing. With the model-fitting approach the $\boldsymbol{D}$ is estimated that best fits the data [cf. Kerr, Atkin, Stasser, Meck, Holt & Davis, 1976]. The results of the model-fitting exercise may serve as input to the model-testing approach which has its basis in theory. With the model-testing approach, the $\boldsymbol{D}$ matrix is fully specified and its predictions are compared to the outcomes of group decisions to determine whether the specified decision scheme can be rejected as having produced the data [cf. Laughlin & Earley, 1982].

A variety of social decision schemes have been proposed and tested. These include 'weight of opinion' schemes such as:

Proportionality: The probability of selecting an alternative, A, is the proportion of members for whom A is the first choice.

Equiprobability: All alternatives that are the first choice of one or more members are equally likely to be chosen.

Majority: If A is the first choice of at least half (or 2/3) of the group it will be chosen.

Plurality: The first-choice alternative of the largest number of members will be chosen.

Other schemes depend upon characteristics of the alternatives as well as individual preferences and are only appropriate when the alternatives possess the requisite properties. For example:

Compromise or arithmetic mean or averaging: If the alternatives are located on an interval scale, the arithmetic mean of alternatives that are the first choice of one or more members will be chosen.

Truth wins: If one or more members prefer A to all other alternatives and it is the correct choice, it will be chosen.

(The latter scheme is more appropriate for problem-solving than decision-making or choice tasks.) In the context of decisions involving risk additional schemes have been considered:

Highest expected value: The alternative with the highest expected value among those that are the first choice of one or more members will be chosen.

Extreme member or most (least) risky wins: The most (least) risky of the set of alternatives that are the first choice of one or more members will be chosen.

Neutral member: The most neutral of the set of alternatives that are the first choice of one or more members will be chosen.

Risk-supported (conservative-supported or caution-supported) wins: The most (least) risky of the set of alternatives that are the first choice of two (or some other number) or more members will be chosen.

Variations on these schemes incorporating secondary schemes for contingencies (e.g. no majority and ties) have also been considered.

Research investigating the appropriateness of different social decision schemes in a wide variety of decision-making contexts has found that the equiprobability model performs well in tasks with high uncertainty or ambiguity (members do not know the probabilities with which various outcomes will occur if an alternative is selected) while moderately uncertain tasks are associated more with plurality schemes and low-uncertainty tasks with majority schemes [Davis, 1982]. Examples of low-uncertainty tasks are provided by mock juries [Davis, Kerr, Atkin, Holt & Meek, 1975; Davis, Kerr, Stasser, Meek & Holt, 1977; Gelfand & Solomon, 1975, 1977] and many kinds of risky choice [Castore, Peterson & Goodrich, 1971; Davis, Kerr, Sussman & Rissman, 1974; Laughlin & Earley, 1982] in which majority schemes appear to be better predictors than others. The difference between the schemes used in high and low-uncertainty tasks may be because when there is certainty members are more confident in their opinions and, thus, hold their preferences more firmly. When many members are not easily swayed, a more decisive scheme is required. There is also some evidence that tasks in which members become personally involved require more decisive schemes for resolution [Kerr, Davis, Meek & Rissman, 1975], perhaps for the same reason.

Laughlin & Earley [1982] suggested that the distinction made earlier between intellective (problem-solving) and judgmental (decision-making) tasks relates to the decision scheme used. Because people engaged in tasks that are closer to the intellective end of the continuum are likely to produce more arguments and more compelling arguments favoring the 'best' answer, they expect truth-wins and truth-supported-wins schemes to be used. In risky choice, risk-supported and caution-supported schemes and stronger choice shifts are expected. More judgmental tasks, on the other hand, should result in a balance of arguments less strongly favoring risk or caution, making majority schemes more appropriate and producing weaker shifts. Although they did not evaluate the arguments used in group discussion, they did find that the risk- and caution-supported models predicted best where there were strong shifts and that the majority rule predicted best where shifts were weaker.

McGuire, Kiesler & Siegel [1987] hypothesized that the risky choices examined in prospect-theory research fall under Laughlin's definition of intellective tasks because they offer defensible or compelling alternatives (which may or may not be correct). Thus, they expected and found that when these tasks involved face-to-face discussions they were characterized by 'norm wins' schemes rather than majority schemes. In this case the norm was the prospect theory finding risk-aversion for gains and risk-seeking for losses.

In their studies of risky group choice, Crott, Zuber & Schermer [1986; Crott & Zuber, 1983] compared the performance of several Condorcet functions (those that consider the members' entire preference rankings of the alternatives) to the proportionality, equiprobability, majority, and arithmetic-mean decision schemes (which consider only each group member's first choice). They found that the Condorcet models performed consistently better than the social decision schemes, suggesting that when examining risky choice it is important to use models that consider more than just the members' most preferred alternatives.

Another model that takes into account members' rankings of all alternatives was proposed by Harnett [1967] and based on Siegel's [1957] work on aspiration levels. He incorporated not only each member's preference ranking, but also a ranking of the relative distances between adjacently ranked alternatives. Harnett defined 'level of aspiration' as that represented by the more preferred of the two alternatives between which there is the largest difference in preference (of all adjacent pairs). An individual is said to be 'satisfied' by alternatives at or above this aspiration level and dissatisfied by those below it. This model predicts that the group will choose the alternative that satisfies the largest number of members. (This is equivalent in spirit to approval voting, discussed earlier.) Harnett's tests of this model provided some support, especially when unanimity was the formal rule and when there was no clear majority.

Castore, Peterson & Goodrich [1971] compared Harnett's model, Luce & Raiffa's [1957] modified-majority-rule model, and a mean rule in the risky-choice setting. The modified majority-rule model also uses the members' rankings of the alternatives. The magnitude of an index, $V(x)$, determines the expected group ranking and is the number of times x 'wins' in paired comparisons with each other alternative across all group members, less the number of times x 'loses'. Harnett's model and the modified-majority-rule model performed equally well, always predicting the direction of choice shifts, although the models did not always predict as extreme a shift as was made by the groups. Castore, Peterson & Goodrich hypothesized that the models' ability to predict shifts was due to an interesting characteristic of the data; in most cases, subjects' second choices were riskier than their first choices. If a majority was not found on first choices the groups may have moved to the second, riskier, choices.

A variety of other models have been used to predict jury decisions. (Work using social decision schemes was mentioned earlier.) Many of these models depend on the binary characteristic of jury decisions (the two alternatives being guilt or acquittal) and the formal rule for the decision (consensus or a quorum), making them less useful for modeling less structured and formal decisions. An example is a binomial model that predicts the probability that a jury will convict (or acquit) based on the required quorum and the probabilities that individual jurors will vote to convict [Penrod & Hastie, 1979]:

$$P_G(j) = \sum_{i=Q}^{n} \binom{n}{i} P_i(j)(1 - P_i(j))^{n-1}. \tag{5}$$

Here, $P_G(j)$ is the probability that the n-member jury (G for group) will vote for alternative j (either conviction or acquittal), $P_i(j)$ is the probability that member i will vote for j, and Q is the minimum number of votes required to convict.

3.3. *Marketing*

Although considerable research has been conducted on decisions made by families, organizations, and buyers and sellers, few models have been proposed and fewer tested. In this section we will review models that have been applied to these problems in research on families, organizations, buyers and sellers, and others.

3.3.1. *Families*

Many choices made by families are made with the influence of more than one family member. In particular, decisions involving larger financial commitments and products or services that will be used by more than one member tend to be the result of a group choice. Sheth's [1974] theory of family buying decisions is a comprehensive conceptual model of family choice based on the Howard-Sheth [1969] theory of buyer behavior. Although not testable in this form, it has provided a useful framework for research on family purchasing by suggesting relationships that should be considered in the creation of empirical models.

The empirical models that have been proposed for modeling family choice have been primarily variations on a weighted linear model in which the weights reflect the influence of the family members (usually spouses) and determine how strongly each member's preferences are reflected in the group preference or choice:

$$P_G(j) = \sum_{i} W_i P_i(j). \tag{6}$$

In this representation, $P_G(j)$ is the group's preference for alternative j or the probability that the group will choose that alternative, W_i is member i's influence in the group or the probability that member i will end up making the choice for the group, and $P_i(j)$ is member i's preference for alternative j or the probability that member i would choose j acting independently. When the $P(j)$'s are interpreted as probabilities this model is known as the weighted probability model.

In their examination of post-choice satisfaction, Curry & Menasco [1979; Curry & Woodworth, 1984] suggested an equal-weight variation on this model, equivalent to social decision scheme's compromise model, in which spouses' preferences are averaged. In their other model one spouse capitulates, effectively allowing his or her influence weight to go to zero.

Kriewall [1980] also used a weighted linear model. She estimated influence weights for parents and a child in each family using data on preferences for colleges (for the child to attend) and then modeled influence weights as a function of several family-member characteristics. Results indicated that the following factors contributed to influence: sex role, education, volunteer status, occupational status, academic status, and income. Krishnamurthi [1981] used a similar approach in his investigation of MBA job choices. He estimated an equal-weight model, a model in which the weights reflect the relative influence of the individuals, and models that weight each individual's preferences not only by general relative influence, but also by preference intensity at the attribute level (conflict resolution models). These three types of models had some predictive ability, although there were no significant differences among them in their ability to predict actual choices.

A model suggested by Steckel, Lehmann & Corfman [1988] combines Kriewall's two-stage estimation procedure into one stage (omitting the estimation of influence weights), by using influence-related characteristics as instrumental variables and assuming systematic variation of the weights across individuals and groups:

$$W_i = \frac{1}{n} + \sum \alpha_k T_{ki}. \tag{7}$$

In this model the weights are functions of individual characteristics. The variable T_{ki} is the amount of characteristic k possessed by member i (in an n-member group) relative to that possessed by the remaining member(s) of the group and α_k is the impact of characteristic k on influence. (As this study was not conducted using families, discussion of the results appears in a later section.)

Models estimated by Corfman & Lehmann [1987] continued in this spirit, but they incorporated preference intensity as one of a large number of determinants of relative influence:

$$P^*_{\mathrm{G}}(j) = \beta_0 + \sum_k \beta_k T_{ki}. \tag{8}$$

Here, $P^*_{\mathrm{G}}(j)$ is the probability that the group will choose alternative j, which is member i's preferred alternative. Corfman & Lehmann proposed that T_{ki} be either the difference between the amounts of a trait spouses possess or the proportion (although there was no significant difference in predictive ability between these representations). Of the 17 traits they examined, the following had significant main effects on infuence: preference intensity, decision history (whose choices had been favored in preceding decisions), expertise, sex role, bargaining skill, sociability, desire to support the relationship, and desire to win and control. As preference intensity had by far the strongest effect, situations in which spouses had equally intense preferences and those in which one had stronger preferences than the other were examined separately. Results indicated that when one spouse had more intense preferences than the other, his or her preferences drove the decision. When preferences were equally intense, who had 'won' in the preceding decision was used to determine whose preferred alternative would be chosen the next time. Corfman & Lehmann also estimated the weighted probability model using Steckel, Lehmann & Corfman's [1988] instrumental-variable approach and found that its predictive ability was markedly worse. (When $P_G(j)$ and $P_i(j)$ are viewed as probabilities, Equation (6) is the weighted probability model.)

Taking a different approach, Curry, Menasco & Van Ark [1991] have applied three of the normative solutions discussed earlier to the multiattribute dyadic-choice problem (Harsanyi's additive model, Nash's cooperative solution concept, and Gupta & Livne's [1988] reference-point solution). The conflict they model is due to differential weighting of attributes by two parties selecting a single, multi-attribute option from a set of feasible alternatives. A unique feature of their analysis is that they provide the solution in terms of the attribute values and not just in terms of the utilities as is usual in the literature. The authors argue that 'solution points are therefore one step closer to management activities such as product positioning and new product design'. Further, they derive solutions for the cases where the conflict outcome is at (0, 0) and where there is an exogenously specified cut-off value for each attribute (e.g. any alternative rated less than 3 on attribute one and 5 on attribute two is unacceptable). Results of a husband–wife dyadic-choice experiment show successful prediction of the attribute values of the dyad's first choice and rankings of the alternatives. They also found that the 'reference outcome plays a distinct role from that of (0, 0) conflict point and a "locally shifted" conflict point (a point in which a previous agreement serves as a conflict outcome)'.

3.3.2. *Organizations*

The structure of organizations and the relationships among their members ensures that most purchase decisions are made with the influence of more than one person. The group of people who influence the outcome of a purchase decision has come to be known as the 'buying center' [Wind, 1967, 1978]. The degree of involvement of the members of this group varies, however, from the case in which a purchasing agent takes the preferences of other buying-center members into account to true group decision-making. Although several conceptual models of organizational buying have been proposed [e.g. Robinson Stidsen, 1967; Robinson, Faris & Wind, 1967; Webster & Wind, 1972; Sheth, 1973; Bonoma, Zaltman & Jonston, 1977; Thomas, 1980] little empirical modeling of the group-choice phase of the process has been published.

Choffray & Lilien's [1978, 1980] industrial market response model was the first attempt to develop an operational model of organizational buying. In their model the decision process incorporates four submodels, the last of which concerns the group decision. They proposed four classes of models for this stage: weighted probability, voting, minimum endorsement, and preference perturbation models. Special cases of the weighted probability model are the autocracy model in which $W_i = 0$ for all but one member of the group and the equiprobability model in which all W_i's are equal. The voting model is the same as the plurality social-decision scheme; let $x_{ij} = 1$ if i prefers j to the other alternatives, 0 otherwise:

$$\text{If } z_j = \sum_i x_{ij}, \text{ then } P_G(0) = \Pr\left[z_0 = \max_j (z_j) \right]. \tag{9}$$

The minimum endorsement model says that to be chosen by the group, an alternative must be preferred by at least a prespecified number of group members. Thus, the majority social-decision scheme is a special case of this model. If that minimum equals the number of group members, it becomes the unanimity model. Given that the group has reached consensus, the following is the probability that the group chooses alternative 0:

$$P_G(0) = \frac{\prod_i P_i(0)}{\sum_j \prod_i P_i(j)} \tag{10}$$

The preference perturbation model is the only one of these models that incorporates more preference information than just the members' first choices. This model is essentially a truncated version of the city-block distance approach to producing consensus rankings [Kemeny & Snell, 1962]. As it is not concerned with producing an entire group ranking of the alternatives, it stops once it has found the single alternative that 'perturbs' individual preferences the least, i.e. would require the smallest number of preference shifts in the members' rankings to make the alternative the first choice of all members. If γ_w is the group's pattern of preference structures (w indicates a particular set of n individual preference rankings) and $Q(j|\gamma_w)$ is the perturbation required under pattern γ_w to make alternative j preferred by all members, then the following assumption is made:

$$\frac{P_G(j|\gamma_w)}{P_G(I|\gamma_w)} = \frac{Q(I|\gamma_w)}{Q(j|\gamma_w)}. \tag{11}$$

If $Q(I|\gamma_w) = 0$, then $P_G(I|\gamma_w) = 1$ and $P_G(j|\gamma_w) = 0$. The group choice is, thus, determined by:

$$P_G(0) = \sum_w P_G(0|\gamma_w) \Pr(\gamma_w). \tag{12}$$

The only test of the models suggested by Choffray & Lilien in an organizational purchasing context was performed by Wilson, Lilien & Wilson [1991]. They proposed and tested a contingency paradigm which suggested that different models from Choffray & Lilien's set are appropriate in different buying situations as defined by the type of task (new task versus modified rebuy) and degree of 'perceived risk' (a combination of technical uncertainty and financial commitment required). They concluded that situational factors do have an impact on the types of choice schemes used by buying centers. Specifically, they found that decisions with low perceived risk were characterized well by the autocracy model, compromise decisions schemes (especially the voting model) were better predictors of decision outcomes with moderate perceived risk, and the majority model was the best predictor of the decisions with high perceived risk. This is counter to results of studies discussed earlier which found that majority schemes were most associated with low-uncertainty tasks. This difference may be because the subjects responded more to the expenditure component of Wilson, Lilien & Wilson's perceived risk manipulation than to the technical-uncertainty component.

Steckel [1990] tested two group decision-making models in a different kind of organizational task—the choice of a corporate acquisition. The models he tested were the Borda solution and the Core. Two aspects of the task were manipulated: the incentive structure (individual or group) and whether the consequences of choosing particular alternatives were certain or uncertain. Groups with individual incentives more often reported used a majority rule, while those with a group incentive reported searching for consensus. The Core predicted better than the Borda solution under all conditions.

Rao & Steckel [1989] compared three group-choice models using experiments involving an organizational task (the choice of faculty employment candidates) and a task involving ad hoc groups (a restaurant choice). Two of the models were from group decision theory, additive and multilinear [Keeney & Kirkwood, 1975; Keeney & Raiffa, 1976], and the third was a variation on the weighted linear model which incorporates a polarization term:

$$P_G = \sum_i W_i P_i(j) + \phi(\bar{P}_i(j) - K). \tag{13}$$

The polarization term is the difference between the mean preference of the individuals in the group and a neutral value, K, multiplied by the shift parameter, Φ. Now $P_G(j)$ shifts upward for values of the group mean higher than K. In their experiments the polarization model slightly outperformed the additive model which outperformed the multilinear model.

Steckel & O'Shaughnessy [1989] proposed a weighted linear model for choice between two alternatives which splits an individual's power into two components, constructive and destructive power:

$$P_G(j) = \frac{1}{2} + \sum_i \delta_i X_i + \sum_i \sigma_i Y_i. \tag{14}$$

Here, δ_i and σ_i represent i's constructive and destructive power, respectively, and X_i and Y_i represent i's liking of the first alternative relative to the second and i's dislike for the first alternative relative to the second.[6] They do not test this model, but assume that the form is appropriate and use it as a basis for the estimation of power.

3.3.3. Other groups

While one tends to think of families and organizations when group choice in marketing is mentioned, other groups also make joint consumption decisions. In the following studies ad hoc groups and groups of friends were studied. (See also Rao & Steckel [1989] discussed earlier.)

Three such problems were examined by Corfman, Lehmann & Steckel [1990; Steckel, Lehmann & Corfman, 1988]: the choice of a musical selection, a stock-market investment, and a restaurant. In the 1988 study on music and stocks (mentioned earlier) they estimated a weighted probability model in which the weights were functions of opinion leadership and decision history, both of which were significant. In the 1990 study they estimated the model in Equation (8), and found that for all three decision tasks, preference intensity was the most important predictor. Expertise and decision history were also important. Further anaysis of the differences between decisions in which preference intensities were either equal or unequal supports the process suggested by Corfman & Lehmann's [1987] study.

Buss [1981] also used variations on the weighted probability model in his study using groups of friends and strangers, and compared them with equal-weight models: Borda-up, Borda-down, plurality, and random models. (The nature of the task is not clear from the paper.) Rather than estimate or model the weights, Buss used member perceptions of influence, communication effectiveness, and preference intensity. The Borda models and the weighted probability model using preference intensity outperformed the others in predicting first choices. This suggests that it may be important to consider both the members' entire preference rankings and their preference intensities.

3.3.4. Buyer–seller negotiations

Negotiations between buyers and sellers can occur over a large variety of issues including price, quantity, delivery, terms, promotional support, product configuration, materials, warranties, and service. Much modeling of buyer–seller negotiations has made use of various cooperative game-theoretic models of bargaining, especially the Nash solution. Although these models were developed as normative models, because they choose 'fair' solutions they are reasonable starting points for modeling outcomes of actual negotiations in which fairness is an important motivation. Researchers in fields other than marketing have conducted experiments to test the axioms and resulting solution concepts [e.g. Bartos, 1974; Heckathorn, 1978; Nydegger, 1977; Nydegger & Owen, 1974; Rapoport & Perner, 1974; Roth &

[6] X_i takes the value 1 if i prefers the first alternative to the second, 0 if i is indifferent, and -1 if i prefers the second. $Y_i = -X_i$.

Malouf, 1979; Svejnar, 1986]. Generally, experimental tests indicate that, although the cooperative bargaining models have some predictive ability, they have a number of shortcomings when such factors as imperfect information, information-sharing strategies, multiple issues, reference points, interpersonal comparisons of utility, future negotiations, profit goals and compensation, asymmetric power structures, bargaining skill, and experience are introduced. As discussed in Section 3.1, some of these factors have been added to axiomatic models.

In their investigation of the strategic use of preference information in bargaining, Chatterjee & Ulvila [1982] addressed the situation in which bargainers have agreed to the principles that yield a Nash solution. Although they did not examine whether bargainers naturally gravitate toward an 'optimal' solution, they observed that even when this kind of solution is the goal, information-sharing strategies can prevent bargainers from arriving at it.

A study by Bazerman, Magliozzi & Neale [1985] demonstrated that experience in a market results in settlements that are increasingly close to the Nash solution. This generally occurred because the profits of the less profitable party increased with experience, while the other party's profits remained relatively constant. This 'learning' process appeared to occur even faster for negotiators who had been given difficult profit constraints.

Eliashberg, LaTour, Rangaswamy & Stern [1986] simulated negotiations in a price-setting context and tested the predictive ability of Nash's theory and two group-utility functions from group decision theory: additive and multilinear functions. They found that all three models predicted well, even when power was unequal and only partial information on utilities was initially available, and that Nash's theory performed better than the decision theory models.

The Nash model has also been used to predict outcomes of multiple-issue negotiations. Neslin & Greenhalgh [1983, 1986] tested the Nash model's predictive ability in three issue negotiations between buyers and sellers. They found that this solution had some predictive ability (42% of the settlements represented the Nash solution in the 1986 study). Further, situational power (dependence) and bargaining skill had no effect on the settlements: Nash solutions were reached less often when both bargainers viewed the interaction as a one-shot deal, and Nash solutions were reached more often when the seller was on commission.

Noting the ambiguous predictive ability of Nash in these studies, Gupta [1989] observed that although multiple issues can be represented in the Nash framework, some essential characteristics of multiple-issue bargaining are not captured (e.g. logrolling and the role of reference points) and independence of irrelevant alternatives is assumed, which is often not appropriate. Two proposed solutions to this bargaining problem that take reference points into account are the Gupta–Livne [1988] model and Curry, Menasco & Van Ark's [1991] attribute-based formulation, both described earlier. The Gupta–Livne prediction was tested in manufacturer–retailer bargaining experiments [Gupta, 1989; Gupta & Livne, 1989]. In Gupta [1989], only in cases in which the negotiators had equal power did the model predict the agreements accurately, but in those cases it clearly outperformed both the local Nash and Kalai–Smorodinsky models. In the unequal-power conditions, using an empirically derived reference point resulted in significantly improved predictions. In Gupta & Livne [1990], where the reference point was provided by the previous agreement between the two parties, substantial support for the model's predictions was reported. As discussed earlier, support for the special role of the reference outcome has also been reported by Curry, Menasco & Van Ark [1991] in the context of husband–wife dyadic choice.

4. Dimensions of choice situations

Existing research on mathematical models of group choice and negotiations suggests numerous directions for future research. There are two basic levels at which this work might proceed. The first is a micro-level focus on the specification of group-choice models for specific applications. Some suggestions for future research at this level have been made in the preceding discussion. The second is a macro-level focus on integrating what we know and creating classifications of models appropriate in different contexts. The latter approach involves the development of typologies or contingency paradigms for models that classify them according to the situations in which they are the best reflections of group-choice behavior [cf. Frazier & Rody, 1991; Kohli, 1989; Wilson, Lilien & Wilson, 1991]. Enough modeling of group-choice behavior has been done to allow us to begin to make generalizations about the contexts in which particular models will be the best predictors of group choice. Further, research on determinants of influence in a variety of settings suggests when certain variables should be incorporated into group-choice models. In order to take advantage of what we have learned and structure future research in a useful way, this broader focus is essential. We organize this section around this classification goal and discuss dimensions that should prove useful in developing model classification schemes.

The dimensions that might be considered in developing typologies fall into two categories: task characteristics and group characteristics. Although others could be proposed, those listed below seem particularly promising candidates for inclusion in model typologies.

Task characteristics:

Intellective vs. judgmental
Risk vs. non-risky alternatives
Low vs. high uncertainty
Feedback on previous decisions available vs. not available
High vs. low importance
Low vs. high perceived risk
Information on members' valuations complete vs. incomplete
New vs. familiar
Low vs. high time pressure
Group choice dependent on vs. independent of members' outside alternatives
Resource allocation vs. discrete choice vs. ranking vs. rating
Single vs. multiple issues or attributes

Group characteristics:

Two-person vs. small vs. large
Primary vs. institutional
Individual vs. group vs. task goals dominant
Decision rule imposed vs. flexible
Cohesive vs. non-cohesive
Existing vs. newly formed
Ongoing vs. terminal
Members have equal vs. unequal power

One of the problems with attempting to integrate theory concerning the distinctions implied by these dimensions with results of empirical studies, is that few studies have examined variations along these dimensions while controlling for other factors. Thus, for example, models that predict well under high levels of uncertainty in one study may perform poorly in another study due to differences in the tasks and groups examined. The discussion that follows draws heavily on theory and intuition, uses empirical evidence for support when it exists, and makes some observations about findings that appear to contradict theory and each other. Examples of models that may be appropriate in different choice contexts appear in Tables 3.3 and 3.4.

Table 3.3
Choice-context dimensions and examples of models: task characteristics

Task characteristic	Requirements	Examples of models
Intellective task	Allow 'best' choice.	Truth-wins models WLM[1] with expertise
Judgmental task	Incorporate member preferences.	Normative models, majority, plurality, WLM
	Incorporate influence.	Asymmetric Nash, Gupta–Livne, WLM with power sources
Risky choice	Spread responsibility.	Majority, plurality, approval voting
	Avoid individuals' less preferred alternatives.	Lexical maximin, preference perturbation
	Incorporate risk attitude.	Keeney & Kirkwood [1975]
	Limit degree of risk.	Extreme member wins
	Incorporate more than just most preferred alternative.	Any model using rankings or ratings (e.g. not proportionality, plurality, majority)
Risky choice with high uncertainty	Reflect lack of confidence in ability to choose well	Normative models, equiprobability and other decision schemes
Incomplete information on members' valuation of alternatives	Reflect uncertainty about valuations.	Noncooperative bargaining models with incomplete information
Important task	Incorporate preference strengths.[2]	Group value function, Nash, WLM

Table 3.3 (cont'd)

Task characteristic	Requirements	Examples of models
	Incorporate concern about other's preferences.	Eliashberg & Winkler [1981], WLM with preference intensity
	Incorporate influence.	Asymmetric Nash, Gupta–Livne, WLM with power sources
	Spread responsibility.	Group utility function, majority, plurality, approval voting
	Avoid individuals' less preferred alternatives.	Lexical maximin, preference perturbation
Unimportant task	Simple rule.	Social welfare rules, majority, plurality
	Indiscriminate or assign responsibility.	Equiprobability Autocracy
High task-familiarity	Incorporate influence.	Gupta–Livne, asymmetric Nash, WLM with power sources
Low task-familiarity	Incorporate member ability.	WLM with expertise
	Incorporate characteristics of risky decisions.	(See risky decisions.)
High time pressure	Simple and decisive rules.	Social welfare rules, majority, plurality, compromise
	Assign responsibility.	Autocracy
	Reflect use of faster-acting power sources.	WLM with coercion and rewards (vs. those requiring persuasion)
	Incorporate cost of time.	Noncooperative bargaining models, process theories of bargaining
Group choice dependent on members' outside alternatives	Predicted outcome a function of conflict outcome.	Bargaining models
Group choice independent of members' outside alternatives	Predicted outcome independent of conflict outcome.	Social welfare rules, decision-theoretic models, social decision schemes, WLM
Allocate resource	Divide resource among members or alternatives.	Bargaining models, any model with probability of choice as dependent variable (interpret as proportion)
Choose from among discrete alternatives	Select single alternative.	Most models
	Allow 'compromise' over series of decisions.	WLM with decision history, logrolling models
Provide ranking of alternatives	Rank alternatives in set.	Borda, consensus ranking, modified majority model
Provide ratings of alternatives	Rate alternatives.	Nash, Rawls, decision-theoretic models, compromise decision scheme, any model with probability of choice as dependent variable (interpret as rating)
Multiple issues or attributes	Reflect interdependence of decisions.	Curry, Menasco & Van Ark [1991], Gupta–Livne, Nash
	Allow logrolling.	Logrolling models

[1]Weighted linear models.
[2]Input to group decision is a rating versus a ranking.

Table 3.4
Choice-context dimensions and examples of models: group characteristics

Group characteristic	Requirements	Examples of models
Two-person groups	Need not be able to accommodate models, unanimity model, WLM.	Most models, including bargaining larger (but not proportionality, plurality, majority)
	Accommodate coalitions.	Coalition models
	Decisive.	Majority, plurality
	Incorporate impersonal power sources.	WLM with legitimate and expert power
Primary groups	Reflect importance of equity and allow compromise.	Group value functions, consensus ranking models, cooperative bargaining models, consensus decision scheme, compromise decision scheme, WLM with decision history
	Incorporate preference strengths.	Group value functions, Nash, WLM
	Incorporate concern about other's preferences.	WLM with preference intensity, Eliashberg & Winkler [1981]
	Incorporate personal power sources	WLM with referent, reward, coercive, etc. power
	Incorporate personal and relationship goals.	WLM with conflict attitude, importance of winning, desire to support relationship, sex roles, status, etc.
Institutional groups	Incorporate impersonal power sources.	WLM with legitimate and expert power
	Incorporate personal goals.	WLM with importance of winning and control, etc.
Individual goals dominate	Reflect member concern with impact of decision on self.	Noncooperative bargaining models, process models of bargaining, WLM with bargaining skill, coercion, rewards, and personal goals (e.g. competitiveness, conflict attitude, etc.)
Group goals dominate	Reflect member concern with impact of decision on group, e.g.	
	Equity, compromise, risk attitude, and efficiency	Social welfare rules, decision-theoretic models, consensus ranking models, cooperative bargaining models, consensus decision scheme, compromise decision scheme, WLM with decision history
	Preference strengths	Group value functions, cooperative bargaining models, WLM
	Relationship goals	WLM with desire to support relationship, sex roles, etc.
Decision quality dominates	Reflect member concern with quality of decision, e.g.	

Table 3.4 (cont'd)

Group characteristic	Requirements	Examples of models
	Find 'best' answer.	Truth wins, WLM with expertise
	Choose fair answer.	(See equity and compromise models above.)
Cohesive groups	Reflect importance of equity and allow compromise.	Social welfare rules, group value function, consensus ranking models, cooperative bargaining models, compromise decision scheme, WLM with decision history
	Incorporate preference strengths.	Group value function, Nash, WLM
	Incorporate concern about other's preferences.	Eliashberg & Winkler [1981], WLM with preference intensity
	Incorporate 'nice' power sources.	WLM with expert, reward, referent, etc. power
	Predict decisions that do not need to be self-enforcing.	Models other than noncooperative bargaining models
Existing groups	Incorporate outcomes of prior decisions.	Logrolling models, Gupta–Livne, WLM with decision history
	Incorporate more characteristics of primary groups.	(See primary groups.)
New groups	Incorporate impersonal power sources.	WLM with legitimate and expert power
Ongoing groups	Reflect importance of equity and allow compromise.	Cooperative bargaining models, compromise decision scheme, WLM with decision history
	Incorporate concern about other's preferences.	Eliashberg & Winkler [1981], WLM with preference intensity
	Incorporate 'nice' power sources.	WLM with expert, reward, referent, etc. power
Terminal groups	Incorporate more aggressive power sources.	WLM with coercive power, bargaining skill, etc.
Members have equal power	Weight members equally.	Normative models, social decision schemes
Members do not have equal power	Reflect relative power of members.	Gupta–Livne model, asymmetric Nash model, WLM with power sources

4.1. Task characteristics

4.1.1. Intellective vs. judgmental tasks

As specified in the Introduction, our concern is with decision-making rather than problem-solving tasks. However, decision-making tasks can fall on the intellective/judgmental dimension anywhere short of being completely intellective. The location of a task on this dimension will depend on (1) whether there is an objectively correct answer, (2) if there is, when this answer can be confirmed as correct (either upon its discovery accompanied by an 'aha' reaction or following implementation of the group decision), and (3) if there is not a correct answer, whether the group, nevertheless, perceives that there is one. As an example of (2), if the goal of an investment group is to select the set of investments that will yield the highest returns, there is a correct answer. However, this answer will not be available until after (perhaps, long after) the decision is made, making the task more judgmental. As an example of (3), the choice rule used by a management team is likely to depend upon whether they believe there is a correct strategy. If they believe there is, they are more likely to use or try to use group choice rules appropriate for intellective tasks.

In tasks closer to the intellective end of the spectrum, choice rules in the spirit of truth wins or truth-supported wins may be used and the judgments of experts are likely to be given more weight in the identification of 'truth'. Feedback on past decisions will also be important for learning about task performance and for providing evidence concerning member expertise and ability. (See Bordley [1983], for a model based on historical accuracy.) In judgmental tasks, preferences are the issue. When alternatives are discrete, majority and plurality rules and turn-taking may be used as non-judgmental ways of reaching solutions. When alternatives are continuous, compromises may be reached. When power is unequal and exercised, strength of preference will probably play a role and, although expertise may still be an important issue, other sources of power, such as bargaining skill and reward power, are likely to become relatively more important.

4.1.2. Risk and uncertainty

The definitions of decisions under uncertainty and risk vary in literature on group decision-making. To facilitate discussion and comparisons among studies, the following definitions will be used here. Both decisions under uncertainty (ambiguity) and risk are those for which members do not know with certainty what will happen if they select particular alternatives. The difference is that in the case of decisions under risk, the members know the probabilities associated with the possible consequences of selecting an alternative, while with decisions under uncertainty, they are not aware of these probabilities [Davis, 1982]. A task's degree of uncertainty is associated with whether these probabilities are known or not. (If a decision is not perceived as a decision under risk, it cannot be a decision under uncertainty.) Two ways of interpreting an alternative's degree of risk have been used. In one, an alternative is considered riskier when it has higher variance (e.g. $p = 0.5$ of either \$100 or \$10 would be considered more risky than either $p = 0.1$ of \$10 and $p = 0.9$ of \$100, or $p = 0.1$ of \$100 and $p = 0.9$ of \$10, which have equal variance). The other interpretation adds a distinction, saying that an alternative is more risky when a more preferred consequence has a lower probability of occurring than a less preferred consequence, even when the alternatives have equal variance (e.g. $p = 0.1$ of \$100 and $p = 0.9$ of \$10 would be considered more risky than $p = 0.1$ of \$10 and $p = 0.9$ of \$100). We will adopt this additional distinction.

In the realm of decisions under risk, tasks can vary in their uncertainty. Very-high-uncertainty tasks should tend to make group members equal because ability to select a best alternative is uniformly low and there are no bases for intense preferences. This is probably why equiprobability rules have often performed well in these situations. Sources of influence not associated with the quality or nature of the choice itself may, however, be important in these situations because winning or getting one's way can become the more important goal for individuals. Feedback on the consequences of past decisions is valuable in uncertain tasks. When feedback is available, a task may become more certain or groups may perceive it as being more certain and behave accordingly, even though the conclusions they draw may be spurious. In tasks with moderate to high levels of uncertainty, expertise and information power that might improve predictions of probabilities should play important roles. Groups making decisions under risk with no uncertainty have been observed to use majority schemes [Davis, 1982]. One reason for this may be that these schemes spread responsibility across the members of the majority, which may be desirable in high-risk contexts. It also appears that models that incorporate more than just the members' most preferred alternative predict better than 'first choice' models [Crott, Zuber & Schermer, 1986]. Models that avoid least preferred (most or least risky?) alternatives (lexical maximin, preference perturbation), incorporate risk attitude [Keeney & Kirkwood, 1975], and limit the degree of risk (extreme members decision scheme) should also perform better in risky choices.

4.1.3. Task importance and perceived risk

When decisions are perceived as being unimportant, simple rules that give members equal weight are more likely to be used, one individual may be permitted or assigned to make the decision for the group, and there is less motivation to exercise power (unless, as suggested above, being powerful takes over as the goal for one or more members). When decisions are important, especially in judgmental tasks, individual preference intensities and power sources tend to play an important role. On the other hand, when tasks are more intellective, there may be a desire to use choice rules that spread responsibility, such as majority and plurality rules. If one can assume task importance leads to involvement, similar observations may be made about the involvement dimension.

Perceived risk is generally thought of as having two components: uncertainty (implying, therefore, some degree of risk) and the importance of the decision (more important decisions having higher variances because the differences between the possible outcomes are larger). The little work that has been done on modeling group decisions in situations that vary in their perceived risk is difficult to integrate with some of the observations about uncertainty and task importance just made. This is partly because other task factors may have strong effects and because the effects of uncertainty and task importance cannot be separated in these studies. In situations with high perceived risk, Wilson, Lilien & Wilson [1991] found that majority and voting rules were the best predictors and Kohli [1989] found that expert and information power were important, while reward and coercive power and status were not. One partial explanation is that the highest levels of uncertainty encountered in the cited studies were probably not extreme, hence, the importance of expertise and information. As suggested earlier, the motivation for the use of majority and voting rules may have been a desire to spread risk when making important decisions. In Wilson, Lilien & Wilson's study, compromise models (voting, equiprobability, preference perturbation and weighted probability models) performed best at moderate levels of perceived risk and the autocracy model at the lowest level of perceived risk. The latter finding is consistent with the observation made about unimportant decisions that are delegated to a single member. In an organizational setting, especially, this kind of efficiency makes sense.

4.1.4. Information on valuation of alternatives

Models of group decision-making typically assume that the group members know which alternatives each prefers and how much. However, there are cases in which members may not have this information and may choose not to reveal it to each other explicitly. Noncooperative bargaining models that allow incomplete information (either one-sided or two-sided uncertainty) are designed to model this situation.

4.1.5. Task familiarity

Two aspects of task familiarity are important to consider. When tasks are new to the group they may or may not be new to the members. As recognized by Wilson, Lilien & Wilson [1991], task familiarity and perceived risk are not independent. This is probably why their subjects used the responsibility-spreading models (majority models spreading responsibility the most and voting models to a lesser degree) in tasks that were new to both the members and the group, and models representing compromise, in familiar tasks. In new tasks it may also be appropriate to model the choice at the attribute level because this is where the group's attention will usually be focused [Krishnamurthi, 1981; Curry & Menasco, 1979]. When the task is new to the group, but familiar to one or more members, the expertise and information they possess are likely to be important. When the task is familiar to the group, members are likely to possess the same amounts of expertise, and other power sources will play larger roles. Exceptions occur when the relevant expertise is very specialized and not easily transferred. In these cases, the more expert member(s) will be given greater influence, or even complete responsibility [Wilson, Lilien & Wilson, 1991], even when the task is familiar.

4.1.6. Time pressure

When a group is facing pressure to make a decision quickly, simple and decisive choice rules that give members equal weight, such as plurality and pure compromise, may be used. Alternatively, one member or a small number of members may quickly emerge as leaders based on expertise or seniority (legitimate power) and be given responsibility for the decision, suggesting the appropriateness of the autocracy model and consideration of expert and information power [Isenberg, 1981; Spekman & Moriarty, 1986]. When preferences are intense or the decision is important, time pressure may result in the use of more forceful power sources, like coercion and the offering of rewards, rather than persuasion which often takes more time [Kohli, 1989]. Further, the noncooperative modeling approach, which explicitly accounts for time costs, may prove especially useful.

4.1.7. Dependence of group choice on members' outside alternatives

Typically, group choice models account for the possibility of breakdown in decision-making or the decision not to decide as one of the set of alternatives the group considers choosing. The value of that alternative is assumed to be the same for all members. However, there are cases (more often negotiations) in which members have alternatives to a group choice or negotiation that are not equal, giving more power to those with more valuable alternatives. The effects of this kind of power should be reflected in the outcome predicted by the chosen model. Bargaining models are designed to accommodate this situation and model the final outcome as a function of the conflict outcome. Any model that weights members to reflect their influence over a decision can also be modified to reflect power derived from the existence of outside alternatives.

4.1.8. Nature of choice

Bargaining models are designed for *resource allocation* among group members and any model whose dependent variable is a probability may also be useful here, because the probability can be interpreted as the proportion of a resource to be awarded to an alternative or to a member. When alternatives are *discrete* they may still be ordered in a way that allows some kind of compromise to be made (e.g. a low- vs. moderate- vs. high-priced product), but when they are not compromise must occur over a series of decisions in the form of turn-taking or equalizing gains over a period of time. Thus, models that incorporate the outcomes of preceding decisions [Corfman & Lehmann, 1987] and logrolling [Coleman, 1973] are appropriate.

A ranking or rating of all alternatives may be required when a group is making an analysis of a set of alternatives for informational purposes, such as expert ratings of appliance brands or suppliers, or when the alternatives are one or few of a kind and the group's preferred alternative(s) may end up being unavailable, as in home purchases and hiring decisions. Consensus ranking approaches [Kemeny & Snell, 1962; Bowman & Colantoni, 1973] are designed for cases in which group *rankings* are required. However, most other models can be adapted to provide not only the group's first choice, but its second and third, etc., by eliminating each alternative from the set after it is chosen. Models that have probability of choice as the dependent variable may also be used to create rankings. Decision-theoretic models, the compromise decision scheme, and any model with probability of choice as the dependent variable (e.g. many weighted linear models) can be used to provide joint *ratings* of alternatives in a set.

In some situations groups will need to develop a group preference function. This occurs when a group wishes to establish its priorities and develop a rule for use in future choices, possibly before it is known exactly which alternatives will be available. Decision-theoretic models may be useful here, as will models that allow the estimation of group part worths [e.g. Krishnamurthi, 1981].

4.1.9. Number of issues

While some collections of decisions to be made by a group can be treated sequentially and somewhat independently, some issues are so closely related that they cannot be modeled separately. For example, for a two-career couple with children, the choice of a town to move to, each job, a house to buy, and school(s) for the children cannot be decided independently. Buyers and seller also often negotiate multiple, related issues including price, quantity, terms, and delivery. Examples of appropriate models for multiple issues include Coleman's [1973], Curry, Menasco & Van Ark's [1991] and Gupta's [1989] models. Most noncooperative bargaining models as currently formulated are *inappropriate* for studying multiple-issue negotiations.

4.2. Group characteristics

4.2.1. Group size

Bargaining models are designed for the smallest groups–those with two members (although some can be generalized for larger groups, e.g. the Nash and Gupta–Livne models). Many of the social decisions schemes are not helpful for two-member decisions because they require that an alternative be advocated by more than one member (those based on proportionality, majority, or plurality). Most of the models we have reviewed are appropriate for small groups. It is the larger groups that often require special models due to the role of coalitions in their joint decisions. Decisive rules (e.g. majority) may be used in larger groups because consensus is more difficult to reach. When members have differential power in a large group's decision, legitimate and expert power are likely to play important roles because they are effective across a wider range of other members. Also, because behavior in a large group is visible to a larger number of people, these groups are often characterized by preference for the use of socially acceptable, impersonal power over such approaches as coercion or rewards [Kohli, 1989].

4.2.2. Primary vs. institutional groups

Primary groups are 'held together by common traits and sentiments and tend to be spontaneous' [Faris, 1953, p. 160]. Families, cultural groups, and cliques are examples. Institutional groups, such as purchasing departments and juries, exist to perform functions other than those that bind the members to the group and, thus, tend to be externally formed, externally controlled, and more heterogeneous. In primary groups the people are often more important than the task and there tends to be greater trust, liking and empathy. Therefore, preference intensity can be an important power source, equity is more important, and compromise or effort to equalize gains over time is often visible [Corfman & Lehmann, 1987]. Institutional groups may have some of these characteristics, but because the task is usually more important than the people, at least initially they tend to rely more on impersonal power sources, such as legitimate power and expertise. Informal power may evolve as well, perhaps based on expertise or referent power, resulting in increasing power for influential members (in contrast to the preference-based turn-taking observed in families).

4.2.3. Dominant goal or reward structure

Whether the members of a group are more concerned about the benefits of a group choice to themselves as individuals, or care more about the welfare of other members and the group itself, or whether the performance of the task is paramount, will affect the appropriateness of models chosen. The choices of groups whose members are more focused on their own personal rewards, as often happens in resource-allocation tasks, may be better modeled by noncooperative bargaining models (which are less concerned than other normative models with a decision's equity), and weighted linear models that incorporate power sources that are not necessarily relationship-preserving (e.g. rewards and coercion) and personal goals like winning and controlling. On the other hand, groups whose members care about each other and the health of the group will be more interested in equity (making many normative models potentially useful) and relationship goals (suggesting that they be incorporated into weighted linear models). Groups whose members care most about the quality of the decision must establish criteria for making this judgment. Intellective tasks may be evaluated externally, making truth wins and WLM models with expertise useful. Judgmental tasks may be deemed of high quality if they are fair, suggesting the use of many normative models and models that incorporate decision history.

4.2.4. Decision rule imposed vs. flexible

In some situations a formal group-decision rule may be imposed on a group either from the outside or by agreement among members that one will be adopted. Possibilities include majority, plurality, approval voting, consensus and autocracy rules. Rather than simplify the problem, as it would appear on the surface, this adds interesting complexity to the modeling problem. In these situations, unless group interaction is prohibited or impossible, the choice becomes at least a two-stage process. In the first stage members discuss alternatives and their preferences, and a variety of influence processes may operate to change opinions and positions on the issue (perhaps without opinion or preference change). Thus, the input to the decision rule is not as it would have been before the group's interaction. If preferences or opinions are sufficiently strongly held, a model that reflects the formal decision rule will still predict well.

4.2.5. Cohesiveness

Groups may become cohesive or viscid [Hemphill & Westie, 1950] through experience together, communication, liking and respect which build stronger bonds. Members of cohesive groups are characterized by the ability to work well together, concern about each other's preferences, and trust. Their concern for equity in judgmental tasks, suggests the use of models that incorporate the outcomes of past decisions. In task-oriented groups, expertise and legitimate power should be incorporated and are likely to play more important roles than less socially acceptable power sources [Kohli, 1989]. Trust among group members makes the self-enforcing (equilibrium) solutions of the noncooperative bargaining models unnecessary. In these groups, the members are motivated to implement the decision even when it does not represent their individual preferences.

4.2.6. Group history

The less familiar members are with each other, the more likely they are to behave in socially acceptable ways [Bormann, 1975]. As it is more acceptable to use impersonal power sources, expertise and legitimate power are more likely to be used than coercion and aggression, for example [Kohli, 1989]. For groups that are not newly formed, the processes and outcomes of past decisions are often important and should be included in models. Turn-taking, equalizing of gains, and logrolling may be motivators for the outcome of the current decisions. Time also allows institutional groups to evolve informal power structures and develop characteristics of primary groups, which would alter their decision-making processes. For example, levels of trust and loyalty are determined and may affect willingness to influence other members and use particular sources of power.

4.2.7. Group future

When a group will continue to exist and make decisions following the decision being studied, awareness of future dependence is likely to make the group more cooperative and concerned with equity. In these cases, models with cooperative normative foundations may be useful [Neslin & Greenhalgh, 1986] and 'destructive' power sources are less likely to be used. Terminal groups have far less incentive to nurture the relationship any more than necessary to resolve the current issue. In these cases models of noncooperative bargaining and coalition formation may be appropriate.

4.2.8. Power allocation

In groups whose members have roughly equivalent amounts of influence over the decision, normative models and social decision schemes may be very useful. However, when members have differential amounts of influence this must be reflected in the chosen model. As discussed earlier, the Gupta–Livne and the asymmetric Nash models may be adapted to reflect unequal power and many have formulated weighted linear models that incorporate sources of influence.

4.3. Conclusions

The potential applications of this classification approach are many, although few appear in the marketing literature. As suggested by Wilson, Lilien & Wilson's [1991] and Kohli's [1989] work, the decision-making process in buying centers can vary considerably due to differences in aspects of the task and group. Between them they explored the nature of the buying task, perceived risk, time pressure, buying-center size, familiarity and viscidity, and individual power bases and influence attempts. Further investigation of these and other dimensions will provide us with better understanding of how the buying center operates in different contexts and should lead both to better decision-making in buying centers and more effective selling to them. A similar set of dimensions should be used to structure the investigation of buyer–seller negotiations and will result in similar benefits. When this approach is taken to the study of family choice the relevant dimensions will change and the group characteristics will vary less. The benefits of greater understanding of family choice in different settings are better family decisions and improved strategies or advertising, promotion, distribution and design of products and services typically selected with the input of more than one family member.

In this section we have described and discussed a set of dimensions that should prove useful in the development of model typologies. While our discussion has been largely one-dimensional, there are undoubtedly many interesting interactions to explore. For example, the relationships between group cohesiveness and task riskiness, group size and time pressure, and task importance and uncertainty, may imply different models for different combinations of characteristics. Existing research provides some guidance for the development of these typologies, but careful observation and experimentation are necessary before we can begin to complete the picture. We recommended that future studies focus on exploring small numbers of task and group dimensions, developing theory concerning model performance in each context, and testing the models. Rather than focusing on developing models for single situations, we hope that researchers will concentrate on work generalizes from one context to another due to understanding of the factors or dimensions that are driving the ability of models to predict.

5. Applications

The examples in Sections 5.1, 5.2 and 5.3 are provided to show how specific group tasks might be positioned on relevant dimensions and how this information can be used as a guide to modeling the group choice or negotiation. The three examples were chosen because they are areas in which further work would be interesting and valuable and, more importantly, because they are situations that are not typically modeled as group decisions. We hope also to illustrate the dangers of assuming that many common choices are made by individuals when they are, in fact, made by multiple decision-makers. These examples represent different stages of development. They progress in terms of existing work and remaining questions vary from fairly formal to very open and in need of greater definition.

5.1. Repeat buying in households

Repeat purchase behavior has often been studied in the context of a household's purchases of non-durable goods. Based on theories of consumer behavior, households are often expected to display *variety-seeking* or *reinforcement* (loyalty to last brand) behavior. Empirically, several authors [e.g. Givon, 1984; Kahn, Kalwani & Morrison, 1986; Bawa, 1990] have relied on household-purchase panel data to propose and test models of variety-seeking and reinforcement behaviors. Typically, based on each household's string of purchases the household's preferences are summarized by a transition matrix:

$$P_{\mathrm{HH}} = \begin{pmatrix} p_{AA} & p_{AB} \\ p_{BA} & p_{BB} \end{pmatrix}$$

where p_{qr} is the probability of buying brand r if brand q was bought on the previous occasion. The general first-order transition matrix, P can reflect a variety of preference structures:

(i) strict preference for $A(B)$	p_{AA}(or p_{BB}) > 0.5 and p_{BA}(or p_{AB}) > 0.5,
(ii) variety-seeking	$p_{AA} < 0.5$ and $p_{BB} < 0.5$, and
(iii) reinforcement	$p_{AA} > 0.5$ and $p_{BB} > 0.5$.

Furthermore, if $p_{AA} = p_{BA}$ and $p_{AB} = p_{BB}$, the behavior is zero-order.

Such empirical analyses, contrary to theoretical expectations, have generally concluded that households are 'indifferent to variety' [Givon, 1984]. However, Kahn, Morrison & Wright [1986] and Kahn, Kalwani & Morrison [1986] have suggested that these findings may be due to errors in model specification. Households usually have more than one member and the resulting purchases may reflect some resolution of the conflict among individual preferences. For example, it may be that individual members of the household are indeed variety-seeking or last-brand loyal; however, the process of resolving conflicts among the individuals may lead to a household transition matrix that *appears* to represent a zero-order process. Thus, a completely specified model must account for individual preferences ($P_i(j)$ in Equation (6)) *and* the conflict-resolution mechanism adopted by the household (analogous to W_i in equation (6)).

Because the focus of such studies is on detecting first-order preferences (e.g. variety-seeking or reinforcement), Gupta & Steckel [1992] represent individual preferences with separate transition matrices P_{H} and P_{W}, for two-member households. But, as we have seen in the preceding discussion, there are many possible conflict-resolution mechanisms. The possibilities can be narrowed, however, on the basis of the task and group characteristics:

Task characteristics: Repeat purchases of non-durables can be classified as primarily judgmental, low-uncertainty, familiar tasks in which one or more of several discrete alternatives must be chosen.

Group characteristics: The family is an ongoing, small, primary and cohesive group.

Given these characteristics, and the relative importance that each individual places on the choice, the household may be expected to resolve the conflict in preferences in the following ways. First, suppose the decision is considered important by both members. Given the group characteristics listed above, and because the alternatives available are typically discrete, we may expect an effort to equalize gains over time through a *turn-taking* mechanism (i.e. $P_{HH} = 1 \cdot P_H + 0 \cdot P_W$ on occasion 1, $P_{HH} = 0 \cdot P_H + 1 \cdot P_W$ on occasion 2, and so on). In terms of Equation (6), the W_i's change predictably from purchase occasion to purchase occasion. A second possibility arises if the weights are constrained to be the same on each purchase occasion (i.e. $P_{HH} = w_H \cdot P_H + w_W \cdot P_W$ on every purchase occasion). The household compromises on each purchase occasion, and the relative preference intensities are reflected through the W's. Gupta & Steckel examine the case $W_H = W_W = 0.5$, labeled *strict compromise.* Note that if one of the family members places low importance on the choice, then the household's preferences will coincide with those of the member with higher preference intensity (e.g. if H places low importance on the choice $P_{HH} = 0 \cdot P_H + 1 \cdot P_W$). In this case the household essentially behaves as a single individual and the current approach for analyzing purchases should be sufficient. Finally, Gupta & Steckel examine a conflict-resolution mechanism suggested by Kahn, Morrison & Wright [1986], labeled *decoupled superpositioning.* Consider the case in which both members place moderate-to-high importance on the choice (ruling out capitulation). However, instead of being constrained to make a single joint choice (as in turn-taking or strict compromise), each individual purchases according to his or her own preferences, as and when the need arises. This may be the case for a product category such as toothpaste, where consumption is not joint and the family budget permits each member to satisfy his/her own preferences. For such a household, the observed purchase string is a superpositioning of decoupled, individual buying processes. Following Kahn, Morrison & Wright [1986] assume that the individual interpurchase times are independent, identical and exponentially distributed. Then, in terms of Equation (6), the household behaves as if a given individual's weight (say W_H) is 1 on some purchase occasions and 0 on others. However, unlike the predictable weight changes under turn-taking, W_H is 1 or 0 depending on the exponentially distributed interpurchase times. That is, decoupled superpositioning is a more 'random' form of turn-taking.

Having enumerated these possibilities, the central question addressed by Gupta & Steckel is, 'given only the household level purchase string, is it possible to infer the conflict resolution mechanism (turn-taking, strict compromise, or decoupled superpositioning), and the individual transition matrices?' The following example briefly demonstrates their approach.

Example. Suppose the two individual transition matrices are:

$$P_H = \begin{matrix} & A & B \\ A & 1 & 0 \\ B & 0 & 1 \end{matrix}, \qquad P_W = \begin{matrix} & A & B \\ A & 0 & 1 \\ B & 1 & 0 \end{matrix}.$$

Next, suppose the conflict-resolution mechanism is turn-taking and the first purchase is A. Then, because H always chooses the last brand purchased and W always switches, the resulting purchase string will be:

household's choice	*A A B B A A B B A A B B A A* ...
chosen by	H WH WH WH WH WH WH

The resulting transition matrix is:

$$P_{\mathrm{HH}}=\begin{pmatrix}0.5 & 0.5\\ 0.5 & 0.5\end{pmatrix}. \quad \square$$

First, note that the same household transition matrix would result under any of the other conflict-resolution mechanisms, or even under simple coin-tossing. But, also note that each run in the household's string is of length 2! Such a pattern of run lengths could not have resulted under any of the other conflict-resolution mechanisms. Recognizing this, Gupta & Steckel suggest an approach based on analyzing the *distribution of run lengths*. For two-member households, their results show that:

(i) It is possible to distinguish strict turn-taking from other conflict-resolution processes. Further, under strict turn-taking, it is possible to accurately infer the underlying individual transition matrices.
(ii) When household purchases are decoupled, it is possible to recover the individual transition matrices if both members seek variety or are reinforcers, or one family member is variety-seeking and the other is a reinforcer. This result also implies that it is possible to recover the individual transition matrices whenever the family uses any conflict-resolution process that is less random than decoupling.[7]
(iii) Classification is more accurate for longer purchase lengths.

Gupta & Steckel's work shows that careful modeling of the conflict-resolution mechanism can enable us to gain more precise insights than are possible when the group processes are ignored. Future research should:

(i) develop more powerful tests and statistical theory for discriminating among the various processes,
(ii) empirically apply this approach to various product categories and examine the results against those expected on the basis of the theory of variety-seeking behavior,

[7]Recall that under decoupling, knowing who made the previous purchase provides no information about who will make the current purchase. Under strict turn-taking the identity of the current purchaser is known with certainty. Other conflict-resolution processes can, therefore, be represented paramorphically by varying the probability of who makes the next purchase. The ability to distinguish the least informative case (decoupling) from the equivalent zero-order process suggests, therefore, the ability to also distinguish any other more systematic conflict-resolution process.

(iii) attempt to classify products according to conflict-resolution processes (this should be especially helpful in validating and enriching the contingency approach discussed earlier in this section).

5.2. *Interdependent decisions in marketing channels*

In many markets it is common to observe that members of the distribution channel are independently owned. In such conventional channel systems, typically, each party attempts to maximize its own profits (that is, each member behaves in a *locally* optimal manner). Also, it is often the case that if mechanisms for coordination among channel members could be found, system-wide efficiency could be increased. Further, such efficiency gains usually require that at least some members behave in a *locally suboptimal* manner. For such situations, the marketing channels literature has largely focused on the following questions:

(a) What mechanisms, initiated by which channel member, are likely to lead to greater channel efficiency?
(b) Under what conditions is coordination likely to increase the channel's efficiency?

However, important and related questions about the process by which channel members choose how to increase efficiency, and how to share in the joint gains have been less well studied. To understand how the group choice literature can add to the marketing literature by providing models suitable for examining these questions, consider the manufacturer's problem of choosing quantity discounts. That is, how will the buyer–seller dyad arrive upon a quantity-discount schedule that helps increase the profits of both?

Most previous research on quantity discounts focuses on a single decision-maker, the seller, attempting to maximize his own profits [e.g. Lal & Staelin, 1984; Dada & Srikanth, 1987]. The normative results of such an approach are appropriate if the underlying process is one where the seller presents a discount schedule to the buyer who then decides whether or not to avail himself of it. However, as Buffa [1984], Banerjee [1986] and Kohli & Park [1989] observe, questions of pricing and lot-sizing are often settled through negotiations between the two parties. Consequently, models of cooperative or noncooperative bargaining, discussed above, should be useful in developing more realistic descriptions. Kohli & Park's (KP) modeling approach makes an important contribution in this regard.

In KP's formulation, the buyer and the seller jointly attempt to agree upon the quantity-discount schedule. First, based upon the costs and profits of the two parties, the set of Pareto-optimal discount policies is determined. Then, the joint agreement is predicted by applying cooperative game-theoretic solution concepts to choose one policy from this set.

In terms of our classification scheme, KP's model treats the quantity-discount problem as an intellective, single-issue, one-time decision between two parties who are certain about their own payoffs and those of the other. On the basis of our classification scheme, the following extensions of their research seems promising:

(i) KP assume bargaining over a single product. Often, however, the same buyer may purchase multiple products from the seller. KP's results could be used to make separate predictions of the discount schedule for each of the products. However, it will often be possible to increase the efficiency of the system even further by coordinating the purchases. In such cases the profits earned from uncoordinated purchasing would no longer be Pareto-optimal, and other discount schemes that help increase the gains of both parties could be found. Models of integrative, multiple-issue bargaining [e.g. Gupta, 1989] could be used to predict how the parties would share in the additional gains from coordination. The no-discount and uncoordinated purchasing policies would represent the conflict and reference outcomes respectively. The final outcome would be expected to be Pareto-superior to both of these outcomes.

(ii) For simplicity, KP assumed that the payoffs are known with certainty and that the game is played in a single period. Often, however, buyers and sellers transact business year after year with uncertainty about their own and others' future costs. Also, this uncertainty is often resolved at the end of each year, making the relative gains from the current year's discount policy more apparent to both sides. For such situations, models in which past outcomes can be expected to influence future negotiations, and in which equity has an important role to play may provide a better description [e.g. Corfman & Lehmann, 1987].

(iii) In deriving the expected discount policy, KP assumed only that it be Pareto-optimal. KP then answer the question of which among the several Pareto-optimal policies will be chosen by separately applying various solution concepts. But, is it possible to rule out some of these solution concepts and get a more definite prediction?

It may be possible to do so by making other assumptions, in addition to Pareto-optimality, to which bargainers can reasonably be expected to adhere. For example, suppose that the buyer is able to reduce her costs and thus increase her profitability for every possible discount policy. Then, it may be reasonable to expect that the chosen discount policy will be such that the buyer's profits do not decrease. But this assumption is the same as Kalai & Smorodinsky's *individual monotonicity* axiom (A5). Consequently, we should not expect the dyad to agree upon the discount policy represented by the Nash outcome. Or, in times of increasing sales and profits, it may be reasonable to assume that the previous agreement within the same dyad would play the role of a reference point over which both parties can Pareto-improve. In this case, the Gupta–Livne solution might be appropriate.

(iv) KP's analysis assumes a single buyer and seller. Suppose, now, that there are multiple buyers, each with an idiosyncratic utility function. Further, suppose it is possible for the buyers to form a cooperative and bargain with the seller as a coalition. What quantity-discount structure can be expected to emerge? How will the gains from coalition formation be shared among its members? Models of coalition formation could provide useful insights. Alternately, by representing the agreements that *might* be reached with other buyers as the seller's outside options, Binmore, Shaked & Sutton's [1989] noncooperative bargaining model with outside options may also prove useful.

5.3. Strategic decision-making

While many models for strategic decision-making have been developed, most of these are normative models, and very few treat the selection of a strategy as a group decision. Typically, models of organizational decisions (other than purchasing decisions) have assumed, at least implicitly, that there is a single decision-maker, although it is clear that many of these decisions are made by groups. For example, many studies of competitive behavior have used the prisoner's dilemma to represent the situation [e.g. Burke, 1988; Corfman & Lehmann, 1992]. Investigations using this game invariably involve only two people, each one representing a competitor. Conclusions have been drawn about how individuals behave in these games and what individual and situational characteristics affect behavior. However, we must not assume that the outcomes would be the same if groups were playing the competitive roles. The polarization literature alone implies that group behavior may be quite different from individual behavior in these settings.

Let us take the example of a small group of managers setting advertising budgets in a competitive environment, framed as a prisoner's dilemma with two alternatives – a high budget and a low budget. This task is probably viewed by management as a fairly intellective task. Although the success of a strategy cannot be known before its implementation, a 'correct' answer is a strategy that results in acceptable profits. This suggests that 'truth wins' rules may be used, with truth revealed through the input of experts and those in possession of pertinent information. If the task is familiar, expertise may be shared and, thus, play a less important role. This is also a risky and moderately uncertain task, because the probabilities associated with possible competitor actions are not known. Further, the decision is important. Thus, majority and voting rules may be used to spread responsibility and, again, expertise and information are likely to be important power sources when not possessed by all members. Because feedback on the outcomes of similar past decisions is likely to be available, the group can learn about the competition and improve its predictions, making the task less uncertain and encouraging the use of compromise models (e.g. weighted probability). Feedback is also likely to reinforce the influence of true experts. The fact that this is an ongoing institutional group makes the use of impersonal power sources (e.g. legitimate and expert power) more likely, although primary ties and informal power structures may have evolved, resulting in the use of personal and, perhaps, destructive power sources.

Given that we want a model for a small group to make a single choice between discrete alternatives and that it is important to examine the roles of expertise, legitimacy and, perhaps, other sources of power, a variation on the weighted linear model would be a good place to start. If expertise is shared by the members or competitor actions are extremely uncertain (resulting in high perceived risk), majority and plurality models may do an adequate job of predicting. Although the prisoner's dilemma structures the alternatives as discrete, in reality they lie on a continuous dimension making compromise a possibility if judgments conflict. If we allow continuous alternatives, the weighted Nash model might be appropriate.

6. Conclusions

It should be clear from this review that there is a wealth of research on group choice in other disciplines that researchers in marketing have only begun to tap. Opportunity to benefit from and extend this work exists in a number of areas. Normative models of group choice and bargaining could be further explored for their appropriateness as foundations for descriptive modeling. Examples are modeling the weights in the asymmetric Nash model [Neslin & Greenhalgh, 1983] or the reference alternative in the Gupta–Livne [1988] solution to reflect relative imbalances in power, information and relationship factors. Social decision schemes should be further explored for their usefulness in describing management decision-making behavior in common contexts. Wilson, Lilien & Wilson [1991] have begun this task in the buying center. This paper does not review the wealth of research in social psychology on determinants of influence in group decision-making and bargaining [e.g. French & Raven, 1959; Kelley & Thibaut, 1978; Rubin & Brown, 1975; Tedeschi, Schlenker & Bonoma, 1973]. However, this work would be valuable input to the development of models and model typologies.

Above all, we feel research on group choice and negotiations should proceed with a focus on what makes different models better descriptors of choice behavior than others in different contexts. This approach is a good way to take advantage of existing research and provides structure for further investigation.

A final goal of this paper was to illustrate the importance and prevalence of group choice in marketing. Few choices are made by individuals truly independent of others and many are explicitly joint. Our examples in Section 5, were designed to illustrate the hazards of assuming that most choices are independent. As we discussed, purchase histories can be misinterpreted if they are assumed to belong to a single individual and actually reflect the preferences of multiple family members, buyers and sellers often negotiate issues that have been assumed to be set by one party and either accepted or rejected by the other, and strategy is more often formulated by formal or informal management teams than by individuals, which may result in inaccurate choice predictions for them.

References

Admati, A.R., and M. Perry (1987). Strategic delay in bargaining. *Rev. Econom. Studies* 54, 345–364.

Ali, I., W.D. Cook and M. Kress (1986). Note: Ordinal ranking and intensity of preference: A linear programming approach. *Management Sci.* 32(12), 1642–1647.

Arrow, K.J. (1950). A difficulty in the concept of social welfare. *J. Political Economy* 58, 328–346.

Arrow, K.J. (1951). *Social Choice and Individual Values*, Cowles Commission Monograph No. 12, Wiley, New York.

Ashenfelter, O., and D.E. Bloom (1984). Models of arbitrator behavior: Theory and evidence. *Amer. Econom. Rev.* 74(1), 111–124.

Banerjee, A. (1986). A joint economic lot-size model for purchaser and vendor. *Decision Sci.* 17, 292–311.

Bartos, O.J. (1974). *Process and Outcome Negotiations*, Columbia University Press, New York.

Bawa, K. (1990). Modeling inertia and variety-seeking tendencies in brand choice behavior. *Marketing Sci.* 9 (Summer) 263–278.

Bazerman, M.H. (1985). Norms of distributive justice in interest arbitration. *Indust. Labor Relations Rev.* 38(4), 558–570.

Bazerman, M.H., T. Magliozzi and M.A. Neale (1985). Integrative bargaining in a competitive market. *Organ. Behavior Human Decision Processes* 35, 294–313.

Binmore, K.G., A. Rubinstein and A. Wolinsky (1986). The Nash bargaining solution in economic modeling. *Rand J. Econom.* 17, 176–188.

Binmore, K.G., A. Shaked and J. Sutton (1985). Testing noncooperative bargaining theory: A preliminary study. *Amer. Econom. Rev.* 75, 1178–1180.

Binmore, K.G., A. Shaked and J. Sutton (1989). An outside option experiment. *Quart. J. Econom.* 104, 753–770.

Bishop, R.L. (1964). A Zeuthen–Hicks theory of bargaining. *Econometrica* 32, 410–417.

Black, D. (1958). *The Theory of Committees and Elections*, Cambridge University Press, London/New York.

Blin, J.M., and A.B. Whinston (1974). A note on majority rule under transitivity constraints. *Management Sci.* 20(11), 1439–1440.

Bonoma, T.V., G. Zaltman and W.J. Johnston (1977). Industrial buying behavior, Marketing Science Institute Monograph. Report 77–117.

Bordley, R.F. (1983). A Bayesian model of group polarization. *Organ. Behavior Human Performance* 32, 262–274.

Bornmann, E.G. (1975). *Discussion and Group Methods: Theory and Practice, 2nd ed.*, Harper and Row, New York.

Bowman, V.J., and C.S. Colantoni (1973). Majority rule under transitivity constraints. *Management Sci.* 19(8), 1029–1041.

Brock, H.W. (1980). The problem of utility weights in group preference aggregation. *Operations Res.* 28(1), 176–187.

Buffa, E.S. (1984). *Meeting the Competitive Challenge: Manufacturing Strategy for U.S. Companies*, Irwin, Homewood, IL.

Burke, M. (1988). The dynamic effects of competitor signals on managers' choices in an iterated prisoner's dilemma, Working Paper, FSB 8801, Fuqua School of Business, Duke University, Durham, NC.

Buss, W.C. (1981). A comparison of the predictive performance of group-preference models, in K. Bernhardt (ed.), *The Changing Marketing Environment: New Theories and Applications*, Educators Conference Proceedings, Vol. 47, American Marketing Association, Chicago, pp. 174–177.

Camerer, C.F. (1990). Behavioral game theory, in R.M. Hogarth (ed.), *Insights in Decision Making*, University of Chicago Press, Chicago, pp. 311–336.

Castore, C.H., K. Peterson and T.A. Goodrich (1971). Risky shift: Social value or social choice? An alternative model. *J. Personality and Social Psychology* 20(3), 487–494.

Chatterjee, K., and L. Samuelson (1988). Bargaining under two-sided incomplete information: The unrestricted offers case. *Oper. Res.* 36(4), 605–618.

Chatterjee, K., and J.W. Ulvila (1982). Bargaining with shared information. *Decision Sci.* 13 (July), 380–404.

Choffray, J., and G.L. Lilien (1978). Assessing response to industrial marketing strategy. *J. Marketing* 42 (April), 20–31.

Choffray, J., and G.L. Lilien (1980). *Market Planning for New Industrial Products*, Wiley, New York.

Coddington, A. (1968). *Theories of the Bargaining Process*, Aldine, Chicago, IL.

Coleman, J.S. (1973). *The Mathematics of Collective Action*, Aldine, Chicago.

Cook, W.D., and M. Kress (1985). Ordinal ranking with intensity of preference. *Management Sci.* 31 (1), 26–32.

Cook, W.D., and L.M. Seiford (1978). Priority ranking and consensus formation. *Management Sci.* 24(16), 1721–1732.

Corfman, K.P., and D.R. Lehmann (1987). Models of cooperative group decision-making: An experimental investigation of family purchase decisions. *J. Consumer Res.* 14 (June), 1–13.

Corfman, K.P., and D.R. Lehmann (1991). The importance of others' welfare: A model and application to the bargaining relationship, Working Paper, Leonard N. Stern School of Business, New York University.

Corfman, K.P., and D.R. Lehmann (1992). The prisoner's dilemma and the role of information in competitive marketing strategy, Working Paper, Leonard N. Stern School of Business, New York University.

Corfman, K.P., D.R. Lehmann and J.H. Steckel (1990). Longitudinal patterns of group decisions: An exploratory analysis. *Multivariate Behavioral Res.* 25 (July), 249–273.

Cramton, P.C. (1984). Bargaining with incomplete information: An infinite horizon model with continuous uncertainty. *Rev. Econom. Studies* 51, 579–593.

Cramton, P.C. (1991). Dynamic bargaining with transaction costs. *Management Science* 37(10), 1219–1233.

Crawford, V.P. (1990). Explicit communication and bargaining outcomes. *Amer. Econom. Rev.* 80(2), 213–219.

Cross, J.G. (1965). A theory of the bargaining process. *Amer. Econom. Rev.* 55(1), 69–94.

Crott, H.W., and J.A. Zuber (1983). Biases in group decision making, in R.W. Scholz (ed.), *Decision Making under Uncertainty*, North-Holland, New York, pp. 229–252.

Crott, H.W., J.A. Zuber and T. Schermer (1986). Social decision schemes and choice shifts: An analysis of group decisions among bets. *J. Exp. Social Psychol.* 22 (January), 1–21.

Curry, D.J., and M.B. Menasco (1979). Some effects of differing information processing strategies on husband–wife decisions. *J. Consumer Res.* 6 (September), 192–203.

Curry, D.J., M.B. Menasco and J.W. Van Ark (1991). Multiattribute dyadic choice: Models and tests. *J. Marketing Res.* 28(3), 259–267.

Curry, D.J., and G. Woodworth (1984). A structural theory of the effects of product attributes in joint decisions, Working Paper Series No. 84–24, University of Iowa.

Dada, M., and K.N. Srikanth (1987). Pricing policies for quantity discounts. *Management Sci.* 33, 1247–1252.

Davis, J.H. (1973). Group decision and social interaction: A theory of social decision schemes. *Psychol. Rev.* 80 (March), 97–125.

Davis, J.H. (1982). Social interaction as a combinatorial process in group decision, in H. Brandstatter, J.H. Davis and G. Stocker-Kreichgauer (eds.), *Group Decision Making*, Academic Press, New York, pp. 27–58.

Davis, J.H., N.L. Kerr, R.S. Atkin, R. Holt and D. Meek (1975). The decision processes of 6- and 12-person mock juries assigned unanimous and 2/3 majority rules. *J. Personality Social Psychol.* 32, 1–14.

Davis, J.H., N.L. Kerr, G. Stasser, D. Meek and R. Holt (1977). Victim consequences, sentence severity, and decision processes in mock juries. *Organ. Behavior Human Performance* 18, 346–365.

Davis, J.H., N.L. Kerr, M. Sussman and A.K. Rissman (1974). Social decision schemes under risk. *J. Personality Social Psychol.* 30(2), 248–271.

Deutsch, M. (1973). *The Resolution of Conflict*, Yale University Press, New Haven, CT.

Dyer, J., and R.K. Sarin (1979). Group preference aggregation rules based on strength of preference. *Management Sci.* 25(9), 822–832.

Dyer, J., and R.K. Sarin (1982). Relative risk aversion. *Management Sci.* 28(8), 875–886.

Eliashberg, J. (1986). Arbitrating a dispute: A decision analytic approach. *Management Sci.* 32(8), 963–974.

Eliashberg, J., S.A. LaTour, A. Rangaswamy and L.W. Stern (1986). Assessing the predictive accuracy of two utility-based theories in a marketing channel negotiation context. *J. Marketing Res.* 23 (May), 101–110.

Eliashberg, J., and R.L. Winkler (1981). Risk sharing and group decision making. *Management Sci.* 27(11), 1221–1235.

Faris, R.E.L. (1953). Development of the small group research movement, in M. Sherif and M.O. Wilson (eds.), *Group Relations at the Crossroads*, Harper and Brothers, New York, pp. 155–184.

Fishburn, P.C. (1986). Empirical comparisons of voting procedures. *Behavioral Sci.* 31, 82–88.

Frazier, G.L., and R.C. Rody (1991). The use of influence strategies in interfirm relationships in industrial product channels. *J. Marketing* 55 (January), 52–69.

French, J.R.P., and B. Raven (1959). The basis of social power, in D. Cartwright (ed.), *Studies in Social Power*, University of Michigan Press, Ann Arbor, pp. 150–167.

Fudenberg, D., D. Levine and J. Tirole (1985). Infinite horizon models of bargaining with one-sided incomplete information, in A.E. Roth (ed.), *Game Theoretic Approaches to Bargaining Theory*, Cambridge University Press, Cambridge, pp. 73–98.

Fudenberg, D., and J. Tirole (1983). Sequential bargaining with incomplete information. *Rev. Econom. Studies* 50, 221–247.

Gelfand, A.E., and H. Solomon (1975). Analyzing the decision-making process of the American jury. *J. Amer. Statist. Assoc.* 70, 305–309.

Gelfand, A.E., and H. Solomon (1977). An argument in favor of 12-member juries, in S.S. Nagel (ed.), *Modeling the Criminal Justice System*, Sage, Beverly Hills, CA.

Gibbard, A. (1973). Manipulation of voting schemes: A general result. *Econometrica* 41, 587–601.

Gibbard, A. (1977). Manipulation of schemes that mix voting with chance. *Econometrica* 45, 665–681.

Givon, M.U. (1984). Variety seeking through brand switching. *Marketing Sci.* 3 (Winter), 1–22.

Grossman, M., and M. Perry (1986). Sequential bargaining under asymmetric information. *J. Econom. Theory* 39, 120–154.

Guillbaud, G.T. (1966). Theories of the general interest, and the logical problem of aggregation, in P.F. Lazarsfeld and N.W. Henry (eds.), *Readings in Mathematical Social Science*, Science Research Associates, Inc., Chicago, pp. 262–307.

Gul, F., and H. Sonnenschein (1988). On delay in bargaining with two-sided uncertainty. *Econometrica* 56(3), 601–611.

Gul, F., H. Sonnenschein and R. Wilson (1986). Foundations of dynamic monopoly and the Coase conjecture. *J. Econom. Theory* 39, 155–190.

Gupta, S. (1989). Modeling integrative multiple issue bargaining. *Management Sci.* 35(7), 788–806.

Gupta, S., and R. Kohli (1990). Designing products and services for consumer welfare: Theoretical and empirical issues. *Marketing Sci.* 9(3), 230–246.

Gupta, S., and Z.A. Livne (1988). Resolving a conflict situation with a reference outcome: An axiomatic model. *Management Sci.* 34(11), 1303–1314.

Gupta, S., and Z. A. Livne (1990). Testing the emergence and effect of the reference outcome in an integrative bargaining situation. *J. Marketing Lett.* 1(2), 103–112.

Gupta, S., and J.H. Steckel (1992). Conflict resolution and repeat buying in households, Working Paper, School of Business Administration, University of Michigan, Ann Arbor, MI.

Güth, W., R. Schmittberger and B. Schwarz (1982). An experimental analysis of ultimatum bargaining. *J. Econom. Behavior and Organization* 3, 367–388.

Güth, W., and R. Tietz (1987), Ultimatum bargaining for a shrinking cake. An experimental analysis, Mimeo.

Harnett, D.R. (1967). A level of aspiration model for group decision making. *J. Personality Social Psychol.* 5(1), 58–66.

Harsanyi, J.C. (1955). Cardinal welfare, individualistic ethics, and interpersonal comparisons of utility. *J. Political Economy* 63, 309–321.

Harsanyi, J.C. (1956). Approaches to the bargaining problem before and after the theory of games. *Econometrica* 24, 144–157.

Harsanyi, J.C. (1977), *Rational Behavior and Bargaining Equilibrium in Games and Social Situations*, Cambridge University Press, Cambridge.

Harsanyi, J.C., and R. Selten (1988). *A General Theory of Equilibrium Selection in Games*, MIT Press, Cambridge, MA.

Heckathorn, D. (1978). A paradigm for bargaining and a test of two bargaining models. *Behavioral Sci.* 23, 73–85.

Hemphill, J.K., and C.M. Westie (1950). The measurement of group dimensions. *J. Psychol.* 29 (April), 325–342.

Howard, J.A., and J.N. Sheth (1969). *The Theory of Buyer Behavior*, Wiley, New York.

Isenberg, D.J. (1981). Some effects of time pressure on vertical structure and decision-making accuracy in small groups. *Organ. Behavior Human Performance* 27 (February), 119–134.

Kahn, B.E., M.U. Kalwani and D.G. Morrison (1986). Measuring variety-seeking and reinforcement behavior using panel data. *J. Marketing Res.* 23 (May), 89–100.

Kahn, B.E., D.G. Morrison and G.P. Wright (1986). Aggregating individual purchases to the household level. *Marketing Sci.* 5(3), 260–268.

Kahneman, D., J.L. Knetsch and R.H. Thaler (1986a). Fairness and the assumptions of economics. *J. Business* 59, S285–S300.

Kahneman, D., J.L. Knetsch and R.H. Thaler (1986b). Fairness as a constraint on profit seeking: Entitlements in the market. *Amer. Econom. Rev.* 76, 728–741.

Kalai, E. (1985). Solutions to the bargaining problem, in L. Hurwicz, D. Schmeidler and H. Sonnenschein (eds.), *Social Goals and Social Organizations*, Cambridge University Press, Cambridge, pp. 77–105.

Kalai, E., and M. Smorodinsky (1975). Other solutions to Nash's bargaining problem. *Econometrica* 43, 513–518.

Kaneko, M., and K. Nakamura (1979). The Nash social welfare function. *Econometrica* 47, 423–435.

Keeney, R.L. (1976). A group preference axiomatization with cardinal utility. *Management Sci.* 23(2), 140–145.

Keeney, R.L., and C.W. Kirkwood (1975). Group decision making using cardinal social welfare functions. *Management Sci.* 22(4), 430–437.

Keeney, R.L., and H. Raiffa (1976). *Decisions with Multiple Objectives: Preferences and Value Tradeoffs*, Wiley, New York.

Kelley, H.H., and J.W. Thibaut (1978). *Interpersonal Relations: A Theory of Interdependence*, Wiley, New York.

Kemeny, J.G., and L.J. Snell (1962). Preference ranking: An axiomatic approach, in J.G. Kemeny and L.J. Snell (eds.), *Mathematical Models in the Social Sciences*, Ginn, New York, pp. 9–23.

Kerr, N.L., R.S. Atkin, G. Stasser, D. Meek, R.W. Holt and J.H. Davis (1976). Guilt beyond a reasonable doubt: Effects of concept definition and assigned decision rule on the judgments of mock jurors. *J. Personality Social Psychol.* 34, 282–294.

Kerr, N.L., J.H. Davis, D. Meek and A.K. Rissman (1975). Group position as a function of member attitudes: Choice shift effects from the perspective of social decision scheme theory. *J. Personality Social Psychol.* 31, 574–593.

Kirkwood, C.W. (1979). Pareto-optimality and equity in social decision analysis. *IEEE Trans. Systems, Man and Cybernet.* SMC-9(2), 89–91.

Kohli, A. (1989). Determinants of influence in organizational buying: A contingency approach. *J. Marketing* 53 (July), 50–65.

Kohli, R., and H. Park (1989). A cooperative game theory model of quantity discounts. *Management Sci.*, 35(6), 693–707.

Kriewall, M.A.O. (1980). Modeling multi-person decision processes on a major consumption decision, Unpublished Dissertation, Stanford University, Stanford, CA.

Krishnamurthi, L. (1981). Modeling joint decision making through relative influence, Unpublished Dissertation, Stanford University, Stanford, CA.

Lal, R., and R. Staelin (1984). An approach for developing and optimal discount policy. *Management Sci.* 30, 1524–1539.

Laughlin, P.R. (1980). Social combination processes of cooperative problem-solving groups on verbal intellective tasks, in M. Fishbein (ed.), *Progress in Social Psychology*, Erlbaum, Hillsdale, N.J.

Laughlin, P.R., and P.C. Earley (1982). Social combination models persuasive arguments theory, social comparison theory, and choice shift. *J. Personality Social Psychol.* 42, 273–280.

Luce, R.D., and H. Raiffa (1957). *Games and Decisions*, Wiley, New York.

MacCrimmon, K.R., and D.M. Messick (1976). A framework for social motives. *Behavioral Sci.* 21, 86–100.

McGuire, T.W., S. Kiesler and J. Siegel (1987). Group and computer-mediated discussion effects in risk decision making. *J. Personality Social Psychol.* 52(5), 917–930.

Miller, C.E., and S.S. Komorita (1986). Changes in outcomes in coalition bargaining. *J. Personality Social Psychol.* 51(4), 721–729.

Murnighan, J.K. (1978). Models of coalition behavior: Game theoretic, social psychological, and political perspectives. *Psychol. Bull.* 85(5), 1130–1153.

Nash, J.F. (1950). The bargaining problem. *Econometrica* 18 (April), 155–162.

Nash, J.F. (1953). Two person cooperative games. *Econometrica* 21, 128–140.

Neelin, J., H. Sonnenschein and M. Spiegel (1988). A further test of noncooperative bargaining theory. *Amer. Econom. Rev.* 78, 824–836.

Neslin, S.A., and L. Greenhalgh (1983). Nash's theory of cooperative games as a predictor of the outcomes of buyer–seller negotiations: An experiment in media purchasing. *J. Marketing Res.* 20 (November), 368–379.

Neslin, S.A., and L. Greenhalgh (1986). The ability of Nash's theory of cooperative games to predict the outcomes of buyer–seller negotiations: A dyad-level test. *Management Sci.* 32 (April), 480–498.

Nydegger, R.V. (1977). Independent utility scaling and the Nash bargaining model. *Behavioral Sci.* 22, 283–289.

Nydegger, R.V., and G. Owen (1974). Two-person bargaining: An experimental test of the Nash axioms. *Intern. J. Game Theory* 3(4), 239–249.

Ochs, J., and A.E. Roth (1989). An experimental study of sequential bargaining. *Amer. Econom. Rev.* 79(3), 355–384.

Osborne, M.J., and A. Rubinstein (1990). *Bargaining and Markets*, Academic Press, Boston.

Penrod, S., and R. Hastie (1979). Models of jury decision making: A critical review. *Psychol. Bull.* 86(3), 462–492.

Perry, M. (1986). An example of price formation in bilateral situations: A bargaining model with incomplete information. *Econometrica* 50, 97–109.

Plott, C.R. (1976). Axiomatic social choice theory: An overview and interpretation. *Amer. J. Political Sci.* 70(3), 511–596.

Pruitt, D.G. (1981). *Negotiation Behavior*, Academic Press, New York.

Raiffa, H. (1982). *The Art and Science of Negotiation*, Belknap/Harvard, Cambridge, MA.

Rao, V., and J.H. Steckel (1989). A polarization model for describing group preferences, Working Paper, New York University.

Rapoport, A., and J. Perner (1974). Testing Nash's solution of the cooperative game, in A. Rapoport (ed.), *Game Theory as a Theory of Conflict Resolution*, Reidel, Dordrecht, pp. 103–115.

Rawls, J. (1971). *A Theory of Justice*. Belknap, Cambridge, MA.

Robinson, P.J., C.W. Faris and Y. Wind (1967). *Industrial Buying and Creative Marketing*, Allyn and Bacon, Boston.

Robinson, P.J., and B. Stidsen (1967). *Personal Selling in a Modern Perspective*, Allyn and Bacon, Boston.

Roth, A.E. (1977). Individual rationality and Nash's solution to the bargaining problem. *Math. Oper. Res.* 2(1), 64–65.

Roth, A.E. (1979). *Axiomatic Models of Bargaining*, Springer, Berlin/New York.

Roth, A.E. (1985). Toward a focal point theory of bargaining, in A.E. Roth (ed.), *Game-Theoretic Models of Bargaining*, Cambridge University Press, New York, pp. 259–268.

Roth, A.E., and M.W.K. Malouf (1979). Game theoretic models and the role of information in bargaining. *Psychol. Rev.* 86, 574–594.

Roth, A.E., J.K. Murnighan and F. Schoumaker (1988). The deadline effect in bargaining: Some experimental evidence. *Amer. Econom. Rev.* 78, 806–823.

Rubin, J.Z., and B.R. Brown (1975). *The Social Psychology of Bargaining and Negotiation*, Academic Press, New York.

Rubinstein, A. (1982). A perfect equilibrium in a bargaining model. *Econometrica* 50, 97–109.

Rubinstein, A. (1985). A bargaining model with incomplete information about time preferences. *Econometrica* 53, 1151–1172.

Sarin, R.K. (1982). Strength of preference in risky choice. *Oper. Research*, 30(5), 982–997.

Satterthwaite, M.A. (1975). Strategy-proofness and Arrow's conditions: Existence and correspondence theorems for voting procedures and social welfare functions. *J. Econom. Theory* 10, 187–217.

Schelling, T.C. (1960). *The Strategy of Conflict, 2nd ed.*, Harvard University Press, Cambridge, MA, 1980.

Selten, R. (1972). Equal share analysis of characteristic function experiments, in H. Sauermann (ed.), *Beitrage zur Experimentellen Wirtschaftsforschung, 3*, Mohr, Tubingen, pp. 130–165.

Sen, A.K. (1977). Social choice theory: A re-examination. *Econometrica* 45, 53–89.

Sen, A.K. (1982). *Choice, Welfare and Measurement*, MIT Press, Cambridge, MA.

Sheth, J.N. (1973). A model of industrial buyer behavior. *J. Marketing* 37 (October), 50–56.

Sheth, J.N. (1974). *Models of Buying Behavior*, Harper and Row, New York.

Shubik, M. (1982). *Game Theory in the Social Sciences: Concepts and Solutions*, MIT Press, Cambridge, MA.
Siegel, S. (1957). Level of aspiration and group decision making. *Psychol. Rev.* 64, 253–263.
Sobel, J., and I. Takahashi (1983). A multi-stage model of bargaining. *Rev. Econom. Studies* 50, 411–426.
Spekman, R.E., and R.T. Moriarty, Jr. (1986). An exploratory investigation of perceived time pressure and its effect on industrial buying behavior, Paper Presented at the European Marketing Academy Conference (June), Helsinki.
Srinivasan, N., and K.W. Wen (1991). Price negotiations in new car purchases: A game theoretic experimental approach, Working Paper, University of Connecticut, Storrs, CT.
Steckel, J.H. (1990). Committee decision-making in organizations: An experimental test of the core. *Decision Sci.* 21 (Winter), 204–215.
Steckel, J.H., D.R. Lehmann and K.P. Corfman (1988). Estimating probabilistic choice models from sparse data: A method and application to groups. *Psychol. Bull.* 103 (January), 131–139.
Steckel, J.H., and J.O'Shaughnessy (1989). Towards a new way to measure power: Applying conjoint analysis to group decisions. *Marketing Lett.* 1(1), 37–46.
Sutton, J. (1986). Non-cooperative bargaining theory: An introduction. *Rev. Econom. Studies* 53, 709–724.
Svejnar, J. (1986). Bargaining power, fear of disagreement, and wage settlement: Theory and evidence from U.S. industry. *Econometrica* 54(5), 1055–1078.
Tedeschi, J.T., B.R. Schlenker and T.V. Bonoma (1973). *Conflict, Power and Games*, Aldine, Chicago.
Thomas, R.J. (1980). Correlates of interpersonal purchase influence in organizations, Unpublished Dissertation, University of Pennsylvania.
Van Damme, E. (1986). The Nash bargaining solution is optimal. *J. Econom. Theory* 38, 78–100.
Vincent, D. (1989). Bargaining with common values. *J. Econom. Theory* 48, 47–62.
Webster, F.E., Jr. and Y. Wind (1972). *Organizational Buying Behavior*, Prentice-Hall, Englewood Cliffs, NJ.
Weg, E., and R. Zwick (1991). On the robustness of perfect equilibrium in fixed cost sequential bargaining under an isomorphic transformation. *Econom. Lett.* 36, 21–24.
Wilson, E.J., G.L. Lilien and D.T. Wilson (1991). Formal models of group choice in organizational buying: Developing and testing a contingency paradigm. *J. Marketing Res.* 28 (November), 452–466.
Wilson, R. (1969). An axiomatic model of logrolling. *Amer. Econom. Rev.* 3, 331–341.
Wind, Y. (1967). The determinants of industrial buyers' behavior, in P.J. Robinson and C.W. Faris (eds.), *Industrial Buying and Creative Marketing*, Allyn and Bacon, Boston.
Wind, Y. (1978). Organizational buying center: A research agenda, in T.V. Bonoma and G. Zaltman (eds.), *Organizational Buying Behavior*, American Marketing Association, Chicago.
Zwick, R., A. Rapoport and J.C. Horward (1992). Two-person sequential bargaining with exogenous breakdown, *Theory and Decision* 32(3), 241–268.

J. Eliashberg and G.L. Lilien, Eds., *Handbooks in OR & MS, Vol. 5*

Chapter 4

Competitive Marketing Strategies: Game-Theoretic Models*

K. Sridhar Moorthy
William E. Simon Graduate School of Business Administration, University of Rochester, Rochester, NY 14627, USA

1. Introduction

The competitive marketing strategies of firms has long been a favorite subject in the popular business literature. See, for example, Sloan [1963], McDonald [1975], Louis & Yazjian [1980] and Ries & Trout [1986]. But it has been only about ten years or so since marketing academics first displayed a serious interest in competition. The number of competition-oriented papers published in this period would eclipse the corresponding number from several previous decades. The study of competition has moved from the vague exhortations that we used to find – firms must consider the 'competitive environment' when planning marketing strategies; products must be designed to 'fill the holes in the market' – to a much richer discussion of the dynamics of competition, the tradeoffs faced by companies in pursuing competitive marketing strategies, and the role of information in shaping those strategies. Finally, academic research in competitive strategy is almost as exciting as competition itself.

The relatively late arrival of competition on the academic marketing scene is surely correlated with the development of game theory as an analytical tool. While game theory has a long history, for too long was it confined to the study of toy problems. Over the last fifteen years or so, however, powerful advances in game theory have taken place in the area of dynamic games. This has enriched the theory, and made it more applicable to the modeling of real-world competitive strategies. This is not to say that game theory is the only way to understand competition.[1] The 'perfect competition model' of classical, 'pre-game-theory'

*I would like to thank Josh Eliashberg, Gary Lilien and three anonymous referees for their comments on an earlier version of this paper.

[1] Nor is game theory limited to the modeling of competition. Vertical relationships, such as those between a manufacturer and a distributor or that between a sales manager and a salesperson, have also been analyzed using game theory. In this paper, however, we will focus on 'horizontal competition' – where the actions of one firm take demand away from another's product – and our discussion of vertical relationships is limited to the effect of horizontal competition on vertical relationships.

economics applies to some competitive situations. Mostly though, competition in the modern world takes place among a few competitors, whose interests are interdependent, and where each competitor's actions affect the others. Such situations are characterized by strategic competition, and non-cooperative game theory is a good way to study them. The good news is that the reader doesn't have to take my word for it. Empirical evidence is on the way.

The purpose of this chapter is to review the key developments in our understanding of competitive marketing strategies. Product, price, advertising, and distribution competition are all addressed. While the emphasis is on models, I will survey the empirical literature as well. There is a significant amount of empirical work to report, but the ratio of theoretical to empirical work is nevertheless unpleasantly large. Hopefully, the next edition of this survey will offer more balanced coverage.

I will begin with a short account of some concepts which are essential in interpreting the models to be reviewed. After these preliminaries, I will review in turn what we know about competitive strategy in each marketing-mix variable, and the connections among them. This organization reflects the way the papers themselves are positioned, but one of the main points I want to get across is that competition on one marketing-mix variable invariably depends on the choices made on the others. So, for example, when discussing product competition, price competition comes in; when discussing price competition, product differentiation comes in, etc. In each of the surveys empirical results are discussed alongside the theory. Concluding remarks appear in Section 7. Throughout, my emphasis is on the marketing content of the models surveyed, not the technical details.

2. Preliminaries

The generic competitive strategy problem has several competitors, $1,\ldots,n$, each of which is choosing some marketing-mix variables to maximize its objective function. The objective function is usually profits, which we denote by π^i for firm i. The marketing-mix variables of choice could be product(s) – one or more attributes of the product(s) – price(s), advertising budget(s), advertising schedule(s), number of salespeople, distribution channel structure(s), etc. Let us denote firm i's marketing strategy by s_i, where $s_i = (s_{i1},\ldots,s_{im})(m \geqslant 1)$.

In general, a strategy is a function of whatever information the firm possesses at the point of decision-making. In game-theoretic terms, a strategy is thus a complete specification of the firm's actions in all the contingencies it may find itself in. For example, in the so-called Stackelberg game where one firm moves and commits to its strategy before the others – with the others observing the first firm's move – the strategies of the followers must consider every possible move of the leader. So, whereas the leader's strategy is merely an m-tuple, the followers' strategies are m-dimensional functions. Once strategies are defined with the dynamics built in, the strategy choices themselves must be considered simultaneous.

The competitive situation arises because firm i's demand function D_i is a function not only of its own strategy s_i, but also competitive strategies s_j ($j \neq i$). Denote $\{s_j\}_{j \neq i}$ by s_{-i}. Then firm i's competitive strategy problem can be written as

$$\max_{s_i \in S_i} \pi_i(s_i, s_{-i}). \tag{1}$$

Observe that while each firm's demand function could depend on a large number of marketing variables, i.e. m could be large, not all of these variables may be involved in a particular competitive situation. The constraint set S_i may be such that all except one or two variables are fixed at certain values. For example, some of the literature reviewed here models price competition only; the implicit assumption is that the competitors have already fixed their product, advertising, distribution, etc. This may not be unrealistic either. Most price competition does take place under conditions where other marketing-mix variables are fixed because product, advertising and distribution are harder to change than prices. In what follows, we will assume that m reflects only those variables which are being currently set and treat the rest as parameters of the demand function D_i.

The constraint set S_i also sometimes serves the purpose of capturing the technological constraints on the firms' choices. For example, in Hauser [1988], even though each firm is ostensibly competing on two product attributes and price – i.e. three strategic variables – the two product attributes are restricted to lie on the circumference of a circle. The usual way of handling such constraints is to substitute for one of the variables in terms of the others, reducing the dimensionality of the strategy space by one. In what follows, we will assume that m reflects these substitutions as well.

2.1. Best-response functions

To analyze a problem such as (1) we first compute each firm's best-response (or reaction) function for each of its strategic variables and then find the intersection of these functions as the Nash equilibrium. In practice, this means computing the first-order conditions for each firm, and then solving these equations simultaneously. It is the last step in this process – the solving for the equilibrium from the first-order conditions – that gives strategic content to the competition. Up to that point, the analysis is 'decision-theoretic' – each firm is treating its competitors' strategies as given, and computing its best response. The best-response function simply documents the firm's best response for each possible strategy combination of its competitors.

For example, Hauser & Shugan's [1983] analysis of defensive strategies is decision-theoretic. There are two firms, defender and attacker; the attacker moves first. Hauser & Shugan's methodology is to analyze the defender's best-response function. This analysis tells us what the defender should do for every possible action of the attacker. It doesn't tell us, however, what the defender *will do in equilibrium*. In order to determine that we need to calculate the attacker's optimal strategy *anticipating* the defender's responses, and plug this into the defender's best-response function.

Most of the competition-oriented empirical work in marketing is devoted to estimating best-response functions [Lambin, Naert & Bultez, 1975; Leeflang & Wittink, 1992; Green & Krieger, 1991].

The first-order conditions governing each firm's choice of marketing strategy can be written as

$$\frac{\partial \pi_i}{\partial s_{ik}}(s_i, s_{-i}) = 0 \quad \text{for } k = 1,\dots,m, i = 1,\dots,n. \tag{2}$$

Assuming that the profit functions π_i are strictly quasi-concave with respect to s_i [see Avriel, 1976, p. 145], these first-order conditions have unique solutions, and the best-response functions $s^*_{ik}(s_{-i})$ are well-defined. A question which arises immediately is whether these best-response functions are increasing, decreasing, or flat. If s^*_{ik} is increasing with respect to s_{jk}, then we say that firm i is a *strategic complement* of firm j with respect to the strategy variable k; if s^*_{ik} is decreasing with respect to s_{jk}, then i is a *strategic substitute* of j with respect to k; and if s^*_{ik} is constant with respect to s_{jk}, then i is *strategically independent* of j with respect to the variable k. In the case of $m = 1$, these properties are characterized by $\partial^2\pi_i/\partial s_i \partial s_j > 0$, < 0, and $= 0$, respectively. If $m > 1$, then such a characterization is not possible because of the inter-relationships among firm i's own choice variables. Note that firm i may be a strategic complement (substitute, independent) of firm j with respect to some variable, but firm j may not have the same relationship with respect to firm i.

Bulow, Geanakoplos & Klemperer [1985] have noted the importance of the strategic dependence concept for competitive strategy. The nature of competitive response is determined by the nature of strategic dependence. Will an aggressive move by one firm elicit an aggressive or a defensive response by its competitors? Or no response? In the case of strategic complementarity (substitutability), an aggressive move elicits an aggressive (defensive) response, but with strategic independence, there is no response at all. Clearly, strategic independence is the least interesting competitive situation. But note that even in this case the firm's *profits* are dependent on the strategies chosen by its competitors.

To illustrate these concepts, suppose $n = 2$, $m = 1$, and $D_i(p_i, p_{3-i}) = p_i^{-\alpha} p_{3-i}^{\beta}$ ($\alpha > 1, \beta > 0$), where p_i is firm i's price ($i = 1, 2$). Let each firm's marginal costs be constant at c, and assume there are no fixed costs. Then each firm's profit function is given by $(p_i - c)p_i^{-\alpha} p_{3-i}^{\beta}$. Differentiating this with respect to p_i and solving for p_i^* we get $p_i^* = c\alpha/(\alpha - 1)$. In other words, the two firms are strategically independent of each other. On the other hand, if $D_i = 1 - p_1 + \theta p_2$ $(0 < \theta < 1)$, then firm i's best-response function is $(1 + c + \theta p_{3-i})/2$ and the two firms are strategic complements. Finally, with the same demand function and a unit cost function given by $cQ - dQ^2$ $(1 > d > 0.5)$, firm i's best-response function is $(1 + c - 2d + \theta p_2(1 - 2d))/2(1 - d)$, which is decreasing in p_2. Here, the economies of scale are so great that the best response to a price increase by a competitor is to reduce one's price in order to exploit the lower marginal costs.

2.2. Nash equilibrium

The best-response function begs the question of what strategy combination to assume for the competitors. The Nash equilibrium answers that by requiring that each firm's strategy be the best response to the other's strategies. A *Nash equilibrium* is an n-tuple of strategies $(s_1^*, \ldots, s_n^*)$, such that for each firm i, s_i^* is a best response to s_{-i}^*. A Nash equilibrium is a *pure-strategy* Nash equilibrium if each firm's equilibrium strategy is a pure strategy, i.e. a strategy chosen with probability one. If a Nash equilibrium involves randomization among pure strategies, then the equilibrium is a *mixed-strategy* Nash equilibrium. Dasgupta & Maskin [1986] characterize the sufficient conditions for the existence of pure-strategy and mixed-strategy Nash equilibrium.

Often a pure-strategy Nash equilibrium will not exist in a game. Then the analyst can either resort to a mixed-strategy equilibrium or else look for an ε-Nash equilibrium in pure strategies. An ε-Nash equilibrium is an n-tuple of pure strategies such that, for every $\varepsilon > 0$, no firm can gain more than ε by deviating unilaterally from its equilibrium strategy. The force of the ε-equilibrium concept comes from the fact that ε can be arbitrarily small. Essentially, an ε-equilibrium says that while a firm can gain by deviating unilaterally from its equilibrium strategy, it won't gain a lot. For all practical purposes, therefore, the firms will stay at the ε-Nash equilibrium.

2.3. Perfect Nash equilibrium

There are several ways to refine the Nash equilibrium concept to increase its predictive power. The prediction problem arises when there are several Nash equilibria in the same game. Which Nash equilibrium will the firms play? By using the idea of perfection we can eliminate certain Nash equilibria in a reasonably convincing way. One kind of perfection is *subgame perfection* which applies to competitive situations with sequential moves. Subgame perfection requires that at *every* stage in the competition, the Nash equilibrium prescriptions regarding what each firm should do in the future must be in Nash equilibrium from that point on. We can thus rule out Nash equilibria sustained by incredible threats or promises. Another refinement of Nash equilibrium, *sequential equilibrium*, says that at *every* stage in the game, the Nash equilibrium prescriptions from that point on must be 'justifiable' on the basis of some beliefs held by the various firms about the things they are uncertain about at that point. These beliefs are required to satisfy Bayes's law if equilibrium behavior has been observed up to that point.

For more information on these and other concepts of game theory, see Gibbons [1992] and Fudenberg & Tirole [1991]. For a lively discussion of the foundations of game theory see Kreps [1990], Smith [1990], Rubinstein [1991] and Binmore [1992].

3. Price competition

3.1. Nature of competition: prices versus quantities

Given the connection between quantity and price via the demand function, the choice of which variable to compete on has been the subject of much debate in the economics literature. Cournot [1838] argued for quantity as the choice variable; Bertrand [1883] argued for price as the choice variable. Note that this distinction has an impact only at the equilibrium level; in single-firm decision-making under certainty, the choice of variable is moot. For example, we can write the monopolist's problem as

$$\max_{p} pD(p) - C(D(p))$$

or as

$$\max_{q} D^{-1}(q)q - C(q)$$

and we would get the same optimal price, quantity and profits. In an oligopoly, also, when computing the best-response functions it doesn't matter which variable is actually chosen. For a given conjecture regarding the other firms' strategies – prices or quantities – one can typically invert the demand function for a given firm to get quantity or price. But when solving for the equilibrium, it does matter that each firm's conjecture about the other firms' strategy variable is the one they actually set. As Klemperer & Meyer [1986] show, with two firms, this leads to four *kinds* of equilibria: (price, price), (price, quantity), (quantity, price), (quantity, quantity). For example (price, quantity) is the equilibrium that results when firm 1 chooses price while conjecturing that firm 2 sets quantity and firm 2 sets quantity while conjecturing that firm 1 sets price.

With uncertainty and increasing or decreasing marginal costs, even a monopolist will prefer to set price or quantity. The reason is, with increasing or decreasing marginal costs, the monopolist's profit function is concave or convex, respectively, so risk-averse and risk-seeking behavior come into the picture. As intuition suggests, a monopolist would prefer to set quantity (and let the market determine price) when marginal costs are increasing in quantity and prefer to set price (and vary his production) when marginal costs are decreasing in quantity. In the oligopoly case, the same intuition carries through. The four types of equilibria are cut down to just two: with increasing marginal costs, we get (quantity, quantity) as the only equilibrium type; with decreasing marginal cost, we get (price, price) as the only equilibrium type. The case of capacity constraints corresponds to increasing marginal costs. Kreps & Sheinkman [1983] show that in a two-stage game where capacities are chosen first and prices second, the Nash-equilibrium prices resemble those that will prevail in a one-stage quantity-competition game.

Competition is more muted in quantity competition than in price competition. In other words, equilibrium profits are higher when quantity is the choice variable. To see a simple illustration of this, assume two firms, linear demand $1-p$, and constant, equal marginal costs $c<1$. The Bertrand equilibrium is $p_1 = p_2 = c$, but the Cournot equilibrium is $q_1 = q_2 = (1-c)/3$. Whereas the Bertrand equilibrium yields zero profits, the Cournot equilibrium yields $(1-c)^2/9$ to each firm.

Whether price competition or quantity competition is the right way to model competition is ultimately an empirical question. With price competition, the implicit assumption is that each firm should take the other's price as given: the other firm's quantity is flexible because, presumably, quantity is easy to change. With quantity competition, prices are considered flexible and the target is a certain quantity sold. In production situations with long lead times and perishable products (which cannot be inventoried), e.g. fruits and vegetables, the Cournot model seems appropriate. Similarly for airline competition: here the maximum number of seats on a route needs to be fixed a priori and cannot be changed easily. Brander & Zhang's [1990] study of the competition between American Airlines and United Airlines on Chicago-based routes concludes that this competition is better represented by the Cournot model than by the Bertrand model. Klemperer & Meyer [1986], however, observe that airlines competing on shuttle routes (e.g. Pan Am and Eastern on the New York–Boston route) compete Bertrand-style on prices because they can add or subtract seat capacity relatively easily due to the frequency of flights and the smaller size of the airplanes.

Both Bertrand competition and Cournot competition can be subsumed under the same first-order conditions by using *conjectural variations* in quantities. Let $D(q_i; q_j)$ denote the (inverse) demand function of firm i; here j denotes collectively all the other firms. Then i's profit function is

$$\Pi_i = q_i D(q_i; q_j) - C(q_i)$$

and its first-order condition can be written as

$$D - \mathrm{MC} + q_i\left(\frac{\partial D}{\partial q_i} + \frac{\partial D}{\partial q_j} R_{ji}\right) = 0,$$

with $R_{ji} = \partial q_j / \partial q_i$ as the conjectural variation. So Cournot competition is simply $R_{ji} = 0$ for all i, j and Bertrand competition is $R_{ji} = -1$ for all i, j. Collusive behavior, i.e., maximization of joint profits, entails $R_{ji} = 1$.

The conjectural-variation formulation is used extensively in empirical work. See, for example, Slade [1987] and Brander & Zhang [1990].

3.2. *Price competition when demand and costs are dynamic*

Dockner & Jorgensen [1988] study the open-loop price equilibria in a differential game with diffusion effects on the demand side and learning effects on the cost side. These equilibria generally have properties similar to the monopoly solution. Learning effects on the cost side lead to decreasing prices; diffusion effects lead to rising prices; saturation effects lead to decreasing prices. When diffusion and learning cost are present in the same model, it is difficult to draw general conclusions on the nature of the equilibrium price path.

Markets with positive network externalities are an important subset of dynamic demand situations. The necessary condition for positive network externalities is that the utility of consumption increases with the number of other users. This encompasses a large set of applications, e.g. telecommunication networks (e.g. fax services, electronic mail) where there is a direct connection between utility and number of subscribers, and experience goods, where word-of-mouth from early users reduces the risk of purchase for later users. The monopoly analysis of markets with positive network externalities is due to Oren & Smith [1981] and Dhebar & Oren [1985]. They show that optimal price trajectories are increasing over time, and that the steady-state network size is larger, and price lower, as consumers' expectations about network growth (during the transient stage) become more optimistic.

Katz & Shapiro [1985] examine a static model of price competition among rival networks. Consumer's expectations about network size are required to be rational, i.e. fulfilled in equilibrium. The price competition among the firms is modeled as a Cournot game. The other innovation here is the introduction of the distinction between compatible and incompatible networks. With compatible networks, the consumers are concerned only about the total network size, the sum of the outputs of the individual firms; with incompatible networks, the consumer is concerned about each network's expected size, individually. The interesting results have to do with the choice between compatibility and incompatibility. Compatibility allows each firm to draw on its competitors' network, in the sense of making the consumer's adoption decision easier; on the other hand, compatibility also increases the intensity of competition. Katz & Shapiro show that firms with small networks or weak reputations will favor compatibility whereas firms with larger networks and stronger reputations won't.

Xie & Sirbu [1992] use the Bass [1969] model as the basis for their analysis of price competition among networks. Again, the interesting results concern the compatibility–incompatibility choice. They show that the Nash equilibrium in prices with compatible symmetric networks (same starting conditions, same constant marginal costs) yields greater profits to each firm than the corresponding incompatible equilibrium. In fact, the profits in the compatible equilibrium may be greater than the monopoly profits. This suggests that an incumbent may welcome the entry of a compatible competitor, especially if the incumbent's installed base is currently low. The later entrant, too, benefits from compatibility, especially when the incumbent's installed base is large. The equilibrium pricing trajectories are increasing for the most part (until saturation effects take hold), as in Dockner & Jorgensen [1988].

For more on competition among positive-externality networks see the March 1992 special issue of *Journal of Industrial Economics*.

3.3. Promotional competition

Much of the recent price-competition research in marketing has been on 'promotional competition'. Shilony [1977], Varian [1980], Narasimhan [1988] and Raju, Srinivasan & Lal [1990] have modeled promotions as the outcome of randomized pricing strategies. Each of the competitors chooses a price randomly from a certain distribution with the highest price in the support of the distribution serving as the regular price and any price below that serving as a deal price. All of these models assume that only one price is available from a brand at any given time; in other words, the deals in these papers are in the nature of shelf-price reductions (and not coupons, for example).

In Shilony's [1977] model, each brand has a loyal market segment of (say) size 1, provided its price is within c of the lowest-priced brand. But if a brand is more than c higher than the lowest-priced brand, then it will have no customers. Thus, brand loyalty is not absolute – if the 'other' brand is sufficiently lower-priced, then customers will switch from their favorite brand. Each customer is assumed to have a reservation price of 1 for all the brands. Shilony shows that no pure-strategy equilibrium can exist in this model if $c < (n-1)/n$. (If $c \geqslant (n-1)/n$, a pure-strategy Nash equilibrium exists with all firms pricing at 1.) To see why, assume for simplicity that $n = 2$. If the pure-strategy equilibrium involves unequal prices for the two firms and the price difference between the two firms is more than c, say $p_2 > p_1 + c$, then the higher-priced firm will reduce its price so that the price difference between the two firms is exactly c; on the other hand, if the price difference between the firms is less than or equal to c, then the lower-priced firm will raise its price to $\min\{1, p_2 + c\}$. This leaves only one possibility for a pure-strategy equilibrium: $p_1 = p_2 = 1$. But now, either firm would prefer to price at $1 - c - \varepsilon$, capturing both segments, and gaining a profit increase of $2(1 - c - \varepsilon) - 1 = 1 - 2c - 2\varepsilon$ (remember $c < 1/2$). Hence there is no pure-strategy equilibrium when $c < 1/2$. Shilony shows that a mixed-strategy equilibrium exists in his model when $c < 1/2$, which he then interprets as showing the existence of sales. The regular price is 1 here, and any price below that in the support of the mixed-strategy is a promotion. Both brands promote equally often given that they are identical, and the frequency of sales can be higher or lower than the frequency of charging the regular price, depending on c.

Varian [1980] assumes that consumers are of two types: informed and uninformed. The informed consumers know the lowest-priced store in the market and patronize that store; the uninformed choose a store at random. Each consumer has the same reservation price r. Again, it is easy to see that a pure-strategy Nash equilibrium can't exist here. If the equilibrium involves the same price for all the firms, then, depending on whether the other firms' price is equal to marginal cost or higher, either one of the firms will raise its price to r (content to capture its share of the uninformed) or else lower it slightly to capture all of the informed and a share of the uninformed. On the other hand, if the pure-strategy equilibrium involves different prices for the different firms, then a lower-priced firm can always gain by increasing its price up to, but not at, the price of its nearest competitor. Varian computes the mixed-strategy equilibrium and shows that it is a continuous distribution with no mass-points. The top price in the support of the distribution is r and the lowest price is $p^* = k/(I + k/r)$ where I is the number of informed consumers and k is the fixed cost (the marginal cost is zero). The density of the distribution is higher near r than near p^*, signifying that the frequency of 'regular prices' is higher than the frequency of promotions. (Given the absence of mass-points, however, there is no single regular price here.) Villas-Boas [1990] estimates Varian's equilibrium price distribution on IRI coffee data and finds good fits.

Narasimhan's [1988] model is quite similar to Varian's. He models consumers as being of three types: loyal to brand L, loyal to brand S, and deal-prone. In the basic model, all consumers have a reservation price r for any of the products, but whereas the deal-prone consumers will choose the cheapest product, the loyal consumers always choose their favorite brand. The deal-prone consumers here play the role of Varian's informed consumers: they generate price competition among the firms.

The only difference between brands L and S is the size of their loyal segments, α_ℓ and α_s; the 'larger' brand has the larger loyal following, i.e. $\alpha_\ell > \alpha_s$. The profit function of the two firms is:

$$\Pi_i(p_i, p_j) = \begin{cases} \alpha_i p_i + \beta p_i & \text{for } p_i < p_j, \\ \alpha_i p_i + (1/2)\beta p_i & \text{for } p_i = p_j, \\ \alpha_i p_i & \text{for } p_i > p_j. \end{cases} \tag{3}$$

Once again, it is straightforward to show that no pure-strategy equilibrium will exist. A mixed-strategy equilibrium does exist, however, and it involves the following distribution functions for the two firms:

$$F_\ell(p) = \begin{cases} 1 + \dfrac{\alpha_s}{\beta} - \dfrac{\alpha_s r(\alpha_s + \beta)}{(\alpha_\ell + \beta)\beta p} & \text{for } \dfrac{\alpha_s r}{\alpha_\ell + \beta} \leqslant p < r, \\ 1 & \text{for } p = r, \end{cases} \tag{4}$$

$$F_s(p) = 1 - \frac{\alpha_\ell (r - p)}{\beta p} \quad \text{for } \frac{\alpha_s r}{\alpha_\ell + \beta} \leqslant p \leqslant r. \tag{5}$$

The larger brand has a higher average price than the smaller brand, but it promotes less frequently (because it has a mass-point at r). In fact, the smaller brand doesn't have a regular price – its price is below r all the time. The average discount on promotion is, however, the same for both brands. Both brands price above marginal cost all the time.

These results change somewhat if the switching segment is not indifferent between the two brands. If the switching segment has a slight preference for the smaller brand (modeled as in Shilony – the larger brand will have to offer a price advantage of at least $l > 0$ in order to get the switching segment's custom), then the larger brand still promotes less often, but its average discount on promotion is greater. However, if the switching segment has a slight preference for the larger brand, then the larger brand promotes more often, but it offers smaller average discounts on promotion.

Note that having *both* loyal and switching segments is crucial to Narasimhan's results. If there were no loyal segments, then a pure-strategy Nash equilibrium exists with one firm priced at l plus marginal cost and the other at marginal cost, i.e., neither firm offers promotions. (If the switching segment prefers neither brand, i.e., $l = 0$, then both firms price at marginal cost all the time.) If there were no switching segments, then, too, there are no promotions: both firms price at reservation price all the time.

Raju, Srinivasan & Lal [1990] generalize Shilony's model in the following way. Instead of assuming that both brands have the same loyalty, they allow for a (relatively) strong brand and a weaker brand. (In contrast to Varian and Narasimhan, neither brand has any absolutely loyal customers here.) The strong brand's loyal customers are harder to lure away than the weaker brand's loyal customers: the price discounts required are l_s and l_w with $l_s > l_w$. Compared to the Narasimhan (and Varian) models, competition is more muted here. In fact, if the required price discounts – which are parameters of the model – are sufficiently large relative to r, a pure-strategy price equilibrium at r exists here. But if even one of the brands is relatively weak (say $l_w < r/2$), then a mixed-strategy equilibrium is the only possibility. Again, this equilibrium features a higher frequency of promotion by the weaker brand, and prices above marginal cost. Raju, Srinivasan & Lal provide some empirical evidence in support of this finding. In a sample of 59 pairs of national and store brands from a grocery store, they find nearly half of them to involve more frequent promotions by the store brand; in less than 30% of the pairs, the store brand promotes less often. (In the remaining pairs, there is no statistical difference in frequency of promotion.)

The Shilony, Narasimhan, and Raju, Srinivasan & Lal models can be interpreted as special cases of the Hotelling [1929] model considered in the next section. (See Gal-Or [1982] and Osborne & Pitchik [1987] for a study of the mixed-strategy equilibrium in Hotelling's model.) In all these models, the probability of charging a price lower than r – the frequency of promotion – can be higher or lower than the probability of charging the regular price, depending on the parameters. But (in general) there is a tradeoff between frequency and depth of promotions: the greater the maximum depth of promotion, the lower the frequency. At least one of the firms ends up getting the same expected profits as if it charged r all the time (and the other firm responded optimally), but, of course, charging r all the time is not an equilibrium strategy. In Narasimhan [1988], in fact, one brand gets its max-min payoff in equilibrium, i.e. the same expected profits that it could *guarantee* for itself by pricing at r all the time. In other words, strategic competition is crucial to these models; a firm competing non-strategically with 'fringe' competitors would not promote in these models.

One paper which doesn't rely on mixed strategies to motivate promotions is

Rao [1991]. He models the competition between a strong brand (national brand) and a weaker brand (called a store brand) in three stages: regular-price choice, promotion-depth choice, and frequency-of-promotion choice. (Promotions are once again in the sense of shelf-price reductions.) Consumers are assumed to be of two types: completely deal-oriented (they always choose the lower-priced brand) and those with some national-brand loyalty (these consumers are like those in Raju, Srinivasan & Lal's model). The national-brand-loyal consumers are assumed to be heterogeneous in loyalty; in fact, Rao assumes a continuous distribution of brand-loyalties. The main result is that an equilibrium in pure strategies exists and it involves only the national-brand promoting. The finding that store brands don't promote in equilibrium – or even promote less often – doesn't get much support in the empirical work of Raju, Srinivasan & Lal [1990] as noted above. Furthermore, the existence of a pure-strategy equilibrium is driven largely by technical considerations, not marketing considerations. Essentially it boils down to this: given that frequency of promotion is chosen separately – as a distinct strategy variable – there is no need to further randomize on prices. The three-stage formulation further implies that the firms can commit to various aspects of their strategy sequentially. For example, it is assumed that the national brand knows the store brand's regular price when choosing its promotion depth, and further, that it knows the store brand's promotion depth (and regular price) when choosing its frequency of promotion. Most national brands, however, seem to set all elements of their promotion schedule – depth, frequency and timing – simultaneously, and well in advance of execution, and store brands typically *react* to the national brand's promotions. The leadership issue is relevant because Deneckere, Kovenock & Lee [1992] have shown that in Narasimhan's [1988] model, if one of the firms is the price leader, then there are no promotions.

3.4. Competition with switching costs

In many markets, there are significant switching costs for consumers in moving from one brand to a competing brand. One source of this switching cost is *learning cost*: for experience goods, if the experience with one brand is satisfactory, then the consumer will be reluctant to try another, unless special incentives are given. Another kind of learning cost arises when the consumer has to learn how to use a brand, e.g. switching among different brands of software. Yet another source of switching costs is transaction costs, e.g. switching between banks, switching between stores, etc. A result of all these switching costs is brand loyalty.

Klemperer [1987] shows that the non-cooperative equilibrium in an oligopoly with switching costs may be the same as the *collusive* outcome in an otherwise identical market without switching costs. To see this, suppose there are two firms A and B producing identical products. Let q consumers have reservation prices at least as much as $f(q)$ for the product they purchased earlier (or were exposed to by word-of-mouth from other purchasers). Denote $f^{-1}(\cdot)$ by $h(\cdot)$. Further suppose that a fraction of the market σ^A – A's customers – must incur a switching cost to buy B's product and the fraction σ^B $(=1-\sigma^A)$ – B's customers – must pay the same switching cost to buy A. (In a two-period model these fractions would simply be the respective firms' market shares from period 1; see below.) Let $\Gamma(w)$ be the proportion of a firm's customers whose cost of switching to the other firm's product is less than or equal to w; $\Gamma(0) = 0$.

Without loss of generality assume $p^A \leqslant p^B$. Then the demand functions of the two firms are:

$$q^A = \sigma^A h(p^A) + \sigma^B \Gamma(p^B - p^A) h(p^B) + \sigma^B \int_{r=p^A}^{p^B} \Gamma(r - p^A)[-\mathrm{d}h(r)], \tag{6}$$

$$q^B = \sigma^B(1 - \Gamma(p^B - p^A))h(p^B). \tag{7}$$

Firm A sells to those of its own customers with reservation prices less than or equal to p^A, to those of B's customers with reservation prices greater than or equal to p^B and switching costs less than or equal to $(p^B - p^A)$, and to B's customers with reservation prices in the range (p^A, p^B) and reservation price minus switching cost greater than or equal to p^A. As for firm B, its demand consists of those of its previous customers with switching costs greater than or equal to $(p^B - p^A)$. Note that B will not get any of A's customers because its price is at least as high as A's. Assuming that the two firms have the same constant marginal cost c, the first-order conditions describing A's price choice is:

$$\sigma^A h(p^A) + \sigma^B \Gamma(p^B - p^A) h(p^B) + \sigma^B \int_{r=p^A}^{p^B} \Gamma(r - p^A)[-\mathrm{d}h(r)]$$
$$+ [p^A - c]\Bigg[\sigma^A h'(p^A) - \sigma^B \gamma(p^B - p^A) h(p^B)$$
$$+ \sigma^B \int_{r=p^A}^{p^B} -\gamma(r - p^A)[-\mathrm{d}h(r)]\Bigg] = 0, \tag{8}$$

where γ is the density function corresponding to Γ. At a symmetric equilibrium $p^A = p^B = p^*$ with $\sigma^A = \sigma^B = 1/2$, and (8) reduces to

$$\tfrac{1}{2}[h(p^*) + (p^* - c)(h'(p^*) - \gamma(0)h(p^*))] = 0. \tag{9}$$

If $\gamma(0) = 0$, this becomes

$$h(p^*) + (p^* - c)h'(p^*) = 0. \tag{10}$$

This last equation is, however, nothing but the first-order condition of a *monopolist* choosing price in an industry with no switching costs. In other words, with switching costs and the condition $\gamma(0) = 0$, the two firms' equilibrium-pricing behavior resembles what they would have done if they colluded to maximize joint profits in a market with no switching costs. The condition $\gamma(0) = 0$ says that the density of consumers with zero switching costs is zero; if all consumers had a switching cost greater than zero it will be satisfied.

But what about the first-period competition? If switching costs produce a lock-in effect, then getting customers in the first period to choose your brand becomes all the more important. Klemperer [1987] argues that the first-period competition will be more vigorous than if there were no switching costs – each firm goes for a larger market share. In fact, in the constant, equal marginal costs case, the competition is so fierce in the first period that each firm prices below cost (but, of course, prices at the monopoly level in the second period).

If we think of switching costs as a way of modeling loyalty (cf. the Raju, Srinivasan & Lal [1990] model), one may wonder whether Klemperer's model of price competition is also providing a theory of price promotions. The Klemperer results do suggest another way to motivate price promotions, but in contrast to the mixed-strategy models reviewed in the previous section, here there is an explicit dynamic structure. The firms promote in the first period, and charge regular (monopoly) prices in the second. The purpose of the promotion is very much like in the 'textbooks': to get the consumer to try the product, hoping that s/he will like the product enough to become loyal to it.

Beggs & Klemperer [1992] extend the Klemperer [1987] analysis to an infinite-periods market in which new consumers arrive each period and a fraction of the old leave. The desire to attract the new consumers who arrive each period may be thought of as reducing the ability of the firms to exploit the old consumers. Nevertheless, Beggs & Klemperer conclude that prices and profits are higher in the steady-state equilibrium with switching costs than without. This feature of the equilibrium also leads to the surprising prediction that entry is easier in a market with switching costs than in one without.

Gerstner & Hess [1990] present a theory of retail bait-and-switch which is based on the switching costs between retail stores which arise after a consumer has already entered a store. The idea is that consumers choose retail stores based on advertised retail prices. Consumers also have search costs for determining the prices of unadvertised brands. The firms' equilibrium strategy turns out to have a bait-and-switch feature. Each store deliberately understocks the advertised brand, but offers a rain check to those who are unserved. Consumers, however, have travel costs, so the people who are unserved would rather switch to a competing unadvertised brand, even if that brand doesn't present as good a value as the advertised brand. This provides the leverage to the store to raise its margins on these unadvertised brands. (Note that consumers are not fooled by the retailers' strategies: in equilibrium they correctly anticipate the out-of-stock percentage and the price of the unadvertised brand.) Competition on the advertised brand, however, lowers its price to below cost. The net effect on profits is that in equilibrium every retailer makes zero profits. Similar ideas underlie models of loss-leader pricing such as Hess & Gerstner [1987], Lal & Matutes [1992] and Simester [1992].

Borenstein [1991] provides empirical evidence on the effect of switching costs on store price competition. He examines the retail margins for leaded and unleaded gasoline, and finds them to be generally higher for leaded gasoline. Moreover, the difference in margins is negatively correlated to the availability of leaded gasoline. Borenstein's hypothesis is that as the availability of leaded gasoline has decreased, the switching costs of leaded-gasoline consumers have increased. Correspondingly, the monopoly power of leaded-gasoline stations has increased.

3.5. *Implicit collusion and price wars*

There are several papers in the literature that model implicit collusion in prices. This literature originates in Stigler [1964] and Friedman [1971] and continues with Abreu [1986], Green & Porter [1984], Abreu, Pearce & Stacchetti [1986], Slade [1989] and Lal [1990]. The basic idea is that firms in an oligopoly could collude implicitly by threatening to punish price-cutters by cutting prices themselves; if future profits are sufficiently important, the threat of punishment will deter would-be cheaters from cheating. The reason we call this implicit collusion and not explicit collusion is that no legally binding agreements among the firms are required to implement the collusion. The collusion is self-enforcing in the sense of Nash equilibrium.

Let us consider Friedman's model first. Suppose there are two identical competitors, each of whom has a single-period profit function π and a discount factor $d \in (0, 1]$ on next-period profits. They compete with each other infinitely often, choosing a price each period. The one-period competition has the prisoner's dilemma structure: both would be better off cooperating and choosing the jointly-optimal price p^{o}, but if either firm believes the other is holding to that price, then it will be better off 'cheating' and charging a lower price p^{c}. The only Nash equilibrium of the one-period game is p^{n}, and

$$\pi(p^{\mathrm{c}}, p^{\mathrm{o}}) > \pi(p^{\mathrm{o}}, p^{\mathrm{o}}) > \pi(p^{\mathrm{n}}, p^{\mathrm{n}}).$$

In the infinitely repeated game, p^{n} each period by both firms is still a Nash equilibrium. But another, more interesting, equilibrium emerges as well when $d \geqslant (\pi(p^{\mathrm{c}}, p^{\mathrm{o}}) - \pi(p^{\mathrm{o}}, p^{\mathrm{o}}))/(\pi(p^{\mathrm{c}}, p^{\mathrm{o}}) - \pi(p^{\mathrm{n}}, p^{\mathrm{n}}))$:

Price at p^{o} as long as competitor has not deviated from it.

Price at p^{n} every period after deviation.

To see why this is an equilibrium, observe that if either firm contemplates deviating from p^{o} in any period, then it will gain $\pi(p^{\mathrm{c}}, p^{\mathrm{o}}) - \pi(p^{\mathrm{o}}, p^{\mathrm{o}})$ immediately but it will lose $\pi(p^{\mathrm{o}}, p^{\mathrm{o}}) - \pi(p^{\mathrm{n}}, p^{\mathrm{n}})$ every period after that. Deviation is not worthwhile if and only if

$$\pi(p^{\mathrm{c}}, p^{\mathrm{o}}) - \pi(p^{\mathrm{o}}, p^{\mathrm{o}}) \leqslant d(\pi(p^{\mathrm{o}}, p^{\mathrm{o}}) - \pi(p^{\mathrm{n}}, p^{\mathrm{n}}))[1 + d + d^2 + \cdots], \tag{11}$$

i.e.

$$d \geqslant \frac{\pi(p^{\mathrm{c}}, p^{\mathrm{o}}) - \pi(p^{\mathrm{o}}, p^{\mathrm{o}})}{\pi(p^{\mathrm{c}}, p^{\mathrm{o}}) - \pi(p^{\mathrm{n}}, p^{\mathrm{n}})}. \tag{12}$$

Note that this collusive equilibrium is subgame-perfect. The condition on the discount factor essentially says that the 'future' has to be sufficiently important for collusion to be sustained non-cooperatively. If the discount factor is small, then either firm may be tempted to cheat because the 'punishment' doesn't have enough 'bite'.

(Various ways of reducing the temptation to cheat on the one hand and increasing the severity of punishments on the other have been proposed in the literature. One way to resist the temptation to cheat is to bind oneself to a 'most-favored-customer' pricing policy [Cooper, 1986]. Such a policy requires that a discount offered in the future be retrospectively made available to current customers. Bernheim & Whinston [1990] argue that multimarket contact between the firms will increase the severity of possible punishments and thus the likelihood of collusion.)

One issue which remains after this analysis is whether the two equilibria identified above are the only ones – in which case we would have strong grounds for choosing the collusive equilibrium – or are there any others. Unfortunately, the answer here is that there are many equilibria. The so-called 'folk theorems' in game theory say that in an infinitely repeated game with sufficiently patient players, *any* set of feasible, individually rational payoffs from the one-period game (the payoffs which give each player at least as much as what he can guarantee himself) can be achieved in some Nash equilibrium of the repeated game [Fudenberg & Tirole, 1991]. In other words, there are lots of Nash equilibria of the repeated game. The intuition is that infinitely repeated play gives players *many* opportunities to devise creative punishments to enforce virtually any set of payoffs, provided they care about the future. Given this abundance of riches, the question arises whether we can determine a unique equilibrium which enforces the collusive outcome with the *cheapest* punishments. Abreu [1986] rigorously investigates this question and shows the existence of firm-specific punishments which keep the competitors at their collusive prices in a least-cost way. These optimal punishments are of a 'stick-and-carrot' nature: an extremely low price for everyone immediately after a defection, but then everyone returns to the collusive price until the next episode of cheating and punishment. The 'stick' is more severe here than in the Friedman scheme, but it lasts only one period.

Lal [1990] applies these ideas in his study of price promotions. His model has two national brands competing against a local brand. Each national brand has a loyal segment of consumers, but there are also brand-switchers who choose either the local brand or the cheaper national brand, depending on the price difference. There is no pure-strategy Nash equilibrium in the one-period game involving the two national brands (with the local brand behaving as a Stackelberg follower). However, optimal collusion between the national brands against the local brand – with the local brand continuing to behave as a Stackelberg follower – involves one national brand charging the regular price (the reservation price of its loyal consumers) and the other national brand charging a price low enough to leave the optimal amount of market share for the local brand. The main insight here is that, to the extent it is optimal to promote to take share away from the local brand, it is in the national brands' collective interest to have only one national brand promoting. Both national brands promoting is too 'heavy-handed' – it leaves 'too much money on the table'. Lal further shows that the collusion between the national brands can be implemented non-cooperatively (à la Abreu) in an infinite replication of the one-period game if the national brands' discount factor on future profits is large enough. While the implementation is not unique – the folk theorem says that there is an infinite number of ways for the two national brands to achieve the collusive outcome non-cooperatively – an attractive implementation, which has the virtue of giving each national brand a nearly equal share of the joint profits (the national brand which begins the game with a promotion has a slight advantage), is the alternate promotions strategy where the national brands take turns promoting. Only one national brand promotes each period, but some national brand is always on promotion.

Green & Porter [1984] have extended this argument to situations where competitors' past behavior cannot be read with certainty. The reason for the noise could be a stochastic component to market demand. While each firm knows its own past output and the market price (we are assuming a homogeneous product here), it doesn't know whether a low price is due to some firm 'cheating' (by 'overproducing') or 'adverse market conditions'. The collusive equilibrium now involves a trigger price, such that only if the market price dips below the trigger price, is punishment action taken. This leads to the phenomenon of periodic 'price wars', (precipitated by the stochastic demand shocks) followed by price increases. Note that this contrasts with the prediction of the Friedman [1971] model: there are no price wars unless some firm cheats, and that is not supposed to happen in equilibrium.

Rotemberg & Saloner [1986] have argued that collusion is harder to sustain under 'boom' conditions than under 'bust' conditions (in contrast to Green & Porter). The key to their formulation is stochastic demand. In each period, demand can be low, the demand function is $D_1(\cdot)$, or high, the demand function is $D_2(\cdot)$, with probability 1/2. Now $D_2(p) > D_1(p)$ for all p, so D_2 corresponds to 'boom times'. Each firm is supposed to observe the state of demand before making its pricing decision. The collusive price is obviously higher under D_2 than under D_1, but the temptation to cheat is also higher under D_2. The one-period gain from cheating is higher, and subsequent punishments do not hurt as much because they are based on 'average demand conditions' – some of the punishments will be administered under 'bust' conditions in which the firm is not going to make as much profit anyway. The main result is that as long as the discount factor is in some intermediate range $[1/2, \delta_0]$, the collusive arrangement that can be sustained has the firms charging *below* the monopoly price p_2^{m} (corresponding to D_2) during boom times and at the monopoly price p_1^{m} (corresponding to D_1) during bust times. In fact, the collusive price in booms may be lower than the collusive price in busts, leading to countercyclical prices, i.e., 'price wars' during booms, no 'price wars' during busts.

A slightly different argument for price wars is offered by Slade [1989]. She suggests that price wars may be provoked in a collusive arrangement by exogenous demand shocks which permanently change the structure of demand in *unknown* ways (cf. Rotemberg & Saloner). The competitors would like to collude at the new jointly optimal price, but this price is hard to find given the changed circumstances. Price wars become a way to learn about demand. Once the new demand structure is learnt – which should take only as many periods as there are parameters to learn – the competitors settle in an implicitly collusive equilibrium held together by the threat of punishments.

3.6. *Empirical results on implicit collusion and price wars*

Green & Porter's model has been tested by Porter [1983] in his seminal study of the Joint Executive Committee railroad cartel of the 1980s. Porter starts with a constant elasticity demand function for the cartel:

$$\log Q_t = \delta_0 + \delta_1 \log p_t + \delta_2 L_t + \varepsilon_{dt}, \tag{13}$$

where p_t is the price charged by the cartel in week t (as measured by a weekly poll of the cartel members), Q_t is the total amount of grain in tons shipped by rail from Chicago to the East Coast, and L_t is a dummy variable which accounts for the seasonal competition from water shipping (it is equal to 1 if the Great Lakes were open to navigation). The firms' quantity-setting behavior is captured by a modified MR = MC relationship:

$$p_t(1 + \theta_t/\delta_1) = \mathrm{MC}(q_t), \tag{14}$$

where q_t is a given firm's output, and $p_t(1 + \theta_t/\delta_1)$ its 'perceived marginal revenue' – the ordinary MR of a monopolist, augmented by θ_t, a competitiveness index. As θ_t approaches zero, we approach Bertrand competition; as θ_t approaches 1, we approach monopoly (i.e., collusive behavior); and as θ_t approaches market share, we approximate Cournot competition. The marginal cost in the above equation is represented as

$$\mathrm{MC} = a_i \gamma q_t^{\gamma - 1}, \tag{15}$$

and is to be interpreted as the marginal cost of the average firm in the industry. The critical question is whether θ_t varies over time to reflect periods of successful collusion followed by periods of price wars. In order to answer this, Porter estimates the intersection of the demand and supply equations, (13) and (14) respectively, under the collusion and price-war regimes. But since the collusive and price-war regimes have to be picked up from the data (and not identified exogenously), he specifies two versions of the supply equation (14):

$$p_t(1 + \theta_r/\delta_1) = \mathrm{MC} \quad \text{during price wars}, \tag{16}$$

$$p_t(1 + \theta_c/\delta_1) = \mathrm{MC} \quad \text{during collusion}, \tag{17}$$

and postulates a probability π for the first regime. Then, π along with the other parameters of the demand and supply equations are estimated by an iterative maximum-likelihood procedure. Porter finds that 'reversions to non-cooperative behavior did occur in the JEC, with a significant decrease in market price in these periods'. The market prices during these periods of non-cooperative behavior correspond better to Cournot quantity-setting behavior than to Bertrand price-setting behavior. In other words, while the market price is lower during price wars than under collusion, it is not as low as Bertrand competition would imply.

What triggers the price wars cannot be answered conclusively. Porter argues that they were due to unanticipated drops in the market share of some firm (as opposed to unanticipated decreases in total demand). But it is also possible that they were due to other external demand and supply shocks not modeled by Porter. In fact, Rotemberg & Saloner suggest that the price wars in the JEC cartel coincided with boom times in railroad grain shipping. They produce Table 4.1 as evidence. The first column is the index of non-adherence to the cartel-optimal prices estimated by Porter [1983]. The rest of the data are self-explanatory. Rotemberg & Saloner observe that the three years in which cartel non-adherence was most serious – 1881, 1884 and 1885 – were also the years when the railroad shipments were the highest and competition from lake-shipping was the weakest. In other words, these were boom years for the railroads, yet cartel non-adherence was the highest. This is consistent with Rotemberg & Saloner's theory, but not with Green & Porter's.

Bresnahan [1987] studies the competition in the US automobile industry in the years 1954, 1955 and 1956. The industry is modeled as a differentiated-products industry with multiple products per firm. The focus is on pricing behavior, taking as given the product positions of the various cars. Two alternative price-conduct modes are studied: (1) Bertrand price competition, and (2) implicit collusion. Bresnahan exploits the fact that if two firms are close substitutes in some region of the product space, then the price–cost margins for those products are likely to vary considerably depending on whether the firms are colluding or not. On the other hand, if the firms' products are considerably differentiated, then pricing conduct shouldn't matter as much – collusion as well as competition should produce similar price–cost margins. To see this, consider a firm i's first-order conditions

Table 4.1
Joint Executive Committee railroad cartel in the 1880s; Data from Rotemberg & Saloner [1986]

Year	Estimated non-adherence	Rail shipments (million bushels)	Fraction shipped by rail	Total grain production (billion tons)	Days lakes closed April 1–December 31
1880	0.00	4.73	22.1	2.70	35
1881	0.44	7.68	50.0	2.05	69
1882	0.21	2.39	13.8	2.69	35
1883	0.00	2.59	26.8	2.62	58
1884	0.40	5.90	34.0	2.98	58
1885	0.67	5.12	48.5	3.00	61
1886	0.06	2.21	17.4	2.83	50

for price choice when it is competing with firm j and when it is colluding with firm j:

$$\frac{\partial \Pi_i}{\partial p_i} = q_1 + (p_i - \mathrm{MC}(s_i))\frac{\partial q_i}{\partial p_i} = 0, \tag{18}$$

$$\frac{\partial \Pi_i}{\partial p_i} = q_i + (p_i - \mathrm{MC}(s_i))\frac{\partial q_i}{\partial p_i} + (p_j - \mathrm{MC}(s_j))\frac{\partial q_j}{\partial p_i} = 0. \tag{19}$$

Here q_i denotes i's sales quantity, and s_i and s_j are the two firms' qualities. Note that the additional term under collusive price-setting arises because firm i internalizes the effect of product i's price on product j's sales. This term will be larger when the two products are close substitutes ($s_i \approx s_j$), than when they are highly differentiated. In the mid-1950s, the high-quality end of the automobile range was more differentiated than the low-quality end; see Bresnahan [1981] below. This enables Bresnahan to conclude that the 1954 and 1956 data are consistent with collusive pricing, while the 1955 data are consistent with Bertrand price competition. Putting these results in conjunction with the fact that 1955 was also a boom year for the auto industry – automobile production was 45% higher than in the two surrounding years, and GNP growth was 7% as opposed to a fall of 1% in 1954 and a rise of 2% in 1956 – we get further evidence consistent with Rotemberg & Saloner's [1986] theory. [See also Domowitz, Hubbard & Peterson, 1987.]

Slade [1987] tests Slade's [1989] theory of price wars on retail gasoline-pricing data from Vancouver. She focuses on the data from periods of price wars – the other periods are characterized by constant prices – to determine the precise mode of punishment administered to 'cheating' retailers. Her data support a continuous-reaction-function model – a given firm's price changes are related continuously to rivals' previous-period price changes – rather than the discontinuous punishments characteristic of Friedman's Bertrand–Nash punishments. The ultimate price equilibrium is less collusive than joint-profits maximization, but more collusive than non-cooperative single-period behavior.

4. Product competition

Hotelling [1929] (with refinements by D'Aspremont, Gabszewicz & Thisse [1979]) is the pioneering study of strategic product competition. It has served as the paradigm for much of the theoretical work in marketing, so we will examine it in some detail. The principal aim is to explain firms' product choices in a competitive context: why sometimes firms differentiate their products and sometimes they don't.

4.1. Hotelling's model

Hotelling's model is as follows. There are two identical firms, each of which has to decide on a product location (in attribute space) and a price. The attribute space is assumed to be the interval $[a, b]$, and consumers' ideal-points are distributed uniformly along this interval. Consumers whose ideal point is t evaluate a product s by using the utility function $u(t, s) = R - (t - s)^2$; their consumer surplus if the product is priced at p is, therefore, $R - (t - s)^2 - p$.[2] Clearly, if all products were priced the same, then a consumer in segment t would most prefer the product t.

Each firm has to decide on a product first, and then a price. This sequence of decision-making is not only realistic – pricing decisions are less permanent than product decisions – it also enables a pure-strategy equilibrium to exist. (If the firms' product and price decisions were modeled as simultaneous, then for every product–price choice of its opponent, a firm could always find a product–price pair for itself which would give it all of the market.) Analytically, it means that each firm, when choosing its product, must anticipate the effect its product will have on *both* firms' prices. In other words:

(1) For each possible choice of product by the two firms, we should be looking for prices with the property that neither firm would want to change its price unilaterally.
(2) The product choices should be such that neither firm would want to deviate from its product choice unilaterally, while anticipating the price equilibrium in the first step.

Where should the firms locate taking into account consumer preferences, costs, and price competition? Let us begin by simplifying the problem even more by assuming that all product positions cost the same to deliver, say c. Suppose the two manufacturers' products are s_1 and s_2, with $s_1 < s_2$, and their prices are p_1 and p_2. Firm 1 will get those segments for which the consumer surplus is higher with firm 1's offering than with firm 2's offering (provided the consumer surplus is non-negative). That is, a segment t will choose firm 1 if and only if

$$[R - (t - s_1)^2 - p_1] \geqslant \max\{0, [R - (t - s_2)^2 - p_2]\}.$$

Ignoring the non-negative consumer-surplus restriction for the moment, this implies, after some rearranging of terms, that segment t will choose firm 1 if and only if

$$t < t^{\mathrm{i}} \doteq \frac{(p_2 - p_1)}{2(s_2 - s_1)} + \left(\frac{s_1 + s_2}{2}\right),$$

where t^{i} is the segment which is indifferent between the two firms. Note that if

[2] Hotelling [1929] actually used a linear utility function $R - |t - s|$. But as D'Aspremont, Gabszewicz & Thisse [1979] show, a price equilibrium doesn't exist in Hotelling's model when the two firms' products are close to each other. D'Aspremont, Gabszewicz & Thisse then introduce the quadratic utility function in the text, but without a finite reservation price R.

$p_1 = p_2$, then $t^i = (s_1 + s_2)/2$, i.e., anyone whose ideal-product is to the left of the midpoint between the two firms' products will go with firm 1. Also, $t^i < a$ implies that no consumer prefers firm 1 to firm 2 and $t^i > b$ implies that no consumer prefers firm 2 to firm 1. Therefore, firm 1's market share is $(t^i - a)/(b - a)$, provided $t^i \geqslant a$ and firm 2's market share is $(b - t^i)/(b - a)$, provided $t^i \leqslant b$. Assuming $t^i \in [a, b]$, the two firms' profits are given by (ignoring the total market size N which is just a scaling factor in the absence of fixed costs)

$$\Pi_1 = \left(\frac{t^i - a}{b - a}\right)(p_1 - c), \qquad \Pi_2 = \left(\frac{b - t^i}{b - a}\right)(p_2 - c).$$

Differentiating these with respect to p_1 and p_2, respectively, and simplifying, we get the following first-order conditions:

$$(p_2 - c) - 2(p_1 - c) + (s_2^2 - s_1^2) - 2a(s_2 - s_1) = 0, \tag{20}$$

$$-2(p_2 - c) + (p_1 - c) - (s_2^2 - s_1^2) + 2b(s_2 - s_1) = 0. \tag{21}$$

From (20), it is clear that the larger p_2 is, the higher the p_1 that firm 1 will choose; similarly, (21) implies that firm 2 responds to a price increase by firm 1 by increasing its own price. The two firms are strategic complements in their pricing. Solving for p_1 and p_2 we get

$$p_1^* - c = \frac{2(s_2 - s_1)}{3}\left[b - 2a + \frac{s_2 + s_1}{2}\right], \tag{22}$$

$$p_2^* - c = \frac{2(s_2 - s_1)}{3}\left[2b - a - \frac{s_2 + s_1}{2}\right]. \tag{23}$$

The market shares for the two firms at these equilibrium prices are

$$m_1^* = \frac{1}{3(b - a)}\left[b - 2a + \frac{s_2 + s_1}{2}\right], \tag{24}$$

$$m_2^* = \frac{1}{3(b - a)}\left[2b - a - \frac{s_2 + s_1}{2}\right]. \tag{25}$$

Now we come to the product choices. We substitute (22)–(25) in the two firms' profit functions and get

$$\Pi_1 = \frac{2(s_2 - s_1)}{9(b - a)}\left[b - 2a + \frac{s_2 + s_1}{2}\right]^2, \tag{26}$$

$$\Pi_2 = \frac{2(s_2 - s_1)}{9(b - a)}\left[2b - a - \frac{s_2 + s_1}{2}\right]^2. \tag{27}$$

Differentiating Π_1 with respect to s_1 we find that it is decreasing in s_1 for $s_2 \leqslant b$ and $s_1 \geqslant a$. In other words, for any $s_2 \leqslant b$, firm 1's best response is a. Similarly, for any $s_1 \geqslant a$, firm 2's best response is b. Therefore, (a, b) is the unique product equilibrium.

Substituting these products into (22) and (23), we get the equilibrium margins

$$p_1^* - c = (b - a)^2 = p_2^* - c. \tag{28}$$

The equilibrium market-shares are 1/2 for each firm. Hence, each firm's equilibrium profit is

$$\Pi_1^* = \frac{(b - a)^2}{2} = \Pi_2^*.$$

Remarks. (1) There is another product equilibrium with exactly the same product positions as above, but with the identities of the two firms reversed.

(2) In the analysis above, the alternative to buying either of the two firms' products is not to buy in the product class at all. We normalized this alternative as giving zero surplus to the consumers. So our equilibrium is valid if it doesn't give negative surplus to the consumers. Does it? To answer this, consider the segment which gets the *least* consumer surplus in the equilibrium. This segment is $(b + a)/2$, the segment in the middle of the market. (The equilibrium products are farthest from this segment's ideal product.) This segment's consumer surplus from either firms equilibrium offering is $R - c - [5(b - a)^2/4]$, which is non-negative if $R \geqslant c + [5(b - a)^2/4]$. So our results are valid provided R is in this range.

(3) What if $R < c + [5(b - a)^2/4]$? In this case, if the firms were to choose the products a and b and price according to (28), then they would lose segments in the middle of the market. This effect will temporize their desire to move 'far apart'.

(4) How does competitive strategy differ from a monopolist's strategy? If a monopolist were to introduce one product, then he would place it at $(b + a)/2$ and price it at $R - (b - a)^2/4$ if he wants to cover the market. With two products, the products will be positioned at $(3a + b)/4$ and $(3b + a)/4$ and priced at $R - (b - a)^2/16$; each product will serve half the market. Compared to the duopoly, the monopolist's two products are closer to each other, and each product fills the 'hole' in the market left by the other. The monopolist internalizes the competition between the two products, so for the same two product positions, the price competition between them will be less severe than in the duopoly situation. Therefore, the monopolist would like to push his two products closer to the center with the idea of increasing the prices he can charge for his two products.

4.2. Extensions

As noted earlier, there have been a number of extensions of Hotelling's work. These extensions can be seen as exploring the role of each of Hotelling's assumptions. These assumptions (some explicit, others implicit) are:

(1) Each segment has a distinct ideal-point.
(2) The disutility from moving away from the ideal-point is quadratic in the distance.
(3) All product positions cost the same to deliver.
(4) The distribution of ideal-points is uniform.
(5) Consumers' utility functions are deterministic.
(6) Each firm competes with the other on only one side. This assumption comes from Hotelling's assumption that the market is linear. If, instead, the market is thought of as circular, then, potentially, there can be competition on two sides [Salop, 1979].
(7) There is only one attribute (besides price) on which firms can differentiate themselves.
(8) There are only two competitors.
(9) Firms choose their products simultaneously.
(10) Firms compete on prices (instead of quantities) after choosing their products.

Economides [1986] shows that the maximal differentiation result is sensitive to how the consumers' utility functions are modeled. If the disutility from choosing a less-than-ideal product is given by td^{α} where d is the distance from the ideal-point, then a pure-strategy Nash equilibrium exhibits maximal differentiation for $\alpha \in [1.67, 2]$, but less than maximal differentiation for $\alpha \in [1.26, 1.67]$. Neven [1986] relaxes Assumption 4 by allowing distributions of ideal points *concentrated* in the center. As might be expected, this results in an equilibrium where the products are closer to the center than in Hotelling's model.

Shaked & Sutton [1982] relax Assumption 1. The product attribute here is interpreted as quality, but could stand for any attribute on which consumers' preferences are increasing. All consumers have the same ideal-point – the maximum feasible level of quality. But consumers differ in their importance weight for quality (versus price); for example, segment t evaluates a product of quality s and price p at $ts - p$. Shaked & Sutton find that the equilibrium involves one firm choosing the maximum feasible quality and the other firm choosing a quality below that.

Moorthy [1988a] modifies Shaked & Sutton's model to incorporate different costs for different products. This modification is especially important when the product attribute is interpreted as quality. In a heterogeneous ideal-points model such as Hotelling's, where the product attribute is like store location, e.g. ice-cream flavors, it may be reasonable to assume that different attribute levels cost the same to deliver. But when the product attribute is something like quality, it is unrealistic to assume that higher quality doesn't cost more to deliver. So Moorthy assumes that firms' marginal costs are increasing in the level of the attribute, say αs^2. It is easy to see that in this setting, if the entire product spectrum were available and priced at marginal cost, then each segment would choose a different quality level – its efficient quality level $t/2\alpha$. (In the Hotelling model, also, each segment has a distinct efficient product, but this is entirely due to the variation in consumers' ideal-points. In the Shaked & Sutton model, on the other hand, without the variation in costs, every segment has the same efficient product – the highest feasible quality.) Moorthy also finds that the prospect of price competition induces the competitors to differentiate their products. In fact, price competition induces the two competitors to move their products farther apart than a monopolist producing two products would.

Hauser [1988] studies two- and three-firm product and price competition in Hauser & Shugan's [1983] DEFENDER consumer model. The chief characteristic of this model is that even though the products are characterized by two attributes besides price, effectively the two product attributes can be collapsed into one because of a technology relationship between the two attributes. For example, even though a car manufacturer may want to choose a gas-mileage level and a horse-power level independently, technology determines a one-to-one relationship between gas-mileage and horse power. Hauser represents this technology relationship by imposing the restriction that the firms' product choices must lie on the boundary of a circle. That is, if x and y are the two product attributes, then $x^2 + y^2 = k^2$. Consumer preferences are such that each consumer maximizes $w_1(x/p) + w_2(y/p)$. Substituting for x in terms of y this becomes

$$w_1\left(\frac{\sqrt{k^2 - y^2}}{p}\right) + w_2\left(\frac{y}{p}\right),$$

which has a maximum with respect to y at

$$k\left(\frac{w_2}{\sqrt{w_2^2 + w_1^2}}\right).$$

Each consumer type (w_1, w_2), has a different ideal-point in y (holding price constant). A homogeneous ideal-point model has become a heterogeneous ideal-point model with the collapsing of two product attributes into one! Unlike Hotelling's model, however, a monopolist is indifferent among all product positions because consumers' willingness to pay doesn't go down with distance from the ideal-point. Therefore, price competition is the only force controlling the positions of the competing firms. As one might expect, the product equilibrium involves maximum separation among the competitors' products. With two firms, each occupies a corner of the quarter-circle; with three firms, two firms take the corners, and the third is in the middle.

Carpenter [1989] investigates a two-dimensional version of Hotelling's [1929] model, but given the generality of his consumer model, very little can be said about the product equilibrium. Two recent papers with more positive results on two-dimensional competition are Ansari & Steckel [1992] and Vandenbosch & Weinberg [1992]. The former adopts a two-dimensional version of the Hotelling model. The utility function is given by $R - w_1(t_1 - s_1)^2 - w_2(t_2 - s_2)^2$, and consumers' types (t_1, t_2) are distributed uniformly on $[a, b] \times [a, b]$. The product space is $[0, 1] \times [0, 1]$. The interesting result is that the product equilibrium only involves differentiation on the more important attribute; on the other attribute, both firms choose the same position – the center. For example, if $w_1 > w_2$, then the product equilibrium involves one of the firms choosing (0, 1/2), and the other choosing (1, 1/2). The Vandenbosch & Weinberg paper obtains similar results in a 'vertical differentiation' model.

Another noteworthy study is that of De Palma, Ginsburgh, Papageorgiou & Thisse [1985]. They modify the consumer preferences in Hotelling's model into a logit model, i.e., change Assumption 5. A consumer of type t_i chooses a product s_1 over s_2 if and only if $[R - |t_i - s_1| - p_1] + \mu\varepsilon_i > [R - |t_i - s_2| - p_2] + \mu\varepsilon_i$ where the ε_i are assumed to be i.i.d. Weibull-distributed random variables with mean zero and variance 1. The interpretation is that there is a significant stochastic component to consumers' preferences, so that even if both firms' products are the same but their prices aren't, the higher-priced firm may nevertheless get a positive market share. With this change, De Palma, Ginsburgh, Papageorgiou & Thisse show that if the stochastic component is large – μ is large – then there is a Nash equilibrium with *both* firms choosing a position in the center. This result may explain the proliferation of me-too products in low-involvement product classes.

Moorthy [1985] analyzes *simultaneous* product and quantity competition in a model which is otherwise similar to Moorthy [1988a]. In quantity competition, each firm takes its competitor's quantity sold as given when choosing its price (or quantity). The main effect of quantity competition turns out to be a reduction in the intensity of price competition; equilibrium prices are higher for the same product locations. As a result, the equilibrium product locations are closer to each other than in Moorthy [1988a]. Bonanno [1986] examines *sequential* product and quantity competition in Shaked & Sutton's [1982] model. Firms choose their products first, and then they compete on quantities (in the sense noted above). With price competition in the second stage, we noted earlier that product differentiation is the equilibrium result. With quantity competition, however, both firms choose the same product – the highest feasible quality. A similar result is obtained if *collusion in prices* follows product choices. Friedman & Thisse [1990] show, in Hotelling's model, that collusion in prices induces firms to come together at the center of the market.

The main insight arising from all these models is that competitive strategy is a reconciliation of two forces. One force, price competition, moves the competitor's product positions apart. The other force, going after the location which best trades off consumer reservation prices, segment size, and costs, brings them closer to each other. In the Hotelling model with $R \geqslant c + [5(b-a)^2/4]$ both forces operate, and the net result is that the equilibrium product locations straddle the monopolist's optimal location (the center), but are far apart. If $R < c + [5(b-a)^2/4]$, however, the equilibrium products are closer to the center. In the Hauser [1988] model, the second force doesn't impose any restrictions on product locations – any location would be equally good for a monopolist. Therefore, effectively, only the first force operates, pushing the two competitors far apart. By contrast, in Moorthy's [1988a] model, both forces operate, so the equilibrium products straddle the monopolist's best product. Finally, in De Palma's [1985] model, essentially only the second force operates because the randomness in consumers' behavior leads to muted price competition even with identical products. Then, given that the center is the best location for a monopolist, agglomeration in the center is an equilibrium.

4.3. Product-line competition

In the real world, firms compete on product lines, not single products. For example, Honda produces Honda Civic, Honda Accord and Honda Prelude not to mention the Acura line, and these cars compete with an even larger line of Ford cars. In product-line competition, one of the central questions is, should firms 'specialize' in one segment of the market or the other, or should they 'interlace' their products among their competitors' products? Brander & Eaton [1984] analyze a simple model to evaluate this issue. Four possible products are available to be chosen by two firms: 1, 2, 3, 4. These products are ordered on some attribute. So one firm can choose (1, 2) and the other (3, 4) or one firm can choose (1, 3) and the other (2, 4). The first would be a specialization equilibrium, the second an interlacing equilibrium. Brander & Eaton find that specialization is a more profitable equilibrium for both firms than interlacing. The reason is, with specialization, one product of each firm is relatively shielded from price competition.

Moorthy [1987b], however, casts some doubt on the efficacy of specialization. In a model where product qualities are freely chosen (as opposed to the Brander–Eaton formulation where product choices are fixed *a priori*) along with quantities, he finds that specialization might force at least one of the firms to choose a relatively less attractive specialization. Given that not all areas of the attribute space are equally attractive, specialization necessarily entails all the firms fighting to specialize in the most attractive area. So the dominance of specialization over interlacing is muted; at least one of the firms may prefer interlacing to specialization.

Klemperer [1992] frames the issues in product-line competition as the choice between interlacing and competing 'head-to-head' with identical product lines. Consumers in his model seek variety – they will choose multiple products. And they would rather buy all of their product requirements from one supplier than two (if both offer the same product lines), i.e. they attach value to one-stop shopping. Under these circumstances, having identical product lines may be better because it mutes the price competition between the suppliers.

4.4. Empirical work on competitive product differentiation

Two testable propositions come out of the quality-differentiation models of Moorthy [1988a] and Shaked & Sutton [1982]:

(1) The higher-quality product carries a higher margin in equilibrium.
(2) The closer the product qualities of the competitors, the lower their price–cost margins.

Both of these predictions are verified by Bresnahan [1981] in his study of automobile pricing in the years 1977–1978. The demand functions for the lowest-quality car s_1, a car s_i with lower-quality (s_h) and higher-quality (s_j) neighbors, and the highest-quality car s_n are, respectively ([cf. Moorthy, 1988a]:

$$q_1 = \delta\left[\frac{p_2 - p_1}{s_2 - s_1} - \frac{p_1 - p_0}{s_1 - s_0}\right],$$
$$q_i = \delta\left[\frac{p_j - p_i}{s_j - s_i} - \frac{p_i - p_h}{s_i - s_h}\right], \tag{29}$$
$$q_n = \delta\left[t_{\max} - \frac{p_n - p_{n-1}}{s_n - s_{n-1}}\right],$$

where p_0 and s_0 represent the price and 'quality' of the lower-end product class which is bought when automobiles are not bought, δ is the density of consumer types, and $t_{\max}$ is the most quality-sensitive consumer type. ($t_{\max}$ and δ are to be estimated from the data.) Bresnahan uses the manufacturers' prices to the dealers (for the basic model without options) as his prices, and estimates quality hedonically using surrogates such as length, weight, horse power, etc. (vector z):

$$s = \sqrt{\beta_0 + \sum_j z_j \beta_j}. \tag{30}$$

Here the β's are parameters of the hedonic function to be estimated from the data, and s is interpreted as the quality of the least-cost car that can be produced from z.

To complete the specification, Bresnahan assumes that the cost function for the firms is:

$$C(s, q) = F(s) + \mathrm{MC}(s)q \tag{31}$$

where the marginal-cost function MC(s) is assumed to be the log-linear function μe^s.

Since the profit function is $(p_i - \mathrm{MC}(s_i))q_i - F(s_i)$, the first-order conditions characterizing the firms' pricing behavior are given by equations of the form:

$$q_i + (p_i - \mathrm{MC}(s_i))\frac{\partial q_i}{\partial p_i} = 0, \tag{32}$$

$$q_i + (p_i - \mathrm{MC}(s_i))\frac{\partial q_i}{\partial p_i} + (p_i + 1 - \mathrm{MC}(s_{i+1}))\frac{\partial q_{i+1}}{\partial p_i} = 0, \tag{33}$$

where the first equation corresponds to a single-product firm and the second to a firm making the adjacent qualities s_i and s_{i+1}.

The price equilibrium is obtained by solving simultaneously the demand equations (29) and the supply equations (32) and (33). Bresnahan finds that

(1) The highest-quality car had about 1.5 times the quality of the lowest-quality car.

(2) Typical mark-ups ranged from 4% for the lowest quartile of the product quality distribution to 24% for the highest quartile in 1977 (similar results for 1978).

(3) There was much more bunching of cars at the low-quality end than at the high-quality end (explaining (2)).

4.5. *Sequential entry, defensive strategy, first-mover advantages*

In many real situations, firms choose their products sequentially, not simultaneously as in the discussion above. One firm enters an industry first with a product, then another firm enters with another product, and so on. Among the questions this raises are: does the first-mover have an advantage by virtue of seizing the most attractive product locations? How does the sequential-entry industry's equilibrium product configuration compare with that of a simultaneous-entry industry? How will a first-mover's strategy change if he anticipates a second entrant and makes defensive preparations?

Let us examine how the equilibrium changes in the Hotelling model when one firm chooses its product before the other, i.e. we examine the Stackelberg equilibrium. The prices are still chosen simultaneously after *both* have chosen their products. This assumption is realistic for the reasons given earlier: because products are more costly to change than prices, commitments are easier to sustain with products than with prices.

Recalling our earlier results, if the first mover chooses a product to the left of $(b + a)/2$, then the second mover will choose b; on the other hand, if the first mover chooses a product to the right of $(b + a)/2$, then the second mover will choose a. At $(b + a)/2$, however, the second mover will be indifferent between a and b. Clearly, from the first mover's point of view, either end of the product space is equally good. A position in the middle, which may seem like an attractive position to pre-empt given the monopolist's preference for it, turns out not to be so attractive after all. The reason is the limited maneuverability of the second mover: because of the exogenous bounds on the product space, the second mover cannot move beyond a or b even if he wants to. Unable to push the second mover beyond $[a, b]$, the first mover prefers the ends to the middle. The first entrant's profits end up being the same as either firm's profits in the simultaneous-moves equilibrium. There is no first-mover advantage.

These results are not true in general, however. In Moorthy's [1988a] model, there is a first-mover advantage, and the first mover's equilibrium position is close (but not identical) to the monopolist's optimal position. In both models, the first mover's product location is not the same as that of a monopolist choosing a single product. In other words, the first mover's product is different depending on whether or not it foresees the second firm's entry. For example, when he doesn't foresee the second entrant, the first mover chooses $(b + a)/2$ in Hotelling's model. Then, surprised by the entry at a or b, he wishes he had chosen b or a, respectively. On the other hand, with foresight, the first mover would have prepared to defend. He would have chosen a or b, forcing the second entrant to choose b or a, respectively.

For other analyses of sequential-entry and defensive strategies see Prescott & Visscher [1977], Lane [1980], Hauser & Shugan [1983], Kumar & Sudharshan [1988], and Choi, DeSarbo & Harker [1990]. In the Prescott–Visscher and Lane papers, entry involves a fixed cost of K. Because of the fixed cost and the finite size of the market, at most a finite number of firms, say n (to be determined endogenously from the equilibrium product and price computations), can profitably coexist in the market. Each successive entrant up to n, chooses a product for himself given the products of the earlier entrants and *anticipating* the products of the remaining entrants and the equilibrium prices that will prevail after all n entrants have entered. The equilibrium shows that the early entrants take up the 'prime' locations in attribute space, leaving the less prime locations for the later entrants. Table 4.2 from Prescott & Visscher [1977] is illustrative.

As the entry cost increases, the number of firms that enter either goes down or stays the same. Even when it stays the same, however, the product positions of the entrants change. A higher entry cost encourages the entrants to choose positions farther apart without inviting further entry – and positions farther apart are preferred because they reduce price competition and increase profits. As the entry cost goes down, the profits of all entrants go down. The product qualities chosen and the profits obtained go down with order of entry: the first entrant always chooses the highest-quality product (here 0.500) and makes the most profit.

Schmalensee [1978] applies this reasoning to the ready-to-eat cereal industry, carrying the logic one step further. The early entrants can 'fill' the product space with their own products, leaving practically no opportunities for later entrants. (This argument was ultimately rejected by the Federal Trade Commission in its complaint against the big cereal manufacturers.)

All of these entry-deterrence stories depend on the assumption that the n entrants' costs of repositioning their products, or withdrawing from the market completely, are higher than the profits they would make if any more entrants were accommodated. Otherwise, the $(n+1)$st firm can simply enter and force the withdrawal or repositioning of at least some of the earlier entrants' products to accommodate

Table 4.2
Equilibrium in the Prescott–Visscher [1977] model

Fixed entry cost K	Equilibrium number of firms	Order of entry	Products	Margins	Quantities	Profits
0.300	2	1	0.500	0.548	6.101	3.041
		2	0.590	0.350	3.899	1.064
0.200	2	1	0.500	0.311	6.062	1.685
		2	0.551	0.202	3.938	0.595
0.160	3	1	0.500	0.356	5.555	1.818
		2	0.564	0.185	3.569	0.500
		3	0.833	0.236	0.875	0.040

him; cf. Judd [1985]. Exit and repositioning costs will be high if product introduction involves *sunk* costs, e.g. advertising, that cannot be salvaged. Judd's analysis emphasizes that a multiproduct incumbent may be at a disadvantage in deterring the entry of a single-product entrant if exit is not costly. Essentially, the presence of another, differentiated product in the incumbent's product line represents an opportunity to avoid a price war in the product closest to where the entrant enters. Given these 'opportunity profits', the incumbent will withdraw the product being attacked, accommodate the entry, and enjoy higher profits on the products remaining. (In Hauser & Shugan [1983], this possibility leads to a price *increase* for the incumbent after entry.)

In Eliashberg & Jeuland [1986] the defensive preparations are in the form of market penetration. They compare the pricing behavior of a far-sighted incumbent who anticipates entry at T with that of a 'myopic' incumbent who is surprised by the entry. The consumer side of their model combines saturation effects (as with a durable good) and downward-sloping demand. Both incumbent and entrant have the same product. Eliashberg & Jeuland show that the optimal pricing policy is declining throughout the time horizon because of saturation effects and, in the duopoly period, also because of competition effects. (Consumers do not have expectations in this model.) The onset of competition leads to a sudden drop in price, after which the price declines continuously once more. The interesting differences are between the two types of incumbent. The prices are lower in the pre-entry period when the incumbent anticipates the entry at T, because he would like to begin the duopolistic period with a larger penetration of the market. He would rather sacrifice some profit in the monopoly period in the interests of leaving less market to fight over in the duopoly period, than begin the duopoly period with a large market remaining to be served. The profit reward from anticipating entry and making defensive preparations obviously depends on the timing of entry vis-à-vis the entire time horizon. Fershtman, Mahajan & Muller [1990], however, argue that the advantages of early entry may not be durable. In a model with dynamic costs and brand loyalty, they show that long-term market shares do not depend on the order of entry or length of the monopoly period if cost and brand-loyalty advantages dissipate progressively.

In the Hauser–Shugan and Kumar–Sudharshan papers, the concept of defensive strategy is different from the one used by the above writers. (The only differences between these papers are that Kumar & Sudharshan use the Lane consumer model instead of the DEFENDER model, and they have multiple defenders instead of one.) They view defense as the *response* to attack, not as preparations before attack. Thus, the first mover in their model is the attacker, not the defender(s), but because they focus only on the defender(s)' strategies (see my comments above in Section 2), it is really immaterial whether the game is considered a simultaneous-move game with both the attacker and the defender(s) moving simultaneously or a sequential-move game with the defender(s) moving second. In either case, only the defender(s)' best-response function need be examined. Hauser & Shugan consider various kinds of defender responses: price (lowered because of increased competition – exception is when the incumbent serves multiple segments prior to entry, but is induced to cede the price-sensitive segment to the entrant), awareness advertising (decreased because margins decrease – see below), distribution expenditures (decreased because margins decrease – see below), repositioning advertising (increased to reposition brand toward greater product differentiation from the entrant).

Choi, DeSarbo & Harker [1990] provide a procedure for computing the Stackelberg equilibrium when the leader is the new entrant (as in Hauser–Shugan and Kumar–Sudharshan), and the followers are various incumbents. The leader announces a product position and a price; the followers then play a Nash equilibrium in prices taking the leader's position and price as given. This formulation has the weakness that the leader is assumed to be able to commit to a price. Horsky & Nelson [1992] also provide a methodology for determining the optimal product-positioning of a new entrant into an existing oligopolistic market. Again, the incumbents are assumed to be able to react on prices only. But, unlike Choi, DeSarbo & Harker, here the entrant's price is determined as part of the Nash equilibrium in prices. The entrant chooses his product position anticipating the price equilibrium that will prevail after he has entered. Their calculations imply that a new car entering optimally into a car market consisting of twelve existing mid-sized cars will get the second-highest market share and the third-highest profit.

Carpenter & Nakamoto [1989] provide a different perspective on first-mover advantages. They argue, and provide experimental evidence for the view, that first movers gain a durable competitive advantage by molding consumer preferences to their product. Either the consumers' importance weights for the product attributes change to favor the first mover or else their ideal-points move toward the pioneer's product. A me-too strategy by a later entrant doesn't succeed in wresting away the first mover's market share lead because consumers continue to view the pioneer's product as distinctive. Carpenter & Nakamoto offer this argument as essentially a psychological phenomenon. But economic explanations are also possible. Later entrants with a 'me-too' strategy may never be able to catch up with the pioneer because they suffer from a familiarity disadvantage. This disadvantage may be especially important if there are hidden attributes on which the later entrants are unable to provide direct evidence that they are 'me-too'. Consumers may use familiarity as the basis for assessing performance on these attributes.

4.6. Empirical work on first-mover advantages and defensive strategy

Bresnahan & Reiss [1990] use the technology of qualitative-choice models to study the entry decisions of automobile dealers in geographically isolated rural markets. The entry decision leads to inequality restrictions on profits: for example, in a monopoly market, $\Pi_i^{\mathrm{M}} \geqslant 0$ for the incumbent dealer i, but $\Pi_j^{\mathrm{D}} < 0$ for all potential entrants j; in a duopoly market with two dealers i and j, $\Pi_i^{\mathrm{D}}, \Pi_j^{\mathrm{D}} \geqslant 0$, but $\Pi_k^{\mathrm{T}} < 0$ for all potential entrants (here T denotes triopoly). Bresnahan & Reiss focus on the transition from monopoly to duopoly, and they consider both simultaneous-move and sequential-move competition. The results suggest that monopoly dealers do not block the entry of a second dealer. Furthermore, the post-second-dealer-entry competition does not cause a significant drop in price–cost margins: the ratio of duopoly variable profits to monopoly variable profits ranges from 0.62 to 0.66, which is consistent with differentiated-products competition, not homogeneous-products competition (of any kind – prices or quantities).

Robinson [1988] provides some empirical evidence on the post-entry strategies of incumbents. His data are from the Strategic Planning Institute's survey of new entrants asking them for their *perceptions* of the reactions of incumbents. Product, distribution, marketing-expenditure and price reactions are asked for. On a reaction index which goes from −4 (most accommodating reaction) to 4 (most aggressive reaction), Robinson finds that most entrants' surveyed report a passive response (reaction index 0) up to two years after entry. Reaction is more aggressive in the second year after entry than in the first year after entry. Across the marketing-mix variables, reaction is most aggressive in price (price decreases) and most passive in product. The limited reaction of incumbents to entry is consistent with the view – but doesn't prove – that incumbents anticipate new entry and make defensive preparations on the things they can commit to, i.e. product. To develop stronger evidence for this, however, one needs to examine the pre-entry behavior of incumbents as well. Cubbin & Domberger [1988] focus on the advertising responses of incumbents in several consumer goods classes. They find no response in 61% of the cases, and when there is a response, it is generally an increase-in-advertising response. They also find that 'dominant' incumbents are more likely to respond than non-dominant firms and response is more likely in static markets than growing markets.

Robinson & Fornell [1985] and Kalyanaram & Urban [1992] analyze the sources of market pioneering advantages in mature, consumer goods industries. They find no residual effect of order of entry on market share after accounting for marketing effort: quality, product-line breadth, advertising intensity, price. This is what we would expect from the theoretical work discussed above. From Prescott & Visscher [1977] and Schmalensee [1978] we know that quality and product-line breadth could be used as sources of advantage by market pioneers. Furthermore, Fershtman, Mahajan & Muller's [1990] work points out the importance of brand-loyalty and cost advantages. The latter are probably reflected in the price. Hence, controlling for quality, product-line breadth, advertising, and price, leaves no net market-share advantage for pioneering. Urban, Carter, Gaslain & Mucha [1986] find a significant market-share advantage for pioneers in consumer goods, but they only control for product positioning, advertising expenditures, and time lags between successive entries.

Glazer [1985] cites evidence suggesting that first entrants are not more successful than later entrants. He examines the success and failure of newspapers in Iowa during the period 1836–1976. In eighteen of the Iowa markets, a first and second entrant existed simultaneously for some length of time. In thirteen of these markets, he finds that the first entrant survived longer than the second entrant counting from the date of arrival of the second entrant. This seems to say that successful first entrants do far better than second entrants. But a different type of analysis suggests otherwise. Glazer constructs a sample of equal numbers of first and second entrants with the second entrants separated from the first by five years (obviously the second entrant corresponding to a first is not necessarily from the same city). The distribution of entry dates is therefore similar for both first and second entrants. Glazer finds that 25 years after founding, there is no statistically significant difference in the survival rates of first and second entrants: 32% of first entrants survived, 39% of second entrants survived. This suggests that if one looks at *all* market pioneers – not just the successful ones – then it is not clear that innovation always triumphs. (Golder & Tellis [1993] provide similar findings.)

5. Advertising competition

Two types of advertising competition have been studied, competition on budgets and competition on advertising schedules. As always, the results depend on how consumer behavior is modeled.

5.1. Competition in advertising spending

One early analysis of advertising-budged competition is the so-called Lanchester model. Market share is assumed to be an increasing function of advertising-spending share ('share of voice') – for simplicity we will assume market share equals share of voice – but the total market is fixed in size, and prices are fixed and equal as well. Note, in particular, the absence of price competition.

The sales-response function can be written as

$$s_i = N\left(\frac{A_i}{A_i + A_{3-i}}\right), \quad i = 1, 2. \tag{34}$$

Note that (34) can also be interpreted as the steady-state sales-response function under constant advertising by both firms if we model the sales increase in each period as

$$\dot{s}_i = A_i s_{3-i} - A_{3-i} s_i.$$

Also, it is easy to model differential advertising effectiveness by putting coefficients ρ_i in front of the advertising terms. For other enhancements of the Lanchester model see Carpenter, Cooper, Hanssens & Midgley [1988].

Going back to the static, symmetric formulation, the only choice variable is the advertising budget.

$$\max_{A_i} (p - c)N\left(\frac{A_i}{A_i + A_{3-i}}\right) - A_i, \quad i = 1, 2,$$

where N is the total market size. The first-order conditions are:

$$(p-c)N\frac{A_{3-i}}{(A_1+A_2)^2}-1=0,\quad i=1,2. \tag{35}$$

Solving for A_i,

$$A_i=\sqrt{(p-c)NA_{3-i}}-A_{3-i},\quad i=1,2 \tag{36}$$

which means that the best response of either firm to an increase in the other's budget is to increase its budget provided the other's budget is below $(p-c)N/4$; otherwise, an increase in spending induces a decrease in spending. (The two firms are strategic complements in advertising if $A_{3-i}<(p-c)N/4$, strategic substitutes otherwise.) When $A_{3-i}=(p-c)N$, firm i's best response is to reduce spending to zero. Essentially, as the rival's advertising spending increases beyond a certain level, advertising becomes less productive for the firm – the costs increase faster than the additional revenues. Solving (36), the equilibrium is

$$A_i=\frac{(p-c)N}{4},\quad i=1,2.$$

Observe that each firm's market share in equilibrium is a half, the same as it would have been if they had spent nothing on advertising. If they could collude, they would in fact agree to spend nothing on advertising. In other words, the firms face the familiar prisoner's dilemma: unable to trust the other firm to hold its spending level down, each firm ends up spending more than is collectively optimal. (This feature of the model changes when advertising increases total market size; see Friedman [1983] below.) One implication is that government regulations that have the effect of increasing the cost of advertising (or decreasing the effectiveness of advertising) will increase the firms' equilibrium profits by reducing their advertising spending.

Hauser & Shugan [1983], Kumar & Sudharshan [1988] and Carpenter [1989] find that price competition leads to reduced advertising spending. Hence their recommendation that the optimal defensive advertising strategy is to reduce awareness advertising. To see why, let us examine Hauser & Shugan's profit function (Kumar & Sudharshan's and Carpenter's models are similar):

$$(p-c)N_aM_a(p)A(k_a)-k_a.$$

Here A, a number between 0 and 1, is an increasing function of the firm's expenditure on awareness advertising k_a, and M_a is the firm's market share. Note that competitors' advertising has no effect on the firm's market share or on A; hence competitors' advertising has no effect on the firm's profits. Advertising competition is not being modeled here. The marginal revenue from advertising is proportional to $(p-c)N_aM_a$. This quantity goes down with price competition because prices go down. Hence advertising has to be reduced. In fact, if the firms' products were not differentiated, then, because the equilibrium margins will be zero, there would be no incentive to advertise at all.

In the Reiss [1991] model, symmetric firms end up choosing asymmetric advertising levels in equilibrium. Advertising determines top-of-mind awareness here, and top-of-mind awareness determines the brand examined first in the store. In other words,

$$\text{probability of examining brand } i \text{ first} = \frac{A_i}{A_i + A_{3-i}}, \quad i = 1, 2$$

where A_i is firm i's advertising budget. Consumers are supposed to be of two types: (1) those who are very price-sensitive and will search for the lowest-priced brand regardless of which brand they examine first, and (2) those who go with the brand which comes to their mind first. (In the Lanchester model that we evaluated above, essentially all consumers were of the second kind.) Both advertising and price competititon are modeled here. Reiss shows that the two-stage competition, with advertising expenditures chosen before prices, leads to one firm advertising more and pricing higher than the other. The firm with the higher advertising level captures a high share of the less-price-sensitive consumers at a relatively high price; the other firm captures all of the price-sensitive consumers, and some of the less-price-sensitive consumers, at a relatively low price.

Friedman [1983] generalizes the Nerlove–Arrow [1962] monopoly model to a differentiated, symmetric oligopoly. Firms choose 'advertising goodwill' levels (via advertising spending) and quantities. Friedman shows that an open-loop equilibrium (i.e. an equilibrium where the strategies of each firm are a function of time alone) exists, and, in an example where the profit functions are quadratic in goodwill and quantities, he computes the steady state of the equilibrium. The interesting comparative-statics are with respect to w, an index of the cooperative vs competitive nature of advertising spending. As the advertising becomes more cooperative, each firm's spending benefits the others; in fact, the perfectly cooperative case is one where the firm's spending levels are completely interchangeable in their profit functions. In contrast, the perfectly competitive case is one where advertising only affects market share (as in the Lanchester model above). The comparative-statics reveal that steady-state goodwill levels and quantities supplied are higher, the more cooperative the advertising effects; however, the effect on steady-state price is ambiguous because goodwill and quantity sold have opposite effects on price.

Horsky & Mate [1988] examine the advertising equilibrium when two firms compete over time in a durable-good market with saturation and word-of-mouth effects. Competitive advertising spending affects a given firm's profits by reducing the number of customers available. The equilibrium results are similar to the monopoly case: advertising spending decreases over time for two reasons. First, advertising is most effective in 'feeding' the word-of-mouth process early in the product life-cycle than later. Second, as the market saturates, the diminishing returns to advertising spending come into effect, so it is not worth spending as much. One implication of these results is that if one firm starts with an installed base of customers – because it entered earlier – then the second firm can never catch up (unless it has a superior product which increases the effectiveness of its advertising and word-of-mouth). The word-of-mouth advantage from being first in the market is decisive.

5.2. *Empirical work on advertising competition*

Chintagunta & Vilcassim [1992] model the competition between Coke and Pepsi as a dynamic Lanchester game. They compute the open-loop and closed-loop Nash equilibria, and compare them to a period-by-period optimization of each firm's profits given the actual spending level of its competitor. They find that the closed-loop equilibrium fits best overall, although the open-loop policy does reasonably well. In absolute terms, the fit of either equilibrium strategy to the actual expenditure pattern is not very good, suggesting that the Lanchester model may be omitting something important in the way advertising affects market share in this industry. One possible omission is 'advertising goodwill'.

Carpenter, Cooper, Hanssens & Midgley [1988] generalize the Lanchester model above to include differential advertising effects across brands as well as asymmetric cross-effects. In addition, they allow for lagged advertising effects. Their data are from an Australian household-product class which is mature and non-seasonal. Monthly price, advertising and sales data from eleven brands are analyzed. Demand analysis shows that price effects on market share are instantaneous whereas advertising has contemporaneous as well as one-period lagged effects. Carpenter, Cooper, Hanssens & Midgley find that the equilibrium strategies differ *considerably* from the actual strategies chosen. This may be because they ignore the lagged advertising effects when computing the equilibrium price and advertising strategies.

Roberts & Samuelson [1988] consider advertising dynamics explicitly in their study of the advertising competition among cigarette manufacturers. Their analysis controls for prices and the number of brands offered by each manufacturer, and allows for advertising to have market-share *and* market-size effects. The choice of advertising spending in each period is modeled as a choice of goodwill level, considering the goodwill levels prevailing in the market at the start of the period. (The modeling of advertising goodwill is as in Nerlove & Arrow [1962].) Two modes of competition are examined: naive competition where each firm maximizes the discounted sum of future profits without taking into account the effect of current spending on the goodwill level chosen by its competitors in the next period, and sophisticated competition where firms anticipate the effect of their current spending on rivals' future spending. Note that this distinction is not the same as the open-loop–closed-loop distinction. The open-loop–closed-loop distinction speaks to whether or not firms take into account the 'state of the world' – which includes the history of the game up to that point – in choosing their actions each period. On that criterion, both naive and sophisticated equilibria are closed-loop equilibria.

Roberts & Samuelson find that advertising primarily has market-size effects (especially in the low-tar cigarette market), not market-share effects. (In other words, Lanchester-type models are not good descriptors of demand in the case of cigarettes.) The number of brands, however, has an important effect on market share: the more the number of brands, the greater the firm's market share. Finally, the competition in advertising spending suggests sophisticated rather than naive behavior on the part of the cigarette manufacturers.

Gruca & Sudharshan [1990] examine the reaction of incumbents to new entry and find that the evidence contradicts the predictions of Hauser & Shugan [1983] and Kumar & Sudharshan [1988]. They study the optimal price, advertising and distribution response of the incumbents in the Pittsfield, Massachusetts and Marion, Indiana coffee markets to the introduction of a new brand, Master Blend, by General Foods. General Foods and Procter and Gamble were the major competitors in this category, together accounting for 65.5% of the market in Pittsfield and 95.6% of the market in Marion. The data are for the two-year period April 1980 to April 1982; Master Blend was introduced nationally in March 1981. Gruca & Sudharshan find that prices of all the incumbent brands decreased after entry. Advertising expenditures by the Procter and Gamble brands increased, whereas it decreased for the General Foods brands. (Given the established nature of the Procter and Gamble brands, it is difficult to claim that these increases were due to repositioning.) The latter decrease could, however, be due to the fact that General Foods owned the new brand as well. (Total advertising spending by General Foods increased after the new brand's introduction.) These results suggest that competition in advertising budgets has the prisoner's dilemma feature predicted by the Lanchester model. (Robinson [1988] as well as Cubbin & Domberger [1988] also find that, to the extent incumbents react to a new entrant in terms of marketing expenditures, they do so by increasing these expenditures rather than decreasing them.)

5.3. Competition in media scheduling

Villas-Boas [1993] studies the competition in timing of advertising spending. Suppose two competitors with the same advertising budget are trying to decide how to schedule their advertising spending. Should the competitors' media schedules be in-phase or out-of-phase? Villas-Boas shows that the Markov equilibrium strategy of each firm is to use an out-of-phase pulsed media schedule. (A Markov strategy is one which depends only on the current state of the world, not on the entire history of the game.)

His model is as follows. There are two firms, each of whom makes two decisions each period: (i) first whether to advertise at level $\bar{u}$ or zero, and (ii) then determine its price. Advertising expenditures affect the consideration probability of the brand according to a response function which is sufficiently S-shaped that only $\bar{u}$ and zero are the 'possible' advertising levels. In fact, with a $\bar{u}$ spending level, maximum consideration is reached (say 1). Each firm knows the consideration levels prevailing at the start of the period. Dynamics are introduced via a decay function for consideration: from $t-1$ to t, consideration will fall from C_{t-1} to $(1/2)C_{t-1}$. In other words, depending on whether firm i advertises (at level $\bar{u}$) or not in period t, its consideration in period t will be either 1 or $(1/2)C_{t-1}$. (Consideration is like Nerlove & Arrow's [1962] 'goodwill': it depreciates unless it is replenished with advertising.) Each firm's demand function is given by:

$$Q_i = C_i(1-C_j)Q^i(p_i, \infty) + C_iC_jQ^i(p_i, p_j), \tag{37}$$

where $Q^i(p_i, p_j)$ is the demand for i's product at prices p_i and p_j when both brands are considered and $Q^i(P_i, \infty)$ is the monopoly demand for i when only i is considered.

The competition in prices starting with consideration levels C_i, C_j, leads to a (price-equilibrium) profit level $\pi(C_i, C_j)$ for each firm (not counting the advertising expenditure), which must now be taken into account in conjunction with the impact of current advertising on future consideration levels, in deciding how much to advertise this period. A key property of these π functions turns out to be:

$$\pi(1, 1/2) - \pi(1/2, 1/2) > \pi(1, 1) - \pi(1/2, 1). \tag{38}$$

This means that an increase in consideration from 1/2 to 1 is more valuable when the other firm's consideration is low rather than high. (In other words, not accounting for the cost of advertising, the two firms are strategic substitutes in consideration levels. See also the discussion of the Lanchester model above.) Then, assuming that $\pi(1,1) - \pi(1/2, 1) < \bar{u}$ – so that advertising in each period at level $\bar{u}$ is not a dominant strategy for each firm – and the discount factor is large, the unique Markov-perfect equilibrium involves each firm advertising (out-of-phase) in alternate periods at level $\bar{u}$. This result is entirely driven by (38). Given an alternating advertising strategy from its competitor, the firm would rather be out-of-phase than in-phase because advertising expenditures are more productive when the other firm has a lower consideration level. But why is this the only equilibrium? For example, why isn't one firm advertising all the time and the other firm not advertising at all an equilibrium? The reason is, Villas-Boas rules out the possibility of a firm going two consecutive periods without advertising by assuming (reasonably) that this would cause considerable loss of consideration in future periods. Therefore, the firm that didn't advertise last period *will* advertise this period, no matter what the other firm does. Realizing this, of course, the other firm doesn't advertise this period (by the previous-productivity-of-advertising argument). Note that the alternating-advertising strategy also implies a positive correlation between advertising expenditures and prices: when a firm is not advertising, it is price-promoting, and vice versa.

Villas-Boas tests his theory on monthly network advertising spending data in nine product classes, and finds, as expected, a generally negative correlation between each firm's *monthly* spending and the total monthly spending of all its competitors (after accounting for seasonality and trends).

6. Competition in distribution channels

On the one hand, we can model competition in distribution channels as we have modeled product and advertising competition. For example, distribution-channel choice can be viewed as the choice of a distribution-coverage, and the choice variable will be a spending level on distribution. Presumably higher spending levels will lead to more coverage and hence more sales. This is the approach taken by Hauser & Shugan [1983], Kumar & Sudharshan [1988] and Carpenter [1989]. In their models, distribution spending is mathematically identical to (awareness) advertising spending. The distribution results are therefore identical to the awareness advertising results discussed above. Similarly, if we view the choice of a distribution system as giving the manufacturer access to a distinct group of consumers, then the earlier results on product differentiation will reappear. Competing manufacturers will choose different distribution channels under exclusivity arrangements as a way to reduce the (wholesale) price competition between them.

The more interesting issues in channel competition arise from the effect of downstream (retail) competition on relations between the manufacturer and the retailers or the relations between competing manufacturers. Let us consider the first issue first.

6.1. Intrabrand retail competition

Assume a monopolist manufacturer has the choice of giving his retailers exclusive territory rights or not. Exclusive territories will essentially make each retailer a monopolist in his territory, leading to the familiar double-marginalization problem with linear pricing. The retailer's price will be too high, and end-user demand too small, from the channel's point of view [Spengler, 1950]. But now suppose the manufacturer encourages price competition among his retailers. Then the retailer's price to end-users will be bid down to his effective marginal cost. Realizing this, the manufacturers can induce the channel-optimal retail price p^i by selling his product to the retailers at the price $p^i - r$, where r is the retailers' marginal cost. (Then the retailer's effective marginal cost will be $p^i - r + r$, i.e. p^i.) In other words, retail competition becomes one way to 'coordinate' the channel. Of course, there are other ways of coordinating the channel which work with exclusive territories, e.g. two-part tariffs [Moorthy, 1987a], profit-sharing [Jeuland & Shugan, 1983], etc., so the choice between them depends on the strengths and weaknesses of the different schemes in coping with other real-world features not modeled here. For example, price competition at the retail level has the disadvantage of discouraging the provision of non-differentiable fixed-cost retail services.

6.2. Interbrand competition through exclusive retailers

Suppose two competing manufacturers sell their products through exclusive retailers. McGuire & Staelin [1983] have analyzed this situation for a linear demand function.

Let w_1 be manufacturer 1's wholesale price, w_2 manufacturer 2's wholesale price, and p_1 and p_2 the corresponding retail prices. We assume that the manufacturers first set their wholesale prices. Then the retailers react to these prices by setting their retail prices. Given this Stackelberg formulation of the game, we start by looking at the second-stage equilibrium. Each retailer is maximizing a profit function of the form

$$(p_i - w_i - r)(1 - p_i + \theta p_{3-i}), \quad i = 1, 2. \tag{39}$$

Differentiating these profit functions with respect to p_i and solving for the resulting first-order conditions we get the following price equilibrium:

$$p_i = \left(\frac{1}{4-\theta^2}\right)[(2+\theta)(1+r) + 2w_i + \theta w_{3-i}], \quad i = 1, 2. \tag{40}$$

Note that each retailer increases his price when *his* wholesale price increases as well as when the other wholesale price increases.

Each manufacturer's profit function is of the form

$$(w_i - m)[1 - p_i(w_i, w_{3-i}) + \theta p_{3-i}(w_{3-i}, w_i)], \quad i = 1, 2, \tag{41}$$

where the $p_i(w_i, w_{3-i})$ are the *equilibrium* prices from (40) above. Differentiating these profit functions with respect to w_i and solving the resulting first-order conditions we get the wholesale price equilibrium,

$$w_i = \left(\frac{1}{4-\theta-2\theta^2}\right)[m(2-\theta^2) + (4-\theta^2) - (2+\theta)(1+r)(1-\theta)], \quad i = 1, 2. \tag{42}$$

Now the equilibrium profits of each firm can be calculated by substituting these equilibrium prices in the respective profit functions. We do not write these equilibrium profit expressions here because of their algebraic complexity. See McGuire & Staelin [1983] for the case where $m = r = 0$.

The intermediate case where one manufacturer uses an independent exclusive retailer while the other manufacturer is vertically integrated can be analyzed similarly. The equilibrium retail prices are still given by (40), if we substitute the marginal manufacturing cost, m, for the vertically integrated manufacturer's wholesale price. Assuming that manufacturer 1 is the one with the independent channel, the equilibrium retail prices are

$$p_1 = \left(\frac{1}{4-\theta^2}\right)[(2+\theta)(1+r) + 2w_1 + \theta m], \tag{43}$$

$$p_2 = \left(\frac{1}{4-\theta^2}\right)[(2+\theta)(1+r) + 2m + \theta w_1]. \tag{44}$$

As far as wholesale prices are concerned, only the manufacturer with the independent retailer has to make a wholesale-price decision. It is easy to calculate the optimal wholesale price,

$$w_1 = \left(\frac{1}{4-2\theta^2}\right)[m(2+\theta-\theta^2)+(4-\theta^2)-(2+\theta)(1+r)(1-\theta)] \qquad (45)$$

This wholesale price is less than the equilibrium wholesale price when both manufacturers used independent channels because now the 'other' manufacturer's wholesale price is marginal cost. Once again, by substituting this wholesale price in the manufacturer's profit functions, we can compute the equilibrium profits; cf. McGuire & Staelin [1983].

Finally, the case where both manufacturers are integrated can be obtained by substituting m for w_i $(i = 1, 2)$ in (40). Again, the corresponding profit expressions are in McGuire & Staelin [1983].

6.3. *Competition in channel structure*

If we think of each manufacturer as strategically choosing his channel structure – vertical integration or decentralization – in order to better compete with his rival, then we should look at the Nash equilibrium of the 2×2 game in choice of channel structure. How do the equilibrium channel profits compare in the various structures? McGuire & Staelin [1983] find that the channel profits with an independent retailer are higher than with a vertically integrated manufacturer if and only if $\theta \geqslant 0.4323$. Moreover, each manufacturer's profit is higher when both use independent channels than when both are vertically integrated if and only if $\theta \geqslant 0.708$. Looking at the Nash equilibrium in channel structures, both manufacturers choosing vertical integration is a Nash-equilibrium strategy on either profit criterion for all values of θ. In addition, each manufacturer choosing an independent channel is also a Nash equilibrium on the channel-profits criterion for $\theta \geqslant 0.771$ and on the manufacturer-profits criterion for $\theta \geqslant 0.931$.

Note that it is easier to justify independent channels on the channel-profits criterion that on the manufacturer-profits criterion – the critical values of θ for which independent channels beats vertical integration are higher when comparing manufacturer profits than when comparing channel profits. This is because manufacturer profits are a fraction of channel profits when using independent channels but they are equal to channel profits when vertically integrated. Therefore, the main thing to understand here is why the channel profits under independent channels can be higher than the channel profits under vertical integration. Moorthy [1988b] has shown that when a manufacturer switches from vertical integration to an independent channel, not only does he raise his own equilibrium retail price due to the 'double-marginalization' effect discussed above, but he also raises the other manufacturer's equilibrium retail price. Whereas the first effect has negative consequences for channel profits, the second has positive consequences when the products are demand substitutes.

The raising of the other manufacturer's equilibrium retail price when one manufacturer switches to an independent channel is not always the case, nor is it always desirable. It happens only if there is *strategic complementarity* between the two manufacturers at the manufacturing or retail levels: when one firm raises its price, the other must find it optimal to do so as well. For example, if there are economies of scale in retailing costs, then the two firms may be strategic *substitutes* at the retail level, and then, switching to an independent channel may actually lower the other manufacturer's retail price. That will *decrease* channel profits if the two products are demand substitutes (i.e. if $\theta > 0$) and *increase* channel profits if the two products are demand complements (i.e. if $\theta < 0$).

Bonanno & Vickers [1988] and Coughlan & Wernerfelt [1989] have considered the effect of allowing two-part tariffs between the manufacturer and the independent retailer in interbrand competition. The two-part tariff can be interpreted as a franchise-fee system with the fixed payment as the franchise fee; in other words, these papers are looking at the case where each manufacturer can use a 'franchised system' [see Stern & El-Ansary, 1988, p. 332]. With two-part tariffs, the manufacturers can count on the fixed payments for their profits, so they can even choose wholesale prices below their marginal manufacturing cost. This means that, regardless of the strategic relationship between them – strategic complementarity or strategic substitutability – each manufacturer, when he switches to an independent channel, can always move the other manufacturer's retail price in the 'desirable' direction by choosing a wholesale price above or below his marginal manufacturing cost. So choosing an independent channel is always better – regardless of θ. (Coughlan & Wernerfelt emphasize that this result depends critically on the observability of the manufacturer's contracts with the retailers. If secret deals can be made between manufacturers and their retailers, then vertical integration is the only equilibrium. See also Katz [1991].) This suggests that if two-part tariffs can be used, then independent channels are no worse than vertically integrated channels and are probably better.

Empirical evidence on the role of retail competition in determining channel structure is provided by Coughlan [1985]. She looks at the channel structures chosen by new entrants in various international semiconductor markets. All of these markets are characterized by competition from entrenched firms, and Coughlan generally finds a negative correlation between product substitutability and the propensity to vertically integrate.

7. Conclusion

Much progress has been made in the last ten years or so in the study of competitive marketing strategies. Most of this work has been theoretical, using simple models of firm and consumer behavior. These models serve the function of demonstrating rigorously the existence of certain 'effects' – factors which need to be considered in analyzing real-world competition.

Problems arise, therefore, in using these models to recommend competitive strategies for firms, and also in testing our theories. The power of current decision-support systems in competitive strategy is very limited indeed. Most decision-support systems either limit themselves to estimating a demand function for the firm with competitors' marketing efforts as independent variables or, at the most, push themselves to estimating the firm's best-response function. Notably absent are considerations of dynamics, information asymmetries and industry equilibrium. This is not an accident. Decision-support systems are most successful in dealing with OR-type problems which do not have strategic content. For example, a model like Bultez & Naert's S.H.A.R.P. [1988] deals with optimal shelf-space allocation as a 'single-person' decision problem. In such models, either there is no uncertainty in the firm's demand, or even if there is, the uncertainty is of the 'impersonal', non-strategic, kind. This allows the modeler to develop general methodologies which transcend specific situations. Such an approach can hardly work for competitive strategy. As this survey indicates, optimal competitive strategy must necessarily be situation-specific. And the dimensionality of the 'situations space' is large. The optimal competitive strategy depends significantly on the nature of competitors (e.g. whether they are strategic or not, their long-term versus short-term orientation), the history of the industry (how cooperative or competitive it has been, existence of leaders, entry and exit patterns), customer behavior (the presence or absence of 'positive network externalities' and switching costs, high-involvement versus low-involvement), etc. There is no alternative to studying the situation carefully before offering recommendations.

On the empirical testing front, in many – probably most – cases, the theory is not rich enough to be tested as it is. Too many things are left unmodeled, and it is not clear whether the theory's predictions are robust to these unmodeled features. For example, the McGuire–Staelin theory of the effect of retail competitiveness on channel structure assumes exclusive dealing arrangements. Such arrangements, however, are a very small fraction of real-world distribution arrangements, and at present we don't know how non-exclusive distribution will affect the predictions of this theory [Choi, 1991]. Similarly, the punishment story which underlies Lal's [1990] explanation of price promotions by national brands requires the retailer to cooperate in administering the punishment to the errant national brand. What is not clear is whether the explanation is sustainable when retailers' incentives are taken into account. Some of the empirical papers that we have reviewed here [e.g. Bresnahan, 1987] have explicitly addressed the robustness issue by *adapting* the theory to the empirical situation. The researcher picks a situation where the 'bare-bones' model's predictions can be tested, enhances the model to include the additional features of the empirical environment, derives new predictions in this enhanced setting, and then checks whether these predictions hold empirically. (The empiricist must be a theoretician as well!) This process would be greatly aided, of course, if theoretical modelers paid greater attention to the institutional features of the markets they are modeling.

References

Abreu, D. (1986). External equilibria of oligopolistic supergames. *J. Econom. Theory* 39, 191–225.

Abreu, D., D. Pearce and E. Stacchetti (1986). Optimal cartel equilibria with imperfect monitoring, *J. Econom. Theory* 39, 251–269.

Ansari, A., and J. Steckel (1992). Multidimensional competitive positioning, Working Paper, Stern School of Business, New York University.

Avriel, M. (1976). *Nonlinear Programming*, Prentice-Hall, Englewood Cliffs, NJ.

Bass, F. (1969). A new product growth model for consumer durables. *Management Sci.* 15 (January), 215–227.

Beggs, A., and P. Klemperer (1992). Multi-period competition with switching costs. *Econometrica* 60 (May), 651–666.

Bernheim, B.D., and M.D. Whinston (1990). Multimarket contact and collusive behavior. *Rand J. Econom.* 21 (Spring), 1–26.

Bertrand, J. (1883). Théorie mathématique de la richesse sociale. *J. Savants*, 499–508.

Binmore, K. (1992). Foundations of game theory, in J.J. Laffont (ed.), *Advances in Economic Theory: Sixth World Congress*, Cambridge University Press, Cambridge.

Bonanno, G. (1986). Vertical differentiation with Cournot competition. *Econom. Notes* 15, 68–91.

Bonanno, G., and J. Vickers (1988). Vertical separation. *J. Indust. Econom.* 36 (March), 257–266.

Borenstein, S. (1991). Selling costs and switching costs: Explaining retail gasoline margins. *Rand J. Econom.* 22 (Autumn), 354–369.

Brander, J.A., and J. Eaton (1984). Product line rivalry. *Amer. Econom. Rev.* 74 (June), 323–334.

Brander, J.A., and A. Zhang (1990). Market conduct in the airline industry: An empirical investigation. *Rand J. Econom.* 21 (Winter), 567–583.

Bresnahan, T.F. (1981). Departures from marginal-cost pricing in the American automobile industry: Estimates from 1977–1978. *J. Econometrics* 11, 201–227.

Bresnahan, T.F. (1987). Competition and collusion in the American automobile oligopoly: The 1955 price war, *J. Indust. Econom.* 35 (June), 457–482.

Bresnahan, T.F., and P.C. Reiss (1990). Entry in monopoly markets. *Rev. Econom. Studies* 57, 531–553.

Bulow, J., J. Geanakoplos and P. Klemperer (1985). Multimarket oligopoly: Strategic substitutes and complements, *J. Political Economy* 93, 488–511.

Bultez, A.V., and P.A. Naert (1988). S.H.A.R.P.: Shelf space for retailers' profit. *Marketing Sci.* 7 (Summer), 211–231.

Carpenter, G.S. (1989). Perceptual position and competitive brand strategy in a two-dimensional, two-brand market, *Management Sci.* 35 (September), 1029–1044.

Carpenter, G.S., L.G. Cooper, D.M. Hanssens and D.F. Midgley (1988). Modeling asymmetric competition. *Marketing Sci.* 7 (Fall), 393–412.

Carpenter, G.S., and K. Nakamoto (1989). Consumer preference formation and pioneering advantage. *J. Marketing Res.* 26 (August), 1285–1298.

Chintagunta, P.K., and N.J. Vilcassim (1992). An empirical investigation of advertising strategies in a dynamic oligopoly. *Management Sci.*, to appear.

Choi, S.C. (1991). Price competition in a channel structure with a common retailer. *Marketing Sci.* 10 (Fall), 271–296.

Choi, S.C., W.S. DeSarbo and P.T. Harker (1990). Product positioning under price competition. *Management Sci.* 36 (February), 175–199.

Cooper, T.E. (1986). Most-favored-customer pricing and tacit collusion. *Rand J. Econom.* 17 (Autumn), 377–388.

Coughlan, A. (1985). Competition and cooperation in marketing channel choice: Theory and application. *Marketing Sci.* 4 (Spring), 110–129.

Coughlan, A., and B. Wernerfelt (1989). Credible delegation by oligopolists: A discussion of distribution channel management. *Management Sci.* 35 (February), 226–239.

Cournot, A. (1838). *Recherches sur les Principes Mathématiques de la Théorie des Richesses*, Paris.

Cubbin, J., and S. Domberger (1988). Advertising and post-entry oligopoly behavior. *J. Indust. Econom.* 37 (December), 123–140.

Dasgupta, P., and E. Maskin (1986). The existence of equilibrium in discontinuous economic games. 1: Theory. *Rev. Econom. Studies* 53, 1–26.
D'Aspremont, C., J. Gabszewicz and J. Thisse (1979). On Hotelling's 'Stability in competition'. *Econometrica* 47, 1145–1150.
Deneckere, R., D. Kovenock and R. Lee (1992). A model of price leadership based on consumer loyalty. *J. Indust. Econom.* 40 (June), 147–155.
De Palma, A., V. Ginsburgh, Y.Y. Papageorgiou and J.F. Thisse (1985). The principle of minimum differentiation holds under sufficient heterogeneity. *Econometrica* 53 (July), 767–781.
Dhebar, A., and S. Oren (1985). Optimal dynamic pricing for expanding networks. *Marketing Sci.* 4 (Fall), 336–351.
Dockner, E., and S. Jorgensen (1988). Optimal pricing strategies for new products in dynamic oligopolies. *Marketing Sci.* 7 (Fall), 315–334.
Domowitz, I., R.G. Hubbard and B.C. Peterson (1987). Oligopoly supergames: Some empirical evidence on prices and margins. *J. Indust. Econom.* 35 (June), 379–398.
Economides, N. (1986). Minimal and maximal product differentiation in Hotelling's duopoly, *Econom. Lett.* 21, 67–71.
Eliashberg, J., and A. Jeuland (1986), The impact of competitive entry in a developing market upon dynamic pricing strategies. *Marketing Sci.* 5 (Winter), 20–36.
Fershtman, C., V. Mahajan and E. Muller (1990). Marketing share pioneering advantage: A theoretical approach. *Management Sci.* 36 (August), 900–918.
Friedman, J.W. (1971). A noncooperative equilibrium for supergames. *Rev. Econom. Studies* 38, 1–12.
Friedman, J.W. (1983). Advertising and oligopolistic equilibrium. *Bell J. Econom.* 14 (Autumn), 464–473.
Friedman, J.W., and J.-F. Thisse (1990). Infinite horizon spatial duopoly with collusive pricing and noncollusive location choice, Working Paper, Virginia Polytechnic Institute, Blacksburg, VA.
Fudenberg, D., and J. Tirole (1991). *Game Theory*, The MIT Press, Cambridge, MA.
Gal-Or, E. (1982). Hotelling's spatial competition as a model of sales. *Econom. Lett.* 9, 1–6.
Gerstner, E., and J. Hess (1990). Can bait and switch benefit consumers? *Marketing Sci.* 9, 114–124.
Gibbons, R. (1992). *Game Theory for Applied Economists*, Princeton University Press, Princeton, NJ.
Glazer, A. (1985). The advantages of being first. *Amer. Econom. Rev.* 75 (June), 473–480.
Golder, P.N. and G. Tellis (1993). Pioneer advantage: Marketing logic or marketing legend? *J. Marketing Res.* 30 (May), 158–170.
Green, P.E., and A.M. Krieger (1991). Modeling competitive pricing and market share: Anatomy of a decision support system, MSI Working Paper No. 91–106, Cambridge, MA.
Green, E., and R. Porter (1984). Noncooperative collusion under imperfect price information. *Econometrica* 52, 87–100.
Gruca, T.S., and D. Sudharshan (1990). Defensive marketing strategies: An empirical examination using a brand share attraction model with coupled response functions, Working Paper, University of Illinois, Urbana-Champaign, Ill.
Hauser, J. (1988). Competitive price and positioning strategies. *Marketing Sci.* 7 (Winter), 76–91.
Hauser, J., and S. Shugan (1983). Defensive marketing strategies. *Marketing Sci.* 3 (Fall), 319–360.
Hess, J., and E. Gerstner (1987). Loss leader pricing and rain check policy. *Marketing Sci.* 6 (Fall), 358–374.
Horsky, D., and K. Mate (1988). Dynamic advertising strategies of competing durable good producers. *Marketing Sci.* 7 (Fall), 356–367.
Horsky, D., and P. Nelson (1992). New brand positioning and pricing in an oligopolistic market. *Marketing Sci.* 11 (Spring), 133–153.
Hotelling, H. (1929). Stability in competition. *Econom. J.* 39, 41–57.
Jeuland, A., and S. Shugan (1983). Managing channel profits. *Marketing Sci.* 2 (Summer), 239–272.
Judd, K. (1985). Credible spatial preemption. *Rand J. Econom.* 16 (Summer), 153–166.
Kalyanaram, G., and G. Urban (1992). Dynamic effects of the order of entry on market share, trial penetration, and repeat purchases for frequently purchased consumer goods. *Marketing Sci.* 11 (Summer), 235–250.
Katz, M. (1991). Game-playing agents: Unobservable contracts as precommitments. *Rand J. Econom.* 22 (Autumn), 307–328.

Katz, M., and C. Shapiro (1985). Network externalities, competition and compatibility. *Amer. Econom. Rev.* 75 (June), 424–440.

Klemperer, P. (1987). Markets with consumer switching costs. *Quart. J. Econom.* 102 (May), 375–394.

Klemperer, P. (1992). Equilibrium product lines: Competing head-to-head may be less competitive. *Amer. Econom. Rev.* 82 (September), 740–755.

Klemperer, P., and M. Meyer (1986). Price competition vs. quantity competition: The role of uncertainty. *Rand J. Econom.* 17 (Winter), 618–638.

Kreps, D.M. (1990). *Game Theory and Economic Modelling*, Clarendon Press, Oxford.

Kreps, D., and J.A. Sheinkman (1983). Cournot pre-commitment and Bertrand competition yield Cournot outcomes. *Bell J. Econom.* 14, 326–337.

Kumar, K.R., and D. Sudharshan (1988). Defensive marketing strategies: An equilibrium analysis based on decoupled response function models. *Management Sci.* 23 (July), 405–415.

Lal, R. (1990). Price promotions: Limiting competitive encroachment. *Marketing Sci.* 9 (Summer), 247–262.

Lal, R., and C. Matutes (1992). Consumer expectations and loss-leader pricing in retail stores, Working Paper, Stanford University, Stanford, CA.

Lambin, J.-J., P.A. Naert and A.V. Bultez (1975). Optimal marketing behavior in oligopoly. *Eur. Econom. Rev.* 6, 105–128.

Lane, W.J. (1980). Product differentiation in a market with endogenous entry, *Bell J. Econom.* 11 (Spring), 237–260.

Leeflang, P.S.H., and D.R. Wittink (1992). Diagnosing competitive reactions using (aggregated) scanner data. *Inter. J. Res. Marketing*, to appear.

Louis, J.C., and H.Z. Yazijian (1980). *The Cola Wars*, Everest House, New York.

McDonald, J. (1975), *The Game of Business*, Doubleday, New York.

McGuire, T., and R. Staelin (1983). An industry equilibrium analysis of downstream vertical integration. *Marketing Sci.* 2 (Spring), 161–192.

Moorthy, K.S. (1985). Cournot competition in a differentiated oligopoly. *J. Econom. Theory* 36, 86–109.

Moorthy, K.S. (1987a). Managing channel profits: Comment. *Marketing Sci.* 6 (Fall), 375–379.

Moorthy, K.S. (1987b). Product line competition. *Ann. Télecomm.* 42 (November–December), 655–663.

Moorthy, K.S. (1988a). Product and price competition in a duopoly. *Marketing Sci.* 7 (Spring), 141–168.

Moorthy, K.S. (1988b). Strategic decentralization in channels. *Marketing Sci.* 7 (Fall), 335–355.

Narasimhan, C. (1988). Competitive promotional strategies. *J. Business* 61, 427–450.

Nerlove, M., and K. Arrow (1962). Optimal advertising under dynamic conditions. *Economica* 22, 129–142.

Neven, D.J. (1986). On Hotelling's competition with non-uniform customer distribution. *Econom. Lett.* 21, 121–126.

Oren, S., and S. Smith (1981). Critical mass and tariff structure in electronic communications markets. *Bell J. Econom.* 12 (Autumn), 467–487.

Osborne, M.J., and C. Pitchik (1987). Equilibrium in Hotelling's model of spatial competition. *Econometrica* 55 (July), 911–922.

Porter, R. (1983). A study in cartel stability: The joint executive committee, 1880–1886. *Bell J. Econom.* 14, 301–314.

Prescott, E.C., and M. Visscher (1977). Sequential location among firms with foresight. *Bell J. Econom.* 8, 378–393.

Raju, J.S., V. Srinivasan and R. Lal (1990). The effects of brand loyalty on competitive price promotional strategies. *Management Sci.* 36, 276–304.

Rao, R. (1991). Pricing and promotions in asymmetric duopolies. *Marketing Sci.* 10 (Spring), 131–144.

Reiss, P. (1991). Price and advertising strategies that segment 'top-of-mind' shoppers. Working Paper, Stanford University, Stanford, CA.

Ries, A., and J. Trout (1986). *Marketing Warfare*, McGraw-Hill, New York.

Roberts, M.J., and L. Samuelson (1988). An empirical analysis of dynamic, nonprice competition in an oligopolistic industry. *Rand J. Econom.* 19 (Summer), 200–220.

Robinson, W.T. (1988). Marketing mix reactions to entry. *Marketing Sci.* 7 (Fall), 368–385.

Robinson, W.T., and C. Fornell (1985). The sources of marketing pioneer advantages in consumer goods industries. *J. Marketing Res.* 22 (August), 297–304.

Rotemberg, J.J., and G. Saloner (1986). A supergame-theoretic model of price wars during booms. *Amer. Econom. Rev.* 76 (June), 390–407.

Rubinstein, A. (1991). Comments on the interpretation of game theory. *Econometrica* 59 (July), 909–924.

Salop, S. (1979). Monopolistic competition with outside goods. *Bell J. Econom.* 10, 141–156.

Schmalensee, R. (1978). Entry deterrence in the ready-to-eat breakfast cereal industry. *Bell J. Econom.* 9 (Autumn), 305–327.

Shaked, A., and J. Sutton (1982). Relaxing price competition through product differentiation. *Rev. Econom. Studies* 49, 3–13.

Shilony, Y. (1977). Mixed pricing in an oligopoly. *J. Econom. Theory* 14, 373–388.

Simester, D. (1992). Signalling and commitment using retail prices. Working Paper, MIT, Cambridge, MA.

Slade, M. (1987). Interfirm rivalry in a repeated game: An empirical test of tacit collusion. *J. Indust. Econom.* 35, 499–516.

Slade, M. (1989). Price wars in price-setting supergames. *Economica* 56, 295–310.

Sloan Jr., A.P. (1963). *My Years with General Motors*, Doubleday, New York.

Smith, V.L. (1990). Experimental economics: Behavioral lessons for microeconomic theory and policy. 1990 Nancy L. Schwartz Memorial Lecture, Kellogg Graduate School of Management, Northwestern University, Evanston, Ill.

Spengler, J. (1950). Vertical integration and anti-trust policy. *J. Political Economy* 58 (August), 347–352.

Stern, L., and A. El-Ansary (1988). *Marketing Channels*, Prentice-Hall, Englewood Cliffs, NJ.

Stigler, G. (1964). A theory of oligopoly. *J. Political Economy* 72, 44–61.

Urban, G., T. Carter, S. Gaslain and Z. Mucha (1986). Market share rewards to pioneering brands: An empirical analysis and strategic implications. *Management Sci.* 32 (June), 645–659.

Vandenbosch, M., and C. Weinberg (1992). Product and price competition in a two-dimensional vertical differentiation model, Working Paper, University of British Columbia, Vancouver, BC.

Varian, H. (1980). A model of sales. *Amer. Econom. Rev.* 70, 651–659; erratum, March 1981.

Villas-Boas, J.M. (1990). A competitive rationale for price promotions: Evidence from the retail coffee market, Working Paper, MIT, Cambridge, MA.

Villas-Boas, J.M. (1993). Predicting advertising pulsing policies in an oligopoly: A model and empirical test. *Marketing Sci.* 12 (Winter), 88–102.

Xie, J., and M. Sirbu (1992). Price competition in the presence of positive demand externalities, Working Paper, University of Rochester, Rochester, NY.

Part III
Tools and Methods for Market Analysis

J. Eliashberg and G.L. Lilien, Eds., *Handbooks in OR & MS, Vol. 5*

Chapter 5

Non-Spatial Tree Models for the Assessment of Competitive Market Structure: An Integrated Review of the Marketing and Psychometric Literature

Wayne S. DeSarbo

Department of Marketing, Graduate School of Business, Univeristy of Michigan, Ann Arbor, MI 48109-1234, U.S.A.,

Ajay K. Manrai and Lalita A. Manrai

College of Business and Economics, University of Delaware, Newark, DE 19716-2710 U.S.A.

1. Introduction

Competitive market structure refers to a configuration of competing products/brands which are perceived as substitutes by consumers. It is usually conceptualized for identifying levels of competition among brands in a well-defined product-market. It requires the simultaneous determination of customer segments, products/brands, and conditions of purchase/use [Shocker, Stewart & Zahorik, 1986, 1990; Day, Shocker & Srivastava, 1979; Urban, Hauser & Dholakia, 1987; Grover & Srinivasan, 1987; Grover & Rao, 1988; Jain, Bass & Chen, 1990; Ramaswamy & DeSarbo, 1990; Zahorik, 1992]. The definition of a product-market in terms of the set of products/brands to be included often depends on managerial judgment. Once the relevant product-market is appropriately defined, however, the problem of determining competitive market structure involves partitioning the set of products/brands into subsets or submarkets such that products/brands within a submarket are closer substitutes of one another than of products/brands in a different submarket. The assessment of such product-market configurations plays a useful role in a variety of tactical and strategic marketing decisions. A knowledge of competitive market relationships is important for initiating such tactical decisions as those involving price discounts, advertising, sales promotion and sales force allocation. The product-market boundaries can reveal competitive dynamics in a market, and thus assist in making strategic moves such as the identification of new product opportunities, as well as in the process of design, development and launch of new products in the marketplace. Several other strategic decisions such as positioning and repositioning of existing products, the definition of the business, and antitrust considerations are also guided by the nature and intensity of competition as revealed by such competitive-market-structure analyses.

As an example, consider an approach based on product/brand substitutability to identify hierarchical product-market structure called the Hendry system [see Butler & Butler, 1976; Kalwani & Morrison, 1977]. In this methodology, a competitive hierarchical market structure is employed in which each brand competes more directly with brands located in the same partition than with brands located in a different partition of a hierarchy. This idea of competition entails the assumption that consumers make brand choices in a category by choosing one partition and then eliminating the brands in other partitions at each level of the hierarchy. This notion of a hierarchical consumer choice process involving sequential elimination of alternatives has been widely supported in the marketing literature [cf. Bettman, 1974; Gensch, 1987; Hauser, 1986; Lehmann & Moore, 1986; Manrai & Sinha, 1989]. Consider, for example, Panel A of Figure 5.1 which depicts a hypothetical hierarchical tree structure to describe a market for luxury automobiles. This hierarchy divides the automobile market by body style, country of origin, and make of the automobile. This market structure suggests that consumers would first decide among body styles, then on country of origin, and finally on make/brand. The automobiles would be more substitutable if they are on the same branch of the hierarchy than if they are on different branches; e.g. Lexus and Acura are closer competitors than BMW and Mercedes. Furthermore, Corvette competes more closely with Cyclone, Porsche and BMW than with Cadillac or Mercedes in this example. Note, this inference is driven by the sequence of decisions that the consumer is assumed to make in constructing this particular hierarchy. In this example, Corvette competes more closely with Cyclone, Porsche and BMW because both Cadillac and Mercedes are eliminated from the set of alternatives if the consumers decide for a sporty car at the first stage of selection process. Now consider, for example, a different scenario in which the consumer is assumed to first decide on the country of origin before deciding on the body styling. The hierarchical tree structure will change to that shown in Panel B of Figure 5.1. The revised market structure reverses our earlier conclusion. Assuming that the consumer initially opts for an American car, Corvette competes more closely with Cyclone and Cadillac than with Porsche, BMW or Mercedes as all the European cars are eliminated at the time the consumer decides for American cars. It is possible that the different consumer segments use varying sequences of decision-making, and therefore market structure may vary with segments. Clearly, the hierarchical structure is useful as it contains information on product categorization based on relevant product attributes (e.g. country of origin, body style and make/brand, etc.), and the sequence in which these attributes are considered in making a product/brand selection. As previously stated, marketers have usefully applied this approach to some key strategic marketing areas, such as assessing the nature of competition, new product planning and market opportunity identification [cf. Lilien & Kotler, 1983; Srivastava, Leone & Shocker, 1981; Urban, Hauser & Dholakia, 1987].

A large number of approaches for determining competitive market structure exist in the marketing and psychometric literature. These techniques include both spatial and non-spatial methods. The spatial methods typically represent brands

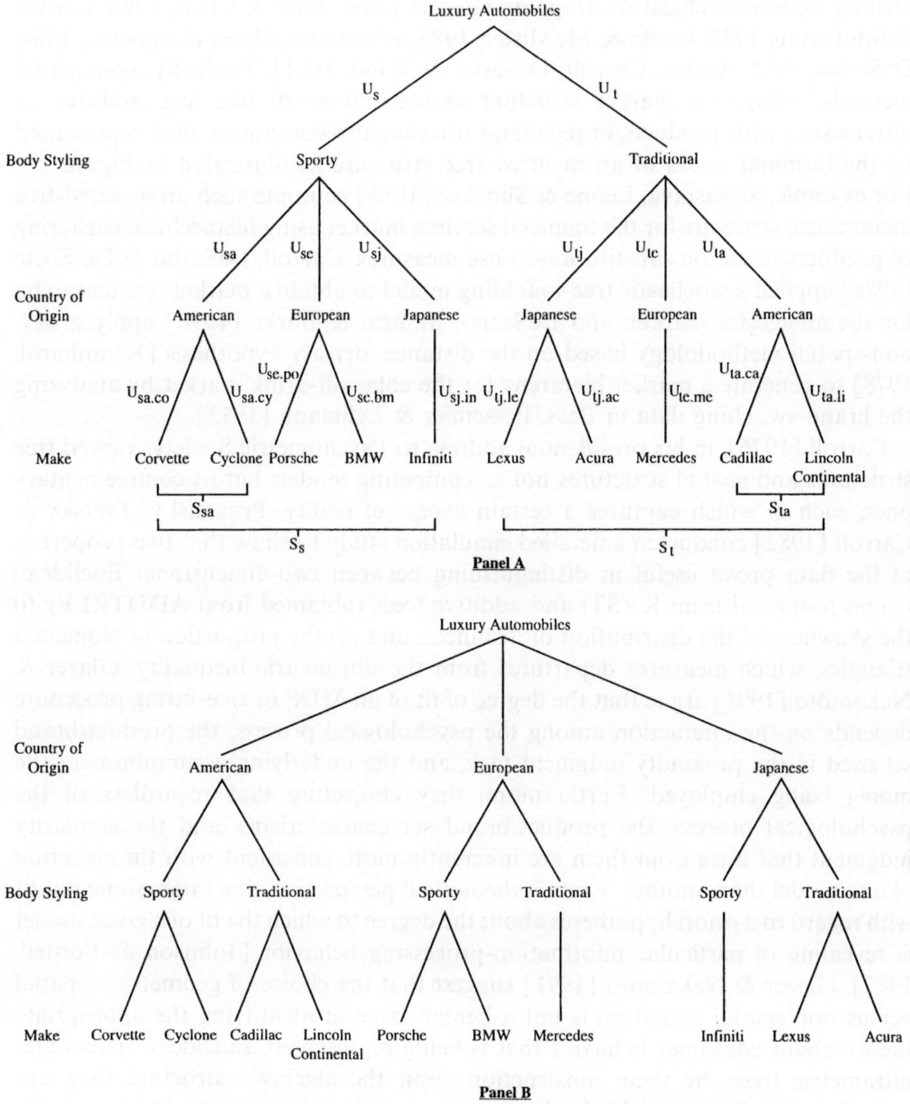

Fig. 5.1. Hypothetical product-market hierarchy for luxury automobiles.

as points and customers as points or vectors in a multidimensional attribute space [Eliashberg & Manrai, 1992; Green, Carmone & Smith, 1989; DeSarbo & Rao, 1984, 1986; Lehmann, 1972], while non-spatial methods represent brands and customers as terminal nodes of some tree structure [Kannan & Wright, 1991a; DeSarbo, Manrai & Burke, 1990; Fraser & Bradford, 1992; Rao & Sabavala, 1981; Kalwani & Morrison, 1977]. There are also other non-spatial approaches that identify non-hierarchical overlapping clusters [Jain, Bass & Chen, 1990; Grover & Srinivasan, 1987; Lattin & McAlister, 1985; Srivastava, Alpert & Shocker, 1984; DeSarbo, 1982; Arabie, Carroll, DeSarbo & Wind, 1981]. Typically, non-spatial methods estimate a market structure as some form of tree (e.g. additive or ultrametric) with products/brands (and occasionally consumers also) represented by the terminal nodes of an inverted tree structure as illustrated in Figure 5.1. For example, Srivastava, Leone & Shocker [1981] compute such an inverted-tree hierarchical structure for the financial services market using hierarchical clustering of products based on substitution-in-use measures. Carroll, DeSarbo & De Soete [1988] applied a stochastic tree-unfolding model to obtain a market tree hierarchy for the analgesics market, and DeSarbo, Manrai & Burke [1990] apply a new non-spatial methodology based on the distance–density hypothesis [Krumhansl, 1978] to generate a market hierarchy for the cola soft-drink market by analyzing the brand-switching data in Bass, Pessemier & Lehmann [1972].

Carroll [1976], in his presidential address to Psychometric Society, viewed tree structures and spatial structures not as competing models but as complementary ones, each of which captures a certain aspect of reality. Pruzansky, Tversky & Carroll [1982] conducted a detailed simulation study to show that two properties of the data prove useful in distinguishing between two-dimensional Euclidean planes (obtained from KYST) and additive trees (obtained from ADDTREE): (i) the skewness of the distribution of distances, and (ii) the proportion of elongated triangles, which measures departures from the ultrametric inequality. Glazer & Nakamoto [1991] argue that the degree of fit of an MDS or tree-fitting procedure depends on the interaction among the psychological process, the product/brand set used in the proximity judgment task, and the underlying assumptions of the model being employed. Furthermore, they conjecture that regardless of the psychological process, the product/brand set characteristics and the similarity judgment that arise from them are inherently more consistent with the structure of one model than another. From a theoretical perspective, this raises some doubt with regard to a priori hypotheses about the degree to which the fit of a given model is revealing of particular information-processing behavior [Johnson & Fornell, 1987]. Glazer & Nakamoto [1991] suggest that the choice of geometries (spatial versus non-spatial structure) is not a benign issue in identifying the appropriate theory about consumer behavior that is being represented. Euclidean spaces and ultrametric trees, by their construction, limit the algebraic structure they can represent. Furthermore, the fundamental properties of these two structures are incompatible and a set of distances that satisfy one model cannot satisfy the other. Thus, there is a high risk of overinterpretation of such solutions in terms of psychological meaning. Shepard [1980], in his invited lecture to the US-USSR symposium on 'Normative and descriptive models of decision-making', proposed that it would be a mistake to ask which of these various scaling, tree-fitting, or clustering methods is based on *the correct model*. Shepard [1980] provides a set of illustrative applications to demonstrate that different models may be more appropriate for different sets of brands or types of data. Even for the same set of data, he proposes that different methods of analysis may be better suited to bringing out different but equally informative aspects of the underlying competitive market structure.

In recent years, one has witnessed a more rapid proliferation of non-spatial methods as compared to spatial methods in the marketing and psychometric literature. Such non-spatial approaches include traditional hierarchical clustering methods [Johnson, 1967], ultrametric trees [Carroll, 1976], additive trees [Novak, 1991; Cunningham, 1978; Sattath & Tversky, 1977], multiple trees [Carroll & Pruzansky, 1975], hybrid models [Carroll & Pruzansky, 1980], two-mode tree-unfolding models [Furnas, 1980], network models [Hutchinson, 1989], preference trees [Tversky & Sattath, 1979], Simple Stochastic Tree UNfolding (SSTUN) models [DeSarbo, De Soete, Carroll & Ramaswamy, 1988], General Stochastic Tree UNfolding·(GSTUN) models [Carroll, DeSarbo & De Soete, 1989], and, more recently, latent class stochastic tree models [Ramaswamy & DeSarbo, 1990]. A detailed review of the non-spatial tree approaches for the assessment of competitive market structure does not exist in the marketing literature.

The goal of this chapter, therefore, is to fill in gap in the marketing literature by providing a detailed technical review of several non-spatial tree approaches for determining competitive market structure. We encourage the reader interested in the spatial approaches to refer to the detailed reviews provided in the marketing and psychometric literature, including Carroll & Arabie [1980], Young [1984], Hoffman & Franke [1986], Gifi [1990], Elrod [1991], Elrod & Winer [1991], and Hoffman & De Leeuw [1991]. We begin with a taxonomy of methodologies for determining non-spatial market structures. In the section we discuss hierarchical-clustering-based models, ultrametric, additive, asymmetric two-mode, and stochastic-preference/choice trees, as well as some of the recent generalizations of these models (e.g. generalized networks).

2. Non-spatial tree models for the assessment of competitive market structure

2.1. *A taxonomy of non-spatial methodologies*

Methodologies for the non-spatial assessment of competitive market structure can be differentiated with respect to the input data required to generate the particular representation and the specific model characteristics that underlie the representation. Modifying the framework used by DeSarbo, De Soete, Carroll & Ramaswamy [1988], we further decompose these two major classification themes below into those involving data characteristics and those involving model characteristics:

2.1.1. *Data characteristics*

Type/level of data. There are essentially two types of data: behavioral and judgmental. Behavioral data indicate the actual choices/purchases of customers (past or current), whereas judgmental data provide insights into future intention patterns. The former are usually gathered from consumer panels, stores, and laboratory shopping environments, whereas the latter are primarily survey-based. Concerning data level, data can be collected at the individual consumer, household, segment (e.g. aggregated data for heavy/medium/light users), or aggregate level (e.g. brand sales data). In general, individual-level data with results extended to the segment level are desired, although constraints on data collection/availability and the nature of the product class itself may restrict the actual level selected.

Measure of competitive relation. A number of approaches have used brand-switching to infer competitive structure based on the assumption that if a relatively high degree of switching exists between any pair of brands, they must be substitutable and hence this switching is indicative of the nature of competition between the two brands. Switching measures are typically obtained from panel data. One problem with using behavioral switching data occurs in product classes in which variety-seeking is prevalent and where situational and environmental influences on consumer choice (e.g. unavailability, price promotions), are substantial. For example, Lattin & McAlister [1985] employ behavioral consumption data to help mitigate this problem.

Level of analysis/customer preference heterogeneity. As mentioned, data can be collected with respect to different levels of aggregation. Most of the current approaches have analyzed competitive relationships among products in a market at the aggregate level. Here, the model is typically specified at the aggregate level and estimated with data aggregated over customers. Hence, differences in individual demand are ignored. There are also model/methodologies that are conducted at the segment level of analysis. This is typically accomplished in one of two ways: (1) by segmenting customers a priori on some basis and deriving a perceptual structure within each segment, or (2) by specifying stochastic models of choice for different segments and fitting these models to aggregated switching data. Individual-level models, or individual-level models aggregated to the segment or market level, have also been proposed in the marketing literature.

2.1.2. Model characteristics

Type of representation. The structure of a market can be represented in a variety of ways. As mentioned earlier, continuous spatial representations typically embed products in some coordinate space so that either the angle between brands or a specified distance measure (usually Euclidean) between brands in the space represents the observed 'competitiveness' among them. Customer's preferences can be embedded via vectors or ideal-points to provide a joint space representation of products and customers. Of the non-spatial representations, the most widely used is hierarchical (or ultrametric) tree portrayal of the competitive structure (see Figure 5.1). In the usual representation, the brands appear as terminal nodes of a tree, and a metric is defined in which the distance between a pair of products is the height of their 'lowest common ancestor' node (the first internal node at which they meet as one proceeds 'up' the hierarchy). The behavioral justification for such hierarchical structures arises from the fact that they provide a schematic representation of the process of choosing from a set of products. Typically, an aggregate, discrete tree representation is estimated assuming homogeneity in the hierarchical choice process across individuals. Alternatively, additive tree representations can also be utilized to portray competition market structure where distance in the additive tree is represented by the length of the path connecting pairs of brands. Such representations are not as restrictive as hierarchical or ultrametric trees in that they allow brands in different clusters to be closer than brands in the same cluster. In fact, a hierarchical or ultrametric tree can be shown to be a special case of an additive tree. Finally, more general network structures allow for competitive market structures to be wheels, grids, or any shape – they do not have to correspond to nested tree structures.

Incorporation of marketing-mix variables. Competitive market structure analysis has traditionally focused on identifying product partitions based on product features. Few approaches, however, have attempted to directly incorporate other marketing-mix variables such as price and advertising, thereby assessing the impact of marketers' decisions within and across the estimated structure.

Type of analysis. There are two basic types of market analysis: confirmatory and exploratory. In a confirmatory approach, a managerially relevant market structure is first defined a priori, and then formulated into a mathematical statement based on theoretical considerations. Statistical criteria are then used to ascertain if the market (i.e. the observed data) satisfies the (theoretical) mathematical definition. Thus, depending on the theoretical considerations employed, different models can be formulated to *test* competitive market structures. Typically, individual responses are aggregated to test hypothesized aggregate product partitionings, which may then be followed by an allocation of customers to partitions (using specific allocation rules) if the structure is accepted. In an exploratory approach, the complete competitive structure of the market is derived from the *data*.

One-mode vs. two-mode structures. Some types of data collected for use in market-structure studies (e.g. brand-switching data) may be non-symmetric. As such, some models of market structure ignore asymmetry and present a portrayal of the respective set of brands based on either a portion or averaging of the collected data. On the other hand, some non-spatial methods utilize the entire, full data array and accommodate asymmetry by estimating brand locations for each mode of the data (e.g. in brand-switching data, estimating a location for each brand at times t and $t+1$).

Error specification. Most non-spatial models can be written in the form of:

$$\delta_{ij} = d_{ij} + e_{ij}, \tag{1}$$

where δ_{ij} is the observed proximity data between brands i and j, d_{ij} is the model-predicted distance between brands i and j, and e_{ij} is error. In many non-spatial methodologies, there are no parametric assumptions about the stochastic nature of e_{ij}, while in others, there are.

Table 5.1 provides a summary of these different criteria (Table 5.1A) as well as a taxonomy of several of the methods to be discussed based on these criteria (Table 5.1B). We choose to utilize the last criterion, error specification, as a major way of organizing most of the non-spatial methods to be discussed, while we discuss these other criteria in the text.

2.2 Deterministic models

2.2.1 Models based on hierarchical clustering

Hierarchical market definition is one of the major approaches cited by Urban & Hauser [1980], Wind (1982) and Urban, Hauser & Dholakia [1987] for representing competitive market structure. We have seen the implications of such a representation in Figure 5.1. There are a number of different approaches for deriving such hierarchical tree representations by using either judgmental or behavioral data [cf. Day, Shocker & Srivastava, 1979]. Bettman [1974] suggests that such a structure be constructed on the basis of an observation or measurement of the sequence of issues considered and decisions made by consumers. For example, in Figure 5.1, the researcher would determine if actual consumers first choose between body styling, and then, conditional on that primary choice, select within a country of origin. Unfortunately, as noted by Urban & Hauser [1980], the in-depth interviews necessary to obtain such information in the field can be unwieldy in practice. (Perhaps the most useful approach in using judgmental data to derive hierarchical market structures is the one suggested by Srivastava, Leone & Shocker [1981] who utilize product-use data and a substitution-in-use framework with iterative multiple regression and clustering.)

Given the difficulties and associated expense of collecting such judgmental data (e.g. decision protocols, product usage, proximities) via consumer surveys, attention has more recently been placed towards developing procedures that utilize existing behavioral data sets (e.g. switching data). One of the earliest of such approaches previously discussed was the Hendry model [Butler & Butler 1976; Kalwani & Morrison, 1977], which derives such a hierarchy based on consumers switching between brands of frequently purchased consumer products. Managerial judgment is used to establish a number of hypothetical hierarchical partitionings, and switching patterns are examined for each structure (confirmatory analyses). The hierarchical partitioning which fits the empirical data 'best' (i.e. the switching constant for each brand within a partition is identical and equal to the switching constant describing aggregate switching behavior in that group) is selected as the one for the respective market. The criterion used to define such trees implies that switching should be high within a branch and low between branches. Figure 5.2, taken from Wind [1982], displays the two types of hierarchical partitions traditionally tested in the Hendry system: a form-primary market (Panel A) and a brand-primary market (Panel B). In a form-primary market, a consumer first selects a form (e.g.

cup, stick, liquid), and then chooses a brand among the set of brands offered in the particular form. On the other hand, in a brand-primary market, consumers exhibit higher brand-loyalty by selecting first the brand, and then the form. Note, other hierarchical partitions involving form-primary and brand-primary structures, attributes, etc. are also testable. (The mathematical details are available in Butler & Butler [1976] and Kalwani & Morrison [1977].) Other, more recently proposed methods for testing competitive market structures include Urban, Johnson & Hauser [1984], Grover & Dillon [1985], Novak & Stangor [1987], Vilcassim [1989], Kumar & Sashi [1989] and Kannan & Wright [1991b] which will be briefly discussed later in this review paper.

Rao & Sabavala [1980, 1981] were among the first to propose the application of hierarchical clustering methods to brand-switching data. They empirically derive an approximation of consumer's hierarchical choice processes from panel data by determining sequentially partitioned subsets of brands among which there exist varying degrees of switching. The Rao & Sabavala [1981] aggregate choice process

Table 5.1
A: Criteria of non-spatial approaches to competitive market structure assessment

- I. Data characteristics
  - A. Type
    1. Behavioral
    2. Judgmental
  - B. Measure of competitive relation
    1. Perceptions
    2. Switching
    3. Preference/Choice
  - C. Level of aggregation
    1. Individual
    2. Segment
    3. Market
- II. Model characteristics
  - A. Representation
    1. Hierarchical/ultrametric
    2. Additive
    3. Networks
    4. Latent class
  - B. Accommodate marketing-mix effects?
    1. No
    2. Yes
  - C. Type of analysis
    1. Confirmatory
    2. Exploratory
  - D. Mode of analysis
    1. One mode
    2. Two mode
  - E. Error specification
    1. Deterministic
    2. Stochastic

Table 5.1
B: A taxonomy of non-spatial approaches

Method	Type of data	Level of aggregation	Measure of competitive relation	Representation	Type of analysis	Market mix?	Mode of analysis	Error specification
1. Rao & Sabavala [1981]	Behavioral	Segment	Switching	Hierarchical	Exploratory	No	One-mode	Deterministic
2. Carroll & Pruzansky [1975]; De Soete [1984]	Judgmental or behavioral	Any	Perceptions or switching	Hierarchical	Exploratory	No	One-mode	Deterministic
3. Sattath & Tversky [1977]; Cunningham [1974, 1978]; Carroll & Pruzansky [1975]; De Soete [1983a, 1983b]	Judgmental or behavioral	Any	Perceptions or switching	Additive	Exploratory	No	One-mode	Deterministic
4. Carroll, Clark & DeSarbo [1984]	Judgmental or behavioral	Individual or segment	Perceptions or switching	Hierarchical or additive	Exploratory or confirmatory	No	Two-mode (symmetric)	Deterministic
5. DeSarbo, Manrai & Burke [1990]	Judgmental or behavioral	Any	Perceptions or switching	Hierarchical	Exploratory or confirmatory	No	Two-mode	Deterministic
6. De Soete, DeSarbo, Furnas & Carroll [1984a, 1984b]	Judgmental or behavioral	Any	Perceptions, switching, or preference	Hierarchical or aditive	Exploratory	No	Two-mode	Deterministic

7. Hutchinson [1989]; Klauer & Carroll [1989, 1991]; Corter & Tversky [1986]	Judgmental or behavioral	Any	Perceptions or switching	Network	Exploratory	No	Two-mode	Deterministic
8. Tversky & Sattath [1979]; Moore, Pessemier & Lehmann [1986]	Judgmental	Any	Preference/ choice	Hierarchical	Confirmatory	No	Two-mode	Stochastic
9. Moore & Lehmann [1989]	Judgmental	Individual	Preference/ choice	Hierarchical	Confirmatory	No	Two-mode	Stochastic
10. DeSarbo, De Soete, Carroll & Ramaswamy [1988]; Carroll, DeSarbo, & De Soete [1987, 1988, 1989]	Judgmental	Individual or segment	Preference/ choice	Hierarchical	Exploratory or confirmatory	No	Two-mode	Stochastic
11. Ramaswamy & DeSarbo [1990]	Behavioral	Individual (derives segments)	Choice	Hierarchical	Exploratory	No	Two-mode	Stochastic
12. Currim, Meyer & Le [1988]	Behavioral	Individual	Choice	Hierarchical	Exploratory	No	Two-mode	Deterministic with a probabilistic splitting criterion

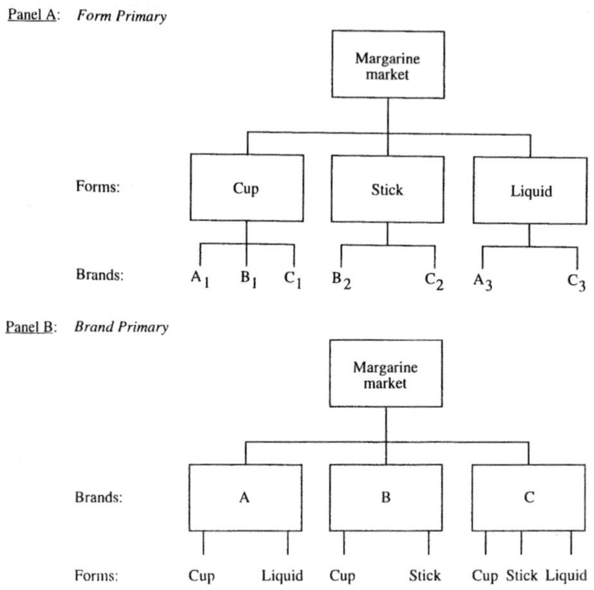

Fig. 5.2. Hypothetical hierarchical market partitioning (taken from Wind [1982]).

can thus be described as a hierarchical, non-overlapping structure consisting of several nested partitions, where a brand may belong to only one partition at a given level. Since their methodology describes repetitive choice situations, the appropriate applications are for frequently purchased products and services. The Rao & Sabavala [1981] methodology is developed from the following four assumptions:

A1. On a given choice occasion, a consumer sequentially partitions the total set of brands on the basis of subjective or objective attributes to some point where a brand is selected from the remaining partition.

A2. For each individual in a market segment, the 'structure' of the decision model is the same with respect to the set of attributes, and the order in which these attributes occur is the same, although preferred features (or levels) on attributes may vary. For this segment, one may represent the hierarchical choice process by a tree.

A3. There is a stochastic component in the individual choice process, so that it is possible to follow different paths through the hierarchy on different choice occasions even though the consumer's preferences remain stable over time. The degree of switching between any two items on consecutive choice occasions in proportional to the choice shares of those items. The constant of proportionality is a parameter of the structure, and varies from one level of the structure to another.

A4. The level in the hierarchy represents the degree of competition between the partitions. If this competition manifests itself in brand-switching behavior by individuals over choice occasions then the interpretation is that switching is least at the highest level in the hierarchy and greatest at the lowest level.

Given that the focus of this review piece is upon the construction of non-spatial tree methods for representing market structure, we choose to focus upon the identification phase of the Rao & Sabavala procedure. The identification stage of the methodology consists of three stages. In the first stage, we take consumer panel data that report product-purchase information over extended time periods and construct a two-period transition matrix from one purchase occasion to the next for a segment of homogeneous consumers. Let us denote this matrix as $\mathbf{N} = ((n_{ij}))$, where n_{ij} is the number of consumers who purchase brand i on the first choice-occasion and brand j on the next. Rao & Sabavala [1981] use a simple average of consecutive two-period transition frequency matrices that represents the structure under 'average' market conditions over the period of time studied (although consecutive pairs of purchases overlap and are not statistically independent).

In the second stage of this identification stage, Rao & Sabavala (1981) transform $\boldsymbol{N}$ into a flow measure. Citing potential problems such as the comparability of brands across the rows of $\boldsymbol{N}$ due to different market shares, the authors define a flow measure, f_{ij}, as the proportionality constant in the switching relationship. Let:

n_{ij} = number of consumers who switched from brand i on the first choice-occasion to brand j on the second,

$n_{i.}$ = number of consumers who purchased brand i on the first choice-occasion,

$n_{j.}$ = number of consumers who purchased brand j on the second choice-occasion,

$n.$ = number of consumers in this homogeneous population.

The measure f_{ij} is defined as:

$$f_{ij} = \frac{n_{ij} n_{..}}{n_{i.} n_{.j}} \tag{1}$$

This measure may be interpreted as the ratio of the actual number of consumers switching from i to j to the expected number switching from i to j, under switching defined by independence between the two consecutive choice-occasions and by choice probabilities given by the shares of i and j, respectively. Note that f_{ij} is a similarity index which can range from zero to infinity. Also, f_{ij} is not symmetric, and Rao & Sabavala [1981] suggest utilizing the upper- or lower-triangular half of $\boldsymbol{F} = ((f_{ij}))$ as input.

The third stage of the identification phase involves the application of standard hierarchical clustering procedures [Johnson, 1967] on $\boldsymbol{F}$. An important premise to this methodology is that the proximity matrix $\boldsymbol{F}$ is composed of an 'exact hierarchical tree structure' ($\boldsymbol{T} = ((t_{ij}))$) plus measurement and sampling error ($\boldsymbol{E} = ((e_{ij}))$):

$$f_{ij} = t_{ij} + e_{ij}. \tag{2}$$

This suggests that if brands i and j are linked together at a higher level in the tree than some other pair k, l, then $f_{ij} < f_{kl}$. At the terminal branches of the hierarchical tree, all brands are disjoint. These conditions thus require that certain inequalities must bold among the elements of $\boldsymbol{F}$:

$$f_{ij} \leqslant \max(f_{ik}, f_{jk}), \tag{3}$$

for all brands i,j and k. This condition is known as the ultrametric inequality. Johnson [1967] shows that satisfaction of (3) for all triples produces a hierarchical clustering or tree. Note that this also imposes the condition that when brand clusters link together at any level in the hierarchical tree, then the similarity of any two brands in this aggregate cluster is the same, and that the node of the tree when they join has a height-value associated with it. Rao & Sabavala [1981] suggests using 'single-linkage', 'complete-linkage', or 'average-linkage' hierarchical cluster analysis on either the lower- or upper-triangular half of $\boldsymbol{F}$ [see Johnson, 1967]. Note that such procedures iteratively merge brands and groups of brands at each stage that are most similar. Differences between these three methods occur with respect to how similarity is defined with respect to, say, a brand and an already formed group of brands. Dubes & Jain (1979) provides an excellent summary of these and many other forms of hierarchical clustering (e.g. centroid method, Ward's [1963] method, median method).

As an illustration of the Rao & Sabavala [1981] identification phase, we use the example given in DeSarbo & De Soete [1984] for eight brands of soft drinks. Bass, Pessemier & Lehmann [1972] present an experiment with 280 students and secretaries who were required to select a 12-ounce can of soft drink four days a week for three weeks from among: Coke, 7-Up, Tab, Fresca, Pepsi, Sprite, Diet Pepsi and Like. (Note that Like was a diet lemon–lime drink at the time this study was performed.) Table 5.2 presents the asymmetric transition matrix ($\boldsymbol{N}$) for the two periods measured. A flow matrix, $\boldsymbol{F}$, was then calculated as suggested in Rao & Sabavala [1981] and an average-linkage hierarchical clustering analysis

Table 5.2
Bass, Pessemier & Lehmann [1972] transition matrix ($\boldsymbol{N}$) for eight brands of soft drinks

		Period $t+1$							
		Coke	7-Up	Tab	Like	Pepsi	Sprite	Diet Pepsi	Fresca
	Coke	50	9	1	3	11	4	1	3
	7-Up	8	20	0	3	6	4	1	2
	Tab	1	1	1	2	1	0	1	1
	Like	1	2	1	2	3	1	2	1
Period t	Pepsi	12	9	1	2	36	5	2	3
	Sprite	2	3	1	1	3	6	1	2
	Diet Pepsi	1	1	2	1	1	1	3	1
	Fresca	4	2	1	2	3	2	1	4

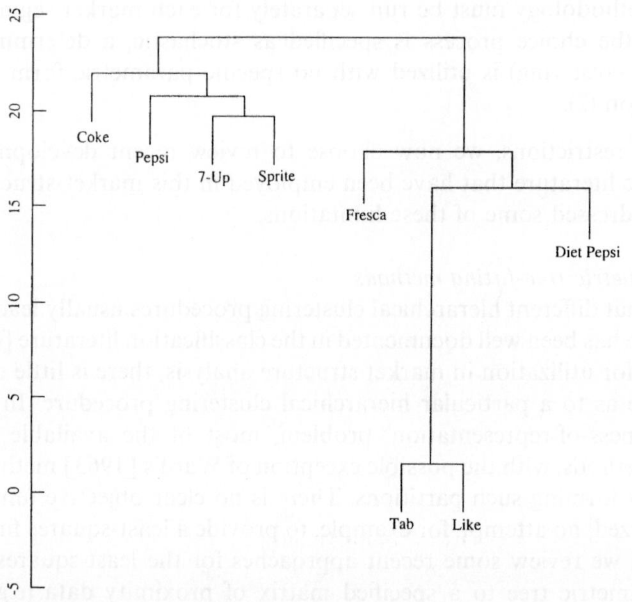

Fig. 5.3. Hierarchical clustering analysis of upper-triangular half of normalized Table 5.2 for the Bass, Pessemier & Lehmann [1972] soft-drink brand-switching matrix (taken from DeSarbo & De Soete [1984]).

was performed on the upper-triangular half of $\boldsymbol{F}$. Figure 5.3 presents the resulting hierarchical tree structure. Two major clusters emerge: one with non-diet items including Coke, Pepsi, 7-Up and Sprite, and the other with mostly diet brands (at the time the study was conducted) such as Diet Pepsi, Fresca, Like and Tab. A weak secondary split is seen as between colas and lemon–lime-tasting drinks. Thus, these consumers tend to primarily weight diet–non-diet as the most important attribute in their choice processes among these brands of soft drinks.

The major contribution of the Rao & Sabavala [1981] methodology is that it provides an empirically driven mechanism for estimating (internally) hierarchical market structures from behavioral data. Unlike the Hendry approach, the researcher does not need to generate prior configurations of market structures to test in advance of examining the data. However, note that the Rao & Sabavala [1981] methodology is somewhat restrictive in that:

(a) the results would typically vary according to the specific type of hierarchical clustering utilized;

(b) none of these hierarchical clustering methods has least-squares properties with the input data;

(c) only half of the $\boldsymbol{F}$ matrix is utilized in these analyses and the asymmetry of $\boldsymbol{F}$ is ignored;

(d) the ultrametric inequality places rather strict constraints on the nature of inter- and intra-cluster distances;

(e) the methodology must be run separately for each market segment; and,

(f) while the choice process is specified as stochastic, a deterministic model (hierarchical clustering) is utilized with no specific parametric form specified on e_{ij} in Equation (2).

Given these restrictions, we now choose to review recent developments in the psychometric literature that have been employed in this market-structure context and have addressed some of these limitations.

2.2.2. Ultrametric tree-fitting methods

The fact that different hierarchical clustering procedures usually lead to different tree structure has been well documented in the classification literature [cf. Hartigan, 1975]. And, for utilization in market structure analysis, there is little or no theory to guide one as to a particular hierarchical clustering procedure. In addition to this 'uniqueness-of-representation' problem, most of the available hierarchical clustering methods, with the possible exception of Ward's [1963] method, are mere heuristics for forming such partitions. There is no clear objective function that is being optimized; no attempt, for example, to provide a least-squares fit to the data. In this light, we review some recent approaches for the least-squares fitting of a unique ultrametric tree to a specified matrix of proximity data (e.g. $\boldsymbol{F}$). (Note, similarities can easily be converted to dissimilarities by the simple device of inverting the scale by, for example, subtracting all values from the largest value.)

Recall, that an ultrametric tree is a rooted tree in which a non-negative weight is attached to each node such that (a) the terminal nodes have zero weight, (b) the root has the largest weight, and (c) the weights attached to the nodes on the path from any terminal node to the root constitute a strictly increasing sequence. The distance between two nodes i and j, denoted d_{ij}, is defined as the maximum of the weights associated with the nodes on the path connecting i and j. It is easy to show that these distances satisfy the ultrametric inequality:

$$d_{ij} \leqslant \max(d_{ik}, d_{jk}) \tag{4}$$

for all i, j, k.

Ultrametric trees are useful for representing dissimilarity data, mainly because they define a hierarchical clustering on the object set. If $\boldsymbol{\Delta} = ((\delta_{ij}))$ be a square symmetric matrix containing the pairwise non-negative dissimilarities between n brands, then an ultrametric tree τ is a representation of $\boldsymbol{\Delta}$ whenever its terminal nodes correspond in a one-to-one fashion with the N brands, *and* whenever for each pair of brands (i,j), d_{ij}, the ultrametric distance between the two nodes corresponding to i and j, approximately equals δ_{ij}. If $d_{ij} = \delta_{ij}$ for all (i, j), then τ constitutes an exact ultrametric tree representation of $\boldsymbol{\Delta}$.

Hartigan [1967], Jardine, Jardine & Sibson [1967] and Johnson [1967] all show that a necessary and sufficient condition for the existence of an exact ultrametric tree representation is the ultrametric inequality. That is, if $\boldsymbol{\Delta}$ satisfies

$$\delta_{ij} \leqslant \max(\delta_{ik}, \delta_{jk})$$

for all i, j, k, an exact ultrametric tree representation can be constructed. Moreover, this exact representation is unique.

Unfortunately, real dissimilarity data almost never perfectly satisfy this property. Therefore, a number of psychometricians have proposed methodologies which construct a 'best fitting' ultrametric tree representation of a given dissimilarity matrix. Such an ultrametric tree representation can be constructed by minimizing the following least-squares loss function:

$$L(D) = \sum_{i<j}^{N}\sum (\delta_{ij} - d_{ij})^2. \tag{5}$$

Hartigan [1967] attempts to minimize (5) by performing a number of local operations on a tree. Chandon, Lemaire & Ponget [1980] develop a branch-and-bound algorithm which, for a given $\boldsymbol{\Delta}$, finds an ultrametric tree representation that minimizes (5) globally. Due to their combinatorial nature, however, these algorithms can only be applied to very small data sets ($n \leqslant 10$). A different approach was suggested by Carroll & Pruzansky [1975, 1980] who presented a mathematical-programming procedure for minimizing (5) which we describe in detail below.

Given a data matrix $\boldsymbol{\Delta} \equiv ((\delta_{ij}))$, of dissimilarities (distances measured up to at least an interval scale), we wish to approximate that matrix, in a least-squares sense, by a matrix $\boldsymbol{D} = ((d_{ij}))$ satisfying the ultrametric inequality. We shall assume, here and elsewhere, that $\boldsymbol{\Delta}$ is symmetric and that its diagonals are undefined, so we may deal, in effect, with only an upper- (or lower-) triangular half-matrix. The Carroll & Pruzansky [1975, 1980] approach is to attempt to minimize $|\boldsymbol{D} - \boldsymbol{\Delta}|^2$ with the constraints mentioned, by use of a *penalty function* approach. In this approach, they use an iterative procedure known as the method of gradients or steepest descent to minimize $\alpha|\boldsymbol{D} - \boldsymbol{\Delta}|^2 + \beta P(\boldsymbol{D})$, where $\alpha, \beta \geqslant 0$ and $\alpha + \beta = 1$. Here $P(\boldsymbol{D})$ is a function of $\boldsymbol{D}$ which measures the degree of departure of $\boldsymbol{D}$ from satisfaction of the ultrametric inequality. Typically, Carroll & Pruzansky [1975, 1980] initialize $\alpha = 2\beta$, continue the gradient-method minimization procedure to convergence, then increase β relative to α, continuing this process of increasing β until the constraints are satisfied (within some criterial tolerance level). They then set $\alpha = 0$, $\beta = 1$, as a final step, to assure that the constraints are perfectly satisfied. $P(\boldsymbol{D})$ which is the function measuring departure from the ultrametric inequality, is defined as

$$P(\boldsymbol{D}) = c/v, \tag{6}$$

where

$$c = \sum_{i}\sum_{\substack{j \\ i<k \\ j\neq i,k}}\sum_{k}^{N} w_{ik}^{j}(d_{ij} - d_{jk})^2, \tag{7}$$

$$w_{ik}^{j} = \begin{cases} 1 & \text{if } d_{ik} \leqslant \min(d_{ij}, d_{jk}), \\ 0 & \text{otherwise.} \end{cases} \tag{8}$$

$$v = \sum_{i<j}^{N} (d_{ij} - \bar{d})^2, \tag{9}$$

$$\bar{d} = \frac{2}{n(n-1)} \sum_{i<j}^{N}\sum d_{ij}. \tag{10}$$

Here, $P(\boldsymbol{D})$ simply sums the squares of differences between pairs of distances that should be equal if the ultrametric inequality were perfectly satisfied (namely the differences between the two largest sides of every triangle) and divides this sum of squared discrepancies by a normalizing factor (proportional to the variance of the $d'\bar{s}$). Note that $P(\boldsymbol{D})$ is so defined as to be invariant under any *positive* linear transformation of $\boldsymbol{D}$ (i.e., addition of a constant and/or multiplication by a positive constant). This means, in particular, that the positivity condition on distances is not enforced. In effect, this automatically allows for estimation of an additive constant.

Given $\boldsymbol{\Delta}$, Carroll & Pruzansky [1975, 1980] define the overall loss function $L(\alpha, \beta, \boldsymbol{D})$ as:

$$L(\alpha, \beta, \boldsymbol{D}) = \alpha\frac{a}{b} + \beta\frac{c}{v}, \tag{11}$$

where α, β, c and v are as previously defined, while

$$a = |\boldsymbol{D} - \boldsymbol{\Delta}|^2 \equiv \sum_{i<j}^{N}\sum (d_{ij} - \delta_{ij})^2, \tag{12}$$

$$b = |\boldsymbol{\Delta} - \bar{\boldsymbol{\Delta}}|^2 = \sum_{i<j}^{N}\sum (\delta_{ij} - \bar{\delta})^2, \tag{13}$$

$$\bar{\delta} = \frac{2}{n(n-1)} \sum_{i<j}^{N}\sum \delta_{ij}. \tag{14}$$

Given the definition of $L(\alpha, \beta, \boldsymbol{D})$ for specified values of α and β, which we shall simply refer to as L below, the gradient of L, ∇L, with respect to elements of $\boldsymbol{D}$, can be specified as

$$\nabla L_{ij} \equiv \frac{\partial L}{\partial d_{ij}} = \frac{\alpha}{b}\left(\frac{\partial a}{\partial d_{ij}}\right) + \beta\left(\frac{v\dfrac{\partial c}{\partial d_{ij}} - c\dfrac{\partial v}{\partial d_{ij}}}{v^2}\right), \tag{15}$$

where

$$\frac{\partial a}{\partial d_{ij}} = 2(d_{ij} - \delta_{ij}), \tag{16}$$

$$\frac{\partial c}{\partial d_{ij}} = 2\sum_k [(w^j_{ik} + w^i_{jk})d_{ij} - w^j_{ik}d_{jk} - w^i_{jk}d_{ik}], \tag{17}$$

$$\frac{\partial v}{\partial d_{ij}} = 2(d_{ij} - \bar{d}). \tag{18}$$

An external-penalty-function method [cf. Rao, 1984] is employed where steepest-descent-gradient search is utilized to iteratively estimate the d_{ij} which come as close to the data (δ_{ij}) as possible, but satisfy the ultrametric inequality.

De Soete [1984] has modified this Carroll & Pruzansky [1975, 1980] methodology by using a computationally more efficient penalty function, adopting an exact sequential unconstrained minimization technique (SUMT), and applying a numerically more stable nonlinear minimization method for solving the unconstrained subproblem. De Soete's [1984] methodology also attempts to minimize (5) subject to all i, j, k triples of distances satisfying (4). Adopting a sequential unconstrained minimization technique, this constrained minimization problem can be transformed into a series of unconstrained minimization problems by sequentially minimizing the augmented function:

$$\Phi(\boldsymbol{D},\rho) = L(\boldsymbol{D}) + \rho P(\boldsymbol{D}) \quad (\rho > 0), \tag{19}$$

for an increasing sequence of values of ρ. The $\Phi(\boldsymbol{D},\rho)$ is a linear combination of the loss function $L(\boldsymbol{D})$ and a penalty function $P(\boldsymbol{D})$ which enforces the ultrametric inequality of $\boldsymbol{D}$. And $P(\boldsymbol{D})$ is defined as

$$P(\boldsymbol{D}) = \sum_{\Omega} (d_{ik} - d_{jk})^2, \tag{20}$$

with

$$\Omega = \{(i,j,k) \mid d_{ij} \leqslant \min(d_{ik}, d_{jk}) \text{ and } d_{ik} \neq d_{jk}\}. \tag{21}$$

That is, Ω is the set of ordered triples for which $\boldsymbol{D}$ violates the ultrametric inequality.

Using r as the iteration index, the exact penalty-function algorithm for solving this can be described as follows:

(i) Initialize r: $r = 1$. Determine $\boldsymbol{D}^{(0)}$, the initial estimate of $\boldsymbol{D}$. Define $\rho^{(1)} = L(\boldsymbol{D}^{(0)})/P(\boldsymbol{D}^{(0)})$.

(ii) Minimize $\Phi(\boldsymbol{D}, \rho^{(r)})$ starting from $\boldsymbol{D}^{(r-1)}$ to obtain $\boldsymbol{D}^{(r)}$.

(iii) Test for convergence: if

$$\sum_{i<j}^{N}\sum (d^{(r)}_{ij} - d^{(r-1)}_{ij})^2 \tag{22}$$

is less than some small constant stop, otherwise continue.

(iv) Update ρ: $\rho^{(r+1)} = 10 \times \rho^{(r)}$. Increment r by one and go back to step (ii).

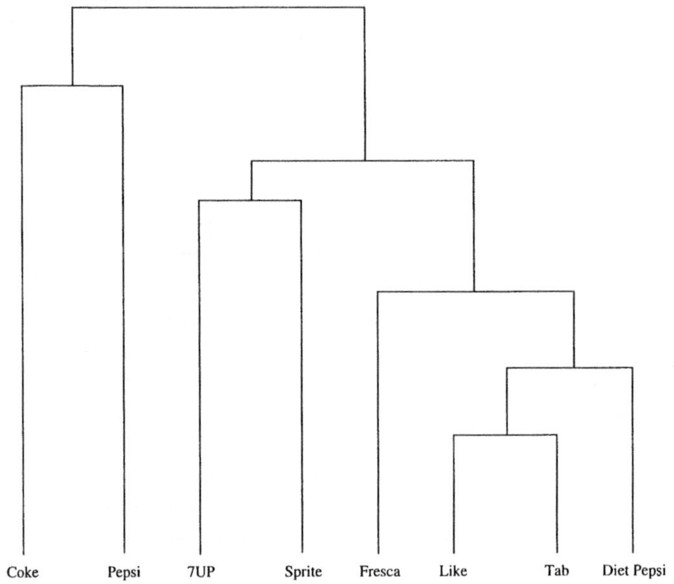

Fig. 5.4. Ultrametric tree representation for the Bass, Pessemier & Lehmann [1972] soft-drink brand-switching data (taken from DeSarbo, Manrai & Burke [1990]).

The initial value of ρ is determined in such a way that the two components of $\Phi(\boldsymbol{D}, \rho)$ have initially an equal contribution. De Soete [1984] uses Powell's [1977] conjugate gradient procedure with automatic restarts. This method has been successfully applied to nonlinear optimization problems involving a large number of unknowns [cf. Dixon, 1980]. According to De Soete [1984], convergence usually occurs within five to six major iterations.

DeSarbo, Manrai & Burke [1990] apply a modification of the Carroll & Pruzansky [1975, 1980] and De Soete [1984] procedure to the flow matrix ($\boldsymbol{F}$) derived from the soft-drink switching data in Table 5.2. Figure 5.4 presents the estimated ultrametric tree which accounts for 73.9% of the variance of $\boldsymbol{F}$ derived from Table 5.2. Indeed, a rather different portrayal of market structure is seen as compared to Figure 5.3. Here, the four diet drinks appear to form a fairly compact group. To the left of this group is the non-diet, lemon–lime group with 7-Up and Sprite. And, to its left is the non-diet, cola group with Coke and Pepsi. The tree here indicates that switching tends to occur predominantly within these three major groups. That is, these 280 consumers are most likely to switch between Coke and Pepsi, between 7-Up and Sprite, or between the four diet drinks: Fresca, Like, Tab and Diet Pepsi. Thus, ultrametric representations of market structure can be generated to 'best-fit' a given set of input data, and a corresponding measure of goodness-of-fit can be generated to examine how restrictive these ultrametric inequality constraints are with respect to a given set of proximity data.

2.2.3. *Additive tree-fitting methods*

Thus far, we have presented hierarchical structures for representing market structures based primarily on theoretical notions of how consumers process attributes in their decision-making or choice judgments. As witnessed in the previous section, this hierarchical structure imposes rather strict inequality constraints in the estimation of either hierarchical clustering solutions or least-squares optimal ultrametric trees (vis-à-vis satisfaction of the ultrametric inequality). The ultrametric inequality implies that given two disjoint clusters, all intra-cluster distances are smaller than all inter-cluster distances, and that all the inter-cluster distances are equal. Distance between brands in such a representation is defined as the heights of their 'lowest common ancestor' node, i.e., the first internal node at which the two brands meet as one proceeds up the hierarchical tree.

Consider the synthetic proximity matrix presented in Panel A of Figure 5.5 between four brands: A, B, C and D. The corresponding hierarchical clustering solution to this data is shown in Panel B. According to this hierarchical tree, brand D should be equally distant from the other three brands A, B and C. Yet, the column of data under D in Panel A clearly demonstrates that this is not the case.

Brand:		B	C	D
	A	5.1	5.7	7.3
Brand:	B		4.7	5.8
	C			5.0

Panel A: Synthetic Dissimilarities for Four Brands

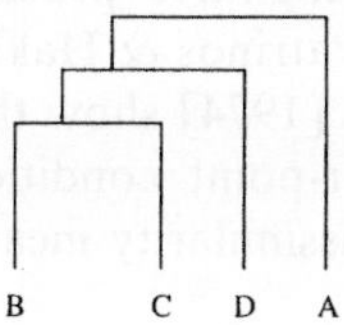

Panel B: Hierarchical Clustering Representation

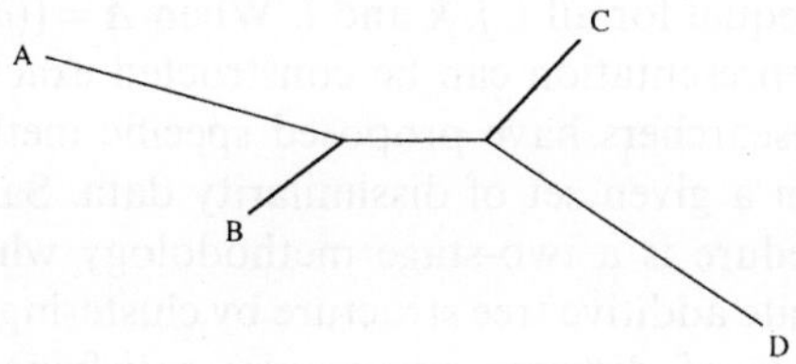

Panel C: Additive Tree Representation

Fig. 5.5. Ultrametric vs. additive tree representations.

Several psychologists have found that empirical proximity data is often not well represented by such hierarchical structures due to these severe constraints placed on the data [cf. Carroll & Chang, 1973; Carroll, 1976; Cunningham, 1978; Sattah & Tversky, 1977; Holman, 1972; De Soete, 1983a, 1983b].

Such limitations of hierarchical structures have led several researchers to explore more general structures called additive trees (also called weighted trees, free trees, path-length trees, or unrooted trees). Panel C of Figure 5.5 displays a fitted additive tree to the synthetic dissimilarities presented in Panel A. Note that the clustering of brands obtained in Panels B and C appear different. In addition, in an additive tree, unlike the hierarchical/ultrametric tree, intra-cluster distances may exceed inter-cluster distances. For example, in Panel C, brands B and C belong to different clusters although they are the two closest brands. In an additive tree, a non-negative weight is attached to each link such that the distance between any pair of nodes is the sum of the weights associated with the links that connect the two nodes. Unlike an ultrametric tree which has a natural 'root' node (typically the topmost node where all branches connect), an additive tree has no unique root, and it is not necessary to think of it as being vertically organized into a tree; a brand outside a cluster is not necessarily equidistant from all brands inside the cluster as in an ultrametric tree. For example, in Panel C, brands C and D are both closer to B than to A. Thus, the differences between these two representations stem from the fact that the external nodes are all equally distant from the root in an ultrametric tree, but not necessarily so for an additive tree. This greater flexibility of the additive tree often permits a better representation of the input data. (Note that an additive tree with a distinguished root node which is equidistant from all external nodes is an ultrametric tree. Thus, an ultrametric tree is a special case of the more general additive tree).

Many psychometricians have examined the formal properties of such additive trees and their role in representing cognitive processes [cf. Bunemann, 1974; Dobson, 1974; Hakimi & Yau, 1964; Patrinos & Hakimi, 1972; Turner & Kautz, 1970]. Bunemann [1974] and Dobson [1974] show that the following condition, called the additive inequality or four-point condition, is both necessary and sufficient for the representation of a dissimilarity measure by an additive tree:

$$\delta_{ij} + \delta_{kl} \leqslant \max(\delta_{ik} + \delta_{jl}, \delta_{il} + \delta_{jk}) \tag{23}$$

for all i, j, k and l, or equivalently, whenever the two longest of $(\delta_{ij} + \delta_{kl})$, $(\delta_{ik} + \delta_{jl})$ and $(\delta_{il} + \delta_{jk})$ are equal for all i, j, k and l. When $\boldsymbol{\Delta} = ((\delta_{ij}))$ satisfies (23) perfectly, an additive tree representation can be constructed exactly.

A number of researchers have proposed specific methodologies for estimating additive trees from a given set of dissimilarity data. Sattath & Tversky's [1977] ADDTREE procedure is a two-stage methodology which first attempts to find the most appropriate additive tree structure by clustering brands so as to maximize the number of sets of distance quadruples satisfying the additive inequality. Conditional on the additive-tree topology, regression is utilized to solve for the branch lengths. While the entire two-stage ADDTREE procedure is not totally 'least-squares' with respect to both additive tree structure and branch lengths, the procedure is quite efficient in accommodating larger-sized data sets.

Cunningham [1974, 1978] is the first attempt to use a least-squares criterion to find an additive tree. Cunningham [1978] presents a non-iterative algorithm meant to minimize:

$$L(D) = \sum_{i<j}^{N}\sum (\delta_{ij} - d_{ij})^2. \tag{24}$$

His procedure is based on the assumption that for all i, j, k and l, the optimal additive-tree distances (d_{ij}) satisfy

$$d_{ij} + d_{kl} \leqslant d_{ik} + d_{jl} \leqslant d_{il} + d_{jk}, \tag{25}$$

whenever

$$\delta_{ij} + \delta_{kl} \leqslant \delta_{ik} + \delta_{jl} \leqslant \delta_{il} + \delta_{jk}. \tag{26}$$

However, these conditions need not always hold, especially when the data contain much error. Thus, this linearly constrained procedure need not necessarily produce truly 'least-squares' additive-tree distances. In addition, several numerical problems have been known to occur with the procedure [cf. Carroll, Clark & DeSarbo, 1984].

Carroll & Pruzansky [1975, 1980] generalize their penalty function method to the estimation of additive trees. Farris [1972] and Hartigan [1975] show that, given an additive tree, it is possible to convert it into an ultrametric tree by a simple operation, given only that one knows distances from the root node to each of the nodes corresponding to objects. Letting d_{iR} represent the distance from the ith object to the root node and d_{ij} be the distance from i to j, it is easy to show that

$$\bar{d}_{ij} = d_{ij} - d_{iR} - d_{jR} \tag{27}$$

satisfies the ultrametric inequality; $\bar{d}_{ij}$, will not, however, satisfy the positivity condition for distances. This can be rectified easily, however, by adding a sufficiently large constant K, so that d^*_{ij}, defined as

$$d^*_{ij} = d_{ij} - d_{iR} - d_{jR} + K \equiv d_{ij} - c_i - c_j, \tag{28}$$

where $c_i = d_{iR} - K/2$, will satisfy both the ultrametric inequality *and* positivity.

An equivalent statement is that

$$d_{ij} = d^*_{ij} + c_i + c_j, \tag{29}$$

which states that the matrix $\boldsymbol{D}$ is decomposable into a $\boldsymbol{D}^*$ that satisfies the ultrametric inequality plus an additive residual, which we shall simply call $\boldsymbol{C} \equiv \|c_i + c_j\|$ (with the understanding that diagonals of $\boldsymbol{C}$ are undefined, or zero if defined). Thus,

$$\boldsymbol{\Delta} = \boldsymbol{D} + \boldsymbol{E}, \tag{30}$$

where $\boldsymbol{D}$ is an additive distance matrix and $\boldsymbol{E}$ is error, and

$$\boldsymbol{D} = \boldsymbol{D}^* + \boldsymbol{C}, \tag{31}$$

where $\boldsymbol{D}^*$ satisfies the ultrametric in equality and $\boldsymbol{C} \equiv \| c_i + c_j \|$. Thus

$$\boldsymbol{\Delta} = \boldsymbol{D}^* + \boldsymbol{C} + \boldsymbol{E}. \tag{32}$$

Since $\boldsymbol{D}^*$ is an ultrametric distance matrix, Carroll & Pruzansky [1975, 1980] fit an additive tree by simply adding an additional step to their penalty-function-based procedure described earlier, in which the constants c_i are estimated by least-squares procedures. That is, given an estimate of $\boldsymbol{D}^*$, define

$$\boldsymbol{\Delta}^{**} = \boldsymbol{\Delta} - \boldsymbol{D}^*, \tag{33}$$

and fit $\boldsymbol{\Delta}^{**}$ by $\hat{\boldsymbol{C}} \equiv \| \hat{c}_i + \hat{c}_j \|$ such that $|\boldsymbol{\Delta}^{**} - \hat{\boldsymbol{C}}|^2$ is minimized. The solution is

$$\hat{c}_i = \frac{1}{N-2} \sum_{j \neq 1}^{N} \delta_{ij} - \frac{1}{(N-1)(N-2)} \sum_{j<l}^{N}\sum \delta_{jl}. \tag{34}$$

Finally, De Soete [1983a, 1983b] generalizes his penalty-function approach to fitting an ultrametric tree to fitting additive trees using the additive inequality condition explicitly in attempting to minimize Equation (24). In order to simplify the notation, it is assumed that the data are normalized such that

$$\sum_{i<j}^{N}\sum (\delta_{ij} - \bar{\delta})^2 = 1, \tag{35}$$

where $\bar{\delta}$ is defined as in (14). De Soete [1983a, 1983b] wants to find a set of distances $\boldsymbol{D}$ which are closest to the data in a least-squares sense and which satisfy the four-point condition perfectly. This constrained optimization problem is solved by sequentially minimizing the unconstrained function

$$F(\boldsymbol{D}, \rho) = L(\boldsymbol{D}) + \rho P(\boldsymbol{D}) \tag{36}$$

for an increasing sequence of values of ρ. The first component of $F(\boldsymbol{D}, \rho)$ is given in (24) and measures the departure from the data, while the second part, $P(\boldsymbol{D})$, is a penalty function that expresses how strongly $\boldsymbol{D}$ violates the additive inequality condition. $P(\boldsymbol{D})$ is defined as

$$P(\boldsymbol{D}) = \sum_{\Omega} (d_{ik} + d_{jl} - d_{il} - d_{jk})^2, \tag{37}$$

where

$$\Omega = \{(i, j, k, l) | i, j, k, l \text{ distinct and } d_{ij} + d_{kl} \leqslant \min(d_{ik} + d_{jl}, d_{il} + d_{jk})\}. \tag{38}$$

Using r as the iteration index, De Soete's [1983a, 1983b] algorithm for obtaining least-squares estimates for the additive distances can be summarized as follows:

(i) Initialize: $r = 1$,

$$\boldsymbol{D}^{(0)} = \{\delta_{ij} + \varepsilon_{ij} | i < j\}, \quad \text{where} \quad \varepsilon_{ij} \sim \mathrm{N}(0, \sigma_\varepsilon^2), \quad \rho^{(0)} = L(\boldsymbol{D}^{(0)})/P(\boldsymbol{D}^{(0)}).$$

(ii) Minimize $F(\boldsymbol{D}, \rho^{(r)})$ starting from $\boldsymbol{D}^{(r-1)}$ to obtain $\boldsymbol{D}^{(r)}$.

(iii) Test for convergence: If

$$\left[\sum_{i<j}^{N}\sum (d_{ij}^{(r)} - d_{ij}^{(r-1)})^2 \right]^{1/2} \tag{39}$$

is less than some small constant stop, otherwise continue.

(iv) Update ρ: $\rho^{(r+1)} = 10 \times \rho^{(r)}$.
Increment r and go back to step (ii).

De Soete [1983a, 1983b] uses Powell's [1977] conjugate gradient procedure with automatic restarts to minimize $F(\boldsymbol{D}, \rho^{(r)})$ in phase (ii). This method requires only the first-order partial derivatives of $F(\boldsymbol{D}, r)$ with respect to the elements in $\boldsymbol{D}$:

$$\frac{\partial F}{\partial d_{st}} = -2(\delta_{st} - d_{st}) + 2\rho \sum_{\Omega} \{(e_{st,ik} + e_{st,jl} - e_{st,il} - e_{st,jk})(d_{ik} + d_{jl} - d_{il} - d_{jk})\}, \tag{40}$$

where the indicator variable $e_{st,ij}$ is defined by

$$e_{st,ij} = \begin{cases} 1 & \text{when } s = i \text{ and } t = j, \\ 0 & \text{otherwise.} \end{cases} \tag{41}$$

Once least-squares estimates of the additive distances are obtained by the procedure outlined above, the additive tree can be constructed in a straightforward way [cf. Cunningham, 1978; Dobson, 1974]. Novak [1991] has recently generalized these approaches with his 'log-linear tree' formulation for estimating market structures from brand-switching data.

Figure 5.6 portrays the rooted additive tree estimated for the soft-drink switching data, $\boldsymbol{F}$, from use of the Sattath & Tversky [1977] ADDTREE procedure. The resulting additive tree is somewhat similar to the fitted ultrametric tree presented in Figure 5.4. Diet versus non-diet is the major attribute which impacts switching behavior, with cola versus non-cola distinctions secondary. Here,

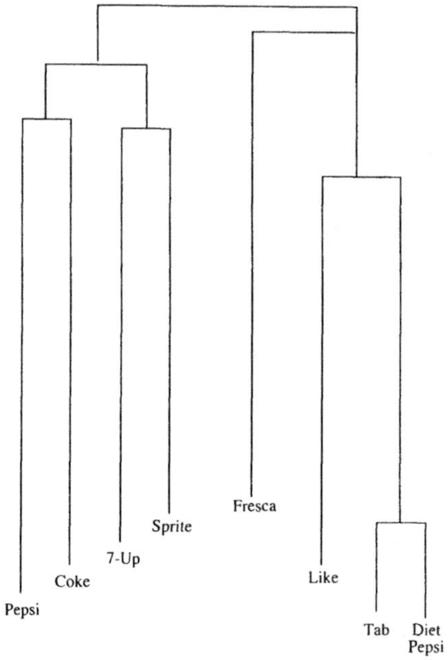

Fig. 5.6. Additive tree representation of the soft-drink $\boldsymbol{F}$ matrix for the Bass, Pessemier & Lehmann [1972] soft-drink brand-switching data.

however, the non-diet, lemon–lime soft drinks (7-Up and Sprite) are represented closer to the non-diet colas (Coke and Pepsi) than to the diet soft drinks, unlike in the ultrametric tree where the reverse was represented. Note that this additive tree accounts for 85.1% of the variance in $\boldsymbol{F}$, 11.4% more than the ultrametric tree in Figure 5.4.

2.2.4. Generalizations and extensions

Rao & Sabavala [1981] suggest performing a hierarchical clustering methodology by market segment in case different hierarchical choice processes were evident by market segment. Unfortunately, such switching matrices may not be available by market segment, or the appropriate market-segmentation scheme may not be precisely known. Here, application of the Carroll & Pruzansky [1975, 1980] multiple-tree-structures procedure may be beneficial. Carroll & Pruzansky [1980] attempt to fit $\boldsymbol{\Delta}$ (or $\boldsymbol{F}$ in our context) with a number of hierarchical tree structures:

$$\boldsymbol{\Delta} = \boldsymbol{D}_1 + \boldsymbol{D}_2 + \cdots + \boldsymbol{D}_m + \boldsymbol{E}, \tag{42}$$

where each $\boldsymbol{D}_i$ satisfies the ultrametric inequality. They use the penalty-function procedure described in Section 3.2.2 as a component of this (to fit a least-squares $\boldsymbol{D}$ to any $\boldsymbol{\Delta}^*$) and use an *overall alternating least-squares* (ALS) strategy to fit the mixture of tree structures. In particular, given current fixed estimates of all $\boldsymbol{D}$

matrices *except* $\boldsymbol{D}_k$, they define

$$\boldsymbol{\Delta}_k^* = \boldsymbol{\Delta} - \sum_{r \neq k} \hat{\boldsymbol{D}}_r, \tag{43}$$

and use the penalty-function procedure to find a least-squares estimate, $\hat{\boldsymbol{D}}_k$, of $\boldsymbol{\Delta}_k$. Concretely, $\hat{\boldsymbol{D}}_k$ is the output of this penalty-function procedure with $\boldsymbol{\Delta}_k^*$ as input. Assuming this procedure converges to the global minimum, this will result in an exact least-squares solution for $\hat{\boldsymbol{D}}_k$ with the other matrices fixed. As with all ALS (sometimes called, after Wold [1966], NILES or NIPALS) procedures, this methodology continues going around this iterative loop (estimating all $\hat{\boldsymbol{D}}_i$) until convergence occurs. The convergence criterion for this procedure is that $\sum_r^m |\hat{\boldsymbol{D}}_r^T - \hat{\boldsymbol{D}}_r^{T-1}|^2$ be less than some criterial value, where $\hat{\boldsymbol{D}}_r^T$ refers to the Tth estimate of the matrix $\boldsymbol{D}_r$. Carroll & Pruzansky [1980] also generalizes this approach to the fitting of multiple additive trees and 'hybrid' models which combine both tree(s) and a multidimensional scaling space.

If, in fact, the market segments were known and such $\boldsymbol{\Delta}$ (or $\boldsymbol{F}$) matrices could be obtained by segment, the Carroll, Clark & DeSarbo [1984] INDTREES methodology can be utilized for such three-way data. This INDTREES methodology posits a common tree topology for all market segments, but allows the different market segments to have different node heights and/or branch lengths. This provides a 'common thread' through the market segment analyses as opposed to performing separate analyses for each market segment where no communalities are posited.

Let

δ_{ijl} = the input dissimilarity between brands i and j in the lth market segment;
d_{ijl} = the reconstructured dissimilarity (distance) between brand i and j in the lth market segment;
e_{ijl} = the error $(\delta_{ijl} - d_{ijl})$ term for i and j in the lth segment;
$i, j = 1, \ldots, N$ brands;
$l = 1, \ldots, L$ market segment.

Then, the INDTREES model [Carroll, Clark & DeSarbo, 1984] can be simply stated as

$$\delta_{ijl} = d_{ijl} + e_{ijl}, \tag{44}$$

where one wishes to estimate the d_{ijl} which satisfy certain specific constraints depending upon the type and number of trees to be fitted. The INDTREES methodology can fit single or multiple ultrametric or additive trees. We will discuss the fitting of a single ultrametric tree to three-way proximity data because this phase is essential to all other types of trees that can be fitted in INDTREES. It is desired to estimate d_{ijl} to 'best-fit' the δ_{ijl}, and yet satisfy the three-way ultrametric inequality:

$$d_{ijl} \leqslant \max(d_{ikl}, d_{jkl}) \quad \text{for all } i, j, k, l. \tag{45}$$

That is, one estimates one general tree topology for L slices of the input data, but allows different node heights and/or branch lengths for each slice (segment). This can be translated into a constrained optimization problem where one attempts to estimate d_{ijl} in order to minimize

$$T = \sum_{l=1}^{L} \sum_{i<j}^{N}\sum [\delta_{ijl} - d_{ijl}]^2, \tag{46}$$

subject to satisfying the ultrametric inequality constraints in Expression (45). Note that an equivalent statement of the ultrametric inequality in Expression (45) is that all triangles formed by connecting all possible triples of points (d_{ijl}) are acute isosceles. This property can be restated as

$$d_{ikl} \geqslant d_{jkl} \geqslant d_{ijl} \quad \text{iff} \quad d_{ikl} = d_{jkl} \text{ for all } i, j, k, l. \tag{47}$$

In INDTREES, the associated ultrametric trees all have the *same* topology. This is equivalent to requiring the same two pairs of distances of each triple (i, j, k) to be the longest two (and therefore to be equal) for all values of l. Carroll, Clark & DeSarbo [1984] re-express the ultrametric inequality constraints in Expression (47), as well as the requirement of a common topology, in a more convenient mathematical form via the following equality constraints:

$$P_1 = \sum_{l=1}^{L} \left[\sum_{i=1}^{N} \sum_{\substack{j=1 \\ i<k \\ j \neq i,k}}^{N} \sum_{k=1}^{N} w_{ik}^{j} (d_{ijl} - d_{jkl})^2 \right] = 0, \tag{48}$$

and

$$P_2 = \sum_{l=1}^{L} \left[\sum_{i=1}^{N} \sum_{\substack{j=1 \\ i<k \\ j \neq i,k}}^{N} \sum_{k=1}^{N} w_{ik}^{j} (((d_{ikl} - d_{ijl})_+)^2 + ((d_{ikl} - d_{jkl})_+)^2) \right] = 0, \tag{49}$$

where

$$w_{ik}^{j} = \begin{cases} 1 & \text{if } d_{ik\cdot} \leqslant \min(d_{ij\cdot}, d_{jk\cdot}) \\ 0 & \text{otherwise.} \end{cases}$$

$$d_{ij\cdot} = \frac{1}{L} \sum_{i=1}^{L} d_{ijl},$$

$$(\xi)_+ = \max\{0, \xi\}.$$

The equality constraints in Expression (48) force the two largest distances (on average) to be equal while the equality constraints in Expression (49) force the two largest (and therefore equal) distances to be the same for all values of l. Together, *both* Expressions (48) and (49) enforce the ultrametric inequality based on a single tree structure. Note that the indicator function w^j_{ik} is defined in terms of an average two-way squared distance matrix $((d_{ij\cdot}))$. This is just one way of defining the indicator function so as to move toward a 'consensus' or common tree structure. Both Expressions (48) and (49) also restrict the tree topology of each slice or segment to be the same (since the ultrametric inequality constraints are defined for all i, j, k and l) outside of differential branch lengths and node heights for different values of l. The authors present a proof that the conditions enforced by P_1 and P_2 are necessary and sufficient conditions for ultrametricity and topological equivalence of the L trees (segments).

Carroll, Clark & DeSarbo [1984] express the three-way ultrametric tree-fitting problem as a nonlinear equality-constrained optimization problem in attempting to minimize a sum-of-squares loss function (46) subject to the nonlinear equality constraints in (48) and (49). INDTREES utilizes an exterior-penalty-function approach [Rao, 1984] in order to produce an at-least local optimum (minimum) and feasible estimate of d_{ijl}. The optimization problem can thus be restated as:

$$\underset{d_{ijl}}{\text{minimize}} \quad Z = (A + B), \tag{50}$$

where

$$A = T/a, \tag{51}$$

$$a = \sum_{l=1}^{L} \sum_{i<j}^{N} \sum^{N} [\delta_{ijl} - \delta_{\cdot\cdot l}]^2, \tag{52}$$

$$\delta_{\cdot\cdot l} = \frac{2}{N(N-1)} \sum_{i<j}^{N} \sum^{N} \delta_{ijl}, \tag{53}$$

$$B = \lambda^{(r)} \left(\frac{P_1 + P_2}{b} \right), \tag{54}$$

$\lambda^{(r)}$ = a positive penalty parameter at iteration r,

$$b = \sum_{l=1}^{L} \sum_{i<j}^{N} \sum^{N} (d_{ijl} - d_{\cdot\cdot l})^2, \tag{55}$$

$$d_{\cdot\cdot l} = \frac{2}{N(N-1)} \sum_{i<j}^{N} \sum^{N} d_{ijl}. \tag{56}$$

The A term in Expression (50) represents a normalized sums of squares which, when minimized, attempts to provide estimates of d_{ijl} which are as 'close' as possible to the given data δ_{ijl}. Clearly, without constraints placed on d_{ijl}, one could drive this A-term to zero by making $d_{ijl} = \delta_{ijl}$, for all i, j, l. The B-term in Expression (50) designates the magnitude of the violation of the ultrametric inequality constraints incorporated in the analysis. The set effect of the B-term in Expression (50) is to increase Z in proportion to the amount by which the constraints in Expressions (48) and (49) are violated. There will be a penalty for violating the constraints, and the amount of the penalty will increase at a rate based on the amount of violation of the constraints. Carroll, Clark & DeSarbo [1984] employ a standard exterior-penalty-function algorithm using conjugate gradient search methods to estimate d_{ijl}.

Finally, DeSarbo, Manrai & Burke [1990] present a non-spatial operationalization of the Krumhansl [1978, 1982] distance–density model of similarity. This model assumes that the similarity between two brands i and j is a function of both the inter-point distance between brands i and j and the density of other brands in the regions surrounding brands i and j. Note, the various models considered thus far utilize metric distance functions that satisfy the three metric axioms:

1. Minimality: $\delta_{ab} \geqslant \delta_{aa} = 0$.
2. Symmetry: $\delta_{ab} = \delta_{ba}$.
3. Triangle inequality: $\delta_{ab} + \delta_{bc} \geqslant \delta_{ac}$.

However, Tversky [1977], Sjöberg [1972], Parducci [1965], Birnbaum [1974] and others provide empirical evidence demonstrating that some measures of similarity (e.g. identification probabilities in recognition experiments, errors of substitutions, and directional ratings of pairs of objects) violate one or more of these metric axioms. Krumhansl [1978] introduces the distance–density model of similarity which, as she demonstrates, can also account for many violations of these axioms of proximity. DeSarbo, Manrai & Burke [1990] operationalize it in a non-spatial context.

Let

$i, j = 1, \ldots, N$ brands in the set R;
$\delta_{ij} =$ the empirical/observed dissimilarity between brand i and j;
$\Delta = ((\delta_{ij}))$ where $\delta_{ij} \neq \delta_{ji}$ and $\delta_{ii} \neq 0$ in general;
$d_{ij} =$ the predicted ultrametric tree distance between brands i and j, where $d_{ij} = d_{ji}$ and $d_{ii} = 0$.

Then, we can write the 'full' Krumhansl model as

$$\delta_{ij} = d_{ij} + a_i \eta(i) + b_j \eta(j) + e_{ij}, \tag{57}$$

where

$\eta(h) = \sum_{\substack{p \in R \\ p \neq h}} \Psi_{ph}$, a measure of the density of brands around brand h;
$\Psi_{ph} = \max(0, r_h - d_{ph}) = (r_h - d_{ph})_+$;
$r_h =$ a threshold value for object h;
$a_i, b_j =$ multiplicative constants;
$e_{ij} =$ error.

DeSarbo, Manrai & Burke [1990] estimate a_i, b_j, r_h and d_{ij}, given Δ, where d_{ij} satisfies the ultrametric inequality, in order to

$$\text{minimize} \quad Z(a_i, b_j, r_h, d_{ij}) = \sum_i^N \sum_j [\delta_{ij} - \hat{\delta}_{ij}]^2 = \sum_i^N \sum_j e_{ij}^2 \tag{58}$$

$$\text{subject to} \quad d_{ij} \leqslant \max(d_{ik}, d_{jk}) \quad \text{for all } i, j, k, \tag{59}$$

where

$$\delta_{ij} = d_{ij} + a_i \eta(i) + b_j \eta(j). \tag{60}$$

Note that $\eta(h)$ must be greater than zero in order for these parameters to be estimable (e.g. the derivatives of Z with respect to $r(h)$ are undefined otherwise). A sequential unconstrained minimization technique [Fiacco & McCormick, 1968] which combines aspects of exterior and interior or barrier penalty functions is used for estimation where the estimation problem is transformed:

$$\text{minimize} \quad \Phi = Z(a_i, b_j, r_h, d_{ij}) + \lambda P(d_{ij}) - \mu G(r_h, d_{ij}), \tag{61}$$

where the first term on the right-hand side of (61) related to (58) allowing for the recovery of the δ_{ij}, the second term on the right-hand side of (61) is to ensure that the d_{ij} satisfy the ultrametric inequality, and the third term on the right-hand side of (61) ensures that $\eta(h) > 0$ so that the respective parameter derivatives exist. This is equivalent to a strict enforcement of the distance–density hypothesis for all stimuli, that is, $\eta(h) > 0$ for all h. Thus,

$$Z(a_i, b_j, r_h, d_{ij}) = \sum_i^N \sum_j e_{ij}^2, \tag{62}$$

$$P(d_{ij}) = \sum_i^{N-1} \sum_{\substack{j \\ i<j \\ j \neq i,k}}^{N} \sum_k^{N} w_{ik}^j (d_{ij} - d_{jk})^2, \tag{63}$$

$$w_{ik}^j = \begin{cases} 1 & \text{if } d_{ik} \leqslant \min(d_{ij}, d_{jk}), \\ 0 & \text{otherwise,} \end{cases} \tag{64}$$

$$G(r_h, d_{ij}) = \sum_{l=1}^N \log\left[(N-1) r_h - \sum_{\substack{p \in R \\ p \neq h}} d_{ph} + \varepsilon \right], \tag{65}$$

$\lambda > 0$, $\lambda \to \infty$ during iterations,
$\mu > 0$, $\mu \to 0$ during iterations,
$\varepsilon =$ a small positive constant (0.001).

Note how (65) operates to ensure $\eta(h) \geqslant 0$. Give the particular operating definition of density in (57):

$$\eta(h) = \sum_{\substack{p \in R \\ p \neq h}} \Psi_{ph} = \sum_{\substack{p \in R \\ p \neq h}} (r_h - d_{ph})_+, \tag{66}$$

for $\eta(h) > 0$; then expanding, one obtains

$$\sum_{\substack{p \in R \\ p \neq h}} r_h - \sum_{\substack{p \in R \\ p \neq h}} d_{ph} > 0, \tag{67}$$

or

$$(N-1)r_h - \sum_{\substack{p \in R \\ p \neq h}} d_{ph} > 0, \tag{68}$$

or, to accommodate the inequality constraint ($\eta(h) \geqslant 0$) in the SUMT estimation procedure:

$$(N-1)r_h - \sum_{\substack{p \in R \\ p \neq h}} d_{ph} + \varepsilon \geqslant 0, \tag{69}$$

where ε is the small positive constant. Note that this methodology can be utilized to fit an ordinary ultrametric tree ($a = b = r = 0$), a symmetric density model ($a = b$), or an asymmetric model with all parameters free to vary.

DeSarbo, Manrai & Burke [1990] report an analysis of the soft-drink switching data (***F***) reported throughout this chapter thus far. Table 5.3 presents the results of the three different models fitted to this data. As shown, there is an appreciable drop in the error sums of squares in moving from the ultrametric-only tree to the symmetric Krumhansl representation (the same ultrametric tree estimated in the $a = b = r = 0$ model was used in the two subsequent models). However, there is little difference between the Krumhansl symmetric and asymmetric models. This small difference is due to the small amounts of asymmetry relative to the high variance across the diagonal elements in the proximity matrix. The middle portion of Table 5.3 presents the estimated $a = b$ and threshold parameters, as well as the density constants ($\eta(h)$). The lower portion of the table lists the predicted ultrametric distances (d_{ij}) which can be compared to r to examine subsequent density contributions (note that $r > d_{ij}$). In particular, note how Tab and Like have a small predicted ultrametric distance producing a high density contribution. Note that an internal analysis for the symmetric Krumhansl model produced congruent results, where the correlation between the two sets of ultrametric distances was 0.989. Figure 5.4 is the estimated ultrametric tree discussed earlier. This tree was held fixed for the symmetric and asymmetric density models. The estimated density constants ($\eta(h)$) presented in Table 5.3 also reveal some interesting aspects of the

Table 5.3
Krumhansl model results for the Bass, Pessemier & Lehmann [1972] soft-drink brand-switching data (taken from DeSarbo, Manrai & Burke [1990])

Model	Error Sum of squares	V.A.F.
Ultrametric	1186.2	0.739
Symmetric	924.8	0.764
Asymmetric	874.3	0.780

Symmetric models results
$a = b = 0.034$
$r = 23.604$

Density constants: $\eta(h)$		
	Coke:	1.96
	7-Up:	17.05
	Tab:	45.50
	Like:	45.43
	Pepsi:	1.99
	Sprite:	17.05
	Diet Pepsi	33.98
	Fresca:	26.48

Predicted ultrametric tree distances

Soft drink:	Coke	7-Up	Tab	Like	Pepsi	Sprite	Diet Pepsi	Fresca
Coke	0							
7-Up	23.48	0						
Tab	23.48	20.79	0					
Like	23.48	20.79	1.56	0				
Pepsi	22.37	23.48	23.48	23.48	0			
Sprite	23.38	18.07	20.79	20.79	23.48	0		
Diet Pepsi	23.48	20.79	12.99	12.99	23.48	20.79	0	
Fresca	23.48	20.79	16.74	16.74	23.48	20.79	16.74	0

brand-switching data. The largest values are for the four diet sodas, while the smallest values are for Coke and Pepsi. These density constants can, in this context, be interpreted as 'penalties' for not achieving a distinctive market position. That is, brands with higher density constants are more likely to have brand share taken away from them by other brands. Note that the two market leaders, Coke and Pepsi, suffer the least here due to their dominant market position attained as a result perhaps of strong advertising and promotional activity. 7-Up and Sprite have intermediate values indicating that their market position is considerably stronger than the diet drinks, but not as dominant as Coke and Pepsi. It is interesting to note the close grouping of Tab and Like which, at the time of the study, were targeted primarily to a female audience (as were most other diet drinks). These two brands also possess the highest density constants indicating that they (as well as the other two diet drinks to a lesser extent) have not obtained a dominant, unique positioning in the marketplace. Consumers evidently must have perceived

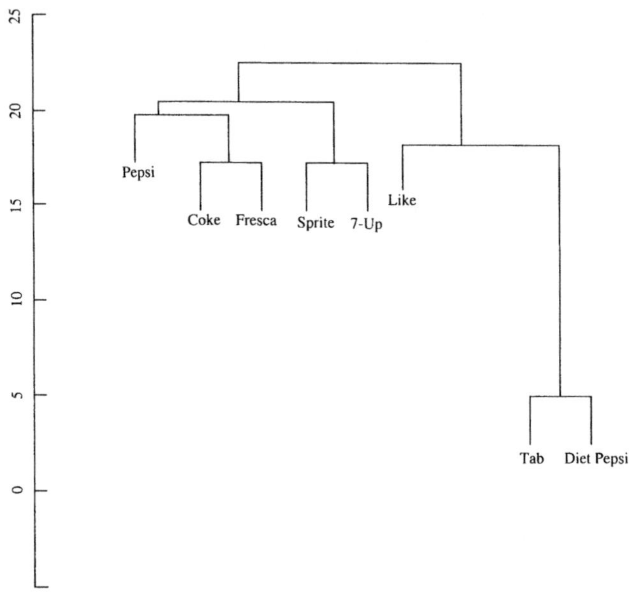

Fig. 5.7. Hierarchical clustering analysis of lower-triangular half of normalized Table 5.2 for the Bass, Pessemier & Lehmann [1972] soft-drink brand-switching data (taken from DeSarbo & De Soete, [1984]).

these four brands of diet drinks similarly (i.e. as diet drinks) and switched freely between them. Perhaps consumers were variety-seeking within a restricted set of brands that were perceived to have the same dominant characteristic (diet) and/or satisfy the same set of needs.

2.2.5. Asymmetric two-mode trees

An important aspect alluded to in the last section concerns asymmetry and its consideration in the various procedures dealt with thus far. In fact, only the DeSarbo, Manrai & Burke [1990] non-spatial operationalization of Krumhansl's [1978] distance–density model accommodates an analysis of a full brand-switching or flow matrix (as opposed to merely an upper- or lower-triangular half of such a matrix). Empirically speaking, brand-switching, for example, is often asymmetric and depending upon its extent, a consideration of only one half of $\boldsymbol{F}$ can lead to different non-spatial representations of market structure. For example, DeSarbo & De Soete [1984] perform the Rao & Sabavala [1981] analysis on the flow matrix ($\boldsymbol{F}$) calculated from the soft-drink switching data presented in Table 5.2. Figure 5.3 presents the derived hierarchical clustering results for the upper-triangular half of $\boldsymbol{F}$, while Figure 5.7 presents the derived hierarchical clustering results for the lower-triangular half of $\boldsymbol{F}$. As seen, somewhat different market-structure portrayals occur, especially concerning the location of Fresca, Diet Pepsi and Like. It appears that both triangular halves of $\boldsymbol{F}$ contain different information, and most of the techniques discussed thus far do not take into account the full information in the entire $\boldsymbol{F}$ matrix (including the main diagonals which reflect brand-loyalty).

One way to accommodate all the information in $\boldsymbol{F}$ is to portray both the row and column brands separately in the tree, i.e. a two-mode representation. Furnas [1980] examines the necessary and sufficient conditions for, and the resulting uniqueness of, such two-mode tree representations. As already mentioned, ultrametric distances (i.e. distances associated with ultrametric trees) must obey the ultrametric inequality: $d_{ij} \leqslant \max(d_{ik}, d_{jk})$. In the case of full or rectangular distance matrices, however, it is not possible to test the ultrametric inequality since one of the three distances will be missing for every triple. Furnas [1980] shows that, for rectangular matrices with a distance measure defined only between items of different classes (A, with elements represented by letters early in the alphabet and Z represented by letters late in the alphabet), the following two-class ultrametric inequality condition is necessary and sufficient for representation as an ultrametric tree:

$$t_{az} \leqslant \max(t_{ax}, t_{bx}, t_{bz}), \tag{70}$$

where t represents distances in the two-class ultrametric tree. When this inequality is satisfied, the representation is unique up to the internal structure of purely one-class subtrees. Necessary and sufficient conditions for unfolding path-length or additive trees are much more complicated (Furnas [1980] presents a bounded deterministic algorithm for this) and will not be given here. It suffices instead to note that overall distances in a path-length or additive tree can be decomposed into the sum of an ultrametric part and an additively decomposable part [see Carroll & Pruzansky, 1980] which can be represented by a 'star' or 'bush' tree (an additive tree having only one interior node). (The same is true for rectangular submatrices of distances from a path-length or additive tree, and the analytic techniques discussed here make use of this decomposition.)

Given Furnas's [1980] contribution, De Soete, DeSarbo, Furnas & Carroll [1984a, 1984b] develop exterior-penalty-function procedures for estimating either ultrametric or additive two-mode tree structures. For the ultrametric case, their procedure can be summarized as follows:

(a) Transform the data matrix $\boldsymbol{\Delta}$ into a matrix $\boldsymbol{T}$ best approximating $\boldsymbol{\Delta}$ in a least-squares sense, where $\boldsymbol{T}$ satisfies the two-class ultrametric inequality. An alternative statement of the two-class ultrametric inequality which can be shown to be equivalent to Expression (70) is that for every quadruple of points comprised of two from each class, the two largest of the four defined distances must be equal, i.e., given t_{il}, t_{ik}, t_{jl} and t_{jk} (the only four distances among i and j in class one and k and l in class two defined by the rectangular proximity data), the two largest of those four distances must be equal. This problem is reformulated by De Soete, DeSarbo, Furnas & Carroll [1984a, 1984b] as that of solving the optimization problem:

$$\min\left\{L(T) = \sum_{i=1}^{N} \sum_{k=1}^{M} (\delta_{ik} - t_{ik})^2\right\}, \tag{71}$$

subject to the condition that $\boldsymbol{T}$ satisfies the two-class ultrametric inequality. To do this, an exterior-penalty-function approach [Rao, 1984] is utilized to convert the constrained problem into a series of unconstrained ones. The augmented function

$$\Phi(\boldsymbol{T},\rho) = L(\boldsymbol{T}) + \rho P(\boldsymbol{T}), \tag{72}$$

with $\rho > 0$, is minimized for an increasing sequence of values of ρ, where the penalty part of Expression (72), $P(\boldsymbol{T})$, is defined as

$$P(\boldsymbol{T}) = \sum_{i=2}^{N}\sum_{j=1}^{i-1}\sum_{k=2}^{M}\sum_{l=1}^{k-1}(u_{ijkl} - v_{ijkl})^2, \tag{73}$$

where

$$u_{ijkl} = \max(t_{il}, t_{ik}, t_{jk}, t_{jl}), \tag{74}$$

and

$$v_{ijkl} = \begin{cases} \max(t_{il}, t_{jk}, t_{jl}) & \text{if } u_{ijkl} = t_{ik} \\ \max(t_{ik}, t_{jk}, t_{jl}) & \text{if } u_{ijkl} = t_{il} \\ \max(t_{il}, t_{ik}, t_{jl}) & \text{if } u_{ijkl} = t_{jk} \\ \max(t_{il}, t_{ik}, t_{jk}) & \text{if } u_{ijkl} = t_{jl}. \end{cases} \tag{75}$$

The specific steps of a penalty-function algorithm have already been discussed earlier.

(b) Construct a square $(N + M) \times (N + M)$ matrix $\boldsymbol{D}$ which satisfies the ordinary one-class ultrametric inequality. $\boldsymbol{D} = ((d_{ab}))$, for $a, b = 1,\ldots, N + M$, is symmetric ($d_{ab} = d_{ba}$) and is defined for $a \neq b$. Because of symmetry, we need only define d_{ab} for $a > b$. Now $\boldsymbol{D}$ can be thought of as the matrix having $\boldsymbol{T}$ as the $N \times M$ submatrix consisting of the last N rows and the first M columns. The problem is to fill in the (lower half of the symmetric) $M \times M$ and $N \times N$ submatrices comprising the first M rows and columns and the last N rows and columns respectively. This is accomplished by use of the following equations [Furnas, 1980]:

$$d_{ab} = \begin{cases} t_{(a-M)b} & \text{if } M+1 \leqslant a \leqslant M+N \\ & \quad \text{and } 1 \leqslant b \leqslant M, \\ \min\limits_{i=1,\ldots,N}[\max(t_{ia}, t_{ib})] & \text{if } 1 \leqslant a \leqslant M \\ & \quad \text{and } 1 \leqslant b \leqslant M, \\ \min\limits_{k=1,\ldots,M}[\max(t_{(a-M)k}, t_{(b-M)k})] & \text{if } M+1 \leqslant a \leqslant M+N \text{ and} \\ & \quad M+1 \leqslant b \leqslant M+N. \end{cases} \tag{76}$$

If necessary, a positive constant is added to the d_{ab} so that they satisfy the triangle inequality.

(c) Using standard hierarchical clustering methods [e.g. Johnson, 1967], the ultrametric tree representation of both row and column elements is obtained from $\boldsymbol{D}$.

For estimating an additive tree, as discussed in Carroll [1976], Carroll & Pruzansky [1980], Carroll, Clark & DeSarbo [1984], based on the work of Farris [1972] and Hartigan [1975], given an ultrametric tree, it is possible to convert it into an additive tree by adding a trivial 'star' or bush' tree (i.e. an additive tree having only one interior node) to it. The algorithm here is thus based on the fact that any set of path-length tree distances can be decomposed into a set of ultrametric distances plus a set of additive constants for each of the row and column elements. The numerical problem can be stated as

$$\text{minimize}\left\{L(\boldsymbol{T}, r_i, c_k) = \sum_{i=1}^{N}\sum_{k=1}^{M}(\delta_{ik} - t_{ik} - r_i - c_k)^2\right\}, \tag{77}$$

subject to the condition that $\boldsymbol{T}$ satisfies the two-class ultrametric inequality. Once $\boldsymbol{T}$ is estimated via the penalty-function algorithm, the additive constants are estimated in closed from via

$$\hat{r}_i = \frac{\sum_{k=1}^{M}(\delta_{ik} - t_{ik})}{M} - \frac{1}{2}\frac{\sum_{j=1}^{N}\sum_{k=1}^{M}(\delta_{jk} - t_{jk})}{NM},$$

$$\hat{c}_k = \frac{\sum_{i=1}^{N}(\delta_{ik} - t_{ik})}{N} - \frac{1}{2}\frac{\sum_{i=1}^{N}\sum_{l=1}^{M}(\delta_{il} - t_{il})}{NM}, \tag{78}$$

as generalized from Carroll & Pruzansky [1980]. Once the $\hat{r}_i$ and $\hat{c}_k$ constants are estimated, the algorithm cycles back to the ultrametric tree estimation phase in estimating $\boldsymbol{T}$; given, $\hat{r}_i$ and $\hat{c}_k$. This alternating least-squares procedure [Wold, 1966] continues cycling back and forth over these two major phases until convergence in the loss function and/or t_{ik} values is reached. Once the final estimates of $\boldsymbol{T}$ and the r_i and c_k are obtained, $\boldsymbol{D}$ is reconstructed from $\boldsymbol{T}$, and the appropriate additive constants are added. The additive tree is recovered from this tree [see Dobson, 1974] by defining the length of every branch to be the difference in height values of the two nodes connected by that branch (thus defining the heights of terminal nodes to be zero), and then adding the constants $\hat{r}_i$ and $\hat{c}_k$ to the lengths of the 'leaves' of the tree (branches connecting the terminal nodes to the first non-terminal or internal node).

DeSarbo & De Soete [1984] fit a two-mode ultrametric tree to the flow matrix ($\boldsymbol{F}$) derived from the data in Table 5.2. The resulting tree, shown in Figure 5.8, accounted for 89.1% of the variance in the *complete* $\boldsymbol{F}$ matrix. The brands underlined represent the row items (in period t) and the brands not underlined (in period $t+1$) represent the column items. Here too, we see a diet (Diet Pepsi, Tab, Like

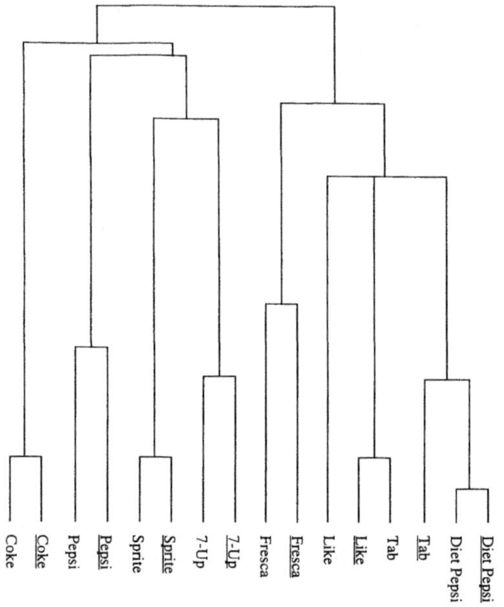

Fig. 5.8. Hierarchical tree estimated from the complete non-symmetric flow matrix for the Bass, Pessemier & Lehmann [1972] soft drink brand switching data (taken from DeSarbo & De Soete [1984]).

and Fresca) and non-diet (Sprite, Pepsi, 7-Up and Coke) market structure/choice process. But Figure 5.8 provides some interesting additional information. Note the variance of the heights at which the same row and column brands are joined together. For example, Diet Pepsi, Sprite and Coke join at relatively low heights, while Fresca, Like and Tab join at much greater heights. The height at which similar row and column brands join is inversely related to the degree of repeat-trial or brand-loyalty of the brand in the normalized transition matrix. For example, while Coke_t and Coke_{t+1} join at a low height (reflecting the large main diagonal element in the table), Tab_t and Tab_{t+1} join at a much greater height. Note that Tab_t and Like_{t+1} join at a very low height, indicating a strong propensity to switch from Tab in period t to Like in period $t+1$. Thus, the non-symmetric analysis in Figure 5.8 is an efficient way to display the structure in non-symmetric transition matrices without having to ignore over half of the data or having to average/smooth it.

2.2.6. Generalized network structures

Hierarchical and additive trees often provide parsimonious portrayals of market structure as demonstrated in the past five subsections of this review chapter. However, such approaches, being limited to trees, can lead to inadequate representations when the input judgmental or behavioral (proximity) data are better described by more general graphs such as grid or wheel patterns. While it is not obvious what particular choice process leads to such market structures, it may be desirable to consider alternative methods of representation such as network models which include ultrametric and additive trees as special cases, and allow for a more general class of network structures.

Corter & Tversky [1986] developed extended similarity trees (EXTREE) which generalize traditional additive trees by including marked segments that correspond to overlapping clusters. Extended trees can provide accurate representations of proximity data (e.g. $\boldsymbol{F}$) when such data are consistent with the distinctive features model of Restle [1959] where the distance between two brands, x and y, is a function of the attributes that are present in brand x and missing from brand y, and the attributes present in y but missing from x. The EXTREE algorithm first constructs an additive tree structure from the data via ADDTREE. In the second stage, the procedure estimates the weights of the marked features and selects a subset to be included in the model. The final stage consists of the simultaneous estimation of all parameters and the elimination of inconsequential features.

More recently, interest has arisen in the development of methods that yield representations of proximity data by means of the minimum-path-length metric for more general graphs than trees [cf., Feger & Bien, 1982; Feger & Droge, 1984; Orth, 1988; Klauer, 1989; Klauer & Carroll, 1989; Hutchinson, 1989]. Hutchinson [1989] proposes the NETSCAL procedure that represents non-symmetric proximity data as network distances. His algorithm determines which nodes are to be directly connected by an arc and estimates the lengths of each arc. The NETSCAL algorithm [Hutchinson, 1989] proceeds in two steps. The first step determines the links to be included in the directed network and is based on the Theorem 5.1 below [see Hutchinson, 1989, Corollary 1].

Theorem 5.1. *A link is called* redundant *if its deletion does not change the minimum-path-length distances, and networks that do not contain redundant links are called* irreducible. *Let G be an irreducible directed network with a positive minimum path-length distance d_G that is known at least ordinally. If a pair of objects* (x, y) *satisfies*

$$d_G(x, y) \leqslant \min\{\max[d_G(x, z), d_G(z, y)]: z \neq x, y\}, \tag{79}$$

then (x, y) *is a link of G.*

Using Hutchinson's [1989] ordinal criterion of Theorem 5.1 with raw data, the set of links of the representing network in NETSCAL is determined, completing the first phase. In the second step, link weights are derived. For this purpose, the raw data are first subjected to a linear transformation so that the highest proximity is set equal to zero and the lowest proximity equal to one, yielding normalized data values $\delta(x, y)$. The values $\delta(x, y)$ corresponding to links (x, y) determined in the first step, are then subjected to a generalized power transformation to yield link weights $\rho(x, y)$ [see Hutchinson, 1989, Equation (7)]:

$$\rho(x, y) = a + b[\gamma + \delta(x, y)]^{\lambda}. \tag{80}$$

With these link weights, the minimum-path-length distance can be determined and is given as a function of the coefficients a, b, γ and λ of the transformation function. Using an iterative direct search algorithm and linear regression, the coefficients are chosen to maximize goodness-of-fit, defined by a least-squares criterion [Hutchinson, 1989, p. 31]. Thus, NETSCAL has a non-metric first phase to determine network structure, and a metric second phase to determine the network distance.

While links identified through the use of the ordinal criterion of Theorem 5.1 must be non-redundant links of the irreducible network G, according to Klauer & Carroll [1991], the theorem is far from providing *sufficient* criteria for identifying the links of the irreducible network. Klauer [1989] provides stronger criteria such as the so-called 'necessary links criterion' that identify additional necessary links. Thus, even if the order of the network distances is known without errors, use of Hutchinson's [1989] criterion according to Klauer & Carroll [1991] is likely to miss links actually present in the underlying network, and therefore, to underestimate the number of links present in this network.

Klauer & Carroll [1989, 1991] discuss two methodologies for fitting directed graphs to symmetric and non-symmetric proximity data based on a penalty-function approach to impose additivity constraints upon parameters (the latter is termed MAPNET). For a user-specified number of links, MAPNET seeks to derive the connected network that renders the least-squares approximation of the proximity data with this specified number of links, allowing for linear transformations of the data. Note, it is well known that any non-symmetric distance function d satisfying the triangle inequality can be represented as the minimum-path-length metric of a directed and connected graph. For example, consider the network G^* that contains all possible links (x, y), $x, y \in E$, and set $t(x, y) = d(x, y)$. It follows that $d_{G^*} = d$. If only networks with smaller numbers of links are admitted, restrictions are imposed on the metrics that can be represented. It is possible, for example, to remove one link, if and only if there is a triple (x, y, z), $x \neq y$, $z \neq x$, $y \neq z$, such that $d(x,z) = d(x, y) + d(y,z)$. The distance $d(x,z)$ can then be expressed as the length of a path from x to z via y and the link (x,z) may therefore be removed without affecting the minimum-path-length metric. These observations can be generalized to the case where $M - L$ links are to be removed, or, equivalently, a network with L links is desired according to the Theorem 5.2 below which is due to Klauer & Carroll [1991]:

Theorem 5.2. *A positive function d satisfying the triangle inequality can be represented as the minimum-path-length distance of a connected and directed network G with L links, if and only if there are M − L distinct pairs of objects,* (x_i, z_i), *as well as third points* y_i *with* $x_i \neq y_i$, $z_i \neq x_i$, $y_i \neq z_i$, $i = 1, \ldots, L$ *such that* $d(x_i, z_i) = d(x_i, y_i) + d(y_i, z_i)$. *Thus, M − L links can be removed if M − L different triples can be found that satisfy the triangle inequality as an equality.*

The above theorem provides the basis for the MAPNET algorithm. In MAPNET, a loss function is minimized using a conjugate gradient algorithm [Powell, 1977] that is the weighted sum of an A-, B- and C-part. The A-part is simply a normalized measure of the sum of squared errors. Minimizing the A-part is equivalent to maximizing the variance accounted for. The B-part is designed to move the derived distances toward satisfying the triangle inequality and constitutes a classical continuous and differentiable penalty function for imposing inequality constraints [Ryan, 1974]. The C-part, finally, consists of a penalty function designed to push the derived distances to satisfy the condition specified in the theorem. These loss and penalty functions are straightforward extensions of corresponding functions discussed by Klauer & Carroll [1989] in the context of symmetric proximity data.

An EXTREE analysis of the $\boldsymbol{F}$ matrix for the soft-drink data is presented in Figure 5.9. This EXTREE representation accounts for 95% of the variance in $\boldsymbol{F}$. As observed in the figure, four distinct, overlapping feature sets are estimated: C, D, E and H. These estimated feature sets do not correspond to the diet versus non-diet, cola versus non-cola factorial nature underlying the eight brands, although the estimated tree structure does somewhat. The marked features in the tree (whose basic structure is quite similar to the ADDTREE solution presented earlier) provide an interesting way to model distinctive features. Here, for soft drinks sharing the same feature (e.g. C: Tab, Like, 7-Up), one would estimate distance between them as the ordinary sum of the path-lengths connecting them

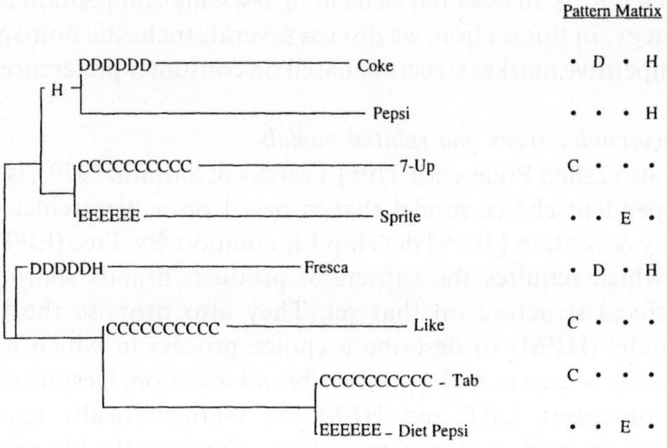

Final Set of Marked Features:

Feature	Brands Sharing Feature
C	[Tab, Like, 7-Up,]
D	[Coke, Fresca,]
E	[Sprite, Diet-Pepsi,]
H	[Coke, Pepsi, Fresca,]

Fig. 5.9. EXTREE representation of the soft-drink $\boldsymbol{F}$ matrix for the Bass, Pessemier & Lehmann [1972] soft-drink brand-switching matrix.

ignoring the marked C segments. However, for brands not sharing a common feature set, one would add the lengths of the respective marked segments to the path-length distances. The four feature sets estimated by EXTREE embellish the distinctive switching patterns for these eight brands of soft drinks discussed in previous analysis. For example, there is some propensity for Fresca drinkers to switch to Coke and Pepsi (and vice versa since this is a symmetric analysis by definition).

2.3. Stochastic models

The analysis of consumer preference and choice plays a major role in optimal product positioning, market segmentation, and competitive strategy formulation [Eliashberg & Manrai, 1992; Manrai & Manrai, 1992; Manrai & Sinha, 1989; Hauser & Shugan, 1983; Wind, 1982]. An examination of the empirical literature suggests that choice behavior is often inconsistent, hierarchical and context-dependent [Kahn, Moore & Glazer, 1987]. Luce [1959] and several others conceptualize choice as a probabilistic process and use the concept of choice probability as a basis of measurement of preference intensity. Furthermore, the choice probability depends not only on the values of alternatives but also on their similarity and comparability [Manrai & Sinha, 1989; Batsell & Polking, 1985; Currim, 1982; Tversky, 1972]. An analysis of structural relations among the alternatives, therefore, is an essential element of assessing competition and designing marketing strategy. In this section, we discuss several stochastic non-spatial models to estimate competitive market structure based on consumer preference and choice.

2.3.1. Preference/choice trees and related models

PRETREE, also called Preference Tree [Tversky & Sattath, 1979], is a probabilistic, context-dependent choice model that is based on a hierarchical elimination process. Tversky & Sattath [1979] develop Elimination-By-Tree (EBT) as a special case of EBA, which requires the subsets of products/brands sharing aspects to form a hierarchical structure on that set. They also propose the Hierarchical-Elimination model (HEM) to describe a choice process in which a prespecified elimination process is used to make product/brand selection. Despite the differences in the choice processes, EBT and HEM are mathematically equivalent, and therefore both are referred to as preference trees. Consider the hierarchical market structure presented in the hypothetical example described in Figure 5.1, Panel A; we now assume a set of utility values associated at each branch. We use the following simple notation. The utility is represented by U, and at any branch of the tree structure, it is subscripted by the first letter of the automobile category located at the node in the first level of the hierarchy (e.g. U_s for sporty automobiles and U_t for automobiles with the traditional body style); a second subscript is appended by using first letter of the automobile category located at the node in the second level of the hierarchy (e.g. U_{sa} for sporty American automobiles, U_{se} for sporty European automobiles, and U_{sj} for sporty Japanese automobiles). Finally, the first two letters of the automobile make are appended following a period for branches in the third level of the hierarchy. As an illustration, $U_{\mathrm{sa.co}}$ at a branch in the third level (e.g., at the bottom part of the tree structure) designates utility of Corvette which is an American sporty automobile. Using this notation, the probability of choosing a Corvette paired against a Cadillac as suggested by EBT or HEM is

$$P(\text{Corvette; Corvette, Cadillac}) = \frac{U_{\mathrm{s}} + U_{\mathrm{sa}} + U_{\mathrm{sa.co}}}{U_{\mathrm{s}} + U_{\mathrm{sa}} + U_{\mathrm{sa.co}} + U_{\mathrm{t}} + U_{\mathrm{ta}} + U_{\mathrm{ta.ca}}}. \tag{81}$$

PRETREE can be regarded as an intermediate model that is much less restrictive than Luce's [1959] constant-ratio model, since it is compatible with the similarity hypothesis; yet it is much more parsimonious than the general EBA model. This is because PRETREE has $2N - 2$ rather than the $2^N - 2$ parameters in EBA.

Tversky & Sattath [1979] apply this tree model to several sets of individual and aggregate choice probabilities to construct tree representation for these data, and test PRETREE against Luce's constant-ratio model (CRM). They show that the following trinary and quaternary conditions are necessary and sufficient for the representation of error-free data on binary choice probabilities as a preference tree. The trinary condition employs a probability ratio:

$$R(\text{Corvette, Cyclone}) = P(\text{Corvette; Corvette, Cyclone})/ P(\text{Cyclone; Corvette, Cyclone}), \tag{82}$$

and suggests the following inequality:

$$\text{If } R(\text{Corvette, Cyclone}) \geqslant 1, \text{ then}$$
$$R(\text{Corvette, Cyclone}) \geqslant R(\text{Corvette, Porsche})/R(\text{Cyclone, Porsche}) \geqslant 1. \tag{83}$$

The quaternary condition suggests the following relation among four alternatives; which asserts that the measure of preference for Corvette over Cyclone relative to Porsche and BMW is the same:

$$\frac{R(\text{Corvette, Porsche})}{R(\text{Cyclone, Porsche})} = \frac{R(\text{Corvette, BMW})}{R(\text{Cyclone, BMW})}. \tag{84}$$

However, for observed data which often contains error, Tversky & Sattath [1979] note that the construction of the most appropriate tree structure, the estimation of link lengths, and the evaluation of the adequacy of the tree model pose complex computational and statistical problems. In the data-analysis phase, Tversky & Sattath [1979] begin with the paired comparison choice data and a hypothesized tree structure, derived from a priori consideration or inferred from other data (e.g.

proximity data). They use Chandler's [1969] iterative program, STEPIT, to obtain maximum-likelihood estimates for both the CRM and PRETREE models, and compare the two models via a likelihood-ratio test. They also perform an estimate-free comparison of the two models by comparing the trinary inequality condition discussed in (83) above with the following product rule shown by Luce [1959] for three alternatives:

$$P(\text{Corvette; Corvette, Cyclone})\cdot P(\text{Cyclone; Cyclone, Porsche})\cdot P(\text{Porsche; Porsche, Corvette}) = P(\text{Corvette; Corvette, Porche})\cdot P(\text{Porsche; Porsche, Cyclone})\cdot P(\text{Cyclone; Cyclone, Corvette}), \quad (85)$$

that is,

$$R(\text{Corvette, Cyclone})\cdot R(\text{Cyclone, Porsche})\cdot R(\text{Porsche, Corvette}) = 1. \quad (86)$$

Tversky & Sattath [1979] analyze several data sets reported in the literature and examine the trinary inequality which provides an estimation-free comparison of CRM and PRETREE. They show that in all data sets, CRM is violated in the direction implied by the similarity hypothesis and the assumed tree structure. The statistical tests for the correspondence between models and data indicate that PRETREE offers an adequate account of the data that is significantly better than the account offered by CRM.

2.3.2. Estimation and extensions of preference trees

Moore, Pessemier & Lehmann [1986] proposes an alternative method for the estimation of a PRETREE structure obtained from paired comparison data. The authors estimate the utility measures associated with the branches and the overall fit of the model through the method of maximum likelihood. As discussed before (see Figure 5.1, Panel A and Equation (81)), one considers only the branches that directly link each brand to the node at which they are first joined. For expositional simplicity, consider Z_{ij} as the sum of the utility measures of the branches that directly link brand i (Corvette in our example) to the node at which i and j (Cadillac in our example) are first joined, then the probability of choosing i over j, P_{ij}, is:

$$P_{ij} = \frac{Z_{ij}}{Z_{ij} + Z_{ji}}. \quad (87)$$

Note that P_{ij} is the same as P(Corvette; Corvette, Cadillac) in Equation (81); whereas $Z_{ij} = U_s + U_{sa} + U_{sa.co}$ and $Z_{ji} = U_t + U_{ta} + U_{ta.ca}$. Using this notation, the authors construct the following likelihood function:

$$L = \prod_{i=1}^{M-1} \prod_{i>j}^{M} \left(\frac{Z_{ij}}{Z_{ij} + Z_{ji}}\right)^{n_{ij}} \left(\frac{Z_{ji}}{Z_{ij} + Z_{ji}}\right)^{n_{ji}}, \quad (88)$$

where M is the number of brands, n_{ij} is the number of times brand i is chosen over brand j (or the number of people who choose brand i over brand j), and the U's are the parameters to be estimated. The logarithm of the likelihood function is:

$$\operatorname{Ln} L = \sum_{i=1}^{M-1} \sum_{i>j}^{M} [n_{ij} \ln Z_{ij} + n_{ij} \ln Z_{ji} - (n_{ij} + n_{ji}) \ln (Z_{ij} + Z_{ji})]. \qquad (89)$$

The input data are the n_{ij}'s, the number of people choosing brand i over brand j. The values of U's that maximize the logarithm of this likelihood function are found through PAR, the derivative-free nonlinear estimation routine in BMDP [Dixon, 1980; Lee & Jennrich, 1984]. Moore, Pessemier & Lehmann [1986] point out three major drawbacks with conventional hierarchical clustering of similarity measures derived from aggregate brand-switching probabilities. These are: (a) the aggregate-level switching probabilities may not be representative of the majority of consumers, thereby leading to incorrect conclusions at the individual or segment level, (b) the choice process cannot be inferred from typical purchase data, and (c) a market structure yielded by the hierarchical clustering method is sometimes influenced largely by the brands with small market share. Using data from a study of cola soft-drinks, they show that PRETREE eliminates all three drawbacks.

Moore & Lehmann [1989] also present a method for estimating individual-level hierarchical structures using the nested-logit model [Dubin, 1986; McFadden, 1986; Maddala, 1983] with paired-comparison preference data. Let S_s and S_{sa} and S_t and S_{ta} represent the similarity or substitutability coefficients $0 \leqslant S. \leqslant 1$ as shown in Figure 5.1, Panel A, If an $S.$ is equal to one, the automobiles are no more substitutable outside than inside a partition, and $S.$ equal to zero implies that the automobiles are perfect substitutes for each other inside a partition when compared to automobiles outside the partition. Using the above-described notation, the ratio of the probability of choice of a Corvette paired against a Cadillac in the nested-logit approach is given by the following expression:

$$\operatorname{Ln}\left[\frac{P(\text{Corvette; Corvette, Cadillac})}{P(\text{Cadillac; Corvette, Cadillac})}\right] = S_s \cdot S_{sa} \cdot U_{sa.co} - S_t \cdot S_{ta} \cdot U_{ta.co}. \qquad (90)$$

The nested-logit approach due to Moore & Lehmann [1989] is attractive as it estimates individual-level market hierarchies in contrast to most applications in which the researcher estimates one decision tree for a sample or segment, then assumes this process holds for each consumer [e.g. Currim, 1982; Dubin, 1986; Urban, Johnson & Hauser, 1984]. It is more akin to Gensch & Svestka's [1984] Maximum Likelihood Hierarchical (MLH) model and Gensch's [1987] HIRACH, both of which estimate the parameters of a hierarchical elimination rule at the individual level. But MLH and HIRACH require measures of relative importance of product attributes to each consumer – something usually unavailable.

Moore & Lehmann [1989] estimate parameters of an individual preference structure by an alternating least-squares (ALS) procedure. The initial parameter estimates are formed like those in a two-step nested multinomial logit using constant-sum paired-comparison data. The lowest branches are estimated first, then they are used as input (i.e. inclusive values) to the regression at the next level of hierarchy. These initial estimates are improved through an ALS procedure. As in Tversky & Sattath [1979], where only the links directly connecting two brands are used, Moore & Lehmann [1989] treat inclusive values in paired comparisons as functions of only the two brands being compared. Consider our example in Figure 5.1, Panel A; in the first iteration, the lowest branches in the tree (i.e. automobile-specific values) are estimated by a logit formulation corresponding to the Luce model for alternatives in the same partition at the lowest level of the tree. Moore & Lehmann's [1989] procedure would perform six regressions (for 2 branches at the highest level in the tree and 3 branches in the second level of the tree) using a generalized least-squares procedure [cf. Cooper & Nakanishi, 1983; Green, Carmone & Wachspress, 1977]. These estimated automobile-specific values form the inclusive values in the next level of paired-comparison logit regression. These regressions are run across all pairs of automobiles that are joined for the first time in the second level of the hierarchy. The procedure continues until initial estimates for all parameters are obtained (both U's and S's in Figure 5.1, Panel A, and Equation (90)). These initial estimates are then refined using an ALS procedure. In the empirical study using perception and preference data, Moore & Lehmann [1989] show that the proposed individual-level nested-logit approach outperforms Luce's [1959] constant-ratio model for most respondents. Furthermore, in simulations, their approach produces estimates that have smaller variances than those of either two-stage maximum-likelihood estimates or generalized least-squares estimates. On account of the high degree of heterogeneity in their sample, they question the practice of building only aggregate-level models and propose separate estimates of competitive market structure at the individual or segment level.

One particular alternative of the general class of overlapping or non-nested feature structures [Shepard & Arabie, 1979] is a factorial structure in which all combinations of certain attribute levels are present in a product category. Elimination-By-Factorials (EBF) due to Moore [1990] represents a compromise between Luce's [1959] CRM model and Tversky's [1972] EBA model. Hauser [1986] makes a theoretical investigation of factorial choice structures and Moore [1990] presents an external-analysis, alternating least-squares (ALS) approach to estimating factorial preference and purchase-intention structures from constant-sum, paired-comparison data which is a modification of Moore & Lehmann [1989]. We use the foregoing notation and market structure in Figure 5.1, Panel A, together with the assumption $U_{sa} = U_{ta}$, $U_{se} = U_{te}$, $U_{sj} = U_{tj}$; (i.e. (i) the utility of a certain country of origin (body style) of automobiles is the same regardless of body style (country of origin); and (ii) when an American sporty automobile is compared with an American traditional-body-styled automobile, the aspect 'American' would not enter into the decision.) Under these assumptions, the probability of choice as suggested by EBF is given as:

$$P(\text{Corvette; Corvette, Cadillac}) = \frac{U_s + U_{sa.co}}{U_s + U_{sa.co} + U_t + U_{ta.ca}}. \tag{91}$$

Moore's [1990] EBF is an interesting and useful development in the light of the position advanced by several researchers that factorial or overlapping structures are more representative of several product classes than the hierarchical structures [e.g. Urban, Johnson & Hauser, 1984]. Arabie, Carroll, DeSarbo & Wind [1981] demonstrate that an overlapping structure is more sensible for measuring the perceptions of breakfast items, while Corter & Tversky [1986] report significantly better fit for the factorial structures in the cases of the perceptions of both furniture and sports as compared to an additive tree structure. Note that most of these approaches are external or confirmatory analyses where the tree structure must be set in advance.

2.3.3. Stochastic ultrametric tree-unfolding approaches

DeSarbo, De Soete, Carroll & Ramaswamy [1988] present a stochastic ultrametric tree-unfolding (SSTUN) methodology for simultaneously assessing competitive market structure and deriving marketing segments. They estimate a joint hierarchical or ultrametric tree representation in a maximum-likelihood framework based on paired-comparison choice data. The tree structure obtained from this methodology represents both brands and consumer segments as terminal nodes, such that a brand which is closer to a consumer segment in the derived tree has a higher probability of getting selected by that consumer segment.

Let $i, j = 1,\ldots,N$ represent consumers/households/segments and $k, l = 1,\ldots, M$ represent competitive brands. Let

$$\delta_{ikl} = \begin{cases} 1, & \text{if consumer } i \text{ prefers brand } k \text{ to brand } l, \\ 0, & \text{otherwise,} \end{cases}$$

and let Z_{ik} denote the latent 'dispreference' or 'disutility' of brand k to consumer/household/segment i, d_{ik} the distance between consumer/household/segment i and brand k defined on a two-mode ultrametric tree whose terminal nodes consist of both consumers/households/segments and brands, and let e_{ik} be an error term. They define a latent, unobservable dispreference or disutility function Z_{ik} as

$$Z_{ik} = d_{ik} + e_{ik}, \tag{92}$$

where it is assumed that:

$$\begin{aligned} &e_{ij} \sim \mathrm{N}(0, \sigma^2), \\ &\mathrm{Cov}(e_{ij}, e_{kl}) = 0 \quad \text{for } k \neq i, \\ &\mathrm{Cov}(e_{ij}, e_{ik}) = 0 \quad \text{for } k \neq j. \end{aligned}$$

Given that a consumer/household/segment is presented with two brands, k and l, the probability that brand k is chosen over brand l is modeled as a stochastic function of the difference of the distances of the consumer/household/segment i from the two brands k and l in the derived ultrametric tree. Thus,

$$\begin{aligned}P(\delta_{ikl}=1) &= P(Z_{ik}<Z_{il})\\ &= P(e_{ik}-e_{il}<d_{il}-d_{ik})\\ &= \Phi\left(\frac{(d_{il}-d_{ik})}{\sqrt{(2\sigma^2)}}\right)\\ &= \Phi(d_{il}-d_{ik}) = p_{ikl},\end{aligned} \tag{93}$$

since one can assume $\sigma = 1/\sqrt{2}$ without loss of generality because the distance terms can absorb the 'free multiplicative constant'. Similarly,

$$\begin{aligned}P(\delta_{ikl}=0) &= P(Z_{ik}<Z_{il})\\ &= 1-\Phi(d_{il}-d_{ik}) = \Phi(d_{ik}-d_{il}),\end{aligned} \tag{94}$$

where $\Phi(\cdot)$ in Equations (93) and (94) denotes the standard normal cumulative distribution function.

The objective is to estimate a two-mode ultrametric or hierarchical tree whose terminal nodes represent both consumers/households/segments and brands, based on collected empirical pairwise choices, which will render information on competitive market structure and segmentation. Let n_{ikl} denote the number of times consumer/household/segment i prefers k to l (if replicated choice judgments are collected; if not, $n_{ikl} = \delta_{ikl}$), and N_{ikl} the number of presentations of the brand-pair (k, l) to consumer/household/segment i (if no replications, $N_{ikl} = 1$). Then, assuming independence over subscripts i, k, and l, one can form a likelihood function:

$$L = \prod_{i=1}^{N} \prod\prod_{k<1}^{M} p_{ikl}^{n_{ikl}}(1-p_{ikl})^{(N_{ikl}-n_{ikl})}, \tag{95}$$

or

$$K = \ln L = \sum_{i}^{N} \sum\sum_{k<1}^{M} [n_{ikl}\ln p_{ikl} + (N_{ikl}-n_{ikl})\ln(1-p_{ikl})]. \tag{96}$$

The objective is to maximize L or K (or, equivalently, to minimize $-L$ or $-K$) with respect to the d_{ik}, subject to the constraint that these d_{ik} satisfy the two-class ultrametric inequality [Furnas, 1980] so that an ultrametric or hierarchical tree can be constructed. DeSarbo, De Soete, Carrol & Ramaswamy [1988] use an exterior-penalty-function approach [Rao, 1984] to convert the above constrained optimization problem into a series of unconstrained ones as discussed in Section 2.2.2 on ultrametric tree-fitting methods. DeSarbo, De Soete, Carroll & Ramaswamy [1988] also provide a technical detail of the five-step estimation algorithm.

DeSarbo, De Soete, Carroll & Ramaswamy [1988] obtain an ultrametric

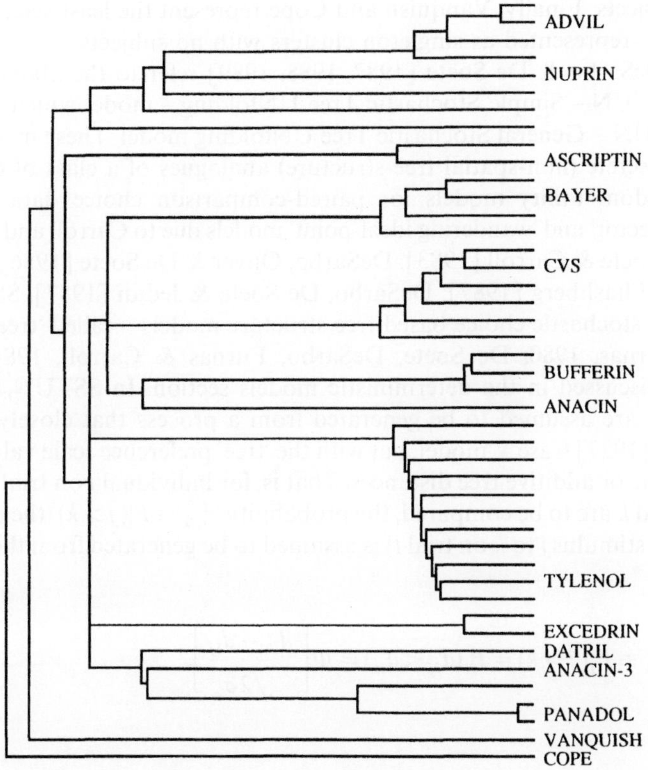

Fig. 5.10. Product-market hierarchy for analgesics based on the SSTUN methodology (taken from DeSarbo, De Soete, Carroll & Ramaswamy [1988]).

hierarchical structure based on data involving paired-comparisons preference judgments by 30 subjects on 14 over-the-counter analgesics. The resulting product-market hierarchy is shown in Figure 5.10. In this figure, the brands are labeled at the terminal nodes of their respective branches, whereas the terminal nodes of the subjects are left blank. Note that the major branch at the top of the tree contains Advil and Nuprin, the two ibuprofen brands, with some six 'ideal points' for six subjects, indicating that these two brands are their most preferred brands. The next set of five brands below these are the aspirin brands. Ascriptin is most preferred by only one subject. Then, the major branch with more popular aspirin brands – Bayer, Bufferin and Anacin – is grouped with four subjects. Note the unique position enjoyed by CVS, a generic brand of aspirin sold at CVS drug stores in the Greater Philadelphia area (where the study occurred) which occupies a sub-branch with five subjects. The next major branch of the tree contains the acetaminophen brands. The first sub-branch contains the most popular brand, Tylenol, with ten subjects. Next is Excedrin with one subject, and followed by less popular acetaminophen brands: Datril, Anacin-3 and Panodol which are grouped with two subjects. Finally, Vanquish and Cope represent the least selected brands and these are represented as singleton clusters with no subjects.

Carroll, DeSarbo & De Soete [1987, 1988, 1989] refer to the above-described model as SSTUN – Simple Stochastic Tree UNfolding – model which is a special case of GSTUN – General Stochastic Tree UNfolding model. These models can be viewed as discrete (non-spatial tree-structure) analogues of a class of continuous (spatial) random utility models for paired-comparison choice data called the 'wandering vector' and 'wandering ideal-point' models due to Carroll and Pruzansky [1980], De Soete & Carroll [1983], DeSarbo, Oliver & De Soete [1986], DeSarbo, De Soete & Eliashberg [1987], DeSarbo, De Soete & Jedidi [1987]. SSTUN and GSTUN are stochastic choice based tree structure models – called 'tree-unfolding models' [Furnas, 1980; De Soete, DeSarbo, Furnas & Carroll, 1984a, 1984b] previously discussed in the deterministic models section. In SSTUN, the paired comparisons are assumed to be generated from a process that closely resembles Thurstone's [1927] Case V model, but with the 'tree' preference scale values defined by ultrametric or additive tree distances. That is, for individual i on trial t, in which stimulus j and k are to be compared, the probability $p^t_{i,jk} \equiv P^t_i(j > k)$ (the probability that i prefers stimulus j to k on trial t) is assumed to be generated from the following process:

$$p^t_{i,jk} \equiv P_i(j > k) = P_i(d_{ij} < d_{ik}) = \Phi\left[\frac{\bar{d}_{ik} - \bar{d}_{ij}}{\sqrt{2}\sigma}\right], \tag{97}$$

with

$$d^t_{ij} = \bar{d}_{ij} + \varepsilon^t_j, \tag{98}$$

$$d^t_{ik} = \bar{d}_{ik} + \varepsilon^t_k, \tag{99}$$

where ε^t_j and ε^t_k are independently normally distributed with mean zero and variance σ^2, and where d_{ij} denotes the (ultrametric or additive) tree distance between the nodes representing subject i and stimulus j. This is exactly equivalent to the Thurstone Case V model with subject i's mean 'discriminal process' equal to d_{ij} and with all subjects having a common variance σ^2 of the discriminal process. Note, in (97) the t superscript may be dropped because $P_{i,jk}$ is independent of t, since the ε_j's are assumed independent both of t and j. A preliminary version of a procedure which uses the De Soete, DeSarbo, Furnas & Carroll [1984a, 1984b] penalty-function procedure for fitting the structural tree-unfolding model as a central component has already been discussed [cf. DeSarbo, De Soete, Carroll & Ramaswamy, 1988].

This version of stochastic tree-unifolding does not, however, utilize the tree structure in any inherent manner in generating the stochastic components. The distances, d_{ij}, in this case (or other numbers assumed related in an inverse linear fashion to preference scale values) could have been generated by any process whatsoever – the structural model and the stochastic component are simply 'grafted' onto one another without any essential theoretical link interconnecting them. Furthermore, this leads to a Thurstone Case V model for each subject, which is known to entail *strong* stochastic transitivity for each subject; i.e. if $P_{i,jk}$ and $P_{i,kl}$ are both equal to or larger than 1/2, then $P_{i,jl} \geqslant \max(P_{i,jk}, P_{i,kl})$. There is considerable evidence in the literature, however, that in many empirical situations, strong stochastic transitivity does not hold. At best, a weaker condition known as moderate stochastic transitivity (in which, under the same conditions, $P_{i,jl} \geqslant \min(P_{i,jk}, P_{i,kl})$) can be expected to hold.

Carroll, DeSarbo & De Soete [1989] show that the SSTUN model is a special case of the GSTUN model. The GSTUN model can be viewed as a special case of a wandering vector model [De Soete & Carroll, 1983; Carroll, 1980] but with a different 'stimulus space' defined for each subject. The GSTUN model starts with a fixed tree (hierarchical in the ultrametric case, or a rootless, non-hierarchical tree, or 'free tree', in the additive case). A matrix associated with that tree is called the 'path matrix', and denoted as $\boldsymbol{P}$. In the case of an additive-tree metric, the matrix can be viewed as defining the unique path connecting every pair of terminal nodes i and j. In the case of an ultrametric, it does not define such a path, but rather defines the 'least common ancestor' node for every pair i and j, which can be viewed as defining the 'path' connecting the two.

In the case of a path-length or additive-tree metric, the path matrix $\boldsymbol{P}$ is a matrix whose rows correspond to pairs of terminal nodes i and j, where (in the present case of the tree-unfolding models) i corresponds to a subject and j to a stimulus. The columns of $\boldsymbol{P}$ correspond to branches in the tree. The general entry in $\boldsymbol{P}$, which is designated as $P_{(ij)q}$ (for the entry in the row corresponding to node pair (i, j) and to branch q) will be 1 if and only if branch q is included in the path connecting i to j, and 0 otherwise. This matrix is, thus, a binary 'indicator' matrix indicating which branches are involved in the path interconnecting each pair of nodes i and j.

Given a set of branch lengths, $h_1, h_2, \ldots, h_Q$, which are represented as a Q-dimensional (column) vector $\boldsymbol{h}$, the distances d_{ij} $(i = 1, \ldots, I, j = 1, \ldots, J)$, which can be 'packed' into another column vector of $I \times J$ components, $\boldsymbol{d}$, can be defined via the matrix equation

$$\boldsymbol{d} = \boldsymbol{P}\boldsymbol{h}. \tag{100}$$

Furthermore, it is assumed that, for individual i, the distribution of $\boldsymbol{h}$ is

$$\boldsymbol{h}_i \sim \mathrm{N}(\boldsymbol{\mu}_i, \boldsymbol{\Sigma}_i); \tag{101}$$

then, on a particular paired-comparisons trial in which subject i is comparing stimulus j to stimulus k,

$$\begin{aligned} P_{i,jk} &\cong P_i(j > k) \\ &= P(d_{ij} < d_{ik}) \\ &= P(d_{ij} - d_{ik} < 0) \\ &= P(s_{i,jk} > 0), \end{aligned} \tag{102}$$

where $s_{i,jk} = d_{ik} - d_{ij}$. Under the assumptions that are made in this general stochastic tree-unfolding model, the distribution of $s_{i,jk}$ is:

$$s_{i,jk} \sim \mathrm{N}(d_{ik} - d_{ij}, \delta^2_{(ij)(ik)}), \tag{103}$$

where

$$d_{ij} = p_{(ij)}\mu_i, \tag{104}$$

$$d_{ik} = p_{(ik)}\mu_i, \tag{105}$$

$$\delta^2_{(ij)(ik)} = (\boldsymbol{p}_{(ij)} - \boldsymbol{p}_{(ik)})\boldsymbol{\Sigma}(\boldsymbol{p}_{(ij)} - \boldsymbol{p}_{(ik)})', \tag{106}$$

and $\boldsymbol{p}_{(ij)}$ and $\boldsymbol{p}_{(ik)}$ are the row vectors corresponding to the (i, j) and (i, k) rows of the path matrix, $\boldsymbol{P}$, respectively. Since $\boldsymbol{\Sigma}_i$ is a covariance matrix, it is positive definite (or semidefinite) so that $\delta^2_{(ij)(ik)}$ is the squared generalized Euclidean distance between rows (i, j) and (i, k) of $\boldsymbol{P}$ in the metric of $\boldsymbol{\Sigma}_i$. Consequently,

$$p_{i,jk} = \Phi\left[\frac{d_{ik} - d_{ij}}{\delta_{(ij)(ik)}}\right], \tag{107}$$

where $\boldsymbol{\Phi}$ denotes the standard normal distribution function. Since δ is a (Euclidean) metric, Model (107) is a moderate utility model [see Halff, 1976]. It should be evident that exactly the same development will hold for the ultrametric case, except that the rows of the path matrix $\boldsymbol{P}$ correspond to Q internal nodes (rather than Q branches) with $p_{(ij)q}$ being 1 if and only if node q is the lowest common ancestor of i and j. It is clear, however, if one considers the structure of the path matrix, $\boldsymbol{P}$, that the distribution of the choice probabilities for subject i are dependent only on the distribution of those components of $\boldsymbol{h}$ that affect the distances from the node for subject i to the stimulus nodes. Those distributional parameters for subject i involving components of $\boldsymbol{h}$ not affecting these distances are indeterminate without further constraints. Carroll & De Soete [1990] present a mathematical-programming procedure to fit a quasi-Poisson case of GSTUN and some of its extensions. This may be gainfully applied to obtain product-market structures as it could jointly estimate and portray consumers and products/brands as terminal nodes of an additive tree.

Ramaswamy & DeSarbo's [1990] SCULPTRE is a stochastic revealed preference model which estimates competitive market structure from panel data using constrained maximum-likelihood estimation. SCULPTRE allows for the presence of preference segments and explicitly represents the ideal-point for each segment as a terminal node on an ultrametric tree as also the brands. In ultrametric trees, brands/segments are represented by terminal nodes of identical height. These are similar to the graphical output from a hierarchical clustering procedure. The customer segments in SCULPTRE are latent classes – their sizes and locations on the tree are estimated simultaneously with the brand locations. In this model, the disutility that a segment has for a brand is considered to be proportional to the distance between the segment and brand nodes. Note that the distance between two nodes in an untrametric tree is defined as the height of the first internal node at which the two meet. The probability of choice of a brand by a segment is defined in this model as proportional to the exponentiated negative disutility that the segment has for that brand. Mathematically, the likelihood function that Ramaswamy & DeSarbo [1990] optimize is given as;

$$L=\prod_h \sum_s \alpha_s \frac{\left(\sum_j x_{hj}\right)!}{\prod_j x_{hj}!} \prod_j \frac{\exp(-d_{sj}x_{hj})}{\left[\sum_k \exp(-d_{sk})\right]^{x_{hj}}}, \tag{108}$$

where

$h = 1,\ldots,H$ households;
$r,s = 1,\ldots,S$ segments or latent classes;
$j,k = 1,\ldots,J$ products;
x_{hj} = the observed number of choices of product j for household h in a given time period;
d_{sj} = the distance between segment s and product j defined on a hierarchical product-market tree whose terminal nodes consist of both segments and products;
α_s = proportion of households in the sample that belong to segment s.

Ramaswamy & DeSarbo [1990] characterize three types of distances; namely, product–product, segment–product and segment–segment distances to produce a hierarchical ultrametric tree structure jointly representing brands and customer segments. The optimization problem is solved subject to the four-point rectangular (or two-class ultrametric) inequality, which is a necessary and sufficient condition [cf. Furnas, 1980] for constructing an exact hierarchical tree representation with two classes; i.e. products/brands and customer segments (see Expression (70)).

Ramaswamy & DeSarbo [1990] use an exterior-penalty-function approach [Rao, 1984] to convert the constrained estimation problem into a series of unconstrained ones and employ Akaike's [1973, 1974] information criteria to select number of segments. Their augmented function is

$$F(\boldsymbol{D},\alpha,\theta) = -k(\boldsymbol{D},\alpha) + \theta P(\boldsymbol{D}), \tag{109}$$

where

$\boldsymbol{D}$ = matrix of segment–product distances to be estimated,
α = vector of mixing proportions,
k = kernel of the negative of the logarithm of the likelihood function in Equation (108)

$$= -\sum_h \log\left\{\sum_s \alpha_s \prod_j \frac{\exp(-d_{sj}x_{hj})}{\left[\sum_k \exp(-d_{sk})\right]}\right\}, \tag{110}$$

and the penalty function $P(\boldsymbol{D})$ is structured along the lines of (73)–(75). In the analysis of the Elrod & Winer [1991] data, Ramaswamy & DeSarbo [1990] find a six-segment solution and report prediction on the holdout purchases better than any of the mapping methods presented in Elord & Winer [1991]. They attribute the superior performance of SCULPTRE to its ability to capture the preference of multiple segments. Considering the relative distances of the brands from each

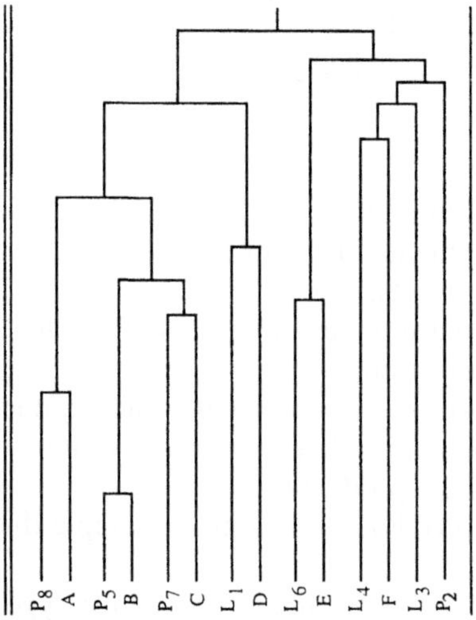

PANEL A: Based on SCULPTURE, Ramaswamy, & DeSarbo (1990)
A, B,... are segments and L_1, P_2,... are brands of detergents.

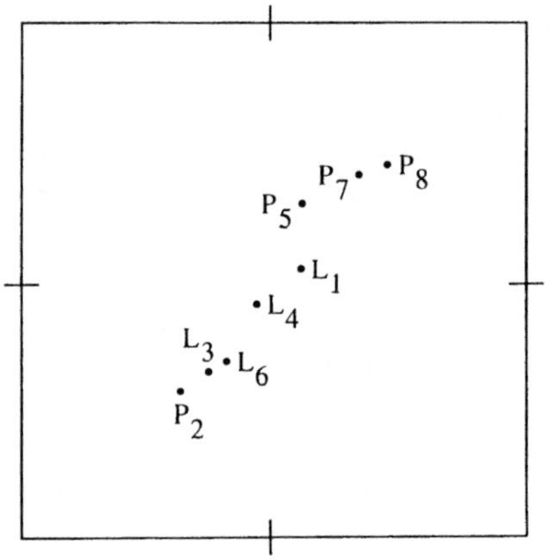

PANEL B: Based on Choice Map, Elrod & Winer (1991)
L_1, P_2,... are brand positions. The average ideal-point estimated for the entire sample is not shown here because the authors do not indicate it.

Fig. 5.11. Non-spatial and spatial product-market structures for detergent market (taken from Ramaswamy & De Sarbo [1990]).

of the segment locations (in Figure 5.11, Panel A), it appears that four of the six segments (A, B, D, E) have relatively strong preferences for a single brand (P_8, P_5, L_1, L_6, respectively). Of these four segments, D with strong affinity for brand L_1 seems to be somewhat more vulnerable given its position between major brands of liquids and powders. The remaining two segments, C and F, do not have relatively strong preferences for any single brand. Segment C has relatively strong preferences for powders P_5 and P_7, whereas segment F has a weak preference for all brands. The results from the same data used by Elrod's Choice Map [Elrod & Winer, 1991] are reproduced in Figure 5.11, Panel B. Note that the proximity between product positions in Figure 5.11, Panel B is similar to that in the hierarchical product-market tree in Figure 5.11, Panel A. One fundamental difference between the two approaches is with respect to estimation of consumer heterogeneity. Choice Map estimates the parameters of a unimodal distribution of preferences and infers an average ideal-point for the entire population. However, the product-market tree derived from SCULPTRE allows for the presence of preference segments and explicitly defines and represents the 'ideal-point' for each segment. This difference may be the source of superior predictive validity of SCULPTRE as compared to Choice Map and other spatial approaches compared in Elrod & Winer [1991].

2.3.4. *Tree models based on concept learning systems*

Currim, Meyer & Le [1988] propose a different approach to inferring hierarchical product-market structures. The method departs from other methods of estimating tree structures from choice data by allowing the tree structure to be estimated at the individual level with available data and without a need to prespecify the form of the decision policy. They use an inductive learning algorithm, CLS, Concept Learning System [Quinlan, 1983], similar to AID by Morgan & Sonquist [1963], CART due to Breiman, Friedman, Olshen & Stone [1984], and CHAID by Perreault & Barksdale [1980]. CLS is a non-parametric classification procedure for inferring 'if–then' rules to relate a set of predictor variables (such as product attributes) to a discrete outcome criterion (such as choice). CLS works with discrete panel data and it produces tree structures by successively partitioning choice data by product attributes that best discriminate selected from rejected choice alternatives. Currim, Meyer & Le [1988] summarize the four-step algorithm as follows:

(1) For each product attribute x, define a splitting criterion $C(x)$ which is a measure of the ability of that attribute to discriminate chosen from unchosen options. Based on information theory [e.g. Shannon, 1948], $C(x)$ is a measure of the classification power of x or its entropy. Formally, let $j = 1, \ldots, N_x$ be the number of levels associated with attribute x ($N \geqslant 2$), and let $f_{j|x}$ be the number of choice options having level j of x. $C(x)$ is defined as:

$$C(x) = -\sum_{j=1}^{N_x} f_{j|x}[p(\text{chosen}\,|\,j,x)\log_2 p(\text{chosen}\,|\,j,x) + p(\text{unchosen}\,|\,j,x)\log_2 p(\text{unchosen}\,|\,j,x)], \qquad (111)$$

where p (chosen$|j, x$) is the probability (estimated from the sample proportion) of an option being chosen that has level j of attribute x, and p (unchosen$|j, x$) is the probability that it is not chosen given j and x.

(2) Define that attribute with the smallest criterion as the starting attribute or primary 'root' of the decision tree. Then, partition the data into N_x splits, where N_x is number of levels associated with attribute x. For example, if color were the starting attribute, we would partition the data into several sets containing just those options that are red, just those that are blue, and so on. If there is a tie in determining the attribute with the lowest criterion value, the starting attribute is selected at random.

(3) Within each split, recalibrate the discrimination criterion for each remaining attribute and define the attribute that best descriminates chosen from unchosen options as the root of a secondary branch of the decision tree.

(4) Continue to apply this heuristic to successive splits of the data until either all instances have been classified or a stopping criterion is reached (e.g. until there is no longer a significant increase in the proportion of explained choices).

CLS is part of a more general consumer-modeling system that, after having estimated a tree structure for each individual in a sample, assists in performing further analysis to summarize consumer-choice strategies by way inferring relative importance of attributes in choice, assesses heterogeneity in choice strategies to identify market segments, and can be utilized in the prediction of market share due to changes in marketing-mix variables. Currim, Meyer & Le [1988] apply the CLS algorithm and consumer-modeling system to UPC scanner panel data and provide illustrations of various types of analyses that may be obtained from the system. The results of the CLS modeling system are compared with the results obtained by logit analysis [Cooper, 1988; Guadagni & Little, 1983] and they report that the two are comparable in terms of aggregate predictive validity and the diagnostic information they yield about the primary determinants of choice behavior. The interesting and differentiating aspect of CLS is its ability to represent interactive or contingent attribute effects at the household level that are precluded in logit modeling due to data sparsity. The strongest advantage of logit modeling, which CLS cannot match, is its parsimony in capturing simple compensatory decision rules and the presence of a rich theoretical basis that supports detailed hypothesis-testing. CLS is a particularly attractive approach, if one has a reason to believe that individual-level decisions are made through non-compensatory conditional processes or if one wants to study patterns of heterogeneity in non-additive decision rules.

3. Discussion, related literature, and directions for future research

As far as we are aware, this chapter represents the first attempt in marketing to assemble the vast literature dealing with a variety of non-spatial tree models for the assessment of competitive market structure. We present a taxonomy of the non-spatial approaches using two major dimensions, namely data and model characteristics. The data characteristics include: type of data (behavioral or judgmental), level of aggregation (individual, segment, or market), and measure of competition relation (perceptions, switching, or preference/choice). The model characteristics include representation (hierarchical/ultrametric, additive, networks, or latent class), type of analysis (confirmatory or exploratory), ability to accommodate marketing-mix effects, various modes of analysis, and error specifications. We analyzed the brand-switching data on eight brands of soft drinks collected by Bass, Pessemier & Lehmann [1972] using various methodologies for assessment of non-spatial tree-type competitive market structure and discussed insights provided by various methods and their limitations. We also discussed stochastic tree models.

Most approaches discussed in this review chapter do not incorporate the influence of competitive marketing-mix variables (such as advertising, pricing, etc.) as seen in Table 5.1B. Kamakura & Russell [1989], Russell & Bolton [1988], Moore & Winer [1987], Clarke [1978] and Houston [1977] present econometric approaches to account for the influence of marketing-mix variables. According to their standard economic approach, two brands are considered to be in the same market if their cross-elasticities of demand with respect to some marketing-mix variables are large. Marketers have also applied the economic approach in the development of as well as in the testing of competitive market structures [e.g. Vilcassim, 1989; Clements & Selvanathan, 1988; Cooper, 1988; Shugan, 1987; Vanhonacker, 1985; Clarke, 1973]. Most of these approaches address issues of determination of market structure and estimation of the market response function in a joint framework. Typically, a spatial representation of market structure is also obtained from most of these approaches (with the exception of Clements & Selvanathan [1988] and Vilcassim [1989] which produce hierarchical market structures). Recently, researchers have proposed a new class of techniques, referred to as latent structure analysis (LSA) [cf. Jain, Bass & Chen, 1990; Grover & Srinivasan, 1987; Grover & Dillon, 1985], which also perform such simultaneous estimation.

Another important set of related literature concerns the testing of competitive market structures. Charnes, Cooper, Learner & Phillips [1984] present an information-theoretic approach via the minimum discrimination information statistic which may be gainfully applied to statistical testing of hypothesized competitive market structures. Novak & Stangor [1987] in extending Urban, Johnson & Hauser's [1984] work on modeling of aggregate data, in the form of forced switching matrix, presents a two-sided multivariate statistical approach for testing competitive market structures. Recently, Kannan & Wright [1991b] presented a one-sided multivariate statistical test and demonstrated that it is an improvement on the Novak & Stagnor [1987] procedure in judging a hypothesized competitive market structure. Kumar & Sashi [1989] and Grover & Dillon [1985] also present probabilistic models for testing hypothesized hierarchical market structures. The former works with brand-switching data and the latter uses scanner panel data. The basis of partitioning the market in Kumar & Sashi's [1989] approach is identical to the criterion used by Urban, Johnson & Hauser [1984] for forming submarkets. A unique aspect of Kumar & Sashi's [1989] approach is that each hypothesized model of competitive market structure becomes the null model, while in Urban, Johnson & Hauser [1984], each model of interest is tested against the constant null hypothesis of no structure. Kumar & Sashi's [1989] method does not require any assumption of homogeneity in brand-switching behavior at either the individual or the segment level as is done by Grover & Dillon [1985]. Kumar & Sashi's [1989] method generalizes both Grover & Dillon [1985] and Urban, Johnson & Hauser [1984] in terms of utilizing complete brand-switching data to perform simultaneous tests of hypotheses about brand-loyal and brand-switching customers. This is not possible in either of the other two approaches as both exclude data on brand-loyal customers. An important limitation of Kumar & Sashi's [1989] approach is its inability to partition the market into overlapping clusters as suggested by Grover & Srinivasan [1987] and Srivastava, Alpert & Shocker [1984]. This limitation is, however, common to most other testing methods such as Kannan & Wright [1991b], Vilcassim [1989], Novak & Stangor [1987], Grover & Dillon [1985], Urban, Johnson & Hauser [1984].

In contrast to most of these approaches, which either identify or test market structures, Kannan & Wright [1991a] and Allenby [1989] present econometric approaches for both identifying and testing competitive market structures. Allenby [1989] postulates that a product category may be partitioned into clusters of similar brands, such that brands within a cluster have cross-price elasticities that follow proportional-draw and influence constraints. First, he estimates a matrix of unconstrained cross-price elasticities by regressing log shares against log prices of all brands and then obtains measures of pairwise proximity for all pairs of brands on the basis of these estimates. The proximity measures are subjected to metric MDS to identify clusters. Allenby's [1989] approach overcomes a major limitation of Russesll & Bolton's [1988] approach in which a prior assumption about the composition of submarkets is made. Allenby [1989] also proposes a method of testing the partitioning of brands into clusters by estimating market attraction models that impose the implied restriction on cross-elasticities. Kannan & Wright [1991a] use a nested-logit model to test existence of hypothesized multiple structured markets and nature of brand competition within each market hierarchy by including marketing-mix variables. They also present a segmentation algorithm based on iterative nested-logit estimation procedure.

Clearly, recent gains in developing these quantitative techniques have been impressive, but further work is needed to overcome the difficulties met by some of the existing methods. While the studies due to Lehmann & Moore [1986] and Jain & Rao [1991] compare some of the approaches for the assessment of competitive market structures, a more comprehensive study comparing the various competing techniques is needed. It would be managerially useful to compare these techniques in terms of their ability to recover true market structures. Because the true structure is rarely (if ever) known with certainty in most real-world situations, such a comparative study would necessarily involve application of Monte Carlo simulation techniques. Furthermore, specifications of conditions under which a particular approach is preferable also need to be established. A related issue to investigate would be the extent to which results obtained from various approaches are convergent, and the situations under which such convergence occurs.

Most approaches to market structure analysis have been based on the assumption that the market of interest is homogeneous in its perceptions of market structure, which has caused some researchers to argue that the insights yielded about competition may be inappropriate [e.g. Lehmann & Moore, 1986; Kahn, Morrison & Wright 1986; Grover & Dillon, 1985]. Future research should explore the extent to which the individual-level hierarchical models offered by Currim, Meyer & Le [1988] and Moore & Lehmann [1989] might be used to overcome this limitation. Currim, Meyer & Le's [1988] Concept Learning System approach provides a quick and simple tool for assessment of non-spatial market hierarchies which is easy to implement and has theoretical links to established literature in tree-structure modeling. The usefulness of alternative sophisticated rule-learning algorithms might be explored. These, which are being developed within artificial intelligence, include Michalski's [1983] STAR and INDUCE procedures and may help in overcoming some of the shortcomings of CLS.

All approaches to market structure analysis using panel data (see Kannan and Wright [1991a] and several others cited earlier in the paper) could have a problem of model misspecification since the purchase history reflects the choice of a household, and not an individual. This suggests that there could be a set of purchases by a household for different individuals or for different usage occasions. Grover & Dillon [1985] reduced the impact of this problem by considering non-substitutable products as different markets by analyzing the ground- and instant-coffee markets separately. Kahn, Morrison & Wright [1986] address this issue more directly and provide some comforting arguments in support of using household-level data for market structure analysis. However, we feel the issue needs consideration in future research to find better methods for handling this potential problem.

A major limitation of econometric approach of the type described in Russell & Bolton [1988] is the assumption of composition of submarkets. Though Allenby [1989] proposes a procedure to develop a submarket classification by analyzing the unconstrained cross-price elasticities, the approach is susceptible to measurement problems such as multicollinearity that affect scanner data. Future research is needed in this direction to resolve the issue.

An important limitation of most statistical testing methods [Kannan & Wright, 1991a, 1991b; Kumar & Sashi, 1989; Vilcassim, 1989; Novak & Stangor, 1987; Grover & Dillon, 1985; Urban, Johnson & Hauser, 1984] is their inability to allow assessment and testing of market partitioning into overlapping clusters as suggested in Grover & Srinivasan [1987] and Srivastava, Alpert & Shocker [1984]. Future research is needed to develop models and testing procedures to overcome this problem in existing methods.

Finally, more work is needed to develop a dynamic approach for assessment of competitive market structure and testing its stability over time. It will be managerially insightful to capture the connection between market structure and marketing-mix variables by conducting more studies similar to the recent work of Kannan & Wright [1991a]. The nature of this connection also needs to be studied in a dynamic framework.

References

Akaike, H. (1973). Information theory and an extension of the maximum likelihood principle, in B.N. Petrov and F. Csaki (eds.), *2nd International Symposium on Information Theory*, Akademiai Kaido, Budapest, pp. 267–281.

Akaike, H. (1974). A new look at statistical model identification, *IEEE Trans. Automat. Control* 6, 716–723.

Allenby, G.M. (1989). A unified approach to identifying, estimating and testing demand structures with aggregate scanner data. *Marketing Sci.* 8, 265–280.

Arabie, P., J.D. Carroll, W. DeSarbo and Y. Wind (1981). Overlapping clustering: A new methodology for product positioning. *J. Marketing Res.* 18, 310–317.

Bass, F.M., E.A. Pessemier and D.R. Lehmann (1972). An experimental study of relationships between attitudes, brand preferences, and choice. *Behavioral Sci.* 17, 532–541.

Batsell, R.R., and J.C. Polking (1985). A new class of market share models. *Marketing Sci.* 4, 177–198.

Bettman, J.R. (1974). Toward a statistics for consumer decision net models. *J. Consumer Res.* 1, 71–80.

Birnbaum, M.H. (1974). Using contextural effects to derive psychological scales. *Perception and Psychophysics* 15, 89–96.

Breiman, L., J.H. Freidman, R.A. Olshen and C.W. Stone (1984). *Classification and Regression Trees*, Wadsworth International, Belmont, CA.

Bunemann, P.A. (1974). A note on the metric properties of trees. *J. Combin. Theory* 17, 48–50.

Butler, D.H., and R.F. Butler (1976). Development of statistical marketing models, in *Speaking of Hendry*, Hendry Corporation, Croton-on-Hudson, NY, pp. 125–145.

Carroll, J.D. (1976). Spatial, non-spatial, and hybrid models for scaling. *Psychometrika* 41, 439–463.

Carroll, J.D., and P. Arabie (1980). Multidimensional scaling. *Ann. Rev. Psychol* 31, 607–649.

Carroll, J.D., and J.J. Chang (1973). A method for fitting a class of hierarchical tree structure models to dissimilarities data and its application to some 'body parts' data of Miller's. *Proc. 81st Annual Convention of the American Psychological Association* 8, 1097–1098.

Carroll, J.D., L. Clark and W.S. DeSarbo (1984). The representation of three-way proximities data by single and multiple tree structure models. *J. Classification* 1, 25–74.

Carroll, J.D., W.S. DeSarbo and G. De Soete (1987). Stochastic tree unfolding (STUN) models. *Commun. and Cognition* 20, 63–76.

Carroll, J.D., W.S. DeSarbo and G. De Soete (1988). Stochastic tree unfolding (STUN) models: Theory and application, in H.H. Bock (ed.), *Classification and Related Methods of Data Analysis*, Elsevier, Amsterdam, pp. 421–430.

Carroll, J.D., W.S. DeSarbo and G. De Soete (1989). Two classes of stochastic unfolding models, in G. De Soete, H. Feger and K.C. Klauer (eds.), *New Developments in Psychological Choice Modelling* North-Holland, Amsterdam, pp. 161–176.

Carroll, J.D., and G. De Soete (1990). Fitting a quasi-poisson case of the GSTUN (general stochastic tree unfolding) model and some extensions, in *Knowledge, Data and Computer-Assisted Decisions*, M. Schader & W. Gaul (eds.), Springer, Berlin and Heidelberg.

Carroll, J.D., and S. Pruzansky (1975). Fitting of hierarchical tree structure (HTS) models, mixtures of HTS models, and hybrid models, via mathematical programming and alternating least squares, Paper presented at US–Japan Seminar of Multidimensional Scaling, 20–24 August, University of California at San Diego, La Jolla, CA.

Carroll, J.D., and S. Pruzansky (1980). Discrete and hybrid scaling models, in E.D. Lantermann and H. Feger (eds.), *Similarity and Choice*, Hans Huber, Bern, pp. 48–69.

Chandler, J.P. (1969). STEPIT – finds local minima of a smooth function of several parameters. *Behavioral Sci.* 14, 81–82.

Chandon, J.L., L. Lemaire and J. Pouget (1980). Construction de l'ultramétrique la plus proche d'une dissimilarité au sens des moindres carrés, *RAIRO, Rech. Oper.* 14, 157–170.

Charnes, A., W.W. Cooper, D.B. Learner and F.Y. Phillips (1984). An MDI model and an algorithm for composite hypotheses testing and estimation in marketing. *Marketing Sci.* 3, 55–72.

Clarke, D.G. (1973). Sales-advertising cross elasticities and advertising competition. *J. Marketing Res.* 10, 250–261.

Clarke, D.G. (1978). Strategic advertising planning: Merging multidimensional scaling and econometric analysis. *Manag. Sci.* 24, 1687–1699.

Clements, K.W. and E.A. Selvanathan (1988). The Rotterdam demand model and its application in marketing. *Marketing Sci.* 7, 60–75.

Cooper, L.G. (1988). Competitive maps: The structure underlying asymmetric cross elasticities. *Management. Sci.* 34, 707–723.

Cooper, L.G., and M. Nakanishi (1983). Two logit models for external analysis of preference. *Psychometrika* 48, 607–620.

Corter, J.E., and A. Tversky (1986). Extended similarity trees. *Psychometrika* 51, 429–451.

Cunningham, J.P. (1974). Finding the optimal tree realization of a proximity matrix. Paper presented at the Mathematical Psychology Meetings, August, Ann Arbor, MI.

Cunningham, J.P. (1978). Free trees and bidirectional trees as a representation of psychological distance. *J. Math. Psychol.* 17, 165–188.

Currim, I.S. (1982). Predictive testing of consumer choice models not subject to independence or relevant alternatives. *J. Marketing Res.* 19, 208–222.

Currim, I.S., R.J. Meyer and N.T. Le (1988). Disaggregate tree-structured modeling of consumer choice data. *J. Marketing Res.* 25, 253–265.

Day, G.S., A.D. Shocker and K. Srivastava (1979). Consumer oriented approaches to identifying product markets. *J. Marketing* 43, 8–20.

DeSarbo, W.S. (1982). GENNCLUS: New models for general nonhierarchical clustering analysis. *Psychometrika* 47, 446–459.

DeSarbo, W.S., and G. De Soete (1984). On the use of hierarchical clustering for the analysis of nonsymmetric proximities. *J. Consumer Res.* 11, 601–610.

DeSarbo, W.S., G. De Soete, J.D. Carroll and V. Ramaswamy (1988). A new stochastic ultrametric tree unfolding methodology for assessing competitive market structure and deriving market segments. *Appl. Stochast. Models Data Anal.* 4, 185–204.

DeSarbo, W.S., G. De Soete and J. Eliashberg (1987). A new stochastic multidimensional unfolding model for the investigation of paired comparison consumer preference/choice data. *J. Econom. Psychol.* 8, 357–384.

DeSarbo, W.S., G. De Soete, and K. Jedidi (1987). Probabilistic multidimensional scaling models for analyzing consumer choice behavior. *Commun. and Cognition* 20, 93–116.

DeSarbo, W.S., A.K. Manrai and R. Burke (1990). A non-spatial methodology for the analysis of two-way proximity data incorporating the distance-density hypothesis. *Psychometrika* 55, 229–253.

DeSarbo, W.S., R.L. Oliver and G. De Soete (1986). A probabilistic multidimensional scaling vector model. *Appl. Psychol. Measurement* 10, 79–80.

DeSarbo, W.S., and V.R. Rao (1984). GENFOLD2: A set of models and algorithms for the GENeral unFOLDing analysis of preference/dominance data. *J. Classification* 1, 147–186.

DeSarbo, W.S., and V.R. Rao (1986). A constrained unfolding methodology for product positioning. *Marketing Sci.* 5, 1–19.

De Soete, G. (1983a). Algorithms for constructing least-squares ultrametric and additive tree representations of dissimilarities data (in Dutch), Unpublished Dissertation, University of Ghent, Belgium.

De Soete, G. (1983b). A least-squares algorithm for fitting trees to proximity data. *Psychometrika* 48, 621–626.

De Soete, G. (1984). A least squares algorithm for fitting an ultrametric tree to a dissimilarity matrix. *Pattern Recognition Lett.* 2, 133–137.

De Soete, G., and J.D. Carroll (1982). A maximum likelihood method for fitting the wandering vector model. *Psychometrika* 48, 553–567.

De Soete, G., J.D. Carroll and W.S. DeSarbo (1987). Least squares algorithms for constructing constrained ultrametric and additive tree representations of symmetric proximity data. *J. Classification* 4, 155–174.
De Soete, G., W.S. DeSarbo, G.W. Furnas and J.D. Carroll (1984a). Tree representations of rectangular proximity matrices, in E. Degreef and J. Van Buggenhaut (eds.), *Trends in Mathematical Psychology*, North-Holland, Amsterdam.
De Soete, G., W.S. DeSarbo, G.W. Furnas and J.D. Carroll (1984b). The estimation of ultrametric and path length trees from rectangular proximity data. *Psychometrika* 49, 289–310.
Dixon, W.J. (1980). *BMDP: Biomedical Computer Programs*, University of California Press, Los Angeles.
Dobson, J. (1974). Unrooted trees for numerical taxonomy. *J. Appl. Probab.* 11, 32–42.
Dubes, R., and A.K. Jain (1979). Validity studies in clustering methodologies. *Pattern Recognition* 11, 235–254.
Dubin, J.A. (1986). A nested logit model of space and water heat system choice. *Marketing Sci.* 5, 112–124.
Eliashberg, J.E., and A.K. Manrai (1992). Optimal positioning of new product-concepts: Some analytical implications and empirical results. *Eur. J. Oper. Res.* 63(3), 376–397.
Elrod, T. (1991). Internal analysis of market structure: Recent developments and future prospects. *Marketing Lett.* 2, 253–267.
Elrod, T., and R.S. Winer (1991). An empirical comparison of mapping methods based on panel data, Working Paper, University of Alberta, Edmonton.
Farris, J.S. (1972). Estimating phylogenetic trees from distance matrices. *Amer. Naturalist* 106, 645–668.
Feger, H., and W. Bien (1982). Network unfolding. *Social Networks* 4, 257–283.
Feger, H., and U. Droge (1984). Ordinal network scaling. *Kölner Z. Soziol. Sozialpsychol.* 3, 417–423.
Fiacco, A.V., and G.P. McCormick (1968). *Nonlinear Programming: Sequential Unconstrained Minimization Techniqies*, Wiley, New York.
Fraser, C., and J.W. Bradford (1982). Competitive market structure analysis: Principal partitioning of revealed substitutability. *J. Consumer Res.* 10, 15–30.
Furnas, G.W. (1980). Objects and their features: The metric representation of two class data, Unpublished Doctoral Dissertation, Stanford University, Stanford, CA.
Gensch, D. (1987). A two-stage disaggregate attribute choice model. *Marketing Sci.* 6, 223–239.
Gensch, D., and J. Svestka (1984). A maximum-likelihood hierarchical disaggregate model for predicting choices of individuals. *J. Math. Psychol.* 28, 160–178.
Gifi, A. (1990). *Nonlinear Multivariate Analysis*, Wiley, New York.
Glazer, R., and K. Nakamoto (1991). Cognitive geometry: An analysis of structure underlying representation of similarity. *Marketing Sci.* 10, 205–228.
Green, P.E., F.J. Carmone and S.M. Smith (1989). *Multidimensional Scaling: Concept and Applications*, Allyn and Bacon, Needham Heights, MA.
Green, P.E., F.J. Carmone and D.P. Wachspress (1977). On the analysis of qualitative data in marketing research, *J. Marketing Res.* 14, 52–59.
Grover, R., and W.R. Dillon (1985). A probabilistic model for testing hypothesized hierarchical market structure. *Marketing Sci.* 4, 312–335.
Grover, R., and V.R. Rao (1988). Inferring competitive market structure based on a model of inter-purchase intervals. *Internat. J. Res. Marketing* 5, 55–72.
Grover, R., and V. Srinivasan (1987). Simultaneous approach to market segmentation and market structuring. *J. Marketing Res.* 24, 139–153.
Guadagni, P.M., and J.D.C. Little (1983). A logit model of brand choice calibrated on scanner data. *Marketing Sci.* 2(3), 203–238.
Hakimi, S.L., and S.S. Yau (1964). Distance matrix of a graph and its realizability. *Quart. App. Math.* 22, 305–317.
Halff, H.M. (1976). Choice theories for differentially comparable alternatives. *J. Math. Psychol.* 14, 244–246.
Hartigan, J.A. (1967). Representation of similarity matrices by trees. *J. Amer. Statist. Assoc.* 62, 1140–1158.
Hartigan, J.A. (1975). *Clustering Algorithms*, Wiley, New York.
Hauser, J.R. (1986). Agendas and consumer choice. *J. Marketing Res.* 23, 119–212.

Hauser, J.R., and S.M. Shugan (1983). Defensive marketing strategies. *Marketing Sci.* 2, 319–360.
Hoffman, D.L., and J. De Leeuw (1991). Interpreting multiple correspondence analysis as an MDS method, Workinx Paper, School of Management, University of Texas at Dallas.
Hoffman, D.L., and G.R. Franke (1986). Correspondence analysis: Graphical representation of categorical research in marketing research. *J. Marketing Res.* 23, 213–227.
Holman, E.W. (1972). The relation between hierarchical and Euclidean models for psychological distances. *Psychometrika* 37, 417–423.
Houston, F.M. (1977). An econometric analysis of positioning. *J. Business Admin.* 9, 1–12.
Hutchinson, J.W. (1989). NETSCAL: A network scaling algorithm for non-symmetric proximity data. *Psychometrika* 54, 25–52.
Jain, D., F.M. Bass and Y.M. Chen (1990). Estimation of latent class models with heterogeneous choice probabilities: An application to market structuring. *J. Marketing Res.* 27, 94–101.
Jain, D.C., and R.C. Rao (1991). Latent class models to infer market structure: A comparative analysis, Working Paper, Northwestern University, Evanston, IL.
Jardine, C.J., N. Jardine and R. Sibson (1967). The structure and construction of taxonomic Hierarchies. *Math. Biosci.* 1, 173–179.
Johnson, M.D., and C. Fornell (1987). The nature and methodological implications of the cognitive representation of products. *J. Consumer Res.* 14, 214–228.
Johnson, S.C. (1967). Hierarchical clustering schemes. *Psychometrika* 32, 241–254.
Kahn, B., W.L. Moore and R. Glazer (1987). Experiments in constrained choice. *J. Consumer Res.* 14, 96–113.
Kahn, B., D.G. Morrison and G.P. Wright (1986). Aggregating individual purchases to the household level. *Marketing Sci.* 5, 260–280.
Kalwani, M.U., and D.G. Morrison (1977). A parsimonious description of the Hendry system. *Management Sci.* 23, 467–477.
Kamakura, W.A., and G.J. Russell (1989). A probabilistic choice model for market segmentation and elasticity structure. *J. Marketing Res.* 26, 379–390.
Kannan, P.K., and G.P. Wright (1991a) Modeling and testing structured markets: A nested model approach. *Marketing Sci.* 10, 58–82.
Kannan, P.K., and G.P. Wright (1991b). On 'Testing competitive market structures'. *Marketing Sci.* 10, 338–347.
Klauer, K.C. (1989). Ordinal network representation: Representation proximities by graphs. *Psychometrika* 54, 737–750.
Klauer, K.C., and J.D. Carroll (1989). A mathematical programming approach to fitting general graphs. *J. Classification* 6, 247–270.
Klauer, K.C., and J.D. Carroll (1991). A comparison of two approaches to fitting directed graphs to nonsymmetric proximity matrices. *J. Classification* 8, 251–268.
Krumhansl, C.L. (1978). Concerning the applicability of geometric models to similarity data: The interrelationship between similarity and spartial density. *Psychol. Rev.* 85, 445–463.
Krumhansl, C.L. (1982). Density vs. feature weights as predictors of visual identification: Comment on Appelman and Mayzner. *J. Exp. Psychol. General* 111, 101–108.
Kumar, A., and C.M. Sashi (1989). Confirmatory analysis of aggregate hierarchical market structure: Inferences from brand-switching behavior. *J. Marketing Res.* 26, 444–453.
Lattin, J.M., and L. McAlister (1985). Using a variety-seeking model to identify substitute and complementary relationships among competing products. *J. Marketing Res.* 22, 330–339.
Lee, S.Y., and R. Jennrich (1984). The analysis of structural equation models by means of derivative free nonlinear least squares, *Psychometrika* 49, 521–528.
Lehmann, D.R., and W.L. Moore (1986). Two approaches to estimating hierarchical models of choice, Working Paper, Graduate School of Business, Columbia University, New York.
Lehmann, R.D. (1972). Judged similarity and brand-switching data as similarity measures. *J. Marketing Res.* 9, 331–334.
Lilien, G.L., and P. Kotler (1983). *Marketing Decision Making: A Model-Building Approach*, Harper and Row, New York.
Luce, R. (1959). *Individual Choice Behavior*, Wiley, New York.

Maddala, G.S. (1983). *Limited-Dependent and Qualitative Variables in Econometrics*, Cambridge University Press, Cambridge.

Manrai, A.K, and L.A. Manrai (1992). Role of travel-experience and country-popularity in determining consumer perceptions and preferences of European countries, Working Paper, University of Delaware, Newark, DE.

Manrai, A.K., and P.K. Sinha (1989). Elimination-by-cutoffs. *Marketing Sci.* 8, 133–152.

McFadden, D. (1986). The choice theory approach to marketing research. *Marketing Sci.* 5, 275–297.

Michalski, R.S. (1983). A theory and methodology of inductive learning, in R.S. Michalski, J.G. Carbonell and T.M. Mitchell (eds.), *Machine Learning: An Artificial Intelligence Approach*, Tioga Publishing, Palo Alto, CA, pp. 83–134.

Moore, W.L. (1990). Factorial preference structures. *J. Consumer Res.* 17, 94–104.

Moore, W.L., and D.R. Lehmann (1989). A paired comparison nested logit model of individual preference structure. *J. Marketing Res.* 26, 420–428.

Moore, W.L., E.A. Pessemier and D.R. Lehmann (1986). Hierarchical representation of market structure and choice process through preference trees. *J. Business Res.* 14, 371–386.

Moore, W.L., and R.S. Winer (1987). A panel-data based method for merging joint space and market response function estimation. *Marketing Sci.* 6, 25–47.

Morgan, J.N., and J.A. Sonquist (1963). Problems in the analysis of survey data, and a proposal. *J. Amer. Statist. Assoc.* 58, 415–434.

Novak, T.P. (1991). Log-linear trees: models of market structure in brand switching data, Working Paper, Cox School of Business, Southern Methodist University, Dallas, TX.

Novak, T.P., and C. Stangor (1987). Testing competitive market structures: An application of weighted least squares methodology to brand switching data. *Marketing Sci.* 6, 82–97.

Orth, B. (1988). Representing similarities by distance graphs: Monotonic network analysis (MONA), in H.H. Bock (ed.), *Classification and Related Methods of Data Analysis*, North-Holland, Amsterdam, pp. 489–494.

Parducci, A. (1965). Category judgment: A range-frequency model. *Psychol. Rev.* 72, 407–418.

Patrinos, A.N., and S.L. Hakimi (1972). The distance matrix of a graph and its tree realization. *Quart. Appl. Math.* 30, 255–269.

Perreault, W.D., and H.C. Barksdale (1980). A model-free approach to analysis of complex contingency data in marketing research. *J. Marketing Res.* 18, 503–515.

Powell, M.J. (1977). Restart procedures for the conjugate gradient method. *Math. Programming* 12, 241–254.

Pruzansky, S., A. Tversky and J.D. Carroll (1982). Spatial versus tree representations of proximity data. *Psychometrika* 47, 3–24.

Quinlan, J.R. (1983). Learning efficient classification procedures and their application to chess end games, in *Machine Learning: An Artificial Intelligence Approach*, R.S. Michalski, J.G. Carbonell and T.M. Mitchell (eds.), Tioga Publishing, Palo Alto, CA, pp. 463–482.

Ramaswamy, V., and W.S. DeSarbo (1990). SCULPTRE: a new methodology for deriving and analyzing hierarchical product-market structures from panel data. *J. Marketing Res.* 27, 418–427.

Rao, S.S. (1984). *Optimization: Theory and Applications, second edition*, Wiley, New York.

Rao, V.R., and D.J. Sabavala (1980). Methods of market strucrure/partitioning analysis using panel data, in *Market Measurement and Analysis: Proceedings of ORSA/TIMS Special Interest Conference*, B. Montgomery and D.R. Wittink (eds.), Marketing Science Institute Report 80–103, Cambridge, MA.

Rao, V.R., and D.J. Sabavala (1981). Inference of hierarchical choice processes from panel data. *J. Consumer Res.* 8, 85–96.

Restle, F. (1959). A metric and an ordering on sets. *Psychometrika* 24, 207–220.

Russell, G.J., and R.N. Bolton (1988). Implications of market structure for elasticity structure. *J. Marketing Res.* 25, 229–241.

Ryan, D.M. (1974). Penalty and barrier functions, in *Numerical Methods for Constrained Optimization*, P.E. Gill and W. Murray (eds.), Academic Press, New York, pp. 175–190.

Sattath, S., and A. Tversky (1977). Additive similarity trees. *Psychometrika* 42, 319–345.

Shannon, C.E. (1948). A mathematical theory of communication. *Bell Systems Tech. J.* 27, 379–423.

Shepard, R.N. (1980). Multidimensional scaling, tree-fitting, and clustering. *Science* 210, 390–398.

Shepard, R.N., and P. Arabie (1979). Additive clustering: Representation of similarities as combinations of discrete overlapping properties. *Psychol. Rev.* 86, 87–123.

Shocker, A.D., D.W. Stewart and A.J. Zahorik (1986). Mapping competitive relationships: Practices, Problems, and Promise, Working Paper, Owen Graduate School of Management, Vanderbilt University, Nashville, TN.

Shocker, A.D., D.W. Stewart and A.J. Zahorik (1990). Market structure analysis: Practice, Problems, and Promise. *J. Managerial Issues* 2, 9–56.

Shugan, S.M. (1987). Estimating brand positioning maps using supermarket scanning data. *J. Marketing Res.* 24, 1–18.

Sjöberg, L.A. (1972). A cognitive theory of similarity. *Goteborg Psychol. Rep.* 2, 10–30.

Srivastava, R.K., M.I. Alpert and A.D. Shocker (1984). A customer-oriented approach for determining market structures. *J. Marketing* 48, 32–45.

Srivastava, R., R. Leone and A. Shocker (1981). Market structure analysis: Hierarchical clustering of products based on substitution in use, *J. Marketing* 45(3), 38–48.

Thurstone, L.L. (1927). A law of comparative judgment. *Psychol. Rev.* 34, 273–286.

Turner, J., and W.J. Kautz (1970). A survey of progress in graph theory in the Soviet Union. *Siam Rev.* 12, 1–68 (Supplement).

Tversky, A. (1972). Elimination by aspects: A theory of choice. *Psychol. Rev.* 79, 281–299.

Tversky, A. (1977). Features of similarity. *Psychol. Rev.* 84, 327–352.

Tversky, A., and S. Sattath (1979). Preference trees. *Psychol. Rev.* 86, 542–573.

Urban, G.L., and J.R. Hauser (1980). Market definition and entry strategy, in *Design and Marketing of New Products*, Chapter 5, Prentice-Hall, Englewood Cliffs, NJ.

Urban, G.L., J.R. Hauser and N. Dholakia (1987). *Essentials of New Product Management*, Prentice-Hall, Englewood Cliffs, NJ.

Urban, G.L., P.L. Johnson and J.R. Hauser (1984). Testing competitive marketing structures. *Marketing Sci.* 3, 83–112.

Vanhonacker, W.R. (1985). Structuring and analyzing brand competition using scanner data, Working Paper, Graduate School of Business, Columbia University, New York.

Vilcassim, N. (1989). Note: Extending the Rotterdam model to test hierarchical market structures. *Marketing Sci.* 8(2), 181–190.

Ward, J.H. (1963). Hierarchical groupings to optimize an objective function. *J. Amer. Statist. Assoc.* 58, 236–244.

Wind, Y. (1982). *Product Policy: Concepts, Methods, and Strategy*, Addison-Wesley, Reading, MA.

Wold, H. (1966). Estimation of principal components and related models by iterative least squares. in P.R. Krishnaiah (ed.), *Multivariate Analysis*, Academic Press, New York.

Young, F.W. (1984). Scaling. *Ann. Rev. Psychol.* 35, 55–81.

Zahorik, A.J. (1992). Non-hierarchical brand switching model for inferring market structure. *Eur. J. Oper. Res.* (to appear).

J. Eliashberg and G.L. Lilien, Eds., *Handbooks in OR & MS, Vol. 5*

Chapter 6

Market-Share Models*

Lee G. Cooper

Anderson Graduate School of Management, University of California at Los Angeles, Los Angeles, CA 90024-1481, USA

1. Introduction

The topic of market-share models overlaps substantially with Roberts and Lilien's discussion of choice models (This Handbook, Chapter 2), since consumer choice underlies the process of market-share formation; with Gatignon's discussion of marketing-mix models (This Handbook, Chapter 15), since market-share models should be useful in planning the marketing mix for a brand in light of competitive forces, with the Hanssens and Parsons discussion of enconometric and time-series models (This Handbook, Chapter 9), since market-share models deal with market response over time as well as over geography and over competitors, and with the Blattberg and Neslin discussion of sales-promotion models (This Handbook, Chapter 12), since market-share models have been used extensively to analyze the effects of retail promotions. What this chapter contributes to management science in marketing beyond that offered by these other chapters is hopefully an understanding of how increasingly rich specification of market-share models can guide the systematic study of market and competitive structures.

By *market and competitive structures* we mean the complex pattern of competitive interplay within a market. Take the cereal market as an example. The presweetened cereals such as Frosted Flakes or Honey Nut Cheerios serve a predominantly different segment than the mainly unsweetened cereals such as Cheerios, Kellogg's Corn Flakes, or Wheaties. Substitution *within* these submarkets is likely to be more frequent than *between* them. But we cannot treat them as totally separate markets since dramatic price reductions for Cheerios might entice consumers to switch from the presweetened segment and sweeten at home. Even within the unsweetened cereals, we expect more substitution within varieties of corn flakes, than between corn flakes and wheat flakes, or more substitution within varieties

*This chapter relies heavily on the developments in Chapters 2 and 3 of Cooper & Nakanishi [1988]. The numerous contributions of Masso Nakanishi to this work are gratefully acknowledged. I also thank M.J. Snyder for her assistance with the numerical illustration, A.C. Nielsen for providing the data used in the numerical illustration, and the reviewers for their many helpful comments.

of granolas than between granolas and single-grain cereals. Media advertising for one of Kellogg's brands may help other Kellog brands, have little effect on other premium national brands, and hurt each store's private-label brand. In return the large price differential between a store's private-label brand and the corresponding national brand (e.g. Honey Nut Cheerios and Honey Nut Tasteeos–two to one according to a recent *Wall Street Journal* story, Gibson [1991]) can create long-term cross-competitive influences within this dyad that are not felt throughout the market.

Three basic principles motivate the specification of the market-share models discussed in this chapter. Market-share models should be *competitive, descriptive* as well as predictive, and *profit-oriented*, Being fundamentally *competitive* implies that we cannot know the effect or effectiveness of a marketing action without accounting for the actions of competitors. Say we try an eight-week promotion for a bar soap that combines a newspaper feature with a high-value coupon and a low feature price, and observe only a 10% gain over baseline sales. Management's reaction to such a disappointing response would be very different if all other brands were sitting quietly at shelf price, than if the other national brands were temporally exhausting demand with four-for-the-price-of-three multipacks. While single-brand sales models can be specified to include the actions of particular competitors, only market-share models include competition as a fundamental part of their composition. Market-share models are models for understanding how the marketing efforts of every brand impact the results in a competitive marketplace. Only by *describing* the influence of each marketing instrument can we gain a basis for marketing planning. *Prediction* alone is not enough. Time-series models that forecast the future from the past sales provide no insight into how those sales were generated. The emphasis on being *descriptive* also embraces the need to understand the areas in which consumer choice probabilities are synonymous with market shares as well. Part of the goal of *description* transcends what can be done by market-share models alone. Managers need to understand that their efforts have (potentially) competitive effects and (potentially) market-expansive effects. In sales-response models these effects are comingled, but by combining *descriptive* market-share models for the competitive effects with *descriptive* category-volume models for the market-expansive effects, managers obtain a much richer understanding of the market. The *profit-oriented* goal of market-share analysis urges us to ask how the firm's allocations of resources to aspects of the marketing mix produce bottom-line results. It reminds us that maximizing market share is not the same as maximizing profits. Systematically understanding how the actions available to a brand impact the market results of all competitors would be a very important gain for marketing science.

We begin by discussing the fundamental relations between marketing effort and market shares. In this context we discuss the derivation of the basic theorem that relates marketing effort to market share. We then develop, present and discuss five alternative market-share models, and evaluate them in terms of how we expect market-share elasticities to behave. We then discuss the relations between the aggregate concept of *market share* and the disaggregate concept of *choice probability*, with special emphasis on the threats to parameter stability in market-share models. The topic then shifts to the sources and representation of asymmetries in markets and competition, and the issue of the distinctiveness of marketing activities. A numerical example illustrates the diagnostic richness of these models. A concluding section discusses some of the challenges that market-share models must confront in the next decade.

2. Market share and marketing effort

We use the term *market share* to signify the share of total market sales (in quantity sold) for a product in a given period and in a given geographical area. This concept of market share is more explicitly stated in the following manner:

$$s_i = \frac{Q_i}{Q} \tag{1}$$

where

s_i = the market share of brand i,
Q_i = the sales of brand i's product,
Q = the total sales for the market,
$Q = \sum_{j=1}^{m} Q_j$,
m = the number of competing brands.

The quantity Q in the above equation is commonly called the *industry sales*, *primary demand*, all commodity volume (ACV), or simply *the market*. Market shares are temporally and spatially specific. They are defined and measured only for a specific period and a specific geographical area, but the time or occasion subscript is dropped in these preliminary developments for notational convenience. It does not make much sense for one to talk about a brand's share in general; one must say instead a brand's share of the Chicago trading area in 1990, that of the New York market in 1991. This is because both the numerator and denominator of Equation (1) are time- and area-specific, and will have to be matched for the same period and geographical area for this ratio to make sense.

Kotler [1984] sets up the basics for using market-share models in brand planning by asserting that a brand's market share is proportional to the *marketing effort* supporting it. We may represent this by:

$$s_i = k \cdot M_i \tag{2}$$

where

M_i = the marketing effort of brand i,
k = a constant of proportionality.

This simplest representation asserts that the greater the brand's marketing effort, the greater should be its market share.

Setting aside for the time being the question of how one might measure marketing effort, one must know the value of the proportionality constant, k, before Equation (2) is useful. But since market shares for an industry must sum to one, i.e.

$$\sum_{i=1}^{m} s_i = 1,$$

we know that

$$\sum_{i=1}^{m} k \cdot M_i = 1$$

or

$$\sum_{i=1}^{m} M_i = \frac{1}{k}.$$

Hence

$$k = \frac{1}{\sum_{i=1}^{m} M_i}.$$

By substituting this value of k in Equation (2), we have

$$s_i = \frac{M_i}{\sum_{j=1}^{m} M_j}. \tag{3}$$

This last equation says that the market share of brand i is equal to the brand's share of the total marketing effort, a statement which certainly seems plausible. Equation (3) is what Kotler calls the *fundamental theorem* of market share [Kotler, 1984, p. 231].

On important variation on this fundamental theorem indicates if brands tended to differ in terms of the effectiveness of their marketing effort; one may write

$$s_i = \frac{\alpha_i \cdot M_i}{\sum_{j=1}^{m} \alpha_j \cdot M_j} \tag{4}$$

where α_i is the effectiveness coefficient for brand i's marketing effort. This implies that, even if two brands expend the same amount of marketing effort, they may not have the same market share. If one brand's marketing effort is twice as effective as that of the other, the former will achieve a market share twice as large as the other's share.

Specification and measurement of what goes into *marketing effort* is an important topic. Kotler assumes that a brand's marketing effort is a function of its marketing mix, both past and current. Mathematically, we may write

$$M_i = f(P_i, A_i, D_i, \ldots) \tag{5}$$

where

P_i = the price of brand i's product,
A_i = the advertising expenditures of brand i,
D_i = the distribution efforts (e.g. the percent of stores carrying brand i).

There are wide choices in the specification of the functional form for Equation (5). For example, if we believe that components of the marketing mix interact we may choose a multiplicative function

$$M_i = P_i^p \cdot A_i^a \cdot D_i^d$$

where p, a, d are parameters to be estimated reflecting the importance of each component of the marketing mix. If one substitutes this expression in (3) or (4), the resultant market-share model will be the simplest version of an MCI (multiplicative, competitive-interaction) model. Or if we choose an exponential function

$$M_i = \exp(p \cdot P_i + a \cdot A_i + d \cdot D_i),$$

the market-share model is the simplest version of the multinomial logit (MNL) model.

2.1. Market-share theorem

Kotler's *market-share-as-share-of-marketing-effort* representation makes a lot of intuitive sense, but there are other ways to derive such a representation. We will review some of them in a later section, and only look here at one important theorem derived by Bell, Keeney & Little [1975].

Bell, Keeney & Little (BKL) consider a situation where, in purchasing a product, consumers must choose one brand from a set of alternative brands available in the market. They posit that the only determinant of market shares is the *attraction* which consumers feel toward each alternative brand, and make the following assumptions about attractions. Letting $\mathscr{A}_i$ be the attraction of brand i ($i = 1, 2, \ldots, m$) and s_i be its market share,

Axiom A1. $\mathscr{A}_i \geqslant 0$ for all i and $\sum_{i=1}^{m} \mathscr{A}_i > 0$ (i.e., attractions are nonnegative and their sum is positive).

Axiom A2. $\mathscr{A}_i = 0 \Rightarrow s_i = 0$. (The symbol $\Rightarrow$ should be read 'implies', i.e., zero attraction implies zero market share.)

Axiom A3. $\mathscr{A}_i = \mathscr{A}_j \Rightarrow s_i = s_j$ $(i \neq j)$ (i.e., equal attraction implies equal market share).

Axiom A4. When $\mathscr{A}_j$ changes by Δ, the corresponding change in s_i $(i \neq j)$ is independent of j (e.g. a change in attraction has a symmetrically or proportionally distributed effect on competitive market share).

From those four *axioms* they show that the following relationship between attractions and market shares may be derived:

$$s_i = \frac{\mathscr{A}_i}{\sum_{j=1}^{m} \mathscr{A}_j}. \tag{6}$$

The first three axioms are not controversial. But, as will be developed later, Axiom A4 has been the subject of much critical discussion. While Equations (3) and (6) represent two rather distinct schools of thought regarding the determinants of market shares (a brand's marketing effort for the former and consumer attraction for the latter), few would argue the fact that these equations are extremely similar. An additional assumption that the attraction of a brand is proportional to its marketing effort (which has intuitive appeal) is all that is required to reconcile these two equations.

BKL also show that a slightly different set of assumptions also yield Equation (6). Let C be the set of all alternative brands from which consumers make their choice.

Axiom B1. $\mathscr{A}_i \geqslant 0$.

Axiom B2. The attraction of a subset $S(\subseteq C)$ is equal to the sum of the attractions of elements in S.

Axiom B3. $\mathscr{A}_i$ is finite for all i and nonzero for at least one element in C.

Axiom B4. If the attractions of subsets $S^{(1)}$ and $S^{(2)}$ are equal, their market shares are equal.

The last axiom establishes the relationship between attractions and market shares. BKL observe that, if we add an assumption that

$$\sum_{i=1}^{m} \mathscr{A}_i = 1$$

in lieu of B4, $\mathscr{A}_i$ in this set of axioms satisfies the assumptions for probabilities in a finite (discrete) sample space. Because of this BKL suggest that attractions may be interpreted as *unnormalized probabilities*. However, this in turn suggests that if attractions were to follow axioms B1 through B4, by normalizing the $\mathcal{A}_i$'s through (6), market shares (s_i) may be interpreted as probabilities. This confuses an *aggregate* concept (*market shares*) with an *individual* (or *disaggregated*) concept (*probabilities*). When the market is homogeneous (i.e. not composed of systematically different consumer segments), market shares and choice probabilities may be used interchangeably. But, as is discussed later, in other circumstances we must be careful not to use these concepts interchangeably.

2.2. *Alternative models of market share*

The previous sections gave the rationales behind the MCI model and its close cousin, the MNL model. We now give explicit specifications to the simplest versions of those models.

MCI model:

$$\mathcal{A}_i = \exp(\alpha_i)\cdot \prod_{k=1}^{K} X_{ki}^{\beta_k}\cdot \varepsilon_i, \tag{7}$$

$$s_i = \frac{\mathcal{A}_i}{\sum_{j=1}^{m} \mathcal{A}_j}.$$

MNL model:

$$\mathcal{A}_i = \exp\left(\alpha_i + \sum_{k=1}^{K} \beta_k\cdot X_{ki} + \varepsilon_i\right), \tag{8}$$

$$s_i = \frac{\mathcal{A}_i}{\sum_{j=1}^{m} \mathcal{A}_j},$$

where

s_i = the market share of brand i,
$\mathcal{A}_i$ = the attraction of brand i,
m = the number of brands,
X_{ki} = the value of the kth explanatory variable X_k for brand i (e.g. prices, product attributes, expenditures for advertising, distribution, sales force),
K = the number of explanatory variables,
β_k = a parameter to be estimated,
α_i = a parameter for the constant influence of brand i,
ε_i = an error term.

In what follows we will use *attraction*, rather than *marketing effort*, to describe $\mathcal{A}_i$, because it is a more accepted terminology, keeping in mind that this implies the assumption that attraction is proportional to marketing effort.

The MCI and MNL models are not the only models of market shares. The *linear model* assumes simply that a brand's market share is a linear function in marketing-mix variables and other relevant variables. The *multiplicative* and *exponential models* represent market shares as a product of a number of variables (shrunk or stretched by appropriate parameters). Although there are other more complicated market-share models, for our purposes at present we need only define these three alternative models.

Linear model:

$$s_i = \alpha_i + \sum_{k=1}^{K} \beta_k \cdot X_{ki} + \varepsilon_i. \tag{9}$$

Multiplicative model:

$$s_i = \exp(\alpha_i) \cdot \prod_{k=1}^{K} X_{ki}^{\beta_k} \cdot \varepsilon_i. \tag{10}$$

Exponential model:

$$s_i = \exp\left(\alpha_i + \sum_{k=1}^{K} \beta_k \cdot X_{ki} + \varepsilon_i \right). \tag{11}$$

The five models – MCI, MNL, linear, multiplicative and exponential – are closely related to each other. For example, if we take the logarithm of both sides of either the multiplicative or exponential model, we will have a linear model (linear in the parameters of the respective models, and not in variables). In other words, while the conceptual difference may be great, the mathematical difference between the linear model and the multiplicative and exponential models is merely in the choice of transformations for variables, that is, whether or not the logarithmic transformation is applied to the explanatory variables. (The specification for the error term may be different in those three models, but this is a technical issue that will not be addressed here.)

The most interesting relationship is, however, the one between the MCI and multiplicative models (and the corresponding relationship between the MNL and exponential models). The multiplicative model, of course, assumes that market shares are a multiplicative function in explanatory variables, while in the MCI model attractions are multiplicative in variables and market shares are computed by normalizing attraction (making the sum of market shares to be equal to one). Obviously, the key difference between the two is normalization. In this connection, Naert & Bultez [1973] proposed the following important conditions for a market-share model:

(1) Estimated market shares from the model are nonnegative.
(2) The estimated market shares sum to one over all the competitors.

These conditions, commonly known as the *logical-consistency requirements*, are clearly not met by either the multiplicative or the exponential model, but are met by their respective normalized forms (i.e., MCI and MNL) – a clear advantage for MCI and MNL models. Note that the linear model does not satisfy the logical-consistency requirements.

Why, then, are the MCI and MNL models not used more extensively? The answer is that for a time both of those models were considered to be intrinsically nonlinear models, requiring estimation schemes that were expensive in analysts' time and computer resources. This, however, turned out to be a hasty judgment because Nakanishi [1972; Nakanishi & Cooper, 1974] showed that those models may be changed into a linear model (in the model parameters) by a simple transformation. Using the MCI model, for example, we can first take the logarithm of both sides.

$$\log s_i = \alpha_i + \sum_{k=1}^{K} \beta_k \log X_{ki} + \log \varepsilon_i$$
$$- \log\left\{\sum_{j=1}^{m}\left(\alpha_j \prod_{k=1}^{K} X_{kj}^{\beta_k}\varepsilon_j\right)\right\}.$$

If we sum the above equation over i $(i = 1, 2, \ldots, m)$ and divide by m, we have

$$\log \tilde{s} = \bar{\alpha} + \sum_{k=1}^{K} \beta_k \log \tilde{X}_k + \log \tilde{\varepsilon} - \log\left\{\sum_{j=1}^{m}\left(\alpha_j \prod_{k=1}^{K} X_{kj}^{\beta_k}\varepsilon_j\right)\right\}$$

where $\tilde{s}$, $\tilde{X}_k$ and $\tilde{\varepsilon}$ are the geometric means of s_i, X_{ki} and ε_i, respectively. Subtracting the above from the previous equation, we obtain

$$\log\left(\frac{s_i}{\tilde{s}}\right) = \alpha_i^* + \sum_{k=1}^{K} \beta_k \log\left(\frac{X_{ki}}{\tilde{X}_k}\right) + \varepsilon_i^* \tag{12}$$

where

$$\alpha_i^* = (\alpha_i - \bar{\alpha}), \qquad \varepsilon_i^* = \log(\varepsilon_i/\tilde{\varepsilon}).$$

The last equation is linear in model parameters α_i^* $(i = 1, 2, \ldots, m)$ and β_k $(k = 1, 2, \ldots, K)$. (In addition, there is another parameter σ_ε^2, the variance of ε_i, to be estimated, but this parameter does not concern us here.) This transformation is called the *log-centering* transformation. The importance of this transformaton is that it leads to ways to estimate the parameters of the original nonlinear model using linear-regression techniques. Note also that if we apply the inverse of this transformation to the estimates that result from a linear regression we must obtain market-share estimates that satisfy the logical-consistency conditions. That is,

$$\hat{s}_i = \frac{\exp \hat{y}_i}{\sum_{j=1}^{m} \exp \hat{y}_j}$$

where $\hat{s}_i$ is the estimate market share for brand i and $\hat{y}_i$ is the estimated dependent variable from the *reduced form* of the regression model. This is known as the *inverse log-centering transformation.*

If we apply the log-centering transformation to the MNL model, we obtain the following linear form:

$$\log\left(\frac{s_i}{\tilde{s}}\right) = (\alpha_i - \bar{\alpha}) + \sum_{k=1}^{K} \beta_k (X_{ki} - \bar{X}_k) + (\varepsilon_i - \bar{\varepsilon})$$

where $\bar{\alpha}$, $\bar{X}_k$ and $\bar{\varepsilon}$ are the arithmetic means of α_i, X_{ki} and ε_i, respectively. If we let $\alpha_i^* = (\alpha_i - \bar{\alpha})$ and $\varepsilon_i^* = (\varepsilon_i - \bar{\varepsilon})$,

$$\log\left(\frac{s_i}{\tilde{s}}\right) = \alpha_i^* + \sum_{k=1}^{K} \beta_k (X_{ki} - \bar{X}_k) + \varepsilon_i^* . \tag{13}$$

Both Equations (12) and (13) are linear functions of the model parameters, and hence can be called *log-linear* models. The multiplicative and exponential models are also log-linear models. In other words, both the MCI and MNL models are really special cases of log-linear models. Compare the *reduced forms* of these models.

Linear model:

$$s_i = \alpha_i + \sum_{k=1}^{K} \beta_k X_{ki} + \varepsilon_i .$$

Multiplicative model:

$$\log s_i = \alpha_i + \sum_{k=1}^{K} \beta_k \log X_{ki} + \log \varepsilon_i .$$

Exponential model:

$$\log s_i = \alpha_i + \sum_{k=1}^{K} \beta_k X_{ki} + \varepsilon_i .$$

MCI model:

$$\log\left(\frac{s_i}{\tilde{s}}\right) = \alpha_i^* + \sum_{k=1}^{K} \beta_k \log\left(\frac{X_{ki}}{\tilde{X}_k}\right) + \varepsilon_i^* .$$

MNL model:

$$\log\left(\frac{s_i}{\tilde{s}}\right) = \alpha_i^* + \sum_{k=1}^{K} \beta_k (X_{ki} - \bar{X}_k) + \varepsilon_i^*.$$

In all five equations the right-hand side is linear in both α_i or α_i^* $(i = 1, 2, \ldots, m)$ and β_k $(k = 1, 2, \ldots, K)$. The left-hand side is a market share, the logarithm of a market share, or a log-centered form of a market share. Ignoring the differences in the specification of the error term (ε_i, $\log \varepsilon_i$ or ε_i^*), note that the number of parameters in the five formulations are the same, one would expect that those models would be just as accurate in predicting the *dependent variable*, namely, the left-hand side of each equation. Which one, then, makes the most accurate prediction of market shares? Many studies on predictive accuracy of market-share models [Brodie & De Kluyer, 1984; Ghosh, Neslin & Shoemaker, 1984; Leeflang & Reuyl, 1984; Naert & Weverbergh, 1981, 1985] found the logical-consistency property of the MCI and MNL models to produce only marginally better predictions than the linear and multiplicative models. Whey then all this fuss about the MCI and MNL models? First, these tests did not include the more sophisticated versions of the models specified later in this chapter. And second, as was stated in the Introduction, we do not believe that predictive accuracy is the only important criterion for judging the value of a model. We would rather find the answer in the *construct validity* (i.e. intrinsic meaningfulness) of those models. Is the model *descriptive* in a way that facilitates brand planning? Is the model *profit-oriented* so that the revenue implications can be investigated? Do the elasticities make managerial sense? This latter issue is addressed in the next section.

2.3. Market-share elasticities

Simply stated, *market-share elasticity is the ratio of the relative change in a market share corresponding to a relative change in a marketing-mix variable.* Expressed mathematically,

$$e_{s_i} = \frac{\Delta s_i / s_i}{\Delta X_{ki} / X_{ki}} = \frac{\Delta s_i}{\Delta X_{ki}} \cdot \frac{X_{ki}}{s_i} \tag{14}$$

where s_i is the market share and X_{ki} is the value of the kth marketing-mix variable, for brand i. The symbol Δ indicates a change in respective variables. There is nothing conceptually difficult in market-share elasticity. For example, if a brand's share increased 10% (say from 30 share points to 33) corresponding to a price reduction of 5%, the above equation would give a (price) elasticity of -2; or if advertising expenditures were increased by 3% and as a result the share increased by 1%, the (advertising) elasticity would be 0.33; and so forth. We should really use $e_{s_i}^{(k)}$ to denote the elasticity of share with respect to a particular instrument k, but drop the superscript for notational convenience.

There is no way to estimate elasticities directly from empirical data without adopting a model. This may not be intuitively clear because the formula for computing elasticities (14) appears to contain only those terms which may be empirically measurable. But note that the Δs_i term in Equation (14) must correspond to the change in a specific marketing-mix variable, ΔX_{ki}. Suppose that one observed that a brand's share increased 3% in a period. How does one know how much of that increased share is due to price reduction? Or due to increased advertising? To assess those so-called *partial effects* one needs a market-share model.

The reader may be cautioned at this point that the estimated values of elasticities vary from one model to another, and hence one must choose the model that conceptually fits the situation best. To illustrate, we will derive the share elasticity with respect to X_{ki} for the simplest version of each model. For that purpose, however, one needs another concept of share elasticity which is slightly different from the one defined by (14). Technically, (14) is called the *arc elasticity*. This is because both Δs_i and ΔX_{ki} span a range over the market-response curve which gives the relationship between market shares and marketing-mix variables. The other elasticitiy formula is called the *point elasticity* and takes the following form:

$$e_{s_i} = \frac{\partial s_i}{\partial X_{ki}} \cdot \frac{X_{ki}}{s_i}. \tag{15}$$

Note that the only difference between the two formulas is that $(\Delta s_i/\Delta X_{ki})$ in Equation (14) is replaced by $(\partial s_i/\partial X_{ki})$ in (15). Formula (15) utilizes the slope of the market-response curve at a specific value of X_{ki}. The reason for using the point-elasticity formula rather than the arc formula is that the former gives much simpler expressions of share elasticity. We may add that (15) is a close approximation of (14) for a small value of ΔX_{ki}, that is, when the change in X_{ki} is very small. The point elasticity for each model is given below.

Linear model:

$$e_{s_i} = \beta_k X_{ki}/s_i.$$

Multiplicative model:

$$e_{s_i} = \beta_k.$$

Exponential model:

$$e_{s_i} = \beta_k X_{ki}.$$

MCI model:

$$e_{s_i} = \beta_k(1 - s_i).$$

MNL model:

$$e_{s_i} = \beta_k(1 - s_i)X_{ki}.$$

Though the five market-share models are similar in the sense that they are either linear or log-linear models, the share elasticities implied from the models are quite different. One may wish to disqualify some models on the basis of those expressions on some a priori grounds.

Market-share elasticities should have the following properties:

(1) Since $Q_i = Q \cdot s_i$, we can show that $e_{Q_i.x} = e_{Q.x} + e_{s_i.x}$,
(2) If s_i is an increasing function in $X, e_{s_i.x} \to 0$ as $s_i \to 1$. This is because, as $s_i \to 1$, $Q_i \to Q$ and therefore $e_{Q_i.x} \to e_{Q.x}$ in property (1) above.
(3) If s_i is a strictly increasing function in $X, e_{s_i.x} \to 0$ as $X \to \infty$. This is derived from property (2) above, since as $X \to \infty$, $s_i \to 1$. If s_i is an increasing function in X but approaches a constant (<1) as $X \to \infty$, then $e_{s_i.x} \to 0$ (since $\mathrm{d}s_i/\mathrm{d}X \to 0$).

The first property is a strict mathematical consequence of the relation of brand sales to market share and industry sales. While none of the currently considered models fails to satisfy this condition, it should be kept in mind for evaluating other alternatives. The second property reflects that a brand's share elasticity should approach zero as the share for that brand approaches one. The multiplicative model implies that share elasticity is constant regardless of the share level, and therefore seems rather inappropriate as a market-share model.

The third property reflects the generally accepted view that it becomes harder to gain market shares as a brand increases its marketing effort. In other words, one would expect market-share elasticity to approach zero as X_{ki} goes to infinity (or minus infinity, depending on the variable in question). But the exponential model implies an opposite: share elasticity may be increased indefinitely as the value of X_{ki} increases. This is an uncomfortable situation, especially if variable X_{ki} is a promotional variable (such as advertising expenditures, number of salesmen, etc., since it implies ever-increasing market-share returns for increasing promotional expenditures. In addition, the exponential model has the same problem as the multiplicative model: for a fixed value of X_{ki}, e_{s_i} is constant for all levels of s_i.

Note that the elasticity expression for the linear model reflects that share elasticity declines as the share increases, but, when the share approaches one, the elasticity does not approach zero. In fact, share elasticity approaches 1 as X_{ki} increases to infinity (or minus infinity, as the case may be). Thus the linear model produces a highly unreasonable share-elasticity expression.

Considering what we expect from share elasticities, one may conclude that the linear, multiplicative and exponential models are not proper market-share models for use in marketing decision-making. This leaves us the MCI and MNL models as feasible alternatives. Figure 6.1 shows the change in share elasticity over the positive range of X_{ki} values.

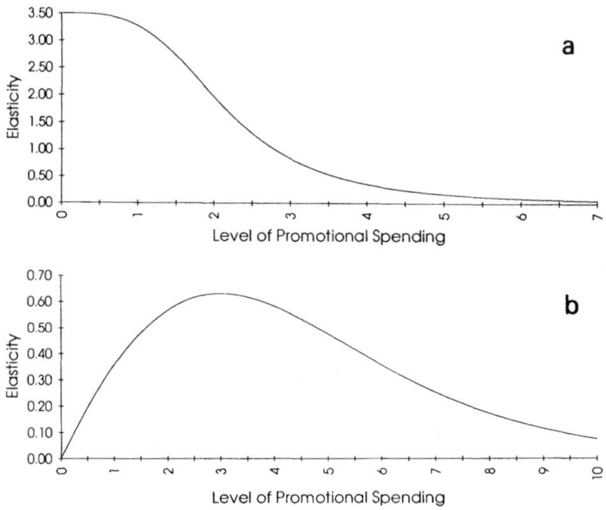

Fig. 6.1. Share elasticities for (a) MCI and (b) MNL models.

The share is assumed to increase as X_{ki} increases. Accounting for this share increase, the share elasticity for the MCI model monotonically declines as X_{ki} increases (Figure 6.1a), while that for the MNL model increases to a point and then declines. Which expression is a better one for share elasticity depends on the nature of the explanatory variable X_{ki}. The relevant issue is how share elasticity should behave for low values of the variable. If X_{ki} is product price, for example, it is more likely that share elasticity is fairly large even when price is near zero. Hence, one would be inclined to use the MCI model for price. On the other hand, if the variable is advertising expenditure, it is not unreasonable to assume that, at an extremely low level of expenditure, advertising is not very effective. This assumption, of course, leads to the adoption of the MNL model for advertising expenditure. Gruca & Sudharshan [1991], however, point out some issues when using MNL forms of variable as a basis for resource allocation. For firms with less than half of the market, the MNL formulation of an advertising variable implies that it is optimal to increase spending as much as possible. While these authors advise using the MCI version for advertising, another interpretation is possible. It might in fact be optimal for a firm to allocate as much to advertising as possible until it gains 50% of the market. In any case, careful consideration of the nature of each explanatory variable could rightfully lead to a mixture of MCI and MNL variables within a single market-share model. The general attraction framework encompasses both MCI and MNL models.

General attraction model:

$$\mathscr{A}_i = \exp(\alpha_i + \varepsilon_i) \prod_{k=1}^{K} f_k(X_{ki})^{\beta k}, \tag{16}$$

$$s_i = \frac{\mathscr{A}_i}{\sum_{j=1}^{m} \mathscr{A}_j},$$

where f_k is a monotone transformation of X_{ki}. If one chooses an identity transformation for k (that is, $f_k(X_{ki}) = X_{ki}$), (16) becomes the MCI model; if f_k is an exponential function (that is, $f_k(X_{ki}) = \exp(X_{ki})$), then (16) becomes the MNL model. But there is no reason for one to have to choose either the identity or exponential transformation for all f_k's in (16). Depending on the nature of variable X_k, one should be free to choose either the identity or exponential transformation (or any other appropriate monotone transformation, for that matter). This is why in (16) f_k has subscript k.

3. Market shares and choice probabilities

So far we have chosen to treat market shares as an aggregate quantity, namely, the ratio of a firm's (brand) sales to the relevant industry sales. But, since aggregate sales are composites of many purchases made by individual buyers (consumers and industrial buyers), market-share figures must be related to individual buyers' choices of various brands. In analyzing the relationships between market shares and individual choice probabilities, we will have to consider the variability of two factors – *choice probabilities* and *purchase frequency* for individual buyers – over the population of buyers in the market. Let us first define those two concepts.

Suppose that each buyer purchases a number of units of the product per period. We will assume that the *purchase frequency* (i.e. the number of purchases per period) by an individual buyer is a random variable that has a statistical distribution. We shall call this distribution an individual *purchase-frequency distribution*, since it is defined for each buyer in the market. The specific form of this distribution does not concern us here except that it has its own mean (*mean purchase frequency*).

Let us assume, not unreasonably, that a buyer does not always purchase the same brand from a set of alternative brands. In additon, it is assumed that a buyer's choice of a brand at one *purchase occasion* is made independently from his/her previous purchase and the buyer's selection is governed by probabilities specific to each brand (i.e. each buyer's brand selection in a period follows a zero-order Bernoulli process). While this *zero-order assumption* has been debated for the last thirty years [Frank, 1962; Kuehn, 1962], and it is a more reasonable assumption for the *household* than for the individual within a household [Kahn, Morrison and Wright, 1986], it is a palatable starting point for these developments [Bass, Givon, Kalwani, Reibstein & Wright, 1984; Givon 1984]. The probabilities for alternative brands in the industry are called *individual choice probabilities*.

Whether or not the buyer's behavior is truly probabilistic or deterministic is not an issue here. A buyer's choice behavior may be largely deterministic, but the environmental conditions surrounding purchase occasions may be such that they involve probabilistic elements that, from the viewpoint of an outside observer, make the buyers' choices appear probabilistic. We also posit that the attractions of alternative brands affect choice probabilities. This is to be consistent with our position that brand attractions are the determinants of market shares.

We distinguish four cases regarding the homogeneity (or heterogeneity) of the buyer population with respect to *individual choice probabilities* and *purchase frequencies.*

Case 1: Homogeneous purchase frequencies and choice probabilities
If mean individual-purchase frequencies are equal for all buyers and the brand selection of every buyer in the market is governed by the same set of choice probabilities, it is rather obvious that the market share of a brand will be approximately equal to the choice probability for the brand. (Actually, it is the expected value of the market share of a brand which will be equal to the choice probability for the brand.) In this case market shares may be interpreted as individual choice probabilities. For example, if the market share for a brand is 30 share points, one may say that each buyer chooses this brand with a 0.3 probability.

Case 2: Homogeneous purchase frequencies and heterogeneous choice probabilities
The interpretation of market shares will have to be changed a little if each buyer has a different set of choice-probability values for alternative brands. We still assume that mean purchase frequencies are equal for all buyers in the market. Under those assumptions it is easy to show that the expected value of a brand's market share is equal to the (population) average of choice probabilities for that brand. In other words, a market share of 30 share points may be interpreted as meaning that the average of the choice probabilities across the buyer population is 0.3.

Case 3: Heterogeneous purchase frequencies and homogeneous choice probabilities
This is the case where, while a common set of choice probabilities is shared by all buyers, mean purchase frequencies vary over buyers and have a statistical distribution over the buyer population. In this case the expected value of a brand's market share is still equal to its choice probability.

Case 4: Heterogeneous purchase frequencies and choice probabilities
In this case both choice probabilities and purchase frequencies are assumed to be variable over the buyer population. We need to distinguish further two cases within this.

(a) Uncorrelated case: choice probabilities and purchase frequencies are uncorrelated (i.e. independently distributed) over the buyer population.
(b) Correlated case: choice probabilities and purchase frequencies are correlated over the buyer population.

If purchase frequencies and choice probabilities are uncorrelated, the expected value of market shares is, as is shown below, still equal to population averages of choice probabilities (as in the case of homogeneous purchase frequencies). Turning to the correlated case, one finds that market shares are no longer directly related to choice probabilities. Case 4(b) is perhaps more realistic for many products, since one often hears that so-called *heavy users* and *light users* exhibit remarkably different purchase behavior. Heavy users are said to be more discriminating in taste, to be more price-conscious, and to tend to purchase *family-size* or economy packages. It is not surprising, then, to find heavy users, preferring some brands or brand/size combinations to those preferred by light users. If there were differences in the value of choice probability for a brand between heavy and light users, individual purchase frequencies and choice probabilities would be correlated and the market share for the brand will be biased toward the choice probability values for heavy users simply because they purchase more units of the brand. Thus market shares and choice probabilities generally do not coincide in this case. The results above may be stated more formally. The expected value of unit sales for brand i is obtained by averaging (over the buyer population) individual purchase frequencies multiplied by the individual's choice probability for the brand. Hence the expected value of market share for brand i is given by:

$$\text{market share}_i = \frac{\text{average number of units purchased for brand } i}{\text{average purchase frequency (for all brands)}}$$

or

$$\mathrm{E}(s_i) = \frac{1}{\bar{\mu}} \int_0^{\infty} \int_0^1 \mu \pi_i g(\mu, \pi_i)\, \mathrm{d}\pi_i \mathrm{d}\mu \tag{17}$$

where

$\mathrm{E}(s_i)$ = the expected value of market share for brand i,
μ = the mean purchase frequency per period (per individual),
$\bar{\mu}$ = the population mean of μ,
π_i = the individual choice probability for brand i,
$g(\mu, \pi_i)$ = the joint density function for μ and π_i.

Equation (17) shows that the expected value of market share for brand i is a weighted average of choice probabilities (weights are individual mean purchase frequencies) divided by average (over individuals) mean purchase frequency $\bar{\mu}$. From (17) we directly obtain the following result.

$$\mathrm{E}(s_i) = \bar{\pi}_i + \mathrm{cov}(\mu, \pi_i)/\bar{\mu}$$

where

$\bar{\pi}_i$ = the population mean of π_i,
$\mathrm{cov}(\mu, \pi_i)$ = the covariance of μ and π_i.

This is because, by definition, $\mathrm{cov}(\mu, \pi_i) = \bar{\mu}\mathrm{E}(s_i) - \bar{\mu}\bar{\pi}_i$. This equation shows that in general $\mathrm{E}(s_i)$ is not equal to $\bar{\pi}_i$. Since $\mathrm{cov}(\mu, \pi_i)$ may be positive or negative, one cannot say if market shares are greater or smaller than population mean of the

Table 6.1
Relations between market shares and choice probabilities

Choice probabilities	Purchase frequencies	
	Homogeneous	Heterogeneous
Homogeneous	Case 1: $E(s_i) = \pi_i$	Case 3: $E(s_i) = \pi_i$
Heterogeneous	Case 2: $E(s_i) = \bar{\pi}_i$	Case 4(a) Uncorrelated: $E(s_i) = \bar{\pi}_i$ Case 4(b) Correlated: $E(s_i) = \bar{\pi}_i + \text{cov}(\mu, \pi_i)/\bar{\mu}$

choice probabilities. But if μ and π_i are positively correlated, $E(s_i)$ is greater than $\bar{\pi}_i$. If the correlation is negative, $E(s_i)$ is less than $\bar{\pi}_i$. Note also that, if $\text{cov}(\mu, \pi_i) = 0$ (that is, if there is no correlation between the market share and choice probability), then the expected market share and the average choice probability are equal. In other words, in the uncorrelated case the expected value of a brand's market share is equal to its average choice probability ($\bar{\pi}_i$). The foregoing results are summarized in Table 6.1.

It is apparent from the table that the only case where we are uncertain of the correspondence between market shares and choice probabilities is Case 4(b). This fact might tempt one to look at this case as an exception or anomaly, but it is probably the most prevalent condition in the market. A practical implication of the preponderance of Case 4(b) is that, for the purpose of market-share forecasts, it is not sufficient for one to be able to predict the choice behavior of individuals accurately; rather it becomes necessary for one to be able to predict choice probabilities for each different level of purchase frequencies.

Of course, the situation cannot be changed by merely assuming that μ and π_i are uncorrelated over the buyer population (Case 4(a)). Since μ and π_i are arithmetically related, that is, $\pi_i = \mu_i/\mu$ where μ_i is the expected number of units of brand i purchased by an individual, and $\sum_{i=1}^{m} \mu_i = \mu$ where m is the number of alternative brands in the industry, the assumption that $\text{cov}(\mu, \pi_i) = 0$ (for all i) implies a very restrictive form of joint distribution for μ and π_i. Indeed, it may be shown that μ is distributed as a gamma function and the π_i's are jointly distributed as a Dirichlet distribution. No other distributional assumption will give $\text{cov}(\mu, \pi_i) = 0$. (See Cooper & Nakanishi [1988, pp. 52–54] for the proof of this result.)

What does all this argument about the relationship between purchase frequencies and choice probabilities suggest to analysts and marketing managers? If the correlation between purchase frequencies and choice probabilities is suspect, there may be an aggregation problem. One should segment the market in terms of purchase frequencies and analyze each segment separately. One may discover that marketing instruments have different effects on different segments and may be able to allocate marketing resources more efficiently. Also forecasting of brand sales and market shares will become more accurate if market shares are forecast for each segment and weighted by the mean purchase frequencies for the segments to obtain the estimate of overall market shares. Segmentation analysis of this type, however, requires more refined data than the usual aggregate market-share data, such as consumer-diary or scanner-panel data. Such data are currently available in the *single-source* data sets, and an illustration integrating the aggregate store data and the information in the associated consumer panels is presented later.

3.1. Individual choice probabilities

The focus of this section is to relate individual choice probabilities to attractions of alternative brands. We can of course assume that the choice probability for a brand is proportional to its attraction, and obtain a result similar to *Kotler's fundamental theorem* discussed earlier. But there are other more axiomatic approaches to deriving choice probabilities, and here we will be dealing with two basic models which are closely related to each other. It may be added that the terms *attraction* and *utility* will be used interchangeably in this section.

3.1.1. Constant-utility models

The simplest model for choice probabilities is the constant-utility model which is also called the Luce model or Bradley–Terry–Luce model. Its basic assumption (or *axiom*) may be stated as follows.

Axiom 1. Let an object, x, be an element of the choice set (i.e. set of choice alternatives), C, and also of a subset of C, S (i.e. $S \subseteq C$). The probability that x is chosen from C is equal to the product of the probability that x is chosen from S and the probability that (an element of) S is chosen from C.

Luce [1959] calls this assumption the *individual choice axiom*, which may be expressed mathematically as:

$$\Pr(x|C) = \Pr(x|S)\Pr(S|C)$$

where $\Pr(x|C)$ is read as 'the probability that x is chosen from C'.

This *axiom* for choice probabilities leads to results similar to that of the market-share theorem for market shares. If we let

$$u_x = \frac{\Pr(x|C)}{\Pr(z|C)}$$

for an arbitrary object in C, then for two objects x and y in C

$$\frac{u_x}{u_y} = \frac{\Pr(x|C)}{\Pr(y|C)}$$

and this ratio does not change with the choice of z. Also, since

$$\sum_{y \in C} \Pr(y|C) = \Pr(x|C) \sum_{y \in C} \frac{u_y}{u_x} = 1$$

we have

$$\Pr(x|C) = u_x \Big/ \sum_{y \in C} u_y.$$

The quantity u_x is called the *constant utility* of object x, and presumably determined for each individual as a function of marketing activities for x.

This model formed a basis of various models of individual choice behavior [Huff, 1962; Haines, Simon & Alexis 1972; Nakanishi & Cooper, 1974] and was also implicitly adopted for many market-share models. But this model exhibits the so-called *independence from irrelevant alternatives* (IIA) property which produces some quite counterintuitive results. From the axiom we have

$$\frac{\Pr(x|C)}{\Pr(y|C)} = \frac{\Pr(x|S)}{\Pr(y|S)}$$

for any subset of S of C which contains both x and y. Since this relationship must hold for set $\{x, y\}$,

$$\frac{u_x}{u_y} = \frac{\Pr(x|\{x,y\})}{\Pr(y|\{x,y\})}.$$

This ratio is independent of the choice of z. Since z is supposedly irrelevant to the odds of choosing x over y, this has been called the *independence of irrelevant alternatives* (IIA) property. The classic counterexamples are from Debreu [1960]. Although Debreu proposed a record-buying situation, the issues are often more clearly illustrated using a transportation-choice example. Suppose a person is indifferent between riding on a red bus (RB) or a blue bus (BB) if offered just these two alternatives, but prefers riding a taxi (T) four-to-one over a red bus, if offered this pair, or four-to-one over a blue bus, if offered that pair of alternatives. The choice axiom would summarize this case by noting that $\Pr(\text{RB}|\{\text{RB},\text{BB}\}) = 0.5$, $\Pr(\text{T}|\{\text{T},\text{RB}\}) = 0.8$, and $\Pr(\text{T}|\{\text{T},\text{BB}\}) = 0.8$. While it seems clear that the probability of choosing a taxi shouldn't decrease if it is offered in a choice set along with both a red bus and a blue bus (i.e. $\Pr(\text{T}|\{\text{RB},\text{BB},\text{T}\})$ should still be 0.8), the choice axiom insists that $\Pr(\text{T}|\{\text{RB},\text{BB},\text{T}\}) = 0.67$ and $\Pr(\text{RB}|\{\text{RB},\text{BB},\text{T}\}) = 0.16$. The choice axiom forces this so that the *ratio* of the utility of RB to T is *constant* regardless of the choice set in which they are offered.

The concept of *constant utility* for a brand and the IIA property are really two sides of the same coin. If we think of *utility* is an inherent property of a brand that doesn't change regardless of the context in which a choice is made, we will be trapped by the IIA property into counterintuitive positions. There are two ways out of this problem. First, we can explicitly consider how the context in which choices are made affects the attractions of the alternatives. This is the path we follow in discussing the *temporal distinctiveness* of marketing efforts. Second, we can consider *utility* to be a random variable, rather than a constant. This is the topic of the next section.

3.1.2. Random-utility models

A choice model can be based on the assumption that the attractions an individual feels toward various objects (in our application, brands in an industry) on each purchase occasion are random variables, and the individual selects the brand that happens to have the largest utility value among the alternatives on that occasion. This *random-utility model* is defined as follows. Let $U_1, U_2, \ldots, U_m$ be the utilities for alternative brands where m is the number of brands in the choice set, C, of all competing brands in the industry, and let $g(U_1, U_2, \ldots, U_m)$ be the joint density function for them. The probability that brand i is chosen on a purchase occasion is given by

$$\Pr(i \mid C) = \Pr(U_i \geqslant U_j \text{ for all } j \in C).$$

In order to evaluate this probability, however, one must evaluate an integral function. For three brands, the probability that brand 1 is chosen is given by the following integral:

$$\Pr(1 \mid C) = \int_{-\infty}^{\infty} \int_{-\infty}^{u_1} \int_{-\infty}^{u_1} g(u_1, u_2, u_3)\, \mathrm{d}u_3\, \mathrm{d}u_2\, \mathrm{d}u_1. \tag{18}$$

Similarly, $\Pr(2 \mid C)$ and $\Pr(3 \mid C)$ are given by suitably changing the upper limits of integration. Integral (18) may be defined for any number of choice objects (e.g. brands).

A large number of variants of random utility models may be created from this definition by selecting different specifications for g. However, the usefulness of random-utility models is limited because, unless the density function g is so very special as to give an analytical solution, the evaluation of this integral will in general require numerical integration. For example, if g is a joint-normal density (known as a probit or multivariate-probit model), there is no analytical (or closed-form) solution to this integeral. The probit model is a reasonable model for many applications, but its use has been hampered by the fact that the evaluation of (18) for a large number of objects involves tedious numerical integration.

There is one noted exception, however, to the need for cumbersome numerical integration of (18). McFadden [1974] showed that, if the joint distribution for random utilities $\{U_1, U_2, \ldots, U_m\}$ is a so-called multivariate *extreme-value distribution* of type I, then Integral (18) has a closed-form solution. A multivariate extreme-value distribution takes the following form:

$$G(u_1, u_2, \ldots, u_m) = \prod_{i=1}^{m} \exp[-\exp(\alpha_i - u_i)]$$

where $\alpha_i (i = 1, 2, \ldots, m)$ are parameters. This distribution is convenient because the maximum value among a sample of random utilities $\{u_1, u_2, \ldots, u_m\}$ from this distribution is also distributed as an extreme-value distribution of the following form:

$$F(u_{\max}) = \exp\left[-\exp(-u_{\max}) \sum_{i=1}^{m} \exp(\alpha_i)\right]$$

where $u_{\max}$ is a realization of a new random variable,

$$U_{\max} = \max(U_1, U_2, \ldots, U_m).$$

Using this property, the distribution function for random variable

$$U_{\max^*_i} = \max\{U_j\text{: for all } j \neq i\}$$

is given by

$$F(u_{\max^* i}) = \exp\left[-\exp(-u_{\max^* i}) \sum_{j \neq i}^{m} \exp(\alpha_j)\right].$$

Then the probability that brand i is chosen at a purchase occasion is given by

$$\Pr(i|C) = \Pr(U_i > U_{\max^* i})$$

$$= \int_{-\infty}^{\infty} \int_{-\infty}^{u_i} \mathrm{d}G(u_i)\mathrm{d}F(u_{\max^* i})$$

$$= \int_{-\infty}^{\infty} \exp[-\exp(\alpha_i - u_i)] \exp(\alpha_i - u_i)$$

$$\cdot \exp\left[-\exp(u_i) \sum_{j \neq i}^{m} \exp(\alpha_j)\right] \mathrm{d}u_i = \exp(\alpha_i) \Big/ \sum_{j=1}^{m} \exp(\alpha_j). \tag{19}$$

If we let the attraction of brand i, $\mathscr{A}_i$, be equal to $\exp(\alpha_i)$, this expression is similar to an MNL model. Indeed the foregoing argument has been used to derive MNL models for individual-choice behavior. However, one may derive an expression similar to more straightforward attraction models in Equation (6), if, instead of an extreme-value distribution of type I, one chooses an extreme-value distribution of type II, namely,

$$G(u_1, u_2, \ldots, u_m) = \sum_{i=1}^{m} \exp[-\mathscr{A}_i u_i^{-b}]$$

where $\mathscr{A}_i$ ($i = 1,2,\ldots,m$) are parameters. To show this, first note that the distribution function for random variable

$$U_{\max *i} = \max\{U_j\text{: for all } j \neq i\}$$

is given by

$$F(u_{\max *i}) = \exp\left[-u_{\max *i}^{-b} \sum_{j \neq i}^{m} \mathscr{A}_j\right].$$

Using this,

$$\begin{aligned} \Pr(i|C) &= \Pr(U_i > U_{\max *i}) \qquad (20) \\ &= \int_{-\infty}^{\infty} \int_{-\infty}^{u_i} \mathrm{d}G(u_i)\mathrm{d}F(u_{\max *i}) \\ &= \int_{-\infty}^{\infty} \exp[-\mathscr{A}_i u_i^{-b}](\mathscr{A}_i b u_i^{-b-1})\exp\left[-u_i^{-b} \sum_{j \neq i}^{m} \mathscr{A}_j\right] \mathrm{d}u_i \\ &= \mathscr{A}_i \bigg/ \sum_{j=1}^{m} \mathscr{A}_j. \end{aligned}$$

Thus individual-level versions of MCI models as well as MNL models are derivable if extreme-value distributions are assumed for the joint distribution of random utilities. So if we substitute an extreme-value distribution of type II, then what McFadden showed for MNL models can be generalized to MCI models.

Although both Equations (19) and (20) are derived for individual choice probabilities, one may derive an attraction model for aggregate market shares, if the definition of distribution functions is slightly changed. Suppose that random utilities for alternative brands, $U_1, U_2, \ldots, U_m$, are jointly distributed over the population of individual buyers, rather than within an individual. Each individual has a set of realized values for utilities, $u_1, u_2, \ldots, u_m$, and will select that brand which has the maximum utility value among m brands. Cast in this manner, the problem is to find the proportion of buyers who will purchase brand i, but Equations (19) and (20) give precisely this proportion (that is, market share) for two extreme-value functions.

Although random-utility models in general do not have the IIA property, it should be noted that some random-utility models do. Yellott [1977] proved that a random-utility model is equivalent to a constant-utility model (and hence possesses the IIA property) if and only if the joint distribution for random utilities follows a multivariate extreme-value distribution. The basic forms of MNL and MCI models belong to this special case. But we wish to emphasize that it is possible to construct attraction models of probabilistic choice which do not have the IIA property. We will discuss two such models – the *fully extended* and *distinctiveness* models – later in this chapter.

4. Asymmetries in markets and competition

Up to this point we have dealt with the simplest attraction models and the foundations that underlie them. These models have been symmetric in that a change in the market share of one leads to symmetrically distributed changes in the market shares of the other brands (i.e. each brand gains or loses from the actions of others in proportion to its market share). An even cursory observation of competitive interactions in the marketplace reveals that some firms (brands) are capable of exerting inordinately strong influence over the shaping of demand and competition, while other firms (brands) are not. On-package ads such as General Mills' Total Corn Flakes claim "more nutritious and better tasting than Kellogg's Corn Flakes" are offered in the managerial belief that going after specific competitors can have a disproportionate impact [Gibson, 1991]. Split-cable ad tests have shown some companies how to choose ads that will give more market-share boost for the same media buck. Recent work by Blattberg & Wisniewski [1989] emphasizes how national brands can draw market shares from regional brands much more readily than vice versa, and how regional brands can draw from economy brands more easily than economy brands can fight back. Further, all brands do not receive the same return from advertising or promotional expenditures. Such cases illustrate both differential effectiveness of brands and asymmetries in market and competitive structures. Differential effectiveness among brands reflects that firms (brands) have different degrees of effectiveness in carrying out their marketing activities. That such differences exist in real markets is obvious, but differential effectiveness alone does not create or reflect asymmetries. Shares will still be gained or lost according to the rules of the symmetric market. There are two fundamental sources of asymmetries. First, asymmetries are reflected in stable differential cross-effects between brands. Brands are differentially effective not only with respect to their own shares and sales, but also with respect to their ability to influence the shares and sales of other brands (that is, *clout*). Furthermore, brands seem to differ in the degree to which they are influenced by other brands' actions (that is, *vulnerability*). The second source of asymmetries derives from the *temporal distinctiveness* that a brand achieves in the marketplace by differentiating itself from the competition. We will first deal with differential effect and differential cross-effects, and look at market and competitive structure in terms of the patterns of clout and vulnerability of the competitors. Then we will address the issues concerning the temporal distinctiveness of marketing activity.

4.1. Differential effectiveness

In the initial discussion of differential effectiveness a solution at that time was to include some parameters in market-share models to take account of the overall *marketing effectiveness* of each brand. In the general specification of an attraction model,

$$\mathscr{A}_i = \exp(\alpha_i + \varepsilon_i) \sum_{k=1}^{K} f_k(X_{ki})^{\beta_k},$$

$$s_i = \mathscr{A}_i \Big/ \sum_{j=1}^{m} \mathscr{A}_j,$$

the parameters α_i $(i = 1, 2, \ldots, m)$ represented the marketing effectiveness of each brand. But the inclusion of the α's in attraction models, does not account fully for differential effectiveness among brands. The differential effectiveness may be specific to each marketing instrument, such as a brand that has a particularly effective pricing policy or an effective advertising campaign. The α_i's do not appear directly in the elasticity formulas for a particular marketing instrument, X_k (namely, $e_{s_i} = \beta_k(1 - s_i)$ for MCI models and $e_{s_i} = \beta_k X_{ki}(1 - s_i)$ for MNL models). The *marketing-effectiveness parameters* may reflect differences in *brand equity*, the *brand franchise*, or *brand loyalty* – literally, they are the constant component of each brand's attraction, but have nothing directly to do with elasticities. As a result, elasticity formulas for simple-effects attraction models do not reflect differential effectiveness.

If we wish to modify market-share elasticities to account for differential effectiveness, this may be achieved in only one way, that is, by specifying parameters β_k's in such a manner that each brand has a special parameter, β_{ki}, for variable X_k. The attraction model becomes:

$$\mathscr{A}_i = \exp(\alpha_i + \varepsilon_i) \prod_{k=1}^{K} f_k(X_{ki})^{\beta_{ki}}, \tag{21}$$

$$s_i = \mathscr{A}_i \Big/ \sum_{j=1}^{m} \mathscr{A}_j.$$

This modification does not change the basic structure of direct and cross-elasticities for attraction models. The self-elasticities, for example, are

MCI model:

$$e_{si} = \beta_{ki}(1 - s_i).$$

MNL model:

$$e_{s_i} = \beta_{ki} X_{ki}(1 - s_i).$$

As variable X_{ki} increases, the elasticity decreases for MCI models, but it increases and then decreases for MNL models. (The cross elasticities are given in the next section.) By expanding the parameterization of the model we are now able to capture brand-by-brand differences in market responsiveness to each element of the marketing mix. If all brands are equally effective then $\beta_{ki} = \beta_{kj} = \beta_k \; \forall \, i,j$, and the elasticity expressions reduce to those for simple-effects attraction models.

4.2. *Differential cross-elasticities*

If we are interested in knowing what effects other brands' actions will have on a brand's share, or what effects a brand's marketing actions will have on other brands' shares, then we need to consider *cross elasticities*. Suppose that brand j changed variable X_{kj} by a small amount ΔX_{kj}. The cross elasticity of brand i's $(i \neq j)$ share with respect to variable X_{kj} may be verbally expressed as 'the ratio of the proportion of change in market share for brand i corresponding to the proportion of change in variable X_k for brand j,' and is defined as follows:

$$e_{s_i \cdot j} = \frac{\Delta s_i / s_i}{\Delta X_{kj} / X_{kj}} = \frac{\Delta s_i}{\Delta X_{kj}} \cdot \frac{X_{kj}}{s_i}. \tag{22}$$

Note that $e_{si \cdot j}$ has two subscripts: the first indicates the brand that is influenced and the second, the brand that exerts influences. This is an *arc* cross-elasticity formula and the corresponding *point* cross-elasticity is defined as:

$$e_{s_i \cdot j} = \frac{\partial s_i / s_i}{\partial X_{kj} / X_{kj}} = \frac{\partial s_i}{\partial X_{kj}} \cdot \frac{X_{kj}}{s_i}. \tag{23}$$

Point cross-elasticities for differential-effects attraction models are as follows:

MCI model:

$$e_{s_i \cdot j} = -\beta_{kj} s_j.$$

MNL model:

$$e_{s_i \cdot j} = -\beta_{kj} X_{kj} s_j.$$

Let us consider what the above formulas imply. For the raw-score versions of both MCI and MNL models cross elasticities with respect to variable X_{kj} are constant for any brand $i (i \neq j)$. This means that the relative changes of other brands' shares (i.e. $\partial s_i / s_i$) caused by brand j's actions are the same for any brand, though actual changes in shares (i.e. ∂s_i) are different from one brand to another, depending on the current share level for each brand (i.e. s_i).

Table 6.2 shows the pattern of direct and cross elasticities we might get from a differential-effects attraction model. The direct elasticities are on the diagonal of

Table 6.2.
Elasticities for a differential-effects model

Brand	1	2	3	4	5	6
1	−1.2	0.6	0.5	0.1	0.3	0.7
2	0.3	−1.7	0.5	0.1	0.3	0.7
3	0.3	0.6	−0.9	0.1	0.3	0.7
4	0.3	0.6	0.5	−0.8	0.3	0.7
5	0.3	0.6	0.5	0.1	−1.6	0.7
6	0.3	0.6	0.5	0.1	0.3	−1.7

this matrix and the cross elasticities are off the diagonal – showing how the brand indicated by the column exerts influence on the brand indicated by the row. The diagonal entries can differ between columns due to different market shares between columns as well as due to differing parameters β_{kj}. The off-diagonal entries can also differ between columns due to different market shares as well as due to differing parameters β_{kj}. But within each column the off-diagonal entries are identical. This reflects the symmetry of Axiom 4 of the market-share theorem discussed earlier. It is a pattern that tells us that the differential-effects attraction model developed so far is an IIA model.

The equality of cross elasticities implied by such attraction models does not fit what we observe in the marketplace. There are brands that seem to be nearly immune from other brands' price changes; some brands seem to be able to ignore promotional activities of other brands with little loss of their shares, while others seem to be particularly vulnerable. It is therefore desirable to specify market-share models that reflect inequality of cross elasticities that we believe exists in the marketplace. As indicated before, there are two ways to attack this problem. On one hand, we could reflect the asymmetries which might arise from the *temporal distinctiveness* of marketing efforts. This is pursued in the section on the distinctiveness of marketing activities. The other way involves extending the parameters of the attraction model to reflect asymmetries due to *systematic and stable cross-competitive effects.* Fortunately, this can be accomplished with relative ease within the framework of attraction models as shown below.

The fully extended attraction model

$$\mathscr{A}_i = \exp(\alpha_i + \varepsilon_i) \prod_{k=1}^{K} \prod_{j=1}^{m} f_k(X_{kj})^{\beta_{kij}}, \tag{24}$$

$$s_i = \mathscr{A}_i \Big/ \sum_{j=1}^{m} \mathscr{A}_j,$$

where β_{kij} is the parameter for the cross-competitive effect of variable X_{kj} on brand i.

Equation (24) is called an attraction model with differential cross-competitive effects or a *fully extended* attraction model to distinguish it from the differential-effects attraction model shown in Equation (21). The most important feature of the fully extended model is that the attraction for brand i is now a function not only of the brand's own actions (variables X_{ki}'s, $k = 1, 2, \ldots, m$) but also of all other brands' actions (variables X_{kj}'s, $k = 1, 2, \ldots, K$; $j = 1, 2, \ldots, m$). The β_{kij}'s for which i is different from j are the *cross-competitive effects* parameters, which partly determine cross elasticities. The β_{kij}'s for which j equals i (i.e., β_{kii}) are *direct-effects* parameters and are equivalent to the β_{ki}'s in the differential-effects model (21). This notation is cumbersome, but it is necessary to keep track of who is influencing whom. Note that the fully extended model has many more parameters (with $m^2 \times K$ β_{kij}'s and m α_i's) than the original attraction model (with $K + m$ parameters) and the differential-effects model (with $mK + m$ parameters). But even for extremely large markets these parameters are possible to estimate by the procedures discussed in Cooper & Nakanishi [1988, Chapter 5]. Since we get $(m - 1)$ independent observations from each store each week, scanner data provides enough degrees of freedom to overdetermine most models. For example, there are around 100 brands of cereal. If we track price, feature, display, coupon and brand-specific effects we have to estimate around 40 100 parameters. While this is a daunting numerical task that no one has yet undertaken, data from only ten stores over a year's time provide enough independent observations (51 480) to overdetermine a solution. This, of course, assumes homogeneity of parameters across stores. If differences in store format (e.g. every-day low-price versus advertised specials) indicate this assumption is questionable, then data from only ten stores per format would still overdetermine a solution. When other, less obvious, forms of heterogeneity across stores exist, methods for discovering latent classes in other marketing arenas may be adaptable to the current context [cf. Kamakura & Russell, 1989; Ramaswamy & DeSarbo, 1990].

4.3. *Properties of fully extended attraction models*

The fully extended attraction model is not an IIA because the choice between two brands can be affected by the cross-competitive influences of the other brands available in the market. To see what market and competitive structures can be revealed by the fully extended model (24), let us look at the direct and cross elasticities for this model.

MCI model:

$$e_{s_i \cdot j} = \beta_{kij} - \sum_{h=1}^{m} s_h \beta_{khj}.$$

MNL model:

$$e_{s_i \cdot j} = \left(\beta_{kij} - \sum_{h=1}^{m} s_h \beta_{khj}\right) X_{kj}.$$

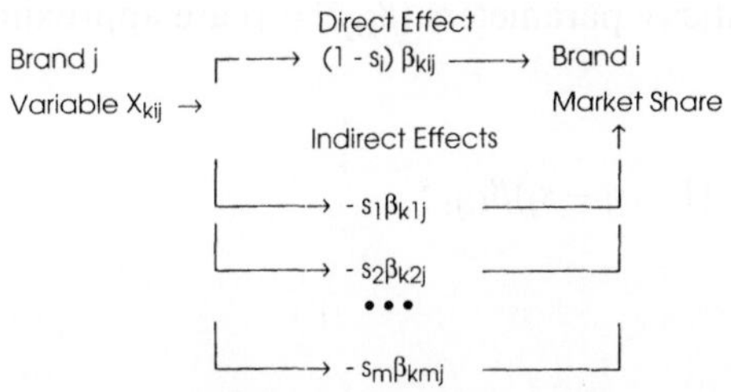

Fig. 6.2. Cross elasticities in the fully extended model.

These formulas apply to both direct and cross elasticities. If i is equal to j, then we have the direct elasticities for brand i, otherwise we have the cross elasticity, $e_{s_i \cdot j}$ of market share for brand i with respect to changes in marketing variable X_{kj} for brand j, and it is given by β_{kij} minus the weighted average of β_{khj}'s over h, where the weights are the market shares of respective brands (s_h) [cf. McGuire, Weiss & Houston, 1977]. Figure 6.2 describes the effects that influence market shares according to the fully extended model.

Assume that variable X_{kj} is the price for brand j. Then parameter β_{kij} for which i is not equal to j is likely to have a positive value. When brand j reduces its price the share of brand i tends to decrease. This effect of brand j's price change on brand i's share is shown in Figure 6.2 as a *direct competitive effect*. Note that a direct competitive effect is weighted by the complement of brand i's share (as we show below). When brand i's share is large, brand i is less affected directly by the moves by brand j. The influence of brand j's price change is not limited to the direct competitive effect on brand i, however. When brand j reduces its price, its own share should increase. Furthermore, the market shares of brands 1 through m (other than brands i and j) will also receive a negative effect, which in turn should have a positive effect on brand i's share. Influences of these kinds are *indirect competitive effects* shown in Figure 6.2.

In order to examine formally the points raised above, rewrite the cross-elasticity formula for MCI models as follows:

$$e_{s_i \cdot j} = (1 - s_i)\beta_{kij} - s_j\beta_{kjj} - \sum_{h \neq i,j}^{m} s_h\beta_{khj}.$$

The first term, of course, represents the direct competitive effects. The second term shows the indirect competitive effects through brand j. The last term consists of indirect competitive effects through all other brands. If X_{kj} is brand j's price, one expects that $\beta_{kjj} < 0$ and $\beta_{kij} > 0$ (for $i \neq j$). Since the first and last terms are expected to be positive and the second term negative, we do not know the sign of $e_{s_i \cdot j}$. It is dependent on the relative size of $(1 - s_i)\beta_{kij} - s_j\beta_{kjj}$ and $\sum_{h \neq i,j}^{m} s_h\beta_{khj}$.

Consider the following special cases.

Case 1: All cross-elasticity parameters (β_{kij}, $i \neq j$) are zero. In this case, $e_{s_i \cdot j} = -s_j\beta_{kjj}$. This is the same as the cross-elasticity formula for the differential-effects MCI models.

Case 2: All cross-elasticity parameters ($\beta_{kij}, i \neq j$) are approximately equal. In this case,

$$\sum_{h \neq i,j}^{m} s_h \beta_{khj} \approx (1 - s_i - s_j)\beta_{kij}.$$

Then

$$e_{s_i \cdot j} \approx s_j(\beta_{kij} - \beta_{kjj}).$$

This suggests that $e_{s_i \cdot j}$ has the same sign as β_{kij}.

Case 3: β_{kij} is nearly zero, but

$$\sum_{h \neq i,j}^{m} s_h \beta_{khj} > s_j \beta_{kjj}.$$

In this case $e_{s_i \cdot j}$ may have a sign different from β_{kij}.

Case 3 is an interesting situation because, in this case, it is possible that brand i even gains share when brand j reduces its price. For Case 3 to occur brand j's share should be relatively small, but the impact of its actions on brands other than i must be large. (This brings to our mind an image of an aggressive small brand j which is frequently engaged in guerilla price-wars.) In addition, brand i must be reasonably isolated from the rest of the market, implying that it is a *niche*-er. This case illustrates the richness of market and competitive structures that can be revealed by the fully extended attraction models.

It may be added that if $i = j$, we may write

$$e_{s_i \cdot j} = (1 - s_i)\beta_{kii} - \sum_{h \neq i}^{m} s_h \beta_{khi}.$$

The first term represents the direct effect of X_{ki} on brand i's share. The second term gives the sum of all indirect competitive effects on brand i's share. This formula suggests a possibility that, even if the direct effect is negligible (e.g. β_{kii} is small), direct elasticity, $e_{s.i}$, may be sizeable due to the combination of indirect competitive effects. In other words, a brand may be able to increase its share merely by reducing other brands' shares. Simple-effects or differential-effects attraction models do not allow such a possibility. This is another indication of the descriptive richness of the fully extended attraction models.

While issues in estimation are beyond the mandate of this chapter, readers may have noted that not all of the parameters of the fully extended model are identified. McGuire, Weiss & Houston [1977] showed that only the deviations $\beta^*_{kij} = \beta_{kij} - \bar{\beta}_{k \cdot j}$ and the brand-specific parameters α_i are estimable. But Cooper & Nakanishi [1988, p. 145] showed that only β^*_{kij} is needed to estimate all the elasticities.

4.4. Revealing competitive structures

Once cross-elasticity parameters are introduced in market-share models, it becomes possible to specify market and competitive structures on the basis of cross elasticities among brands. An example will serve to illustrate this concept. Suppose that the marketing variable in question is price. One may estimate share elasticities with respect to price using a differential cross-elasticities market-share model. Table 6.3 shows the matrix of direct and cross elasticities among six brands in a hypothetical market.

Some readers familiar with matrices may manage to see the market and competitive structure with a little work. However, we can always graph the pattern of an elasticity matrix using the simplest form of a *competitive map* [Cooper, 1988]. If we think of brands as vectors emanating from the origin of a space, the stronger the cross elasticity between two brands, the more correlated those brands' vectors would be. The closer the competition the smaller the angle between the vectors for two brands. The more complementary two brands are, the more opposite (closer to 180°) these brands should be in the map. If two brands to not compete at all, the vectors should be at right angles to each other. If some subset of brands does not compete with any of the brands in the market, the noncompeting brands should reside at the origin of the space. This space will be a joint space – showing both how brands exert influence (i.e. *clout*) and how they are influenced by other brands' actions (*vulnerability*). The cross elasticities are represented in a competitive map as if they were the *scalar products* of the coordinates of the brands.

$$ {}_iE_j = {}_iV_t' {}_tC_j + {}_i\Delta_j \tag{25}$$

where ${}_iE_j$ is the matrix of cross elasticities, ${}_iV_t$ is a matrix showing the coordinates of the brands on dimensions that describe the vulnerability of the brands, ${}_tC_j$ is a matrix showing the coordinates of the brands on dimensions that describe the clout of the brands, and ${}_i\Delta_j$ is a matrix of errors. Singular-value decomposition can be used to obtain the smallest (least-squares) error for any given choice of the dimensionality of the competitive map.

The two-dimensional competitive map for Table 6.3 is given in Figure 6.3. We expect the marketing actions of a brand to help itself. In a map this would be

Table 6.3.
Elasticities for a fully extended attraction model

Brand	1	2	3	4	5	6
1	−1.2	1.0	0.2	0.2	0.3	1.2
2	0.9	−1.6	0.3	0.4	0.1	1.4
3	0.1	0.2	−0.4	0.6	0.2	0.2
4	0.2	0.3	0.0	−1.7	1.1	0.3
5	0.3	0.5	0.4	1.0	−1.8	0.3
6	0.9	1.0	0.3	0.1	0.2	−0.7

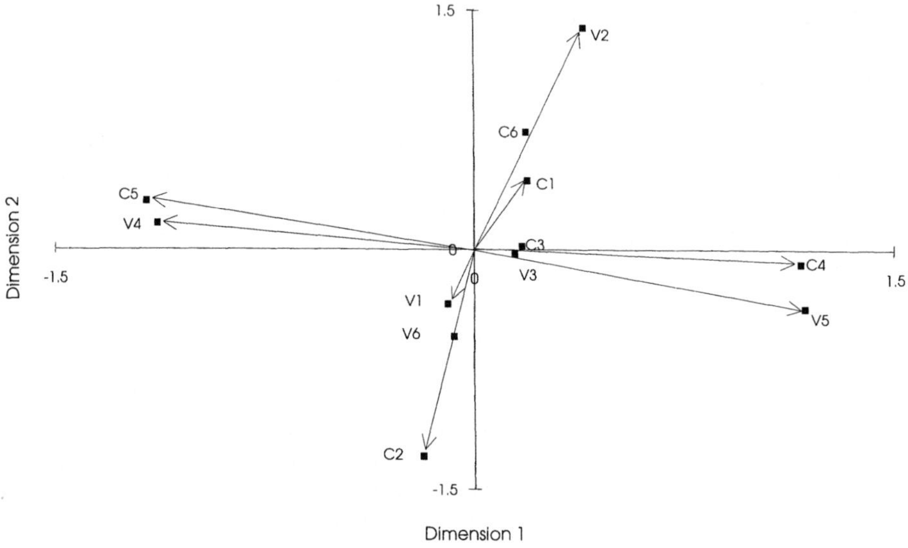

Fig. 6.3. Scaling of elasticities from Table 6.3, based on singular value decomposition.

reflected by having the vector representing the clout for one brand be about 180° from the vector representing vulnerability for that same brand. This occurs throughout Figure 6.3. Note that brand 2 is aligned to exert a good deal of competitive pressure on both brands 1 and 6; but these brands are positioned to return the pressure. Brands 4 and 5 are aligned to compete with each other, but there is not much competition between these two submarkets. Additionally, brand 3 is isolated at the origin – competing with neither group of brands.

This simple version of competitive mapping provides a snapshot of the competitive structure implied by a single matrix of elasticities. Mapping the elasticities for this marketing instrument over time and/or regions can give brand managers a view of what events produce changes in competitive patterns. And the full story on the competitive structure of this market is not known until the elasticities for each marketing instrument are mapped. Some analysts worry that looking at maps for different instruments will reveal brands as substitutes with respect to one instrument and complements with respect to another. This is certainly possible, but not necessarily undesirable. National brands seem to compete fiercely with each other on price maps, but ad maps might show that ads for one premium national brand help other premium national brands (at the expense of regional and private-label brands). Brand managers need to know if such patterns exist, for surely brand planning is affected by such knowledge.

4.5. Hierarchies of market segments

Ambiguities in interpreting the nature of competition from the tables of elasticities may be caused by the aggregation, that is, by not explicitly recognizing segments of buyers in the market. As was already pointed out, the overt pattern of brand grouping does not necessarily give hints about the underlying patterns of buyer demand. There are two possible interpretations on the nature of brand groups in Figure 6.3, for example. One interpretation is that two market segments exist and the cross elasticities reflect the difference in product perception between segments. The buyers who belong to the first segment might have only brands 1, 2 and 6 in their consideration set; those who belong to the second segment might consider brands 4 and 5 as the only relevant alternatives. In this interpretation brand groups correspond one-to-one with market segments of buyers.

The second interpretation of brand groups is that brands tend to be grouped in accordance with different types of buyer needs they serve. Suppose that the consumer uses plain and fruited yogurts for different occasions (e.g. plain yogurt for salad dressings and sauces, but fruited yogurt for desserts and snacks). This will cause the yogurt market to be divided into the plain and fruited brand groups, and minor price differences between the two groups will not affect demand for either. This type of segmentation on the basis of needs or a *benefit* segmentation, does not produce distinct buyer segments in the market, since the same household purchases both plain and fruited yogurts. Of course, if two brand groups serve two entirely isolated buyer needs, they should be treated as two distinct industries rather than one. But if the price of plain yogurt is drastically reduced, buyers might start cutting up their own fruit and the demand for fruited yogurt may be affected. A plain-yogurt brand with an aggressive price policy may have some cross elasticities with fruited brands, or vice versa. Moderate cross elasticites between groups would force one to treat them as a single market.

As in the above example, if the elasticities are measured only for the entire market, if will be impossible to establish the propriety of the above two interpretations solely on the basis of tables such as Table 6.3. In order to evaluate the correctness of these two interpretations, one will need data sets such as consumer panels (either diary or scanner panels). Moreover, it is desirable to have accompanying data on the buyer perception of alternative brands. Lacking such detailed data sets, however, one should at least understand well the aggregate implications of variabilities in elasticities among buyer segments. We will first look at the nature of elasticities in a multisegmented market.

Suppose that there are two segments in the market, containing N_1 and N_2 buyers, respectively. We sill use the notation $q_{i(l)}$ and $s_{i(l)}$ to indicate, respectively, the sales volume and market share of brand i in the lth segment. Since

$$s_i = [q_{(1)}s_{i(1)} + q_{(2)}s_{i(2)}]/q$$

where

$$q_{(l)} = \text{sales volume in segment } l \ (l = 1,2),$$
$$q = \text{total sales volume } (q_{(1)} + q_{(2)}).$$

The point share elasticity of brand i with respect to X_{kj} is given by

$$e_{s_i \cdot j} = [(q_{(1)}/q)(\partial s_{i(1)}/\partial X_{kj}) + (q_{(2)}/q)(\partial s_{i(2)}/\partial X_{kj})](X_{kj}/s_i).$$

This shows that an overall elasticity is the weighted average of corresponding segment elasticities, weights being the relative sales volumes for respective segments. If we write the segment elasticity as $e_{s_i \cdot j(l)}$, then the general expression for $e_{s_i \cdot j}$ is given by

$$e_{s_i \cdot j} = \sum_{l=1}^{L} (q_{i(l)}/q_i) e_{s_i \cdot j(l)} \tag{26}$$

where L is the number of segments and q_i is the sales volume for brand i for the entire market. This expression gives one the means to compute the overall elasticity matrix from matrices for segments. It also hints at ways to redress the problems created by the heterogeneity in purchase frequency discussed earlier. If we segment the market into heavy users and light users, and parameterize an attraction model in each segment, we still can compute the overall elasticities from the segment elasticities.

We could achieve this segmentation by using panel data in each trading area to identify the heavy users and the light users in a category. The problem then becomes how to obtain an estimate of the market-level aggregate sales of a brand for each segment, when we have only the corresponding sales in the panel. Simple aggregation of the contemporaneous panel sales is not a good idea. Early research indicated that data aggregated this way did not allow for good estimation of cross-competitive effects. Panel data in a particular week is too sparse, even with large panels, to allow for reliable estimation of cross-competitive effects.

A simple remedy for this is to think that each panel segment has a long-term attraction to a brand as well as a contemporaneous attraction that incorporates the impact of the immediate promotional environment. Using long-term average sales in the panel segment and contemporaneous sales in each panel segment, we wish to develop weights that split the total sales for a brand in a period (S_{jt}) into parts that correspond to each segment. In the two-segment case we want to estimate weights $W_{\mathrm{L}jt}$ and $W_{\mathrm{H}jt}$ for that light- and heavy-user segments respectively, such that

$$W_{\mathrm{L}jt} + W_{\mathrm{H}jt} = 1,$$
$$W_{\mathrm{L}jt} \times S_{jt} = S_{\mathrm{L}jt},$$
$$W_{\mathrm{H}jt} \times S_{jt} = S_{\mathrm{H}jt}.$$

This way the segment sales we estimate add up to the known aggregate sales in the market. The theoretical relations could be specified in a simple linear model as below:

$$S_{\mathrm{L}jt} = \gamma_j \bar{P}_{\mathrm{L}j.} + \lambda_{\mathrm{L}j} P_{\mathrm{L}jt},$$
$$S_{\mathrm{H}jt} = \gamma_j \bar{P}_{\mathrm{H}j.} + \lambda_{\mathrm{H}j} P_{\mathrm{H}jt},$$

where

$S_{\mathrm{L}jt}$ = the aggregate sales for brand j in period t in the light-user segment,
$S_{\mathrm{H}jt}$ = the aggregate sales for brand j in period t in the heavy-user segment,
$P_{\mathrm{L}jt}$ = the panel sales for brand j in period t in the light-user segment,
$P_{\mathrm{H}jt}$ = the panel sales for brand j in period t in the heavy-user segment,
γ_j = a parameter expressing the influence of long-term panels sales for brand j in each segment,
$\lambda_{\mathrm{L}j}$ = a parameter expressing the influence of the contemporaneous marketing environment on the relation between panel sales for brand j in period t and the corresponding aggregate sales for the light-user segment,
$\lambda_{\mathrm{H}j}$ = a parameter expressing the influence of the contemporaneous marketing environment on the relation between panel sales for brand j in period t and the corresponding aggregate sales for the heavy-user segment.

The weights we desire could be based on a simple linear model such as

$$S_{jt} = \hat{\gamma}_j(\bar{P}_{\mathrm{L}j.} + \bar{P}_{\mathrm{H}j.}) + \hat{\lambda}_{\mathrm{L}j}P_{\mathrm{L}jt} + \hat{\lambda}_{\mathrm{H}j}P_{\mathrm{H}jt} + e_{jt}. \tag{27}$$

We then obtain estimates of the required weights from

$$\hat{W}_{\mathrm{L}jt} = \hat{S}_{\mathrm{L}jt}/\hat{S}_{jt}, \tag{28}$$

$$\hat{W}_{\mathrm{H}jt} = \hat{S}_{\mathrm{H}jt}/\hat{S}_{jt}. \tag{29}$$

A similar segmentation scheme could be developed for any number of mutually exclusive and exhaustive segmentation. With minor modification a scheme based on fuzzy segments could be developed. We end up with an estimated brand-sales vector for each segment. For all practical purposes we may calibrate segment models just as we do for the aggregate market sales. In this way information (such as manufacturer's coupon redemption) that has previously been the exclusive domain of panel data, can be incorporated into aggregate (store-level) attraction models. A numerical illustration of this is given in Section 5.

4.6. Distinctiveness of marketing activities

Fully extended attraction models have advanced our ability to reflect the complexity of market and competitive structures, but there are other aspects of competition which have not been properly dealt with even in the fully extended models. We will turn to some of the more critical issues in this section and the next one. Here we will take up the issue of *distinctiveness* of marketing activities by competing brands.

The main thesis of this section is that a brand's marketing actions must be distinct to be effective. Even casual observations bear out this proposition. Price reduction by a brand would have more effect on market shares when other brands' prices are kept high than it would when all competitors match the price reduction.

The market-share impact of one brand's promotion would be significantly greater when the brand is alone in promotion than it would when all brands engage in promotional activities.

If it is the differences between brands, rather than the absolute levels of marketing activities that materially affect buyers' preference, then we will have to bring the distinctiveness of marketing activities among brands into the market-share models. Attraction models handle the distinctiveness issue quite naturally.

Cooper & Nakanishi [1988, pp. 70–72] showed that one may express the variables in MCI and MNL models in a *deviation* form without changing the properties of the models. In other words, we may express a variable either as

$$X_{ki}^* = X_{ki}/\tilde{X}_k \quad \text{or} \quad X_{ki}^* = X_{ki} - \bar{X}_k$$

and substitute X_{ki}^* for X_{ki} in MCI or MNL models, respectively. This property of attraction models does not change if we move from the simple-effects form to differential-effects models and fully extended models, or if monotone transformations (f_k) other than identity or exponential are used. Substituting

$$f_k^*(X_{ki}) = f_k(X_{ki})/\tilde{f}_k(X_k),$$

where $\tilde{f}_k(X_k)$ is the geometric mean of $f_k(X_{ki})$ over i, for $f_k(X_{ki})$ in an attraction model, will not change the nature of the model. Thus, the variables in attraction models may be replaced by some equivalent form of deviations from the industry mean, and those models operate, in essence, on the principle of distinctiveness. If X_k is price in an MCI model, each brand's price may be expressed as deviations from the average price for the industry. If all brands charge the same price, X_{ki}^* will be equal to one, and price will not affect the shares of brands. Only when the prices for some brands deviate from the industry mean do they influence market shares of themselves and others.

The handling of distinctiveness by attraction models becomes technically difficult when the variable in question is qualitative. Product attributes are example of qualitative variables – a make of refrigerator may or may not have an ice-maker; or an automobile model may or may not have an automatic transmission. Such variables take only two values, typically, one if the product (or brand) has an attribute and zero if it does not. Of course, one may compute the industry average for a binary (two-valued) variable (which is the same as the proportion of products or brands that have the attribute) and subtract it from the value for each product/brand. But by this operation the transformed variable may take either positive or negative values, and hence it may be used only with an MNL model. In order to incorporate binary variables in an MCI model a simple, but effective, transformation – the *index of distinctiveness* – was developed [Nakanishi, Cooper & Kassarjian, 1974].

Suppose that X_k is a variable associated with the possession or nonpossession of an attribute. Let the proportion of products (or brands) in this industry which have the attribute be r. If there are ten brands and two brands have the attribute, r will be 0.2. The value of the index of distinctiveness for each brand is determined by the following simple operation.

If brand i has the attribute, $X_{ki} = 1/r$.

If brand i does not have the attribute, $X_{ki} = 1 - r$.

Thus if r equals 0.2, those brands with the attribute are given the value of 5 and those without the attribute will be given the value of 0.8. Note that the smaller r, the greater the value of X_k for those brands that have the attribute. This represents, in essence, the effect of the distinctiveness of a brand. If a brand is the only one which has the attribute the index value $(1/r)$ becomes maximal.

This index has a rather convenient property that it is ratio-wise symmetrical to the reversal of coding a particular attribute. If we reversed the coding of possession and nonpossession of an attribute in the previous numerical example, r would be 0.8, and the value of X_k for those brands with the attribute would be 1.25 ($= 1/0.8$) and that for the brands without the attribute would be 0.2 ($= 1/5$). In other words, those brands without the attribute become distinctive in the reverse direction.

The index of distinctiveness shown above transforms a binary variable such that it is usable in an MCI model. Cooper & Nakanishi [1983] found that this index is a special case of a more general transformation applicable not only for qualitative variables but also for any quantitative variable. First, convert any variable X_{ki} to a standardized score by the usual formula:

$$z_{ki} = (X_{ki} - \bar{X}_k)/\sigma_k$$

where

$\bar{X}_k$ = the arithmetic mean of X_{ki} over i,
σ_k = the standard deviation of X_{ki} over i.

Since standardized z-scores (z_{ki}'s) may take both positive and negative values, they may be used in an MNL model in the form of $\exp(z_{ki})$, but cannot be used in an MCI model. To create a variable usable in the latter model transform z-scores in turn in the following manner:

$$\zeta_{ki} = (1 + z_{ki}^2)^{1/2}, \quad \text{if } z_{ki} \geqslant 0,$$
$$\zeta_{ki} = (1 + z_{ki}^2)^{-1/2}, \quad \text{if } z_{ki} \leqslant 0. \tag{30}$$

This new transform, ζ_k, (to be called the *zeta-score* for X_k) takes only positive values and has a property that it is ratio-wise symmetrical when the positive and the negative directions of variable X_k are reversed. For example, let the value of ζ_{ki} be 2.5. If X_{ki} is multiplied by -1, ζ_{ki} will take a value of 0.4 ($= 1/2.5$). It may be easily shown that the zeta-score includes the index of distinctiveness as a special case for binary variables. For a binary variable X_k, $\bar{X}_k = r$ and $\sigma_k = r(1-r)$. Hence

$$z_{ki}^2 = (1-r)/r \quad \text{if } X_{ki} = 1,$$

$$z_{ki}^2 = r/(1-r) \quad \text{if } X_{ki} = 0.$$

Substitution of the equivalent of z_{ki}^2's in the zeta-score formula yields squared roots of distinctiveness indices.

We can think of brands as point masses in space. The zeta-score is based on the ratio of the noncentral moment of inertia about brand i to the central moment of inertia – thus reflecting how an object stands out from a group. This ratio is not affected by a general linear transformation of X_k, making it an appropriate transformation of interval-scale ratings – thus allowing interval-scale rating to be used in MCI as well as MNL models. The ratio has a minimum value of one for brands at the center (i.e., the mean of X_k), and increases as a particular brand gets farther away from the center. To translate this ratio into a usable index we invert it at the mean of the underlying variable. This allows us to tell if a brand is distinctively high or distinctively low in an attribute compared to the other brands in the competitive offering. (Instead of thinking of brands as point masses in space, we could think of brands as points in space with masses equal to their market shares. This leads to a new, and as yet untested, version of distinctiveness that has great appeal to this one-time student of physics.) Figure 6.4 gives the comparison of the zeta-score with the $\exp(z_{ki})$ transform.

Although the shapes of the two transforms are quite similar, the choice between the two may be made by the form of the elasticities. The direct and cross elasticities for the $\exp(z_{ki})$ transforms are given by

$$E = (I - JD_s)BSD_X$$

and those for the zeta-transforms are given by

$$E = (I - JD_s)BSD_z$$

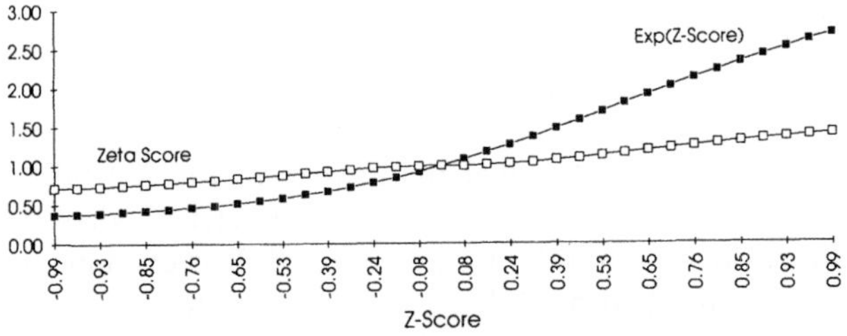

Fig. 6.4. Comparison of zeta and exp z.

where

$S =$ the $m \times m$ matrix with elements $\{\partial z_{kj}/\partial X_{ki}\}$, i.e.,

$$S = \frac{1}{\sigma_k}\left[I - \frac{1}{m}J - \frac{1}{m}ZZ' \right],$$

$D_s =$ an $m \times m$ diagonal matrix with the ith diagonal element s_i,
$D_X =$ an $m \times m$ diagonal matrix with the ith diagonal element X_{ki},
$\sigma_k =$ the standard deviation of X_k over i,
$J =$ an $m \times m$ matrix of 1's,
$Z =$ an $m \times 1$ vector of standardized scores (i.e. $z_{ki} = (X_{ki} - \bar{X}_k)/\sigma_k$),
$D_z =$ an $m \times m$ diagonal matrix with the ith diagonal element $|z_{ki}|/(1 + z_{ki}^2)$.

Figure 6.5 compares the elasticities of the zeta-score with the $\exp(z_{ki})$ transform. The dip in the middle of the elasticity plot for zeta-scores corresponds to the flat portion of the zeta-score function depicted in figure 6.5. With zeta-scores, change is always depicted as slower in the undifferentiated middle portion of the distribution. Consider what this might imply for a frequently purchased branded good (FPBG). If it establishes an initial *sale price* about one-half a standard deviation below the average price in the category, the price is distinctively low and market-share change is relatively rapid. If the price drops further from this point, market share increases, but at a slower and slower rate. Bargain-hunting brand-switchers have already been attracted to the brand, and little more is to be gained from further price cuts. If the price increases from this initial sale price, market share drops rapidly at first, as the value of being distinctively low-priced is dissipated. At the undifferentiated position at the middle of the price distribution, market share is changing least rapidly as minor changes on either side of the average price go largely unnoticed. This indistinct region is similar to what DeSarbo, Rao, Steckel, Wind & Columbo [1987] represent in their friction-pricing model and similar to what Gurumurthy & Little [1986] discuss in their pricing model based on Helson's adaptation-level theory. On the high-priced side an analogous series of events happen. Small price increases around the average price are not noticed, but once the brand price is high enough to be distinguished from the mass, the loss of market share becomes more rapid. At some point, however, the change in market share must decline, as the brand loses all but its most loyal following.

In many categories of FPBG's the brands pulse between a relatively high self-price and a relatively low sale-price. In such cases the middle of the elasticity curve is vacant and the values of the elasticities for zeta-scores and exp(z-scores) might be quite similar. The exp(z-score) elasticities might be most descriptive of the path of market-share change from aggregate advertising expenditures, with increasing market-share growth as the expenditures move from zero up to the industry average, and diminishing growth rate for additional expenditures.

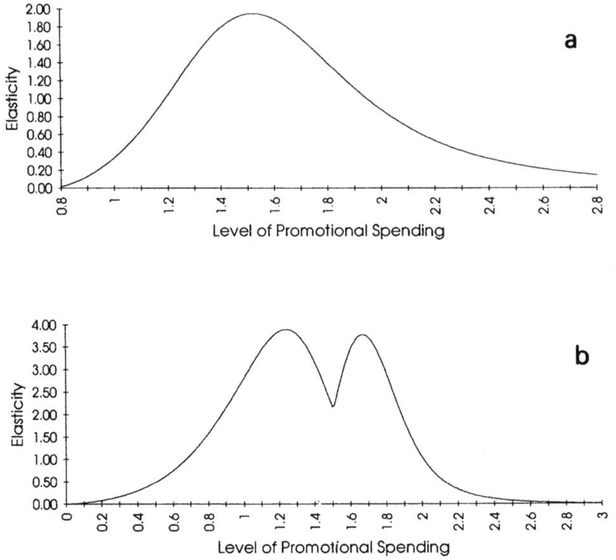

Fig. 6.5. Comparison of (a) zeta-score and (b) exp (z-score) elasticities.

Zeta-scores or exp(z-scores) explicitly model the *temporal distinctiveness* of brands by separating the underlying importance of a feature from the particular pattern of shared features in any given choice context (i.e. its *salience*). If two brands are both *promoted* in a store they do not each get the same boost in market share as if they were promoted alone. By specifically modeling such contextual effects we overcome the limitations imposed by the IIA (context-free) assumption of Luce choice models discussed earlier. Since the IIA assumption does not recognize that the value of a major promotion is somehow shared by all the brands on sale in that time period, the parameters of a raw-score (Luce-type) model will always reflect both the underlying value of the feature and the particular pattern of shared features in the contexts used for calibration. By using a distinctiveness index explicitly to model the changing pattern of feature-sharing from one period to the next, the parameters of the market-share model are free to reflect the underlying value of a feature. In forecasting, one again uses either zeta-scores or exp(z-scores) to help translate the underlying value of a feature to the particular pattern of shared features in new periods. So while the models in Nakanishi & Cooper [1974] were IIA models, as indicated above, the first real application of MCI models [Nakanishi, Cooper & Kassarjian, 1974] found a way out of the counterintuitive results imposed by the IIA assumption. All we need to do is provide a representation of how the context in which choices are made affects those choices.

The dramatic swings in market shares from week to week that analysts observe in scanner records of store sales encourages us to apply distinctiveness transformations in each time period to produce a generalized attraction model:

$$\mathscr{A}_{it} = \exp(\alpha_i + \varepsilon_i) \prod_{k=1}^{K} \prod_{j=1}^{m} f_{kt}(X_{kjt})^{\beta kij},$$

$$s_{it} = \mathscr{A}_{it} \Big/ \sum_{j=1}^{M} \mathscr{A}_{jt}.$$

Here f_{kt} has two subscripts to indicate not only a choice of functional form for the representation of an explanatory variable (i.e. MCI versus MNL representations), but also the kind of distinctiveness transformation to be applied within each period (i.e. zeta-scores or exp(z-scores)). Transformations such as exp(z-scores) and zeta-scores in each time period or choice situation not only highlight the distinctiveness of brands but serve to standardize variables. This reduces the collinearity otherwise inherent in the differential-effects forms of market-response models [cf. Cooper & Nakanishi, 1988, Chapter 5].

5. A numerical illustration from single-source data

The last decade has witnessed a tremendous explosion of research on how to use scanner data to learn about consumer and market response. The intense efforts at developing methods to deal with scanner data have fallen into two separate camps. On one hand, there has been extensive development of discrete choice (mainly logit-based) models and methods for understanding individual-level choice processes [Bawa & Ghosh, 1991; Bawa & Shoemaker, 1987; Bucklin & Lattin, 1991; Carpenter & Lehmann, 1985; Currim, Meyer & Le, 1988; Currim & Schneider, 1991; Elrod, 1988; Fader & McAlister, 1990; Grover & Srinivasan, 1989; Guadagni & Little 1983; Gupta, 1988, 1991; Jain & Vilcassim, 1991; Kalwani, Yim, Rinne & Sugita, 1990; Kamakura & Russell, 1989; Kannan & Wright, 1991; Krishnamurthi & Raj, 1991; Lattin & Bucklin, 1989; Meyer & Cooper, 1987; Moore & Winer, 1987; Neslin, 1990; Neslin, Henderson & Quelch, 1985; Pedrick & Zufryden, 1991; Ramaswamy & DeSarbo, 1990; Tellis, 1988; Vilcassim & Jain, 1991; Wheat & Morrison, 1990a; Winer, 1986, 1989; and Zufryden, 1984, 1987]. On the other hand, there have been substantial efforts to develop market-response models and methods that address both the vast size and detail of store-tracking data [Abraham & Lodish, 1987; Allenby, 1989, 1990; Bemmaor & Mouchoux, 1991; Blattberg & Wisniewski, 1989; Bolton, 1989; Bultez & Naert, 1988; Cooper, 1988; Cooper & Nakanishi, 1988; Doyle & Saunders, 1990; Kumar & Leone, 1988; Russell & Bolton, 1988; Shugan, 1987; Vilcassim, 1989; and Walters & MacKenzie, 1988]. The few efforts that have tried to use both panel and store data have been like Wheat & Morrison [1990b] which uses the percentage of times deals occur (computed from store-level data) in a panel-data investigation of purchase-timing models, or like Pedrick & Zufryden [1991] where store-level causal variables are used in panel-level modeling efforts. In spite of the common modeling frameworks (i.e. discrete MNL models and aggregate MNL models) used in some of these undertakings referenced above, no work has focused on bridging between these two research streams.

There are very pragmatic reasons for attempting to merge the two traditions. Consumer panels contain information that is missing from the store-tracking data. Panel data tell for example about brand-usage frequency, about redemption of manufacturers' coupons, and about television-advertising exposures – information that is simply not available in store-tracking databases. If such data are not incorporated into market-response models, the diagnostic value of the models is necessarily impaired, and the forecasting ability of the models may also be affected.

This section proceeds by:

(1) developing a segmentation scheme that divides the consumer panel into mutually exclusive and exhaustive groups based on usage frequency;
(2) aggregating panel variables to the segment level;
(3) estimating the store-level sales for each segment (for each brand);
(4) calibrating an asymmetric market-share model for the store-level sales of each segment;
(5) combining segment-level market-share models into a single forecast;
(6) calibrating and forecasting from an aggregate market-share model; and
(7) comparing forecasts and diagnostics.

5.1. Developing a segmentation scheme

While there are many useful bases for segmenting consumer panels [cf. Wind, 1978], one of the most fruitful areas for investigation of market-share models concerns differences in usage frequency. As pointed out earlier, parameters from aggregate market-share models will not reflect the individual choice processes if the heavy users in a category systematically purchase different brands than the light users (Case 4(b)).

Without a consumer panel to go along with store-tracking data a model-developer would not know if there was a correlation between brand choice and usage frequency. But with single-source databases come both the knowledge of the problem (if it exists) and the opportunity to address it through segmentation.

The problematic correlation between brand choice and purchase frequency can be detected with a simple χ^2 test on expected purchase frequencies. The theoretical market shares can be estimated from the long-term sales data in the store-tracking data or the panel (using the overall panel would eliminate any rejections due to the panel failing to track the store). The market shares times the total number of purchases in each panel segment provides the expected purchase frequency for each brand, while the observed purchase frequency is readily obtainable for each panel segment. The great size of the panels may make it very likely that trivial differences will be confirmed as statistically significant. Only experience over diverse categories will tell if extremely conservative testing procedure (i.e. extreme type-one error rates) should be invoked.

But before we can test for the correlation between brand choice and purchase frequency, we have to decide who are the heavy users and who are the light users. Cooper [1989a, 1989b] split Nielsen's single-source panels into heavy- and light-user segments in 19 different ways (depending on different definitions of how heavy the heavy users had to be). All but the most extreme definitions led to groups that were significantly discriminable on the basis of actionable variables such as income, number of members in the family, number of years at the same residence, number of TV's in the household, hours-per-week worked by the male head-of-household (HOH), highest degree obtained by male HOH, and number of hours-per-week worked by female HOH. Given this latitude, we decided to define heavy users as those panel households that purchased the top half of the total volume in the category. We know that in general it is tougher to predict more extreme events. This specification of segment membership means we will have ultimately to forecast less extreme volumes than with any other split.

In the catsup category 50% of volume is purchased by the top 20% of the households. In the yogurt category the top 10% of the households purchased 50% of the volume. We expect the concentration to vary from one category to another. Further, in any historical period the record of which households have purchased the most in a category is an imperfect indicator of who are the *real* heavy users. But since Schmittlein, Cooper & Morrison [1993] have shown that the longer the term on which manifest concentration is estimated the closer the manifest concentration is to the *true concentration*, our approach is to use all available panel data to classify households into heavy- and light-user segments.

Using the approximately 50–50 split of volume to define segments in the catsup market, the market and segment shares for Heinz, Hunts, Del Monte, and a combination of the private-label and generic catsups appear in Table 6.4. That the store shares for Heinz and Del Monte are slightly higher than either panel-segment share or that the store shares for the private-label and generic brands are slightly higher, indicates that to a minor extent the panels do not track the stores. While such minor discrepancies should not harm the overall analysis, in such a case the expected frequencies for the χ^2 should (and did) come from overall panel sales. The χ^2 for the independence of segment and share is 372 with 3 degrees of freedom. The significance indicates that we are in a Case 4(b) situation and segmentation should be undertaken. This extreme significance, however, is due

Table 6.4.
Store and segment market shares

Brand	Store share (%)	Heavy-segment share (%)	Light-segment share (%)
Heinz	67.40	68.79	68.25
Hunts	15.80	15.98	15.31
Del Monte	7.60	8.15	8.52
PvtGeneric	9.20	7.08	7.91

mainly to the large size of the panel, since the Φ coefficient is only 0.019 for this same cross tabulation.

5.2. *Aggregate panel variables to the segment level*

The kinds of variables that would be useful to incorporate from the panel file into a market-response analysis are relatively obvious. We aren't interested in the number of toasters or dogs in the household, not only because we have no hypotheses as to why certain brands would differentially benefit from the various levels, but more fundamentally because these kinds of variables do not vary across weeks to any appreciable degree. They would act like segment-specific constants or intercepts.

The obvious candidates for inclusion are those variables we wished were in the store-tracking database to begin with. Highest on this list would be information on manufacturer's coupon redemptions. While store-coupon redemptions have been reported, and used in market-share analysis [cf. Cooper & Nakanishi, 1988], manufacturer-coupon redemptions have not. It may be that inclusion of this information will alter our understanding of price or store-coupon sensitivity.

A less obvious, but no less important, variable is commercial exposures. GRP's or TRP's could be recorded in a store-tracking databse. But it is not obvious how commercial exposures would be routinely included in anything but a panel database. In the catsup category both manufacturer coupons and commercial exposures were initially aggregated for each segment. But in the catsup category too few brands engaged in TV advertising to obtain meaningful results. Thus only manufacturer coupons are used in this first application.

5.3. *Estimating the store-level sales for each segment (for each brand)*

There are three basic assumptions that lead to the estimation Equations (27)–(29).

(1) The long-term average panel sales for a brand has an influence on contemporaneous store sales. This implies that even if there are no sales in the panel segment for a particular brand in a given week there still might be sales in the corresponding store segment. The higher the historic average sales the more likely it is that there will be sales in the store segment *ceteris paribus*, even in the absence of sales in the panel segment.

(2) The contemporaneous panel sales for a brand has an influence on contemporaneous store sales. Of course, we expect the contemporaneous brand sales in a panel segment to be positively related to brand sales for the corresponding store segment. Each panel segment can have its unique sensitivity, i.e. the regression weight that relates contemporaneous panel sales for the heavy panel segment to contemporaneous store sales for the heavy store segment may be different from the regression weight that relates the corresponding sales figure for the light segments in the panel and in the store.

(3) The sensitivity of contemporaneous store sales to long-term panel sales is

the same within brand across segments. There is no reason that would force us to speculate that long-term historic sales for a brand affects one segment differently than another. We do, of course, expect different levels of average sales across segments, but this restriction is much more specific than that. It merely says that the sensitivity of contemporaneous sales to historic sales for a brand is the same for each panel segment. This amounts to a necessary restriction on the intercept for the regression model.

The regression model in (27) was estimated using the Nielsen single-source database tracking catsup sales in Sioux Falls, SD, for 138 weeks. Table 6.5 presents the regression-model results for Heinz, Hunts, Del Monte, control (private-label) brands, generic catsup, and aggregation of all other branded catsups, and an aggregation of all catsup called ALLBRAND in the analysis. The top 20% of users in this market purchased approximately 53% of the catsup volume. These households constituted the heavy-users segment in the panel.

The models have very high R-square values (except for the aggregate of all other branded catsup), but one must be careful to recognize that since the normal intercept is suppressed, R-square is more like a congruence coefficient than the coefficient of multiple determination we expect. All of these models are highly significant when compared to the simulation results for congruence coefficients reported by Korth & Tucker [1975]. All of the parameters are also statistically significant. These tables also report the split of the baseline volume into the average historical weekly volume (in ounces) for each panel segment.

Table 6.5.
Summary of regression analyses – Sioux Falls panel

Brand	R-square	F(3, 138)	Alpha baseline	Beta light	Beta heavy	Average volume	
						Light	Heavy
Heinz	0.976	1827	8.596	15.137	10.562	2403	2784
(*t*-values)			10.811	5.248	3.429		
Hunts	0.965	1233	8.273	11.786	15.617	539	647
(*t*-values)			11.98	5.837	8.761		
Del Monte	0.923	539	5.024	14.287	13.298	300	330
(*t*-values)			6.095	6.746	7.314		
Control-brands	0.967	1315	13.381	8.623	14.585	233	243
(*t*-values)			17.993	5.173	10.519		
Generic	0.931	604	26.599	11.813	6.014	45	44
(*t*-values)			17.95	7.504	3.11		
All others	0.578	62	10.496	4.737	6.843	3	3
(*t*-values)			6.401	4.301	6.283		
All brands	0.983	2645	9.719	8.545	14.798	3524	4050
(*t*-values)			11.01	3.268	5.024		

5.4. *Calibrating an asymmetric market-share model for the store-level sales of each segment*

Remember we have created one sales stream that we believe corresponds to the part of total brand sales that was purchased by the entire light-users segment, and a corresponding sales stream for the entire heavy-users segment. Except for the aggregated information from the panel file (which in this illustration concerned only the redemption of manufacturer's coupons), the causal environment encountered by these segments is the same. So we calibrated an asymmetric MCI model using the procedures outlined in Cooper & Nakanishi [1988, p. 168] and Carpenter et al. [1988]. Basically these procedures estimate all differential effects and brand-specific intercepts, search among the residuals for potentially significant cross effects, and finally re-estimate all effects using weighted least squares. Given the tiny shares of the aggregate representing all other branded catsups, this aggregate was dropped from the analysis. The private-label and generic catsups were combined into an aggregate simply called Private Labels. Each brand was represented by a brand-specific intercept (Int) and a differential effect for line ads (Ad-L), major ads (Ad-M), end-of-aisle display (D-EA), front-aisle display (D-FA),

Table 6.6.
Summary of market-share model – light-users segment

Brand	Int	Ad-L	Ad-M	D-EA	D-FA	D-IN	D-AO	Cp-S	Cp-M	Price
Heinz	2.00	0.14	+NS	+NS	0.29	+NS	+NS	0.57	−NS	−0.49
Cross effects	Heinz is less influenced by Del Monte's D-FA, Heinz is more influenced by Hunt's Cp-M, Heinz's D-AO has more influence on private labels, than predicted by the symmetric model.									
Hunts	−NS	0.26	0.36	0.22	−NS	0.24	0.28	0.72	0.16	−NS
Cross effects	Del Monte's Price has more influence on Hunts, Heinz is more influenced by Hunt's Cp-M, Del Monte's D-EA has more influence on Hunts, Private labels' D-EA has less influence on Hunts, Hunt's Price has more influence on private labels, than predicted by the symmetric model.									
Del Monte	0.00	−NS	0.29	0.75	1.09	0.15	0.38	−NS	0.51	−0.61
Cross effects	Heinz is less influenced by Del Monte's D-FA, Del Monte's Price has more influence on Hunts, Del Monte's D-EA has more influence on Hunts, Private labels' Price, D-EA and Cp-M have more influence on Del Monte, than predicted by the symmetric model.									
Private labels	−0.62	−NS	0.17	0.35	+NS	0.27	+NS	0.68	+NS	−0.73
Cross effects	Heinz's D-AO has more influence on private labels, Private labels' D-EA has less influence on Hunts, Hunt's Price has more influence on private labels, Private labels' Price, D-EA and Cp-M have more influence on Del Monte, than predicted by the symmetric model.									

in-aisle display (D-In), an aggregate of all other displays (D-AO), percent of brand volume sold on store coupon (Cp-S), and price (Price). Manufacturer's coupon (Cp-M) was represented as the percent of panel-segment sales on which a manufacturer's coupon was redeemed. All variables were represented as exp(z-scores).

Tables 6.6 and 6.7 report the parameters estimated for the market-share models for the light and heavy segments, respectively. Both models fit very well in calibration. The light-segment R-square is 0.824 ($F^{52}_{3210} = 288$). The heavy segment R-square is 0.828 ($F^{48}_{3214} = 323$). One would hope that this would be the case since the cross-competitive effects are selected so that they are very likely to be significant in the calibration data set (approximately two-thirds of the store weeks are used for calibration). The models also fit quite well in cross calibration in which the specification developed in the calibration dataset is applied to the remain one-third of the store weeks. Here the R-squares were 0.803 and 0.814 respectively. And finally the models also cross-validated quite well. The cross validation used the parameter values form the calibration dataset to forecast market shares for the untouched data in the final one-third of the store weeks. Here we form a single composite for each segment and perform a simple regression on the appropriately transformed (log-centered) dependent measure. The R-squares are 0.756 and 0.766 respectively for models with one predictor and 1607 degrees of freedom. The comparison to the aggregate model is discussed in Section 5.7. The cross effects are described verbally, by comparison with what would be expected from a symmetric market-share model [cf. Bell, Keeney & Little, 1975]. In symmetric market-share models, when one brand loses share the other brands are represented as if

Table 6.7.
Summary of market-share-model – heavy-users segment

Brand	Int	Ad-L	Ad-M	D-EA	D-FA	D-IN	D-AO	Cp-S	Cp-M	Price
Heinz	2.30	0.15	+NS	0.07	0.22	0.03	+NS	0.61	0.11	−NS
Cross effects	Heinz is less influenced by Del Monte's D-FA and private labels' Cp-M than predicted by the symmetric model.									
Hunts	−NS	0.21	0.34	0.21	+NS	0.24	0.25	0.71	0.16	−0.50
Cross effects	Hunts is less influenced by private labels' Price than predicted by the symmetric model.									
Del Monte	0.00	−NS	0.44	0.78	1.07	+NS	0.32	−NS	0.26	−1.13
Cross effects	Del Monte's D-FA has less influence on Heinz, Private labels' D-EA has more influence on Del Monte, and Del Monte's Price has less influence on private labels than predicted by the symmetric model.									
Private labels	−0.87	+NS	0.22	0.38	−NS	0.35	0.16	0.54	−NS	−1.30
Cross effects	Heinz is less influenced by private labels' Cp-M, Hunts is less influenced by private labels' Price, Private labels' D-EA has more influence on Del Monte, and Del Monte's Price has less influence on private labels than predicted by the symmetric model.									

they gain share strictly in proportion to their prior market shares. Further interpretation is deferred to the section below where diagnostics are also compared.

5.5. Combining segment-level market-share models into a single forecast

Combining the segment-level forecasts mentioned in the previous section into a single market-share forecast is relatively straightforward since we already have the weights from Equations (28) and (29). Combined forecast of market share for each brand merely applies these weights to the estimated brand shares from the segment models.

The variance accounted for (VAF) in the forecast period of the combined forecast is over 71%. This is a strong indication of very good forecasting ability. The root-mean-squared error (RMSE) of 0.128 might seem high, but we must remember that there are tremendous swings in market share when looked at on a week-by-week and store-by-store basis.

5.6. Calibrating and forecasting from an aggregate market-share model

Excluding the manufacturer's coupons, the procedures for specification of the aggregate market-share model were the same as those for the segment-level models. The R-square in calibration was 0.845 ($F^{45}_{3217} = 390$), in cross calibration

Table 6.8.
Summary of market-share model – aggregate market

Brand	Int	Ad-L	Ad-M	D-EA	D-FA	D-IN	D-AO	Cp-S	Cp-M	Price
Heinz	2.06	0.17	0.07	0.08	0.20	+NS	0.13	0.60		−0.70
Cross effects	Heinz is less influenced by Del Monte's D-FA, Heinz is less influenced by Hunt's Price, than predicted by the symmetric model.									
Hunts	−NS	0.26	0.35	0.19	+NS	0.29	0.22	0.84		−0.40
Cross effects	Heinz is less influenced by Hunt's Price, Del Monte's Price has more influence on Hunts, Private labels' D-IN has less influence on Hunts, than predicted by the symmetric model.									
Del Monte	0.00	−NS	0.38	0.75	1.08	+NS	0.33	−NS		−0.57
Cross effects	Heinz is less influenced by Del Monte's D-FA, Del Monte's Price has more influnce on Hunts, Private labels' Price and D-EA have more influence on Del Monte, than predicted by the symmetric model.									
Private labels	−0.79	−NS	0.19	0.35	−NS	0.39	0.17	0.61		−0.84
Cross effects	Private labels' D-EA has more influence on Hunts, Hunt's Price has more influence on private labels, Private labels' Price, D-EA and Cp-M have more influence on Del Monte, than predicted by the symmetric model.									

was 0.816, and in cross validation was 0.772 – just slightly higher in all cases than the corresponding values for the segment-level models.

The parameter values are reported in Table 6.8. Here too the cross effects are described verbally, in relation to what we expect from a symmetric market-share model. Further interpretation of the parameters is postponed to the next section.

5.7. *Comparing forecasts and diagnostics*

Table 6.9 compares the summary statistics on model calibration, cross calibration, cross validation, and forecasts. The similarities are remarkable. Although a slight edge might seem to go to the aggregate model (there are no statistical tests to compare these R-square values), when it comes to forecasting, the models are identical to three decimal places.

The *condition index* is also reported for the models in each of the calibration datasets. This number is the ratio of the largest singular value (square root of the eigenvalue) to the smallest singular value in the sum-of-squares-and-crossproducts (SSCP) matrix for the (reduced-form) regression model. This index is discussed by Belsley, Kuh & Welsch [1980] as an indicator of the degree of collinearity in the regression system. These authors indicate that condition indices over 100 can cause 'substantial variance inflation and great potential harm to regression estimate' [p. 153]. Indices from 21 to 35 are moderate at worst and give further evidence that asymmetric market-share models that use exp(z-scores) [cf. Cooper & Nakanishi, 1988, pp. 141–143] are exempt from the warnings concerning collinearity first given by Bultez & Naert [1975].

We may begin the comparison of the diagnostic value of this approach by looking at the parameter values listed in Table 6.10. This table shows only the differential-effect parameters for the three models calibrated earlier. There are no statistical tests for the equality of parameters across equations of this sort. What

Table 6.9.
Comparison of market-share models

	Light-users segment R-square	Heavy-users segment R-square	Aggregate market R-square
Calibration	0.824	0.829	0.845
D.F.	52–3210	48–3214	45–3217
Condition index	32.5	34.8	21.6
Cross calibration	0.803	0.814	0.816
D.F.	51–1558	47–1562	44–1565
Cross validation	0.756	0.766	0.772
D.F.	1–1607	1–1607	1–1607
Forecast accuracy		*Combined*	*Aggregate*
	RMSE	0.128	0.128
	VAF	0.711	0.711

Table 6.10.
Brand summary – across models

Brand	Int	Ad-L	Ad-M	D-EA	D-FA	D-IN	D-AO	Cp-S	Cp-M	Price
Heinz										
Aggregate	2.06	0.17	0.07	0.08	0.20	+NS	0.13	0.60		−0.70
Heavy users	2.30	0.15	+NS	0.07	0.22	0.03	+NS	0.61	0.11	−NS
Light users	2.00	0.14	+NS	+NS	0.29	+NS	+NS	0.57	−NS	−0.49
Hunts										
Aggregate	−NS	0.26	0.35	0.19	+NS	0.29	0.22	0.84		−0.40
Heavy users	−NS	0.21	0.34	0.21	+NS	0.24	0.25	0.71	0.16	−0.50
Light users	−NS	0.26	0.36	0.22	−NS	0.24	0.28	0.72	0.16	−NS
Del Monte										
Aggregate	0.00	−NS	0.38	0.75	1.08	+NS	0.33	−NS		−0.57
Heavy users	0.00	−NS	0.44	0.78	1.07	+NS	0.32	−NS	0.26	−1.13
Light users	0.00	−NS	0.29	0.75	1.09	0.15	0.38	−NS	0.51	−0.61
Private labels										
Aggregate	−0.79	−NS	0.19	0.35	−NS	0.39	0.17	0.61		−0.84
Heavy users	−0.87	+NS	0.22	0.38	−NS	0.35	0.16	0.54	−NS	−1.30
Light users	−0.62	−NS	0.17	0.35	+NS	0.27	+NS	0.68	+NS	−0.73

we are undertaking is not a statistical comparison, but rather a comparison of how differently these models would be interpreted by managers having to develop brand plans in a competitive environment.

For convenience the parameters have been grouped into four classes. Those with no border are relatively stable across analyses. Note that 28 of the 40 groups (70%) fall into this stable class, which is reassuring in many ways. The brand-specific intercepts, line-ad parameters, front-aisle display parameters, and store-coupon effects all seem stable within brands across analyses.

The solid, dark lines highlight parameter groups with major differences in levels (although no changes in the pattern of statistical significance across analyses). For Del Monte the aggregate price parameter is −0.57, but the introduction of the manufacturer's coupon and segmentation leads to a heavy-user segment that is very price-sensitive ($\beta_{Hj\cdot\mathrm{Price}} = -1.13$) and somewhat coupon-sensitive ($\beta_{Hj\cdot\mathrm{Coupon}} = 0.26$), while the light-user segment is much less price-sensitive ($\beta_{Lj\cdot\mathrm{Price}} = -0.61$) and more opportunistic users of manufacturer's coupons ($\beta_{Lj\cdot\mathrm{Coupon}} = 0.51$) for *private-label* brands the manufacturer's coupon effect is not significant in either segment (as should be the case), but the segmentation still leads to major differences in the price parameter – with the heavy-user segment being much more price-sensitive than the light-user segment.

The dotted lines highlight groups in which the analyses reveal differences in the patterns of significance across analyses. In the aggregate analysis of Heinz there is a significant price effect. Segment-level analysis indicates that the heavy-user segment is not price-sensitive, but is sensitive to manufacturer's coupons, while the light-user segment is somewhat price-sensitive and not affected by manufacturer's coupons. For Hunts we see both segments are somewhat sensitive to the presence of manufacturer's coupons, but all of the price sensitivity that appears in the aggregate is due to the sensitivity of the heavy-users segment.

Particularly for Heinz (the dominant brand in the category) we see diagnostically different patterns comparing the segment analyses and the aggregate analysis. Major ads and other displays appear effective in the aggregate, but have no significant effect in either segment. The end-of-aisle displays that seem effective in the aggregate analyses influence the heavy users but not the light users. All of these differences lead us to believe that segment-based analyses provide a diagnostically richer picture of this brand and of the market – without a sacrifice in forecast accuracy.

5.8. Conclusion

The goal of this section was to illustrate a method for bridging the too-long-separate traditions of individual-choice modeling and market-response modeling. We have shown that some kinds of information in panel databases can be used to segment otherwise aggregate market-response models, and other kinds of information can be integrated into these segment models to provide a diagnostically richer representation of market and competitive influences. And we have shown that these diagnostically rich, asymmetric market-share models can be estimated without the fear of collinearity.

This was a modest effort involving segmentation by usage frequency and the integration of a single variable from the panel database. But the underlying methods are so simple and robust that more venturesome applications seem readily doable.

6. Issues facing attraction models

This section deals with three issues that attraction models need to confront in the coming decade. The first feals with the tension between tactical and strategic uses of these models. The second concerns incorporating effects with greatly varying temporal impacts. And the third concerns new areas of application.

6.1. Strategy versus tactics

Resource-allocation decisions are typically made at the brand (or strategic-business-unit) level. Optimal allocation rules are elasticity-based. So we need models calibrated at this level to support strategic decisions. Promotion-planning involves decisions such as what combinations of brand versions and sizes should be co-promoted. Should fruited 4 oz. yogurts be promoted with plain yogurt of all sizes? Which topping combination of frozen pizza is best to feature in an ad? Such questions require very detailed specification of market-share models. Cross effects may relate to aggregates of versions and sizes within a brand line. Current illustrations of market-share models are between these two extreme levels of specification.

What is needed is a way of specifying and estimating attraction models in great detail (to satisfy tactical requirements), and a means of aggregating elasticities over versions and sizes of a brand to satisfy strategic requirements. As computations become amazingly cheaper, estimating detailed models becomes more practical. But aggregating elasticities over brand versions or sizes (without estimating a more aggregate model) involves mathematical developments that have yet to be undertaken. Specification of a more aggregated model for strategy than for tactics seems an obvious alternative, but there is no guarantee that the complex of competitive forces that appears in detailed models will appear in models with more aggregated competitors. Detailed study of the competitive structures revealed by models of the same underlying data, at different levels of brand aggregation is needed.

6.2. *Differences in temporal impact*

Scanner data have helped us grow accustomed to calibrating models at the weekly level. The promotional environment is largely constant throughout a week within a trading area. Models that account for the huge swings in sales (and shares) that accompany promotions are useful for planning coupons, displays and newspaper features. But what about advertising? TV ads are much slower in showing any effect they might have. If they are effective, the impact is spread out over a much longer time period. In the numerical illustration of the previous section, advertising effects are probably lumped into the brand-specific effects α_i. So effects that are *slow* with respect to the periodicity of a calibrated model might show up as the *constant* component of a brand's attraction. This makes evaluating advertising effectiveness very difficult.

We are greatly aided in the search for a remedy, by the proof in Cooper & Nakanishi [1988, pp. 78–85] that distributed-lag models can be specified for both explanatory variables and lagged market-share effects without losing the logical-consistency property of attraction models, if the specification is done in the *log-centered* form of the variables. But even with this capability we might face a situation in which each week there are very weak, lagged advertising effects from the prior twelve (or more) weeks of advertising. With the possibility of differential lagged effects and cross-competitive lagged effects, the number of possible parameters could become unmanageable for dynamic forces that we expect to be weak in each time period.

Another alternative might be to estimate the brand-specific parameters as *sequentially varying parameters* with their values varying *systematically* as functions of advertising expenditures. Chapter 9 by Hanssens and Parsons discusses such models.

6.3. *New application areas*

The rapid evolution of single-source, scanner databases, with their rich description of the competitive influences affecting all brands in a market, has given new momentum to the study and development of attraction models. The trend is bound to continue and strengthen as manufacturers and retailers come to grips with the complexities of what it means to manage in an information-rich environment. But the new areas of application are likely to be far removed from the brand-management context that has dominated the discussion in this chapter so far.

Attraction models have their roots in the interface between marketing and geography [cf. Huff, 1962, 1963; Haines, Simon & Alexis, 1972]. How shoppers in neighborhood *j* were attracted to retail center *i*, was the type of problem broached in these early studies. But the Huff model was an IIA model incapable of reflecting asymmetries in attraction. We believe that some of the most challenging problems to which attraction models can be applied return to these roots, but in a much more mature form.

For example, the nations of the world can be thought of as centers of attraction. The asymmetric flows of trade between nations could be represented by extended attraction models. Even at an aggregate level implied by investigating the balance of trade in gross dollars (or other monetary units), asymmetric attraction models provide a framework for valuing the various forces that are theorized to drive trade imbalances (e.g. differences in labor rates, tariff barriers, barriers in the distribution channels). The relative values of currencies themselves could be represented with asymmetric attraction models. If these representations are *descriptive* as well as predictive, we would enrich the empirical basis for understanding currency markets.

There are fundamental inadequacies, however, in representing the asymmetric flows of resources between countries in terms of capital. Some capital has its roots in largely renewable resources, while other capital is generated by the depletion of finite and fixed resources. The implications of the differences in the resource base are grave, but glossed over by purely aggregate representations of capital flows. For example, the trade surpluses that most *first-world* countries have with many *third-world* countries drains capital from the third world. It makes a considerable difference if this need for capital is sated by the export of rapidly renewable resources (e.g. coffee, sugar beet, or other cultivated agricultural commodities), versus the diminishing supply of exotic hardwoods from the world's rainforests. It even makes a difference if the agricultural land is claimed by the destruction of rainforests as opposed to balanced reuse of existing agricultural lands.

The weighty and complex problems we face in establishing a sustainable balance of resource flows between nations requires modeling techniques rich enough to capture the diversity of the causal influences driving these problems. In the hands of creative researchers, asymmetric attraction models can help us understand the forces driving imbalance, and perhaps help provide insight into what can be done.

References

Abraham, M.M., and L.M. Lodish (1987). PROMOTER: An automated promotion evaluation system. *Marketing Sci.* 6(2), 101–123.

Allenby, G.M. (1989). A unified approach to identifying, estimating and testing demand structures with aggregate scanner data. *Marketing Sci.* 8(3), 265–280.

Allenby, G.M. (1990). Hypothesis testing with scanner data: The advantage of Bayesian methods. *J. Marketing Res.* 27 (November), 379–389.

Bass, F.M., M.M. Givon, M.U. Kalwani, D. Reibstein and G.P. Wright (1984). An investigation into the order of the brand choice process. *Marketing Sci.* 3 (Fall), 267–287.

Bawa, K., and A. Ghosh (1991). The covariates of regularity in purchase timing. *Marketing Lett.* 2(2), 147–157.

Bawa, K., and R.W. Shoemaker (1987). The effects of direct mail coupon on brand choice behavior. *J. Marketing Res.* 24 (November), 370–376.

Bell, D.E., R.L. Keeney and J.D.C. Little (1975). A market share theorem. *J. Marketing Res.* 12 (May), 136–141.

Belsley, D.A., E. Kuh and R.E. Welsch (1980). *Regression Diagnostics: Identifying Influential Data and Sources of Collinearity.* Wiley, New York.

Bemmaor, A.C., and D. Mouchoux (1991). Measuring the short-term effect of in-store promotion and retail advertising on brand sales: A factorial experiment. *J. Marketing Res.* 28 (May), 202–214.

Blattberg, R.C., and K.J. Wisniewski (1989). Price induced patterns of competition, *Marketing Sci.* 8(4), 291–309.

Bolton, R.N. (1989). The relationship between market characteristics and promotional price elasticities. *Marketing Sci.* 8(2), 153–169.

Brodie, R., and C.A. De Kluyver (1984). Attraction versus linear and multiplicative market share models: An empirical evaluation. *J. Marketing Res.* 21 (May), 194–201.

Bucklin, R.E., and J.M. Lattin (1991). A two-state model of purchase incidence and brand choice. *Marketing Sci.* 10(1), 24–39.

Bultez, A.V., and P.A. Naert (1975). Consistent sum-constrained models. *J. Amer. Statist. Assoc.* 70 (September), 529–535.

Bultez, A.V., and P.A. Naert (1988). SH.A.R.P.: SHelf Allocation for Retailer's Profit, *Marketing Sci.* 7(3) 211–231.

Carpenter, G.S., L.G. Cooper, D.M. Hanssens and D.F. Midgley (1988). Modeling asymmetric competition, *Marketing Sci.* 7(4), 393–412.

Carpenter, G.S., and D.R. Lehmann (1985). A model of marketing mix, brand switching, and competition. *J. Marketing Res.* 22 (August), 318–329.

Cooper, L.G. (1988). Competitive maps: The structure underlying asymmetric cross elasticities. *Management Sci.* 34(6), 707–723.

Cooper, L.G. (1989a). Integrating scanner-panel and store-level data. Seventh Marketing Science Conference, Duke, March.

Cooper, L.G. (1989b). Toward integrating scanner-panel and store-level data. Joint UCLA–USC Marketing Colloquium, May, UCS, Los Angeles.

Cooper, L.G., and M. Nakanishi (1983). Standardizing variables in multiplicative choice models. *J. Consumer Res.* 10 (June), 96–108.

Cooper, L.G., and M. Nakanishi (1988). *Market-Share Analysis: Evaluating Competitive Marketing Effectiveness.* Kluwer Academic Publishers, Boston.

Currim, I.S., R.J. Meyer and N.T. Le (1988). Disaggregate tree-structured modeling of consumer choice data. *J. Marketing Res.* 25 (August), 253–265.

Currim, I.S., and L.G. Schneider (1991). A taxonomy of consumer purchase strategies in a promotion intense environment. *Marketing Sci.* 10(2) 91–110.

Debreu, G. (1960). Review of R.D. Luce's *Individual Choice Behavior: A Theoretical Analysis, Amer. Econom. Rev.* 50(1), 186–188.

DeSarbo, W.S., V. Rao, J.H. Steckel, Y. Wind and R. Columbo (1987). A friction model for describing and forecasting price changes. *Marketing Sci.* 6(4), 299–319.

Doyle, P., and J. Saunders (1990). Multiproduct advertising budgeting. *Marketing Sci.* 9(2), 97–113.

Elrod, T. (1988). Choice Map: Inferring a product-market map from panel data, *Marketing Sci.* 7(1), 21–40.

Fader, P.S., and L. McAlister (1990). An elimination by aspects model of consumer response to promotion calibrated on UPC scanner data. *J. Marketing Res.* 7 (August), 322–332.

Frank, R.E. (1962). Brand choice as a probability process. *J. Business* 35, 43–56.

Ghosh, A., S. Neslir, and R. Shoemaker (1984). A comparison of market share models and estimation procedures. *J. Marketing Res.* 21 (May), 202–210.

Gibson, R. (1991). Cereal giants battle over market share. *Wall Street J.* December 16, B1–2.

Givon, Moshe M. (1984). Variety seeking through brand switching. *Marketing Sci.* 3 (Winter), 1–22.

Grover, R., and V. Srinivasan (1989). An approach for tracking within-segment shifts in market shares. *J. Marketing Res.* 26 (May), 230–236.

Gruca, T.S., and D. Sudharshan (1991). Equilibrium characteristics of multinomial logit market share models. *J. Marketing Res.* 28 (November), 480–482.

Guadagni, P.M., and J.D.C. Little (1983). A logit model of brand choice calibrated on scanner data. *Marketing Sci.* 2(3), 203–288.

Gupta, S. (1988). Impact of sales promotion on when, what, and how much to buy. *J. Marketing Res.*, 25 (November), 342–356.

Gupta, S. (1991). Stochastic models of interpurchase time with time dependent covariates. *J. Marketing Res.* 28 (February), 1–15.

Gurumurthy, K., and J.D.C. Little (1986). A pricing model based on perception theories and its testing on scanner panel data. Working Paper Draft, Massachusetts Institute of Technology, May.

Haines, G.H., Jr. L.S. Simon and M. Alexis (1972). Maximum likelihood estimation of central-city food trading areas. *J. Marketing Res.* 9 (May), 154–159.

Huff, D.L. (1962). *Determination of Intraurban Retail Trade Areas*, Los Angeles: Real Estate Research Program. University of California, Los Angeles.

Huff, D.L. (1963). A probabilistic analysis of consumer spatial behavior, in W.S. Decker (ed.), *Emerging Concepts in Marketing.* American Marketing Association, Chicago, pp. 443–461.

Jain, D.C., and N.J. Vilcassim (1991). Investigating household purchase timing decisions: A conditional hazard function approach. *Marketing Sci.* 10(1), 1–23.

Kahn, B.E., D.G. Morrison and G.P. Wright (1986). Aggregating individual purchases to the household level. *Marketing Sci.* 5(3), 260–268.

Kalwani, M.U., C.K. Yim, H.J. Rinne and Y. Sugita (1990). A price expectations model of customer brand choice. *J. Marketing Res.* 27 (August), 251–262.

Kamakura, W.A., and G.J. Russell (1989). A probabilistic choice model for market segmentation and elasticity structure. *J. Marketing Res.* 26 (November), 379–390.

Kannan, P.K., and G.P. Wright (1991). Modeling and testing structured markets: A nested logit approach. *Marketing Sci.* 10(1), 58–82.

Korth, B., and L.R. Tucker (1975). The distribution of chance coefficients from simulated data. *Psychometrika*, 40(3), 361–372.

Kotler, P. (1984). *Marketing Management: Analysis, Planning, and Control, 5th Edition.* Prentice-Hall, Englewood Cliffs, NJ.

Krishnamurthi, L., and S.P. Raj (1991). An empirical analysis of the relationship between brand loyalty and consumer price elasticity. *Marketing Sci.* 10(2), 172–183.

Kuehn, A.A. (1962). Consumer brand choice – a learning process. *J. Advertising Res.* 2 (December), 10–17.

Kumar, V., and R.P. Leone (1988). Measuring the effect of retail store promotions on brand and store substitution. *J. Marketing Res.* 25 (May), 178–185.

Lattin, J.M., and R.E. Bucklin (1989). Reference effects of price and promotion on brand choice behavior. *J. Marketing Res.* 26 (August), 299–310.

Leeflang, P.S.H., and J.C. Reuyl (1984). On the predictive power of market share attraction models. *J. Marketing Res.* 21 (May), 211–215.

Luce, R.D. (1959). *Individual Choice Behavior: A Theoretical Analysis.* Wiley, New York.

McFadden, D. (1974). Conditional logit analysis of qualitative choice behavior. in P. Zarembka. *Frontiers in Econometrics.* Academic Press, New York, pp. 105–142.

McGuire, T.W., D.L. Weiss and F.S. Houston (1977). Consistent multiplicative market share models. in B.A. Greenberg and D.N. Bellinger (eds), *Contemporary Marketing Thought.* American Marketing Association, Chicago, pp. 129–134.

Meyer, R.J., and L.G. Cooper (1987). A longitudinal choice analysis of consumer response to a product innovation, in R. Golledge and H. Timmermans (eds), *Decision Making and Choice Behaviour: Behavioural Modeling*. Croom-Helm, London, pp. 424–451.

Moore, W.L., and R.S. Winer (1987). A panel-based method for merging joint space and market response function estimation. *Marketing Sci.* 6(1), 25–42.

Naert, P.A., and A. Bultez (1973). Logically consistent market share models. *J. Marketing Res.* 10 (August), 334–340.

Naert, P.A., and M. Weverbergh (1981), On the prediction power of market share attraction models. *J. Marketing Res.* 18 (May), 146–153.

Naert, P.A., and M. Weverbergh (1985). Market share specification, estimation and validation: Toward reconciling seemingly divergent views. *J. Marketing Res.* 22 (November), 453–461.

Nakanishi, M. (1972). Measurement of sales *promotion effect at the retail level*–a new approach. *Proceedings, Spring and Full Conference*, American Marketing Association. Chicago, pp. 338–343.

Nakanishi, M., and L.G. Cooper (1974). Parameter estimation for a multiplicative competitive interaction model – least squares approach. *J. Marketing Res.* 11 (August), 303–311.

Nakanishi, M., L.G. Cooper and H.H. Kassarjian (1974). Voting for a political candidate under conditions of minimal information. *J. Consumer Res.* 1 (September), 36–43.

Neslin, S.A. (1990). A market response model for coupon promotions, *Marketing Sci.* 9(2), 125–145.

Neslin, S.A., C. Henderson, and J. Quelch (1985). Consumer promotions and the acceleration of product purchase. *Marketing Sci.* 4 (Spring), 147–165.

Pedrick, J.H., and F.S. Zufryden (1991). Evaluating the impact of advertising media plans: A model of consumer purchase dynamics using single-source data. *Marketing Sci.* 10(2), 111–130.

Ramaswamy, V., and W.S. DeSarbo (1990). SCULPTURE: A new methodology for deriving and analyzing hierarchical product-market structure from panel data. *J. Marketing Res.* 27 (November), 418–427.

Russell, G.J., R.N. Bolton (1988). Implications of market structure for elasticity structure. *J. Marketing Res.* 25 (August), 229–241.

Schmittlein, D.C., L.G. Cooper and D.G. Morrison (1993). Truth in concentration in the land of 80/20 laws. *Marketing Sci.* 12(1), forthcoming.

Shugan, S.M. (1987). Estimating brand positioning maps from supermarket scanning data. *J. Marketing Res.* 24 (February), 1–18.

Tellis, G.J. (1988). Advertising exposure, loyalty, and brand purchase: A two-stage model of choice. *J. Marketing Res.* 25 (May), 134–144.

Vilcassim, N.J. (1989). Extending the Rotterdam model to test hierarchical market structures. *Marketing Sci.* 8(2), 181–190.

Vilcassim, N.J., and D.C. Jain (1991). Modeling purchase timing and brand switching behavior incorporating explanatory variables and unobserved heterogeneity. *J. Marketing Res.* 28 (February), 29–41.

Walters, R.G., and S.B. MacKenzie (1988). A structural equation analysis of the impact of price promotions on store performance. *J. Marketing Res.* 25 (February), 51–63.

Wheat, R.D., and D.G. Morrison (1990a). Estimating purchase regularity with two interpurchase times. *J. Marketing Res.* 27 (February), 87–93.

Wheat, R.D., and D.G. Morrison (1990b). Assessing purchase timing models: Whether or not is preferable to when. *Marketing Sci.* 9(2), 162–170.

Wind, Y. (1978). Issues and advances in segmentation research. *J. Marketing Res.* 15, 317–337.

Winer, R.S. (1986). A reference price model of brand choice for frequently purchased products. *J. Consumer Res.* 13(2), 250–271.

Winer, R.S. (1989). A multi-stage model of choice incorporating reference prices. *Marketing Lett.* 1(1), 27–36.

Yellott, J.I. (1977). The relationship between Luce's choice axiom, Thurstone's theory of comparative judgments, and the double exponential distribution. *J. Math. Psychology*, 15, 109–144.

Zufryden, F.S. (1984). Modeling purchase patterns on the basis of incomplete and biased consumer purchase diary and UPC panel data. *Intern. Res. Marketing*, 1, 199–213.

Zufryden, F.S. (1987). A model for relating media exposure to purchase incidence behavior patterns. *Management Sci.* 33(10), 1253–1266.

J. Eliashberg and G.L. Lilien, Eds., *Handbooks in OR & MS, Vol. 5*

Chapter 7

Pretest Market Forecasting*

Glen L. Urban

Sloan School of Management, Massachusetts Institute of Technology, Cambridge, MA 02139, USA

In the last twenty years major advances have been made in the development and implementation of models and measurement methodologies to allow forecasting of new product sales before test market and/or market introduction. The potential to reduce failure rates and accurately make forecasts has been proven when good models have been used, careful measurement and estimation has been conducted, and plans are carefully implemented. The initial breakthroughs occurred in the consumer packaged-goods field where over 6000 applications have been conducted by numerous market research firms worldwide. New model structures are being applied to consumer durable goods and are showing encouraging results. The state of the art is on forecasting major breakthrough innovations in consumer, industrial and service industries.

In this paper we indicate the criteria for good premarket methods, review the state of the art of models and measurement methods for packaged goods, consumer durables, industrial and service innovations, and close with advice on how to most effectively use the models. Emphasis is on models documented in the academic literature, but commercial methods are cited when adequate information is available.

1. Criteria for pretest market analysis

A managerial decision to use a pretest market analysis is justified if sufficiently accurate predictions can be achieved, the timing of the analysis is before large investment commitments are necessary, useful diagnostics for improvement are generated, and the cost of the analysis is reasonable. In these situations failures can be reduced, time-to-market can be shortened, and products improved to increase customer satisfaction.

*Adapted from Urban & Hauser [1993, Chapter 16].

1.1. Accuracy

Since the final product environment may change before full-scale launch and measurement error will be present, pretest markets cannot predict perfectly, but they should be sufficiently good for a GO/NO GO market decision. This means that a pretest market should reject poor products with a high probability of being correct. Also, good products should have a high probability of being identified correctly. A reasonable criterion to achieve these managerial goals is that predictions are within 25% of long-run sales 75% of the time. For most consumer brands, this would imply the predicted share should be about two points above the minimum share required for a GO decision in order to assure a 75% chance of success in the test market. Such accuracy can be obtained as we report below.

1.2. Managerial diagnostics

Many new products (35–50%) are identified as failures at the pretest stage even after careful design work. One could merely drop these products, but usually there are opportunities to improve the physical product, advertising copy, or marketing mix. A pretest market model and measurement system should provide actionable diagnostics on why the product succeeded or failed, how it could be improved, and what the share implications are of such improvements. When a product is rated as 'good' after the pretest analysis, diagnostics generate information to improve the product further. Such improvement is important because the better the product is, the less likely it is to be vulnerable to competitive entries. The diagnostics to improve quality should be many and linked to operational variables that can be changed.

1.3. Timeliness

The premarket forecasting must be done early enough before the launch that major expenditures can be stopped if the analysis indicates the product is likely to be a failure. In packaged goods the big expenditures are for test market (12–18 months before launch) and national launch. For consumer durables there are two significant points – before commitment to production capacity (e.g. in automobiles 36–48 months before launch) and before committing to specific levels of launch expenditure (e.g. 12 months before launch). In industrial products, the investment in production is the milestone (often 1–2 years before introduction). In services, the investment points may include large fixed costs (e.g. new computers for credit services) or are concentrated at launch time (e.g. a new health service for the very old).

The pretest market model should provide results fast enough for managerial action; furthermore, the use of a pretest market should not significantly delay full-scale launch. A good analysis should improve the average time-to-market by preventing inferior products from getting to launch. Three months is a typical time for a pretest analysis.

1.4. Cost

One gains little if the pretest market is very costly in dollars and/or time. The cost of a pretest market should be well below the expected gains (from \$ 75 000 to \$ 100 000 is an attainable cost for pretest market analysis in packaged goods and about two or three times this amount for consumer-durable and industrial products), and it should be compared to the value generated.

2. Alternative approaches – packaged goods

The input to a premarket analysis is the physical product, advertising copy, packaging, price, selling channels of distribution strategy, service policies, and the advertising and promotion budget. The output is a forecast of sales and diagnostics. To fulfill the above criteria, the pretest market must be based on careful measurement and models of consumer response. Table 7.1 lists a number of alternative approaches. Each approach has its relative strengths and weaknesses; you may wish to combine two or more approaches to enhance accuracy. At least one available model uses such a convergent approach by combining trial/repeat and attitude-change models.

In this paper we describe how these approaches have been used in frequently purchased packaged goods, consumer durables, and industrial and service industries. The procedures were invented in the packaged-goods industry and have diffused into the other marketing domains where the unique aspects of these markets have led to new models and market research approaches.

The high failure rates and attendant losses in test markets (\$ 1.5–3 million investment) and national launches (\$ 10–50 million investment) led innovative packaged-goods firms to develop methods to reduce the risks of failure in test scores. As the models developed they used simulated test-market measures, models based on trial/repeat behavior, and analyses of attitude change.

2.1. Judgment and past-product experience

One approach to pretest forecasting is to examine past experience to determine which measurable characteristics of a new product determines its success. For

Table 7.1
Alternative modeling approaches to premarket analysis

Judgment and past-product experience
Trail/repeat measurement
Test-market models
Stochastic models
Home delivery
Laboratory measurement
Attitude-change models
Convergent

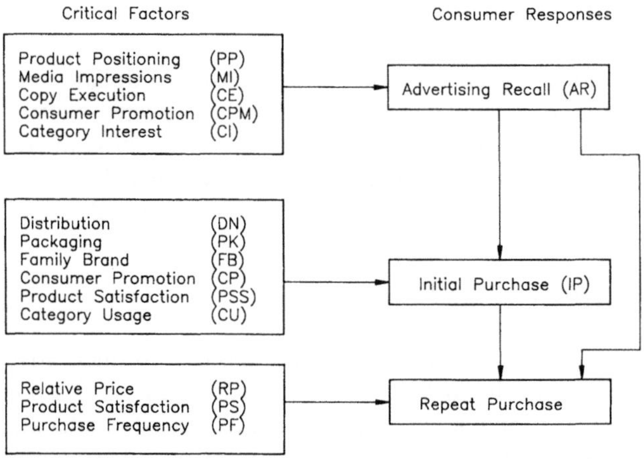

Fig. 7.1. Model based on past product experience (adapted from [Claycamp & Liddy, 1969, p. 415]).

example, Figure 7.1 suggests one set of critical factors that affect advertising recall, initial purchase, and repeat purchase. These particular factors are used in a model developed by Claycamp & Liddy [1969] some years ago for packaged goods. To develop such a model, one gathers these measures (both the cirtical factors and consumer response) and uses statistical analysis (regression) of past-product results to estimate the relationships between the cirtical factors and consumer response. For the new product, the critical factors are measured and the regression equation is used to forecast consumer response.

The advantage of this approach is that once that regression equation is estimated, the model can produce predictions rapidly and at a low cost. It makes use of previous experience. Because the media and distribution plans appear in the model, alternative plans can be tried and the best one chosen. The approach also has a number of disadvantages. Besides its sensitivity to expert judgment, the model is extremely sensitive to the past products used to estimate the model. Since the model has no underlying theory of the consumer response (beyond a causal diagram), the regressions may not be appropriate for categories that are significantly different from those used to estimate the model. Finally, since few direct measures are taken from the consumer, the model may miss important consumer concerns.

The Claycamp & Liddy model is based on data obtained from 58 new-product introductions that covered 32 different types of packaged goods. The regressions were run on 35 of those introductions, 50% of which were foods; the other 23 were saved for predictive testing. Two regression equations were estimated, one for advertising recall and one for initial purchase. No results are reported for repeat purchase. The regressions explained over 70% of the variation in the data and were significant at the 1% level. The largest effect on advertising recall were produced by product positioning (PP), copy and advertising ($\sqrt{MI*CE}$), consumer promotion (CP) and category interest (CI), in that order. Trial was affected most by packaging (PK), family branding (FB), and advertising recall (AR). When the model was tested on 23 new products, 15 of 23 fell within 10 percentage points of observed advertising recall, and 20 of 23 fell within 10 percentage points of the observed trial. The correlations of actual and predicted were 0.56 for recall and 0.95 for trial.

This approach is interesting because it indicates that studying past products is useful. But the levels of correlation indicate that past relationships may not be sufficient. The model is limited because no experience with the repeat-purchase sector has been reported. Without a valid repurchase model, the new-product share cannot be predicted. The pioneering Claycamp & Liddy model has led to recent research to develop more measures and stronger models to predict market share.

2.2. *Trial/repeat measurement*

Long-run sales are based on both trial and repeat. Accurate forecasts of long-run sales can be made if the pretest analysis predicts the percentage of consumers who will try the product (cumulative trial) and the precentage of those who will become repeat-users (cumulative repeat). A series of models have been developed which present the new product to consumers in a reasonably realistic setting and take direct consumer measures which are used to forecast trial-and-repeat purchases. The advantage of this approach is that it is based on direct observation of consumer response to the new product. The disadvantage is that errors are introduced because the direct measures may not be representative of what would happen in a test market or a full-scale launch.

2.2.1. *Test-market models*

Since premarket analysis for consumer packaged goods was initially directed at reducing the failure rate in the test market, we begin by considering models that were developed for test markets. We adapt them to pretest market forecasts. The approach is to estimate the key trial-and-repeat parameters based on concept and product tests and then use the test-market model structure to forecast sales. Three examples are NEWS [Pringle, Wilson & Brody, 1982], SPRINTER [Urban, 1970] and TRACKER [Blattberg & Golanty, 1978]. For example, Figure 7.2 shows the NEWS model logic. The advertising-to-brand-awareness translation is obtained from statistical studies of past brand launches. Promotion and distribution response are similarly based on past experience and the marketing plan for the new brand. NEWS estimates the trial from the 'definitely-will-repurchase' intent measure from a home-use test. The research measures plus judgment define the parameters used in the model.

In premarket analysis, trial-and-repeat behavior must be estimated. The initial approaches developed 'norms' or rules based on experience with past products. In the trial-and-repeat models two translations are necessary. One transforms stated trial intent (usually on a five-point scale) into ultimate penetration and the other transforms repeat intent (also usually on a five-point scale) into cumulative

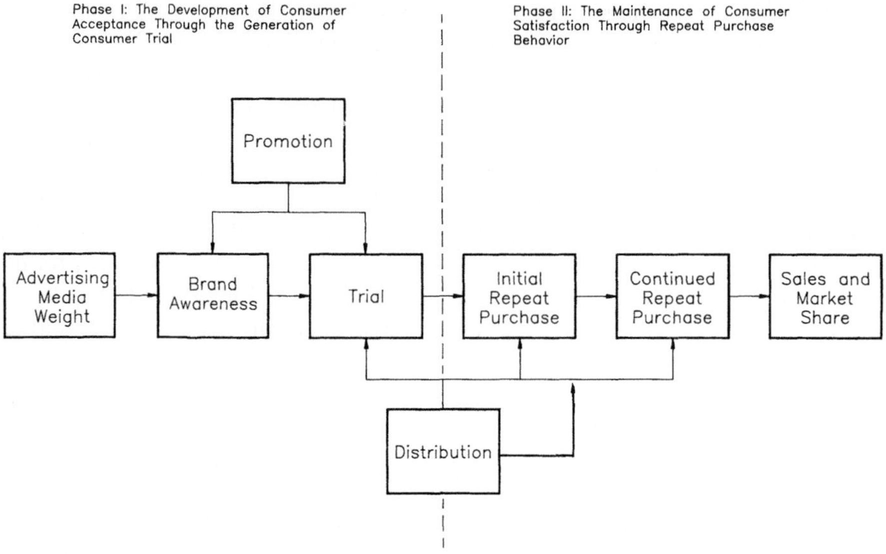

Fig. 7.2. The new product introduction process [Pringle, Wilson & Brody, 1982]).

repeat. In the NEWS model, the top box, 'definitely will buy', is used, but other modelers weigh the top two or three boxes based on their statistical derivation of rules derived from past new-product launches and category-purchase incidence. The translations represent 'norms' to translate stated intent into predicted behavior. These norms depend heavily on the analogy of the new product to past new products. In packaged goods these analogies are quite close and the norms work surprisingly well.

2.2.2. *Stochastic models*

In this approach, regressions based on previous purchasing experience are used to identify how the direct measures relate to trial-and-repeat dynamics. A number of alternative equations are possible. We illustrate the approach by describing parts of one stochastic model developed by Eskin & Malec [1976].

Their equation for cumulative trial is derived from past-product trial rates. The cumulative trial one year (α_1), depends on product-class penetration (PCP, percent of households buying at least one item in the product class during one year), the total consumer direct promotional expenditures (SPN) for the new product, and the distribution (DIS, weighted percent of stores stocking the new product). Trial is then given by

$$\alpha_1 = \alpha(\mathrm{PCP})^{b_1}(\mathrm{SPN})^{b_2}(\mathrm{DIS})^{b_3} \tag{1}$$

where α, b_1, b_2 and b_3 are parameters. After taking logs of both sides of this equation, a linear regression is used to estimate b_1, b_2 and b_3 based on past experience from past new products. This equation is similar to that of Claycamp & Liddy, but it does not include judged variables like the product position, copy effectiveness, or packaging. However, both models fit trial well. The model would be made more useful for diagnostic purposes if more trial variables were included and it was strengthened by direct measures of propensity to try.

Equation (1) gives cumulative trial, but it is important to predict the growth of trial. Figure 7.3 shows the most common form of growth. The stochastic models predict this growth. The equation used by Eskin & Malec for this curve is

$$R_t(0) = \alpha_1(1 - \gamma_1^t) \tag{2}$$

where

$R_t(0)$ = the percentage of consumers who have tried the new product by time t,
α_1 = the cumulative trial given by Equation (1),
γ_1 = a parameter to be estimated ($0 \leqslant \gamma_1 \leqslant 1$).

Eskin & Malec model the first repeat in a similar way except that (i) the cumulative repeat is estimated from a direct measure of intent to buy after usage, and (ii) the decay parameter is based on a hypothesis of consumer response and is a function of the frequency of purchase. First repeat, $R_t(1)$, is given by

$$R_t(1) = \alpha_2(1 - \gamma_2^t). \tag{3}$$

Similar equations are used for the second repeat purchase, and the third, etc.

To use this model for a new product, penetration is observed for the category, promotion and distribution are obtained from the introduction plan, and these values are substituted in Equation (1) to give α_1. Trial over time is given by a curve similar to Figure 7.3. Intent to buy is measured for those who have tried

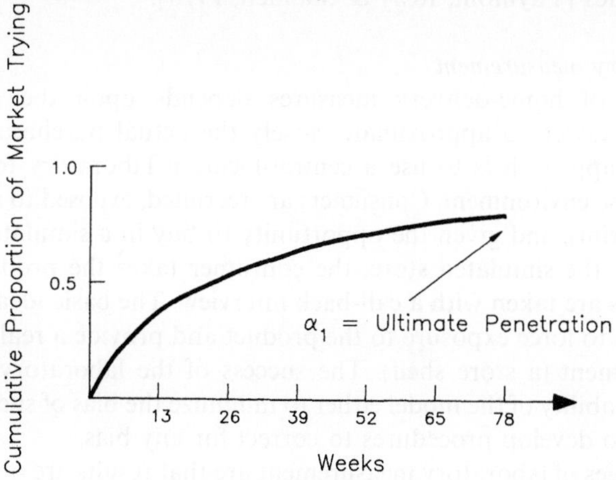

Fig. 7.3. Trial growth.

the product and cumulative repeat is determined. Equations predict first repeat, second repeat, third repeat, etc. Total sales come from summing trial and the various repeat classes. (See Eskin & Malec [1976] for details, and Silk & Kalwani [1982] for extensions.)

Stochastic models are attractive because of their explicit modeling of trial-and-repeat dynamics. Using past-purchasing data from new-product introductions in the model helps achieve good forecasting accuracy.

2.2.3. Home-delivery measures

Another approach to forecasting with a trial/repeat model is based on direct measures of trial and repeat in a sample of households served by a home delivery service. The measurement of trial and repeat is done in a panel (1000 households) which is visited each week by a salesperson. Based on information in a color catalog published each month and a biweekly promotion sheet describing price promotion, the consumer orders from a wide range of frequently purchased consumer products. The products are delivered on the same day and purchase records are computerized.

When a new product is to be tested, an ad is placed in the monthly catalog and trial-and-repeat purchase is observed. From this data a share of market for the product is forecasted by multiplying cumulative trial times the share of purchases the new brand receives from those who have tried it [Parfitt & Collins, 1968].

The advantage of this approach is that it is based on a home-delivery panel that approximates the actual product launch. The direct measures of trial are obtained based on exposure to real advertising, and realistic repeat-purchasing environments enhance forecasting accuracy. One disadvantage of this approach is that the panel must be run long enough to get good estimates, probably longer than other pretest market approaches. Therefore, costs are relatively high.

This panel approach has been used both to analyze existing product promotion [Charlton & Pymont, 1975; Charlton, Ehrenberg & Pymont, 1972] and to forecast new-product sales [Paymont, Reay & Standen, 1976].

2.2.4. Laboratory measurement

The success of home-delivery measures depends upon the ability of the home-delivery service to approximate closely the actual purchase environment. An alternative approach is to use a central-location laboratory to approximate the trial-purchase environment. Consumers are recruited, exposed to advertisements (television or print), and given the opportunity to buy in a simulated retail store. After buying in the simulated store, the consumer takes the product home and repeat measures are taken with a call-back interview. The basic idea of laboratory measurement is to force exposure to the product and provide a realistic purchase-choice environment (a store shelf). The success of the laboratory measurement depends on the ability of the model either to minimize the bias of such a laboratory simulation or to develop procedures to correct for any bias.

The advantages of laboratory measurement are that results are obtained rapidly and at a relatively low cost. The measures of trial and repeat are based on direct consumer response in a realistic purchase environment. Such measures have the potential for producing highly accurate forecasts. The disadvantage of such measurement is that the laboratory abstracts reality. The simulated store is not an actual store, measures are taken shortly after exposure to advertising, and the measurement may influence consumer behavior. While each of these problems can be overcome, they represent potential systematic biases that must be considered carefully.

One laboratory measurement model was based on a procedure development by Yankelovich, Skelly & White [1981] called LTM. They adjusted the observed trial-and-repeat rates based on judgment derived from past experience. For example, the observed trial is reduced by 25% due to 'inflation' in the laboratory. Another adjustment is a 'clout' factor that varies from 0.25 to 0.75 depending on introductory spending. Predictions of market share are made by multiplying trial and repeat by the frequency of purchase where frequency is adjusted based on a judged 'frequency factor' which reflects departures of new products from known frequency of purchase patterns. The Yankelovich, Skelly & White approach is interesting because it blends direct observation with managerial judgment, but the predictions are very dependent upon the judgmental input.

Another laboratory measurement model is the trial/repeat component of a model developed by Silk & Urban [1978] called ASSESSOR. They use the stochastic-model formulation to estimate market share for the brand by multiplying the ultimate cumulative trial by the share of purchases from those who have tried.

Trial comes about in one of two ways: direct trial or receipt and use of free samples. The direct trial, given ad exposure and availability, is the proportion of respondents who purchase the new brand in the laboratory on their simulated shopping trip. The predicted awareness from advertisements is based on the planned advertising budget. The predicted availability is based on planned sales-force and promotional activity directed at the retail trade. These parameters are obtained from judgment or from regression equations. Direct trial is the product of trial in the lab times awareness and distribution. The amount of trial from free samples depends on the number of samples that will be sent and the observed use in the laboratory simulation. If the probability of a consumer's direct trial is independent of the probability of receipt and use of a sample, the total trial is the sum of both sources of trial less their overlap.

The long-run share for those who have tried is modeled as a stochastic model, similar to the Eskin & Malec structure. Estimates of the repeat-purchase probabilities are derived from measurements obtained in the post-usage survey. The proportion of respondents who make a mail-order repurchase of the new brand when given the opportunity to do so is taken as an estimate of new-product repeat.

The advantages of the Silk & Urban formulation are that it is based on theoretical models of consumer response and that most consumer-response estimates come from direct measurement. The disadvantage is that this component of their model is still a laboratory simulation and thus subject to all the criticisms discussed above.

2.2.5. Summary of trial/repeat measurement

Trial and repeat purchase models are the most logical way to represent consumer response to a new frequently purchased brand. Direct measures of trial and repeat are important inputs to forecasting and many of the models discussed above are based firmly in consumer theory. Judgments need to be applied to any model, but direct measures and explicit models promote consistency, methodological rigor, and forecasting accuracy.

2.3. Attitude-change models

In product design, forecasts of purchase potential can be made based on estimates of consumer preferences for the new product. The advantage of this approach is that response is predicted directly and intervening effects such as awareness and availability are incorporated directly in the model. The attitude-based pretest-market analysis models use this basic approach of estimating behavior from consumer preferences. Consumer attitudes (preference or beliefs about product attributes) are measured first for existing products. The consumer is then given the new product and, after use, attitudes are measured for the new product.

The advantage of this approach is that the indirect attitude measures avoid some of the laboratory effects inherent in the direct trial-and-repeat measures. For example, attitudes toward existing products are often measured prior to laboratory exposure and are more representative of the attitudes of the consumer population. This is in contrast to the direct measures of trial which are highly dependent upon the closeness with which the laboratory approximates the real world. The disadvantage of attitude measures is that they are not direct measures. Predictions depend upon the accuracy and completeness of the model used to estimate choice behavior from the measured attitudes.

One early attitude model, called COMP, was developed by Burger, Gundee & Lavidge [1981]. The measurement to support this model is done by an initial interview to measure attitudes and an interview after consumers are exposed to advertisements and products in a simulated store. A call-back interview measures attitudes after use of the new brand.

An alternative attitude model is the second component of the pretest-market forecasting model published by Silk & Urban [1978] using the logit modeling procedure. They augment their first component with measures of preference. Their preference measure is developed from a constant-sum paired-comparison task in which consumers allocate a fixed number of 'chips' among each pair of products in their consideration set. A scaling technique developed by Torgerson [1958] transforms the constant-sum measures into ratio-scaled preferences. A variation of the logit model is then used to estimate behavior from the preferences.

To forecast the purchase probability for the new product (brand b), preference measures for the new and existing products are obtained after the consumer has experienced a period of trial usage of the new product. The new product is assumed to be in the consumer's consideration set and the logit model is used to forecast the unadjusted purchase probability for the new product.

The unadjusted purchase probability is forecast assuming the new product will be in the consideration set. In order to calculate an expected market share for the new brand, Silk & Urban take into account that the new brand will not necessarily become an element of the consideration set of brands for all consumers when it becomes available in the market. To do this, they obtain estimates of the percent of consumers who will consider the new product and multiply the consideration percent by the average unadjusted purchase probability.

For existing brands, the observed consideration levels are used to adjust the logit-based purchase probabilities. (Recall that the purchase probabilities for the existing brands change when the new product is introduced.) These estimates are important to the new-product manager because they indicate which established brands are likely to retaliate to defend their share.

Both the Burger, Gundee & Lavidge and Silk & Urban models base their estimates on some form of perference measures and both correct for awareness and availability. The predictions in both cases are the probabilities of purchase. The models differ in the specific equations and estimation procedures used. In particular, Silk & Urban use stronger preference measures (constant-sum), behavioral-based statistical techniques (logit), and limit their measurements to the cosideration set. Both models assume that the brand enters an established category.

2.4. *Convergent measures and models*

Judgment, trial/repeat, and attitude models each have their strengths and their weaknesses. An emerging view on pretest market analyses is to use more than one method in parallel and compare the results. For example, one might use the Eskin & Malec model to develop estimates based on trial-and-repeat measures and compare this to predictions obtained from Burger's attitude-change model. If the models agree, then the product manager has more faith in the predictions. If they disagree, then by comparing and reconciling results, any biases in measurement or structural problems in models can be identified and corrected. The advantage of a such a convergent approach is potentially greater accuracy and more confidence in the resulting forecasts. Furthermore, a combination of approaches gives a more comprehensive indication of how to improve the new product. The disadvantage of a convergent approach is the slightly greater cost. Costs do not double, however, because inputs for more than one model can often be obtained in the same set of consumer measures.

We return to the ASSESSOR model to illustrate the specific measures and analyses used in a convergent approach based on a trial/repeat and attitude model. This model is selected because it is completely documented in refereed academic journals and represents all the critical premarket modeling issues underlying the other models.

ASSESSOR is designed to aid management in evaluating new products once a positioning strategy has been developed and executed to the point where the product, packaging, and advertising copy are available and an introductory marketing plan (price, promotion and advertising) has been formulated. Given these inputs, the system is specifically intended to:

(1) Predict the new brand's equilibrium of long-run market share and unit sales volume over time.
(2) Estimate the sources of the new brand's share – 'cannibalization' of the firm's existing brand(s) and 'draw' from competitors' brands.
(3) Produce actionable diagnostic information for product improvement and develop advertising copy and other creative materials.
(4) Permit low-cost screening of selected elements of alternative marketing plans (advertising copy, price, and package design).

Figure 7.4 shows the overall structure of the system developed to meet these requirements. The critical task of predicting the brand's market share and sales volume is approached through the trial/repeat and attitude models described earlier. Convergent results strengthen confidence in the prediction while divergent outcomes signal the need for further analyses to identify sources of discrepancies and to provide bases for reconciliation. The measurement inputs required for both models are obtained from a research design involving laboratory and usage tests. The key outputs are a market-share prediction plus diagnostic information which is used to make a decision as to the brand's future.

2.4.1. Research design and measurement

The measurement inputs required to develop the desired diagnostic information and predictions for ASSESSOR are obtained from a research design structured to parallel the basic stages of the process of the consumer response to a new product. Table 7.2 outlines the essential features of the design and identifies the main types of data collected at each step. To simulate the awareness-trial stages of the response process, a laboratory-based experimental procedure is employed wherein a sample of consumers are exposed to advertising for the new product

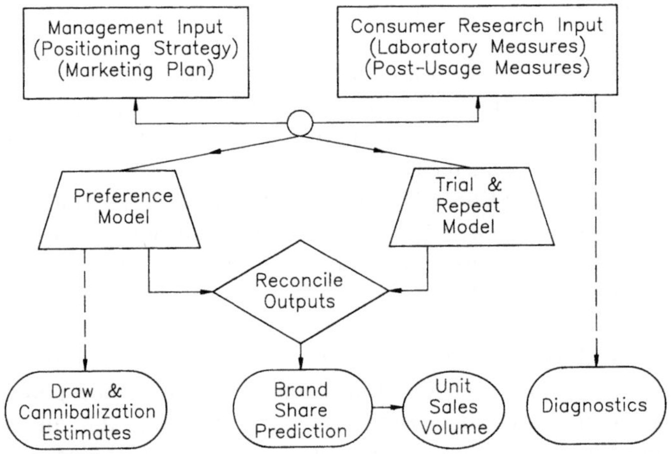

Fig. 7.4. ASSESSOR model (adapted from [Silk & Urban, 1978], and [Urban & Katz, 1983]).

Table 7.2.
ASSESSOR research design and measurement

Design	Procedure	Measurement
O_1	Respondent screening and recruitment (personal interview)	Criteria for target-group identification (e.g. product-class usage)
O_2	Pre-measurement for established brands (self-administered questionnaire)	Composition of 'relevant set' of established brands, attribute weights and ratings, and preferences
X_1	Exposure to advertising for established brands and new brand	
$[O_3]$	Measurement of reactions to the advertising materials (self-administered questionnaire)	Optional, e.g. likability and believability ratings of advertising materials
X_2	Simulated shopping trip and exposure to display of new and established brands	
O_4	Purchase opportunity (choice recorded by research personnel)	Brand(s) purchased
X_3	Home use/consumption of new brand	
O_5	Post-usage measurement (telephone interview)	New-brand usage rate, satisfaction ratings, and repeat-purchase propensity; attribute ratings and preferences for 'relevant set' of established brands plus the new brand

O = Measurement; X = Advertising or product exposure
[a]Silk & Urban [1978, p. 174, Table 1]

and a small set of the principal competing products already established in the market. Following this, consumers enter a simulated shopping facility where they have the opportunity to purchase quantities of the new and/or established products. The ability of the new product to attract repeat purchases is asssessed by one or more waves of follow-up interviews with the same respondents. These interviews are conducted after sufficient time has passed for consumers to use or consume a significant quantity of the new product at home.

The laboratory phase of the research is executed in a facility located in the immediate vicinity of a shopping center. 'Intercept' interviews (O_1) are conducted with shoppers to screen and recruit a sample number of consumers representative of the target market for the new product. Fieldwork is done at several different locations chosen to attain heterogeneity and obtain quotas desired in the final sample. Studies typically employ samples of approximately 300 persons.

Upon arriving at the laboratory facility location, respondents are asked to complete a self-administered questionnaire that constitutes the 'before' measurement (O_2). Individually, respondents then proceed to a separate area where they are shown a set of advertising materials (X_1) for the new brand and for the leading established brands. Ordinarily, respondents are exposed to 5–6 commercials, one per brand, and the order in which they are presented is rotated to avoid systematic position effects. Measurement of reactions to the advertising materials (O_3) occurs next if such information is desired for diagnostic purposes.

The final stage of the laboratory experiment takes place in a simulated retail store where participants have the opportunity to make a purchase. When first approached, they are told that they will be given a fixed amount of compensation for their time – typically about ten dollars, but always more than the sum needed to make a purchase. In the lab they are informed that they may use the money to purchase any brand or combination of brands in the product category they choose, with any unexpended cash to be kept by them. They then move to an area where quantities of the full set of competing brands, including the new one, are displayed available for inspection (X_2). Each brand is priced at a level equal to the average price at which it is being regularly sold in mass retail outlets in the local market area. The brand (or brands) selected by each participant is (are) recorded by one of the research personnel (O_4) at the checkout counter. Although respondents are free to forgo buying anything and retain the full ten-dollar sum, most do make a purchase. To illustrate, the proportion of participants making a purchase observed in two separate studies of deodorants and antacids were 74% and 64% respectively. Those who do not purchase the new brand are given a quantity of it free after all buying transactions have been completed. This procedure parallels the common practice of affecting trial usage through the distribution of free samples. A record is maintained for each respondent as to whether the respondent 'purchased' or was given the new brand so as to be able to assess whether responses on the post-usage survey are differentially affected by trial purchase vs. free sampling. (Remember, samples are given to those who *do not* try as a result of the advertising.)

The post-usage survey (O_5) is administered by telephone after sufficient time has passed for usage experience to have developed. The specific length of the pre–post measurement interval is determined by the estimated usage rate for the new product. Respondents are offered an opportunity to make a repurchase of the new brand (to be delivered by mail) and respond to essentially the same set of perception and preference measurements that were utilized in the 'before' of pre-measurement step (O_2), except that they now rate the new brand as well as established ones.

2.4.2. *Model structure*

As shown in Figure 7.4, ASSESSOR uses both the trial/repeat and an attitude model as described earlier. The basic input to estimate the preference model is obtained from measurement O_2. The measurements for prediction are obtaind from O_5. The inputs for the trial probability are obtained from O_5. The models are estimated and their outputs are compared.

If the product is entering an established category, the sales volume is obtained by multiplying the share from the preference model by the forecasted total category sales. The preference model is a logit model:

$$L_{ij} = \frac{(P_{ij})^{\beta}}{\sum_{l=1}^{M_i} (P_{il})^{\beta}} \tag{4}$$

where P_{ij} is consumer i's preference for produce j, L_{ij} is the estimate of the probability that consumer i will purchase product j, and β is a parameter to be estimated. The sum in the denominator is over all products in consumer i's evoked set M_i. The estimate L_{ij} is equal to zero if j is not in i's evoked set. The constant, β, is estimated by a maximum-likelihood analysis of individual last purchases and preferences, and M_i is the number of brands in the evoked set of consumer i.

To forecast the purchase probability, L_{ib}, for the new product (brand b), preference measures for the new and existing products are obtained after the consumer has experienced a period of trial usage of the new product. The new product is assumed to be in i's evoked set and Equation (4) is used to forecast L_{ib} for the new product.

The purchase probability is forecast assuming the new product will be in the evoked set. In order to calculate an expected market share for the new brand, Silk & Urban take into account that the new brand will not necessarily become an element of the relevant set of brands for all consumers when it does in fact become available in the market. To do this, they obtain estimates of the percent of consumers who will evoke the new product (E_b). The market share, M_b, of the new product is then given by

$$M_b = E_b \sum_i \frac{L_{ib}}{N} \tag{5}$$

where N is the sample size. The preference model share is compared to the asymptotic sales from the trial-and-repeat model. If the brand is creating a completely new category, the preference model cannot be used and the trial/repeat model is used alone to generate the forecast of sales growth and dynamics. In most cases (95% of the applications) brands enter established categories or segment an existing category so that both models are useful.

2.4.3. Convergence

The expression for market share developed from the individual preference-purchase probability model is structurally similar to that defined in terms of trial and repeat purchase levels. In the former case, market share is the product of the relevant set proportion, and the average conditional probability of purchasing the new brand. In the latter case, market share is the product of the cumulative trial proportion and repeat-purchase share.

The submodels and measures used to arrive at estimates of these conceptually similar quantities are quite distinct. Whereas the trial and repeat proportions are based upon direct observations of these quantities obtained under controlled conditions, the relevant set proportion and the average conditional purchase probability are estimated indirectly from other measures.

Finding that the two models yield outputs that are in close agreement serves to strengthen confidence in the prediction. On the other hand, divergent forecasts trigger a search for and evaluation of possible sources of error or bias that might account for the discrepancy. The first step is to compare the relevant set proportion and trial estimates. Lack of agreement here implies that the assumptions concerning awareness and retail availability are not compatible with those made implicitly or explicitly in estimating the relevant set proportion. After reconciling the trial and relevant set estimates, attention is focused on the values of the conditional purchase probability and the repeat rate. In the end, some judgment may have to be exercised in order to reconcile differences that arise, but that process is facilitated by careful consideration of the structural comparability of the two models.

2.4.4. Predictions and marketing plans

Prediction of a new brand's market share reflects the estimated parameters and the plans for the marketing program to be employed in the future test market or launch. Frequently at this pretest market stage, the new-product team is interested in evaluating variations in the introductory marketing mix for the new brand. The trial/repeat model is used to perform rough simulations of the effects of marketing-mix modifications. The changes or alternatives management wishes to consider are approximated by judgmentally altering parameter levels. For example, increasing the level of advertising spending is represented by raising the awareness probability and therefore the estimated trial. Differences in sampling programs are estimated by changing the number of samples or their probability of usage. Other types of changes, such as in advertising copy or price, that affect the conditional first-purchase probability are measured by expanding the research design shown in Table 7.2. to observe the differential effects on trial purchases due to alternative price or copy treatments.

After examining the impact of strategic changes in this manner, profitability measures are calculated for the market-share estimates. Based on these inputs and the forecasted share, the new-product team can decide whether or not to proceed to test-market the new brand.

2.5. *Summary of alternative approaches and commercial services*

This section has covered a number of generic, alternative approaches for forecasting new packaged-goods sales. By understanding the basic approach behind various available models, you can better assess each model and select the model that is most appropriate for your use. Alternatively, if your new-product development program is sufficiently large, you can build upon these basic ideas and customize a pretest market analysis to best fit the needs of your organization.

The 1980s saw the emergence of many commercial pretest-market services based on the approaches discussed above. ASSESSOR was initially marketed by Management Decision Systems, Inc. (MDS) and then by Information Resources Inc. (as the result of a merger with MDS) and subsequently by M/A/R/C, Inc. and Macro Strategies, Inc. In this period the model evolved from the original formulation to allow dynamic forecasting of volume and use of consumer-panel and UPC-scanner data. Yankalovich, Skelly & White dropped their LTM model and adopted a new model called LITMUS [Blackburn & Clancy, 1980]. Probably the largest selling service was marketed by Burke Market Research and was called BASES. This service initially was positioned against ASSESSOR with a full proposition test called BASES III, but was later modified to produce concept forecasts at a lower cost and accuracy based on trial-and-repeat intent norms. BASES I tested concepts and BASES II tested concept and product. Many other services have been developed in the USA and Europe (to name a few: DESIGNER by Novaction, Inc.; ESP by NPD; SENSOR by Research International; ENTRO by M/A/R/C; CRITERION by Custom Research, Inc., and a pretest marketing model by Market Simulations Inc.). The commercial services could originally be divided into share (preference models) or sales volume (trial-and-repeat models with intent norms), but now many services use convergent models based on share structures and trial and depth of repeat dynamics. Consultants have moved between market research firms so most commercial pretest services are quite similar in model structure today.

3. Accuracy of pretest market forecasting

In this section we review evidence of the accuracy of pretest models as well as suggesting guidelines for using pretest forecasts. While many commercial services have been used, the available published evidence on the predictive accuracy of pretest models is not large and a number of issues make the available evidence difficult to judge. There are commercial services who say 'they have never missed' or are '97% correct'. Some of the claims are difficult to substantiate. In one case a client sued the supplier for failure to predict sales accurately.

Many services provide lists of 'predicted' and 'actual' share. However, one must be careful in interpreting them [Tauber, 1977]. For example, Eskin & Malec report 'forecasted' and actual results for their model. The authors clearly state that the model forecast is based not on estimates of repeat (α_2), but on the actual value from the test market. Despite this warning, a casual reader may not realize this severely restricts implications of validity from this particular data.

In some cases the 'predicted' is not the original prediction, but one adjusted for 'differences' between test market and pretest market. For example, after the test, it may have been discovered that advertising spending was less than planned or that a new competitor has entered the market. Although it is logical to make some adjustments, looking for reasons to make predicted sales agree with actual sales is dangerous. This may occur unintentionally if one only looks at differences and then tries to find reasons why they do not agree. If changes are allowed, they should be pursued with equal vigor in cases where actual and predicted agree as well as when they disagree. Then revision may result in higher or lower differences between predicted and actual. Another bias can occur if the product is tested concurrently with test market rather than prior to test market. It takes a high level of discipline not to be influenced by the concurrent experience. If a service claims an almost perfect record of forecasting, you should examine whether their analysis is biased, either explicitly or implicitly.

Other difficulties occur because 'actual' share is itself subject to measurement error and because 'actual' long-run share may not stabilize in a 9–12-month test market. When we take these cautions into account, we find that many commercial models claim success, but that not all have used rigorous predictive testing procedures.

3.1. Published validation data

Two sets of data have passed the scrutiny of academic reviews [Pringle, Wilson & Brody, 1982; Urban & Katz, 1983]. One found a 67% success rate in test market after use of ASSESSOR compared to the success rate of 35.5% [*Nielsen Researcher*, 1979] for products that did not have a formal pretest-market model analysis. On the other side of the error possibilities, 3.8% of the products that failed in ASSESSOR succeeded in test market.

Figure 7.5 shows a plot of actual versus predicted market share for 44 products where validation data was available for ASSESSOR. The correlation is 0.95 and is an encouraging result. Table 7.3 puts the correlation in better perspective. The table shows the original forecasts and the forecasts after 'adjustment' for differences between the original business plan and the actual execution of advertising, promotion and distribution in the test market. The average pretest-market share forecast was 7.77 whereas the average test-market share was 7.16. Thus a positive bias of 0.61 share point is present and is significant at the 10% level ($t = 2.0$). The

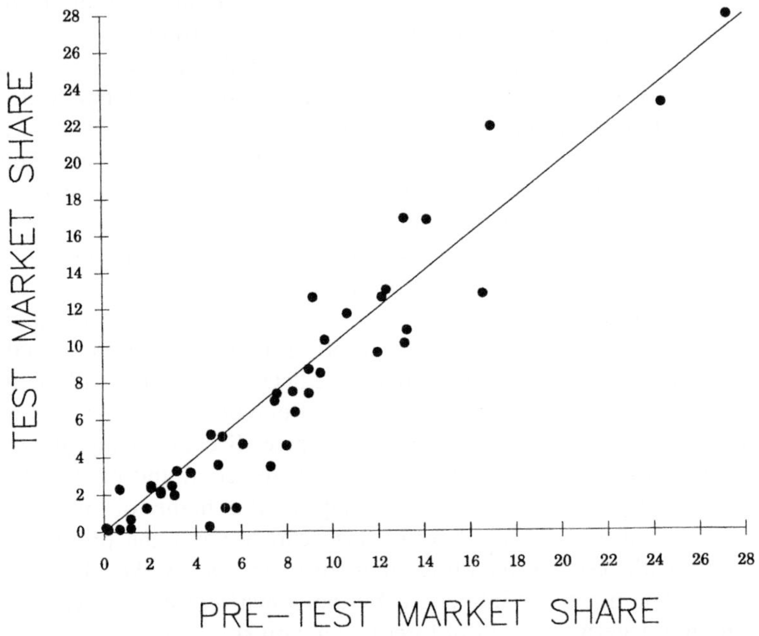

Fig. 7.5. Comparison of pre-test-market and test-market shares [Urban & Katz, 1983, p. 223].

Table 7.3.
Comparison of pretest-market, adjusted, and test-market shares [Urban & Katz, 1983, p. 223]

	Overall ($n=44$)	Health and beauty aids ($n=13$)	Household ($n=11$)	Food ($n=20$)
Average test-market share	7.16	7.35	10.14	5.40
Pre-test versus test-market share				
Mean difference	0.61	0.43	0.61	0.73
Mean absolute difference	1.54	1.66	1.37	1.56
Standard deviation of differences	1.99	2.08	1.71	2.06
Adjusted versus test-market share				
Mean difference	−0.01	−0.29	−0.15	0.25
Mean absolute difference	0.83	0.88	1.04	0.68
Standard deviation of differences	1.12	1.09	1.23	1.02

average absolute deviation is 1.54 share points and the standard deviation is 1.99 share points.

As expected, the comparisons between adjusted and test-market shares show less error – mean deviation of −0.01, average absolute deviation of 0.83, and standard deviation of 1.12. The correlation of the adjusted predictions with test-market shares is 0.98. Adjustments were made in 36 of the 44 cases. In most of these the adjustments improved the accuracy, but in 6 of the cases the deviation increased. The systematic overprediction for lower share values shown in Figure 7.5 was reduced substantially by the adjustments.

The validation sample consists of 13 health and beauty aid (HBA) products, 11 household cleaning products, and 20 food products. Table 7.3 reports the individual category results. The absolute differences are small and none of the paired comparisons of means or variances are significantly different at the 10% level. Similar levels of accuracy are observed across these product categories.

Similar predictive results have been reported for NEWS [Pringle, Wilson & Brody, 1982], where it was found, on a pretest unadjusted basis, a mean bias of +1.33 share points and a standard deviation of 1.48.

3.2. *Managerial use of validation data*

One way to interpret this predictive accuracy is to consider how the test-market decision should be made. If the pretest share forecast is much higher than the minimum required share or cut-off criteria, a GO decision is appropriate. If the predicted share is much less than the required share, a NO decision is appropriate. The greater the amount by which the forecast exceeds the required share, the higher is the probability of success in test market.

For example, suppose that the minimum required share was 6.0% and the model predicted 9.1%. Then, accounting for about a 0.6% bias in the model, the predicted share minus the required share is 1.25 standard deviations above the average model bias. (Number of standard deviations = (9.1 − 6.0 − 0.6)/2.0 = 1.25.) We use a cumulative normal table to translate the number of standard deviations to a probability of achieving the minimum required share. For example, 1.25 standard deviations translates to a 90% probability of achieving or exceeding the target.

Now a difficult question is raised. How much risk should be taken in test market? If we require a 95% chance of success, we will need almost a 4-share-point margin of forecast over actual. Few products will meet this margin so, although we will have few failures, we will also have few successes. In the final analysis each new-product team must make this tradeoff implicitly or explicitly. The accuracy of forecasts is higher after adjustment (the standard deviation of adjusted and actual share is 1.0 share point, rather than 2.0 for initial versus actual), so if management is sure it could execute the test as planned, the risks will be lower. The accuracy also varies according to the type of product. If the new product fits well into an established category the accuracy is higher. If the product is revolutionary and creates a whole new category, variance is higher. If the brand is going to have a small share (less than 2%), larger samples are needed to achieve the indicated accuracies.

Pretest market forecasts are not perfectly valid, but pretest market analysis can be used by management to control effectively the risk of test-market failure.

3.3. Value of pretest market forecasting of packaged goods

The value of a pretest market forecast depends upon the costs of failure, the accuracy of the forecast, and the rewards of success. It also depends upon the GO/NO GO cutoffs set for both the pretest-market analysis and the test-market experiment. For example, if the GO/NO GO cutoff is set too low, then everything will pass the pretest-market analysis and, hence, it will provide little value. By the same token, if the cutoff is set too high, all products will be eliminated, thus eliminating any possibility of success.

There are many ways to set cutoffs. One formal method was proposed by Urban & Katz [1983]. They use decision analysis [Raiffa & Schlaifer, 1961; Rao & Winter, 1981] to select the cutoffs that lead to the greatest expected profit. For example, suppose that a typical reward function is:

- $55 million introductory expense for advertising, promotion, plant and equipment. A loss that is incurred at a 0.00 share;
- a break-even profit at a 5.75% share;
- a profit of $80 million at a 10% share; and
- a profit of $190 million at a 20% share.

Suppose further that the cost of a test market is $1.5 million and the cost of a pretest-market analysis is $50 000. From published data for 50 new brands (*Nielsen Researcher*, 1979], the accuracy of a test market is that 50% of the observations of first-year national share are within 10% of the test-market share. (This data is consistent with that of Gold [1964].) If we combine these data with the pretest-market accuracy reported in Table 7.3, then Urban & Katz suggest that the best cutoffs are a cutoff share of 4.5% for pretest-market analysis and a cutoff share of 5.5% for a test-market experiment. The resulting expected profit is $28.4 million compared to an expected profit with no testing of $16.7 million. The value of testing is $11.7 million!

Of course we can consider other strategies. For example, we might use pretest-market analysis but skip the test-market experiment. In this case it pays to be somewhat more conservative with a cutoff share of 6.0%. The resulting expected profit is $28.0 million. Thus, if the test market is to be skipped, the value of the pretest market analysis is $11.3 million, not a bad return on an investment of $50 000. If we skip the pretest market and use only test markets, then we can achieve an expected profit of $28.1 million with a cutoff of 6% share. Putting it all together we see that both the pretest-market analysis and the test-market experiment provide dramatic returns if used singly or together.

If we plan to test-market a product we still gain an incremental expected profit of over $300 000 by using pretest analyses–the $50 000 investment seems to be justified. If we use a pretest-market analysis, the incremental gains from test market are still $400 000. The investment of $1.5 million is justified, but there is risk. If the test market delays introduction without providing useful diagnostic information, some new-product teams may prefer to be more conservative with the pretest-market cutoff and choose to skip test markets.

Naturally, the above calculations are for an average return of an average new-product project in an average category. Each case will be different. The potential for greater losses will raise the screen while the potential for higher rewards will lower the screen. If both are raised, the screen may stay the same. Similarly, if the penalties of delaying are great, there will be justifiable pressure to skip test market although it is unlikely that there will be a justification for skipping both the pretest and test-market analyses.

We suggest that the formal analyses be reapplied to your specific situation. However, the following guidelines may help. A test market may not be required if (1) there is a large penalty for reaching the market 12 months later, (2) entry costs are low and losses at small share levels are small, (3) a small market is entered and potential gains and losses are both small, (4) pretest-market sample sizes are large (greater accuracy), accurate awareness and distribution estimates can be made, and the firm's marketing plan will be executed faithfully. Time penalties are increasing and markets are being increasingly subsegmented so it can be expected that test marketing may not be necessary for many consumer packaged goods. For example, in Europe, some markets tend to be small and the associated rewards are small in relation to the fixed cost of test marketing. This is compounded by the difficulty of finding a representative test-market city and controlling the marketing execution.

3.4. *Summary of packaged-goods pretest-market forecasting*

Test-market failure can be reduced, better introductory market strategies (e.g. advertising, sampling) can be identified, competitive environments can be understood, and improved financial and production plans can be made.

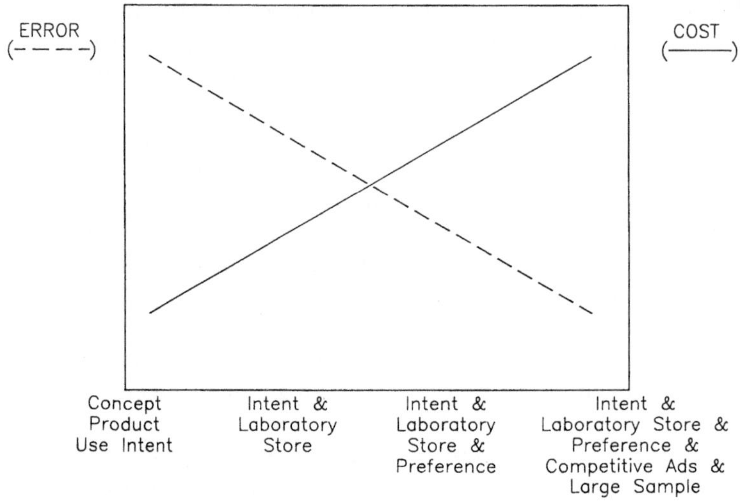

Fig. 7.6. Estimated error and cost tradeoffs.

Pretest-market forecasting has been accepted as standard procedure by major packaged-goods firms. Proven techniques are available and if *used correctly* they can generate value, reduce risk, and improve products. Over 6000 premarket model applications were done worldwide in the period from 1972 to 1992.

The number of alternatives is large and they vary by cost and accuracy (see Figure 7.6). The cost goes up when one includes a simulated store, competitive ad exposures, and larger samples, but errors decrease as measured by the standard deviation of difference between actual and predicted sales. Each firm must make its own tradeoff of cost and accuracy, but given that a good design effort has been carried out with preliminary 'what if' forecasts of market potential based on concept tests, it makes sense to do a full proposition test with high accuracy.

Investing more in pretest eliminates the need for test market when time penalties for delay are high and large introductory budgets are not required. In cases where the risk of large losses is present, a test market is appropriate even after a large-scale pretest-market forecasting analysis. In either case, in packaged goods, tools are available to produce accurate forecasts and managerial diagnostics on a timely and relatively low-cost basis.

4. Durable consumer products

Premarket forecasting models were invented in the consumer packaged-goods field but they have been modified and transferred to the durable-goods industry. This has not been easy because durable goods are very different in price and consumers use a different information-gathering and decision process. Word-of-mouth communication must be included and norms for translating intent are almost impossible to derive. In this section we use automobile purchasing to demonstrate the durable modeling differences and new measurement and premarket analysis procedures based on published documentation of a premarket forecasting model for consumer durables. Then we discuss applications to other durable goods, the industrial sector, and services.

4.1. The case of automobiles

Automobiles represent a very large market. Sales in the 1992 model year were over 100 billion dollars in the US and over 300 billion worldwide. A new car can contribute over 1 billion dollars per year in sales if it sells a rather modest 100 000 units per year at an average price of $12 000 per car. Major successes generate several times this in sales and large associated profits.

These potential rewards encourage firms to allocate large amounts of capital to design, production and selling of a new model. Ford spent 3 billion dollars developing the Taurus/Sable line. General Motors routinely spends 1 billion dollars on a new model such as the Buick Electra. Most of this investment occurs before launch; if the car is not a market success, significant losses result.

Rates of failure are not published for the auto industry, but many cars have fallen short of expectations. Most failures are not as dramatic as the Edsel which was withdrawn from the market, but significant losses occur in two ways. When sales are below forecasts there is excess production capacity and inventories. In this case, capital costs are excessive and prices must be discounted or other marketing actions undertaken to clear inventories. Losses also occur when the forecast of sales is below the market demand. In this case not enough cars can be produced, inventories are low, and prices are firm. The car is apparently very profitable, but a large opportunity cost may be incurred. Profits could have been higher if the forecast had been more accurate and more production capacity had been planned.

For those readers unfamiliar with the US automobile industry we describe a few facts that will become important in developing pretest-market models.

4.2. Consumer response

4.2.1. Search and experience

In automobiles, consumers reduce risk by searching for information and, in particular, visiting showrooms. Typically 75% of buyers test-drive one or more cars. The marketing manager's task is to persuade the consumer to consider the automobile, get the prospect into the showroom, and facilitate purchasing with test drives and personal selling efforts.

4.2.2. Word-of-mouth communication/magazine reviews

One source of information about automobiles is other consumers. Another is independent magazine reviews such as *Consumer Reports* and *Car and Driver*. Given the thousands of dollars involved in buying a car, the impact of these sources is quite large.

4.2.3. Importance of availability

Of domestic sales, 80% are 'off the lot', i.e. purchased from the dealer's inventory. Many consumers will consider alternative makes and models if they cannot find a car with the specific features, options, and colors they want.

4.3. Managerial issues

4.3.1. No test market

Building enough cars for test marketing (say, 1000 cars) requires a full production line that could produce 75 000 units. Once this investment is made, the 'bricks and mortar' are in place for a national launch and the major element of risk has been borne. Therefore, test marketing is not done in the auto industry.

4.3.2. Replacing existing model of car

Occasionally the auto industry produces an entirely new type of car (for example, Chrysler's introduction of the Minivan), but the predominant managerial issue is a major redesign of a car line such as the introduction of a down-sized, front-wheel-drive Buick Electra to replace its larger, rear-wheel-drive predecessor.

When the management issue is a redesign, the sales history of its predecessor provides important information for forecasting consumer response to the replacement. Even when no direct replacement is planned, say, the introduction of the two-seated Buick Reatta, the sales history of related cars such as the Toyota Supra provide anchors to forecasts.

4.3.3. Production constraints

The production capacity level must be set before any actual market sales data can be collected. Once the production line has been built, production is limited to a rather narrow range. The maximum is the plant capacity (e.g. two shifts with the machines in the plant and their maintenance requirements) and the minimum is one eight-hour shift of production unless the plant is shut down completely.

The need to make production commitments early in the new-product development process produces a two-stage sequence of decisions. First, a market strategy is developed, advanced engineering specification and designs are created, consumer reaction is gauged, and a GO or NO GO production commitment is made. Because of the long construction times, this usually occurs three or more years before introduction. As market launch nears (18 months or less), the second set of decisions is made. A premarket forecast is generated and a revised marketing plan (e.g. targeting, positioning, advertising copy and expenditure, price, promotion, and dealer training) is formulated. In the first decision, production level is a variable, but in the pre-launch forecasting phase the capacity constraints are taken as given.

4.3.4. 'Price' forecasting problem

Production capacity is based on the best information available at the time, but as engineering and manufacturing units develop the prototype cars, details change as do external conditions in the economy. At the planned price and marketing levels consumers may wish to purchase more or fewer vehicles than will be produced. The number of vehicles that would be sold if there were no production constraints is known as 'free expression'. Naturally, free expression is pegged to a price and marketing effort.

If the free-expression demand at a given level of price and marketing effort is less than the production minimum, the company and its dealers must find a way to sell more cars (e.g. target new markets or change price, promotion, dealer incentives and advertising). If the forecast is in the range, marketing variables can be used to maximize profit with little constraint. If free-expression demand is above the maximum production, then opportunities exist to increase profit by adjusting price, by reducing advertising, or by producing cars with many optional features.

4.4. Measurement

In keeping with the magnitude of the investment and the potential profit impact of pre-launch decision, analyses are based on a heavy commitment to measurement to get consumer-based estimates of the relevant inputs. Since norms to translate intent are usually not available, a control group is necessary to calibrate biases. Usually the control group sees the existing car model which is being replaced. The control group does not see the new-model car. If the car does not replace an old one, the most similar existing car (or cars) is used for control purposes.

If cost were not an issue one would select a random sample of consumers and gauge their reactions to the test and control vehicles. However, there are a large number of automobiles available (over 300), the automobile market is highly segmented (luxury, sport, family, etc.), and automobile purchases are infrequent, so stratified sampling is done by grouping consumers by the car model that they purchased previously. Once selected, consumers are contacted via telephone, screened on interest in purchasing an automobile in the next year, and recruited for the study. Consumers who agree to participate are scheduled to come to a central location, a clinic, for a one-hour interview. They are paid for their participation. If both spouses participate in the decision to buy a new car, both are encouraged to come.

Upon arrival some consumers are assigned randomly to the test-car group and some to the control-car group. They are next presented with a list of the 300 or so automobile lines available and asked which they would consider seriously. The consideration set commonly consists of about three cars; the median is five cars. In addition, they indicate the cars they feel would be their first, second, and if appropriate, third choices and rate these cars on probability scales and on a constant-sum paired comparison of preferences. Consumers are shown advertisements and they rate the new car on the same probability and preference scales as the cars they now consider.

In the market, after advertising exposure, some consumers will visit showrooms for more information, others will seek word-of mouth or magazine evaluations. Thus the sample is split. For example, one-half of each test/control treatment cell might see videotapes which simulate word-of-mouth and evaluations which represent consumer-magazine evaluations (e.g. *Consumer Reports*); the other half are allowed to test-drive the car to which they are assigned. The video treatment can be divided into positive- and negative-exposure cells. Probability and constant-sum paired-comparison preference measures are taken for the stimulus car and the respondents' top three choices among cars now on the market. The half which saw the videotapes and magazine abstracts now test-drive the car; the half which test-drove are now exposed to the videotape and magazine information. Again probability and preference measures are taken.

4.5. Flow models

The experimental condition must now be translated to market response. This means we must predict how many consumers will see advertisements, hear word-of-mouth, visit dealers, etc. One technique to make such forecasts is the use of flow models. The flow-model approach has been used successfully in the test-market and launch analyses of frequently purchased consumer goods [Urban, 1970] and innovative public-transportation services [Hauser & Wisniewski, 1982]. The modeling concept is simple. Each consumer is represented by a behavioral state that describes a level of information about the potential purchase. The behavioral states are chosen to represent consumer behavior as it is affected by the managerial decisions being evaluated. For example, Buick used the set of behavioral states shown in Figure 7.7 to represent information flow/diffusion theory customized to the automobile market.

In each time period, consumers flow from one state to another. For example, in the third period a consumer, say Judy Smith, might have been unaware of the new car. If, in the fourth period, she talks to a friend who owns one, but she does not see any advertising, she 'flows' to the behavioral state of 'aware via word-of-mouth'. We call the model a 'macro-flow' model because we keep track, probabilistically, of the market. We do not track individual consumers. The flow probabilities are estimated from the clinic or industry norms, but supplemented by judgment when all else fails. For example, after consumers see the concept boards which

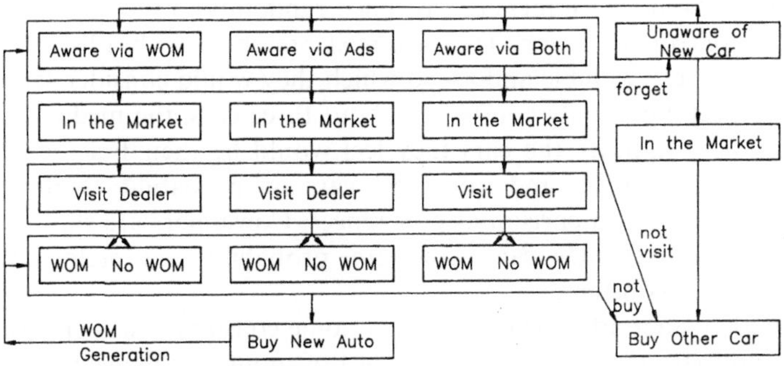

Fig. 7.7. Behavioral states macro-flow model for a new automobile (from [Urban, Hauser & Roberts, 1990, Fig. 2, p. 409]).

simulate advertising, they are asked to indicate how likely they would be to visit a dealer.

In some cases the flow rates (percent of consumers/period) are parameters, say, $X\%$ of those who are aware via advertisements visit dealers in any given period. In other cases, the flows are functions of other variables. For example, the percent of consumers, previously unaware, who become aware in a period is clearly a function of advertising expenditures. For example, consider advertising flows. At zero advertising this flow from the unaware to the aware state is 0%; at saturation advertising we expect some upper bound, say α. We also expect this flow to be a concave function of advertising spending. Similarly, word-of-mouth flows will be given by response curves that depend upon the number of consumers who buy the car in each month.

4.6. *Managerial application of flow model*

Table 7.4 reports forecasts for a new compact auto based on the macro-flow model. The forecasted sales based on the initial marketing strategy were well below goals. The projected shortfall in sales put pressure on management to develop strategies that would improve free-expression sales. To improve sales, the new-product team simulated three marketing strategies. The first strategy was a doubling of advertising in an attempt to increase advertising awareness (the model was run with advertising spending doubled). Table 7.4 indicates this would increase sales somewhat, but not enough. Given its cost, this strategy was rejected.

The next strategy considered was a crash effort to improve the advertising copy to encourage more dealer visits. Assuming that such copy would be attainable, the macro-flow analysis was used to simulate 40% more dealer visits. (The model was run with dealer-visit flow-parameters multiplied by 1.40 for ad-aware conditions.) The forecast was much better and actually achieved the sales goals in year 2. Although a 40% increase was viewed as too ambitious, the simulation did highlight the leverage of improved copy that encouraged dealer visits. The new-product team decided to devote resources toward encouraging dealer visits. The advertising agency was directed to begin work on such copy, especially for the identified segment of women currently driving small cars.

The final decision evaluated was the effect of incentives designed to increase the conversion of potential buyers who visit dealer showrooms. The team simulated a

Table 7.4.
Sales forecasts and strategy simulations (in units) [from Urban, Hauser & Roberts, 1990, p. 415]

Year	Base case	Advertising spending doubled	Advertising copy improved 40%	Dealer incentives improved 20%
1	281 000	334 000	395 000	340 000
2	334 000	370 000	477 000	406 000
3	282 000	330 000	405 000	345 000
4	195 000	225 000	273 000	234 000

Table 7.5.
Sales forecasts for two-car strategy (in units) [from Urban, Hauser & Roberts, 1990, p. 416]

Year	New model	Old model	Combined sales
1	181 000	103 000	284 000
2	213 000	89 000	301 000
3	174 000	80 000	245 000
4	121 000	84 000	205 000

20% increase in conversation (all dealer-visit flow parameters were multiplied by 1.2). The leverage of this strategy was reasonable but not as high as the improved advertising copy. This simulation coupled with management's realization that an improvement would be difficult to achieve on a national level (competitors could match any incentive program) led management to a more conservative strategy which emphasized dealer training.

The net result of the sales analysis was that management decided to make an effort to improve dealer training *and* advertising copy, but that any forecast should be conservative in its assumptions about achieving the 40% and 20% improvements.

The shortfall in projected sales, dealer pressure to retain the popular rear-wheel-drive car, and indications that production of the new car would be delayed, caused the new-product team to decide to retain both the old and new cars. Initial thinking was that the total advertising budget would remain the same but be allocated 25/75 between the old and new cars. Evaluation of this strategic scenario required a two-car macro-flow model.

The forecasts for the two-car strategy were done by extending the model flows to include new and old model competition with the above advertising and dealer's incentives tactics shown in Table 7.5. The combined sales were forecast to be higher than a one-car strategy in years 1 and 4, but lower in years 2 and 3. Overall the delayed launch caused a net sales loss of roughly 48 000 units over four years. This is not dramatic, especially given potential uncertainty in the forecast. However, the two-car strategy did not achieve the sales goal and made it more difficult to improve advertising copy and dealer training. Once the production decision had been made and the production delays were unavoidable, management was forced to retain the two-car strategy. The macro-flow analysis suggested that it be phased out as soon as was feasible.

This chain of events illustrates the value of a flexible macro-flow model. The world is not static. Often, unexpected events occur (dramatic sales shortfalls, production delays) that were not anticipated when the initial model was developed.

4.7. *Validation*

Validations of durable-goods forecasts face all of the difficulties that are faced by validations of pretest-market predictions. Managers have the incentive to sell cars, not provide a controlled laboratory validation. Not only do they have seek to modify and improve the marketing strategy as the product rolls out, but they often face unexpected production constraints. For example, in the launch of the new automobile model described above, advertising was adjusted versus the plan, industry sales were above the economic forecasts, there was a special interest-rate incentive program at the end of the first year, and there was a reduced availability of the most popular engine in the first half of the second year.

Once these adjustments were taken into account, Urban, Hauser & Roberts [1990] report that the forecasts agree with the actual sales at a level that is sufficient for strategy formulation. However, unlike pretest markets for frequently purchased packaged goods, we do not yet have sufficient experience with durable-goods pre-launch forecasts to determine statistical predictive capabilities. However, based on initial results across five car studies, we believe that such models provide forecasts that are sufficient to evaluate the magnitude of the new-product opportunity and we believe that simulations based on the macro-flow models are sufficiently accurate to set marketing strategies for the roll-out.

4.8. Other durable-goods applications

Pre-launch forecasts have also been applied to cameras, home computers and personal telecommunication devices. Most of the products have not been on the market long enough to carry out the actual versus predicted comparison and in many of those where the experience exists, changes between test and launch conditions cloud the assessment of validity. Figure 7.8 provides one case of a new photographic product where the launch was carried out according to plan. In this case there is close agreement on the sales level and the cannibalization from the

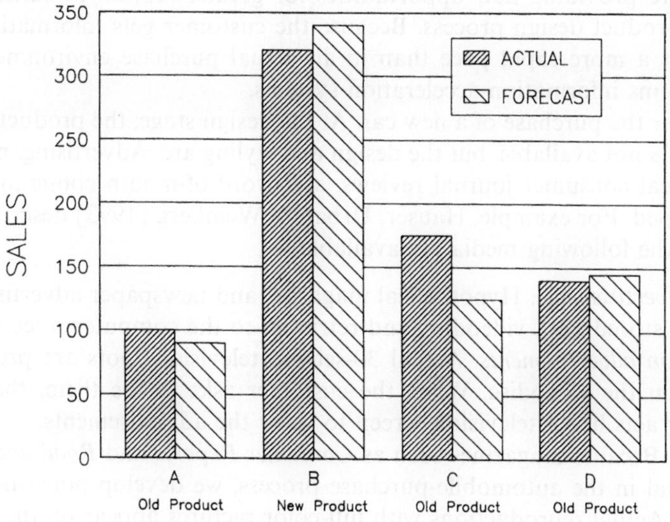

Fig. 7.8. Four product line sales after one year.

other products in the line. The forecasts were based on a simulated retail purchase opportunity. Validation conclusions will have to wait for more data, but initial results show some grounds for confidence in the premarket predictions.

4.9. Extensions

One extension to the premarket model described in this section is to include the key behavioral phenomena of categorization and consideration. This involves modifying Figure 7.7 by dividing awareness into categories of awareness. Categories are divided by having customers group cars into similar categories and indicating which ones they would consider. The advantage of this extension is that management can identify with whom they are competing and develop copy to generate the (1) correct categorization, (2) high consideration, and (3) high choice given that a car is considered [see Urban, Hulland & Weinberg, 1993, for more details].

Recently a number of researchers have been experimenting with multi-media computer systems in an effort to provide realistic stimuli to customers. A multi-media computer system combines images from a videodisc (or other media) to provide full-motion, realistic visual images on a computer screen. The computer interface allows the customer to interact with the images to produce a more realistic purchase environment. This means that not just the product can be simulated, but the full marketing environment including brochures, print advertisements, television advertising, word-of-mouth, shopping visits, and even personal selling. While no system will ever be a perfect substitute for the final environment that the customer sees when making a purchase and no system will be fully able to model the 'in-use' system or the full effects of customer-satisfaction feedback, these multi-media systems are providing new opportunities for greater realism at earlier stages of the new-product design process. Because the customer gets information in these systems at a more rapid pace than in an actual purchase environment, we call these systems information-acceleration systems.

Consider the purchase of a new car. At the design stage, the production version of the car is not available, but the design and styling are. Advertising, print media, hypothetical consumer journal reviews, and word-of-mouth communication can be developed. For example, Hauser, Urban & Weinberg [1993] describe a system in which the following media are available:

- *Print advertisements.* Hypothetical magazine and newspaper advertisements are created, stored on a videodisc, and retrieved to the computer screen.
- *Television advertisements.* Actual 30-second television spots are produced and stored on the videodisc. When the customer asks to see them, the computer monitor acts like a television screen to show the advertisements.
- *Articles.* Because magazines such as *Consumer Reports* and *Road and Track* are influential in the automobile-purchase process, we develop potential magazine articles. Actual reproductions with full-color pictures appear on the screen and the customer can read them at his or her own pace.

- *Interviews.* To simulate word-of-mouth we produce videotapes of unrehearsed interviews with actual customers (or actors). To make the situation more realistic, four-to-six 'word-of-mouth' customers are available. When the customer viewing the word-of-mouth selects a source he or she sees another computer screen and can select topics upon which to query the source. In this way the interviews become interactive and more realistic.
- *Showroom.* The showroom or shopping environment is simulated with tapes of the actual (prototype) car. The customer can 'walk around' the car by clicking on the arrows. The car rotates as if the customer were actually walking around the car. If the customer 'opens the door', he/she sees interior shots which change as he/she moves around the interior. Similarly, he/she can open the trunk and look under the hood.

We have not yet developed an actual drive simulator on the computer, but prototype cars can be used to augment the multi-media computer. For example, a 1992 Geo Storm may be retrofitted with solar power and electric motors in 1992 to simulate a new 1996 'Supernova' drive experience. Eventually drive simulators (analogous to flight simulators) may eliminate the need for prototypes.

If we integrate the notions of leading-edge users into the multi-media 'information accelerator', we have all the ingredients for forecasting more-radical innovations. The leading edge users give responses based on their advanced-use experience and knowledge and we capture this information to accelerate the other potential customers to the point in time where the middle majority of the market are ready to consider purchases. With a model of diffusion from leading edge to majority users, a time-path forecast can be generated.

With a multi-media computer system measures of attitude, intent, and purchase probability information are based on more realistic stimuli. After the design is complete and the product proceeds to the production stage this same methodology can be used to obtain more accurate forecasts based on final advertising, pricing, promotion, product and distribution strategies.

5. Industrial and services products

While premarket-forecasting methods have begun to be implemented in durable consumer-goods industries, almost no formal premarket models exist for industrial products and services. Some obvious directions for possible application are to pursue the use of information-acceleration methods for services and the integration of lead-user analysis with flow models for industrial and high-technology products.

If a new industrial product is technology-driven and revolutionary, information-acceleration methods could be used to 'accelerate' the majority of the market to where the lead users are now positioned. This could be done with technical articles and conference papers written for the research study that would represent the likely real articles that would be written after the product was on the market and the technology window was reached. Word-of-mouth communication could be created by filming lead-user comments on the technology and the (hypothetical) new products that would be produced. Sales brochures could be created based on the core benefit proposition and the price and service to be delivered in the market. The product-use experience could be simulated by prototypes. For example, new composites for auto bodies could be supplied from the lab at the specification level of a new production process. Advanced workstations could be simulated by using mainframes to reflect the desktop power that would be available at the time of launch. With these stimuli the future scenario could be represented and measures taken of willingness to buy, preference versus competition, and attribute ratings. The measures would then be input to a flow model of the buying process and forecasts of alternative strategies generated. This has not been done yet, but the path of marketing progress suggests that it soon will be. Industrial models will have to capture the multi-person aspects of the decision-making process. If it is successful, industrial new-product managers would have a tool for effective premarket forecasting.

Services are probably easier to test with an information accelerator than industrial products because it is often easier to represent customer use. For example, telecommunication services can be simulated by expensive means now and provided by low-cost means later. Consider a low-cost personal communications network (PCN) service that provide users with a small (1/2″ × 2″ × 4″) personal phone that can be used while walking (but not driving) in a metropolitan area. This use could be simulated by a currently available cellular phone with a filter added to restrict transmission while the user is moving at more than 5 m.p.h. Another example is a comprehensive personal investment, legal and banking service which could be simulated by a trained team of people backed by a workstation and modem at the user's home. In addition to use-experience simulation, the other forms of personal and interpersonal communication would be added to the market-research computer system to allow model-based premarket forecasts of market sales volumes.

6. Summary

Pretest-market models provide a low-cost and rapid method to test the combined product, advertising, price, promotion, selling and distribution plan. The 'full proposition' analyses are sufficiently accurate to identify most winners and eliminate most losers. They provide an effective way to control the risks of failure and supply actionable managerial diagnostics to improve the product. The output is a high-quality product that meets customer needs and reaches the market quickly.

Pretest-market models are an accepted practice for most frequently purchased products, but are relatively new for consumer durables. They are now being developed and tested for really new industrial products and services. Since pretest markets are extremely valuable in reducing risk and increasing the expected benefit of new products, we expect that proven models will soon be available for all products and services. Research on premarket forecasting in these new industries should be the highest priority for future work.

References

Baldinger, A.L. (1988). Trends and issues in STMs: Results of an ARF pilot project. *J. Advertising Res.* 28(5), pp. RC3–R7.

Blackburn, J.D., and K.J. Clancy (1980). LITMUS: A new product planning model, in R.P. Leone (ed.), *Proceedings: Market Measurement and Analysis*, The Institute of Management Sciences, Providence, RI, pp. 182–193.

Blattberg, R., and J. Golanty (1978). TRACKER: An early test-market forecasting and diagnostic model for new product planning. *J. Marketing Res.* 15(2), 192–202.

Burger, P.C., H. Gundee and R. Lavidge (1981). COMP: A comprehensive system for the evaluation of new products, in Y. Wind, V. Mahajan and R.N. Cardozo (eds.), *New-Product Forecasting: Models and Applications*, Lexington Books, D.C. Heath, Lexington, MA, pp. 269–284.

Charlton, P., A.S.C. Ehrenberg and B. Pymont (1972). Buyer behavior under mini-test conditions. *J. Market Res. Soc.* 14(3), 171–183.

Charlton, P., and B. Pymont (1975). Evaluating marketing alternatives. *J. Market Res. Soc.* 17(2), 90–113.

Chatterjee, R., J. Eliashberg, H. Gatignon and L.M. Lodish (1988). A practical Bayesian approach to selection of optimal market testing strategies. *J. Marketing Res.* 25(4) (November), 363–375.

Claycamp, H., and L.E. Liddy (1969). Prediction of new product performance: An analytical approach. *J. Marketing Res.* 6(3), 414–420.

Eskin, G.J., and J. Malec (1976). A model for estimating sales potential prior to the test market. *Proceedings 1976 Fall Educators' Conference*, American Marketing Association, Chicago, pp. 230–232.

Gold, J.A. (1964). Testing test market predictions. *J. Marketing Res.* 1 (August), 8–16.

Hauser, J.R., and K.J. Wisniewski (1982). Dynamic analysis of consumer response to marketing strategies. *Management Sci.* 28(5), 455–486.

Hauser, J.R., G.L. Urban and B. Weinberg (1992). Time flies when your're having fun: How consumers allocate their time when evaluating products, Working Paper #3439-92, MIT Sloan School of Management, Cambridge, MA (February).

Keeney, R.L., and H. Raiffa (1976). *Decision Analysis with Multiple Objectives*, Wiley, New York.

Levine, J. (1981). Pre-test-market research of new packaged-goods products – A user orientation, in Y. Wind, V. Mahajan and R.N. Cardozo (eds.), *New-Product Forecasting: Models and Applications*, Lexington Books, D.C. Heath, Lexington, MA, pp. 285–290.

Nielsen Researcher (1979). New product success ratios, in *The Nielsen Marketing Service*, Northbrook, IL, pp. 7–9.

Parfitt, J.H., and B.J.K. Collins (1968). Use of consumer panels for brand share prediction, *J. Marketing Res.* 5(2), 131–146.

Pringle, L.G., R.D. Wilson, and E.I. Brody (1982). NEWS: A decision-oriented model for new product analysis and forecasting. *Marketing Sci.* 1(1), 1–30.

Pymont, B.C., D. Reay and P.G.M. Standen (1976). Towards the elimination of risk from investment in new products: Experience with micro-market testing, Paper presented at the 1976 ESOMAR Congress, Venice, Italy (September).

Raiffa, H., and R. Schlaifer (1961). *Applied Statistical Decision Theory*, Harvard University Press, Boston.

Rao, V.R., and F.W. Winter (1981). A Bayesian approach to test market selection. *Management Sci.* 12 (December), 1351–1368.

Robinson, P.J. (1981). Comparison of pre-test-market new-product forecasting models, in Y. Wind, V. Mahajan and R.N. Cardozo (eds.), *New-Product Forecasting: Models and Applications*, Lexington Books, D.C. Heath, Lexington, MA, pp. 181–204.

Shocker, A.D., and W.G. Hall (1986). Pretest market-models: A critical evaluation. *J. Product Innovation* 3(2), 86–107.

Silk, A.J., and M.U. Kalwani (1982). Structure of repeat buying for new packaged goods. *Marketing Sci.* 1 (Summer), 243–287.

Silk, A.J., and G.L. Urban (1978). Pre-test-market evaluation of new packaged goods: A model and measurement methodology. *J. Marketing Res.* 15 (May), 171–191.

Tauber, E.M. (1977). Forecasting sales prior to test market. *J. Marketing* 41 (January), 80–84.

Torgerson, W.S. (1958). *Theory and Method of Scaling*, Wiley, New York.

Urban, G.L. (1970). SPRINTER mod III: A model for the analysis of new frequently purchased consumer products. *Oper. Res.* 18(5), 805–853.

Urban, G.L., and J.R. Hauser (1993). *Design and Marketing New Products, 2nd ed.*, Prentice-Hall, Englewood Cliffs, NJ.

Urban, G.L., J.R. Hauser and J.H. Roberts (1990). Prelaunch forecasting of new automobiles: Models and implementation. *Management Sci.* 36(4), 401–421.

Urban, G.L., J.S. Hulland and B.D. Weinberg (1993). Pre-market forecasting of new consumer durables: Modeling categorization, elimination, and consideration phenomena. *J. Marketing* 57 (April), 47–63.

Urban, G.L., and G.M. Katz (1983). Pre-test-market models: Validation and managerial implications. *J. Marketing Res.* 20 (August), 221–234.

Yankelovich, Skelly & White, Inc. (1981). LTM estimating procedures, in Y. Wind, V. Mahajan and R.N. Cardozo (eds.), *New-Product Forecasting: Models and Applications*, Lexington Books, D.C. Heath, Lexington, MA, pp. 249–268.

J. Eliashberg and G.L. Lilien, Eds., *Handbooks in OR & MS, Vol. 5*

Chapter 8

New-Product Diffusion Models*

Vijay Mahajan

Department of Marketing, University of Texas at Austin, Austin, TX 78712-1176, USA

Eitan Muller

Recanati Graduate School of Business Administration, Tel-Aviv University, Ramat Aviv, Israel 69978

Frank M. Bass

School of Management, University of Texas at Dallas, Richardson, TX 75083-0688, USA

1. Introduction

The diffusion of an innovation has traditionally been defined as the process by which that innovation "is communicated through certain channels over time among the members of a social system" [Rogers, 1983, p. 5]. As such, there are four key elements in the diffusion process: innovation, channels of communication, time, and the social system.

As a theory of communications, diffusion theory's main focus is on communication channels. Communication channels are the means by which information about an innovation is transmitted to or within the social system. These means consist of both the mass media and interpersonal communication channels. Individual members of a social system have different propensities for relying on mass media or interpersonal channels for seeking information about the innovation. Interpersonal communication, including nonverbal observations, are important influences in determining the speed and shape of the diffusion process in a social system.

Since its introduction to marketing in 1960s [King, 1963; Frank, Massy & Morrison, 1964; Silk, 1966; Arndt, 1967; Robertson, 1967; Bass, 1969], the diffusion theory perspective has been of interest to scholars of consumer behavior, marketing management, and management and marketing science. Researchers in consumer behavior, for example, have been concerned with evaluating the applicability of hypotheses developed in the general diffusion area to consumer research (for a review of this literature, see Gatignon & Robertson [1985]). The marketing-management literature, on the other hand, has been concerned with examining

*This paper is an updated and extended version of the paper that appeared in *Journal of Marketing* 54 (January 1990), 1–26.

the implications of these hypotheses for targeting prospects for a new product and for developing marketing strategies for penetrating the various adopter categories [see, for example, Kotler & Zaltman, 1976; Engle, Blackwell & Miniard 1986, Chapter 20; McKenna, 1985, Chapter 4]. Researchers in management and marketing science have contributed to the cumulative development of diffusion theory by suggesting analytical models for describing and forecasting the diffusion of an innovation in a social system. More recently, this literature has also been concerned with developing normative guidelines as to how an innovation should be diffused in a social system.

This paper is concerned with the contributions of management and marketing science literature to our cumulative understanding of the dynamics of innovation diffusion. The main impetus underlying these contributions is a new-product growth model suggested in the late 1960s by Bass [1969]. The Bass model and its revised forms have been successfully demonstrated for forecasting innovation diffusion in retail service, industrial technology, agriculture, and the educational, pharmaceutical and consumer-durables markets [Bass, 1969; Dodds, 1973; Nevers, 1972; Lawton & Lawton, 1979; Tigert & Farivar, 1981; Akinola, 1986; Lancaster & Wright, 1983; Kalish & Lilien, 1986a). Only a few of the companies that have used the model are Eastman Kodak, RCA, IBM, Sears and AT&T [Bass, 1986].

Since the publication of the Bass model in 1969, research on the modeling of the diffusion of innovations in marketing has resulted in a body of literature consisting of several dozen articles, books and assorted other publications. The major contributions to this literature in the 1970s were reviewed by Mahajan & Muller [1979]. In addition to discussing the basics of the diffusion models, the review included an evaluation of contributions made by ten published articles to that date. The voluminous diffusion-modeling research in the 1980s has further contributed to our understanding of the structural, estimation and conceptual assumptions underlying the diffusion models. Although some of these recent developments have been documented in Mahajan & Peterson [1985] and Mahajan & Wind [1986b], the present paper complements these efforts by presenting a critical evaluation of the cumulative developments since Bass [1969] and Mahajan & Muller (1979). To complement the evaluation of analytical developments, developments related to estimation of the diffusion-model parameters are included in the Appendix.

2. The basic first-purchase diffusion models

In their review article, Mahajan & Muller [1979] stated that the objective of a diffusion model is to present the level of spread of an innovation among a given set of prospective adopters over time. The purpose of the diffusion model is to depict the successive increase in the number of adopters and predict the continued development of a diffusion process already in progress. In the product-innovation context, diffusion models focus on the development of a life-cycle curve and serve the purpose of forecasting first-purchase sales of innovations. That is, the first-purchase diffusion models assume that, in the product-planning horizon being considered, there are no repeat buyers and purchase volume per buyer is one unit. The number of adopters define the unit sales for the product. Diffusion models, by definition, are concerned with representing the growth of a product category.

The best-known first-purchase diffusion models of new-product diffusion in marketing are those of Bass [1969], Fourt & Woodlock [1960] and Mansfield [1961]. These models were proposed in the 1960s and attempted to describe the penetration and the saturation aspects of the diffusion process. After briefly reviewing the original formulations of these models, we review here the recent developments that further evaluate their basic structure.[1]

2.1. The Bass model

The main impetus underlying the diffusion research in marketing is the Bass model. Figure 8.1a describes the communication structure underlying the Bass model.

Subsuming the models proposed by Fourt & Woodlock [1960] and Mansfield [1961], the Bass model assumes that potential adopters of an innovation are influenced by two means of communication – mass-media communication and word-of-mouth communication. In its development, it further assumes that the adopters of an innovation comprise two groups. The first group is influenced only by the mass-media communication (external influence) and the second group is influenced only by the word-of-mouth communication (internal influence). Bass termed the first group 'innovators' and the second group 'imitators'. Unlike the Bass model, the model proposed by Fourt & Woodlock [1960] assumes that the diffusion process is primarily driven by the mass-media communication or external influence. On the other hand, the model proposed by Mansfield [1961] assumes that the process is primarily driven by the word-of-mouth communication or internal influence.

Figures 8.1 and 8.2 show plotted the conceptual and the analytical structure underlying the Bass model. As noted in Figure 8.1a, the Bass model conceptually assumes that 'innovators' or buyers who adopt exclusively because of the mass-media communication or external influence are present at any stage of the diffusion process. Figure 8.2 shows the analytical structure underlying the Bass model. As depicted, the noncumulative adopter distribution peaks at time T^*, which is the point of inflection of the S-shaped cumulative adoption curve.

[1] Related to the Mansfield model is the imitation model suggested by Fisher & Pry [1971] and the Gompertz curve. For applications of the Gompertz curve and its comparison with the Mansfield model, see Hendry [1972], Dixon [1980] and Ziemer [1992].

A number of other growth models have also been proposed in the marketing, economics and the technological substitution literature to depict the growth phenomenon (e.g. the Weibull distribution). Since some of these models either do not explicitly consider the diffusion effect in their formulations or combine other models, they are not included in this review. For applications of such models to new product growth situations, see DeKluyver [1982], Sharif & Islam [1980], Meade [1984], Lee & Lu [1987] and Skiadas [1985, 1986].

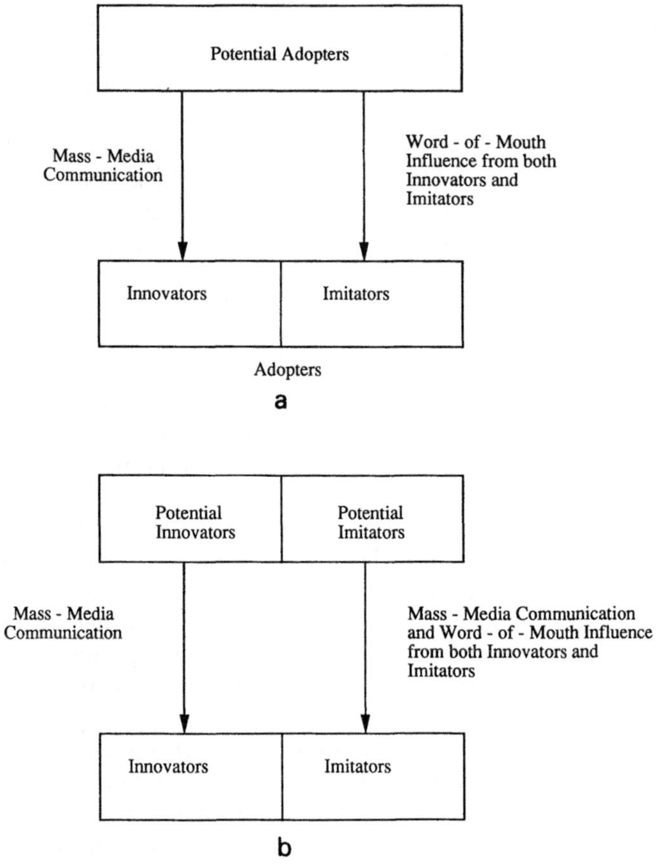

Fig. 8.1. Communication influence in diffusion models: (a) The Bass model; (b) Extension of the Bass model by Tanny and Derzko [1988].

Furthermore, the adopter distribution assumes that an initial *pm* (a constant) level of adopters buy the product at the beginning of the diffusion process. Once initiated, the adoption process is symmetric with respect to time around the peak time T^*, up to $2T^*$. That is, the shape of the adoption curve from time T^* to $2T^*$ is the mirror image of the shape of the adoption curve from the beginning of the diffusion process up to time T^* [Mahajan, Muller & Srivastava, 1990].

The Bass model derives from a hazard function (the probability that an adoption will occur at time t given that it has not yet occurred). Thus, $f(t)/(1 - F(t)) = p + qF(t)$ is the basic premise underlying the Bass model. The density function of time to adoption is given by $f(t)$ and the cumulative fraction of adopters at time t is given by $F(t)$. This basic premise states that the conditional probability of adoption at time t (the fraction of the population that will adopt at time t) is increasing in the fraction of the population that has already adopted. Therefore, the basic premise states that part of the adoption influence depends on imitation

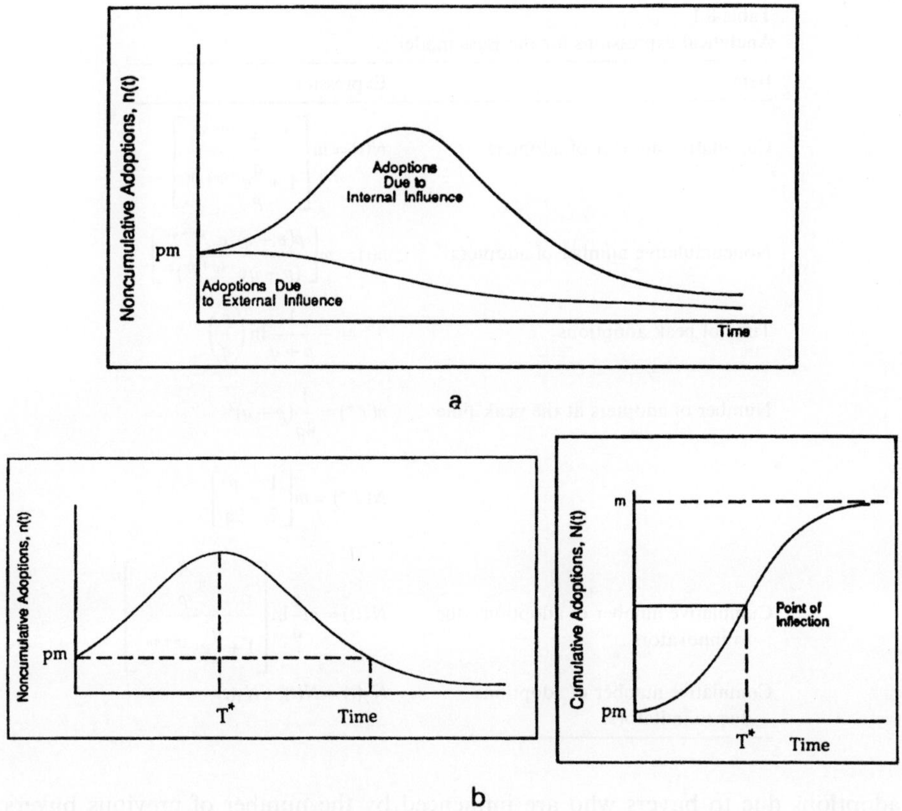

Fig. 8.2. The basic new product diffusion model: (a) Adoptions due to external influences in the Bass model; (b) Analytical structure of the Bass model.

or 'learning' and part of it does not. The parameter q reflects that influence whereas the parameter p reflects an influence that is independent of previous adoption. If q is zero, $f(t)$ will follow the negative exponential distribution. If m is the potential number of ultimate adopters, then the number of adopters at time t will be $mf(t) = n(t)$ and the cumulative number of adopters at time t will be $mF(t) = N(t)$. The basic premise of the Bass model may be manipulated, along with the definitions just provided to yield:

$$n(t) = \frac{\mathrm{d}N(t)}{\mathrm{d}t} = p(m - N(t)) + \frac{q}{m}N(t)(m - N(t)). \tag{1}$$

The first term, $p(m - N(t))$, in Equation (1) represents adoptions due to buyers who are not influenced in the timing of their adoption by the number of people who have already bought the product. Bass [1969] referred to p as the 'coefficient of innovation'. The second term $(q/m)N(t)(m - N(t))$, in Equation (1) represents

Table 8.1
Analytical expressions for the Bass model

Item	Expression
Cumulative number of adopters	$N(t) = m\left[\dfrac{1 - e^{-(p+q)t}}{1 + \dfrac{q}{p}e^{-(p+q)t}}\right]$
Noncumulative number of adopters	$n(t) = m\left[\dfrac{p(p+q)^2 e^{-(p+q)t}}{(p + qe^{-(p+q)t})^2}\right]$
Time of peak adoptions	$T^* = -\dfrac{1}{p+q}\ln\left(\dfrac{p}{q}\right)$
Number of adopters at the peak time	$n(T^*) = \dfrac{1}{4q}(p+q)^2$
	$N(T^*) = m\left[\dfrac{1}{2} - \dfrac{p}{2q}\right]$
Cumulative number of adoptions due to innovators	$N_1(t) = m\dfrac{p}{q}\ln\left[\dfrac{1 + \dfrac{q}{p}}{1 + \dfrac{q}{p}e^{-(p+q)t}}\right]$
Cumulative number of adoptions due to imitators	$N_2(t) = N(t) - N_1(t)$

adoptions due to buyers who are influenced by the number of previous buyers. Bass [1969] referred to q as the 'coefficient of imitation'. Note in Equation (1) that at time $t = 0$, $n(0) = pm$.

Equation (1) is a first-order differential equation. This equation can be integrated to yield the S-shaped cumulative adopter distribution, $N(t)$. Once $N(t)$ is known, further differentiation yields expressions for the noncumulative number of adopters, $n(t)$, and the time (T^*) and the magnitude ($n(t^*)$ and $N(t^*)$) of the peak of the adoption curve. Table 8.1 provides expressions for these items.

Given the basic structure of the Bass diffusion model, three questions can be raised: (i) How does the Bass model compare with the classical normal distribution model proposed by Rogers [1983]? (ii) Is the Bass model complete in capturing the communication structure between the two assumed distinct groups of innovators? (iii) How can the Bass model, that captures diffusion at the aggregate level, be linked to the adoption decisions at the individual level? Recent developments that deal with these three questions, respectively, are presented in the following three subsections.

2.2. *Unbundling of adopters*

Rogers has articulated that because of the interpersonal interaction (or word-of-mouth effect), the adoption curve should exhibit a normal distribution [1983,

p. 244]. In fact, using two basic statistical parameters of the normal distribution – mean and standard deviation, Rogers [1983] has proposed an adopter categorization scheme dividing adopters into five categories of innovators, early adopters, early majority, late majority and laggards.

To establish the linkage between the Bass model and the classical normal distribution model, a comparison between the two approaches has been provided by Mahajan, Muller & Srivastava [1990]. In their comparison, they highlight two points. First, they argue that adopters termed innovators by the Bass model should not be called innovators since they are not necessarily the first adopters of an innovation, as defined by Rogers. Following Lekvall & Wahlbin [1973], and noting Mahajan & Muller [1979] and Mahajan & Peterson [1985], they suggest that since the Bass model captures the spread of an innovation due to the mass media (external sources of information) and interpersonal (internal sources of information) communication channels, the Bass model coefficients p and q should be referred to as the coefficient of external influence and the coefficient of internal influence, respectively. (We will use these labels in the remainder of this paper.) They also provide an explicit expression to estimate the total number of adoptions due to external influence at any time in the diffusion process. This expression is also included in Table 8.1.

Second, they suggest that since one standard deviation away from the mean of the normal distribution represents its points of inflection (the analytical logic underlying the categorization scheme proposed by Rogers), the same analytical logic can be used to develop adopter categories for the Bass model. This scheme also yields five adopter categories with the number of buyers (pm) that initiate the Bass model being defined as innovators. Examining the diffusion of personal computers, Mahajan, Muller & Srivastava [1990] have shown how the adopter categories based on the Bass model can be used to study differences among their profiles.

2.3. Innovators versus imitators

Irrespective of the term 'innovators' used to label buyers that adopt due to external influence in the Bass model, a question can be raised as to whether the Bass model really captures the communication structure between two assumed groups of adopters of 'innovators' and 'imitators'. Emphasizing this argument, Tanny & Derzko [1988] suggest that the communication structure assumed in the Bass model is not complete. As depicted in Figure 8.1b, they propose an extension of the Bass model that assumes that (a) potential adopters are divided into two distinct groups of potential innovators (say m_1) and potential imitators (say m_2), (b) both potential-innovator and potential-imitator groups are influenced by the mass-media communication, and (c) *only* the potential-imitator group is influenced by word-of-mouth influence due to innovators and imitators. In order to appreciate the linkage between the Bass model and its extension proposed by Tanny & Derzko [1988], consider the following rate equations proposed by them:

$$\text{innovators: } \frac{\mathrm{d}N_1(t)}{\mathrm{d}t} = p_1(m_1 - N_1(t)), \tag{2}$$

$$\text{imitators: } \frac{dN_2(t)}{dt} = p_2(m_2 - N_2(t)) + q_2(N_1(t) + N_2(t))(m_2 - N_2(t)). \quad (3)$$

If we assume that $p_1 = p_2$, i.e. the coefficient of external influence is the same for both groups, the total adoptions can be represented by summing the above two rate equations (and noting that $m_1 + m_2 = m$ and $N(t) = N_1(t) + N_2(t)$):

$$\begin{aligned}\frac{dN(t)}{dt} &= p(m_1 + m_2 - N_1(t) - N_2(t)) + q_2 N(t)(m_2 - N_2(t)) \\ &= p(m - N(t)) + q_2 N(t)(m_2 - N_2(t)). \quad (4)\end{aligned}$$

Note that Equation (4) is identical to the Bass model, Equation (1), except for the fact that Equation (4) considers the word-of-mouth influence on the potential adopters that are 'potential imitators' rather than on all of the 'potential adopters' as is done in the Bass model. In their empirical work on some of the consumer durables analyzed by Bass [1969], Tanny & Derzko [1988] report that they did not find satisfactory results for their proposed extension (the model either reduced to the Bass model or it failed to provide estimates for the additional model coefficients). These empirical results are not surprising since as the diffusion process progresses, the population of 'potential adopters' mostly comprises 'potential imitators', justifying the parsimonious model suggested by Bass.

2.4. Diffusion models from individual adoption decisions

A key aspect of the Bass model is that it deals with the market in the aggregate. The typical variable that is measured is the number of adopters that purchase the product by a certain time t. The emphasis is on the total market response rather than an individual customer. This is a convenient approach from a practical point of view but it raises the following issue: can the diffusion model be built by aggregating demand from consumers who behave in a neoclassical microeconomic fashion? That is, assume that potential adopters are smart and they are not just carriers of information. They, therefore, maximize some objective function such as expected utility or benefit from the product taking into account the uncertainty associated with their understanding of its attributes, its price, pressure from other adopters to adopt it, and their own budget. Since the decision to adopt the innovation is individual-specific, all potential adopters do not have the same probability of adopting the product in a given time period. The question now is, given the heterogeneity among potential adopters in terms of their probability to adopt the product at any time t, can we develop the adoption curve at the aggregate market level? Development of a model that answers this question can potentially assist in ascertaining the effect of marketing mix and other variables on demand for the product via their effect on individual consumers.

In recent years, attempts have been made by Hiebert [1974], Stoneman [1981], Feder & O'Mara [1982], Jensen [1982], Oren & Schwartz [1988], Chatterjee &

Eliashberg [1990] and Lattin & Roberts [1989] to develop diffusion models by specifying adoption decisions at the individual level. Figure 8.3 outlines a flow chart that characterizes the general logic underlying the development of these models. These models assume that, at any time *t*, a potential adopter's utility for an innovation is based on his uncertain perception of the innovation's performance, value, or benefits. The potential adopter's uncertain perceptions about the innovation, however, change over time as he learns more about the innovation from external sources (e.g. advertising) or internal sources (e.g. word-of-mouth). Therefore, due to this learning, whenever his utility for the innovation becomes greater

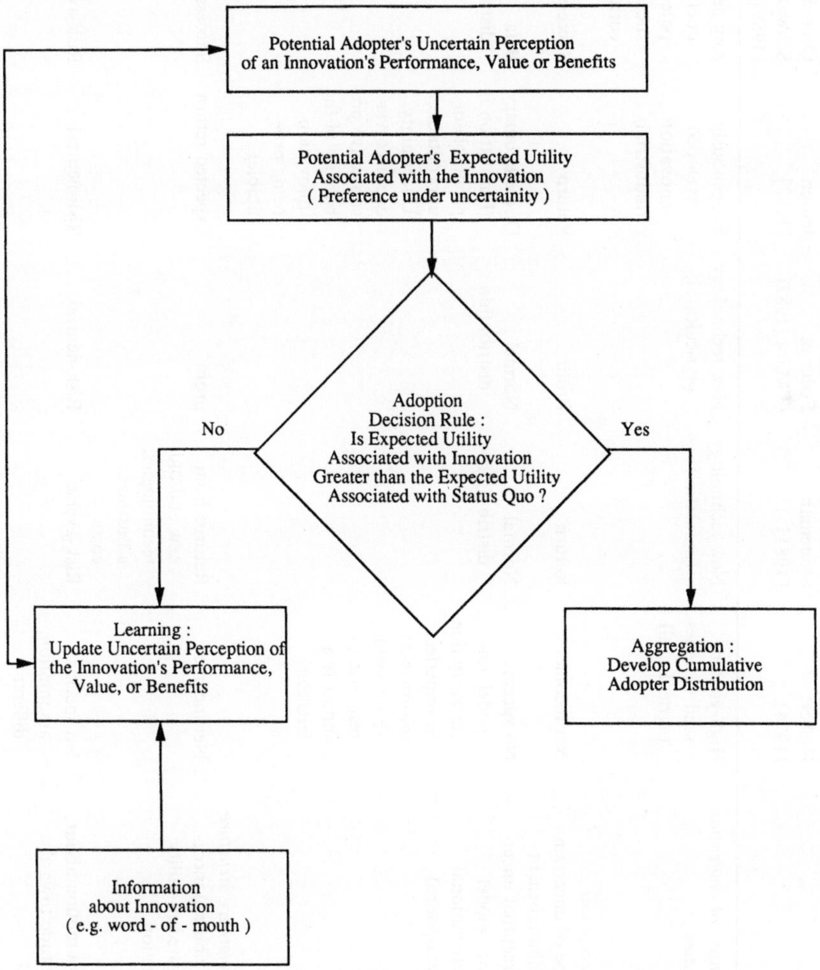

Fig. 8.3. A general modeling structure for diffusion models based on individual adoption decisions.

Table 8.2
Characteristics of diffusion models based on individual adoption decisions

	Hiebert [1974]	Stoneman [1981]	Feder & O'Mara (1982)	Jensen [1982]	Oren & Schwartz [1988]	Chatterjee & Eliashberg [1990]	Lattin & Roberts [1989]
I. *Nature of innovation studied*	High-yielding seed varieties (agricultural)	New technology (industrial)	New technology (agricultural)	Exogenously developed innovation (industrial)	Any new product that is potential substitute for current product	Durables	Durables
II. *Perceptions*							
(a) Type of uncertain attribute/benefit	Net income	Return	Profit	Return	Success rate	Performance	Benefit
(b) Perceptual uncertainty model (distributional assumptions)	No specific model: uncertainty due to imperfect information about yield response to inputs (e.g. fertilizer)	Normal distribution	Normal distribution	Discrete: binary (Innovation is profitable or unprofitable. Uncertainty captured via subjective probability of the innovation being profitable)	Beta distribution	Normal distribution	Normal distribution
III. *Preference structure*							
(a) Attribute(s) incorporated in utility function	Net income	Returns from new and old technologies, adjustment costs	profit	Expected return	Success rate	Performance. price	Benefit
(b) Assumption about attitude toward risk	No specific assumption: different attitudes considered	Risk-averse	Risk-neutral	Risk-neutral	Risk-averse	Risk-averse	Risk-averse

IV. *Adoption decision rule*	Maximize expected utility (partial adoption of innovation possible)	Maximize utility to determine proportion of output produced on new technology	Expected profit from new technology exceeds profit from current technology	Expected return from adoption is greater than expected value of continuing waiting for additional information	Expected utility for new product exceeds expected utility for current product	Expected utility for new product exceeds expected utility for status quo	Expected utility for new product exceeds expected utility for status quo
V. *Learning*							
(a) Learning model	Not explicit: learning reduces uncertainty	Bayesian	Bayesian	Bayesian	Bayesian	Bayesian	Bayesian
(b) Source of information		Previous experience with new technology	Internal (previous adopters)	External	Internal (previous adopters)	Both internal and external	Internal (previous adopters)
VI. *Aggregation*							
Heterogeneity criterion on which aggregation is done across potential adopters	No aggregation	Not applicable: considers only intrafirm diffusion	Mean of initial perceptions about profitability	Initial subjective probability of innovation being profitable	Risk-aversion parameter (Note: Model assumes constant flow of consumers so that aggregation yields market share rather than cumulative penetration)	(i) Initial perceptions (both expectation and degree of uncertainty) (ii) Perceived reliability of information (iii) Risk-aversion parameter (iv) Price/performance tradeoff	Difference in the mean of perceptions about benefit from status quo

than the status quo (he is better off with the innovation), he adopts the innovation. Aggregation across the various potential adopters yields the cumulative adoption curve.

Table 8.2 contrasts the various individual-level diffusion models on several dimensions. Of all the models compared in Table 8.2, only three models provide explicit functions for aggregate diffusion models. Depending upon the assumptions made about the distribution of parameters that measure heterogeneity across individuals, the model by Chatterjee & Eliashberg [1990] yields several basic diffusion models. If it is assumed that risk-aversion across the potential adopters follows a negative exponential distribution, the model by Oren & Schwartz [1988] reduces to the Mansfield model. Assuming that the perceived differences in the potential benefits of the product, across potential adopters, follow a uniform distribution, Lattin & Roberts [1989] suggest the following model:

$$N(t) = a + bN(t-1) - \frac{d}{c + N(t-1)} \tag{5}$$

where a, b, c and d are constants. Using the data on several consumer durables, Lattin & Roberts [1989] indicate that their model provides a better fit to the data than the Bass model. Their model, however, contains four parameters (as compared to three in the Bass model) and, unlike the Bass model, it does not provide $N(t)$ as an explicit function of time, limiting its ability for long-term forecasting.

3. Refinements and extensions of the Bass diffusion model

There are several assumptions that underlie the Bass model. For the most part, these are simplifying assumptions that provide parsimonious analytical representation of the diffusion process. Recognition of these assumptions, however, is important to properly understand and interpret the dynamics of innovation diffusion captured by the Bass model. These assumptions are briefly highlighted below.

3.1. The diffusion pattern is symmetric with a fixed inflection point

The basic structure of a diffusion model can be characterized in terms of two mathematical properties – point of inflection and symmetry. The point of inflection on a diffusion curve occurs when the maximum rate of diffusion is reached. If the diffusion pattern after the point of inflection is the mirror image of the diffusion pattern before the point of inflection, the diffusion curve is characterized as being symmetric. For example, as depicted in Figure 8.1B, the adopter distribution for the Bass model peaks at time T^*, which is the point of inflection of the S-shaped cumulative adoption curve, and is symmetric with respect to time around the peak time T^* up to time $2T^*$. Furthermore, the Bass model assumes that the maximum penetration rate cannot occur after the product has captured 50% of the market potential. In practice, as well as in theory, the maximum rate of diffusion of an innovation should be able to occur at any time during the diffusion process. Additionally, diffusion patterns can be expected to be nonsymmetric as well as symmetric.

Easingwood, Mahajan & Muller [1983] have suggested that the flexibility in the diffusion models can be achieved by recognizing an important assumption underlying the diffusion models. Most of the diffusion models assume that the impact of the word-of-mouth effect on potential adopters remains constant throughout the entire diffusion span. This assumption is tenuous since, for most innovations, the word-of-mouth is likely to increase, decrease, or remain constant over time [Hernes, 1976]. Easingwood, Mahajan & Muller [1983] suggest that the time-varying nature of the word-of-mouth effect can be incorporated in the Bass model by specifying the coefficient of internal influence as systematically varying over time as a function of penetration level. That is,

$$w(t) = q\left[\frac{N(t)}{m}\right]^{\alpha} \tag{6}$$

where α is a constant and $w(t)$ is the time-varying coefficient of external influence. Substitution of Equation (6) into the Bass model, Equation (1), yields the non-uniform-influence (NUI) model suggested by them (in terms of the cumulative fraction of adopters):

$$\frac{\mathrm{d}F(t)}{\mathrm{d}t} = (p + qF^{\delta}(t))(1 - F(t)), \tag{7}$$

where $F(t) = N(t)/m$ and $\alpha + 1 = \delta$. When $p = 0$ (i.e., coefficient of external influence is zero), Equation (6) or (7) yields a flexible extension of the Mansfield model termed nonsymmetric responding logistic (NSRL) by Easingwood, Mahajan & Muller [1981] (an interesting alternative interpretation of the NSRL model in terms of experience curve and price elasticity has been provided by Sharp [1984]).

In addition to the NUI and NSRL models, Table 8.3 reports salient characteristics of nine other diffusion models proposed in the diffusion literature. The following observations are warranted from this table:

- In addition to the NUI and NSRL models, there are only two models that offer complete flexibility in capturing diffusion patterns (i.e. point of inflection can occur from 0% to 100% penetration and the diffusion patterns can be symmetric or nonsymmetric). These are the models proposed by Von Bertalanffy [1957] (an identical model has been proposed by Nelder [1962] and Bewley & Fiebig [1988]).
- Like the NUI and NSRL models proposed by Easingword, Mahajan & Muller [1981, 1983], the model by Von Bertalanffy also expresses the coefficient of internal influence as systematically changing over time as a function of penetration level, i.e.

Table 8.3
Flexibile diffusion models

Model	Model equation ($\mathrm{d}F/\mathrm{d}t =$)	Model solution ($F =$)	Point of inflection (F^*)	Symmetry(10)	Coefficient of internal influence	Illustrated reported applications
1. Bass [1969](1)	$(p+qF)(1-F)$	$\dfrac{1-\mathrm{e}^{-(p+q)t}}{1+\dfrac{q}{p}\mathrm{e}^{-(p+q)t}}$	0.0–0.5	NS	Constant	Consumer durables, retail service, agricultural, educational and industrial innovations, electronics, photographic products, industrial processes.
2. Gompertz curve(2) [see Hendry, 1972; Dixon, 1980]	$qF\ln\left(\dfrac{1}{F}\right)$	$\exp[-\exp(-(c+qt))]$	0.37	NS	Constant	Consumer durables, agricultural innovations.
3. Mansfield [1961]	$qF(1-F)$	$\dfrac{1}{1+\mathrm{e}^{-(c+qt)}}$	0.5	S	Constant	Industrial, high-technology and administrative innovations.
4. Floyd [1962]	$qF(1-F)^2$		0.33	NS	Decreasing to zero	Industrial innovations.
5. Sharif & Kabir [1976](3)	$\dfrac{qF(1-F)^2}{1-F(1-\sigma)}$		0.33–0.5	S or NS	Constant or decreasing to zero	Industrial innovations.
6. Jeuland [1981](4)	$(p+qF)(1-F)^{1+\gamma}$		0.0–0.5	S or NS	Constant or decreasing to zero	Consumer durables.
7. Non-uniform influence. (NUI) [Easingwood, Mahajan & Muller, 1983]	$(p+qF^{\delta})(1-F)$		0.0–1.0	S or NS	Increasing, decreasing or constant	Consumer durables, retail service and education .innovations.

Nonsymmetric responding logistic (NSRL, $p=0$ in NUI) [Easingwood, Mahajan & Muller, 1981]	$qF^{\delta}(1-F)$		0.0–1.0	S or NS	Increasing, decreasing, or constant	Medical innovations.
8. Nelder [1962](5)(6) [see McGowan, [1986]	$qF(1-F^{\phi})$	$\frac{1}{[1+\phi e^{-(c+qt)}]^{1/\phi}}$	0.0–1.0	S or NS	Decreasing to a constant	Agricultural innovations.
Von Bertalanffy(7) [1957] [see Richards, 1959]	$\frac{q}{1-\theta}F^{\theta}(1-F^{1-\theta})$	$(1-e^{-(c+qt)})^{1/(1-\theta)}$	0.0–1.0	S or NS	Decreasing to a constant	
9. Stanford Research(8) Institute [e.g., Teotia & Raju, 1986]	$\frac{q}{t}F(1-F)$	$\frac{1}{1+\left(\frac{T^*}{t}\right)^q}$	0.0–0.5	NS	Decreasing to zero	Energy-efficient innovations.
10. Flexible logistic(9) Growth (FLOG) [Bewley & Fiebig, 1988]	$q[(1+kt)^{1/k}]^{\mu-k}$	$\frac{1}{1+e^{-((c+qt)\mu,k)}}$	0.0–1.0	S or NS	Increasing, decreasing, or constant	Telecommunication innovation.

(1) The model is symmetric around the peak time T^* up to $2T^*$.
(2) c is a constant; (3) $0 \leqslant \sigma \leqslant 1$; (4) $\gamma \geqslant 0$.
(5) The model suggested by Nelder [1962] is identical to the model originally suggested by Von Bertalanffy [1957]. The equivalence between the two can be shown by substituting $\phi = \theta - 1$ in the Von Bertalanffy model.
(6) c is a constant, model reduces to Mansfield model for $\Phi = 1$ and the Gompertz curve as Φ approaches zero.
(7) c is a constant, $\theta \geqslant 0$; model reduces to the Mansfield model when $\theta = 2$ and the Gompertz curve as θ approaches 1.
(8) The model is not invariant to the choice of time scale. A linear transformation of time t is required to make it time-scale-independent. T^* is time of 50% penetration. [See Bewley and Fiebig, 1988.]
(9) μ and k are constants and $t(\mu, k) = \{[(1+kt)^{(1/k)}]^{\mu} - 1\}/\mu$, $\mu \neq 0$, $k \neq 0$, $= (1/k)\log(1+kt)$, $\mu = 0$, $k \neq 0$, $= (e^{\mu t} - 1)/\mu$, $\mu \neq 0$, $k = 0$, $= t$, $\mu = 0$, $k \neq 0$.
(10) Note: S = symmetric, NS = nonsymmetric.

$$w(t) = \frac{q(1 - F^{\phi})}{(1 - F)} \tag{8}$$

where ϕ is a constant. Unlike the NUI and NSRL models, however, the differential equation used to specify the diffusion process by the Von Bertalanffy model possesses a closed-form solution enabling the representation of cumulative adoption as an explicit function of time. This model, however, assumes that the word-of-mouth effect decreases over time. The NUI and NSRL models can accommodate the word-of-mouth effect that increases, decreases, or remains constant over time.

As compared to the models suggested by Easingwood, Mahajan & Muller [1981, 1983] and Von Bertalanffy [1957], the FLOG (flexible logistic growth) model suggested by Bewley & Fiebig [1988] expresses the systematically variation in the coefficient of internal influence as a function of time, i.e.,

$$w(t) = q[(1 + kt)^{1/k}]^{\mu - k} \tag{9}$$

where k and μ are constants. The FLOG model provides a closed-form solution, and like the NUI and NSRL models, can accommodate the word-of-mouth effect that increases, decreases, or remains constant over time.

Although there is some evidence to suggest that, as compared to the basic diffusion models (such as the Bass model), the flexible models provide a better fit to the diffusion data [see Rao, 1985; Lattin & Roberts, 1989; McGowan, 1986; Easingwood, 1987, 1988], this advantage is obtained by incorporating additional parameters, thus making it more difficult to use these models in the absence of diffusion time-series data. (Using the historical data on existing products, however, Easingwood [1989] has demonstrated how the NUI model can be used to develop analogical parameter estimates for a new product.)

3.2. Market potential of the new product remains constant over time

The Bass model assumes that the market potential (m) of a new product is determined at the time of introduction and remains unchanged over its entire life [Mahajan & Peterson, 1978, 1982; Sharif & Ramanathan, 1981; Kalish, 1985]. From a theoretical perspective, there is no rationale for a static potential-adopter population. Instead, a potential-adopter population continuously in flux is to be expected.

Extensions of the Bass model that deal with this assumption have attempted to relax this assumption by specifying the market potential as a function of relevant exogenous and endogenous variables – controllable as well as uncontrollable – that affect the market potential. Examining the diffusion of a durable, Kalish [1985], for example, specified the dynamics of the market potential as a function of price of the product and the reduction of uncertainty associated with the product with its increased adoption. Assuming full product awareness in the population, he specified.

$$m(t) = m_0 \exp\left\{ -dP(t)\left[\frac{a+1}{a+N(t)/m_0}\right]\right\} \tag{10}$$

where a and d are constants, m_0 is the size of the market potential at the time of product introduction, $P(t)$ is the product price and the term $[(a+1)/(a+N(t)/m_0)]$ represents the effect of market penetration in increasing the size of market potential due to the word-of-mouth effect. Other applications have represented the market potential as a function of growth in the number of households [Mahajan & Peterson, 1978], population growth [Sharif & Ramanathan, 1981], product profitability [Lackman, 1978], price [Chow, 1967; Kamakura & Balasubramanian, 1988; Jain & Rao, 1990], growth in the number of retailers making the product available to potential customers [Jones & Ritz, 1987], and income distribution, price and product uncertainty [Horsky, 1990].

3.3. Diffusion of an innovation is independent of all other innovations

The Bass model assumes that the adoption of an innovation does not complement, substitute for, detract from, or enhance the adoption of any other innovation (and vice versa) [Peterson & Mahajan, 1978]. In reality, however, an innovation is not introduced into a vacuum nor does it exist in isolation. Other innovations exist in the marketplace and may have an influence (positive or negative) on the diffusion of an innovation.

The consideration of simultaneous diffusion of multiple innovation is especially critical for product innovations where the diffusion of an innovation is contingent upon the diffusion of another innovation (e.g. compact-disc software and compact-disc hardware) or where the diffusion of an innovation complements the diffusion of another innovation (e.g. washers and dryers).

Following the contingent diffusion model suggested by Peterson & Mahajan [1978], Bayus [1987], for example, has provided an interesting empirical study that examines the diffusion-dependence between compact-disc software and compact-disc hardware. In the contingent diffusion model, the market potential of the dependent product is contingent upon the diffusion of the primary product. That is, in the Bass-model representation of its growth, Equation (1), its market potential is specified as $(N_1(t) - N_2(t))$ where $N_1(t)$ is the cumulative number of adopters of the primary product (e.g. compact-disc hardware) and $N_2(t)$ is the cumulative number of adopters of the contingent product (e.g. compact-disc software).

3.4. Nature of an innovation does not change over time

Manufacturers of high-technology products usually achieve diffusion in the marketplace by offering successive generations of an innovation. Each generation is positioned to be better than its predecessors on relevant product attributes. Assessment of market penetration, therefore, is critical for successive generations of a high-technology product. In addition to creating its own demand, each generation of the product cannibalizes the diffusion of its predecessors. This important application of diffusion models for assessing technological substitution has been successfully demonstrated by Norton & Bass [1987] for the growth of two basic types of integrated circuits: memory and logic circuits. If τ_2 represents the time of the introduction of the second generation, Norton & Bass [1987] suggest that the word-of-mouth effect within each generation and substitution effect across successive generations can be represented by the following extension of the Bass model:

$$S_1(t) = m_1 F_1(t) - m_1 F_1(t) F_2(t - \tau_2), \tag{11}$$

$$S_2(t) = m_2 F_2(t - \tau) + m_1 F_1(t) F_2(t - \tau_2), \tag{12}$$

where Equation (11) represents the diffusion equation for the first-generation product and Equation (12) represents the second-generation product, S_1 and S_2 are their shipments at time t, $F_1(t)$ and $F_2(t)$ are fractions of adoptions for each generation and are given by the Bass-model solution of Equation (1) in Table 8.1. In Equations (11) and (12), the term $m_1 F_1(t) F_2(t - \tau_2)$ represents the cannibalization or substitution effect.

3.5. *The geographical boundaries of the social system do not change over the diffusion process*

In spite of the fact that the diffusion of an innovation occurs simultaneously in space and time, research on these two dimensions of diffusion has seldom been integrated in marketing. For example, the new-product rollout is clearly a popular option used by many firms to diffuse their products from market to market over time (both in the national and the international markets). Such a new-product launch strategy enables a firm to capitalize on the word-of-mouth communication, referred to as the neighborhood effect [Brown, 1981; Gore & Lavaraj, 1987], across markets. It is, therefore, necessary to simultaneously assess the market penetration within a market and across markets.

One application that addresses diffusion from a joint space and time perspective has been reported by Mahajan & Peterson [1979]. In examining the adoption of tractors in 25 states in the central agricultural-production region of the United States over the period 1920–1964, they extend the Bass model by assuming that (a) the innovation is initially introduced in one market and (b) the relative number of total adoptions is greater in those markets that are closest to the market of innovation origination (i.e. the neighborhood effect diminishes with the increased distance from the market of innovation origination, decreasing the size of market potential across markets).

3.6. *The diffusion process is binary*

As depicted in Figure 8.1a, the Bass model assumes that potential adopters of an innovation either adopt the innovation or they do not adopt it. As a consequence of this assumption, the Bass model does not take into account stages in the adoption process (e.g. awareness, knowledge, etc.). Some of the attempts to extend the two-stage models to incorporate the multistage (or polynomial) nature of the diffusion process include models by Midgley [1976], Dodson & Muller [1978], Sharif & Ramanathan [1982], Mahajan, Muller & Kerin [1984] and Kalish [1985]. Most of these extensions tend to characterize stages in which positive, negative, or neutral information is communicated about the product. The implementation of the above models to innovation diffusion is rather cumbersome since they require detailed information about the customer flow across the various stages. In empirical applications, the developers of these models, therefore, either collapse the various stages (Kalish [1985] assumes full product awareness), attempt to derive the population in various stages by decomposing the time-series diffusion data [Midgley, 1976; Sharif & Ramanathan, 1982] with too many parameters to be estimated with the limited available data [Silver, 1984], or trace the innovation diffusion with the panel data [Mahajan, Muller & Kerin, 1984; Mahajan, Muller & Sharma, 1984].

3.7. Diffusion of an innovation is not influenced by marketing strategies

Since the pioneering work of Robinson & Lakhani [1975] that incorporated the impact of price in the Bass model, several efforts have been made to systematically study the impact of marketing-mix variables such as price, advertising, promotion and personal selling, and distribution on the product growth (efforts related to price and advertising are extensively reviewed by Kalish & Sen [1986]). Since the Bass model contains three parameters (coefficients of external influence and internal influence, and the market potential), the impact of marketing-mix variables has been incorporated into the Bass model by representing these parameters as functions of relevant variables. Attempts have been made to represent the market potential as a function of price [e.g. Kalish, 1983, 1985] and distribution growth [Jones & Ritz, 1987]. Other attempts to incorporate marketing-mix variables have been concerned with representing the coefficients of external influence and internal influences as a function of diffusion-influencing variables. Although analytically very elegant, most of these modeling efforts lack empirical validation [Mahajan & Wind, 1986a]. They have, however, been useful in establishing working hypotheses to examine the likely impact of marketing-mix variables on innovation diffusion. Since these hypotheses are presented in the next section, we briefly comment here on studies that have provided some empirical support for their extensions.

Two empirical studies by Horsky & Simon [1983] and Simon & Sebastian [1987] have examined the impact of advertising on innovation diffusion. Studying the diffusion of a new banking service, Horsky & Simon [1983] argue that since advertising provides information to innovators, the coefficient of external influence in the Bass model should be represented as a function of advertising expenditures (with diminishing returns). The empirical results provided a good fit to the diffusion data used by them, supporting their argument. Studying the diffusion of new telephones in West Germany, Simon & Sebastian [1987] suggest that, though advertising may influence innovators (and hence the coefficient of external influence) in the early stage of the product life-cycle, it is more likely to influence the coefficient of imitation in the intermediate life-cycle stage of a new product since the objective of the advertising content in the intermediate stage is to influence potential customers through evaluation by customers and social pressure. Furthermore, the advertising effect is cumulative over time. They report a good fit to the diffusion data used by them, supporting their arguments regarding the incorporation of cumulative effect of advertising into the coefficient of imitation.

The question about the inclusion of price into the Bass model intrigued diffusion analysts in the 1970s and 1980s. As pointed out earlier, examining the diffusion of an (unmentioned) durable, Kalish [1985] has suggested that price impacts the market potential of a product (see Equation (10)). Recent empirical studies, employing data on several consumer durables, by Kamakura & Balasubramanian [1988] and Jain & Rao [1990], however, conclude that price affects the rate of diffusion (via the coefficients of external influence and internal influence) rather than the market potential.

3.8. Product and market characteristics do not influence diffusion patterns

The Bass model does not explicitly consider the impact of product and market characteristics on diffusion patterns. Empirical studies in the innovation diffusion literature, however, have reported that product and market characteristics have a substantial impact on innovation diffusion patterns [Rogers, 1983; Tornatzky & Klein, 1982]. Three empirical studies – Srivastava, Mahajan, Ramaswami & Cherian [1985], Kalish & Lilien [1986b] and Gatignon, Eliashberg & Robertson [1989] – have attempted to incorporate product and market characteristics into the Bass model. All of these studies incorporate the impact of these characteristics in the diffusion model by expressing the coefficients of external influence and/or internal influence as a function of these characteristics. Whereas the studies by Srivastava, Mahajan, Ramaswami & Cherian [1985] and Kalish & Lilien [1986b] examine the impact of product characteristics on diffusion patterns, the study by Gatignon, Eliashberg & Robertson [1989] studies the impact of market characteristics on the diffusion of a product across markets. Only the study by Kalish & Lilien [1986b], however, explicitly considers the changing consumers' perception of the product characteristics as the product is accepted over time. They achieve this by defining the coefficient of imitation as changing over time due to changes in the product characteristics.

3.9. There are no supply restrictions

The Bass model is a demand model. If the demand for a product cannot be met because of supply restrictions, such as the unavailability of product due to limitations on the production capacity or difficulties encountered in setting up distribution systems, the excess unmet demand is likely to generate a waiting line of potential adopters [Simon & Sebastian, 1987]. In such a situation, the adopter distribution is the same as the supply distribution and it will be inappropriate to apply the Bass model to these adoption data. It is, therefore, necessary to extend the Bass model to integrate the demand-side dynamics with the supply-side restrictions.

A model that captures the innovation-diffusion dynamics in the presence of supply restrictions has been suggested by Jain, Mahajan & Muller [1991]. Their model conceptualizes the diffusion process as a three-stage diffusion process: potential adopters → waiting adopters → adopters. Jain, Mahajan & Muller [1991] have demonstrated the application of their model on the diffusion of new telephones in Israel.

3.10. There is only one adoption by an adopting unit

The objective of a diffusion model is to represent the level or spread of an innovation among a given set of prospective adopters. For a great many product innovations, the increase in the number of adopters may consist of first-time buyers as well as repeat buyers. The Bass model, however, captures only the first-time buyers.

In recent years, five empirical studies have been reported that capture the repeat/replacement dynamics of innovation diffusion. Two of these studies by Lilien, Rao & Kalish [1981] and Mahajan, Wind & Sharma [1983] include repeat-purchase in the Bass model to study diffusion of ethical drugs. The other two studies by Olson & Choi [1985] and Kamakura & Balasubramanian [1987] include product replacements in the Bass model to assess long-term sales for consumer durables. Norton & Bass [1987] assume that adopters continue to buy and that the average repeat-buying rate over the population of adopters is constant.

4. Uses of diffusion models

Innovation diffusion models have traditionally been used in the context of sales forecasting. However, as pointed out by Mahajan & Wind [1986a] and Kalish & Lilien [1986b], sales forecasting is only one of the objectives of diffusion models. In addition to forecasting, perhaps the most useful uses of diffusion models are for *descriptive* and *normative* purposes. Since diffusion models provide an analytical approach to describe the spread of a diffusion phenomenon, they can be used in an explanatory mode to test specific diffusion-based hypotheses. Furthermore, since the diffusion models are designed to capture the product life-cycle of a new product, for normative purposes, they can be used as the basis of how a product should be marketed. Our objective here is to assess the use of diffusion models for these two objectives.

4.1. Descriptive uses

Table 8.4 provides a listing of nine illustrative studies that have used the diffusion-modeling framework to test hypotheses. Two of these studies, by Srivastava, Mahajan, Ramaswami & Cherian [1985] and Rao & Yamada [1988], use diffusion

Table 8.4
Illustrative descriptive applications of diffusion models

Study by	Hypothesis tested	Diffusion model used	Remarks
Bass [1980]	As a result of learning and accumulated experience, declining pattern of costs and prices should result for technological innovations.	Bass	The study reports results for 6 durables. The hypothesis is generally confirmed for most of these products. Similar results are provided by DeKluyver [1982].
Olshavsky [1980]	Product life-cycles of consumer durables are shortening due to rapidly accelerating technological developments.	Mansfield	The study uses data from 25 consumer durables. The hypothesis is tested by examining the relationship between the coefficient of imitation and the time of the introduction of an innovation. The study confirms the hypothesis.
Kobrin [1985]	The pattern of oil-production nationalization across countries is a 'social interaction' phenomenon.	Bass	The study examines the pattern of the number of countries per year that nationalized oil production from 1960 to 1979. Supplementing the quantitative results with detailed qualitative analyses, the study confirms the hypothesis.
Srivastava, Mahajan, Ramaswami & Cherian [1985]	Potential adopter's perceptions of innovation attributes explains the diffusion pattern of a product.	Bass	The study examines the diffusion of 14 investment alternatives. In order to explain the diffusion patterns across investment alternatives, the coefficient of imitation is expressed as a function of perceived product attributes. Two attributes of perceived information cost and perceived likelihood of loss of principal/negative return explain those differences. The study confirms the hypothesis.
Mahajan, Sharma & Bettis [1988]	The adoption of the M-form organizational structure by the US firms resulted from an imitation behavior.	Bass	The study examines the adoption of the M-form organization structure among 127 US firms from 1950 to 1974. The study questions the validity of the hypothesis.
Modis & Debecker [1988]	There is a relationship between the number of new computer models and the number of new computer manufacturers.	Mansfield	The study uses data on the number of new models introduced and the number of new manufacturers that emerged in the computer market from the

			beginning of 1958 up to the end of 1984. The study is also done for personal computers. By examining the relationship between the growth patterns of the number of new computer models and the number of new computer manufacturers, the study concludes that, on the average, a new computer manufacturer emerges for every five new models that appear on the market. For the personal-computer market, the figure is around six.
Rao & Yamada [1988]	Potential adopter's perceptions of innovation attributes explain the diffusion pattern of a product.	Lilien, Rao & Kalish [1981]	The study examines the diffusion of 21 ethical drugs using the repeat-purchase diffusion model suggested by Lilien, Rao & Kalish. The model coefficients are expressed as a function of six perceived attributes of ethical drugs. The study confirms the hypothesis.
Takada & Jain [1991]	Cultural differences among countries will lead to different diffusion patterns.	Bass	The study examines the diffusion of eight consumer durables in Japan, Korea and the United States. By testing the differences between the coefficients of innovation and imitations across the three countries, the study concludes that among the three countries analyzed, a product is adopted in Korea at a much faster rate than in either the US or in Japan. No significant differences are found between the diffusion patterns in Japan and the US.
Gatignon, Eliashberg & Robertson [1989]	Three dimensions explain the differences in the diffusion patterns across countries – level of cosmopolitanism of a country, mobility, and the role of women in the society.	Bass	The study examines the diffusion of six consumer durables in 14 European countries. The coefficients of imitation and innovation are expressed as a function of variables measuring the three hypothesized dimensions and their impact on the two coefficients is determined simultaneously across products and across countries. The study confirms the hypothesis.

models to test hypotheses related to the impact of perceived product attributes on diffusion patterns. Three studies, by Kobrin [1985], Takada & Jain [1991] and Gatignon, Eliashberg & Robertson [1989], respectively, use diffusion models to test hypotheses related to innovation diffusion across countries. Studies by Bass [1980], Olshavsky [1980] and Modis & Debecker [1988] use diffusion models to test hypotheses related to the life-cycle dynamics of a new product. Finally, the study by Mahajan, Sharma & Bettis [1988] evaluates the hypothesis that any S-shaped curve need not be a result of the imitation process.

The above studies clearly demonstrate how the diffusion models can be used to evaluate hypotheses related to the dynamics of innovation diffusion.

4.2. Normative uses

Although diffusion models are concerned with representing the growth of a product category, the growth of the product category can be influenced by the individual or by the collective actions of competitors that have long-term effect on the growth or decline of the market. Alternatively, even if there is only one firm in the industry, it needs to consider the life-cycle dynamics over time to determine optimal marketing-mix strategy for maximizing its profitability. To highlight this point, consider the following scenario.

A firm is introducing a new product. It has a patent protecting the product and the firm is planning the product's introduction and subsequent growth for the time period in which it is monopolist. The firm has conducted the necessary marketing research studies and it knows the relevant demand parameters of the segment it serves. In the static case of no growth, economic theory tells us that the firm should equate the marginal revenues it gets (via either changing production or changing price) to its marginal costs at that output or price. The firm realizes that taking growth into account, if it just equates marginal costs to marginal revenues *at each point of time*, it is not maximizing the long-run profit but rather short-term instantaneous profits. The firm, therefore, realizes that its current actions (price-setting, for example) has an effect not only on its current profits but on its position and profits in the future. It wants, therefore, to *find the optimal pricing strategy throughout the product lift-cycle*, so as to maximize net present value of future stream of net cash flow.

This is, of course, a much simplified scenario of the real problem a firm faces, since it has to concern itself not only with pricing, but with all the marketing-mix variables that are relevant for the product growth such as advertising expenditures, distribution channels, subsequent new-product introductions, and the like. In addition it has to consider the fact that its actions might trigger a response from one or more of its competitors. This response, again, has an effect not only on its current profits and market share, but on its position and profits in the future.

The firm thus chooses a vector of strategies (advertising, price and distribution), so as to maximize total discounted profits over the planning horizon, i.e.

$$\text{maximize} \int_0^T \pi(N(t), u(t))\mathrm{e}^{-rt}\,\mathrm{d}t \tag{13}$$

where $N(t)$ is the vector of sales or market shares of all firms in the market and $u(t)$ is their strategies. The firms' sales growth (in a vector form) is given by

$$dN/dt = g(N(t), u(t)) \tag{14}$$

for some growth function g.

The dynamic optimization (or game) formulation outlined in Equations (13) and (14) is the general framework that has been used by several authors in the 1980s to develop optimal marketing-mix strategies especially for price and advertising. Most of these studies use the Bass model, and its extensions incorporating marketing-mix variables, in Equation (14) to represent the life-cycle dynamics over time. They usually consider a single marketing-mix variable, such as price, to isolate its effects on product growth.

For example, in pricing over time the firm has two opposing strategies: one, known as skimming, is a strategy that calls for charging a high initial price and dropping the price gradually later on. This will help the firm to discriminate among its consumers based on their price elasticity. It skims the cream of the market by having the consumer with high reservation price purchase the product earlier. The second strategy, called penetration, is the exact opposite of the above. The firm starts with a low introductory offer to get the word-of-mouth mechanism to start operating. Then it increases the price gradually. Given that competitors might react differently to each of the above strategies, what should the firm do in practice? Skim, penetrate, or have a combined strategy? And why should it employ such strategy? These are exactly the issues involved in this section.

Table 8.5 provides a summary of some of the major results derived by various studies for optimal strategies for three variables: pricing, advertising and product-introduction time. We have summarized these results for two industry settings – monopoly and oligopoly. The major results reported for each study respond to the issue raised in the study. For example, the study by Wilson & Norton [1989] deals with the issue of timing of a second-generation product. Fearing cannibalization, a monopolist has an option of either shelving it or introducing it later at some 'optimal' time. What should he do? The analytical results obtained by Wilson & Norton [1989] suggest that, in most cases, it is a 'now or never' decision. That is, the monopolist either introduces the product without any delay or he delays its introduction indefinitely. To further comment on the normative uses of diffusion models reported in Table 8.5, the following discussion is organized around dynamic pricing, dynamic advertising, timing and technological substitution, discounted profits vs. market share, price leadership, competitive price paths, and competitive advertising paths.

4.3. *Dynamic pricing*

It is clear that price can have an effect on the coefficient of innovation (say a), on the coefficient of imitation ($b = q/m$), and on the market potential (m).

If we assume that the market potential m is defined in such a way that it includes all potential buyers at the *lowest* conceivable price (say at a price that is equal to

Table 8.5
Optimal marketing-mix strategies for innovation diffusion
A. *Industry setting: Monopoly*

Issue and marketing-mix variable	Major assumptions/comments	Major normative results	Illustrative references
Price How should a monopolist price a new product over its life-cycle	1. Price interacts with diffusion (rate of adoption). 2. Demand saturation effect causes decline in price over time and diffusion effect causes price to increase over time. The experience effect (learning by doing) causes a decline in price over time.	For a long planning horizon, if the imitation effect is dominating, price first increases and then decreases.	Robinson & Lakhani [1975], Dolan & Jeuland [1981], Kalish [1983], Clarke, Darrough & Heineke [1982]
	Price has a multiplicative cycle effect on diffusion and interacts with experience curve.	Price declines over time.	Kalish [1983], Bass & Bultez [1982]
	Price affects market potential.	Price declines over time.	Kalish [1983]
How should a monopolist price over time a new product that can be copied?	Monopolist produces a new product that can be copied. Market potential is affected by price.	If the product is not protected gainst copying, price is initially high and then decreases as copying increases.	Nascimento & Vanhonacker [1988]
How should a monopolist price a repeat-purchased product over its life-cycle?	Price affects market potential.	1. Price increases monotonically over time. 2. With experience effect, price may first increase (strong imitation effect) then decrease (strong experience effect).	Feichtinger [1982], Jorgensen [1983, 1986], Kalish [1983], Jeuland & Dolan [1982]
How should a monopolist price over time a new product or service whose consumption value increases with the expansion of the 'network' of adopters referred to as a network externality (e.g. electronic mail)?	Price and cumulative adoption effects market potential.	Price increases over time.	Dhebar & Oren [1985]

Advertising			
How should a monopolist advertise a new product over time?	Advertising affects the coefficients of innovation and/or imitation. Three types of response functions can be used to represent this effect: linear, concave (diminishing returns), S-shape (increasing and then diminishing returns).	1. Linear response function implies a blitz followed by a constant maintenance level. 2. If advertising affects only the innovators, concave response function implies a policy where advertising decreases over time, gradually approaching the maintenance level. If advertising affects imitators, concave response function implies a policy where advertising increases over time. 3. S-shaped response function implies a high-intensity blitz level followed by a pulsing policy.	Horsky & Simon [1983], Dockner & Jorgensen [1988], Mahajan & Muller [1986].
Timing			
When should a monopolist introduce a product if both positive and negative word-of-mouth affect the diffusion process? How should the product be advertised over time?	Members in a social system pass through three stages in innovation decision process – unaware, potential customers, and adopters. Both potential customers and adopters circulate positive as well as negative word-of-mouth.	Optimal timing calls for advertising before the product is introduced and withdrawal of a product after the end of advertising period	Mahajan, Muller & Kerin [1984]
When should a monopolist introduce a second-generation product? Should the firm shelve it or introduce it as soon as it is available?	No pricing or advertising effect.	In most cases, the optimal timing decision is 'now or never'. If optimal introduction time exists, it occurs early in the life-cycle of the first product.	Wilson & Norton [1989]
B. *Industry setting: Oligopoly*			
Price			
How will firms in an oligopoly price their products over their life-cycle?	Price has a multiplicative effect on diffusion. Demand saturation causes decline in price. Diffusion	Monopoly results extend to the oligopoly case: If imitation effect is strong, price	Thompson & Teng [1984], Clarke & Dolan [1984], Dockner & Jorgensen [1988]

cont'd

Table 8.5 (cont'd)

Issue and marketing-mix variable	Major assumptions/comments	Major normative results	Illustrative references
	effect causes price increase. Experience effect causes a decline in price.	increases initially, and if planning horizon is long, it decreases towards the end of planning horizon.	
How does an industry set price of a new product class over time?	Market price is a function of quantities set by oligopolists.		Rao & Bass [1985]
Advertising			
How would firms in an oligopoly advertise their products over time?	Advertising affects innovators or imitators: linear or concave advertising response.	1. In many cases, advertising starts with a high level that decreases to a constant-maintenance policy. 2. Emphasis on final market shares causes an increase in advertising towards the end of the planning horizon. 3. In some cases, advertising may increase. Moreover, in some cases advertising for one competitor may increase while that of the second competitor may decrease, or both may increase.	Deal [1979], Teng & Thompson [1983], Thompson & Teng [1984], Erickson [1985]
Timing			
Does the order of entry affect long-term market share? How would anticipation of entry affect investment decision of a monopolist?	Multiplicative price effect on diffusion.	1. Order of entry has no long-term effects on final market shares 2. The monopolist who does not foresee entry overcapitalizes as opposed to the far-sighted monopolist who anticipates entry.	Fershtman, Mahajan & Muller [1990]
How would anticipation of entry affect pricing decision of a monopolist?	Multiplicative price effect on diffusion	Far-sighted monopolist who anticipates entry reduces price as compared to a surprised monopolist who does not foresee entry.	Eliashberg & Jeuland [1986]

the marginal cost of producing the product) then market potential is not affected by price, by definition. If, however, we define the market potential so as to include all potential buyers at the *current* price then its size varies with price. The marketing literature is divided on this issue. Most researchers, such as Robinson & Lakhani [1975], Bass [1980], Dolan & Jeuland [1981], Bass & Bultez [1982], Kalish & Lilien [1986a] Thompson & Teng [1984], Mahajan & Muller [1990] and Eliashberg & Jeuland [1986], have preferred an approach similar to the first, while Kalish [1983], Rao & Bass [1985], Horsky [1990] and Kalish & Lilien [1986b] have preferred the other.

An assumption, that is not usually critical to the analysis but simplifies formalization of the problem considerably is that the effect of price on both coefficients of innovation and imitation is the same, that is, $a(p) = ag(p)$ and $b(p) = bg(p)$. In addition, the most commonly used function is negative exponential, i.e. $g(p) = \mathrm{e}^{-\varepsilon p}$ for some elasticity parameter ε. The resultant equation is as follows:

$$\mathrm{d}N/\mathrm{d}t = (a + bN)(m - N)\mathrm{e}^{-\varepsilon p}. \qquad (15)$$

Formally the firm chooses a price path $p(t)$ that maximizes its long-run discounted profits, subject to Equation (15). Since instantaneous profits are $(p - c)\mathrm{d}N/\mathrm{d}t$, where c is the average cost of the production, total long-term discounted profits (J) are given by the equation

$$J = \int_0^T (p - c)\mathrm{d}N/\mathrm{d}t\,\mathrm{e}^{-rt}\,\mathrm{d}t \qquad (16)$$

where r is the discount rate and T is the planning horizon.

The main results of such a model are as follows: if T is relatively short, price will be increasing throughout the planning horizon T. If, however, T is long enough, price will have a diffusion-based pattern of first increasing and then decreasing. For a formal proof see Kalish [1983]. The intuitive explanation is as follows.

The firm would like to price-discriminate over time and thus employ a skimming price policy. It realizes, however, that a high initial price will negatively affect the diffusion rate for its product. Thus it starts with an initial low price and increases it gradually as the word-of-mouth process builds up. Only after this process has reached its peak can the firm resort to price discrimination over time for the remaining population, and thus reduces the price gradually. If the time horizon is too short for the word-of-mouth process to reach its maximum, the firm cannot take advantage of the later strategy and so the price path remains monotonic.

Specifically, break down Equation (15) into its components as follows:

$$\mathrm{d}N/\mathrm{d}t = a(m - N)\mathrm{e}^{-\varepsilon p} + bN(m - N)\mathrm{e}^{-\varepsilon p}. \qquad (17)$$

The first part of the equation is the *demand-saturation* effect while the second is the *diffusion effect* [see Rao & Bass, 1985]. The demand-saturation part of the equation causes the downward 'pull' on the price while the diffusion part is responsible for the upward pull. Since the initial periods are critical to the diffusion part, price starts low so as to encourage later diffusion. As demand becomes more saturated it takes over in terms of its importance and price declines so as to take advantage of possible price discrimination while there is still enough demand 'left over' to make this profitable. With a long time-horizon, the period in which price increases is very prolonged. Since this is rarely seen in practice, the model has to take into account one of the major factors affecting price – the experience, or learning-by-doing, effect.

If the firm reduces its cost of production as it 'learns by doing' (the so-called learning-by-doing – LBD – effect), then cost will decrease and this will have a downward effect on the price. If this effect is large, price might decrease throughout the planning horizon. In addition, the above results are robust with respect to the functional form of the price function (Kalish [1983]). The fact that the price pattern is first increasing, then decreasing was also obtained by Narashimhan [1989] in a model that incorporates price expectations of fully rational consumers.

The empirical investigation of price effect conducted by Horsky [1990] suggests, however, that incorporating price into the population potential has better empirical support than the multiplicative model.

The model thus becomes the following:

$$\mathrm{d}N/\mathrm{d}t = (a + bN)(m(p) - N). \tag{18}$$

The results of the maximization problem is surprisingly similar to the previous one. Price first increases (provided the word-of-mouth coefficient b is large enough) and then decreases, see Kalish [1983] and Horsky [1990]. As before, an experience effect will tend to lower prices and therefore the combined effect might be a price decline throughout the planning horizon. It is important to realize that in both cases the *diffusion effect* (i.e. the word-of-mouth activity) is the one force that causes a price increase, while both the demand-saturation and experience effects cause a price decline. The net effect depends on the relative sizes and forces of these effects.

4.4. Dynamic advertising

The discussion that exists on the effect of the decision variable in the pricing literature did not appear at all in the advertising literature. Though the models and their treatment of advertising are not equivalent, in general they incorporated advertising into the coefficient of innovation since it is the 'external' coefficient that supplies information independently of the word-of-mouth (internal) activities. Such are the models by Dodson & Muller [1978], Dockner & Jorgensen [1988], Horsky & Simon [1983], Thompson & Teng [1984], Mahajan, Muller & Kerin [1984] and Kalish [1985]. Simon & Sebastian [1987] did incorporate advertising into the coefficient of imitation. Their coefficient of innovation, however, turned out to be negative, thus making generalizations from their work difficult. A comparison of some of the above models and the similarity between their treatments of advertising effects is found in Mahajan, Muller & Sharma [1984].

A typical approach is found in Horsky & Simon [1983].

The firm chooses a path of advertising A so as to maximize total discounted profits subject to the following equation:

$$\mathrm{d}N/\mathrm{d}t = (f(A) + bN)(m - N). \tag{19}$$

The parameter of innovation is thus a function of advertising, that in the Horsky & Simon case is chosen to be logarithmic, i.e. $f(A) = \alpha + \beta \ln(A)$ for some parameters α and β. In this model, as indeed in most of the works on advertising, it was found that the optimal path is monotonically decreasing through time. In most other works, however, an exponential decay (forgetting) parameter is added to the model so as to take into account the fact that sales will suffer if advertising is suddenly stopped altogether. This is formally done by adding a decay parameter δ to Equation (19) to arrive at the following:

$$\mathrm{d}N/\mathrm{d}t = (f(A) + bN)(m - N) - \delta N.$$

Three cases can be distinguished with respect to the shape of the advertising response function $f(A)$:

(a) The advertising response function is linear. In this case the optimal policy is to advertise at a maximal level until x reaches some desirable level, and then to maintain that level A^*. This maintenance level of A^* satisfies the requirement that $\dot{x} = 0$. For a formal proof see, for example, Mahajan, Muller & Kerin [1984].

(b) The advertising response function is concave. In this case the optimal policy is to start with a high level of advertising and to *gradually decrease* the level of the spending to the maintenance level of A^*. Horsky & Simon [1983] show this for a specific concave function (logarithmic) and no decay; thus their maintenance level is zero.

(c) The advertising response function is S-shaped. In this case, with the additional requirement that $b = 0$, i.e., no word-of-mouth communication, Mahajan & Muller [1986] show that in order to maintain advertising at a desired level the firm should theoretical pulse at an infinite frequency (chatter) between the two levels of $\hat{A}$ and zero. Since such a theoretical policy is clearly not feasible, the practical optimal policy is to pulse between these two levels. What Mahajan & Muller show is that very little is lost in terms of profits by pulsing instead of chattering, i.e. a relatively small number of pulses regain most of the optimal theoretical chattering policy. Mahajan & Muller also conjectured that for a pulsing policy, the total response is an increasing function of the number of cycles in the planning horizon. This conjecture was proven analytically by Sasieni [1989], who also proved that the optimal policy is to start with a high level of advertising and decrease it gradually. Maintenance then follows the one prescribed by Mahajan & Muller.

Mahajan & Muller also conjectured that given a small cost associated with each pulse over and above the regular advertising costs, the optimal policy would be pulsing and not chattering. This was indeed proved by Hahn & Hyun [1991].

4.5. Timing and technological substitution

Timing of a new-product introduction is a subject that has been neglected in marketing in general and in diffusion theory in particular. There are several issues to be considered: sequential vs. simultaneous introductions, shelving time of new products or technologies, advertising timing, and the like. The lack of works on the subject, we think, is not because of lack of interest. It is a dynamic issue in nature, and only recently has diffusion theory, which is the one dynamic area of marketing that could deal with such phenomena, started looking at normative issues and using diffusion models as tools to tackle these issues.

Optimal advertising timing in a specific context of negative word-of-mouth has been dealt with by Mahajan, Muller & Kerin [1984].

The marketer of a product, e.g. a movie, knows about negative reaction to its film. The only positive information in the market about the movie is carried by its advertising. How should the marketer time its advertising? The answer is as follows:

> The marketer starts advertising before it introduces the product and ends before it withdraws it.

The intuition behind this policy is as follows. Since the producer/marketer knows that the word-to-mouth mechanism will be against the product and it does not start until consumers have actually adopted it, the producer does not introduce the product initially, but instead builds a stock of potential customers by advertising well before the product introduction. In that way only positive information is circulated. Once the desired level of potential customers has been achieved, the producer introduces the product. The word-of-mouth process takes time to be effective, since it is proportional to the number of people who have adopted the product (penetration level). Therefore, for some time the producer enjoys a relatively stable adoption level (the level of the flow depends on the effectiveness of the producer's advertising blitz). Gradually, the word-of-mouth process starts building up, and consequently the number of potential customers drops.

When the level of potential customers drops to a prespecified level that depends on the profit schedule with relation to the adoption level, the producer withdraws the product since, at that level, its gross operating profits (revenues net of all costs except advertising) is zero. Naturally, since the marginal value of an additional potential customer at that time is zero, and since advertising is related to this marginal value, it is worthwhile to stop advertising *before* product withdrawal time, but after sales have reached their peak.

A critical issue in the introduction of a new technology is the market timing/entry decision. A too-early entry runs the risk of poor performance by the product because of pushing a 'half-baked' innovation into the market. A late introduction is costly in terms of lost sales and possibly loss of a monopoly position. This is the subject of the work of Kalish & Lilien [1986b] that was applied to the innovative photovoltaic program of the US Department of Energy.

They used a diffusion model in which the market potential is a function of price, as in Kalish [1983], the coefficient of innovation is a function of advertising, as in Horsky & Simon [1983], and the coefficient of imitation is a function of the product's perceived performance. Using *prelaunch* data using experts' estimates and survey questionnaire, they arrived at the conclusion that entry should have been delayed by as much as 6 years. This late introduction (assuming no competition entered in the meantime) would have given additional sales up to three times at the specified target year (10 years from the early introduction).

Since the cost of introduction of a new product commits large amount of funds, launching of a new product requires careful planning to ensure desired market success of a new product [Lilien & Yoon, 1990].

One of the most critical issues in launching of a new product and especially a new generation of an existing technology is its introduction time. This is the subject of research of two papers: Wilson & Norton [1989] use an extension of the diffusion model by Kalish [1985] to study the optimal-timing decision for a second generation of a product. Their optimal-timing rule calls for the firm to either introduce the new generation simultaneously with the first, or not to introduce the second generation at all. They very aptly called this the 'now or never' rule. Mahajan & Muller [1990] use an extension of the Bass model that includes cannibalization and leap-frogging to study the optimal-timing decision of a second generation of a product. They came up with a modified version of the Wilson & Norton result: the firm should either introduce the second generation as soon as it is available or delay its introduction until the first generation is in its maturity stage.

The difference between the two results lies in the models' setting. In Wilson & Norton the firm does not maximize net present value of a stream of net cash flow as in Mahajan & Muller but rather profits at the introduction time of the second generation. Therefore, the 'bang-bang' property of the 'now or never' result is smoothed to a 'now or at maturity' result of Mahajan & Muller.

Another key timing issue involves international penetration of new products.

In understanding the diffusion of an innovation across countries, an important concept of diffusion theory relevant to predicting the global diffusion is the nature of communication that about the innovation between two countries [Eliashberg & Helsen, 1987]. The ability of change agents or adopters of an innovation in one country, called the lead market, to communicate with the potential adopters in the second country, referred to as the foreign market, provides an additional external source of information to the second country which influences the rate of adoption among its potential adopters [Gatignon, Eliashberg & Robertson, 1989]. The potential adopters in the second country observe the success of the product in the lead market. If it is successful, the risk associated with the innovation is reduced. This reduction in risk is translated into higher adoption rate in the second country. That is, it is the *lead effect* that creates an important source of information about the innovation from the lead market to the foreign market. The lead effect (if it creates positive information about the product) works in the favor of a manufacturer and influences the lead time – the time interval between the timings of the new-product introduction in the lead market and the foreign market. The equations that describe the diffusion in two countries where one country leads the other are as follows:

Let $N(t)$ and $M(t)$ denote cumulative adoption of the product in the two countries and α and β denote the coefficients of innovation and imitation in the second country. While the diffusion in the lead country follows a standard Bass process, in the second country the diffusion equation is as follows:

$$\mathrm{d}M/\mathrm{d}t = (\alpha + \beta M/m_2 + \delta N/m_1)(m_2 - M) \tag{20}$$

where m_1 and m_2 are the market potential of the product in the two countries and δ is the lead coefficient.

Mahajan, Muller & Kalish [1990] incorporated the concept of lead effect into a competitive environment in which the main issue is whether to follow a *sequential* strategy (called 'waterfall') in which the firm introduces its product in one market after the other, or a *simultaneous* strategy (called 'sprinkler') in which the firm introduces the product in all markets at once. What they found is that today's market conditions that include globalization of markets and more intense competition favor the sprinkler strategy over waterfall. The reason is that the more intense the competition, the more is lost by waiting and introducing the product sequentially, in terms of market share and profits, than is gained via the lead-effect mechanism (δ).

4.6. *Discounted profits vs. market share*

The objective functions in most works in the diffusion area are long-term profits, usually discounted. The reasonability of this assumption is the question posed by Deal [1979]. The framework he uses is similar to Eliashberg & Jeuland [1986] in that a duopoly is described with x and y denoting sales of firm 1 and 2, respectively. Deal uses advertising as the control variable and includes a decay factor such as in Equation (6). The objective function, however, is composed of the terms: profits, aggregated up to the planning horizon T, and market share at that time. Firm 1, for instance, maximizes the following expression:

$$w_1 x(T)/(x(T) + y(T)) + \int_0^T ((p_1 - c_1)x(t) - u_1^2(t))\mathrm{d}t, \tag{21}$$

where w_1 is the weight factor of the market-share portion of the objective function, p_1 and c_1 are the price and cost (assumed constant) and u_1^2 is the cost of having the effect of u_1.

The numerical analysis performed by Deal shows the problematic nature of such an objective function. Consider the symmetric situation in which the firms are equal in all parameters. The result is an equal market share and a profit index of, say, 100. Now retain all parameters at their current, equal value, and increase the weight parameter of the market share of firm 2 only (i.e. w_2). As this parameter is increased to 10, 20 and 30 times its original value, the market share of firm 2 indeed increases from 50% to 66, 71 and 76%. The profits of firm 2, however, deteriorate rapidly. For every \$100 profits at a symmetric situation, profits decline to about \$70, \$35 and to a loss of \$36. Clearly this firm would not retain its leadership for long with such losses while the second firm remains at the \$100 original profits.

Objectives such as sales or market share make sense in the short run only because they presumably signal higher profits in the long run. Thus, objective functions such as the one in Equation (20) are reasonable long-term objectives if we can translate the market share term to long-term profitability. This translation would tell us the 'correct' weight term w_1 in this function. Since to the best of our knowledge, this has not been done, long-term profits remain the one subjective used in the diffusion (and dynamic economics) literature.

4.7. *Price leadership*

The standard solution or 'equilibrium' concept used in almost all of the works on competition in marketing is the Nash (or open-loop) equilibrium concept. Each firm chooses a price path or advertising path so as to maximize long-term discounted profits, given the second firm's price path.

This constitutes an equilibrium in the following sense: the price path will not, in general, be constant. Along the price path a player can decide at each point of time whether to stick to his or her original planned path or to deviate (by reducing the price, for example). If the player does not have any incentive *unilaterally* to deviate, and so does the second player, the price paths constitute an equilibrium.

Although this has a clear intuitive appeal, this approach has one drawback – it does not indicate *how* these price paths were chosen to begin with. The firms pick the exact price paths such that each path is a best response against the other price. The mechanism that leads to such a simultaneous choice is ignored. Two notable exceptions are the papers by Clarke & Dolan [1984] and Thompson & Teng [1984]. In both works the idea of a price leader is presented. The leader announces a price (that can change in time) and the followers adhere to the announced price. This is somewhat troublesome, since the follower can clearly do better. In what it does, it does not solve any maximization problem, it just follows the price leader. If it would behave rationally, a different price path would have been followed. Only if all the parameters of the problem of the follower and the leader were identical is such behavior optimal.

Another approach is given by Clarke & Dolan. The leader (either by size or by the fact that it is the incumbent firm) announces a price and the follower chooses the price that maximizes its profits given the leader's price. This makes the follower's decision a rational one, and describes well circumstances under which there exists a natural price leader.

4.8. Competitive price paths

Recall that in the monopoly case, the price path has an overshooting, diffusion-based pattern that was caused by two opposing effects: the diffusion part of the diffusion Equation (17) that causes a penetration (increasing) policy and a demand part that causes a skimming (decreasing) policy. The combination of these two forces formed the overshooting pattern.

This result extends to the oligopoly market structure as well, as is shown by Rao & Bass [1985], Mahajan & Muller [1986], Clarke & Dolan [1984], Thompson & Teng [1984], Eliashberg & Jeuland [1986], Nascimento & Vanhonacker [1988], and Dockner & Jorgensen [1988].

For example, Rao & Bass treat two separate cases: one in which the diffusion equation has only a demand-saturation effect and one in which it has only a diffusion effect. Indeed, in the first case prices decline over time while in the second prices increase through time. In Eliashberg & Jeuland, only demand saturation is modeled and so prices decline over time. In Thompson & Teng, price indeed declines in most cases, but since a simulation technique was used we cannot be certain that it has exhausted all possibilities. The results, however, were reported to be similar to the monopoly case. In Dockner & Jorgensen, the results of the monopoly case were extended analytically to the oligopoly case with striking similarities both in the patterns and in the causes, i.e. diffusion vs. market-saturation effects.

Mahajan & Muller [1991] show the optimal price paths to have indeed the overshooting pattern in a duopoly situation in which one duopolist produces one main primary product (such as computer hardware) and the other produces a contingent product (such as software). In addition, they found the following: a monopolist pricing the two products, prices the primary product as well as the contingent product *lower* than two firms independently producing each of the two products. Moreover, contrary to common belief, the monopolist makes more money from the primary product than from the contingent product.

Eliashberg & Jeuland [1986], who consider an oligopoly with a process involving only a market-saturation mechanism, indeed found an increasing market-price pattern as expected. They considered a case in which one player (newcomer) entered late and compared two incumbents – a surprised incumbent monopolist who has not known or has not considered the fact that a newcomer will enter versus a far-sighted monopolist who has planned ahead. The price of the far-sighted monopolist is always *lower* than that of the surprised monopolist.

The reason is as follows: the surprised monopolist expects a longer monopoly period than the far-sighted one and therefore follows a slower penetration strategy than is optimal, thus charging a higher price. The far-sighted monoplist overestimates competition and acts as if it would be at a strong disadvantage during the duopoly period. It thus wishes to leave a small fraction of the market at the end of the monopoly period. It thus prices lower and therefore penetrates faster.

We thus conclude that much of our intuition concerning optimal pricing carries over from the monopoly situation to the oligopoly market structure.

4.9. Competitive advertising paths

While we could end the section on competitive pricing with an encouraging note, we find it more difficult doing so when dealing with competitive advertising. Of the three main recent works on advertising in an oligopoly, no clear picture emerges. In Erickson [1985], Deal [1979] and Thompson & Teng [1984], various, very different policies emerged as equilibrium policies.

Erickson presents three types of paths that were found in the simulation as equilibrium strategies: advertising of one firm increasing while that of the rival decreased, one at a zero level and one decreasing, and both increasing. Unfortunately, no clear classification was presented as to when and why one policy prevails over another.

A few policies are also found in Thompson & Teng and Deal. Both present one possible explanation for these policies: a firm that places much emphasis on market share (as opposed to profits) will tend to increase advertising toward the end of the planning horizon so as to achieve higher market share at this point of time. A firm that places emphasis on profits more than final market share will tend to start with a high level of advertising, and later on to rely on the carry-over effect and decrease advertising spending.

Fershtman, Mahajan & Muller [1990] investigated a problem that is the counterpart of the Eliashberg & Jeuland [1986] paper to the case of advertising. As in Eliashberg & Jeuland they considered a case in which a newcomer entered late and compared two incumbents – a surprised one who has not considered the fact that a newcomer will enter and a far-sighted monopolist who has planned ahead for such a contingency. The advertising level of the surprised monopolist is always *larger* than that of the far-sighted monopolist. The reason is that the surprised monopolist plans to accumulate advertising (in a form of goodwill) to reach a final level that is higher than he/she is going to reach eventually. This is so since the steady-state level of advertising of a monopolist is higher than that of each of the oligopolists, and so the surprised monopolist plans an advertsing path as if he/she were going to remain a monopolist for the duration of the game and thus *overcapitalizes*.

5. Conclusions and discussion

After a review of the emerging literature on innovation-diffusion modeling in marketing, it is important to highlight research issues which must be addressed in order to make these models theoretically more sound and practically more effective and realistic. Such research possibilities are summarized in Table 8.6 and brief explanatory comments on these research possibilities are provided below.

Table 8.6
A research agenda

Research areas	Research possibilities
Basic diffusion models	• Empirical studies on the profiles of adopters whose purchase decisions are influenced by external information sources. • Analytical procedures that can assist in linking sales data to number of adopters for multiunit-adoption innovations. • Effect of consumer expectations on product-category growth. • Exploration of recent developments in hazard models as a unifying theme for comparing diffusion models. • Understanding of diffusion processes at the micro (individual) level.
Refinements and extensions	• Approaches (such as hazard models) for incorporating the effect of marketing-mix variables such as price. • Optimal product designs from multiattribute diffusion models. • Diffusion of generations of technology and timing issues related to successive generations of an innovation. • Contingent products – hardware/software effects. • Entry/exit effects on product-category growth. • Nature of supply/distribution restrictions. • Effect of market interventions on growth patterns. • Effect of rollout strategy in multiple markets on product-category growth. • Negative word-of-mouth via multistage diffusion models. • Modeling and predicting product take-off.
Use of diffusion models	• Empirical comparison with other sales forecasting time-series models. • Conditions under which diffusion models work or do not work. • Empirical studies related to hypothesis testing (descriptive studies). • Empirical evidence for working hypotheses generated by normative use of diffusion models. • Validation: results of actual implementation of diffusion models.

5.1. Basic diffusion models

Although several assumptions underlying the Bass model have been of concern in 1980s [Mahajan & Wind, 1986b], we believe that five issues need further investigation.

5.1.1. Adoptions due to internal influence

One of the key features of the Bass model is that it explicitly considers the influence of internal (word-of-mouth) as well as external sources of communication on innovation diffusion. As depicted in Figure 8.2a, the Bass model assumes that adopters whose purchase decisions are influenced by external sources of information are present at any stage of the diffusion process. Such adopters, however, should not be labeled innovators since innovators, by definition, are characterized as the first adopters of an innovation [Mahajan, Muller & Srivastava, 1990]. The question now is what are the characteristics of adopters who, despite a large product penetration in the marketplace, are predominantly influenced by external sources? How do they differ from innovators and other adopter categories on those characteristics? Since within a certain time period in the diffusion process, the Bass model implies presence of adopters due both to internal influence and external influence, how do those two groups differ from each other?

In an empirical study, Feick & Price [1987] suggest that in any social system, there are individuals who assimilate and disseminate information on products (and therefore influence others) and tend to rely on external sources of information. They label these individuals 'market mavens'. Based on their empirical results, they conclude, however, that 'the concepts of the market maven and the innovative consumer are distinct' [1987, p. 90]. Given the study by Feick & Price [1987], research questions can be raised about the linkage between market mavens and adopters who buy due to external influence in the Bass model.

5.1.2. Multiple adoptions

The Bass model has been developed to represent the conversion of potential adopters to adopters. It explicitly assumes that each potential adopter buys only one unit of the product. On the other hand, there are innovations that are bought in multiple units by the potential adopters (e.g. adoption of multiple units of scanners by a supermarket, adoption of multiple units of personal computers by a firm). For these innovations, it is necessary to link the sales data with the number of adopters by using a function that explicitly takes into consideration the multiple-unit-adoption behavior of the potential adopters [see Norton & Bass, 1987].

5.1.3. Effect of consumer expectations

For certain innovations (e.g. computers), consumer expectations about an innovation's future characteristics (e.g. price) influence purchase intensions [see, for example, Winer, 1985; Holak, Lehmann & Sultan, 1987]. For such innovations, in addition to influencing the nature of the adoption curve, consumer expectations can also influence the optimal marketing-mix strategy used by a firm. For example, incorporating consumer expectations related to price in the Bass model, Narasimhan [1989] suggests that the optimal pricing strategy for a monopolist cycles over time.

Given its importance in understanding diffusion dynamics, we expect to see a lot more theoretical and empirical work in the coming years explicitly incorporating consumer expectations in the Bass model.

5.1.4. Exploration of recent developments in hazard models

The different diffusion models can be viewed as making different assumptions about the 'hazard rate' for non-adopters, as a function of time. (The hazard rate being the likelihood that an individual who has remained a non-adopter through time t becomes an adopter in the next instant of time.) The Bass model specifies this as a linear function of previous adopters. Since the publication of the Bass model, however, a great deal of work developing and applying hazard models has appeared in statistics, biometrics, and econometrics literatures [e.g. Cox & Oakes, 1984; Kalbfleisch & Prentice, 1980]; for possible marketing applications of hazard models, see Helsen & Schmittlein [1989]; for interpretation of diffusion models as hazard models, see Lavaraj & Gore [1990]. The key developments in hazard models over the last decade have been in the area of understanding covariate effects on the hazard rate (and consequently on duration times). This is particularly important since attempts to incorporate marketing-mix variables (and other covariate effects) in diffusion models have to date been quite limited in scope, and *ad hoc* in their choice of model specifications for those effects. Exploration of recent developments in the hazard-modeling framework may provide a unifying theme for understanding of covariate/marketing-mix effects in diffusion models.

5.1.5. Understanding of diffusion processes at the micro (individual) level

Diffusion models based on individual-level adoption decisions offer a major opportunity to study the actual pattern of social communication, and its impact on product perceptions, preferences and ultimate adoption. The empirical evidence provided by Chatterjee & Eliashberg [1990] on the developments of aggregate diffusion models from the individual-level adoption decisions, although limited, is encouraging. Further empirical work on such models may suggest dynamics at the individual level may assist in developing the aggregate diffusion models prior to launch.

5.2. Refinements and extensions

In Table 8.6, we have listed ten possibilities for further refinement and extension of the Bass model. They are briefly discussed below.

(1) In their review of diffusion models Mahajan & Muller [1979] concluded that it is not clear how the marketing-mix variables should be incorporated into the Bass model. The few empirical studies reported in the 1980s still don't provide conclusive guidelines on this question. Despite the arguments made in favor of including price in the market potential, empirical studies on consumer durables by Kamakura & Balasubramanian [1988] and Jain & Rao [1990] suggest that price affects the rate of diffusion (by influencing the coefficients of external influence and internal influence). Similarly, regarding the inclusion of advertising in the Bass model, the two reported empirical studies favor different alternatives – Horsky & Simon [1983] recommend that it be included in the coefficient of external influence whereas Simon & Sebastian [1987] report that they find better results by including it in the coefficient of internal influence. It is interesting to note, however, that although both of these studies examine the effect of advertising on the diffusion of a service (a banking service by Horsky & Simon [1983] and the telephone service by Simon & Sebastian [1987]), they are conducted in two different markets (the USA and West Germany) and under different market conditions (there was a supply problem with the availability of telephones in West Germany). Whether these differences had an impact on the reported results is an open empirical question.

Given the importance of including marketing-mix variables in understanding diffusion dynamics, we do anticipate to see more empirical work including on other marketing-mix variables such as distribution.

(2) Several empirical studies (see Table 8.4) have incorporated product attributes in the Bass model. A natural extension of these studies is to develop procedures to determine optimal product design to obtain the desired penetration rate.

(3) For high-technology products the time interval between successive generations of technologies has been decreasing. Norton & Bass [1987] have shown how diffusions of successive generations interact within the context of the Bass model. Forecasting possibilities stemming from this work appear to be promising. Extensions involving pricing of generations of technology would appear to be desirable and feasible.

When should a firm introduce a second-generation product? Although the analytical results provided by Wilson & Norton [1989] suggest the answer 'now or never', their results exclude the impact of other variables such as price. Their study, however, deals with an important question. Further theoretical and empirical work dealing with this question will be very timely.

(4) For high-technology products the product offering of a firm generally includes both hardware and software (e.g. Nintendo hardware (key pad) and Nintendo software (video games) for children). Therefore, given the contingency nature of the relationship, it is important to develop diffusion models that examine the diffusion of the entire bundle of product offerings. In addition to forecasting, normative questions may relate to its optimal pricing and distribution. For example, how should a monopolist (e.g. Nintendo) manufacture and distribute its hardware and software? Should it keep a monopoly on both of them? Should it keep a monopoly on hardware and create a oligopoly for software so as to increase demand for the hardware in which it is a monopolist?

(5) How does the number of competitors and rivalry among them influence the growth of a product category? Does the growth affect the entry/exit patterns of competitors? Answers to these questions are within the domain of the diffusion-modeling framework and provide a linkage with the strategic planning literature. Theoretical and empirical work on these questions will further enhance the utility of diffusion models.

(6) It was pointed out earlier that supply restrictions influence diffusion patterns. For certain type of products (e.g. drugs), it may be desirable to retard the diffusion process by controlling their supply and distribution. Further empirical and theoretical work, therefore, on this linkage would enable management to control the life-cycle of a product by managing the supply.

(7) Market interventions (e.g. patent violations) represent externalities that can influence the growth pattern of a new product. Although the use of intervention analysis is well established in the time-series analysis literature, no attempt seems to have been made to conduct intervention analysis with the diffusion models [Mahajan, Sharma & Wind, 1985]. Theoretical and empirical work in this area could assist in assessing the impact (e.g. assessment of patent-violation damages in a legal case) of market interventions on the product like-cycle.

(8) Although the integration of the time and spatial dimensions has been of interest to geographers, their integration is equally important im marketing to evaluate the alternative product-distribution strategies across markets. Such

extensions of the Bass model could assist in evaluating the impact of how and where a product is made available on the growth of a new product.

(9) The diffusion literature has consistently emphasized the importance of negative word-of-mouth on the growth of a new product [Mahajan, Muller & Kerin, 1984]. The multistage extensions of the Bass model do offer an avenue to consider its impact on the growth pattern. These extensions, however, lack empirical validation. Data collection and estimation procedures need to be developed to make these extensions practically viable.

(10) Not all new products are accepted by consumers at the time of their introduction. Some products are much slower than others in being accepted by potential adopters. That is, they differ in terms of how long it takes them to 'take off'. The take-off phenomenon is not explicitly considered by the Bass model. The Bass model assumes the presence of a certain number of consumers before take off (i.e. pm). Extensions of the Bass model that explicitly consider this phenomenon will be useful in explaining and predicting the take-off behavior of a new product.

5.3. *Use of diffusion models*

One of the critical uses of diffusion models has been for forecasting the first-purchase sales volume curve. In recent years, questions have been raised, however, about the forecasting accuracy of diffusion models [Bernhardt & MacKenzie, 1972; Heeler & Hustad, 1980]. We tend to sympathize with such findings and re-echo here the plea by Mahajan & Wind [1986a] and Bass [1986] that further empirical work is needed to identify conditions under which diffusion models work or do not work. For example, as pointed out earlier, recent work by Jain, Mahajan & Muller [1991] suggests that it is inappropriate to use the Bass model in international settings where the supply for the product is restricted. Furthermore, since the diffusion models capture the dynamics of innovation diffusion for the first-time buyers, it is not clear that the same diffusion dynamics are applicable to replacement sales. Therefore, the use of diffusion models for such adoption data may not be appropriate [see, for example, Bayus, 1988; Bayus, Hong & Labe, 1989]. Finally, diffusion models are imitation models. Any S-shaped curve, however, may not be a result of the imitation process and alternative time-series models may be more appropriate for such data [Mahajan, Sharma & Bettis, 1988]. Even in the presence of the imitation effect, it may be necessary to systematically examine various diffusion models to identify the one that best describes the data [Rust & Schmittlein, 1985]. There is also a growing body of literature on 'chaos theory' suggesting that for certain parameter values, diffusion models generate persistent chaotic behavior within predictable boundaries [Gordon & Greenspan, 1988]. Understanding of such phenomenon may be essential to decipher the impact of changes which affect the diffusion dynamics.

The use of diffusion models to test diffusion-based hypotheses is very encouraging. The illustrative empirical studies documented in Table 8.4 clearly attest to their potential use for such applications. We anticipate seeing a lot more empirical work in the future that will use a diffusion-modeling framework to test hypotheses related to life-cycle dynamics. Examples include the following questions. How does the number of competitors change over the life-cycle of a product? How does the number of brands available in a market influence the growth of a product? How does the rivalry among competitors in an industry affect the life-cycle of a product?

The use of diffusion models to derive normative results for the dynamics of innovation diffusion received a lot of attention in the 1980s. However, as summarized in Table 8.5, these results are simply working hypotheses. Furthermore, the nature of these results is contingent upon the assumptions made in the analytical derivation of such results. For most of these studies, the analytical elegance surpasses the empirical validation of the derived results. Empirical evidence is required to find out if and when the firms use the derived normative strategies.

Finally, it is important to acknowledge that a number of firms have used diffusion models for forecasting the demand of a new product. By sharing their experiences, industry users can contribute to the further validation of diffusion models.

Appendix

The use of the Bass model for forecasting the diffusion of an innovation requires the estimation of three parameters – the coefficients of external influence (p), the coefficient of internal influence (q), and the market potential (m). Although the estimate for the market potential of a new product can be derived from the diffusion time-series data, recent applications of diffusion models report better forecasting results by using exogenous sources of information (such as market surveys, secondary sources, management judgments, or other analytical models) for estimating m [see, for example, Teotia & Raju, 1986; Souder & Quaddus, 1982; Mesak & Mikhail, 1988; Heeler & Hustad, 1980].

In the 1980s, a number of estimation procedures were proposed to estimate the Bass-model parameters. Meta-analyzing the results of 15 such diffusion studies, Sultan, Farley & Lehmann [1990] report average values of 0.03 and 0.38 for the coefficients of external influence and internal influence, respectively. Their analyses further suggest that the values of these coefficients are influenced by the type of the estimation procedure used to estimate them. For a practitioner, the main questions are which of the several estimation procedures should be used and why. Answers to these questions partially depend upon the amount of data available to estimate these parameters. We review here estimation procedures that are designed to develop estimates both in the absence of and in the presence of the time-series diffusion data. A brief analytical description of these procedures is given in Table 8.A1.

A.1. No prior data are available

If no data are available, parameter estimates can be obtained by using either management judgments or the diffusion history of analogous products.

One procedure that exclusively employs management judgments to estimate the diffusion parameters is an algebraic estimation procedure suggested by

Table 8.A1
Estimation procedures for the Bass diffusion model

Procedure type	Procedure type description	Proposed by	Analytical description
Algebraic estimation procedures	These procedures are based on information obtained from management or other analogous products. No prior diffusion data for the product under consideration are required.	Mahajan & Sharma [1986]	The procedure requires information from management on three items: (1) the potential market size (m), (2) the timing of the occurrence of the noncumulative adoption curve (T^*), and (3) the adoption level at the peak time (n^*). Once peak is guessed, the following expressions can be used to estimate the coefficient of external influence (p) and internal influence (q): $$p = \frac{n^*(m-2N^*)}{(m-N^*)^2}, \quad q = \frac{n^*m}{(m-N^*)} \quad \text{and} \quad T^* = \frac{(m-N^*)}{2n^*} \ln\left[\frac{m}{m-2N^*}\right]$$ The last equation is solved numerically for N^* to obtain p and q from the other two equations.
		Lawrence & Lawton [1981]	This procedure requires information on three items: (1) the potential market size (m), (2) the number of adoptions in the first time period ($N(1)$) and (3) an estimate of the sum of the coefficients of external influence and internal influence ($p + q = s$). Knowing these items, the following expression can be used to estimate p and q. Let $$\frac{q}{p} = \frac{m(1-e^{-s}) - N(1)}{N(1)e^{-s}} = r \text{ (say)},$$ $$p = \frac{s}{1+r} \quad \text{and} \quad q = \frac{sr}{1+r}.$$
Product/market attribute-based analogical estimation procedures	These procedures use product and/or social-system characteristics to explain parameters of diffusion patterns of existing products. Once a regression	Srivastava, Mahajan, Ramaswami & Cherian [1985]	This procedure requires information on the market potential (m) and estimates of diffusion parameters based on historical diffusion patterns of existing products as a function of perceived product attributes (relative advantage, compatibility, complexity, trialability and observability), i.e., $$p_i = f(x_{1i}, x_{2i}, \ldots, x_{ki}, \ldots),$$ $$q_i = f(x_{1i}, x_{2i}, \ldots, x_{ki}, \ldots),$$

model is developed explaining these relationships, characteristics of a new product and/or a market can be used to project life-cycle of a new product. These procedures, therefore, require historical diffusion data on existing products but not on the new product under consideration.		where p_i and q_i are the coefficients of external influence and internal influence, respectively, of a new product i and x_{ki} is the perceived value of product i on attribute k. The coefficients are first obtained by fitting the Bass model to the historical data of existing products and attribute values are obtained from consumer surveys. Once p and q have been expressed as a function of product attributes, perceived values of various attributes of a new product are used to estimate its diffusion-model parameters. The procedure has been illustrated for predicting the diffusion of new investment alternatives for consumers.
	Gatignon, Eliashberg & Robertson [1989]	This procedure is conceptually similar to the procedure by Srivastava et al. It, however, expresses the coefficients of external influence and internal influence of existing products in various markets as a function of market characteristics (rather than product attributes), i.e., $$\frac{\mathrm{d}N_{ij}(t)}{\mathrm{d}t} = (p_{ij} + q_{ij}N_{ij}(t))(m_j - N_{ij}(t)),$$ $$p_{ij} = f(y_{1j}, y_{2j}, \ldots y_{qj}, \ldots),$$ $$q_{ij} = f(y_{1j}, y_{2j}, \ldots y_{qj}, \ldots),$$ where p_{ij} and q_{ij} are the coefficients of external influence and internal influence, respectively, for product i in market j, y_{qj} is the qth attribute of market j, $N_{ij}(t)$ is the cumulative number of adopters of product i in market j, and m_j is the market potential of market j. A simultaneous generalized least-squares procedures is used on the above three equations to estimate p_{ij} and q_{ij} as a function of market characteristics. Once estimated, market characteristics of a new market can be used to estimate these parameters for a new product. The procedure has been illustrated for forecasting the diffusion of consumer durables in European countries based on three country characteristics: cosmopolitanism, mobility, and role of women.

Table 8.A1 (cont'd)

Procedure type	Procedure type description	Proposed by	Analytical description
		Sultan, Farley & Lehmann [1990]; Montgomery & Srinivasan [1989]	This procedure meta-analyzes the values of the coefficients of external influence and internal influence by expressing the inter-study differences in terms of product/market characteristics. Sultan, Farley & Lehmann express those differences in terms of six variables: type of innovation (consumer durable, industrial/medical, and other), country (USA or Europe), marketing-mix variables included (yes/no), other parameters included (yes/no), estimation procedure (ordinary least squares, maximum likelihood, nonlinear least squares), and repeat use of data across studies (yes/no for each product). Controlling differences in possible errors due to the model specifications, the estimation procedures, and the different analysts developing these estimates, Montgomery & Srinivasan meta-analyze the values of the coefficient of internal influence (and peak time and market potential) by expressing differences across 61 products as a function of five variables: price, nature of innovation (convenience, yes/no), year of introduction, number of households in the introductory year, and multiple product-use (yes/no). Once the meta-analysis model has been estimated, it can be used to forecast parameters for a new product.
Time-invariant parameter estimation procedures	These procedures require historical time-series data on the product diffusion.	Bass [1969] (ordinary least squares)	Let $X(i)$ be the incremental number of adopters in time interval $i\,(t_{i-1}, t_i)$, $i = 1, 2, \ldots, T$. This procedure uses a discrete regression analog of the diffusion model to estimate p, q and m. That is, $X(i) = p(m - N(t_{i-1})) + (q/m)N(t_{i-1})(m - N(t_{i-1})) + \varepsilon(i),$ $X(i) = pm + (q-p)N(t_{i-1}) - (q/m)N^2(t_{i-1}) + \varepsilon(i),$ $X(i) = \alpha_1 + \alpha_2 N(t_{i-1}) + \alpha_3 N^2(t_{i-1}) + \varepsilon(i),$ where $\alpha_1 = pm, \alpha_2 = (q-p), \alpha_3 = -(q/m)$. Once regression coefficients are estimated, p, q and m can be obtained by noting that $\hat{p} = (\alpha_i/\hat{m})$, $\hat{q} = -\alpha_3\hat{m}$ and

			$\hat{m} = \dfrac{(-\alpha_2 - \sqrt{\alpha_2^2 - 4\alpha_1\alpha_3})}{2\alpha_3}.$
		Schmittlein & Mahajan [1982] (maximum likelihood)	Let $p + q = s$ and $q/p = r$ and hence $p = s/(1+r)$ and $q = sr/(1+r)$. Let M be the sample size of adopters and non-adopters and c be the probability of eventually adopting a product. Then the estimated market potential $m = cM$ or $c = m/M$. Let T equal the number of time intervals for which the diffusion data are available and $X(i)$ be the number of individuals who adopt in time interval $i(t_{i-1}, t_i)$, $i = 1, 2, \ldots, T$. This procedure first obtains the maximum-likelihood estimates of s and r by using optimization algorithms to maximize the following likelihood functions: $L = [1 - F(t_{T-1})]^{X(T)} \prod_{i=1}^{T-1} [F(t_i) - F(t_{i-1})]^{X(i)},$ where from the Bass model $F(t) = \dfrac{c(1 - e^{-st})}{(1 + re^{-st})}$ and $X(T) = M - X(1) = X(2) \cdots - X(T-1) = \sum_{i=1}^{T-1} X(i).$ Once s and r are estimated, p and q can be obtained. Formulae for the estimation of standard errors of p and q are given in the original source. A copy of the program is available from the authors.
		Srinivasan & Mason [1986] (nonlinear least squares)	This procedure suggests that if $X(i)$ is the number of adopters in the time interval $i\ (t_{i-1}, t_i)$, then $X(i) = m[F(t_i) - F(t_{i-1})] + \mu_i$ where μ_i is the additive error term and $F(t)$ is from the Bass model, i.e., $F(t) = \dfrac{1 - e^{-(p+q)t}}{1 + \dfrac{q}{p} e^{-(p+1)t}}.$ Any standard nonlinear regression package can be used to estimate p, q and m.
Time-varying estimation procedures	These procedures assume that parameters of the diffusion models	Sultan, Farley & Lehmann [1990]	This procedure suggests a Bayesian updating formula to develop new (or posterior) parameter estimates as additional data become available. The parameter estimates developed from a meta-analysis of earlier-

Table 8.A1 (cont'd)

Procedure type	Procedure type description	Proposed by	Analytical description
	change over time. The procedures provide mechanisms to update parameter estimates as new data become available.	(Bayesian estimation procedure)	introduced products serve as the initial (or prior) estimates of the new product. The updating procedure provides a weighted average of these prior estimates and estimates that are developed from the actual data of the new product. (Any procedure, such as nonlinear-estimation procedure, can be used to develop these estimates.) The values of these weights vary over time and depend upon the variation in the estimates that are obtained from the actual data. As estimates for the parameters stabilize (i.e., the variance in zero), the updating formula reduces the weight of prior estimates to zero. For example, the formula for the coefficients of innovation (p) is: $P_{\text{new}} = w_1 p_{\text{meta}} + w_2 p_{\text{data}}$ $w_1 = \dfrac{\dfrac{1}{\text{Var}(p_{\text{meta}})}}{\dfrac{1}{\text{Var}(p_{\text{meta}})} + \dfrac{1}{\text{Var}(p_{\text{data}})}}$ $w_2 = \dfrac{\dfrac{1}{\text{Var}(p_{\text{data}})}}{\dfrac{1}{\text{Var}(p_{\text{meta}})} + \dfrac{1}{\text{Var}(p_{\text{data}})}}$ where Var is the variance. A similar formula can be written for the coefficient of imitation.
		Bretschneider & Mahajan [1980]	This procedure uses a feedback filter or adapter to update parameters in the discrete regression analog of the Bass model. The filter calculates an adjustment to the existing value of a parameter based on the error or the difference between the actual and the predicted value of the noncumulative number of adopters. For the Bass model, the discrete regression analog is given by:

$$n(t+1) = pm + (q-p)N(t) - \frac{q}{m}N^2(t)$$

$$= \alpha_1 + \alpha_2 N(t) + \alpha_3 N^2(t)$$

where α's are regression coefficients and can be converted into p, q and m. As additional data become available, α's are updated by using the filter. For example, the time-varying estimate for α_2 at time $(t+1)$ is given by

$$\hat{\alpha}_2(t+1) = \hat{\alpha}_2(t) + A(e_t)$$

where $A(e_t)$ is the adjustment based on the error between the actual and the predicted values of $\hat{n}(t)$ and is given by

$$A(e_t) = |\alpha_2(t)| \cdot \frac{e_t}{\hat{n}_t} \cdot \frac{N(t)}{\bar{N}(t)} \cdot K$$

where K is the learning factor between the zero and one, and determines the speed of adaptation, and $\bar{N}(t)$ is an average of the independent variable, $N(t)$, associated with α_2. An experimental scheme is used to calculate this average: $\bar{N}(t) = wN(t) + (1-w)\bar{N}(t-1)$ where w is between zero and one, and depends upon the 'forgetting rate' of past observations or the cumulative number of adopters. Similar formulae can be written for other coefficients α_1 and α_3 in the discrete regression analog of the Bass model.

Mahajan & Sharma [1986]. The implementation of this procedure requires information from management on three items: (1) the market size (m), (2) the time of the peak of the noncumulative adoption curve, and (3) the adoption level at the peak time (n^*). That is, the key information required by the estimation procedure is the peak of the noncumulative adoption curve. Knowing this information the coefficients of external influence and internal influence can be estimated. Although the algebraic estimation procedure has been implemented in actual applications by some firms (e.g. Institute for the Future), Bass [1986] has very appropriately questioned the desirability of this procedure, suggesting that one of the key outputs of the diffusion model is the prediction of the timing and magnitude of the peak. Therefore, if one can guess these items there is no need to estimate model parameters.

An alternative algebraic estimation procedure has also been suggested by Lawrence & Lawton [1981]. This procedure also involves obtaining information from management on three items: (1) the potential market size (m), (2) the number of adoptions in the first time period, and (3) an estimate of the sum of the coefficients of external influence and internal influence, i.e. $p + q$ value. Although it may be possible for management to guess the adoption level for the first time period, how does one guess $p + q$ value! A record of the parameter values of earlier new products may provide a basis, by analogy, for guessing $p + q$. From an analysis of the diffusion patterns of several products, Lawrence & Lawton [1981], for example, recommend using a value of 0.66 for industrial-product innovations and a value of 0.50 for consumer-product innovations (for an application of this procedure to consumer durables, see De Kluyver [1982]). Such a recommendation, however, may be too general and does not consider idiosyncratic characteristics of a particular diffusion situation. Thomas [1985], therefore, has recommended that, for a new product under consideration, its parameters may be estimated by taking a weighted sum of the parameters of the analogous products where weights are determined by establishing the similarity/dissimilarity relationships between the new product and the various analogous products on five bases of comparisons: environmental situation (e.g. socioeconomic–ecological–political environment), market structure (e.g. barriers to entry, number and type of competitors), buyer behavior (e.g. buying situation, choice attributes), marketing-mix strategy, and characteristics of innovation (e.g. relative advantage, complexity). In fact, in order to consider idiosyncratic characteristics of a new product in a particular social system, recent analogical approaches estimate its coefficients of external influence and internal influence from regression models that express a historical empirical relatonship between these coefficients and product or market attributes of several existing products. Once this relationship has been established, the values for the coefficients of a new product can be estimated by knowing its characteristics. Four such approaches for the Bass model have been suggested by Srivastava, Mahajan, Ramaswami & Cherian [1985], Gatignon, Eliashberg & Robertson [1989], Sultan, Farley & Lehmann [1990] and Montgomery & Srinivasan [1989].

In studying parameter estimates of the Bass model Lawrence & Lawton [1981] have found that $p + q$ ranged from 0.3 to 0.7 over several innovations. They note that first-year sales, S_1, may be expressed as $m(l - e^{-(p+q)})/(1 + (q/p)e^{-p+q)})$ and hence q/p may be expressed as $(m(1 - e^{(p+q)}) - S_1)/S_1 e^{-(p+q)}$. It is possible to use judgment in guessing m and S_1. From a strategic viewpoint probably the most critical forecast deriving from the Bass model is the time of peak of adoptions, T^*. This value is given by $(1/(p-q))\ln(q/p)$. Because $p+q$ varies over a relatively narrow range and has a mode around 0.5, for consumer products, guesses of $p+q$, m and S_1 may provide good estimates of T^*. Lawrence & Lawton [1981, p. 535] have reported good success using this method for a substantial number of cases.

A.2. Availability of data

Since the Bass model contains three parameters (p, q and m), adoption data for a minimum of three time periods is required to estimate these parameters. Empirical studies, however, have documented that estimates of these parameters, and hence the adoption forecasts, are sensitive to the number of data points used to estimate them [see, for example, Tigert & Farivar, 1981; Hyman, 1988]. In fact, these studies suggest that stable and robust parameter estimates for the Bass model are obtained only if the data under consideration include the peak of the non-cumulative adoption curve [Heeler & Hustad, 1980; Srinivasan & Mason, 1986]. Given these concerns, attempts have also been made in recent years to develop estimation procedures that update parameter estimates as additional data become available after the initiation of the diffusion process. These procedures include Bayesian estimation procedures and adaptive filtering approaches that provide time-varying parameter estimates. We will first discuss procedures that are specifically designed to provide time-invariant parameter estimates.

A.2.1. Time-invariant estimation procedures

One of the earliest procedures suggested to estimate the diffusion parameters is the ordinary least-squares (OLS) procedure suggested by Bass. The OLS procedure involves estimation of the parameters by taking the discrete or regression analog of the differential equation formulation of the Bass model, i.e. Equation (1). In fact, rearrangement of Equation (1) yields:

$$N(t+1) - N(t) = pm + (q-p)N(t) - (q/m)N^2(t),$$
$$n(t+1) = \alpha_1 + \alpha_2 N(t) + \alpha_3 N^2(t), \tag{A1}$$

where

$\alpha_1 = pm$, $\alpha_2 = q - p$, and $\alpha_3 = -q/m$.

That is, regression analysis is used to estimate α_1, α_2 and α_3 in Equation (A1). Once α's are known, p, q and m can be estimated. If there is a reason to believe that all data points in the diffusion time series should not have an equal weighting in the least-squares procedure, discounted least squares may be used for estimating

α's (for an application of discounted least squares to the discrete analog of the Bass model, see Young and Ord (1985]).

The OLS procedure, however, suffers from three shortcomings. As pointed out by Schmittlein & Mahajan [1982], these shortcomings are: (i) because of the likely multicollinearity between independent variables in Equation (A1), i.e, $N(t)$ and $N^2(t)$, the procedure may yield parameter estimates which are unstable or possess wrong signs; (ii) the procedure does not directly provide standard errors for the estimated parameters p, q and m (and, hence, statistical significance of these estimates cannot be assessed); and (iii), there is a time-interval bias since discrete time-series data are used for estimating a continuous model (i.e. the solution of the differential equation specification of the Bass model given in Table 8.1).

To overcome these shortcomings, Schmittlein & Mahajan [1982] have suggested a maximum-likelihood estimation procedure to estimate the parameters. Their procedure estimates the parameters directly from the solution of the differential-equation specification of the Bass model. This procedure, however, is also not without limitations. For example, Srinivasan & Mason [1986] have pointed out that since the maximum-likelihood procedure considers only sampling errors and ignores all other errors such as the effects of excluded marketing variables that influence the diffusion process, it underestimates the standard errors of the estimated parameters, resulting in possible wrong inferences about the statistical significance of the parameters. To overcome this shortcoming, they suggest a formulation by means of which estimates of p, q and m can be obtained by using any appropriate nonlinear regression packages (a similar formulation has also been suggested by Jain & Rao [1990]). This formulation also uses the solution to the differential-equation specification of the Bass model for parameter estimation.

From the above descriptions, it is clear that, at the present time, both the maximum-likelihood and the nonlinear estimation procedures offer better choices than the OLS procedure. Although empirical comparison of these estimation procedures (along with the algebraic estimation procedure suggested by Mahajan & Sharma [1986]) provided by Mahajan, Mason & Srinivasan [1986] suggests an overall superiority of the nonlinear estimation procedure, the maximum-likelihood procedure performs equally well when survey-type diffusion data are used to estimate the parameters because of the dominance of sampling errors [Srinivasan & Mason, 1986; Mahajan, Mason & Srinivasan, 1986]. It should be pointed out that parameter estimation for diffusion models is not a matter of the same significance as that conventionally encountered, because by the time sufficient observations have developed for reliable estimation, it is too late to use the estimates for forecasting purposes. Thus estimation is primarily a matter of historical interest. The estimates may be used for model-testing purposes and for comparison across products. Considered in this context, the methods often do not yield estimates that differ greatly.

A.2.2. Time-varying estimation procedures

Time-varying estimation procedures are designed to update parameter estimates as new data become available.[2] The updating of parameters is achieved either with the Bayes procedure or with feedback filters.

These procedures have been applied in the various diffusion settings by Sultan, Farley & Lehmann [1990], Lenk & Rao [1990] and Bretschneider & Mahajan [1980]. Each of these procedures has two elements in common: (a) the procedure requires an initial estimate of the diffusion-model parameters before the diffusion data become available and (b) it specifies an updating formula to upgrade the initial estimates as additional diffusion data become available.

The Bayesian estimation procedure advocated by Sultan, Farley & Lehmann [1990] uses statistical results of their meta-analysis study to develop initial estimates for the coefficients of external influence and internal influence for a new product. For each of these two coefficients, it updates the initial estimates by taking a weighted sum of its two values: the initial estimate and the estimate that is developed from the actual data (by using any procedure such as the nonlinear estimation procedure of Srinivasan & Mason [1986]). The weights in the updating formula are expressed as a function of the variation in the parameter estimates from the actual data such that as these time-varying estimates stabilize, the weight for the initial estimate based on the meta-analysis goes to zero. A Bayesian estimation procedure has also been reported by Lenk & Rao [1990]. Their procedure explicitly considers the between-product and within-product variations in establishing initial estimates for the new product.

An alternative approach to updating the diffusion-model parameters for the Bass model has been demonstrated by Bretschneider & Mahajan [1980]. This approach estimates the time-varying values of the Bass-model parameters by updating the regression coefficients in the discrete analog of the Bass model, Equation (A1). The updating formula is based on a feedback filter suggested by Carbone & Longini [1977]. This feedback filter estimates an adjustment to the

[2] The idea that coefficients of a market response model should change over time is not new in marketing. In fact, several theoretical approaches that assist in developing market response models where model coefficients exhibit a time-varying behavior have been applied and documented in the marketing literature [see, for example, Wildt and Winer, 1978; Mahajan, Bretschneider & Bradford, 1980]. Two of such approaches have also been examined in the context of diffusion models: the systematic parameter-variation methods and the random coefficient methods. The systematic parameter variations assume a priori the time path of the model coefficients. These methods have a generated new set of diffusion models that have been termed flexible diffusion models [Mahajan & Peterson, 1985] and are reviewed in this paper.

In the random coefficient methods, the random parameters are assumed to constitute a sample from a common multivariate distribution with an estimated mean and variance–covariance structure. Following Karmeshu & Pathria [1980a, 1980b] the applicability of these methods to the Bass diffusion model has been explored by Eliashberg, Tapiero & Wind [1987]. They consider the coefficients of innovation (p) and imitation (q) in the Bass model as stochastic, and hence time-varying, by assuming that $\tilde{p} = p + \varepsilon_p(t)$ and $\tilde{q} = q + \varepsilon_q(t)$, where p and q denote constant means, and ε_p and ε_q denote normally distributed error terms surrounding those means such that their means are zero and the variances are constant. Their empirical results suggest that their stochastic formulation of the Bass model does as well as the deterministic version of the Bass model. There are other types of stochastic diffusion models. These models, however, are not included in this paper. Reviews of such models can be found in Bartholomew [1982], Eliashberg & Chatterjee [1986] and Boker [1987].

current values of parameters at time t based on the error between the actual and the predicted values of the noncumulative number of adopters at time t. Although the procedure provides time-varying estimates for the diffusion-model coefficients, it suffers from the same shortcomings as the ordinary least-squares procedure.[3]

References

Akinola, A.A. (1986). An application of Bass model in the analysis of diffusion of cocoa-spraying chemicals among Nigerian cocoa farmers. *J. Agricul. Econom.* 37, 395–404.

Arndt, J. (1967). Role of product-related conversations in the diffusion of a new product. *J. Marketing Res.* 4 (August), 291–295.

Bartholomew, D.J. (1982). *Stochastic Models for Social Processes, 3rd edition*, Wiley, New York.

Bass, F.M. (1969). A new product growth model for consumer durables. *Management Sci.* 15 (January), 215–227.

Bass, F.M. (1980). The relationship between diffusion rates, experience curves, and demand elasticities for consumer durable technological innovations. *J. Business* 53, S51–S67.

Bass F.M. (1986). The adoption of a marketing model: Comments and observations, in V. Mahajan and Y. Wind (eds), *Innovation Diffusion of New Product Acceptance*, Ballinger, Cambridge, MA, 27–33.

Bass, F.M., and A.V. Bultez (1982). A note on optimal stragegic pricing of technological innovations. *Marketing Sci.* 1 (Fall), 371–378.

Bayus, B.L. (1987). Forcasting sales of new contingent products: An application to the compact disc market. *Appl. Management* 4 (December), 243–255.

Bayus, B.L. (1988). Accelerating the durable replacement cycle with marketing mix variables. *J. Product Innovation Management* 5 (September), 216–226.

Bayus, B.L., S. Hong and R.P. Labe, Jr. (1989). Developing and using forecasting models for consumer durables, *J. Product Innovation Management* 6 (March), 5–19.

Bernhardt, I., and K.M. MacKenzie (1972). Some problems in using diffusion models for new products. *Management Sci.* 19 (October), 187–200.

Bewley, R., and D.G. Fiebig (1988). A flexible logistic growth model with publications in telecommunications. *Inter. J. Forecasting* 4, 177–192.

Boker, F. (1987). A stochastic first purchase diffusion model: A counting approach. *J. Marketing Res.* 24 (February), 64–73.

Bretschneider, S.I., and B. Bozeman (1986). Adaptive diffusion models for the growth of robotics in New York State Industry. *Technol. Forecasting Social Change* 30 (September), 111–121.

Bretschneider, S.I., and V. Mahajan (1980). Adaptive technological substitutions models. *Technol. Forecasting Social Change* 18 (October), 129–139.

Brown, L.A. (1981). *Innovation Diffusion: A New Perspective*, Methuen, New York.

Carbone, R., and R.L. Longini (1977). A feedback model for automated real estate assessment. *Management Sci.* 24 (November), 241–248.

Chatterjee, R., and J. Eliashberg (1990). The innovation diffusion process in a heterogeneous population: A micromodeling approach. *Management Sci.* 36 (September), 1057–1079.

Chow, G.C. (1967). Technological change and the demand for computers. *Amer. Econom. Rev.* 57 (December), 1117–1130.

Clarke, D.G., and R.J. Dolan (1984). A simulation model for the evaluation of pricing strategies in a dynamic environment. *J. Business* 57 (January), S179–S200.

[3] For another application of this approach to the diffusion of robotics in the state of New York, see Bretschneider & Bozeman [1986]. It should also be pointed out that other feedback filters can also be used to estimate time-varying diffusion parameters. For example, the use of the Kalman filter to estimate the time-varying coefficients for the Mansfield model has been reported by Meade [1985].

Clarke, F.H., M.N. Darrough and J.M. Heineke (1982). Optimal pricing policy in the presence of experience effects. *J. Business* 55, 517–530.

Cox, D.R., and D. Oakes (1984). *Analysis of Survival Data*, Chapman and Hall, London.

Deal, Kenneth R. (1979). Optimizing advertising expenditures in a dynamic duopoly. *Oper. Res.* 27 (July–August), 682–692.

DeKluyver, C.A. (1982). A comparative analysis of the Bass and Weibull new product growth models for consumer durables. *New Zealand J. Oper. Res.* 10, 99–130.

Dhebar, A., and S.S. Oren (1985). Optimal dynamic pricing for expanding networks. *Marketing Sci.* 4 (Fall), 336–351.

Dixon, R. (1980). Hybrid corn revisited. *Econometrica* 48, 1451–1461.

Dockner, E., and S. Jorgensen (1988). Optimal advertising policies for diffusion models of new product innovations in monopolistic situations. *Management Sci.* 34 (January), 119–130.

Dodds, W. (1973). An application of the Bass model in long-term new product forcasting. *J. Marketing Res.* 10 (August), 308–311.

Dodson, J.A., and E. Muller (1978). Models of new product diffusion through advertising and word-of-mouth. *Management Sci.* 24 (November), 1568–1578.

Dolan, R.J., and A.P. Jeuland (1981). Experience curves and dynamic demand models: Implications for optimal pricing strategies. *J. Marketing* 45 (Winter), 52–62.

Easingwood, C.J. (1987). Early product life-cycle forms for infrequently purchased major products. *Intern. J. Res. Marketing* 4, 3–9.

Easingwood, C.J. (1988). Product life-cycle patterns for new industrial products. *R & D Management* 18, 23–32.

Easingwood, C.J. (1989). An analogical approach to the long term forecasting of major new product sales. *Intern. J. Forecasting* 5, 69–82.

Easingwood, C.J., V. Mahajan and E. Muller (1981). A nonsymmetric responding logistic model for technological substitution. *Technol. Forecasting Social Change* 20, 199–213.

Easingwood, C.J., V. Mahajan and E. Muller (1983). A nonuniform influence innovation diffusion model of new product acceptance. *Marketing Sci.* 2 (Summer), 273–296.

Eliashberg, J., and R. Chatterjee (1986). Stochastic issues in innovation diffusion models, in V. Mahajan and Y. Wind (eds.), *Innovation Diffusion Models of New Product Acceptance*, Ballinger, Cambridge, MA, 151–203.

Eliashberg, J., and K. Helsen (1987). Cross-country diffusion process and market entry timing, Working Paper, Marketing Department, The Wharton School, University of Pennsylvania.

Eliashberg, J., and A.P. Jeuland (1986). The impact of competitive entry in a developing market upon dynamic pricing strategies. *Marketing Sci.* 5 (Winter) 20–36.

Eliashberg, J., C.S. Tapiero and Y. Wind (1987). Innovation diffusion models with stochastic parameters: Forecasting and planning implications. Working paper No. 87–003. The Wharton School, University of Pennsylvania.

Engle, J.E., R.D. Blackwell and P.W. Miniard (1986). *Consumer Behavior*. Dryden Press, Hinsdale, IL.

Erickson, G.M. (1985). A model of advertising competition. *J. Marketing Res.* 22 (August), 297–304.

Feder, G., and G.T. O'Mara (1982). On information and innovation diffusion: A Bayesian approach. *Ameri. J. Agricul. Econom.* 64 (February), 145–147.

Feichtinger, G. (1982). Optimal pricing in diffusion model with concave price-dependent market potential. *Oper. Res. Lett.* 1, 236–240.

Feick, L.F., and L.L. Price (1987). The market maven: A diffuser of marketplace information. *J. Marketing* 51 (January), 83–97.

Fershtman, C., V. Mahajan and E. Muller (1990). Market share pioneering advantage: A theoretical approach. *Management Sci.* 36 (August), 900–918.

Fisher, J.C., and R.H. Pry (1971). A simple substitution model for technological change. *Technol. Forecasting Social Change* 2 (May), 75–88.

Floyd, A. (1962). Trend forecasting: A methodology for figure of merit, in J. Bright (ed.), *Technological Forecasting for Industry and Government: Methods and Applications*, Prentice-Hall, Englewood Cliffs, NJ, pp. 95–105

Fourt, L.A., and J.W. Woodlock (1960). Early prediction of market success for grocery products. *J. Marketing* 25 (October), 31–38.

Frank, R.E., W.F. Massy and D.G. Morrison (1964). The determinants of innovative behavior with respect to a branded, frequent purchased food product, in L.G. Smith (ed.), *Proceedings of the American Marketing Association*, American Marketing Association, Chicago, pp. 312–323.

Gatignon, H., J. Eliashberg and T.S. Robertson (1989). Modeling multinational diffusion patterns: An efficient methodology. *Marketing Sci.* 8 (Summer), 231–247.

Gatignon, H., and T.S. Robertson (1985). A propositional inventory for new diffusion research. *J. Consumer Res.* 11 (March), 849–867.

Gordon, T.J., and D. Greenspan (1988). Chaos and fractals: New tools for technological and social forecasting. *Technol. Forecasting Social Change* 34 (August), 1–26.

Gore, A.P., and V.A. Lavaraj (1987). Innovation diffusion in a heterogeneous population. *Technol. Forecasting Social Change* 32 (September), 163–167.

Hahn, M., and J.-S. Hyun (1991). Advertising cost interactions and the optimality of pulsing. *Management Sci.* 37 (February), 157–169.

Heeler, R.M., and T.P. Hustad (1980). Problems in predicting new product growth for consumer durables. *Management Sci.* 26 (October), 1007–1020.

Helsen, K., and D.C. Schmittlen (1989). Analyzing duration times in marketing research. Working paper, marketing department, The Wharton School, University of Pennsylvania.

Hendry, I. (1972). The three parameter approach to long range forecasting. *Long Range Planning* 51 (March), 40–45.

Hermes, G. (1976). Diffusion and growth – the non-homogeneous case. *Scand. J. Econom.* 78, 427–436.

Hiebert, L. (1974). Risk, learing and the adoption of fertilizer responsive seed varieties. *Amer. J. Agricul. Econom.* 56 (November), 764–768.

Holak, S., D.R. Lehmann and F. Sultan (1987). The rule of expectations in the adoption of innovative consumer durables: Some preliminary evidence. *J. Retailing* 63 (Fall), 243–259.

Horsky, D. (1990). A diffusion model incorporating product benefits, price, income and information. *Marketing Sci.* 9 (Fall) 342–365.

Horsky, D., and L.S. Simon (1983). Advertising and the diffusion of new products. *Marketing Sci.* 1 (Winter), 1–18.

Hyman, M.R. (1988). The timeliness problem in the application of bass-type new product growth models to durable sales forecasting. *J. Business Res.* 16, 31–47.

Jain, D.C., V. Mahajan and E. Muller (1991). Innovation diffusion in the presence of supply restrictions. *Marketing Sci.* 10 (Winter), 83–90.

Jain, D.C., and R.C. Rao (1990). Effect of price on the demand for durables. *J. Business Econom. Statist.* 8 (April), 163–170.

Jensen, R. (1982). Adoption and diffusion of an innovation of uncertain profitability. *J. Econom. Theory* 27, 182–193.

Jeuland, A.P. (1981). Parsimonious models of diffusion of innovation: Part A, derivations and comparisons. Working paper, Graduate School of Business, University of Chicago.

Jeuland, A.P., and R.J. Dolan (1982). An aspect of new product planning: Dynamic pricing, in A.A. Zoltners (ed.) *TIMS Studies in the Management Sciences, Vol. 18: Marketing Planning Models*. Elsevier, New York, pp. 1–21.

Jones, J.M., and C.J. Ritz (1987). Incoporating distribution into new product diffusion models. Working paper, marketing department, University of North Carolina, Chapel Hill, NC.

Jorgensen, S. (1983). Optimal control of a diffusion models of new product acceptance with price-dependent total market potential. *Optimal Control Appl. Methods* 4, 269–276.

Jorgensen, S. (1986). Optimal dynamic pricing in an oligopolistic market – A survey. *Lecture Notes in Economics and Mathematical Systems* 265, 179–237.

Kalbfleisch, J.D., and R.L. Prentice (1980). *The Statistical Analysis of Failure Time Data*, Wiley, New York.

Kalish, S. (1983). Monopolist pricing with dynamic demand and production cost. *Marketing Sci.* 2 (Spring), 135–160.

Kalish, S. (1985). A new product adoption model with pricing, advertising and uncertainty. *Management Sci.* 31 (December), 1569–1585.

Kalish, S., and G.L. Lilien (1986a). Applications of innovation diffusion models in marketing, in V. Mahajan and Y. Wind (eds.), *Innovation Diffusion Models of New Product Acceptance*, Ballinger, Cambridge, MA, pp. 235–280.

Kalish, S., and G.L. Lilien (1986b). A market entry timing model for new technologies. *Management Sci.* 32 (February), 194–205.

Kalish, S., and S.K. Sen (1986). Diffusion models and the marketing mix for single products, in: V. Mahajan and Y. Wind (eds.), *Innovation Diffusion Models of New Product Acceptance*, Ballinger, Cambridge, MA, 87–116.

Kamakura, W.A., and S.K. Balasubramanian (1987). Long-term forecasting with innovation diffusion models: The impact of replacement purchase. *J. Forecasting* 6, 1–19.

Kamakura, W.A., and S.K. Balasubramanian (1988). Long-term view of the diffusion of durables. *Intern. J. Res. Marketing* 5, 1–13.

Karmeshu and R.K. Pathria (1980a). Stochastic evolution of a nonlinear model of diffusion of information. *J. Math. Sociology* 7, 59–71.

Karmeshu and R.K. Pathria (1980b). Diffusion of information in a random environment. *J. Math. Sociology* 7, 215–227.

King, C.W., Jr. (1963). Fashion adoption: A rebuttal to the trickle down theory, in: S.A. Greyser (ed.), *Proceedings of the American Marketing Association*, American Marketing Association, Chicago, pp. 108–125.

Kobrin, S.J. (1985). Diffusion as an explanation of oil nationalization or the domino effect rides again. *J. Conflict Resolution* 29 (March), 3–32.

Kotler, P., and G. Zaltman (1976). Targeting prospects for a new product. *N. Advertising Res.* 16 (February), 7–20.

Lackman, C.L. (1978). Gompertz curve forecasting: A new product application. *J. Marketing Res. Soc.* 20 (January), 45–47.

Lancaster, G.A., and G. Wright (1983). Forecasting the future of video using a diffusion model. *Eur. J. Marketing* 17, 70–79.

Lattin, J.M., and J.H. Roberts (1989). Modelling the role of risk-adjusted utility in the diffusion of innovations, Working paper 1019, Graduate School of Bussiness, Stanford University, Stanford, CA.

Lavaraj, U.A., and A.P. Gore (1990). On interpreting probability distributions fitted to times of first adoption. *Technol. Forecasting Social Change* 37 (July), 355–370.

Lawrence, K.D., and W.H. Lawton (1981). Applications of diffusion models: Some empirical results, in: Y. Wind, V. Mahajan and R.C. Cardozo (eds.), *New Product Forecasting*, Lexington Books, Lexington, MA, pp. 529–541.

Lawton, S.B., and W.H. Lawton (1979). An autocatalytic model for the diffusion of educational innovations. *Educational Adminis. Quart.* 15, 19–53.

Lee, J.C.O., and K.W. Lu (1987). On a family of data-based transformed models useful in forecasting technological substitution. *Technol. Forecasting Social Change* 31 (March), 61–78.

Lekvall, P., and C. Wahlbin (1973). A study of some assumptions underlying innovation diffusion functions. *Swedish J. Econom.* 75, 362–377.

Lenk, P.J., and A.G. Rao (1990). New models from old: Forecasting product adoption by hierarchical bayes procedures. *Marketing Sci.* 9 (Winter), 42–53.

Lilien, G.L., A.G. Rao and S. Kalish (1981). Bayesian estimation and control of detailing effort in a repeat purchase diffusion environment. *Management Sci.* 27 (May), 493–506.

Lilien, G.L., and E. Yoon (1990). The timing of competitive market entry: An exploratory study of new industrial products. *Management Sci.* 36 (May), 568–585.

Mahajan, V., S.I. Bretschneider and J.W. Bradford (1980). Feedback approaches to modeling structural shifts in market response, *J. Marketing* 44 (Winter), 71–80.

Mahajan, V., C.H. Mason and V. Srinivasan (1986). An evaluation of estimation procedures for new product diffusion models, in: V. Mahajan and Y. Wind (eds.), *Innovation Diffusion Models of New Product Acceptance*, Ballinger, Cambridge, MA, 203–234.

Mahajan, V., and E. Muller (1979). Innovation diffusion and new product growth models in marketing. *J. Marketing* 43 (Fall), 55–68.

Mahajan, V., and E. Muller (1986). Advertising pulsing policies for generating awareness for new products. *Marketing Sci.* 5 (Spring), 89–106.

Mahajan, V., and E. Muller (1990). Timing, diffusion and substitution of successive generations of durable technological innovations: The IBM mainframe case. Working paper No. 71/90, Israeli Institute of Business Research, Tel Aviv University, Tel Aviv, Israel.

Mahajan, V., and E. Muller (1991). Pricing and diffusion of primary and contingent products, *Technol. Forecasting Social Change* 39 (May), 291–308.

Mahajan, V., E. Muller and S. Kalish (1990). Waterfall and sprinkler new product strategies for competitive global markets. Working paper, Graduate School of Business, The University of Texas at Austin, Austin, TX.

Mahajan, V., E. Muller and R.A. Kerin (1984). Introduction strategy for new products with positive and negative word-of-mouth. *Management Sci.* 30 (December), 1389–1404.

Mahajan, V., E. Muller and S. Sharma (1984). An empirical comparison of awareness forecasting models of new product acceptance, *Marketing Sci.* 3 (Summer) 179–197.

Mahajan, V., E. Muller and R.K. Srivastava (1990). Using innovation diffusion models to develop adopter categories. *J. Marketing Res.* 27 (February), 37–50.

Mahajan, V., and R.A. Peterson (1978). Innovation diffusion in a dynamic potential adopter population. *Management Sci.* 24 (November), 1589–1597.

Mahajan, V., and R.A. Peterson (1979). Integrating time and space in technological substitution models. *Technol. Forecasting Social Change* 14, 231–241.

Mahajan, V., and R.A. Peterson (1982). Erratum to: Innovation diffusion in a dynamic potential adopter population. *Management Sci.* 28 (September), 1087.

Mahajan, V., and R.A. Peterson (1985). *Models for Innovation Diffusion*, Sage, Beverly Hills, CA.

Mahajan, V., and S. Sharma (1986). Simple algebraic estimation procedure for innovation diffusion models of new product acceptance. *Technol. Forecasting Social Change* 30 (December), 331–346.

Mahajan, V., S. Sharma and R.A. Bettis (1988). The adoption of the M-form organizational structure: A test of imitation hypothesis. *Management Sci*, 34 (October), 1188–1201.

Mahajan, V., S. Sharma and Y. Wind (1985). Assessing the impact of patent infringement on new product sales. *Technol. Forecasting Social Change* 28 (August), 13–27.

Mahajan, V., and Y. Wind (1986a). Innovation diffusion models of new product acceptance: A reexamination, in: V. Mahajan and Y. Wind (eds.), *Innovation Diffussion Models of New Product Acceptance*, Ballinger Cambridge, MA.

Mahajan, V., and Y. Wind (1986b). *Innovation Diffusion Models of New Product Acceptance.* Ballinger, Cambridge, MA.

Mahajan, V., Y. Wind and S. Sharma (1983). An approach to repeat purchase diffusion models. *Proceedings American Marketing Educator's Conference*, American Marketing Association, Chicago, pp. 442–446.

Mansfield, E. (1961). Technical change and the rate of imitation. *Econometrica* 29 (October), 741–766.

McGowan, Ian (1986). The use of growth curves in forecasting market development. *J. Forecasting* 5, 69–71.

McKenna, R. (1985). *The Regis Touch*, Addison-Wesley, Reading, MA.

Meade, N. (1984). The use of growth curves in forecasting market development: A review and appraisal. *J. Forecasting* 3, 429–451.

Meade, N. (1985). Forecasting using growth curves: An adaptive approach. *J. Oper. Res. Soc.* 36, 1103–1115.

Mesak, H.I., and W.M. Mikhail (1988). Prelaunch sales forecasting of a new industrial product. *Omega*, 16, 41–51.

Midgley, D.F. (1976). A simple mathematical theory of innovative behavior. *J. Consumer Res.* 3 (June), 31–41.

Modis, T., and A. Debecker (1988). Innovation in the computer industry. *Technol. Forecasting Social Change* 33 (May), 267–278.

Montgomery, D.B., and V. Srinivasan (1989). An improved method for meta analysis: With application to new product diffusion models. Working Paper, Graduate School of Business, Standord University Stanford, CA.

Narasimhan, C. (1989). Incorporating consumer price expectations in diffusion models. *Marketing Sci.* 8. (Fall), 343–357.

Nascimento, F., and W.R. Vanhonacker (1988). Optimal strategic pricing of reproducible consumer products. *Management Sci.* 34 (August), 921–937.

Nelder, J.A. (1962). An alternative form of a generalized logistic equation. *Biometrics* 18 (December), 614–616.

Nervers, J.V. (1972). Extensions of a new product growth model. *Sloan Management Rev.* 13 (Winter), 78–79.

Norton, J.A., and F.M. Bass (1987). A diffusion theory model of adoption and substitution for successive generations of high technology products. *Management Sci.* 33 (September), 1069–1086.

Olshavsky, R.W. (1980). Time and the rate of adoption of innovations. *J. Consumer Res.* 6 (March), 425–428.

Olson, J.A., and S. Choi (1985). A product diffusion model incorporating repeat purchases. *Technol. Forecasting Social Change* 27, 385–397.

Oren, S.S., and R.G. Schwartz (1988). Diffusion of new products in risk-sensitive markets. *J. Forecasting* 7 (October–December), 273–287.

Peterson, R.A., and V. Mahajan (1978). Multi-product growth models, in: J. Sheth (ed.), *Research in Marketing*, JAI Press, Greenwich, CT, pp. 201–231.

Rao, A.G., and M. Yamada (1988). Forecasting with a repeat purchase diffusion model. *Management Sci.* 34 (June), 734–752.

Rao, R.C., and F.M. Bass (1985). Competition, strategy, and price dynamics: A theoretical and empirical investigation. *J. Marketing Res.* 22 (August), 283–296.

Rao, S.K. (1985). An empirical comparison of sales forecasting models. *J. Product Innovation Management* 2 (December), 232–242.

Richards, F.J. (1959). A flexible growth function for empirical use. *J. Exp. Botany* 10, 290–300.

Robertson, T.S. (1967). Determinants of innovative behavior, in: R. Moyer (ed.), *Proceedings of the American Marketing Association*. American Marketing Association, Chicago, pp. 328–332.

Robinson, B., and C. Lakhani (1975). Dynamic price models for new product planning. *Management Sci.* 10 (June), 1113–1122.

Rogers, E.M. (1983). *Diffusion of Innovations 3rd edition*. The Free Press, New York.

Rust, R.T., and D.C. Schmittlein (1985). A Bayesian cross-validated likelihood method for comparing alternative specifications of quantitative models, *Marketing Sci.* 4 (Winter), 20–40.

Sasieni, M.W. (1989). Optimal advertising strategies. *Marketing Sci.* 8 (Fall), 358–370.

Schmittlein, D.C., and V. Mahajan (1982). Maximum likelihood estimation for an innovation diffusion model of new product acceptance. *Marketing Sci.* 1 (Winter), 57–78.

Sharif, M.N., and M.N. Islam (1980). The Weibull distribution as a general model for forecasting technological change. *Technol. Forecasting Social Change* 18, 247–256.

Sharif, M.N., and C. Kabir (1976). A generalized model for forecasting technological substitution. *Technol. Forecasting Social Change* 8, 353–364.

Sharif, M.N., and K. Ramanathan (1981). Binomial innovation diffusion models with dynamic potential adopter population. *Technol. Forecasting Social Change* 20, 63–87.

Sharif, M.N., and K. Ramanathan (1982). Polynomial innovation diffusion models. *Technol. Forecasting Social Change* 21, 301–323.

Sharp, J.A. (1984). An interpretation of the non-symmetric responding logistic model in terms of price and experience effects. *J. Forecasting* 3, 453–456.

Silk, A.J. (1966). Overlap among self-designated opinion leaders: A study of selected dental products and services. *J. Marketing Research* 3 (August), 255–259.

Silver, S.D. (1984). A simple mathematical theory of innovative behavior: A comment. *J. Consumer Res.* 10 (March), 441–444.

Simon, H., and K.-H. Sebastian (1987). Diffusion and advertising: The German Telephone Company. *Management Sci.* 33 (April), 451–466.

Skiadas, C.H. (1985). Two generalized rational models for forecasting innovation diffusion. *Technol. Forecasting Social Change* 27, 39–62.

Skiadas, C.H. (1986). Innovation diffusion models expressing asymmetry and/or positively or negatively influencing forces. *Technol. Forecasting Social Change* 30 (December), 313–330.

Souder, W.E., and M.A. Quaddus (1982). A decision-modeling approach to forecasting the diffusion of longwall mining technologies. *Technol. Forecasting Social Change* 21, 1–14.

Srinivasan, V., and C.H. Mason (1986). Nonlinear least squares estimation of new product diffusion models, *Marketing Sci.* 5 (Spring), 169–178.

Srivastava, R.K., V. Mahajan, S.N. Ramaswami and J. Cherian (1985). A Multi-attribute diffusion model for forecasting the adoption of investment alternatives for consumers. *Technol. Forecasting Social Change* 28 (December), 325–333.

Stoneman, P. (1981). Intra-firm diffusion, Bayesian learning and profitability. *Econom. J.* 91 (June), 375–388.

Sultan, F., J.U. Farley and D.R. Lehmann (1990). A meta-analysis of diffusion models. *J. Marketing Res.* 27 (February), 70–77.

Takada, H., and D. Jain (1991). Cross-national analysis of diffusion of consumer durable goods in Pacific Rim countries. *J. Marketing* 55 (April), 48–54.

Tanny S.M., and N.A. Derzko (1988). Innovators and imitators in innovation diffusion modeling. *J. Forecasting* 7 (Oct.–Dec.) 225–231.

Teng, J.-T., and G.L. Thompson (1983). Oligopoly models for optimal advertising. *Management Sci.* 29 (September), 1087–1101.

Teotia, A.P.S., and P.S. Raju (1986). Forecasting the market penetration of new technologies using a combination of economic cost and diffusion models. *J. Product Innovation Management* 3 (December), 225–237.

Thomas, R.J. (1985). Estimating market growth for new products: An analogical diffusion model approach. *J. Product Innovation Management* 2 (March), 45–55.

Thompson, G.L., and J.-T. Teng. (1984). Optimal pricing and advertising policies for new product oligopoly models. *Marketing Sci.* 3 (Spring), 148–168.

Tigert, D., and B. Farivar (1981). The Basss new product growth model: A sensitivity analysis for a high technology product. *J. Marketing* 45 (Fall), 81–90.

Tornatzky, L.G., and R.J. Klein (1982). Innovation characteristics and innovation adoption-implementation: A meta-analysis of findings, *IEEE Trans. Engrg. Management.* EM-29, 28–45.

Von Bertalanffy, L. (1957), Quantitative laws in metabolism and growth, *Quart. Rev. Biology.* 32, 217–231.

Wildt, A.R., and R.S. Wincr (1978). Modeling structural shifts in market response: An overview, in: S.C. Jain (ed.), *Educator's Proceedings.* 5. American Marketing Association, Chicago, pp. 96–101.

Wilson, L.O., and J.A. Norton (1989). Optimal entry time for a product line extension. *Marketing Sci.* 8 (Winter), 1–17.

Winer, R.S. (1985). A price vector model of demand for consumer durables: Preliminary development. *Marketing Sci.* 4 (Winter) 74–90.

Young, P., and J.K. Ord (1985). The use of discounted least-squares in technological forecasting. *Technol. Forecasting Social Change* 28, 263–274.

Ziemer, D.R. (1992) A decision support system to aid scenario construction for sizing and timing marketplaces. *Technol. Forecasting Social Change* 42 (November), 223–250.

J. Eliashberg and G.L. Lilien, Eds., *Handbooks in OR & MS, Vol. 5*

Chapter 9

Econometric and Time-Series Market Response Models*

Dominique M. Hanssens
Anderson Graduate School of Management, University of California at Los Angeles, Los Angeles, CA 90024-1481, USA

Leonard J. Parsons
School of Management, Georgia Institute of Technology, Atlanta, GA 30332-0520, USA

1. Introduction

Marketing managers need to know how their markets will respond, both in the short run and in the long run, to the actions they take. The heart of marketing management practice then is understanding the market mechanism governing a particular market. The key component of such a mechanism is a sales-response function, how unit sales are affected by the controllable actions of the firm, the uncontrollable activities of competitors, and autonomous events in the environment. When a firm wants to describe a more complete model of a market mechanism, multiple relations may arise. Not only will there be a sales-response function, but there also may be competitive reaction functions, vertical market structures, cost functions, and other behavioral relations. A market mechanism specifies the connections among these relations as well as among individual variables.

Various elements constitute a market-response model. In any given situation, the model builder may or may not have advance knowledge of these factors. For example, the analyst may be able to identify the elements of the marketing mix, but know very little about the functional form of the model. It is the task of careful empirical analysis, using econometric and time-series methods, to advance the model builder to a higher state of knowledge. *Econometrics* is the application of statistical and mathematical techniques for the measurement (estimation and testing) of structural relations in predominantly nonexperimental situations. The major technique used in econometrics is regression analysis and its extensions.

*This chapter is a condensation and update of Hanssens, Parsons & Schultz [1990]. We would like to acknowledge the contributions of our collaborator in that original work, Randall L. Schultz of the University of Iowa. We thank Albert Bemmaor [ESSEC), Peter Leeflang (Groningen), Gary Russell (Toronto) and reviewers for their thoughtful comments.

Time-series analysis is the application of one of a wide range of techniques, including univariate and multivariate time series analysis, to examine data that evolve over time. The underlying observations are usually obtained at regular intervals.

Our knowledge about the modeling environment can be organized in the following way:

- level 0: only the information set (i.e. a collection of relevant variables) is known;
- level 1: the causal ordering among variables is known; and
- level 2: the functional form, causal ordering and lag structure are known.

Econometric-time series techniques (ETS) are not appropriate to situations with less than level-0 knowledge. We must start with an information set developed from subject-matter theory or directly from managers. For example, the concept of the marketing mix leads to a commonly used information set in market-response modeling consisting of product sales, price, distribution, sales force, and communication efforts. Once a level-0 prior knowledge is obtained, econometric-time series methods can make substantial contributions in moving the marketing scientist up the knowledge hierarchy.

At level 0, empirical methods should be used to establish the direction of causality among marketing variables. This can only be accomplished with time-series data because it requires the temporal ordering of events. At level 1, the model builder is not ready to estimate parameters or predict sales. The functional form and dynamic structure of the model must first be specified. The latter may require a different set of techniques involving time-series analysis – univariate techniques for lag structure specification and multiple time-series methods. At level 2, the model builder estimates the parameters of a fully specified model using econometric techniques. The analyst may verify the adequacy of the model via testing procedures. The model may then be used for forecasting and/or marketing planning.

We will first look at how we might model the market mechanism from an econometric point of view. Our perspective is primarily, but not exclusively, *static* in nature; that is, actions and responses take place in the same time interval. We will examine how to describe how different marketing phenomena may be captured with specific functional forms. These functional forms, of course, may also be used in dynamic models. By initially only discussing static models, we are simplifying our discussion. (Space limitations preclude us from addressing the numerous practical problems such as multicollinearity that plague applied researchers trying to implement market-response models.) We will then turn to extending this static analysis to capture the *dynamics* of the process, especially by gaining insights from time-series analysis. Again to simplify our discussion, we will focus on linear time-series models. A market mechanism, however, may be both dynamic and nonlinear. The dynamic structure of marketing variables themselves will first be addressed, to be followed by discussions of leads and lags among marketing variables and the assessment of the direction of causality. Dynamic properties of sales-response functions will be discussed in more detail. Marketing generalizations that have been uncovered as well as empirical evidence on the shape of the sales response function will be reported. We would usually now step to the normative domain once we have a response model estimated. However, we will not go on to discuss what we do with our modeling results in this review. The interested reader is referred to 'Improving marketing decisions' in Hanssens, Parsons & Schultz [1990] as well as recent articles such as Levy & Simon [1989], Luhmer, Steindl, Feichtinger, Hartl & Sorger [1988a, 1988b], Sasieni [1989], Doyle & Saunders [1990], Cooil & Devinney [1992], Feinberg [1992], Mantrala, Sinha & Zoltners [1992] and Mesak [1992]. Finally, current research issues will be noted.

2. Market mechanisms

The core relation in the market mechanism is the *sales-response function.* The dependent variable in a sales response function should be a quantity, rather than a monetary measure, of sales. One reason for this is that we need quantity sales forecasts for planning purposes. Another is to avoid spurious correlation arising from price possibly being on both sides of the sales-response function, e.g. revenue (= price × quantity sold) = f(price). For a discussion of the complexities caused by the use of composite dependent variables such as revenue, see Farris, Parry & Ailawadi [1992] and Ailawadi & Farris [1992].

Sometimes a firm might find it advantageous to decompose its sales-response function into two relations: an *industry demand function* and a *market-share model.* The first relation would describe how various factors influence industry sales; the second how various factors, which may or may not include some or all of those factors affecting industry sales, influence the firm's market share. Many firms evaluate their relative success in terms of selective demand position or market share. Three reasons for this are suggested. One is that the product category is simply mature and the primary demand has a zero growth rate; e.g. the frequently purchased, inexpensive, consumable good studied by Beckwith [1972], or the product category within the hypnotics and sedative segment of the British pharmaceutical market described by Leeflang, Mijatovich & Saunders [1992]. Another is that trends in primary demand are frequently out of the control of the firm and affect the industry as a whole. The third is that marketing instruments, in particular advertising, may have minimal impact on total industry sales. Instead, the setting of managerial decision variables serves to allocate this total amount among the competing firms. In many cases, however, a single relation between a firm's sales and both its own actions and environmental variables will be preferred. One practical problem with market-share models is defining the relevant market, i.e. industry boundaries. Decomposition, like many design alternatives in response modeling, depends on the nature of the response problem.

A firm often must be able to forecast the levels of competitors' marketing instruments. If the competitors make their decisions without regard to the firm's actions, then time-series analysis might be used to project future values for their marketing activities. If the competition reacts to the firm's actions, then *reaction functions* should be specified. If both the firm and its competitors are simultaneously trying to optimize their results in light of their opponents' likely behaviors, then optimal control theory and game theory might be appropriate.

Most firms do not sell directly to their customers. Usually one or more intermediaries exist in a channel of distribution. For example, a channel for a consumer packaged good might look like this:

$$\text{Factory} \xrightarrow[\text{shipments}]{} \begin{array}{c}\text{Chain/distributor}\\ \text{warehouse}\end{array} \xrightarrow[\text{withdrawals}]{} \begin{array}{c}\text{Retail}\\ \text{store}\end{array} \xrightarrow[\text{sales}]{} \text{Customer}$$

Each channel member has its own sales-response function. For example, Blattberg & Levin [1987] study the effectiveness and profitability of trade promotions using a market mechanism containing two relations – one for shipments and another for consumer sales. Factory shipments respond to trade promotions. Shipments increase sharply during the interval when an allowance is given on product purchases, then fall markedly after the promotion is over. A similar pattern occurs just before a major price increase as the trade stocks up on a product at the existing price. Peaks and valleys in retail sales occur in response to the presence or absence of temporary sales promotions such as price features, special displays, and coupons. Findley & Little [1980] note that dynamics of warehouse withdrawals tend to be smoother than factory shipments and retail sales. They argue that this smoothing is mainly due to the buffer effect of retail inventories.

In many applications, a product's cost per unit, exclusive of marketing costs, is assumed to be constant. This is a satisfactory approximation in most circumstances. However, there are times when more attention should be given to the *cost function.* For instance, price promotions typically cause both consumer sales and factory shipments to be uneven. Irregular factory shipments often mean higher production and/or inventory costs. Another exception occurs in the case of technological innovations, including consumer durables. For these products, total unit costs usually decline as experience with producing product is gained [Hall & Howell, 1985]. Total unit costs also tend to decline in response to competitive entry. As new brands enter a market, the resultant growth of industry output forces price downward; and consequently, costs must be reduced if profitability is to be maintained [Devinney, 1987].

The design of response models involves variables, relations, functional forms, and data. Variables represent the building blocks of a response study. An analysis of price elasticity, for example, would require at least two variables: price and unit sales. Relations deal with the connections among variables. To answer a question about the magnitude of price elasticity, it would be necessary to examine the special relation of price to unit sales. Functional forms refer to the nature of a relation. One form of a relation between price and sales could be linear; a form such as this would give both mathematical and substantive meaning to the relation. Finally, data are the actual realizations of variables. We will focus on market-level data primarily, but note that Wittink & Porter [1991] and Wittink, Porter & Gupta [1991] recommend using store-level data (when available) rather than market-level data for estimating sales-response functions because of aggregation bias present in market-level results. (Their comment is consistent with Bolton's [1989] finding that 'elasticity estimates exhibit substantial variability across stores'.) Taken together, these things provide the materials for building a response model. Let us now examine the formulation and estimation of response models.

3. Static models

A firm may simply be interested in how its advertising and price affect its sales. This firm needs to know about a single relation – its sales-response function. Its sales, the dependent variable, are determined, in part, by a set of explanatory variables, advertising and price. The set of explanatory variables might be expanded to include environmental variables as well as other decision variables of the firm. The environmental variables may represent competitive actions and autonomous phenomena such as macroeconomic variables.

A relation is made concrete by specifying its functional form. A functional form should exhibit the same properties the relation is known to possess. Possible properties of a sales-response function include what happens to sales when marketing effort is zero or very large; rate of change in sales as marketing activity increases, e.g. diminishing returns to scale; threshold effects such as a minimum advertising investment; parameter variation such as might occur over different market segments; and asymmetric response such as a different response by competitors to a decrease in price or to an increase in price. Reaction functions, since they usually represent decision rules, may be less complex. In discussing static models, we cover the shape of the sales-response function, specification of market-share models, and econometric estimation in marketing.

3.1. Shape of the sales-response function

The shape of the sales-response function may exhibit increasing, constant, or decreasing returns to scale, might be different depending on whether marketing effort is increasing or decreasing, and might change in response to changes in the environment. (Many of the functional forms of the market-response function we will cover as well as other forms are discussed in Naert & Leeflang [1978, Chapter 5], Saunders [1987], and Lilien, Kotler & Moorthy [1992, Appendix C].) Constant returns to scale occur when any unit change in marketing effort generates an equal incremental change in sales. This is true of a linear model:

$$Q = \beta_0 + \beta_1 X_1 + \beta_2 X_2 + \cdots + \beta_k X_k \tag{3.1}$$

where Q is unit sales, X_i is the ith explanatory variable, and β_i is the ith parameter. Linear relations are used by Banks [1961] and Lambert [1968] to study the impact of managerial decision variables and market share and volume, respectively; by Moriarty [1985] to examine promotional effects on intra- and inter-brand performance; by Blattberg & Neslin [1990, pp. 197–204] to illustrate using regression analysis to investigate the effects on instant coffee sales of promotion: feature, display, and price-cut activities; and by Leeflang, Mijatovic & Saunders [1992] to investigate (dynamic) promotional effects on market share.

When sales always increase with increases in marketing effort, but each additional unit of marketing effort brings less in incremental sales than the previous unit did, a sales-response curve is said to exhibit *diminishing returns to scale.* A functional form that meets this requirement, for certain parameter values, is the *multiplicative model*:

$$Q = e^{\beta_0} X_1^{\beta_1} X_2^{\beta_2} \cdots X_k^{\beta_k}, \quad \beta_i < 1. \tag{3.2}$$

This model has the attractive property that the power coefficient of the marketing instrument can be directly interpreted as that instrument's short-term elasticity. Taking the natural logs of both sides makes the model linear. Bass & Parsons [1969], Lambin [1976], and many others employ multiplicative models for sales response to advertising of frequently purchased branded goods. (While increases in most marketing decision variables such as advertising expenditures, sales calls, deal discounts, and retail availability lead to higher sales, increases in price lead to lower sales. Consequently, to make it comparable with other marketing variables, price is sometimes expressed in the response function in reciprocal form – one over price. In passing, we note that deal discount is often modeled using a percentage discount from regular price (RP − DP)/RP.) Gopalakrishna & Williams [1992] use a multiplicative model in a planning and performance assessment of industrial trade shows. A special case of the multiplicative model when there is only a single instrument and β_1 lies between 0 and 1 is the *fractional-root model*, which itself is known as the *square-root model* when the fraction equals one-half.

Another concave sales-response function is the *semi-logarithmic model*:

$$Q = \beta_0 \ln X. \tag{3.3}$$

Constant *absolute* increments in sales require constant *percentage* increases in marketing effort. Wildt [1977] and Lambin [1969] use the semi-log model for sales response to advertising for branded consumer products; and Doyle & Saunders [1990] for merchandise lines of a leading European variety store. Simon [1982] elaborates upon this model in his study of wearout and pulsation.

Although sales response to most marketing variables exhibits diminishing returns to scale, sales response to decreases in price may exhibit *increasing returns to scale.* An *exponential model*,

$$Q = Q^o e^{-\beta_0 X}, \quad \beta_0 > 0, \tag{3.4}$$

is employed by Cowling & Cubbin [1971] to explain the United Kingdom market for cars in terms of quality-adjusted price, by Blattberg & Levin [1987] to assess the effect of trade promotions on factory shipments, by Krishnamurthi & Raj [1988] to model household purchase quantity as a function of price, by Blattberg

& Wisniewski [1989] to explore asymmetric patterns of price competition, and by Bolton [1989] to estimate retail-level price elasticities and cross-elasticities for waffles, bleach, tissue and ketchup.

Sometimes a response function might be *S-shaped*. More precisely, we are discussing 'nicely convex–concave' functions. Initially, sales may exhibit increasing returns to scale and then diminishing returns to higher levels of marketing effort. Bemmaor [1984] considers & *log-reciprocal model* in his study of the advertising threshold effect:

$$Q = \exp\left(\beta_0 - \frac{\beta_1}{X}\right), \quad \beta_0 > 0. \tag{3.5}$$

Even when marketing effort is zero, a firm might still have sales due to loyal buyers, captive buyers or impulse buyers. This would be a minimum sales potential, or *base sales*, Q_o. Most functional forms can be modified appropriately by simply adding a positive constant as Metwally [1980] does to a log-reciprocal model. There is also a finite achievable upper limit to sales no matter how much marketing effort is expended. Buyers become insensitive to the marketing stimuli or find themselves purchasing at their capacities or capabilities. This maximum sales potential is called *saturation*, Q^o. Many commonly used sales-response functions work well despite not formally modeling saturation even though it must exist. This is because firms do not find it profitable to be operating very near saturation; and so these functional forms are adequate for the actual operating range, especially for frequently purchased consumer goods. A saturation level is explicitly represented in the *modified exponential model*:

$$Q = Q^o(1 - \mathrm{e}^{-\beta X}). \tag{3.6}$$

This functional form is used by Buzzell [1964] in his analysis of the optimal number of salespeople, by Shakun [1965] for the study of advertising expenditures in coupled markets, by Holthausen & Assmus [1982] in a probe of advertising budget allocation across territories, by Rangan [1987] in an investigation of the effects of channel effort, and by Mantrala, Sinha & Zoltners [1992] in an assessment of resource allocation rules. A *logistic model* can take into account market saturation while depicting an S-shaped function:

$$\ln\left(\frac{Q - Q_o}{Q^o - Q}\right) = \ln \beta_0 + \sum_{j=1}^{J} \beta_j X_j. \tag{3.7}$$

Johansson [1973] used survey data to estimate the minimum sales level and the saturation level for a new woman's hairspray in one version of a logistic model with market share as the dependent variable. His estimate of minimum sales was the proportion of repeaters and his estimate of saturation was the trial proportion. When a priori information is not available, we must use a functional form that allows the intercept and saturation level to be estimated. One such functional form was used by Little [1970] in his ADBUG model:

$$Q = Q_o + (Q^o - Q_o)\frac{X^{\beta_2}}{\beta_3 + X^{\beta_2}}. \tag{3.8}$$

An additional phenomenon has been theorized – *supersaturation.* Supersaturation occurs when higher levels of marketing effort result in lower sales than lower levels of effort were able to achieve; that is, the marginal rate of change is negative. Perhaps this might occur when too much marketing effort causes a negative response; for example, a buyer might feel that an excessive number of visits by a salesperson is intolerable. The simplest functional form that represents this effect is the *quadratic model*:

$$Q = \beta_0 + \beta_1 X - \beta_2 X^2. \tag{3.9}$$

Some positive amount of marketing effort might be necessary before any sales impact can be detected. For example, the expenditure of only one thousand dollars in a highly competitive mass market is unlikely to show a sales effect. The minimum effort to show an effect is called a *threshold.* This might be modeled by simply adding a positive constant to a marketing instrument. The fact that the quantity sold must be nonnegative (ignoring the possibility that returned product exceeds product sales) implies some functional forms have thresholds built into them, for example, the *saturation model with decreasing returns*:

$$Q = \beta_0 - \beta_1 X^{-\beta_2}. \tag{3.10}$$

A special case ($\beta_2 = 1$) of this, the *reciprocal model,* is applied by Ward [1975] to the processed-grapefruit industry.

One marketing decision variable may moderate or enhance another. A fast-food company may advertise on local television just before the drop of coupons in newspapers. The combination of variables is more effective than would be predicted from each variable separately. The power model can be extended to take into account all the *interactions* among marketing decision variables. A very general way for representing interactions is the *transcendental logarithmic (translog) model*:

$$\begin{aligned} \ln Q = {} & \beta_0 + \beta_1 \ln X_1 + \beta_2 \ln X_2 + \beta_3 \ln X_3 \\ & + \beta_{12} \ln X_1 \ln X_2 + \beta_{13} \ln X_1 \ln X_3 \\ & + \beta_{23} \ln X_2 \ln X_3 + \beta_{11} (\ln X_1)^2 \\ & + \beta_{22} (\ln X_2)^2 + \beta_{33} (\ln X_3)^2. \end{aligned} \tag{3.11}$$

The translog functional form is a quadratic approximation to any continuous function. The elasticities of the marketing instruments vary with changes in the entire marketing mix. (A constant-elasticity model is a special case.) Jagpal, Sudit

& Vinod [1982] estimate a translog model for Lydia Pinkham sales and advertising. The full interaction model can quickly become unwieldy when all the possible interactions among marketing decision variables are taken into account. Because of small sample sizes or estimation problems, this model is usually simplified by having some of the parameters equal each other, and often equal 1 or 0 as well. Prasad & Ring [1976], for example, look at four main effects plus only the six pairwise interactions. A special case of the translog model is the *multiplicative nonhomogeneous model* (when $\beta_{11} = \beta_{22} = \beta_{33} = 0$). Jagpal, Sudit & Vinod [1979] illustrate this model with Palda's [1964] Lydia Pinkham data. Jagpal [1981] also uses it in his investigation of cross-product media advertising effects for a commercial bank. In turn, the most popular sales-response function, the multiplicative model is a special case of the multiplicative nonhomogeneous model in which only the highest-order interaction is retained. Hanssens & Levien [1983] specify multiplicative functional forms for the relationships in their econometric model of recruitment marketing in the US Navy.

Interaction among marketing variables may also be modeled by making the parameters of one marketing variable a function of other marketing variables, e.g. the price elasticity a function of advertising. More formally, the parameter vector β in some models such as $\boldsymbol{q} = f(\boldsymbol{\beta}, \boldsymbol{X})$ may exhibit variation and this *coefficient variation* may be systematic. Systematic variation implies that the parameter vector can be expressed as a function of other parameters $\boldsymbol{\alpha}$ and observable variables $\boldsymbol{Z}$. This set of variables may include some of the variables in $\boldsymbol{X}$. An application to sales-call elasticities is given in Parsons & Vanden Abeele [1981].

The deterministic relationship can be made stochastic by adding a disturbance term. When this relationship is linear and it is embedded in a linear response function, the resultant model has an heteroscedastic disturbance term. Such a model is used by Gatignon [1984] to investigate the influence of advertising on a market's price sensitivity and by Gatignon & Hanssens [1987] to examine factors influencing sales-force effectiveness.

Our discussion of functional forms has emphasized the specification of a functional relation between two or more variables. Such a functional relation does not explain everything. After all, it is only a model incorporating the salient features of some marketing phenomenon. Moreover, only the deterministic part of the underlying mechanism has been specified. There may be some inherent randomness in the marketplace; for instance, unpredictable variety seeking by customers. Consequently, any specification of a relationship must be expanded to include a *random disturbance* term that captures *equation error*, i.e. the difference between actual observations of a dependent variable and those predicted by a particular functional relationship, i.e. add v to, or multiply e^{v} times, the functional form of choice as appropriate. Typically $v = \omega$, where ω is white noise.

In situations where the data represent observations from a combination of a cross-section and a time series, the disturbance term is sometimes partitioned into three components. The components are the individual or cross-section effect, the temporal effect, and the remaining effects which vary over both individuals and time periods. Parsons [1974] and Moriarty [1975] use variants of this variance-components formulation. Parsons studied the advertising, retail availability, and sales of new brands of ready-to-eat cereals. Moriarty studied regional fluctuations in the effectiveness of marketing decision variables for a single brand.

Discrimination among alternative models is impossible if they are *observationally equivalent*. This occurs when two or more theories yield exactly the same implications about observable phenomena in all situations. Under such conditions no sample, no matter how large, can resolve the issue. We will use the term observational equivalence loosely to cover any observed space in which the models under consideration are not observationally distinguishable. Saunders [1987, pp. 27–29] applies different functional forms to same data sets and all fit quite well. He concludes:

> "It is evident that good fit does not mean that an expression [functional form] gives the right shape. This is particularly true if an expression is used to fit data that only covers a small portion of the curve. In such cases it is not safe to draw conclusions about the shape that an expression gives beyond the limits of the data."

This warning should be kept in mind when implementing marketing policies based upon an estimated sales response function.

3.2. Specification of market-share models

When the dependent variable in a response function is market share, an additional complication is introduced. A desirable property of any market-share model is that it be *logically consistent*. This means that the model produces an estimate of a brand's market share that lies between 0 and 1 when market share is expressed as a fraction. Furthermore, the sum of these estimated market shares for all brands in any given period must equal one. Violations of the range and/or sum constraints expose the internal inconsistencies of a model.

A model that must be logically consistent is one based upon the definition of market share. This model is called an *attraction* model [Bell, Keeney & Little, 1975]:

$$\mathrm{MS}_i = \frac{Q_i}{\sum_{j=1}^{N} Q_j} = \frac{f_i(X, v_i; \beta_i)}{\sum_{j=1}^{N} f_j(X, v_j; \beta_j)}. \tag{3.12}$$

By including competitors' marketing instruments in the set of explanatory variables X for each sales-response function, *cross-competitive* (market-share) *effects* can be modeled. When the multiplicative form is used for each individual sales response function, the model is known as the *MCI* (*multiplicative competitive interaction*) model [Cooper & Nakanishi, 1988; Houston, Kanetkar & Weiss, 1991]:

$$\mathrm{MS}_{ti} = \frac{\beta_0 \prod_{k=1}^{K} X_{tik}^{\beta_k} v_{ti}}{\sum_{j=1}^{N} \beta_0 \prod_{k=1}^{K} X_{tjk}^{\beta_k} v_{ij}}. \tag{3.13}$$

The MCI model also assumes all brands have the same coefficients. In effect, a prototype brand rather than a specific brand is being estimated. The assumption that each firm has the same coefficient is relaxed in the *differential-effects MCI* model:

$$\mathrm{MS}_{ti} = \frac{\beta_{0i} \prod_{k=1}^{K} X_{tik}^{\beta_{ik}} v_{ti}}{\sum_{j=1}^{N} \beta_{0j} \prod_{k=1}^{K} X_{tjk}^{\beta_{jk}} v_{tj}}. \tag{3.14}$$

Carpenter, Cooper, Hanssens & Midgley (1988) point out that differential effects can arise for four reasons: (1) differences in marketing effectiveness; (2) differences in competitive vulnerability, i.e. relative positions in the market structure; (3) differences in marketing objectives; and (4) differences in timing of marketing efforts. The differential-effects MCI model is used by Urban [1969] in studying interdependencies among brands in a firm's product line, by Bultez & Naert [1975] in investigating competitive marketing activities in the market for an inexpensive European consumer durable, and by Carpenter, Cooper, Hanssens & Midgley [1988] in exploring an Australian household-product market. Vanden Abeele, Gijsbrechts & Vanhuele [1991] propose and empirically evaluate a *cluster-asymmetry market-share model*. It represents competitive cross-effects at the level of clusters of market contenders and does so through the attraction of the competitors rather than through the instruments which determine these attractions. A variant of this model is used by Bultez, Gijsbrechts, Naert & Vanden Abeele [1989] in their analysis of the retail assortment for the canned dog-food category of a Belgian hypermarket. Foekens, Leeflang & Wittink [1992] put forth and empirically test a *hierarchical market-share model*. It assumes that customers choose items according to brand attributes which are considered in hierarchical order. Competition between and within branches can be modeled separately allowing for heterogeneous competitive effects. Both the cluster model and the hierarchical model, unlike the differential-effects MCI model, require some type of a priori structuring of competition (with the benefit of reducing the number of parameters in the model to be estimated).

We have argued that a desirable property of market-share models is that they be logically consistent. Attraction models meet this requirement. However, they do so at a cost. They are not very parsimonious and are often 'overparameterized', that is, they may contain a large number of parameters relative to the size of the sample and variability in the data. As a result, linear or multiplicative market-share models are often used in practice despite not being logically consistent in most situations.

This state of affairs has led to a series of studies on the estimation and testing of market-share models [Naert & Weverbergh, 1981, 1985; Brodie & De Kluyver, 1983; Ghosh, Neslin & Shoemaker, 1984; Leeflang & Reuyl, 1984]. Most studies emphasize assessing the degree of heterogeneity in the parameters of a model. Hypotheses that some of the parameters are equal are tested and the descriptive and predictive power of the alternative models are examined. The studies differ on whether the linear, multiplicative, or attraction model is 'best'. This suggests that the answer may well be criterion as well as product-specific.

3.3. Econometric estimation in marketing

Our focus is on finding estimates of the unstandardized parameters in a sales response function, or, more generally, in a market mechanism. This information will allow a marketing manager to evaluate the possible consequences of a marketing action. In this setting the use of standardized parameter estimates, sometimes called beta weights, is not appropriate. Wittink [1983a] demonstrates that 'beta weights are meaningless for applications involving managerial decision making' by showing that 'although beta weights allow for comparisons between predictor variables when the variables are measured in different units, they have no actionable interpretation to managers'.

To make estimation as easy as possible and to ensure that any resultant parameter estimates have desirable statistical properties, simplifying assumptions are made about the error structure. Again, discussion of such detail is omitted in this review. Rather we will simply point out who in marketing use the various possible econometric estimation methods.

There are numerous applications of econometrics to a *single linear* estimating *equation* in marketing. We are talking about an equation that is linear in its parameters. Certain models can be specified as nonlinear, but can be transformed into a linear-in-parameters estimating equation. Some examples of *ordinary least squares* estimation include Wierenga [1981] in relating the number of visitors in a recreational park to advertising effort, Wildt, Parker & Harris [1987] in analyzing sales contests, and Hagerty, Carman & Russell [1988] in estimating elasticities with PIMS (Profit Impact of Market Strategies) data.

Utilization of econometrics for *multiple-equation systems* is somewhat less common. Ordinary least squares estimation of a *recursive model* is employed by Aaker & Day [1971] to study the communications process and by Moore & Winer [1987] to integrate information from joint space maps into market response models. *Disturbance-related equations regression* is applied by Beckwith [1972], Wildt [1974], Houston & Weiss [1974], Picconi & Olson [1978], Takada [1986] and Nguyen [1985] to analyze the response of competing brands to advertising expenditures, by Reibstein & Gatignon [1984] to study the response of competing brands to prices, by Parker & Dolich [1986] to understand retail strategy using cross-sectional rather than time-series data, by Allenby [1989] to estimate price cross-elasticities, and by Blattberg & George [1991] and Hill, Cartwright & Arbaugh [1990, 1991] to develop shrinkage estimates of price and promotion elasticities. Clarke [1973] uses an extension of the disturbance-related-equations regression procedure that takes into account autocorrelated disturbances in his investigation of sales–advertising cross-elasticities. Nakanishi & Cooper [1974], Bultez & Naert [1975], Naert & Weverbergh [1981], Brodie & De Kluyver [1983], Ghosh, Neslin & Shoemaker [1984] and Leeflang & Reuyl [1984] use ordinary least squares, *generalized least squares*, and *iterative generalized least squares* in conducting methodological comparisons of estimation methods for market-share models. The method of *two-stage least squares* is the most popular of the simultaneous-equation estimating procedures. This method is applied by Farley & Leavitt [1968] to a model of the distribution of branded personal products in Jamaica; By Bass [1969] and Rao [1972] to models of the sales–advertising relationship of cigarettes; by Bass & Parsons [1969] to the analysis of sales and advertising of ready-to-eat cereals; by Dalrymple & Haines [1970] in an investigation of market period demand–supply relations for a firm selling fashion products; by Samuels [1970/71] to advertising and sales of household cleansers; by Cowling [1972] to the advertising and sales of various products; and by Albach [1979] to pricing and sales of prescription drugs. *Three-stage least squares* is used by Schultz [1971] in a study of the airline industry, by Houston [1977] in an econometric analysis of positioning, and, in two studies based on business-level (PIMS) data, by Carpenter [1987] in an investigation of competitive marketing strategies and Tellis & Fornell [1988] in an examination of the relationship of advertising and product quality over the product life-cycle. *Iterative three-stage least squares* is employed by Lancaster [1984] to explore the relation of competitive-brand advertising to industry, brand and rival retail sales and market share in seven mature nondurable-product categories. *Constrained three-stage least squares* is conducted by Neslin [1990] in estimating a market-response model for coupon promotions.

Linear models are computationally easy to estimate. Unfortunately, most marketing phenomena are *nonlinear*. For example, a sales-response function is believed to exhibit diminishing returns to scale over most, if not all, of its range. Many nonlinear functional forms, however, can be transformed into linear ones for estimation purposes. Those that cannot be transformed must be estimated by nonlinear methods. Fortunately, more and more statistical and econometric procedures use nonlinear estimation because computation has become feasible. Marketing has lagged behind on this issue.

Transformations are often used to convert linearizable nonlinear structural models into linear estimating equations. Consider the most common sales-response function, the multiplicative (3.2), with a multiplicative disturbance. A linear estimating equation for this function can be found by taking the logarithms of both sides of the relationship. For example, Di Benedetto [1985] applies this transformation to a multiplicative dynamic-adjustment model of sales response to marketing-mix variables. A problem arises when an observation on a variable, especially the dependent variable, is zero ($\ln[0] = -\infty$). To get around this problem, many researchers add 1 to each observation ($\ln[1] = 0$). Rao, Wind & DeSarbo [1988, p. 132], for example, recommend adding a small positive number to all entries. Young & Young [1975] recommend dropping such observations rather than arbitrarily setting the log-value of the dependent variable to be zero. Alternatively, when independent variables such as promotion are zero (i.e. there are often periods when no promotion is offered), researchers are now replacing the X's in the multiplicative model by e^X's, and the resultant sales-response function is written as

$$Q = e^{\beta_0}(e^{X_1})^{\beta_1}(e^{X_2})^{\beta_2}\cdots(e^{X_k})^{\beta_k} = \exp\left(\beta_0 + \sum_{i=1}^{k} \beta_i X_i\right). \quad (3.15)$$

This is a *generalized exponential model*, cf. (3.4). Applications include Cooper & Nakanishi [1988], Vanden Abeele, Gijsbrechts & Vanhuele [1990] and Foekens, Leeflang & Wittink [1992].

Some functional forms are intrinsically nonlinear. For instance, if the multiplicative sales-response function has an additive error instead of a multiplicative error, the relationship cannot be transformed and its parameters must be found by *nonlinear estimation.* The least squares principle can be applied to nonlinear models although the computations will be more complex. *Nonlinear least squares* (NLS) in general provides biased estimates of the parameter vector β. A more serious problem is that the distribution of β is usually unknown even if the distribution of the disturbance term is known. We must rely on asymptotic results arising from approximations we have to make. Under suitable conditions, the NLS estimator is consistent and asymptotically normally distributed. When the error term follows the standard normal distribution, the maximum-likelihood estimator is the same as the least squares estimator as is the case for linear models. Nonlinear regression is used by Horsky [1977] to estimate market-share response to advertising in the cigarette industry, by Metwally [1980] to estimate sales response to advertising of eight Australian products, by Parker [1992] to investigate price-elasticity dynamics over the adoption life-cycle, and by Gopalakrishna & Chatterjee [1992] to study the impact of the industrial communications mix of a firm marketing electrical cables.

The coefficients in the standard linear model are assumed to be constant. This may well not be true if micro-units in a cross-section study respond differently or if the environment changes over time. Thus we have *nonconstant coefficients.* If the changes are systematic and deterministic, OLS regression can be used. However, if the systematic changes also incorporate a random disturbance, then *estimated* (a.k.a. approximate or feasible) *generalized least squares* (EGLS) must be used because the error term will be heteroscedastic. Gatignon [1984] extends this approach to take into account constraints on some of the parameters in his model.

4. Dynamic models

Marketing for a firm rarely takes place in a static environment. Customers and competitors anticipate or react to the firm's actions. Their adjustment processes are one basis for believing market mechanisms should be dynamic. We will discuss, in order, three major scenarios in market-response modeling for which a dynamic approach is appropriate. In each case we will discuss the modeling issues, make a brief reference to estimation issues, and conclude with some applications and findings in the marketing literature. A much more extensive treatment of these issues may be found in HPS [Hanssens, Parsons & Schultz, 1990].

4.1. The dynamic structure of marketing variables by themselves

There are a number of scenarios in model-based planning and forecasting which make it desirable to analyze a marketing time-series strictly as a function of its own past. Thse scenarios can be organized in three categories:

(1) We have developed a planning model relating, say, product prices to product sales. However, price may be determined partially from market factors outside the control of the firm, so it is necessary to forecast prices separately. These predictions are then used to obtain sales estimates. We refer to such situations as 'forecasting exogenous variables'.

(2) Our product line is so large that building individual planning models for each product is prohibitive. Nevertheless, separate forecasts for each are needed. Perhaps the company will invest in a comprehensive marketing-mix model for the four or five leading products and use extrapolative methods to handle the remaining two hundred or so items. This would be an example of 'forecasting performance variables'.

(3) Sometimes it is useful to decompose a marketing time-series, say price, into a systematic, predictable part and a random, unpredictable part. For example, product sales may react differently to predictable price changes, say those due to inflation adjustments, than to unpredictable price 'shocks', say surprise deals offered by the manufacturer. This decomposition of the price variable produces a smooth, predictable price series and a residual price series which is uncorrelated over time (white noise). This is an example of 'prewhitening' a marketing time-series.

The three scenarios apply only when marketing data over time are available. Furthermore, we will assume that the data are collected in regular intervals (e.g. weekly or quarterly) and that they are sufficiently long for statistical modeling (e.g. a minimum of 30 uninterrupted observations). Under these assumptions we can apply principles of *univariate time-series analysis* in order to obtain extrapolative forecasts.

The time-series analyst examines the behavior of data over time as a function of deterministic and stochastic elements:

(1) Deterministic elements whose outcome is perfectly predictable at any point of time. An example is the linear trend model on an arbitrary variable Z:

$$Z_t = \beta_0 + \beta_1 t, \tag{4.1}$$

where t is a time counter. For every new period, a fixed value β_1 is added to the base level β_0 of the time series.

(2) Random or stochastic components whose effect cannot be predicted with certainty. If the random component is correlated over time, it may contribute to forecasting, although imperfectly. It is referred to as a systematic time-series component. If it is uncorrelated, however, it is strictly an error term and is of no use for forecasting. These terms are known as 'white noise', 'shocks', or 'innovations'.

For example:

$$Z_t = \beta_2 Z_{t-1} + \omega_t, \tag{4.2}$$

where $E(\omega_t) = 0$, $E(\omega_t^2) = \sigma_\omega^2$ and $E(\omega_t \omega_{t-k}) = 0$ for all $k \neq 0$.

The first right-hand term is a systematic effect of the last period on the current period and is useful for forecasting. The second term is white noise and, while it may affect the current Z significantly, it cannot be used for estimating future Z.

In conclusion, situations exist in model-based planning and forecasting where strictly extrapolative predictions of marketing variables are needed. Such models are developed using principles of modern time-series analysis, which pay particular attention to the deterministic, systematic, and pure random elements in marketing data. The most popular of these techniques is due to Box & Jenkins. In essence, this method finds the linear filter that converts time-series data to a series of uncorrelated, random shocks called white noise. Once estimated, the filter may be used to generate optimal extrapolative forecasts, in the sense that all the systematic information present in the history of a time series has been effectively utilized. We refer to HPS, Chapter 4, for a detailed discussion.

4.2. Leads and lags among marketing variables

Few managers would disagree that their marketing actions are effective in more than just the period in which they are taken. This dynamic aspect of marketing is exhibited in two ways: (1) lagged effects, i.e. sales changes, competitive reactions, and other forms of marketing behavior may be noticeable in one or more periods after the original stimulus occurs; and (2) lead effects, i.e. consumers or competitors may anticipate a marketing stimulus and adjust their behavior before the stimulus actually occurs. There has been a great deal of empirical research on lagged effects in marketing and virtually none on lead effects. However, since the methods used in modeling leads and lags are the same, we can discuss them together. (This statement is only correct in a time-series (Box–Jenkins) sense; it is not correct in a traditional econometric sense. In traditional econometrics, lags have a known (and, hence, deterministic) stimulus whereas leads have an unknown (and, hence, stochastic) stimulus.) Furthermore, as the quality of marketing data continues to increase with advances in management information systems, the accurate modeling of marketing dynamics becomes more important. For example, ignoring lagged advertising effects on sales may be more serious on monthly than on annual data if the true advertising duration is a few months.

An important distinction in marketing dynamics is between *pulse* and *step* actions in marketing. A pulse action is turned on and off by the marketer, e.g. an advertising campaign or a price promotion. A step action has more of a permanent character, for example, the launching of a new product in the line or the tapping of a different distribution channel. Although dynamic effects are expected to occur in both cases, the literature has for all practical purposes only investigated pulse actions.

Moreover, these studies have generally focused on two marketing-mix elements: advertising and price (in particular, price promotions), although, in principle, all marketing-mix variables can have dynamic effects. We will therefore focus our discussion on advertising and price dynamics. We will also address competitive reactions.

4.2.1. Advertising dynamics

There are various reasons why advertising's effect on sales may be distributed over time. The most important ones are:

- The advertising may not get noticed by the customer until some time after its expenditure. For example, Montgomery & Silk [1972] found lagged journal advertising effects on prescription drug sales of up to six months. This may be caused by physicians delaying the reading of their professional journals.
- An advertising-induced purchase may be followed by subsequent purchases *if the product is satisfactory*. Likewise, the positive word-of-mouth resulting from the initial purchase may bring new customers into the market. (Givon & Horsky [1990] address the problem of untangling the effects of purchase reinforcement and advertising carryover.)
- In some instances, competitive reaction to an advertising campaign may be slow. If the advertising is effective, it may affect sales performance until competitive retaliation takes place.
- Advertising may gradually build up customer loyalty and thus be responsible for more than the immediately observable short-term sales fluctuations.

The literature on advertising dynamics has addressed two important questions: (1) What are the cumulative advertising effects and (2) does advertising wear out? We address each of these issues in turn.

Cumulative advertising effects. It is difficult to specify the advertising dynamics in a market from marketing or psychological theory alone. Although several approaches are possible, three simple yet intuitively appealing models have been used most frequently. These models all recognize that sales or market-share data are typically autocorrelated, but they differ in opinion on whether or not advertising is causing the autocorrelation in sales, i.e., whether or not an advertising carryover effect exists. Among the most popular models are

(1) *The autoregressive current effects model (ACE)*: This model argues that advertising only has contemporaneous effects on sales:

$$Q_t = \beta_0 + \beta_1 A_t + v_t. \tag{4.3}$$

However, other factors such as consumer inertia and habit formation cause sales to fluctuate smoothly over time, which is represented by the autoregressive process of the error term:

$$v_t = \rho v_{t-1} + \omega_t \tag{4.4}$$

where ω_t is white noise. The implied advertising carryover effect in the ACE model is zero, so that the short- and long-run impact is the same $(=\beta_1)$.

(2) *The distributed lag model (Koyck)*: This model arises when advertising has an infinitely long effect on sales, but with an exponentially decaying pattern over time. The short-term effect is β_1 and subsequent-period effects are $\lambda\beta_1$, $\lambda^2\beta_1$, $\lambda^3\beta_1, \ldots, \lambda^N\beta_1$,

$$Q_t = \beta_0 + \beta(1-\lambda)\sum_{\tau=0}^{\infty} \lambda^\tau A_{t-\tau} + \omega_t \tag{4.5}$$

where λ is the carryover effect of advertising and must be less than 1. This model is estimated by applying the Koyck transformation, to yield

$$Q_t = \beta_0(1-\lambda) + \lambda Q_{t-1} + \beta_1 A_t + \xi_t \tag{4.6}$$

where $\xi_t = \omega_t - \lambda\omega_{t-1}$ and ω_t is white noise. The implied long-term effect of advertising $(N \to \infty)$ is $\beta_1/(1-\lambda)$ and $\theta\%$ of the long-run impact of advertising occurs in $\log(1-\theta)/\log(\lambda)$ periods [e.g. Russell, 1988].

(3) *The partial adjustment mode (PAM)*: This response pattern occurs when consumers can only partially adjust to advertising or other marketing stimuli. However, they do gradually adjust to the desired consumption level, which causes the advertising effects to be distributed over time:

$$Q_t = \beta_0(1-\lambda) + \lambda Q_{t-1} + \beta_1 A_t + \omega_t. \tag{4.7}$$

The partial adjustment model is very similar to the Koyck scheme, except for the structure of the error term. The implied long-term advertising effect is also $\beta_1/(1-\lambda)$.

Selection among these alternative specifications is done by *nesting*, a process in which the parameters of lower-order equations are contained within the parameters of higher-order ones. For details on this process, see Bass & Clarke [1972], Weiss & Windal [1980], and especially Leeflang, Mijatovic & Saunders [1992].

The standard linear model assumes that disturbances are independent. The alternative hypothesis may be that two disturbances s periods apart are correlated. The correlation between these disturbances is called the *autocorrelation* coefficient, ρ. In the presence of first-order autocorrelation, a two-step estimation procedure is required. The first step involves obtaining an estimate of ρ by means or ordinary least squares (OLS) estimation. The second step requires that this estimate of ρ be used in an estimated generalized least squares (EGLS) regression. Marketing applications include Simon [1982] and Vanhonacker [1984].

The Koyck model has been the most frequently used among the three most popular models. In an important survey of 70 empirical studies of advertising carryover effects using the Koyck model, Clarke [1976] concluded that:

> "the published econometric literature indicates that 90% of the cumulative effects of advertising on sales of mature, frequently purchased low-priced products occurs within 3 to 9 months of the advertisement. The conclusion

that advertising's effect on sales lasts for months rather than years is strongly supported".

Clarke's conclusion is a very interesting one, as it gets to the heart of a key advertising management question: How long do the economic effects of advertising last? However, when we try to answer the question with econometric techniques, there is a tendency to find different advertising durations for different data intervals, i.e. there may be a *data-interval-bias problem.* In particular, Clarke finds that researchers using annual data tend to discover multiple-year advertising effects, which is in conflict with his empirical generalization. This report has spurred an active interest in the data-interval-bias problem which is covered in more detail in HPS. The data-interval-bias problem is not a data problem; rather it is a modeling (specification) problem. See Vanhonacker [1991] for an autocorrelation test of the Koyck scheme.

Advertising wearout. More recent attention has focused on asymmetric patterns in the dynamic sales response to advertising. Little [1979]'s five phenomena of advertising response include three dynamic aspects:

(1) different rise and decay rates;
(2) changing effectiveness over time;
(3) hysteresis, i.e. the response may fall off with constant advertising.

Different rise and decay rates of sales response to advertising are also known as the *wearout* phenomenon. Advertising wearout may occur for two reasons. First, for consumer or industrial durables, there may be a fixed number of potential customers actively looking to buy the product at any point in time. As an advertising campaign is launched, the sales rate increases immediately, but then tapers off because customers leave the market as soon as they purchase the product (i.e. a market-depletion effect). Second, for frequently purchased products, we often observe impulse-response buying, i.e. an immediate reaction to new advertising which disappears even while the advertising is still running (i.e. an adaptation effect). Either way, the response dynamics may be asymmetric, which must be accommodated by a special function.

Simon [1982] proposes a differential-stimulus response model to incorporate the wearout effect. The differential stimulus is the difference between current and previous advertising or zero, whichever is greater:

$$Q_t = \beta_0 + \beta_1 A_t + \beta_2 \max(A_t - A_{t-1}, 0). \tag{4.8}$$

Sales and advertising may be measured in logarithms to incorporate decreasing returns to scale. The wearout hypothesis is tested by a positive coefficient for β_2. This implies that, whenever an advertising campaign is new, there will be an extra response effect above and beyond the level stimulus effect (β_1). Simon tested the model successfully on three frequently purchased products. Also, Hanssens & Levien [1983] found differential stimulus effects in print and television advertising for the US Navy manpower recruitment program.

The managerial implications of advertising wearout are interesting. Simon [1982] argues that the advertising budget should be allocated to pulsing and constant-spending budgets and that the share of pulsing increases with the differential-stimulus effect. The most profitable advertising strategy is one of 'alternating pulsation', i.e. a pulse in every other period. We do not know, though, what the best length of a pulsing period is.

In conclusion, several empirical studies have demonstrated the existence of dynamic effects of advertising on sales performance. The lag lengths of the effects are several months, although the generalization can only be made for mature, low-priced, frequently purchased products [Clarke, 1976]. Furthermore, advertising wearout has been observed in several cases. Both phenomena have important managerial implications for the optimal timing of advertising efforts.

4.2.2. Price dynamics

Price-setting is complex, involving cost, demand, competitive, and organizational considerations. In many instances the resulting price is stable over time, perhaps indicating that an equilibrium has been reached. In other cases there is frequent use of temporary price changes such as price promotions or seasonal price hikes. Empirical research on price dynamics has focused mostly on the latter.

The simplest form of consumer response to a price change is the zero-order model, i.e. sales are a function of the current price only, which implies a static response function. Zero-order price response has been observed on several occasions, even when dynamic price effects were specifically tested. For example, price response for eleven brands of an Australian household product was found to be strictly zero-order [Carpenter, Cooper, Hanssens & Midgley, 1988].

Zero-order price response implies that there is no transient component in the sales–price relation. Buyers are reacting to current prices only; they are not taking advantage of temporary price-cuts by stocking up on the product, nor are they anticipating future price movements. Thus, competitors are operating along a static demand curve and can only influence the level, not the timing of their customer's purchases.

If consumers deviate at all from this myopic behavior, dynamic price response should occur. The most common form is *stockpiling*, i.e. moving future purchases to the present to take advantage of a temporary price-cut. This leads to an asymmetric response function not unlike Simon's differential-stimulus model.

A more sophisticated dynamic consumer response is to *anticipate a future price-cut* and thus to reduce purchasing levels until the price reduction occurs. This scenario is described by Doyle & Saunders [1985] as 'regret reduction'. Their empirical example on a European supplier of natural gas and gas appliances did reveal such anticipations, not at the customer level, but rather at the sales-force level. Salespeople were taking advantage of planned promotion campaigns by enticing customers to switch their purchases into the promotion period so that they would receive higher commission rates.

Dynamic price response was studied more formally by Winer [1985], using a vector-price model which distinguishes between five price concepts: anticipated price, price uncertainty, unanticipated inflation or deflation, and reservation price. In an empirical test of seven consumer durables, several of the price concepts were statistically significantly related to probability of purchase. Similarly, a price expectations effect was found to exist in an analysis of coffee buying [Winer, 1986]. These and other studies highlight the importance of using dynamic models for assessing consumers' price-responsiveness.

Price dynamics have also been studied at the firm level. In particular, DeSarbo, Rao, Steckel, Wind & Colombo [1987] developed a friction model for describing and predicting price changes. The model posits, first, that in the absence of major frictions, companies will tend to hold their price constant. However, upward tensions such as inflation and downward tensions such as competition may build up in price-setting to a point where a threshold is exceeded, which prompts the firm to adjust its price (upward or downward). The resulting threshold model of price movements over time is estimated using maximum likelihood. An application to weekly mortgage interest-rate setting revealed that an individual bank will adjust its interest rate in response to the previous weeks' changes in the cost of money and competitive rates.

4.2.3. Reaction functions

Construction of the sales-response function is just one step in marketing programming. If competitors react to our actions, we must develop competitive reaction functions. In a path-breaking article, Bass [1969] presented a model of a market mechanism for cigarettes that contained sales-response functions and the corresponding advertising decision rules for the filter and non-filter segments. The advertising decision-rule equations indicated how one segment's sales influenced the other segment's advertising expenditure decision in the same year. This study was followed by a major investigation of the ready-to-eat cereal market [Bass & Parsons, 1969]. Again there was a four-equation model of the market mechanism. This time there was a pair of relationships describing the behavior of a particular brand and another pair for all other brands combined. A major empirical result was that competitive advertising activities seemed to stimulate primary demand in this market. The advertising decision rules were based on marketing actions and results in the previous bimonthly period. Samuels [1970/71] tested a model very similar to that of Bass & Parsons with data from three markets: scouring powders, toilet soaps and household cleansers. Wildt [1974] studied retail price advertising as well as network advertising as a managerial decision rule. Since three firms accounted for the majority of sales in the industry, his market mechanism contained nine equations.

Lambin [1970] and Lambin, Naert & Bultez [1975] investigated a small electrical appliance from the Stackelberg leader–follower perspective. They constructed the followers' reaction functions for advertising, price and quality. They found that while the competition did react to a change in one marketing instrument by the leader with a change in the same instrument, the competition also changed other elements in their marketing mix. For instance, the competition might only partially match a price-cut and, instead, increase their advertising outlays In the discussion of their results, Lambin, Naert & Bultez raised the possibility of kinked demand curves coming about if the competition did not react when it would result in increased market share. However, they did not address this in their ordinary least squares estimation of the reaction functions.

Parsons & Schultz [1976] describe the general form of these models, which they call *models with endogenous competition.* Our interest is in a typical decision rule for a firm. The level of a particular decision variable for a specific competitor may be affected by the firm's own managerial decision variables, by the managerial decision variables of each of its competitors, by its own and its competitors' past sales, and by autonomous environmental conditions including seasonality. What is important to recognize is that the reaction function of the economist can be, and often is, embedded in the more general construct of the decision rule.

Hanssens [1980b] incorporated the phenomenon of the level of one marketing instrument affecting, or being affected by, levels of other marketing instruments within the same firm into a generalized reaction matrix. This matrix is partitioned so that the main diagonal blocks represent simple competitive reaction. The off-diagonal blocks represent multiple reaction. The diagonal elements represent intra-firm effects and the off-diagonal ones represent inter-firm effects. Hanssens noted that in an oligopoly the inter-firm reaction elasticities should be zero if the firm is a follower (Cournot–Bertrand reaction function) and nonzero if the firm is a leader (Stackelberg reaction function).

Most of what little evidence we have on reaction elasticities is due to Lambin [1976], Metwally [1978] and Leeflang & Wittink [1992]. Leeflang & Wittink conclude:

> "Our findings show that simple competitive reaction functions would fail to capture systematic effects due to marketing variables. At the same time, simple reactions do account for a disproportionate number of reaction effects. Importantly, the estimated competitive reactions appear to be very complex".

Whether a recursive or nonrecursive model is necessary to represent the system containing both sales-response functions and reaction functions depends largely on the data interval. As the data interval lengthens, more mix movements would appear to be simultaneous. Temporal interrelationships can be identified using time-series analysis [Hanssens, 1980a; Leeflang & Wittink, 1992]. The functional form of reaction functions examined has been restricted to either linear or multiplicative. That firms react to either an absolute change or a relative change in competitive behavior seems reasonable; however, no attempt has been made to show which of these is true.

4.3. Assessing the direction of causality

Determining the direction of causality may be straightforward when only two variables are involved, but real-world marketing systems are often so complex that the causal chains cannot be easily established a priori. For example, in competitive markets causal relations may exist in many directions among the following variables: product sales, industry sales, market share, profits, marketing efforts, competitive marketing efforts, and environmental conditions. Although in this case we would have a good idea of the elements in the information set (level 0), it would be difficult to posit one structural marketing model from prior insight alone.

This section discusses ETS (econometric and time-series analysis) model-building techniques for the data-driven assessment of causality in marketing systems. We introduce the concept of Granger causality, discuss empirical testing procedures, and summarize the use of these techniques in marketing models to date.

4.3.1. The concept of Granger causality

It is difficult to establish a workable definition of causality in nonexperimental research. As far as statistical analysis is concerned, we often hear the remark that 'correlation does not imply causation'. But when we adopt a stochastic view of time-series behavior, temporal ordering of events can be used to make an empirical distinction between leading and lagging variables. That distinction is at the basis of a well-known definition of causality due to Granger [1969].

Suppose a marketing system is defined by a two-variable information set (X, Y). In an attempt to forecast Y, we could build a univariate model, i.e., considering the past of Y alone, or we could combine the past of Y and the past of X in a bivariate model. Now, X is said to *Granger cause* Y if the mean squared forecast error (MSFE) of Y using the bivariate model is smaller than the MSFE of the univariate model. Formally:

For the information set containing X and Y, X is said to Granger cause Y if:

$$\mathrm{MSFE}(Y_t | Y_{t-1},\ldots, Y_{t-k}, X_{t-1},\ldots, X_{t-m}) < \mathrm{MSFE}(Y_t | Y_{t-1},\ldots, Y_{t-k}), \tag{4.9}$$

where k and m are positive integers indicating the maximum memory length in Y and X.

There are three distinctive components to Granger's definition:

- It stresses the importance of an adequately formulated information set.
- The empirical detection of causality between X and Y is valid only insofar as no major factors Z are missing from the information set. The 'null' model against which forecasting performance is evaluated is a powerful rival. For example, univariate time-series models have been shown to outperform complex econometric models of the US economy [Nelson, 1972].
- The ultimate test is done out-of-sample. Thus, statistical significance of transfer-function parameters alone is not sufficient to establish Granger causality.

Granger causality applies well in a marketing context. For example, monthly time series of the number of airline passengers on a route have often been found to follow an ARIMA (0,1,1) $(0,1,1)_{12}$ process – known as the airline model – which predicts future passenger levels remarkably well. This model may be written as

$$\begin{aligned}\hat{z}_t &= z_{t-1} + z_{t-12} - z_{t-13} - \theta_1[z_{t-1} - \hat{z}_{t-1}] \\ &\quad - \theta_{12}[z_{t-12} - \hat{z}_{t-12}] + \theta_{13}[z_{t-13} + \hat{z}_{t-13}]\end{aligned} \tag{4.10}$$

where z_t is passengers at time t, $\hat{z}_t$ is time t passengers predicted at time $t-1$, and θ_i are forecasting parameters ($i = 1, 12, 13$). The marketing question 'does manipulating the air fares affect demand?' might be poorly answered by merely correlating or regressing passenger and air-fare series. Granger's definition would assess whether or not air-fare information improves the prediction of passenger levels beyond what is achieved by extrapolation. If the airline pricing managers act rationally and forecast demand accurately, the air fares may follow a rigid seasonal pattern with little extra variation. In that case we may well find that they do not Granger cause passenger demand, but, instead, are caused by (perfectly anticipated) passenger movements. One extension of the definition includes present as well as past values of X in the prediction of Y. This is known as 'Granger instantaneous causality' and is more difficult to measure empirically [Layton, 1984].

4.3.2. Test procedures

Although the concept of Granger causality was developed in economics, it did not achieve recognition until time-series methods for its execution became available. Several procedures have been proposed, including the double prewhitening technique and two regression-based methods due to Granger & Sims.

The double prewhitening method, first proposed by Haugh [1976] and later extended by Haugh & Box [1977], Pierce [1977] and Pierce & Haugh [1977], establishes the direction of causality between two series by cross-correlating the residuals of univariate time-series models fitted to each. How does this method relate to the definition of Granger causality? In the first stage, the predictive power of each series' past is removed via the prewhitening operation. Then, by cross-correlating the residuals at various lags, the method scans the data for any additional sources of covariation. If a significant cross-correlation exists at positive or negative lags, it contributes to Granger causality in that direction. If the spike occurs at lag 0, it contributes to Granger instantaneous causality, but the direction of the effect cannot be established by itself. The main restriction of double prewhitening, though, lies in the fact that both stages are typically carried out on the same sample, so there is no true forecasting test. That limitation prompted Ashley, Granger & Schmalensee [1980] to develop a supplementary test for the out-of-sample performance of univariate vs. bivariate time-series models.

The double prewhitening method has been instrumental in stirring controversial debates of cause and effect in the macroeconomic and financial economics literature. For example, Pierce [1977] reported a lack of relations among several key interest and money indicators previously thought of as highly interrelated. In marketing it was first used to establish primary demand vs. market-share effects of airline flight-scheduling and advertising and to sort out various patterns of competitive reactions among airlines [Hanssens, 1977, 1980b]. Causality testing has also been extensively discussed in Bultez, Leeflang & Wittink [1991]. A more comprehensive overview of causality tests in marketing may be found in HPS, Chapter 5.

Regression models have been used as well, in particular techniques attributed to Granger [1969] and Sims [1972]. By regressing current Y against lagged Y and lagged X [Granger], or against past and future X [Sims], we may test for causality without the preliminary step of univariate time-series analysis. Regression-based causality tests were first used in marketing to determine the causal ordering of advertising and aggregate consumption. Using the Sims method, Jacobson & Nicosia [1981] established a contemporaneous relation between annual advertising and personal consumption in the UK. They also found that advertising affected next year's consumption, and vice versa. Their regression results were confirmed by a double-prewhitening test on the same data.

4.4. Shape of the sales response function revisited

While we have already introduced some dynamic properties of sales-response functions such as asymmetry in response and coefficient variation, we now wish to discuss them in more detail. Asymmetry in response occurs when the magnitude of response to a change in a marketing instrument is different depending on whether the change is an increase or a decrease. This is different from asymmetry in competitive effects, that is, a change in a brand's marketing effort affecting each competitive brand differentially. Coefficient variation occurs when a coefficient changes over time, e.g. an advertising elasticity over the product life-cycle.

4.4.1. Asymmetry in response

The magnitude of sales response to a change in a marketing instrument might be different, depending on whether the change is upward or downward. The effect is beyond any that might be explained by the nonlinearity of the sales-response function. Sales might rise quickly under increased advertising, but stay the same or decline slowly when advertising is removed. As noted previously, this phenomenon has been termed 'hysteresis'. One explanation is that higher advertising expenditures create more customers through greater reach as well as greater frequency. Under the customer holdover paradigm, these new customers subsequently repurchase the product. Thus, if advertising is cut back, sales will fall by less than would be the case in the absence of this effect. (Sasieni [1989] observes that 'In 20 years of studying response data [he] can recall only one example of hysteresis and that concerned price rather than advertising.') Sales response to price may also be asymmetric because of habit formation. The sales-response function will be kinked. A price rise would be less elastic than a price fall. This is termed 'addiction asymmetry'.

Asymmetry in response is usually captured by *rachet models*. There are two types of rachet models. The first is saw-toothed in appearance. The sales-response function is kinked at the prevailing level of a marketing instrument, irrespective of past changes in the instrument. Segments of the adjustment path for increases in level are parallel; segments for decreases are also parallel to each other. The second resembles a bird's footprint in appearance. Purchasing habits that were developed by the use of a product under a condition of record-breaking marketing activity will not be broken easily if marketing effort recedes. Rachet or rachet-type models have been used by Parsons [1976] for advertising carryover effects, by Young [1983] in a cigarette sales-price investigation, and by Simon [1982] in his ADPULS model of the advertising wearout phenomenon [see (4.8)]. A continuous-time version of ADPULS is discussed by Luhmer, Steindl, Feichtinger, Hartl & Sorger [1988a, 1988b]. Asymmetric models may be considered a special case of coefficient variation.

Asymmetry can arise in frequently purchased branded goods because of the phenomenon of fast learning and slow forgetting on the part of consumers. Asymmetry in response to advertising has been addressed by Parsons [1976], Haley [1978], Little [1979] and Simon [1982]. Haley reported on some experiments that showed an immediate sales response to increased advertising. In addition, these experiments indicated that even though the advertising was maintained at the new and higher levels, the magnitude of response gradually became less and less. Little offered two explanations for this. One is that advertising causes prospects to try a product. Only a portion of these new triers became regular purchasers. Consequently, sales taper off from their initial gain to a lower level. (It might be argued that this is not a response phenomenon at all. Rather it might be considered a sampling problem, or more generally, an aggregation problem, because time-series observations are derived from different populations.) The second explanation is that the advertising copy is wearing out. We believe another possible explanation would be competitive reaction.

Asymmetry in response to price has been discussed by Moran [1978]. He provides a summary of some price research that has been conducted in a variety of consumer-product categories. He argues that the only way to analyze a price elasticity is in terms of relative price. Relative price expresses a brand's price relative to the average price for the product category in which it competes. One of his major findings is that a brand's upside demand elasticity and downside elasticity can differ. He conjectures that one reason these elasticities might differ is that consumer segments are not equally informed about what is going on. For instance, an unadvertised price change is more likely to be noticed by current customers. We must note that Moran was working with data that are obsolete now that scanner data are available, and that price promotion and price effects are different.

Russell [1992] provides a generalization of much of the work on brand price competition. His model, the *Latent Symmetric Elasticity Structure* (LSES), assumes that the market-share cross-price-elasticity η_{ij}, the percentage change in the share of brand i with respect to a 1% change in the price of brand j, is equal to the product of the (asymmetric) clout factor of brand j and a symmetric index of the substitutability of the brand pair (i,j). His empirical work shows that clout factors depend upon both market share and average price while the pattern of substitution indices is influenced by the brand's average price level. Assuming that price is correlated with quality, this work suggests that both the pattern of asymmetry (explained by the clout factors) and the draw pattern from price promotions (explained by substitution indices) depend on quality levels. Also see Bucklin, Russell & Srinivasan [1992].

4.4.2. Time-varying coefficients

The effectiveness of each controllable marketing instrument is frequently treated as having the same value over time. However, market response to managerial decision variables might change because of the impact of marketing actions by either a company or its competitors or because of shifts in the environment. For example, Simon & Sebastian [1987] allow the 'innovation' or 'imitation' coefficients in the *Bass market-growth model* to vary systematically with advertising.

If structural changes occur at *known* points in time, the changes in the coefficients of the relevant variables can be represented by dummy variables. A dummy variable takes the value 1 when a phenomenon or characteristic is present and takes the value 0 when it is absent. Palda [1964] assumes that restrictions placed upon Lydia Pinkham's advertising copy by the Food and Drug Administration in 1914 and again in 1925 and by the Federal Trade Commission in 1940 could be captured by dummy variables. These dummy variables affect only the intercept of the sales response function. A somewhat more appropriate approach might have been to use the dummy variables to model changes in the slope coefficient, i.e. the effectiveness of advertising.

Unfortunately the timing of a structural change is rarely known. The parameters in a response function might vary between each time period rather than only between a few time periods. If the parameters follow some random process, the parameter variation is said to be *stochastic*. Any model of stochastic parameter variation that assumes an autoregressive process is called a *sequentially varying parameter model*. If the parameters themselves are functions of observable variables, the parameter variation is said to be *systematic*. Coefficients can also vary over cross-section units.

Specific models, e.g. *switching models*, have been developed for situations where sample observations are generated by two or more distinct regimes. A switch from one regime to another may depend on time, but alternatively, it might depend on a threshold value for some variable or occur stochastically. In the two-regime case, the switching model can be written as

$$\begin{aligned} &\text{Regime 1: } Q = f(\mathbf{X}_1;\beta) \text{ if condition holds,} \\ &\text{Regime 2: } Q = f(\mathbf{X}_2;\alpha) \text{ if condition does not hold.} \end{aligned} \tag{4.11}$$

Bemmaor [1984] tests for the existence of an advertising threshold effect using the stochastic version of this model. The first-regime condition is 'with probability θ' while the second-regime condition is 'with probability $1-\theta$'. Lee & Brown [1985] study the impact for Florida Department of Citrus coupon promotional programs on the demand for frozen concentrated orange juice. Separate sales-response functions were estimated for coupon users and nonusers. The probability of a household redeeming a coupon was itself a function of household characteristics, market conditions, and properties of various promotional programs. The modeling of changing market environments is critically reviewed by Wildt & Winer [1983].

One source of dynamic systematic variation in marketing is the product life-cycle. Marketing theory states that the demand elasticities of managerial decision variables change over the product life-cycle. The theory has been interpreted to say that the advertising elasticity is highest at the growth stage of a product life due to the need to create increased product awareness, and lowest during maturity, with elasticities increasing slightly through saturation and decline stages of the product life-cycle [Mahajan, Bretschneider & Bradford, 1980]. The theory supposedly conjectures that the price elasticity increases over the first three stages – introduction, growth and maturity – and decreases during the decline stage [Mickwitz, 1959]. Very early in the product life-cycle the demand curve may be relatively inelastic as consumers purchase a product to learn about its unknown quantities [Tonks, 1986]. Over time as information accumulates consumers become more price-conscious. General economic principles predict that the presence of close substitutes causes high elasticities. Thus, as a product matures, price elasticities should increase (become more negative) because of the availability of close substitutes. Toward the very end of the product life-cycle, the demand curve may (again) become inelastic as only 'diehard' brand-loyal customers remain.

Empirical evidence on changes in the efficiency of various marketing instruments at different stages of the product life-cycle is sparse. Indications are that advertising elasticities generally fall as products pass through their life-cycles [Parsons, 1975; Arora, 1979]. A naive model of this process would be

$$\varepsilon_A = \alpha_1 e^{-\alpha_2 t} + \alpha_3. \tag{4.12}$$

Using 'moving-window' regressions, Leeflang, Alsem & Reuyl [1991] investigate the competition among suppliers of advertising media in the Dutch advertising market. They find that the cross-elasticity of television advertising on newspaper advertising declined over a 20-year period ending up not significantly different from zero.

Simon [1979] in an empirical study of 35 brands in seven different markets found price elasticities seem to decrease markedly during the introduction and growth stages, reaching a minimum in the maturity stage, after which they may experience an increase during the decline stage. For industrial chemicals, Lilien & Yoon [1988, p. 273] conclude:

> "The level of price elasticity tends to be lower during the later stages of the product life cycle (maturity and decline) than during the earlier stages (introduction and growth). There is no clear tendency of shift in the level of the price elasticity between the introduction and growth stages. Over the latter two stages of the product life cycle (maturity and decline), price elasticity shows a tendency to be stable".

Although these results may be tentative due to methodological problems, e.g. Shoemaker's [1986] comment on Simon [1976], nonetheless, these empirical findings do seem inconsistent with current marketing theory. Snell & Tonks [1988] provide more conventional results in their examination of eight products in the UK chocolate confectionery industry. They report that, with only a few exceptions, elasticities become larger (more negative) over the product life-cycle.

5. Empirical findings and marketing generalizations

A marketing manager's central concern is how selective marketing activities of a brand affect its sales. The manager would like to draw on accumulated wisdom about the shape of the response function. The manager also recognizes that sales effects come through changes in selective demand, through changes in primary demand, or both. As a consequence, the manager might well want to couple a model of industry demand with a market-share model. Whether interested in the brand level or the industry level, the manager would like to know what marketing generalizations have been discovered. This is especially helpful for a manager confronting a new market/product situation.

5.1. *Empirical evidence on the shape of the response function*

The shape of response to a particular nonprice marketing instrument, with the remainder of the marketing mix held constant, is generally concave. Sales always increase with increases in marketing effort, but exhibit diminishing returns to scale. Sometimes the sales response function might be S-shaped with effort. Initially sales may exhibit increasing returns to scale and then diminishing returns to higher levels of marketing effort. Jones [1984] emphasizes that 'nowhere is it suggested that increasing returns are anything but limited and temporary'. The temporary increasing-return phenomenon may be localized in the introductory stage of the product life-cycle and related to increasing distribution coverage, i.e. an improvement in the conversion of demand into sales [cf. Steiner, 1987]. The shape of the response function might be different depending on whether marketing effort is increasing or decreasing, that is, response may be asymmetric. The shape of the response function also might vary with changes in the environment.

The preponderance of empirical evidence favors the strictly concave sales response to nonprice marketing-decision variables. This is especially true for mass-media advertising of frequently purchased goods. For instance, Lambin [1976, p. 95], after doing an analysis of 107 individual brands from 16 product classes and 8 different countries of Western Europe, concludes that 'the shape of the advertising response curve is concave downward, i.e. that there is no S-curve and no increasing returns in advertising a given brand by a given firm'. Earlier, Simon [1970, pp. 8–22] had surveyed the evidence then available on the shape of the response function and found that 'both sales and psychological [nonsales measures of behavior] suggest that the shape of the advertising-response function is invariably concave downward, i.e. that there is no S-curve'. Reviews by Simon & Arndt [1980] and Aaker & Carman [1982] also indicate diminishing returns to advertising.

There are several reasons to expect diminishing returns to increased advertising expenditures [Jagpal, Sudit & Vinod, 1979]. For one, the fraction of unreached prospects is progressively reduced as advertising increases. Consequently, most of the impact of additional advertising messages at high levels of advertising takes place by means of increased frequency. Moreover, after a small number of exposures, perhaps as few as three, increased frequency has very limited marginal effectiveness. Grass & Wallace [1969] among others report on the satiation effects of television commercials. Ottesen [1981] proposed a *theory* of the individual's purchase-response function, and on the basis of this theory, he concludes: 'as advertising effort is being increased, returns in sales must generally be expected to diminish'.

An S-shaped sales response to advertising has long been conjectured [Zentler & Ryde, 1956]. However, this proposition has not been tested explicitly. Two studies explore the proposition that the relation between *market share* and advertising is S-shaped. Johansson [1973] found for a women's hairspray that the advertising effect was concave rather than the proposed S-shape. Rao & Miller [1975] adopt an ad hoc procedure to develop S-shaped response functions for five Lever brands. The work of Ambar Rao & Miller seems suspect, however, since they discard markets that were 'out of line'. This means that for the two brands they discuss in detail, 27% and 20% respectively, of the markets were omitted. Eastlack & Rao [1986] also apply Rao & Miller's methodology. A linear sales response to radio gross-ratings points and television gross-ratings points was estimated for each Selling Areas Marketing, Inc. (SAMI) market. Gross-ratings points (GRP's) refers to the total number of exposures generated by an advertising schedule. It is a measure of delivered advertising. Inspection of per-capita estimates of marginal response to radio GRP levels revealed no significant response below 180 GRP's (an indication of a threshold), a sharp increase in response as GRP's increased between 180 and 230, a slight (almost flat) decline in response as GRP's increased from 230 to 340 (an indication of saturation), and low response to a few observations with GRP's above 400 (an indication of supersaturation?). These two works, unfortunately (because of their ad hoc nature), are the only published support for an S-shaped response function. The possibility of an S-shaped relation between market share and communications (advertising plus personal selling) for an industrial product is considered by Gopalakrisna & Chatterjee [1992]. Their empirical evidence implies a concave response function [p. 191, fn. 3]. Broadbent [1984, p. 310] in a discussion of an advertising stock model reports that "The uncertainty in the data also makes it difficult – we would say from our experience impossible – to prove or disprove the reality of an S-shaped or step function."

The lack of evidence for an S-shaped curve has an important implication for the timing of advertising expenditures. An advertiser might want to choose between two alternative policies, a constant spending rate per period or a pulsed expenditure. Ambar Rao [1970, p. 55] defines a pulsing policy as a pattern of advertising where periods with high advertising intensity alternate with very little or no advertising. A sufficient condition [Rao, 1970, p. 5] for adopting a pulsing policy would be that the sales-response function be S-shaped and the budget constraint be binding. The budget constraint has to require that the alternative constant-rate policy be in the region of increasing returns to scale. But most empirical evidence says that a typical brand has a concave sales-response function; consequently, the S-shape cannot be used to justify a pulsing policy.

The relationship between *market share* and *share of retail outlets* seems to be S-shaped. Cardwell [1968] reports that in marketing gasoline incremental new outlets were substantially below average in gallonage until a certain share of market was achieved. Above this critical market-share, performance improved markedly. Lilien & Rao [1976] also postulate an S-shaped relationship between share of market and share of outlets. Neither study provides empirical evidence supporting its claims. Naert & Bultez [1975] do an analysis of the effect of market share on the distribution network of a major brand of gasoline in Italy. Their results support the S-shaped hypothesis at the market-share level. However, when the hypothesis is tested at the aggregate brand-switching level, it is rejected. In any event, the relationship between market share and share of outlets may be simply an expression of the difference between demand and sales. In general, an S-shape for market share may be an artifact of its being constrained to lie between zero and one. The underlying sales-response function may not be S-shaped.

If support for S-shaped sales response is weak, *even less support exists for the threshold effect*. Although many marketing managers believe that a threshold effect operates within their market [Corkindale & Newall, 1978], Simon [1970, p. 22] expresses the opinion that "threshold effects ... constitute a monstrous myth". Even though the argument might be made at the individual level that a prospect might be unaware of a brand or unwilling to buy it until several advertising messages have been received, little evidence of this threshold phenomenon in aggregate sales-response functions has been found. Corkindale & Newall [p. 373] note that 'Little generalisable evidence of either phenomena [threshold and wearout levels of expenditure] seems to exist. This is mostly because managers and their agencies avoid operating at or near the supposed limits.'

A most interesting attempt to identify a threshold effect in an aggregate sales response is by Bemmaor [1984]. A market-share response function is partitioned into two regimes – above and below the threshold [see (4.1)]. A multiplicative function describes each segment. A random shift between these two regimes was postulated. For the product studied, the best fit occurs when the estimate of the proportion of observations above the threshold was 73%. The corresponding threshold advertising share was deduced to be about 18%. Thus, these results indicate decreasing returns to scale but with a discontinuity.

The existence of a saturation level is universally accepted. Nonetheless, the saturation level is rarely explicitly modeled and measured. The usual procedure is to represent response by a function that allows any given level to be surpassed, but requires increasing effort to exceed each higher level. This approach is probably adequate for use in decision models focusing on short-run marketing tactics; however, when interest is in long-term strategy, the saturation ceiling should be estimated. One industry sales-response function in which the saturation level was explicitly modeled was Ward's [1975] study of canned, single-strength grapefruit juice. He used a reciprocal model. Saturation sales, Q^0, were estimated to be 69.82 million gallons. The highest sales observed to date were 53.77 million gallons.

The notion of a supersaturation effect, excessive marketing effort causing reduced sales, has been promulgated by Ackoff and his colleagues [Waid, Clark & Ackoff, 1956; Rao, 1970; Ackofff & Emshoff, 1975] and is being incorporated into marketing theory [Enis & Mokwa, 1979]. A possible explanation could involve the content of the advertising message. If the message is inappropriate, more exposure to the 'wrong' message could have a negative effect. This could also be the case with the 'wrong' advertising-copy execution. In particular, some advertisements may be very irritating after too many exposures. Still, *the argument for supersaturation in advertising is unconvincing*. Campaigns such as Wisk's 'Ring around the collar' have been very much disliked by viewers, but, nonetheless, have been very successful in terms of sales. The only empirical evidence even tangentially bearing on the existence of such an effect comes from Ackoff's Budweiser study. While previous research, such as that of Parsons & Bass [1971], has shown that reducing advertising expenditures may increase profits even though sales are lost, the Budweiser study is the only research in which reducing advertising not only increased profits but also increased sales. Haley [1978] did report on another beer test in which those areas where advertising was stopped showed better results than the remaining areas. However, subsequent investigation revealed that local distributors, upon finding their advertising support dropped, invested their own funds in advertising. Their efforts more than offset the cuts made by the manufacturer. Participants in the Budweiser study have asserted that adequate controls were maintained in their work; consequently, their results remain an anomaly. Even if supersaturation does exist, it is well outside the usual operating ranges for marketing instruments since management has little incentive to operate even at saturation. Of course, a firm could operate in this region by mistake.

A more plausible argument for supersaturation might be made for marketing-decision variables other than advertising. For example, a reduction in sales-force size might lead to more effort, and consequently sales, if territories and hence potential were realigned and salespeople were more highly motivated because of this. Also, it was recently reported in the business press that a major computer manufacturer increased its sales by decreasing the number of retail outlets carrying its personal computers. The explanation was that with fewer dealers there was less price competition, higher retail prices and hence increased margins, and thus more funds available to each retailer to support direct sales effort. These examples still may not justify the theoretical existence of supersaturation. They may only demonstrate that it could be empirically found if the model is misspecified by ignoring sales-force motivation and/or territory alignment. Whatever the case, there have been no empirical studies of supersaturation for sales-force or distribution variables.

One source of systematic parameter variation is the interaction of the marketing decision variables with each other. Advertising expenditures often influence the magnitude of price elasticity [Moran, 1978; Sunoo & Lin, 1978]. Conventional wisdom is that advertising decreases price-sensitivity. Schultz & Vanhonacker [1978] provide some empirical support for this proposition, yet Wittink [1977a] gives some evidence that relative price becomes more elastic as advertising share increases. The implication is that advertising tends to increase the price-competitiveness of the brand investigated. This supports earlier findings [Eskin,

1975; Eskin & Baron, 1977] that a high advertising effort yields a higher price elasticity than a low advertising effort. Farris & Albion [1980] suggest that the concept of vertical market structures might reconcile what appears to be conflicting evidence. They posit that the relationship between advertising and price depends on whether price is measured at the factory level or at the consumer level. Krishnamurthi & Raj [1988] found that, for a well-established brand, increased noninformational advertising of the mood type decreased price sensitivity. Popkowski, Peter & Rao [1990] postulated a model in which local advertising makes demand more price sensitive while national advertising makes demand less price-sensitive. They reported empirical evidence supporting their model.

Moreover, many secondary dimensions of marketing variables are only operative when the primary dimension of the variable is present. If no advertising expenditure is made, the advertising copy can have no impact on sales. Samples and handouts are distributed in conjunction with a sales call. Parsons & Vanden Abeele [1981] demonstrated that the effectiveness of the calls made by the sales force of a pharmaceutical manufacturer for an established ethical drug varied systematically as a function of collateral material, such as samples, used.

Systematic variation might occur over individuals or territories. Moran [1978] found that the price elasticities for a brand varied from market to market and from segment to segment. Wittink [1977b] tested one brand to evaluate whether demographic variables explained differences in the estimated parameters of the sales response functions for various territories. He found that they did not. Elrod & Winer [1979] had only somewhat better luck in relating household characteristics to the estimated parameters in purchasing response functions for different households. Gatignon & Hanssens [1987] reported that marketing effectiveness in Navy recruiting is inversely related to environmental conditions, in particular, civilian employment rate.

5.2. *Marketing generalizations*

Guidance for marketing action comes from regularities in aggregate response behavior across markets. Of course, marketing is very product-market-specific and these generalizations are not too precise. We begin with brand-level generalizations, then turn to industry-level generalizations.

5.2.1. *Brand-level generalizations*

Many brand-level generalizations relate to *short-term elasticities.* One of the first marketing generalizations [Leone & Schultz, 1980] is that *the elasticity of selective advertising on own-brand sales is positive but low.* This is supported by the meta-analyses conducted by Aaker & Carman [1982] and Assmus, Farley & Lehmann [1984]. The value for the advertising elasticity with unit sales appears to be of the order of 0.10.

There is a growing body of information on price elasticities. *The elasticity of price on own-brand sales is negative and elastic.* A meta-analysis conducted by Tellis [1988] found a mean own-price elasticity of about −2.5. (The magnitude of cross-price elasticities is roughly 0.5, e.g. Bolton [1989].) Some argue that Tellis's own-price elasticities appear too low. If a simple constant-elasticity model is used, a −2.5 elasticity would imply that grocery markups should be 67%. One never sees these types of markups. The reason is that the retailer worries about lost customers, which is not analyzed by Tellis. The large discrepancy in the magnitudes between these two own elasticities – advertising and price – has led to a debate about whether or not price is a superior tactic to advertising [Broadbent, 1989; Tellis, 1989; Sethuraman & Tellis, 1991].

Blattberg & Neslin [1989] propose some generalizations about sales promotions. One is that *sales promotions have a dramatic immediate impact on brand sales.* This proposition is supported by the work of Chevalier [1975], Gupta [1988] and Moriarty [1985, p. 42]. A second generalization is that *short-run promotional cross-elasticities are asymmetric.* They mean that the effect of Brand A's promotion on Brand B's sales is not the same as the effect of Brand B's promotion on Brand A's sales. Blattberg & Wisniewski [1989] found that higher-price, higher-quality brands steal share from brands in the tier below as well as from other brands in the same price-quality tier. However, lower-tier brands do not steal a significant share from the tiers above. A third generalization is that *each promotional tool has its own impact and may, in addition, interact with other promotional tools.* Blattberg & Neslin point out that promotions are often composed of two or more promotional tools; e.g. price-cut, feature and display may be used together. It may, however, be difficult to estimate the separate effects of each tool because of the high correlations among these variables, i.e. multicollinearity. Blattberg & Neslin [1989] and Guadagni & Little [1983] provide support for this proposition. The last generalization is that *promotional price-cut elasticities are larger than those for regular-price elasticities.*

Another marketing generalization identified by Schultz & Leone is that *increasing store-shelf (display) space has a positive impact on sales of nonstaple grocery items.* They found support for this statement in the works of Pauli & Hoecker [1952], Mueller, Kline & Trout [1953], *Progressive Grocer* [1963, 1964], Cox [1964, 1970], Kotzan & Evanson [1969], Frank & Massy [1970], Kennedy [1970] and Curhan [1972, 1974a, 1974b]. Criticisms of these studies have been made by Peterson & Cagley [1973] and Lynch [1974]. They raise the possibility that the relationship between sales and shelf space should be expressed in terms of a simultaneous system of (nonlinear) equations.

Another possible marketing generalization might be that *personal selling has a direct and positive influence on sales.* Lambert [1968] found that sales volume of medical X-ray film in a district was related to the number of salespeople employed by the company in the district as well as to a product-mix measure and a selling-price index. However, the direction of causality is not clear. Waid, Clark & Ackoff [1956] in their analysis of the lamp division of General Electric indicated that the number of calls was the only variable to influence dollar sales. Turner [1971] refined the concept of calling effort by defining it as the product of the number of calls and the number of people seen per call. Calling effort was shown to have a significant impact on the actual sales to individual customers. Beswick & Cravens

[1977] reported that dollar sales of one firm's high-priced consumer goods were determined by the salesperson's percentage of time spent in a geographic area and variables representing potential, workload, company experience, salesperson experience, and sales manager experience. They could not estimate the elasticity of selling effort precisely. It could be increased by about 50% without changing the reported R^2 because of the flat response surface arising from the high correlations among the independent variables in their nonlinear model. Parsons & Vanden Abeele [1981] found the sales-call elasticity of an established Belgian ethical drug to be positive, but inelastic.

Little information exists on product and distribution elasticities because changes occur rarely, or slowly, for established products. Thus, their effects are usually represented in sales response functions as part of the constant intercept. Although these effects cannot be identified, this does not mean they are unimportant. For additional discussion of brand generalizations, see Erickson [1990]. Having seen what is known about brand sales, we now turn to industry sales.

5.2.2. Industry-level generalizations

Models of industry demand have also been constructed to assess the impact of trade-association or government efforts and to address public policy questions. For example, wool producers might want to determine the effectiveness of advertising the 'Wool Mark'. In the same vein, public-health officials might want to evaluate the relationship between cigarette advertising and children's cigarette consumption. These would be examples of 'primary' advertising.

Nerlove & Waugh [1961] discovered that the advertising and promotion expenditures of the two largest organized groups of growers, the Florida Citrus Commission and Sunkist Growers, had a marked impact on the sales of oranges in the United States. Ball & Agarwala [1969] determined that generic advertising for tea in the United Kingdom slowed the downward sales trend, but could not reverse the slide. McGuiness & Cowling [1975] decided that advertising had a positive, statistically significant impact on cigarette sales in the United Kingdom, and that this impact was only partially offset by the amount of publicity given to the health effects of smoking. Lambin [1976] found that in only four out of ten product markets did industry advertising increase industry sales. Simon & Sebastian [1987], using a model with systematic parameter variation, showed that advertising influenced the diffusion of new telephones in West Germany. Their advertising (goodwill) elasticity attained a maximum of 2.14%, then declined nonmonotonically to 0.89% within five years. These and other studies lead to the generalization that *primary advertising has a direct and positive influence on total industry (market) sales* [cf. Leone & Schultz, 1980].

Industry sales are less price-elastic than individual brand sales. Industry price-elasticities are typically less than one in absolute magnitude (inelastic) whereas brand price-elasticities are typically larger than one in absolute magnitude (elastic). Neslin & Shoemaker [1983] found that the presweetened segment of the ready-to-eat cereal market in the United States was much more price-sensitive than the market as a whole. If industry elasticities are less than one (inelastic), then why do firms not raise price? The answer is they do when they can – such as in the case of oligopolies with a leader, e.g. ready-to-eat cereal with Kellogg. With what we know now, where might we go next with our research agenda?

6. Research issues

While we know quite a bit about advertising and something about price, our empirical base on other marketing instruments is woefully small. A better grasp of marketing instruments other than advertising is needed. For instance, marketing managers would like to know when and to what degree excessive price-promotion changes customers' perceptions of the normal price of a product and of its quality. Also, managers would like to know how to assess the impact of a salesperson's effort, especially since empirical evidence has indicated that territory workload and potential are significant determinants in sales differences among territories, whereas sales effort may have little, if any, effect. Ryans & Weinberg [1979] conjecture that it might be useful to construct a two-stage model of sales-force performance. The first part would specify the factors that influence the amount of effort a salesperson puts forth and the second would represent the relationship of sales to sales-force effort.

Some empirical results, such as those involving the product life-cycle, seem to be in conflict with marketing theory. Other empirical results, such as those for the price–advertising interaction, have been contradictory. Consider, for example, the relationship between the demand elasticity and relative price. Moran [1978] states that the farther a brand's price is from the category average in either direction, the lower its demand elasticity is, whereas Simon [1979] says that the magnitude of price elasticity increases for increasing positive and negative deviations of a brand's price from the average price of brands competing with it. Parker [1992] found no consistent pattern of price-elasticity dynamics over the adoption life-cycle for 19 consumer durables. We will now focus our attention on major emerging trends in ETS.

6.1. Emerging trends in econometric modeling

While the use of econometrics in marketing is now mature, nonetheless there are exciting prospects for new advances. Major developments relate to definition of variables, under-researched mix elements, model identification, Bayesian estimation based on meta-analysis, combining different functional forms, level of aggregation, discretization of data, and efficiency frontiers.

6.1.1. Definition of variables

How should we measure marketing instruments properly? For example, in many, but not all, sales-response models, 'advertising' is measured in monetary units, e.g. dollars, but consumers do not react to dollars. In a similar vein, is an unpromoted temporary price-cut a 'promotion'? How temporary should a price-cut be to be classified as a 'promotion'? Should price be price/weight, or price paid, or price/delivered benefit (e.g. price/'cleaning power' for detergents)? These and related questions need to be addressed to refine our assessments of the effects of marketing instruments.

6.1.2. Under-researched mix elements

While advertising and price have been widely studied, and price promotion is currently under intense scrutiny with the availability of scanner data, distribution and sales-force effort have been little studied. Farris, Olver & De Kluyver [1989] propose an interesting approach to modeling the relation between distribution and market share. Total market share is broken down into share due to uncompromised demand and share due to compromised demand from buyers whose preferred brand is unavailable. These two share variables are then modeled as different functions of distribution. Distribution is made operational by using PCV, the weighted (by-product-category volume) fraction of stores stocking the brand. (They note that many retail audit services report ACV, which is weighed by all-commodities volume; and that these two measures (PCV and ACV) may not be equal.) More research on this approach, and distribution in general, is needed. Very few studies have been able to separate out the effects of sales-force effort from the overwhelming influences of potential and workload. Yet sales-force effort is often crucial to the successful marketing of products and services.

6.1.3. Model identification

We do not want to leave the false impression that you only need to grab some data set to obtain parameter estimates of the functional form of your model. Econometric techniques explain the impact of *variation* in the explanatory variables on a dependent variable. But what if an explanatory variable does not vary much? For example, a brand manager of the leading brand in the soap market knows that if he increases price, brand unit sales will go down dramatically. If he decreases it, he will lose money. Consequently, the price of the brand is likely to remain relatively constant over a several-year time horizon. What can an econometrician say about the price parameter in this circumstance? Very little. We need to know the conditions to be met for a model to be identifiable from the data.

6.1.4. Bayesian estimation based on meta-analysis

Farley & Lehmann [1986] believe that Bayesian applications of meta-analysis are a promising area for research when data are sparse or when preliminary estimates are needed such as in the case of new products. The results from meta-analysis can be considered prior estimates; and then Bayesian regression can be used to get modified estimates for the market-response function. In this spirit, Russell, Hagerty & Carman [1991] apply a Bayesian methodology to estimate firm-level marketing-mix elasticities when sparse data prevent classical regression procedures from recovering elasticity estimates. Elasticity estimates for over 2200 firms in the PIMS database are recovered by using the elasticities of 197 firms found earlier [Hagerty, Carman & Russell, 1988] as prior information.

6.1.5. Separate response functions

Most research on market-response functions assumes that each of the marketing-mix instruments follows the *same* response function. In particular, each instrument is usually assumed to follow a power function, which, in turn, can be combined multiplicatively with other instruments to directly form the multiplicative sales-response function. However, each instrument could follow a different functional form. In MARMIX, a computer-based model-building package designed to help managers in setting annual marketing budgets, De Kluyver & Pessemier [1986] permit separate response functions for the marketing-mix elements to be estimated. These separate functions are then combined in an additive model if independence among the different elements in the marketing mix is assumed, or in a multiplicative model if interaction among these elements is expected. Moore & Pessemier [1992] discuss more recent refinements of MARMIX. Work in this direction has just begun.

6.1.6. Level of aggregation

The 'market' in 'market response' refers to a group of heterogeneous individuals. One problem that has not been addressed is the lack of recognition of individual heterogeneity in a changing population over time. Moreover, while we have discussed store-level versus market-level aggregation, nothing much has been said about the individual level where response actually occurs.

We do want to call attention to econometric developments as they relate to the total number of purchases by a customer in a particular time period. *Purchase incidence* has been modeled as a Poisson-distributed variable, in which heterogeneity among customers is captured by allowing their purchase rates to vary following a gamma distribution. Parsons [1987] and Rosenquist & Strandvik [1987] have proposed representing heterogeneity directly by relating explanatory variables to purchase incidence using *Poisson regression*:

$$\Pr\{N_t = k|\lambda\} = \frac{e^{-\lambda}\lambda^k}{k!}, \quad k = 0, 1, 2, \ldots \tag{6.1}$$

where N_t is the number of purchases at time interval t and λ is a parameter.

Explanatory variables are introduced by making the parameter of the Poisson distribution, λ, a function of them:

$$\lambda = f(X, \alpha) \tag{6.2}$$

where α's are the parameters. This is but another example of (deterministic) systematic parameter variation. The functional form of this relationship is usually linear or log-linear, but could be nonlinear. Estimation is usually done by maximum likelihood estimation (MLE) based on the Poisson distribution, but Bayesian and pseudo-MLE methods have been put forward as well. The Poisson distribution has been criticized because of its property that the variance equals the mean:

$$\lambda = \mathrm{E}(N_t) = \mathrm{Var}(N_t) > 0. \tag{6.3}$$

Extensions have been proposed to relax this assumption. Modified count data models include *hurdle models* and *with-zeros models.*

Despite the research noted earlier, more work needs to be done on the impact of aggregation on the functional form of the response function and the parameter estimates. Areas of interest include individual- versus aggregate-level estimation, weekly versus monthly estimation, cross-section versus time-series versus cross-section-and-time-series estimation.

6.1.7. Discretization of data

The process being modeled is inherently continuous, yet we usually build models based upon discrete data. A number of the response phenomena might be artifacts of this discretization.

The main issue in the specification of a dynamic model is whether to formulate a continuous-time model using differential equations, a discrete-time model using difference equations, or a mixed model using differential–difference equations. Before discussing this issue, it is necessary to make a distinction between instantaneous variables and flow variables. An *instantaneous* (*stock*) *variable* is a variable that is measurable at a point in time. Prices, distribution coverage and interest rates are examples of instantaneous variables in marketing. A *flow variable* is a variable that is not measurable at a point in time. Unit sales and advertising expenditures are examples of flow variables in marketing. The rate of change in an instantaneous variable is also treated as a 'flow' variable.

The primary advantage of a continuous model is that *its estimated parameters are independent of the observation period.* This does not hold for a discrete model. A discrete model estimated on weekly data will be different from one estimated on annual data. The two primary advantages of a discrete model are that it can capture discontinuous phenomena and that most econometric techniques have been developed for estimating it. Some work on this topic has been done by Houston & Parsons [1986] and Rao [1986].

6.1.8. Efficiency frontiers

We have discussed various specifications of sales-response functions and have noted the presence of equation error. Random disturbances are assumed to occur around the estimated sales-response function. These errors occur on both sides of the estimated function. Thus, the traditional econometric approach may be considered to produce an 'average' sales-response function. This is sufficient for many purposes. However, in other cases such as that of marketing productivity, it is inadequate.

Consider sales-force productivity. Econometric methods are often used to either set quotas or to assess the performance of a salesperson in a territory in order to take into account the many factors, such as potential and workload, involved. A sales manager does not want to use 'average' performance as a standard, but rather wants people to strive to achieve the best that can be achieved in their territories. Therefore, a need arises to estimate the sales-response function that expresses the 'maximum' sales achievable from the effort of the sales force given the environments in which its members operate. This function is called a *frontier* sales-response function.

Observations will either lie on a frontier or fall below it. The result is a model with a one-sided distribution of errors:

$$Q = f(X, \beta) - v \quad \text{where } v \geqslant 0. \tag{6.4}$$

These errors represent *inefficiency*. Distributions used include the half-normal, exponential, truncated-normal, and the gamma. Estimation is done by corrected least squares or maximum likelihood.

One-sided distributions, however, have their weaknesses. Measurement error in the dependent variable would be a major problem in the analysis. Moreover, as might be expected, outliers can dominate the estimated sales-response function. This has led some to add a traditional two-sided error term to the model as well:

$$Q = f(X, \beta) - v + \omega = f(X, \beta) + v. \tag{6.5}$$

We now have a *frontier model with composed error*. For a recent review of econometric estimation of frontiers, see Bauer [1990]. Marketing researchers working in this area include Parsons [1991] and Horsky & Nelson [1991].

6.2. Emerging trends in time-series modeling

Although a lot has been written on distributed-lag relationships among marketing variables, we know remarkably little about the long-term effects of marketing actions on sales and other performance variables. A key reason for this is that our market-response models typically assume that the data are generated as stable (usually normal) distributions around a fixed mean. Therefore, if long-term movements in the data are present (such as an upward trend followed by a downturn), our models are not well equipped to represent their underlying causes. Addressing long-term effects is one emerging trend. Another one is the untangling of the effects of purchase reinforcement and advertising carryover.

6.2.1. Long-term effects

Recent developments in long-term time-series model-building, especially *unit-root* testing and *cointegration modeling*, offer substantial promise for gaining new insights on the long-run effects of marketing efforts. In this section we briefly review the key aspects of long-term modeling. For a complete application we refer to Powers, Hanssens, Hser & Anglin [1991].

Temporary and permanent components. It is often observed that marketing and other socioeconomic time-series move smoothly over time. Suppose such is the case for a hypothetical brand's sales Q and that a simple first-order Markov model or autoregressive process can be used to represent this phenomenon:

$$Q_t = \varphi Q_{t-1} + c + \omega_t \tag{6.6}$$

or, using lag operator notation,

$$(1 - \varphi L)Q_t = c + \omega_t, \qquad (6.7)$$

where ω_t is white noise. The time series of sales has the simple properties of a constant mean and a constant variance. Furthermore, successive substitution of lagged sales in Model (6.7) ultimately produces the expression

$$Q_t = c + \omega_t + \varphi\omega_{t-1} + \varphi^2\omega_{t-2} + \cdots \qquad (6.8)$$

in which current sales levels are explained as the sum of an infinite number of random shocks in the past. With $|\varphi| < 1$, the effect on any shock ω on Q eventually dies out, i.e. the time series Q_t consists of strictly *temporary* components. If the series drifts away from its mean, it must eventually return.

If $\varphi = 1$ the situation changes drastically. Now the infinite-shock representation of the model is

$$Q_t = c + \omega_t + \omega_{t-1} + \omega_{t-2} + \cdots \qquad (6.9)$$

and it is clear that *any* shock in the past, however distant, has a *permanent* effect on sales. The reduced form of such a model is

$$Q_t = Q_{t-1} + c + \omega_t \qquad (6.10)$$

which is commonly known as the random-walk model, and may be 'without drift' ($c = 0$) or 'with drift' ($c \neq 0$). The properties of the random walk are that it has no fixed mean and that its population variance is infinite, i.e. the variance grows without bounds as the time series expands. In contrast to a temporary-effects model, this model does *not* imply that the series must return to any previous value. It may wander in any direction for as little as one period or as many as one hundred or more periods. In fact, the expected time of return to any observed value is infinite. The best-known example of a random walk is the behavior of stock-market prices.

In practice we may observe time series with a mixture of temporary and permanent components. The statistical distinction between the two involves the presence or absence of *unit roots* in the characteristic equation of the time series. For example, in the model above, the characteristic equation is

$$1 - \varphi z = 0, \qquad (6.11)$$

which has a unit root only if $\varphi = 1$. Consequently, testing for the presence of permanent components in time series is equivalent to testing for the presence of unit roots in the time-series model underlying the data. Such tests are far from trivial, because the statistical properties of the data are different in the presence as opposed to the absence of unit roots. See Dickey, Bell & Miller [1986] for a comprehensive review.

Implications of unit-root testing. Unit roots in a time series of brand sales imply that the sales fluctuations are more than just temporary deviations from a constant mean. For example, sales may grow for long periods of time, and at different rates of growth, they may suddenly peak and even take on a downward course, as would be typical of a product life-cycle. These developments are typically not deterministic, for example, a growth trend may stop at any time, and it is precisely this type of sales evolution that is realistic in the marketplace and of obvious managerial relevance. On the other hand, stationary data (without unit roots) are perhaps less interesting since the long-run outlook of sales in a stationary system is known from the sample.

Unfortunately, it is difficult to build models on data with unit roots. Since the population mean is undefined and the variance is infinite, traditional statistical inference runs into problems because the basic assumptions of the general linear model are violated. Time-series analysts solve this problem by transforming the data prior to model-building: first-order differencing removes linear trend, second-order differencing removes quadratic trend, and seasonal differencing removes seasonality. Granger [1980] refers to the original series as 'integrated of order 1', or $I(1)$, and the differenced series as $I(0)$. In general, if a time series requires kth-order differencing in order to become stationary, i.e if it has k unit roots in its characteristic equation, then the series is said to be $I(k)$.

While differencing the data to obtain stationarity is common practice in time-series model-building, the resulting model in changes operates only the short run: temporary fluctuations in Y can be traced to temporary fluctuations in X. Such models do not make inferences about the long-run behavior of Y in function of that of X. Consequently, as soon as the forecasting horizon is extended, the predictive power of such models drops considerably.

The equilibrium relationship. Several literatures, most notably economics, statistics, engineering and management, use concepts such as 'equilibrium', 'steady state' and 'long-term relationship'. Although individual definitions may vary somewhat, we can say, in general, that in an equilibrium relation between X and Y, there will be no change in either Y or X; furthermore, there will be a relationship $Y = cX$. Formally:

$$Y_t - Y_{t-1} = 0, \tag{6.12a}$$

$$X_t - X_{t-1} = 0, \tag{6.12b}$$

$$Y_t = cX_t, \tag{6.12c}$$

or, in words, there are no pressures for either sales or marketing to move away from present levels, and there is some constant ratio between the two. In practice, of course, there will be random perturbations from equilibrium, but they will be strictly zero-order. For example, the *first-order differences* of the data may be white noise:

$$Y_t - Y_{t-1} = (1 - L)Y_t = \omega_{yt}, \tag{6.13a}$$

$$X_t - X_{t-1} = (1 - L)X_t = \omega_{xt}. \tag{6.13b}$$

The steady-state relationship between X and Y prevents the individual series from wandering away too far from each other. As a simple example, consider the relationship between production levels and retail sales. The equilibrium between the two is maintained by an inventory position which is acceptable to both parties in the exchange (the marketer and the consumers). If, for some external reason, retail sales suddenly start to move upward, then inventories are depleted and production must eventually catch up. Thus, while individual series may well be nonstationary (sales in the example), equilibrium implies that the (scaled) *difference* between the two is not allowed to permanently deviate from zero.

We are therefore in a position to formally incorporate an equilibrium relationship in a market-response model or other system. Following a recent definition by Engle & Granger [1987], two series X and Y are said to be *cointegrated* if they are each $I(k)$, but there exists a linear combination of the two series which is stationary:

$$Z_t = X_t + cY_t \sim I(0), \tag{6.14}$$

where c is called the integrating constant. The definition is conceptually appealing. In the absence of cointegration, any arbitrary linear combination of two nonstationary time-series will also be nonstationary. Also, in the seasonal time-series that are characteristic of many marketing situations, it will typically be the case that the combination of two seasonal series is itself seasonal. But if the series are cointegrated, then a powerful result emerges, namely that the (scaled) deviation between the two is stationary. If more than two series are involved, the concept may be extended to that of a *cointegrating vector*.

Testing for an equilibrium. The definition of cointegration is not only intuitively appealing, it also allows for empirical testing on time-series data. Having established, for example, that X and Y are each $I(1)$:

$$\Delta Y_t = \omega_{yt}, \quad \text{so } Y_t \text{ is } I(1), \tag{6.15a}$$

$$\Delta X_t = \omega_{xt}, \quad \text{so } X_t \text{ is } I(1). \tag{6.15b}$$

If X and Y are cointegrated, then the time series of residuals,

$$u_t = Y_t - bX_t, \tag{6.16}$$

should be $I(0)$. Engle & Granger [1987] propose to estimate the 'equilibrium regression'

$$Y_t = a + bX_t + u_t \tag{6.17}$$

by ordinary least squares and to subject the residuals $\hat{u}_t$ to a Dickey–Fuller test. Rejection of the null hypothesis of nonstationary residuals is evidence that the time series are in fact cointegrated. A few comments about the 'equilibrium regression' are in order. At first glance it is a naive equation, estimated by a basic method (OLS) which does not reflect the state of the art in applied econometric modeling. The residuals are likely to be ill-behaved, for example, they may be highly autocorrelated. But the essence of the equation is not the common hypothesis test on b or an overall goodness-of-fit test, but rather the challenge of taking two or more nonstationary time-series and finding a linear combination of them that is stationary. Stock [1987] has shown that, under the hypothesis of cointegration, the OLS estimate has three desirable properties: it is consistent, it has a bias of order T-1, and it has a variance of order T-2. Thus for all but unduly small samples the OLS estimate provides a reliable estimate of the cointegrating vector.

In conclusion, we may formulate two conditions for the existence of a long-run or equilibrium relationship between sales levels and marketing support. First, the sales series must contain at least one permanent component. Secondly, these permanent components must be related to each other. If these conditions are not met, we may still observe strong relationships between the series, including distributed-lag relationships, but these would only affect the temporary behavior of the series. For example, sales promotion may increase market share in the same period and decrease it in the next period (due to consumer stockpiling), but eventually sales will return to their average levels. However, if an equilibrium relation is present, then the use of sales promotions may eventually cause market shares to grow to higher levels.

To date, cointegration models have been used in marketing to assess the long-term market structure of the private aircraft industry [Dekimpe & Hanssens, 1991] and to measure the long-run impacts of public demarketing efforts to curb narcotics abuse [Powers, Hanssens, Hser & Anglin, 1991]. Several other areas of research in marketing stand to benefit from this approach, for example, product life-cycle theory and brand-equity research.

6.2.2. Untangling purchase reinforcement and advertising carryover

We have already noted that at least some of the impact of advertising in one time period may be carried over into future periods. The argument is that past advertising is remembered by those who see it and, as a result, a brand builds 'goodwill'. This goodwill influences brand choice. This approach may be too simplistic in that it ignores purchase experience. Advertising may create the initial purchase, but customers will buy a brand again only if they find it acceptable in use. Thus, an alternative to an advertising carryover approach is a *current advertising effects with purchase feedback* approach. In reality we would expect both to be operating. Thus, Givon & Horsky [1990] propose a model to estimate simultaneously the relative magnitude of the two approaches. Their empirical work indicates that purchase reinforcement dominates over advertising carryover in affecting the evolution of market share. Dekimpe & Hanssens [1993] propose a new measure called 'persistence' to assess these effects in the long run.

7. Discussion

Marketing has seen a rapid expansion in the widespread use of quantitative methods. Correlation and regression analysis were among the first techniques used as marketing research emerged as a discipline after World War II [cf. Ferber, 1949]. In the early 1970s regression analysis became econometrics. Simultaneous-equation systems could be estimated almost as easily as single regression equations [e.g. Bass & Parsons, 1969]. While econometrics as a whole continues to flourish as new and more sophisticated estimation techniques and associated computer software have become available, simultaneous-equation systems have not become widely prevalent. One explanation is that an applied researcher may find little difference in practice between parameter estimates obtained from a technically correct simultaneous-equation technique and those obtained from a corresponding 'sinner' single-equation technique. Notwithstanding this possibility, allied social-science disciplines have experienced a recent resurgence in the use of simultaneous-equation models not yet seen in marketing. For example, simultaneous-equation models currently comprise more than 40% of the econometric articles in agricultural economics [Debertin & Pagoulatos, 1992, p. 8]. Perhaps what is being indicated is a need for more theory in marketing.

Knowledge about the nature of market mechanisms has increased appreciably. For example, not long ago managers had little but their own subjective impressions of the effectiveness of their advertising. Managers would say things like 'I know I am wasting half my advertising spending... I just don't know which half'. Today managers of heavily advertised brands can measure the short-run effects of advertising spending with reasonable accuracy. This research stream has progressed to the point where we now have a good handle on the average advertising elasticity of a frequently purchased branded good. Even managers of industrial products have at least a benchmark against which to evaluate their advertising effort [Lilien, 1979; Lilien & Ruzdic, 1979]. Our task now is to understand the more subtle variations in marketing's impact.

Although the shape of the sales-response function is almost surely concave over realistic operating ranges, we should be alert to the possibility of other shapes. Johansson [1979], for example, has suggested one approach for identifying whether or not a relationship under analysis is S-shaped. In general, because different combinations of phenomena such as threshold and saturation effects might be present in a particular market, we should not think in terms of a single aggregate response function. A specific response function should be constructed for each product/market situation. A table of response functions and their characteristics is given by Doyle & Saunders [1990]. We present in Table 9.1 selected applications of the use of different response functions for each of the marketing-mix elements.

The research developments reviewed herein share an important common theme: market-response models are becoming closer to the behavioral and managerial realities of marketing. For example, the simplistic linear and logarithmic approximations buyer response to marketing are being replaced by more behaviorally realistic functions that take into account the managerial objectives of marketers.

Table 9.1.
Selected marketing-mix applications of functional forms

Fuctional form	Marketing mix			
	Advertising	Price	Promotion	Sales force
Linear	Banks [1961]	Eastlack & Rao [1986]	Blattberg & Neslin [1990]	Lambert [1968]
Multiplicative	Bass & Parsons [1969], Lambin [1976]	Popkowski, Peter & Rao [1990]		Parsons & Vanden Abeele [1981]
Semi-logarithmic	Lambin [1969], Wildt [1977], Simon [1982]		Bemmaor & Mouchoux [1991]	
Exponential		Cowling & Cubbin [1971], Bolton [1989]	Blattberg & Wisniewski [1989]	
Log-reciprocal	Metwally [1980], Bemmaor [1984]			
Modified exponential	Shakun [1965], Holthauser & Assmus [1982]			Buzzell [1964] Rangan [1987]
Logistic	Johansson [1973]			
Reciprocal	Ward [1975]			
Translog	Jagpal, Sudit & Vinod [1982]			
Multiplicative nonhomogeneous	Jagpal, Sudit & Vinod [1979], Jagpal [1981]			

As data-processing and parameter-estimation technology evolves, implementing these more sophisticated models becomes easier.

Another emerging trend may have even more far-reaching implications. As the environment of marketing becomes more information-intensive, a new marketing strategy evolves around information technology [Glazer, 1991]. For example, many service organizations such as banks, credit-card companies and airlines use their extensive customer databases as strategic assets to develop cross-selling and other customer-loyalty-focused marketing strategies. The sheer size of these databases necessitates the use of market-response models in order to understand the driving forces of purchasing behavior and to predict the likely outcomes of alternative marketing strategies. For example, financial institutions need to know which factors contribute to customer loyalty and how promotional strategies can enhance this loyalty. Therefore, market-response models are becoming an inherent part of marketing strategy. We expect continuing managerial payoff of the ETS approach in marketing.

References

Aaker, D.A., and J.M. Carman (1982). Are you overadvertising? *J. Advertising Res.* 22 (August/September), 57–70.

Aaker, D.A., and G.S. Day (1971). A recursive model of communication processes, in D.A. Aaker (ed.), *Multivariate Analysis in Marketing: Theory and Application*, Wadsworth, Belmont, CA, pp. 101–114.

Ackoff, R.L., and J.R. Emshoff (1975). Advertising research at Anheuser-Busch, Inc. (1963–68). *Sloan Management Rev.* 16 (Winter), 1–15.

Ailawadi, K.L., and P.W. Farris (1992). Tests of significance in regression models with composite-component relationships. Darden School Working Paper 92-05, University of Virginia.

Albach, H. (1979). Market organization and pricing behavior of oligopolistic firms in the ethical drugs industry. *KYKLOS* 32(3), 523–540.

Allenby, G.M. (1989). A unified approach to identifying, estimating, and testing demand structures with aggregate scanner data. *Marketing Sci.* 8(3), 265–280.

Arora, R. (1979). How promotion elasticities change. *J. Advertising Res.* 19 (June), 57–62.

Ashley, R., C.W.J. Granger and R. Schmalensee (1980). Advertising and aggregate consumption: An analysis of causality. *Econometrica* 48 (July), 1149–1167.

Assmus, G., J.U. Farley and D.R. Lehmann (1984). How advertising affects sales: A meta analysis of econometric results. *J. Marketing Res.* 21 (February), 65–74.

Ball, R.J., and R. Agarwala (1969). An econometric analysis of the effects of generic advertising on the demand for tea in the UK. *Br. J. Marketing* 4 (Winter), 202–217.

Banks, S. (1961). Some correlates of coffee and cleanser brand shares. *J. Advertising Res.* 1 (June), 22–28.

Bass, F.M. (1969). A simultaneous equation regression study of advertising and sales of cigarettes. *J. Marketing Res.* 6 (August), 291–300.

Bass, F.M., and D. Clarke G. (1972). Testing distributed lag models of advertising effect. *J. Marketing Res.* 9 (August), 298–308.

Bass, F.M., and L.J. Parsons (1969). A simultaneous equation regression analysis of sales and advertising. *Appl. Econom.* 1 (May), 103–124.

Bauer, P.W. (1990). Recent developments in the econometric estimation of frontiers. *J. Econometrics* 46 (October/November), 39–56.

Beckwith, N.E. (1972). Multivariate analysis of sales responses of competing brands to advertising. *J. Marketing Res.* 9 (May), 168–176.

Bell, D.E., R.E. Keeney and J.D.C. Little (1975). A market share theorem. *J. Marketing Res.* 12 (May), 136–141.

Bemmaor, A.C. (1984). Testing alternative econometric models on the existence of advertising threshold effect. *J. Marketing Res.* 21 (August), 298–308.

Bemmaor, A.C., and D. Mouchoux (1991). Measuring the short-term effect of instore promotion and retail advertising on brand sales: A factorial experiment. *J. Marketing Res.* 28(2), 202–214.

Beswick, C.A., and D.A. Cravens (1977). A multistage decision model for salesforce management. *J. Marketing Res.* 14 (May), 135–144.

Blattberg, R.C., and E.I. George (1991). Shrinkage estimation of price and promotion elasticities: Seemingly unrelated equation. *J. Amer. Statist. Assoc.* 86, 304–315.

Blattberg, R.C., and A. Levin (1987). Modelling the effectiveness and profitability of trade promotions. *Marketing Sci.* 6 (Spring), 124–146.

Blattberg, R.C., and S.A. Neslin (1989). Sales promotion: The long and short of it. *Marketing Lett.* 1(1), 81–97.

Blattberg, R.C., and S.A. Neslin (1990). *Sales Promotion: Concepts, Methods, and Strategies*. Prentice-Hall, Englewood Cliffs, NJ.

Blattberg, R.C., and K.J. Wisniewski (1989). Price-induced patterns of competition. *Marketing Sci.* 8(4), 291–309.

Bolton, R.N. (1989). The robustness of retail-level price elasticity estimates. *J. Retailing* 65(2), 193–219.

Broadbent, S. (1984). Modelling with adstock. *J. Marketing Res. Soc.* 26 (October), 295–312.

Broadbent, S. (1989). What is a 'small' advertising elasticity?. *J. Advertising Res.* 29(4), 37–39, 44.
Brodie, R., and C.A. De Kluyver (1983). Attraction versus linear and multiplicative market share models: An empirical evaluation, Krannert Graduate School of Management, Purdue University, January. A shorter version appears in *J. Marketing Res.* 21 (May 1984), 194–201.
Bucklin, R., E. Gary, J. Russell, and V. Srinivasan (1992). A relationship between price elasticities and brand switching probabilities in heterogeneous markets. Working Paper, April.
Bult, J.R., P.S.H. Leeflang and D.R. Wittink (1991). Testing causality between marketing variables using scanner data. Working Paper 436, Institute of Economic Research, Faculty of Economics, University of Groningen.
Bultez, A., E. Gijsbrechts, P. Naert and P. Vanden Abeele (1989). Asymmetric cannibalism in retail assortments. *J. Retailing* 65(2), 153–192.
Bultez, A.V. and P.A. Naert (1975). Consistent sum-constrained models. *J. Amer. Statist. Assoc.* 70 (September), 529–535.
Buzzell, R.D. (1964). *Mathematical Models and Marketing Management*, Harvard University, Division of Research, Boston, pp. 136–156.
Cardwell, J.J. (1968). Marketing and management science – a marriage on the rocks? *California Management Rev.* 10 (Summer), 3–12.
Carpenter, G.S. (1987). Modeling competitive marketing strategies: The impact of marketing-mix relationships and industry, *Marketing Sci.* 6 (Spring), 208–221.
Carpenter, G.S., L.G. Cooper, D.M. Hanssens and D.F. Midgley (1988). Modeling asymmetric competition. *Marketing Sci.* 7 (Fall), 393–412.
Chevalier, M. (1975). Increase in sales due to instore display. *J. Marketing Res.* 12 (November), 426–431.
Clarke, D.G. (1973). Sales-advertising cross-elasticities and advertising competition. *J. Marketing Res.* 10 (August), 250–261.
Clarke, D.G. (1976). Econometric measurement of the duration of advertising effect on sales. *J. Marketing Res.* 13 (November), 345–357.
Cooil, B. and T.M. Devinney (1992). The return to advertising expenditure. *Marketing Lett.* 3(2), 137–145.
Cooper, L.G., and M. Nakanishi (1988). *Market Share Analysis: Evaluating Competitive Marketing Effectiveness*, Kluwer Academic Publishers, Boston, MA.
Corkindale, D. and J. Newall (1978). Advertising thresholds and wearout. *Eur. J. Marketing*, 12(5), 328–378.
Cowling, K. (1972). Optimality in firms' advertising policies: An empirical analysis, in K. Cowling (ed.), *Market Structure and Corporate Behavior: Theory and Empirical Analysis of the Firm*, Gray-Mills, London, pp. 85–103.
Cowling, K., and J. Cubbin (1971). Price, quality and advertising competition: An econometric investigation of the United Kingdom car market, *Economica* 38 (November), 378–394.
Cox, K.K. (1964). The responsiveness of food sales to shelf space changes in supermarkets. *J. Marketing Res.* 1 (May), 63–67.
Cox, K.K. (1970). The effect of shelf space upon sales of branded products. *J. Marketing Res.* 7 (February), 55–58.
Curhan, R.C. (1972). The relationship between shelf space and unit sales in supermarkets. *J. Marketing Res.* 9 (November), 406–412.
Curhan, R.C. (1974a). Shelf space elasticity: Reply, *J. Marketing Res.* 11 (May), 221–222.
Curhan, R.C. (1974b). The effects of merchandising and temporary promotional activities on the sales of fresh fruits and vegetables in supermarkets. *J. Marketing Res.* 11 (August), 286–294.
Dalrymple, D.J., and G.H. Haines, Jr. (1970). A study of the predictive ability of market period demand–supply relations for a firm selling fashion products. *Appl. Econom.* 1 (January), 277–285.
Debertin, D.L., and A. Pagoulatos (1992). Research in agricultural economics 1919–1990: Seventy-two years of change. *Rev. Agricul. Econom.* 14(1), 1–22.
Dekimpe, M.G. and D.M. Hanssens (1991). Assessing the evolution of competitive relationships: Do long-run market equilibrium really exist? Working Paper, Anderson Graduate School of Management, UCLA.

Dekimpe, M.G., and D.M. Hanssens (1993). The persistence of marketing effects on sales, Working Paper, Anderson Graduate School of Management, UCLA.

De Kluyver, C., and E.A. Pessemier (1986). Benefits of a marketing budgeting model: Two case studies. *Sloan Management Rev.* 28(1), 27–38.

DeSarbo, W.S., V.R. Rao, J.H. Steckel, J. Wind and R. Colombo (1987). A friction model for describing and forecasting price changes. *Marketing Sci.* 6 (Fall), 299–319.

Devinney, T.M. (1987). Entry and learning. *Management Sci.* 33 (June), 706–724.

Di Benedetto, C.A. (1985). A multiplicative dynamic-adjustment model of sales response to marketing mix variables. *Modelling, Simulation, and Control C: Environmental, Biomedical, Human and Social Systems* 4 (Autumn), 7–18.

Dickey, D.A., W.R. Bell, and R.B. Miller (1986). Unit roots in time series models: Tests and implications. *Amer. Statist.* 40 (February), 12–26.

Doyle, P. and J. Saunders (1985). The lead effect in marketing. *J. Marketing Res.* 22 (February), 54–65.

Doyle, P. and J. Saunders (1990). Multiproduct advertising budgeting. *Marketing Sci.* 9(2), (Spring), 97–113.

Eastlack, Jr., J.O. and A.G. Rao (1986). Modeling response to advertising and pricing changes for 'V-8' Cocktail Vegetable Juice. *Marketing Sci.* 5 (Summer), 245–259.

Elrod, T., and R.L. Winer (1979). Estimating the effects of advertising on individual household purchasing behavior, in N. Beckwith et al. (ed.), *Proceedings*, American Marketing Association, Chicago, pp. 83–89.

Engle, R.F., and C.W.J. Granger (1987). Co-integration and error correction: Representation, estimation, and testing. *Econometrica*, 55(2), (March), 251–276.

Enis, B.M., and M.P. Mokwa (1979). The marketing management matrix: A taxonomy for strategy comprehension, in O.C. Ferrell, S.W. Brown, and C.W. Lamb (eds.), *Conceptual and Theoretical Developments in Marketing*. American Marketing Association, Chicago, pp. 485–500.

Erickson, G.M. (1990). Assessing response model approaches to marketing strategy decisions, in G. Day, B. Weitz and R. Wensley (eds.), *The Interface of Marketing and Strategy*, JAI Press, Greenwich, CT, pp. 353–385.

Eskin, G.J. (1975). A case for test market experiments. *J. Advertising Res.* 15 (April), 27–33.

Eskin, G.J. and P.H. Baron (1977). Effect of price and advertising in test-market experiments. *J. Marketing Res.* 14 (November), 499–508.

Farley, J.U., and H.J. Leavitt (1968). A model of the distribution of branded products in Jamaica. *J. Marketing Res.* 5 (November), 362–369.

Farley, J.U., and D.R. Lehmann (1986). *Meta-analysis in Marketing: Generalization of Response Models*, Lexington Books, Lexington, MA.

Farley, J.U., D.R. Lehmann, and T.A. Oliva (1990). Are there laws in production: A meta-analysis of Cobb-Douglas 1921–1980, Working Paper, The Wharton School, University of Pennsylvania, Philadelphia, PA.

Farris, P.W., and M.S. Albion (1980). The impact of advertising on the price of consumer products. *J. Advertising Res.* 44 (Summer), 17–35.

Farris, P.M., J. Olver and C. De Kluyver (1989). The relationship between distribution and market share. *Marketing Sci.* 8(2), (Spring), 107–128.

Farris, P.W., M.E. Parry, and K.L. Ailawadi (1992). Structural analysis of models with composite dependent variables. *Marketing Sci.* 11(2), (Winter), 76–94.

Feinberg, F.M. (1992). Pulsing policies for aggregate advertising models. *Marketing Sci.* 11(3), (Summer), 221–234.

Ferber, R. (1949). *Statistical Techniques in Market Research*, McGraw-Hill, New York.

Findley, J.J., and D.C. Little (1980). Experiences with market response analysis. Working Paper. The Sloan School of Management, Massachusetts Institute of Technology, Cambridge, MA, March.

Foekens, E., P.S.H. Leeflang, and D.R. Wittink (1992). Asymmetric market share modeling with many competitive items using market level scanner data. Working Paper no. 471, Institute of Economic Research, Faculty of Economics, University of Groningen.

Frank, R.E., and W.F. Massy (1970). Shelf position and space effects on sales. *J. Marketing Res.* 7 (February), 59–66.

Gatignon, H. (1984). Competition as a moderator of the effect of advertising on sales. *J. Marketing Res.* 21 (November), 387–398.

Gatignon, H., and D.M. Hanssens (1987). Modeling marketing interactions with applications to salesforce effectiveness. *J. Marketing Res.* 24 (August), 247–257.

Ghosh, A., S. Neslin, and R. Shoemaker (1984). A comparison of market share models and estimation procedures. *J. Marketing Res.* 21 (May), 202–210.

Givon, M., and D. Horsky (1990). Untangling the effects of purchase reinforcement and advertising carryover. *Marketing Sci.* 9(2), 171–187.

Glazer, R. (1991). Marketing in an information-intensive environment: Strategic implications of knowledge as an asset. *J. Marketing* 55(4), 1–19.

Gopalakrishna, S., and R. Chatterjee (1992). A communications response model for a mature industrial product: Application and implications. *J. Marketing Res.* 29(2), 189–200.

Gopalakrishna, S., and J.D. Williams (1992). Planning and performance assessment of industrial trade shows: An exploratory study. *Intern. J. Res. Marketing* 9(3), 207–224.

Granger, C.W.J. (1969). Investigating causal relation by econometric models and cross-spectral methods. *Econometrica* 37, 424–438.

Granger, C.W.J. (1980). Long memory relationships and the aggregation of dynamic models. *J. Econometrics* 14, 227–238.

Grass, R.G., and W.H. Wallace (1969). Satiation effects of TV commercials. *J. Advertising Res.* 9 (September), 3–8.

Guadagni, P.M. and J.D.C. Little (1983). A logit model of brand choice calibrated on scanner data. *Marketing Sci.* 2 (Summer), 203–238.

Gupta, S. (1988). Impact of sales promotion on when, what and how much to buy. *J. Marketing Res.* 25 (November), 242–355.

Hagerty, M.R., J.M. Carman, and G. Russell (1988). Estimating elasticities with PIMS data: Methodological issues and substantive implications. *J. Marketing Res.* 25 (February), 1–9.

Haley, R.I. (1978). Sales effects of media weight. *J. Advertising Res.* 18 (June), 9–18.

Hall, G., and S. Howell (1985). The experience curve from the economist's perspective. *Strategic Management J.* 6, 197–212.

Hanssens, D.M. (1977). An empirical study of time-series analysis in marketing model building, Unpublished Ph.D. thesis, Krannert Graduate School of Management, Purdue University.

Hanssens, D.M. (1980a). Bivariate time series analysis of the relationship between advertising and sales. *Appl. Econom.* 12 (September), 329–340.

Hanssens, D.M. (1980b). Market response, competitive behavior, and time series analysis. *J. Marketing Res.* 17 (November), 470–485.

Hanssens, D.M., and H.A. Levien (1983). An econometric study of recruitment marketing in the US Navy. *Management Sci.* 29 (October), 1167–1184.

Hanssens, D.M., L.J. Parsons, and R.L. Schultz (1990). *Market Response Models: Econometric and Time Series Analysis*, Kluwer, Boston.

Haugh, L.D. (1976). Checking the independence of two covariance-stationary time series: A univariate residual cross-correlation approach. *J. Amer. Statist. Assoc.* 71 (June), 378–385.

Haugh, L.D. and G.E.P. Box (1977). Identification of dynamic regression (distributed lag) models connecting two time series. *J. Amer. Statist. Assoc.* 72 (March), 121–129.

Hill, R.C., P.A. Cartwright, and J.F. Arbaugh (1990). Using aggregate data to estimate micro-level parameters with shrinkage rules. *Proceedings of the Business and Economic Statistics Section.* American Statistical Association, Washington, DC, pp. 339–344.

Hill, R.C., P.A. Cartwright, and J.F. Arbaugh (1991). Using aggregate data to estimate micro-level parameters with shrinkage rules: More results. *Proceedings of the Business and Economic Statistics Section.* American Statistical Association, Washington, DC.

Holthausen, D.M., Jr. and G. Assmus (1982). Advertising budget allocation under uncertainty. *Management Sci.* 28 (May), 487–499.

Horsky, D. (1977). Market share response to advertising: An example of theory testing. *J. Marketing Res.* 14 (February), 10–21.

Horsky, D., and P. Nelson (1991). Determination of sales potential for salesforce districts, TIMS Marketing Science Conference, University of Delaware/Dupont.

Houston, F.S. (1977). An econometric analysis of positioning. *J. Business Admin.* 9 (Fall), 1–12.

Houston, F.S., V. Kanetkar, and D.L. Weiss (1991). Simplified estimation procedures for MCI and MNL models: A comment. Working paper, University of Toronto.

Houston, F.S., and L.J. Parsons (1986). Modeling cumulative advertising as a continuous function, TIMS/ORSA Marketing Science Conference, University of Texas, Dallas.

Houston, F.S., and D.L. Weiss (1974). An analysis of competitive market behavior. *J. Marketing Res.* 11 (May), 151–155.

Jacobson, R., and F.M. Nicosia (1981). Advertising and public policy: The macroeconomic effects of advertising. *J. Marketing Res.* 18 (February), 29–38.

Jagpal, H.S. (1981). Measuring joint advertising effects in multiproduct firms. *J. Advertising Res.* 21(1), 65–69.

Jagpal, H.S., E.F. Sudit, and H.D. Vinod (1979). A model of sales response to advertising interactions. *J. Advertising Res.* 19 (June), 41–47.

Jagpal, H.S., E.F. Sudit, and H.D. Vinod (1982). Measuring dynamic marketing mix interactions using translog functions. *J. Business*, 55 (July), 401–415.

Johansson, J.K. (1973). A generalized logistic function with an application to the effect of advertising. *J. Amer. Statist. Assoc.* 68 (December), 824–827.

Johansson, J. K. (1979). Advertising and the S-curve: A new approach. *J. Marketing Res.* 16 (August), 346–354.

Jones, J.P. (1984). Universal diminishing returns – true or false? *Intern. J. Advertising* 3(1), 27–41.

Kennedy, J.R. (1970). The effect of display location on the sales and pilferage of cigarettes. *J. Marketing Res.* 7 (May), 210–215.

Kotzan, J.A., and R.V. Evanson (1969). Responsiveness of drug store sales to shelf space allocation. *J. Marketing Res.* 6 (November), 465–469.

Krishnamurthi, L., and S.P. Raj (1988). A model of brand choice and purchase quantity price sensitivities. *Marketing Sci.* 7(1), 1–20.

Lambert, Z.V. (1968). *Setting the Size of the Sales Force.* Pennsylvania State University Press, State College, Pittsburgh, PA.

Lambin, J.-J. (1969). Measuring the profitability of advertising: An empirical study. *J. Indust. Econom.* 17 (April), 86–103.

Lambin, J.-J. (1970). Advertising and competitive behavior: A case study. *Appl. Econom.* 2 (January), 231–251.

Lambin, J.-J. (1976). *Advertising, Competition, and Market Conduct in Oligopoly Over Time.* North-Holland, Amsterdam.

Lambin, J.-J., P.A. Naert, and A. Bultez (1975). Optimal marketing behavior in oligopoly. *Euro. Econom. Rev.* 6, 105–128.

Lancaster, K.M. (1984). Brand advertising competition and industry demand. *J. Advertising* 13(4), 19–24.

Layton, A.P. (1984). A further note on the detection of Granger instantaneous causality. *J. Time Series Anal.* 5(1), 15–18.

Lee, J., and M.G. Brown (1985). Coupon redemption and the demand for concentrated orange juice: A switching regression. *Amer. J. Agricul. Econom.* 67, 647–653.

Leeflang, P.S.H., K.H. Alsem, and J.C. Reuyl (1991). Diagnosing competition for public policy: A case study. Working Paper no. 207, Marketing Studies Center, Anderson Graduate School of Management, UCLA.

Leeflang, P.S.H., G.M. Mijatovic, and J. Saunders (1992). Identification and estimation of complex multivariate lag structures: A nesting approach. *Appl. Econom.* 24, 273–283.

Leeflang, P.S.H., and J.C. Reuyl (1984). On the predictive power of market share attraction models. *J. Marketing Res.* 21 (May), 211–215.

Leeflang, P.S.H., and D.R. Wittink (1992). Diagnosing competitive reactions using (aggregated) scanner data. *Intern. J. Res. Marketing* 9(1), 39–57.

Leone, R.P., and R.L. Schultz (1980). A study of marketing generalizaton. *J. Marketing* 44 (January), 10–18.

Levy, H., and J.L. Simon (1989). A generalization that makes useful the Dorfman–Steiner theorem with respect to advertising. *Managerial and Decision Econom.* 10(1), 85–87.

Lilien, G.L. (1979). ADVISOR 2: Modeling marketing mix decisions for industrial products. *Management Sci.* 25 (February), 191–204.

Lilien, G.L., P. Kotler, and K.S. Moorthy (1992). *Marketing Models*, Prentice-Hall, Englewood Cliffs, NJ.

Lilien, G.L., and A.G. Rao (1976). A model for allocating retail outlet building resources across market areas. *Oper. Res.* 24 (January–February), 1–14.

Lilien, G.L., and A.A. Ruzdic (1982). Analyzing natural experiments in industrial markets, in Andris A. Zoltners (ed.). *Planning Models*, North-Holland, New York, pp. 241–269.

Lilien, G.L., and E. Yoon (1988). An exploratory analysis of the dynamic behavior of price elasticity over the product life cycle: An empirical analysis of industrial chemical products, in T.M. Devinney (ed.). *Issues in Pricing*, Lexington Books, Lexington, MA, pp. 261–287.

Little, J.D.C. (1970). Models and managers: The concept of a decision calculus. *Management Sci.* 16 (April), 466–485.

Little, J.D.C. (1979). Aggregate advertising models: The state of the art. *Oper. Res.* 27 (July–August), 629–667.

Luhmer, A., A. Steindl, G. Feichtinger, R.F. Hartl, and G. Sorger (1988a). ADPULS in continuous time, in G. Feichtinger (ed.). *Optimal Control Theory and Economic Analysis 3*, North-Holland, Amsterdam, pp. 73–76.

Luhmer, A., A. Steindl, G. Feichtinger, R.F. Hartl, and G. Sorger (1988b). ADPULS in continuous time. *Eur. J. Oper. Res.* 34, 171–177.

Lynch, M. (1974). Comment on Curhan's 'The relationship between shelf space and unit sales in supermarkets'. *J. Marketing Res.* 11 (May), 218–220.

Mahajan, V., S.I. Bretschneider, and J.W. Bradford (1980). Feedback approaches to modeling structural shifts in market response. *J. Marketing* 44 (Winter), 71–80.

Mantrala, M.K., P. Sinha, and A.A. Zoltners (1992). Impact of resource allocation rules on marketing investment-level decisions and profitability. *J. Marketing Res.* 29(2), 162–175.

McGuiness, T., and K. Cowling (1975). Advertising and the aggregate demand for cigarettes. *Eur. Econom. Rev.* 6, 311–328.

Mesak, H.I. (1992). An aggregate advertising pulsing model with wearout effects. *Marketing Sci.* 11(3), 310–326.

Metwally, M.M. (1978). Escalation tendencies of advertising. *Oxford Bull. Econom. Statist.* 40 (May), 153–163.

Metwally, M.M. (1980). Sales response to advertising of eight Australian products. *J. Advertising Res.* 20 (October), 59–64.

Mickwitz, G. (1959). *Marketing and Competition.* Centraltrykeriet, Helsinki, pp. 87–89.

Montgomery, D.B., and A. Silk (1972). Estimating dynamic effects of market communications expenditures. *Management Sci.* 18, B-485–501.

Moore, W.L., and E.A. Pessemier (1992). *Product Planning and Management: Designing and Delivering Value*, McGraw-Hill, New York.

Moore, W.L., and R.S. Winer (1987). A panel-data based method for merging joint space and market response function estimation. *Marketing Sci.* 6 (Winter), 25–42.

Moran, W.T. (1978). Insights from pricing research, in E.L. Bailey (ed.), *Pricing Practices and Strategies*, The Conference Board, New York, pp. 7–13.

Moriarty, M.M. (1975). Cross-sectional, time-series issues in the analysis of marketing decision variables. *J. Marketing Res.* 12 (May), 142–150.

Moriarty, M.M. (1985). Retail promotional effects on intra- and interbrand sales performance. *J. Retailing* 61 (Fall), 27–48.

Mueller, R.W., G.E. Kline, and J.J. Trout (1953). Customers buy 22% more when shelves are well stocked. *Progressive Grocer* 32 (June), 40–48.

Naert, P.A., and A.V. Bultez (1973). Logically consistent market share models. *J. Marketing Res.* 10 (August), 334–340.

Naert, P.A., and P.S.H. Leeflang (1978). *Building Implementable Marketing Models.* Martinus Nijhof, Leiden.

Naert, P.A., and M. Weverbergh (1981). On the predictive power of market share attraction models. *J. Marketing Res.* 18 (May), 146–153.

Naert, P.A., and M. Weverbergh (1985). Market share specification, estimation, and validation: Toward reconciling seemingly divergent views. *J. Marketing Res.* 22 (November), 453–467.

Nakanishi, M., and L.G. Cooper (1974). Parameter estimation for a multiplicative competitive interaction model – A least squares approach. *J. Marketing Res.* 11 (August), 303–311.

Nakanishi, M., and L.G. Cooper (1982). Simplified estimation procedures for MCI models. *Marketing Sci.* 1 (Summer), 314–322.

Nelson, C.R. (1972). The prediction performance of the FRB-MIT-PENN model of the US economy. *Amer. Rev.* 62, 902–917.

Nerlove, M., and F. Waugh (1961). Advertising without supply control: Some implications for the study of the advertising of oranges. *J. Farm Econom.* 43 (4 Part I), 813–837.

Neslin, S.A. (1990). A market response model for coupon promotions. *Marketing Sci.* 9(2), 125–145.

Neslin, S.A., and R.W. Shoemaker (1983). Using a natural experiment to estimate price elasticity: The 1974 sugar shortage and the ready-to-eat cereal market. *J. Marketing* 47 (Winter), 44–57.

Nguyen, D. (1985). An analysis of optimal advertising under uncertainty. *Management Sci.* 31 (May), 622–633.

Ottesen, O. (1981). A theory of short-run response to advertising. in Jagdish N. Sheth (ed.). *Research in Marketing*, Vol. 4, JAI Press, Greenwich, CT, 181–222.

Palda, K.S. (1964). *The Measurement of Cumulative Advertising Effects.* Prentice-Hall, Englewood Cliffs, NJ.

Parker, P. (1992). Price elasticity dynamics over the adoption lifecycle. *J. Marketing Res.*29(3), 358–367.

Parker, T.H., and I.J. Dolich (1986). Toward understanding retail bank strategy: Seemingly unrelated regression applied to cross-sectional data. *J. Retailing* 62 (Fall), 298–321.

Parsons, L.J. (1974). An econometric analysis of advertising, retail availability, and sales of a new brand. *Management Sci.* 20 (February), 938–947.

Parsons, L.J. (1975). The product life cycle and time-varying advertising elasticities. *J. Marketing Res.* 9 (November), 476–480.

Parsons, L.J. (1976). A rachet model of advertising carryover effects. *J. Marketing Res.* 13 (February), 76–79.

Parsons, L.J. (1987). Poisson regression, TIMS Marketing Science Conference, Centre HEC-ISA, France.

Parsons, L.J. (1991). Estimation of a frontier production function for a sales force. TIMS Marketing Science Conference, University of Delaware/DuPont, Wilmington, DE.

Parsons, L.J., and F.M. Bass (1971). Optimal advertising expenditure implications of a simultaneous-equation regression analysis. *Oper. Res.* 19 (May–June), 822–831.

Parsons, L.J., and R.L. Schultz (1976). *Marketing Models and Econometric Research*, North-Holland, New York.

Parsons, L.J., and P. Vanden Abeele (1981). Analysis of sales call effectiveness. *J. Marketing Res.* 18 (February), 107–113.

Pauli, H., and R.W. Hoecker (1952). Better utilization of selling space in food stores: Part I: Relation of size of shelf display to sales of canned fruits and vegetables. Marketing Research Report No. 30, United States Government Printing Office, Washington, DC.

Peterson, R.A., and J.W. Cagley (1973). The effect of shelf space upon sales of branded products: An appraisal. *J. Marketing Res.* 10 (February), 103–104.

Picconi, M.J., and C.L. Olson (1978). Advertising decision rules in a multibrand environment: Optimal control theory and evidence. *J. Marketing Res.* 15 (February), 82–92.

Pierce, D.A. (1977). Relationships – and the lack thereof – between economic time series, with special reference to money and interest rates. *J. Amer. Statist. Assoc.* 72 (March), 11–22.

Pierce, D.A., and L.D. Haugh (1977). Causality in temporal systems. *J. Econometrics*, 5, 265–293.

Popkowski, L., T.L. Peter, and R.C. Rao (1990). An empirical analysis of national and local advertising effect on price elasticity. *Marketing Lett.* 1(2), 149–160.

Powers, K., D.M. Hanssens, Y.-I. Hser, and M.D. Anglin (1991). Measuring the long-term effects of public policy: The case of narcotics use and property crime. *Management Sci.* 27(6), 627–644.

Prasad, V.K., and L.W. Ring (1976). Measuring sales effects of some marketing-mix variables and their interactions. *J. Marketing Res.* 13 (November), 391–396.

Progressive Grocer (1963, 1964). The Colonial study. 42 (September), 43 (March).

Rangan, V.K. (1987). The channel design decision: A model and an application. *Marketing Sci.* 6 (Spring), 156–174.

Rangaswamy, A., and L. Krishnamurthi (1991). Response function estimation using the equity estimator. *J. Marketing Res.* 28 (February), 72–83.

Rao, A.G. (1970). *Quantitative Theories in Advertising*. Wiley, New York.

Rao, A.G., and P.B. Miller (1975). Advertising/sales response functions. *J. Advertising Res.* 15 (April), 7–15.

Rao, R.C. (1986). Estimating continuous time advertising-sales models. *Marketing Sci.* 5(2), 125–142.

Rao, V.R. (1972). Alternative econometric models of sales–advertising relationships. *J. Marketing Res.* 9 (May), 177–181.

Rao, V.R., J. Wind, and W.S. DeSarbo (1988). A customized market response model: Development, estimation, and empirical testing. *J. Acad. Marketing Sci.* 16 (Spring), 128–140.

Reibstein, D.J., and H. Gatignon (1984). Optimal product line pricing: The influence of cross-elasticities. *J. Marketing Res.* 21 (August), 259–267.

Rosenquist, G., and T. Strandvik (1987). Purchase incidence models with explanatory variables. TIMS Marketing Science Conference, Centre HEC-ISA, France.

Russell, G.J. (1988). Recovering measures of advertising carryover from aggregate data: The role of the firm's decision behavior. *Marketing Sci.* 7 (Summer), 252–270.

Russell, G.J. (1992). A model of latent symmetry in cross elasticities. *Marketing Lett.* 3(2), 157–169.

Russell, G.J., M.R. Hagerty, and J.M. Carman (1991). Bayesian estimation of marketing mix elasticities using PIMS priors. Working Paper, University of California at Berkeley, March.

Ryans, A.B., and C.B. Weinberg (1979). Territory sales respone. *J. Marketing Res.* 16 (November), 453–465.

Samuels, J.M. (1970/71). The effect of advertising on sales and brand shares. *Eur. J. Marketing* 4 (Winter), 187–207.

Sasieni, M.W. (1989). Optimal advertising strategies. *Marketing Sci.* 8(4), 358–370.

Saunders, J. (1987). The specification of aggregate market models. *Eur. J. Marketing* 21(2), 5–47.

Schultz, R.L. (1971). Market measurement and planning with a simultaneous-equation model. *J. Marketing Res.* 8 (May), 153–164.

Schultz, R.L., and W.R. Vanhonacker (1978). A study of promotion and price elasticity, Institute Paper No. 657, Krannert Graduate School of Management, Purdue University, March.

Sethuraman, R., and G.J. Tellis (1991). An analysis of the tradeoff between advertising and price discounting. *J. Marketing Res.* 28(2), 160–174.

Shakun, M.F. (1965). Advertising expenditures in coupled markets – a game-theory approach. *Management Sci.* 11 (February), B42–47.

Shoemaker, R.W. (1986). Comment on 'Dynamics of price elasticity and brand life cycles: An empirical study'. *J. Marketing Res.* 23 (February), 78–82.

Simon, H. (1979). Dynamics of price elasticity and brand life cycles: An empirical study. *J. Marketing Res.* 16 (November), 439–452.

Simon, H. (1982). ADPULS: An advertising model with wearout and pulsation. *J. Marketing Res.* 19 (August), 352–363.

Simon, H., and K.-H. Sebastian (1987). Diffusion and advertising: The German telephone campaign, *Management Sci.* 33 (April), 451–466.

Simon, J.L. (1970). *Issues in the Economics of Advertising*, University of Illinois Press, Urbana, IL.

Simon, J.L., and J. Arndt (1980). The shape of the advertising function. *J. Advertising Res.* 20 (August), 11–28.

Sims, C.A. (1972). Money, income and causality. *Amer. Econom. Rev.* 62 (September), 540–552.

Snell, A., and I. Tonks (1988). The sweet taste of information: A study of the demand for new brands in the UK confectionery industry. *Appl. Econom.* 20(8), 1041–1055.

Steiner, R.L. (1987). The paradox of increasing returns to advertising. *J. Advertising Res.* 27 (February–March), 45–53.

Stock, J.H. (1987). Asymptotic properties of least squares estimators of cointegrating vectors. *Econometica* 55(5) (January), 1035–1056.

Sunoo, D., and L.Y.S. Lin (1978). Sales effects of promotion and advertising. *J. Advertising Res.* 18 (October), 37–40.

Takada, H. (1986). Analysis of competitive marketing behavior using multiple time series analysis and econometric methods, Working Paper, Graduate School of Management, University of California, Reverside, Working Paper.

Tellis, G.J. (1988). The price sensitivity of selective demand: A meta-analysis of econometric models of sales. *J. Marketing Res.* 25 (November), 391–404.

Tellis, G.J. (1989). Interpreting advertising and price elasticities. *J. Advertising Res.* 29(4), 40–43.

Tellis, G.J., and C. Fornell (1988). The relationship between advertising and product quality over the product life cycle: A contingency theory. *J. Marketing Res.* 25 (February), 64–71.

Tonks, I. (1986). The demand for information and the diffusion of a new product. *Intern. J. Indust. Organization* 4(4), 397–408.

Turner, R.E. (1971). Market measures from salesmen: A multidimensional scaling approach. *J. Marketing Res.* 8 (May), 165–172.

Urban, G.L. (1969). A mathematical modeling approach to product line decisions. *J. Marketing Res.* 6 (February), 40–47.

Vanden Abeele, P., E. Gijsbrechts and M. Vanhuele (1991). Specification and empirical evaluation of a cluster-asymmetry market share model. *Intern. J. Res. Marketing* 7(4), 223–247.

Vanhonacker, W.R. (1984). Estimation and testing of a dynamic sales response model with data aggregated over time: Some results for the autoregressive current effects model. *J. Marketing Res.* 21 (November), 445–455.

Vanhonacker, W.R. (1990). Estimating dynamic response models when data are subject to different aggregation. *Marketing Lett.* 1(2) (June), 125–137.

Vanhonacker, W.R. (1991). Testing the Koyck scheme of sales response advertising: An aggregation-independent autocorrelation test. *Marketing Lett.* 2(4), 379–392.

Waid, C., D.F. Clark, and R.L. Ackoff (1956). Allocation of sales effort in the Lamp Division of General Electric Company. *Oper. Res.* 4 (December), 629–647.

Ward, R.W. (1975). Revisiting the Dorfman–Steiner static advertising theorem: An application to the processed grapefruit industry. *Amer. J. Agricul. Econom.* (August), pp. 500–504.

Weiss, D.L., and P.M. Windal (1980). Testing cumulative advertising effects: A comment on methodology. *J. Marketing Res.* 17 (August), 371–378.

Wierenga, B. (1981). Modelling the impact of advertising and optimising advertising policy. *Eur. J. Oper. Res.* 8, 235–248.

Wildt, A.R. (1974). Multifirm analysis of competitive decision variables. *J. Marketing Res.* 11 (November), 50–62.

Wildt, A.R. (1977). Estimating models of seasonal market response using dummy variables. *J. Marketing Res.* 14 (February), 34–41.

Wildt, A.R., J.D. Parker and C.E. Harris (1987). Assessing the impact of sales force contests: An application. *J. Business Res.* 15 (April), 145–155.

Wildt, A.R., and R.S. Winer (1983). Modeling and estimation in changing market environments. *J. Business* 56 (July), 365–388.

Winer, R.S. (1985). A price vector model for demand for consumer durables: Preliminary developments. *Marketing Sci.* 4 (Winter), 74–90.

Winer, R.S. (1986). A reference price model of brand choice for frequently purchased products. *J. Consumer Res.* 13 (September), 250–256.

Wittink, D.R. (1977a). The influence of advertising on price sensitivity. *J. Advertising Res.* 16 (April).

Wittink, D.R. (1977b). Exploring territorial differences in the relationship between marketing variables. *J. Marketing Res.* 14 (May), 145–155.

Wittink, D.R. (1983). Standardized regression coefficients: Use and misuse, Graduate School of Management, Cornell University, Ithaca, NY, September.

Wittink, D.R. (1988). *The Application of Regression Analysis*, Allyn and Bacon, Boston, MA.

Wittink, D.R., and J.C. Porter (1991). Pooled store-level data versus market aggregates: A comparison of econometric models. Working paper, Johnson Graduate School of Management, Cornell University, Ithaca, NY.

Wittink, D.R., J.C. Porter, and S. Gupta (1991). Biases in parameter estimates from linearly aggregated data when the disaggregate model is nonlinear. Working paper, Johnson Graduate School of Management, Cornell University, Ithaca, NY.

Young, K.H., and L.Y. Young (1975). Estimation of regression involving logarithmic transformation of zero values in the dependent variable. *Amer. Statist.* 29 (August), 118–120.

Young, T. (1983). The demand for cigarettes: Alternative specifications of Fujii's model. *Appl. Econom.* 15 (April), 203–211.

Zentler, A.P., and D. Ryde (1956). An optimal geographic distribution of publicity expenditure in a private organization. *Management Sci.* 4 (July), 337–352.

Part IV
Elements of the Marketing Mix

J. Eliashberg and G.L. Lilien, Eds., *Handbooks in OR & MS, Vol. 5*

Chapter 10

Conjoint Analysis with Product-Positioning Applications

Paul E. Green
Marketing Department, Suite 1450, Steinberg Hall–Dietrich Hall, Wharton School, University of Pennsylvania, Philadelphia, PA 19104, USA

Abba M. Krieger
Statistics Department, Suite 3000, Steinberg Hall–Dietrich Hall, Wharton School, University of Pennsylvania, Philadelphia, PA 19104, USA

1. Introduction

The OR/MS researcher is no stranger to MAUT (multiattribute utility theory). Even a small sampling of the literature [Keeney & Raiffa, 1976; Bell, Keeney & Raiffa, 1977; Starr & Zeleny, 1977; Zionts, 1978; Hwang & Yoon, 1981; Bell, Raiffa & Tversky, 1988] yields a plethora of research, both descriptive and prescriptive, on the topic.

The work of Keeney and his associates typifies the OR/MS point of view. Their applications of multiattribute preference measurement usually entail one or a small group of key decision makers, faced with high-stake (and often high-risk) decisions involving broad social and environmental issues. Examples include water-resource planning, air pollution, the environmental impact of nuclear power stations, and aircraft safety regulations.

About the same time that Keeney and his associates were researching MAUT another well-known OR/MS researcher, Thomas Saaty, was developing his own approach to the problem: AHP (analytic hierarchy process). This research culminated in a book [Saaty, 1980] and several applications and examples, including transport planning in the Sudan, issues related to political candidacy, strategies for academic promotion and tenure, optimal land use, and school selection; also, see Dyer [1990].

Both Keeney's MAUT and Saaty's AHP typically focus on small numbers of decision makers faced with high-level decisions. Data collection may be arduous and time-consuming. In most cases the analyses are tailor-made. Suffice it to say that both groups of researchers identify closely with the OR/MS field and many of their publications appear in this literature.

OR/MS researchers are probably less knowledgeable (if familiar at all) with the more plebeian methodology of conjoint analysis, a multiattribute utility-measurement approach applied primarily by marketing researchers. Conjoint researchers are usually concerned with the more day-to-day decisions of consumers – what brand of soap, automobile, phone service, photocopy machine to buy (or lease). While, in principle, conjoint methodology can be (and sometimes is) used to measure corporate administrators' multiattribute values, in most applications this is not the case.

Whereas the Keeney and Saaty approaches often entail a single administrator, or small group of decision makers, conjoint studies typically deal with hundreds or even thousands of respondents. Not surprisingly, the measurement methods of conjoint analysis are considerably more routinized and streamlined to deal with the larger scope of the task. Utility measurements must be obtained in a matter of minutes rather than hours. Conjoint analysis methods may seem crude by Keeney standards; this notwithstanding, thousands of conjoint studies, both in the U.S. and abroad, have been implemented. There is little question about either conjoint's popularity or its grass-roots orientation.

The primary purpose of this paper is to provide the OR/MS researcher with an overview of conjoint's origins, foundations and progress, culminating in prescriptive models for optimal product-positioning. Its evolution has moved beyond initial preoccupation with utility measurement and buyer-choice simulations to interest in product design, market segmentation and competitive strategy. These latter topics should be of especial interest to OR/MS researchers.

We first describe the essentials of MAUT and the specific niche occupied by conjoint analysis. We then provide a non-technical discussion of the evolution of conjoint analysis and the various research paths that marketing researchers have taken in developing this pragmatic approach to multiattribute utility measurement. In particular, we describe two important trends:

(1) The development and diffusion of packaged PC software designed to make conjoint analysis easily and inexpensively accessible to industry practitioners.
(2) The scaling up of conjoint studies from their earlier focus on narrowly defined tactical problems to higher-level, strategic issues.

We then describe the role of buyer-choice simulators in conjoint analysis. Capsule descriptions of various conjoint applications are also presented.

Our second principal objective focuses on prescriptive modeling – namely the development of optimal product-positioning and segmentation models, based on conjoint input data. This is a more recent area of research and one where industry applications do not seem to have kept pace with academic modeling developments. We discuss progress in this aspect of conjoint analysis and describe, in detail, some of our own research on this topic. We conclude the paper with some brief comments about where research in optimal positioning and segmentation appears to be heading.

2. Compositional versus decompositional preference models

The two principal ways of constructing multiattribute utility functions entail what are known as compositional and decompositional models. Compositional models go back to the late 1770s [see Dawes & Corrigan, 1974], when Benjamin Franklin wrote to this friend, Joseph Priestly, on September 19, 1772:

> "I cannot, for want of sufficient premises, advise you *what* to determine, but if you please I will tell you *how*... My way is to divide half a sheet of paper by a line into two columns; writing over the one *Pro*, and over the other *Con*. Then, doing three or four days' consideration, I put down under the different heads short hints of the different motives, that at different times occur to me *for* or *against* the measure. When I have thus got them all together in one view, I endeavor to estimate the respective weights... [to] find at length where the balance lies... And, though the weight of reasons cannot be taken with the precision of algebraic quantities, yet, when each is thus considered, separately and comparatively, and the whole matter lies before me, I think I can judge better, and am less liable to make a rash step; and in fact I have found great advantage for this kind of equation, in what may be called *moral* or *prudential algebra*."

As would be gathered from the text, Franklin is advocating a precursory approach to today's two-stage self-explicated model, in which:

(1) The decision maker rates the desirability of each of a set of possible levels of each of a set of attributes on (say) a 0–10 scale.
(2) Following this, the decision maker rates the importance of each attribute on (say) a 0–10 scale.
(3) The utility of any option composable from the set of attributes is found as the sum of the appropriately weighted desirabilities with both sets of inputs supplied by the decision maker.

Examples of the two-stage, self-explicated model include the compositional technique of Edwards and his colleagues [Edwards & Newman, 1982; Gardiner & Edwards, 1975] and the approach of Hoepfl & Huber [1970].

Decompositional models also have a long history. As early as 1923, Henry A. Wallace (former Vice President under Roosevelt) proposed that one method of determining 'what is on the corn judge's mind' is to build a linear model of the judge by regressing his overall ratings of corn quality on various characteristics of the corn he rates [see Dawes & Corrigan, 1974]. Almost 40 years later, Hoffman [1960] independently proposed linear models to represent expert judgment. Parameter estimation techniques involved multiple regression, or analysis of variance (ANOVA).

Since Hoffman's development of the decompositional 'paramorphic' model, a large number of researchers from the behavioral sciences have extended these initial ideas. An excellent summary of this (and related) work appears in the book by Hammond, McClelland & Mumpower [1980].

Norman Anderson's [1970] functional measurement approach is also decompositional. He estimates parameters within the context of an ANOVA model. Multiattribute stimuli composed from full factorial designs are used for the evaluative task. In Anderson's approach emphasis centers on alternative model testing as much as (if not more than) on parameter estimation.

Conjoint analysis is also primarily decompositional, although recent developments (described later) have centered on various hybrid approaches that combine input from both compositional and decompositional elicitation procedures. Unlike paramorphic and functional measurement approaches (that use either full factorial designs or random samples of profiles), conjoint utilizes highly fractionated factorials where only main effects (and, sometimes, a limited number of two-way interactions) are estimated orthogonally.

In sum, in compositional models, parameters are explicitly estimated by the decision maker. In decompositional models, parameter values are derived (using techniques like multiple regression and ANOVA) from the decision maker's holistic, evaluative responses to profile descriptions designed by the researcher. Both approaches are 'deterministic' in the sense that standard gamble elicitation techniques are not employed. Only a few examples of this latter approach have been noted in marketing research [e.g. Hauser & Urban, 1979; Roberts & Urban, 1988]; the standard gamble method has never achieved popularity in industry-based marketing studies.

2.1. Model representations

Whatever preference/choice elicitation technique is used, a variety of models have been proposed for characterizing a decision maker's multiattribute utility function. We first represent each alternative (or choice option) as an ordered M-tuple. In vector notation, an alternative x is represented as

$$x = (x_1, x_2, \ldots, x_M)$$

where $x_1, x_2, \ldots, x_j, \ldots, x_M$ refer to the level (or state) of the jth attribute, describing x. If an attribute is categorical (i.e. refers to a p-state unordered polytomy), we assume that it is non-redundantly coded by means of $p-1$ dummy variables.

Next, we assume that the decision maker values some levels or states more than others. We posit a value or utility function:

$$U(x_1, x_2, \ldots, x_M) = f[u_1(x_1), u_2(x_2), \ldots, u_M(x_M)] \tag{1}$$

where each u_j is a part-worth function defined over all relevant values of the jth attribute; $f[\cdot]$ is an appropriate function that aggregates part-worths over attributes.

We let x' denote another option. We assume that

$$U(x) \leqslant U(x') \quad \text{if and only if} \quad x \leqslant_0 x' \tag{2}$$

where

$\leqslant_0$ denotes is 'not preferred to'.

2.2. *Additive models*

The additive model, which is used quite frequently in MAUT, is defined as

$$U(x_1, x_2, \ldots, x_M) = \sum_{j=1}^{M} w_j u_j(x_j) \tag{3}$$

where, typically, w_j and $u_j(\cdot)$ are obtained from two-stage, self-explicated techniques, as described earlier.

Alternatively, the researcher could show the decision maker a subset of profile descriptions, constructed orthogonally from the full Cartesian product set. The decision maker is then asked to rate each full profile on (say) a 0–100 likelihood-of-purchase scale. It is up to the researcher to estimate the part-worth utilities, according to some decompositional, regression-like procedure.

In this case, profile x can be described by dummy variables d_{ij} where d_{ij} is 1 if attribute j is at level i and 0 otherwise. The model is:

$$U(x_i, \ldots, x_M) = b_0 + \sum_{j=1}^{M} \sum_{i=1}^{L_j} b_{ij} d_{ij} \tag{4}$$

where b_0 denotes the intercept (if relevant), b_{ij} denotes the partial regression coefficient to be applied to the dummy-coded state d_{ij}, and L_j is the number of levels for attribute j. Note, here, that the separate w_j's and u_j's of Equation (3) are absorbed into the b_{ij} coefficients of Equation (4), and are not estimated separately.

2.3. *Configural models*

In addition to additive utility models, various configural models (where utility for the whole is not a simple aggregation of part-worths) have been proposed. For example, in MAUT, the multilinear utility model is sometimes employed:

$$\begin{aligned} U(x_1, x_2, \ldots, x_M) = {} & \sum_{j} w_j u_j(x_j) + \sum_{k>j} w_{jk} u_j(x_j) u_k(x_k) \\ & + \sum_{l>k>j} w_{jkl} u_j(x_j) u_k(x_k) u_l(x_l) \\ & + \cdots + w_{12\cdots M} u_1(x_1) u_2(x_2) \cdots u_M(x_M) \end{aligned} \tag{5}$$

which involves two-way cross-products, triple products, and so on. In practice, however, marketing researchers rarely go beyond configural models that entail a selected set of two-way interaction terms; again, the main effects and interaction terms are typically estimated by dummy-variable regression or fixed-effects ANOVA models.

Although behavioral scientists have posited a variety of noncompensatory models (e.g. lexicographic, conjunctive, disjunctive, elimination by aspects), conjoint analysts have made little use of these, to date. Noncompensatory models typically entail go/no-go or pass/fail decisions. Conjoint analysts are more interested in a continuum of evaluations, such as those elicited by likelihood-of-purchase rating tasks.

More general surveys of MAUT models and elicitation techniques can be found in Fishburn [1967, 1968], Farquhar [1977] and Fischer [1979].

3. Basic ideas of conjoint analysis

The seminal paper that touched off marketers' interest in conjoint analysis was actually written by a mathematician and a statistician [Luce & Tukey, 1964]. The authors were primarily interested in the conditions under which measurement scales for both dependent and independent variables exist, given only: (a) order information on the joint effects of the independent variables, and (b) a hypothesized composition rule. Luce & Tukey's paper soon led to several theoretical extensions [Krantz, 1964; Tversky, 1967] and algorithmic contributions [Kruskal, 1965; Carroll, 1969; Young, 1969]. Luce & Tukey called their approach *conjoint measurement.*

Researchers in marketing, however, are more interested in parameter estimation and scaling and soon adopted the name *conjoint analysis* to emphasize the distinction. Marketing researchers quickly noted the applicability of conjoint analysis to the multiattribute preference-measurement problem [Green & Rao, 1969; Green & Carmone, 1970]. The first detailed paper on the applicability of conjoint methodology to consumer behavior appeared in 1971 [Green & Rao, 1971], and was soon followed by various extensions and applications [Green, Carmone & Wind, 1972; Srinivasan & Shocker, 1973; Johnson, 1974].

To illustrate the basic concepts of conjoint analysis, assume that a pharmaceutical firm that sells liquid dietary supplements (for use in hospitals) wishes to examine the possibility of modifying its current product. One of the first steps in designing a conjoint study is to develop a set of attributes and levels that sufficiently characterize the competitive domain. Focus groups, in-depth consumer interviews, and internal corporate expertise are some of the sources used to structure the sets of attributes and levels that guide the rest of the study.

Table 10.1 shows an illustrative set of nine attributes employed in an actual study (to be discussed later). Note that the number of levels within an attribute range from 3 to 4, for a total of 32 levels. However, the total number of possible combinations of levels is 82 944.

As noted earlier, conjoint analysts make extensive use of highly fractionated factorial designs [Addelman, 1962; Green, 1974] to reduce the number of stimulus descriptions to a small fraction of the total number of combinations. For example,

Table 10.1
Attribute levels for liquid dietary supplement study (source: Green & Krieger [1991b])

Source of protein
1. Amino acids
2. Meat, eggs (natural)
3. Casein
4. Soy/caseinate

Percent calories from protein
1. 24
2. 18
3. 12
4. 6

Caloric density (calories/millilitre)
1. 2.0
2. 1.5
3. 1.0

Incidence of diarrhea, cramps (side effects), % of patients
1. 5
2. 10
3. 15
4. 20

Percent of patients disliking taste
1. 5
2. 15
3. 25
4. 35

Flavor base
1. Fruit juice
2. Chocolate-flavored milk
3. Unflavored

Convenience of preparation
1. Ready-to-use liquid
2. Powder–to be mixed with water
3. Powder–to be mixed in blender

Health professionals' endorsement
1. Most recommend
2. Most are neutral
3. Most are neutral to negative

Therapy-cost per patient per week ($)
1. 40
2. 50
3. 60
4. 70

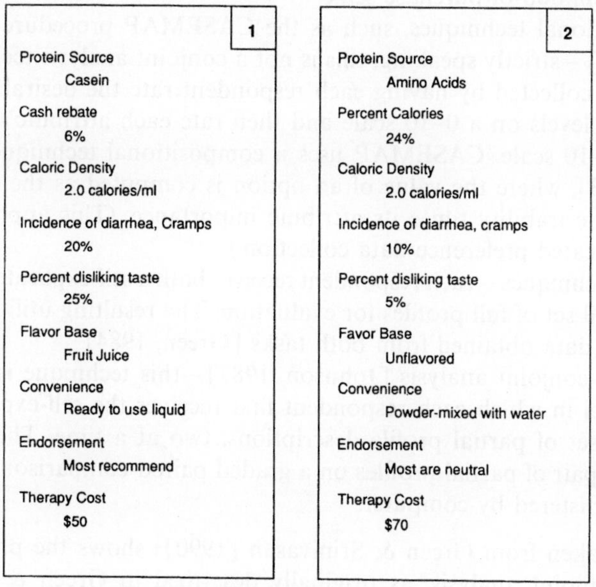

Fig. 10.1. Illustrative full profile prop cards.

in the preceding problem an orthogonal array of only 64 profiles (less than 0.1% of the total) is sufficient to estimate *all* attribute-level main effects on an uncorrelated basis. Since the study designers used a hybrid conjoint design [Green, 1984], each respondent received only 8 (balanced) profile descriptions, drawn from the 64 profiles.

Figure 10.1 shows two illustrative prop cards, used in the study. After the respondent sorts the prop cards in terms of preference, each is rated on a 0–100 likelihood-of-acquisition scale.

In small conjoint studies (e.g. six or seven attributes, each at two or three levels) the respondent receives all of the full profiles, ranging in number from 16 to 32 prop cards. In these cases the prop cards are sorted into four to eight ordered categories before likelihood-of-purchase ratings are obtained for each separate profile, within group.

3.1. Types of conjoint data collection

There are five major types of data-collection procedures that have been implemented for conjoint analysis:

(1) Tradeoff tables – each respondent sees a sequence of tables, involving two attributes each. The respondent is asked to rank the cell descriptions of each two-way table in terms of preference; other attribute levels are assumed to be equal across the options of interest.

(2) Full-profile techniques – each respondent sees a full set of prop cards, as illustrated in Figure 10.1. After initial sorting into ordered categories, each is rated on a 0–100 likelihood-of-purchase scale.

(3) Compositional techniques, such as the CASEMAP procedure [Srinivasan & Wyner, 1989] – strictly speaking, this is not a conjoint analysis technique since preferences are collected by having each respondent rate the desirability of each set of attribute levels on a 0–10 scale and then rate each attribute's importance on a similar 0–10 scale. CASEMAP uses a compositional technique [Wilkie & Pessemier, 1973], where the value of an option is computed as the sum of each attribute-level desirability times its attribute importance. (This approach is also called self-explicated preference data collection.)

(4) Hybrid techniques – each respondent receives both a self-explicated evaluation task and a small set of full profiles for evaluation. The resulting utility function is a composite of data obtained from both tasks [Green, 1984].

(5) Adaptive conjoint analysis [Johnson, 1987] – this technique is also a type of hybrid model in which each respondent first receives the self-explication task followed by a set of partial profile descriptions, two at a time. The respondent evaluates each pair of partial profiles on a graded paired-comparisons scale. Both tasks are administered by computer.

Table 10.2 (taken from Green & Srinivasan [1990]) shows the principal steps involved in conjoint analysis, as originally described in Green & Srinivasan's [1978] review paper. With the benefit of the ensuing years, we comment on the

Table 10.2
Steps involved in conjoint analysis (source: Green & Srinivasan [1990])

Steps	Alternative methods
1. Preference model	Vector model; ideal-point model; part-worth function model; mixed model.
2. Data-collection method	Full profile: two-attribute-at-a-time (tradeoff table).
3. Stimulus-set construction	Fractional factorial design; random sampling from a multivariate distribution; Pareto-optimal designs.
4. Stimulus presentation	Verbal description (multiple-cue stimulus card); paragraph description; pictorial or three-dimensional model representation; physical products.
5. Measurement scale for the dependent variable	Rating scale; rank order; paired comparisons; constant-sum paired comparisons; graded paired comparisons; category assignment.
6. Estimation method	Metric methods (multiple regression); nonmetric methods (Linmap, Monanova, Prefmap, Johnson's tradeoff table algorithm); choice-probability-based methods (logit; probit).

trends that have taken place in the various alternatives listed under each of the six steps of Table 10.2.

3.2. Preference model

As noted from Table 10.2, Green & Srinivasan originally listed four models for measuring buyers' multiattribute preference functions. First, we let $j = 1, 2, \ldots, M$ denote the set of M attributes that are used in the study design. We let x_{ij} denote the level of the jth attribute for the ith stimulus ($i = 1, 2, \ldots, r$). We first assume that x_{ij} is inherently continuous. The *vector* model posits that the preference s_i for the ith stimulus is given by

$$s_i = \sum_{j=1}^{M} w_j x_{ij} \tag{6}$$

where the $\{w_j\}$ denote a respondent's weights for the M attributes.

The *ideal-point* model posits that preference s_i is negatively related to the weighted squared distance d_i^2 of the location $\{x_{ij}\}$ of the ith stimulus from the individual's ideal-point for attribute $j(I_j)$, where d_i^2 is defined as

$$d_i^2 = \sum_{j=1}^{M} w_j (x_{ij} - I_j)^2. \tag{7}$$

The *part-worth* model posits that

$$s_i = \sum_{j=1}^{M} f_j(x_{ij}) \tag{8}$$

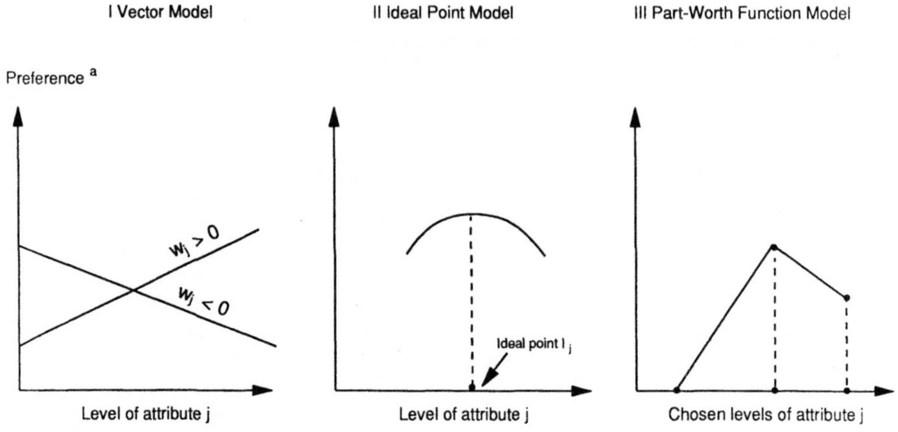

[a]Preference for different levels of attribute j while holding the values for the other attributes constant.

Fig. 10.2. Alternative models of preference (source: Green & Srinivasan [1978]).

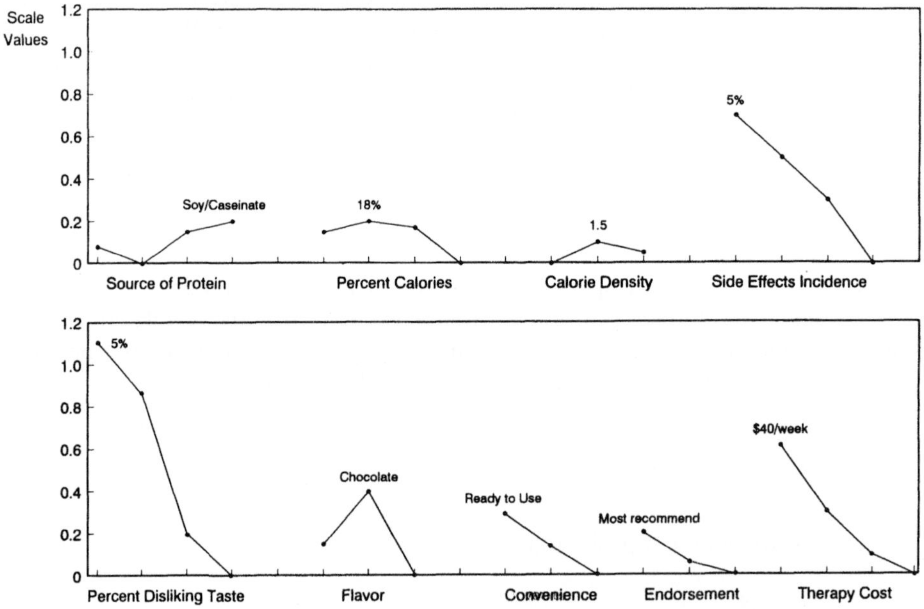

Fig. 10.3. Average part-worths from hybrid conjoint model (source: Green & Krieger [1991]).

where f_j is a function denoting the part-worth of different levels of x_{ij} for the jth attribute. In practice, $f_j(x_{ij})$ is estimated for a selected set of levels of x_{ij}.

The *mixed* model combines features of all three preceding models. Figure 10.2 illustrates the three basic models. While the part-worth model is the most general of Equations (6), (7) and (8), it also entails more parameters to estimate. Currently, the part-worth model has emerged as the most popular conjoint model, particularly insofar as industry applications are concerned.

Figure 10.3 shows illustrative (averaged) part-worths for each of the attribute levels described in Table 10.1. As noted, part-worths are often scaled so that the lowest part-worth is zero, within each attribute. Strictly speaking, part-worth functions are evaluated at discrete levels for each attribute. However, in most applications, analysts interpolate between levels of continuous attributes, such as price (when the part-worths enter buyer-choice simulators). Note that the scaling (vertical axis) is common across all attributes. This enables the researcher to obtain the overall utility of any profile, composable from the basic attribute levels, as the sum of the appropriate part-worths.

3.3. Data collection

Conjoint data collection currently emphasizes the full-profile procedure, at the expense of the two-attribute-at-a-time, or tradeoff matrix. Reasons for this emphasis are varied but appear to relate to growing practitioner interest in replacing simple liking or preference judgments with more behaviorally oriented constructs, such as intentions to buy, likelihood of trying, chances of switching to the new option, and so on. Full-profile descriptions of buyer options are much more relevant for this objective since they deal with a complete description of the product/service.

A related advantage of the full-profile method is that the practitioner can bypass the intermediate step of linking preference ratings or rankings (required in the tradeoff matrix approach) to more behaviorally oriented choice measures. Hence, the once heated debate about which data-collection method is 'superior' (full-profile or tradeoff table) is now largely of historical and academic interest. Currently, tradeoff tables receive little application.

3.4. Stimulus set construction

Fractional factorial designs and other kinds of orthogonal plans that either exclude or markedly limit the measurement of orthogonal interaction effects currently dominate the applications scene. This trend has been helped immeasurably by the recent appearance of microcomputer software [Herman, 1988] for preparing a wide variety of orthogonal main-effects plans.

If two or more attributes are highly correlated environmentally, then Green & Srinivasan's suggestion of making up 'superattributes' also appears to be popular in industry studies. If this device is not feasible, it is not unusual to depart from fully orthogonal design requirements and permit some attributes to be correlated. In cases where the price attribute ranges widely, researchers sometimes embed price in the profile description (i.e. allow it to depend completely on the rest of the profile). If so, all non-price part-worths reflect the presence of price (which is not estimated separately).

3.5. Stimulus presentation

While some industry studies still employ paragraph descriptions, profile cards (with terse attribute-level descriptions) are, by far, the more popular stimulus-presentation method. Increasing use of pictorial materials is to be noted; these kinds of props not only make the task more interesting to the respondent, but provide easier and less ambiguous ways of conveying information. Pictorial materials are virtually indispensable in conjoint studies associated with appearance and esthetics, such as package design and product styling. Moreover, conjoint methodology is increasingly being applied to the design of physical products (e.g. foods and beverages, fragrances, personal care products, and so on). As such, conjoint methods are being adapted to provide a type of discrete-level analog to response-surface modeling [Moskowitz, Stanley & Chandler, 1977].

3.6. Measurement scale for the dependent variable

As suggested above, historical interest in ranking-type judgments has given way to the almost universal use of ratings scales (e.g. likelihood of purchase). Even techniques that feature paired comparisons of profiles now employ *graded* paired judgments (expressing degree of preference of profile A versus B on some type of rating scale). Constant-sum judgments are also becoming more popular in presentation sets that require consideration of the full competitive array of options [Mahajan, Green & Goldberg, 1982]. Alternatively, the respondent may simply be asked to choose the item that she/he would most likely buy; this procedure yields quantal choice data and the opportunity to apply multinomial logit or probit models [Louviere & Woodworth, 1983]; competitive-set models are typically applied to data that are pooled across individuals.

3.7. Estimation method

With the swing toward behavior-intentions ratings scales (as opposed to preference rankings), it is not surprising that several of the earlier nonmetric regression techniques, such as MONANOVA [Kruskal, 1965], have given way to OLS regression as the major estimation technique. Attribute levels are simply recoded into dummy variables and entered into a standard multiple-regression program. As shown by many researchers [Green, 1975; Cattin & Wittink, 1976; Carmone, Green & Jain, 1978], OLS regression does a respectable job in mimicking the output of nonmetric techniques, without the associated dangers of solution degeneracy or local optima, associated with nonmetric methods. However, the LINMAP nonmetric program [Shocker & Srinivasan, 1977] still continues to be popular.

Logit and probit models are finding increasing industry application [Currim, 1982; Kamakura & Srivastava, 1984] as well. In most instances these models have been applied to aggregate-level data, requiring the need for relatively large numbers of observations [Malhotra, 1983]. To the extent that logit and probit models ignore data heterogeneity, there is some question as to whether models using high levels of data aggregation retain the original spirit of conjoint analysis, with its stress on the retention of individual part-worth differences. In this chapter we do not consider conjoint-based logit modeling, since our emphasis is on models that emphasize individual utility functions. McFadden [1986] provides an excellent overview of choice-based utility functions, including the role of conjoint analysis.

A relatively recent version of decompositional preference measurement, called experimental choice analysis, has been proposed by Louviere and his colleagues [e.g. Louviere & Woodworth, 1983]. This approach employs the stimulus design methodology of conjoint (and extends it to the design of sets of choice options). However, the methodology differs in terms of dependent variable and estimation techniques. In experimental choice analysis the respondent typically chooses his/her most preferred option from the set. Alternatively, if the respondent is asked to rank the multiattribute items, the rank are 'exploded' into a derived set of choices [Chapman & Staelin, 1982].

Experimental choice analysis also uses probabilistic choice modeling (e.g. the multinomial logit in its various forms) to estimate part-worths at an aggregate level. While Chapman [1984] has applied the logit to individual respondent preference data, the number of stimulus evaluations needed to obtain stable parameter estimates is prohibitive in commercially designed conjoint studies. Typically, experimental choice analysts pool data across subjects and introduce respondent-based covariates to capture inter-group differences.

As Louviere, the major developer of this approach, has said [Louviere, 1991, p. 292]:

> "it is probably fair to say that individual analyses of choice rarely will be practical with discrete choice experiments, at least not if one wishes to have statistical confidence in one's results."

A similar viewpoint is expressed by Batsell & Louviere [1991]. Still, experimental choice analysis has come into its own as a marketing research tool for situations where data-pooling across individuals is not a problem for the study's sponsor.

3.8. Segmentation and part-worth estimation

Recently, researchers have attempted to combine aspects of clustering and part-worth estimation to improve reliability by the partial pooling of data across respondents. Hagerty [1985] was the first to do this by means of a factor-analytic approach that weights respondents according to their similarity to other respondents' evaluations.

Following this, Kamakura [1988] developed a hierarchical clustering approach that solves simultaneously for respondent clusters and averaged part-worths within cluster. Ogawa [1987] and DeSarbo, Oliver & Rangaswamy [1989] address similar questions.

While attempts to improve upon individually based parameter estimation are laudable, empirical comparisons with individually estimated part-worths have yet to show dramatic improvements for data-pooling. For example, Green & Helsen [1989] found that neither the Hagerty nor the Kamakura proposals led to higher predictive validities than traditional, individual-level conjoint-parameter estimation. In fact, both aggregation methods performed more poorly than the traditional conjoint model.

3.9. The Cattin and Wittink industry surveys

A definitive documentation of industry usage of conjoint analysis is contained in the two surveys by Cattin & Wittink [1982] and Wittink & Cattin [1989]. Their more recent survey indicates that the number of conjoint studies completed in 1981 to 1985 is approximately 1500. Some of the highlights of their second study show that:

(1) Consumer goods account for 59% of the studies, industrial goods 18%, and financial, government, transportation and other goods account for the remainder.
(2) New product/concept evaluation, competitive analysis, price, and market segmentation represent the principal types of applications.
(3) Personal interviewing is the most popular data-gathering procedure, although computer-interactive methods are gaining momentum.
(4) Typical sample sizes are 300–400 respondents; typical product profiles are composed of approximately eight attributes.

A considerably more complete analysis of their findings can be found in the original papers.

In sum, the original conjoint *measurement* theme [Luce & Tukey, 1964], which emphasized model-testing based on ordinal observations, has moved to an increased emphasis on robust, metric procedures that are more in the spirit of policy-capturing models [Hoffman, Slovic & Rorer, 1968]. The full factorial designs associated with conjoint measurement have been replaced with highly fractionated designs [Green, 1974] that enable the practitioner to maintain an extraordinarily high leverage of response predictions to the number of calibration stimuli.

4. Trends in conjoint analysis

Until the mid-1980s conjoint analysis applications displayed an aura of the arcane. Several consulting firms offered their particular version of the methodology, often accompanied by strident claims regarding its superiority over others.

Things changed with the introduction of microcomputer software packages that put conjoint methodology in the hands of non-specialist analysts – both those working for marketing-research supplier firms and those in industry research departments.

4.1. Microcomputer software packages

Two principal conjoint software packages are currently available for applications researchers:

(1) Bretton-Clark's package of CONJOINT DESIGNER, CONJOINT ANALYZER, SIMGRAF, LINMAP and BRIDGER.
(2) Sawtooth Software's ADAPTIVE CONJOINT ANALYSIS and PRICE VALUE ANALYSIS programs.

Bretton-Clark's package [Herman, 1988] is the more traditional of the two. It has a module for constructing orthogonal arrays (CONJOINT DESIGNER) and a module for estimating part-worths and for running new-product simulations (CONJOINT ANALYZER). Newer additions to the package include nonmetric part-worth estimation (LINMAP), a more sophisticated simulator (SIMGRAF), and BRIDGER, for dealing with large numbers of conjoint attributes. Data are collected by conventional pencil-and-paper questionnaires.

Sawtooth's ADAPTIVE CONJOINT ANALYSIS package [Johnson, 1987] utilizes the PC to collect conjoint data and uses a somewhat different procedure to estimate part-worths. (Its PRICE VALUE ANALYSIS package, however, does contain an option for preparing pencil-and-paper questionnaires.) Otherwise, the packages are quite similar in their components.

Bretton-Clark's and Sawtooth's packages play an increasingly important role in industry's utilization of conjoint. Their appearance has served to define the state of conjoint practice (which is not far different from the kinds of studies carried out in the mid-1970s). More recently, a bigger player in the marketplace, SPSS, Inc. [1990], has introduced a PC software package that is virtually identical in design to Bretton-Clark's. Similarly, another software developer, Intelligent Marketing Systems [1991], has designed a package that also utilizes the full-profile approach found in the Bretton-Clark software.

Bretton-Clark's and Sawtooth's software have played a critical role in diffusing conjoint methods throughout industry. However, neither package has incorporated any type of optimal product or product-line design model. Their software limits users to simulating outcomes related to a small set of new-product candidates in a buyer-choice simulator.

4.2. From research department to board room

The second major trend, which also started around the mid-1980s, has been the 'upward mobility' of conjoint analysis applications. In its first 15 years of application most studies were initiated for tactical reasons, e.g. to determine whether a price change should be implemented, or what set of benefits to promote in a new ethical drug. Studies were done by marketing-research suppliers, and typically presented to corporate marketing-research managers.

Times have changed. For example, over the past several years McKinsey and Company has sponsored over 200 applications of conjoint analysis. The results are being used in high-level marketing and competitive-strategy planning [Allison, 1989]. Recently, McKinsey used a conjoint study (on behalf of AT & T) as evidence for seeking legal redress from foreign producers' incursions on the U.S. business-communications market (through alleged price-dumping practices).

Nor is McKinsey the only general management-consulting firm becoming interested in conjoint analysis. Booz-Allen, Arthur D. Little, The Boston Consulting Group, and Bain and Company are some of the large, general-line consulting firms that have added conjoint analysis to their research tool box. We expect the trend to continue.

5. Conjoint simulators and sensitivity analysis

Probably the main reason for the high popularity of conjoint analysis in industry is the fact that most applications of conjoint are initiated primarily for obtaining a matrix of consumers' part-worths; this is then entered into a buyer-choice simulator. It is no accident that both the Bretton-Clark and Sawtooth Software packages include built-in simulators. Moreover, marketing consulting firms frequently offer their clients a choice-simulator program as part of the research contract.

Ironically, relatively little academic research has been reported on choice simulators. Much of what is known about them has been assembled informally. We first describe the more or less common characteristics of commercial choice simulators. We then discuss extensions of present-day simulators to deal with several sensitivity-analysis questions that can help the marketing researcher/manager better understand the input data.

5.1. Characteristics of buyer-choice simulators

First-generation choice simulators were quite primitive by today's standards. Most of them were limited to an input matrix of individuals' part-worths and a set of user-supplied product profiles. Each buyer was assumed to choose the product with the highest utility (max-utility choice rule). The simulator's output typically consisted of the proportion of choices received by each product (i.e. its 'market' share). Capability for performing sensitivity analyses or obtaining segment-based information was limited and cumbersome.

Today's choice simulators are considerably more versatile. Table 10.3 shows a list of various features that current conjoint simulators may display. The list is not meant to be exhaustive. As noted from the table, three kinds of simulations can be provided: (a) single-product; (b) multiple (competitive) products; and (c) a 'bundle' of the firm's products, against a backdrop of competitive products. Choice rules include the max utility, Bradley–Terry–Luce (BTL) and logit rules. Output

Table 10.3
Characteristics of consumer-choice simulators

Product simulation flexibility
– Single product (versus status quo)
• Likelihood-of-purchase (averaged response)
• Proportion of respondents whose predicted likelihood of purchase exceeds a user-supplied criterion level
– Multiple products (sponsor and competitors): share received by each
– Sponsor's product bundle (versus competitors' products): share received by bundle and its separate components
Choice rules for the multiple-product and bundle cases
– Max-utility rule
– Share of utility (BTL) rule
– Logit rule
Other substantive features of choice simulators
– Interpolation of part-worths
– Base-case entry with adjusted current-product comparisons
– Confidence intervals around output measures
• Parametric intervals
• Nonparametric (bootstrapped) intervals
– Frequency tabulations and histograms of responses
– Replicated cases in a single run
– Inclusion of price and cost parameters
– Brand-switching matrices
– Derived attribute-level importances (based on choice data)
Consumer characteristics
– Respondent background data for market segment summaries
– Respondent importance weights
– Respondent perceptual distributions
– Individual/respondent output file (for additional analyses)
Sensitivity features
– Runs through all levels of a single attribute
– Flexibility for fixing attribute levels at user-present values (in all runs)
Cosmetic features
– Menu-driven
– Graphics output
• Pie charts and histograms of market share; part-worth graphs
• Averaged part-worths for total sample and segments

can be organized by respondent background characteristics, and limited sensitivity-analysis capabilities are sometimes included.

A few trends occurring in the design of choice simulators should be pointed out. First, there is growing interest in the simulation of a base-case scenario/profile. Inclusion of a base-case profile (in both data collection and choice simulation) provides a useful benchmark for subsequent comparative analysis. If the base-case scenario includes competitive products (with known market shares), the simulator-based shares may even be adjusted, by multiplicative constants, to known shares, prior to running comparative analyses.

A second trend entails the compilation of various kinds of market-segmentation summaries, in which shares of choices may be automatically cross-tabulated against selected segments. More detailed kinds of outputs are also being requested by the users of choice simulators. Outputs may include sales-dollar volume and gross profits, in addition to the usual share data.

Finally, the simulators themselves are becoming more user-friendly, with menu-driven features and opportunities for simulating a large number of different new-product configurations in a single run of the simulator. As noted earlier, most of the major consulting firms now offer a microcomputer-based simulator to their clients, along with part-worth utility matrices and respondent background data. The client is then encouraged to try out various simulations, as future needs arise.

5.2. Sensitivity analysis

Rather surprisingly, the full potential for incorporating a wide variety of sensitivity-analysis features in conjoint choice simulators does not appear to have been realized by commercial software packages. Simulators can be adapted to examine systematically the interplay of part-worth utilities, choice rule, product profiles, status quo product-utilities, costs and revenues.

Table 10.4 describes some of the sensitivity analyses that can be easily programmed into present-day choice simulators [Green & Krieger, 1988]. User-supplied inputs include a matrix of respondents' part-worths, a vector of status quo product-utilities, a set of product descriptions (which could entail a single new-product concept or a bundle of new-product concepts), and a matrix of respondent background characteristics, such as one's current brand, demographics, and so on.

Table 10.4
Illustrative outputs of sensitivity analysis simulator

Preliminary detail-proportion of sample selecting each attribute level as displaying the highest part-worth, by attribute
Sensitivity analyses (assuming a bundle of two or more new products): compute bundle share (and individual item shares), given:
– Deletion of each item of bundle, in turn
– Change levels of each attribute of each product, holding all others fixed at initial levels
– Fixing or restricting range of levels of each attribute across all items in the bundle
– Raising or lowering of all status quo utilities by a fixed (user-supplied) percentage
– Selection of a specified segment (based on background-variable categories or cluster-based segments)
– Random selection of K bundles (up to 1000) where random bundles can be constrained to include user-specified profiles and/or restricted attribute-level variation
Additions to basic sensitivity analyses
– Inclusion of attribute-level returns to the user's product line
– Inclusion of price versus utility relationship for adjusting respondent utilities to price increases/decreases
– Inclusion of effect on firm's existing products (cannibalization) due to new-product(s) introduction

Basic sensitivity analyses usually assume a maximum-utility choice rule (e.g. choice of some item from the bundle versus one's status quo product) with the output indicating share of choices received by the bundle, as well as individual shares received by bundle members. As noted from Table 10.4, each of the six illustrative analyses represents a set of straightforward sensitivity calculations. If the user can also estimate financial returns (compared to a base case) at the product *attribute* level, sensitivity analyses can be extended to yield sales and profit data. Although experience with more sophisticated types of simulators (e.g. as described in Table 10.4) is still limited, we have found that the results provide the user with a useful set of summaries about data interrelationships that one cannot obtain from typical commercial choice simulators.

Whither conjoint analysis? Judging by recent events (e.g. introduction of PC software packages, increases in higher-level industry applications), conjoint analysis

Table 10.5
Future directions in conjoint analysis (source: Green & Srinivasan [1990])

Research
- Statistical methodology for choosing among alternative conjoint models.
- Empirical studies for determining the extent to which varying numbers of levels within attributes lead to biases in attribute importances and market-share estimates.
- Theoretical and empirical studies in the design of compensatory models (with selected interactions) for mimicking noncompensatory decision processes.
- Studies in the robustness of orthogonal designs in predicting choices in correlated attribute environments.
- Methodologies for data-pooling that increase conjoint reliability while maintaining individual differences in part-worths.
- Methodologies for coping with large numbers of attributes and levels within attribute.
- Models for dealing with multivariate responses [e.g. Louviere & Woodworth, 1983; Green & Krieger, 1989] in explicit competitive set evaluations.
- Extensions of choice simulators to encompass flexible sensitivity analyses and optimal product and product-line search.

Practice
- Extension of conjoint methodology to new application areas, such as litigation, employee benefit packages, conflict resolution (e.g. employer/employee negotiations), corporate strategy, and social/environmental tradeoffs.
- Application of newly developed models for optimal product and product-line design, including models that combine conjoint analysis with multidimensional scaling; for a review, see Green & Krieger [1989].
- Descriptive and normative studies for measuring customer satisfaction, perceived product and service quality.
- Models and applications of conjoint analysis to simulated test marketing services that include ongoing prediction validation and the establishment of adjustment 'norms' for converting survey responses to market forecasts.
- Extension of conjoint models and applications to include marketing-mix strategy variables, such as advertising, promotion and distribution.
- Models and applications that combine survey-based data (e.g. conjoint analysis) with single-source behavioral data obtained from scanning services and split-cable TV experiments.
- New computer packages that exploit recent developments in hybrid modeling, multivariate response analysis and optimal product search.

appears to have a bright future. Table 10.5 (taken from Green & Srinivasan [1990]) represents a partial listing of those authors' speculations about where the field may be heading, both with respect to research and application.

6. Applications of conjoint analysis

Over the past 20 years conjoint has been applied to virtually every industry sector, both in the U.S. and abroad. Every major marketing-research supplier offers this service and a few firms specialize in conjoint (and related) techniques.

Table 10.6 lists a wide variety of conjoint applications, ranging from consumer nondurables to large complex industrial machinery. Some idea of the range of possibilities may be gained from the capsule applications that follow.

6.1. Designing bar soaps

In a consumer-products study, researchers related the psychological images of physical characteristics of actual bars of soap to end-use appropriateness; this study was conducted for the laboratory and marketing personnel of a large,

Table 10.6
Sample list of conjoint applications

Consumer nondurables	*Other products*
1. Bar soaps	1. Automotive styling
2. Hair shampoos	2. Automobile and truck tires
3. Carpet cleaners	3. Car batteries
4. Synthetic-fiber garments	4. Ethical drugs
5. Gasoline pricing	5. Toasters/ovens
6. Panty-hose	6. Cameras
7. Lawn chemicals	7. Apartment design
Financial services	*Other services*
1. Branch bank services	1. Car-rental agencies
2. Auto insurance policies	2. Telephone services and pricing
3. Health insurance policies	3. Employment agencies
4. Credit-card features	4. Information-retrieval services
5. Consumer discount cards	5. Medical laboratories
6. Auto retailing facilities	6. Hotel design
7. High-tech maintenance service	
Industrial goods	*Transportation*
1. Copying machines	1. Domestic airlines
2. Printing equipment	2. Transcontinental airlines
3. Facsimile transmissions	3. Passenger train operations
4. Data transmission	4. Freight train operations
5. Portable computer terminals	5. International Air Transportation Association
6. Personal computer design	6. Electric car design

diversified soap manufacturer. Although the designing of a bar of soap (by varying weight, size, shape, color, fragrance type and intensity, surface feel, and so on) may seem like a mundane exercise, the extent of industry knowledge about the importance of such imagery is woefully meager.

The researchers formulated actual bars of soap in which color, type of fragrance, and intensity of fragrance were constructed according to a factorial design. All other characteristics of the soap were held constant. Respondents examined the soaps and assigned each bar to the end-use that they felt best matched its characteristics: moisturizing facial soap, deep-cleaning soap for oily skin, women's deodorant soap, or men's deodorant soap. The data were then analyzed by conjoint analysis, leading to a set of psychophysical functions for each of the physical characteristics.

The study showed that type of fragrance was the most important physical variable contributing to end-use appropriateness. Rather surprisingly, the type of fragrance (medicinal) and color (blue) that appeared best suited for a man's deodorant soap were also found to be best for the deep-cleaning soap. Deep-cleaning soap had previously been classed, for marketing purposes, as a facial soap in which floral fragrances predominated. On the other hand, fragrance intensity played a relatively minor role as a consumer cue for distinguishing among different end-uses.

In brief, this study illustrated the feasibility of translating changes in various physical variables into changes in psychological variables. Eventually, more-detailed knowledge of these psychological transformations could enable a laboratory technician to synthesize color, fragrance, shape, and so forth to obtain soaps that conjure up almost any desired imagery. Moreover, in other product classes, such as beers, coffees and soft drinks, it appears possible to develop a psychophysics of taste in which such elusive verbal descriptions as 'full-bodied' and 'robust' are given operational meaning in terms of variations in physical or chemical characteristics.

6.2. *New-concept descriptions*

In many product classes, such as automobiles, houses, office machines, and computers, the possible design factors are myriad and expensive to vary physically for evaluation by the buying public. In cases such as these, the researcher usually resorts to verbalized and/or pictorial descriptions of the principal attributes of interest.

In an early application of conjoint to automobile preferences researchers found that gas mileage and country of manufacture were highly important attributes in respondent evaluations of car profiles. Somewhat surprising, however, was the finding that even large-car owners (and those contemplating the purchase of a large car) were more concerned with gas economy than owners of that type of car had been historically. Thus, while fully expecting to get fewer miles per gallon than they could get in compact cars, they felt quite strongly that the car should be economical compared with others in its size class.

6.3. *Airline services*

One of the most interesting application areas for conjoint analysis is in the transportation industry, particularly airlines and other forms of passenger travel, where the service aspect is important to consumer choice. As a case in point, a large-scale study of consumer evaluations of airline services was conducted in which part-worths were developed for some 25 different service attributes such as on-ground services, in-flight services, décor of cabins and seats, scheduling, routing and price. Moreover, each part-worth was developed on a route (city-pair) and purpose-of-trip basis.

As might be expected, the part-worth functions for each of the various types of airline service differed according to the length and purpose of the flight. However, in addition to obtaining consumers' evaluations of service profiles, the researchers also obtained information concerning their perceptions of each airline on each of the service attributes for which the consumers were given a choice.

These two major pieces of information provided the principal basis for developing a buyer simulation of airline services over all major traffic routes. The purpose of the simulation was to estimate the effect on share of choices that a change in the service configuration of the sponsor's services would have, route by route, if competitors did not follow suit. Later, the sponsor used the simulator to examine the effect of assumed retaliatory actions by its competitors. A procedure was also designed to update the model's parameters periodically by the collection of new field data.

Each new service configuration was evaluated against a base-period configuration. In addition, the simulator showed which competing airlines would lose business and which would gain business under various changes in perceived service levels. Thus, in addition to single, ad hoc studies, conjoint analysis was used in the ongoing monitoring (via simulation) of consumer imagery and preference evaluations over time.

6.4. *The Courtyard by Marriott study*

The largest conjoint study (that we know of) involved the design of a new hotel concept – Courtyard by Marriott. The study entailed 50 attributes, organized under seven facets:

- external factors (e.g. location);
- rooms;
- food;
- lounge;
- services;
- leisure;
- security.

A total of 167 different attribute levels were involved. Figure 10.4 shows only one of the seven facets, the one dealing with rooms. In total, there were nine

Most Frequently Used Hotel Chain ____

"X" the TRIANGLE (△) in the block that comes closest to describing your current hotel (ONLY "X" ONE)

"X" the CIRCLE (○) in the block(s) that you find to be completely unacceptable

(YOU MAY "X" NONE, ONE, OR MORE THAN ONE)

"X" the SQUARE (□) in the block that represents what you want and are willing to pay for (ONLY "X" ONE)

FEATURES	ALTERNATIVE DESCRIPTIONS				
Entertainment □	Color TV* (.00) △○□	Color TV with movies which are 9 months ahead of HBO, $5 each (.00) △○□	Color TV with 30 channel cable (.25) △○□	Color TV with HBO movie channel, sports news channel (.40) △○□	Color TV with free in-room movies (choice of 3) (2.50) △○□
Entertainment/ Rental □	None (.00) △○□	Rental cassettes available for use with in-room Atari or Intelevision (.40)+ △○□	Rental cassettes available. In-room stereo cassette player (1.35)+ △○□	Rental movies. In -room video cassette player (BetaMax). (1.35)+ △○□	
Size & Furniture □	Small--typical size motel/hotel room △○□	Somewhat larger--1 foot longer △○□	Much larger-- 2 1/2 feet longer △○□	Small suite-- 2 rooms △○□	Large suite-- 2 rooms △○□
Quality of Decor (in standard room) □	Similar to Days Inn and other budget motels △○□	Similar to older Holiday Inn, Ramada, Roadway △○□	Similar to newer and better Holiday Inns △○□	Similar to newer and better Hilton and Marriott △○□	Similar to Hyatt Regency and Westin "Plaza" hotels △○□
Heat/Cooling □	Through wall unit full control of heating and cooling year round △○□	Through wall unit (soundproofed). Full control of heating & cooling year round △○□	Either central heating or cooling (not both), depending on season △○□	Full control of central heating and cooling year round △○□	

↑ IMPORTANCE RANKING

*Costs shown illustratively (in parentheses) for first two attributes

This is the stimulus card for the second facet. Each respondent received cards corresponding to all facets.

Source: Wind *et al.* (1989)

Fig. 10.4. Illustrative stimulus card for room description (first five attributes) (source: Wind, Green, Schifflet & Scarbrough [1989]).

attributes, with three to five levels each [Wind, Green, Shifflet & Scarbrough, 1989].

A hybrid conjoint design was used. In the self-explicated task each respondent saw descriptions of each of the seven facets (illustrated by Figure 10.4). Following this, respondents were shown five full profiles (see Figure 10.5), each describing a

ROOM PRICE PER NIGHT IS $ 44.85

BUILDING SIZE, BAR/LOUNGE

Large (600 rooms) 12-story hotel with:

- Quiet bar/lounge
- Enclosed central corridors and elevators
- All rooms have very large windows

LANDSCAPING/COURT

Building forms a spacious outdoor courtyard

- View from rooms of moderately landscaped courtyard with:
  - many trees and shrubs
  - the swimming pool plus a fountain
  - terraced areas for sunning, sitting, eating

FOOD

Small moderately priced lounge and restaurant for hotel guests/friends

- Limited breakfast with juices, fruit, Danish, cereal, bacon and eggs
- Lunch--soup and sandwiches only
- Evening meal--salad, soup, sandwiches, six hot entrees including steak

HOTEL/MOTEL ROOM QUALITY

Quality of room furnishings, carpet, etc. is similar to:

- Hyatt Regencies
- Westin "Plaza" Hotels

ROOM SIZE & FUNCTION

Room 1 foot longer than typical hotel/motel room

- Space for comfortable sofa-bed and 2 chairs
- Large desk
- Coffee table
- Coffee maker and small refrigerator

SERVICE STANDARDS

Full service including:

- Rapid check in/check out systems
- Reliable message service
- Valet (laundry pick up/deliver)
- Bellman
- Someone (concierge) arranges reservations, tickets, and generally at no cost
- Cleanliness, upkeep, management similar to:
  - Hyatts
  - Marriotts

LEISURE

- Combination indoor-outdoor pool
- Enclosed whirlpool (Jacuzzi)
- Well-equipped playroom/playground for kids

SECURITY

- Night guard on duty 7 p.m. to 7 a.m.
- Fire/water sprinklers throughout hotel

"X" the ONE box below which best describes how likely you are to stay in this hotel/motel at this price:

Would stay there almost all the time	Would stay there on a regular basis	Would stay there now and then	Would rarely stay there	Would not stay there
☐	☐	☐	☐	☐

Fig. 10.5. Illustrative full profile description of hotel offering (source: Wind, Green, Schifflet & Scarbrough [1989]).

potential hotel offering. Within each facet of the profile, a set of levels (chosen by Marriott's study team) was listed. The master design consisted of 50 profile cards, similar in make-up to that shown in Figure 10.5.

Attributes and levels were chosen in accordance with Marriott's desire to develop a new hotel chain for a segment of travelers who were interested in good value (with a reasonable number of amenities). Interest centered on the features that the new hotel chain should have, its physical layout and location, and its price. Respondents included business and non-business travelers. Pictorial materials (colored slides and photographs) were used, wherever possible, to portray various layout and design features.

6.4.1. Results

The study clearly suggested that some business and pleasure travelers were dissatisfied with current hotel offerings. Some hotels cost too much and offered features not valued by the traveler while others that cost less offered too few of the desirable features. Both types of hotels also lacked the personalization of features that travelers seek. A new hotel concept, tuned to travelers' needs at an acceptable price, seemed to be the most viable product for Marriott to consider.

Respondents' dissatisfaction with hotels that cost too much for value given suggested the positioning of 'a special little hotel at a very comfortable price'.

The study provided detailed guidelines for the selection of features and services. Some of the specific attributes Marriott selected for inlcusion were amenities such as shampoo and hair-conditioner; in-room kitchen facilities (either coffee makers or coffee makers and refrigerators); and a 'limo' to the airport. Marriott postponed installation of complete exercise rooms but weight rooms were included. The computer simulation provided additional insight into the value of various features and services. The simulation output included:

- The likely share of nights any hotel concept (presented as a specific combination of features and services) would get by any target segment(s).
- The source of business – the hotels from which the new hotel would be most likely to draw business, including the likelihood of cannibalization of the existing Marriott chain.
- The characteristics of the segment attached to each specific configuration of attributes and services.

6.4.2. Implementation

Development team members from several corporate departments were involved in the design of the study and provided expertise in the direct translation of the research results into final product design. The resulting hotel followed almost to the letter the recommendations of the study. Every one of the features and services offered was among the highest valued by the survey respondents.

6.4.3. Validation

Internal cross-validation of the conjoint analysis was implemented by using a leave-one-out procedure. The researchers predicted each individual's actual first choice (among the five full profiles evaluated) from model parameters computed across the rest of the sample. Each person's data were held out and predicted, one respondent at a time. Predictions covered not only first choice but also the ranking of each respondent's five test profiles.

The leave-one-out procedure indicated that approximately 40% of first choices were predicted (versus 20% by chance). Given the complexity of the profiles (and respondent heterogeneity), this performance, while not outstanding, was statistically significant. Predictions of the market-share level were much higher: mean absolute deviations of four to five share points were obtained from a bootstrap resampling procedure.

The most effective validation of the study results is the success of the Courtyard by Marriott. As of 1989 (six years after initial construction) there were 175 hotels open, under construction, or under contract. In 1988 the actual market share of Courtyard by Marriott was within four percentage points of the share predicted by the conjoint simulation.

6.4.4. Financial impact

The Courtyard by Marriott chain has been a success, growing from 3 test hotels in 1983 to 90 hotels in 1987 (with total sales exceeding $200 million). The chain is expected to grow to 300 hotels by 1994 (with sales exceeding $1 billion). Courtyard by Marriott contributes significantly to Marriott's overall growth goals and related stock values. It has also created 3000 new jobs. By 1994, that figure is expected to reach 14000.

7. From simulator to product optimizer

One of the most significant events in recent conjoint research has been the emphasis placed on the development of optimal products. At best, most conjoint choice simulators (including those offered by commercial software packages) show the user which of a limited set of simulated profiles is 'best' in the sense of largest market share. Bearing in mind that the full array of possible profiles may number in the hundreds of thousands (or even millions), limiting one's considered set to a dozen or so simulated profiles is unduly (and regretfully) restrictive. Clearly, there appears to be a need for optimal-product selection procedures.

Following the initial research by Shocker & Srinivasan [1974], Zufryden [1981] was the first to propose a formal representation of the optimal-product design problem in a conjoint context. He formulated the problem as a zero-one integer programming model in which the researcher maximizes the (weighted) number of choices (versus one's status quo product) going to the new product. The choice rule is of the (deterministic) max-utility type. Subsequently, Zufryden extended his single-product conjoint model to encompass the product-line optimization case [Zufryden, 1982].

Green, Carroll & Goldberg [1981] took a different path in approaching the (single) product-positioning problem. While also using conjoint analysis as the primary data-collection tool, their POSSE model employed response-surface methodology in an effort to model the simulator's output. They constructed a consumer-choice simulator that accommodated large numbers of experimentally designed stimulus profiles that, one by one, were entered into the simulator. Using one of a variety of choice functions, the simulator then computed market share, dollar volume, and contribution to overhead and profit. Depending upon the nature of the control variables (continuous or discrete product attributes), different kinds of response 'surfaces' could be modeled and 'optimized'. Their approach also considered various sensitivity calculations after the optimizing procedure was completed.

Their model has received a fair amount of real-world application to commercial research problems. Even at that, however, the original software package has been markedly reduced in complexity, so as to fit response 'surfaces' with ANOVA-like models (that make extensive use of two-way interactions in addition to main effects). The optimizing procedure employs branch-and-bound, implicit enumeration that guarantees an optimum, albeit an optimum related to a function of the simulator's output.

In retrospect, an unexpected outcome of Green, Carroll & Goldberg's research has been the *simplification* of an initially highly complex set of computer programs that had the potential capability of doing more extensive analyses than could be supported by either data or managerial interest. The present version of their methodology is considerably simplified from the original; sensitivity analysis and segmentation questions have turned out to be at least as important as the optimization step itself.

7.1. Other research

Researchers in multidimensional scaling [e.g. Pessemier, 1975; Bachem & Simon, 1981; Albers & Brockhoff, 1977; Albers, 1979; Gavish, Horsky & Srikanth, 1983; Sudharshan, May & Gruca, 1988; Sudharshan, May & Shocker, 1987; DeSarbo & Rao, 1984, 1986; Eliashberg & Manrai, 1989] have also made important contributions to optimal-product and product-line design.

Similarly, several researchers [e.g. Green & Krieger, 1985, 1989, 1991; Kohli & Krishnamurti, 1987, 1989; Kohli & Sukumar, 1990; Dobson & Kalish, 1988; McBride & Zufryden, 1988; Gupta & Kohli, 1990] have made contributions to conjoint-based product-line optimization.[1]

Having provided a brief history of general contributions to optimal product design, we now focus on some of our own research on this topic. We discuss a model that considers strategies for modifying a firm's product-attribute levels, including pricing. A case example is used to motivate the discussion. The case is based on a real-world application that is disguised here for purposes of maintaining corporate confidentiality.

[1] In preparing the normative sections of this chapter (optimal product positioning), we have drawn extensively on Green & Krieger [1991].

8. The SIMOPT model

SIMOPT (SIMulation and OPTimization model) is an optimal product-positioning model that can be used for either the single-product or the product-line case. Its principal inputs are a matrix of K buyers' part-worths and a set of competitive product profiles. The part-worths may come from any conjoint procedure, including the commercially distributed programs of Sawtooth Software or Bretton-Clark. In particular, part-worths obtained from hybrid conjoint models [Green, 1984] are appropriate. Moreover, the part-worths may contain two-way interaction terms as well as main effects.

In addition to input matrices of buyer part-worths and competitive-supplier profiles, the model has options for including:

(1) buyer 'importance' weights (reflecting buyers' frequency and/or amount of purchase);
(2) demographic or other background attributes;
(3) demographic weights for use in market-segment selection and market-share forecasting;
(4) current market-share estimates of all supplier (brand) profiles under consideration (used in model calibration); and
(5) costs/returns data, measured at the individual-attribute level.

8.1. Choice rule (alpha)

SIMOPT uses a general choice rule, based on share of utility [Pessemier et al., 1971; Moore, Pessemier & Little, 1979]. This rule is called the alpha rule, and is capable of mimicking the more traditional Bradley–Terry–Luce (BTL), logit, or max-utility choice rules. The alpha rule assumes that the probability π_{ks} of buyer k selecting brand s is given by

$$\pi_{ks} = \frac{U_{ks}^{\alpha}}{\sum_{s=1}^{S} U_{ks}^{\alpha}} \tag{9}$$

where U_{ks} is the utility of buyer k for brand s; α (which is typically at least 1.0) is chosen by the user; and S is the number of suppliers. If $\alpha = 1$, the model mimics the BTL share-of-utility rule; as α approaches infinity the model mimics the max-utility choice rule. We employ a separate computer program, called ALPH, to find the optimal value of alpha (see Appendix).

8.2. Individuals' part-worths

The primary data input to the SIMOPT model consists of a matrix of K individuals' part-worths. In the simple case where no interaction effects are included, the general entry is

$p_{i,j}^{(k)}$ = part-worth for level i of attribute j for individual k;
$i = 1, \ldots, L_j$; $j = 1, \ldots, M$;
$a^{(k)}$ = intercept term for individual k;

where L_j denotes the number of levels for attribute j, and M is the number of attributes. Each row vector of part-worths enables the user to compute a utility for any product/supplier profile for any individual k. A profile is defined by its levels $(i_1, \ldots, i_M)$. The utility of this profile to individual k is given by

$$U_k(i_1, \ldots, i_M) = \sum_{j=1}^{M} p_{i,j}^{(k)} + a^{(k)}. \tag{10}$$

We assume that in any given run of SIMOPT, each supplier is represented by a profile vector $\boldsymbol{i}_s$; $s = 1, 2, \ldots, S$. Hence, we can compute

$$U_{k,s} \equiv U_k(\boldsymbol{i}_s)$$

as the utility of individual k for supplier s. The 'market share' of individual k for supplier s is

$$\pi_{k,s} = \frac{U_k^{\alpha}(\boldsymbol{i}_s)}{\sum_{s=1}^{S} U_k^{\alpha}(\boldsymbol{i}_s)} \tag{11}$$

for a specified value of α.

Once we have computed the $\pi_{k,s}$, we can combine them into a total market share by using $\sum_{k=1}^{K} W^{(k)} \pi_{k,s}$ where $W^{(k)}$, the weight for individual k, is non-negative, with $\sum_{k=1}^{K} W^{(k)} = 1$.

8.3. *Market segments*

The individual weights can be further modified by considering various market segments. We assume that an input matrix of demographic (or general background) classification variables is available. We let

$D_n^{(k)}$ = the demographic category of individual k for variable n; $n = 1, 2, \ldots, N$, where N denotes the total number of demographic variabls.

We also have weights E_n, one weight for each of the N demographics; $E_n \geqslant 0$; $\sum_{n=1}^{N} E_n = 1$.

In SIMOPT we can specify the number of demographics H we want to use, which demographics, $t_1, t_2, \ldots, t_H$, and the level for each demographic l_h (more than one level within demographic can be included). We then have

$$V_t^{(k)} = W^{(k)} \sum_{h=1}^{H} I_h^{(k)} E_{t_h} \tag{12}$$

where

$$I_h^{(k)} = \begin{cases} 1 & \text{if } D_{t_h}^{(k)} = l_h, \\ 0 & \text{otherwise,} \end{cases}$$

and

$$V^{(k)} = \frac{V_t^{(k)}}{\sum_{k=1}^{K} V_t^{(k)}}.$$

The overall market share for supplier/product s is given by

$$M_s^* = \sum_{k=1}^{K} V^{(k)} \pi_{k,s}.$$

(Note that M_s^* implicitly depends on the profiles of each of the S suppliers.)

8.4. *Initial supplier profiles and market shares*

Initial conditions for applying the model entail a set of initial supplier profiles and initial market shares I_s. These initial supplier profiles are associated with market shares M_s^{*b} and, hence, multipliers given by $f_s \equiv I_s / M_s^{*b}$.

The adjusted market shares are then given by

$$\hat{M}_s = \frac{f_s M_s^*}{\sum_{s=1}^{S} f_s M_s^*}. \tag{13}$$

8.5. *Costs/returns*

Finally, the model can incorporate costs/returns and can optimize over this measure (as well as over market share). First, we let:

$$R_{i,j} = \text{return for level } i \text{ of attribute } j$$

(Note: the default value is $R_{i,j} = 1/M$ for all j and i.) We can then compute the return for any brand/supplier profile as

$$T(i_1, i_2, \ldots, i_M) = \sum_{j=1}^{M} R_{i_j, j}. \tag{14}$$

Hence, for each supplier we have a total return:

$$T_s \equiv T(\boldsymbol{i}_s).$$

This gives us a respective adjusted and unadjusted return for each supplier of

$$O_s^* = M_s^* T_s, \quad \hat{O}_s = \hat{M}_s T_s,$$

with the default value of $T_s = 1$.

9. SIMOPT's features

The model's outputs consist of market shares or dollar contributions to overhead and profits for each supplier. In the latter case, direct (or variable) costs/returns have to be estimated at the individual-attribute level for each supplier – a daunting task in most real-world settings.

In any given run of the model, the user obtains market share (return) for each supplier on both an unadjusted and adjusted (for initial share) basis. Outputs can be obtained for both the total market and for any segment defined by the user from the available demographic variables.

The user is then able to perform four types of analysis:

(1) A sensitivity analysis. This shows how shares (returns) change for all suppliers as one varies the levels within each attribute, in turn.

(2) An optimal attribute-level analysis. If this option is chosen, the model computes the best attribute profile for a given supplier, conditioned on specified attribute levels for all competing suppliers.

(3) A cannibalization analysis. The user can also specify one or more ancillary products. If so, the model finds the optimal profile that maximizes share (return) for the set of chosen products (that can include the firm's existing products). This profile can be compared to the best product for a given supplier that does not take into acccount interactions with the firm's existing products.

(4) A Pareto frontier analysis. In most real-world problems the marketing strategist is not only interested in finding the 'best' product in terms of (say) return but also wishes to get some feel for the tradeoff between return and market share. SIMOPT provides a capability to trace out the (Pareto) frontier of all profiles that are undominated with respect to return and share. The user can then find out what the potential value may be in giving up some amount of return for an increase in market share.

Through a sequential series of new-product additions the user can examine the effect of adding/deleting products in the firm's line.

10. An empirical application

We now turn to an actual study using the model. The context has been changed (to maintain sponsor cofidentiality), but all data have remained intact. We return to the dietary food-supplement product, first introduced in Table 10.1 and Figure 10.1.

10.1. Study background

The Beta company is a national pharmaceutical firm that sells both prescription and over-the-counter drugs. One of its products is a liquid dietary supplement that is primarily sold to hospitals. The product is taken orally and is used to provide nutrition in cases where disorders of the mouth, esophagus, or stomach preclude the ingestion of solid foods.

Beta's product competes with the counterpart products of Gamma and Delta, the remaining major suppliers to this market. (All other suppliers account for less than 5% of total sales.) Each of the competitive dietary items can be described in terms of nine attributes: source of protein; percent calories from protein; caloric density; incidence of side effects; percent of patients disliking taste; flavor base; convenience of preparation; endorsement by health professionals; and patient cost per weekly therapy.

Beta's management was interested in both new-product additions and the associated question of market segmentation.

10.2. Study design

A national marketing-research study was designed to measure hospital dietitians' tradeoffs across the nine attributes (see Table 10.1 for detailed descriptions) that were believed, on the basis of earlier focus groups and in-depth interviews, to be the primary criteria by which dietitians judged competing products in this field.

A national sample of hospitals, stratified by type of hospital and number of beds, was selected. A mail–telephone–mail interview was administered, in which a hybrid conjoint approach [Green, 1984] was used to collect and analyze the data; all respondents (dietitians) received an honorarium for their participation. A total of 356 interviews was obtained. A part-worth vector was obtained for each respondent, along with a classification-attribute vector, containing the following respondent background characteristics:

(1) hospital type:
  (a) technical/specialty,
  (b) general,

   (c) government,
   (d) other;
(2) size:
   (a) fewer than 100 beds,
   (b) 100–499 beds,
   (c) 500 beds and over;
(3) decision authority:
   (a) user, but does not recommend to buying committee,
   (b) user and recommends,
   (c) member of buying committee,
   (d) head of buying committee,
(4) years of experience:
   (a) less than 5,
   (b) 5–10,
   (c) 11–15,
   (d) 16 years and over.

Direct costs of manufacturing and distribution at the individual-attribute level were estimated by Beta personnel. The estimates were admittedly crude (particularly for the attributes: patient taste and health professionals' endorsement). However, management was satisfied that the costs were reasonable enough to justify the use of a return measure (contribution to overhead and profit) rather than a market-share measure. (Market shares were, of course, also computed in each run of SIMOPT.) Each respondent was weighted by the size category of hospital with which s/he was associated.

10.3. Research questions

For illustrative purposes, we consider the following research questions:

(1) How sensitive is Beta's market share and return to changes in specific product attributes, such as source of protein, percent calories from protein, etc.?
(2) Given no change in competitors' offerings, what is Beta's optimal product-profile from a return viewpoint?
(3) Suppose Beta decides to keep its (optimized) current product and add a second one. What is its optimal additional product, given the tradeoff between cannibalization and competitive draw?
(4) Suppose Beta decides to design an optimal product for a prespecified market segment, while maintaining its current (optimized) product. What should this product be and what is the overall return to Beta?
(5) Assume that Delta decides to retaliate to Beta's (optimized) current product. What is Delta's best profile?

Of course, many other strategic questions could be raised. The preceding ones are only illustrative, but should serve to show the flexibility and practicality of the model.

10.4. Some preliminaries

Before addressing the research questions shown above, we briefly consider some descriptive aspects of the problem. First, Table 10.7 shows the current profiles of the three major competitors: Beta, Gamma and Delta. Also shown is the current market-share for each. As can be noted, in none of the nine attributes do we find the same level for each of the three suppliers. We also note that the experimental design attributes of Table 10.1 contain many levels for which there are no current realizations. (This was done deliberately in order to examine the potential market for new attribute levels, as well as different combinations of old ones.)

Figure 10.3 shows, illustratively, averaged part-worths across the 356 respondents. To reduce clutter, only the best (average) level is labeled; Table 10.1 shows the labels for all levels. In line with convention, Figure 10.3 is constructed so that the lowest part-worth for each attribute is set to zero. We note visually (from the range of variation) that the major attributes appear to be side effects: incidence, taste, and patient-therapy cost.

Before starting the various runs of SIMOPT a further step remained. We had to calculate the value of the decision constant, alpha in Equation (9), that when applied to product utilities at the individual-respondent level would best approximate the actual current shares, shown in Table 10.7. The ALPH program (see Appendix) was used for this purpose. The best-fitting value of alpha was 4.3. This value is fairly close to a BTL rule (in which alpha is 1.0) but will lead to somewhat greater sensitivity to profile changes than BTL.

10.5. Sensitivity analysis

We now turn to the first of the research questions. How salient is each attribute in terms of changes in Beta's return and share, as SIMOPT cycles through the

Table 10.7
Current attribute levels for three major competitors (source: Green & Krieger [1991])

	Beta	Gamma	Delta
Source of protein	Meat, eggs (natural)	Amino acids	Soy/caseinate
Percent calories from protein	6	6	12
Caloric density/millilitre	1.0	2.0	2.0
Incidence of diarrhea, cramps (side effects) (%)	10	15	10
Percent disliking taste	15	5	5
Flavor base	Chocolate	Fruit juice	Unflavored
Convenience of preparation	Ready to use	Mixed with water	Mixed in blender
Health professionals' endorsement	Most are neutral	Most recommend	Most neutral/negative
Therapy-cost per patient per week ($)	40	40	50
Current market share (%)	36	35	29

levels of each? If the researcher has no recourse to a simulator/optimizer, a common practice is to find the relative part-worth ranges for each attribute. Of course, this measure need not agree with the individual-attribute importance obtained by summarizing variation in market share for Beta, given that all other attributes remain fixed at Beta's current levels.

Nor should either of these measures necessarily agree with an importance measure based on relative ranges in return for Beta. This latter measure reflects not only changes in Beta's share but also reflects differential returns associated with the direct cost structure estimated at the attribute level by Beta's management.

Figure 10.6 illustrates the ambiguity of attribute-importance measures. The first bar shows relative attribute importances for the conventional measure that is

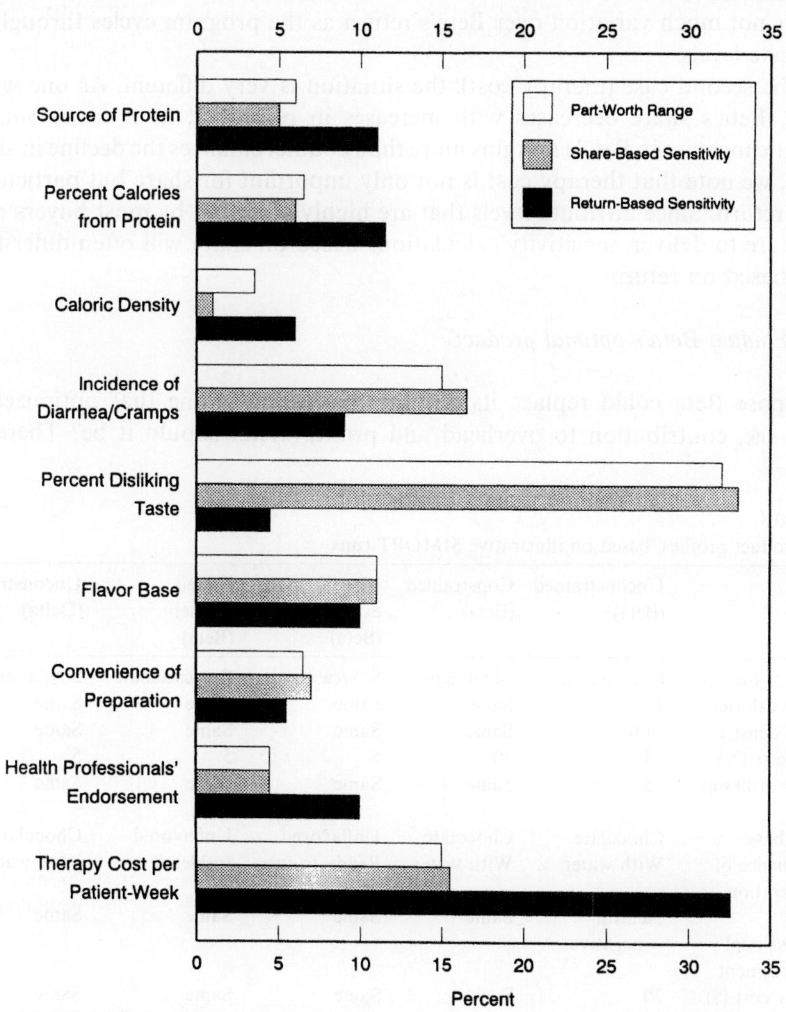

Fig. 10.6. Attribute importance based on three different methods (source: Green & Krieger [1991]).

computed from averaged part-worths. Since part-worths *are* ultimately related to share, the bar lengths for the first and second criteria are fairly close in most instances.

In contrast, both of these importance measures show some major disparities when compared to the return-based sensitivity measure, particularly, for:

(1) percent disliking taste;
(2) therapy-cost per patient per week.

As noted from Figure 10.4, taste is highly salient from a part-worth viewpoint and relatively large gains in share are associated with taste improvements. However, the cost structure for achieving these improvements is such that the share gains are just about counterbalanced by the associated costs of improvement; hence, there is not much variation over Beta's return as the program cycles through the four taste levels.

In the second case (therapy cost), the situation is very different. As one would expect, Beta's share decreases with increases in price but, as it turns out, the dramatic increase in Beta's margins more than counterbalances the decline in share. Hence, we note that therapy cost is not only important for share but particularly so for return. Since attribute levels that are highly preferred by most buyers often cost more to deliver, sensitivity calculations based on share will often differ from those based on return.

10.6. Finding Beta's optimal product

Suppose Beta could replace its current product with one that optimized its return (i.e. contribution to overhead and profit). What should it be? There are

Table 10.8
New-product profiles, based on illustrative SIMOPT runs

	Unconstrained (Beta)	Constrained (Beta)	Line extension (Beta)	Added segment (Beta)	Unconstrained (Delta)
Source of protein	Soy/caseinate	Meat/eggs	Soy/caseinate	Soy/caseinate	Soy/caseinate
Percent calories	12	Same	Same	Same	Same
Caloric density	1.0	Same	Same	Same	Same
Side effects (%)	5	10	5	5	5
Percent disliking taste	5	Same	Same	Same	Same
Flavor base	Chocolate	Chocolate	Unflavored	Unflavored	Chocolate
Convenience of preparation	With water	With water	Ready to use	In blender	With water
Health professional's endorsement	Neutral/ negative	Same	Same	Same	Same
Therapy cost ($)	70	Same	Same	Same	Same
Return ($)	17.34	13.42	12.71 alone	12.06 alone	16.34

two principal ways that one might approach this problem. One way would be to find the best product-profile for Beta by assuming that the firm is free to modify any or all attribute levels (unconstrained optimum). More realistically, however, the firm may be committed to one or more attribute levels for reasons of technology, customer expectations, historical inertia, or whatever. If so, SIMOPT could find an optimal profile, conditional on a set of user-specified constraints.

We first use the model to find the unconstrained optimum. Table 10.8 shows the results. Currently, Beta's return is \$2.94 per patient-week of therapy. Under the optimal profile (given no competitive retaliation) return would increase to \$17.34. As Panel II of Figure 10.7 shows, Beta's share would also increase from 36% to 45%.

More realistically, if the optimization is constrained to keep: (a) meat/eggs as the protein source, and (b) a 10% incidence of side effects, Table 10.8 shows that

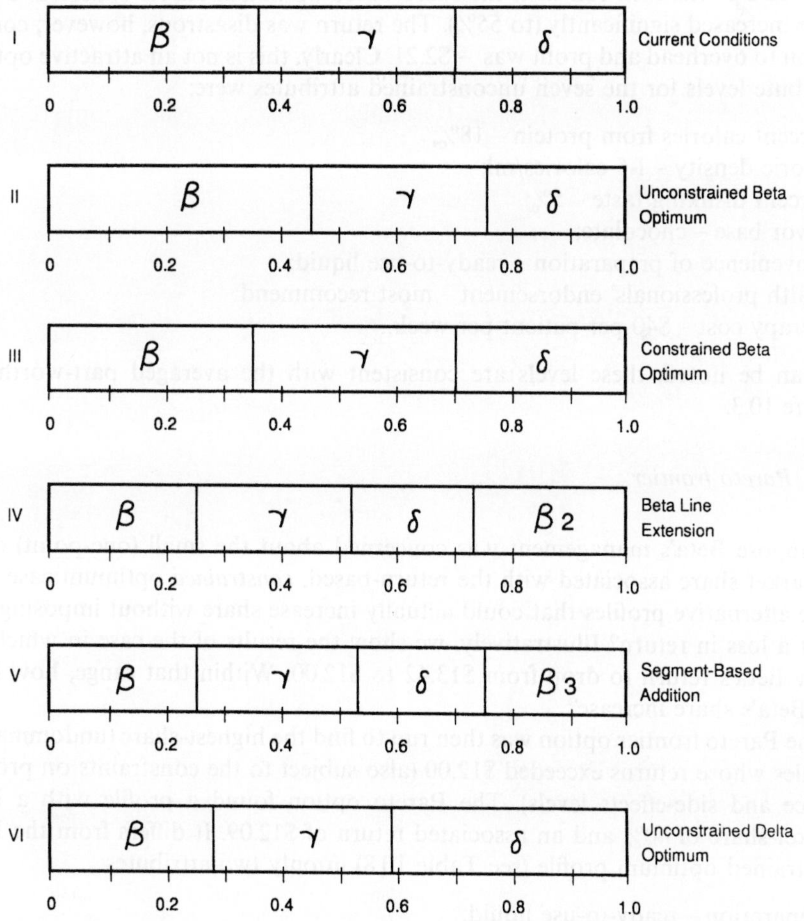

Fig. 10.7. Competitive market share under different marketing strategies (source: Green & Krieger [1991]).

the constrained optimum yields a return of \$13.42. Panel III of Figure 10.7 shows that Beta's associated market share is 35%, a one-point *decrease* from Beta's current share. However, given more favorable attribute-level costs, it is still to Beta's advantage to reduce share slightly (assuming that the costs of changing over to the new attribute levels justify the shift).

We also note that the constrained optimum maintains the same levels (Table 10.8) of the remaining attributes that were formed in the unconstrained case. Apparently, attribute 'interactions' are not sufficiently strong to lead to different levels for the unconstrained attributes. What if we elected to optimize Beta's market share instead of its return? To illustrate this option we again imposed the two constraints:

- meat/eggs as the protein source;
- a 10% incidence of side effects.

SIMOPT was then run with the share-based optimization. As expected, Beta's share increased significantly (to 55%). The return was disastrous, however; contribution to overhead and profit was −\$2.21. Clearly, this is not an attractive option. Attribute levels for the seven unconstrained attributes were:

- percent calories from protein – 18%;
- caloric density – 1.5 calories/ml;
- percent disliking taste – 5%;
- flavor base – chocolate;
- convenience of preparation – ready-to-use liquid;
- health professionals' endorsement – most recommend;
- therapy cost – \$40 per patient per week.

As can be noted, these levels are consistent with the averaged part-worths of Figure 10.3.

10.7. Pareto frontier

Suppose Beta's management was concerned about the small (one-point) drop in market share associated with the return-based, *constrained* optimum case. Are there alternative profiles that could actually increase share without imposing too great a loss in return? Illustratively, we show the results of the case in which we allow Beta's return to drop from \$13.42 to \$12.00. Within that range, how high can Beta's share increase?

The Pareto frontier option was then run to find the highest-share (undominated) profiles whose returns exceeded \$12.00 (also subject to the constraints on protein source and side-effects levels). The Pareto option found a profile with a Beta market-share of 40% and an associated return of \$12.09. It differs from the Beta constrained optimum profile (see Table 10.8) in only two attributes:

- preparation – ready-to-use liquid;
- health professionals' endorsement – most recommend.

10.8. Line extension

Next, we consider the case where Beta maintains its current (constrained optimal) product but considers a line extension, for which no attribute-level constraints are imposed. SIMOPT was run for this option, leading to a fourth product, called Beta 2, whose share and return were 28% and $12.71, respectively.

Table 10.8 shows the associated profile (line extension) for Beta, which can be compared to Beta's constrained optimum profile. As noted, the line extension differs in source of protein, side effects, flavor base, and convenience of preparation from the (optimized) current product. Panel IV of Figure 10.7 shows the associated market-shares for all four competitive products.

The line extension cannibalizes the (optimized) Beta product; the latter product's share drops to 25% and its return drops to $9.48. However, for both products combined the share is 53% and the return is $23.19. (This does not contain any adjustment for the cost of adding the second Beta product.)

10.9. Segment-based addition

This time we consider a segment-based line addition for Beta. First, given the (constrained) optimal Beta we found the best product for respondents satisfying the conditions:

- technical/specialty hospitals;
- fewer than 100 beds;
- head of buyer committee;
- 16 years (and over) business experience.

This product profile is shown in Table 10.8. With the exception of convenience of preparation (in blender), it is the same profile as that of the line extension.

Next, this profile is added to Beta's line and is made available to *all* buyers, along with the (constrained) optimized Beta. In this case the return associated with the segment-oriented addition (called Beta 3) is $12.06, somewhat less than that of the line extension. The combined share and return are 50% and $21.18, respectively, which are also lower than their line-extension counterparts. Panel V of Figure 10.7 shows the competitive shares for this case.

10.10. Delta's retaliatory optimization

As our last illustrative case we consider a retaliatory move by Delta. We assume that Delta observes that Beta has modified its current product to that shown in Table 10.8, under the (constrained) optimal Beta column. Given no retaliation by Beta or Gamma, what is Delta's unconstrained optimal product?

Unfortunately, we do not know Delta's direct costs at the attribute level. Under the simplifying assumption that they are the same as Beta's, the SIMOPT model finds that Delta's return increases from its current $8.73 to $16.34 (see Table 10.8). However, its new profile is identical to Beta's (unconstrained) optimal profile. As

Panel VI of Figure 10.7 shows, Delta's share increases to 42% (from the 29% starting condition).

What can be concluded from this result? Apparently the part-worths are reasonably homogeneous across buyers; we could have already suspected this, given the close results between Beta's line extension and the added segment cases. To check this conjecture, we correlated the part-worths across all pairs of the 356 respondents. The average correlation was 0.72.

10.11. Dynamic changes

As might be surmised, we could continue to examine actions and reactions on the part of all suppliers – Beta, Gamma and Delta – up to the point where equilibrium might be reached. By 'equilibrium' is meant that market shares stabilize and there is no inducement for any supplier to change its product profile, conditional on the profiles of all the others. If respondent part-worths are very homogeneous, there will be a tendency for suppliers to gravitate toward the same product profile and toward equal market shares.

However, several factors militate against this outcome occurring in the real world:

(1) There are costs associated with changing one's present product position, including the possible alienation of currently loyal buyers.
(2) Suppliers may exhibit different cost structures at the individual-attribute level; these will differentially affect the optimum.
(3) In practice, suppliers are not perfectly free to change all attributes to any desired level. Clearly, one's brand name (and all that is implied in terms of goodwill, reputation, etc.) is a fixed attribute level, at least in the short run.
(4) Buyers do not adjust instantaneously to differences in product offerings; their part-worths may also be altered by earlier competitive moves.
(5) Certain product offerings may be incompatible with a supplier's image and its historical behavior.
(6) Product-profile changes do not consider the associated time and costs of communication and distribution to buyers.
(7) Buyers may build up loyalties to pioneering products, particularly if consumer learning is required (e.g. witness the strong consumer loyalty to Lotus 1-2-3).

In short, the preceding exercise of looking at the implications of supplier action and reaction should be considered more as a diagnostic (rather than predictive) tool for examining the consequences of fixing various attribute levels (or effecting lower attribute-level costs) on profile optimization.

If the market is highly heterogeneous in terms of its part-worth functions, suppliers may pursue differentiated strategies. The model would recognize this condition by finding optimum profiles that differ markedly across suppliers, particularly if supplier loyalties also interact with various product-attribute preferences.

10.12. *Practical implications*

As we have tried to show by means of both formal presentation and numerical example, SIMOPT has been designed as a practical model that can be operationalized by market-based, conjoint data. We believe its value lies in its versatility for considering:

(1) market share and/or profit-return optimization for main effects or main effects and two-way interactions;
(2) total market and/or individual-segment forecasts;
(3) sensitivity analysis as well as optimal profile seeking;
(4) cannibalization issues related to product complementarity and line-extension strategies;
(5) calibration of results to existing market conditions;
(6) constrained optimization, through fixing selected attribute levels for any or all suppliers;
(7) a decision parameter (alpha) that can be used to mimic any of the principal conjoint choice rules (max utility, logit, BTL);
(8) sequential competitive moves, such as line extensions or competitor actions/reactions; and
(9) detailed information on who chooses which product under any specified set of conditions.

Like any model, SIMOPT no doubt will be modified and extended as further information about its performance and user reception is obtained. Perhaps its most significant contribution lies in illustrating how current conjoint-based simulators can be extended beyond their traditional application to estimating market shares for a few user-selected profiles.

11. Conclusions

In this paper we have tried to show the evolution of conjoint analysis from a basic preference-measurement tool to its incorporation in product/service positioning simulators and optimizers. The OR/MS specialist should be particularly interested in the present normative aspects of conjoint modeling.

Much more remains to be done (as is illustrated in Table 10.5). In particular, we need additional research dealing with product-positioning models that consider competitive action and reaction strategies. Another broad area for future development is the incorporation of other marketing control variables (e.g. advertising, sales promotion, distribution) in the positioning models.

Unlike many measurement and modeling methodologies, conjoint analysis has enjoyed a 'grass-roots' tradition in which both academic and industry researchers have made contributions since its inception. The availability of specialized conjoint software packages and the intensity of interest shown by general management-consulting firms augurs well for the continued development and application of conjoint techniques. Conjoint analysis has, indeed, become a mainstream methodology that is being increasingly employed in high-level, strategic decision-making.

Appendix

This appendix has been prepared to deal with two aspects of the SIMOPT models:

(1) ALPH, the model used to find the optimal value of alpha in equation (9);
(2) the divide-and-conquer heuristic, used to find optimal products and product lines in SIMOPT.

A.1. The ALPH model

For any value of α, we obtain from Equation (9) a set of predicted market shares $\hat{\Pi}_1(\alpha),\ldots,\hat{\Pi}_S(\alpha)$. We also assume that we have *external* market shares $\Pi_1,\ldots,\Pi_S$. The problem is to find α such that the vector $\hat{\boldsymbol{\Pi}}=(\hat{\Pi}_1(\alpha),\ldots,\hat{\Pi}_S(\alpha))$ is as close as possible to $\boldsymbol{\Pi}=(\Pi_1,\ldots,\Pi_S)$.

There are many possible distance metrics between two probability measures that can be considered. The ones most commonly employed are:

(1) chi-squared:

$$d_C(\hat{\Pi},\Pi)=\sum_{s=1}^{S}(\hat{\Pi}_s-\Pi_s)^2/\Pi_s; \tag{15}$$

(2) entropy:

$$d_E(\hat{\Pi},\Pi)=\sum_{s=1}^{S}\Pi_s \ln \Pi_s/\hat{\Pi}_s; \tag{16}$$

(3) Kolmogorov–Smirnov:

$$d_K(\hat{\Pi},\Pi)=\max_s|\Pi_s-\hat{\Pi}_s|; \tag{17}$$

(4) absolute:

$$d_A(\hat{\Pi},\Pi)=\sum_{s=1}^{S}|\Pi_s-\hat{\Pi}_s|. \tag{18}$$

The problem is to find the α that minimizes the distance function.

Clearly, if there is an α such that $\hat{\Pi}(\alpha)=\Pi$, then all four distances would lead to the same α, since all distances are non-negative and equal to zero when $\Pi=\hat{\Pi}$.

When no such α exists, then the choice of an α that minimizes distance depends on the metric that is used. In practice, α does not vary widely across d_C, d_E, d_K, or d_A. The differences arise because in comparing α_1 to α_2, $\hat{\Pi}_1(\alpha_1)$ could be closer to Π_1 than $\hat{\Pi}_1(\alpha_2)$, but $\hat{\Pi}_2(\alpha_1)$ could be further from Π_2 than $\hat{\Pi}_2(\alpha_2)$. Which is viewed as superior would then depend on the metric.

Since there is no strong theoretical basis for choosing among d_C, d_E, d_K and d_A, on practical grounds we choose the distance metric that has useful mathematical properties. It can be shown that d_C, d_K and d_A are *not* unimodal in α. Although the value of α that minimizes each of the three distance metrics can be found by a numerical search procedure, this is time-consuming and not very elegant. In contrast, we show below that d_E *is* convex in α so there is only one local optimum.

In our context, the predicted market shares are:

$$\hat{\Pi}_s(\alpha) = \sum_{k=1}^{K} V^{(k)} f^{\alpha}(U_{ks}) \Big/ \sum_{t=1}^{S} f^{\alpha}(U_{kt}),$$

where $f(U_{ks})$ allows for a location and scale transformation of the utilities. Hence,

$$d_E(\hat{\Pi}(\alpha), \Pi) = \sum_{s=1}^{S} \Pi_s \ln \Pi_s / \hat{\Pi}_s(\alpha) = \sum_{s=1}^{S} \Pi_s \ln \Pi_s - \sum_{s=1}^{S} \Pi_s \ln \hat{\Pi}_s(\alpha).$$

But $\ln \hat{\Pi}_s(\alpha) = -\ln \sum_{k=1}^{K} V^{(k)} \sum_{t=1}^{S} f^{\alpha}(U_{kt})/f^{\alpha}(U_{ks})$. So, showing that d_E is convex in α is equivalent to showing the convexity of $h_s(\alpha)$ where

$$h_s(\alpha) = \ln \sum_{k=1}^{K} V^{(k)} \sum_{t=1}^{S} (w_{kt}/w_{ks})^{\alpha} \tag{19}$$

and $w_{ks} \equiv f(U_{ks})$.

Proposition 10.1. *The function $h_s(\alpha)$ is convex in α.*

Proof. Let $x_{kst} = w_{kt}/w_{ks}$. Then,

$$\frac{\mathrm{d}h_s(\alpha)}{\mathrm{d}\alpha} = \frac{\sum_{k=1}^{K} V^{(k)} \sum_{t=1}^{S} x_{kst}^{\alpha} \ln x_{kst}}{\sum_{k=1}^{K} V^{(k)} \sum_{t=1}^{S} x_{kst}^{\alpha}}.$$

Similarly,

$$\frac{\mathrm{d}^2 h_s(\alpha)}{\mathrm{d}^2\alpha} = \left\{\left[\sum_{k=1}^{K} V^{(k)} \sum_{t=1}^{S} x_{kst}^{\alpha}\right]\left[\sum_{k=1}^{K} V^{(k)} \sum_{t=1}^{S} x_{kst}^{\alpha} (\ln x_{kst})^2\right]\right.$$

$$-\left[\sum_{k=1}^{K} V^{(k)} \sum_{t=1}^{S} x_{kst}^{\alpha} \ln x_{kst}\right]^2\Bigg\}\Bigg/\left[\sum_{k=1}^{K} V^{(k)} \sum_{t=1}^{S} x_{kst}^{\alpha}\right]^2$$

$$= \sum_{k=1}^{K}\sum_{t=1}^{S} p_{kt}(\ln x_{kst})^2 - \left(\sum_{k=1}^{K}\sum_{t=1}^{S} p_{kt} \ln x_{kst}\right)^2 \tag{20}$$

where

$$p_{kt} = V^{(k)} x_{kst}^{\alpha} \Bigg/ \sum_{q=1}^{K} V^{(q)} \sum_{r=1}^{S} x_{qsr}^{\alpha}.$$

But $\mathrm{d}^2 h_s(\alpha)/\mathrm{d}^2\alpha \geqslant 0$, since the right-hand side of (20) can be viewed as the variance of $\ln x_{kst}$ for fixed s, where the probability mass function on (k, t) is p_{kt}. □

We opt for entropy as the 'best' measure of distance for our problem. It has nice mathematical properties and, in practice, often leads to results that are similar to the other metrics. Typically, we use entropy as our preferred measure in the ALPH program, although all four measures, noted above, can be computed. Finally, the model has the capability of determining how sensitive the results are to the choice of α.

A.2. The divide-and-conquer heuristic

To find the best product profile(s), conditional on specified competitive product configurations, the model employs a divide-and-conquer heuristic. We now discuss the nature of this heuristic.

In implementing the heuristic, we want to find the levels $(i_1^*, \ldots, i_M^*)$ that maximize share or return for the supplier of interest, possibly in an environment in which the supplier has more than one product in the product class. The objective we want to maximize can be written in the form $\Phi(i_1, \ldots, i_M)$ where i_m denotes the attribute level for attribute m; $m = 1, \ldots, M$.

The levels $(i_1^*, \ldots, i_M^*)$ that maximize Φ can be found by complete enumeration. The number of possible solutions is $B = \prod_{m=1}^{M} i_m$. In practice, B could be large, although with high-speed computing if $B \leqslant 1\,000\,000$, this is certainly a viable approach. Alternatively, we can divide the attributes into subsets. To see how this approach works, assume that we divide the M attributes into two subsets, so that attributes 1 to M_1 define subset 1 and attributes $(M_1 + 1)$ to M define subset 2.

We begin the process by finding levels $(i_1, \ldots, i_M)$ that are reasonable first approximations to $(i_1^*, \ldots, i_M^*)$. One approach is to average the part-worths within each level of each attribute and choose the level, within attribute, that has the highest average. Label these levels as $[i_1^{(0)}, \ldots, i_M^{(0)}]$. We find $[i_1^{(p)}, \ldots, i_M^{(p)}]$ from $[i_1^{(p-1)}, \ldots, i_M^{(p-1)}]$ in two steps:

(1) Find $(i_1^{(p)}, \ldots, i_{M_1}^{(p)})$ by choosing the levels for attributes $1, \ldots, M_1$ that maximize $\Phi[i_1, \ldots, i_{M_1}, i_{M_1+1}^{(p-1)}, \ldots, i_M^{(p-1)}]$

(2) Find $[i^{(p)}_{M_1+1},\ldots,i^{(p)}_M]$ by choosing the levels for attributes $M_1+1,\ldots,M$ that maximize $\Phi[i^{(p)}_1,\ldots,i^{(p)}_{M_1},i_{M_1+1},\ldots,i_M]$.

If $\Phi(i^{(p)}) = \Phi(i^{(p-1)})$, then stop. Since Φ cannot decrease at each iteration, this approach leads to a local optimum.

Of course, the procedure can be extended to an arbitrary number of subsets. It should be pointed out that the effect of increasing the number of subsets is to reduce the amount of computation at the risk of not finding the global optimum.

There is no foolproof way of knowing whether this 'divide-and-conquer' approach has produced the global optimum except by checking it with complete enumeration. In applications where we have applied this technique, the optimum *was* found. If we were to simulate data that are independently and identically distributed, then, intuitively, divide-and-conquer would work very well. Environments in which there are many interactions among attributes are ones in which the divide-and-conquer heuristic could potentially lead to a suboptimal solution.

SIMOPT is designed so that the user can specify the subset compositions. In general, subsets should be formed so as to minimize the correlation of part-worths *across* subsets of attributes. Intuitively, attributes that are more closely related to each other should be assigned to the same subset and attributes that are more nearly independent should be assigned to different subsets. This suggests that we might like to cluster attributes based on distances between attributes.

We need a distance measure between attributes that reflects the extent to which individuals' part-worths for levels of one attribute are related to the part-worths for levels of the other attribute. We propose two reasonable, albeit ad hoc, measures. Consider two attributes with I and J levels respectively. We can create an $I \times J$ contingency table with entry n_{ij} indicating the number of individuals whose preferred levels are i for the first attribute and j for the second attribute. The distance between the two attributes can be defined as a (1 – P-value) of the chi-squared test; we use P-values for calibration when the number of levels differ across attributes and a (1 – P-value) so that similar attributes have small distances.

Another possibility is to create an $I \times J$ matrix where the (i, j) entry is the squared correlation between the part-worths of level i of the first attribute and level j of the second attribute. Then, $1 - \bar{R}^2$ defines another measure where $\bar{R}^2$ is the average of the IJ entries in this matrix. (In either case the SIMOPT model contains an option where the user can choose the make-up of the subsets in the divide-and-conquer heuristic; as noted above, the subsets can be designed in several different ways.)

References

Addelman, S. (1962). Orthogonal main-effect plans for asymmetrical factorial experiments. *Technometrics* 4, 21–46.

Albers, S. (1979). An extended algorithm for optimal product positioning. *Eur. J. Oper. Res.* 3, 222–231.

Albers, S., and K. Brockhoff (1977). A procedure for new product positioning in an attribute space. *Eur. J. Oper. Res.* 1, 230–238.

Allison, N. (1989). Conjoint analysis across the business system. *1989 Sawtooth Software Conference Proceedings*. Sawtooth Software, Ketchum, ID, pp. 183–196.

Anderson, N.H. (1970). Functional measurement and psychophysical judgment. *Psychol. Rev.* 77, 153–170.

Bachem, A., and H. Simon (1981). A product positioning model with costs and prices. *Eur. J. Oper. Res.* 7, 362–370.

Batsell, R.R., and J.J. Louviere (1991). Experimental analysis of choice. *Marketing Lett.* 2, 199–214.

Bell, D.E., R.L. Keeney and H. Raiffa, eds. (1977). *Conflicting Objectives in Decisions*, Wiley, New York.

Bell, D.E., H. Raiffa and A. Tversky, eds. (1988). *Decision Making: Descriptive, Normative, and Prescriptive Interactions*. Cambridge University Press, New York.

Carmone, F., P.E. Green and A.K. Jain (1978). The robustness of conjoint analysis: Some Monte Carlo results. *J. Marketing Res.* 15, 300–303.

Carroll, J.D. (1969). Categorical conjoint measurement, Meeting of Mathematical Psychology, Ann Arbor, MI.

Cattin, P., and D.R. Wittink (1976). A Monte Carlo study of metric and nonmetric estimation methods for multiattribute models. Research Paper No. 341, Graduate School of Business, Stanford University, Stanford, CA.

Cattin, P., and D.R. Wittink (1982). Commercial use of conjoint analysis: A survey. *J. Marketing* 46, 44–53.

Chapman, R.G. (1984). An approach to estimating logit models of a single decision maker's choice behavior. *Adv. Consumer Res.* 11, 656–661.

Chapman, R.G., and R. Staelin (1982). Exploiting rank ordered choice set data within the stochastic utility model. *J. Marketing Res.* 19, 288–301.

Currim, I.S. (1982). Predictive testing of consumer choice models not subject to independence of irrelevant alternatives. *J. Marketing Res.* 19, 208–222.

Dawes, R.M., and B. Corrigan (1974). Linear models in decision making, *Psychol. Bull* 81, 95–106.

DeSarbo, W.S., R.L. Oliver, and A. Rangaswamy (1989). A simulated annealing methodology for clusterwise linear regression. *Psychometricka* 54, 707–736.

DeSarbo, W.S., and V.R. Rao (1984). GENFOLD 2: a set of models and algorithms for the general unfolding analysis of preference/dominance data. *J. Classification* 1, 147–186.

DeSarbo, W.S., and V.R. Rao (1986). GENFOLD 2: a new constrained unfolding model for product positioning, *Marketing Sci.* 5, 1–19.

Dobson, G., and S. Kalish (1988). Positioning and pricing a product line. *Marketing Sci.* 7, 107–125.

Dyer, J.S. (1990). Remarks on the analytic hierarchy process. *Management Sci.* 36, 249–258.

Edwards, W., and J.R. Newman (1982). *Multiattribute Evaluation*, Sage, Beverly Hills, CA.

Eliashberg, J., and A. Manrai (1992). Optimal positioning of new products: Some analytical implications and empirical results. *Eur. J. Oper. Res.* 63, 376–397.

Farquhar, P.H. (1977). A survey of multiattribute utility theory and applications. *TIMS Studies in the Management Sciences* 6, 59–89.

Fischer, G.W. (1979). Utility models for multiple objective decisions: do they accurately represent human preference? *Decision Sci.* 10, 451–479.

Fishburn, P.C. (1967). Methods of estimating additive utilities. *Management Sci.* 13, 435–458.

Fishburn, P.C. (1968). Utility theory. *Management Sci.* 14, 335–378.

Gardiner, P.C., and W. Edwards (1975). Public values: Multiattribute-utility measurement for sound decision making. In: M.F. Kaplan and S. Schwartz (eds.), *Human Judgment and Decision Processes*, Academic Press, New York.

Gavish, B., D. Horsky, and K. Srikanth (1983). An approach to the optimal positioning of a new product, *Management Sci.* 29, 1277–1297.

Green, P.E. (1974). On the design of choice experiments involving multifactor alternatives. *J. Consumer Res.* 1, 61–68.

Green, P.E. (1975). On the robustness of multidimensional scaling techniques. *J. Marketing Res.* 12, 73–81.

Green, P.E. (1984). Hybrid models for conjoint analysis: an expository review. *J. Marketing Res.* 21, 155–159.

Green, P.E., and F.J. Carmone (1970). *Multidimensional Scaling and Related Techniques in Marketing Analysis.* Allyn and Bacon, Boston.

Green, P.E., F.J. Carmone, and Y. Wind (1972). Subjective evaluation models and conjoint measurement. *Behavioral Sci.* 17, 288–299.

Green, P.E., D.J. Carroll, and S.M. Goldberg (1981). A general approach to product design optimization via conjoint analysis. *J. Marketing* 45, 17–37.

Green, P.E., and K. Helsen (1989). Cross-validation assessment of alternatives to individual-level conjoint analysis: a case study. *J. Marketing Res.* 26, 346–350.

Green, P.E., and A.M. Krieger (1985). Models and heuristics for product line selection. *Marketing Sci.* 4, 1–19.

Green, P.E., and A.M. Krieger (1988). Choice rules and sensitivity analysis in conjoint simulators. *J. Acad. Marketing Sci.* 16, 114–127.

Green, P.E., and A.M. Krieger (1989). Recent contributions to optimal product positioning and buyer segmentation. *Eur. J. Oper. Res.* 41, 127–141.

Green, P.E., and A.M. Krieger (1991). An application of a product positioning model of pharmaceutical products. Working Paper, Wharton School, University of Pennsylvania, Philadelphia, PA.

Green, P.E., and V.R. Rao (1969). Nonmetric approaches to multivariate analysis in marketing. Working Paper, Wharton School, University of Pennsylvania, Philadelphia, PA.

Green, P.E., and V.R. Rao (1971). Conjoint measurement for quantifying judgmental data. *J. Marketing Res.* 8, 355–363.

Green, P.E., and V. Srinivasan (1978). Conjoint analysis in consumer research: issues and outlook. *J. Consumer Res.* 5, 103–123.

Green, P.E., and V. Srinivasan (1990). Conjoint analysis in marketing: new developments with implications for research and practice. *J. Marketing* 54, 3–19.

Gupta, S., and R. Kohli (1990). Designing products and services for consumer welfare: theoretical and empirical issues. *Marketing Sci.* 9, 230–246.

Hagerty, M.R. (1985). Improving the predictive power of conjoint analysis: the use of factor analysis and cluster analysis. *J. Marketing Res.* 22, 168–184.

Hammond, K.R., G.H. McClelland, and J. Mumpower (1980). *Human Judgment and Decision Making.* Praeger, New York.

Hauser, J.R., and G.L. Urban (1979). Assessment of attribute importance and consumer utility functions: von Neumann–Morgenstern theory applied to consumer behavior. *J. Consumer Res.* 2, 579–619.

Herman, S. (1988). Software for full-profile conjoint analysis. *Proceedings of the Sawtooth Software Conference on Perceptual Mapping. Conjoint Analysis, and Computer Interviewing.* Sawtooth Software: Ketchum, ID, pp. 117–130.

Hoepfl, R.T., and G.P. Huber (1970). A study of self-explicated utility models. *Behavioral Sci.* 15, 408–414.

Hoffman, P.J. (1960). The paramorphic representation of human judgment. *Psychol. Bull.* 57, 116–131.

Hoffman, P.J., P. Slovic, and L.G. Rorer (1968). An analysis of variance model for the assessment of configural cue utilization in clinical judgment. *Psychol. Bull.* 69, 338–349.

Hwang, C., and K. Yoon (1981). *Multiple Attribute Decision Making: Methods and Applications.* Springer, New York.

Intelligent Marketing Systems, Ltd. (1991). *Consurv: Conjoint Analysis Software Manual.* Edmonton, Alberta, Canada.

Johnson, R.M. (1974). Trade-off analysis of consumer values. *J. Marketing Res.* 11, 121–127.

Johnson, R.M. (1987). Adaptive conjoint analysis. *Sawtooth Software Conference on Perceptual Mapping, Conjoint Analysis, and Computer Interviewing.* Sawtooth Software, Ketchum, ID, pp. 253–266.

Kamakura, W. (1988). A least-squares procedure for benefit segmentation with conjoint experiments. *J. Marketing Res.* 25, 157–167.

Kamakura, W., and R.K. Srivastava (1984). Predicting choice shares under conditions of brand interdependence. *J. Marketing Res.* 21, 420–434.

Keeney, R.L., and H. Raiffa (1976). *Decisions with Multiple Objectives: Preferences and Value Tradeoffs.* Wiley, New York.

Kohli, R., and R. Krishnamurti (1987). A heuristic approach to product design. *Management Sci.* 33, 1525–1533.

Kohli, R., and R. Krishnamurti (1989). Optimal product design using conjoint analysis: computational complexity and algorithms. *Eur. J. Oper. Res.* 40, 186–195.

Kohli, R., and R. Sukumar (1990). Heuristics for product-line selection using conjoint analysis. *Management Sci.* 36, 1464–1478.

Krantz D.H. (1964). Conjoint measurement: the Luce–Tukey axiomatization and some extensions. *J. Mathematical Psychol.* 1, 248–277.

Kruskal, J.B. (1965). Analysis of factorial experiments by estimating monotone transformations of the data. *J. Royal Statist. Soc. Ser. B* 27, 251–263.

Louviere, J.J. (1991). Experimental choice analysis: introduction and overview. *J. Business Res.* 23, 291–297.

Louviere, J.J., and G. Woodworth (1983). Design and analysis of simulated consumer choice on allocation experiments: an approach based on aggregate data. *J. Marketing Res.* 20, 350–367.

Luce, R.D., and J.W. Tukey (1964). Simultaneous conjoint measurement: a new type of fundamental measurement. *J. Mathematical Psychol.* 1, 1–127.

Mahajan, V., P.E. Green, and S.M. Goldberg (1982). A conjoint model for measuring self- and cross-price/demand relationships. *J. Marketing Res.* 19, 334–342.

Malhotra, N.K. (1983). A comparison of the predictive validity of procedures for analyzing binary data. *J. Business Econom. Statist.* 1, 326–336.

McBride, R.D., and F.S. Zufryden (1988). An integer programming approach to optimal product line selection. *Marketing Sci.* 7, 126–140.

McFadden, D. (1986). The choice theory approach to market research. *Marketing Sci.* 5, 275–297.

Moore, W.L., E.A. Pessemier, and T.E. Little (1979). Predicting brand choice behavior: a marketing application of the Schönemann and Wang unfolding model. *J. Marketing Res.* 16, 203–210.

Moskowitz, H.R., D.W. Stanley, and J.W. Chandler (1977). The eclipse method: optimizing product formulation through a consumer generated ideal sensory profile. *Canadian Inst. Food Sci. Technol. J.* 10, 161–168.

Ogawa, K. (1987). An approach to simultaneous estimation and segmentation in conjoint analysis. *Marketing Sci.* 6, 66–81.

Pessemier, E.A. (1975). Market structure analysis of new product and market opportunities. *J. Contemporary Business* 4, 35–67.

Pessemier, E.A., P. Burger, R. Teach, and D. Tigert (1971) Using laboratory brand preference scales to predict consumer brand purchases. *Management Sci.* 17, 371–385

Roberts, J.H., and G.L. Urban (1988). Modeling multiattribute utility, risk, and belief dynamics for new consumer durable brand choice. *Management Sci.* 34, 1–19.

Saaty, T.L. (1980). *The Analytic Hierarchy Process.* McGraw-Hill, New York.

Shocker, A.D., and V. Srinivasan (1974). A consumer-based methodology for the identification of new product ideas. *Management Sci.* 20, 921–937.

Shocker, A.D., and V. Srinivasan (1977). LINMAP (Version II): a FORTRAN IV computer program for analyzing ordinal preference (dominance) judgments via linear programming techniques and for conjoint measurement. *J. Marketing Res.* 14, 101–103.

SPSS, Inc. (1990). *SPSS Categories*, SPSS, Inc., Chicago.

Srinivasan, V., and A.D. Shocker (1973). Linear programming techniques for multidimensional analysis of preferences. *Psychometrika* 38, 337–369.

Srinivasan, V., and G.A. Wyner (1989). CASEMAP: Computer-assisted self-explication of multiattribute preference. In W. Henry, M. Menasco, and H. Takada (eds.), *New Product Development and Testing*, Lexington Books, Lexington, MA, 91–112.

Starr, M.K., and M. Zeleny (1977). *Multiple Criteria Decision Making*, North-Holland, Amsterdam.

Sudharshan, D., J.H. May, and T. Gruca (1988). DIFFSTRAT: an analytical procedure for generating optimal new product concepts for a differentiated-type strategy. *Eur. J. Oper. Res.* 36, 50–65.

Sudharshan, D., J.H. May, and A. Shocker (1987). A simulation comparison of methods for new product location. *Marketing Sci.* 6, 182–201.

Tversky, A. (1967). A general theory of polynomial conjoint measurement. *J. Math. Psychol.* 4, 1–20.

Wilkie, W.L., and E.A. Pessemier (1973). Issues in Marketing's use of multiattribute attitude models. *J. Marketing Res.* 10, 428–441.

Wind, J., P.E. Green, D. Schifflet and M. Scarbrough (1989). *Courtyard by Marriott*: designing a hotel facility with consumer-based marketing models, *Interface* 19, 25–47.

Wittink, D.R., and P. Cattin (1989). Commercial use of conjoint analysis: an update. *J. Marketing* 53, 91–96.

Young, F.W. (1969). Polynomial conjoint analysis of similarities: definitions for a special algorithm, Research Paper No. 76, Psychometric Laboratory, University of North Carolina.

Zionts, S. (1978). *Multiple Criteria Problem Solving*, Springer, New York.

Zufryden, F.S. (1982). Product line optimization by integer programming. *Proceedings of the Annual Meeting of ORSA/TIMS*, San Diego.

Zufryden, F.S. (1977). A conjoint-measurement-based approach for optimal new product design and product positioning. In: A.D. Shocker (ed.), *Analytical Approaches to Product and Market Planning.* Marketing Science Institute, Cambridge, MA, pp. 100–114.

J. Eliashberg and G.L. Lilien, Eds., *Handbooks in OR & MS, Vol. 5*

Chapter 11

Pricing Models in Marketing*

Vithala R. Rao

529 Malott Hall, Cornell University, Ithaca, NY 14853-4201, USA

1. Introduction

A justifiable case can be made for the predominant significance of the pricing decision in the total array of all marketing-mix decisions for branded products and services. These decisions are important not only for the firm but also for various intermediaries in the distribution channel. While prices can be decided purely on cost or demand considerations, their effectiveness is vastly improved when they are set in consonance with various other aspects of the brand's marketing strategy (for example, such aspects as target market, firm's objectives, competitive positioning, functional versus emotional benefits offered by the product, and the like). Further, price decisions need to be made for transactions at different levels in the channel, because the definition of 'price' differs considerably from one distribution level to another and even from one consumption situation to another.

Even though decisions on price are often difficult to make, firms should find them to be easier to implement. Further, competitors can react more quickly to appeals based on price as compared to those based on product benefits and imagery. As an example, one may think about the extensive price-promotion activity in various markets (e.g. coffee, automobiles) without any change in either the product quality or advertising appeals.

Several pressures (both upward and downward) operate on the firm in the process of arriving at a thoughtful and deliberate pricing decision (or strategy). Upward pressures include unique product features, company reputation (or brand equity), product costs and supply of raw material, while factors such as availability of substitutes, price controls and competition operate as downward pressures. Over the last two decades, business firms have designed and implemented a wide range of innovative pricing strategies (over and above the traditional cost-plus pricing and value pricing) in an effort to cope with various competitive and other external forces (see Tellis [1986] for a taxonomy of these strategies).

*The author thanks three anonymous reviewers and Professors Pradeep K. Chintagunta, Barry L. Bayus and Edward L. McLaughlin for their valuable comments on a previous draft, Lynn Brown, Willie Myles and Tim Castagna for bibliographic assistance, and Professors Jehoshua Eliashberg and Gary L: Lilien for their encouragement in preparation of this chapter.

While marketing researchers have investigated various topics in pricing for quite some time (see Monroe [1990] and Simon [1989] for a discussion), the 1982 conference on pricing at the University of Rochester kindled the interest of academicians in investigating theoretical and empirical issues related to pricing decisions. Several developments support this assessment: an increasing number of journal articles that deal with pricing have appeared in marketing journals, recent completion of at least seven doctoral theses [Dash, 1982; Rao, 1986; Nascimento, 1987; Wruck, 1989; Yim, 1989; Yoo, 1986; Roy, 1990] in marketing that focus almost exclusively on pricing questions, publication of advanced texts on pricing [e.g. Simon, 1989] and an edited volume of special papers on pricing issues [see DeVinney, 1988], and an increasing interest on pricing decisions on the part of marketing executives in industry.

In the case of new products, the pricing decision is closely related to the product-design decision. The latter decision problem has been well studied using the methodology of conjoint analysis. Interestingly, conjoint analysis has also been employed to study the effects of price on choice behavior at the individual and aggregate levels and has also contributed to the measurement of price effects. More recently, the product-design problem has naturally been extended to the study of developing multiple products or bundles. Accordingly, a subset of pricing models in marketing have focused on the issue of pricing multiple products.

Two dominant trends in the development of pricing models in marketing can be identified.[1] First, marketing academics have been utilizing game theory and optimal control concepts in their investigations of pricing issues. In this vein, researchers have constructed theoretical microeconomic models that abstract various real-world strategies such as bundling and discounting in order to examine their implications. The second trend has been the use of behavioral theories such as adaptation-level theory, information processing and prospect theory to examine how individuals react to particular pricing strategies, bundling and discounts. The transaction utility model derived from prospect theory [Thaler, 1985] has significantly contributed to the latter trend. A major part of this behavioral research uses experimental data or data collected via scanner panels.

A few developments – theoretical and empirical – have come to be generally accepted in the development of pricing models. First, a number of consumer behavior constructs such as the use of reservation price, consideration set of alternatives for choice, and existence of brand loyalty are well accepted by model builders. Consumer heterogeneity has been incorporated into certain models in terms of such variables as differential search costs, differential knowledge, expectations, and the deterministic or stochastic nature of the choice process. Second, phenomena such as cost-declines due to experience (or learning effects) and adoption and diffusion of new products among consumers over time are well

[1] An area in which these two identified trends can be found is that of price-promotion research. In addition to theoretical work using game-theoretic models, researchers in this area have developed and empirically tested models for determining the effects of price promotions using the data bases collected from scanner panels.

accepted in the context of building dynamic models. However, it must be pointed out that all models do not necessarily utilize all of these constructs. Accordingly, a growing trend in developing pricing models has been to offer better theoretical explanations to observed firm behavior as well as to develop more precise models for determining optimal strategies.

Against this background, this paper will attempt to review and synthesize various pricing models in marketing that have appeared in the literature. See Rao [1984], Nagle [1987] and DeVinney [1988] for earlier reviews on this subject. Several caveats need to be stated with regard to the coverage of topics in this review. First, this review is mainly restricted to the literature that has appeared since the previous review by this author. Further, this review will be restricted to five topics[2] in pricing research: static models for single products, dynamic pricing models for single products, pricing multiple products or bundling, behavioral aspects of pricing and selected issues on measurement of price effects. Also, the main focus is on models appearing in marketing journals or developed by marketing academics. (Given the academic training in microeconomics of some marketing scholars, the distinction between a 'marketing-oriented' pricing model and an 'economics-oriented' pricing model has become quite blurred, however.) No attempt is made here to ensure complete coverage of the literature, but rather the review focuses on the more recent research of interest to management-science researchers and practitioners.

There are two interesting implications here for normative pricing models. First, consumer reference prices can be incorporated into pricing models and such models do indicate different profit-maximizing price levels than when price alone is included [Winer, 1988]. Second, there appears to be a need to develop demand functions which allow for both an impact of price deviations (beyond the usual price effect) and for the possibility of greater changes in volume-for-price increases than for promotional-price decreases (e.g. perhaps a kinked demand curve).

The remainder of this paper is organized as follows. The next section lays out a framework for reviewing various pricing models. Section 3 covers static models of pricing for single products. The fourth section reviews the developments in dynamic pricing models for single products, where the focus in on the time paths for pricing products under different market conditions. The problems of pricing multiple products are reviewed in Section 5. Models that cover the behavioral aspects of pricing are reviewed in the sixth section. Some efforts of measurement of effects of price are reviewed in the seventh section. Finally, Section 8 provides a summary and offers a number of directions for future research.

[2] Marketing researchers have investigated several other topics in pricing. These have been covered in other chapters in this edited volume. In particular, the reader may refer to Chapter 4 by Moorthy for game-theoretic price-promotion models, Chapter 12 by Blattberg and Neslin for empirical models on sales promotion, and Chapter 9 by Hanssens and Parsons for econometric models for the measurement of price effects and price changes. Chapter 15 by Gatignon deals with the modeling of interactions between price and other marketing-mix variables.

Table 11.1
A schema of factors for the description of pricing models

Firm-specific factors		Customer-specific factors	
• *Number of firms:*	• One • More than one	• *Sources of heterogeneity:*	• None considered • Price-sensitivity • Reservation prices • Transaction costs • Search behavior • Other
• *Objectives:*	• Maximize profit • Maximize profit subject to target market share or revenue share • Maximize market share subject to target profit • Other	• *Rule for choice:*	• Deterministic • Probabilistic
• *Production costs:*	• No experience effects considered • Experience effects considered • Joint costs considered	• *Basis for choice:*	• Relative to reservation price • Relative to reference price • Relative to expected price • Brand utility relative to price • Other
• *Focus for setting prices*	• One product • Line of related products • Product bundles	• *Effects of diffusion: (awareness, adoption, etc.)*	• Not considered • Included

Other factors[1]	
• *Macroeconomic effects*	• Not included • Included
• *Source of dynamic effects:*	• Carryover • Price change response • Experience curve
• *Channel:*	• Not included • Included
• *Technology:*	• Assumed to be constant • Changing
• *Uncertainty of demand:*	• Not included • Included
• *Governmental factors (regulation. etc.):*	• Not considered • Considered

[1] These include environmental factors and those that cannot be easily classified into firm-specific and customer-specific factors.

2. A general framework for pricing

Our review of pricing models will be from the viewpoint of a firm that has to decide upon the prices for its products. Actual price per unit charged by a firm generally lies between the average cost per unit (at which the firm makes no profit at all or even a loss) and a highest price at which the demand for the product is zero. Firms adopt several rules to find a price point intermediate between these two so as to reach some prespecified objective. It is not clear that the actual prices set by firms are optimal with respect to the specified objective.

Marketing scientists attempt to develop mathematical models to derive prices that are optimal for a predefined objective. In doing so, they consider various factors that are relevant to the firm, customers (or demand situation), and several environmental factors. A general schema for these factors is developed in Table 11.1. The various terms used here are quite self-explanatory. Over the years, models have appeared that cover a variety of situations described by combinations of these factors. Our review in this chapter will be confined to a few selected models to provide a perspective of some recent pricing research in the marketing area.

First, we will separately consider models for pricing single products and multiple products. While the models in the literature can be organized on several dimensions, two factors seem to be quite significant. These are exclusion or inclusion of carryover effects and exclusion or inclusion of competitive effects. To enable use of a specific terminology, a taxonomy based on only two of the factors identified above is shown in Table 11.2 for models of pricing single products. We will focus in this review on both static (or single-period) models and dynamic models for single products; we will not cover either nonoptimal or nonequilibrium models.[3]

Table 11.2
A taxonomy of pricing models for single products

Carryover effects	Effects of competition: Not included	Effects of competition: Included
Not included (static or single-period)	• Optimal[1] • Nonoptimal	• Equilibrium[1,2] • Nonequilibrium
Included (dynamic or multiple-period)	• Optimal[1] (steady state; time path) • Nonoptimal	• Equilibrium[1] (steady state; time path) • Noneequilibrium

[1] Denotes the types of models reviewed in this chapter.
[2] Many of these models are reviewed in the chapter on game-theoretic models (Chapter 4, this Handbook) and are, therefore, not emphasized in this chapter.

[3] Pricing rules such as cost-plus, charging going rate, following the competition, and charging to attain a target rate of return belong to this class of nonoptimal or nonequilibrium models. For details on these, see the texts on pricing by Simon [1989] and Monroe [1990].

With respect to the case of multiple products, we will focus only on the static models covering the models for pricing a line of interrelated products of a firm and models for pricing a bundle of products (or bundling). The literature is not well developed for the case of dynamic pricing models for multiple products.

Mathematical models reviewed for single or multiple products make assumptions on various behavioral aspects (e.g. information search) of consumers in the marketplace. An examination of the degree to which these assumptions are appropriate has been of concern to some researchers in marketing. This concern has led to a large body of research on pricing in marketing. Selected topics in this general area of behavioral aspects are also reviewed in this chapter.

Inplementation of any optimal pricing model requires measures of such constructs as price-elasticity, willingness-to-pay (or reservation price), and competitive responses. A brief review of some newer methods for these measurement issues is also provided in this chapter.

3. Static models for pricing single products

In this section we will review static models for pricing single products, i.e. models for setting the prices of a product one period at a time. We will consider optimal pricing rules when competition is ignored and when competitive effects are included. Models of competition in which the effects of competition will have reached an equilibrium are beyond the scope of this chapter.[4] When the model describes the situation of a new product with no existing substitutes, the situation is akin to that which ignores competitive effects (or, in general, that of a monopolist).

3.1. Models ignoring competition

Our discussion will cover the optimal pricing rule for a monopolist and an extension when consumer heterogeneity is included in the pricing model.

3.1.1. Optimal-pricing rule

To lay the groundwork for various efforts in the literature, we begin with a basic result for the optimal price per unit of a product that maximizes a firm's profit in a given period. This result can be derived for any case by solving the general condition that marginal revenue should equal marginal cost. When applied to a monopoly (for example, for a new product), this condition yields the rule for optimal price (P^*) for a single product as:

$$P^* = \frac{\varepsilon}{1+\varepsilon}\cdot \mathrm{MC} \tag{1}$$

[4] See Chapter 4 by Moorthy for a discussion.

where ε is the price elasticity of demand (assumed to be less than -1) and MC is the marginal cost function per unit. This rule is for one period; presumably price changes should follow this rule as conditions change over time. Several problems do occur in estimating the revenue (demand) and cost (supply) functions in a particular situation.

Various assumptions are needed for this innocuous pricing rule. These include: (1) the firm desires to maximize its profits; (2) competition is nonexistent or passive; (3) customers are homogeneous with respect to their response to price changes; and (4) customers do not incur any transaction costs. Given the fact that this rule is based on an aggregate demand function, there is no direct connection made between the way a customer makes a choice for the product and the aggregate demand. As indicated earlier, the decision construct that a customer chooses a product with a price that is below his/her reservation price has received considerable popularity in the literature. It is possible to relate this construct to an aggregate demand function by postulating heterogeneity among customers with respect to their reservation prices.

Further, various factors relevant in the marketing environment for a brand are also ignored in this rule; these factors include: consideration of a competing set of products for the brand in question, variation of these competing sets across individual consumers, and interactions of price effects with those of other elements of marketing mix (e.g. advertising, channels used), and dynamics over time. Several extensions to this model have been the subject of various studies. See Rao [1984] for a review of papers on how optimal price can be set for different levels of distribution channel and on quantity discounts. More recently, Dolan [1987] reviewed the literature on quantity discounts and identified areas for future investigation.

3.1.2. Consumer heterogeneity

Consumer heterogeneity can be described in three important ways: heterogeneous reservation prices, different price-sensitivities, and different choice rules. As we argued before, an aggregate demand function can be derived from choice behavior of consumers who are heterogeneous in their reservation prices. In this context, the choice rules are deterministic and are identical across consumers.

It is well known that discriminatory pricing rules are optimal for a monopolist when there are distinct groups of customers (or market segments) having different price-sensitivities, or alternatively, whose subaggregate demand functions are distinct (see Simon [1989] and Nagle [1987] for a discussion of these models). In this differentiated pricing model, it is assumed that market segments do not overlap or are assumed to be perfectly sealed.

Introducting the concept of "overlapping markets" (i.e. segments of consumers that are not perfectly sealed), Gerstner & Holthausen [1986] derive conditions under which a monopolist will find price differentiation to be the most profitable pricing strategy. In their model, the firm is assumed to know the distribution of transaction costs across consumers. They show that zero leakage between segments is not essential for differentiated pricing to be optimal (as assumed in a standard model of price discrimination).

3.2. Models considering competition

3.2.1. Optimal-pricing rule

When a firm faces competiton in the market, it should set its price so that it is optimal after taking into consideration competitive reactions. This reaction can be summarized by a reaction function specific to each competitor in the market or by an aggregate form of the reaction function. Using the aggregate form, we can write the average price of all competitiors to a firm, $\bar{P}$, as $\bar{P} = f(P)$. Incorporating this into a demand function for a product and optimizing the profit function leads to the following rule for optimal price:

$$P^* = \frac{\varepsilon + r\eta}{1 + \varepsilon + r\eta} \cdot \mathrm{MC} \tag{2}$$

where $r = (\partial \bar{P}/\partial P) \cdot (P/\bar{P})$ is the price-reaction elasticity of the competitor price with respect to firm's price and $\eta = (\partial Q/\partial \bar{P} \cdot (\bar{P}/Q)$ is the cross-price elasticity of the firm's demand with respect to competitor's price. (See Simon [1989] for an extended discussion of this approach.) It is easy to see that Equation (2) reduces to (1) when there is no competitive reaction (i.e. r is equal to zero).

Issues do arise as to how to define the appropriate set of competitors[5] and how to measure the reaction and cross-price elasticities for implementing this rule. Also, this rule does not fully reflect the interdependent behavior of competitors as would be possible in an equilibrium analysis of a competitive game.

3.2.2. Pricing in quality-sensitive markets

We will now consider an approach to determine the optimal price of a new product competing in quality-sensitive markets as developed by Smith [1986].[6] It incorporates two factors essential to a new product's success: its quality and price relative to its competitors and the sensitivity of the market to a product's penetration level, as measured by cumulative sales at a point in time. It illustrates how the consumer-surplus concept can be used to develop a demand function. Smith expresses the consumer-preference behavior for a combination of products in terms of the inverse of the function of number of customers willing to purchase a product of a given quality at a particular price. This inverse function, $w(s, n)$ is the maximum willingness-to-pay of consumer n for a product of quality s. Given that k products (s_i, P_i), $i = 1, \ldots, k$ are offered, the normative choice behavior, in the absence of income effects, is that each customer n would select the product that maximizes $\{w(s_i, n) - P_i\}$. Then, the total potential market for product i is: $M_i(Pi) = z_i - z_{i-1}$ where z_i's are determined by the equations: $w(s_i, z_i) - P_i = w(s_{i+1}, z_i) - P_{i+1}$, $i = 1, \ldots, k$. The market penetration effects are captured by a scaling function, $F_i(y)$, defined as the fraction of potential purchasers of product i who would be willing

[5] Marketing scientists have contributed extensively to the problem of identifying market partitions or subsets of competing brands; see Allenby [1989] and Grover & Rao [1988].

[6] The basic assumptions of this model are essentially the same as those of Moorthy [1984].

to purchase the product when the market penetration is reported to be y. Thus, the equilibrium condition in the market is: $y_i = M_i(P_i)F_i(y_i)$. Using this model, the optimal price of the product that maximizes firm's profit is given by:

$$\frac{c(y)}{P} = 1 - [1 - e_D(y)]/e_D(P) \tag{3}$$

where $e_D(y) = yF'(y)/F(y)$; $e_D(P)$ is the price-elasticity of potential demand and $c(y)$ is the marginal cost of production at the penetration level, y. This expression is a modified form of the classical monopoly pricing rule given in Equation (1). In this extension, the optimal price depends on product cost, qualities of the product and its competing items, penetration levels, and market potential. Using this model, Smith derives formulae for maximum sustaining price and the price differential between a firm's new product and its competitors'. If the elasticity of potential demand is constant (at e), then he shows that the change in new product's price should never be larger than $(1 - e)/(2 - e)$ times the competitor's price change. This general approach seems to be applicable to markets characterized by price and performance tradeoffs (such as computers and electronic-document delivery systems).

3.2.3. Equilibrium analysis of price and quality

Tellis & Wernerfelt [1987] show that the equilibrium correlation between price and (objective) quality of competitive products increases with the level of consumer information on prices and qualities of various sellers in a market. Further, they show that this correlation can be negative even when there is a sufficiently low level of consumer information. Given the information problem for consumers, they predict that price–quality correlation will be much stronger in markets for durables, unpackaged goods, and products sold over a wide price range. Using data from various prior studies covering over 1200 product markets, they show empirical evidence for their theoretical results of the equilibrium correlation. They find the distribution of price–quality correlation to be unimodal and moderately skewed, with a mean of 0.27, and a median of 0.31. The mean price–quality correlation was 0.30 for durables (with a range of 0.17 to 0.43 according to the relative price range of the product) and 0.30 for unpackaged goods (with a range of 0.18 to 0.44 according to the relative price range of the product).

3.2.4. Objectives other than profit

Interesting and perhaps easy-to-implement extensions to the basic marginal-revenue-equals-marginal-cost rules are those provided by Saghafi [1988]. He develops formulae for optimal price for a firm operating in a competitive market that seeks to maximize profits subject to a target on share of revenue or quantity sold. His formulae depend upon the self-price-elasticities for the product and competition, the cross-price-elasticity between the two products and the price-reaction elasticity of the product, x, with respect to competition, y, defined as $(\partial P_y/\partial P_x)(P_x/P_y)$ and the marginal cost of x.

3.3. Summary

This brief review provides a flavor of the static models for one product. Our review of this vast subject matter is necessarily brief. An important omission in this area of research is the lack of consideration for pricing objectives other than profit (except for the Saghafi paper referred to above); examples of such objectives include minimizing costs subject to achieving a target market-share by the end of a prespecified planning horizon. It is easy to observe that valid measures for price-elasticity, reaction elasticity, cross-price elasticity are required for implementing them in practice, in addition to costs. Recent developments in marketing research such as conjoint analysis [e.g. Mahajan, Green & Goldberg, 1982] offer some help in this direction. Further, the results from static optimal-pricing models are highly useful in evaluating the benefits of more complex models of dynamic pricing.

4. Dynamic pricing models for single products

Two dynamic factors – diffusion of innovations and cost declines due to accumulated volume of production – contribute to different time paths of prices of new products (see Table 11.1). The last fifteen years or so have witnessed considerable research on this topic of determining optimal dynamic price-paths for new products. Various researchers such as Robinson & Lakhani [1975], Bass [1980], Dolan & Jeuland [1981], Jeuland & Dolan [1982] and Kalish [1983] have addressed the basic question: which is the best dynamic price policy (skimming or penetration) for a new product (so as to maximize net present value) considering such factors as the nature of the new product (e.g. is the 'innovation' effect more important than the 'imitation' effect?), the functional form for the model of diffusion that incorporates price, and the discount factor for future stream of profits? It is fair to say that the research stream in this area up until 1982 or so dealt with the price policy of a monopolist in the market. The major result of this research is that optimal price, $P^*(t)$ at time t is given by $P_m(t) + \Delta P(t)$ where $P_m(t)$ is the optimal monopoly price shown in Equation (1) and $\Delta P(t)$ is an adjustment that depends upon various factors such as parameters of a diffusion model (e.g. coefficients of imitation and innovation in the Bass-type model and repeat-buying probability), market potential for the new product, and cost dynamics. Conditions for skimming and penetration strategies are derived in this stream of research (see Rao [1984] for a summary).

Over the last nine years or so, this topic of dynamic pricing has been a haven for mathematically oriented marketing researchers. Using the techniques of dynamic optimization, various researchers pursued the problem of determining dynamic pricing policy for a new product covering a range of relevant related issues. These efforts include: (i) incorporation of price expectations among consumers [Yoo, Dolan & Rangan, 1987; Moorthy, 1988; Narasimhan, 1989]; (ii) marketing-mix effects [Kalish, 1985]; (iii) market-structure issues of oligopolistic markets [Rao & Bass, 1985; Dockner & Jorgensen, 1988; Eliashberg & Jeuland,

1986; Chintagunta, Rao & Vilcassim, forthcoming]; (iv) externality effects [Dhebar & Oren, 1985]; and (v) product interdependencies due to primary and contingent products [Mahajan & Muller, 1991] and overlapping replacement cycles of a durable product [Bayus, 1992]. We will briefly review these selected efforts.

4.1. Price expectations

Yoo, Dolan & Rangan [1987] develop a model for the sales of a new durable product (first-time buyers or potential adopters) by incorporating the effect of price into the Bass model of diffusion and postulating a process of consumer price expectations in the future. Their resulting model takes the following form for sales at time t:

$$S(t) = [Mf(P^*(t)) - X(t)][a + bX(t)]$$

where a and b are respectively the coefficients of innovation and imitation, $X(t)$ is cumulative sales up to t, M is the market potential for the product at a very low price, and $P^*(t)$ is the price expected by consumers at time t. If consumers fully consider future prices which they predict with complete confidence, then the predicted price is the total utility derived from the product by buyers at time t. This utility is shown to be $P(t) + [P(t) - P(t+1)]/\lambda$, where λ is the consumer's utility discount factor. Nine variations of this formulation arise when three processes of consumer price expectations (leading to $P^*(t)$) and three functional forms – exponential, uniform and Weibull – for f are used to represent the distribution of the $P^*(t)$ across the population. The three price-expectation processes are myopic (no future is included in $P^*(t)$), full expectations ($P^*(t)$ is equal to the utility of the product), and partial expectations, resulting in the expressions for $P^*(t)$ as:

$$P^*(t) = \begin{cases} P(t) & \text{for a myopic process;} \\ P(t) + \dfrac{P(t) - P(t+1)}{\lambda} & \text{for full expectations;} \\ [1 - x(t)]P(t) + x(t)\left[P(t) + \dfrac{P(t) - P(t+1)}{\lambda}\right] & \text{for partial expectations.} \end{cases}$$

Here, $x(t) = X(t)/M$. Using various empirical and simulation analyses, the authors conclude that the hypothesis of partial expectations seems more valid than the others in some product categories and that the relatively simple uniform distribution for f seems to describe consumer heterogeneity in $P^*(t)$ quite well. The authors also show that firms lose much by following a myopic price strategy rather than the optimal strategy applicable over time, and that the optimal price path is steady for a few periods and declining thereafter.

Narasimhan [1989] had modeled the same problem using the assumption that consumers form expectations for future prices, with perfect foresight. Using a general function to capture the diffusion process for a new durable product and allowing new consumers to enter the market each period, he arrives at the conclusion that the equilibrium price path for the new product is cyclical, with unequal cycle lengths and price being highest at the beginning of the cycle and declining monotonically until the end of the cycle. Thus, in both of these efforts, incorporation of price expectations will lead to a dynamic price policy of skimming (with some variations) for a new durable product.

4.2. Marketing-mix effects

Kalish [1985] has formulated a two-step process of consumer behavior – awareness and adoption – toward a new product and used the following optimization of a firm's net present value of cash flows to determine dynamic price path for an innovation:

$$\text{maximize} \quad \int_0^T e^{-rt}[(P_t - c_t)S_t - A_t]\,dt$$

where c_t is the average cost at time t, r is the discount rate, P_t is the price, A_t is the advertising expenditure, and S_t is the sales rate at t. In his formulation, S_t is described by the adoption process and product awareness over time. Awareness is influenced by advertising and word-of-mouth effects. The number of potential adopters at any time is a function of price. Using this model, Kalish has developed the following two major propositions on the dynamic price paths for new products:

(a) the dynamic price path for a durable good is monotonically decreasing unless (1) the effectiveness of adopters in generating awareness is high and/or (2) the reduction of uncertainty about the new product among adopters is high; and
(b) for repeat-purchase goods, price is monotonically increasing if and only if advertising is decreasing and if the production cost is constant.

While Kalish's model is quite rich, it does leave out the effects of competition. Further, the rate of adoption is exogenous to the model. Implementation of this model in any particular application requires specifying and estimating functional forms for the number of potential adopters.

Using the household production framework, Horsky [1990] develops a diffusion model for a new durable product that incorporates product benefits, price, income and information. He derives a logistic equation for adoption that depends on income and price at the aggregate level. Also, some potential consumers may delay purchase of the durable due to various factors such as expected future price decreases, suspicion of quality, and lack of awareness. His results show that the product life-cycle phenomenon can be explained jointly or separately by the effects of income and price and the effects of awareness, uncertainty, and price expectation. He demonstrates that if the word-of-mouth-type effects are weak, a price-skimming strategy is optimal for monopolists and also is likely to be relevant for oligopolists.

4.3. Market-structure issues

Rao & Bass [1985] explore how competition affects the dynamic pricing of new products. Their analysis includes the dynamic effects of diffusion, market saturation and cost reductions. Assuming an undifferentiated oligopoly for the structure of the market, they formulate the ith firm's problem as:

$$\underset{q_{it}}{\text{maximize}} \quad V_i = \int_0^{\infty} e^{-rt}(P_t - c_{it})q_{it}\,dt$$

$$\text{subject to} \quad \frac{dx_{it}}{dt} = q_{it}$$

where

$$c_{it} = C(x_{it}); \quad P_t = g(X_t, Q_t); \quad \text{and } x_{io} \text{ is given.}$$

Here, x_{it} is the accumulated volume for the ith firm with output of q_{it} at time t, and X_t and Q_t represent accumulated output of the industry and current output respectively. Owing to lack of differentiation, each firm has the opportunity to maximize its net present value with respect to its output decision. A dynamic Nash equilibrium analysis implies the following necessary condition for each firm in the industry:

$$P_t(1 + m_{it}/\eta_t) = r\int_t^{\infty} c_{it}\exp(-r(\tau - t))d\tau - \int_t^{\infty} q_{i\tau}\rho_{x\tau}\exp(-r(\tau - t))d\tau \tag{4}$$

where $\eta_t = (\partial Q_t/\partial P_t)/(Q_t/P_t)$ is the elasticity of demand, $\rho_{x\tau} = \partial P_t/\partial X_t$, and m_{it} is the ith firm's share of current output, Q_t. Using this general condition, the authors study the dynamic path of the industry price for various special cases of only demand saturation, only demand diffusion and only cost reduction. They find that the equilibrium price path is declining for the cases of market saturation and cost-learning and increasing for demand-diffusion effects. They also provide some numerical results for the duopoly case.

Dockner & Jorgensen [1988] deal with the determination of optimal dynamic-pricing policies in an oligopolistic market using differential game theory and open-loop Nash equilibrium concepts. They analyze four classes of models: (1) demand depends on prices only; (2) demand depends on prices and own-firm adoption effects; (3) demand depends on prices and industry-adoption levels; and (4) demand depends on prices and adoption effects of all firms. Their general conclusion is that when imitation and/or cost-learning effects are the dominating factors, the myopic oligopolists will price higher than dynamic oligopolists. If saturation effects dominate over the planning period, the dynamic oligopolists will use a discrimination policy and price higher than myopic oligopolists. Using a similar methodology, Chintagunta, Rao & Vilcassim [forthcoming] analyze a duopolistic market where accumulated consumption experience of a brand is a dominant determinant of its sales or market share. They demonstrate that penetration price paths seem to be optimal for 'frequently' purchased goods.

Eliashberg & Jeuland [1986] consider the natural evolution of a market structure in which a monopoly market becomes a duopoly due to a new entrant. They analyze the monopolist pricing strategies for maximizing undiscounted profits for three situations – nonmyopic, myopic and 'surprised' – using the Nash-equilibrium analysis of a two-period game. While a nonmyopic monopolist predicts competitive entry, the myopic monopolist totally discounts the period of duopoly. The surprised monopolist is a first entrant who has a longer time-horizon than the nonmyopic monopolist, but does not foresee the competitive entry. In their model, sales functions for the two situations (monopoly and duopoly) consist of the effects of growth, diffusion and price, but no cost dynamics are included. Their major results indicate that the three pricing strategies may be quite different and that it is optimal for the nonmyopic firm to price its product at a higher level than the myopic monopolist. Further, their simulation results indicate that the 'surprised' monopolist may price higher than a nonmyopic monopolist with the same planning horizon during the monopoly period because he underestimates the competition. Finally, they show that products having higher prices will exhibit a more rapid rate of decline in price. These results are particularly relevant for a firm whose monopoly for its new product is protected for a period of time due to patent or other factors.

4.4. *Externality effects*

Dhebar & Oren [1985] develop a model for determining the optimal dynamic price-path for a new product or service (such as electronic mail) whose consumption value increases with the expansion of the 'network' of adapters.[7] Thus, externalities are essentially a form of diffusion. Let $x \in [0, 1]$ be the size of the subscriber set and index h reflect an attribute such as income for a marginal consumer. Dhebar & Oren denote $W(h, x)$ as the willingness-to-pay function for the marginal consumer when the subscriber-set size is x. They assume that the decision to subscribe will depend upon the consumer's anticipated subscriber-set size, $[\alpha h + (1 - \alpha)x]$. Thus, the number of nonsubscribers wishing to subscribe when the price is P for the service is given by:

$$d^{\alpha}(x, P) = \max\{h : 0 \leqslant h \leqslant 1, W(h, [\alpha h + (1 - \alpha)x]) = P\}.$$

Here α may be thought of as the 'awareness' parameter that can be influenced through product advertising and promotional campaigns. The demand for subscribers adjusts as long as $d^{\alpha} > x \geqslant 0$ and the network expansion stops when

[7] Their premise can be considered to be different from that of the dynamic pricing models reviewed above which implicitly assume that the consumption value of a product is constant over time. Further, one may consider that the Dhebar & Oren paper shows a way of deriving functions in Dockner & Jorgensen's framework.

$d^{\alpha} = x$. Denoting the growth of the network by a general function, $\dot{x} = G(d^{\alpha}(x, P), x)$ where x is the cumulative number of adopters and d is the potential market, the optimal pricing policy for a monopolist can be obtained by solving the optimization problem:

$$\text{maximize} \quad \int_0^{\infty} \mathrm{e}^{-rt}[Pu - c(x)]\mathrm{d}t$$

$$\text{subject to} \quad \dot{x} = G(d^{\alpha}(x, P), x), x(0) = x_0,$$

$$0 \leqslant P \leqslant W(x, x).$$

The optimal price path is given by the equations:

$$u(x^*) + rv^{\alpha}(x^*) = 0$$

where

$$u^{\alpha}(x^*) = P^*\left[1 + \frac{x^*(1 - d_x^{\alpha *})}{P^* d_x^{\alpha *}}\right] - c_x^*$$

and

$$u^{\alpha}(x^*) = \frac{x^*}{G_d(x^*, x^*)} d_x^{\alpha *}. \tag{5}$$

Dhebar & Oren conclude that a greater level of consumer awareness and information with regard to network growth potential will result in larger equilibrium networks and lower prices. In general, the price path will be monotonically increasing and will consist of initial subsidy region, with the subsidy terminating when the subscription price and marginal cost functions intersect. Their results are intuitive and offer important extensions to the dynamic-pricing problem for a new product.

4.5. Product interdependence

Several situations exist in which certain products (called contingent products) must be used with another (primary) product (for example, television and video-cassette recorder). In these cases, the price policies of primary and contingent products depend on one another. Mahajan & Muller [1991] look at the problem of determining optimal pricing policies for contingent products for different conditions of contingent-product relationships. Their basic model involves two differential equations describing the rate of demand for the primary (X) and contingent (Y) products as follows:

$$\begin{aligned} \dot{x}(t) &= (a_1 + b_1 x(x))(N - x(t))\exp(-\varepsilon_1 P_1(t)); \quad x(0) = x_0 > 0, \\ \dot{y}(t) &= (a_2 + b_2 y(t))(x(t) - y(t))\exp(-\varepsilon_2 P_2(t)); \quad y(0) = 0, \end{aligned} \tag{6}$$

where $x(t)$ and $y(t)$ are respectively the cumulative number of adoptions for the primary and contingent products with respective prices P_1 and P_2 and a_1, b_1, a_2, b_2 are parameters for the demand-growth functions for X and Y. Using the maximization of the net present value of profit as the objective function, they test various propositions for pricing contingent products under different forms of production integration. For example, they conclude that an integrated firm that produces both products should price either product lower than the prices of two firms that independently produce the two products. Further, they conclude that an integrated firm will make more profit from the primary product than from the contingent product. A related problem was investigated by Nascimento [1987] and Nascimento & Vanhonacker [1988] who derived optimal strategic pricing policies for consumer reproducible goods such as computer software and pre-recorded music tapes. They conclude that when the product is not protected against copying, skimming pricing strategies tend to be optimal.

A related issue is examined by Bayus [1992] who derives optimal dynamic-pricing policies for durable products with overlapping replacement cycles where the replacement component is significant (as in the case of color television versus black-and-white television). He formulates the following model of demand for the second-generation product:

$$\dot{x}(t) = [N - x(t)][1 - \theta(q, t)]Z(x)g(P) + [N - x(t)]\theta(q, t)h(P, q)$$

where $x(t)$ is the cumulative sales of the second-generation product, $P(t)$ and $q(t)$ are the prices of the second- and first-generation products, and $\theta(q, t)$ is the proportion of installed base of the first-generation product that will make a 'normal replacement' at time t. The function $h(P, q)$ is the proportion of households making a normal replacement that purchase a second-generation product, while $g(P)$ considers the effect of price on the growth of the demand for the second-generation product. The term $Z(x)$ captures the diffusion process of the second-generation product. Using the present value of firm profits from the first- and second-generation products over the period after the second-generation product becomes available, Bayus derives a wider set of optimal pricing strategies for the second-generation product (i.e. the new product) under different scenarios of replacement behavior than previously obtained. For example, if replacements are an important factor in the sales of a new product, the optimal price path for the second-generation product will be decreasing over time. A similar problem of optimal pricing of successive generations of product advances is looked at by Padmanabhan & Bass [forthcoming].

4.6. *Summary*

This section describes various advances in the determination of optimal dynamic price-paths for products under various conditions. The literature indicates an impressive array of situations analyzed and a high level of technical sophistication in the analytical methods employed. Bearing the risk of oversimplification, these varied and technically sophisticated analyses can be summarized by the following statement: a skimming pricing policy is optimal for situations in which consumers expect lower prices in the future, when the word-of-mouth effects are weak for diffusion of demand, when the market is becoming saturated, and when costs decline according to learning effects. In addition to the cost learning curve, three aspects of consumer behavior – expectations, word-of-mouth and replacements – seem to be relevant in the determination of optimal price paths. While it is almost impossible to empirically validate the results obtained in this stream of research, it may be possible to use the results as a general guide in setting price policies over time. For this purpose, one ought to look for a model whose assumptions correspond most closely with the practical situation under consideration. Also, the normative results in the literature can be compared to those obtained from numerical simulations [Parker, 1992].

5. Multiple-product pricing models

5.1. Optimal prices for a product line

Given the significance of the introduction of new, related products for a firm's continued growth and success, pricing a product line is an important area of research. Equation (1) for optimal monopoly price ignores any effects due to the interdependence of demand and costs of the product with others. Assuming only one other product, B, in the line and no cost dependencies, the optimal price, P_A^*, for a product A (assuming that the sales are in the elastic portion of the demand curve) can be shown to be

$$P_A^* = \frac{\varepsilon_A}{1+\varepsilon_A}\cdot \mathrm{MC}_A - \left(\frac{\eta_{AB}}{1+\varepsilon_A}\right)\frac{Q_N(P_B - \mathrm{MC}_B)}{Q_A} \tag{7}$$

where ε_A and η_{AB} are self- and cross-price-elasticities for product A; Q_A and Q_B are sales quantities of A and B; and MC_A and MC_B are marginal cost functions of A and B, respectively. A and B are substitutes if η_{AB} is positive and complements if η_{AB} is negative. The extension of (7) to a set of B-type products (denoted by $B_1, B_2, \ldots, B_J$) is quite immediate; the formula for optimal price P_A^* can be shown to be:

$$P_A^* = \frac{\varepsilon_A}{1+\varepsilon_A}\cdot \mathrm{MC}_A - \sum_{j=1}^{J}\left(\frac{\eta_{AB_j}}{1+\varepsilon_A}\right)\frac{Q_{B_j}(P_{B_j} - \mathrm{MC}_{B_j})}{Q_A} \tag{8}$$

where η_{AB_j} is the cross-price elasticity of demand of jth related product (B_j) with respect to the price of A, MC_{B_j} and Q_{B_j} are respectively the marginal cost and the sales quantity of B_j. Implementation of this result presents several empirical problems for estimating the required elasticities and the problem of allocation of joint costs. Mahajan, Green & Goldberg [1982] show how conjoint analysis can be used for estimating self- and cross-price–demand relationships. Reibstein & Gatignon [1984] report another empirical effort in which econometric methods are used to measure self- and cross-elasticities for eggs of different sizes using sales data at the store level with a multiple exponential specification of the demand function and logarithms of errors distributed according to a multivariate normal distribution; they also discuss how optimal prices for the line of eggs may be set using these estimates according to Equation (8) above.

5.2. Current directions

Three main directions may be identified in recent models on the pricing of multiple products. These are: (i) models for optimal prices or margins for a multi-product firm that use an aggregate model of demand [Juhl & Kristensen, 1990; Little & Shapiro, 1980]; (ii) models for pricing bundles of products derived from distributions of reservation prices for individual items [Hanson & Martin, 1990; Cready, 1991; Schmalensee, 1984]; and (iii) models of pricing (and positioning) a product line of partial substitutes [Moorthy, 1984; Dobson & Kalish, 1988; Oren, Smith & Wilson, 1984]. Related research by Lal & Matutes [1989] who analyze the complete information game of pricing by two duopolistic firms that offer an assortment of goods is of tangential interest to the problem of multiproduct pricing. Further, the experimental finding by Petroshius & Monroe [1987] that consumers' evaluations of a product (model) within a product line is influenced by the range of prices of items in the line may offer opportunities for enriching the analytical models for pricing multiple products. We will briefly comment on a subset of these papers.

5.2.1. Aggregate demand models

Maximizing the profit function, $\sum_{i=1}^{n}(P_i - c_i)q_i$ for a multiproduct firm with n products with respective costs, prices and quantities denoted by c_i, P_i and q_i will yield the set of equations for determining the vector of optimal gross margins, $\boldsymbol{g}' = (g_1, \ldots, g_n)$, where $g_i = (P_i - c_i)/P_i$:

$$\boldsymbol{g} = -(\boldsymbol{R}\boldsymbol{E}^{-1}\boldsymbol{R}^{-1})'\boldsymbol{K} \tag{9}$$

where $\boldsymbol{R}$ is a diagonal matrix of revenue shares ($r_i = P_i x_i / \sum_j P_j x_j$), $\boldsymbol{E}$ is the matrix of self- and cross-elasticities, and $\boldsymbol{K}$ is the $(n \times 1)$ unity vector. This equation system is the same as that shown in (8), but in a different form. Given that one needs n^2 estimates of self- and cross-elasticities, the problem of determining optimal gross margins becomes quite difficult to solve in practice. Generally, these estimates are obtained from time-series data using methods similar to those employed by Reibstein & Gatignon [1984]. But, Juhl & Kristensen [1990] suggest a parameterization of the $\boldsymbol{E}$-matrix which will permit a reduction in the number of parameters and which in addition will allow estimation of parameters from cross-sectional data. They assume that the utility function of the aggregate consumer is strongly separable in the subutilities of the goods. Accordingly, their method requires only the estimates of the income elasticities for the n goods and not all n^2 elasticities. The authors implement their procedure to determine the optimal pricing policy of a Danish textile company for two product lines of curtains and tablecloths.

Little & Shapiro [1980] develop a two-stage theory of price-setting that postulates maximizing behavior on the part of customers and stores. In their model, once in the store, customers purchase goods to maximize utility; this process determines the short-run response to prices. The store's problem then is to maximize short-run profit subject to a constraint that a given level of customer utility be delivered. The utility level becomes a policy parameter for the store which in part determines the long-run attractiveness of the store to the customers. Their model is quite comprehensive in dealing with the customer–store interaction and is a stepping stone to a theory of pricing a bundle of goods at the level of a supermarket, which includes interactions among various products. In their model, optimal prices for n goods in a store are obtained by solving the following equation:

$$P_k = \frac{\varepsilon_k - \sum_{i \neq k} [(P_i - c_i)/c_k][S_i/S_k]\eta_{ik}}{1 + \varepsilon_k - z_k} \cdot c_k; \quad k = 1, 2, \ldots, n \tag{10}$$

where ε_k is self-price-elasticity for the kth product; $k = 1, 2, \ldots, n$; η_{ik} is cross-price-elasticity for products i and k; $i \neq k \neq 1, 2, \ldots, n$; c_k is marginal cost of the kth product to the store; S_k is quantity of the kth product bought by the customers from the store; and z_k is a measure for the store of the effect of utility constraint for the customers at the set of prices $(P_1, \ldots, P_n)$. However, the equation system (10) is hard to solve owing to the interdependence of the equations. The authors comment upon the measurement issues involved in estimating the cross-elasticities. As anticipated by the authors, the advent of scanner data has enabled estimation of these elasticities. Two aspects of their model that offer future research possibilities are inclusion of the phenomenon of customers' desire to seek variety in shopping and the stores' decision process with regard to acceptance or rejection of new products.

5.2.2. *Optimal bundle pricing*

Although bundling is a widespread phenomenon, research on how to find optimal bundle prices is of recent vintage. Three distinct strategies of bundling are considered in the literature: (a) pure bundling, in which only the bundle of products is offered; (b) mixed bundling, in which the bundle components are sold separately but at a premium relative to the price of the bundle; and (c) premium bundling, which is similar to mixed bundling, but bundles are sold at a *premium* (rather than at a discount) relative to prices of individual components.

The first two cases of bundling have been considered by Adams & Yellen [1976] with the use of examples and by Schmalensee [1984] who presents a formal model for two-item bundles by assuming a bivariate normal distribution of reservation prices of the two products. Cready [1991] considers the case of premium bundling and examines the conditions of the correlation between the reservation prices of the two products in order for premium bundling to be advantageous to a monopolist. In fact, his analysis suggests that premium bundling may be desirable when the overall correlation in reservation prices is positive and pronounced negative correlation exists among those consumers with relatively low (but not below-cost) reservation prices. This result is in contrast to mixed bundling, where an overall negative correlation in reservation prices is desirable [Adams & Yellen, 1976], but not necessary [Schmalensee, 1984].

Schmalensee's formulation provides a flavor of the bundle-pricing models. Given a bivariate distribution of reservation prices for two goods priced at P_1 and P_2, with respective constant marginal costs C_1 and C_2, the profit function for a monopolist marketing the two products can be described in terms of areas under the joint distribution for the two cases of unbundled, pure bundled and mixed bundled sales. Let the price of bundle be $P_B = P_1 + P_2 - 2\phi$. If the parameter ϕ is positive, there are advantages in offering a bundle. If ϕ is equal to zero, we will have the case of unbundling. (Although not considered by Schmalensee, negative values of ϕ will lead to premium bundling described earlier.) Schmalensee analyzed various conditions under which the two strategies of pure bundling and mixed bundling are desirable. Among his main results are: (i) mixed bundling is generally more profitable than either unbundled sales or pure bundling since it combines the advantages of both, (ii) pure bundling makes buyers worse off than unbundled sales and is more profitable when the average reservation prices are high enough, and (iii) a bundling strategy which treats goods symmetrically is most attractive distribution of reservation prices.

5.2.3. Mathematical-programming models

Under the assumption that a firm wishes to pursue the policy of bundling n products (e.g. components), Hanson & Martin [1990] formulate the problem of deriving optimal prices for L bundles and solve it using mixed integer linear-programming methods. Assuming M consumer segments of sizes $N_1, \ldots, N_M$, the objective function for the firm is

$$\text{maximize} \quad \sum_{k=1}^{M} \sum_{i=1}^{L} N_k Z_{ki}$$

where Z_{ki} denotes the marginal revenue generated from a customer in segment k if that consumer selects bundle i priced at P_i. Their formulation assumes that customers select bundles to maximize consumer surplus, defined as the difference between bundle-specific reservation price and the bundle price. We may note extensive data inputs are required for implementing this formulation – reservation prices of all relevant customer segments for each of the bundles, the size of the various segments, and the costs of supplying a customer of a specific segment with a particular bundle. Much of these data can be collected using various marketing-research and cost-accounting methods.

Building on the theory developed by Moorthy [1984], Dobson & Kalish [1988] developed a decision support system to tackle the problem of pricing and positioning a line of related products by a monopolist using the techniques of mathematical programming. Their formulation relevant to pricing of multiple products assumes that a set of m products has been targeted to m customer segment. The problem, then, is to find profit-maximizing prices $P_1, P_2, \ldots, P_m$ so as to maximize $\sum_{i=1}^{m} q_i(P_{k_i} - c_{k_i})$ subject to the constraints $u_{ik_i} - P_{k_i} > u_{ij} - P_j \forall i,j$, where the ith customer segment with demand q_i is targeted to the k_ith product with variable cost c_{k_i}. The indices k_i are defined by $x_{k_i} = 1$, $x_{ij} = 0$, $j \neq k_i$ where x_{ij} denotes the indicator variable taking value 1 or 0 depending upon whether the ith segment is assigned to the jth product. This formulation can also be extended to the case when more than one segment is assigned to a product. The authors offer several heuristics to solve the twofold problem of positioning and pricing with several simplifications to solve the subproblem of pricing a line of products. A related issue of setting prices for a line of products has been tackled by Oren, Smith & Wilson [1984] using nonlinear pricing methods which capture the role of price breaks designed to achieve market segmentation.

5.3. Summary

This section describes various attempts at modeling the problem of pricing multiple products and bundling. The practice of bundling offers significant opportunities for a multiproduct firm. While bundling has been studied using mathematical models, this area offers significant opportunities for study using behavioral experimental methods. It is a safe conjecture to make that results from such experimental work will enable sharpening of the premises used in model building and model formulations for bundling and multiple-product pricing. Also, opportunities exist to deal with the issue of cost interdependence in this general area. Further, this topic is of great practical interest in such industries as automobiles and computers. An issue that has not been investigated in this literature is the ability of a customer with respect to consuming the bundle that is offered; this problem arises, for example, in the pricing of season tickets for theater or concert performances. Venkatesh & Mahajan [forthcoming] develop a probabilistic model to deal with the pricing of season tickets for musical performances that incorporates not only a consumer's reservation price but also time availability to attend the performances.

6. Behavioral pricing models

Pricing studies that emphasize behavioral aspects have been more frequent since about 1980. Owing to its interdisciplinary nature, this segment of research on pricing has drawn from various developments in behavioral decision theory (e.g. prospect theory and its derivative, transaction utility theory [Thaler, 1985]). The basic model of consumer choice which postulates that an individual will choose the brand that maximizes consumer surplus (i.e. reservation price less brand price) has been augmented in several directions.

First, consumers' search costs and their search processes have been included in the model [Kolodinsky, 1990; Urbany, 1986; Urbany, Bearden & Weilbaker, 1988]. Next, models have been developed to describe the construct of reference price and its different operationalizations [e.g. Winer, 1985, 1986; Urbany & Dickson, 1990; Kalwani, Yim, Rinne & Sugita, 1990]. The asymmetry of effects of deviations of a brand price from a consumer's reference price is an interesting concept which has important implications for the demand curve. This concept has been empirically tested by Gurumurthy & Little [1987], and Kalwani, Yim, Rinne & Sugita [1990] using scanner data, and Kalwani & Yim [1992] using experimental data. The asymmetry of effects has been explicitly incorporated in a microeconomic model of brand choice [Putler, 1992]. Finally, the relationships between brand price, brand quality (objective or perceived), and brand value have been investigated for possible inclusion in a choice model [e.g. Lichtenstein & Burton, 1989; Zeithaml, 1988; Curry & Riesz, 1988; Rao and Monroe, 1989].

The most important recent augmentations are the addition of consumer time costs and price search (which introduces the premise that consumers may be uninformed about prices; [e.g. Kolodinsky, 1990]), the asymmetry of effects of price deviations from a consumer's reference price [e.g. Gurumurthy & Little, 1987; Kalwani, Yim, Rinne & Sugita, 1990], and the possibility that consumers use price as a cue for product quality and value [e.g. Lichtenstein & Burton, 1989]. These behavioral subtleties in how consumers respond to price may have important implications for how normative pricing decisions should be modeled. The following sections briefly review how consumer choice has been modeled to account for these issues and what the implications are for models of pricing decisions.

6.1. Search costs and search processes

Using a 'joint production' model that combines aspects of household production and economics of information, Kolodinsky [1990] formulated a model to explain the variation in time spent in a price-information search on groceries by dual-earner households. In particular, she incorporated a variable for capturing one's enjoyment of search time. Her empirical results of analyzing survey data using two-stage least squares procedures indicate that variables such as enjoyment of search, income, age, price of search time, presence of young children, daily use of microwave oven, and percentage of brand items in the market basket are significant variables in explaining variation in time spent in the price-information search.

Using a normative model, Ratchford [1980] shows how a monetary value can be placed on the benefits of search for a consumer who maximizes expected utility, with application to durable products. Urbany [1986] tests experimentally various propositions on search behavior, derived from Stigler's economics of information theory [1961] and finds that buyers are heterogeneous in the way they value the search cost–benefit relationship. It is, therefore, important to include this heterogeneity while developing a purchase decision model. Further experiments by Urbany, Bearden & Weilbaker [1988] show the effects of the advertised regular price of a brand and plausible reference prices on consumer perceptions and price-search behavior. Their results should help in developing a process model of the effects of reference prices and search on final patronage of brands.

It is well known that consumers may not have adequate information on all available brands.[8] As such, firms may take consumer ignorance (i.e. which determines price-elasticity) into account when setting prices. Wilde & Schwartz [1979] and Salop & Stiglitz [1977] present models for examining seller pricing behavior as a function of consumer research.

6.2. *Models with reference price*

Winer [1985] proposed and empirically tested the following model for the probability of purchase of a durable good (PR_{it}) by household i in period i:

$$\begin{aligned}\mathrm{PR}_{it} = f_1(&\text{order of durable acquisition}_{it}, \text{ age of durable}_{it}, \text{ wealth}_{it},\\ &\text{need for convenience}_{it}, \text{ confidence}_{it}, \text{ stage of family life-cycle}_{it},\\ &\mathrm{EP}_{it}, \mathrm{SD}_{it}, \mathrm{SS}_{it}, \mathrm{RP}_{it}, \mu_{1it})\end{aligned}$$

where EP_{it}, SD_{it}, SS_{it} and RP_{it} are respectively expected price, consumer uncertainty about expected price, sticker shock and reservation price about the durable good, and μ_{1it} is an error term. The four price-related variables were operationalized as: $\mathrm{EP}_{it} = (P^{\mathrm{e}}_{i,t+1} - P^{\mathrm{r}}_{i,t})/(y_{it} \times P^{\mathrm{r}}_{it})$; $\mathrm{SD}_{it} = (\sigma^{\mathrm{e}}_{it+1})/(y_{it} \times P^{\mathrm{r}}_{it})$; $\mathrm{SS}_{it} = (\boldsymbol{P}_{it} - P^{\mathrm{r}}_{it})/(y_{it} \times P^{\mathrm{r}}_{it})$; and $\mathrm{RP}_{it} = (P^{\mathrm{v}}_{i,t+1} - P^{\mathrm{r}}_{it})/(y_{it} \times P^{\mathrm{r}}_{it})$; where $\boldsymbol{P}_{it}$ is the vector of observed market prices until period t of the good, P^{r}_{it} is the current reference (or perceived) price for the durable, $P^{\mathrm{e}}_{i,t+1}$ is the mean of the distribution of expected price for the period $(t+1)$ with a standard deviation of $\sigma^{\mathrm{e}}_{i,t+1}$, P^{v}_{it} is the maximum price the household is willing to pay, and y_{it} is the current level of household income. Winer developed these operationalizations using various findings in related literature. Further, Winer proposed a second model to describe the price expectation process as:

$$P^{\mathrm{e}}_{i,t+1} = f_2(P^{\mathrm{e}}_{it}, P^{\mathrm{s}}_{i,t+1}, \text{ other variables describing the household}, \mu_{2it})$$

where $P^{\mathrm{s}}_{i,t+1}$ refers to the signals about prices in $(t+1)$ and μ_{2it} is an error term. In a similar manner, he proposed models for reference price (P^{r}_{it}) uncertainty ($\sigma^{\mathrm{e}}_{i,t+1}$) and reservation price (P^{v}_{it}). Winer based his empirical analysis on the data from the 1977 Survey of Consumer Credit of the Survey Research Center of the University of Michigan. Although the constructs of expected price, reservation price and uncertainty were formally proposed, he could not estimate the corresponding

[8] In an exploratory study for twenty products, Urbany & Dickson [1990] find that no more than one-half of their 59 subjects could estimate the normal price ranges and that respondents were incorrect in categorizing prices about one-third of the time.

models owing to lack of measurements. But, he used some proxies for them in the model of purchase probability. Further, he approximated P_{it}^{r} (reference price) by the actual price paid by the household. Winer [1986] used a similar formulation for predicting brand purchase for a frequently purchased consumer product (coffee) where he incorporated the effects of prior purchase and advertising as well.

Focusing on a frequently bought product (coffee), Kalwani, Yim, Rinne & Sugita [1990] developed a two-stage model to understand how consumers use price information in choosing among alternative brands. The first stage investigated how expected prices are formed. Variables such as past price, frequency of brand promotion, and customer characteristics were shown to affect these expectations. In the second stage, brand choice (specified as a conditional logit model) was assumed to depend on the brand's retail price and whether or not that price compares favorably with the brand's expected price. The authors also tested the hypothesis of symmetry in consumer response to positive deviations ('losses') and negative deviations ('gains') of the retail price and expected price. Their empirical results based on coffee scanner panel data were consistent with the predictions of prospect theory (i.e. consumers were found to react more strongly to price losses than to price gains).

The above findings on the effects of reference price effects were incorporated by Putler [1992] into a theoretical economic model of consumer choice. The corresponding consumer problem of utility maximization under a budget M was specified as:

$$\text{maximize} \quad (\boldsymbol{x}, \boldsymbol{L}, \boldsymbol{G})$$

subject to $\sum_{i=1}^{n} P_i x_i = M$, $L_i = I_i x_i (P_i - \mathrm{RP}_i)$, and $G_i = (1 - I_i) x_i (\mathrm{RP}_i - P_i)$ where n is the number of goods and the ith good's quantity and price are respectively x_i and P_i, and L_i and G_i are defined to represent total losses and gains from the transaction for the ith good. Here, RP_i is the reference price of the ith good and I_i is an indicator variable representing the purchase of the ith good taking the value 1 if $\mathrm{RP}_i > P_i$ and 0 otherwise. Putler derived several implications of this model and empirically tested them using weekly retail egg-sales data from southern California. His analysis assumed that the reference price for a good came from an extrapolative expectations process. While the null hypothesis of no effect on reference price on demand was rejected, the results on the presence of asymmetry of gain and loss effects were mixed.

There are two interesting implications here for normative pricing models. First, consumer reference prices can be incorporated into pricing models and such models do indicate different profit-maximizing price levels than when price alone is included [Winer, 1988]. Second, there appears to be a need to develop demand functions which allow for both an impact of price deviations (beyond the usual price effect) and allow for the possibility of greater changes in volume for price increases than for proportional price decreases (e.g. perhaps a kinked demand curve).

6.3. *Price–quality relationships*

Understanding how quality and value perceptions are affected by market prices has been a subject of extensive study and of lasting interest to various researchers in marketing. Zeithaml [1988] proposed a 'means–end' model to synthesize the empirical and theoretical evidence on this topic. She attempted to provide answers to such questions as 'What do consumers mean by quality and value?', 'How are perceptions of quality and value formed?', 'Are they similar across consumer and products?' and 'How do consumers relate quality, price, and value in their deliberation about products and services?'. Her research was exploratory using data generated in the form of protocols and means–end maps for individual consumers.

Using longitudinal data from *Consumer Reports* for 62 durable-product forms, Curry & Reisz [1988] examined the price behavior as the products traverse their product life-cycle. Developed from product life-cycle theory, dynamic pricing policy, and certain economic models that consider the level of consumer information about quality among brands in a product group, they developed three hypotheses: (1) real prices decline over time among brands competing in a specific product form; (2) these prices also converge; and (3) the correspondence over time between price and product quality becomes more precise. Their analysis confirmed the first two hypotheses, but not the third.[9] The data also suggested that price and quality levels tended to correspond less strongly over time.

Using four survey-based studies and data from *Consumer Reports*, Lichtenstein & Burton [1989] found a positive relationship between consumer's price–quality perceptions and price–objective-quality relationships present in the marketplace. Further, they found a high degree of heterogeneity among consumers with respect to the correlation between price–perceived-quality and price–objective-quality; it was lower for individuals who rely on a fixed price–perceived-quality schema or who believe that no price–perceived-quality exists than for other individuals. They also found that the correlation between price–perceived-quality and price–objective-quality was higher for nondurable goods than for durable goods. While these results have obvious implications for model builders and pricing managers, the authors do not offer a defensible measurement of price–quality relationship.

Past studies on the price–perceived-quality were experimental and the reported results naturally depended on the nature of manipulation. Using the methodology of meta-analysis, Rao & Monroe [1989] investigated the influence of price and brand name and/or store name on buyers' evaluations of product quality. While they found that the price–perceived-quality effect varied positively with the strength of the price manipulation, they found no association with the price level used in the experiments for the test products.

[9] The data envelopment analysis (DEA) methodology implemented by Kamakura, Ratchford & Agarwal [1988] may be appropriate for answering the question whether the market price is more than the minimum price for a given bundle of product (objective) attributes. It can consequently answer the question of the existence of a price–quality relationship.

6.4. Summary

The various behavioral studies reviewed in this section present reasons why consumer choice might vary from the standard 'consumer surplus' explanation. They offer bases for developing defensible mathematical models for pricing as well as in developing appropriate measures for various constructs. The methodological paper by Kohli & Mahajan [1991] is a step in this direction. One inescapable fact does emerge from this extensive research; that is that the behavioral relationships are contingent upon various factors. Several questions such as how consumer reference prices are formed, how they affect choice of brands, versatility of asymmetry of price effects need to be explored further. Also, the way in which firms can design appropriate pricing policies using these studies requires careful thought and investigation.

7. Measurement of price effects

The response of demand to changes in price, measured by price-elasticity (in one form or another), is an essential input to the implementation of most pricing models reviewed in this chapter. This measurement is naturally dependent on the nature – historical or cross-sectional – of data available. Econometric techniques relevant for estimating elasticities for time-series data become less suitable for cross-sectional data obtained through surveys or experiments. Experimental data have often been employed for estimating the expected price response of demand for new products; the underlying methodology, which came to be known as conjoint analysis, essentially develops a utility function for an individual in terms of the various product attributes including price. In this situation, price plays two distinct roles – allocative and informational – and the measurement procedures may need to separately estimate the two effects.

Our review on measurement of price effects will be confined to a review of four research efforts: a discussion of the results of meta-analysis of price-elasticity studies that use time-series data [Tellis, 1988]; a survey-based procedure for measuring willingness-to-pay function (or inverse demand function) for multiattributed products [Cameron & James, 1987]; a conjoint procedure to measure self- and cross-price/demand relationships for existing brands [Mahajan, Green & Goldberg, 1982]; and a methodology designed to estimate the two roles of price [Gautschi & Rao, 1990].

7.1. Price-elasticity meta-analysis

Tellis [1988] conducted a meta-analysis of several econometric studies that estimated the price-elasticity of selective sales or market share using literature search covering the 1960–1985 period. The analysis involved 367 suitable price-elasticities from about 220 different brand/markets. His main conclusions were that the price-elasticity was significantly negative with a mean of -1.76 and, in absolute value, eight times that of the advertising-elasticity (of 0.22) obtained from a prior meta-analysis. Further, the price-elasticity was found to be positive in 50 cases. In addition, factors such as brand life-cycle, product category, estimation method used, and country of data contributed to the variation of the estimated price-elasticity of selective demand. For example, price-elasticity of selective demand was found to be lower for detergents (−2.77) and durable goods (−2.03) compared to other categories; lower for markets in Australia/New Zealand (−2.07) and U.S.A. (−1.91) compared to Europe (−1.62); and less for early stages of life-cycle by 0.78. Among the factors contributing to the bias in the estimate of price-elasticity were the omission of distribution-coverage variable or quality measure in the model of market response, the use of only cross-sectional data, and the procedure used for temporal aggregation. Despite these problems, existing studies in the literature report a reasonable measure of price-elasticity for established brands as estimated from time-series data.

7.2. Measurement of willingness-to-pay

Cameron & James [1987] presented an alternative pre-test-market procedure – labeled closed-ended contingent valuation surveys – to estimate the willingness-to-pay function for a product (new or established). This method involves eliciting from a random sample of individuals a binary ('yes/no') response of purchase of a product described by its characteristics and a threshold amount (in dollars) randomly assigned to each individual. Letting $I_i(=1$ or $0)$ be the response at the threshold t_i and x_i be the product description given to the ith individual, they formulated the probit model for the underlying latent variable for the valuation, y_i as: $y_i = x_i'\beta + u_i$ and $I_i = 1$ if $y_i > t_i$ and 0 otherwise. Assuming a normal distribution with zero mean and unknown variance σ^2 for u_i, they estimate the parameters β and σ^2 and their variances using the methods. The authors had implemented this procedure with data from a sample of recreational salmon anglers on their willingness to pay randomly assigned additional dollars to fish under identical conditions to their most recent fishing trip. This approach seems to offer significant potential to determine price response using a survey method.

7.3. Measurement of self- and cross-price relationships

Mahajan, Green & Goldberg [1982] developed and implemented a conjoint-based approach to measure own- and cross-price/demand relationships. In this approach, respondents evaluate the likelihood of buying a brand under the scenario of posted prices for it and other competing brands. Further, the brand prices are varied according to a fractional factorial design. A logit model is fitted to the responses using the generalized least squares method. The estimated parameters are then used to determine the own- and cross-price/demand relations. The authors implemented the method to a nondurable good and the results were deemed face valid. While this method is appealing, it will need to incorporate the variation in the consideration sets of respondents.

7.4. *Allocative and informational effects*

Given the fact that price plays two roles – allocative and informational effects – in an individual's utility function, a conjoint-analysis procedure in which price is used as an attribute is likely to confound these two effects. In fact, estimated price effect can be thought of as net of these two effects of price, which may partially account for the finding of positive price-elasticity by Tellis. Gautschi & Rao [1990] proposed a method to reduce the confounding of the two effects of price; it requires that two preference orderings on the set of choice alternatives, X (unconstrained and constrained preferences) be obtained from each individual. Denote by $U(\boldsymbol{b}^*)$ a preference ordering obtained under no budget constraint and denote by $U(\boldsymbol{b})$ a constrained preference ordering obtained under the budget constraint $\boldsymbol{b}$. Their procedure may be illustrated for the situation with one product feature, Z_1, and price, P, and linar functions for the two preferences. Possible functional forms would be $U(\boldsymbol{b}^*) = \alpha_0 + \alpha_1 Z_1 + \alpha_2 P + \varepsilon \boldsymbol{b}^*$; and $U(\boldsymbol{b}) = \beta_0 + \beta_1 Z_1 + \beta_2 P + \varepsilon \boldsymbol{b}$. The difference equation becomes $U(\boldsymbol{b}) - U(\boldsymbol{b}^*) = (\beta_0 - \alpha_0) + (\beta_1 - \alpha_1)Z_1 + (\beta_2 - \alpha_2)P + (\varepsilon \boldsymbol{b} - \varepsilon \boldsymbol{b}^*)$. In this case, one need only estimate $U(\boldsymbol{b}^*)$ and the difference, $U(\boldsymbol{b}) - U(\boldsymbol{b}^*)$ constraining $(\beta_1 - \alpha_1)$ to zero. The main allocative effect of price is then revealed by the estimate of $(\beta_2 - \alpha_2)$. The signaling effect is reflected in the estimate of α_2. The authors had implemented this method for a set data on laptop computers with face-valid results.

7.5. *Summary*

This section delved into some methods for measuring the effects of price. This review should be of interest to model builders to ensure that theoretical constructs are being appropriately translated at the empirical level of inquiry. Undoubtedly, greater correspondence will increase the usefulness of normative models. Also, certain measurement issues such as measurement of price-response functions and reference prices still remain.

8. Directions for future research

This chapter attempts to bring together a set of diverse efforts in the recent literature on the modeling of price decisions and related questions in marketing. There has been an impressive growth in the array of topics investigated in the literature. Various trends in the development of pricing models should be evident from the foregoing review. First, one trend has been to develop theoretical models to describe observed pricing strategies in the marketplace and to derive conditions under which certain strategies are optimal. This trend is clearly evident when one considers the area of dynamic pricing models. Another trend is an attempt to develop pricing models in which certain aspects of consumer behavior (e.g. asymmetric response to price increases versus price decreases) are incorporated. This development is quite recent and does offer a large potential. A third dominant direction is the use of game-theoretic models for developing equilibrium pricing strategies. (We have reviewed only a small subset of this research to reduce the potential overlap with other chapters in this volume, as noted earlier.)

A few observations on the substantive and other findings may be appropriate. Briefly, it is clear that the simple rule of optimal pricing for a monopolist requires significant modifications as we incorporate competitive effects, carryover effects, quality effects, consumer search behavior, etc. Next, the literature seems to have delved deeply into the conditions under which skimming (or penetration) price policies are optimal for a new product. Third, attempts have been made to study the problem of pricing multiple products; in this endeavor, the focus has been on the demand interdependencies and not as much attention has been paid to the supply or cost sides. Fourth, there seems to be a general acceptance of the use of reservation price in the derivation of a demand model. While this concept appears in several ways (e.g. reference price, expected price, just price, etc.), no consensus has yet emerged as to how consumers (individuals) form these prices for products, particularly for new products. Finally, the research effort seems to delve deeply into narrower substantive topics rather than extend the domain of pricing research to tackle hitherto relatively less explored areas; this situation is troublesome when one considers the overriding importance of the price variable in the marketing mix for a product.

These summary comments lead naturally to a discussion of various gaps in the literature and future research directions. It is hoped that the ensuing discussion will foster more fruitful research on pricing. When one examines the schema shown in Table 11.1 in light of the literature reviewed in this chapter, it becomes evident that marketing research in pricing is in its early stages. In the opinion of this author, fruitful research opportunities exist in several areas. These include an extensive study on how pricing decisions are made in practice, methodologies to validate the results of normative pricing models, pricing models that incorporate emerging knowledge of individual-level choice behavior, pricing models for maximizing or meeting objectives other than profits, pricing models that integrate channel behavior, newer ways of determining optimal bundle prices, pricing under demand uncertainty, descriptive and normative models of competitive price reactions, and a miscellany of substantive issues. We will elaborate on each of these.

8.1. Descriptive studies on pricing practices

Benefits of knowing more about the decision processes of how industry managers go about determining (and changing) prices for their products [see Hulbert, 1981] are quite apparent. However, issues such as discount structures, variation of prices across different levels of channels, and reactions to competitive price-moves do call for further empirical investigation; such studies could also determine the degree to which current economic theories or models available in the literature are being employed by practitioners and the role of market forces in setting prices of products. These studies should also attempt to look at issues of price-setting for one product as well as a line of related products and at various levels of the distribution channel;

attention also has to be paid to the problems and procedures relating to the implementation of price policies. A good description of practice should lead to improved theoretical work. This could be accomplished by undertaking a comprehensive study of price-setting in selected industries; such a study could determine which of the various pricing strategies identified by Tellis [1986] are in use and the business conditions under which each is being used.

8.2. *Methodologies for validation*

Building upon a descriptive study, it may be feasible to identify the degree to which observed business situations depart from the assumptions made in various normative models. Accordingly, one may be able to find new ways of testing the predictions made from optimal models of observed firm behavior. This approach also may enable an assessment of the costs and benefits of departure from normative prescriptions.

8.3. *Incorporating knowledge of consumer behavior*

As is evident from this review, the construct of maximizing consumer surplus has been the overriding rule for consumer behavior in the determination of optimal prices. The growing body of consumer research reveals that actual behavior significantly departs from such 'rational' considerations. For example, not only is choice behavior probabilistic, but various noncompensatory models are relevant in describing consumer choice. (See Table 11.1 for a range of alternatives for sources of heterogeneity and choice rules.) It is, therefore, important to develop pricing models that could incorporate such departures. Further, as behavioral research explores the process of formation of reference prices, optimal pricing models should be developed to incorporate that knowledge.

8.4. *Objectives other than profit*

Opportunities exist to extend the work of Saghafi [1988] in determining optimal or near-optimal pricing policies when businesses pursue objectives other than maximizing profit (see Table 11.1). See Diamantopoulos [1991] for an integrative essay on pricing that uses industrial organization theory. In this regard, concern for the environment may become significant in the future.

8.5. *Integration of channel behavior*

The interdependence of a channel intermediary's pricing strategies and the firm's own strategies raises several issues that need further study. For example, how should the retailer decide on the optimal number of weeks of forward buying when the manufacturer offers a price promotion and what should the retailer's policy be in passing on the price reduction to consumers? Vilcassim & Chintagunta [1992] develop a normative model for tackling these questions and demonstrate how they can be empirically analyzed using the logit framework. These are but a small number of research questions with regard to channels.

8.6. Pricing bundles

The research reviewed in this chapter on the problem of deciding optimal prices for bundles of products utilizes the distribution of reservation prices for individual items in the bundle. These normative models begin with a predefined set of items to be 'bundled'. But, when one looks at the problem from a multiattribute perspective, a model can be constructed that relates the reservation price of the bundle to interactions among the attributes of the items in the bundle using such approaches as the balance model for subsets [Farquhar & Rao, 1976]. Such a model can be used in identifying optimal characteristics of the bundle and its price so as to maximize the contribution to the firm.

8.7. Pricing under demand uncertainty

A limited amount of research in pricing exists in the literature that considers various aspects of demand uncertainty (e.g. random coefficients in a demand model, stochastic error term, probabilistic choice behavior and the like). While Jagpal & Brick [1982] developed a general model for marketing-mix decision under conditions of uncertainty, the field seems quite open for further investigations. The advantages of considering demand uncertainty by a monopolist in high-tech markets are explored by Raman and Chatterjee [1992].

8.8. Models of competitive reactions

Various research issues remain to be investigated in the area of competitive pricing. These questions include: When would a competitor react to a price change by a rival firm? How large a price change will be implemented by a competitor in reaction to a price change by a rival? What would the reactions be when there is more than one rival in the industry? What roles to various factors (e.g. management culture, inflation, profit expectations) play in the competitive pricing behavior? What are the dynamics of competitive behavior? Is the reaction to a rival's price change restricted to change only in price or other marketing-mix tools utilized by a firm? Existing techniques of analysis (e.g. game theory, semi-Markov chains, reaction functions) may naturally be utilized in this research effort. The friction model developed by DeSarbo, Rao, Steckel, Wind & Colombo [1987] may be extendable to this general research problem. Further, the recent work by Slade [1989, 1992] that analyzes price wars in the gasoline market using the equilibrium analysis of supergames promises to be a productive direction for the analysis of competitive reactions. Also, the descriptive work of Urbany & Dickson [1991] should provide ways of designing behavioral experiments in this area. Further, model validation may not present much difficulty since data on competitive price movements are generally in the public domain or are easily collected with the help of conjoint-type experiments.

8.9. Miscellaneous substantive issues

Opportunities exist for developing pricing models that cover several substantive situations such as warranties, services, high-technology products and international markets. Further, there is a clear need to incorporate the effects of macroeconomic factors such as inflation into the optimal pricing models.

References

Adams, W.J., and J.L. Yellen (1976). Commodity bundling and the burden of monopoly. *Quart. J. Econom.* 90 (August), 475–498.

Allenby, G.M. (1989). A unified approach to identifying, estimation and testing demand structures with aggregate scanner data. *Marketing Sci. 8* (Summer), 265–280.

Bass, F.M. (1980). The relationship between diffusion rates, experience curves, and demand elasticities for consumer durable technological innovations. *J. Business* 53 (July), S51–S67.

Bayus, B.L. (1992). The dynamic pricing of next generation consumer durables. *Marketing Sci.* 11(3), 251–265.

Cameron, T.A., and M.D. James (1987). Estimating willingness to pay from survey data: An alternative pre-test-market evaluation procedure. *J. Marketing Res.* 24 (November), 389–395.

Chintagunta, P., V.R. Rao and N.J. Vilcassim (forthcoming). Equilibrium pricing and advertising strategies for nondurable experience products in a dynamic duopoly. *Managerial Decision Econom.*

Cready, W.M. (1991). Premium bundling. *Econom. Inquiry*, 29 (January), 173–179.

Curry, D.J., and P.C. Riesz (1988). Prices and price/quality relationships: A longitudinal analysis. *J. Marketing*, 52 (January), 36–50.

Dash, M. (1982). Pricing and advertising policies for an innovation, Ph.D. Dissertation, New York University.

DeSarbo, W.S., V.R. Rao., J.H. Steckel., J. Wind., and R. Colombo (1987). A friction model for describing and forecasting price changes. *Marketing Sci.* 6(4), 299–319.

DeVinney, T. (ed.) (1988). *Issues in Pricing: Theory and Research.* Lexington Books, Lexington, MA.

Dhebar, A., and S.S. Oren (1985). Optimal dynamic pricing for expanding networks, *Marketing Sci.* 4(4), 336–351.

Diamantopoulos, A. (1991). Pricing: Theory and evidence – A literature review, in M.J. Baker, (ed.), *Perspectives on Marketing Management*, Wiley, London, 1, 63–192.

Dobson, G., and S. Kalish (1988). Pricing and positioning a product line. *Marketing Sci.* 7(2), 107–125.

Dockner, E., and S. Jorgensen (1988). Optimal pricing strategies for new products in dynamic oligopolies. *Marketing Sci.* 7(4), 315–334.

Dolan, R.J. (1987). Quantity discounts, managerial issues and research opportunities. *Marketing Sci.* 6 (Winter), 1–22.

Dolan, R.J., and A.P. Jeuland (1981). Experiences curves and dynamic demand models: implications for optimal pricing strategies. *J. Marketing*, 45 (Winter), 52–73.

Eliashberg, J., and A.P. Jeuland (1986). The impact of competitive entry in a developing market upon dynamic pricing strategies. *Marketing Sci.* 5(1), 20–36.

Farquhar, P., and V.R. Rao (1976). A balance model for evaluating subsets of multiattributed items. *Management Sci.* 22 (January), 528–539.

Gautschi, D.A., and V.R. Rao (1990). A methodology for specification and aggregation in product concept testing. In A. De Fontenay, M.H. Shugard and D.S. Sibley (eds.), *Telecommunications Demand Modelling: An Integrated View*, North-Holland, Amsterdam, 37–63.

Gerstner, E., and D. Holthausen (1986). Profitable pricing when market segments overlap. *Marketing Sci.* 5(1), 55–69.

Grover, R., and V.R Rao (1988). Inferring competitive market structure based on a model of interpurchase intervals. *Intern. J. Res. Marketing*, 5 (December), 55–72.

Gurumurthy, K., and J.D.C. Little (1987). A pricing model based on perception theories and its testing on scanner panel data. Working Paper, Sloan School of Management, MIT, Cambridge, MA, July.
Hanson, W., and R.K. Martin (1990). Optimal bundle pricing. *Management Sci.* 36(2), 155–174.
Horsky, D. (1990). A diffusion model incorporating product benefits, price, income and information. *Marketing Sci.* 9(4), 342–365.
Hulbert, J. (1981). Descriptive models of marketing decisions. in R.L. Schultz and A.A. Zoltners (eds.), *Marketing Decision Models*, North-Holland, New York, 19–54.
Jagpal, H.S., and I.E. Brick (1982). The marketing-mix decision under uncertainty. *Marketing Sci.* 1 (Winter), 79–92.
Jeuland, A.P., and R.J. Dolan (1982). An aspect of new product planning: dynamic pricing. In A.A. Zoltners (ed.), *Marketing Planning Models*, TIMS Studies in the Management Sciences, 18, North-Holland, New York, 1–21.
Juhl, H.J., and K. Kristensen (1989). Multiproduct pricing: A microeconomic simplification. *Intern. J. Res. Marketing* 6(3), 175–182.
Kalish, S. (1983). Monopolist pricing with dynamic demand and production costs. *Marketing Sci.* 2(2), 135–160.
Kalish, S. (1985). A new product adoption model with price, advertising, and uncertainty. *Management Sci.* 31(12), 1569–1585.
Kalwani, M.U., and C.K. Yim (1992). Consumer price and promotion expectations: An experimental study. *J. Marketing Res.* 29 (February), 90–100.
Kalwani, M.U., C.K. Yim., N.J. Rinne and Y. Sugita (1990). A price expectations model of customer brand choice. *J. Marketing Res.* 27 (August), 251–262.
Kamakura, W.A., B.T. Ratchford and J. Agarwal (1988). Measuring market efficiency and welfare loss. *J. Consumer Res.* 15 (December), 289–302.
Kohli, R., and V. Mahahan (1991). A reservation-price model for optimal pricing of multiattribute products in conjoint analysis. *J. Marketing Res.* 28 (August), 347–354.
Kolodinsky, J. (1990). Time as a direct source of utility: The case of price information search for groceries. *J. Consumer Affairs* 24(1), 89–109.
Lal, R., and C. Matutes (1989). Price competition in multimarket duopolies. *J. Econom.* 20(4), 516–537.
Lichtenstein, D.R., and S. Burton (1989). The relationship between perceived and objective price quality. *J. Marketing Res.* 26 (November), 429–443.
Little, J.D.C., and J.F. Shapiro (1980). A theory of pricing non-featured products in supermarkets. *J. Business*, 53 (July), S199–S209.
Mahajan, V., P.E. Green and S. Goldberg (1982). A conjoint model for measuring self- and cross-price/demand relationships. *J. Marketing Res.* 19 (August), 334–342.
Mahajan, V., and E. Muller (1991). Pricing and diffusion of primary and contingent products. *Technol. Forecasting Social Change*, 39 (May), 291–307.
Monroe, K.B. (1990). *Pricing: Making Profitable Decisions, 2nd edition*, McGraw-Hill, New York.
Moorthy, K.S. (1984). Market segmentation, self selection and product line design. *Marketing Sci.* 3, 262–282.
Moorthy, K.S. (1988). Consumer expectations and pricing of durables. In T. DeVinney (ed.), *Issues in Pricing: Theory and Research*, Lexington Books, Lexington, MA, 99–114.
Nagle, T. (1987). *The Strategy and Tactics of Pricing.* Prentice-Hall, Englewood Cliffs, NJ.
Narasimhan, C. (1989). Incorporating consumer price expectations in diffusion models. *Marketing Sci.* 8(4), 343–357.
Nascimento, F.M. (1987). Studies in strategic pricing decisions, Ph.D. Dissertation, Columbia University, New York.
Nascimento, F.M., and W.R. Vanhonacker (1988). Optimal strategic pricing of reproducible consumer products. *Management Sci.* 34(8), 1568–1578.
Oren, S., S.A., Smith, and R. Wilson (1984). Pricing a product line. *J. Business* 57 (January), 2, S73–S100.
Padmanabhan, V., and F.M. Bass (forthcoming). Optimal pricing of successive generations of product advances. *Intern. J. Res. Marketing.*
Parker, P. (1992). Pricing strategies in markets with dynamic elasticities. *Marketing Lett.* 3(3), 227–237.

Petroshius, S.M., and K.B. Monroe (1987). Effect of product-line pricing characteristics on product evaluations, *J. Consumer Res.* 13 (March), 511–519.

Putler, D.S. (1992). Incorporating reference price effects into a theory of consumer choice. *Marketing Sci.* 11(3), 287–309.

Raman, K., and R. Chatterjee (1992). Optimal monopolist pricing in uncertain markets with demand and cost dynamics. Working paper, University of Florida, Gainesville, FL (September).

Rao, A.R. (1986). The impact of product familiarity on the price-perceived quality relationship. Ph.D. Dissertation, Virginia Polytechnic Institute and State University.

Rao, A.R., and K.B. Monroe (1989). The effects of price, brand name, and store name on buyers' perceptions of product quality: An integrative review. *J. Marketing Res.* 26 (August), 351–357.

Rao, R.C., and F.M. Bass (1985). Competition, strategy, and price dynamics: A theoretical and empirical investigation. *J. Marketing Res.* 22 (August), 283–296.

Rao, V.R. (1984). Pricing research in marketing: The state of the art. *J. Business* 57 (1, Pt. 2), S39–S60.

Ratchford, B.T. (1980). The value of information for selected appliances. *J. Marketing Res.* 17(1), 14–25.

Reibstein, D.J., and H. Gatignon (1984). Optimal product line pricing: The influence of elasticities and cross-elasticities. *J. Marketing Res.* 21 (August), 259–267.

Robinson, B., and C. Lakhani (1975). Dynamic pricing models for new product pricing, *Management Sci.* 21 (June), 1113–1122.

Roy, A. (1990). Optimal pricing with demand feedback in a hierarchical market. Ph.D. Dissertation, University of California, Los Angeles.

Saghafi, M.M. (1988). Optimal pricing to maximize profits and achieve market-share targets for single-product and multiproduct companies. In T. DeVinney (ed.), *Issues in Pricing: Theory and Research*, Lexington Books, Lexington, MA, 239–253.

Salop, S., and J. Stiglitz (1977). Bargains and ripoffs: A model of monopolistically competitive price dispersion. *Rev. Econom. Studies* 44(3), 493–510.

Schmalensee, R. (1984). Gaussian demand and commodity bundling. *J. Business* 57 (January), Part 2, S211–S230.

Simon, H. (1989). *Pricing Management*, North-Holland, Amsterdam.

Slade, M.E. (1989). Price wars in price-setting supergames. *Econometrica* 56 (August), 295–310.

Slade, M.E. (1992). Vancouver's gasoline price-wars: An empirical exercise in uncovering supergame strategies. *Rev. Econom. Studies*, 59(2), 257–276.

Smith, S.A. (1986). New product pricing in quality sensitive markets. *Marketing Sci.* 5(1), 70–87.

Stigler, G. (1961). Economics of information. *J. Political Economy* 69, 213–225.

Tellis, G.J. (1986). Beyond the many faces of price: An integration of pricing strategies. *J. Marketing* 50 (October), 146–160.

Tellis, G.J. (1988). The price elasticity of selective demand: A meta-analysis of econometric models of sales. *J. Marketing Res.* 25 (November), 331–341.

Tellis, G.J., and B. Wernerfelt (1987). Competitive price and quality under asymmetric information. *Marketing Sci.* 6(3), 240–253.

Thaler, R. (1985). Mental accounting and consumer choice. *Marketing Sci.* 4(3), 199–214.

Urbany, J.E. (1986). An experimental examination of the economics of information. *J. Consumer Res.* 13 (September), 257–271.

Urbany, J.E., W.O. Bearden and D.C. Weilbaker (1988). The effect of plausible and exaggerated reference prices on consumer perceptions and price search. *J. Consumer Res.* 15 (June), 95–110.

Urbany, J.E. and P.R. Dickson (1990). Consumer knowledge of normal prices: An exploratory study and framework. Report #90–112, Marketing Science Institute.

Urbany, J.E., and P.R. Dickson (1991). Competitive price-cutting momentum and pricing reactions. *Marketing Lett.* 2 (November), 393–402.

Venkatesh, R., and V. Mahajan (forthcoming). A probabilistic approach to pricing a bundle of products or services. *J. Marketing Res.*

Vilcassim, N.J., and P.K. Chintagunta (1992). Investigating retailer pricing strategies from household scanner panel data. Working Paper, Cornell University, Ithaca, NY, February.

Wilde, L.L., and A. Schwartz (1979). Equilibrium comparison shopping. *Rev. Econom. Studies* 46(3), 543–554.

Winer, R.S. (1985). A price vector model of demand for consumer durables: Preliminary developments. *Marketing Sci.* 4 (Winter), 74–90.
Winer, R.S. (1986). A reference price model of brand choice for frequently purchased products. *J. Consumer Res.* 13 (September), 250–256.
Winer, R.S. (1988). Behavioral perspective on pricing: Buyers' subjective perceptions of price revisited. In T. DeVinney (ed.), *Issues in Pricing: Theory and Research*, Lexington Books, Lexington, MA, 35–57.
Wruck, E.G. (1989). Dynamic pricing implications of uncertain demand. Ph.D. Dissertation, Cornell University, Ithaca, NY.
Yim, C.K. (1989). Price expectations and optimal sales promotion policies. Ph.D. Dissertation, Purdue University, Lafayette, IN.
Yoo, P.H. (1986). Dynamic pricing for new consumer durables. Ph.D. Dissertation, Harvard University, Cambridge, MA.
Yoo, P.H., R.J. Dolan and V.K. Rangan (1987). Dynamic pricing strategy for new consumer durables. *Z. Betriebwirtschaft* 57 (October), 1024–1043.
Zeithaml, V.A. (1988). Consumer perceptions of price, quality, and value: A means–end model and synthesis of evidence. *J. Marketing* 52 (July), 2–22.

J. Eliashberg and G.L. Lilien, Eds., *Handbooks in OR & MS, Vol. 5*

Chapter 12

Sales Promotion Models*

Robert C. Blattberg

Kellogg Graduate School of Management, Northwestern University, Evanston, IL, USA

Scott A. Neslin

Amos Tuck School of Business Administration, Dartmouth College, Hanover, NH, USA

1. Introduction

In the last ten years sales promotion has become a major research topic for both academics and practitioners. In packaged-goods industries, both AC Nielsen and Information Resources now offer procedures to measure the impact of sales promotions on retailer sales. On the academic side numerous articles have been written discussing the theory and measurement of promotions. As a bridge between academics and practitioners, the Marketing Science Institute has sponsored four special-interest conferences on sales promotion. The time is therefore opportune to summarize the numerous models now available in the area of sales promotions. The purpose of this chapter is to fulfill that need. In this introductory section, we offer a brief history of promotion modeling, present an overview of relevant data and methodologies, and define the major types of promotion. We then outline the rest of the paper.

1.1. Early promotional models

The earlies attempts to measure promotional effects were stochastic brand-choice models in which the 'baseline' (normal sales in the absence of promotions) was determined from a simple stochastic model, usually a Markov model. For example, Hinkle [1964] developed a Markov model which incorporated promotional effects into the switching matrix, and was able to relate choice probabilities to promotional activity [see also Herniter & McGee, 1961; Maffai, 1960]. Kuehn & Rohloff [1967] developed a path-breaking article in which they used a linear learning model to determine baseline sales and then contrasted the actual sales to the stochastic model's prediction to estimate the impact of promotions. Later research along

*The authors express their appreciation to Josh Eliashberg, Gary Lilien, and two anonymous reviewers for very helpful comments and suggestions on earlier drafts of this paper.

these lines included Lilien [1974] which added a price component to the linear learning model. Rao & Thomas [1973] developed an optimization model which incorporated many of the phenomena now being studied in the promotion literature such as the pre-promotion dip, the trough after the deal, and deal wearout caused by the frequency of promotions. Strang [1975] investigated the relationship between sales promotion and the brand franchise. He found an association between increased sales promotion and a declining franchise.[1] An important descriptive study in the 1970s was conducted by Chevalier & Curhan [1976], who analyzed the pass-through of trade promotions at the retail level. This pioneering article revealed the need to consider the role of the retailer in sales promotion.

This early literature provided the antecedents to much of the current work on promotions but since the mid-1980s there has been a plethora of articles on the subject. Two of the major reasons for this growth are the availability of scanner data and the increasing importance of the promotion budget in the marketing mix.

1.2. An overview of data and methodologies

There are two basic types of data used to analyze sales promotions: household panel data and sales-per-period data. The unit of analysis for household data is the purchase occasion, while for sales-per-period data it is weekly or perhaps monthly sales. Household data consist of purchase histories for a panel of households. These data have traditionally been collected using diaries or surveys, but in the packaged-good area, they are now collected using supermarket scanner equipment. The scanners link a household's purchase at the checkout counter with an ID number for that household stored on a computer file. Over time, a purchase history is compiled. The benefits of household data are the ability to study phenomena such as brand-loyalty or repeat purchasing, and the potential to segment the market by demographic characteristics. Sales-per-period data represent retail sales or factory shipments pertaining to a market area, an account, or even specific stores. Such data are directly relevant to managers because managers need to track weekly or monthly sales. They also are more readily available than household data.

Figure 12.1 lists modeling approaches used to analyze sales promotions. A fundamental distinction can be made between descriptive and prescriptive models. Descriptive models *measure* the effects of sales promotion. Prescriptive models utilize a descriptive model to make a *normative recommendation* on a managerial course of action. For example, a descriptive model is needed to measure the effect of a retail price cut on brand sales; a prescriptive model would be used to recommend the specific price cut the retailer should implement.

Among descriptive models, regression and time-series analysis employ sales-per-period data, whereas choice and purchase incidence models employ household data. Among prescriptive models, decision calculus [Little, 1970] emphasizes manage-

[1]An interesting issue in interpreting this research is whether sales promotion causes the brand to decline, or whether managers use sales promotion to attempt to rescue a declining brand.

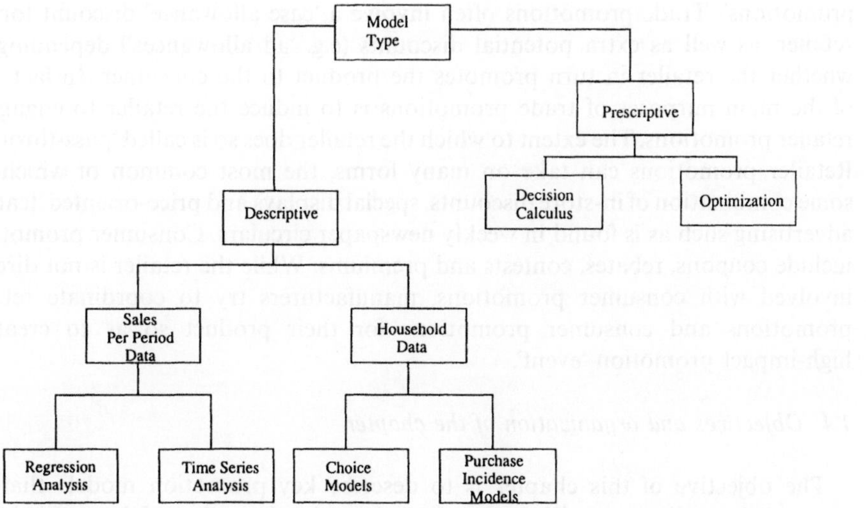

Fig. 12.1. Types of models, data, and methodologies for analyzing sales promotion.

ment involvement in the development of the descriptive model, and typically evaluates a limited set of alternatives. Optimization models take a descriptive model, embed it within a profit function, and use calculus or mathematical programming to derive the optimal course of action.

1.3. The major types of sales promotion

Figure 12.2 portrays the major types of sales promotion. There are three 'actors': manufacturers, retailers and consumers. Promotions developed by the manufacturer and targeted at retailers are called 'trade promotions'. Promotions developed by the manufacturer and targeted at consumers are called 'consumer promotions'. Promotions developed by the retailer and targeted at consumers are called 'retailer

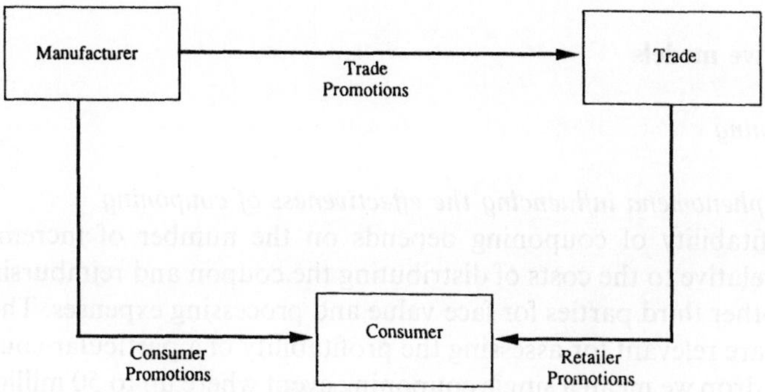

Fig. 12.2. Major types of sales promotion.

promotions'. Trade promotions often involve a 'case allowance' discount for the retailer, as well as extra potential discounts (e.g. 'ad allowances') depending on whether the retailer in turn promotes the product to the consumer. In fact, one of the main purposes of trade promotions is to induce the retailer to engage in retailer promotions. The extent to which the retailer does so is called 'pass-through'. Retailer promotions can take on many forms, the most common of which are some combination of in-store discounts, special displays and price-oriented 'feature' advertising such as is found in weekly newspaper circulars. Consumer promotions include coupons, rebates, contests and premiums. While the retailer is not directly involved with consumer promotions, manufacturers try to coordinate retailer promotions and consumer promotions for their product so as to create a high-impact promotion 'event'.

1.4. Objectives and organization of the chapter

The objective of this chapter is to describe key promotion models that are currently in the literature. We have written from the viewpoints of the sophisticated practitioner who needs to develop a model, and the researcher who wishes to contribute to the field. Because of space limitations we cannot provide a description of all of the models but will attempt to describe key types of models covering the breadth of the promotion literature. We cover the most important phenomena and models relevant to couponing, retailer promotions and trade promotions.

Section 2 covers descriptive models, and is organized in subsections devoted to coupons, trade promotions and retailer promotions. The general format of each subsection is to begin with a discussion of the phenomena that determine the overall impact or profitability of the particular promotion. We then discuss attempts to model these phenomena. Section 3 covers prescriptive models. We describe a selection of models that can be applied to couponing, trade promotions and retailer promotions. Much of the research to date has been descriptive modeling and has been driven by the availability of data. As a result, the models we review may not cover all the managerial issues. In summarizing the chapter in Section 4, we will compare the work that has been done with the work that needs to be done.

2. Descriptive models

2.1. Couponing

2.1.1. Key phenomena influencing the effectiveness of couponing

The profitability of couponing depends on the number of incremental sales generated relative to the costs of distributing the coupon and reimbursing retailers as well as other third parties for face value and processing expenses. The following definitions are relevant for assessing the profitability of a particular coupon 'drop'. By coupon drop we mean a single couponing event where up to 50 million coupons are distributed at one time using the same vehicle, face value, etc.

If we let

D = number of coupons distributed,
f = face value per coupon,
c = processing cost per coupon,
d = distribution cost per 1000 coupons distributed,
r = percentage of distributed coupons redeemed (redemption rate),
i = incremental sales per redemption generated by the coupon drop,
p = profit margin per unit,
Π = incremental profit generated by the coupon drop,

the profitability of a coupon drop can then be calculated as

$$\Pi = \text{incremental benefits} - \text{incremental costs}$$
$$= D \cdot r \cdot i \cdot p - D \cdot d - D \cdot r \cdot (f + c). \qquad (2.1)$$

The first term represents the profit contribution generated from incremental sales. The quantity $D \cdot r$ represents the number of coupon redemptions, which are then multiplied by incremental unit sales per redemption (i) and profit contribution per unit (p) to yield profit contribution. The second term represents distribution costs. These costs are fixed in that they do not vary as a function of redemption rate. The third term represents redemption costs. The number of redemptions ($D \cdot r$) is multiplied by the variable cost per coupon redemption (face value plus processing costs) to yield these variable costs.

As an example, assume a Sunday free-standing insert coupon drop is implemented using 50 000 000 coupons (D) with a face value (f) of \$0.25. Assume distribution costs (d) are \$8 per thousand and processing cost (c) is \$0.10 per redeemed coupon. Assume also that 3% of the coupons will be redeemed. On the benefits side, assume 50% of redeemed coupons are incremental sales (i) and profit contribution is \$1.00 per unit. The profitability of this coupon drop would be:

$$\Pi = 50\,000\,000 \times 0.03 \times 0.50 \times \$1.00 - 50\,000\,000/1000 \times \$8$$
$$- 50\,000\,000 \times 0.03 \times (\$0.25 + \$0.10)$$
$$= \$750\,000 - \$400\,000 - \$525\,000$$
$$= -\$175\,000.$$

In this case, although the coupon drop generates \$750 000 in incremental profit contribution, incremental costs were \$925 000 and this results in a loss of \$175 000.

From Equation (2.1) and the above calculation, we see that the key phenomena to be modeled are redemption rates and incremental sales. The other quantities are known specifications of the coupon drop (such as number distributed, face value, etc.) that do not have to be modeled. While the above example shows the importance of the magnitude of redemption rates, the timing of those redemptions is also important for budget control. We now review models of both these aspects of coupon redemptions, and then discuss models of incremental sales.

2.1.2. Magnitude of redemption rates

Regression can be used to predict redemption rates for future coupon drops by modeling the historical relationship between redemption rates and various explanatory factors.[2] Three steps in developing these models are: (1) deciding which factors to include, (2) collecting the desired data, and (3) estimating the model. Table 12.1 suggests which explanatory factors should be considered for inclusion in the model. Most of these are self-explanatory but three warrant discussion: size of the coupon drop, brand-loyalty, and recency of previous coupon drops. As size of the drop increases, there are relatively more coupons available compared to the limited number of coupon users. This decreases the percentage of coupons that are redeemed. The assumed positive effect of brand-loyalty reflects the finding that a brand's loyal customers are more likely than non-loyal customers to redeem its coupons [e.g. Bawa and Shoemaker, 1987]. The negative effect hypothesized for recency of previous drop is because coupons for the second of two closely bunched coupon drops might either be ignored or lost before they are used.

While Table 12.1 presents a comprehensive list of potential variables to include in a redemptions model, lack of available data (e.g. for competitive activity) often constrains redemption models to a subset of these factors. This has important implications for the forecast accuracy of these models.

The general redemption model can be specified as:

$$r_i = f(\boldsymbol{M}_i, \mathrm{FV}_i, \boldsymbol{C}_i, \boldsymbol{B}_i, \boldsymbol{X}_i) \tag{2.2}$$

where

r_i = redemption rate for the ith coupon drop,
$\boldsymbol{M}_i$ = vector of distribution vehicle variables for the ith coupon drop,
FV_i = face-value measure for the ith coupon drop,
$\boldsymbol{C}_i$ = vector of other coupon characteristics for the ith coupon drop,
$\boldsymbol{B}_i$ = vector of brand characteristics for the ith coupon drop,
$\boldsymbol{X}_i$ = vector of other variables including region of the country.

The critical issues in modeling redemption rates are: (1) functional form to use for the redemption-rate model, (2) whether to develop a separate model for each type of distribution vehicle (e.g. free-standing insert, direct mail, etc.) (3) how to operationalize face-value discount, (4) what variables to include in the model, and (5) model-specificity by brand or region.

Regarding functional form, an important consideration is that redemption rates by definition must be between zero and one. Using a linear model potentially

[2]Redemption rates vary by distribution vehicle and product category. They usually range between 0 and 10%, except for in-pack or on-pack coupons, where redemption rates are higher [see Nielsen Clearing House, 1990].

Table 12.1
Potential factors to include in redemption-rate forecasting models

Factor	Hypothesized relationship to redemption rate
Coupon characteristics	
1. Distribution vehicle	Different across vehicles
2. Region of distribution	Different across regions
3. Size of coupon drop	−
4. Purchase requirements	−
5. Absolute face value	+
6. Face value relative to price	+
7. Recency of previous coupon drop	−
8. Overlay (accompanying contest, premium, etc.)	+
9. Attractiveness of design	+
10. Expiration date	−
Brand characteristics	
11. Brand market-share	+
12. Brand distribution	+
13. Lateness in product life-cycle	−
14. Brand-loyalty	+
15. Brand image	+
Other factors	
16. Competitive couponing	−
17. Brand advertising	+
18. Retailer promotions	+
19. Seasonality	Depends on product and season
20. Product-class penetration	+

Sources: Factors 1, 3, 4, 5, 6, 12, 15, 16, 17 and 18 are discussed in Ward & Davis [1978]. Factors 1, 2, 3, 4, 5, 6, 9, 11, 12, 13, 14, 15, 16, 17, 18, 19 and 20 are discussed in Reibstein & Traver [1982]. Factor 10 is discussed in Neslin Clearing House [1990]. Also see Blattberg & Neslin [1990, pp. 293–294].

results in predictions outside this range. It is possible to redefine the dependent variable using the logit transformation, $\ln(r_i/(1-r_i))$, or any other transformation that serves to constrain predicted redemption rates between zero and one.

Distribution vehicle is relatively easy to add to the model through dummy variables and usually explains a significant portion of variance in redemption rates. However, the more difficult question is whether to use a separate model for each vehicle. The justification for this is that variables such as face value may have a very different effect by vehicle. For example, if redemption rates for FSI (free-standing insert) coupons are much more sensitive to face value than in-pack or on-pack coupons, then a separate model would need to be built for each vehicle type.

Face value can be operationalized by either the absolute or relative savings. The advantage of relative savings is that a 10-cent coupon on a 10-dollar item is much less appealing to consumers than a 10-cent coupon on a 25-cent item. However, both save the consumer 10 cents. Which measure is a better predictor, absolute or relative savings, is not known and needs to be investigated thoroughly before settling on a final model. It is also possible to justify including both measures in a model. Absolute savings might measure a type of 'acquisition utility' while relative savings might represent 'transaction utility' [Thaler, 1985].

Distribution vehicle and face value should be included in any redemption model. They are managerially relevant and tend to have high predictive ability. Expiration date has also become a more important issue recently, and has been shown to have an important effect on redemption rates and timing, as well as incremental sales [Nielsen Clearing House, 1990; Little, 1991]. As Table 12.1 indicates, there are a host of other variables that could also be included in redemption-rate models. For example, competitive factors may be important yet they are very difficult to incorporate because data are difficult to obtain. For this reason, most coupon-redemption models do not include competitive activity. The question of whether it is worthwhile to undertake the additional effort needed to include more variables in the model can be resolved by testing the base model in terms of forecasting ability. If the base-case model is accurate enough, there is no need to obtain additional data.

A challenging estimation problem is the specificity of the model in terms of brand and region. One's first instinct is to develop brand-specific, region-specific models so as to avoid aggregation bias [Blattberg & Neslin, 1990, p. 183; Theil, 1971, pp. 556–567]. However, there are rarely enough data for a specific brand in a specific region to fit the model. If data are aggregated across regions and brands, one should include area and brand dummy variables to pick up at least some of the variation due to regional and brand differences.

Reibstein & Traver [1982] developed a redemption model for a single brand across regions. A total of 140 coupon drops were available for analysis. The following variables were included in the model:

$$X_{ij} = \begin{cases} 1 & \text{if coupon vehicle } i \text{ was used for coupon drop } j, \\ 0 & \text{otherwise,} \end{cases}$$

$i = 1$ for magazine on-page,
$i = 2$ for magazine pop-up,
$i = 3$ for Sunday supplement,
$i = 4$ for free-standing insert,
$i = 5$ for direct mail,
$i = 6$ for in-package.

One vehicle, run-of-press newspaper, was not given its own dummy variable, so the coefficients for the included vehicle dummy variables represent increases or decreases in redemption rate relative to ROP newspaper.

X_{7j} = coupon face-value in cents for drop j, normalized so that the mean is 0;[3]

X_{8j} = 'discount ratio' of coupon value to brand price for drop j, normalized so that the mean is 0;

[3]Variables X_7 through X_{10} are normalized so as to facilitate interpretation of the regression coefficients.

X_{9j} = size of coupon drop j, operationalized as the square root of the reciprocal of number of coupons distributed per household, normalized so that the mean is 0. Given this operationalization, larger values of X_{9j} correspond to smaller coupon drops;

$X_{10,j}$ = market share for the brand in the region where drop j was distributed, normalized so that the mean is 0;

Y_j = redemption rate achieved by drop j, expressed as a percentage.

The estimated model was

$$Y_j = 5.039 + 1.151X_{1j} + 8.198X_{2j} + 2.102X_{3j} + 7.415X_{4j} + 10.05X_{5j} + 36.26X_{6j} + 0.1939X_{7j} + 20.68X_{8j} - 1.072X_{9j} + 0.02464X_{10,j} \quad (2.3)$$

The R^2 for the model was 0.919 and all variables were significant at the 0.01 level except for discount ratio (X_{8j}) which was significant at the 0.10 level, and magazine on-page (X_{1j}) which was not significant at the 0.10 level.

The model predicts that a newspaper coupon using average face value, average discount ratio, average distribution size, and in a region where the brand achieves average market share, would achieve a 5.039% redemption rate. Variables X_{1j}–X_{6j} show how different vehicles increase the redemption rate. For example, a direct-mail coupon would improve redemption rate to 5.039 + 10.05 = 15.09%.[4]

The coefficients for absolute face value and the ratio of face value to price are both significantly positive, suggesting that consumers take into account both the absolute and percentage savings when using coupons. Size of the coupon drop has the hypothesized negative effect (recall that larger value of X_{9j} implies smaller coupon drops, so a positive sign means a negative effect of drop size). The coefficient for market share is positive as expected although the effect does not seem to be large for this brand: An increase of 10 share points over average market share only increases redemption rate of 0.25 percentage points (10 × 0.02464).

Reibstein & Traver report a median absolute *percentage* prediction error (|(predicted-actual)|/actual) of 23.5%. On a base of 5% redemption rate, this would amount to a one-percentage-point error in redemption rate. Reibstein & Traver tried a logit transformation to investigate whether functional form would improve prediction, but it did not. This suggests that achievement of highly accurate redemption-rate predictions is a non-trivial task. Given the availability of data, it is difficult to add more variables to the regression model. As an alternative, Blattberg & Hoch [1990] recently report increased accuracy when managerial judgment is combined with regression-based predictions.

[4]These redemption rates are much higher than current levels that are generally published [e.g. Nielsen Clearing House, 1990]. However, the ordering among the vehicles is generally consistent with published redemption rates.

2.1.3. Redemption timing

While redemption rate (r) is the key aspect of redemption included in Equation (2.1), the timing of these redemptions can be important for gauging the timing of sales impact as well as the timing of the firm's financial liability for redeemed coupons. There are two aspects to redemption timing: (1) the timing of actual consumer use of coupons ('redemption at retail') and (2) the timing of firm liability for the value of the coupon. Examples of redemption-at-retail models include Ward & Davis [1978] and Neslin [1990]. Neslin modeled redemptions at retail in time t as a function of coupon distribution in time t and redemptions at retail in time $t-1$ (see Section 2.1.4, Equation 2.5c). His results indicated that redemptions at retail for free-standing-insert coupons are greatest in the first week of distribution, and then decline after the first week [see also Manufacturers Coupon Control Center, 1988].[5]

The timing of redemption liability is very different than the timing of redemption at retail because a number of processing steps follow the initial redemption by the consumer. The retailer receives the coupon from the customer, sends it to a retail clearing house which pays the retailer, and then the retail clearing house sends it to a manufacturer house which sends it to the manufacturer for payment. This results in a redemption-liability pattern that is much more elongated and peaks significantly later than the consumer-redemption curve (see Figure 12.3).

One way to think of coupon-redemption timing models is that they are equivalent to 'survival' models in which the 'life' of the coupon is the time before redemption. Once one conceptualizes coupon-redemption timing models in this form, numerous modeling avenues are available. One is to use exponential regression or related estimation procedures (see Lawless [1982, pp. 282–294] in which the parameter(s)

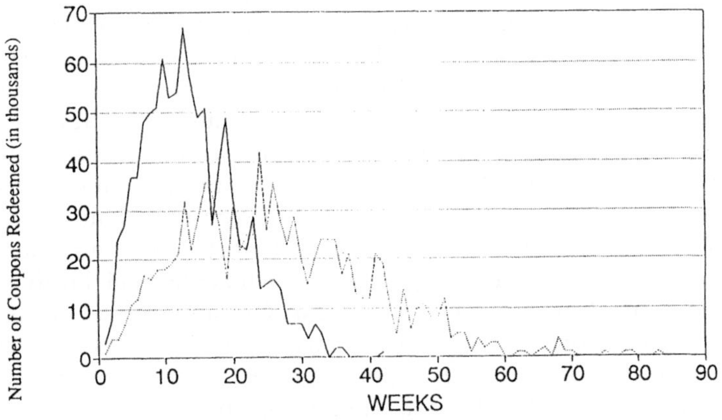

Fig. 12.3. An illustration of the timing of coupon financial liability (—— 12 weeks duration, ······ 24 weeks duration).

[5]Note that in other applications the definition of the starting day for a weekly redemptions database could result in smaller numbers of redemptions in the first 'week' compared to the second 'week'.

of a distribution, e.g. the exponential, are a function of a series of explanatory variables. Let T be the survival time for a given coupon and assume the p.d.f. for T is:

$$f(t|\boldsymbol{x}) = \delta_x^{-1} \exp(-t/\delta_x), \quad t > 0, \tag{2.4}$$

where $\boldsymbol{x}$ is a vector of regressor variables and $\delta_x = \mathrm{E}(T|x)$. Thus, the expected time for the coupon to be redeemed depends upon explanatory variables such as face value and duration. These variables are incorporated into the model through the parameter δ_x. One can model δ_x using various functional forms such as $\delta_x = \exp(\boldsymbol{x}\beta)$ which ensures that $\delta_x > 0$.

One important use of this redemption-timing model is to predict the final redemption rate only a few weeks after the distribution date. The general methodology is to (1) assume a particular redemption pattern based on the coupon vehicle, etc., (2) use the probabilities associated with the assumed distribution to determine what percentage of the ultimately redeemed coupons have been redeemed by this time, (3) determine how many coupons have been redeemed after a given number of weeks, and then (4) extrapolate the known number of redemptions at this point to the total number. No articles have been published that use this approach, but the general concept has been used by a coupon clearing house.

2.2.4. Incremental sales impact of couponing

Regression and logit models have been used to measure incremental sales from couponing. Chapman [1986] used regression analysis and market-level weekly sales data to analyze the results of a couponing experiment for a pizza restaurant. His dependent variable was sales per household in a particular census tract in a particular week. To measure the effect of coupon distribution on sales, he defined a dummy variable to signify the week in which coupons were distributed. He then included this variable plus five lags of it in the model. The lags capture the fact that coupons redeem over an extended period of time, so the sales impact will be evidenced not only in the week of distribution, but in the succeeding weeks as well. Chapman found that the impact was significant in all six weeks. The impact was highest in the week of distribution, and generally declined over the next five weeks.

The Chapman analysis shows that a relatively simple regression model can be used to measure the impact of coupons on sales. The key modeling requirement is to take into account lagged effects of coupon distribution. Note also that the model links coupon distribution directly to sales. There is no separate equation for coupon redemptions.

Neslin [1990] developed a detailed regression model of couponing that traces the translation of coupon distribution to coupon redemptions, and coupon redemptions to brand sales. Neslin's model assumes that redemptions at retail will be highest in the week of distribution, and decrease exponentially in succeeding weeks. To translate these redemptions into sales, his model incorporates two key issues:

- There is a simultaneous relationship between coupon redemptions and sales. Redemptions determine sales in that a certain percentage of coupon redemptions represent incremental sales. However, sales also determine redemptions in that a certain percentage of consumers induced by other causes to buy the product will also bring along the coupons that they might have stored for the brand.

- Coupon redemptions will generate incremental sales to the extent that the brand's coupons are redeemed by consumers who otherwise are not loyal users of the brand. We can quantify this by examining the degree to which market share among *non-coupon-redeemers* changes in weeks of heavy coupon redemption. If market share among non-redeemers decreases drastically in weeks of heavy redemptions, we can conclude that the coupon has drawn a large number of loyal users. The loyals have been taken away from the pool of consumers not redeeming the coupon, resulting in small market share among non-redeemers. If, however, the market share among non-redeemers does not decrease as drastically or even increases, then coupons draw more consumers who otherwise would not have bought the brand, leaving the brand's loyal customers and hence a high market share among those not redeeming the coupon.

To specify his model, Neslin defined the following terms:

MS_t = market share for the brand in time t,
AMS_t = adjusted market share – market share among non-redeemers in week, t,
r_t = percentage of category sales that are coupon redemptions for the brand in time t,
D_t = face value of coupons distributed in time t,
$\varepsilon_t, \varepsilon_t'$ = 'error terms' or other factors influencing sales or redemptions in time t.

The above ideas are then captured in the following multi-equation model:

$$\mathrm{MS}_t = r_t + (1 - r_t)\mathrm{AMS}_t, \tag{2.5a}$$

$$\mathrm{AMS}_t = \alpha + \beta r_t + \varepsilon_t, \tag{2.5b}$$

$$r_t = \eta + \varphi \mathrm{MS}_t + \lambda r_{t-1} + \psi D_t + \varepsilon_t'. \tag{2.5c}$$

Equation (2.5a) is an identity that defines market share in terms of share based on redemptions and share among non-redeemers. Equation (2.5b) represents the idea that share among non-redeemers should change as the number of coupon redemptions changes. If coupons draw predominantly loyal users, the coefficient β will be negative; if coupons draw non-loyals, β will be positive. The coefficient α is important because it represents the brand's baseline market share, or share that would be achieved without couponing. The appearance of redemptions on the right-hand side of Equation (2.5b), and the appearance of market share on the right-hand side of Equation (2.5bc) reflect the simultaneity of redemptions and sales. Equation (2.5c) includes a distribution variable signifying the time at which coupons are distributed, and a lagged redemptions variable which, if $\lambda < 1$, results in declining redemptions at retail in the periods after distribution (see section 2.1.3).

Neslin extended his model to include the effects of competitive coupons. The extended model quantifies the extent to which competitive coupons draw the brand's loyal versus non-loyal customers. He also included retailer promotions and showed how to calculate incremental sales per redemption based on the extended model. Data were available for seven brands of coffee over a 58-week period. Neslin estimated his model using a constrained three-stage least squares procedure. The key results were that (1) incremental sales per redemption ranged between 0.208 and 0.534 across brands, with a median of 0.398, and (2) brand vulnerability to competitive coupons varied from brand to brand. Putting together these results, Neslin was able to show the extent to which certain brands are able to achieve higher market share in a coupon environment than they would in a world without coupons, while other brands lose share in a coupon environment.

Logit choice models have also been used to evaluate couponing. Little [1991] has used a logit model to extrapolate a baseline during a coupon drop. The logit model includes coupon-distribution variables so that the model accurately describes sales in the periods prior to the coupon drop. Starting at the drop date, the coupon-distribution variable is set equal to zero so that the model predicts sales that would have occurred had there been no couponing in this period. Incremental sales are then calculated as the difference between baseline and actual sales during several weeks beginning with the drop date. This procedure allows Little to calculate incremental sales per coupon drop.

In summary, both logit and regression models have been used to measure incremental sales from couponing. We are not aware of any research that has compared the accuracy of these two techniques. Logit requires household data while regression generally requires weekly sales data (Neslin's regression model also required weekly redemptions which he obtained from household data), so the choice of approach might well depend on the availability of data. An interesting issue emerges here regarding 'event analysis' versus 'average effects', and this issue actually applies to all types of promotions. Little's work calculates incremental sales for each coupon event, whereas Neslin estimates regression coefficients representing the average response to couponing. The issue is not regression versus logit, because Neslin's model could be used to calculate a baseline and perform an event analysis, and Little's model could be used to measure average effects. The issue is what questions management needs to answer. If the question is one of overall effectiveness, average response is relevant. If particular events are being evaluated, event analysis is needed. Obviously, one can obtain the former knowing the latter, but the latter requires more analysis to examine individual events.

2.2. *Trade promotions*

2.2.1. *Key phenomena influencing the effectiveness of trade promotions*

The ultimate success of a trade promotion depends on retailers passing through the discounts they get from manufacturers to consumers in the form of retailer promotions. The degree of pass-through and the incremental sales generated by retailer promotions are the primary sources of incremental benefits. On the cost side, manufacturers incur a reduced margin on sales that would have occurred even had the trade deal not been offered. These sales are of two forms. First are sales that would have occurred during the trade-deal period obviously, since the brand is being sold on discount during this period, these are sales that would have occurred anyway but now are being sold at lower margin. Second, however, are sales representing the 'forward-buy' of retailers. These sales represent product that is warehoused by the retailer to be used after the trade-deal period to satisfy normal demand. Because of forward-buying, the manufacturer loses margin on sales that would have occurred after the trade-deal period. To quantify these effects, we define the following:

w = regular wholesale price per case,
c = costs of goods sold per case,
d = wholesale price discount offered to the retailer per case,
b = average weekly baseline sales level per retailer that would occur without the trade deal (cases),
f = average number of weeks' baseline sales forward-bought per retailer.
p = percentage of retailers who promote the brand as a result of the trade deal,
i = incremental sales among retailers that promote the brand (% of baseline b),
N = number of retailers,
Π = incremental profit from the trade deal.

Incremental profits can be calculated in terms of incremental sales generated by the trade deal minus decreased margins on product that would have been sold anyway. These quantities can be represented as follows:

$$\begin{aligned}\Pi &= \text{incremental profits} - \text{reduced margin}\\ &= (w - c - d)\cdot N\cdot p\cdot b\cdot i - d\cdot(N\cdot(b + b\cdot f)).\end{aligned} \qquad (2.6)$$

The first term represents the benefits of incremental sales from retailers who pass through the trade deal into retailer promotions. Total incremental sales generated by the trade deal are $N\cdot p\cdot b\cdot i$. The profit margin from these incremental sales is $(w - c - d)$. In order to gain these benefits, however, the manufacturer incurs reduced margin on sales that would have occurred anyway. This sacrificed margin equals the trade-deal discount (d) times the number of sales that would have occurred anyway (baseline sales plus sales forward-bought by the retailer $(b + b\cdot f)$[6]).

[6]Implicitly we are assuming that the trade deal is in effect for one week and all retailers order in that week. This would have to be adjusted for the case when the trade deal is in effect for several weeks and not all retailers buy in a week. This could be done by using a term such as $n\cdot b\cdot g$, where n is the number of weeks' duration of the trade deal, and g is the fraction of retailers who buy in any week.

For example, assume regular wholesale price (w) is \$24 per case, costs of goods sold (c) is \$14 per case, and a trade is offered consisting of \$2.50 per case "off-invoice' (d). Assume baseline sales are 100 cases per week per retailer, that 40% of retailers pass through retailer promotions as a result of the trade deal (p), and that the average promoting retailer generates five times normal baseline sales (i). Assume, though, that the average retailer forward-buys four additional weeks of baseline sales for use in satisfying demand after the trade deal is no longer in effect (f). Finally, assume there are 1500 retailers (N accounts). Incremental profit generated by the trade deal would then be:

$$\begin{aligned}\Pi &= (\$24 - \$14 - \$2.50) \times 1500 \times 0.50 \times 100 \times 5 \\ &\quad - \$2.50 \times (1500 \times (100 + 100 \times 4)) \\ &= \$2\,812\,500 - \$1\,875\,000 \\ &= \$937\,500.\end{aligned}$$

In this example, although the manufacturer sacrificed \$1 875 000 in profit margin on sales that would have occurred even without the promotion, enough incremental sales were generated by the 50% of retailers who passed through the trade deal to offset this cost and generate a \$937 500 profit.

Based on Equation (2.6) plus the above example, the key quantities to be modeled are the size of the forward-buy, the amount of pass-through, and incremental sales generated by retailer promotions. In the next section, we discuss the determinants of pass-through. Following that, we combine discussion of forward-buying and incremental sales.

2.2.2. Pass-through

In a pioneering study, Chevalier & Curhan [1976] found a surprisingly low level of pass-through, and it appears to have decreased since that time [Curhan & Kopp, 1986]. Curhan & Kopp [1986] and Walters [1989] have investigated the factors which determine pass-through. Curhan & Kopp studied buyers' overall ratings of specific trade promotions and the actual level of retailer promotion accorded the brand. To determine which variables predict these measures, they began with 30 variables which they then factor-analyzed into eight factors:

- *Item importance*: Item's regular sales volume; importance of the promoted category.
- *Promotional elasticity*: Buyer's estimate of retail sales sensitivity to retailer promotion.
- *Manufacturer brand support*: Concurrent usage of coupons, advertising, point-of-purchase material by manufacturer.
- *Manufacturer reputation*: Manufacturer's overall product quality; quality of sales presentation.
- *Promotion wearout*: Degree to which the item or category has recently been 'over'-promoted.

- *Sales velocity*: Sales volume and market share of brand.
- *Item profitability*: Gross margins, reasonable deal requirements.
- *Incentive amount*: Amount of deal allowance, percent of regular cost.

Curhan & Kopp then used discriminant analysis to identify which variables best discriminated between retailers' high versus low overall ratings of a trade promotion and between trade deals that achieved some level of pass-through versus those that received no pass-through. Using standardized discriminant coefficients, they found item importance and item profitability were the most important predictors for overall rating, and item profitability and manufacturer's reputation were the two most influential predictors for performance. The two factors most closely linked to trade-promotion policy–incentive amount and promotion wearout–had relatively little influence on actual trade performance. However, Walters [1989] undertook a similar investigation of pass-through and found that the design of the trade deal and time since the last trade deal were more important predictors of pass-through than brand market-share or category sales volume. In conclusion then, the list of factors generated by Curhan & Kopp appears to be appropriate, but the ordering of these factors as predictors of pass-through is less well resolved.

2.2.3. Sales impact and profitability of trade dealing

Abraham & Lodish [1987] developed a procedure called 'PROMOTER' which uses time-series analysis to estimate a baseline. There are four primary steps: (1) adjustment of the data for trend, seasonality and 'exceptional' events, (2) elimination of data points influenced by the trade promotion, (3) extrapolation of the data points not influenced by promotion into the promotion period, and (4) computation of the promotion effect as the difference between this baseline and actual sales. The model Abraham & Lodish use is:

$$S_t = [T_t \cdot \mathrm{SI}_t \cdot X_t] \cdot [b_t + p_t + e_t] \tag{2.7}$$

where

S_t = sales in time t,
T_t = trend in sales not due to promotion,
SI_t = seasonal index of consumer demand,
X_t = exception index representing the effects of special factors or events,
b_t = base level of sales excluding trend, seasonality and exceptional events,
p_t = promotion effect,
e_t = random 'noise'.

Trend and seasonality can be estimated in a variety of ways. One method used is the X11 time-series analysis procedure [see Makridakis, Wheelwright & McGee, 1983]. Judgment is used to estimate the effect of exceptional events. For example, if the brand suddenly experienced a 50% decrease in distribution in period t, then X_t would equal 0.5 for that period. After trend, seasonality and exceptional events are estimated, 'adjusted sales' are computed by dividing Equation 2.7 by $T_t \cdot \mathrm{SI}_t \cdot X_t$. The next steps are illustrated in Table 12.2, for a case where a trade deal takes place in period 5.

Table 12.2
Example of a trade deal

Time period	Adjusted sales	Periods influenced by promotion	Data available for baseline computation	Computed baseline	Promotion effect
1	50	no	50		
2	55	no	55	52.3	
3	52	no	52	53.3	
4	53	no	53	53.3	
5	85	yes		53.3	31.7
6	35	yes		52.7	−17.7
7	55	no	55	52.9	
8	52	no	50	53.0	
9	54	no	54	53.3	
10	56	no	56		

Promotions periods can be identified by examining the promotion calendar for the brand, but periods influenced by promotion must be identified based on judgment. In the above example, the judgment has been made that due to forward-buying, the impact of the promotion will be felt in period 6 as well as period 5. Periods 5 and 6 are therefore not used in computing the baseline. In this example, the baseline is computed by taking a three-period moving average of non-contaminated data points. For example, averaging adjusted sales for periods 1, 2 and 3 yields 52.3 ((50 + 55 + 52)/3) and this is estimated baseline sales for period 2. The average of periods 2, 3 and 4 yields the baseline for period 3. We then average periods 3, 4 and 7 (skipping periods 5 and 6). The resulting figure, 53.3, applies to period 5, the middle of periods 3, 4 and 7. We then average the baselines for periods 3 and 5 to yield the baseline for period 4 ((53.3 + 53.3)/2 = 53.3). Once the baseline is computed, it is a simple matter to estimate the promotion effect by subtracting the baseline from adjusted sales. In this example, we see a clear positive promotion effect followed by a negative effects caused by forward-buying. The net impact of the promotion is 31.7 − 17.7 = 20 incremental sales.

The two critical requirements in this methodology are the availability of seasonality, trend and exception estimates for adjusting the data, and the identification of periods not influenced by promotion. These requirements will be easier to fulfill in a promotion environment where seasonality is not confounded with promotion, and when the promotion calendar has periods free of promotional influence.

Blattberg & Levin [1987] model the process by which the manufacturer sells to the retailer, the retailer promotes and sells to the consumer, and the retailer forward-buys from the manufacturer. This is captured in the following equations:

$$S_t = f_1(T_t, I_{t-1}), \tag{2.8a}$$

$$P_t = f_2(T_t, Z_t), \tag{2.8b}$$

$$R_t = f_3(P_t, Z_t), \tag{2.8c}$$

$$I_t = I_{t-1} + S_t - R_t, \tag{2.8d}$$

where

T_t = trade-deal discount at time t,
I_t = ending retailer's inventory at time t,
S_t = manufacturer's shipments to retailers at time t,
P_t = retailer promotion at time t,
R_t = retailer sales to consumers at time t,
Z_t = other factors such as consumer advertising at time t.

To see how the model works suppose the following relationships were estimated:

$$S_t = k_1 \exp\{\alpha T_t - \beta(I_t - \mathrm{TI}_t)/TI_t\}, \tag{2.9a}$$

$$P_t = k_2 T_t, \tag{2.9b}$$

$$R_t = k_3 \exp\{\delta P_t\}, \tag{2.9c}$$

where TI_t = target inventory, the retailer's desired inventory, at time t.

Let $k_2 = 1$, $k_1 = k_3 = 100$, $\delta = 0.2$, $\alpha = 10$, $\beta = 1.5$, $\mathrm{TI}_t = 200$ for all t. Figure 12.4 displays shipments and inventory patterns implied by the model, assuming a trade deal in week 3 and a more substantial trade deal in period 13. The figure shows that, due to forward-buying, shipments are zero after the trade deal until the inventory level declines toward the target level. Figure 12.5 shows retail consumer sales and factory shipments. One can see that shipments lead retailer sales. Eventually, shipments and retailer sales are equal but the adjustment period is long and depends upon how much the retailer forward-buys.

The particular graphs shown in Figures 12.4 and 12.5 are a function of the parameters of the model. For example, if in Equation (2.9a), α is small, then the retailer will forward-buy less. If in Equation (2.9b) k_2 is small, then less of the trade deal is passed through to the consumer. If in Equation (2.9c) k_3 is small,

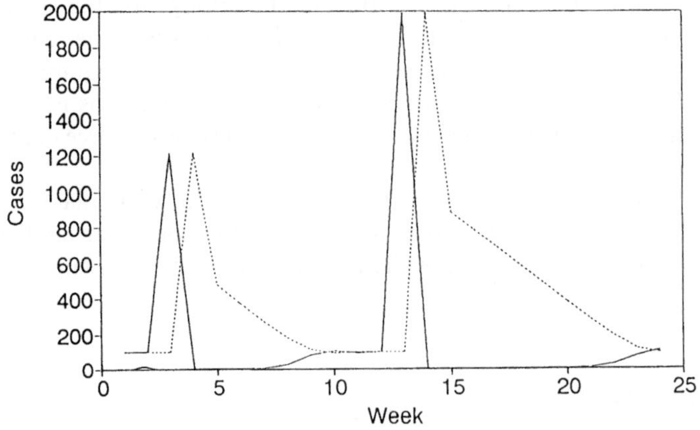

Fig. 12.4. Simulated shipments and inventory levels (—— shipments, ······ inventory).

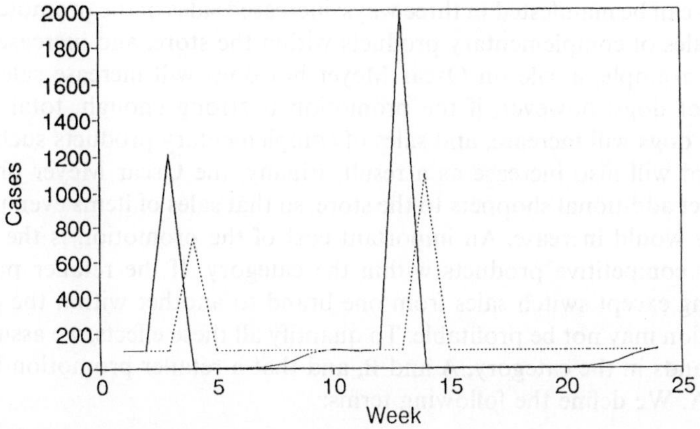

Fig. 12.5. Simulated shipments and consumer sales (—— shipments, ······ consumer sales).

then the consumer is less responsive to whatever level of promotions retailers make available.

To compute baseline retail sales for Blattberg & Levin's model, one notes that when no promotions are run, $P_t = 0$, so baseline retail sales equals k_3. In the absence of promotion, we assume that retail sales equals shipments, so that $R_t = S_t$ and baseline shipments also equals k_3. Depending on the values of k_1, β and TI_t, this implies an equilibrium retailer inventory level. Specifically, $R_t = S_t$ implies that, in the absence of promotion, $k_3 = k_1 \exp\{-\beta(I_t - \mathrm{TI}_t)/\mathrm{TI}_t\}$. If $k_1 = k_3$, as in the above example, then $\exp\{-\beta[(I_t - \mathrm{TI}_t)/\mathrm{TI}_t]\} = 1$ or $I_t = \mathrm{TI}_t$. For our example, $\mathrm{TI}_t = 200$ so $I_t = 200$.

The Blattberg & Levin model differs from Abraham & Lodish's approach in that the former considers both factory shipments and retail sales. In a heavy-promotion environment, it may be impossible to identify periods where factory shipments are unaffected by promotion, and hence one must compute the baseline from retail data. Also as Abraham & Lodish point out, one must be careful when just using factory-shipments data because deal-to-deal buying can depress the baseline. Blattberg & Levin use shipments data but only as part of a multi-equation system which incorporates shipments and retail sales. As a structural model, the Blattberg & Levin model is more complicated and requires more data than Abraham & Lodish's technique. However, once the parameters have been estimated, the model allows the simulation of alternative promotion policies, in addition to the evaluation of previous promotions. The decision to use one approach versus the other would depend on the needs of the researcher to manager.

2.3. Retailer promotions

2.3.1. Key phenomena influencing the effectiveness of retailer promotions

We take the retailer's point of view in identifying the crucial phenomena for determining the effectiveness of retailer promotions. The benefits of retailer promotions can be manifested in three ways: increased sales of the promoted brand, increased sales of complementary products within the store, and increase in store traffic. For example, a sale on Oscar Meyer hot dogs will increase sales of that brand of hot dogs; however, if the promotion is strong enough, total category sales of hot dogs will increase, and sales of complementary products such as buns and mustard will also increase as a result. Finally, the Oscar Meyer promotion might attract additional shoppers to the store, so that sales of items even unrelated to hot dogs would increase. An important cost of the promotion is the decrease in sales for competitive products within the category. If the retailer promotion does nothing except switch sales from one brand to another within the category, the promotion may not be profitable. To quantify all these effects, we assume there are two brands in the category, A and B, and that a retailer promotion is offered on Brand A. We define the following terms:

b_{A} = weekly baseline retail unit sales for Brand A,
m_{A} = normal retailer margin per unit for Brand A,
m_{B} = normal retailer margin per unit for Brand B,
d = trade-deal discount available for Brand A,
r = reduction in retail price for Brand A incurred by promoting Brand A,
η = increase in retail sales from promoting Brand A (% of b_{A}),
η_s = increase in sales of Brand A due to brand-switching (% of b_{A}),
η_c = increase in sales of Brand A due to increase category sales (% of b_{A}),
η_t = increase in sales of Brand A due to store-switching (% of b_{A}), $(\eta = \eta_s + \eta_c + \eta_t)$,
π_c = incremental store profits from increased sales of complementary products (per incremental category unit sold),
π_s = incremental store profits from store-switching (per incremental sale due to store-switching),
A = cost of promoting Brand A,
Π = profitability of the retailer promotion.

Profit contribution from the retailer promotion consists of increased sales of Brand A, incremental profit from increased category sales and store traffic, lost profit from other brands in the category (Brand B), and the cost of promoting Brand A. These factors can be quantified as follows:

$$\Pi = (m_{\mathrm{A}} + d - r)\cdot b_{\mathrm{A}}\cdot\eta + \pi_c\cdot b_{\mathrm{A}}\cdot(\eta_c + \eta_t) + \pi_s\cdot b_{\mathrm{A}}\cdot\eta_t - m_{\mathrm{B}}\cdot(b_{\mathrm{A}}\cdot\eta_s) - A. \tag{2.10}$$

The first term represent profit from selling more of Brand A. A total of $b_{\mathrm{A}}\cdot\eta$ more units of Brand A are sold, at a margin of $(m_{\mathrm{A}} + d - r)$. The next term represents incremental profit for complementary categories within the store. Since a total of $(b_{\mathrm{A}}\cdot(\eta_c + \eta_t))$ more category units are being sold, this is multiplied by π_c to capture profit from incremental sales of complementary products. The third term represents the benefits of incremental traffic generated by promoting Brand A. A total of $b_A \cdot \eta_t$ additional customers are attracted to the store by this promotion, and each of them generates an average of π_s in profit by purchasing other categories in the store. From these benefits, we must subtract the fourth term, which represents decreased profit from sales of competing brands within the category (Brand B in this case). Since a total of $b_A \cdot \eta_s$ unit sales are incremental to Brand A but come at the expense of Brand B sales, we multiply these units times the profit margin of Brand B to capture these costs of within-category switching. Finally, we subtract out the cost (A) of promoting Brand A.

For example, assume that baseline sales and normal margin are 1000 and \$0.19 for Brand A and normal margin is \$0.30 for Brand B. Assume that a \$0.20 trade discount is available for Brand A and that the retailer passes through all of this discount in a price reduction ($r = d = \$0.20$). Next, assume that sales of Brand A will double as a result of this retailer's promotion ($\eta = 2$) and that most of it is due to brand-switching ($\eta_s = 1.5$, $\eta_c = 0.3$ and $\eta_t = 0.2$). Finally, assume store profits from incremental complementary sales is \$0.1 per unit of Brand A associated with increased category sales, and that incremental store profits from incremental store traffic is \$2 per incremental unit of Brand A associated with increased traffic. We then can calculate:

$$\begin{aligned} \Pi &= (\$0.19 + \$0.20 - \$0.20) \times 1000 \times 2 + \$0.10 \times 1000 \times (0.3 + 0.2) \\ &\quad + \$2 \times 1000 \times (0.2) - \$0.30 \times (1000 \times 1.5) - \$20 \\ &= \$380 + \$50 + \$400 - \$450 - \$20 \\ &= \$360. \end{aligned}$$

We see that although the promotion of Brand A generated \$380 in increased profit for that brand, this was at the expense of \$450 in lost profit from Brand B. The net so far would be a loss, because the promotion switched a lot of sales from the more-profitable Brand B to the less-profitable Brand A. However, the benefits of incremental sales for complementary products (\$50) and especially benefits of increased traffic (\$400) served to bring the total profit generated by the retailer promotion into the positive range.

Equation (2.10) plus the above example illustrate the importance of several key phenomena in calculating the effectiveness of a retailer promotion. The most important phenomena relate to the sales impact of retailer promotions, including: (1) brand-switching and category sales, (2) effects on sales of complementary products, and (3) effects on store-switching. These topics are covered in the following sections.

2.3.2 The sales impact of retailer promotions

There have been many models developed to study how retailer promotions affect sales. These models employ logit, regression and time-series analysis. We will review examples of each of these approaches.

2.3.2.1. Brand-choice models. Guadagni & Little [1983] were the first to apply logit modeling to the study of sales promotion. As described by Guadagni & Little, the logit model assumes that utility for a choice alternative 'm' (U_m) can be represented as the sum of deterministic and random components, V_m and ε_m respectively. Thus, $U_m = V_m + \varepsilon_m$. The deterministic component represents measureable phenomena such as household purchase history and the retail environment. The random component represents unmeasurable phenomena; it is assumed that the ε_m's are independent and follow a Gumbel type II extreme-value distribution:

$$F(x) = \mathrm{P}(\varepsilon_m \leqslant X) = \exp[-\exp(-x)], \quad -\infty < x < \infty. \tag{2.11}$$

Assuming that at purchase occasion 't', the consumer purchases the alternative with highest utility from a set S of choice alternatives, one can derive the probability brand k is chosen at purchase occasion t as

$$\mathrm{P}_{kt} = \frac{\exp(V_{kt})}{\sum_{j \in S} \exp(V_{jt})}. \tag{2.12}$$

We have now subscripted deterministic utility by purchase occasion because market environment and household variables vary from occasion to occasion. Guadagni & Little model the deterministic component of utility (V_{mt}) as a function of promotional and household variables. Consider the case of modeling choice among M brand sizes at purchase occasion t. Guadagni & Little define the following variables:

$$X_{1mp} = \text{'brand-size constant' for } p = 1, \ldots, M-1$$
$$= \begin{cases} 1 & \text{if } m = p, \\ 0 & \text{otherwise,} \end{cases}$$

$$X_{2mt} = \text{'promotion'}$$
$$= \begin{cases} 1 & \text{if brand } m \text{ was on promotion at purchase occasion } t, \\ 0 & \text{otherwise,} \end{cases}$$

$$X_{3mt} = \text{'promotional price-cut'}$$
$$= \begin{cases} \text{amount of price per ounce} & \text{if promotion is in effect at purchase occasion } t, \\ 0 & \text{otherwise,} \end{cases}$$

$$X_{4mt} = \text{'price'}$$
$$= \text{price per ounce of brand } m \text{ at purchase occasion } t,$$

$$X_{5mt} = \text{'previous promotion purchase'}$$
$$= \begin{cases} 1 & \text{if household bought brand-size } m \text{ on promotion at the previous purchase occasion before occasion } t, \\ 0 & \text{otherwise,} \end{cases}$$

$$X_{6mt} = \text{'second-previous promotion purchase'}$$
$$= \begin{cases} 1 & \text{if household purchased brand-size } m \text{ on promotion at the second-previous purchase occasion before occasion } t, \\ 0 & \text{otherwise,} \end{cases}$$

$$X_{7mt} = \text{'brand-loyalty'}$$
$$= \begin{cases} \alpha X_{7mt-1} + (1-\alpha)\delta_1(t) \text{ with } \delta_1(t) = 1 & \text{if household bought brand associated with brand-size } m \text{ on purchase occasion } t-1 \text{ (previous purchase),} \\ 0 & \text{otherwise,} \end{cases}$$

$$X_{8mt} = \text{'size-loyalty'}$$
$$= \begin{cases} \gamma X_{8mt-1} + (1-\gamma)\delta_2(t) \text{ with } \delta_2(t) = 1 & \text{if household bought size associated with brand-size } m \text{ on purchase occasion } t-1 \text{ (previous purchase),} \\ 0 & \text{otherwise,} \end{cases}$$

V_{mt} = household's deterministic component of utility for brand-size m at purchase occasion t.

Given thse definition, the equation for V_{mt} is

$$V_{mt} = \sum_{p} \alpha_p X_{1mp} + \sum_{j=2}^{8} \beta_j X_{jmt}. \tag{2.13}$$

The coefficients (α_p) for the brand-choice constants (X_{1mp}) are intercept terms in the model that are specific to each brand-size. They represent the average baseline utility across all consumers and purchase occasions for brand-size m. The baseline utility depends on product characteristics and consumer tastes that are assumed to remain constant over time. Note that if there are M brand-size being considered, only $M-1$ brand-choice constants are needed. The coefficients (α_p) for the $M-1$ brand-sizes are interpreted relative to the Mth brand-size.

The variable X_{2mt}–X_{8mt} represent factors that cause deviations from baseline utility. The promotion and price variables (X_{2mt} through X_{4mt}) are defined fairly simply. The promotion variable X_{2mt} represents special features or displays, while the variable X_{3mt} represents price cuts from regular price, which in turn is represented by X_{4mt}. The prior-promotion purchase variables (X_{5mt} and X_{6mt}) represent the effects on current choice of buying brand-size m on promotion on previous purchase occasions. The motivation for including these variables is behavioral theories that posit a potential negative effect of promotion purchasing on future purchases (see Blattberg & Neslin, 1990, pp. 29–40].

The brand- and size-loyalty variables (X_{7mt} and X_{8mt}) are designed to represent learning or habit formation based on previous purchases of a particular brand or size. The behavioral notion is that buying brand-size m can build 'loyalty' to the brand or the size associated with brand-size m. The 'smoothing constants' α and γ govern the nature of the learning process. High values for these coefficients imply that learning takes place slowly, with only minor changes induced by the previous purchase. Low values for these coefficients imply that the consumer switches loyalty quickly to whichever brand or size was purchased on the previous purchase occasion. The smoothing parameter also assures that the loyalty variables will be between 0 and 1, and sum to 1 across all brand-sizes for a given household.

The key results from Guadagni & Little's application of their model to coffee data are

(1) The promotion, price-cut and regular-price variables were all statistically significant at the 0.05 level.

(2) The magnitudes of the price-cut and regular-price coefficients were quite similar, suggesting that price cuts from regular price yield the same immediate response as an equal permanent change in regular price. However, since price cuts are often accompanied by features or displays which are captured in the promotion variable, the net immediate effect of a price cut is typically stronger than that of a change in regular price.

(3) The prior-promotion coefficients were both negative and significant at the 0.10 level. This reflects the finding that average repeat rates for deal purchases are lower than for non-deal purchases (see Neslin & Shoemaker [1989] for further discussion).

(4) Both the brand- and size-loyalty variables were highly significant. The smoothing parameters α and γ were estimated as 0.85 and 0.75 respectively. Suggesting that there is a fair amount of carryover in loyalty from purchase to purchase, irrespective of which brand was bought last time. See Fader & Lattin [1992] and Fader, Lattin & Little [1992] for recent developments on defining and estimating loyalty effects.

An important recent addition to the logit literature is the inclusion of reference prices. A reference price is a subjective standard to which the consumer compares an available price in order to judge the worthwhileness of that price. The reference price may be based on the consumer's previous purchases, or even on the currently available prices for competitive products. (See Blattberg & Neslin [1990; pp. 40–47, 50–52] for discussion of the behavioral basis for reference prices.) Winer [1986], Lattin & Bucklin [1989] and Kalwani, Rinne & Sugita [1990] have made important contributions in this area. Winer defines an 'extrapolative expectations hypothesis' model as follows:

$$P^r_{ijt} = \delta_0 + \delta_1 P^0_{ijt-1} + \delta_2 \mathrm{TREND} + \varepsilon_{ijt} \tag{2.14}$$

where

P^r_{ijt} = household i's reference price for product i at purchase occasion t,

P^0_{ijt-1} = the price household i observed for brand j at purchase occasion $t-1$,

TREND = trend term counting the number of purchase occasions.

The first variable in Equation (2.14) says that consumers extrapolate previously available prices in forming a reference-price standard. An implicit assumption here is that consumers notice prices of all brands in their consideration set, even if they do not actually purchase all the brands. The second variable in Equation (2.14) allows reference prices to have a general upward or downward trend.

In order to estimate Equation (2.14), Winer assumed that, on average, the reference price at purchase occasion t will equal the actual available price at purchase occasion t ($P^r_{ijt} = P^0_{ijt}$ on average). He then used P^0_{ijt} as the dependent variable in Equation (2.14) and ran a regression with P^0_{ijt-1} and TREND as independent variables. The predicted dependent variable from this regression is used as an estimate of reference price. Winer then adjusted each brand's actual and reference price relative to the category average and included two price terms in his choice model: a relative price term based on currently available price, and a reference price term reflecting the difference between relative reference price and relative available price. He found a significant positive coefficient for the reference price term, meaning that an available price below the reference price gives an additional boost to purchase probability.

Winer's reference-price model has been altered by subsequent researchers. For example, Kalwani, Rinne & Sugita [1990] added terms to reflect the frequency of promotion for the brand and the deal-proneness of the household, and the actual purchases made in particular stores by the household. Lattin & Bucklin [1989] used a somewhat different formulation. They modeled reference price as an exponentially smoothed function of previous reference price, updated by the most recently available price.

A number of other researchers have extended Guadagni & Little's model. One issue that has received a great deal of attention is household heterogeneity. The logit model is typically estimated across households, so implicitly assumes that the parameters for each household are the same. This obviously is not true. The question is, does this then generate a heterogeneity bias, i.e. do some of the estimated coefficients not estimate what they are purporting to represent? Important recent work on these topis include Jones & Landwehr [1988], Kamakura & Russell [1989], Chintagunta, Jain & Vilcassim [1991], Kim [1992], Fader & Lattin [1992] and Fader [1992]. For example, Chintagunta, Jain & Vilcassim add a household-specific, brand-specific constant, α_{ij}, to Equation (2.13). They interpret α_{ij} as household i's preference for brand j. They then assume α_{ij} is constant over time but varies across consumers. They find that in terms of model fit and prediction, the best way to represent this variation is by a 'semi-parametric' probability distribution which assumes α_{ij} takes on a limited number of support point values, each with non-zero probability.

2.3.2.2. Regression models. We review regression model used to study the effects of retailer promotions on brand sales–Blattberg & Wisniewski [1988]–and briefly discuss a related model, Wittink, Addona, Hawkes & Porter [1987]. Blattberg & Wisniewski's [1988] model clearly separates the impact of regular price from that of promotion price, and estimates the separate effects of features and displays as well. Their model also includes competitive and psychological pricing effects.

Let

S_{it} = weekly retail sales (store or chain level) for item i at time t,
R_{it} = the regular (shelf) price of item i at time t,
P_{it} = the observed price (actual paid by the consumer) for item i at time t,
D_{it} = the deal discount for item i at time $t((R_{it} - P_{it})/R_{it})$,
CP_{jt} = the price of a competitive item j at time t with j not equal to i,
X_{it} = a dummy variable which equals 1 if a display is run for item i at time t,
Y_{it} = a dummy variable which equals 1 if a feature ad is run for item i at time t,
L_{it} = a variable representing deal decay, equaling k^{j-1} with j being the time since the beginning of the deal and $0 < k < 1$,
M_{it} = a dummy variable which equals 1 if 'N items for' pricing is used for item i at time t
$\mathrm{E9}_{it}$ = a dummy variable equalling 1 if the promotional price ends in 9 for item i at time t.

The model is:

$$S_{it} = \exp\{\alpha_1 - \alpha_2 R_{it} + \alpha_3 D_{it} + \textstyle\sum \delta_j \mathrm{CP}_{jt} + \alpha_4 X_{it} + \alpha_5 Y_{it} + \alpha_6 L_{it} + \alpha_7 M_{it} + \alpha_8 \mathrm{E9}_{it}\}. \tag{2.15}$$

The functional form in Equation (2.15) was tested by Blattberg & Wisniewski and found along with a log–log formulation to provide a better prediction and be more robust than a linear formulation.

Blattberg & Wisniewski estimated their model using store-level scanner data and uncovered several interesting findings:

(1) Certain items heavily cannibalized other items in the category and therefore were less advantageous to promote.

(2) Asymmetric competition exists, whereby the number of sales Brand A attracts from Brand B when Brand A promotes is not the same as what Brand B attracts from brand A when Brand B promotes [see Blattberg & Wisniewski, 1989]. The particular form of asymmetry discovered by Blattberg & Wisniewski was that high-quality brands tend to attract consumers from lower-quality brands, but not the reverse. For example, national brands tended to draw from store brands but store brands did not draw from national brands. Blattberg & Wisniewski label this a 'price tier' form of asymmetry, because levels of quality are often reflected in price points. Blattberg & Wisniewski argue that this arises because of the shape of the consumer-preference distribution. Other authors have developed different reasons for other forms of asymmetry. For example, Allenby & Rossi [1991] argue that asymmetry is due to an income effect. Hardie, Johnson & Fader [1992] use a generalization of prospect theory to generate asymmetry.

(3) Cross-elasticities for any given brand are small relative to own promotional effects. However, with more than one competitor promoting, each in a different week, the cumulative effect of the cross-elasticities becomes large.

(4) The end-9 effect was significant, indicating that promotional prices ending in 9 add an extra boost to sales.

(5) The decay effect was significant, indicating that response to a retailer promotion is highest in its first week, and then declines.

(6) Display and feature advertising have a highly significant effect on sales, though multicollinearity is a serious problem in separating the display, feature-advertising and price-discount effect.

(7) '*N* items for' promotions were found to be highly significant though the number of occurrences was small.

Wittink, Addona, Hawkes & Porter [1987] also developed a model that describes the effects of retailer promotions on brand sales. Their model is estimated using pooled store-level data. It is necessary to adjust for price and sales differences by store, otherwise cross-sectional variation can become confounded with time-series variation. To accomplish this Wittink et al. used a price index created by determining the median price for the store over the total time period and then indexing each week's prices relative to this median price. They used a similar procedure for sales data. The details of their model are given in Blattberg & Neslin [1990, p. 370].

One difference between Wittink, Addona, Hawkes & Porter and Blattberg & Wisniewski is that Wittink et al. do not separate the retailer-deal effect from the regular-price effect. One could argue that deal prices and regular prices should yield different responses because deals are short-term and are usually communicated to the consumer at the point of purchase. This would suggest that different variables should be defined for deal response and regular-price response (e.g. the Guadagni & Little logit model discussed earlier). The problem with separating these two effects is that it may lead to strange 'optimal' pricing and promotional practices with the model implying that it is optimal to price infinitely high and offer infinitely large price promotions.

Time-series models. Abraham & Lodish [1992] have adapted their PROMOTER methodology (Section 2.2.3) to analyze retailer promotions. Similar to the regression models reviewed above, their procedure uses store-level weekly-sales data. Figure 12.6 shows an example of store-level data for Tropicana refrigerated orange juice, 64 oz. container. The advantage of store-level data is that price and promotion are defined more accurately. This is compared to market-level weekly-sales data aggregated across stores, where data from stores with different prices and promotion schedules have to be combined to form one aggregate measure of price and promotion. Store-level data therefore avoid aggregation-bias problems [Blattberg & Neslin, 1990, pp. 182–185; Wittink, Porter & Gupta, 1993].

Abraham & Lodish define a baseline to be an estimate for each store-week of what the sales of an item would have been had *only* the item's retailer promotion not been run. They assume all other elements of the marketing mix, including competitive marketing activity, would have been held fixed. Their procedure is similar to PROMOTER although it differs in ways reflecting the problem of analyzing retailer promotions as opposed to trade promotions. In particular: (1)

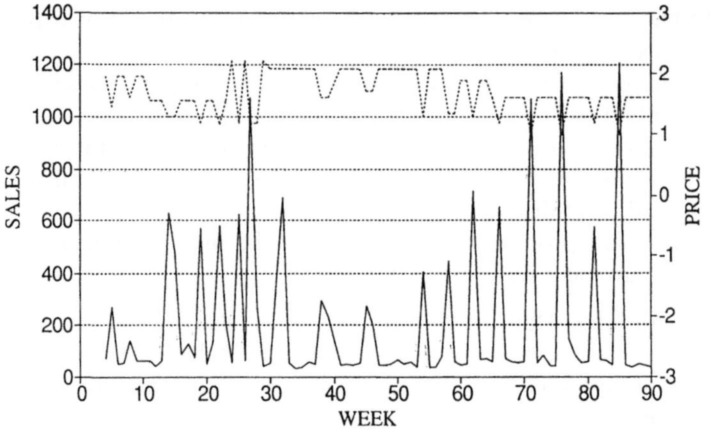

Fig. 12.6. Refrigerated organge sales data store level data for Tropicana 64 ounce (——sales, ······ price).

it can adjust for out-of-stock conditions, (2) it attempts to adjust the baseline for extraneous factors such as couponing and competitive activity that takes place concurrently with the item's retailer promotion, (3) it calculates the effects of specific retailer promotions such as features and displays, and (4) it differs in its estimation of seasonality, detection of promotion periods, and usage of specific smoothing techniques.

The Abraham & Lodish procedure determines periods in which there are no promotions and then computers a baseline by extrapolating sales from these preiods. It works in a manner very similar to regression analysis except that it removes promotion data points whereas regression adjusts for them using an explanatory variable for promotions. Abraham & Lodish use 'resistant' time-series smoothing techniques which are not vulnerable to outliers. Similar methods exist using regression models and are known as robust regression. Thus, the time-series methods used by Abraham & Lodish are closely related to the regression procedures used by Blattberg & Wisniewski and Wittink, Addona, Hawkes & Porter discussed in the privious section.

An advantage of the Abraham & Lodish procedure is that it has been programmed as an *automated* promotion-evaluation system, requiring little analyst time. This enables it to be a practical tool for analyzing promotions for a multitude of brands and categories. Among the limitations of the procedure are that it does not take into account potentially important factors such as purchase acceleration (see next section), store-switching (see Section 2.3.4), and competitive response.

2.3.3. Category sales, purchase acceleration and purchase incidence models

The η_c term in Equation (2.10) implicitly assumes that increased category sales not attributable to increased store traffic represent an increase in primary demand (consumption) for the category. This is why increased category sales is part of what determines incremental purchasing of complementary categories. However, there is strong evidence that much of what appears to be incremental category purchases is accelerated purchases, that is, sales of the category that would have occurred anyway. Accelerated purchasing is 'forward-buying' by consumers. Consumers stock up on the category because of a price break and use their inventory to satisfy their needs once the retailer price returns to normal.

Purchase acceleration complicates the calculation of retailer-promotion profitability because it means that some portion of increased category sales must be substracted from profit, since these represent sales that would have occurred anyway.[7] In this section, we discuss the measurement of purchase acceleration.

Purchase acceleration can manifest itself in terms of decreased interpurchase times and/or increased purchase quantity. Both of these are aspects of consumer stockpiling. Neslin, Henderson & Quelch [1985] developed a multi-equation regression model that described how promotions influence timing and quantity. Their model is shown in Figure 12.7. The model shows the interrelationships among four variables: purchase quantity, interpurchase time, inventory on hand after the previous purchase, and sales promotion. If, after the previous purchase, the household has a larger-than-usual inventory on hand, it will either wait longer before purchasing again, purchase a smaller quantity when purchasing again, or some combination of both. Also, for a given level of previous inventory, the longer a household goes without purchasing, the larger the quantity that will be purchased.

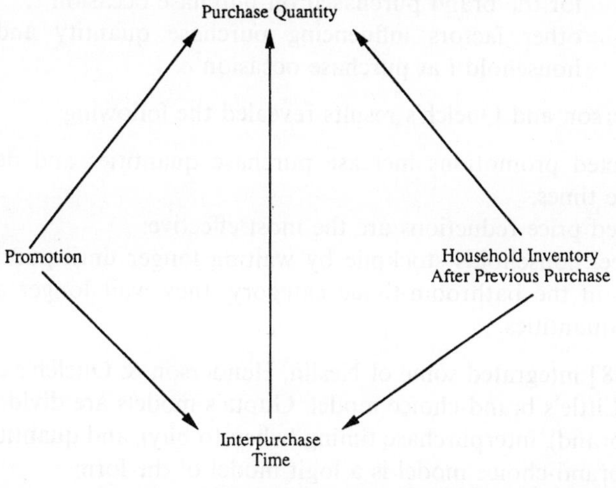

Fig. 12.7. A framework for analyzing purchase acceleration (Source: Neslin, Henderson & Quelch [1985]).

[7] Note, however, that from the standpoint of retailer profit, only the portion of accelerated sales not representing store-switching would have to be subtracted. Store-switching, even accelerated store-switching, is profitable to the retailer (although not necessarily for the manufacturer) and would be captured by the η_t and π_s terms in Equation 2.10.

quantities, because, as described by Blattberg, Eppen & Lieberman [1981], the promotion provides an economic incentive for the household to stockpile. Purchasing earlier and purchasing larger quantities are two forms of stockpiling. Figure 12.7 also shows how it can potentially be inaccurate to compare promotion quantities to non-promotion quantities as an estimate of quantity stockpiling. This is because the promotion may decrease interpurchase times which tends to decrease quantity. As a result, a simple comparison of promotion to non-promotion quantities may underestimate the degree to which promotion has increased purchase quantities.

Based on Figure 12.7, Neslin, Henderson & Quelch then estimated the following recursive model:

$$Q_{ic} = \beta_0 + \beta_1 I_{i,c-1} + \beta_2 E_{ic} + \beta_3 P_{ic} + \varepsilon_{ic}, \tag{2.16a}$$

$$E_{ic} = \delta_0 + \delta_1 I_{i,c-1} + \beta_4 P_{ic} + \varepsilon'_{ic}, \tag{2.16b}$$

where

Q_{ic} = purchase quantity bought by household i on purchase occasion c,
E_{ic} = elapsed (or 'interpurchase') time for household i between purchase occasion c and purchase occasion $c-1$,
$I_{i,c-1}$ = household inventory of the product category immediately after purchase occasion $c-1$,
P_{ic} = zero–one indicator for whether or not a promotion was present for the brand purchased on purchase occasion c,
$\varepsilon_{ic}, \varepsilon'_{ic}$ = other factors influencing purchase quantity and timing for household i at purchase occasion c.

Neslin, Henderson and Quelch's results revealed the following:

(1) as expected promotions increase purchase quantities and decrease interpurchase times;
(2) advertised price reductions are the most effective;
(3) for coffee, households stockpile by waiting longer until purchasing again, whereas in the bathroom-tissue category, they wait longer and purchase smaller quantities.

Gupta [1988] integrated some of Neslin, Henderson & Quelch's concepts with Guadagni & Little's brand-choice model. Gupta's models are divided into brand choice (what brand), interpurchase timing (when to buy), and quantity (how much to buy). The brand-choice model is a logit model of the form:

$$P_{ijn} = \exp(\boldsymbol{b}'\boldsymbol{X}_{ijn}) / \Sigma_m \exp(\boldsymbol{b}'\boldsymbol{X}_{imn}) \tag{2.17}$$

where

P_{ijn} = the probability that person i buys brand j on the nth purchase occasion,
X_{ijn} = the explanatory variables for brand j and consumer i for the nth purchase occasion with response parameters in the vector $\boldsymbol{b}$.

The interpurchase timing model is

$$f_{iw}(t) = \alpha_{iw}^2 t \exp(-\alpha_{iw} t), \tag{2.18a}$$

$$\alpha_{iw} = \exp(-c' Y_{iw}), \tag{2.18b}$$

where

$f_{iw}(t)$ = probability density of interpurchase time t for consumer i in week w,
α_{iw} = scale parameter of Erlang-2 distribution,
Y_{iw} = vector of explanatory variables that may affect the mean time, with response parameters c.

The quantity model is:

$$P(Q_{in} \leqslant k) = \exp(\delta_k - \beta' Z_{in})/(1 + \exp(\delta_k - \beta' Z_{in})) \tag{2.19}$$

where

Q_{in} = quantity purchased by the ith household on occasion the nth purchase occasion,
Z_{in} = vector of explanatory variables for the ith household on the nth purchase occasion.

Gupta's empirical findings showed that promotions decrease the mean, thereby shortening interpurchase times, and that larger household inventory tends to elongate interpurchase times. Gupta's purchase-quantity model is called 'ordered logit', and predicts the integer number of units that are purchased by the household. He found that promotions have a small but statistically significant positive impact on purchase quantity.

Gupta illustrated the value of his model by decomposing promotional elasticity into switching effects (from the logit choice model), timing acceleration (from the interpurchase timing model), and quantity stockpiling (from the ordered logit model). He found for his particular data that 85% of the elasticity was due to brand-switching, 13.6% was due to timing acceleration, and 2% was due to purchasing larger quantities. The finding reinforces the notion of promotion as a switching device, although quantity stockpiling might have been underemphasized because there was not a wide variety of sizes available in the category and market being studied. In addition, Gupta's empirical findings are for only one product category in one particular market area. Since this is a heavily promoted product category, it is possible that consumers did not have to accelerate or purchase extra quantities.

More recent research has used hazard functions to characterize timing effects of promotion. Examples of this research are Helsen & Schmittlein [1989] and Vilcassim & Jain [1991]. The hazard function is the probability that a purchase will occur at time t, *conditional* on no purchase having been made up to that point in time. The hazard function is then decomposed into two parts:

$$h(t \mid x, \theta) = h_0(t) g(x, \theta) \tag{2.20}$$

where $h(t|x,\theta)$ is the hazard functions at period t, x is a set of covariates, and θ a set of parameters. The function h_0 is called the 'baseline' hazard function, and $g(x,\theta)$ allows this hazard function, and hence the probability distribution for the likelihood of purchasing in a given time interval to be influenced by a promotional event. By using this methodology, which has a one-to-one relationship with a purchase timing model (e.g. Poisson or Erlang-2), it is possible to determine how covariates such as promotion affect the likelihood of purchasing in a given period. Vilcassim & Jain [1991] used hazard functions to show: (1) interpurchase times occur at 7, 14 and 21 days; (2) the more recently a purchase occurs, the less likely it is that the next purchase occurs, i.e. time of last purchase has a negative effect on the probability of purchasing; and (3) after some point in time if no purchase occurs, the likelihood of a purchase occurring in the next time interval declines.

The Neslin, Henderson & Quelch, Gupta, and hazard models use household data to measure acceleration. Purchase acceleration is much less commonly found when regression models are used with weekly-sales data. For example, Blattberg & Wisniewski and Wittink, Addona, Hawkes & Porter did not find evidence of purchase acceleration. This is an important issue that remains unanswered. Why do household-level models find evidence of consumer stockpiling, whereas weekly-sales regression models do not find this evidence? Acceleration can have a critical impact on the profitability of promotions, and if acceleration is really there yet weekly-sales regression models do not find it, these models will provide inaccurate estimates of promotion profitability. There are various reasons as to why regression models might not be able to detect acceleration effects, although the issue has not been systematically investigated. These reasons [see Blattberg & Neslin, 1990] include: (1) competitive effects flatten the baseline in non-promotion periods, (2) quantity and timing acceleration mask each other because they imply different lag structures, (3) repeat-purchase effects are positive and cancel out negative acceleration effects, (4) acceleration induces consumption and so accelerated sales are really incremental sales, (5) many consumers buy deal-to-deal, and (6) the acceleration effect is too weak to be detected. Recently, Neslin & Schneider [1992] have suggested that the difficulty in detecting acceleration effects may be due to consumer flexibility in managing household inventory. Also recently, Krishna [1992] has proposed that consumer expectations of promotion may cause sales to dip before as well as after the promotion, so that sales in non-promotion periods never approach true baseline sales.

The few instances of acceleration being detected in weekly-sales data are Leone [1987], Doyle & Saunders [1985] and Thompson & Noordewier [1991]. These three studies use time-series analysis. Leone [1987] utilized a time-series baseline method called intervention analysis which is capable of modeling very complex lag structures. This is important for detecting acceleration because acceleration in fact is a lagged effect of promotion. The intervention-analysis model takes on the following form:

$$S_t = \frac{\omega(B)}{\delta(B)} X_t + \frac{\theta(B)}{\phi(B)} a_t \tag{2.21}$$

where

S_t = sales in period t,
X_t = zero–one indicator variable for presence of promotion in period t,
a_t = random 'error' in time t.

The functions $\omega(B)$, $\delta(B)$, $\theta(B)$ and $\phi(B)$ are polynomials in the 'backwards shift' operator B. For example, $BX_t = X_{t-1}$, $B^2X_t = X_{t-2}$, etc. A polynomial $\omega(B) = 1 - \omega_1 B - \omega_2 B^2$ would imply a lag structure of $X_t - \omega_1 X_{t-1} + \omega_2 X_{t-2}$. Obviously, in taking ratios of these polynomials, i.e. $\omega(b)/\delta(B)$, very flexible lag structures can be represented [see Blattberg & Neslin, 1990, pp. 254–263].

Leone analyzed a retailer promotion for cat food, in particular, an unusual '5 for $1.00' sale. He estimated that the immediate impact of the promotion was to increase sales by 494 cans, but that sales decreased by 295 cans in the week after the promotion. This means that 295 of the 494-can increase in sales represent sales borrowed from the next week.

Doyle & Saunders [1985] examined the possibility that promotions might not only cause consumers to buy earlier than they otherwise would have, but also delay purchases. The situation was retail sales of a furniture product. The retailer implemented a promotion that involved increasing salesperson commission rates during the promotion period. Doyle & Saunders found a significant 'lead' effect of commission rates. The direction of this effect was that if commission rates are increased in period t, sales increase in periods $t-1$ and $t-2$, i.e., the periods before the commission-rate increase. The possible explanation for this is that salespeople were motivated to urge shoppers to defer their purchases until the promotion period. Doyle & Saunders computed that 'almost 40% of the incremental sales from the campaign are transitory effects-delayed purchases caused by the anticipatory behavior of salespersons' [1985, p. 61].

Thompson & Noordewier [1991] provided another example of using time-series analysis to examine the effects of promotion and also use intervention analysis. Their application was to analyze the major rebate programs U.S. manufacturers instituted during the end of year in 1985, 1986 and 1987. Their findings were quite interesting because they found a strong immediate effect of promotion and that a good portion of that increase was due to accelerated sales. Thompson & Noordewier discuss several potential reasons for this decline, including consumer apathy, a loss in quality of implementing the rebate programs, competitive activities not included in the model, and exhaustion of the deal-prone market segment.

2.3.4. *Complementary-category and store-switching effects*

Mulhern & Leone [1991] and Walters [1991] demonstrated that promotions in one category can increase sales in a complementary category. For example, Mulhern & Leone examined the relationship between promotions for cake mix and cake frosting. They used a regression model that included regular and deal prices for brands in both categories. They found substantial complementary effects and interestingly, these were asymmetric. In particular, promotions for cake mix stimulated sales of frosting, but promotions for frosting were less likely to simulate sales of cake mix. Perhaps the reason for this relates to the consumer decision process. Cake mix is in some sense the 'core' product and one needs frosting to embellish it. It makes sense therefore that cake-mix promotions would help sales of frosting, but not the reverse.

Kumar & Leone [1988] studied brand-switching and store-switching, but we will discuss only the store-switching model. Kumar & Leone focus on a 'primary' store and a 'primary' brand. Their model is:

$$\begin{aligned}\mathrm{Sales}_t(\mathrm{AP}) = {} & \beta_0 + \beta_1\mathrm{PR}_t(\mathrm{AP}) + \beta_2\mathrm{PR}_t(\mathrm{AS}) + \beta_3\mathrm{PR}_t(\mathrm{CP}) + \beta_4\mathrm{PR}_t(\mathrm{CS}) \\ & + \beta_5[\mathrm{F}_t(\mathrm{AP}) - \mathrm{F}_t(\mathrm{AS})] + \beta_6[\mathrm{D}_t(\mathrm{AP}) - \mathrm{D}_t(\mathrm{AS})] \qquad (2.22)\end{aligned}$$

where

$\mathrm{Sales}_t(\mathrm{AP})$ = sales at time t for brand A in the primary store (P),
$\mathrm{PR}_t(\mathrm{AP})$ = brand A's price at time t in the primary store (P),
$\mathrm{PR}_t(\mathrm{CP})$ = brand C's price (the competitive brand) at time t at the primary store,
$\mathrm{PR}_t(\mathrm{AS})$ = brand A's price at time t in the competitive or 'secondary' store (S),
$\mathrm{PR}_t(\mathrm{CS})$ = brand C's price at time t in the competitive store,
$\mathrm{F}_t(\mathrm{AP})$ = brand A's feature advertising activity at time t at the primary store,
$\mathrm{F}_t(\mathrm{AS})$ = brand A's feature advertising activity at time t at the competitive store,
$\mathrm{D}_t(\mathrm{AP})$ = brand A's display activity at time t at the primary store,
$\mathrm{D}_t(\mathrm{AS})$ = brand A's display activity at time t at the competitive store,

for $t = 1,\ldots,60$. The parameters β_2, β_4, β_5 and β_6 represent potential store-switching effects due to price of the primary brand, price of the competitive brand, different feature activity for the two stores, and different display activity for the stores, respectively.

Their results showed significant and important store-switching effects for prices and features, especially for pairs of stores located within the same geographic area. The strong competitive effects found between stores may be related to the product category chosen, disposable diapers. However, Walters [1991] also found store-switching effects in the spaghetti, spaghetti-sauce and cake-mix categories.

Walters & MacKenzie [1988] developed a structural equation model to measure the effect of loss leaders, double couponing and in-store promotions on store traffic, total sales and profitability. They found surprisingly that loss-leader promotions had generally little effect on store traffic, although there is some question as to how to interpret this result because the variables in their model indicated which product category was promoted as a loss leader, not the presence or absence of loss-leader promotions. Their weak loss-leader effects could be due to hardly any weeks being available without loss-leader promotions.

3. Prescriptive models

The ultimate goal of any modeling effort is to influence and hopefully improve managerial decision-making. The models reviewed in Section 2 were designed to measure the effects of promotions, but do not prescribe or help managers decide what course of action to take. In this section, we review models designed for this purpose.

3.1. A retailer category-manager model

Blattberg & Neslin [1990, pp. 455–458] describe a model that can be used by a retailer to optimally specify a retail-price discount for a single brand, where the objective is to maximize profits for the *category* in which that brand belongs. As discussed in Section 2.3.1, a supermarket may want to specify a discount for Maxwell House coffee, but the supermarket's goal is to maximize profit for the store's coffee category. The key issue that makes this problem different from optimizing an item's price is cross-price discount elasticities; that is, how does a price discount for Maxwell House influence sales of other items in the category such as Folgers? To illustrate the approach, we define the following variables and parameters:

q_i = quantity sold of brand i,
D_i = deal discount offered for brand i,
β_{ij} = cross-deal coefficient – how a price discount for brand j affects sales of brand i,
β_{ii} = own-deal coefficient – how a price discount for brand i affects sales of brand i,
k_i = baseline sales for brand i.

We then specify the following demand model:

$$q_i = k_i \exp(\beta_{i1}D_1 + \beta_{i2}D_2 + \beta_{i3}D_3). \tag{3.1}$$

Regular price is not included in the equation because it will not vary and therefore is implicitly included in the baseline k_i. In order to define the retailer's profit equation, let m_i be the retailer gross profit margin for Brand i. Then, the profit equation is:

$$\Pi = \sum m_i q_i - \sum D_i q_i. \tag{3.2}$$

If Brand 1 were to be promoted in a particular week, the goal would be to find the value of D_1 that maximizes Equation (3.2), subject to the demand-model Equation (3.1). Blattberg & Neslin note that this problem does not have a closed-form optimal solution; however, to see how the 'category manager' works, assume the following demand equations:

$$q_1 = 10\,000\exp\{6D_1 - 3D_2 - 3D_3\},$$

$$q_2 = 10\,000\exp\{-3D_1 + 6D_2 - 3D_3\},$$

$$q_3 = 10\,000 \exp\{-3D_1 - 3D_2 + 6D_3\}.$$

Regular retail price for each brand is $1.29 and cost is $1.00 for each brand. A trade deal of $0.20 is offered for Brand 1. What is the optimal deal discount? Table 12.3 (base case) shows the deal discount for the brand and category profitability. The optimal discount is $0.30 although profit is relatively constant in the range of $0.25 to $0.35.

Both own-deal elasticity (β_{ii}) and cross-deal elasticity (β_{ij}) play key roles in determining the optimum retail deal discount. Table 12.3 shows, for example, that if the own-deal coefficient for Brand 1 had been 7 rather than 6, the optimal deal discount would be $0.35 for profit of $18 253. If the coefficient had been 5, the optimal deal discount would be $0.25 for profit of $11 117. It is also interesting to note that in this case, Brand 1 profit would be optimized at $0.30 while category

Table 12.3
Category and brand profitability

Deal discount ($)	Profits ($)	
	Brand 1	Category
Base case ($\beta_{11}=6, \beta_{21}=-3, \beta_{31}=-3$)		
0.00	4 900	10 700
0.05	5 939	10 931
0.10	7 106	11 403
0.15	8 363	12 061
0.20	9 628	12 811
0.25	10 756	13 496
0.30	11 494	13 852
0.35	11 433	13 462
0.40	9 921	11 668
0.45	5 952	7 455
0.50	−2 009	−714
Increased own-elasticity ($\beta_{11}=7, \beta_{21}=-3, \beta_{31}=-3$)		
0.25	13 811	16 551
0.30	15 516	17 874
0.35	16 224	18 253
0.40	14 800	16 547
0.45	9 334	10 838
0.50	−3 312	−2 017
Decreased own-elasticity ($\beta_{11}=5, \beta_{21}=-3, \beta_{31}=-3$)		
0.20	7 883	11 066
0.25	8 377	11 117
0.30	8 515	10 873
0.35	8 056	10 086
Decreased own-elasticity and decreased cross-elasticity ($\beta_{11}=5, \beta_{21}=-0.5, \beta_{31}=-0.5$)		
0.20	7 883	13 131
0.25	8 377	13 495
0.30	8 515	13 507
0.35	8 056	12 925
0.40	6 650	11 399

profit is maximized at \$0.25. Keeping the same own-deal response coefficient ($\beta_{11} = 5$), if the two cross-elasticity coefficients (β_{21} and β_{31}) has been -0.5 rather than -3, the optimal deal discount would be \$0.30 for profit of \$13 507. In these examples, then, it appears that optimal discount is steeper and profits are higher if own-deal elasticities are large and cross-elasticities are low. Blattberg & Neslin also show that the optimal discount is steeper if the promoted brand has higher profit margin for the retailer, compared to other brands in the category. See Bucklin [1987] for other general results.

The above category-manager is relatively simple to implement and the required descriptive model is straightforward to estimate. However, this technique has a few limitations. First, it does not take into account influences on complementary categories or store traffic (see discussion in Section 2.3.1). Second, it does not include acceleration effects. Third, it does not address the issue of how long to promote or whether to use displays or features in addition to a price discount. Despite these limitations, however, the category-manager described here is a usable tool that includes the essential fact that retailers manage category profit and not necessarily brand profit.

3.2. An optimal forward-buy model

The forward-buy decision for the retailer requires balancing the desire to purchase additional inventory at a reduced price versus the increased cost of carrying that inventory for future demand. Blattberg & Neslin [1990, pp. 459–461] define a simple model for this purpose which can be solved for an optimal closed-form solution. The model uses the following terms:

G = amount of trade discount per case offered to retailer by manufacturer,
PC = cost to retailer per case after deducting the trade-deal discount,
P = number of cases per 'pallet' (a pallet is a storage platform for the product),
HC = handling cost per pallet (labor and transportation costs),
SC = storage cost per pallet per month (due to spaçe utilization in warehouse),
CC = cost of capital,
F = baseline weekly demand for product at the retail level (assumed constant),
X = number of cases to be purchased.

The number of cases to be purchased is the decision variable, whereas G and PC are determined by the trade deal. The remaining parameters are presumed known to the retailer. Given these definitions, net profit (NP) can be calculated as total savings from the trade deal minus the carrying costs, storage costs and handling costs of taking advantage of the trade deal:

$$\mathrm{NP} = G \cdot X - (\mathrm{PC}) \cdot (X/2) \cdot (\mathrm{CC}/52) \cdot (X/F) - (X/2) \cdot (1/P) \cdot (\mathrm{SC}/4) \cdot (X/F) - (X) \cdot (1/P) \cdot (\mathrm{HC}) \tag{3.3}$$

Differentiating this equation with respect to X gives the expression[8] for optimal order size X^*:

$$X^* = \frac{52 \cdot F \cdot (G \cdot P - \mathrm{HC})}{(\mathrm{PC} \cdot P \cdot \mathrm{CC} + 13 \cdot \mathrm{SC})}. \tag{3.4}$$

Equation (3.4) says that the forward-buy should be greater if the trade discount is large and weekly demand is large. Less should be forward-bought if holding costs, carrying costs, storage costs and product cost are higher. Therefore, Equation (3.4) seems to capture the trade-off between buying additional product on discount and carrying the inventory for future periods. For example, consider a product class in which the retailer normally buys 150 cases per week ($F = 150$). Assume that 40 cases fit on a pallet ($P = 40$), storage cost per pallet per month is \$4.00 ($\mathrm{SC} = 4$), handling cost per pallet is \$14.00 ($\mathrm{HC} = 14$), and the cost of capital is 15% ($\mathrm{CC} = 0.15$). The regular purchase price is \$25.00 per case and a 10% trade deal is offered ($\mathrm{PC} = \$22.50$, $G = \$2.50$). Using Equation (3.4), the optimal amount to forward-buy would be 1024 cases, roughly 6.8 weeks' supply.

Note that the category-manager presented previously and the above forward-buy model consider the two retailer decisions–retail-price discount and forward-buy–to be independent. However, if the length of the promotion is also a decision variable, the decisions are not independent. Armstrong, Bass & Rao [1991] have recently formulated a decision model for the retailer to jointly decide on the retail-price discount, length of retail promotion, and forward-buy quantity.

3.3. *Economic models and their strategic implications*

The planning models described so far are relatively simple in structure and can easily be programmed, and for these reasons are frequently used by retailers. Economic models provide a general view of how promotions work which assist managers in 'framing' the promotional decision. These models begin with assumptions about consumer behavior and the structure of the market (usually competitive) and then derive the optimal pricing policy for the firm. The importance of these models is that they provide managers with an understanding of conditions under which it is optimal to promote.

Blattberg, Eppen & Lieberman [1981] assume that segments of consumers have differential holding costs, high and low, which induces some low-holding-cost consumers to accelerate and stockpile inventory when a promotion is run. High-holding-cost consumers buy only for current consumption when a deal is offered. The consumer's objective is to minimize holding costs given that he or she will continue to consume c units per period. The total cost is

$$\mathrm{TC}(q) = \int_0^{q/c} h(q - ct)\mathrm{d}t - Dq \tag{3.5}$$

[8] The first-order condition is $G - (\mathrm{PC}) \cdot (\mathrm{CC}/52) \cdot (X/F) - (1/P) \cdot (\mathrm{SC}/4) \cdot (X/F) - (\mathrm{HC}/P) = 0$.

where

h = holding costs,
c = consumption rate,
D = deal discount,
t = time,
q/c = time to consume q units bought at time 0.

The optimal quantity the consumer buys is found by differentiating Equation (3.5) with respect to q, setting it equal to zero and solving for q which results in $q = Dc/h$. When a promotion is offered, higher-holding-cost consumers will not buy for inventory if h is high enough. The retailer has an incentive to offer the deal because its holding cost is higher than the low-holding-cost consumers' and yet lower than the high-holding-cost consumers'. The argument is that dealing is based on differential holding costs between consumer segments and higher holding costs for retailers than one of these segments. [See also Jeuland & Narasimhan, 1985.]

Varian [1980] uses a different argument to show that it is optimal to deal. He assumes that different segments of consumers have different information levels regarding price, and divides them into informed and uninformed consumers. Let

R = the reservation price above which no consumer will buy,
P = the price offered by the store,
I = the number of informed consumers,
M = the number of uninformed consumers,
n = number of stores.

If it is assumed that uninformed consumers shop randomly, the number of uninformed consumers per store is simply $U = M/n$. If the price of an outlet is lower than the competition, Varian assumes that the sales of the store are $I + U$. For the market to have two prices retailers will randomize between R, the reservation price, and P_1, the low price determined by the number of informed consumers. Now $P_1 = C\{I + U\}/(I + U)$ where $C\{I + U\}$ is the unit retailer cost function assumed to be strictly decreasing in the number of customers. By *randomizing*, low-priced stores can attract informed consumers and only their random share of uninformed consumers. Uninformed consumers will not know which stores have the lowest prices. If randomization is not used, even uninformed consumers can find the lowest-priced stores by accidentally shopping at that store one time and then always returning to that store. A deal is offered (a temporary price reduction) so that the uninformed consumers cannot always learn what the lowest price is in the market. Thus, dealing is a way to price-discriminate between the less informed and more informed consumers.

Narasimhan [1988] developed a model to show conditions under which competitive brands would promote in equilibrium. His model assumes three segments: (1) those loyal to Band A, (2) those loyal to Brand B, and (3) switchers who buy the lowest-priced brand. Assuming that the switchers are indifferent between brands if they have the same price, a brand's market share in that case is $\alpha_A + \beta/2$ and

$\alpha_B + \beta/2$ respectively where α_A and α_B denote the percentages of the market loyal to A and B, and β represents the number of switchers. If $\alpha_A + \alpha_B$ is small, then by reducing price to attract the switchers, neither gains enough to overcome the loss in revenue from trying to steal switchers. If the switcher segment is large, each brand will try to attract the segment and if they each use a single price, they will 'cut each other's throat' to attract these buyers. However, by oscillating prices both brands can increase their overall profitability relative to offering a single (low) price. Thus, Narasimhan argues the optimal strategy is to randomly oscillate price (i.e. use price promotions).

Raju, Srinivasan & Lal [1990] utilized a similar argument although emphasized the role of brand-loyalty. If brand-loyalty is very high, it does not pay for firms to lower prices enough to attract each others' loyals, because price will also be lower for their own loyals. If brand-loyalty is very low, no brands command substantial brand-preference and the market prices will be competed down to a low uniform level. However, with a medium level of brand-loyalty, firms find it profitable periodically to attract each others' loyal consumers with promotions. Since high levels of loyalty are difficult to sustain in markets with several brands, they predict, and find some confirming evidence, that promotions are more likely in categories where there are several brands.

Lal [1990a], presented a strategic argument that promotions are a mechanism by which national brands compete with store or private-label brands for a switcher segment. Through tacit collusion, the national brands rotate their promotions so that in any given week, a promotion is offered to the consumer. Then, the price-sensitive consumer who would have bought the private-label brand buys the dealt brand. Because national-brand items are promoted regularly (rotated by week), the consumer never has a reason to buy the private-label brand.

Gerstner & Hess [1990] presented an interesting argument for the existence of 'bait and switch' promotions, where a retailer advertises a brand on sale but does not carry sufficient stock to meet demand. Gerstner & Hess concluded that if retailers implement a rain-check policy, so that shoppers who find the advertised brand out of stock can return at some future date and obtain the item for the advertised price, consumers can benefit from lower prices. The argument is that the advertised price for the 'bait' gets competed downward as stores vie for shoppers, and the alternative items in the store (the items the consumer might switch to) are lowered so that in fact the consumer will switch. As a result of their analysis, Gerstner & Hess recommend changes in the regulation of bait and switch.

How do these models help managers plan? By understanding the conditions when dealing is offered, managers have a structure or 'frame' to judge certain actions they will take. For example, Sears decided to change their retail pricing policies to every-day low-price (EDLP) in 1990. Their theory was that this has been very successful for some grocery chains, so why not for them? Because Sears' customers were buying durable goods and devoted extensive time to learning available prices, the consumers' behavior was different than grocery purchasing where the return from searching was lower. Thus, there were a large number of informed consumers. If Sears management had understood Varian's argument that dealing is offered by retailers to avoid being in the position of having a competitor undercut price once consumers know our price, Sears would have recognized that: (1) competitors would undercut Sears' EDLP prices and (2) the consumer was willing to search for a lower price. Hence, Sears would always lose. After approximately six months, Sears abandoned their EDLP strategy.

In early 1992, Procter and Gamble announced that they are going to eliminate dealing on many of their items and try to return to lower list prices without promotions. If you are a competitor of Procter and Gamble should you match? If there are a large number of switchers in the market, the incentive is to promote to attract these customers. This implies that in this case, it may not be optimal to follow Procter and Gamble's lead.

The models presented above help managers think about the 'strategy' of promotions. By understanding when and why promotions are used, managers can avoid the trap of eliminating promotions when it would be detrimental to their firm.

3.4. A model for coupon decisions

Neslin & Shoemaker [1983] developed a detailed simulation model to be used to help design coupon promotions. The model takes into account several aspects of the coupon program, including vehicle, number of coupons distributed, face value, and timing of the coupon drop. In addition, the model recognizes that coupon promotions are often part of a larger promotion campaign that includes trade deals to retailers, and resultant retailer promotions delivered to consumers. Therefore, the model simulates the effects of the coupon drop and the accompanying trade deal. The entire model consists of nine primary equations. We focus on the equation which is used to compute the impact of the coupon drop on brand sales. Define:

LREDEEM_t = the number of coupons redeemed in week t (note this number is net of any misredemptions [Blattberg & Neslin, 1990, pp. 283–286],

ACC = percentage of coupon redemptions that represent sales accelerated from future periods,

MSU = percentage of unaccelerated coupon redeemers who would have bought the brand even if the coupon had not been available,

MSA = percentage of accelerated coupon redeemers who would have bought the brand even if the coupon had not been available,

$S(X)$ = fraction of accelerated sales drawn from X periods ahead,

$\text{NEWREP}(X)$ = fraction of coupon redemptions that result in incremental sales X periods after the coupon redemption (this represents additional repeat purchases),

COUPGAIN_t = the total increment or decrement in sales that occurs in week t due to current or previous coupon redemptions.

Neslin & Shoemaker derive the following equation for COUPGAIN_t:

$$\text{COUPGAIN}_t = \text{LREDEEM}_t{*}[\text{ACC} + (1 - \text{ACC}){*}(1 - \text{MSU})] + \sum_x \text{LREDEEM}_{t-x}{*}[\text{NEWREP}(X) - \text{ACC}{*}\text{MSA}{*}S(X)] \quad (3.6)$$

The first term in Equation (3.6) represents the immediate effect of coupons on sales in week t. The fraction ACC + (1 − ACC)*(1 − MSU) of coupon redemptions in week t are incremental sales for that week, because all accelerated sales are incremental for that week (they are subtracted from future weeks), and of the unaccelerated sales (1 − MSU)% are incremental because they would not have bought the brand had there not been a coupon available.

The second term in Equation (3.6) represents the effect on sales in week t of coupon redemptions that took place in previous periods $t-1$, $t-2$, $t-3,\ldots$, in general $t-x$. For a given value of X, $\text{LREDEEM}_{t-x}{*}\text{NEWREP}(X)$ redemptions that took place in period $t-x$ result in new repeat-purchases in week t. Of the $\text{LREDEEM}_{t-x}{*}\text{ACC}$ redemptions that were accelerated in period $t-x$, MSA% of them represent sales that would eventually occur anyway, and of those, $S(X)$ were accelerated from week t, and so must be subtracted from week t sales. We sum over $x = 1, 2, \ldots, t-1$ to derive the total impact of previous coupon redemptions on sales in week t.

Equation (3.6) shows the way in which the sales effects of couponing can be decomposed into switching, acceleration and repeat-purchase factors. The model requires estimates of critical parameters such as MSU and ACC in order to be applied. In addition, there are several other parameters such as redemption rates, coupon costs, etc., that are inputs to other equations in the model, and estimates must be provided for these parameters as well. Neslin & Shoemaker employed a decision-calculus approach to calibrating their model [Little, 1970, 1979]. The brand manager for the product provided estimates of all the necessary parameters, sometimes relying on 'hard' market-research results, previous coupon-drop results, or managerial judgment. By having a decision-calculus model, the promotion or brand manager can understand how control variables directly influence the redemption rates and profitability of the promotion.

3.5. *A marketing-mix model*

In pioneering work on using decision calculus to solve marketing problems, Little [1975] developed a comprehensive model called 'BRANDAID' to help plan marketing programs. The model considers virtually all aspects of the marketing mix to be decision variables, including advertising, distribution, pricing, sales force and sales promotion. The promotion module will be the focus of our attention. The following model structure is applicable to any type of promotion, including trade deals, coupons, and other consumer promotions.

Little's model generates sales in time t as the product of several 'effect indices', each index representing the influence of a separate part of the marketing mix. The effect index for promotion is a function of 'promotion intensity', which in turn is a function of promotion expenditures, geographic or target-group coverage, and effectiveness of the promotion (ability of the promotion to influence sales). In order to facilitate comparisons, these factors are assessed for the promotion under consideration as well as for a reference promotion, for example, last year's promotion. To derive promotion intensity, Little therefore defines the following variables:

a_t = promotional intensity in time t,
x_0 = expenditures for the reference promotion,
h_0 = fraction of consumers or sales territories covered by the reference promotion,
k_0 = effectiveness of the reference promotion (degree to which promotion influences sales),
x_t = expenditures for promotion under consideration in time t,
h_t = fraction of consumers or sales territories to be covered by the promotion under consideration in time t,
k_0 = relative effectiveness of the promotion under consideration in time t.

These factors are linked together by the following equation:

$$a_t = \frac{h_t k_t x_t}{h_0 k_0 x_0}. \tag{3.7}$$

Therefore, if in period t expenditures are high, coverage is high, and the promotion is highly effective, relative to the reference promotion, then promotional intensity is high in period t. Promotion intensity is then multiplied by a time pattern 'template' to produce the dynamic effects of the promotion. This template might represent the time pattern for a promotion expected to have both pre- and post-promotion dips. This result is then adjusted for cannibalization of other brands in the firm's product line, yielding an effect index for promotion at time t. This effect index is multiplied by the effect indices for advertising, distribution, sales-force efforts, etc., in time t, to yield brand sales.

BRANDAID is a very comprehensive and complex model, but this is commensurate with its purpose – to help managers devise effective marketing plans. Its contribution is that it models the interactions of promotions with other elements of the marketing mix. Thus, advertising spending can affect promotional effectiveness or promotions can influence distribution. Very few promotional models consider these interactions.

3.6. Concluding comments

In this section, we have reviewed both optimization models and decision-calculus models for helping to plan and manage promotional programs. Decision-calculus models tend to add realism and comprehensiveness, while the optimization models tend to be simpler. Since data may not be available for all the realistic phenomena included in the decision-calculus models, they often rely on judgment for many of their parameters. In addition, since complex models are difficult to solve for a single optimal solution, decision-calculus models emphasize testing alternatives rather than finding a single optimal solution. The reliance on judgment has a potential downside in that these judgments can be biased and self-serving. However, proponents of decision calculus would make the following arguments. First, realism and the use of the manager's judgment incorporate the manager into the model. (See Blattberg & Hoch [1990] for a further discussion of this issue.) The manager gains faith in the model because it becomes less of a 'black box' and assists in organizing and highlighting the assumptions the manager will use to make decisions. Second, as Little demonstrated in his application of BRANDAID, the model can help pinpoint critical factors that need to be investigated statistically. Third, proper use of models involves using them once, evaluating results, and then learning from one's mistakes to refine judgments. For example, in Neslin & Shoemaker's application, it turned out that the manager was wrong about one of the assumptions made about retailer promotions. This became apparent after the actual promotion transpired. The model allowed the analyst to pinpoint which assumption was violated.

For both decision-calculus and optimization models, the key to success is the quality and realism of the descriptive model. This depends on the realism of the model specification, as well as in the case of statistical estimation, the quality of the data, or in the case of judgmental estimation, the quality of experience. We expect there will be more emphasis on normative decision models as research on descriptive models progresses to the point where many issues in descriptive modeling have been addressed. The models in this section illustrate the potential for taking these descriptions and molding them into managerial decisions.

4. Summary and future research

This article has focused on many of the currently available models for analyzing, measuring and planning sales promotions. In this section, we review progress that has been made to date and outline areas where more work is needed. Tables 12.4 and 12.5 summarize the research described in this chapter. The tables are organized by type of promotion and that is how we will structure our discussion. We then end with a general discussion of issues that apply to all types of promotion.

Before proceeding with our detailed discussion, we note from the tables that, in general, (1) descriptive models have received more attention than prescriptive models, and (2) retailer promotions have received more attention than couponing or trade promotions. The emphasis on descriptive models is probably welcome, because these models are a necessary ingredient to prescriptive models. However, we should not lose sight of the fact that impact on practice is the ultimate goal of model-building, and therefore we should eventually see more work on prescriptive models. The emphasis on retailer promotions is probably due to the availability of retailer scanner data. This also raises the point that much of the modeling has concentrated on frequently purchased products. Much more work is needed regarding consumer durables, services, and industrial products.

4.1. Couponing

Table 12.4 shows that regression analysis has been the primary tool used to analyze couponing, and that redemption rates and incremental sales have received the most attention. Based on the table and our discussion in Section 2, we can identify the following topics that need to be addressed:

- Redemption rates: How can we improve the accuracy of redemption-rate forecasting? Our review in Section 2 suggested that it is difficult to forecast redemption rates within one-percentage-point accuracy. On a base of approximately a 4 or 5% redemption rate and considering the expenditure involved, this is a large error. There are two potential approaches to this issue – more detailed data or more sophisticated statistical procedures. Both of these need to be examined.
- Redemption rates: How do factors such as recency of previous coupon drops, design of the coupon, competitive couponing, and use of contest or sweepstake overlays affect redemption rates? These factors need to be examined for two reasons: First, if the factors are significant and improve forecasting, this would tell managers to begin collecting the necessary data on a routine basis. Second, if these factors are significant, the design and scheduling of coupon promotions could be improved.
- Redemption timing: How accurately can we predict ultimate financial liability based on a few weeks into the coupon drop? As described in Section 2, there has been some progress made in this area, but a thorough evaluation needs to be made.
- Redemption timing: How do expiration dates, distribution vehicle and other coupon characteristics affect redemption at retail and timing of liability. Answers would have important implications for the effective design of coupon promotions.
- Incremental sales: How do coupon, brand and market characteristics affect the sales impact of coupons? This has important implications for the design of coupon programs. This requires an examination of the incremental sales generated by several coupon drops. Some progress has been made in this area [Little, 1991].
- Incremental sales: Does couponing have advertising value? The focus of most descriptive and prescriptive couponing models is that coupons generate incremental sales through being redeemed. However, many FSI coupons might be more accurately characterized as advertisements with an attached coupon. As understanding of the advertising value of these coupons would enable a more accurate measurement of the total sales impact of couponing.

Table 12.5 shows that only the decision-calculus model has been developed for

Table 12.4
Summary of descriptive models of sales promotion

Phenomena	Choice/incidence models	Regression analysis	Time-series analysis
Part A – Coupons			
Redemption Rates		Reibstein & Traver [1982]	
		Blattberg & Neslin [1990]	
		Blattberg & Hoch [1990]	
Redemption timing		Ward & Davis [1978]	
		Neslin [1990]	
Incremental sales	Little [1991]	Chapman [1986]	
		Neslin [1990]	
Part B – Trade promotions			
Forward-buying		Blattberg & Levin [1987]	Abraham & Lodish [1987]
Pass-through		Walters [1989]	
		Curhan & Kopp [1986]	
Sales impact		Blattberg & Levin [1987]	Abraham & Lodish [1987]
Part C – Retailer promotions			
Store traffic		Kumar & Leone [1988]	
		Walters [1991]	

Brand-switching	Guadagni & Little [1983] Gupta [1988] Krishnamurti & Raj [1988] Allenby [1989] Keon [1980] Vilcassim & Jain [1991] Lilien [1974] Kuehn & Rohloff [1967]	Walters & Rinne [1986] Walters & MacKenzie [1988] Blattberg & Wisniewski [1988] Blattberg & Wisniewski [1989] Moriarty [1985] Wittink, Addona, Hankes & Porter [1988] Walters [1991]	
Purchase acceleration	Neslin, Henderson & Quelch [1985] Vilcassim & Jain [1991] Currim & Schneider [1991] Gupta [1988] Gupta [1991]	Moriarty [1985] Wittink, Addona, Hawkes & Porter [1987]	Thompson & Noordewier [1991] Leone [1988] Doyle & Saunders [1985]
Repeat purchasing	Guadagni & Little [1983]		
Psychological pricing		Blattberg & Wisniewski [1988]	
Reference prices	Winer [1986] Kalwani, Rinne & Sugita [1990] Lattin & Bucklin [1989]		

Table 12.5
Summary of prescriptive models of sales promotion

Application	Optimization models	Decision-calculus models
Couponing		Neslin & Shoemaker [1983]
Trade promotions		
Forward-buying	Blattberg & Neslin [1990]	
	Armstrong, Bass & Rao [1991]	
Pass-through	Blattberg & Neslin [1990]	
	Armstrong, Bass & Rao [1991]	
	Blattberg & George [1991]	
	Mulhern & Leone [1991]	
Promotion design	Neslin, Powell & Schneider [1993]	Little [1975]
Retailer promotions		
Promotion design	Rao & Thomas [1973]	Dhebar, Neslin & Quelch [1987]
Promotion strategy		Lodish [1982]

planning coupon promotions. Based on this table and our discussion in Section 2.1, we can identify the following additional topics that need to be addressed:

- What is the optimal face value for a coupon? There are numerous design characteristics to specify when planning a coupon promotion, but face value stands out because of its direct impact on financial liability.
- How should multiple-coupon promotions be planned throughout the year? The Neslin & Shoemaker model is for a single promotion event, but promotion calendars are generally specified at the beginning of each planning year. The key to developing a multiple-event coupon-planning model would be an understanding of how one coupon event influences the effectiveness of a subsequent event. The issues discussed above, of how 'time since last coupon' affects redemption rates, and an accurate understanding of redemption timing at retail, would be critical inputs for such a model.

4.2. Trade promotions

Table 12.4 shows that regression and time-series analyses have been used to study trade promotions, and forward-buying, pass-through and total sales impact have all received at least some attention. Based on the table and our discussion in Section 2.2, we can identify the following topics that need further investigation.

- Forward-buying: What determines the degree of forward-buying? The prespective model discussed in Section 3 suggests that deal discount and carrying cost should play key roles, but we need to understand in more detail how retailers decide to forward-buy. For example, how do retailers define the various aspects of carrying costs? How do they tradeoff warehouse space?
- Pass-through: Can manufacturers forecast weekly pass-through as a function of their trade dealing? The research shown in Table 12.4 on pass-through is cross-

sectional in nature. It is not from the viewpoint of a manufacturer trying to plan a promotion calendar. For this purpose, manufacturers need to forecast for a given brand, the amount of pass-through that will be obtained depending on the design and schedule of trade deals.

- Sales impact: How do trade promotions affect retailer behavior beyond pass-through? Most of the models used to measure the impact of trade promotions on sales use sales as the dependent variable. This makes sense for a short-term evaluation. However, the strategic reason for trade dealing is often stated in terms of maintaining distribution, motivating the sales force, or maintaining good retailer relations. This obviously affects sales in the long run. Virtually no work has been conducted in this area.
- Sales impact: Under what circumstances does one need retail-sales data in addition to factory shipments to measure the sales impact of a trade promotion? Blattberg & Levin use both factory shipments and retail sales, whereas Abraham & Lodish show examples using factory shipments. Factory-shipment data are distorted by forward-buying and deal-to-deal buying. This can result in a downward-biased baseline, and therein lies the impetus for also considering retail-sales data. However, complete retail-sales data are less easily available on an account-by-account basis. As an initial study, one could compare differences between baselines inferred using factory shipments versus retail-sales data. If the differences are large, one could then develop procedures for selecting the appropriate data.
- Sales impact: Can the effect of trade promotions be measured from market-level sales data? Market-level data can provide a distorted view of trade-promotion effectiveness if for example a subset of retailers are buying deal-to-deal. In that case, a misleadingly low baseline would be inferred. Analogous to household-level data available for retail purchases is account-specific data for retailer purchases. Measures of incremental sales derived from these data need to be compared to market-level data.
- Sales impact: Related to the preceding two issues, what is the best way to include forward-buying in descriptive models of trade promotions? Abraham & Lodish use judgment to identify periods free of promotion influence, including forward-buying. Blattberg & Levin use an econometric model with lagged terms to measure forward-buying. These approaches need to be compared and possibly combined.

Table 12.5 shows that optimization models have been developed for pass-through and forward-buying, and decision calculus has been used for trade-promotion design. Based on the table and Section 3, we can identify the following topics that need to be addressed involving prescriptive models of trade promotions.

- Forward-buying and pass-through: How much is lost by considering these as separate decisions. Recent work by Armstrong, Bass & Rao [1991] suggests that the two decisions are interdependent if length of the retailer decision is a decision variable. In that case, what is lost by using two separate models as described in Sections 3.1 and 3.2?

- How should trade-deal schedules and discounts be influenced by brand characteristics such as retail carrying cost, pass-through percentage and retail promotion sensitivity? Answers to these questions would give general guidance for how managers should be designing trade deals. Neslin & Schneider [1992] have made some progress in this area.
- How should an annual trade-promotion calendar be developed? Little's work can be used to evaluate a given promotion calendar in the context of a full marketing plan, but work is needed to generate potential promotion calendars. This would include the timing and design of trade promotions. Neslin, Powell & Schneider [1993] have made initial progress in this area, but their work is related more to understanding the factors that influence trade-promotion calendars than to specifying an actual promotion calendar. There are formidable challenges here, because of the several characteristics of trade deals (e.g. deal discount, cooperative advertising money, etc.) and because of dynamic effects.
- Is trade dealing necessary for manufacturers? Trade dealing is a mechanism for generating promotions at the retail level. However, manufacturers can reach consumers directly through promotions such as couponing, and not have to incur the costs of retailer forward-buying. In addition, retailers have their own incentives to promote [e.g. Varian, 1980; Blattberg, Eppen & Liberman, 1981] even in the absence of trade deals. Is it that trade promotions are the manufacturer's way of assuring that *its* brand gets promoted? Much management frustration with promotion centers on trade-promotion expenditures. It is important to generate an understanding as to why this is an efficient mechanism for achieving retail price promotions (see Lal [1990]; Gerstner & Hess [1990] for potential explanations).

4.3. Retailer promotions

Table 12.4 shows a multitude of research on retailer promotions. All methodologies are represented as well as most phenomena. Part of the reason for this is the availability of scanner data. However, while many of the phenomena have been investigated, they are not all clearly understood. The following topics warrant investigation:

- Store traffic: How do retailer promotions affect store traffic and total customer profitability? There has been some research in this area but not enough for clear generalizations to emerge. This is a critical issue for retailers and greatly influences their promotional strategies.
- Brand-switching: Can promotional cross-elasticities be decomposed into a simpler structure? The logit model assumes a simple proportional-draw cross-elasticity based on the independence-of-irrelevant-alternatives assumption. Blattberg & Wisniewski [1989] provide evidence for a price-tier structure. Many other regression models assume no structure. This issue is critical because it determines the net category effect of retailer promotions. Allenby & Rossi [1991] have made some progress on this issue.

- Brand-switching: The logit model assumes proportional draw but, in practice, the independence-of-irrelevant-alternatives assumption will probably be violated, leaving the interpretation of logit-model coefficients in doubt. However, how critical is this assumption in practice? How often is it violated, and what is the effect on estimated coefficients and predictions?
- Purchase acceleration: Why do analyses of household-level data detect acceleration effects, whereas analyses of weekly-sales data generally do not? This is a very important issue because weekly-sales data are more commonly used, and potentially these data are overestimating the incremental sales generated by sales promotion.
- Purchase acceleration and primary demand: How can we disentangle acceleration effects and increases in primary demand? This is especially important for durables. For example, rebates for automobiles may cause consumers to purchase an automobile sooner than they otherwise would have, but if consumers then return to their normal interpurchase time, the rebate has actually increased the rate of purchasing the category and increased primary demand [see Blattberg & Neslin, 1990, pp. 129, 133–134].
- Purchase acceleration: To what extent does purchase deceleration influence brand sales? That is, do consumers wait until promotions become available for acceptable brands? This has obvious implications for the measurement of incremental sales due to retailer promotions.
- Reference price: How do consumers form reference prices? Are they based on previous experience or currently available prices of competitive products? How important are reference prices in the determination of retail sales? There is strong evidence from choice models that reference prices are important, but this needs to be replicated using regression models and possibly some form of promotion profile analysis.
- Psychological pricing: How effective are 'end-9' and '*n*-for' pricing, and what brand or category characteristics determine this effectiveness? Blattberg & Wisniewski show some evidence that psychological pricing is effective, but this needs to be generalized and explained.
- Price image: How does a particular retail-promotion strategy affect the price image of a store? Retailers face major decisions involving their general promotion strategies, e.g. everyday-low-pricer versus steep-discounter, and understanding the effect of these strategies on price image would be a crucial impact to this decision.
- Selecting items to promote: How do retailers select among several products to decide which ones to promote? This is related to the issue of pass-through, but is broader. Do retailers look for a portfolio of products to promote? What are the desirable characteristics of such portfolios?

Table 12.5 shows that very few prescriptive models have been developed for retailer promotions. However, the pass-through models shows in the table also can be viewed as retailer promotion models. One critical need in this area is as follows:

- Promotion design: How should retailers select items to promote? This is a very complex issue because, technically, each brand in the store is a candidate for promotion in any given week, even if a trade deal is not available. It may be that, due to cross-category effects, it becomes worthwhile to promote an item in one category even if no trade deal is available, once a trade deal induces promotion of an item in a related category. Conceptually, this problem could be captured in a large mathematical program, but the program would possibly be too large to solve (there are tens of thousands of items in a store), and looking beyond one week would complicate things even more. In the experience of the authors, retailers currently use a variety of heuristics to decide which terms to promote. The question is whether a model could enhance this decision.

4.4. *Issues applicable across more than one promotion type*

There are both methodological issues and additional phenomena that need to be investigated and are applicable across various types of promotion. We start with the phenomena:

- What are the long-run effects of promotion and how can they be incorporated in planning models? There are many dimensions to this issue, all of which are critical. Three of these dimensions are the effects on competition, consumer response, and the 'brand franchise'. All the models of promotion reviewed in this chapter omit competitive response. For example, a retailer promotion that induces an immediate sales increase of 1000 units but triggers a competitive promotion has not yielded a net increase to the retailer of 1000 units. The reference-price models provide one answer to how consumer response to promotion might change over time as a function of promotion frequency. However, this work needs to be expanded to the long term (e.g. a year or more) and applied to other promotions besides price cuts. For example, do consumers become 'trained' to respond to displays and feature advertising and eventually ignore the actual price discount involved? Inman, McAlister & Hoyer [1990] suggest that this does occur. If so, what are the ramifications for promotion planning and for ethical use of promotions? In the case of brand franchise, very little work has been done but again the issue is critical. Do promotions tarnish brand image in the long run? Do they erode brand-loyalty? If so, how can these effects be averted?
- Should promotions be designed as a limited number of promotion events or as an ever-present series of promotional offers? There are two philosophies here. One is that a sales promotion should be a major, multifaceted event, including several promotional tools as well as advertising. This is the way to break through the information clutter facing the consumer. The other fact is that major promotional events induce a major competitive response, and raise the level of information clutter. In this view, promotions should virtually always be available on an understated basis to the consumers who wish to take advantage of them. This is the way to effectively price-discriminate between price-sensitive and non-price-sensitive market segments.

- How do the various forms of promotion synergize with each other? This is related to the previous point but is more tactical. For example, from the manufacturer's point of view, should a retailer promotion be run coincidentally with a coupon drop? Does this simply duplicate coverage or are there synergies? Does a coupon enhance the likelihood of pass-through? Does a sweepstakes overlay enhance the redemption rate of a coupon? Under what circumstances does a display without a price cut generate as many sales as a price cut alone, or the two combined?
- How do promotions affect repeat purchasing? This is a more intermediate-term version of the question of how promotions influence the brand franchise. The point is that household-level data analyses find evidence for positive, negative, or no effect on next purchase after a promotion purchase, whereas weekly-sales data rarely uncover any repeat-purchase effect [see Blattberg & Neslin 1989]. There has been recent progress in understanding this effect [Ehrenberg, Hammond & Goodhardt, 1992; Davis, Inman & McAlister, 1992; Ortmeyer & Huber, 1991]; however, conflicting findings need to be sorted out and generalizations need to emerge.
- What are the sales effects of consumer promotions besides couponing? Rebates, contests, sweepstakes and premiums have received very little attention in the literature, yet these are very important forms of promotion. The effects of these promotions might be difficult to measure, because they do not deliver an instant price discount to the consumer.

Among the methodological issues that need to be developed as:

- How do baseline procedures compare in terms of accuracy? For example, choice models, regression and time-series analysis can all be used to infer a baseline for a retailer promotion. Do these baselines differ substantially? If so, which is most accurate?
- What is the appropriate level of aggregation for sales-promotion models? This is related to the previous issue, and shows itself in couponing, trade promotions and retailer promotions. Generally speaking, anytime an aggregate model is specified – aggregated over brands, stores, or consumers – and the units in the aggregation respond differently to promotion, the estimated promotion coefficients will be biased in that they will not measure an average promotion response. The question is, how dramatic is this bias? If an assistant brand manager estimates a simple regression model based on aggregate national sales and aggregate measures of price and promotion, how inaccurate is that model *in practice*? If the answer is highly inaccurate, this argues against easy implementation of marketing models. It means careful analysis is needed and the analysis should be done at the most disaggregate level possible (see 'Time-series models' in Section 2.3.2).

4.5. Conclusion

In conclusion, modeling certainly has a place in the understanding and planning of sales promotion, and much progress has been recently made. However, there are still many unanswered questions, even regarding some of the areas that have been thoroughly researched. In addition, we should begin to see a shift toward prescriptive models and hopefully an increase in managerial use of models. The potential need is there, and so is the technology. If it is successful, this chapter, by summarizing the field, will help accelerate progress in the development and implementation of sales-promotion models.

References

Abraham, M.M., and L.M. Lodish (1987). PROMOTER: An automated promotion evaluation system, *Marketing Sci.* 6(2), 101–123.

Abraham, M.M., and L.M. Lodish (1992). An implemented system for improving promotion productivity using store scanner data. Working Paper, The Wharton School, University of Pennsylvania, Philadelphia, PA.

Allenby, G.M. (1989). A unified approach to identifying, estimating and testing demand structures with aggregate scanner data, *Marketing Sci.* 8, 265–280.

Allenby, G.M., and P.E. Rossi (1991). Quality perceptions and asymmetric switching between brands. *Marketing Sci.* 10 (Summer), 185–205.

Armstrong, M.K., F.M. Bass, and R.C. Rao (1991). Optimal order quantity under trade promotion: A model of forward buying and reduced retail price. Paper Presented at Marketing Science Conference, March 23, Wilmington, DE.

Bawa, K., and R.W. Shoemaker (1987). The effects of a direct mail coupon on brand choice behavior. *J. Marketing Res.* 24(4), 370–376.

Blattberg, R.C., G.D. Eppen, and J. Liberman (1981). A theoretical and empirical evaluation of price deals for consumer nondurables. *J. Marketing* 45(1), 116–129.

Blattberg, R.C., and E. George (1991). Shrinkage estimation of price and promotional elasticities: Seemingly unrelated equations. *J. Amer. Statist. Assoc.* 86, 304–315.

Blattberg, R.C., and S.J. Hoch (1990). Database models and managerial intuition: 50% model + 50% manager. *Management Sci.* 36(8), 887–899.

Blattberg, R.C., and A. Levin (1987). Modeling the effectiveness and profitability of trade promotions. *Marketing Sci.* 6(2), 124–146.

Blattberg, R.C., and S.A. Neslin (1989). Sales promotion: the long and the short of it, *Marketing Lett.* 1 (December), 81–97.

Blattberg, R.C., and S.A. Neslin (1990). *Sales Promotion Concepts, Methods, and Strategies.* Prentice-Hall, Englewood Cliffs, NJ.

Blattberg, R.C., and K.J. Wisniewski (1988). Modeling store-level scanner data. University of Chicago Marketing Paper 43, January.

Blattberg, R.C., and K.J. Wisniewski (1989). Price-induced patterns of competition. *Marketing Sci.* 8(4), 291–309.

Bucklin, R.E. (1987). Pass-through of manufacturer trade promotions by grocery retailers. Working Paper, Stanford University, Stanford, CA, October.

Chapman, R.G. (1986). Assessing the profitability of retailer couponing with a low-cost field experiment. *J. Retailing*, 62(1), 19–40.

Chevalier, M., and R.C. Curhan (1976). Retail promotions as a function of trade promotions: A descriptive analysis. *Sloan Management Rev.* (Fall), 19–32.

Chintagunta, P.K., D.C. Jain, and N.J. Vilcassim (1991). Investigating heterogeneity in brand preferences in logit models for panel data. *J. Marketing Res.* 28 (November) 417–528.

Curhan, R.C., and R.J. Kopp (1986). Factors influencing grocery retailers' support of trade promotions. Report No. 86–114, Marketing Science Institute, Cambridge, MA, July.

Currim, I.S., and L.G. Schneider (1991). A taxonomy of consumer purchase strategies in a promotion intensive environment. *Marketing Sci.* 10(2), 91–110.

Davis, S., J.J. Inman and L. McAlister (1992). Promotion has a negative effect on brand evaluations – or does it? Additional disconfirming evidence. *J. Marketing Res.* 29 (February) 143–148.

Dhebar, A., S.A. Neslin, and J.A. Quelch (1987). Developing models for planning retailer sales promotions: An application to automobile dealerships. *J. Retailing*, 63(4), 333–364.

Doyle, P., and J. Saunders (1985). The lead effect of marketing decisions. *J. Marketing Research*, 22(1), 54–65.

Ehrenberg, A.S.C., K. Hammond, and G.J. Goodhardt (1992). The after-effects of large scale consumer promotions. Working Paper, London Business School; Stern School, New York University.

Fader, P.S. (1992). Integrating the Dirichlet-multinomial and multinomial logit models of brand choice. Working Paper 91-013R, The Wharton School, University of Pennsylvania, Philadelphia, PA.

Fader, P.S., and J.M. Lattin (1992). Accounting for heterogeneity and nonstationarity in a cross-sectional model of consumer purchase behavior. Working Paper 90-025R, The Wharton School, University of Pennsylvania, Philadelphia, PA.

Fader, P.S., J.M. Lattin, and J.D.C. Little (1992). Estimating nonlinear parameters in the multinomial logit model. Working Paper 90-030R, The Wharton School, University of Pennsylvania, Philadelphia, PA.

Gerstner, E., and J.D. Hess (1991). A theory of channel price promotions. *Amer. Econom. Rev.* 81 (September), 872–886.

Guadagni, P.M., and J.D.C. Little (1983). A logit model of brand choice calibrated on scanner data. *Marketing Sci*, 2(3), 203–238.

Gupta, S., (1988). Impact of Sales Promotions on When, What, and How Much to Buy. *J. Marketing Res.* 25(4), 342–355.

Gupta, S, (1991). Stochastic models of interpurchase time with time-dependent covariates, *J. Marketing Res.* 28 (February), 1–15.

Hardie, B.S., E.J. Johnson, and P.S. Fader (1991). Modeling loss aversion and reference dependence effects on brand choice. Working Paper 91-025, The Wharton School, University of Pennsylvania, Philadelphia, PA.

Helsen, K., and D.S. Schmittlein (1989). Analyzing duration times in marketing research. Working Paper, Wharton School, University of Pennsylvania, Philadelphia, PA.

Herniter, J.D., and J.F. Magee (1961). Customer behavior as a markov process. *Oper. Res.* 9, 105–122.

Hinkle, C.L. (1965). The strategy of price deals. *Harvard Business Rev.* 43 (July–August), 75–84.

Inman, J.J., L. McAlister, and W.D. Hoyer (1990). Promotion signal: Proxy for a price cut. *J. Consumer Res.* 17 (June), 74–81.

Jeuland, A.P., and C. Narasimhan (1985). Dealing – temporary price cuts – by seller as a buyer discrimination Mechanism. *J. Business*, 58, 295–308.

Jones, J.M., and J.T. Landwehr (1988). Removing heterogeneity bias from logit model estimation. *Marketing Sci.* 7(1), 41–59.

Kalwani, M.U., H.J. Rinne, and Y. Sugita (1990). A price expectations model of customer brand choice. *J. Marketing Res.* 27(3), 251–262.

Kamakura, W.A., and G.J. Russell (1989). A probabilistic choice model for market segmentation and elasticity structure. *J. Marketing Res.* 26, 379–390.

Keon, J. (1980). The bargain value model and a comparison of managerial implications with the linear learning model, *Management Sci.* 26 (November), 1117–1130.

Kim, B.D. (1992). Estimating the intensity of preference for quality. Ph.D. Thesis, Graduate School of Business, University of Chicago.

Krishna, A. (1992). The normative impact of consumer price expectations for multiple brands on consumer choice behavior. *Marketing Sci.* 11 (Summer) 266–287.

Krishnamurthi, L., and S.P. Raj (1988). A model of brand choice and purchase quantity price sensitivities. *Marketing Sci.* 7(1), 1–20.

Kuehn, A.A., and A.C. Rohloff (1967). Consumer response to promotions. In P.J. Robinson (ed.), *Promotional Decisions Using Mathematical Models*, Allyn and Bacon, Boston, pp. 45–128.

Kumar, V., and R.P. Leone (1988). Measuring the effect of retail store promotions on brand and store substitutions. *J. Marketing Res.* 25(2), 178–185.

Lal, R. (1990a), Price promotions: limiting competitive encroachment. *Marketing Sci.* 9 (Summer) 247–262.

Lal, R. (1990b) Manufacturer trade deals and retail price promotions. *J. Marketing Res.* 27 (November) 428–444.

Lattin, J.M., and R.E. Bucklin (1989). Reference effects on price and promotion on brand choice behavior. *J. Marketing Res.* 26(3), 299–310.

Lawless, J.F. (1982). *Statistical Models and Methods for Lifetime Data*, Wiley, New York.

Leone, R.P. (1987). Forecasting the effect of an environmental change on market performance: An intervention time-series approach. *Inter. J. Forecasting*, 3, 463–478.

Lilien, G.L. (1974). An application of a modified linear learning model of buyer behavior. *J. Marketing Res.* 11, (August) 279–285.

Little, J.D.C. (1970). Models and managers: The concept of a decision calculus. *Management Sci.* 16(8), B466–B485.

Little, J. (1975). BRANDAID: A marketing-mix model, Part 1: Structure; Part II: Implementation. *Oper. Res.* 23(4), 628–673.

Little, J. (1979). Decision support systems for marketing managers. *J. Marketing* 43 (Summer) 9–26.

Little, J. (1991). A look at coupon effectiveness. Paper presented at marketing science institute sales promotion conference, May 16–17, Boston, MA.

Lodish, L. (1982). A marketing decision support system for retailers. *Marketing Sci.* 1(1), 31–56.

Maffai, R.B. (1960). Brand preference and simple Markov processes. *Oper. Res.* 8, 210–218.

Makridakis, S., S.C. Wheelwright and V.E. McGee (1983). *Forecasting: Methods and Applications, 2nd edition*, Wiley, New York.

Manufacturers Coupon Control Center (1988). Coupon distribution and redemption patterns. Manufacturers Coupon Control Center, Wilton, CT.

Moriarty, M. (1985). Retail promotional effects on intra- and interbrand sales performance. *J. Retailing* 61(3), 27–48.

Mulhern, F., and R. Leone (1991). Implicit price bundling of retail products: a multiproduct approach to maximizing store profitability, *J. Marketing* 55 (October) 63–76.

Narasimhan, C. (1988). Competitive promotional strategies. *J. Business* 61, 427–450.

Neslin, S.A. (1990). A market response model for coupon promotions. *Marketing Sci.* 9(2), 125–145.

Neslin, S.A., C. Henderson, and J. Quelch (1985). Consumer promotions and the acceleration of product purchases. *Marketing Sci.* 4 (Spring) 147–165.

Neslin, S.A., S.G. Powell, and L. Schneider (1991). An optimization model for planning advertising and sales promotion. Working Paper, Amos Tuck School of Business Administration, Dartmouth College, Hanover, NH, September.

Neslin, S.A., and L.G. Schneider (1993). Consumer inventory sensitivity and the post-promotion 'dip'. Working Paper, Amos Tuck School of Business Administration, Dartmouth College, Hanover, NH, September.

Neslin, S.A., and R.W. Shoemaker (1983). A model for evaluating the profitability of coupon promotions. *Marketing Sci.* 2(4), 361–388.

Neslin, S.A., and R.W. Shoemaker (1989). An alternative explanation for lower repeat rates following promotion purchases. *J. Markeing Res.* 26(2), 205–213.

Nielsen Clearing House (1990). Coupon distribution and redemption patterns. Chicago, Nielsen Clearing House.

Ortmeyer, G., and J. Huber (1991). Brand experience as a moderator of the negative impact of promotions. *Marketing Lett.* 2, 35–45.

Raju. J., S.V. Srinivasan, and R. Lal (1990). The effects of brand loyalty on competitive price promotions strategies. *Management Sci.* 36, 276–304.

Rao, V.R., and L.J. Thomas (1973). Dynamic models for sales promotion policies. *Oper. Res. Quart.* 24(3), 403–417.

Reibstein, D.J., and P.A. Traver (1982). Factors affecting coupon redemption rates. *J. Marketing,* 46 (Fall), 102–113.

Strang, R.A. (1975). The relationship between advertising and promotion in brand strategy. Marketing Science Insitute Cambridge, MA.

Thaler, R. (1985). Mental accounting and consumer choice. *Marketing Sci.* 4(3), 199–214.

Theil, H., (1971). *Principles of Econometrics*, Wiley, New York.

Thompson, P., and T. Noordewier (1991). Estimating the effects of consumer incentive programs on domestic auto sales, *J. Business Econom. Statist.*, forthcoming.

Varian, H.R. (1980). A Model of Sales, *Amer. Econom. Rev.* 70 (September) 651–659.

Vilcassim, N.J., and D.C. Jain (1991). Modeling purchase-timing and brand-switching behavior incorporate explanatory variables and unobserved heterogeneity, *J. Marketing Res.* 28(1), 29–41.

Walters, R.G. (1989). An empirical investigation into retailer response to manufacturer trade promotions. *J. Retailing*, 65(2), 253–272.

Walters, R.G. (1991). Assessing the impact of retail price promotions on product substitution, complementary purchase, and interstore sales displacement. *J. Marketing*, 55, 17–28.

Walters, R.G., and S.B. MacKenzie (1988). A structural equations analysis of the impact of price promotions on store performance. *J. Marketing Res.* 25(1), 51–63.

Walters, R.G., and H.J. Rinne (1986). An empirical investigation into the impact of price promotions on retail store performance. *J. Retailing*, 62(3), 237–266.

Ward, R.W., and J.E. Davis (1978). A pooled cross-section time series model of coupon promotions. *Amer. J. Agricul. Econom.* 60 (November) 393–401.

Winer, Russell S. (1986). A reference price model of brand choice for frequently purchased products. *J. Consumer Res.* 13 (September), 250–256.

Wittink, D.R., M.J. Addona, W.J. Hawkes, and J.C. Porter (1987). SCANPRO®: A model to measure short-term effects of promotional activities on brand sales, based on store-level scanner data. Working Paper, Johnson Graduate School of Management, Cornell University, Ithaca, NY, May.

Wittink, D.R., J.C. Porter, and S. Gupta (1993). Biases in parameter estimates from a linearly aggregated data when the disaggregated model is nonlinear. Working Paper, Johnson Graduate School of Management, Cornell University, Ithaca, NY.

J. Eliashberg and G.L. Lilien, Eds., *Handbooks in OR & MS, Vol. 5*

Chapter 13

Salesforce Compensation: A Review of MS/OR Advances

Anne T. Coughlan
Associate Professor of Marketing, Kellogg Graduate School of Management, Northwestern University, 2001 Sheridan Road, Evanston, IL 60208-2001, USA

1. Introduction

A firm that has made the significant investment in a direct salesforce has an interest in the continuing motivation and sales performance of its salespeople. Sales management faces two fundamental problems in designing effective reward systems. First, salespeople typically have objectives that differ from those of the firm, necessitating compensation-plan design that aligns salesforce and sales-management objectives. Second, managers who set compensation often lack information that is crucial to setting the right compensation plan, such as how sales respond to the sales effort of different salespeople in different territories, or the relative preference a salesperson has for income versus leisure. While some array of monetary and non-monetary rewards may help solve both problems and result in effective selling performance, research shows that salespeople are much more highly motivated by monetary rewards than by non-monetary ones [Ford, Walker & Churchill, 1981]. This of course does not mean that sales management should abandon non-monetary rewards, since they too generate positive (albeit lower) utility for the salesforce. Nevertheless, the clear importance of monetary rewards for salesforce motivation justifies this chapter's primary focus on management science/operations research approaches to salesforce compensation research.

The problem of designing an 'optimal' salesforce-compensation problem is very complex. On the most fundamental level, the manager must decide what 'optimal' means: is a plan optimal that maximizes the firm's sales or profits? That maximizes salespeople's income or utility? Is a plan optimal that is constrained by certain requirements of the firm, such as the maintenance of a particular form of plan?

Even after deciding what objectives a salesforce-compensation system is designed to attain, management still has to characterize some important aspects of its environment. It must do its best to characterize (a) the preferences and behavior of salespeople, (b) the nature of sales response, and (c) its own preferences and behavior. Some examples will serve to illustrate the rich array of issues raised here. Salespeople may influence sales and profit outcomes only by the exertion of selling effort, or they may be responsible for other decisions as well, such as pricing.

Sales response may be a function of selling effort alone (as seems approximately true in some industrial-product markets), or may also be significantly influenced by product prices and other marketing-mix variables. Sales response for one product may depend critically on sales of another complementary product in the line, or may depend on the team-selling efforts of several people in the salesforce.

The firm itself may have several interrelated decisions to make, including not only the form of the compensation plan (e.g. whether it will include commission pay in addition to salaries), but also levels of incentives (e.g. commission rates) and whether to offer a tailored menu of plans to a heterogeneous salesforce. This set of decisions on the part of the firm abstracts from the greater environment in which it operates: how it responds to competition, what products it chooses to include in its product line, and the like.

By necessity, the literature on salesforce compensation takes many of these issues as given when attacking a particular aspect of the compensation-setting problem. But there is no doubt that all of these issues, and many more, have an impact on salesforce motivation and ensuing firm profits. The common theme pervading all the research in the area is the search for a compensation plan that makes the best use of available information (or elicits extra valuable information when needed) in designing a plan that comes the closest to aligning the incentives of sales management and the salesperson. Fortunately, the marketing literature on salesforce compensation has progressed far enough on some of these issues to merit review, although as we will see in the concluding section of the chapter, there is still a great deal left to accomplish.

Prior survey work in the salesforce-compensation area in marketing includes Coughlan & Sen [1986, 1989]. This chapter differs from both of these earlier papers in several ways. First, it is more up-to-date in the set of articles it surveys. It also presents material more analytically, to highlight MS/OR advances in modeling in the area. Further, it surveys three major approaches to salesforce-compensation modeling, whereas the other two papers concentrate on a subset of these methods: (i) a microeconomics-based approach assuming no uncertainty in sales response; (ii) an agency-theoretic approach; and (iii) a decision support system (DSS) approach. We also summarize empirical evidence for the first two areas as a guide to assessing the reliability and robustness of the theory.

In what follows, we summarize the modeling structures and results in the three major areas of the MS/OR salesforce-compensation literature. After the discussion of microeconomics-based models (i) and agency-theoretic models (ii), we summarize empirical tests of these theories before turning to a discussion of DSS models (iii). In each case, we provide tabular summaries of model structures as well as textual discussion. All models are characterized by their treatment of the salesforce, the sales-response function, and the firm itself. It turns out that in the microeconomics-based approach and the agency-theoretic approach, one can describe a base model from which later publications build and digress. The development of the DSS literature has been less orderly in some sense, but this is because of a focus on solving different particular problems in salesforce compensation. We close with conclusions and directions for future research.

2. Model structure/techniques: Microeconomic approach

The first set of models is united by the common assumption of non-stochasticity of sales response to selling effort. This means that a given amount of selling effort exerted against a particular product *always* produces the same level of sales; there are no environmental or competitive 'wild cards' inducing randomness into the sales-response function. Despite this non-stochasticity, the firm may or may not know the exact form of a given salesperson's sales-response function for a given product. The salesperson is always assumed to know the sales-response function for every product he sells, however.

All the models assume that the firm maximizes profits and the salesperson maximizes his utility. The firm's problem is to design a compensation plan that causes the salesperson to make his decisions (time allocation across products, total selling-time allocation, and/or product price/discount setting) so as to maximize the firm's profits. Essentially, the compensation plan is to be designed to align the salesperson's objectives with those of the firm, despite the basic fact that the salesperson may seem to have different goals in mind than those of the firm.

We can characterize the general form of all the models in this section, and identify how each one is a special case of the general model. In this general model, the firm's profit can be expressed as:

$$\Pi = \sum_{i=1}^{n} \sum_{j=1}^{m} P_{ij} Q_{ij} - \sum_{i=1}^{n} C_i(Q_i) - \sum_{j=1}^{m} S_j, \qquad (1)$$

where each of the m salespeople in the salesforce sells the firm's line of n products and where

P_{ij} = selling price of product i when sold by salesperson j,
$Q_i = \sum_j Q_{ij}$ = number of units of product i sold by all salespeople,
$C_i(Q_i)$ = total variable cost of selling Q_i units of product i,
S_j = salesperson j's total income.

The sales-response function for product i for salesperson j is

$$Q_{ij} = f_i(t_{1j}, t_{2j}, \ldots, t_{nj}, P_{1j}, P_{2j}, \ldots, P_{nj}), \qquad (2)$$

where t_{ij} is the selling time allocated by salesperson j to product i and P_{ij} is the priced charged for product i by salesperson j (providing for the possibility that salespeople in different territories may charge different prices for the same product, although any one salesperson sets product i's price just once for all his customers). Thus, in the most general form, sales response can include cross-price as well as cross-effort effects, and each salesperson may possibly control product prices as well as his own selling effort. All models assume that the firm acts as a Stackelberg leader relative to its salespeople, that is, that the firm knows the form of the salesperson's reaction to any compensation plan it quotes to the salesforce. Note, however, that none of the articles explicitly considers the possibility of team-selling, where sales by salesperson j are a direct function of the effort exerted by other members of the salesforce. Nor do the articles focus attention on salesperson-specific differences in sales-response functions (hence the functional form f_i in Equation 2 typically applies to all m salespeople).

The salesperson's goal is to maximize utility. His decision variables include the allocation of selling time across the n products, and may also include the setting of product prices (or equivalently, discounts off list price) and the choice of total selling time. Formally, utility can be expressed as:

$$U_j = g_j(S_j) - V_j(T_j) \text{ subject to } \sum_{i=1}^{n} t_{ij} = T_j, \tag{3}$$

where

$g_j(\cdot)$ = utility for income,
$V_j(\cdot)$ = disutility for effort,
t_{ij} = time allocated to selling product i by salesperson j,
T_j = total selling time of salesperson j.

This summarizes the most generic form of the salesforce-compensation model, given certainty in the sales-response function. The goal of all the models in this class is to design a compensation plan (specifically, to set the form of S_j) that induces the salesperson to act so as to maximize the firm's profits. We can classify the papers referred to in this section by the ways in which they specify this general model. Tables 13.1, 13.2 and 13.3 summarize assumptions on the salesforce, the sales-response function, and the firm made by each article in the area, using the Farley [1964] paper as a base case.

Farley [1964] was the first paper to model salesforce compensation in this type of framework. His model makes the following four assumptions concerning the salesforce (expressed in our terminology):

F1. The salesforce has one person in it. (Equivalently, the model could represent a multi-person salesforce, where there are no interactions among salespeople's decisions.)

F2. The salesperson's only choice variable is sales-effort allocation across the n products sold.

F3. The salesperson's objective is to maximize income.

F4. There is one constraint on the salesperson's decisions: total selling time is limited to T.

The next three assumptions in Farley [1964] pertain to the sales response function:

F5. There are n products in the product line, with no demand- or cost-side interactions among them.

Table 13.1
Salesforce-compensation models, sales-response-function certainty: assumptions on the salesforce

Source	F1. Salesforce size	F2. Salesperson's choice variables	F3. Salesperson's objective function	F4. Salesperson's constraints
Base case: Farley [1964]	One salesperson (generalizable to n salespeople, no interactions)	Sales-effort allocation across products only	Maximize income	Total selling time of T_j for any salesperson j
Comparison of Farley [1964] with:				
Davis & Farley [1971]	Same	Same	Same	Same
Weinberg [1975]	Same	Sales-effort allocation, and discounts from list price, across products	Same	Same
Tapiero & Farley [1975]	n salespeople, no interactions	Sales-effort allocation across T time periods	Same	Total selling time of T_j per salesperson per time period
Weinberg [1978]	Same	Sales-effort allocation, and discounts from list price, across products	(a) Maximize income subject to time constraint; or (b) minimize time s.t. an income constraint; or (c) maximize income s.t. a minimum marginal return for time spent on each product	(a) Time constraint; or (b) income constraint; or (c) constraint on minimum marginal return for time spent on each product
Srinivasan [1981]	Same	(a) Sales effort and actual selling price across products; or (b) total selling time; or (c) total selling time	(a) Maximize income s.t. time constraint; or (b) achieve 'fair' income; or (c) maximize utility	(a) Time constraint; or (b) 'fair' income constraint; or (c) unconstrained utility maximization

These assumptions are discussed more fully in Section 2 of the paper. Assumptions are noted for the Farley model, and deviations from the Farley assumptions are noted for the other papers in the table.

Table 13.2
Salesforce-compensation models, sales-response-function certainty: assumptions on the sales-response function

Source	F5. Nature of product line	F6. Arguments of sales-response function	F7. Sales-response functional form
Base case: Farley [1964]	n products, no demand or cost interactions	Selling effort on own product only	$Q_i = f_i(t_i), \quad i = 1,2,\ldots,n, \quad f_i' > 0$
Comparison of Farley [1964] with:			
Davis & Farley [1971]	Same	Same	Same; but also, $f_{ij}'' < 0$
Weinberg [1975]	Same	Selling effort on own product and discount off list price	$Q_i = f_i(t_i, P_i), \quad i = 1,2,\ldots,n$; $\partial f_i/\partial t_i, \partial f_i/\partial P_i > 0$; f_i concave
Tapiero & Farley [1975]	Same	Current and possibly past selling effort on own product	$Q_{ij}(t) = F_{ij}'[\int m(t,z)u_{ij}(z)\mathrm{d}z]$, a function of current marginal effort productivity, a 'forgetting function', and effective units of selling effort
Weinberg [1978]	Same	Selling effort on own and other products; discounts on own and other products	$Q_i = f_i(t_1, t_2, \ldots, t_n, P_1, P_2, \ldots, P_n)$, $\partial f_i/\partial t_i, \partial f_i/\partial P_i > 0$
Srinivasan [1981]	Same	Selling effort on own and other products; discounts on own and other products	$Q_i = f_i(t_1, t_2, \ldots, t_n, P_1, P_2, \ldots, P_n)$; cross-product effects not investigated throughout analysis

These assumptions are discussed more fully in Section 2 of the paper. Assumptions are noted for the Farley model, and deviations from the Farley assumptions are noted for the other papers in the table.

Table 13.3
Salesforce-compensation models, sales-response-function certainty: assumptions on firm behavior

Source	F8. Production cost	F9. Firm knowledge	F10. Firm choice variables	F11. Firm objective function
Base case: Farley [1964]	Constant marginal cost, no economies of scale or scope	Knows salesperson's utility function and sales-response function	Commission rates on gross margins of all products	Maximize profit
Comparison of Farley [1964] with:				
Davis & Farley [1971]	Total variable costs across product line are: $C = \Sigma_i C_i(Q_i)$, where $d^2C_i/dQ_i^2 > 0$ (jointly decreasing returns to scale over product line)	Same	Commission rates on sales or gross margins, or set quotas, on all products	Same
Weinberg [1975]	Same	Same	Commission rates on realized gross margins of all products	Same
Tapiero & Farley [1975]	General function of contemporaneous volume of own product; constant marginal cost for parametric results	Same	Commission rates and/or quotas on all products	Same (dynamic horizon)
Weinberg [1978]	Same	Same	Same	Same
Srinivasan [1981]	Same	Knows salesperson's utility function, but not sales-response function	Commission rates on total contribution	Same

These assumptions are discussed more fully in Section 2 of the paper. Assumptions are noted for the Farley model, and deviations from the Farley assumptions are noted for the other papers in the table.

F6. The only argument of the sales-response function for product i is selling time on product i.

F7. The form of the sales-response function is:

$$Q_i = f_i(t_i), \quad i = 1, 2, \ldots, n, \; f'_i > 0. \tag{4}$$

Finally, four assumptions characterize Farley's assumptions on the firm:

F8. Each of the n products has a constant marginal cost of production, with no cross-product cost interactions (that is, there are no economies of scale or scope).

F9. The firm knows both the salesperson's utility function and the form of the sales response function fully.

F10. The firm's choice variables are commission rates paid on gross margins of each of the n products.

F11. The firm's objective is to maximize profit.

Given these specific assumptions, Equations (1) and (3) become:

$$\Pi = \sum_{i=1}^{n} (P_i - K_i) \cdot (1 - B_i) \cdot f_i(t_i), \tag{5}$$

$$U_j = S_j = \sum_{i=1}^{n} (P_i - K_i) \cdot B_i \cdot f_i(t_{ij}), \tag{6}$$

where B_i is the (fractional) commission rate on gross margin paid on product i.

In this framework, Farley's central result is a very simple rule about incentive-aligning compensation: the firm should compensate each salesperson with a commission-only compensation plan, where each commission rate is an equal percentage of the product's gross margin. That is, $B_i = B_j$ for all products i and j. This plan maximizes the firm's profit because it makes the salesperson's utility function a fraction of total system profits, with the remaining fraction going to the firm. Incentives are aligned because the salesperson is in effect made a 'residual claimant' of the firm.

Farley's result does not specify what exact commission rate is the 'right' one, although common sense suggests that total compensation should be at least equal to the salesperson's opportunity cost of time (otherwise, he will leave the firm). Farley also establishes that in general, commissions paid on *sales revenue* are not optimal, because they cause the salesperson to maximize sales, rather than profits.

Davis & Farley [1971] examine the same problem as Farley's [1964] model, with two differences in assumptions:

DF8. Total variable costs across the entire product line are given by:

$$C = \sum_i C_i(Q_i), \qquad \mathrm{d}^2 C_i / \mathrm{d}Q_i^2 > 0 \tag{7}$$

(there are decreasing returns to scale over the entire product line).

DF10. The firm sets commission rates on sales or on gross margins, or it sets quotas, on all products.

This change complicates matters significantly, since now each salesperson's sales of product i affect the marginal cost associated with selling another unit of i, and hence the optimal sales of product i by the rest of the salesforce; the salespeople's actions are truly interdependent. Davis & Farley show that in this situation, *neither* a commission on sales *nor* a commission on gross margins solves the incentive incompatibility problem of the salesforce and the firm. They offer two solutions: the first involves centralized quota-setting by the firm, based on complete knowledge of the sales-response functions for each salesperson and each product.

The problem with this solution, Davis & Farley point out, is its significant information requirements for the firm. It is unlikely that the firm will possess all the relevant information about each salesperson's marginal productivity of selling effort for every product, for example. Thus, they sketch out an alternative solution. This involves an iterative procedure where the firm proposes a set of commission rates to the salesforce, and salespeople respond with desired quotas for each product; then commissions on products that are oversubscribed (i.e. that produce sales beyond the profit-maximizing level in total) are decreased, while those on products that are undersubscribed are increased, until a commission/quota system results that sells the optimal amount of each product. In such a system, salespeople implicitly inform the firm about their sales response functions when they pass information about preferred quotas back to the firm.

Weinberg's [1975] key extension is to examine how salesforce price-setting ability affects optimal commission-based compensation schemes. He thus extends the Farley framework by changing assumptions F2, F6 and F7 (we modify Weinberg's terminology to be consistent with our terminology above):

W5.2. The salesperson's choice variables are sales-effort allocation across all products *and* decimal discounts off the firm's list price for each product.

W5.6. Sales response for product i is a function of the selling effort and decimal discount off list price for product i.

W5.7. Sales response is given formally by:

$$Q_i = f_i(t_i, P_i), \quad i = 1, 2, \ldots, n;$$

$$\partial f_i / \partial t_i > 0, \quad \partial f_i / \partial P_i < 0; \quad f_i \text{ concave.} \tag{8}$$

Note that choosing a decimal discount is tantamount to choosing actual selling price; we therefore represent sales response as a function of selling time and actual price charged.

Weinberg shows that if the salesperson is setting *both* effort allocation among products *and* prices, a set of equal commission rates on gross margins of the products is optimal and will induce the profit-maximizing prices and quantities sold. If the salesperson is setting *only* price, and his effort allocation is dictated by the firm, Weinberg also shows that *any* commissions on gross margins (not necessarily equal rates across products) induce the right discounting by the salesforce. The ability of the salesforce to set price could also be interpreted from a modeling point of view as any salesforce activity that increases demand, e.g. additional customer service or product features that the salesperson can include in order to close a sale, as long as the salesperson is informed of the cost of providing these services.

Tapiero & Farley [1975] also work with the basic Farley [1964] framework, but consider dynamic effects on salesforce compensation as well. They alter Farley's assumptions F2, F4, F6 and F7 as follows:

TF2. Each salesperson chooses selling effort for the n products in the line across T time periods.

TF4. Each salesperson is constrained to spend not more than T_j time selling per period (the direct dynamic analogue to Farley's assumption F4).

TF6. Sales response for product i is a function of current-period selling effort and may also be a function of past selling effort on product i.

TF7. The rate of sales at any time t is given by:

$$Q_{ij}(t) = F'_{ij}\left(\int_{-\infty}^{t} m(t, z)u_{ij}(z)\mathrm{d}z\right), \tag{9}$$

where

F'_{ij} = marginal productivity of an effective current unit of selling effort,
$m(t, z)$ = a 'forgetting function' representing residual effects of sales effort in some past period z on current sales,
$u_{ij}(t)$ = effective units of selling effort in some time z; a mapping between actual hours spent selling and sales response.[1]

Further, while the authors model production costs for product i as a general function of the contemporaneous volume sold of product i, their major results derive from an assumption of constant marginal cost, as in Farley [1984].

The complexity of this problem makes explicit solution in the general case impossible. However, an example with constant marginal costs and a very long planning period for sales performance results in an optimal compensation plan with commission rates proportional to gross margins of the products, with the constant of proportionality varying from product to product.[2] Salespeople allocate more effort to products with larger marginal profit rates and smaller forgetting

[1] The authors actually state in their Equation 2.1 [p. 979] that $u_{ij}(t)$ is equal to the *integral* of past sales efforts, but then go on in Equation 2.2 to argue that F'_{ij} can have u_{ij} as an argument. This seems circular; the implication would be 'double-counting' of the effect of hours of effort in any time z on future sales of product. A more reasonable interpretation of u_{ij} seems to be the one above. This interpretation is also consistent with the authors' example developed in Section 4 of their paper [pp. 982ff.].

[2] However, this result is derived under the assumption that the firm does not pay for commissions to salespeople but rather assigns quotas [cf. Equation 4.1, p. 982]. It is thus unclear whether the same result would prevail if the profit function were reformulated to include commission costs.

rates. However, more interesting cases with nonlinearities in either costs or sales-effectiveness generally require centralized solutions with optimal quota-setting and significant information acquisition by the firm.

Weinberg [1978] returns to Farley's static formulation and assumption, but examines both variations in the salesperson's objective function and demand interactions among products in price and sales-effort effects. He modifies Farley's assumptions F2, F3, F4, F6 and F7 as follows:

W8.2. The salesperson's choice variables are sales-effort allocation across all products *and* decimal discounts off the firm's list price for each product.

W8.3. The model investigates three possible objective functions for the salesperson: (a) to maximize income subject to a time constraint; (b) to minimize selling time subject to an income constraint; or (c) to maximize income subject to a minimum return per unit time.

W8.4. The constraint facing the salesperson varies with the objective function assumed: (a) the salesperson faces a total-selling-time constraint; or (b) he faces an income constraint; or (c) he faces a constraint on minimum return per unit time.

W8.6. Sales of product i are a function of selling effort for *all* n products and *all* n prices.

W8.7. Formally (and using our terminology), the sales-response function is:

$$Q_i = f_i(t_1, t_2, \ldots, t_n, P_1, P_2, \ldots, P_n),$$

where

$$\partial f_i/\partial t_i > 0, \qquad \partial f_i/\partial P_i < 0. \tag{10}$$

Under objective (a), (b) or (c) in W8.3. above, Weinberg shows that an equal-gross-margin commission system as derived in Farley [1964] is optimal. This is intuitively sensible, since (a) is just Farley's problem; (b) is the dual of Farley's problem; and (c) is tantamount to (a) due to the one-to-one relationship between return per unit time and total income.

Finally, Srinivasan [1981] points out that previous models neglect the fact that the compensation plan offered affects not only the allocation of effort across products, but also total sales effort expended by the salesperson. He builds the most comprehensive model to date by also including the ability of the salesperson to set product prices, and considering varying objective functions for the salesperson. His model differs from Farley's in assumptions F2, F3, F4, F6, F7 and F9 as follows (cases (a), (b) and (c) are consistently listed throughout):

S2. Under three different salesperson objective functions, the salesperson chooses, respectively: (a) sales effort and actual selling prices across products; (b) total selling time; and (c) total selling time.

S3. The salesperson's objective function can be: (a) to maximize income subject to a time constraint (the case of a 'fixed total time' salesperson); (b) to achieve 'fair income' (the case of a 'fair income' salesperson); or (c) to maximize utility (a 'utility-maximizing' salesperson).

S4. The constraint facing the salesperson varies with the objective function assumed: (a) the salesperson faces a total-selling-time constraint; or (b) he faces a 'fair income' constraint; or (c) he faces no constraints in the utility-maximization case.

S6. Sales of product i are a function of selling effort for *all* n products and *all* n prices.

S7. The sales response function is formally modeled as in Weinberg [1978] (see Equation (10)).

S9. The firm knows the salesperson's utility function, but not the sales-response function.

In fact, although Srinivasan is the first to express assumption S9, previous models' solutions and results would be the same with this assumption as well. This is because, given certainty in the sales response function, there is a one-to-one mapping between effort and sales: thus, observing sales made by a salesperson is equivalent to observing effort directly, and compensation can therefore be awarded on the basis of output (i.e. commission) to align the firm's and the salesperson's incentives.

Srinivasan shows, as do those before him, that an optimal compensation plan for objective functions (a) and (b) is the equal-gross-margin commission scheme. He uses the notion of opportunity cost of time to derive the exact commission rate that is optimal in case (a), of the fixed-total-time salesperson. For the utility-maximizing salesperson, however, an equal-commission-rate policy is generally suboptimal, since the salesperson is deciding both the allocation of selling time across products and total selling time itself; the equal-commission-rate policy induces too little *total* time allocation when it produces the right *mix* of time allocated across products. Srinivasan derives optimal unequal commission rates in at least one example, where the salesperson's opportunity cost of time is linear in total selling time and where sales response is given by:

$$Q_i = d_i(P_i)\cdot[a_i t_i^{\gamma_i}], \quad 0 < \gamma_i < 1. \tag{11}$$

In this special case, optimal commission rates are equal to the corresponding elasticities of sales response to selling effort: B_i equals γ_i for all i. This result makes intuitive sense, since salespeople should not be induced to aggressively sell products that have low responsiveness to selling effort.

Finally, through various examples, Srinivasan establishes that heterogeneous salesforces are not usually optimally compensated with equal-commission-rate policies, and that there is some profit loss when the firm is constrained to offer only one compensation plan to a heterogeneous salesforce.

Summary of results in microeconomic models of salesforce compensation

Farley's seminal paper shows that with a non-stochastic sales response function, an income-maximizing salesperson, constant marginal costs, and no across-product or across-salesperson interactions, an all-commission compensation plan with commission rates set as an equal percentage of gross margins maximizes the firm's profits. The equal-commission-rate policy is also shown to be optimal when salespeople set prices as well as selling time across products [Weinberg, 1975], and under varying assumptions on the salesperson's objective function [Weinberg, 1978; Srinivasan, 1981]. When salespeople maximize utility and have a nonzero opportunity cost of time, however, unequal commission rates are generally optimal [Srinivasan, 1981]. Dynamic effects of selling effort in one period on sales in later periods also negate the equal-commission-rate policy in general [Tapiero & Farley, 1975], although not necessarily the optimality of all commission-rate policies. True interdependence among salespeople, as in Davis & Farley's [1971] assumption of non-constant marginal costs, also implies that an equal-commission-rate policy is suboptimal; the solution in such situations of interdependence may involve iterative methods with the salesforce to reveal optimal commission–quota combinations.

Thus, in general, the equal-commission-rate result holds only under fairly strict conditions, not the least of which is non-stochasticity of the sales-response function. Also crucially important is a lack of any fundamental interdependence among decisions about effort allocation or pricing. Thus, team-selling situations and situations where products in a line are closely interrelated in demand are outside the scope of this set of models.

Further, the articles generally do not question the underlying focus on commission-only salesforce-compensation plans. Srinivasan [1981] recognizes that his solutions are sufficient, but may be more than necessary, conditions for profit maximization. But in general, the authors do not consider the more basic question of the elements in the optimal salesforce-compensation plan, or indeed, the uniqueness of their optimum plan. Questions of the appropriate mix of commissions, bonuses and salaries are therefore ignored. As we will see below, the all-commission plan is *never* a unique optimum under certainty in the sales-response function. The optimal level of *total* compensation is also generally ignored (one exception being Srinivasan [1981]). Finally, because of the assumption of certainty in the sales-response function, the authors are unable to investigate the effects of differences in risk attitude of the salesforce or variance in the sales-response function on optimal compensation.

Despite these drawbacks, this literature is useful in defining the ultimate goal of salesforce compensation-setting: the aligning of incentives between the firm and its salesforce. The later literature using agency theory continues with this basic focus, and also seeks to answer some of these challenges posed by the first phase of analytical research in the area. We now turn to this literature.

3. Model structure/techniques: Agency-theoretic approach

Concurrent with the development of the microeconomics-based analytic approach to salesforce compensation, a new branch of economic analysis was also being developed: agency theory. Agency theory is designed to analyze problems where a *principal* (e.g. the firm) hires an *agent* (e.g. the salesperson) to perform some action(s) for it (e.g. exert selling effort). In this framework, the responsiveness of output (e.g. sales) to the agent's input (e.g. effort) is assumed to be stochastic,[3] and further, it is assumed that the principal can observe the agent's effort either imperfectly or not at all. Agency theory assumes that the principal and the agent have different attitudes toward risk: typically, the principal is assumed to be risk-neutral and the agent to be risk-averse. Henceforward, we will refer to the principal as the firm, and the agent as the salesperson.

Within the agency-theory literature, models make varying assumptions about the amount of information the firm has about the salesperson's response function. If the firm has complete information about the form of the response functions across various salespeople (e.g. differences in the productivity of their sales effort), but cannot observe effort itself, the firm is said to face a problem of *moral hazard*: there is the risk that the salesperson will shirk in the provision of effort, and that the firm will not be able to tell whether a particular outcome was due to the salesperson's (lack of) effort or to the stochastic element in the response function. If, in addition, the firm does not know a priori which salesperson has which level of productivity, the firm is said to face the problem of *adverse selection* as well: it may incorrectly classify a low-productivity salesperson as a high-productivity one because of a strongly positive draw from the error distribution in the sales-response function. Agency-theoretic models in economics, and their adaptations in marketing, have attacked the problem of optimal compensation under these various conditions.

The assumptions of uncertainty in the sales-response function, differences in risk attitudes, and unobservability of salesperson effort are key in differentiating the agency-theory approach from the microeconomic approach discussed in Section 2 above. In particular, one basic insight from agency theorists concerns the limiting case of certainty in the sales-response function. Under certainty, there is a simple and elegant alternative to the equal-commission-rate structures posited by earlier authors: the so-called 'forcing contract'. This contract promises compensation *exactly* equal to the salesperson's opportunity cost of time if he generates the profit-maximizing levels of sales for the firm (e.g. a strict quota), and zero otherwise. The salesperson will be just willing to do this job for the firm, since it generates (with certainty) income equal to his minimum acceptable level. Thus, the solution both satisfies the salesperson and maximizes the firm's profits. This implies that all the results in the certainty literature are feasible, but not unique, solutions to the firm's salesforce-compensation problem.

But in an agency-theory context, a forcing contract does not solve the incentive-incompatibility problem, because of the uncertainty in the sales-response function and the difference in risk attitudes of the salesperson and the firm. A risk-averse salesperson will be unwilling to undertake risky activities that a risk-neutral firm may find profit-maximizing, if the salesperson is forced to bear all the selling risk (as happens in a forcing-contract plan). The result will be inefficiently high total pay levels (to provide the necessary risk premium to meet the minimum-utility

[3] Or at least, if the sales-response function is not stochastic, its true form is only known to the salesperson, and not to the firm (this means the firm sets compensation *as if* the sales-response function were stochastic). See Rao [1990] for an example of such a model.

requirement of the salesperson) and a misallocation of selling effort toward unduly low-risk selling activities. Agency-theoretic modelling seeks to solve this problem by developing optimal risk-sharing contracts that reduce the risk in the pay plan while still encouraging selling effort. In this section, we first exposit the early models and then describe how later modelling efforts expand upon the initial contributions.

Berger [1972, 1975] develops a model that is a hybrid between the certainty approach profiled in the above section of this paper and the agency-theoretic approach. He posits a Farley-type [1964] model, but allows sales to be stochastic and varies the salesperson's risk attitude. He assumes compensation is via commission only. He shows that Farley's equal commissions on gross margins create compatible incentives when the salesforce is risk-neutral. He further shows that the Farley commission structure aligns the incentives of the firm and either risk-averse or risk-seeking salespeople, as long as the variance of the sales-response function is not a function of sales effort (that is, mean sales vary with effort, but not sales variance). But when sales-response variance is proportional to sales effort, for example, risk-averse salespeople should receive a higher commission rate on a product with a higher variance (holding profit margin constant). Conversely, risk-seeking salespeople should receive a lower commission rate on such a product.

The critical constraints in Berger's approach, which are relaxed in true agency-theoretic approach, are (1) his assumption of commission-only pay; and (2) his restrictive choice of sales-response functions. The basic agency-theory literature in economics (see, for example, Harris & Raviv [1978, 1979], Holmstrom [1979], or Shavell [1979], among many others) focuses on the derivation of an optimal compensation contract form in a moral-hazard context. The first application of this approach in the marketing literature is in the Basu, Lal, Srinivasan & Staelin [1985] model, hereafter referred to as BLSS. The BLSS model is patterned after Holmstrom [1979], but applies the agency-theoretic framework directly to the salesforce-compensation context and develops many specific predictions based on distributional assumptions on the sales-response function and salesperson's utility function. Because of its position as the first application in marketing, we summarize the form of the BLSS model here and use it as a basis for comparison with later models. Tables 13.4, 13.5 and 13.6 summarize the structure of the BLSS model and contrast its assumptions with those of later models in the marketing literature.

BLSS make several assumptions concerning the salesperson's utility function and behavior, the sales-response function, and the firm. The salesperson is characterized by the first five assumptions below (see Table 13.4 for a contrast between these assumptions and those in later papers in the area):

B1. There is only one salesperson. (Equivalently, BLSS could have assumed many salespeople who are completely unrelated in their activities.)

B2. The salesperson is risk-averse.

B3. Selling effort is the salesperson's only choice variable.

B4. The salesperson's objective is to maximize expected utility. Utility is a separable function of income and the disutility for effort:

$$W = U(s) - V(t), \tag{12}$$

Table 13.4
Agency-theoretic models of salesforce compensation: assumptions on the salesforce

Source	B1. Salesforce size	B2. Salesperson's risk attitude	B3. Salesperson's choice variables	B4. Salesperson's objective function	B5. Salesperson's minimum utility constraint
Base case: BLSS [1985]	Single salesperson	Risk-aversion	Sales effort only	Maximize expected utility	Single minimum acceptable utility level, m
Comparison of BLSS [1985] with:					
Lal [1986]	Same	Same	Sales effort and also possibly price	Same	Same
Lal & Staelin [1986]	Multiple salespeople, two possible types	Same	Same	Same	Salespeople of different types may have different mimimum acceptable utility levels
Rao [1990]	Multiple salespeople, a continuum (beta-distributed) of types	Risk-neutral	Same	Same	Same
Dearden & Lilien [1990]	Same	Same	Sales effort only, in each of two time periods	Same	Same
Srinivasan & Raju [1990]	$n = 2$ salespeople; marginal productivity of effort is equal across territories, but means differ	Same	Same	Same; but do not require specific functional form for results	Same ($m_1 = m_2 = m$)
Lal & Srinivasan [1991]	Same	Constant absolute risk-aversion: $U = -\exp[-r(s - V(t))]$, V = monetary disutility for effort	Sales effort only; but continuously adjustable over accounting period	Same	Same

These assumptions are discussed more fully in Section 3 of the paper. Assumptions are noted for the BLSS model, and deviations from the BLSS assumptions are noted for the other papers in the table.

Table 13.5
Agency-theoretic models of salesforce compensation: assumptions on the sales-response function

Source	B6. Nature of product line	B7. Arguments of sales-response function	B8. Sales-response-functional form
Base case: BLSS [1985]	One product in line	Sales are a stochastic function of selling effort	Dollar sales are distributed either gamma or binomial
Comparison of BLSS [1985] with:			
Lal [1986]	Same	Stochastic function of both selling effort and price	No specific parametric assumption on dollar sales distribution
Lal & Staelin [1986]	Same	Stochastic function of selling effort only, but f_h is not equal to f_l, f_h exhibits first-order stochastic dominance over f_l	$x_i = \bar{\alpha}_i(t) + \xi_i$
Rao [1990]	Same	Same	Two examples: $x_i = \theta t^{\eta}$ and $x_i = x_0(1 - \exp(-\theta t))$
Dearden & Lilien [1990]	Same	Same (no lagged effort effects on sales)	Same
Srinivasan & Raju [1990]	Same	Same	No specific functional form required
Lal & Srinivasan [1991]	One product or multiple products; multi-product case assumes independence in demand and cost	Same	$E(x \mid t) = h + kt, \quad h, k > 0$; $x \sim N(h + kt, \sigma^2)$

These assumptions are discussed more fully in Section 3 of the paper. Assumptions are noted for the BLSS model, and deviations from the BLSS assumptions are noted for the other papers in the table.

Table 13.6
Agency-theoretic models of salesforce compensation: assumptions on firm behavior

Source	B9. Production cost	B10. Firm knowledge	B11. Firm choice variables	B12. Firm objective function
Base case: BLSS [1985]	Marginal cost is a constant fraction of price	Firm knows both salesperson's utility function and his sales-effort productivity	Both form and total size of compensation scheme, $s(x)$	Maximize expected profit (i.e. risk-neutral)
Comparison of BLSS [1985] with:				
Lal [1986]	Same	Same	Firm sets $s(x)$ and also decides whether it or the salesperson sets price	Same
Lal & Staelin [1986]	Dollar marginal cost is a constant (set equal to zero)	Firm knows possible types of salespeople and has a prior belief on what proportion of population are h type, but does not know individual salesperson types	Firm chooses a *menu* of $s(x)$ plans and how many of q total territories to leave unstaffed	Same
Rao (1990)	Same	Firm knows distribution of skill levels and form of utility functions, but does not know individual salesperson skill levels	Firm chooses a *menu* of $s(x)$ plans	Same
Dearden & Lilien [1990]	Constant marginal cost in each period, c_2 is decreasing in x_1	Same	Firm chooses $s_i(x)$ in periods $i = 1, 2$	Maximize discounted expected profit stream over two-period horizon
Srinivasan & Raju [1990]	Same	Same; known for each salesperson	Form of compensation plan is constrained to be salary plus commission if sales exceed quota; firm sets salary, commission and quota parameters	Same
Lal & Srinivasan [1991]	Same	Same	Same; optimal scheme shown to be linear in *total* sales over accounting period	Same

These assumptions are discussed more fully in Section 3 of the paper. Assumptions are noted for the BLSS model, and deviations from the BLSS assumptions are noted for the other papers in the table.

where

s = total income to the salesperson,
t = time spent selling,
$U'(s) > 0,\ U''(s) < 0$ (risk-aversion of salesperson),
$V'(t) > 0,\ V''(t) > 0$ (increasing marginal disutility for effort).

B5. The salesperson requires a minimum level of utility equal to m to be willing to work for the firm.

Sales response is characterized by the next three assumptions in BLSS (see Table 13.5 for a listing of these assumptions and their contrast with later models):

B6. Only one product is sold. (Equivalently, many products could be sold as long as they are unrelated in demand or cost and their selling times do not make any total-selling-time constraint binding in the salesperson's effort-allocation decision.)

B7. Sales are affected only by selling time and a stochastic element; no other marketing-mix variables are modeled. The density function of dollar sales conditional on time spent selling is given by $f(x|t)$.

B8. Dollar sales are assumed to be distributed either gamma or binomial.

The firm's behavior is characterized by the last three assumptions (see Table 13.6 for a summary of these assumptions and their comparison with those in later papers):

B9. Marginal cost, c, is a constant fraction of price.

B10. The firm knows the salesperson's utility functional form (Equation (12)), his minimum acceptable utility level, m, and his sales-effort productivity, i.e. $f(x|t)$.

B11. The firm's choice variable is $s(x)$, the compensation plan for the salesperson. This includes both the form of the plan and the total compensation level.

B12. The firm's objective is to maximize expected profit. The profit function is given by;

$$\Pi = \int_0^\infty [(1-c)x - s(x)]f(x|t)\mathrm{d}x. \tag{13}$$

BLSS then use Holmstrom's [1979] model and solution technique to derive their basic result on optimal compensation. The philosophy of the model is similar to that in the certainty models discussed above: the firm sets compensation to maximize profits, constrained by the salesperson's control over selling effort and by a minimum utility constraint expressing the salesperson's opportunity cost of time. Because of the uncertainty inherent in the problem, however, the solution techniques are somewhat different.

Formally, the firm's optimization problem can be expressed as:

$$\begin{aligned} &\underset{s(x)}{\text{maximize}} && \int [(1-c)x - s(x)]f(x|t)\mathrm{d}x, \\ &\text{subject to} && \int [U(s(x))]f(x|t)\mathrm{d}x - V(t) \geqslant m, \\ & && \int [U(s(x))]f_t(x|t)\mathrm{d}x - V'(t) = 0. \end{aligned} \tag{14}$$

The first constraint ensures that the salesperson's expected utility is at least equal to m, the minimum acceptable utility level. If this constraint were violated, the salesperson would leave the firm. The second constraint simply states that the salesperson chooses sales effort, t, to maximize his utility, and the firm takes this utility-maximizing behavior into account in its compensation-setting problem.

Let λ be the Lagrange multiplier for the first constraint, on minimum utility, and let μ be the Lagrange multiplier for the second constraint, on utility-maximizing sales-effort choice. Then Holmstrom's analysis shows that the optimum is characterized by four conditions which are functions of four unknowns: $s(x)$, λ, μ and t:

$$\frac{1}{U'[s(x)]} = \lambda + \mu \frac{f_t(x|t)}{f(x|t)}, \tag{15a}$$

$$\int [(1-c)x - s(x)] f_t(x|t) \mathrm{d}x + \mu \left[\int U[s(x)] f_{tt}(x|t) \mathrm{d}x - V''(t) \right] = 0, \tag{15b}$$

$$\int [U(s(x))] f(x|t) \mathrm{d}x - V(t) = m, \tag{15c}$$

$$\int [U(s(x))] f_t(x|t) \mathrm{d}x = V'(t). \tag{15d}$$

Equation (15a) is derived from the condition $\partial L/\partial s(z) = 0$ (where L is the Lagrangian). Equation (15b) is the condition that $\partial L/\partial t = 0$. Equations (15c) and (15d) derive from the tightness of the minimum-utility constraint and the constraint on t, respectively.

In order to get more specific insights, BLSS parametrize the problem by assuming a utility function exhibiting constant relative risk-aversion:

$$U(s(x)) = \frac{[s(x)]^{\delta}}{\delta}, \quad \delta < 1. \tag{16}$$

As δ approaches 1, the salesperson's risk attitude approaches risk-neutrality. Then for sales distributed either gamma or binomial, BLSS show that the optimal sales-compensation scheme has the form:

$$s(x) = [A + Bx]^{1/(1-\delta)}, \quad A \geqslant 0, \; B > 0. \tag{17}$$

BLSS call A the 'salary parameter' and B the 'commission-rate parameter'. Both are nonlinear functions of the underlying parameters of the problem. They show how this can imply a number of real-world compensation-plan forms, including straight commission, progressive sliding commission, salary only, salary plus commission, salary plus progressive sliding commission, and salary plus commission beyond a sales target, depending on the values of A and B.

This model structure produces many comparative-static results on optimal compensation (see Table 13.7 for a summary of the effects). As uncertainty, marginal cost, or minimum expected utility increase, the model predicts decreased optimal effort exertion; increased optimal salaries; decreased optimal commission rates; decreased profits at the optimum; and an increased ratio of salary to total pay. An increase in uncertainty or marginal cost causes expected salesperson income to fall, but an increase in minimum expected utility causes expected income to rise. Increased sales-effort productivity results in greater effort and greater firm profits, and an increased base sales rate (net of sales due to effort) increases the firm's profits as well. Basu & Kalyanaram [1990] verify these results through a numerical analysis, although their analysis is weakened by forcing a linear regression framework on the inherently nonlinear optimum of the BLSS model.

The BLSS/Holmstrom framework omits many important factors in setting optimal salesforce compensation. Only one salesperson is modeled, selling one product. Thus, the model does not consider any real interactions among salespeople or among products, such as team-selling, product complementarity, or economies of scale and scope. Effort produces concurrent sales; this approach abstracts away from situations of long lead times between initial salesperson contact and final sale. The firm is assumed to know the salesperson's utility function and minimum acceptable utility level, as well as the form of the sales response function; in a real setting, the firm may have to set compensation without this information. Price plays no role in generating sales in the BLSS model, nor do any marketing-mix variables other than selling effort. Later literature speaks to some of these limitations. Nevertheless, this paper makes a fundamental contribution to the literature on salesforce compensation because of its treatment of uncertainty and its specific results on optimal pay plans.

Lal [1986] uses the BLSS framework to examine when it is optimal to delegate pricing authority to the salesforce. He changes assumptions B3, B7, B8 and B11 of the BLSS framework, respectively, as follows (using BLSS terminology rather than Lal's terminology for consistency):

L3. The salesperson may decide how to price the product as well as the selling effort devoted to it.

L7. Stochastic sales are affected by both selling time and price charged. The density function for sales is $f(x|t, p)$, where p is the product price.

L8. No specific parametric distribution is assumed for dollar sales.

L11. The firm sets $s(x)$, the salesperson's compensation plan. It also decides whether to set p itself or to delegate the pricing decision to the salesperson.

This research question is also asked by Weinberg [1975] in the context of sales-response-function certainty, but Weinberg constrains the salesforce-compensation contract to be commission only. As discussed above, Weinberg's solution ignores the additional possibility of a forcing contract on both price and quantity sold. Neither solution is feasible in the agency-theory context.

Lal then considers two cases in which the information endowments of the firm vary: in the first, the firm and the salesperson have symmetric information about

Table 13.7
Comparative-static effects in agency-theory models of salesforce compensation

Effect of:	Effect* on optimal:						
	Effort	Salary	Commission rate	Profit	Expected income	Salary/ expected income	Quota
Increased uncertainty	↓(B, LS)	↑(B, LS)	↓(B, LS)	↓(B, LS)	↓(B, LS)	↑(B, LS)	N/A
Increased marginal cost	↓(B, LS)	↑(B, LS)	↓(B, LS)	↓(B, LS)	↓(B, LS)	↑(B, LS)	N/A
Increased minimum expected utility	↓(B) 0(LS)	↑(B, LS)	↓(B) 0(LS)	↓(B, LS)	↑(B, LS)	↑(B, LS)	N/A
Increased sales-effort effectiveness	↑(B, LS)	?(B) ↓(LS)	?(B) ↑(LS)	↑(B, LS)	?(B) ↑(LS, R)	?(B) ↓(LS)	↑(R)
Increased base sales	?(B) 0(LS)	?(B) ↓(LS)	?(B) 0(LS)	↑(B, LS)	?(B) 0(LS)	?(B) ↓(LS)	N/A
Increased risk-aversion	↓(LS)	↑(LS)	↓(LS)	↓(LS)	↓(LS)	↑(LS)	N/A
Increased disutility for effort	↓(LS)	↑(LS)	↓(LS)	↓(LS)	↓(LS)	↑(LS)	N/A
Increased number of plans offered (menu)	↓(R)	N/A	N/A	N/A	N/A	N/A	N/A
Increased production learning effects	N/A	↓(DL)	↑(DL)	N/A	N/A	N/A	N/A

*↑ = goes up; ↓ = goes down; 0 = no change; N/A = no hypothesis available in literature; ? = ambiguous, depending on distributional assumption on sales response function. After each directional indicator is a notation for papers producing the comparative static result: B = Basu, Lal, Srinivasan & Staelin [1985], DL = Dearden & Lilien [1990], LS = Lal & Srinivasan [1991] and R = Rao [1990].

the sales-response function, while in the second, the salesperson's information about the sales-response function is superior to that of the firm. In the symmetric-information case, the firm knows just as well as does the salesperson what is the best price to set. It can therefore write a compensation contract that rewards the salesperson based on sales output and the optimal price – no matter whether the salesperson or the firm itself sets that price. Via this logic, Lal shows that the firm is indifferent between delegating pricing authority to the salesperson and centralizing price-setting when information is symmetric. However, when the salesperson has superior information to that of the firm, Lal shows that delegating pricing authority to the salesperson cannot make the firm worse off than centralizing pricing decisions inside the firm, and in some examples, can make the firm better off. Intuitively, decisionmaking authority is best relegated to that decisionmaker with the greatest amount of information.

Lal & Staelin [1986] model optimal compensation-setting in a situation where salespeople may differ in their sales-effort productivity, and the firm does not know which are high- and which low-productivity salespeople. They alter assumptions B1, B5, B7, B8, B9, B10 and B11 of the BLSS framework, respectively, as follows:

LSt1. There are multiple salespeople, each of whom is one of two types, corresponding to his sales-effort productivity: h ('high') or l ('low').

LSt5. Salespeople of different types may have different minimum acceptable utilities, so that m_l need not be equal to m_h.

LSt7. The density function of dollar sales conditional on time spent selling is given by $f_i(x_i|t_i)$, where $i = \mathrm{h}, \mathrm{l}$. The functions have the property that f_h first-order stochastic dominates f_l. That is, for any $t_h = t_l$, the cumulative distribution function of f_h is less than or equal to that of f_l for all values of x, and is strictly less for at least one value of x.

LSt8. The sales-response function for salesperson i is:

$$x_i = \bar{\alpha}_i(t) + \xi_i, \tag{18}$$

where $\bar{\alpha}_i' > 0$, $\bar{\alpha}_i'' < 0$. Thus, sales effort is productive at a decreasing rate.

LSt9. Dollar marginal cost is constant and, without loss of generality, set equal to zero.

LSt10. The firm knows that all salespeople are either of type l or type h, but does not know any individual salesperson's type. However, the firm has a prior belief (represented by the probability density function $g(z)$) on z, the number of h-type salespeople in a group of q salespeople. Then P, the expected number of h-types in the group of q salespeople employed by the firm, is $\int zg(z)\mathrm{d}z$.

LSt11. The firm's choice variable is a set of $s(x)$'s, where the set may have more than member (the firm may offer a menu of plans). The firm also must choose q salespeople to staff its q sales territories; or it may choose to leave a subset of the q territories unstaffed.

Given this set of assumptions, Lal & Staelin use a BLSS-style framework to analyze three strategies:

Strategy 1. Offer one contract only, such that only h-type salespeople work for the firm.

Strategy 2. Offer one contract only, such that only l-type salespeople work for the firm.

Strategy 3. Offer a menu of two contracts that are 'truth-revealing', that is, that cause each salesperson to self-select into the contract designed for his type. In this scheme, each salesperson opts for one of the contracts at the start of the sales period, and is paid at the end of the period based on sales outcomes.

Lal & Staelin show first that if $m_h \leqslant m_l$, and for sufficiently high P, Strategy 1 always dominates Strategy 2, because of the equal or less stringent minimum-utility requirements and better expected sales outcomes from the h-type salespeople. However, if h-types demand significantly higher mimimum utilities (and hence pay), or if there are not likely to be many of them in the population, Strategy 2 can actually dominate Strategy 1. Intuitively, h-types may just be too expensive for the firm to hire if m_h is significantly greater than m_l; or there may be too high a risk of leaving profitable sales territories unstaffed if P is too low. Finally, for $m_h \leqslant m_l$, and for sufficiently low P, Strategy 3 (offering a menu of plans) is a superior choice to attracting just one type of salesperson via Strategies 1 or 2. Intuitively, the firm is better off attracting *both* types of salespeople when there are likely to be relatively few h-type salespeople in the population hired to staff and q sales territories.

Lal & Staelin also reinterpret their results with salespeople who vary not in their sales-effort productivity, but in their risk-aversion. Here, h-types are less risk-averse than l-types. The results go through analogously to those discussed above.

Rao's [1990] model is conceptually very similar to that of Lal & Staelin [1986]. Rao looks at the problem of creating optimal compensation plans for a heterogeneous salesforce, but seeks conditions under which these plans are simple linear compensation plans (salary plus commission for achieving sales over quota). Rao's assumptions differ from the BLSS assumptions B1, B2, B7/8 and B10, respectively, as follows:

R1. There are many salespeople, who differ by skill level (that is, marginal productivity of sales effort). The frequency distribution of the skill levels is a beta distribution.

R2. All salespeople are risk-neutral. Equivalently, if the sales-response function is non-stochastic, salespeople can have any risk attitude (because their knowledge of the non-stochastic sales-response function makes risk attitude a moot point).

R7/8. Sales are affected only by selling time and a stochastic element. For any sales response function $x = \psi(t;\theta)$ that can be inverted to yield $t = f(x;\theta)$, Rao assumes that: $\partial f/\partial x > 0$, $\partial f/\partial \theta < 0$, $\partial^2 f/\partial x \partial \theta < 0$, $\partial^2 f/\partial x^2 \geqslant 0$, $\partial^2 f/\partial \theta^2 > 0$, $\partial^3 f/\partial x^2 \partial \theta < 0$ (i.e., the marginal increase in effort required to achieve an incremental unit of sales decreases with increasing skill); and $\partial^3 f/\partial x \partial \theta^2 > 0$ (i.e. the marginal effort required to achieve a unit sales increase is less for a more skilled person – $\partial^2 f/\partial x \partial \theta < 0$ – and this effect is moderated, the higher the base skill-level).

R10. The firm knows the form of the salespeople's utility functions, but does not know any individual salesperson's skill level. However, the firm knows the distribution of skill levels.

Under the above assumptions, Rao shows the existence of a *separating equilibrium*, where pay plans serve to separate lower-skill from higher-skill salespeople. In this optimal (nonlinear) compensation plan for a heterogeneous salesforce, uncertainty induces two types of inefficiencies: first, every salesperson except the *most highly skilled* exerts less effort than if he were in a homogeneous salesforce or if all skill levels were known. Second, every salesperson except the *least skilled* earns more money than if he were in a homogeneous salesforce or if all skill levels were known. The optimal nonlinear plan described here can also be implemented by a menu of linear plans described graphically by the tangents to the optimal convex compensation scheme.

Dearden & Lilien [1990] look at a dynamic variation on Basu, Lal, Srinivasan & Staelin [1985]. Specifically, they model a two-period horizon for the firm and salesforce, where production-learning effects make second-period marginal costs decline as first-period sales increase. Intuitively, the firm now has a reason to increase selling incentives in period 1, because of the positive externality on costs in period 2. The authors' model varies from the BLSS model in assumptions B3, B9, B11 and B12 as follows:

DL3. While selling effort is the salesperson's only choice variable, as in BLSS, now the salesperson has to decide in a two-period horizon how to allocate effort. However, Dearden & Lilien's assumption of a competitive labor market implies that foresighted sales-effort allocation across periods is the same as myopic effort allocation, since the salesperson does not benefit from any of the positive cost externality accruing to the firm in period 2.

DL9. Marginal cost in each period is constant, but that in period 2, is lower, the higher are sales in period 1 ($c_2 = c_2(x_1)$ and c_2' is negative). This reflects production-learning economies.

DL11. The foresighted firm sets s_1 and s_2 in periods 1 and 2, respectively, taking into account the positive externality of period-1 sales on profitability in period 2.

DL12. The firm maximizes its discounted expected profit stream over the two-period horizon.

For the gamma distribution on sales, utility of income given by $U(s_i) = 2\sqrt{s_i}$, and using BLSS's terminology, the optimal compensation scheme has the same form as BLSS's optimal compensation function (Equation (17) above), but the salary parameter A_i and the commission parameter B_i take into account the positive production externality:

$$s(x_i) = \left[\lambda_i + \frac{\mu_i g'(t_i) q}{g^2(t_i)} [x_i - g(t_i)] \right]^2, \tag{19}$$

where $g(t_i)$ is expected sales and $g^2(t_i)/q$ is the variance of sales.[4] This solution is exactly BLSS's solution, but with period-specific subscripts for sales, selling effort and the Lagrange multipliers. This time-dependency gives Dearden & Lilien their main result: the greater is the increase in period-2 discounted expected profit due to an increase in period-1 sales, the *lower* is A_1 and the *higher* is B_1. That is, the greater is the cross-period production cost externality, the greater should be the incentive to sell in period 1 to maximize profit margins in period 2.

Srinivasan & Raju [1990] build upon the basic BLSS model to show how optimal compensation changes when the firm constrains pay to be in the form of salary and commission beyond quota and when sales territories have unequal sales potentials. Thus, they modify assumptions B1, B8 and B11 in the basic BLSS model as follows:

SR1. There are two salespeople in the salesforce, each covering one sales territory.

SR8. No specific functional form of the sales-response function is required for the model's results. However, if the density function for sales conditional on effort is $f_i(x|t)$, $i=1,2$, then the authors assume $f_i(x|t)=f_2(x+n|t)$. This implies that the marginal productivity of the salespeople's effort is equal across the two sales territories, but the means differ.

SR11. The firm is constrained to choose a particular *form* of compensation scheme, given by:

$$s(x)=\begin{cases} A & \text{if } x\leqslant q, \\ A+B(x-q) & \text{if } x\geqslant q. \end{cases} \tag{20}$$

Srinivasan & Raju also do not require any specific functional form on the utility function to derive their results, unlike BLSS. Solving the BLSS problem (Equation (14) above) subject to the constraint (20) on the form of the compensation plan, they derive their main result that the optimal quota-based compensation plan is characterized by:

$$s_2^*(x+n)=s_1^*(x). \tag{21}$$

That is, both salespeople have the same salary. A, and the same commission-rate parameter on sales beyond quota, B, but the salesperson assigned to the higher potential territory has a correspondingly higher base quota.

However, Srinivasan & Raju point out that this solution generates less profit for the firm than does the BLSS result without the compensation-plan constraint. Why, then, would a firm want to use it? The authors respond by appealing to the plan's *equity*, *flexibility* and *simplicity*. They argue that cross-territory differences

[4] This is a corrected version of Dearden & Lilien's Equation (3), p. 184. The original version has typographical errors.

would be compensated unfairly in the straight BLSS solution, with resulting disgruntlement in the salesforce and reduced morale. Although beyond the scope of their model, they argue intuitively that more-satisfied salespeople will generate higher profits in the long run.

Lal & Srinivasan [1991] use a model first developed by Holmstrom & Milgrom [1987] to examine optimal compensation when the salesperson can adjust his effort decision more frequently than the firm can adjust the compensation plan. Holmstrom & Milgrom describe a set of conditions under which optimal compensation is a linear function of *total* sales over the accounting period. We summarize these as deviations from BLSS's assumptions B2, B3, B6 and B8:

LSr2. The utility function exhibits constant absolute risk-aversion, and disutility for effort is expressed in monetary terms so that total utility is not separable in the utility for income and the disutility for effort:

$$W = -\exp[-r(s - V(t))], \tag{22}$$

where r is the constant absolute risk-aversion parameter and $(s - V(t))$ is the net monetary value of income and disutility for effort.

LSr3. As in BLSS, the salesperson chooses only sales effort; but effort is continuously adjustable over the accounting period.

LSr6. The major emphasis is on the single-product case, but the authors consider multiple product lines where products are completely independent in demand and cost (no complementary or substitutability in demand; no economies of scope or scale).

LSr8. Sales at any instant of time (over which the salesperson can vary effort) are distributed normal:

$$\mathrm{E}(x \mid t) = h + kt, \quad h, k > 0;$$
$$x \sim \mathrm{N}(h + kt, \sigma^2). \tag{23}$$

Thus, the mean (but not the variance) of sales is dependent on sales effort. The authors assume h is large enough to guarantee positive sales virtually all the time. With these assumptions, *cumulative* sales as a function of time follow Brownian motion, where the drift is a function of sales effort but the variance is not.

Holmstrom & Milgrom show a very elegant result for this problem: optimal compensation is a *linear* function of *total* sales over the accounting period, and further, the problem can be treated as a static problem due to the lack of time-dependence in the salesperson's effort decisions. This greatly simplifies the analysis and permits Lal & Srinivasan to derive many comparative-static results on optimal compensation, as summarized in Table 13.7. These results are broadly consistent with those in BLSS, differing only in two cases: the effect of changes in minimum utility (m) on optimal effort t and on the optimal commission rate B (both null effects in this model, and both negative in BLSS).

Summary of results in agency-theory models of salesforce compensation

The agency-theory paradigm yields a rich set of hypotheses concerning optimal form of the salesforce-compensation plan (salary, commission, quota, menus of plans), relative emphasis on incentive components in the plan, total pay levels, and their effects on salesforce effort and firm profitability. Several hypotheses concerning the absolute form of the plan emerge. In general, some form of risk-sharing characterizes the optimal compensation plan, because of the salesperson's risk-aversion relative to the firm and the stochastic nature of sales response. This risk-sharing typically takes the form of a combination plan, including both salary and some incentive component. It can be profitable to offer a menu of plans when the salesforce is made up of people of differing abilities and the firm cannot distinguish ability a priori [Lal & Staelin, 1986; Rao, 1990]. The firm may also be incompletely informed about demand responsiveness to price, in which case it can make sense to delegate pricing responsibility to the salesperson and alter compensation accordingly [Lal, 1986]. Constraining compensation to include quotas can increase equity across the salesforce, but may decrease short-term profitability [Srinivasan & Raju, 1990].

Comparative-static results predict the effect of a change in some parameter of the model on optimal pay parameters. These parameters, summarized in Table 13.7, include characteristics of the salesforce (minimum expected utility, sales-effort effectiveness, risk-aversion, disutility for effort), the firm (marginal cost, base sales rates, production-learning effects), and the environment (uncertainty). Interestingly, models tend to produce complementary rather than redundant results, and there is little contradiction among the models in their predictions.

Some issues remain unresolved. The plethora of results comes at the expense of specificity of assumptions about functional forms of the sales-response function and utility function. We have some comfort in the 'convergent validity' provided by the redundant results across some models, but a very general theoretical treatment has yet to generate rich predictions. The agency-theory approach in the marketing literature on salesforce compensation also does not attack such issues as when a commission is preferred to other forms of incentive pay, such as bonuses or contests. The differences in selling consumer and industrial products, or short- versus long-selling-cycle products, is also ill addressed in this literature. Product-line selling and team-selling are not explicitly modeled in the marketing area. Further, the firm and its salespeople are required to have extensive information about the salespeople's utility functions and minimum acceptable utility levels–information that is unlikely to be available in many real-world situations.

Finally, as in any analytical area, we should question the validity of the models by confronting them with empirical evidence and statistical tests. In the next section, we focus on this task.

4. Empirical evidence on salesforce-compensation models

In the salesforce-compensation area, many empirical studies have of course been done. Space constraints prohibit our reviewing them all. Instead, we focus on those studies that speak directly to tests of the theories advanced above. While the empirical literature testing management-science models of salesforce compensation is still rather limited, it gives some flavor for the applicability (and testability) of the theories' predictions.

The microeconomics-based models in Section 2 generally assume that the salesperson maximizes income, while a cornerstone of the agency-theory approach discussed in Section 3 is the assumption of utility maximization. Two early studies provide evidence that an income-maximization assumption is not representative of actual salesperson preferences. Winer's [1973] experimental work finds that salespeople at one company are not 'income maximizers' but rather 'quota achievers'. In another study, Darmon [1974] finds that salespeople seem to minimize effort subject to reaching an income threshold, or maximize 'satisfaction' subject to a time constraint.

These two studies provide some preliminary support for the assumption of utility maximization over income maximization. Later empirical work does not test this underlying 'maintained hypothesis', but instead investigates whether the comparative-static implications of agency-theory models are borne out in real-world practice. The papers differ in the datasets used as well as in the scope of their inquiries. John & Weitz [1988], Oliver & Weitz [1991] and Coughlan & Narasimhan [1992] use cross-sectional data. John & Weitz [1988] survey 161 manufacturing firms with annual sales of at least $50 million. Oliver & Weitz obtain a sample of 367 salespeople responding to a questionnaire on attitudes toward compensation plans. Coughlan & Narasimhan [1992] use secondary data collected by Dartnell Corporation from 286 firms in 39 different industry classifications. Eisenhardt [1988] collects data from 54 specialty stores in a single shopping center, thus focusing on retail salespeople exclusively. Finally, Lal, Outland & Staelin [1990] survey 77 sales-manager – salesperson dyads within a single Fortune 500 firm selling computer equipment and services. There is some debate in the literature about the appropriateness of testing an individual-level theory (such as that in Basu, Lal, Srinivasan & Staelin [1985]) with aggregate, cross-sectional data; Lal, Outland & Staelin maintain that their approach is superior because it holds cross-firm variation constant. However, in some sense, none of these studies can test the BLSS or other agency-theory approaches purely, because all take measurements from multi-person, multi-product salesforces, while BLSS postulate a single salesperson selling a single product. We should thus take the results with some qualification in any case.

Table 13.8 summarizes the evidence these papers provide to test the comparative-static effects in the agency-theory literature. Each paper contains some other evidence as well (e.g. Coughlan & Narasimhan [1992] also tests some hypotheses from the executive-compensation and economics agency-theory literatures), but we will focus here on the evidence directly pertinent to the theories posited above. Some general observations deserve mention immediately. First, Table 13.8 has many empty cells; this is a sign both that the theories have been incompletely tested and that empirical tests of agency theory are rather difficult to accomplish. For example, it is difficult to operationalize measures of risk-aversion or disutility for effort in the salesforce. Second, many results are not statistically significant. This may not be a sign that we should reject the theory overall, but rather a sign

Table 13.8
Empirical evidence on agency-theory models of salesforce compensation

Effect of:	Effect* on optimal:						
	Effort	Salary	Commission rate	Profit	Expected income	Salary/ expected income	Quota
Increased uncertainty		ns(JW) √(LOS)	ns(JW)	ns(JW)	ns(JW, CN)	ns(JW, CN) √(LOS,OW,E)	
Increased marginal cost		ns(JW)	ns(JW)	√(JW)	ns(JW)	ns(JW)	
Increased minimum expected utility		ns(JW)	ns(JW)	ns(JW)	√(JW, CN)	ns(JW) √(CN)	
Increased sales-effort effectiveness		⊗(JW) ns(LOS)	⊗(JW)	√(JW)	ns(JW) √(CN)	⊗(JW) √(LOS,CN)	
Increased base sales		⊗(JW)	⊗(JW)	√(JW)	ns(JW)	⊗(JW)	
Increased risk-aversion		ns(LOS)				ns(LOS) √(OW)	
Increased disutility for effort							
Increased number of plans offered (menu)							
Increased production learning effects							

*ns = not statistically significant at the 90% level; √ = significant at the 90% level and in the hypothesized direction; ⊗ = significant at the 90% level and in the opposite direction from that hypothesized. A blank entry in a cell indicates that no empirical research has addressed that comparative-static effect. Parenthetical notations are references to empirical papers: JW = John & Weitz [1988]; LOS = Lal, Outland & Staelin [1990]; CN = Coughlan & Narasimhan [1992]; OW = Oliver & Weitz [1991]; and E = Eisenhardt [1988]. Thus, for example, the cell in the row for Increased sales-effort effectiveness and the column for Salary/expected income should be read: John & Weitz [1988] find significant evidence contrary to, while Lal, Outland & Staelin and Coughlan & Narasimhan find significant evidence consistent with, the hypothesis that Salary/expected income is negatively affected by increased sales-effort effectiveness.

of insufficient power of the statistical tests or insufficiently precise operationalizations of theoretical constructs.

On a more positive note, those results that are statistically significant tend to be consistent with the theory (the exceptions all being from the John & Weitz [1988] paper). There is considerable strength of support for hypotheses predicting the ratio of salary to total pay across several of the studies. Some support is also found for hypotheses predicting total expected income levels. Hypotheses concerning the effect of sales-effort effectiveness on compensation are not rejected in several studies.

In sum, while empirical results are inconclusive or incomplete in many cases, we certainly cannot reject agency-theory entirely as a predictive paradigm for salesforce compensation. We feel justified in reiterating the familiar refrain that more work is needed, with better empirical proxies for theoretical constructs and a wider range of hypotheses tested. It is unlikely that all the hypotheses will ultimately be tested, however, due to difficulties in measuring some predictive variables in the theory.

The economics-based approach to modeling salesforce-compensation problems profiled in this section of the paper provides directional, as well as some absolute, insights on optimal compensation practice. It typically does not produce point estimates of the right compensation amount or split among various components, however. Precise normative inputs to compensation-setting are instead provided by the literature on decision support systems. We turn in the next section to a brief survey of this literature, and refer the reader to Chapter 16 on decision support systems for a more in-depth treatment of their application not just to the salesforce-compensation issue, but to other marketing problems as well.

5. Decision support systems for salesforce compensation

Decision support systems (or DSSs) differ from analytical economics-based models or empirical tests in several ways. First, they are typically designed for direct managerial implementation: they have a distinctly normative focus, rather than a predictive focus. Second, they capitalize on expert judgments from decision-makers (in our case, the salesforce or sales managers themselves) to parametrize key aspects of the models – for example, the salesperson's utility function or a territory-specific sales-response function. Third, one typically cannot do a statistical test for optimality or robustness of the model, given the case-specific managerial inputs to the problem. Nevertheless, improvements in profit and sales performance observed over the pre-DSS situation are indicators of their usefulness.

In the salesforce-compensation area, DSSs typically marry the economics-based approach with specific managerial inputs to try to get a parametric representation of an otherwise abstract model that is immediately useful and believable to the sales manager. The trend in these models is toward user-friendliness, via easy (usually computerized) interactions between the managers and salespeople and the model itself.

The content and structure of DSSs for salesforce compensation is summarized in Tables 13.9, 13.10 and 13.11. These differ from Tables 13.1–3 and 13.4–6 in several ways. First, there is no easily identified 'base-case' DSS against which to compare later advances in the area. This is because each DSS seeks to remedy a particular information shortage of the firm, and these shortages have no natural progression over time (however, as we will see below, subsets of the DSSs are strongly interrelated). Second, the use of managerial and salesforce inputs to parametrize the models is accounted for in a new column, D13, in Table 13.11 that summarizes how judgmental inputs are used in each particular DSS. Third, DSSs have focused primarily on the setting of quota-bonus plans, assuming salary to be fixed and exogenously given. Thus, in contrast to the general salary-plus-commission plan derivation in the agency-theory literature, the DSS literature to date does not focus at all on the optimal split between salary and incentive pay.

A model by Farley & Weinberg [1975] is an early application of these principles to the salesforce-compensation problem. They assume that the source of asymmetric information between the salesforce and the firm lies in the sales-response function. It takes the form:

$$q_{ij} = k_{ij} + b_{ij}t_{ij}^{\alpha}, \quad 0 < \alpha < 1. \tag{24}$$

While the salesperson knows the sales response function fully, the firm does not know the values of k_{ij} or b_{ij}, either across products (indexed by i) or salespeople (indexed by j). By iteratively proposing sets of commission rates on the product line and asking salesperson j his time allocation and predicted sales for all products, Farley & Weinberg are able to estimate the parameters of the sales-response function. Once these are known, it is relatively straightforward to set commission rates or quotas to maximize the firm's profit. This application assumes that the salesperson's objective is income maximization; thus, any plan that rewards the salesperson more for higher firm profits solves the incentive-incompatibility problem. Clearly, if the salesperson has a more complex set of incentives, this sort of compensation solution may not be optimal.

In Darmon's [1979] model, the firm lacks knowledge of the parameters of the salesperson's utility function, as well as of the sales-response function. Utility functions are estimated via a conjoint-analysis task where the salesperson ranks various combinations of quota and bonus, producing indifference curves relating the salesperson's willingness to trade off greater work time (via a higher quota) for greater income (via a higher bonus). Once the salesperson's indifference curves are estimated, the firm can offer the salesperson that quota–bonus combination that maximizes its profits.

Darmon [1987] extends his 1979 model in three major ways. First, the DSS is put on a personal computer, enhancing its ease of use for the sales manager as well as for the modeler. Second, he explicitly models the problem of heterogeneous salespeople by adding a module onto his earlier DSS to derive a 'consistent' quota–bonus plan that (a) keeps all salespeople at utility levels at least as great as before implementation of the new plan, and (b) minimizes the profit loss due

Table 13.9
Decision support systems for salesforce compensation: assumptions on the salesforce

Source	D1. Salesforce size	D2. Salesperson's risk attitude	D3. Salesperson's choice variables	D4. Salesperson's objective function	D5. Salesperson's constraints
Farley & Weinberg [1975]	Multiple (but same plan for all)	N/A (no uncertainty)	Sales effort only	Maximize commission income	None
Darmon [1979]	Multiple (but same plan for all)	Major focus on risk-neutrality	Sales effort only	Maximize utility, a positive linear function of bonus and negative quadratic function of quota	Total time available for leisure and work
Darmon [1987]	Multiple (but same plan for all)	N/A (no uncertainty)	Sales effort only	Maximize utility, a positive linear function of bonus and negative quadratic function of quota	Total time available for leisure and work
Gonik [1978]	Multiple; each sales-person self-selects into one of menu of plans	N/A	Forecasted sales before start of monitoring period; sales effort during period	Not known	Not known
Mantrala & Raman [1990]	Single or multiple	Major focus on risk-neutrality	Forecasted sales before start of monitoring period; sales effort during period	Maximize expected utility	None
Mantrala, Sinha & Zoltners (1990)	Multiple; each sales-person self-selects into one of menu of plans	Risk-averse	Effort allocation in total and across multiple products	Maximize expected utility	None

Table 13.10
Decision support systems for salesforce compensation: assumptions on the sales-response function

Source	D6. Nature of product line	D7. Arguments of sales-response function	D8. Sales-response-functional form
Farley & Weinberg [1975]	Multiple products; unrelated in demand and cost	Non-stochastic function of sales effort only	$q_{ij} = k_{ij} + b_{ij} t_{ij}^{\alpha}, \quad 0 < \alpha < 1$
Darmon [1979]	Single product	Non-stochastic function of sales effort only	Only implicitly understood through salesperson's choice of quota–bonus pairs
Darmon [1987]	Single product	Non-stochastic function of sales effort only	Only implicitly understood through salesperson's choice of quota–bonus pairs
Gonik [1978]	Single product	Not explicitly modeled; inference is that it is a function of sales effort only	Not modeled
Mantrala & Raman [1990]	Single product	Stochastic function of sales effort only	$q = g(u) + e$, $u =$ effort, $g' > 0, g'' \leqslant 0$
Mantrala, Sinha & Zoltners [1990]	Multiple products; unrelated in demand or cost	Stochastic function of sales effort only	$q_{ij} = \mu_{ij} + (M_{ij} - \mu_{ij})(1 - \exp(-b_{ij} t_{ij}))$, a function of maximum territory potential and selling effort

Table 13.11
Decision support systems for salesforce compensation: assumptions on firm behavior

Source	D9. Cost functions	D10. Firm knowledge	D11. Firm choice variables	D12. Firm objective function	D13. Use of judgmental DSS inputs
Farley & Weinberg [1975]	Arbitrary differentiable variable-cost functions: $C_i = C_i(Q_i)$	Knows salesperson maximizes commission income; does not know sales-response function	Commission rates on sales volumes of all products	Maximize profit	Estimate sales response function
Darmon [1979]	Constant marginal cost	Knows neither territory-specific sales-response functions nor utility functions	Quotas and bonuses	Maintain utility levels of all salespeople; improve profit	Use conjoint analysis of bonus–quota tradeoff to estimate salesperson's utility function and (indirectly) the sales response function
Darmon [1987]	Constant marginal cost	Knows neither territory-specific sales-response functions nor utility functions	Quotas and bonuses	Maintain constant utility levels; minimize profit loss due to deviation from individual-plan optimum	Use conjoint analysis of bonus–quota tradeoffs to estimate salesperson's utility function and (indirectly) the sales response function; PC based for ease in implementation
Gonik [1978]	Not explicitly modeled; losses accrue when actual sales $\neq$ forecast	Not explicitly modeled	Quotas and bonuses as functions of both actual *and* forecasted sales	Maximize profit; minimize costly deviations of sales from forecast	Incentivize more accurate sales forecasts by salesforce
Mantrala & Raman [1990]	Quadratic or asymmetric loss function for actual sales $\neq$ forecast	Must know utility function and sales-response function to implement	Quotas and bonuses as functions of both actual *and* forecasted sales	Maximize expected profit	Incentivize more accurate sales forecasts by salesforce
Mantrala, Sinha & Zoltners [1990]	Constant marginal cost	Knows neither territory-specific sales-response functions nor utility functions	Bonus plan, contingent on prespecified quotas	Maximize expected profit	Estimate utility function via conjoint analysis

to deviation from the optimum under salesperson-specific plans. Third, he allows the sales manager to weight different salespeople and territories differently when maximizing the firm's profits across all salespeople.

Despite these advances, however, Darmon's [1987] DSS has some limitations. One is that the firm must commit to a specific bonus plan before the DSS optimization is done; in fact, sales managers would also like to know what the *optimal* bonus plan is. This model approach does not lend itself to easy solution of this problem. Further, Darmon's model does not provide for a menu of plans to be offered to the salesforce. The agency-theory literature dealing with this issue [Lal & Staelin, 1986; Rao, 1990] indicates that it may be more profitable to design a menu of plans with the self-selection feature.

A somewhat different managerial problem is raised when the salesforce's private information about the sales-response function is used in sales forecasting. Salespeople may suspect that their inputs to the forecasting process will be used 'against' them when the next year's sales quotas are set. They thus may have an incentive to systematically underrepresent their ability to sell in their sales forecasts. Other salespeople may be overconfident of their selling ability, and may therefore systematically overstate territory potential and sales forecasts. But this bias in information can be costly to the firm, either in inventory holding costs (in the case of overstated forecasts) or in lost sales due to insufficient production (in the case of understated forecasts).

Gonik [1978] addresses this problem in a managerially oriented paper describing IBM Brazil's experience. The company's solution to the problem is to create a quota–bonus plan that first gives each salesperson a sales objective, or quota, for his territory. The salesperson then turns in a forecast of his sales in the territory (which may or may not equal the quota). The bonus plan always rewards the salesperson more for achieving higher actual sales. But it also penalizes him for under- or over-forecasting his sales potential. In effect, IBM Brazil has created a menu of plans (differing according to the payouts promised for different forecasts chosen by the salesperson), into which the salesperson self-selects.

Mantrala & Raman [1990] analyze the Gonik quota–bonus scheme more formally. They show that the plan can be represented mathematically as

$$\begin{aligned} B &= \bar{B}(\hat{q}/\bar{q}) && \text{for } q = \hat{q}, \\ B &= B_1 = \bar{B} + \beta(\hat{q} - \bar{q}) + \gamma(q - \hat{q}) && \text{for } q < \hat{q}, \\ B &= B_2 = \bar{B} + \beta(\hat{q} - \bar{q}) + \alpha(q - \hat{q}) && \text{for } q \geqslant \hat{q}, \end{aligned} \tag{25}$$

where

q = actual sales,
$\bar{q}$ = quota set by management,
$\hat{q}$ = sales forecast submitted by the salesperson,
B = actual bonus awarded,
$\bar{B}$ = fixed bonus offered upon exact fulfillment of $\hat{q}$ when $\hat{q} = \bar{q}$,
$\beta = (\bar{B}/\bar{q})$, $\alpha = (\bar{B}/2\bar{q})$ and $\gamma = (3\bar{B}/2\bar{q})$ in the Gonik scheme.

Clearly, Gonik's values for α, β and γ are special cases, and need not hold in all situations. This way of expressing the bonus-payout scheme highlights the penalty/reward rate for choosing forecasts that differ from managerially set quotas (β), the penalty rate for underselling relative to forecast (γ), and the reward rate for overselling relative to forecast (α). The parameters γ and α need not be equal, because the cost to the firm of over-forecasting may not equal the cost of under-forecasting. Indeed, in the Gonik scheme, $\gamma > \beta > \alpha > 0$, so that underselling is penalized more heavily than overselling is rewarded.

Mantrala & Raman show that, when the salesperson can choose both selling effort and his sales forecast, the optimal quota level for the firm to set a priori is affected by the salesperson's effort decision. However, the firm can influence effort and thereby influence the salesperson's forecast, by manipulating the β parameter in the bonus plan. This can be done while maintaining any desired probability of fulfillment of the forecast by further adjusting the α and γ parameters. The major limitation of this approach is the need for managerial information on specific territories' sales potentials and specific salespeople's utility functions. To fully implement the scheme, one must graft on a module like Darmon's conjoint-analysis process to provide these inputs to management.

Two shortcomings of earlier DSS's in the salesforce-compensation area are their inability to let heterogeneous salespeople self-select into the plans that maximize their productivity, and their focus on a single-product line. Mantrala, Sinha & Zoltners [1990] deal with both of these issues in a DSS similar to that of Darmon [1987] in its use of conjoint analysis to estimate utility functions, but using the agency-theoretic approach of offering a total quota–bonus *plan* to the salesforce, and letting them choose among different levels of effort and sales achievement within the plan. The authors apply their system to a pharmaceutical firm selling two products, 'Largex' and 'Smallex' (names are disguised), through a direct salesforce. Interestingly, the application suggests that more aggressive bonus plans would increase sales and profits generated by several of the salespeople. The model also permits investigation of the profitability of different possible bonus schemes with relative computational ease. The authors show a new quota–bonus plan that increases firm profits from \$4.003 million to \$4.41 million, a significant improvement. However, profit improvement can be hampered considerably if management imposes uniformity on the quota–bonus plan across very heterogeneous salespeople.

Summary of decision support systems for salesforce compensation

One of the strongest criticisms of the economics-based approach to modeling salesforce-compensation problems, discussed in Sections 2 and 3 above, is its assumption that the firm knows the salesperson's utility function as well as the form of the sales response function. These assumptions are rarely verified in practice. The DSS literature profiled above helps answer this criticism by proposing salesforce survey techniques that provide information on both utility functions and sales response, sometimes through the same instrument (conjoint analysis). This collapsing of a two-stage informational problem into a one-stage information-gathering procedure is valuable not only for its computational brevity, but also because it provides some concrete evidence in specific applications of the degree of heterogeneity in the salesforce. Later DSS approaches use this information to good advantage by creating quota–bonus schemes that let the salesperson self-select the quota – and thus sales achievement – to which he is willing to commit. DSSs and more theoretical analytical approaches can thus be valuable complements in any specific empirical application.

There is still work left to be done in the DSS area, however. All the applications surveyed here focus on designing quota–bonus schemes, and ignore the issue raised in the agency-theory literature of optimal risk-sharing in a combination plan. The optimal split between salary and incentive is not dealt with at all in the DSS literature.

It remains somewhat difficult to know when one has approached the *optimum optimorum* when applying a DSS as well. Since each application of a DSS is specifically designed for the company and salesforce in question, it is virtually impossible to generalize across different applications of the same DSS to determine optimality of the plans suggested. In many cases, it is up to the model user to evaluate the profits from different bonus formulations before deciding which one to use. If the user happens not to try a particularly advantageous formulation, the DSS will not be able to warn that the resulting solution is not optimal.

Despite these points, DSSs are enormously useful, both in economically generating information to calibrate an abstract problem, and also in guiding the theoretical modeler to sensible assumptions on parameters of his problem.

6. Conclusions and future research directions

The extensive MS/OR literature on salesforce compensation in marketing has attacked a great variety of problems facing sales managers, including how to set commission rates, whether to delegate pricing authority to a salesforce, what mix of salary and incentive compensation to provide to the salesforce, whether or not to offer a menu of compensation plans, and how to elicit valuable information from salespeople about their utility functions and sales response functions. In the case of theoretical models, some predictions have been tested statistically, but as we have noted above, these tests have been incomplete and, in some cases, inconclusive. Based on available empirical results, we cannot reject agency theory as a useful paradigm for compensation-setting, but further research is necessary to increase the level of confidence in the theory and its predictions. On the DSS front, few diagnostics have been presented for the models described in the literature, although those presented suggest the usefulness of the approach as well.

Some questions seem to have been relatively well researched. All approaches agree that salespeople's incentives to exert effort against a product should be greater when the profit results from effort exertion are higher. Increased profitability can of course arise from many sources: lower production costs, greater sales-effort effectiveness, and greater territory potential are some of the reasons. Similarly, it is well understood that salespeople with a higher opportunity cost of time must be promised a greater expected total pay package. In cases of asymmetric information (i.e. where the salesperson is more completely informed than is sales management), it also makes sense to delegate decisionmaking authority to the salesperson – for example, in price-setting. In addition, when a salesforce is made up of people of differing abilities, or people assigned to territories with different sales potentials, it is generally agreed that the firm can do better by tailoring a menu of plans to the salesforce than by forcing all salespeople into one plan.

Some questions remain to be researched in depth. Further research into the dynamic nature of salesforce motivation is in order, particularly for understanding the sale of products with long selling cycles (such as some large-ticket industrial products). In the agency-theory literature in economics, some work has been done on this issue [see, for example, Fudenberg, Holmstrom & Milgrom, 1990], which suggests the value of tying pay horizons (such as bonus and commission award dates) to performance horizons (such as the closing of a sale) to avoid perverse salesforce incentives. But the modeling is presented at a level of abstraction that prohibits a great deal of detail for the salesforce manager. The empirical support for this line of modeling [Coughlan & Narasimhan, 1992] suggests that there may be value in extending the work to apply more closely to the salesforce context.

Another area in which marketing research has lagged is in the advisability of relative pay plans such as sales contests of various sorts. Again, the economics literature has developed some modeling insights in the area [see, for example, Lazear & Rosen, 1981; Holmstrom, 1982; Green & Stokey, 1983; Nalebuff & Stiglitz, 1983], but without much direct application in the salesforce area. Further modeling research could help suggest when such comparative compensation schemes perform better than salesperson-specific incentive schemes, and what intensity of use such schemes should have in the salesforce.

Finally, other theoretical paradigms could be integrated into the MS/OR approach to modeling salesforce compensation. John & Weitz [1989] empirically test some of the predictions of transaction-cost analysis (TCA) for compensation practice, but the theory (originally posited by Williamson [1975]) has eluded quantitative modelers. John & Weitz themselves note that TCA is concerned primarily with issues of salesforce control, while agency theory focuses on issues of salesforce motivation. It seems clear that a holistic approach, incorporating both aspects of effective salesforce management, could be very useful.

References

Basu, A.K., and G. Kalyanaram (1990). On the relative performance of linear versus nonlinear compensation plans. *Intern. J. Res. Marketing* 7(2/3), 171–178.

Basu, A.K., R. Lal, V. Srinivasan and R. Staelin (1985). Salesforce-compensation plans: An agency theoretic perspective. *Marketing Sci.* 4(4), 267–291.

Berger, P.D. (1972). On setting optimal sales commissions. *Oper. Res. Quart.* 23(2), 213–215.

Berger, P.D. (1975). Optimal compensation plans: The effect of uncertainty and attitude toward risk on the salesman effort allocation decision, in E.M. Mazze (ed.), *American Marketing Association 1975 Combined Proceedings*. American Marketing Association, Chicago, pp. 517–520.

Coughlan, A.T., and C. Narasimhan (1992). An empirical analysis of salesforce-compensation plans. *J. Business* 65 (January), 93–122.

Coughlan, A.T., and Subrata K. Sen (1986). Salesforce compensation: Insights from management science. Report No. 86–101, Marketing Science Institute, Cambridge, MA (May).

Coughlan, A.T., and Subrata K.S. Sen (1989). Salesforce compensation: Theory and managerial implications. *Marketing Sci.* 8(4), 324–342.

Darmon, R.Y. (1974). Salesmen's response to financial incentives: An empirical study. *J. Marketing Res.* 11(4), 418–426.

Darmon, R.Y. (1979). Setting sales quotas with conjoint analysis. *J. Marketing Res.* 16(1), 133–140.

Darmon, R.Y. (1987). QUOPLAN: A system for optimizing sales quota–bonus plans. *J. Oper. Res. Soc.* 38(12), 1121–1132.

Davis, O.A., and J.U. Farley (1971). Allocating sales force effort with commissions and quotas. *Management Sci.* 18(4), Part II, P-55–P-63.

Dearden, J.A., and G.L. Lilien (1990). On optimal salesforce compensation in the presence of production learning effects. *Intern. J. Res. Marketing* 7(2–3), 179–188.

Eisenhardt, K.M. (1988). Agency- and institutional-theory explanations: The case of retail sales compensation. *Acad. Management J.* 31(3), 488–511.

Farley, J.U. (1964). An optimal plan for salesmen's compensation. *J. Marketing Res.* 1(2), 39–43.

Farley, J.U., and C.B. Weinberg (1975). Inferential optimization: An algorithm for determining optimal sales commissions in multiproduct sales forces. *Oper. Res. Quart.* 26(2), 413–418.

Ford, N.M., O.C. Walker and G.A. Churchill, Jr. (1981). Differences in the attractiveness of alternative rewards among industrial salespeople: Additional evidence, Report No. 81–107, Marketing Science Institute, Cambridge, MA (December).

Fudenberg, D., B. Holmstrom and P. Milgrom (1990). Short-term contracts and long-term agency relationships. *J. Econom. Theory* 51(1), (June), 1–31.

Gonik, J. (1978). Tie salesmen's bonuses to their forecasts. *Harvard Business Rev.* 56(3), (May–June), 116–123.

Green, J., and N. Stokey (1983). A comparison of tournaments and contracts. *J. Political Economy* 91(3), 349–364.

Harris, M., and A. Raviv (1978). Some results on incentive contracts with applications to education and employment, health insurance, and law enforcement. *Amer. Econom. Rev.* 68 (March), 20–30.

Harris, M. and A. Raviv (1979). Optimal incentive contracts with imperfect information. *J. Econom. Theory* 20 (April), 231–259.

Holmstrom, B. (1979). Moral hazard and observability. *Bell J. Econom.* 10(1), 74–91.

Holmstrom, B. (1982). Moral hazard in teams. *Bell J. Econom.* 13(2), 324–340.

Holmstrom, B., and P. Milgrom (1987). Aggregation and linearity in the provision of intertemporal incentives. *Econometrica* 55 (March), 303–328.

John, G., and B.A. Weitz (1988). Explaining variation in sales compensation plans: Empirical evidence for the Basu *et al.* model, Working Paper, Marketing Department, University of Minnesota, Minneapolis (July).

John, G., and B.A. Weitz (1989). Salesforce compensation: An empirical investigation of factors related to use of salary versus incentive compensation. *J. Marketing Res.* 26(1), 1–14.

Lal, R. (1986). Delegating pricing responsibility to the salesforce. *Marketing Sci.* 5(2), 159–168.

Lal, R., D. Outland and R. Staelin (1990). Salesforce-compensation plans: An empirical test of the agency theory framework, Working Paper, Graduate School of Business, Stanford University, Stanford, CA (May).

Lal, R., and V. Srinivasan (1991). Compensation plans for single- and multi-product salesforces: An application of the Holmstrom–Milgrom model, Working Paper, Graduate School of Business, Stanford University, Stanford, CA (March).

Lal, R., and R. Staelin (1986). Salesforce-compensation plans in environments with asymmetric information. *Marketing Sci.* 5(3), 179–198.

Lazear, E.P., and S. Rosen (1981). Rank-order tournaments as optimum labor contracts. *J. Political Economy* 89(5), 841–864.

Mantrala, M.K., and K. Raman (1990). Analysis of a salesforce-incentive plan for accurate sales forecasting and performance. *Intern. J. Res. Marketing* 7, 189–202.

Mantrala, M.K., P. Sinha, and A.A. Zoltners (1990). Structuring a multiproduct sales quota–bonus plan for a heterogeneous salesforce, Working Paper, College of Business Administration, University of Florida, Gainesville (October).

Nalebuff, B.J., and J.E. Stiglitz (1983). Prizes and incentives: towards a general theory of compensation and competition. *Bell. J. Econom.* 14(1), 21–43.

Oliver, R.L., and B.A. Weitz (1991). The effects of risk preference, uncertainty, and incentive compensation on salesperson motivation, Report Number 91–104, Marketing Science Institute, Cambridge MA (February).

Rao, R.C. (1990). Compensating heterogeneous salesforces: some explicit solutions. *Marketing Sci.* 9(4), 319–341.

Shavell, S. (1979). Risk sharing and incentives in the principal and agent relationship. *Bell J. Econom.* 10(1), 55–73.

Srinivasan, V. (1981). An investigation of the equal commission rate policy for a multi-product salesforce. *Management Sci.* 27(7), 731–756.

Srinivasan, V., and J.S. Raju (1990). Quota-based compensation schemes for multi-territory salesforces. Working Paper, Graduate School of Business, Stanford University, Stanford, CA (September).

Tapiero, C.S., and J.U. Farley (1975). Optimal control of salesforce effort in time. *Management Sci.* 21(9), 976–985.

Weinberg, C.B. (1975). An optimal commission plan for salesmen's control over price. *Management Sci.* 21(8) 937–943.

Weinberg, C.B. (1978). Jointly optimal sales commissions for nonincome maximizing salesforces. *Management Sci.* 24(12), 1252–1258.

Williamson, O. (1975). *Markets and Hierarchies: Analysis and Antitrust Implications.* The Free Press, New York.

Winer, L. (1973). The effect of product sales quotas on salesforce productivity. *J. Marketing Res.* 10(2), 180–183.

J. Eliashberg and G.L. Lilien, Eds.. *Handbooks in OR & MS, Vol. 5*

Chapter 14

Salesforce Operations

Mark B. Vandenbosch

Western Business School, The University of Western Ontario, London, Canada N6A 3K7

Charles B. Weinberg

Faculty of Commerce and Business Administration, The University of British Columbia, Vancouver, B.C., Canada V6T 1Z2

1. Introduction

Salesforce management continues to be of critical importance to business. In many industries, the salesforce represents the company's main link with its customers. Because of this unique position, the salesforce is required to perform a wide range of duties including personal selling, promotion, distribution and technical support. The successful management of this group of individuals can have a significant impact on the success of a business.

Although the expenses incurred through salesforce operations are typically higher than in other marketing areas, the amount of academic research generated in this area has not mirrored this fact. To illustrate this, a five-year search (ending in December 1990) of the ABI-INFORM database was undertaken for five journals: *Management Science, Marketing Science, Journal of Marketing, Journal of Marketing Research* and *Journal of Consumer Research.* The search yielded 47 articles and 79 authors contributing articles related to personal selling and salesforce management compared with 192 articles and 319 authors contributing articles related to advertising. The large imbalance is probably due to a number of factors including access to data and researcher interest. Another contributing factor may be the greater visibility of advertising. In many ways, advertising information is public as both advertising copy and expenditure levels are relatively easy to obtain. On the other hand, the majority of personal selling situations occur in private. This feature makes it difficult to define and measure constructs and outcomes.

Not only did the literature search find there was only limited published research related to salesforce management, very few OR/MS-oriented articles were noted. Of the 47 salesforce articles found in the major journals, only 13 articles (24 authors) are concerned with operations research/management science approaches to salesforce management and only 7 articles (13 authors) are concerned with non-compensation issues. Salesforce-compensation research is reviewed by Coughlan in Chapter 13 of this book and will only be briefly discussed here.

Although there has not been an abundance of recent research in the area of salesforce operations, the impact of the research stream on practitioners has been very high. For example, an application of Lodish's salesforce size, product and market allocation model [Lodish, Curtis, Ness & Simpson, 1988], won the 1987 Franz Edelman Award for Management Science Achievement and the model reported in Rangaswamy, Sinha & Zoltners [1990] has been implemented in over 100 settings in more than 20 countries [Rangaswamy, Sinha & Zoltners, 1990, p. 280]. Personal contact with these and other researchers indicates that salesforce models continue to be implemented.

This chapter is organized as follows. In Section 2, the nature of sales-management decisions and data availability will be discussed. This will be followed in Section 3 by a review of the major contributions in salesforce operations research. A component of this review will be a discussion of the various modeling efforts resulting from a series of navy recruitment studies. Section 4 will outline some potential avenues for future research while Section 5 provides summary comments and conclusions.

2. Decision areas in sales management

Figure 14.1 illustrates the major decision areas in salesforce management. This structure is based in part on conceptualizations in Montgomery & Urban [1969] and Ryans & Weinberg [1981]. The four boxes represent a structuring of how practitioners and researchers have approached sales management decisions. Salesforce-management goals and objectives provide the interface between the three categories of salesforce decisions and the other components of the marketing mix in the context of a strategic marketing plan. The bi-directional arrow indicates that these goals and objectives affect and are affected by the functional-area decisions. Salesforce decisions are broadly distributed into three categories. Organizational decisions define the bounds of the selling activities. Decisions in this area address the structure of the salesforce(s), the magnitude of the effort, and the composition of selling regions or territories. Allocation decisions utilize the structure imposed by the organizational decisions to allocate the available selling resources (time, representatives, dollars) among a variety of key entities (products, segments, customers, etc.). Finally, control decisions address the needs of the individual sales representatives. Compensation schemes, motivation, and performance evaluation are key areas in the successful management of a salesforce.

Figure 14.1 illustrates the interdependencies which exist between these decision areas. For example, the size of the salesforce affects the amount of time, and thus selling effort, which can be allocated across potential customers. However, the total selling effort expended by the salesforce also depends on the level of motivation and the compensation scheme. To complete the circle, individual motivation and compensation depend on territory-design decisions as the nature of the territory

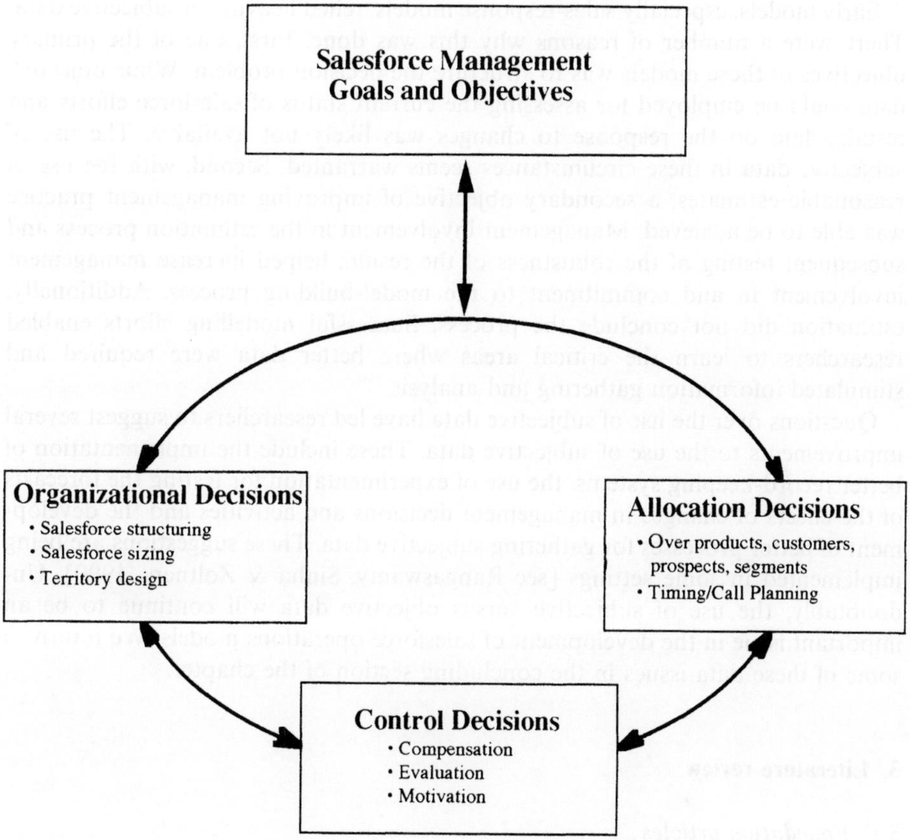

Fig. 14.1. Major decision areas in salesforce management

affects the amount of time an individual sales representative can allocate to selling. Researchers have recognized the importance of these interdependencies and have attempted to address many of these decisions simultaneously. This has been especially true of organizational and allocation decisions. However, control decisions, especially those concerning compensation, have tended to be analyzed in isolation.

2.1. Data issues in sales management

On the surface, it would appear that models of salesforce operations should be able to build on abundant databases. Although there are some instances where objective data is used in model development, it is more often the case that the available objective data is either incomplete or not in the required form.

Early models, especially sales-response models, relied heavily on subjective data. There were a number of reasons why this was done. First, one of the primary objectives of these models was to structure the decision problem. While objective data could be employed for assessing the current status of salesforce efforts and results, data on the response to changes was likely not available. The use of subjective data in these circumstances seems warranted. Second, with the use of reasonable estimates, a secondary objective of improving management practice was able to be achieved. Management involvement in the estimation process and subsequent testing of the robustness of the results helped increase management involvement in and commitment to the model-building process. Additionally, estimation did not conclude the process. Successful modelling efforts enabled researchers to learn the critical areas where better data were required and stimulated information gathering and analysis.

Questions over the use of subjective data have led researchers to suggest several improvements to the use of subjective data. These include the implementation of better record-keeping systems, the use of experimentation for testing the forecasts of the effects of changes in management decisions and activities and the development of better processes for gathering subjective data. These suggestions are being implemented in some settings [see Rangaswamy, Sinha & Zoltners, 1990]. Undoubtably, the use of subjective versus objective data will continue to be an important issue in the development of salesforce operations models. We return to some of these data issues in the concluding section of the chapter.

3. Literature review

3.1. *Foundation articles*

The foundation of salesforce models can be linked to a few key modelling efforts. These original models were developed to aid in understanding important components of the sales-management function. For compensation, the seminal paper was Farley's [1964] article which had the objective of coordinating the efforts of the sales representative with the goals of the firm. This core objective remains the focus of compensation research. (See Coughlan, (Chapter 13), for a discussion of salesforce-compensation research.) Similarly, much of the research in salesforce operations can be traced to three models: CALLPLAN [Lodish, 1971], DETAILER [Montgomery, Silk & Zaragoza, 1971] and GEOLINE [Hess & Samuels, 1971]. Interestingly, these models all appeared in a special issue on marketing-management models in the December 1971 issue of *Management Science*.

CALLPLAN addresses the problem of allocating a salesperson's time across accounts. This model is at the root of many salesforce operations models because it develops a simple yet powerful procedure for estimating sales response to effort. In addition, the modelling framework lends itself well to implementation and has an impressive track record of successful applications. DETAILER presents an alternative form of allocation model. Its contribution results from the fact that the model concentrates on allocations of time or effort across products rather than accounts. Since most sales representatives market a product line, this product-based allocation of effort is of critical importance. In addition, DETAILER was the first salesforce model to incorporate time dynamics into resource-allocation models. The third model, GEOLINE, addresses the territory-design problem. GEOLINE was a pioneer in the use of an 'automatic' procedure for developing territories. Its general approach of grouping small geographic areas to derive compact territories subject to equalization constraints has been carried forward in more recent modelling approaches.

In addition to appearing in the same issue, these models have a number of other features in common. First, each model addresses a significant research problem which is also considered to be important by practitioners. Second, each model discusses implementation issues and presents results of empirical applications. This attention to implementation has carried through to more recent modelling efforts concerning salesforce operations.[1] In addition, each model allows for the inclusion of both subjective judgements and historical data in parameter estimation, thus helping to overcome the problem of limited data availability. Finally, each model obtains insights by concentrating on a limited portion of the sales-management problem. This required the definition and careful specification of those components which were critical to the problem. At times, much can be learned from what is excluded, as the following map paradox illustrates [Hughes & Brecht, 1975]:[2]

> 'That's another thing we've learned from *your* Nation,' said Mein Herr, 'map-making. But we've carried it much further than *you*. What do you consider the *largest* map that would be really useful?
>
> 'About six inches to the mile.'
>
> 'Only *six inches*!' exclaimed Mein Herr. 'We very soon got to six *yards* to the mile. Then we tried a *hundred* yards to the mile. And then came the grandest idea of all! We actually made a map of the country, on the scale of *a mile to the mile*!'
>
> 'Have you used it much?' I enquired.
>
> 'It has never been spread out, yet,' said Mein Herr: 'the farmers objected: they said it would cover the whole country, and shut out the sunlight! So we now use the country itself, as its own map, and I assure you it does nearly as well.'

The following review will describe these three foundation models in more detail and trace their influence in more recent modelling efforts. Table 14.1 provides a synopsis of selected salesforce operations models. The problems addressed by each of these models can be classified into one or more of the decision areas outlined in Figure 14.1. Rather than a chronological description, the review will be organized

[1] Implementation of proposed compensation models appears to be much lower than allocation or organization models. See Coughlan, Chapter 13.

[2] Hughes & Brecht [1975] consider a number of variants of the map paradox. This particular one is attributed to Lewis Carroll's *Sylvie and Bruno Concluded*.

Table 14.1
Synopsis of selected salesforce models

Article	Organization decisions			Allocation decisions		Control decisions
	Salesforce sizing	Territory design	Other	Resources	Entities	
Lodish [1971] Fudge & Lodish [1977]				Sales-representative call time	Prospective customers	
Montgomery, Silk & Zaragoza [1971]				Sales calls	Products	
Hess & Samuels [1971]		Geographic territory design subject to equal activity, contiguity and compactness constraints				
Lodish [1975]		Modify territories to equalize managerial profitability of an hour of effort		Similar to Lodish [1971]	Similar to Lodish [1971]	
Lodish [1976]				Call time available to several sales representatives	Accounts	
Parasuraman & Day [1977]				Call time	Customer groups	
Beswick & Cravens [1977]	Increase selling effort (no, of reps) in each territory to maximize profits.	Hess & Samuels procedure or subjective judgement of managers		Sales time	Individual control units (may be customers, segments or small geographic areas)	Generation of quotas, sales forecasts
Zoltners, Sinha & Chong [1979]				Sales-representative call time	Clients, prospects	
Ryans & Weinberg [1979, 1987]						Environment-adjusted measure of salesperson performance
Lodish [1980] Lodish, Curtis, Ness & Simpson [1988]	Increase salesforce until the marginal profit/rep becomes negative			Call time	Products and market segments	
Zoltners & Sinha [1980]	Unconstrained model allows for selection of optimal level of resource			Arbitrary: any resources	Arbitrary: any entities	
Parsons & Vanden Abeele [1981]						
Zoltners & Sinha [1983]		Grouping of sales coverage units (SCUs) into larger geographic areas subject to any number of constraints		Similar to Zoltners & Sinha [1980]	Similar to Zoltners & Sinha [1980]	
Gelb & Khumawala [1984]		Choice of member of regions and geographic boundaries based on the cost of forgone sales				
Rangaswamy, Sinha & Zoltners [1990]	Increase selling effort until marginal profitability becomes negative		Determination of appropriate numbers of salesforces for firm and which products are to be allocated to each salesforce	Call time	Products and market segments	

Response function			Other factors		Notes
Estimation	Form	Response related to..	Interactions	Time	
Salesperson's best estimate of response	S-shaped or concave	Number of sales calls			
Salesperson and manager judgement	Cubic response with exponential forgetting	Accumulated exposure to products		Carryover effects of past calls	
					Based on a program used for legislative districting; minimize moments of inertia
Similar to Lodish [1971]	Similar to Lodish [1971]	Similar to Lodish [1971]			Considers time required to travel to sub-areas of a region
Sales rep and manager's subjective judgement of ability in an account	Concave, piecewise linear approximation to non-linear function	Sales rep's ability on specific accounts and sales calls	Account effect by sales rep		
Subjective judgement	S-shaped or concave	Accumulated selling effort		Carryover effect of past calls	Considers the ability of reps (effects added)
Historical data, subjective judgement	Exponential (power) function	Salesperson effort (also recognizes the impact of workload, potential, ability etc)	Various company and sales rep characteristics		Given customers and prospects, 1. Use response function to allocate effort optimally. 2. Add sales reps until profit maximizes. 3. Modify territories.
Historical data, subjective judgement	Any functional form, discrete	Call time (also recognizes other variations)			Flexible programming algorithm.
Historical data from three companies	Power function	Representative and territory characteristics	All variables used in the model	Five-year model in Ryans & Weinberg [1987]	Objective to explain the variation in performance among sales reps
Management judgements	Logistic function	Product mentions (details)			Combination of CALLPLAN and DETAILER
Historical data, subjective judgement	Any functional form, discrete	Selected resource(s)	Multiple resources are inter-related as composite strategies	Carryover function allowed	Models discussed: 1. General constrained 2. Unconstrained 3. Multiple-resource 4. Multi-period
Historical data	Power function	Sales calls, samples, handouts, mailings (over time)	Between marketing variables included in model	Lag sales included to show effects of past efforts	Pharmaceutical example objective to assess sales-call effectiveness
Similar to Zoltners & Sinha [1980]	Similar to Zoltners & Sinha [1980]	Similar to Zoltners & Sinha [1980]	Similar to Zoltners & Sinha [1980]	Similar to Zoltners & Sinha [1980]	Two-step iterative procedure: 1. Allocate resources optimally 2. Realign territories
					Mixed integer-program model with managerial judgement
Historical data, subjective judgement	Concave function	Salesperson effort, allocated to substitutes, competitive effort	Effort allocated to substitute products	Scaling parameter to estimate differential carryover efforts	A generalization of Zoltners & Sinha [1980] incorporating a continuous response function

in a manner which better illustrates how researchers have attempted to address interrelationships between these decision areas. First allocation models will be discussed. This is followed by models which primarily address organizational issues. Several of the models described in this section are also concerned with allocation decisions. Finally, modelling efforts which are concerned with control issues, outside of compensation, will be outlined.

3.2. Sales-resource allocation

Sales-management organizations are faced with a number of resource-allocation decisions. These types of decisions, or closely related variants of them, recur at several levels of the organization. At the management level, budgeted selling expenditures must be allocated across divisions or regions; selling effort must be allocated across products and segments; and sales representatives must be allocated across regions, products, and/or segments. At the sales-representative level, individuals must continually allocate their time across customers and prospects while at the same time determining the emphasis to be placed on the various products that they are marketing. Because of the importance of these decisions as well as their abundance, sales-resource allocation has been actively researched.

In all allocation models, one or more sales resources are allocated among several sources of revenue called sales entities [Zoltners & Sinha, 1980]. Potential sales resources are sales budgets, sales representatives, sales calls, sales time and sales effort, while examples of sales entities include sales districts, accounts, prospects, markets and products. Let x_i represent the amount of a sales resource allocated to sales entity i. The effect of this allocation procedure is measured using an entity-level sales-response function which estimates the sales (and thus contribution to profit) which will result from alternative resource-allocation levels. Let $r(x_i)$ represent the sales response function. (By combining the profits generated by a particular allocation scheme with its associated costs, the tradeoffs between alternative allocation policies can be analyzed.) Mathematical search procedures are typically employed to determine good or optimal solutions.[3]

Several of the most influential allocation models are reviewed in the following sections.[4]

3.2.1. CALLPLAN [Lodish, 1971]

The CALLPLAN model was developed to address a key personal selling question: How should a salesperson's time be allocated between customers and prospects in his/her territory? The model provides an interactive call-planning

[3] In this chapter our focus is on the problem structure, the methodological approaches used, and the results obtained – not on the optimization procedures employed. Nevertheless, the considerable advance in optimization techniques and computer systems has increased the scope of problems and the range of response functions that can be utilized.

[4] For purposes of exposition, models are stated as much as possible in a consistent format and, in some cases, are slightly revised.

system which is implemented at the individual representative level and is used to establish call-frequency norms for both customers and prospects. The model allocates a basic resource (sales representative's time) across a number of entities (customers, prospects) while considering the time required to travel to different sub-areas of the territory. Its optimization procedure assumes that sales response is a function of the resource allocated (call-frequency).

The CALLPLAN model has two stages. In the first stage, the expected response at alternative call frequencies is estimated for each customer and prospect in a salesperson's territory. In CALLPLAN, x_i represents the planned call-frequency for customer i. The sales response ($r(x_i)$) is estimated using the salesperson's subjective judgements at five discrete call-frequency levels: (1) no calls (r_0); (2) the saturation call rate (r_∞); (3) current level; (4) 0.5 times the current call rate; and (5) 1.5 times the current call rate.[5] The model thus allows for asymmetric response to increases or decreases from the current sales level.[6] Using these data points, the sales response function for customer i is estimated using the following functional form:

$$r_i(x_i) = r_0 + (r_\infty - r_0)(x_i^\sigma/(\gamma + x_i^\sigma)). \qquad (1)$$

This response function can either be concave or s-shaped (depending on the value of σ) and in Lodish [1971] is estimated using a decision-calculus approach. Interestingly, a recently published model [Rangaswamy, Sinha & Zoltners, 1990] continues to include subjective answers to very similar questions, but the values are based on group consensus rather than on an individual's judgement.

The second stage of the CALLPLAN procedure is the determination of the optimal allocation of time to customers and prospects. The objective function to be maximized considers the contribution of each customer's sales response minus the associated travel costs.[7] Specifically,

[5] For purposes of subjective estimation, the variable x_i is normalized so that at the current number of calls, x_i, is set to 1. Then, once r_0 and r_∞ are estimated, the answer to the question about the current sales level leads to the following form of (1):

$$r(1) = r_0 + (r_\infty - r_0)(1/(\gamma + 1))$$

and the value of γ can be obtained directly. Only σ remains to be determined. However, Lodish [1971] allows for differences in responsiveness to decreases and increases in calling levels. Thus one value of σ, denoted σ_D, is estimated when $0 < x_i < 1$, and another value of σ, denoted σ_I, is estimated when $x_i > 1$. The answers to the questions about the decrease and increase of calling levels yield values of σ_D and σ_I respectively. Similar correspondences between questions asked and parameter values characterize most of the subjectively estimated models discussed in this chapter.

[6] The parameter σ in (1) is given alternative values for an increase or decrease in sales calls.

[7] Lodish [1971] allows for multiple effort periods per response cycle. That is, the response may be based on an annual number of calls which is made up of four quarterly effort periods. No variations in the calls per effort period is allowed in the model. The model estimates the steady-state response when the selected call effort is implemented.

$$\text{maximize} \quad \sum_{i=1}^{I} a_i r_i(x_i) - \sum_{j=1}^{J} \mathrm{NT}_j c_j \tag{2}$$

$$\text{subject to} \quad \sum_{i=1}^{I} t_i x_i + \sum_{j=1}^{J} \mathrm{NT}_j v_j \leqslant T \qquad \text{(time constraint)}$$

$$\mathrm{NT}_j = \max\,\{x_i \text{ such that } g_i = j\} \text{ for } j = 1,\ldots,J \qquad \text{(number of trips)}$$
$$\mathrm{Min}_i \leqslant x_i \leqslant \mathrm{Max}_i \text{ for } i = 1,\ldots,I \qquad \text{(call-frequency range)}$$

where

a_i = adjustment factor for account contribution,
g_i = geographic area where account i is located,
NT_j = number of trips of geographical area j,
c_j = cost per trip to geographical area j,
v_j = time required per trip to geographical area j,
t_i = time spent with customer i,
T = sales representative's total time.

The problem described in (2) maximizes contribution for a sales representative while considering the costs of travelling to different geographic regions. Several constraints impact on this maximization. The time constraint ensures that a salesperson's time is not over-allocated. The number-of-trips constraint ensures that calls to a particular account cannot exceed the number of trips made to that account's geographic region. The final set of constraints puts upper and lower bounds on an account's call-frequency.

A two-step procedure is used to solve this problem. In the first step calls are optimally allocated among the accounts in each of the J geographic areas independently assuming any number of trips from 0 to a prespecified maximum are made to that area. The maximization problem is similar to (2) except that $\sum_{j=1}^{J} \mathrm{NT}_j$ is replaced by l, the number of trips assumed made to the geographic area being analyzed. Step 2 involves allocating the optimal amount of time to spend in each geographic area. The combination of these two steps yields the optimal call-frequency schedule.

Steps 1 and 2 can be solved using a dynamic-programming approach but Lodish recommends a simpler search procedure in which $r_i(x_i)$ is replaced by its linear concave envelope. This simplification appears to provide solutions sufficiently close to the true optimum for most realistic problems [Freeland & Weinberg, 1980]. The exact procedure used in CALLPLAN is developed in Table 14.2.

The CALLPLAN model has become an important allocation model for several reasons. First, the model recognizes the differential impact of call-frequency and focuses on the organization of time to capitalize on these differences. Second, the model incorporates many important constraints which apply to most allocation problems. For CALLPLAN, these include sales representative's time, travel time and cost, and individual differences in productivity. In addition, the model chooses to leave out other factors which are not critical to the problem (e.g. overnight

Table 14.2
Optimal search procedure used in CALLPLAN

A two-step procedure is used to determine the optimal call-planning frequency in CALLPLAN. In step 1, the modified response functions, $r_i'(x_i)$, are constructed. These functions are piecewise-linear concave approximations of the original response functions. Let $x_{i,0} = \text{Min}_i$, the minimum allowable calls for account i. Let $x_{i,1}$ be a value of x_i such that $\{(r_i(x_i) - r_i(\text{Min}_i))/(x_i - \text{Min}_i)\}$ is a maximum over all x_i; $x_i = \text{Min}_i + 1, \ldots, \text{Max}_i$.

In generl, $x_{i,l}$ is the value of x_i such that $\{(r_i(x_i) - r_i(x_{i,l-1}))/(x_i - x_{i,l-1})\}$ is a maximum over all x_i for $x_i = x_{i,l-1} + 1, \ldots, \text{Max}_i$ and $x_{i,L} = \text{Max}_i$.

Let

$$b_{i,l} = \frac{r_i(x_{i,l}) - r_i(x_{i,l-1})}{x_{i,l} - x_{i,l-1}} \quad \text{for } l = 1, \ldots, L.$$

These b's are the slopes of the piecewise-linear approximations. Note that $b_{i1} \geqslant b_{i2} \geqslant b_{iL}$ because of the way the $x_{i,l}$'s were determined.

The approximated function $r_i'(x_i)$ can be defined recursively:

$$r_i(x_i) = r_i(x_{i,0}) + b_{i,1}(x_i - x_{i,0}) \text{ for } \text{Min}_i \leqslant x_i \leqslant x_{i,1},$$

$$r_i'(x_i) = r_i'(x_{i,l-1}) + b_{i,l}(x_i - x_{i,l-1}) \text{ for } x_{i,l-1} \leqslant x_i \leqslant x_{i,l} \text{ and } l = 1, \ldots, L.$$

Note that r_i' has constant or diminishing returns by definition and that at every point at which r' changes slope the approximation is exact, i.e., $r' = r$.

Using the $r_i'(x_i)$'s as the individual account response functions, a near-optimal allocation of sales calls can be made by conducting an incremental analysis of each area, j, for the number of possible trip l. This analysis includes the following steps.

Step 1. Set the maximum calls to each account i in area j to be $\text{Min}\{l, \text{Max}_i\}$.

Step 2. As described above, determine the r_i' piecewise-linear concave approximations with the new maximum calls for each account i in area j.

Step 3. Allocate to each account the minimum calls required.

Step 4. Calculate the incremental ratio (IR_i) for each account, where $\text{IR}_i = a_i b_{i,j}/t_i$. The IR_i is the incremental adjusted sales per time unit spent on account i.

Step 5. Choose the account with the highest incremental ratio and allocate calls to it up to $x_{i,1}$ which is the highest amount of calls which will have a slope of b_{i1}.

Step 6. For this account i, change its slope to be b_{i2} in the IR_i calculation.

Step 7. Choose the account with the highest incremental ratio and allocate calls to it up to the highest number which will still have the slope used in the ratio calculation. Update the time units t, allocated so far. Calculate the objective function value at this allocation. If t is less than the maximum time units which can be allocated to area j go to Step 8, otherwise stop.

Step 8. Change the slope of the chosen account to the next one, recalculate its incremental ratio, go to Step 5.

Once the optimal allocations of calls in each area, j, have been determined, the Step 2 analysis is conducted. A similar routine to Step 1 is employed to allocated time to each of the geographic areas. At each time level, t, the response in each of the j regions is the value of the Step 1 objective function at t time units. Following the Step 2 analysis, the exact call-planning frequency can be determined from the results of Step 1.

Source: Lodish [1971, pp. P30–P31]

accommodations). Finally, the model is relatively simple to apply and has been shown to provide significant improvements in salesperson performance.

Lodish [1974] discusses how the model can be used as an interactive tool in which sales representatives use an iterative procedure to fine-tune estimates and conduct sensitivity analyses. The overall goal of this type of application is to develop an implementable call-planning schedule, which is 'better' than a more ad hoc approach. Numerous applications of the CALLPLAN model have been reported including a controlled field experiment conducted at United Airlines [Fudge & Lodish, 1977]. In the experiment, 10 salespersons used CALLPLAN to develop call-planning schedules while 10 others did not. After 6 months, the CALLPLAN group achieved a significantly higher level of sales increases than the control group. As a result of this initial success, United Airlines continued to use CALLPLAN for several years.

3.2.2 DETAILER [Montgomery, Silk & Zaragoza, 1971]

The DETAILER model represents an alternative form of allocation model. The model considers the situation in which the salesperson sells a number of products and addresses the problem of allocating selling time across products. Like CALLPLAN, DETAILER's objective is to allocate a selling resource (product mentions, also referred to as 'details') over a number of entities (customers).

Montgomery, Silk & Zaragoza assume that a salesperson making N calls (on which up to ρ products can be mentioned) must choose between four levels of coverage for each of the products marketed: (1) N product calls per period (full coverage, product mentioned on all calls); (2) $N/2$ product calls per period (half-coverage); (3) $N/4$ product calls per period (quarter-coverage); and (4) zero calls per period (no coverage). Each coverage policy is assumed to result in a specific 'relative exposure value' (REV) with $\mathrm{REV}(0) = 0$; $0 \leqslant \mathrm{REV}(N/4) = q \leqslant 1$; $\mathrm{REV}(N/2) = 1$; and $\mathrm{REV}(N) = c \geqslant 1$. To incorporate dynamic effects, sales response for a particular product is assumed to be a function of accumulated exposure value and has the following form:

$$Q_t = Q_t^* r(X_t)$$

where

Q_t = unit sales in period t,
Q_t^* = maximum sales potential in period t,
$r(X_t)$ = response to accumulated exposure in period t,
X_t = accumulated exposure in period t, $X_t = \lambda \mathrm{REV}(x_t) + (1 - \lambda) X_{t-1}$,
x_t = detailing level in period t
λ = forgetting parameter.

The authors propose a (non-negative) cubic function to specify $r(X_t)$:

$$r(X_t) = \begin{cases} \beta_0 + \beta_1 X_t^2 - \beta_2 X_t^3 & \text{if } \beta_0 + \beta_1 X_t^2 - \beta_2 X_t^3 \leqslant 1, \\ 1 & \text{otherwise} \end{cases}$$

To parameterize the model, salespersons are asked to estimate the values of q and c by comparing quarter- and full-coverage levels to half-coverage. In addition, λ is estimated by asking salespersons what short-term sales would be with no detailing. Managers are asked to estimate β_0, β_1 and β_2 by making forecasts of sales with different detailing efforts over an extended period of time.[8]

The optimization problem maximizes total gross product-line profits (II) over the planning horizon:

$$\text{maximize} \quad \Pi = \sum_{p=1}^{P} m_p \sum_{t=1}^{T} Q^*_{pt} r(X_{pt}),$$

$$\text{subject to} \quad \sum_{p=1}^{P} x_{pt} \leqslant \rho N \quad \text{for } t = 1, \ldots, T \qquad \text{(detailing capacity)}$$

where m_p = margin for product p.

Though the problem could be formulated as a dynamic program, the authors suggest a heuristic approach which incrementally improves the detailing schedule. The heuristic approach begins with some initial feasible allocation of effort (detailing level) to each product for each period in the planning horizon.[9]

Computation begins by setting all detailing levels to zero in period 1. A marginal analysis is then performed for each product taking account of the future impact of sales effort in $t = 1$ given the allocations made in periods 2,..., T. Effort is allocated to products based upon the marginal response until total detailing capacity is exhausted. Attention is then turned to period 2, only now with the input values from the just completed allocation in period 1. All detailing levels for all products in period 2 are set to zero and the process is repeated with attention once again being given to future efforts. This process is repeated to the end of the planning horizon. Then, the allocations for period 1 are reanalyzed, and so on. When the allocation procedure results in the same plan for two successive passes over all T periods in the planning horizon, the search terminates.

The contributions of DETAILER are three-fold. First, the model was the first to consider the allocation of time across products rather than across customers. Second, the incorporation of dynamic effects added an important component which was lacking in other modelling efforts [e.g. Lodish, 1971]. In addition, the dynamic feature enabled managers to test alternative detailing policies (e.g. pulsing, constant detailing). Finally, like CALLPLAN, the model is relatively simple to apply and has been successfully implemented in multiple settings.

Regrettably, modelling of the time dynamics of changing salesforce allocations has not been actively pursued. Most models focus on sales results in a future

[8] Chakravarti, Mitchell & Staelin [1981] found some limitations in test subjects ability to estimate parameters in a dynamic model where carryover and responsiveness are difficult to separate. Little & Lodish [1981] provide a rejoinder. The success of the experiments in Fudge & Lodish [1977] and McIntyre [1982], both of which contain no time factor, provide support for the view that management estimates are potentially acceptable in cases where actual data are not available.

[9] While the reported final allocations are reasonably robust to the starting solution, Montgomery, Silk & Zaragoza suggest trying several starting points to test the robustness in any given allocation.

period – or planning horizon – when the optimal allocation has been achieved. While most authors are careful to point out the limitations inherent in such an approach, the profit opportunities in dynamic strategies have not been adequately considered. In addition, as noted in the final sections of this chapter, competitive forces and changing market conditions raise concerns about the achievability of stable long-term market conditions.

3.2.3. Extensions and related work

Several researchers have expanded on the CALLPLAN and DETAILER models. Lodish [1976] extends CALLPLAN to address the issue of differential productivity of representatives in a concentrated geographic area. Therefore, travel time is no longer considered. The objective of the model is to assign representatives to accounts in order to maximize profits. The model assumes that different types of representatives are more effective on different types of accounts. Using managerial judgements, a matrix, V_{ik}, of each of the K salespersons' relative effectiveness on each of the I accounts is derived and incorporated into the CALLPLAN maximization problem. The maximization problem becomes:

$$\underset{x_i, y_{ik}}{\text{maximize}} \quad \sum_{i=1}^{I} a_i r_i(x_i) \sum_{k=1}^{K} y_{ik} V_{ik}$$

$$\text{subject to} \quad \sum_{i=1}^{I} y_{ik} x_i \leqslant T_k \quad \text{for } k = 1, \ldots, K \quad \text{(time constraints)}$$

$$\sum_{k=1}^{K} y_{ik} \leqslant 1 \quad \text{for } i = 1, \ldots, I \quad \text{(assignment constraints)}$$

where

y_{ik} = a variable allocating account i to salesperson k.

Lodish solves the problem using a piecewise-linear-approximation approach similar to CALLPLAN. The y_{ik}'s are determined via linear programming. The solution to the optimization problem allocates salespersons to accounts and delivers call-planning schedules simultaneously. Despite the fact that the y_{ik}'s are not 0–1 variables, Lodish reports good model results in a single setting. A limitation of the model is the complexity involved in the development of an effectiveness matrix, especially in large organizations.

Parasuraman & Day's [1977] PAIRS model (purchaser attitudes and interactive response to salesmen) develops a call-planning system which explicitly considers the ability of the sales representative and the carryover effects of sales calls. The response to sales effort is modelled in a manner which is very similar to CALLPLAN with sales representatives judgementally estimating sales response at current calling levels as well as at zero, 1/2 current, 3/2 current and unlimited calling levels. Similar to DETAILER, a decay parameter and a one-period lag term are included to represent the decay and carryover effects of selling effort. As a response function, Parasuraman & Day develop an index describing the 'value' of the selling effort. This index depends on sales calls and the managerial estimates of the representative's selling ability. Selling ability is operationalized as a weighted index of salesperson characteristics. Algebraically, the response function is

$$P_{ik,t} = \lambda_i S_{ik} r_i(x_i) + (1 - \lambda_i) P_{ik,t-1}$$

where

$P_{ik,t}$ = the proportion of potential dollar volume to be obtained from customer i in period t if salesperson k calls on the customer (there may be a number of customers in a segment who have the same response function),

λ_i = parameter representing the extent of 'decay' over time in the purchase proportion of customer i with no selling effort ($0 \leqslant \lambda \leqslant 1$ for all i),

S_{ik} = a scale factor, incorporating selling ability for salesperson k on customer i,

x_i = number of sales calls made on customer i.

Parasuraman & Day's model represents an attempt to bring some of the findings from the personal-selling literature into a formal analytical model. However, it is unclear whether or not the sales representative's selling ability has been included twice. The sales representatives' own estimates of customer response to different levels of effort may already incorporate the ability factor. In addition, development of a valid estimation procedure which considers all possible sales representative–customer-segment pairs appears to be a formidable task. The authors report a limited application of the model in three territories (with one sales rep in each territory) of a consumer-products company. While management appeared supportive of the project, a full-scale implementation was apparently not done.

Zoltners & Sinha [1980] outline a general modelling approach, based on integer programming, to deal with several salesforce-management problems. The modelling approach is conceptually similar to CALLPLAN and its extensions with sales response functions (estimated via subjective judgements and/or historical data) driving the allocation of resources (sales calls, product mentions, etc.) across entities (accounts, prospects, etc.). The major difference between the two methodologies is the solution procedure. Lodish's optimization procedure assumes a piecewise-linear response function while the Zoltners & Sinha approach utilizes a discrete response function estimated over a finite set of feasible allocation levels. Table 14.3 describes the general integer-programming model in more detail.

Zoltners & Sinha outline a number of advantages to integer-programming models. These include: (1) an assurance of a meaningful solution since only feasible strategies are included; (2) the existence of efficient optimization algorithms; (3) the elimination of concavity assumptions regarding the shape of the sales-response function; and, (4) an approach which allows for the incorporation of additional decision variables and constraints. The flexibility that is gained comes from (ever-improving) mathematical-program routines. However, often solutions can be stated only in numeric (and not in analytic) form. Parameter sensitivity testing becomes very important here.

The general model has been modified in a number of ways in applications to

Table 14.3
Zoltners & Sinha [1980] integer-programming allocation model

Zoltners & Sinha's general integer-programming model can be stated as follows. Note the change in terminology as compared to earlier models, resulting from the integer-programming formulation.

Maximize $F(Y)$ — **Objective function**

Resource availability constraints

Subject to $\sum_{j=1}^{J} \sum_{k \in S_{jt}} w_{ijkt} y_{jkt} < W_{it}$ $\quad t = 1, 2, \ldots, T$; for each $i = 1, 2, \ldots, I$;

Feasibility constraints

$\sum_{k \in S_{jt}} y_{jkt} = 1$ $\quad t = 1, 2, \ldots, T$; for each $j = 1, 2, \ldots, J$;

$y_{jkt} = 0$ or 1 $\quad$ for each $k \in S_{jt}$; $j = 1, 2, \ldots, J$; $t = 1, 2, \ldots, T$.

Auxiliary constraints — to specify, as required

where

J = the number of sales entities,
T = the number of time periods,
S_{jt} = the index set of implementable allocation strategies for sales entity j in time period t,
y_{jkt} = the decision variable which is equal to 1 if strategy $k \in S_{jt}$ is selected for sales entity j in time period t,
w_{ijkt} = the amount of ith resource consumed if strategy $k \in S_{jt}$ is implemented for sales entity j in time period t,
Y = the three-dimensional matrix with y_{jkt} as elements,
$F(Y)$ = the expected sales (profit) if strategy Y is used.

The objective function represents the expected sales (or profit) associated with any possible resource allocation to the sales entities. The resource-availability constraints ensure that the final resources allocated to the sales entities do not exceed the resources available in each period. The feasibility constraints ensure that exactly one implementable allocation strategy is chosen for each sales entity. The auxiliary constraints include other restrictions which may be necessary to represent the allocation decision better.

Adopted from: Zoltners & Sinha [1980, p. 249].

a wide variety of situations. Zoltners, Sinha & Chong [1979] apply the general model to develop a salesperson call-planning system similar to CALLPLAN. Because of the flexibility of the integer-programming model, other factors such as salesperson effectiveness and company effort in a territory as described in Beswick & Cravens [1977] and Parasuraman & Day [1977] can be incorporated. However, as noted above, inclusion of factors based on specific salesperson–customer (or territory) pairs can pose difficult modelling and estimation challenges. Often the focus of the model will determine the degree of specificity required.

Zoltners & Sinha [1980] describe the general model as well as four variants. First, an unconstrained model, which maximizes profits in the absence of constraints on the resource(s) is developed to allow for the joint determination of optimal salesforce size and effort allocation. Second, a multiple resource-allocation model, which allocates several resources simultaneously, is developed to account for team-selling situations. In this model variant, each implementable strategy consists of an allocation from all possible resources. A sales-response outcome is then estimated for each strategy. By design, interactions between resources are incorporated in the estimated sales-response outcomes. A third variant of the general model illustrates a multi-period resource-allocation model while the fourth variant allows for a stochastic response outcome. Specialized integer-programming algorithms [e.g., Sinha & Zoltners, 1979] are used to find solutions to the specific variants of the general model. Zoltners & Sinha [1980] do not illustrate these variants with empirical applications.[10]

In addition to the models outlined above, articles by Lodish [1975], Beswick & Cravens [1977], Lodish [1980] and Rangaswamy, Sinha & Zoltners [1990] also represent extensions to the core resource-allocation models. Since these models consider both organizational and allocation decisions, they will be reviewed later in this chapter. Several other resource-allocation models have been suggested in the literature. Most of these models were developed prior to 1980. Interested readers are directed to LaForge, Lamb, Cravens & Mencrief [1989], Lilien & Kotler [1983] and Zoltners & Sinha [1980] for a discussion of these modelling efforts.

Finally, research by Parsons & Vanden Abeele [1981] represents one of the few published attempts to use historical data to estimate sales response to sales calls and other marketing-mix variables. Unlike most allocation models, the response model is calculated across customers and territories in order to determine the company-wide effect of sales calls on sales. The objective of their research is to analyze the effectiveness of sales calls in the presence of potential interacting variables like free samples and information handouts. Using pooled monthly wholesale sales data from a pharmaceutical manufacturer, the authors estimate a response function which includes the number of sales calls made, samples and information handouts given to physicians, and mailings sent to potential customers. The estimated response function (in reduced form) is

$$\begin{aligned}\ln \text{sales}(t) = {} & \beta_0 + \beta_1 \ln(\text{calls}(t)) \\ & + \beta_2 [\ln(\text{samples}(t)) \times \ln(\text{calls}(t))] \\ & + \beta_3 [\ln(\text{handouts}(t)) \times \ln(\text{calls}(t))] \\ & + \beta_4 [\ln(\text{samples}(t)) \times \ln(\text{handouts}(t)) \times \ln(\text{calls}(t))] \\ & + \beta_5 \ln(\text{mailings}(t-1)) \\ & + \beta_6 \ln(\text{sales}(t-1)).\end{aligned}$$

The lagged sales term is included primarily to control for the effect of people refilling prescriptions. Results indicate that sales-call effectiveness improves when samples and handouts are used but they have greater effect when used separately.

[10] It is important to note that later work by Zoltners & Sinha has moved away from integer-programming models in favour of response-function models [see Rangaswamy, Sinha & Zoltners, 1990].

Without further empirical applications, it is difficult to generalize the results. However, Parsons & Vanden Abeele illustrate that estimation of a sales-response function is possible in a sales-management setting and that the effect of potentially important interactions needs to be considered.

3.3. Sales-territory design

Territory-design decisions assign sales entities to individual representatives. Most often, the sales entities are small geographic areas called sales coverage units (SCUs). However, in areas in which travel considerations are minimal, the sales entities may be individual customers and prospects. Territory-design models determine which set of SCU groupings best satisfies management's objectives. These objectives are often dominated by control issues since the sales representatives are to be evaluated on their performance (relative to other representatives) within their assigned territories. Therefore, salesforce managers tend to have a preference for territories which are balanced on key dimensions such as work-load and sales potential.

There have been several approaches to sales-territory design. Key contributions are included in the following review.

3.3.1. GEOLINE [Hess & Samuels, 1971]

GEOLINE was developed to address the problem of territory design. Specifically, the model provided a method of grouping geographic SCUs in a manner which satisfies a number of constraints. The algorithm used in GEOLINE determines compact and contiguous territories which are equalized on a sales-activity constraint. For example, sales activity can represent such factors as sales calls or workload. The goal is to develop balanced territories.

The model assumes that the number of territories is fixed and begins with a starting set of territory centroids defined by its geographic coordinates. Let (E_i, N_i) represent respectively the east/west and north/south coordinates of territory centroid i. Likewise, let (e_j, n_j) represent the east/west and north/south coordinates of SCU j. The measure of compactness used is the moment of inertia which is calculated by multiplying an SCU's estimated sales activity, a_j, by the squared Euclidean distance from the SCU to its allocated territory centroid. That is, $a_j d_{ij}^2 = a_j[(E_i - e_j)^2 + (N_i - n_j)^2]$.

Hess & Samuels assign SCUs to territories in order to minimize the moment of inertia:

$$\text{minimize} \quad \sum_{i=1}^{I} \sum_{j=1}^{J} (a_j d_{ij}^2) y_{ij}$$

$$\text{subject to} \quad \sum_{j=1}^{J} a_j y_{ij} = \left(\sum_{j=1}^{J} a_j \right) \Big/ I \quad \text{for } i = 1, 2, \ldots, I, \quad \text{(equal-activity constraint)}$$

$$\sum_{i=1}^{I} y_{ij} = 1 \quad \text{for } j = 1, 2, \ldots, J, \quad \text{(assignment constraint)}$$

where

y_{ij} = the proportion of SCU j's sales activity assigned to the ith territory centroid.

The equal-activity constraints ensure that the territories are balanced. The assignment constraint ensures that all SCUs are fully covered. As we describe, this does not mean that they are assigned to only one territory – an awkward problem in implementation.

The optimal solution is found using a linear-programming algorithm. This solution results in the activity generated from some SCUs being divided among two or more territories. To assign these SCUs to a single territory, Hess & Samuels use a decision rule which allocates an SCU to the territory to which most of its sales activity is allocated. According to the authors, this adjustment tended to result in small deviations from the equal-activity constraint. However, as Zoltners & Sinha [1983] point out, this rounding procedure (to ensure SCUs are assigned to a single territory) can cause both conceptual and practical problems. This may be particularly troublesome in later models [e.g. Richardson, 1979] which balance territories over multiple attributes.

GEOLINE is iterative in nature. The territory-alignment solution in the first stage is calculated using arbitrary territory centroids. In the second stage, new territory centroids are determined by finding the sales-activity-weighted geographic center of the territories determined in the first stage. The linear-programming solution is then recalculated. The procedure is stopped after a set number of iterations or when two successive passes yield virtually identical solutions.

Hess & Samuels discuss two applications of the GEOLINE model. In a pharmaceutical company, alternative GEOLINE territory alignments were presented to each of 40 district managers. Although district managers had the option of accepting, rejecting, or modifying the GEOLINE results, most managers accepted the model alignments without changes. In a second application, the GEOLINE-model results compared favourable to a manually prepared territory alignment.

The GEOLINE model represented an important contribution to the literature because it was the first model to address the territory-design problem via SCU assignment. The inclusion of the equal-activity constraint addressed management's desire for a balanced set of territories. However, the model also has a number of shortcomings. First, the objective function, which minimizes compactness, does not consider costs or profitability. Second, the approach does not accommodate multiple equalization criteria, like sales potential, workload, etc. Probably the most important limitation of GEOLINE is the fact that the model does not ensure that territories are compatible with the geography of the alignment region. Physical features like mountains, waterways and highways are ignored. If the model develops unrealistic territories (e.g. a territory centre in the middle of a lake), the managerial impact of the model results is limited. The existence of unrealistic territories has been the focus of continuous development. Progress in this area is due to advances in mathematical programming and increased computing power. Beyond these limitations, it is important to note that the way Hess & Samuels structured the problem has had a strong impact on later models. Some of these models have been widely implemented.

3.3.2. Other territory-design models

There have been a number of extensions to the GEOLINE model as well as alternative approaches which concentrate on the maximization of profits.

Lodish [1975] extended the CALLPLAN model to incorporate the territory-design issue. By assuming a constant number of representatives, Lodish maximizes profits by equalizing the marginal profit of an additional hour of sales effort across territories. A CALLPLAN analysis is used to determine the optimal call-planning schedule in the original territories and the marginal profit of an additional hour of sales effort is calculated. By considering the time required to travel to various sub-regions, the territories are arbitrarily modified until the marginal profitability of incremental effort is equalized across territories. This extension broadened the applicability of the CALLPLAN methodology to a more aggregate salesforce-management tool.

Two issues are raised by this modified application of CALLPLAN. First, the response functions for accounts are estimated at the managerial level rather than the individual level. As accounts are moved between territories to equalize marginal profitability, the response functions remain the same. As such, the model is not sensitive to productivity differences among representatives. Second, the assumption of a constant number of sales representatives limits the maximization of profitability. As long as the marginal profit of an additional hour of sales effort is positive, profitability can be improved by increasing the size of the salesforce. Both of these issues were addressed in further extensions of the CALLPLAN methodology [Lodish, 1976, 1980].

In another extension to CALLPLAN, Lodish [1976] considers the assignment of accounts to sales representatives. This model, which is described in more detail in Section 3.2.3, considers a small geographic region in which travel costs are negligible. The assignment of representatives to accounts is based on an evaluation of how effective specific sales representatives are with specific customers. As a result, representatives are matched with customers to which their selling style is most suited.

As noted above, several extensions to the GEOLINE model have been developed to address the limitations of the Hess & Samuels procedure. Segal & Weinberger [1977] incorporate geographic considerations by replacing the Euclidean-distance component of GEOLINE with the shortest path between an SCU and the territory center. Zoltners [1979] and Richardson [1979] both extended the GEOLINE model to incorporate multiple attribute-balancing across territories. A more detailed review of these models is found in Zoltners & Sinha [1983].

The most comprehensive SCU-alignment model is presented in Zoltners & Sinha [1983]. These authors present a model, based on integer programming, which satisfies four key properties which define a good territory alignment: (1) each SCU (or sales entity) is assigned to exactly one sales territory; (2) the sales territories are 'almost' balanced on one or more territory characteristic; (3) the sales territories consist entirely of contiguous SCUs; and (4), the sales territories are compatible with geographic considerations such as highways and non-traversable objects (e.g. lakes, mountains and rivers). A special case of the Zoltners & Sinha model is the GEOLINE model.

The territory-alignment model developed by Zoltners & Sinha [1983] begins with a set of SCUs and a fixed number of territories. Territory centers are exogenous to the model and provided beforehand. To ensure territories are compatible with geographic considerations, the model utilizes a road graph in which SCU nodes are connected (via a line) only to those adjacent SCUs for which there is a connecting road. Using the road graph, the shortest path (measured in travel time) between territory centers and surrounding SCUs can be calculated. The model ensures contiguous territories by imposing the constraint that if SCU j is assigned to territory center i, all SCUs along the shortest path from i to j must also be assigned to territory i.

Zoltners & Sinha [1983] formalize a procedure in which there are K (i.e., $k = 1,\ldots,K$) important attributes (workload, sales potential, travel times) to be considered in the salesforce alignment. Typically, management will choose one of the attributes to minimize ($k = k^*$) and the others to balance.[11] Of course, given the integer assignment of SCUs to territories, the balance constraints can only be approximately met. Constraints which have to be very closely balanced will have a significant impact on the achievement of the objective function.

A general form of the alignment problem can be stated as follows:

$$\text{minimize} \quad \sum_{i=1}^{I}\sum_{j=1}^{J} a_{ijk} y_{ij} \quad \text{for } k = k^* \tag{3}$$

$$\text{subject to} \quad l_{ik} \leqslant \sum_{j=1}^{J} a_{ijk} y_{ij} \leqslant u_{ik} \quad \text{for } i = 1,2,\ldots,I,\ k = 1,2,\ldots,K,\ k \neq k^*, \tag{4}$$

$$y_{ij} \leqslant \sum_{p \in \Gamma_{ij}} y_{ip} \quad \text{for } i = 1,2,\ldots,I,\ j = 1,2,\ldots,J, \tag{5}$$

$$\sum_{i=1}^{I} y_{ij} = 1 \quad \text{for } j = 1,2,\ldots,J, \tag{6}$$

$$y_{ij} = 0 \text{ or } 1 \quad \text{for } i = 1,2,\ldots,I,\ j = 1,2,\ldots,J, \tag{7}$$

where

k = an index for the K relevant territory design attributes,

a_{ijk} = the kth attribute value for SCU j conditioned on the assignment of SCU j to territory center i (this territory-dependence generalizes the GEOLINE procedure),

l_{ik} = the lower limit for the kth attribute for the sales territory centered at i,

[11] The activity being optimized, in fact, can also be subject to a balance constraint. Although not noted by Zoltners & Sinha [1983] in their statement of the model (see (3)), this was apparently recognized by them in their treatment of the activity problem described below. In addition, the activity being optimized can, in turn, be a function of many attributes.

u_{ik} = the upper limit for the kth attribute for the sales territory centered at i,

Γ_{ij} = geographically contiguous set restriction.

This formulation satisfies four key properties of a good sales-territory alignment. Constraints (6) and (7) ensure that SCUs are assigned to only one territory. The constraints in (4) ensure that the sales territories are almost balanced on the k attributes. The closer the values l_{ik} and u_{ik} are to each other, the more balanced the sales territories become. However, the effect of requiring a narrow balance on an attribute in (4) is to make that constraint potentially influential on the overall value of the objective function achieved.[12] The constraints in (5) ensure that the territories are contiguous. Finally, the use of the road graph ensures that sales-territory configurations are compatible with geographic considerations.

The Zoltners & Sinha alignment model starts from a set of preassigned territory centers. While conceptually the model can seek to improve iteratively the integer-program solution as in Hess & Samuels [1971] (by altering the location of territory centers), the computational burden of doing so is considerable. In practice, the authors report that most sales managers have a strong preference for home-base cities.

Following Lodish [1975], Zoltners & Sinha [1983] recognize that defining a territory alignment based on balancing constraints may not place enough emphasis on profit maximization. They propose an iterative procedure which simultaneously optimizes the allocation of effort while designing sales territories. Given a fixed salesforce size, the total time available to the salesforce can be determined. Using current territories, this time can be allocated across SCUs using a resource-allocation model like Zoltners & Sinha [1980] or CALLPLAN. From this information, the workload per SCU can be determined and the Zoltners & Sinha [1983] territory-alignment model can then be used to create territories which minimize travel time while maintaining a balanced workload. Since the new territory alignments are expected to free up more selling time for the salesforce, the new territory alignments are used to re-estimate the resource-allocation model. The authors suggest that good solutions are typically found after a few iterations. Though Zoltners & Sinha do not discuss specific applications in their article, their territory-alignment model (or an updated variant) has been applied in numerous situations. Furthermore, significant advances in the availability of computerized geo-demographic databases have improved the implementability of territory-alignment models.

An alternative territory-alignment model is presented by Gelb & Khumawala [1984]. The primary purpose of their model is to determine how many territories to have and which SCUs to assign to each territory. Less concerned than other models with territory balance, Gelb & Khumawala [1984] introduce the notion of the cost of forgone sales (CFS). CFS is a measure of opportunity cost or profit

[12] To illustrate, assume the objective is to minimize the quarterly travel time and a constraint is the number of nights away from home. If all sales reps had to spend between 4 and 6 nights away from home as compared to between 4 and 10 nights away from home, a higher travel time would likely occur.

forgone from not being able to serve adequately (potential) customers at considerable distance from territory centers. The problem is formulated as a mixed integer-program model that was suitable, at least in the early 1980s, only for medium-sized problems (up to 60 regions) and still required a number of managerial revisions to the computer-generated solutions. (This latter characteristic is reported by most researchers who are concerned with implementation.) Nevertheless, the model led to a territory-realignment plan that was gradually being adopted by the company for which the model was designed.

3.4. *Integrative models addressing organizational and allocation decisions*

The network of interrelationships between sales-management decision areas has been recognized by a number of researchers. Models that consider more than one decision area have primarily combined one or more organizational decisions with a resource-allocation decision. Several of these models have already been reviewed in this chapter. The unconstrained variant of the Zoltners & Sinha [1980] model (see above) considers the salesforce-sizing problem simultaneously with the sales-resource-allocation problem while the models outlined in Lodish [1975], Lodish [1976] and Zoltners & Sinha [1983] consider both territory design and sales-resource allocation. This section reviews three other integrative models that represent significant contributions: Beswick & Cravens [1977], Lodish [1980] and Rangaswamy, Sinha & Zoltners [1990].

Beswick & Cravens [1977] outline a multistage decision model which can be used to address many of the salesforce decisions outlined in Figure 14.1. The model seeks improvements to existing salesforce decisions rather than an optimal solution. The model's stages include: (1) the development of a market-response function; (2) allocation of selling effort and the setting of salesforce size; (3) territory design; (4) comparison with objectives; and (5) forecasting, evaluation and control. The authors suggest a sales-response function which captures many of the influences on sales:

$$\begin{aligned}\text{sales response} = \beta_0 &+ \beta_1 \ln(\text{selling effort}) \\ &+ \beta_2 \ln(\text{workload}) \\ &+ \beta_3 \ln(\text{company experience}) \\ &+ \beta_4 \ln(\text{potential}) \\ &+ \beta_5 \ln(\text{company effort}) \\ &+ \beta_6 \ln(\text{salesperson quality})\end{aligned}$$

Sales response is estimated at the control-unit level by incorporating both managerial judgement and historical data.[13] A control unit is defined as the smallest sub-unit of a market used for analysis (e.g. a customer, a group of customers, or a small geographic area).

At the allocation stage, using a mathematical-programming algorithm, selling

[13] As Beswick & Cravens [1977, p. 140] themselves point out, the observed prediction variables were highly collinear so "it is unwise to place too much confidence in the individual parameter estimates".

effort is increased in each control unit until the marginal return from increased sales equals the marginal cost of increasing the selling effort. Summing the total effort and dividing by the effort possible by a single salesperson yields the required number of sales representatives. The territory-design feature of the model can be implemented using the GEOLINE procedure or via managerial judgement. Changes in the territory alignment and the number of salespersons have implications for the sales response functions. Stage 4 of the Beswick & Cravens model calls for the iterative re-estimation of stages 2 and 3 since territorial variables change each time the territories are realigned. The iterative procedure continues until management is satisfied that its objectives have been met. In stage 5, the authors suggest using the estimates developed in stage 1 as a basis for making important control decisions like setting quotas and evaluating performance.

The Beswick & Cravens model provides a framework which considers problems from each of the sales-management decision areas. The control-unit response function incorporates several representative and company characteristics which have been shown to affect customer sales response. In addition, the iterative procedure suggested in stage 4 of the model considers the interactive effects of these variables. Much of the model's contribution is primarily conceptual in nature. Given the potentially large number of control-unit response functions which need to be estimated, successful model implementation in a large selling organization would require a considerable data-collection effort. (See Rangaswamy, Sinha & Zoltners [1990] and Lodish, Curtis, Ness & Simpson [1988] for examples.)

Lodish [1980] develops a comprehensive model for salesforce sizing and allocation decisions. The model includes elements of both DETAILER and CALLPLAN to study time allocations to products while incorporating market segmentation and salesforce sizing. Like DETAILER, response is assumed to be a function of product details and it is assumed that there are no cross-product sales effects. However, unlike DETAILER, no dynamic effects are incorporated. The model concentrates on the effect of sales calls (actually product mentions) for P products in S segments. The maximization problem can be stated as:

$$\text{maximize} \quad \sum_{p=1}^{P} \sum_{s=1}^{S} m_p r_{ps}(x_{ps})$$

$$\text{subject to} \quad \sum_{p=1}^{P} x_{ps} \leqslant \overline{\mathrm{NC}_s} \cdot \overline{M_s} \qquad \text{(total product mentions in } s\text{)}$$

$$x_{ps} \leqslant \overline{\mathrm{NC}_s} \qquad \text{(calls in } s\text{)}$$

$$\sum_{s=1}^{S} \overline{\mathrm{NC}_s} \cdot A_s \leqslant \mathrm{NC}^* \cdot N \qquad \text{(total call capacity)}$$

where

x_{ps} = average number of mentions for product p in segment s,
$r_{ps}(\cdot)$ = response function for product p in segment s.

The following parameters are determined prior to optimization:

m_p = gross margin for product p,
$\overline{NC}_s$ = average number of calls to a member of segment s,
$\overline{M}_s$ = average number of mentions per call to a member of segment s,
A_s = number of accounts in segment s,
NC^* = maximum number of calls per salesperson,
N = number of salespersons.

The estimation of the response functions and the solution procedure are very similar to the CALLPLAN methodology with a sales-response function being estimated for each product in each of the market segments in which the product is marketed. The major difference here is the incorporation of a consensus-building approach to response-function estimation. In CALLPLAN, the sales representatives use their own judgement to estimate response. In Lodish [1980], response is estimated using judgements from several levels of management in the organization. Through a series of planning meetings, a modified Delphi technique [Dalkey, 1969] is used to create a consensus among management. By tapping the resources of managers with a variety of points of view, more reliable estimates can be expected.

In Lodish [1980], the solution to the allocation problem yields a listing of the average number of product details to be applied to customers in a specific segment. The model assigns product details on the basis of profitability per call. Since the salesforce-sizing decisions is endogenous, details, and thus sales representatives, are added until the marginal profitability becomes zero or negative. As a result, the optimal-salesforce-size and effort-allocation decisions are determined simultaneously.

Lodish's general salesforce sizing and deployment model has yielded a number of successful applications. Its application at Syntex Laboratories won the 1987 Franz Edelman Award for Management Science Achievement (Lodish, Curtis, Ness & Simpson, 1988]. In this particular application, Lodish's model suggested increasing the salesforce from the current level of 433 representatives to over 700 representatives. This level was much higher than company officials expected. However, because of their involvement in model development, Syntex management 'respect[ed] the model results' and began increasing the size of their salesforce [Clarke, 1983, p. 10]. The Syntex application led to a number of important benefits. Not the least of these benefits was a \$25 000 000 increase in annual sales in a high-margin business. In addition, the model suggested a deployment which helped the firm change its focus to product markets with better future potential.

Rangaswamy, Sinha & Zoltners [1990] report a salesforce sizing and allocation model which incorporates a multiproduct salesforce-structuring decision appropriate for firms operating in a repetitive buying situation. Specifically, the objectives of the model are to aid management in: (1) determining the appropriate number of salesforces (different salesforces are assigned to sell different products); (2) establishing the number of representatives in each salesforce; (3) determining which products should be assigned to each salesforce; and (4) ascertaining how the total salesforce effort is to be allocated across products and market segments that buy these products. The model represents the only attempt to address salesforce-structuring issues.

This model represents an extension of earlier research by Zoltners & Sinha [1980] and Lodish [1980]. Continuous (concave) response functions are estimated using historical data and a consensus-based judgement procedure similar to Lodish [1980]. More specifically, in the illustrative application of the model, sales of products in segment s are modelled as a function of number of sales presentations (x_{ps}) allocated to product p in segment s. (More than one product can be presented in a sales call and a product need not be mentioned on every call.) Responsiveness to sales presentations, $r(.)$, depends on the number of presentations of substitute products that the firm sells ($x_{rs}, r \neq p$) and of products sold by competitors (E_{ps}). Algebraically, Rangaswamy, Sinha & Zoltners [1990, p. 288] describe their response function as follows:[14]

$$r_{ps}(\bar{x}_s) = r_{0,ps} + \frac{\Delta_{ps}\alpha_p x_{ps}}{x_{ps} + \sum_{r \in H_p} x_{rs} + E_{ps}}$$

where

$\bar{x}_s$ = a vector representing the firm's sales effort on each product in segment s,
$r_{0,ps}$ = sales that would be generated if no effort were allocated to product p in segment s,
Δ_{ps} = the maximum one-period incremental sales available in market segment s for product p (it is the sales resulting from a very large amount of effort allocated to product p),
H_p = the set of products sold by the firm that are substitutes for product p,
E_{ps} = the estimated total salesforce effort in market segment s allocated by competitors to products that compete with product p (it is assumed that E_{ps} is not affected in the short term by changes in x_{ps}),
α_p = a scaling parameter that is included to reflect management's belief that effort on certain products has a significantly higher long-term effect on sales (over T periods) than does effort spent on other products. (Although sales response is modelled by single-period functions, α_p incorporates the long-term sales effect of repeat purchases resulting from effort in the plan period.)

It is important to note that this model directly separates out the competitive effort (E_{ps}) from market-responsiveness (α_p) unlike previous models which (sometimes implicitly) combined the two. However, no allowance is made for possible competitive response to the firm's changed salesforce strategies. Particularly in the pharmaceutical industry, where literally scores of firms have utilized salesforce marketing models, attention to competitive response seems warranted.

In a typical application, management is interested in a small number of alternative salesforce structures. For example, a firm may wish to determine whether two or three salesforces are required. In addition, for each number of salesforces,

[14] Rangaswamy, Sinha & Zoltners describe some of the variables in their model in dynamic terms. However, since their response function is static, we have restated their variables to be consistent with the terminology used earlier in this paper.

there may be two different allocations of products between the chosen salesforces. This salesforce-structuring problem would require an analysis of four different structures. Rangaswamy, Sinha & Zoltners, [1990, pp. 286–287] exemplify their approach with the following three-salesforce problem where the products are split into the set $\{P_1, P_2, P_3\}$:

$$\underset{x_{ps}, z_{sk}}{\text{maximize}} \quad \sum_{k=1}^{3} \left\{ \left[\sum_{s=1}^{S} \sum_{p \in P_k} m_{ps} r_{ps3}(\bar{x}_s) - C_p x_{ps} \right] - \sum_{s=1}^{S} c_s z_{sk} - c_n N_k \right\}$$

$$\begin{aligned}
\text{subject to} \quad & 0 \leqslant x_{ps} \leqslant z_{sk} \leqslant u_s, && s = 1,2,\ldots,S; \ \forall p \in P_k; \ k = 1,2,3, && \text{(market} \\
& \sum_{p \in P_k} x_{ps} \leqslant b_s z_{sk}, && s = 1,2,\ldots,S; \ k = 1,2,3, && \text{segment} \\
& && && \text{constraints)} \\
& x_{ps} = 0 && \text{for some } p \text{ and } s, && \\
& \sum_{s=1}^{S} h_k(z_{sk}) \leqslant N_k, && k = 1,2,3 && \text{(linking constraints)}
\end{aligned}$$

where

$r_{ps3}(\bar{x}_s)$ = the total long-term sales for product p in segment s resulting from expending effort $\bar{x}_s = \{x_{1s}, \ldots, x_{ps}, \ldots, x_{Ps}\}$ across the P products in the current period under the 3-salesforce structure,

z_{sk} = a decision variable representing the number of sales calls delivered by salesforce k to market segment s,

m_{ps} = the average margin for product p when sold in segment s,

$C_p x_{ps}$ = the product-dependent costs associated with salesforce-effort level of x_{ps},

c_s = the variable cost per call made to market segment s,

c_n = the cost per sales representative,

b_s = the average number of products that can be promoted in a single sales call to market segment s,

$h_k(z_{sk})$ = a non-decreasing function that relates the total number of calls with the requisite number of salespersons,

u_s = the maximum number of calls that can be made to segment s by any one of the salesforces (this is a function of segment size and accessibility),

N_k = the size of salesforce k.

The mathematical-programming solution methodology for this optimization problem is based on the partial decomposability in the model structure. In particular, the market-segment constraints only affect effort deployment in segment s while the linking constraints affect effort deployment across all segments. In order to determine the optimal salesforce structure, the algorithm needs to be repeated for each of the feasible structures. Technical details of the solution algorithm approach are presented in Rangaswamy, Sinha & Zoltners [1990].

Estimation and implementation of the salesforce-structure model are significant tasks. At the outset of the modelling effort, management defines the set of feasible salesforce structures, i.e. the set of possible partitions of products among salesforces to be considered. Then, for each partition, separate market-segment-level response functions are estimated for each product. This approach to response-function specification allows for the subjective incorporation of product-line interdependencies. In addition, a scaling parameter is included to reflect the carryover effects of effort. The maximization problem can be viewed as the problem of determining the best partition of the product line. As with the general salesforce-deployment model outlined in Zoltners & Sinha [1980], almost any number of constraints can be added.

Parameter estimates are obtained through an analysis of historical data and a consensus-building judgement procedure. In one application, estimates for 1200 response functions each with several parameters were required. Several experts in sales and marketing participated in a Delphi exercise. Beginning with an analysis of historical data, a description of future market conditions, pricing assumptions, and a competitive analysis, participants made initial parameter estimates. The Delphi exercise consists of several rounds. Following each round, participants were provided with feedback which described the responses of other participants. With this new information, participants made new judgements. Rangaswamy, Sinha & Zoltners [1990] report that convergence in responses is often observed after two or three rounds.

The salesforce-structuring model developed in Rangaswamy, Sinha & Zoltners [1990] has had a great impact on practitioners; the authors indicate that the model has been implemented over 100 times in over 20 countries. The model has been applied primarily in the pharmaceutical and medical-equipment industries with many companies incorporating the model as a regular feature of their annual review of the salesforce. Rangaswamy, Sinha & Zoltners report that the optimal results of the model are typically modified by managers to account for external circumstances, but the authors report that about 80% of the resource-allocation decisions are implemented in a directional sense.

Recent integrative models represent a considerable advance over earlier work. Reviews of earlier modelling efforts including Comer [1974], Armstrong [1976], Shanker, Turner & Zoltners [1975] and Glaze & Weinberg [1979] are found in Zoltners & Gardner [1980].

3.5. Sales management control

Sales management control is an extremely important component of the sales-management function. Inadequate control procedures can result in significant costs to the firm in terms of salesforce motivation, morale and turnover. Of the many control decisions which must be made, compensation, salesperson evaluation, and the generation of sales quotas are most amenable to management-science techniques. Of these three decisions, compensation issues have generated by far the most research. Contributions to this literature are reviewed by Coughlan in Chapter 13 of this Handbook. The remaining decision areas have received limited attention. Contributions in these areas are discussed next.

Salesperson evaluation is a crucial sales-management issue. If the evaluation system results in inaccurate or inappropriate judgements, the costs to the firm are considerable, if not easily measurable. However, accurate and consistent salesperson evaluations are difficult to do in practice. One of the reasons for this difficulty is the non-comparability of performance results across territories. This is one reason why a key objective of territory-design models, as discussed above, is the development of territories which are equalized on a number of attributes including sales potential and workload. Theoretically, performance results between salespersons are directly comparable in a balanced territory alignment.

An alternative approach to comparing performance results across territories is the development of territory-response functions in which territory sales are a function of salesperson, company and territory characteristics. Ryans & Weinberg's [1979] article is illustrative of this approach. These researchers summarize previous work and develop a framework which provides a basis for explaining the variability in salesperson performance. Their study concentrates on managerially controllable and external, non-psychological variables that affect a sales representative's sales results. These include constructs relating to: (1) company marketing activities; (2) closeness of supervision; (3) field sales manager; (4) salesperson experience; (5) territory characteristics like sales potential, geographic dispersion and manufacturing concentration; and (6) competitor strength. A power-function form is suggested to account for the interdependencies between variables. This function was estimated using multiple regression analysis.

At the organizational level, the statistical results of the response-function estimation yield two types of diagnostic information. First, significant variables in the response function identify company policies or territory characteristics which influence salesperson performance. If a goal of the company is to develop balanced territories, these variables should be considered in a territory-alignment procedure. Second, since the regression procedure partials out variables which are beyond the control of the salesperson, the regression-analysis residuals can be used as an environment-adjusted measure of differential performance between sales representatives. This information can be used in quota-setting and salesperson evaluation. In addition, excellent sales representatives can be identified and their successful sales practices can be spread throughout the firm.

Ryans & Weinberg [1979] estimate their model in three corporate settings so that some limited generalization can be made. It appears that certain variables like sales potential, the concentration of sales potential, salesperson experience, and span of control are worthwhile to include in models of territory-sales response. Ryans & Weinberg [1987] consider territory-sales response over time. They analyze five years of data from a company which participated in the 1979 study. Their results indicate that parameter values seem to be stable over time. This would add credence to the use of such models in salesperson evaluation.

Parsons [1990] argues that the use of regression methods in the development of territory-sales-response models provide estimates of what an 'average' salesperson might achieve in a particular territory. However, management may wish to set its expectations of performance closer to the best that could be achieved. Using a data-envelopment procedure [see e.g. Charnes, Cooper & Rhodes, 1981], Parsons estimates a frontier production function that specifies the maximum output attainable at given levels of input. An application of the approach has been implemented in a pharmaceutical company.

An alternative approach to comparing performance results across salespersons is presented by Claxton, Vandenbosch & Weinberg [1990]. These researchers explore the use of expert systems for salesperson evaluation. In many organizations, the first-level field supervisors are responsible for evaluating the set of (8–12) representatives under their control. These managers are typically ex-salespersons who may not be adequately trained in evaluation procedures. To aid in this process, Claxton, Vandenbosch & Weinberg suggest using the expertise available within the company to develop expert systems to automate certain components of the evaluation process. Specifically, they suggest using an expert system to explain differences in sales-territory difficulty across representatives. Before advocating expert-system development, the authors suggest that the expert-system alternative should be tested against other less costly forms of decision support. They outline an expert-system pre-development test and apply it in a salesperson-evaluation context. Their results suggest that potential improvement can be obtained from either an expert system or a simpler decision support system but their main contribution concerns the establishment of the pre-development process itself.

The procedures outlined above are methods by which sales-performance results can be compared across representatives. However, this research does not explore psychological and interpersonal factors which might help explain variance in salesperson performance. Understanding salesperson performance has been the subject of a considerable amount of research that utilizes theories based on research in psychology and organizational behavior. The range of topics studied in this field of research include models of sales performance [e.g. Churchill, Ford & Walker, 1985], salesperson effectiveness [e.g. Weitz, Sujan & Sujan, 1986], turnover [Darmon, 1990], and motivation [e.g. Teas & McElroy, 1986], among others.

Churchill, Ford, Hartley & Walker [1985], using a meta-analysis technique analyzed the results of 116 published and unpublished articles which studied determinants of salesperson performance. Most of these articles were taken from the psychological literature on personal selling and salesforce management. Churchill et al. found that role perception, that is, a salesperson's perception of the set of activities and behavior that are required of people occupying the position of salesperson, was the best determinant of performance. This was followed by skill level, motivation, personal factors (age, sex, race, etc.), aptitude and organizational/environmental factors respectively. The study found that each of the determinants explained only a relatively small porportion of the variance in salesperson performance. Role perception, with the highest average association with performance, explained, on average, only 9% of the variance. As such, the authors conclude that models of performance which utilize a multiple-determinant perspective are likely to be more successful in assessing future performance of salespersons.

3.6. *Navy recruitment research*

The limited availability of data may explain the lack of modelling research in the area of salesforce operations. In the early 1980s, a series of studies on US

Navy recruitment offered an opportunity to see the progress which can be made in salesforce operations when data restrictions are relaxed. The US Navy, with 43 recruiting districts, over 1300 recruiting stations and about 3400 recruiters, represents one of the largest salesforces in the United States.

Table 14.4 presents a synopsis of the navy recruitment articles which include a salesforce-management component.[15] Morey & McCann [1980], Goldberg [1982] and Hanssens & Levien [1983] carry out an econometric analysis of historical data to estimate the effects of recruiters and advertising on enlistments.

The typical structure used in these models is illustrated by Morey & McCann's response function (adjusted for the size of the labor force in each district):

$$\begin{aligned}\ln \mathrm{EC}_{dt} = {} & A_0 + \alpha_1 \cdot D_1 + \cdots + \alpha_{42} \cdot D_{42} + \beta_1 \cdot M_1 + \cdots + \beta_{11} \cdot M_{11} \\ & + \gamma_1 \cdot \mathrm{YR} + \gamma_2 \cdot \mathrm{GI} + \delta_1 \cdot \ln \mathrm{AD}_{dt} + \delta_2 \cdot \ln \mathrm{NR}_{dt} \\ & + \delta_3 \cdot \ln \mathrm{NL}_{dt} + \delta_4 \cdot \ln \mathrm{EC}_{d,t-1} \\ & + \delta_5 \cdot \ln \mathrm{HS}_{dt} + \delta_6 \ln \mathrm{NU}_{dt}\end{aligned}$$

where

EC_{dt} = total enlistment contracts from district d, period t,
H_{dt} = total number of high-school-graduate contracts from district d, period t,
D = district indicator variable,
M = monthly indicator variable,
YR = year indicator variable,
GI = GI bill expiration indicator variable,
AD_{dt} = total advertising and promotion expenditure in district d, period t,
NR_{dt} = number of recruiters in district d, period t,
NL_{dt} = number of new leads from district d, period t,
HS_{dt} = total high-school seniors in district d, period t,
NU_{dt} = number of unemployed for district d, period t.

Morey & McCann as well as Hanssens & Levien use a log-linear distributed lag model estimated over the same pooled, cross-sectional, time-series data set. The primary difference between these articles is the manner in which the recruitment process is modelled (see Table 14.4). Goldberg uses regression analysis to parameterize a time-series distributed lag model. The results of these studies indicated that the number of recruiters has a significant influence on the number of enlistments (elasticities range from 0.26 to 0.98). Morey & McCann report significant lag effects. In addition, all models estimate that recruiters have a greater influence on enlistments than advertising does.

Carroll, Rao, Lee, Shapiro & Bayus's [1985] study involves a large-scale, one-year field experiment designed to quantify the relationship between enlistment achievement and marketing expenditures. This approach was employed to overcome the limitations of econometric analysis of historical data, limited variability in

[15] Morey & McCann [1983] and Gatignon & Hanssens [1987] also use the navy database but deal with issues not directly related to salesforce management.

Table 14.4
Synopsis of navy recruitment articles

Article	Data	Thrust	Model	Recruiter effects	Advertising effects	Validation
Morey & McCann [1980]	• Monthly from Jan 1976 to Dec 1977 • 43 districts	Determination of the proper allocation of resources between advertising and recruiting	Pooled cross-sectional time series Log-linear distributed lag model	• Significant elasticities, 0.44 for total, 0.58 for high-school grads • Significant lags for two months	• National advertising elasticities 0.19 for total, 0.12 for high-school grads • Significant lag for two months	Partial validation using 1977 data
Goldberg [1982]	• Quarterly 1971–1977 • High-school and upper mental group	Estimation of the effects of recruiters, advertising, unemployment and other factors on navy enlistments	Time-series distributed lag model	• Significant elasticity of 0.98 • No significant lag effects	• National advertising elasticity of 0.25 • Significant lag effects	Predicted actual high-school graduate-enlistments to within 2.1%
Hanssens & Levien [1983]	• Monthly from Jan 1976 to Dec 1977 • 43 districts	Assessment of the relative impact of environmental effects and recruiting effects on navy enlistments	Pooled cross-sectional/time series. Multi-stage log-linear, distributed lag model	• Significant elasticities 0.63 for Delayed Entry Contract 0.26 for Direct Ship Contracts • No significant lag effects	• National advertising elasticity of 0.23 • Local advertising elasticity of −0.059 for national leads • Significant lag effects for one month	Split sample analysis

Carroll, Rao, Lee, Shapiro & Bayus [1985]	• Monthly, 1980 • Controlled experiment • 43 districts	Quantify the relationship between enlistment achievement and marketing expenditures	Cross-sectional/time series Log-linear distributed lag model	• Significant elasticities of 0.357 to 0.577 • Market expansion elasticity of 0.099 • Tenure effects found • Significant lags for up to 4 months	• Non-significant navy national advertising • Significant local advertising elasticity 0.164 for HSG • Significant joint DOD advertising elasticity 0.531 for upper mental groups • Some significant lags found	
Carroll, Lee & Rao [1986]	• Contracts submitted by recruiters • Monthly, May 1977 to Dec 1978 • 3 districts	Analyze recruiter productivity and heterogeneity, learning and delearning effects	Poisson model of recruits with gamma mixing distribution for recruiter productivity			Good prediction of future performance in data set
Yun, Buchanan & Rao [1990]	• Contracts submitted by recruiters • Monthly, May 1977 to Dec 1978 • 3 districts	Development of an early-rotation policy based on recruiter productivity	Binomial incidence of non-zero reporting, Poisson model of non-zero reportings. Beta and gamma mixing distributions over behavioral and Poisson parameters.			An alternative model to the one proposed in Carroll, Lee & Rao [1986]

expenditures, and the lack of key data or data not available in sufficient detail or disaggregation. In the experiment, the level of advertising and the number of recruiters were systematically varied in 36 test markets. In addition, 17 markets were selected as control markets. The experiment included five levels of advertising (+100%, +50%, same, −50%, −100%) and three levels of recruiters (+20%, same, −20%).

Throughout the experiment, data were collected in four areas: enlistment contracts, number of recruiters, advertising levels and environmental variables. Using a pooled cross-sectional time-series distributed lag structure, the effects of the number of recruiters, the nature and amount of advertising, expenditures and environmental variables on enlistments were estimated. Similar to the findings with historical data, the number of recruiters was found to have a significant impact on enlistments with elasticities ranging from 0.357 to 0.577. Recruiter effects were much higher than advertising effects. In fact, the results suggested the elimination of national navy advertising in favor of combined armed-services advertising. The estimated model detected significant lags to the efforts of recruiters for up to 4 months. In addition, navy recruiters were shown to contribute significantly to the growth in Department of Defense enlistments while navy advertising was not.[16]

Carroll, Rao, Lee, Shapiro & Bayus [1985] also found that recruiters experienced significant learning and 'delearning' (fewer actual enlistments in the months preceding the end of the posting) effects. In order to analyze these effects further, Carroll, Lee & Rao [1986] conducted a study of recruiter productivity using data from 345 recruiters who served for six months or more during a 20-month study period. In addition to learning and delearning effects, substantial heterogeneity was found in recruiter productivity. Good recruiters tended to stay good while poor recruiters continued to perform poorly. These findings led to the development of a new management-control and rotation policy which had two main objectives: the reduction of delearning effects and the early identification of poor recruiters. The reduction of the delearning effects was accomplished by altering the quota system. Originally, the navy based its monthly enlistment quotas on entry dates. This allowed recruiters to build up an inventory of delayed-entry enlistment contracts which could be allocated against future quotas. Several months before the end of the posting, recruiters tended to run down this inventory, thus reducing productivity. To remedy this problem, a new quota system, which concentrated more on the date of the contract, rather than on the date of entry, was implemented.

The early identification of poor recruiters was achieved through the development of a stochastic model that allows for heterogeneous productivity. The model assumes that enlistment contracts signed through a particular recruiter is a Poisson random variable and that a gamma mixing distribution describes the variation in recruiter productivity. The combination of these two assumptions results in a negative binomial distribution (of the number of recruits per month) which can be used to forecast the number of enlistments to be obtained by recruiters. By

[16]No test was made of joint service recruiting, that is, a policy which amalgamates the separate services' salesforces into one recruiting salesforce.

estimating the parameters of the negative binomial distribution (NBD), the future productivity of recruiters can be estimated on the basis of the number of contracts signed early in the recruiter's posting. This approach has led the Navy Recruiting Command to implement a new early-rotation policy. Yun, Buchanan & Rao [1990] modify the Carroll, Lee & Rao [1986] early-rotation policy by estimating a model which considers both the quantity of contracts reported and the number of months in which non-zero quantities were reported.

Carroll, Lee & Rao [1986] and Yun, Buchanan & Rao [1990] both recognize that contracts are sometimes not reported as part of purposive behavior by the sales representatives. Unlike models in the sales-compensation literature (see Chapter 13), this purposive behavior is not directly modelled but is considered as a stochastic process. It would be interesting to see what insights could be obtained by adding agency-theory approaches to the problem of recruiter productivity and incomplete reporting. Also, with regard to turnover, see Darmon [1990].

Collectively, the results of the navy-recruitment research have a number of significant implications for salesforce management. First, the results, across several econometric modelling efforts indicated that the effect of recruiters and advertising on enlistments can be measured and that recruiters have a significant impact on the recruitment process. Assuming that armed-forces recruiters are analogous to corporate sales representatives, the results suggest that the salesforce can have a dramatic impact on the success of a firm. More research using 'for profit' companies is required to substantiate this claim. Second, the research on recruiter productivity [Carroll, Lee & Rao 1986; Yun, Buchanan & Rao, 1990] is directly applicable to many salesforces. Early recognition of unproductive sales representatives allows for additional training and sales support in a timely manner. Finally, the navy-recruitment research illustrates the range of modelling approaches which can be applied to a data-rich problem area. This repeated analysis of similar phenomena can lead to a better understanding of the features of a problem that need to be modelled, as generalizations can be made across specific modelling applications. Examples of this process in advertising include Clarke's [1976] meta-analysis of dynamic effects of advertising [see also Weinberg & Weiss, 1982] and Aaker & Carman's [1982] evaluation of applications of advertising-response models.

4. Research opportunities

As was mentioned at the outset of this chapter, there has been considerably less research conducted in the area of salesforce management than in other areas of marketing, notably advertising and, more recently, promotion. When only articles employing operations research/management science techniques are considered, the limited range of salesforce research output is accentuated further. To date, a major limitation has been the availability of data. Unlike researchers who have access to a wide range of data sources (e.g. scanner data), researchers developing salesforce-operations models have had to cope with limited historical data available at selected research sites. Most often these sites have been recruited by the researchers or have resulted from consulting activities. A syndicated data source has not emerged to fill the data void, nor has there been an accumulation of individual site analyses to allow for meaningful generalizations. An exception is the IMS–International panel of 2800 physicians in the US, which estimates sales-effort levels on all pharmaceutical products [Rangaswamy, Sinha & Zoltners, 1990, p. 290].

The data limitation has reduced the number of published salesforce-operations modelling efforts. In addition, the level at which the analyses are conducted has been affected as well. Most of the articles analyzing salesforce operations are conducted at the company level. That is, the contribution of the research is in the methodology it develops for application in different settings. This is true of CALLPLAN, DETAILER, GEOLINE and many of the models which followed. Very little research has been conducted across companies to allow for generalizations of phenomena. This leaves a number of important research questions unanswered. For example, what is the best way to incorporate time dynamics into an allocation system? Should response-function formulations be different for new versus established products? How should modelling approaches be altered for different selling tasks?

Even within the current stream of research, the limited availability of adequate data is restrictive. Many of the salesforce-operations decisions discussed in the previous sections are data-intensive.[17] Allocation decisions are driven by models of sales response to effort. These response models, though often estimated judgementally, can be improved if a sufficient database of historical information is available. With this information in hand, response effects related to other-company factors, salesperson factors, environments factors and time can be measured along with effects related to effort allocations. Territory-design and salesperson-evaluation procedures can also be improved with a comprehensive database. The rapidly expanding computer technology which is currently available allows for dramatic improvement in a company's data-tracking capabilities. To the extent that this information is made available to researchers, salesforce-operations models are likely to become more dependent on econometric methods and expert systems and less dependent on subjective parameter estimates.

We are convinced that research activity would increase if there were greater access to comprehensive data sources. One need only look at the research activity currently being generated in the area of scanner panels or the number of models developed in response to the availability of the navy enlistment area. However, developing adequate data sources is not an easy task. Not only must confidentiality and competitive-advantage concerns be addressed with potential suppliers, these data sources must also be involved in comprehensive data-tracking programs. To aid in this development process, organizations like the Marketing Science Institute

[17]The estimation process in Lodish [1980] and Rangaswamy, Sinha & Zoltners [1990] is so intense that data collection can become a major component of model development. It would seem appropriate to ask whether, in certain cases, a more efficient procedure would be to develop a model of 'the model'. In other words, after the data-intensive model is built, a less data-intensive model might be developed, that while being more of an approximation, would be easier to estimate.

and the American Marketing Association may have important roles to play. On the other hand, much of the data from scanner panels, which has formed the basis for scores of articles dealing with promotions of frequently purchased consumer goods, has been made available from private companies. These firms have recognized that the value in data comes not from vast stores of it, but from the information that can be gleaned from it when talented researchers are provided access to it. Perhaps it is only wishful thinking on our part, but the same enlightened self-interest in terms of data availability can go a long way toward increasing our knowledge of salesforce phenomena.

Regardless of the data limitations facing researchers, salesforce management is an important area of marketing and there exist a number of potentially fruitful avenues of research. We will highlight five areas. Two of the research areas, competition and time dynamics, have been shown to be important in other areas of marketing research (e.g. advertising). Two other areas, integrative models incorporating control issues and relationship marketing, take into account the fact that selling resources are people rather than inanimate objects. Finally, we end with a cautionary note on the impact of globalization on development and implementation of salesforce-operations models.

4.1. Competition

In recent years, a major thrust in marketing models has been the incorporation of competitive reactions, especially in the areas of product-positioning, pricing and advertising. Several salesforce-operations models [e.g., Lodish, 1980; Rangaswamy, Sinha & Zoltners, 1990] incorporate competitive intensity as a component of the response function. However, no current model explicitly considers the effects of competitive reactions. Competition appears to be important in this area and warrants more consideration. Allocation models organize the salesforce in a manner which increases sales output, often at the expense of the competition. Given the relatively widespread use of these models, especially in the pharmaceutical industry, the assumption that competitors will behave as they have in the past becomes increasingly unrealistic. We believe that the incorporation of competitive reactions can aid in answering a number of interesting research questions including the following. What is the overall effect of competitors simultaneously 'optimizing' effort allocations? Do equilibrium call-frequencies result in a prisoner's dilemma type situation where competitors are driven to allocate too much effort for small incremental improvements in sales or do competitors adjust their allocations to prevent this situation? And, how do competitors manage the response-function-estimation task with the knowledge that results can be affected by competitive actions?

4.2. Time dynamics

One of the key features of DETAILER was the incorporation of time dynamics into the modelling approach. As models developed, this feature was dropped from most models. In its place, an estimate of the future effect of current effort is often incorporated [e.g. Lodish, 1980; Rangaswamy, Sinha & Zoltners, 1990]. Although this modification acts as a proxy for carryover sales, it does not allow for the testing of alternative call strategies (e.g. pulsing, blitz, constant-rate). Understanding the nature of response to alternative call strategies can have important implications for the resource allocation as certain strategies may enable companies to improve efficiency. Empirical tests, similar to those completed in advertising [Zielske, 1959; Mahajan & Muller, 1986], would be of value in this area. However, as stated earlier, access to data may prove to be the limiting factor. Another time-dynamics research issue is simply the need for a better understanding of the nature of carryover effects as they relate to sales calls. Is carryover stronger for new or established products? How does salesperson ability affect carryover effects? What is the best method of modelling time dynamics?

4.3. Integrative models incorporating control issues

A significant body of research has been developed in each of the three problem areas defined in Figure 14.1. However, an interesting feature of this research is the fact that control decisions, especially compensation, have not been incorporated into models analyzing organizational or allocation decisions. Given the significant impact of compensation on motivation, the successful implementation of any allocation policy depends on an adequate compensation program. Several organizational decisions, like territory design and the structuring of product-line responsibilities, can also benefit from integrative modelling approaches. For example, most territory-design models develop territories according to one or more equalization rules. Although these procedures devolop 'average' territories, they do not consider the fact that representatives are not average. Territory-design models which consider this feature would provide a contribution to the literature. Development of integrative models which incorporate control issues does not appear to be an easy task as it requires the reformulation of existing approaches. However, we believe that the issues are important enough to warrant the effort.

4.4. Relationship marketing

Many of the salesforce-operations models developed to date operate on the premise that a single representative performs the selling function in a geographic area or to a select number of accounts. However, not all selling situations conform to this premise. One of the more important business-to-business marketing strategies to emerge in recent years is relationship marketing. In relationship marketing, contacts are made between customer and supplier at many levels. One of the key aspects of this type of selling approach is the synergy or interactive effects which can be achieved through the multiple allocation of selling resources. This selling strategy is different than those typically modelled in allocation models. As such, a reformulation of the existing model structures is required. Within the domain of relationship marketing, the allocation of resources to accounts, the measurement of the quality of the relationship, and salesperson-performance evaluation all represent under-researched issues.

4.5. Globalization

With few exceptions [e.g. Rangaswamy, Sinha & Zoltners, 1990; Parsons & Vanden Abeele, 1981], the salesforce-operation models discussed in the previous sections have been developed in North American settings. The current trend towards globalization may have the effect of requiring these types of modelling approaches to be applied in international settings. We caution researchers away from simply applying these modelling approaches, especially in countries where there are strong cultural differences from the country in which the model was developed. In different countries, personal selling may play a different role in the marketing process. For example, supplier trust may be the most important factor in the buying decision. Therefore, several 'sales' calls may have to be made to build trust before a single sale is made. This process has implications for response-function estimation. There is a growing body of literature on doing business in foreign countries [see, for example, Rangaswamy, Eliashberg, Burke & Wind, 1989]. Research on how these cultural differences impact on quantitative modelling techniques would be of interest.

5. Summary

Managers face a number of difficult decision problems when managing the salesforce. These decisions range from the allocation of the selling effort, salesforce sizing and territory design to salesperson evaluation, motivation and compensation. Given the cost of hiring, training and maintaining a salesforce, making effective decisions in each of these areas is imperative. To aid managers, several model-based approaches to addressing many of these issues have been developed. The implementation focus of some of the more successful models has had a profound effect on practicing managers. In fact, few areas of marketing can boast of more implementations of specific models.

Few modifications are expected in the modelling approaches employed by the most successful salesforce-operations models. These models have the flexibility of blending judgemental and objective information and balance the value of optimization with efficient heuristics. However, ample opportunities for research in salesforce operations remain. The five areas outlined in the previous sections – competition, time dynamics, integrative models incorporating control decisions, relationship marketing and globalization – all offer significant research potential. In addition, there is a need for more empirical work which has the objective of identifying important generalizations across settings.

Sales management is a very important management function which has, to date, been relatively under-researched. Though the problems facing managers are well defined, the interactive nature of decision areas and personal factors involved in managing a salesforce present a number of challenges to quantitative model-builders. These characteristics, combined with a foundation of highly successful modelling efforts, should provide the groundwork for a significant research activity in the future.

Acknowledgements

We would like to thank Anne Coughlan, Josh Eliashberg, Gary Lilien, Len Lodish, Len Parsons, Amber Rao, Andy Zoltners, and the anonymous reviewers, for their valuable assistance in the preparation of this chapter.

References

Aaker, D.A., and J.M. Carman (1982). Are you overadvertising? *J. Advertising Res.* 22(4), 57–69.

Armstrong, G.M. (1976). The SCHEDULE model and the salesman's effort allocation. *California Management Rev.* 18(4), 43–51.

Beswick, C.A., and D.W. Cravens (1977). A multistage decision model for salesforce management. *J. Marketing Res.* 14 (May), 135–144.

Carroll, V.P., H.L. Lee, and A.G. Rao (1986). Modelling navy recruiter productivity: A case study. *Management Sci.* 32(11), 1371–1388.

Carroll, V.P., A.G. Rao, H.L. Lee, A. Shapiro, and B.L. Bayus (1985). The navy enlistment marketing experiment. *Marketing Sci.* 4(4), 352–374.

Charkravarti, D., A. Mitchell, and R. Staelin (1981), Judgement based marketing decision models: Problems and possible solutions. *J. Marketing* 45(4). 13–23.

Charnes, A., W.W. Cooper, and E.L. Rhodes (1981). Evaluating program and managerial efficiency: An application of data envelopment analysis to program follow through. *Management Sci.* 27 (June), 668–697.

Churchill, G.A., Jr., N.M. Ford, S.W. Hartley and O.C. Walker, Jr. (1985), The determinants of sales performance: A meta-analysis. *J. Marketing Res.* 22 (May), 103–118.

Churchill, G.A., Jr., N.M. Ford, and O.C. Walker, Jr. (1985). *Sales Force Management, revised edition.* Richard D. Irwin, Homewood, IL.

Clarke, D.G. (1976). Economic measurement of the duration of advertising effects on sales. *J. Marketing* 18, 345–357.

Clarke, D.G. (1983). Syntex Laboratories (A), Case Number 9-584-033, Harvard Business School.

Claxton, J.D., M.B. Vandenbosch, and C.B. Weinberg (1990). An expert system predevelopment test for assessment of sales territory response. *Intern. J. Res. Marketing* 7, 203–215.

Comer, J.M. (1974). ALLOCATE: A computer model for sales territory planning. *Decision Sci.* 5, 323–338.

Dalkey, N.C. (1969). The Delphi method: An experimental study of group opinion. RM-5888 PR, Rand Corporation, Santa Monica, CA.

Darmon, R.Y. (1990). Identifying sources of turnover costs: A segmental approach. *J. Marketing* 54 (April), 46–56.

Farley, J.U. (1964). An optimal plan for salesman's compensation. *J. Marketing Res.* 1 (May), 39–43.

Freeland, J.R., and C.B. Weinberg (1980). S-shaped response functions: Implications for decision models. *J. Oper. Res. Soc.* 31, 1001–1007.

Fudge, W.K., and L.M. Lodish (1977). Evaluation of the effectiveness of a model based salesman's planning system by field experimentation. *Interfaces*, May, 18–27.

Gatignon, H., and D.M. Hanssens (1987). Modeling marketing interactions with application to salesforce effectiveness. *J. Marketing Res.* 24 (August), 247–257.

Gelb, B.D., and B.M. Khumawala (1984). Reconfiguration of an insurance company's sales regions. *Interfaces* 14(6) (November–December), 87–94.

Glaze, T., and C.B. Weinberg (1979). A sales territory alignment program and account planning system. In R. Bagozzi (ed.), *Sales Management: New Developments from Behavioral and Decision Model Research*, Marketing Science Institute, Cambridge, MA.

Goldberg, L. (1982). Recruiters, advertising, and Navy enlistment. *Naval Res. Logist. Quart.* 29 (June), 385–398.

Hanssens, D.M., and H.A. Levien (1983). An econometric study of recruitment in the U.S. Navy. *Management Sci.* 29 (October), 1167–1184.

Hess, S.W., and S.A. Samuels (1971). Experiences with a sales districting model: Criteria and implementation. *Management Sci.* 18(4), Part II, 41–54.

Hughes, P., and G. Brecht (1975). *Vicious Circles and Infinity*. Doubleday, New York.

LaForge, R.W., C.W. Lamb, Jr., D.W. Cravens, and W.C. Moncrief III (1989). Improving judgment-based salesforce decision model application. *J. Acad. Marketing Sci.* 17(2), 167–177.

Lilien, G.L., and P. Kotler (1983). *Marketing Decision Making: A Model Building Approach*, Harper and Row, New York.

Little, J.D.C., and L.M. Lodish (1981). Commentary on judgment-based marketing decision models. *J. Marketing* 45(4) (Fall), 24–29.

Lodish, L.M. (1971). CALLPLAN: An interactive salesman's call planning system. *Management Sci.* 18(4), Part II (December), 25–40.

Lodish, L.M. (1974). 'Vaguely right' approach to sales force allocations. *Harvard Business Rev.* 52 (January–February), 119–124.

Lodish, L.M. (1975). Sales territory alignment to maximize profit. *J. Marketing Res.* 12 (February), 30–36.

Lodish, L.M. (1976). Assigning salesman to accounts to maximize profits. *J. Marketing Res.* 13 (October), 440–444.

Lodish, L.M. (1980). A user oriented model for sales force size, product and market allocation decisions. *J. Marketing* 44 (Summer), 70–78.

Lodish, L.M., E. Curtis, M. Ness and M. K. Simpson (1988). Sales force sizing and deployment using a decision calculus model at the syntex laboratories. *Interfaces*, 18 (January–February), 5–20.

Mahajan, V., and E. Muller (1986). Advertising pulsing policies for generating awareness for new products. *Marketing Sci.* 5 (Spring), 89–106.

McIntyre, S.H. (1982). An experimental study of the impact of judgment-based marketing models. *Management Sci.* 28 (January), 17–33.

Montgomery, D.B., A.J. Silk, and C.E. Zaragoza (1971) A multiple product sales force allocation model. *Management Sci.* 18(4), Part II, 22–31.

Montgomery, D.B., and G.L. Urban (1969). *Management Science in Marketing*, Prentice-Hall, Englewood Cliffs, NJ.

Morey, R.C., and J.M. McCann (1980). Evaluating and improving resource allocation for navy recruiting. *Management Sci.* 26 (December), 1198–1210.

Morey, R.C., and J.M. McCann (1983). Estimating the confidence interval for the optimal marketing mix: An application to lead generation. *Marketing Sci.* 2 (Spring), 193–202.

Parasuraman, A., and R.L. Day (1977). A management-oriented model for allocating sales effort. *J. Marketing Res.* 14 (February), 22–33.

Parsons, L.J. (1990). Assessing salesforce performance with data envelopment analysis, Presented at the 1990 Marketing Science Conference, Urbana, IL.

Parsons, L.J., and P. Vanden Abeele (1981). Analysis of sales call effectiveness. *J. Marketing Res.* 18 (February), 107–113.

Rangaswamy, A., J. Eliashberg, R.R. Burke, and J. Wind (1989). Developing marketing expert systems: An application to international negotiations. *J. Marketing*, 53 (October), 24–39.

Rangaswamy, A., P. Sinha, and A. Zoltners (1990). An integrated model-based approach for sales force structuring. *Marketing Sci.* 9(4), 279–298.

Richardson, R.J. (1979). A territory realignment model–MAPS, Unpublished Paper presented at the New Orleans ORSA/TIMS Meeting, May, 1979.

Ryans, A.B., and C.B. Weinberg (1979). Territory sales response, *J. Marketing Res.* 16 (November), 453–465.
Ryans, A.B., and C.B. Weinberg (1981). Sales force management: Integrating managerial and research perspectives. *California Management Rev.* 24 (Fall), 75–89.
Ryans, A.B., and C.B. Weinberg. Territory sales response models: Stability over time. *J. Marketing Res.* 24, 229–233.
Segal, M., and D.B. Weinberger (1977). Turfing. *Oper. Res.* 25(3), 367–386.
Shanker, R.J., R.E. Turner, and A.A. Zoltners (1975). Sales territory design: An integrated approach. *Management Sci.* 22(3), (November), 309–320.
Sinha, P., and A.A. Zoltners (1979). The multiple choice knapsack problem. *Oper. Res.* 27, 503–515.
Teas, R.K., and J.C. McElroy (1986). Causal attributions and expectancy estimates: A framework for understanding the dynamics of salesforce motivation. *J. Marketing* 50 (January), 75–86.
Weinberg, C.B., and D.L. Weiss (1982). On the econometric measurement of the duration of advertising effect of sales. *J. Marketing Res.* 19 (November), 585–591.
Weitz, B.A., H. Sujan and M. Sujan (1986). Knowledge, motivation and adaptive selling effectiveness. *J. Marketing*, 50 (October), 174–191.
Yun, K., B. Buchanan, and A. Rao (1990). The BB/NBD + 1 model applied to rotation policy. Working Paper, Stern School of Business, New York University.
Zielski, H.A. (1959). The remembering and forgetting of advertising. *J. Marketing* 23 (January), 239–243.
Zoltners, A.A. (1979). A unified approach to sales territory alignment. In R. Bagozzi (ed.), *Sales Management: New Developments from Behavioral and Decision Model Research.* Marketing Science Institute, Cambridge, MA, 360–376.
Zoltners, A.A., and K.S. Gardner (1980). A review of sales force decision models. Working Paper, Northwestern University, Evanston, IL.
Zoltners, A.A., and P. Sinha (1980). Integer programming models for sales resource allocation. *Management Sci.* 26(3), 242–260.
Zoltners, A.A., and P. Sinha (1983). Sales territory alignment – A review and model. *Management Sci.* 29(11), 1237–1256.
Zoltners, A.A., P. Sinha, P.S.C. Chong (1979). An optimal algorithm for sales representative time management. *Management Sci.* 25(12), 1197–1207.

Part V
Interaction, Strategy and Synergy

J. Eliashberg and G.L. Lilien, Eds., *Handbooks in OR & MS, Vol. 5*

Chapter 15

Marketing-Mix Models*

Hubert Gatignon

The Wharton School, University of Pennsylvania, 1460 Steinberg Hall–Dietrich Hall, Philadelphia, PA 19104–6371, USA

1. Introduction

Marketing-mix models are defined as those models that contain more than one marketing decision variable [Lilien & Kotler, 1983].[1] In a *response model*, these variables, which can be any subset of the marketing mix (i.e. variable concerned with the product, advertising, price or distribution), are determinants of the performance of a brand, a business unit or a firm. Performance is typically expressed in terms of sales, market share or profitability. These marketing decision variables can also be part of a *decision model* which represents, in particular, the coordination between the marketing-mix elements, i.e. how management harmonizes a marketing decision variable as a function of other marketing decisions. These are very often considered in conjunction with the competitors' marketing decision variables.

Models concerned with marketing decision variables are basically of two types which differ by their primary objectives. The purpose of the first group of models is to estimate the impact of the marketing decision variables. While this type of model would encompass a large review of econometric models in marketing, we will concentrate on issues which are specific to models which incorporate more than one marketing decision variable, specifically the modeling of interactions between these variables. The second group of marketing-mix models concern models which provide guidelines as to what the level of the marketing-mix variables should be. Again, only normative models which incorporate multiple marketing decision variables will be considered. These decision-oriented models can be divided into four categories as they differ in their calibration approach, as well as in the manner in which the recommendations are obtained. Calibration can be through statistical inference, it can be based on management's subjective assessment, or sometimes no calibration is performed at all. Recommendations can be obtained

*The author thanks Bruce Hardie, Peter Fader, Douglas Bowman and Leonard Lodish for their helpful comments on an earlier draft of this paper.

[1] The reader is referred to Cooper (Chapter 6, this Handbook) for econometric models with a single-mix variable.

from optimization methods or by simulation. According to these two dimensions, four types of normative models are reviewed. The first type follows from the econometric models discussed in the first section. These are simply the optimization rules which are applied to the econometrically estimated model. The second type is represented by decision-calculus models where the parameters are assessed by managerial input. The third type of normative models are empirically based models which intend to provide norms for strategic decision-making. Finally, the fourth type of marketing models to be reviewed here are analytical models which, with or without empirical estimation of market-specific parameters, help understand how markets work and offer normative guidelines as to the optimal allocation of resources across marketing-mix variables.

Therefore, the objective of this paper is to review the literature concerning any of these models which involve more than one marketing decision variable. Section 1 discusses models to estimate the impact of marketing-mix variables and their interactions. The following section reviews normative marketing models. It includes a review of optimal marketing-mix allocation rules based on econometrically estimated models, decision-calculus models, empirically based marketing-mix models developed for the purpose of establishing norms, and analytical models which derive an optimal allocation of resources across the marketing-mix elements.

2. The impact of marketing-mix variables and their interactions

It is well recognized in marketing that marketing efforts do not impact performance (product sales or market share) independently of each other. Instead, marketing-mix activities need to be coordinated because they interact to determine performance. Coordination of marketing-mix activities enables management to take advantage of the complementarity and to avoid the incompatibility between marketing-mix instruments, given constraints imposed on the marketing budget as well as on the marketing-mix variables themselves. The literature contains substantial empirical support for the presence of interactions. Indeed, *advertising effectiveness* is enhanced by the quality of the product [Kuehn, 1962], prior salesperson contact [Swinyard & Ray, 1977], retail availability [Kuehn, 1962; Parsons, 1974] and higher or lower price depending on the advertising medium [Prasad & Ring, 1976]. *Sales-call effectiveness* increases with the use of samples and handouts in medical marketing [Parsons & Vanden Abeele, 1981] and with advertising in the recruiting for the U.S. Navy [Gatignon & Hanssens, 1987]. Consumers' price-sensitivity has been shown to be affected by advertising; while sometimes a positive interaction (i.e. whereby advertising increases price-sensitivity) is reported [e.g. Eskin & Baron, 1977; Wittink, 1977], a negative relation is supported in other studies [e.g. Krishnamurti & Raj, 1985; Lambin, 1976]. One possible explanation for this controversial evidence is the amount of competitive reactions to advertising in the market [Gatignon, 1984a].

In this section, we first present a general framework for modeling marketing-mix interactions with the appropriate estimation methods. Then, we review the evidence about these interactions and the models which were used to provide such evidence.

2.1. *A general method for modeling market response with interactions*

Before specifying a response function, the level of analysis should reflect the heterogeneous nature of a market. Consequently, if a market consists of segments characterized by different response parameters, the response function must be specified at the market-segment level. This requires an *a priori* understanding of the market structure by the modeler, although tests of homogeneity of coefficients can be useful in establishing the nature of the market structure. Another aspect of the market structure which brings important information for modeling the response function concerns the competitive structure of the market. Both segmentation and competitive structure analyses lead to a market definition which should be used for determining the appropriate level of analysis. Given this level of analysis, a market-response model with interactions can be specified.

In this section, we first discuss the general model specification. Then, the question of how to specify the interaction process will be discussed. Finally, the estimation approaches of such models will be presented.

2.1.1. *The general model specification*

As defined earlier, marketing-mix response models contain more than one marketing-mix variable to predict market performance. Therefore, in its general form, a market-response model can be expressed as:

$$y = f_1(X, Z; \beta, \gamma; \varepsilon) \tag{1}$$

where

y = a measure of market performance such as product sales,
X = a set of marketing variables (possibly with lagged effects) hypothesized to influence y,
Z = a set of environmental variables (which could contain the marketing activities of competitors) hypothesized to influence y,
β = the response parameters of the marketing variables,
γ = the response parameters of the environmental variables,
ε = disturbance term (possibly with a specific covariance structure due to time dynamics or due to a competitive model specification).

In Equation (1), the dependent variable can represent sales or market-share measures. Market shares present the advantages of being less sensitive to seasonality than sales and to incorporate competition. Market shares are estimated from sales data. A number of sources of information provide sales data. The reader should refer to Hanssens, Parsons & Schultz [1990] for a detailed discussion of the sources. However, briefly, there are four major sources of sales data. *Warehouse withdrawals* (e.g. SAMI) data have been used, among others, by Wittink [1977] and Pekelman & Tse [1980]. *Store-shelf audit data* (e.g. Nielsen) were analyzed by Gatignon. Anderson & Helsen [1989], Bass & Leone [1983], Bass & Parsons [1969] and Clarke [1973]. *Mail consumer panels* (e.g. MRCA) are the source of sales data for Nakanishi [1973] and McCann [1974]. Consumer panels are also used by Carpenter, Cooper, Hanssens & Midgley [1988] and Krishnamurthi & Raj [1985]. *Store scanner data* (e.g. IRI or Nielsen) are a major source of sales data especially for individual-choice models [e.g., Guadagni & Little, 1983; Bucklin & Lattin, 1991; Lattin & Bucklin, 1989; Bolton, 1989; Gupta, 1988]. In addition, industry-specific publications (often published by governmental agencies) provide sales data on a regular basis, especially for consumer durables [e.g. Bass, 1969; Lambin & Dor, 1989; Gatignon, 1984a; Bowman & Gatignon, 1992].

The marketing-mix variables can also be measured in a number of ways. First of all, marketing-mix measures can be expressed in absolute or in relative terms. For example, price can be expressed in the currency unit or relative to the average price in the market. Similarly, advertising can be expressed in terms of the absolute expenses or relative to competition, in the form of Us versus Them [Lambin, 1970a, 1970b] or Us versus Them + Us [e.g. Metwally, 1975; Lambin, 1972a], or Us versus the industry average [e.g. Weiss, 1968]. The advertising variable is most often represented by advertising expenditures. Expenditures are estimated by commercial monitoring services such as Leading National Advertisers (LNA) for print media and Broadcast Advertising Reports (BAR) for broadcast-media expenditures [e.g. Gatignon, 1984a; Bolton, 1989]. Other advertising weights measures such as GRPs have been used as well [Carpenter & Lehmann, 1985; Krishnamurthi & Raj, 1985; Prasad & Ring, 1976]. Distribution is most often measured in terms of distribution coverage from audit data as the percentage of stores carrying the brand [Lambin, 1970b, 1972a, 1972b; Lambin, Naert & Bultez, 1975; Parsons, 1974]. Stores can be weighted by store total volume (ACV) or by volume of sales in the product category – PCV [Farris, Olver & De Kluyver, 1989; Wildt, 1974]. The raw number of outlets has also been used in Gatignon [1984a] or Bowman & Gatignon [1992]. Salesforce is typically measured by the number of salespersons [Gatignon & Hanssens, 1987], by the number of sales calls [Parsons & Vanden Abeele, 1981], or by the number of minutes spent by the salesforce selling the product [Gatignon, Weitz & Bansal, 1990]. In most aggregate studies price is measured by the manufacturer's list price [Lambin & Dor, 1989; Gatignon, 1984a; Popkowski, Leszczyc & Rao, 1989; Prasad & Ring, 1976; Wildt, 1974] deflated by a retail or consumer price index when the time series is long [Lambin, 1972b; Bass, 1969]. In many cases, especially for models of market shares other than attraction models, a relative measure is used [Lambin, 1970a, 1970b]. In a few studies, the price actually paid is used [Carpenter & Lehmann, 1985; Krishnamurthi & Raj, 1991; Wittink, 1977]. In the case of studies using the PIMS data, the relative price as perceived by management filling out the questionnaire is used [Jacobson & Aaker, 1987; Phillips, Chang & Buzzell, 1983].

Product quality is most often measured from managers' subjective judgments [Lambin, 1970a, 1970b; Lambin, Naert & Bultez, 1975; Jacobson & Aaker, 1987; Phillips, Chang & Buzzell, 1983]. Gatignon, Weitz & Bansal [1990] use an expert (a pharmacist) who is not involved with any particular firm to evaluate pharmaceutical products. These judgments are often made in combination with a consumer survey to find out what are the most important attributes [Lambin, 1970a, 1970b; Lambin, Naert & Bultez, 1975]. Consumer reports can also be used to provide measures of product quality [Bowman & Gatignon, 1992].

The predictor variables (X and Z) in the response function (Equation 1) are assumed to be observed without error. Econometric theory provides valuable insight into the problem of measurement errors [Leamer, 1978] – especially in terms of the bias introduced in the estimators – although the 'estimation of the parameter in models that contain measurement errors and unobservable variables is not as straightforward as in classical models' [Judge, Griffiths, Hill, Luthepohl & Lee, 1985, p. 735]. Issues of proxy or instrumental variable selection as well as models with multiple measures of variables being outside the scope of this paper, we proceed with the assumption that the marketing mix and the environmental variables are observed without error. It should be recognized, however, that some marketing-mix variables such as product quality or advertising-copy quality cannot be objective, readily available measures.

A number of studies have investigated the functional form of the response function f_1 that fits the data the best. However, this choice of the functional form is directly related to the question of how the interactions between the marketing-mix variables are modeled. Gatignon & Hanssens [1987] define an interaction as the process that drives the response parameters of the marketing variables (i.e. β in Equation (1)). More specifically, they define this process as consisting of three elements:

(1) *Marketing variables.* The marketing-mix concept implies that marketing efforts complement each other; for example, selling a product may be easier with stronger advertising support. Thus, we would generally expect a positive interaction among marketing-mix efforts.
(2) *Environmental conditions.* In addition to the main effects shown in Equation 1, changes in environmental conditions over time or differences across markets may affect the effectiveness of the marketing program.
(3) *Stochastic element.* The introduction of a random component is consistent with market-response modeling and represents the unexplained portion of the market-response parameter.

These considerations lead to the specification of a second function which explains the parameter vector β of Equation (1):

$$\beta = f_2(X, Z; \alpha, \delta; v). \quad (2)$$

This system of Equations (1 and 2) is a comprehensive market-response model[2]

[2] A fully comprehensive market model would also contain equations representing the marketing decision functions [Hanssens, Parsons & Schultz, 1990]. These decision functions may affect the estimated response models and may be estimated simultaneously with the response function.

with interactions. Equation (1) is the traditional *response function* and Equation (2), which describes the process that generates marketing impact, is the marketing parameter function or the *process function.* This process function results in a varying-parameter model.

Several special cases of this system of equations correspond to a number of marketing models found in the literature. While these models are reviewed next, let us point out how general the specification of these models is. When the functional form of the response function (Equation (1)) is linear and the process function is linear *without* stochastic element, the classical ANOVA model with interactions results. Indeed, for two marketing-mix variables and no environmental variables the two equations for the response and the process functions are:

$$y = \beta_0 + \beta_1 X_1 + \beta_2 X_2 + \varepsilon, \tag{3a}$$

$$\beta_1 = \alpha_0 + \alpha_1 X_2. \tag{3b}$$

Substituting Equation (3b) into (3a) leads to:

$$y = \beta_0 + \alpha_0 X_1 + \beta_2 X_2 + \alpha_1 X_1 X_2 + \varepsilon. \tag{4}$$

Gatignon & Hanssens [1987] point out three deficiencies with this special case:

(1) The response surface is linear, which is often inappropriate in a marketing context. It should be recognized, however, that the approximation to a linear surface in a region can be appropriate, especially if the system is adaptive over time.
(2) The model ignores a stochastic influence on the response coefficient. Consequently, the model is estimated under a strict constraint as to the variables influencing the coefficient.
(3) The model is observationally equivalent to an interaction model where the direction is reversed, i.e. where β_2 is determined by X_1. This point is critical to the evaluation of the specific role of the marketing-mix variables; for example, it is important to know whether advertising affects price-sensitivity or whether the price level of a product has an impact on the effectiveness of advertising spending.

This indicates that the role of the stochastic element in the process function goes beyond the issue of the completeness of the specification. In fact, the stochastic component contributes in distinguishing the causal mechanism underlying the interaction.

Another special case ignores the process function while the response function is specified as a multiplicative or constant elasticity response model, i.e. for example:

$$y = \beta_0 X_1^{\beta_1} X_2^{\beta_2} e^{\varepsilon}. \tag{5}$$

Marketing interactions are embedded in Equation 5 because the marginal effect of X_1 on y is a function of the level of X_2 and vice versa. These implicit interactions are typically tested globally and indirectly by testing for the functional form of the response function. Moreover, it is not clear, a priori, that the theoretical underlying processes lead to this type of interdependencies between the predictor variables.

2.1.2. Specifying the process functions

A process function describes the way in which marketing effectiveness is created. The specification of such functions is determined a priori, on the basis of theories. Specifically, to accommodate prior knowledge and research findings and to be managerially meaningful, a process function which explains the parameter (response) of the marketing variables should satisfy the following conditions [Gatignon & Hanssens, 1987]:

(1) It should accommodate behavioral hypotheses[3] about marketing interactions. For example, complementarity between salesforce effectiveness and advertising support.
(2) It should be consistent with plausible optimal marketing behavior.
(3) It should be tractable for statistical parameter estimation.

It is not difficult to specify a process function which can test one or more hypotheses and which is estimable. However, since the process function acts on the response function, the resulting (i.e. integrated) function such as in Equation (4) can be very complex. This complexity helps discriminate between the direction or causality of the interactions. For example, assuming a multiplicative response function and a linear process function with two marketing-mix variables, after linearization, the response function becomes

$$\ln(y) = \beta_0 + \beta_1 \ln(X_1) + \beta_2 \ln(X_2) + \varepsilon. \tag{6a}$$

The process functions for the two parameters β_1 and β_2 are

$$\beta_1 = \alpha_{10} + \alpha_{11} X_2 + v_1, \quad \beta_2 = \alpha_{20} + \alpha_{21} X_1 + v_2. \tag{6b}$$

Substituting Equations (6b) into Equation (6a) leads to Equation (7):

$$\begin{aligned}\ln(y) = \beta_0 + \alpha_{10} \ln(X_1) + \alpha_{11} X_2 \ln(X_1) + \alpha_{20} \ln(X_2) + \alpha_{21} X_1 \ln(X_2) \\ + \varepsilon + v_1 \ln(X_1) + v_2 \ln(X_2).\end{aligned} \tag{7}$$

This clearly indicates, as opposed to the ANOVA case illustrated above, that the complexity of the relationships distinguishes between the effect of X_1 on β_2 and the effect of X_2 on β_1. Nevertheless, the specification of marketing process functions should proceed very carefully because of the risk of spurious associations and because of the collinearity which can result in estimating an equation such as Equation (7). Consequently, the process functions should be specified with testable hypotheses in mind, and they should be simple to estimate. Most of all, one should

[3] Behavioral hypotheses can be based on theories, data, and/or expert judgments.

examine the conditions for optimal spending that are implied by the interaction model for robustness.

2.1.3. Estimation of models with interactions

Given the general model described in Equations (1) and (2), how can these equations be estimated? The market model with interactions described above can be estimated by using the general linear model when the response function can be linearized, such as with the power function, and when the process function is linear (possibly after transformation of some of the independent variables). This approach is not overly restrictive, as evidenced by the complex but realistic response models found in the marketing literature which can be estimated after linearization, e.g. the attraction model [Nakanishi & Cooper, 1974, 1982; Cooper & Nakanishi, 1988; Carpenter, Cooper, Hanssens & Midgley, 1988].

The estimation of the model differs somewhat depending on whether the variability of the parameters is explained across the same unit of observation as used in the response function (usually time) or if this variability is due to cross-section variations in which case the response function is expressed in terms of time series of cross-sections. In the first case, the model is a time-varying-parameter model as discussed by Wildt & Winer [1983]. We will only discuss the estimation of models with a stochastic element in the process function since in the absence of such a stochastic term, the ordinary least squares estimator is BLUE.

2.1.4. Estimation of time-varying-parameter models

After linearization of the response function, the model to estimate can be expressed as

$$y_t = x_t' Z_t \alpha + x_t' v_t + \varepsilon_t, \tag{8}$$

where

y_t = a scalar representing the dependent variable of the response function at time t,

x_t = the vector (of dimension k) of independent variables in the response function at time t.

Z_t = a block-diagonal matrix where the block diagonals contain the vector (of dimension p) of predictor variables z_t in the process function repeated in each row (therefore, this matrix has k rows and kp columns),

α = a vector of parameters corresponding to the p predictor variables in the process function for the k response parameters stacked on top of each other (therefore α is of dimension kp),

v_t = a vector (of dimension k) of stochastic terms corresponding to the k response parameters process functions at time t,

ε_t = a scalar corresponding to the stochastic term of the response function at time t.

The estimation procedure leading to a BLUE estimator is a generalized least square procedure which follows several steps [Judge, Griffiths, Hill, Lutkepohl & Lee, 1985]:

(i) The ordinary least squares estimate $\hat{\alpha}$ of α is obtained and the residuals $\hat{\eta}_t$ are computed: $\hat{\alpha} = (A'A)^{-1}A'y$ where the rows of A are $x_t'Z_t$.
(ii) The residuals are squared to form the vector $\hat{\eta}^2$.
(iii) The vector of squared residuals $\hat{\eta}^2$ is regressed on the independent variables x_t' after a transformation is applied to correct for the bias that would be introduced by the fact that the squared residuals are non-negative [Judge *et al.*, 1985]. This leads to the parameter vector $\hat{\pi} = (A'\dot{M}\dot{M}A)^{-1}A'\dot{M}\hat{\eta}$ where $\dot{M}$ is the matrix $M = I - A(A'A)^{-1}A'$ with each of its elements squared.
(iv) The coefficients of the regression in Step (iii) enable the derivation of the elements $\hat{\Omega}$ and $\hat{\sigma}_\varepsilon^2$ of the heteroscedastic covariance of the disturbances in Equation (8): $E[(x_t'v_t + \varepsilon_t)(x_t'v_t + \varepsilon_t)'] = x_t'\Omega x_t + \sigma_\varepsilon^2$ where $\Omega = E[vv']$.
(v) Equation (8) can then be estimated with an estimated generalized least squares procedure: $\hat{\alpha}_2 = (A'\hat{\Sigma}^{-1}A)^{-1}A'\hat{\Sigma}y$ where $\hat{\Sigma} = \mathrm{diag}\{x_t'\hat{\Omega}x_t + \hat{\sigma}_\varepsilon^2\}$.

2.1.5. *Estimation of cross-sectional varying-parameter models*

The estimation of the cross-sections variation model follows a procedure similar to the one used by Swamy with the random-coefficient model [Swamy, 1970] and described in Gatignon [1984a]. The number of time-series observations within each cross-section does not need to be identical in each cross-section as illustrated in Gatignon, Eliashberg & Robertson [1989]. The steps of the estimation procedure are as follows:

(i) The OLS estimators of the parameters in the response equations are first obtained separately for each cross-section i: $\hat{\beta}_i = (X_i'X_i)^{-1}X_i'y_i$.
(ii) These cross-sectional estimates become dependent variables to estimate the parameters of the process function using OLS: $\hat{\alpha}_k = (Z^{*\prime}Z^*)^{-1}Z^{*\prime}\hat{\beta}_k$ for all k's where $\hat{\beta}_k$ is the vector of all cross-section estimates of the k's parameter in Step (i) and Z^* is the matrix of predictor variables for all cross-sections.
(iii) The estimated covariance matrix of residuals is computed from the estimated residuals of Steps (i) and (ii).
(iv) The estimated generalized least squares estimator is the GLS estimator where the covariance matrix of disturbances is derived from the estimates computed in Step (iii) using all observations simultaneously. The structure of the covariance matrix is then derived from the equation

$$y_{it} = x_{it}'Z_i\alpha + \eta_{it}$$

where $\eta_{it} = x_{it}'v_i + \varepsilon_{it}$; $E[\eta_{it}\eta_{it}'] = x_{it}'\Omega x_{it} + \sigma_{\varepsilon i}^2$; $\Omega = E[v_i v_i']$.

Therefore, Ω and $\sigma_{\varepsilon i}^2$ are replaced by their respective estimates to obtain the complete covariance matrix Σ of the pooled vector of disturbances and the EGLS estimator is given by

$$\hat{\alpha}_2 = (\dot{Z}'\hat{\Sigma}^{-1}\dot{Z})^{-1}\ \dot{Z}'\hat{\Sigma}^{-1}y \tag{9}$$

where $\dot{Z}$ is the matrix of products $x_{it}'Z_i$ pooled for all cross-sections and time observations.

When there are no disturbance terms specified in the process function, given the possibility of contemporaneous correlation of the error term in the response function ε_{it}, seemingly unrelated regression should be use to estimate the model parameters. Empirical applications of this methodology can be found in Gatignon [1984a, 1984b], Gatignon & Hanssens [1987] and Gatignon, Eliashberg & Robertson [1989].

2.2. *Review of marketing-mix interactions*

We now review the theoretical and empirical evidence for how the sensitivity of each marketing-mix element varies as a function of other marketing-mix elements. Table 15.1 summarizes the literature on marketing-mix interactions by listing the determinants of the effectiveness of marketing-mix variables which have been studied.[4] We discuss in turn the salesforce, advertising and price issues.

Table 15.1
Evidence about marketing-mix interactions

Effectiveness of	Determinants	References
Salesforce	Other selling efforts	Parsons & Vanden Abeele [1981]
	Advertising	Gatignon & Hanssens [1987]
	Product quality	Gatignon, Weitz & Bansal [1990]
Advertising	Salesforce	Swinyard & Ray [1977]
	Retail availability	Parsons [1974]
	Advertising copy	Winer [1979]
		Gatignon [1984b]
	Price level	Prasad & Ring [1976]
	Advertising media	Prasad & Ring [1976]
Price	Advertising intensity	Comanor & Wilson [1979]
		Ornstein [1977]
		Eskin [1975]
		Eskin & Baron [1977]
		Lambin [1976]
		Wittink [1977]
		Krishnamurthi & Raj [1985]
	Advertising competition	Gatignon [1984a]
	Advertising type	Popkowski Leszczyc & Rao [1989]
	Feature activity	Bolton [1989]
		Bucklin & Lattin [1991]
		Lattin & Bucklin [1989]
		Gupta [1988]
	Display activity	Bolton [1989]
		Bucklin & Lattin [1991]
		Lattin & Bucklin [1989]
		Gupta [1988]
	Advertising media	Prasad & Ring [1976]

[4]Only studies where the marketing-sensitivity parameters are affected by other marketing-mix variables are reviewed.

2.2.1. Salesforce effectiveness

In spite of the importance of a salesforce in terms of the budget spent by companies on personal communications and in spite of the complexity of the selling task [Weitz, 1981], there is little empirical quantitative research attempting to assess the degree to which the effectiveness of a salesforce varies depending on the other marketing activities.

Parsons & Vanden Abeele [1981] provide some empirical evidence of the interaction between salesforce and *other selling efforts*. Using time-series data for a pharmaceutical product, they develop a model of the following form:

$$\beta(t) = \gamma_0 + \gamma_1 \ln(\text{samples}(t)) + \gamma_2 \ln(\text{handouts}(t)) + \gamma_3[\ln(\text{samples}(t)) \times \ln(\text{handouts}(t))]. \tag{10}$$

Although the existence of an error term in that process function is discussed by the authors, the estimation used assumes that the error term is zero. However, although the estimator is inefficient when the error in the process function is not zero, the results (which are unbiased) indicate that all the γ parameters in the process equation above are significant. Therefore, this study demonstrates that samples and handouts make sales calls more effective in terms of generating sales. In addition, when both samples and handouts are used, sales-call effectiveness is not as high as the sum of their individual impacts.

Advertising is shown to enhance the effectiveness of the salesforce by Gatignon & Hanssens [1987]. This result is derived from cross-sectional evidence. Time-series data of navy recruits are modeled for a number of cross-sections (geographical areas or recruiting areas). The coefficient of the number of recruiters in a recruiting area was modeled as a function of local advertising and the propensity to enlist in the area. Local advertising refers here to local media expenditures and recruiter aids such as flyers and posters. The model was estimated with and without a stochastic element in the process function. For both model specifications, while local advertising has a small direct effect on the number of enlistment contracts, it influences positively the effectiveness of the recruiters.

In a study of the impact of the introduction strategy of pharmaceutical products on market share, Gatignon, Weitz & Bansal [1990] hypothesized that *product quality* moderates the effectiveness of the relative marketing effort during the introduction of the brand to the market. Using a linear model for the response function and no error term in the process function, the results were not significant. In fact, the sign indicates a tendency for the marginal returns of the detailing effort to decrease with product quality; product quality appears as a main positive effect on market share.

2.2.2. Advertising effectiveness

Kuehn [1962, p. 2] suggested, based on empirical observations, that 'the return on an advertiser's dollar varies – with when he spends it, with consumer loyalty to his brand, and with the price, cost and availability of his brand relative to competition'. Swinyard & Ray [1977] argue on the basis of experimental data that buyers become more responsive to advertising because of their *prior interaction with a salesperson*. The model is of the form shown in Equation (4), the ANOVA design. The sensitivity to advertising exposures on behavioral intentions is highest when advertising exposure occurs before the personal selling effort.

Although the interaction between advertising and *retail availability* is not modeled explicitly in a process function, Parsons [1974] demonstrates that greater distribution coverage leads to higher sales due to the reinforcement of advertising which creates an impulse for distribution coverage. In a sense, this can be viewed as an interaction because the advertising effect is larger than measured by the coefficient of advertising when sales are modeled as a function of distribution coverage and advertising. Indeed, advertising has a strong impact on distribution coverage when distribution is regressed on advertising (and lagged distribution). However, this is not, strictly speaking, an interaction in the sense that the joint effect of distribution and advertising is not larger (or smaller) than the separate effects of distribution and advertising. In this case, instead, advertising affects sales in two different ways: a direct path in the response function and an indirect path through its effect on distribution, which then affects sales. This is expressed by the two equations:

$$D_t = \alpha_0 + \alpha_1 D_{t-1} + \alpha_2 A_t + \varepsilon_t, \tag{11}$$

$$S_t = \beta_0 + \beta_1 D_t + \beta_2 A_t + v_t. \tag{12}$$

It is important to mention these multiple roles of advertising because the lack of their consideration would lead to an under-estimated effectiveness of advertising. In fact, the total effects of advertising would be represented by inserting Equation (11) into Equation (12):

$$S_t = \beta_0 + \beta_1\alpha_0 + \beta_1\alpha_1 D_{t-1} + \beta_1\alpha_2 A_t + \beta_2 A_t + \beta_1\varepsilon_t + v_t. \tag{13}$$

This total effect could be estimated by the following model:

$$S_t = \gamma_0 + \gamma_1 D_{t-1} + \gamma_2 A_t + \omega_t$$

where

$$\omega_t = \beta_1\varepsilon_t + v_t. \tag{14}$$

However, more noise is introduced in the final model (Equation (14)).

While it is the creative role of the advertising agency to develop *advertising copies* that are effective [Gross, 1972] and while it has clearly been demonstrated that the impact of the advertising copy can be critical [e.g. Bloom, Jay & Twyman, 1977], there is little evidence as to the interaction between advertising quantity and quality. A number of studies demonstrate this interaction using a multiplicative model where the copy effects are interpreted, following Little [1970] and Parsons & Schultz [1976], as an adjustment of advertising expenditures [Arnold, Oum, Pazderka & Snetsinger, 1987; Claycamp & Liddy, 1969]. However, the advertising-spending elasticity is not affected by advertising copy [Arnold, Oum, Pazderka & Snetsinger, 1987]. In fact, Winer [1979] shows that different advertising effectiveness coefficients can be associated with different positioning strategies of Lydia Pinkham, in addition to the different intercepts found by Palda [1964]. Based on this varying elasticity notion, Gatignon [1984b] shows that the effectiveness of the number of exposures to an advertisement is moderated by the advertising copy. The model used for estimating this interaction follows the model described above and used by Gatignon & Hanssens [1987]. The response function models consumers' response to a number of exposures to the same advertisement. This effect of repetition is hypothesized in a process equation to depend on two indices of advertising copy, the extent to which an advertisement (c) can reposition the brand, $E(c)$, and the potential change in the uncertainty (variance) about the brand evaluation, $V(c)$. Therefore, if $\beta(c)$ is the effect of the number of exposures to advertising of copy c in terms of predicting brand attitude, the process function is

$$\beta(c) = \alpha_0 + \alpha_1 E(c) + \alpha_2 V(c) + \varepsilon(c). \tag{15}$$

The results indicate that advertising repetition is more effective for advertisements which intend to, and have the potential to, change perceptions to a greater extent than advertisements which did not resposition the brand. Also, advertising repetition is particularly sensitive when the potential for reducing perception uncertainty is high.

In an ANOVA type of model such as in Equation (4), Prasad & Ring [1976] show that TV advertising response depends on the *price level* of the brand and on the advertising in newspapers. TV advertising is more effective when the price level is lower and when advertising in newspapers is low. This study demonstrates, therefore, the interaction between types of *media*.

2.2.3. Price-sensitivity

The impact of advertising on price-elasticity has been an important issue addressed in economics [Comanor & Wilson, 1979; Ornstein, 1977], although most of the work to establish the interactions of price with other marketing-mix variables does not formally model the price-sensitivity parameter. Two theories have been advanced. The first one, the 'market power' school of thought, contends that advertising reduces price-elasticity [Comanor & Wilson, 1979]. The explanation for this reduction in price-sensitivity comes from the increased brand-loyalty generated by advertising [Ornstein, 1977]. The second theory, the 'advertising as information' school, holds that advertising heightens price-elasticity by exposing consumers to information about alternative brands [Nelson, 1974, 1975]. A number of studies have investigated which theory is supported by data. However, the results do not converge. Eskin [1975] and Eskin & Baron [1977] report negative interactions between advertising and price in an analysis of variance using field-market-test data (the model is therefore of the form shown in Equation (4)).

Lambin [1976] performed an extensive study of European markets, estimating, among other marketing-mix elements, the price-elasticity of brand demand. The price-elasticity estimates for each brand/market were then regressed on several measures of advertising intensity. This modeling approach consists of estimating separately the response and the process function (Equations (6a) and (6b)), where both functions contain an error term. This is equivalent to reporting the estimator $\hat{\alpha}_k$ in Step (ii) of the procedure to estimate a cross-sectional varying-parameter model. The data supports the contention that advertising intensity reduces price-elasticity. Analyzing time series of one brand across territories, Wittink [1977] estimated a model of the form reported in Equation 6 and, taking into account the heteroscedasticity, found the opposite relationship bringing support to the advertising-as-information theory. This direction of the interaction is also supported by an analysis of individual-level panel-diary data during an ADTEL split-cable TV experiment for a frequently purchased consumer product [Krishnamurthi & Raj, 1985]. Their model is of the type of Equations (6) where the process function of the price parameter contains no error term and is purely (constrained to be) determined by a dummy variable which represents whether the period is the pre-test period or the test period. The results indicate that increased advertising leads to a decrease in consumer price-elasticity.

Gatignon [1984a] attempted to resolve the conflict by proposing that the relationship between advertising and price-elasticity depends on whether competitors react to each others' advertising or not. In the absence of reaction, the advertiser can increase brand-loyalty and decrease price-sensitivity. However, in markets where competitors react by advertising their own brand with an increased effort, consumers are faced with 'comparative' information which makes them more price-sensitive. A model of the number of passengers in the airline industry revealed that advertising and competitive reactions interacted to impact price-elasticity. The process equation of price-sensitivity was expressed as a function of the advertising of the airline on the airline route and an interaction term of advertising with an index of competitive advertising reactions. Using the estimation method described in Section 2.1.5, the results indicate a significant impact of advertising and of the interaction term on price-elasticity. Price-elasticity is higher in markets where the airline advertises more and when competitive reactions are higher.

Competitive reactions are only one of the possible explanations for inconsistency in results across studies. A number of factors could potentially explain these differences across studies. For example, Popkowski Leszczyc & Rao [1990] show that local advertising which is typically used to inform consumers about prices increases price-sensitivity, while national advertising decreases price-sensitivity. Their model was estimated with time-series data on the market share of three firms competing in a mature consumer packaged-good category predominantly sold in supermarkets. The price-elasticity coefficient is expressed as a linear function of local and national advertising with lags. This process function is, however, specified deterministically without a stochastic component. Consequently, the estimation constrains the price-elasticity coefficient to be purely determined by these two types of advertising. The estimated coefficients provide strong support for the specification with good fit measures for the model and consistent results for the three firms.

In summary, moderating factors can be:

(1) the competitive reactivity in the market, as demonstrated by Gatignon [1984a];
(2) the nature of the product, especially a low-involvement product such as a frequently purchased consumer good as in Krishnamurthi & Raj [1985];
(3) the media used [Prasad & Ring, 1976]; and
(4) the type of advertising, such as local versus national advertising [Popkowski Leszczyc & Rao, 1990], and the content of the advertisements which may or may not be price-related.

Related to advertising are the notions of feature and display of supermarket products. A featured item sold in a supermarket concerns a brand which is advertised by the retailer, usually with reference to the price. A displayed item indicates that the item is shown in the supermarket outside the normal shelf space, either on an extended shelf, on free-standing platforms or bins, or on end-of-aisle shelves. Bolton [1989] studied the price-elasticity of brands as well as the price-elasticity of the product category as a function of the frequency with which the brand (and the category) is featured or on display.[5] The own-price-elasticity of a category with a higher level of feature frequency has a higher price-elasticity than the low-feature-frequency category. This effect at the brand-category level is consistent with the role of competition, although the role of features might be even more critical because of the price emphasis in such advertisements. Display advertising, which can be considered as another type of advertisement has the opposite effect at the category level: the own-price-elasticity of brands in a category which have a high frequency of being displayed is smaller than in a category with a lower frequency. Displays, therefore, appear as a useful method for enhancing brand-loyalty.

While the emphasis in this review is on aggregate marketing-mix models, research on the impact of feature and display has been mostly at the individual level using quantal choice models, mostly conditional logit models of brand choice. A positive interaction term between price and promotion either through feature or display has been found by Bucklin & Lattin [1991] and Lattin & Bucklin [1989] in their studies of the crackers and the ground-coffee markets respectively. For example, Bucklin & Lattin [1991] model the probability of choosing brand *i* given purchase incidence and given that the consumer is in an opportunistic state (i.e. he or she has not considered a purchase or at least has not decided whether or what to buy) as a logit model:

$$p_t^h(i\,|\,\text{inc and opp}) = \frac{\exp(U_{i|\text{opp}})}{\sum_k \exp(U_{k|\text{opp}})} \tag{16}$$

[5] Although a number of other factors are considered in the research, only the significant interactions are reported here.

with

$$U_{i|\mathrm{opp}} = \alpha_i + \beta_1 \,\mathrm{LOY}_i^h + \beta_3 \,\mathrm{PRICE}_{it} + \beta_4 \,\mathrm{PROMO}_{it} + \beta_5 (\mathrm{PRICE}_{it} \times \mathrm{PROMO}_{it})$$

where

$p_t^h(i \mid \text{inc and opp})$ = the probability of household h choosing brand i given a purchase in the opportunistic state,
$U_{i|\mathrm{opp}}$ = utility of brand i given the consumer is in the opportunistic state,
LOY_i^h = loyalty of household h to brand i,
PRICE_{it} = shelf price of brand i (including discounts) for occasion t,
PROMO_{it} = 1 if brand i is featured or displayed on occasion t and 0 otherwise.

The probability of purchase incidence and brand choice are modeled as a nested logit. The positive interaction indicates either that "the effect of price is less substantial in the presence of feature or display" [Bucklin & Lattin, 1991, p. 33] or that "promotion has a greater effect at higher levels of price" [Lattin & Bucklin, 1989, p. 306]. Moreover, in a study of the IRI ground-caffeinated-coffee data, Gupta [1988] found that promotion through feature or display and price cuts are substitute promotional instruments based on a negative interaction between feature and/or display and price cuts. The nested model of brand choice and purchase incidence is specified similarly to Equation (16). This result indicates either that price cuts are less effective when the item is on promotion or that promotion is less effective (and therefore less necessary), the higher the price cut. As indicated earlier, the direction of the interaction cannot be identified with the additive model where the interaction is represented by a multiplicative term. More research is necessary to discriminate between these alternative explanations.

In this section, we have discussed a general model specification which represents interactions between marketing-mix variables. We have also discussed how to estimate such models. Finally, we have reviewed the evidence concerning how marketing-mix sensitivity parameters vary as a function of other marketing-mix components. It should be noted that the evidence comes from studies which do not involve multiple-product categories (except for Bolton [1989]). Consequently, interactions between marketing-mix variables could differ also due to factors associated with product categories.

3. Normative marketing-mix models

Normative marketing-mix models provide norms as to the allocation of resources to the various marketing-mix elements. We first review the basic norms for allocation of resources, which follow the elasticity of each marketing element [Dorfman & Steiner, 1954]. The rules which are derived from such models are applied using parameter values resulting from the estimation of a response model for the specific brand being analyzed. Then, we consider models where the parameters are not statistically estimated (decision-calculus models). Next, we discuss strategic normative models which are concerned with the long-term profitability of the product or of the 'strategic business unit' and are based on cross-sectional observations. Consequently, the objective is to find, on the average, which factors (strategic actions especially) will lead to the greatest profitability. Finally, analytical marketing-mix models are presented.

3.1. Optimal marketing-mix allocation rules

The Dorfman–Steiner theorem gives the following optimality conditions:

$$\varepsilon_P = (PQ/A)\varepsilon_A = (PQ/D)\varepsilon_D = (P/c)\varepsilon_R \tag{17}$$

where

A = advertising expenditures,
D = distribution expenditures,
P = price,
R = product quality,
Q = quantity sold,
ε = elasticity.

These equalities indicate whether the optimal conditions are met or not and how to change the marketing-mix elements to approach the optimal allocation of marketing resources.[6] Lambin [1970b] derived similar results in terms of market-share elasticities with respect to relative marketing-mix elements (relative advertising, relative price, relative product quality) rather than sales elasticities:

$$P/\eta_{P*} = (A/Q)/\eta_{A*} = x^*(\partial c/\partial x^*)/\eta_{x*}. \tag{18}$$

For two marketing variables, the allocation rule results in expenditures which are directly proportional to their respective elasticities. Gatignon & Hanssens [1987] show that these rules apply even in the conditions of interacting marketing-mix variables. However, while in the absence of marketing-mix interactions the allocation is independent of the budget, Gatignon & Hanssens [1987] demonstrate that marketing interactions create a situation where the allocation ratio changes depending on the total marketing budget. They illustrate this finding by analyzing the salesforce and advertising allocation for different budgets of the U.S. Navy.

Based on the Dorfman–Steiner theorem, the optimal allocation of resources can be derived in theory. However, the elasticities of the various marketing-mix variables are not known with certainty. Only estimates with standard deviations can be obtained. Morey & McCann [1983] provide a confidence interval for the

[6]Sethuraman & Tellis [1991] develop a modified version of the Dorfman–Steiner theorem to account for the fraction of the trade deal that retailers pass on to the consumer and for the fraction of the original demand made at the reduced price.

allocation rule (ratio of expenditures between two marketing-mix variables). In fact, using a general formulation of the marketing-mix model (without specific functional form but possibly with interaction) and maximizing the value of the firm based on the capital-asset-pricing model, Jagpal & Brick [1982] derive a generalization of the Dorfman–Steiner theorem where the elasticities are defined in terms of risk-adjusted elasticities of advertising, personal selling and price. The risk-adjusted elasticities are defined in terms of the risk-adjusted sales:

$$\bar{Q} = \alpha + \beta[E(\tilde{u}) - a_m \operatorname{Cov}(\tilde{u}, \tilde{R}_m)] \tag{19}$$

where

a_m = the market price of risk defined as $[E(\tilde{R}_m) - r_f]/\operatorname{Var}(\tilde{R}_m)$,
$\tilde{R}_m$ = random rate of return of the market portfolio,
r_f = single-period risk-free interest rate (e.g. the rate on a one-year Treasury bill),
$\tilde{u}$ = random element of the sales response function,
$\alpha = \alpha(p, X_1, X_2)$ and $\beta = \beta(p, X_1, X_2)$ are monotonic functions of the marketing variables, i.e. price (p), advertising (X_1) and personal selling (X_2).

Therefore, the risk-adjusted elasticities are $\varepsilon_p = (\partial\bar{Q}/\partial p)(p/\bar{Q})$ and $\varepsilon_{X_i} = (\partial\bar{Q}/\partial X_i)\cdot(X_i/\bar{Q})$ for $i = 1, 2$ (advertising and personal selling respectively).

Based on this model, the following managerial implications result:

(1) If increased advertising and personal selling increase (decrease) price-sensitivity, both optimal advertising and personal spending increase (decrease).
(2) If increased advertising decreases (increases) price-sensitivity but increased personal selling increases (decreases) price sensitivity, optimal advertising increases (decreases) and optimal personal selling decreases (increases).
(3) The role of uncertainty depends on how it enters the demand response equation. In particular, a price increase might not be the best response to increased uncertainty.

Results 1 and 2 conform to the Dorfman–Steiner conditions. Moreover, these results suggest a need for further research about the interaction between salesforce and price given the lack of evidence summarized above (and shown in Table 15.1) about the role of the salesforce as a determinant of price-sensitivity.

The rules discussed above are static. A model that incorporates dynamics in the response function is found in the 'SIMAREX' model of Lambin [1972a]. Subjective estimates are combined with estimates from econometric models and a simulation of marketing-mix decisions is performed.

3.2. Decision-calculus approach to marketing-mix models

An alternative to the analytical derivation of the optimal rules based on econometrically estimated models is to use a marketing-mix model to simulate the market and forecast sales and profits, given a set of marketing-mix decisions [Kotler, 1965]. Although optimization is possible in principle, a major advantage of these models is the ability to represent a greater complexity of market response since no statistical estimation constraints are needed. However, with greater complexity, optimization becomes difficult and often simulation or heuristics appear as the only approach to evaluate and compare the value of particular marketing-mix decisions.

Most decision-calculus models attack the decision problem of one specific marketing-mix variable such as the advertising budget in ADBUDG [Little, 1970], media decisions in MEDIAC [Little & Lodish, 1969] or salesforce time allocation in CALLPLAN [Lodish, 1971]. However, two models investigate the allocation of marketing resources across marketing-mix elements. Lodish [1982] proposes a marketing decision support system for retailers where multiple marketing-mix variables such as national advertising or retail markup are part of the sales-response function. The sales-response model is based on changes in sales from the current-period (reference) sales due to changes in marketing controllable variables (relative to the current or reference level). Each marketing variable has a specific effort represented by an effect index and the total response is specified as a multiplicative function of these indices. For example, the total effect on regular-price sales (RSTOTEFF) is modeled as

$$\text{RSTOTEFF} = e(\text{N.ADV}) \times e(\text{INV}) \times e(\text{SPACE}) \times e(\text{MARKUP}) \times e(\text{RLADV}) \times e(\text{MCHAR})$$

where

RSTOTEFF = total effect on regular-price sales,
N.ADV = level of national advertising,
INV = inventory level,
SPACE = selling space,
MARKUP = average retail markup,
RLADV = advertising placed locally,
MCHAR = quality level of the goods offered,
$e(.)$ = index of effect relative to reference level.

In fact, the model structure is similar to that of Little's BRANDAID model [1975]. BRANDAID [Little, 1975] offers a comprehensive marketing-mix model designed to help brand managers allocate resources to the various marketing-mix elements such as between advertising and promotion expenditures. BRANDAID's model expresses sales at a given time period as a function of a reference level of sales of the brand (dollars per customer per year) s_0, modified by the effects of marketing activities in a multiplicative form:

$$s(t) = s_0 \prod_{i=1}^{I} e(i, t). \tag{21}$$

A submodel is then specified for each marketing-mix variable. For example, the advertising submodel is generated by the dynamic process

$$e(1,t) = \alpha[e(1,t-1)] + (1-\alpha)r[a(t)] \tag{22}$$

where

$e(1,t)$ = advertising-effect index,
α = carry-over effect of advertising per period,
$r[a(t)]$ = long-run sales response to advertising index,
$a(t)$ = advertising rate.

The advertising rate is itself defined as a multiplicative function of the copy effectiveness, the media efficiency and the spending rate, relative to a reference level of these indices:

$$a(t) = \frac{h(t) \cdot k(t) \cdot \chi(t)}{h_0 \cdot k_0 \cdot \chi_0} \tag{23}$$

where

$h(t)$ = copy-effectiveness index,
$k(t)$ = media-efficiency index,
$\chi(t)$ = spending rate,
h_0, k_0, χ_0 = reference values of indices.

Models such as BRANDAID are calibrated using the subjective judgments of managers. This allows greater flexibility in the model specification since the constraints imposed on models for which parameters have to be estimated from statistical inference (for example, linearity for the general linear model) do not need to be imposed. Little [1970] develops the philosophy behind such models which provides results which are typically more robust in extreme values. However, while the model structure is typically richer than econometrically based models [Little, 1980], the validity of the subjectively assessed parameter estimates has been questioned [Chakravarti, Mitchell & Staelin, 1979, 1981; McIntyre, 1982]. Nevertheless, judgmentally calibrated models appear to be an important type of marketing-mix models with successful industry applications [e.g. Lodish, 1981; Little & Lodish, 1981; Larréché & Montgomery, 1977].

3.3. *Strategic empirically based normative models*

The rationale for studying business decisions that are made in practice to develop norms comes from two points of view. The first reason is based on the argument that 'experienced managers make good decisions on average but may display considerable variance in behavior' [Lilien, 1979, p. 192]. This argument proposed by Bowman [1963] is, therefore, based on the need for consistency in managerial decision-making. The second rationale follows Darwinian theory of the survival of species by arguing that studying successful companies or businesses helps identify the practices that lead to survival. These practices are viewed as 'optimal'[7] since,

[7] 'Optimal' is not used in the strict sense since these practices might not be necessarily the best. These practices do, however lead to survival.

otherwise, the enterprise would fail. Two major data bases have been generated to answer the question of allocation of marketing resources (among other, more general, strategic questions) with this approach: the PIMS and the ADVISOR projects.

3.3.1. *PIMS*

A number of studies present different analyses of the PIMS data base. The 'PAR ROI' model predicts ROI as a function of strategic factors, as a function of the competitive position of the strategic business unit, as a function of market and industry factors, and as a function of company factors [Schoeffler, Buzzell & Heany, 1974]. The marketing strategic factors include, in a linear model of ROI, product and service quality, pricing, marketing expenses, and distribution in terms of vertical integration [Buzzell & Gale, 1987]. The simplified model for which the results are published in Buzzell & Gale [1987] contains 22 explanatory variables for which the individual coefficients are at least significant at the 0.05 level:

$$\mathrm{ROI}_{(i)} = \beta_0 + \sum_{k=1}^{22} \beta_k X_k(i) + u(i) \qquad (24)$$

where

$X_1(i)$ = real market growth rate of SBU i,
$X_2(i)$ = rate of price inflation,
$X_3(i)$ = purchase concentration,
$X_4(i)$ = % unionization,
$X_5(i)$ = low importance of low-purchase amount,
$X_6(i)$ = high importance of low-purchase amount,
$X_7(i)$ = low importance of high-purchase amount,
$X_8(i)$ = high importance of high-purchase amount,
$X_9(i)$ = exports–imports (%),
$X_{10}(i)$ = customized products,
$X_{11}(i)$ = market share,
$X_{12}(i)$ = relative quality,
$X_{13}(i)$ = % new products,
$X_{14}(i)$ = marketing, % of sales,
$X_{15}(i)$ = R&D, % of sales,
$X_{16}(i)$ = inventory, % of sales,
$X_{17}(i)$ = fixed capital intensity,
$X_{18}(i)$ = plant newness,
$X_{19}(i)$ = capacity utilization,
$X_{20}(i)$ = employee productivity,
$X_{21}(i)$ = vertical integration,
$X_{22}(i)$ = FIFO inventory validation.

Ordinary least squares is used to estimate the model parameters.

Depending on whether the analysis is pooled or performed on subsamples by type of business (e.g. consumer product manufacturers vs. industrial product manufacturers), the R^2 varies from 0.39 to 0.52. The Strategic Planning Institute's 'PAR ROI' model includes several 'interactive' terms represented by the product of some variables. For example, a variable which is added to Equation (24) is the product of fixed capital intensity and capacity utilization to represent the fact that profits are most sensitive to the rate of utilization when capital intensity is high. Given the value of these factors for a given SBU, a conditional mean ROI can be established as a norm. Deviations from the norm identify results for the SBU which indicate a poor performance vis-à-vis the expectations or supra-returns. Apart from the role of market share which is a strong indicator of profitability [Buzzell, Gale & Sultan, 1975] – although the size of this impact has been contested [Jacobson, 1988, 1990] – perceived product quality appears as a key strategic variable [Phillips, Chang & Buzzell, 1983; Jacobson & Aaker, 1987].

In addition to these studies predicting profitability, the PIMS data base has also been used to describe the determinants of marketing decisions in terms of advertising-and-sales-promotion-to-sales ratio, salesforce-to-sales ratio, or total-marketing-expenditures-to-sales ratio [Buzzell & Farris, 1976]. Predicting the logarithm of the advertising-and-promotions-to-sales ratio as a linear function of other factors of the type mentioned above, Buzzell & Farris [1976] show, based on data from 791 industrial products, that this resource-allocation ratio depends on other marketing variables such as price (relative price) or the nature of the product (e.g. percentage of sales produced to order or purchase frequency). Conditional on these explanatory variables, a norm can then be derived which can serve as a basis of comparison summarizing the strategies (and interaction between marketing-mix elements) which are being followed in practice.

Fornell, Robinson & Wernerfelt [1985] show that the allocation of resources to two marketing-mix variables (advertising and promotion) are not unconditional. In fact, based on an economic theory of habit formation through consumption learning, they demonstrate that brands with more consumption experience should allocate more resources to advertising relative to promotion, compared to brands with less consumption experience. An analysis of consumer businesses in the PIMS data base using partial least squares indicates that, indeed, more advertising than promotion tends to be used for strategic business units which are at a higher level of consumption experience as indicated by proxy indicators such as being the pioneer or not, or having a higher market share.

Formally, the model they developed relates media-advertising expenditures as a percentage of sales revenue (a) and sales promotion expenditures as a percentage of sales revenue (b) to consumer experience. Consumer experience is a formative indicator which is determined by four variables: market share (χ_1), market-share rank (χ_2), relative market share (χ_3), and order of market entry (χ_4). Consumer experience is therefore specified as:

$$\xi = [\pi_1 \pi_2 \pi_3 \pi_4] \begin{bmatrix} \chi_1 \\ \chi_2 \\ \chi_3 \\ \chi_4 \end{bmatrix} \tag{25}$$

where $\pi_1,\ldots,\pi_4$ are parameters to be estimated. A system of three equations is used to test the hypotheses:

$$\begin{bmatrix} b \\ (a+b) \\ (a-b) \end{bmatrix} = \begin{bmatrix} \delta_1 \\ \delta_2 \\ \delta_3 \end{bmatrix} \xi + \begin{bmatrix} \zeta_1 \\ \zeta_2 \\ \zeta_3 \end{bmatrix} \tag{26}$$

where

$\delta_1,\ldots,\delta_3$ = parameters to be estimated,
ζ = consumption experience,
$\zeta_1,\ldots,\zeta_3$ = error terms.

Equations (25) and (26) are estimated simultaneously using PLS. Overall, consumption experience is negatively related to sales promotion and to the combination of advertising and sales promotion. Also, although marginally significant, more advertising than sales promotion appears to be associated with consumption experience.

In the studies mentioned above, the marketing-mix variables are analyzed separately. Carpenter [1987], in a simultaneous-equation model, considers the marketing-mix decisions of relative product quality, promotional intensity (promotion–sales ratio) and price (price–cost margin) as endogenous variables:

$$\begin{aligned} y_1 &= \delta_{12} y_2 + \delta_{13} + \beta_{10} + \beta_{11}\chi_1 + \beta_{12}\chi_2 + \beta_{13}\chi_3 + \beta_{14}\chi_4 \\ &\quad + \beta_{15}\chi_5 + \beta_{16} + \chi_6 + \beta_{17}\chi_7 + u_1, \\ y_2 &= \delta_{21} y_1 + \delta_{23} y_3 + \beta_{20} + \beta_{21}\chi_1 + \beta_{22}\chi_2 + \beta_{23}\chi_3 + \beta_{29}\chi_9 \\ &\quad + \beta_{2,10}\chi_{10} + \beta_{2,11}\chi_{11} + \beta_{2,12}\chi_{12} + \beta_{2,13}\chi_{13} + \beta_{2,14}\chi_{14} + u_2, \\ y_3 &= \delta_{31} y_1 + \beta_{30} + \beta_{31}\chi_1 + \beta_{32}\chi_2 + \beta_{33}\chi_3 + \beta_{37}\chi_7 + \beta_{38}\chi_8 + u_3, \end{aligned} \tag{27}$$

where

y_1 = price–cost margin,
y_2 = promotion–sales ratio,
y_3 = relative product quality,
χ_1 = market-share instability,
χ_2 = competitors' market shares,
χ_3 = market growth,
χ_4 = R&D intensity,
χ_5 = investment–sales ratio,
χ_6 = capacity–market ratio,
χ_7 = buyer concentration,
χ_8 = patent protection,
χ_9 = number of end-users,
χ_{10} = purchase frequently,
χ_{11} = purchase amount,

χ_{12} = sales direct to end-users,
χ_{13} = new-product intensity,
χ_{14} = capacity utilization.

The model is estimated using three-stage least-squares which provides asymptotically efficient estimates. The results indicate clearly that these decisions are interdependent. Three relationships are particularly important.

(1) consistent with the findings mentioned above, higher perceived quality results in higher price–cost margins,
(2) high-quality brands promote less intensely than do low-quality ones, *ceteris paribus*, and
(3) high promotional intensity leads to lower price–cost margins.

3.3.2. ADVISOR

In the ADVISOR project, Lilien & Little [1976] and Lilien [1979] investigate the factors which condition the marketing of industrial products. Specifically, the amount of advertising and marketing resources used by businesses are compared on a cross-section of 110 products (for the advertising and marketing equations) in Lilien [1979].

A multiplicative (log-linear) model specification is used for the marketing spending model:

$$\text{Marketing}_t = \beta_0 \text{Sales}_{t-1}^{\beta_1} \text{Users}^{\beta_2} \prod_i C_{\text{var}_i}^{\beta_i} \prod_j \beta_j^{D_{\text{var}j}} e^{u_t} \qquad (28)$$

where

Marketing = marketing spending,
Sales = sales dollars,
Users = number of customer-individuals the marketing program must reach,
C_{var_i} = continuous, independent variable *i*, transformed to be greater than 1,
D_{var_j} = 0–1 indicator for discrete, independent variable *j*.

Advertising as a percentage of marketing spending is modeled as a logistic transformation as well as the advertising expenditures as a multiplicative model similar to Equation (28) above. A model of change in advertising expenditure was also specified as a multivariate logistic function.

The results indicate that these marketing and advertising resources are not constant across business situations. Among a number of factors which determine these allocation decisions, the results suggest that the nature of the product interacts with the allocation. The fraction of sales made to order, the complexity of the product, and the percentage of sales made directly to the user are significant predictors of the resource-allocation decisions. The distribution channel used in terms of whether the firm was captive or consists of independent units is also analyzed using discriminant analysis. An interaction appears between the product type and the distribution channel. Standardized products are more likely to be sold by independent middlemen, while complex, unique products are typically sold by a captive channel.

While the results from the ADVISOR project are, in general, consistent with the analysis of the PIMS data base [Lilien, 1980], Farris & Buzzell [1980] point out a number of differences in addition to the differences in the philosophy and in the data identified by Lilien [1979]. The results of the PIMS project have also been compared with an analysis of the FTC line-of-business data [Marshall & Buzzell, 1990]. In general, descriptive statistics as well as relationships between variables are very similar. These comparative studies tend to contribute to establishing the validity of the results of the cross-sectional studies.

3.4. Analytical competitive normative models

3.4.1. Marketing-mix competitive strategy of established brands

Carpenter's model [Carpenter, 1989] probably encompasses the most marketing elements: advertising, distribution, price and positioning. Other authors have analyzed price and positioning competition [e.g. Economidies, 1984; D'Aspremont, Gabszewicz & Thisse, 1979; Hauser, 1988; Hotelling, 1929; Moorthy, 1988]. The results obtained by Hauser [1988] using the DEFENDER model show the insights gained for evaluating the strategies that are optimal among a set of competitors (already in the market) [Hauser, 1988]:

(1) firms seek to reposition toward the center of the market,
(2) firms should differentiate maximally from each other, although for four brands or more, this necessitates greater foresight and/or cooperation.

We will concentrate, however, on the results of Carpenter's model because it incorporates a larger number of marketing-mix variables. Based on a model with unimodal taste distribution in a two-dimensional space, the Nash-equilibrium optimal strategies are computed for the two competitors in a duopoly. Carpenter's consumer response model is based on a buyer utility function for a brand which is determined by the brand position in the perceptual space (its distance to the ideal point), price and advertising–distribution spending, and a stochastic component:

$$u_i = v_i(p_i, m_i, D_i) + e_i \tag{29}$$

where

u_i = utility of brand i,
v_i = brand value function,
p_i = price of brand i,
m_i = advertising–distribution,
D_i = distance between ideal point and brand perception,
e_i = random components.

Advertising–distribution also has a positioning role in that brand perceptions are affected by advertising–distribution spending. A maximum-utility brand choice is used conditional on a reservation distance from the ideal point beyond which no brand would be chosen. Formally:

$$\theta_i^* = \begin{cases} 1 & \text{if } D_i \leqslant D_{\min},\ D_j > D_{\min}, \\ \Pr[u_i > u_j] & \text{if } D_i \text{ and } D_j \leqslant D_{\min}, \\ 0 & \text{if } D_i > D_{\min},\ i = 1, 2, \end{cases} \tag{30}$$

where

θ_i^* = probability that buyers with ideal point I^* choose brand i,
$D_{\min}$ = reservation distance from ideal point,
D_i = distance between ideal point and perception of brand i,
u_i = utility of brand i.

Preferences are distributed symmetrically and unimodally according to $f(I^*)$. Therefore, the fraction of all buyers buying brand i is given by

$$\theta_i = \int \theta_i^* f(I^*)\,\mathrm{d}I^*, \quad i = 1, 2. \tag{31}$$

Because the probability of choosing brand i depends on the marketing-mix variables as well as distances, θ_i can be expressed as function of these variables:

$$\theta_i = \theta_i(p_i, p_j, m_i, m_j, D_i, D_j, D_{ij}) \tag{32}$$

where D_{ij} is the distance between perceptions of brands i and j. Carpenter is able to derive a Nash-equilibrium solution by approximating this complex function with a sum of univariate functions:

$$\hat{\theta}_i = \theta_{i1}(D_i) + \hat{\theta}_{i2}(D_{ij}) + \hat{\theta}_{i3}(p_i) + \hat{\theta}_{i4}(m_i) + \hat{\theta}_{i5}(p_j) + \hat{\theta}_{i6} + (m_j), \quad i,j = 1,2; \quad i \neq j. \tag{33}$$

The results are informative regarding how the strategies differ depending on (1) market factors (e.g., price-dominant versus advertising–distribution-dominant), and (2) the position of the brands relative to each other and vis-à-vis the ideal point. In particular, the following results are derived:

Result 1: In markets where a brand is close to the ideal point in comparison to a market where that brand is further away from the ideal point but where the distance between the brands is constant, the brand closer to the ideal point has a higher price and should spend more on advertising and distribution. The other brand also charges more and should spend more on its advertising–distribution if the market is price-dominant. If the market is advertising–distribution-dominant, the other brand charges less and should spend less in the first situation (where the other brand is closer to the ideal point). Therefore, the brand with a positioning advantage should be more aggressive in its advertising–distribution spending and benefit from a better positioning by charging a higher price. The brand with the greater positioning disadvantage spends less on advertising and distribution and must lower its price to compete.

Result 2: The closer the two competitors in a market are positioned (holding their distances to the ideal point constant), the greater the substitutability and the competition, and therefore the lower the price and the advertising–distribution expenditures.

Result 3: The repositioning of both brands to the ideal point to minimize differentiation can be an optimal competitive strategy under certain market conditions related in part to whether the market is price-dominated or advertising–distribution-dominated. In these conditions, prices are higher and advertising–distribution expenses are higher.

These results provide useful insights as to what marketing-mix levels can be anticipated in a market conditional on the market environment. It should be noted, however, that while the pricing results conform to the empirical evidence of the PIMS studies reported earlier, firms might not adhere to some of the advertising results. The empirical competitive-reaction literature shows that advertising rarely declines in competitive markets where brands are direct substitutes [e.g. Gatignon, 1984a] or when a new entry occurs in static markets [Cubbin & Domberger, 1988]. Advertising escalation seems in general more common in practice [Lambin, 1976; Metwally, 1978]. Also, the order-of-entry literature suggests that followers with a positioning inferior to the pioneer can compensate for not being the first in the market with heavy communication expenditures [Bond & Lean, 1977; Whitten, 1978]. Nevertheless, these results point out important directions for future empirical research.

3.4.2. Marketing-mix models of defensive strategy in reaction to a new entry

Hauser & Shugan [1983] developed the DEFENDER model to derive managerial recommendations on how a firm should respond to an attack by a competitive new product. Although the consumer model has been tested empirically [Hauser & Gaskin, 1984] and DEFENDER has been applied in a number of real situations in multiple countries [Hauser, 1988], we only concentrate here on the managerial implications of the model. For a complete description of the model, the reader is referred to the original article by Hauser & Shugan. Briefly, however, market share of brand j among those consumers who evoke a subset of the available brands A_l is a function of the utilities of the brands where the utilities are defined as a linear function of the attribute values per unit price:

$$m_{j|l} = \Pr[(\tilde{w}_1 \chi_{1j} + \tilde{w}_2 \chi_{2j})/p_j > (\tilde{w}_1 \chi_{1i} + \tilde{w}_2 \chi_{2i})/p_i \text{ for all } i \in A_l], \qquad (34)$$

where

$\tilde{w}_1, \tilde{w}_2$ = the relative weights a randomly selected consumer places on attributes 1 and 2, respectively,

χ_{1j}, χ_{2j} = values of brand j on attributes 1 and 2, respectively,
p_j = price of brand j,
A_l = subset of brands evoked,
$m_{j|l}$ = market share of brand j among consumers who evoke A_l.

Hauser & Shugan transform this function by noting that $\tan^{-1}(\tilde{w}_2/\tilde{w}_1)$ represents an angle $\tilde{\alpha}$ of consumer preference and $\tan^{-1}[(\chi_{1j}/p_j - \chi_{1i}/p_i)/(\chi_{2i}/p_i - \chi_{2j}/p_j)]$ is the angle α_{ij} representing the positions of brands i and j. Market share can then be expressed in terms of the distribution of the preference angle $f(\alpha)$:

$$m_{j|l} = \int_{\alpha_{jj-}}^{\alpha_{jj+}} f(\alpha)\,d\alpha$$

where

α_{jj-} = angle between brand j and the brand lower-adjacent to j,
α_{jj+} = angle between brand j and the brand upper-adjacent to j.

The results derived from the model are best described in Hauser [1986]:

Result 1: The incumbent should decrease price from its before-attack level (if consumer tastes are uniformly distributed).

Result 2: A price increase can be the best defense for the incumbent under some distributions of consumer taste.

Result 3: The defensive pricing strategy is independent of the distribution defensive strategy and of the defensive strategy in terms of advertising used for improving brand-awareness. However, the distribution and awareness advertising strategies are conditional on one's pricing strategy.

Result 4: Optimal profits always decrease after the new-competitor entry if market size does not increase dramatically.

Result 5: The best defensive distribution strategy is to cut distribution spending after the entry, unless the market size increases dramatically as the result of the entry.

Result 6: The incumbent should improve its product along the defender's strength (if consumer tastes are uniformly distributed), although under certain conditions, profits are increased by improving the product in the direction of the attacker's strength.

Result 7: The incumbent should cut that portion of the advertising budget whose objective is to improve awareness if the market does not increase dramatically due to the new entry.

Result 8: The incumbent should advertise to reposition its product along the defender's strength (if consumer tastes are uniformly distributed), although under certain conditions, profits are increased by repositioning in the direction of the attacker's strength.

Based on a market-share attraction model and using S-shaped sales-response functions for advertising and distribution expenditures, Kumar & Sudharshan [1988] derive similar implications concerning price reactions as well as for advertising and distribution reactions. If the market size increases due to the entry, the incumbent's advertising and distribution expenditures should be increased. The consumer model determines the unadjusted market-share. Consumers are assumed to be maximizing a utility function:

$$U_\alpha(w_i, Z_i, P_i) = w_i^\alpha z_i^{(1-\alpha)}(Y - P_i) \tag{35}$$

where

(w_i, Z_i) = attribute values for a particular brand,
P_i = price of brand i,
Y = consumers' income (assumed identical for all consumers),
α = weight of w attribute representing the consumer's taste,
U = utility.

The unadjusted demand for brand i is, therefore:

$$Q_i = \int_{i-1}^{\alpha_i} q(\alpha)f(\alpha)\mathrm{d}\alpha = M(\alpha_i - \alpha_{i-1}) = M\beta_i \tag{36}$$

where

Q_i = demand for brand i,
$q(\alpha)$ = quantity purchased assumed to be 1,
$f(\alpha)$ = a continuous function of the distribution of consumer tastes,
α_i = the unique consumer indifferent to brands i and $i+1$,
β_i = unadjusted market share,
$M = \int_0^1 q(\alpha)f(\alpha)\mathrm{d}(\alpha)$ = total demand.

The market share is adjusted for brand-awareness and distribution coverage using an attraction-model specification:

$$\tilde{\beta}_i = \frac{\beta_i A(k_{ai})D(k_{di})}{\sum_{j=1}^{N} \beta_j A(k_{aj})D(k_{dj})}. \tag{37}$$

where

$\tilde{\beta}_i$ = adjusted market-share,
k_{ai} = advertising expenditures of brand i,
k_{di} = distribution expenditures of brand i,
$A(\cdot), D(\cdot)$ = decoupled response functions relating sales to advertising and distribution expenditures respectively.

Both response functions $A(\cdot)$ and $D(\cdot)$ are specified according to the flexible-response model used in ADBUDG [Little, 1970].

3.4.3. Competitive marketing-mix diffusion models for new products

One of the recent extensions of the basic diffusion model [Bass, 1969] is the incorporation of marketing-mix variables [Kalish & Sen, 1986]. Models with price and communication (advertising) for the monopolistic case [e.g. Jeuland, 1981; Kalish, 1985; Spremann, 1981] have been generalized to competitive diffusion models [Thompson & Teng, 1984]. While it is out of the scope of this chapter to describe in detail these models (Chapter 9 by Mahajan, Muller & Bass is devoted to diffusion models), it must be acknowledged that the marketing mix of new products is critical for competing successfully in non-mature markets. Thompson & Teng [1984] conclude that optimal prices and advertising rates start high and steadily decline.

4. Research needs

While marketing-mix modeling is one of the oldest areas of marketing models, which encompasses a broad level of topics surveyed in this chapter, the complexity of the relationships involved justify further investigation using the most advanced modeling techniques. A number of substantive questions remain to be fully addressed. We discuss these first and then suggest a number of methodological issues involved in marketing-mix models.

4.1. Substantive questions

The basic objective for building marketing-mix models is to help management allocate marketing resources to the various marketing-mix variables. While the research reviewed here indicated that much has been done with regard to this question, three areas for further research appear to be needed: (1) the impact of complex interactions on the allocation decisions, (2) the strategic allocation of resources, and (3) the allocation of marketing-mix variables in multi-regional and international markets.

We have provided some evidence for complex interactions between marketing-mix variables. It is clear, however, from this review that interactions whereby a marketing variable affects the market sensitivity to another marketing instrument have been under-researched. Consumer-behavior research is indicative of the complex processes involved in response to a marketing stimulus. Yet, marketing-mix models are often limited to multiplicative effects for representing interactions. It appears that a large amount of research potential exists in developing more complex interaction models which would represent more completely consumer's behavior. This is particularly critical because the allocation of resources among marketing-mix variables is affected by the existence and the nature of these interactions [Gatignon & Hanssens, 1987]. Although the Dorfman–Steiner theorem is general, future research should investigate how the allocation decisions vary depending on the existence and the nature of these interactions.

The strategic allocation of resources has been addressed using cross-sectional evidence. A number of questions are still incompletely answered. The analyses performed to date are for the most part unconditional. Although the PIMS data has been analyzed separately according to discrete categories of variables (e.g. business types), it may be possible to develop a 'contingency theory' of marketing in which the effects of specific marketing expenditures are moderated by other marketing variables as well as environmental factors. For SBUs in particular situations (such as more or less competition, growth, etc.), what are the effects of specific marketing expenditures? Some methodological issues are involved with this question. In particular, strategic issues involve a long-term perspective. Therefore the modeling approach should consider the dynamics underlying the response functions. Models of time series of cross-sectional data should be useful to approach these questions.

One of these questions which is critical in our competitively intense markets is how the allocation strategy of an SBU is affected by competitors' strategies. Using time-series data, it may be possible to understand how an SBU can take into account competitive actions and reactions. This stream of research on competitive dynamics would be directly relevant to management.

The third question concerns the allocation of resources to marketing instruments for firms operating in a multiplicity of countries or regions. Because of the likely interactions between these countries or regions, as well as constraints that might be imposed (for example on pricing), the allocation decisions cannot be made independently within each region or country. Instead, models that represent these interactions should be developed.

4.2. *Methodological developments*

In spite of a long tradition in model-building for measuring the impact of marketing-mix variables and for optimally allocating marketing resources to the marketing mix, much progress has been done in the last decade. A number of methodological issues remain to be addressed more completely.

Some marketing-mix variables are not observed. The measurement of product quality and of advertising quality or copy, for example, are often subjective estimates made by experts. Not only should more objective measures be researched, but the problems associated with error-in-measurement must be investigated in the context of marketing-mix models.

Further efforts should be devoted to model-building with process functions in the context of varying-parameter models. Behavioral theories offer a rich basis for their specification. Some methodological developments of varying-parameter models can be researched in models where there are multiple-response functions, i.e. in a simultaneous system of equations.

While marketing-mix modeling has recently been pursued at the individual level using logit models [Guadagni & Little, 1983] the number of marketing-mix variables is still limited. The role of advertising in choice models must be addressed. The incorporation of all relevant marketing-mix variables should be feasible with the availability of single-source data. Furthermore, modeling interactions in quantal choice models should develop beyond the multiplicative term by incorporating a process function within the choice model.

With the two approaches – aggregate versus individual level of models – the comparison question arises naturally. The issue of consistency in model specification and in terms of the empirical results must be addressed in the context of marketing-mix models.

Finally, with the recent progress in the management of information systems, a real opportunity exists to bring management science to the decision-makers. The development of decision support systems offers potential applications for marketing-mix models to be used regularly by management.

5. Conclusion

Marketing-mix models constitute the essence of the marketing of a product: the coordination of marketing variables into a coherent marketing plan. From an estimation standpoint, marketing models are necessary to estimate the interrelated impacts of the marketing-mix instruments. They also assist in answering a major strategic question, that of how to allocate marketing resources across the marketing mix. Therefore, even though there exists already a vast literature on marketing-mix models, they constitute an essential field with a vast potential for new developments with high managerial demand.

References

Arnold, S.J., T.H. Oum, B. Pazderka, and D.W. Snetsinger (1987). Advertising quality in sales response models. *J. Marketing Res.* 24(1), 106–113.

Bass, F.M. (1969). A new product growth for model consumer durables. *Management Sci.* 15(5), 215–227.

Bass, F.M., and R.P. Leone (1983). Temporal aggregation, the data interval bias, and empirical estimation of bimonthly relations from annual data. *Management Sci.* 29(1), 1–11.

Bass, F.M., and L.J. Parsons (1969). Simultaneous-equation regression analysis of sales and advertising. *Appl. Econom.* 1, 103–124.

Bloom, D., A. Jay and T. Twyman (1977). The validity of advertising pretests. *J. Advertising Res.* 17 (April), 7–16.

Bolton, R.N. (1989). The relationship between market characteristics and promotional price elasticities. *Marketing Sci.* 8(2), 153–169.

Bond, R.S., and D.F. Lean (1977). Sales, promotion, and product differentiation in the prescription drug markets. Federal Trade Commission, Washington, D.C.

Bowman, E.H. (1963). Consistency and optimality in managerial decision-making. *Management Sci.* 9 (January), 310–321.

Bowman, E.H., and H. Gatignon (1992). Order of entry as a moderator of the effect of marketing mix on market share. Working Paper, The Wharton School, University of Pennsylvania, Philadelphia, PA.

Bucklin, R.E., and J.M. Lattin (1991). A two-state model of purchase incidence and brand choice. *Marketing Sci.* 10(1), 24–39.

Buzzell, R.D., and P. Farris (1976). Industrial marketing costs. Working Paper, Marketing Science Institute, Cambridge, MA.

Buzzell, R.D., and B.T. Gale (1987). *The PIMS Principles: Linking Strategy to Performance*, The Free Press, New York.

Buzzell, R.D., B.T. Gale and R.G.M. Sultan (1975). Market share – A key to profitability. *Harvard Business Rev.* January–February, 97–106.

Carpenter, G.S. (1987). Modeling competitive marketing strategies: The impact of marketing-mix relationships and industry structure. *Marketing Sci.* 6(2), 208–221.

Carpenter, G.S. (1989). Perceptual position and competitive brand strategy in a two-dimensional, two brand market. *Management Sci.* 35(9), 1029–1044.

Carpenter, G.S., L.G. Cooper, D.M. Hanssens and D.F. Midgley (1988). Modeling asymmetric competition. *Marketing Sci.* 7(4), 393–412.

Carpenter, G.S., and D.R. Lehmann (1985). A model of marketing mix, brand switching, and competition. *J. Marketing Res.* 22 (August), 318–329.

Chakravarti, D., A. Mitchell and R. Staelin (1979). Judgment based marketing decision models: An experimental investigation of the decision calculus approach. *Management Sci.* 25 (March), 251–263.

Chakravarti, D., A. Mitchell and R. Staelin (1981). Judgment based marketing decision models: Problems and possible solutions. *J. Marketing* 45(4), 13–23.

Clarke, D.G. (1973). Sales–advertising cross-elasticities and advertising competition. *J. Marketing Res.* 10 (August), 250–261.

Claycamp, H.J., and L.E. Liddy (1969). Prediction of new product performance: An analytical approach. *J. Marketing Res.* 6 (November), 414–420.

Comanor, W.S., and T.A. Wilson (1979). The effect of advertising on competition: A survey. *J. Econom. Literature* 17 (June), 453–476.

Cooper, L.G., and M. Nakanishi (1988). *Market-Share Analysis.* Kluwer, Norwell, MA.

Cubbin, J., and S. Domberger (1988). Advertising and lost-entry oligopoly behavior. *J. Indust. Econom.* 37(2), 123–140.

D'Aspremont, C., J.J. Gabszewicz and J.F. Thisse (1979). On Hotelling's stability in competition. *Econometrica* 47 (September), 1145–1150.

Dorfman, R., and P.O. Steiner (1954). Optimal advertising and optimal quality. *Amer. Econom. Rev.* 44 (December), 826–836.

Economidies, N. (1984). The principle of minimum differentiation revisited. *Eur. Econom. Rev.* 24, 345–368.

Eskin, G.J. (1975). A case for test market experiments. *J. Advertising Res.* 15(2), 27–33.

Eskin, G.J., and P.H. Baron (1977). Effects of price and advertising in test-market experiments. *J. Marketing Res.* 14 (November), 499–508.

Farris, P.W., and R.D. Buzzell (1980). A comment on 'Modeling the marketing mix decision for industrial products'. *Management Sci.* 26(1), 97–100.

Farris, P.W., J. Olver and C. De Kluyver (1989). The relationship between distribution and market share. *Marketing Sci.* 8(2), 107–132.

Formell, C., W.T. Robinson and B. Wernerfelt (1985). Consumption experience and sales promotion expenditure. *Management Sci.* 31(9), 1084–1105.

Gatignon, H. (1984a). Competition as a moderator of the effect of advertising on sales. *J. Marketing Res.* 21(4), 387–398.

Gatignon, H. (1984b). Toward a methodology for measuring advertising copy effects. *Marketing Sci.* 3(4), 308–326.

Gatignon, H., E. Anderson and K. Helsen (1989). Competitive reaction to market entry: Explaining interfirm differences. *J. Marketing Res.* 26(1), 44–55.

Gatignon, H., J. Eliashberg and T.S. Robertson (1989). Modeling multinational diffusion patterns: An efficient methodology. *Marketing Sci.* 8(3), 231–247.

Gatignon, H., and D.M. Hanssens (1987) Modeling marketing interactions with application to salesforce effectiveness. *J. Marketing Res.* 24(3), 247–257.

Gatignon, H., B.A. Weitz and P. Bansal (1990). Brand introduction strategies and competitive environments. *J. Marketing Res.* 27(4), 390–401.

Gross, I. (1972). The creative aspects of advertising. *Sloan Management Rev.* 14 (Fall), 83–109.

Guadagni, P.M., and J.D.C. Little (1983). A Logit model of brand choice calibrated on scanner data. *Marketing Sci.* 2(3), 203–238.
Gupta, S. (1988). Impact of sales promotions on when, what, and how much to buy. *J. Marketing Res.* 25(4), 342–355.
Hanssens, D.M., L.J. Parsons and R.L. Schultz (1990). *Market Response Models: Econometric and Time Series Analysis*, Kluwer, Norwell, MA.
Hauser, J. (1986). Theory and application of defensive strategy. In L.G. Thomas III (ed.), *The Economics of Strategic Planning*, Lexington Books, Lexington, MA.
Hauser, J. (1988). Competitive price and positioning. *Marketing Sci.* 7(1), 76–91.
Hauser, J., and S.P. Gaskin (1984). Application of the 'DEFENDER' consumer model. *Marketing Sci.* 3(4), 327–351.
Hauser, J., and S.M. Shugan (1983). Defensive marketing strategies. *Marketing Sci.* 2(4), 319–360.
Hotelling, H. (1929). Stability in competition. *Econom. J.* 39, 41–57.
Jacobson, R. (1988). Distinguishing among competing theories of the market share effect. *J. Marketing* 52 (October), 68–80.
Jacobson, R. (1990). Unobservable effects and business performance. *Marketing Sci.* 9(1), 74–85.
Jacobson, R., and D.A. Aaker (1987). The strategic role of product quality. *J. Marketing* 51 (October), 31–44.
Jagpal, H.S., and I.E. Brick (1982). The marketing mix decision under uncertainty. *Marketing Sci.* 1(1), 79–92.
Jeuland, A.P. (1981). Parsimonious models of diffusion of innovations, Part B: Incorporating the variable of price. Working Paper, University of Chicago, July.
Judge, G.G., W.E. Griffiths, S.C. Hill, H. Lutkepohl and T.C. Lee (1985). *The Theory and Practice of Econometrics, 2nd edition*, Wiley, New York.
Kalish, S. (1985). A new product adoption model with price, advertising, and uncertainty. *Management Sci.* 31(12), 1569–1585.
Kalish, S. and S.K. Sen (1986). Diffusion models and the marketing mix for single products. In V. Mahajan and Y. Wind (eds.), *Innovation Diffusion Models of New Product Acceptance*, Ballinger, Boston, MA.
Kotler, P. (1965). Competitive strategies for new product marketing over the life cycle. *Management Sci.* 12(4), B104–B119.
Krishnamurthi, L., and S.P. Raj (1985). The effects of advertising on consumer price sensitivity. *J. Marketing Res.* 22 (May), 119–129.
Krishnamurthi, L., and S.P. Raj (1991). An empirical analysis of the relationship between brand loyalty and consumer price elasticity. *Marketing Sci.* 10(2), 172–183.
Kuehn, A.A. (1962). How advertising performance depends on other marketing factors. *J. Advertising Res.* 2(1), 2–10.
Kumar, K.R., and D. Sudharshan (1988). Defensive marketing strategies: An equilibrium analysis based on decoupled response function models. *Management Sci.* 34(7), 805–815.
Lambin, J.-J. (1970a). Advertising and competitive behavior: A case study. *Appl. Econom.* 2(4), 231–251.
Lambin, J.-J. (1970b). Optimal allocation of competitive marketing efforts: An empirical study. *J. Business* 43(4), 468–484.
Lambin, J.-J. (1972a). A computer on-line marketing mix model. *J. Marketing Res.* 9 (May), 119–126.
Lambin, J.-J. (1972b). Is gasoline advertising justified. *J. Business* 45 (October), 585–619.
Lambin, J.-J. (1976). *Advertising, Competition and Market Conduct in Oligopoly over Time*, North-Holland, Amsterdam.
Lambin, J.-J., and E. Dor (1989). Part de marche et pression marketing: vers une strategie de modelisation. *Rech. Appl. Marketing* 4(4), 3–24.
Lambin, J.-J., P.A. Naert and A. Bultez (1975). Optimal marketing behavior in oligopoly. *Eur. Econom. Rev.* 6, 105–128.
Larréché, J.C., and D.B. Montgomery (1977). A framework for the comparison of marketing decision models. *J. Marketing Res.* 14 (November), 487–498.
Lattin, J.M., and R.E. Bucklin (1989). Reference effects of price and promotion on brand choice behavior. *J. Marketing Res.* 26(3), 299–310.

Leamer, E.E. (1978). *Specification Searches: ad hoc Inferences with non Experimental Data*, Wiley, New York.

Lilien, G.L. (1979). ADVISOR 2: Modeling the marketing mix decision for industrial products. *Management Sci.* 25(2), 191–204.

Lilien, G.L. (1980). Reply to Farris and Buzzell's comment on Advisor 2 Paper. *Management Sci.* 26(1), 101–105.

Lilien, G.L. and P. Kotler (1983). *Marketing Decision Making: A Model Building Approach.* Harper and Row, New York.

Lilien, G.L. and J.D.C. Little (1976). The ADVISOR project: A study of industrial marketing budgets. *Sloan Management Rev.* 17(13), 17–31.

Little, J.D.C. (1970). Models and managers: The concept of a decision calculus. *Management Sci.* 16 (April), B466–B485.

Little, J.D.C. (1975). BRANDAID: A marketing-mix model. *Oper. Res.* 23 (July–August), 628–673.

Little, J.D.C. (1980). Aggregate advertising models: The state of the art. *Oper. Res.* 28 (January), 629–667.

Little, J.D.C. and L.M. Lodish (1969). A media planning calculus. *Oper Res.* 17 (January–February), 1–34.

Little, J.D.C., and L.M. Lodish (1981). Commentary on 'Judment based marketing decision models. *J. Marketing* 45(4), 24–29.

Lodish, L.M. (1971). CALLPLAN: An interactive salesman's call planning system. *Management Sci.* 17 (February), B293–B306.

Lodish, L.M. (1981). Experience with decision calculus models and decision support systems. In R. Schultz and A. Zoltners (eds.), *Marketing Decision Models*, Elsevier North-Holland, New York.

Lodish, L.M. (1982). A marketing decision support system for retailers. *Marketing Sci.* 1(1), 31–56.

Marshall, C.T., and R.D. Buzzell (1990). PIMS and the FTC line-of-business Data: A comparison. *Strategic Management J.* 11, 269–282.

McCann, J.M. (1974). Market segment response to the marketing decision variables. *J. Marketing Res.* 11 (November), 399–412.

McIntyre, S.H. (1982). An experimental study of the impact of judgment-based marketing models. *Management Sci.* 28(1), 17–33.

Metwally, M.M. (1975). Advertising and competitive behavior of selécted Australian firms. *Rev. Econom. Statist.* November, 417–427.

Metwally, M.M. (1978). Escalation tendencies of advertising. *Oxford Bull.*, 243–256.

Moorthy, K.S. (1988). Product and price competition in a duopoly. *Marketing Sci.* 7(2), 141–168.

Morey, R. and J.M. McCann (1983). Estimating the confidence interval for the optimal marketing mix: An application to lead generation. *Marketing Sci.* 2(2), 193–202.

Nakanishi, M. (1973). Advertising and promotional effects on consumer response to new products. *J. Marketing Res.* 10 (August), 242–249.

Nakanishi, M., and L.G. Cooper (1974). Parameter estimation for a multiplicative competitive interaction model: Least squares approach. *J. Marketing Res.* 11 (August), 303–311.

Nakanishi, M., and L.G. Cooper (1982). Simplified estimation procedures for MCI models. *Marketing Sci.* 1(3), 314–322.

Nelson, P. (1974). Advertising as information. *J. Political Economy* 82 (July–August), 729–754.

Nelson, P. (1975). The economic consequences of advertising. *J. Business*, April, 213–241.

Ornstein, S.I. (1977). *Industrial Concentration and Advertising Intensity.* American Enterprise Institute for Public Policy Research, Washington, DC.

Palka, K.S. (1964). *The Measurement of Cumulative Advertising Effects.* Prentice-Hall, Englewood Cliffs, NJ.

Parsons, L.J. (1974). An econometric analysis of advertising, retail availability and sales of a new brand. *Management Sci.* 20(6), 938–947.

Parsons, L.J., and R.L. Shultz (1976). *Marketing Models and Econometric Research.* North-Holland, New York.

Parsons, L.J., and P. Vanden Abeele (1981). Analysis of sales call effectiveness. *J. Marketing Res.* 18 (February), 107–113.

Pekelman, D., and E. Tse (1980). Experimentation and budgeting in advertising: An adaptive control approach. *Oper. Res.* 28(2), 321–347.
Philips, L.W., D.R. Chang and R.D. Buzzell (1983). Product quality, cost position and business performance: A test of some key hypotheses. *J. Marketing* 47(2), 26–43.
Popkowski, Leszczyc, P.T.L., and R.C. Rao (1989). An empirical analysis of national and local advertising effect on price elasticity. *Marketing Lett.* 1(2), 149–160.
Prasad, V.K., and L.W. Ring (1976). Measuring sales effects of some marketing-mix variables and their interactions. *J. Marketing Res.* 13 (November), 391–396.
Schoeffler, S., R. Buzzell and D. Heany (1974). The impact of stategic planning on profit performance. *Harvard Business Rev.* 52(2), 137–145.
Sethuraman, R., and G.J. Tellis (1991). An analysis of the tradeoff between advertising and price discounting. *J. Marketing Res.* 28(2), 160–174.
Spremann, K. (1981). Hybrid product life cycles and the Nerlove–Arrow theorem. Working Paper, Abt. Wirtschaftswissenschaften, Universität Ulm, Federal Republic of Germany.
Swamy, P.A.V.B. (1970). Efficient inference in a random coefficient regression model. *Econometrica* 38 (March), 311–323.
Swinyard, W.R., and M.L. Ray (1977). Advertising–selling interactions: An attribution theory experiment. *J. Marketing Res.* 14 (November), 509–516.
Thompson, G.L., and J.-T. Teng (1984). Optimal pricing and advertising policies for new product oligopoly models. *Management Sci.* 3(2), 148–168.
Weiss, D.L. (1968). Determinants of market share. *J. Marketing Res.* 5 (August), 290–295.
Weitz, B.A. (1981). Effectiveness in sales interactions: A contingency framework. *J. Marketing* 45 (Winter), 85–103.
Whitten, I.T. (1979). Brand performance in the cigarette industry and the advantage of early entry, 1913–1976. Federal Trade Commission, Washington, D.C.
Wildt, A.R. (1974). Multifirm analysis of competitive decision variables. *J. Marketing Res.* 11 (February), 50–62.
Wildt, A.R., and R.S. Winer (1983). Modeling and estimation in changing market environments. *J. Business* 56 (July), 365–388.
Winer, R.S. (1979). An analysis of the time-varying effects of advertising: The case of Lydia Pinkham. *J. Business* 52(4), 563–576.
Wittink, D.K. (1977). Exploring territorial differences in the relationship between marketing variables. *J. Marketing Res.* 9 (May), 168–176.

J. Eliashberg and G.L. Lilien, Eds., *Handbooks in OR & MS, Vol. 5*

Chapter 16

Marketing Decision Models: From Linear Programs to Knowledge-based Systems*

Arvind Rangaswamy

Marketing Department, Northwestern University, 2001 Sheridan Road, Evanston, IL 60208-2008, USA

'Nothing is more terrible than to see ignorance in action.'
Johann Wolfgang von Goethe

1. Introduction

Decision models are playing an increasingly important role in supporting management decision-making. Several years ago, Little [1979] noted that 'a problem-solving technology is emerging that consists of people, knowledge, software, and hardware successfully wired into the management process'. Even since then, developments in modeling and computer technologies have created new opportunities for marketing scientists to develop decision models that can significantly influence marketing decision-making. The primary objective of this chapter is to provide a critical perspective on one of these new developments, namely, artificial intelligence (AI) modeling, as it compares to decision modeling using conventional OR/MS techniques. Specifically, this chapter:

- summarizes the key contributions of the conventional OR/MS approach to marketing model-building,
- highlights limitations of existing modeling methods, especially in the context of new opportunities generated by computer technologies,
- articulates a role for AI in marketing decision models,
- identifies research opportunities in AI-based decision models.

*This research was supported by a grant from the SEI Center for Advanced Studies in Management, The Wharton School. I would like to thank Raymond Burke, Peter Fader and Mohanbir Sawhney for their comments on an earlier draft of this paper. I would also like to thank the reviewers and the editors for their helpful comments.

Research in decision models is related to the broader area of decision support systems (DSSs), which are defined as 'interactive computer-based systems that help decision makers use data and models to solve unstructured problems' [Scott Morton, 1971]. Much of the DSS research originates in the area of management information systems (MIS) and addresses such issues as design principles of effective DSS, understanding decision styles of managers, evaluating the effects of information technology on organizations, linking models and data, and implementing and managing models. In marketing, DSS is understood to mean computer systems that integrate data, models, statistics and optimization, and enable organizations to convert information into a basis for action [Little, 1979]. Here, we focus on the 'model' component of such systems and limit ourselves to examining issues related to computer-based modeling of marketing *decision situations* rather than on issues related to modeling of decision-makers or their decision-making processes.

We start by defining decision models and characterizing how they differ from theoretical models. We then identify and summarize some key concepts underlying conventional decision models in marketing. Next, we describe and evaluate promising modeling techniques from AI research and identify areas where these approaches can enhance the decision support capabilities that can be delivered to marketing decision-makers. We conclude by noting some potential areas for future research.

2. Key concepts of marketing decision models

2.1. What are decision models?

Models are stylized representations of reality that are easier to deal with and explore for a *specific purpose* than reality itself. Broadly, marketing models may be classified as theoretical or decision models. Theoretical models attempt to precisely and parsimoniously *characterize the world* in which a phenomenon of interest can be shown to occur. Although theoretical models may provide useful decision insights, unlike decision models they do not *directly* help decision-makers to structure a decision situation, evaluate multiple options, or choose an optimal course of action. Decision models generally attempt to *characterize a phenomenon* in terms of variables and relationships of a 'world' as viewed by the model developer (or manager) or as suggested by empirical evidence. This often means that decision models are stated in terms of 'manipulable' variables such as advertising expenditure and price discounts.

To illustrate the distinctions between theoretical and decision models, consider the theoretical model of sales compensation developed by Basu, Lal, Srinivasan & Staelin [1985]. Based on clearly specified axioms about aspects such as a salesperson's preference for leisure and income and the environment in which the sales activities take place, the authors derive several theoretical insights regarding the design of a compensation scheme for individual salespersons. For example, they show that a higher proportion of salary is warranted in a world characterized as having higher uncertainty of sales response to effort. This model could be used for decision-making if the decision situation conforms to the observable scope of the model and the model is robust to 'tractability' assumptions [Moorthy, 1993]. Even then, to use the model as a foundation for decision-making in a particular situation, it must first be suitably 'parameterized' to that decision context. This involves the development of context-specific functional forms, parameter values and, in some cases, other modeling components such as solution procedures. Once these are determined, alternative worlds (e.g. different parameter values) and their corresponding optimal schemes may be explored during the process of, for example, arriving at the salary to be paid to a particular salesperson.

Decision models are the ultimate conceptual tools available to managers. They assist users (managers or their intermediaries) to transform objective or subjective data into actionable insights.[1] The models formalize managers' implicit conceptualizations in order to permit a more systematic evaluation of decision options and their potential consequences.[2]

Decision modeling represents a well-established area of research in the marketing literature. Table 16.1 summarizes several important ideas that have emerged from the OR/MS tradition in marketing model-building over the last three decades. The cited models are not described in any detail here because most of them are well known and descriptions are available in a number of sources including Naert & Leeflang [1978], Schultz & Zoltners [1981], Lilien, Kotler & Moorthy [1992], and in several chapters of this book. The purpose of the table is to highlight some enduring concepts of decision modeling that have resulted from this research stream. The table is organized under four different aspects of decision models, namely, (1) knowledge representation, (2) parameterization, (3) analysis techniques, and (4) modeling philosophy. Each of these areas is elaborated upon next. The later part of this section highlights some limitations of current approaches to model-building.

2.2. *Knowledge representation*

Decision modeling relies on an effective (not necessarily parsimonious) computer representation and manipulation of knowledge relevant to a domain. There are two basic sources of marketing knowledge for decision models: (1) insights and explanations offered by managers and academics, and (2) published research studies. In decision models, knowledge from either source must first be transformed into representations that are suitable for manipulation by computers. In contrast, models used for generating theoretical insights may remain in a symbolic form (e.g. as flow charts or mathematical equations). The representational formalism

[1] *Data* refers to raw values that can be transformed into *information and insights* (i.e. summarized data) by the use of *knowledge*.

[2] More broadly, a decision model may be viewed as a supporting tool that helps managers use data to update their own subjective model of market behavior. (This was suggested by John Little, in conversation.)

Table 16.1
Some useful ideas in the OR/MS tradition from the literature in marketing decision models

Author/model	Decision area/ key issue	Knowledge representation	Parameterization	Analysis techniques	Modeling philosophy
Day [1962]	Media selection	Math program with objective function and matrix of constraints		Optimization using linear programming (LP)	Select/structure marketing problems to be compatible with OR techniques
Green [1963]	Pricing	Decision-tree representation to capture uncertainty in marketing response	Incorporation of empirical and subjective data through Bayesian techniques		
Huff [1964]	Retail-site location	Attraction model based on Luce's choice theory			
		Probability of choice as dependent variable			
Little & Lodish [1969] MEDIAC	Media planning to maximize sales	Long-term effects captured by a parameter representing period-to-period changes		Dynamic programming	
See also DETAILER model of Montgomery, Silk & Zaragoza [1971]				Heuristic approach to obtain near-optimal solutions based on incremental analysis	
		Scaling of a base response function by indices to reflect incremental effects of various influences			
Urban [1969]	Product-line decisions	Response functions that include interdependencies between marketing variables and intensity of competitive			

Little [1970] ADBUDG	Designing, developing and implementing effective decision models	ADBUDG nonlinear response model Anchoring of response model to a reference market situation	Calibration of a chosen response model based on subjective managerial judgments		Articulates the rationale for decision models, their objectives, and the required characteristics Highlights need to focus on the manager's problems rather than on model elegance Use of conversational input/output to model
Urban [1971] SPRINTER (III)	New-product introduction	Response model based on consumer transitions through various purchase states		Simulation of potential outcomes under alternative scenarios	Integration of model, data, statistical analysis and computer resources into an information system for managers Evolutionary model development
Lodish [1970] CALLPLAN	Allocating call time of individual salesperson	Piecewise approximation to nonlinear response function			
Rao & Miller [1975]	Estimating aggregate advertising response		Econometric estimation of aggregate response functions based on natural variations in effort deployment between independent local units		

Table 16.1 (cont'd)

Author/model	Decision area/ key issue	Knowledge representation	Parameterization	Analysis techniques	Modeling philosophy
Little [1975] BRANDAID	Allocating marketing resources across different marketing instruments	Anchoring of response function to a reference market situation in the case of multiple instruments			Developing complex models through modular units
Fudge & Lodish [1977]	Evaluation of the effectiveness of the CALLPLAN model				'Validation-in-use' criterion for evaluating decision models. Compared the relative performance of test group that used the model with a control group that did not.
Silk & Urban [1978] ASSESSOR	Predicting new-product performance		Using laboratory simulation to calibrate model	Using the convergence in predictions of two different model components to assess the credibility of model results	
Bensoussan, Bultez & Naert [1978]	Allocating marketing resources in a competitive environment	Response model based on competitive reactions			
Lilien [1979] ADVISOR	Establishing marketing budgets for industrial products			Evaluation of decision options by comparing them to norms (such as advertising/sales ratio) established from cross-sectional data	
See also Buzzell & Farris [1976]					

Zoltners & Sinha [1980]	Allocation of sales effort across products and markets	Discrete response model		Integer programming (combinatorial optimization)	
Guadagni & Little [1983]	Evaluating effects of marketing instruments on brand choice	Logit model to represent response in a competitive situation	Calibrated on scanner data	Evaluation of decision options based on the model-predicted consequences of that decision in comparison to consequences of status quo	
Abraham & Lodish [1987] PROMOTER	Planning and control of promotional activities	Heuristic response model based on 'if–then' rules depicting quantitative relationships between various variables in the model		Evaluation of the consequences of decision options by comparing them to 'normal' situations	
Rangaswamy, Eliashberg, Burke & Wind [1989] NEGOTEX	Preparing for international commercial negotiations	Heuristic response model based on 'if–then' rules depicting qualitative relationships, between variables that reflect published empirical studies and managerial judgements		Logic programming (backward and forward chaining)	Incorporates qualitative aspects of a decision situation in a formal model Highlights need for decision models to provide explanations of recommendations

Notes: In many cases the underlying concepts originated in other fields. The cited papers are among the early decision-model implementations of these ideas in the marketing domain.
In selecting this list of ideas, we have restricted ourselves to implementable models.

most used in marketing decision models is the 'sales-response function' depicting how sales (or other 'outcome' variables such as consumer choice) are functionally related to various types of activities and events in the marketplace. These activities and events might correspond to those that the firm controls, or those that are controlled by competitors, or they could even be environmental changes.

Response models constitute the core of the traditional decision models. Lilien & Kotler [1983, pp. 66–101] summarize the various functional forms used in marketing models. As summarized in Table 16.1, response functions in decision models have become increasingly sophisticated and are able to accommodate many desirable features such as: (1) simultaneous consideration of the effects of several marketing activities; (2) multiple entities (e.g. products, segments) that are affected by the marketing activities; (3) interdependencies across time, across marketing activities, and across market entities; (4) effects of competitive actions and reactions; and (5) discrete response behavior.

Recent contributions provide further flexibility in representing response behavior. The logit function has emerged as a viable response model for capturing the competitive aspects of marketing decision situations. Another interesting approach is the use of 'heuristics' to represent conditional response behavior. For example, the following are some of the rules that Abraham & Lodish [1987] apply to derive a baseline that helps characterize promotional response.

> 'If an observation t is a negative outlier, and within n periods after the end of a scheduled promotion, then t is a post-promotion period. If so, every observation between t and the end of the prior promotion is a post-promotion period.'
>
> '$w(t) = 0$ if t is a promotion period, a pre- or post-promotion period. $w(t) = f(|r(t)|/\sigma)$ if t is a pseudo-promotion period.' $w(t)$ is a number between 0 and 1 indicating the likelihood that t is a normal period (i.e. without promotion).

In addition to accommodating more complex response behavior, there are other useful aspects of a representation that simplify model implementation. One useful technique is to anchor response functions around the current market situation (e.g. Little, 1970, 1975], an innovation that helps in interpretation by referencing all model results to a 'base scenario' that the manager can understand. The following example from the BRANDAID model [Little, 1975] illustrates this approach:

$$s(t) = s_0 \prod_{i \in I} e(i, t) \tag{1}$$

where

$s(t)$ = sales of product at time t,
s_0 = base sales of product (at current activity levels),
$e(i, t)$ = effect indices of ith marketing activity in tth time period. The index is equal to 1.0 at current activity levels. For example, in

the case of advertising, this is computed as:

$$e(A,t) = \alpha e(A,t) + (1-\alpha) r(a(t)),$$

$r(\cdot)$ = long-run sales response to advertising (as an index),
α = period-to-period carryover effect,
$a(t)$ = index to represent advertising effectiveness in terms of copy-effectiveness ($h(t)$), media efficiency ($k(t)$), and spending rate ($x(t)$) compared to the base levels of these variables:

$$a(t) = \frac{h(t)k(t)x(t)}{h_0 k_0 x_0}.$$

The effectiveness indices represent a measure of the *change* in sales response from a base case. This approach has been successfully employed in many other decision models [e.g. Little & Lodish, 1969; Rangan, 1987]. The use of indices also simplifies model calibration using managerial judgement. For example, it is easier for managers to judge how much more effective a four-color ad will be as compared to a black-and-white execution than it is to guess the absolute level of sales associated with each type of ad.

2.3. Parameterization

Models have to be parameterized to a particular decision context before they can support decision-making. Parameterization may involve specification of functional forms, assignment of values to parameters, and customization of analytical procedures to take advantage of context-specific factors. Even as the decision model is being developed, the researcher should carefully consider the potential functional forms and data availability for model implementation. For example, certain functional forms involving interactions between variables are difficult to parameterize using managerial judgement.

Often, the modeler embeds specific functional relationships directly into the structure of the model. In such cases, parameterization only involves 'calibration' of the model through a choice of appropriate values of model parameters. If calibration is based solely on sample data, such an approach is called 'empirical'. This may involve the estimation of the parameters of response functions from a historical database or from field experiments. The intellectual support for this approach is typically derived from the *Normal theory* in statistics. A comprehensive description of the available techniques is given in Hanssens, Parsons & Schultz [1990]. Some of the factors that limit the use of these methods are the lack of the requisite data and the managerial belief that historical data may not adequately represent future conditions in the decision context of interest.

If the model is calibrated solely by quantifying managerial judgement, such a method is termed 'subjective estimation' [Naert & Weverbergh, 1981]. The intellectual support for this approach is well articulated by Little [1970]. The basic structure of the response function is preselected by the model-developer to satisfy certain desirable characteristics relevant to a class of decision problems (e.g. advertising budgeting). At the time of calibration, it is hoped that managers will tap into their reservoir of experience to help identify model inputs that are appropriate to a particular situation.

The differences between the empirical and subjective estimation approaches have been well documented and are not repeated here [see Bass, 1983; Little, 1983]. Comparisons of the validity of these two approaches suggest that subjective estimation is particularly useful in field settings as opposed to laboratory settings. Fortunately, these are precisely the settings in which it is likely to be used. Based on field studies, Horng [1987] suggests that historical data have an edge over the subjective estimation approach when the market conditions are stable. On the other hand, in contexts such as new products where market experience is limited, the subjective estimation approach is better.

Our experiences with the alternative estimation methods [Rangaswamy, Sinha & Zoltners, 1990] indicate that these two approaches complement each other. In fact, Bayesian estimation provides a formal basis for integrating the empirical and subjective approaches. The limitations in implementing Bayesian estimation in decision models are operational in nature, not theoretical [Naert & Weverbergh, 1981]. Subjective estimation is the only option when empirical data are not available. On the other hand, empirical estimation is the only feasible approach when the response model is very complex. In such cases, difficulties in obtaining multi-parameter priors from managers, or identifying suitable conjugate priors for nonlinear response functions discourage the use of the Bayesian approach.

2.4. Analysis techniques

Most of the decision models in Table 16.1 use representational formalisms and computational techniques of management science. Essentially, OR/MS models enable managers to explore various decision options by computing the consequences of each potential option in numerical terms. These models help focus computer support in areas where human abilities are comparatively limited, namely, the systematic consideration of numerous alternatives that require extensive data-retrieval and computations. Often, the major challenge is in structuring the marketing decision problem to be compatible with available OR/MS approaches. Two broad categories of decision models may be identified within the marketing literature, namely, normative and descriptive models.

2.4.1. Normative decision models

Some managerial decisions may be stated in terms of the following question: 'What is our best course of action in a given situation?' Normative models are designed to help users address such questions by enabling them to explore the optimality of a decision under various scenarios. The managerial question is modeled as a constrained optimization problem where the objective function provides an index to evaluate the goodness of a decision and the constraints summarize the range of allowed variation in the decision options. When the decision options are numerous, the optimization model helps to trim them down to a few effective ones. Examples in marketing are the various mathematical programs for sales-resource allocation [Zoltners & Sinha, 1980], media planning [Little & Lodish, 1969], shelf-space design [Bultz & Naert, 1988], and store location [Ghosh & McLafferty, 1982].

Even when a decision situation can be structured as an optimization problem, available solution methods may be impractical or time-consuming. Therefore, optimization models may not always be suited for interactive modes of decision support. As suggested by the experiences in developing the MEDIAC [Little & Lodish, 1969] and CALLPLAN [Lodish, 1971] models, quick response is an important aspect of providing on-line decision support. Various techniques, such as piecewise approximations to the response functions and heuristic optimization procedures, have been attempted to minimize computational effort and reduce response time. While heuristic procedures enable users to perform a number of quick 'what if' analyses using the optimization model, the results obtained from such procedures might be difficult to interpret without assurance (based on analytical results) that the model converges to an equilibrium point [Geoffrion, 1975]. It is always a good idea to analyze and test heuristic approaches to ensure that they generally converge to solution points that are not counter-intuitive. Otherwise, the model might lose credibility with managers.

Normative decision models are increasingly being referred to as 'prescriptive models' to recognize that such models could prescribe effective courses of action, from among the numerous options available, without being driven by explicit optimization of an objective function. Many of the knowledge-based decision models discussed in later sections are prescriptive in this sense.

2.4.2. Descriptive decision models

Descriptive decision models help to identify, describe and explain the managerially useful variables and relationships associated with a phenomenon. These models are used for: (1) deriving explanations of a phenomenon based on the relationships embodied in the model (e.g. poor new-product sales are due to poor repeat-purchase rates), and (2) predicting possible outcomes when the model is extended to parameter regions other than those used for developing the model (e.g. What will sales be next month?). In the latter context, the models are often referred to as *predictive models*. Many econometric models fall in this category. If used properly, descriptive decision models help managers to understand the extent of support (e.g. range of values of prices) for various actions (e.g. introduce new product) in complex decision situations.

Descriptive models are particularly useful for evaluating the consequences of specific managerial actions. They attempt to provide an answer to the question, 'What will happen if we do *X*?' The user experiments with the model using 'simulations' to learn more about the consequences of potential actions. The ASSESSOR model [Silk & Urban, 1978] is an example of a successful descriptive model that helps managers evaluate the consequences of introducing a new product by predicting its market share and profitability under various advertising and promotion plans.

In problem situations that require complex response surfaces, exact optimization procedures and analytical solutions are often infeasible. Simulation using descriptive models provides an alternative approach for evaluating the consequences of complex interactions between variables.[3] The simulations are symbolic, although sometimes a physical analogue, such as a simulated store, may be employed. Early applications of simulation models in marketing include competitive-response analysis [Amstutz, 1967], forecasting new-product sales [Urban, 1970], and evaluation of media schedules [Gensch, 1973]. The interest in marketing simulation coincided with the growing interest in systems theory. However, because of model complexity (which reduces the interpretability of the results), voluminous data requirements, costs of maintenance, and a general lack of managerial interest, the initial enthusiasm for simulation faded.

Perhaps, the early simulation models were ahead of their time. New modeling concepts combined with flexible computer systems have, in recent years, rekindled the interest in simulation. Two concepts, in particular, are useful for evaluating simulation results: (1) use of multiple models where the results of each model serve as a reference to evaluate the results of the other models [Silk & Urban, 1978], and (2) comparison of results to a base situation [Guadagni & Little, 1983; Abraham & Lodish, 1987]. Other concepts that enhance the interpretation of simulation resuls are: (1) decomposition of results into those due to different modular components [Little, 1975], and (2) comparison of results to norms established from a cross-section of firms [Lilien, 1979].

Using multiple models. Silk & Urban [1978] use two different models to improve the validity of estimates of new-product sales from the ASSESSOR model. The first model, called the trial–repeat model, estimates market share from consumer trial behavior in a laboratory test market and a subsequent survey among triers. The trial–repeat model proposes that the expected long-run market-share for a new packaged-good product ($M(n)$) may be described as

$$M(n) = T \cdot R \tag{2}$$

where

T = cumulative proportion of consumers who try the product,
R = steady-state proportion of those who try who repeat.

The second model, called the preference model, is based on estimating market share for the new product using consumers' stated preferences for the different brands in their relevant sets.

[3] In other fields (e.g., physics, chemistry and biology), simulation is primarily used for studying time-varying phenomena, such as understanding the evolution of the universe by speeding up cosmological processes. Fundamental insights and new theories have evolved from such simulations. For example, the basic concepts of chaos theory originated from computer simulation models.

The use of multiple models is particularly useful if the models and their parameterizations are independent of each other. In the above example, parameterization of both models is done on the same group of individuals. Therefore, the results from the two models are likely to be positively correlated, i.e., they may be expected to converge. In this case, the real value of using two models occurs when the model results diverge and point to different conclusions. Such an outcome suggests more testing before the new brand is launched. On the other hand, if the two models are also parameterized on independent groups of individuals, then converging conclusions may be more informative.

Use of reference points. Consider the following multinomial logit response model proposed by Guadagni & Little [1983] to characterize purchase probabilities for different brands of coffee:

$$p_{il} = \frac{e^{v_{il}}}{\sum_{j \in S_i} e^{v_{ij}}} \tag{3}$$

where

$$e^{v_{ij}} = \prod_{k \in T} e^{b_{kj} x^i_{kj}}$$

l = a particular brand,
v_{ij} = deterministic component of an individual i's utility for brand j,
S_i = choice set of individual i,
p_{il} = probability that individual i will choose brand l,
T = set of attributes/marketing instruments, such as promotion,
x^i_{kj} = observed value of attribute k of brand j for individual i,
b_{kj} = coefficient for attribute k of brand j.

This is a complex model from which it is difficult to obtain closed-form solutions for various response elasticities of interest associated with this model. For example, an interesting managerial question is how market share of rand l responds to a promotion. An analytical solution for this requires a multidimensional integration over a joint probability distribution. Instead, the authors use the following 'simulation': For every purchase occasion calculate the probability of purchase of brand l, and aggregate to obtain average market-share for the brand. This is the reference point. This process is then repeated to compute the average probability of purchase with brand k on a simulated promotion with a median price cut, with all other attributes held constant. Response elasticity is then computed as the percent change in market share over the reference point.

2.5. *Modeling philosophy*

Initial applications of OR/MS models in marketing, such as linear programming (LP) models for media selection [Day, 1962], were based on recognizing similarities in structure between the OR and marketing problems. Often, only technical intermediaries acting on behalf of the managers were involved in the modeling process. As a result, much of the modeler's attention focused on the technical aspects of the problem rather than on the managerial decision-making process. Geoffrion [1987] refers to this as the 'technocentric' view of modeling as opposed to the 'problem-centric' view. With the growth of timeshare systems in the 1970s, there emerged the possibility of more actively involving the manager/intermediary in the decision process through 'conversational' input and output to the model. This was achieved by embedding a dialogue system (primitive by today's standards) on top of the model to allow users to specify input data, assign parameter values, and evaluate alternative scenarios during the decision process. The value of dialogue systems is clear. Without these, managerial users would not be able to use the models in their own decision environments.

In spite of their impressive technical capabilities, early decision models did not have widespread impact. Many of the models were developed for narrow domains and were cumbersome to use. Model-builders preferred to work on decision problems that were compatible with available methods and technologies. The actual importance of the decision to marketing managers was only of secondary concern. These and other factors led Little [1970] to propose the decision-calculus approach. He suggested that unless models become vehicles to engage the manager more actively in the decision-making process, they will continue to have limited appeal. Little proposed new techniques of model-building and criteria for evaluating decision models that were based on an understanding of how managers interact with models. Since then, the 'decision calculus' approach proposed by him has evolved into a model-building paradigm in its own right.

The 1980s witnessed further growth in problem-centered decision models. More elaborate response functions have allowed the model-builder to develop models with greater realism. Simultaneously, technological developments in computer hardware and software now enable users to consider many more scenarios and models during the decision process. Increasingly, models are used as 'consultants' that can actively participate in the decision process rather than as passive entities that take user inputs and convert them into some outputs that are then interpreted by analysts/managers. Instead of being black boxes, these new models are acquiring some shades of grey! AI models represent a further evolution in this direction. As an example, the NEGOTEX model [Rangaswamy, Eliashberg, Burke & Wind, 1989] listed in Table 16.1 highlights how AI models contribute to the decision-modeling literature.

2.5.1. *Validity, value and generalizability of decision models*

Does the model contain a valid representation of the decision situation? There is no simple answer to this question. The criterion commonly used to validate decision models is face validity which is an attempt to answer the question: Does the model give 'sensible' results? Little [1970] refers to this criterion as 'robustness'. Presumably, the user has an exogenous basis (common sense) to judge model output and infer its validity. Sometimes, face validity of a model is assessed by using test cases for which the results are externally known/determined. One simple way to do this is to test whether the model results correspond closely to the known output values when model inputs reflect the current market situation (e.g. current levels of marketing activities). Few decision models have been validated beyond this criterion.

Some models have been tested for their predictive validity, i.e. whether the predictions of the model which drive the decisions were actually realized after the decisions were implemented (see for example, tests of the ASSESSOR model reported in Urban & Katz [1983]). Note that this test is different from predictive validation of theoretical models where there is often no intervening decision to be implemented. In fact, it is difficult to separate out the effect solely due to the decision from several simultaneous activities that are initiated when the decision is implemented. There are several other practical difficulties in conducting predictive validation of decision models. As Urban, Hauser & Roberts [1990] point out, 'Management has an incentive to sell cars, not to provide a controlled laboratory for validation'.

Does face validity or predictive validity justify the development of the model, at least in a post-hoc sense? An additional criterion should be adopted. The basic premise of decision models is that their use will improve the decision process and/or the decision outcomes *in comparison to the approaches the managers currently use*. Therefore, an appropriate test would be 'validation in use', i.e. whether the use of the model leads to better decisions. Unfortunately, few decision models can be rigorously tested on this criterion. In an extensive summary of the tests of DSS effectiveness, Sharda, Barr & McConnell [1988] note that field tests are relatively sparse because it is difficult for the experimenter to control the use of a DSS in an organizational setting. They also report that studies looking at the benefits of DSS have found mixed support and argue that these mixed results are a consequence of the fact that in many cases, the managers were given a 'black box'. There have been only a few validation attempts of this type using control-group–test-group procedures. Validation through field tests of the CALLPLAN model [Fudge & Lodish, 1977] and the target marketing model [Gensch, 1984] and evaluation of the NEGOTEX model in a laboratory experiment by Eliashberg, Gauvin, Lilien & Rangaswamy [1992] represent some of the published studies that have tried formal validation-in-use tests of marketing decision models.

What does generalizability mean in the context of decision models? Broadly, it refers to the ability of the model to be used in a variety of situations – for example, in different product categories. CALLPLAN has been implemented in many different situations and so have many of the pretest market models such as ASSESSOR. In these models, generalizability is achieved by using generalizable variables, relationships and modeling techniques. In other cases, generalizability is achieved by providing a range of tools to the manager who then selects or designs a model most suitable to a particular context. In recent years, the availability of DSS generators [Nunamaker, Applegate & Konsynski, 1988] has greatly improved the generalizability of decision models. DSS generators such as EXPRESS (a product of Information Resources Inc.) and LOTUS-123 (a product of Lotus Corporation) are widely employed by marketing analysts to structure and solve many decision problems.

2.6. Where do we go from here?

Academic contributions in decision modeling have focused primarily on quantitative modeling, measurement and analysis, and have pursued well-defined but narrow domains that are best handled by established quantitative methods. No doubt, these choices have anchored the models on sound theoretical foundations, and have resulted in parsimony in representation and efficiency in computation. Unfortunately, these choices have also restricted the 'expressiveness' of model representations and reduced the potential impact of decision models. Most marketing models appearing in the academic literature have not had the impact on managerial decision-making that is commensurate with their potential. As Keen [1987] notes, although such models are useful, they are not usable. Often, this is not due to any intrinsic limitations of the models. More likely, when delivered to managers, models are often 'inflexible systems' or 'black boxes' that turn even enthusiasts into skeptics.

Conventional modeling approaches have failed to fully recognize the fundamental changes that computers bring to modeling. In particular, new computer technologies allow modelers to define decision environments as they appear to be managers. Computers today can effectively handle many forms of symbolic representations in addition to mathematical equations. With these representational formalisms, the modeler can address neglected problem domains as well as improve user-access and use of existing models in conventional domains. Consider, for example, problems of diagnosis such as, "Why are sales up in Chicago and down in Philadelphia?" Answers to such questions involve logical analyses in addition to numerical computations to systematically evaluate alternative explanations in a process converging towards the most plausible explanation(s). Further, the 'answer' must include some justification for the chosen option. Although conventional decision models have been successful in addressing 'allocation' and 'prediction' problems, they are not well adapted to problems involving 'diagnosis'. To use such models for diagnosis, the user must possess considerable domain expertise as well as prior knowledge of the structure of the underlying model. This is often an unrealistic expectation. Other areas where conventional models are inadequate include: (1) detection of 'exceptions' (e.g. unusual sales patterns) and identifying possible managerial approaches to handle such situations, and (2) 'synthesizing' ways to reach predetermined targets (e.g. desired market-share).

Even apart from limitations in current decision models, changes in the marketing environment and recent strides in computer technologies have created the need for new modeling techniques. In particular, the following trends are noteworthy:

- Marketing managers are joining the growing ranks of professionals who rely on end-user computing to do their jobs. Computing power available to users is also growing. The first computer, ENIAC, had a speed of about 0.0003 mips (million instructions per second), the 8088-based PCs of the early 1980s had a speed of about 0.33 mips, while the 80386-based PCs available today can have a speed in excess of 5 mips. The availability of desktop workstations with a speed of 100 mips is imminent.

With increased computing power, there is a growing demand for computer models that provide greater flexibility in use, more visual outputs, and better integration of models and data. As managers begin to use decision models by themselves without the constant availability of an analyst, some of the skills of the analyst must be somehow made available to the user. Likewise, in this new computing environment, the model must be able to 'explain' its results, which in the past, was also done by the supporting technical staff.

- There is an explosion of marketing data. For example, in the packaged-goods industry, marketing managers have access to 40 times more data with a frequency that is 9 times higher than what they had a few years ago [McCann & Gallagher, 1990]. Much of this data cannot be meaningfully interpreted without some type of automation of the decision-modeling process.
- Marketing decisions increasingly occur in complex environments that may be characterized as competitive, global and dynamic. In such environments, decision-making involves consideration of a greater variety of influences, including those that are essentially qualitative in nature.

New modeling techniques are required to augment existing approaches if decision models are to be designed for use in this environment. Among the many emerging techniques and concepts for enhancing computer-based modeling, AI provides a particularly promising base for broadening the scope and impact of decision models.

3. Artificial intelligence

AI stands for an evolving body of knowledge focusing on concepts and methods to enable computers to do tasks that would be considered to be 'intelligent' if done by machines. A good general introduction to the topic is Winston [1984]. While OR/MS models have focused on problems that are very difficult for humans but comparatively easy for today's computers, AI modeling has focused on problems, such as solving puzzles or understanding language, that are relatively easy for humans but difficult for the von Neumann sequential computer. The areas of research and application of AI have varied from the purely practical, such as designing robots for industrial tasks, to those that border on the very essence of what it means to be a human, namely, solving problems using abstractions and understanding language. In addressing these issues, AI research has produced new formalisms and problem-solving strategies that are relevant to a wide range of problems. Our focus is on understanding the role of AI for developing effective decision models.

There has been some interest in applying AI techniques, expert systems in particular, to develop marketing decision models. Wierenga [1990] summarizes many of the first-generation expert systems developed in marketing. Models such as ADCAD [Burke, Rangaswamy, Wind & Eliashberg, 1990] and Merchandising Analyst [McCann, Tadlaoui & Gallagher, 1990] have been successfully developed. Although these early attempts show promise, they still exist only as prototypes. Nevertheless, the experiences in developing these systems suggest that AI models have the potential to increase decision-effectiveness by delivering *better conceptualizations* of problem situations to the *point of decision-making*. In this section, we discuss some of the basic modeling concepts used in AI. Section 4 explores the potential contributions of AI-based decision modeling.

It is clear that in purely computational tasks, the capabilities of the computer far exceed the cognitive capacities of all but the most gifted humans. (Interestingly, doing computations quickly is not generally considered to be a demonstration of intelligence.) What may be surprising is that in some clearly defined domains that require symbolic and heuristic reasoning, the computer is gaining ground. For example, in chess, the computer can beat most human players including grand masters.[4] On the other hand, computers are abysmal at tasks requiring richness in contextual knowledge such as language understanding and vision where, as of now, human cognitive processing is far superior.

Our primary concern here will be with those AI models that are known as knowledge-based systems. We make a distinction between knowledge-based systems and the more familiar expert systems. The goal of an expert system is to replicate in a computer model the performance levels of a human expert in the chosen domain. We use the term knowledge-based systems to refer to decision models that use AI methods. The goal of such systems is to provide decision support, not necessarily to clone an expert.

All computer-based modeling relies on formalisms for *knowledge representation* and methods for *knowledge processing*. What distinguishes AI models from conventional OR/MS models is the way that knowledge is represented and processed. A basic philosophy of AI modeling is its attempt to develop knowledge-representation techniques that allow knowledge to be specified independent of its particular uses. The 'symbolic' view of modeling often used in AI treats knowledge elements much like conventional computer programs treat data. This design philosophy is not as explicit in the 'algorithmic' view of modeling used in conventional decision models. Although not generally viewed as such, spreadsheet programs such as LOTUS-123 may be considered to be knowledge-based systems. The knowledge-representation scheme used in spreadsheets is a generalized matrix where each cell can contain various types of elements. Items pertaining to a specific domain such as, for example, the 'balance sheet of company XYZ', are simply instantiations[5] of this general representation scheme. The knowledge processing

[4] Recently, the computer program 'Deep Thought' lost to the reigning world champion Kasparov, but only 52 moves! This impressive performance is partly due to the computer's ability to evaluate all positions up to 5 moves ahead and partly due to its heuristics to trim down search paths.

[5] Instantiation', as the term is used in the AI literature, is analogous to the notion of 'parameterization' in conventional decision models.

mechanism is 'constraint propagation' that transmits the consequences of changes made in any cell of the matrix to all other affected cells. Constraint propagation works when there are clearly specified deterministic links between the elements of the matrix (as defined by the user in the case of spreadsheets).

3.1. Some modeling formalisms of AI

3.1.1. Rule-based systems

In these systems, the primary knowledge elements are modular 'if–then' rules that represent conditional relationships between the values of the variables of interest in a chosen domain, and knowledge processing is accomplished by *logical reasoning* (i.e. *matching*) to link the rules to user problems. The variables in the premises (i.e. in the 'if' part of the rules) are instantiated during system-use either by user input, or through database retrieval, or from matching with the conclusions of other rules (i.e. the 'then' part). During run time (or compile time in the case of large knowledge bases), the reasoning mechanism establishes logical linkages between the different rules by backward-chaining (output-driven processing) or by forward-chaining (input-driven processing). This reasoning mechanism creates specific pathways through the knowledge base that help solve the user problem that is posed as a goal to be pursued by the system. Most reported applications in marketing have used this approach.

The primary advantage of using rule-based representations for decision modeling is the ability to construct explanations listing the steps leading to a result, or providing the conceptual support for a recommendation. Another advantage of rule-based systems is that they can process verbal symbols representing terms familiar to users. This 'expressive' representation makes the underlying model more transparent during the decision-making process. The rule formalism also provides a framework for exploring theoretical aspects of knowledge representation.

On the downside, rule-based systems require knowledge to be represented using general principles or heuristics. When there are many exceptions to a heuristic, it becomes tedious to use this approach. Another problem is that it is difficult to transport a knowledge base from one application to another unless the 'lexicon' of each application is defined in an identical manner. This occurs even if much of the knowledge content of the two applications is the same. In conventional models, the availability of relatively uniform mathematical representations obviates this problem to a large extent. For example, FORTRAN subroutines for specific tasks may be readily transported between applications.

3.1.2. Frame-based systems

These systems provide an additional level of flexibility in knowledge representation and processing as compared to rule-based systems. A frame is an entity for grouping knowledge (e.g. rules) into related categories, something that is tedious to accomplish in rule-based systems. Frames contain 'slots' for representing knowledge elements pertaining to an abstract object. The 'values' of slots could be pointers to other frames, an algorithmic procedure, or a variable whose value(s) are inferred from rules in the system. The modeler links a frame to other frames using domain-specific relations, often in a hierarchical scheme.

The primary processing mechanisms of frame-based systems are *message passing* and *inheritance*. A frame is activated when it receives a message from the user or from other frames. A message is a request for a frame to carry out one of its prespecified operations. Each frame is 'awake' at all times during the process but initiates activities only in response to messages it receives. Through inheritance, lower-level frames infer the values of their slots from frames at a higher level in the hierarchy unless the defaults are locally changed. This allows the model-builder to represent objects (e.g. TV and radio commercials) as specializations of other more generic objects (e.g. advertising and communication approaches) and for these representations to be organized into taxonomies. Collectively, these processing strategies are akin to object-oriented programming. When all the slots of a frame are filled with specific values, the frame is instantiated, i.e. a specific instance of the frame is created.

Given their flexibility, frame-based models have the potential to be widely applied in the development of marketing models. Frames allow knowledge to be represented with minimal redundancies as compared to rules. In addition, some of the linkages (i.e. inferences) can be structurally embedded by the modeler, thereby eliminating some unnecessary run-time inferences. This improves system performance compared to the same knowledge represented as a rule base. The structured modeling techniques for OR/MS models proposed by Geoffrion [1987] share much in common with the frame-based representation. The DEALMAKER system [McCann & Gallagher, 1990] and the ADDUCE system [Burke, 1991] are the only reported applications in marketing that use frame representation.

3.1.3. Neural networks

Neural networks are composed of an interlinked set of nodes (neurons) where knowledge is embodied implicitly in the 'threshold values' associated with each node and 'weights' associated with links between the nodes. Each node is a 'signal processor' that first computes a weighted sum of all incoming signals (numerical values) from other linked nodes or from an external source in the case of input nodes. This resultant is then converted into an output signal using a prespecified 'activation' function. Typically, the activation function, e.g. a logistic function, transforms an input signal into an output signal in a bounded range (e.g. $(-1, 1)$). The resulting real number at each node is often further transformed into a binary digit based on a comparison to the threshold. Nodes where the computed value is higher than the threshold are said to be 'active'. The final output of a neural network is a 'pattern' of activation of a subset of nodes called the output nodes.

Starting with a random set of weights, the processing mechanism (*learning*) updates the weights and, sometimes the thresholds associated with the network by minimizing an error measure computed from feedback (usually given by the model developer) regarding the correctness of the output in sample cases. The output of a neural net is a classification – such as recognizing sales as high, medium, or low. Thus, neural nets essentially map input vectors x_i to output vectors y_i, or in other words, the network learns to associate the response y_i with stimulus x_i. For example, x_i's may represent various demographic characteristics and y_i a segment label. Unlike conventional models based on specific analytic functions, in neural nets the relationship between input and output is captured by general nonlinear estimators. There is no requirement that we specify *a priori* functional relationships between input and output. A growing body of research is exploring important formal properties of various types of neural nets [Kosko, 1992].

Neural nets are particularly useful in domains where (1) nothing really is known about the formal relationships between variables, (2) 'machine learning' is desirable due to a need for the system to function in related, but unexpected situations, or (3) there is a need for a response without human participation in the decision (e.g. deciding whether to ship a mail-order catalogue to a customer).

A fundamental problem in using neural nets in decision models is that it is very difficult, if not impossible, to interpret the weights on the neural net in terms of the semantics of the problem domain. Even a 'trained' neural net remains a black box, and consequently, such models are incapable of explaining the rationale for their outputs in terms that are meaningful to managers. Recent research exploring hybrid systems combining rule bases with neural networks offers some hope of resolving this problem [e.g. Romaniuk & Hall, 1991]. Until these issues are resolved, the immediate applications of neural nets in decision models appear to be in prediction tasks that are not driven by conceptual models.

From a theoretical perspective, the philosophies behind the alternative modeling formalisms are quite different. Rule and frame representations are based on the belief that intelligence requires symbol manipulations while neural networks are based on the belief that intelligence requires mimicking brain-like neural processing. Broadly stated, symbol manipulation appears to be effective for emulating higher-order brain functions such as problem-solving while neural processing seems best suited for emulating lower-order brain functions such as perception and pattern recognition. From a practical perspective, a choice among these modeling approaches clearly depends on the domain of application. Given our focus on problem-solving, we will restrict our attention to symbolic knowledge representation and processing.

4. AI and decision modeling

First-order predicate logic provides the theoretical foundation for representing and using knowledge in a symbolic form [Nilsson, 1991]. To highlight the potential contributions of AI techniques to decision modeling, we will develop our arguments primarily using rules to symbolize knowledge. This choice is based on two factors: (1) much of the theoretical discussion in the AI literature and many of the applications use rules to represent knowledge, and (2) in many cases, it is conceptually straightforward to convert a frame-based system into an equivalent rule-based system [see, for example, Thuraisingham, 1989]. Note also that, in principle, a rule-based system can be constructed to mimic a system using any other knowledge representation (i.e. it is 'Turing complete').

4.1. Logic as a modeling language

Much as calculus and matrix algebra provide the foundations for conventional decision models, mathematical logic provides the foundation for AI models. In fact, given any model expressed in the language of predicate logic and given any conclusion that follows from the model, there is a *finite mechanical procedure* for showing that conclusion actually does follow. Thus, inference in classical logic can be embodied as a computable procedure [Robinson, 1965]. Several researchers have noted the potential of using 'logic modeling' for developing decision models [e.g. Bonczek, Holsapple & Whinston, 1981; Kimbrough & Lee, 1988].

Knowledge of the decision process, in addition to numerical algorithm, is often required to obtain useful insights even from quantitative models. Such knowledge might include insights on when and when not to use a particular technique. For example, some response functions may be suitable only for products which are frequently purchased. However, response functions by themselves say nothing about the conditions under which they apply! Logic representation provides a flexible mechanism to ensure that models will not be applied to specific situations without an evaluation of their applicability.

To illustrate this, consider the simple knowledge base given in Table 16.2 consisting of three rules. The first rule specifies a sequence of steps the system must follow in solving a modeling problem. Capital letters (e.g. MODEL) represent variables that are instantiated during run time. The system is initiated by instructing it to seek the goal 'problem_solved'. To do this, it tries to satisfy the premises of

Table 16.2
A simple rule-base to enhance value of ADBUDG model

```
rule-1:
          if   model_name = MODEL and
               input(MODEL) = [INPUT] and
               output(MODEL) = [OUTPUT] and
               constraints_checked(MODEL) = yes and
               estimation_method(MODEL) = EST and
               model_estimation(MODEL,[INPUT],[OUTPUT],EST) = [PARAM] and
               compute(MODEL, [INPUT], [OUTPUT],[PARAM]) = [VALUE]
        then   problem_solved = yes
        else   problem_solved = no.

rule-2:
          if   product_category(adbudg) = appropriate and
               market_segment(adbudg) = appropriate
        then   constraints_checked(adbudg) = yes.

rule-3:
          if   model_name = MODEL and
               not(constraints_checked(MODEL) = yes)
        then   constraints_checked(MODEL) = no.
```

rule-1. To satisfy the first premise of this rule, the system identifies from the user the particular model to be run (e.g. adbudg). In attempting to satisfy the next set of premises, it obtains from the user the list of input and output variables represented by the lists [INPUT] and [OUTPUT] respectively.[6] For example, [INPUT] could be the list [promotion, advertising], and output could be the list [sales]. Next, the system attempts to identify from the user the estimation procedure to be used (e.g. subjective or empirical). The output of the estimation procedure is the list of parameters represented as [PARAM].[7] In order to assess the value of the proposition 'constraints_checked(MODEL)', the system will determine through backward-chaining that it has to use rule-2 (or another rule if a model other than adbudg is chosen by the user). Since adbudg was chosen, the system will then determine whether the product category and market segment to which the model is applied are appropriate (without additional rules in the knowledge base to determine these, the system will directly ask the user about the appropriateness). Only if all the requisite constraints are satisfied, the adbudg model will be executed by initiating compute(adbudg, [promotion, advertising], [sales], [values_of_the_adbudg_parameters]). For our purpose, we may assume that this procedure will access a database to retrieve the appropriate data on promotion, advertising and sales, execute the adbudg model, and return the output in a list called [VALUE]. If the constraints are not satisfied, rule-2 will fail but rule-3 will succeed. But if rule-3 succeeds, rule-1 will fail and the adbudg model will not be executed.

Although the example is intentionally trivial, it is instructive. In this set of rules, the entire conventional ADBUDG model is represented by the term compute(·). The additional elements in the knowledge base, however, enable the system to retrieve the appropriate data, manage the estimation, and check constraints to determine the applicability of the ADBUDG model. If there are other models available in addition to ADBUDG, a separate set of constraints may be specified for each model by adding rules to the system.

In addition to checking these constraints, the rules allow tracking of the sequence of steps by which the system arrives at its results. This sequence may be used to compose an explanation for the results. This aspect is discussed in Section 4.4.

4.2. Models for qualitative analysis

Logic representation enables consideration of the qualitative aspects of a decision situation. In the physical sciences, basic theory can often be represented by parametric equations, the most famous example being $E = mc^2$. In contrast, decision situations in marketing involve reasoning at a qualitative level. For example, the likely options to a price reduction by a competitor might be (1) match the new

[6] For simplicity, assume that the values of the input and output variables exist as a data matrix in an external database.

[7] The number of elements in [PARAM] and the order in which they appear are implicit. These are specified by the model developer.

price, (2) maintain current price, (3) change TV advertising, (4) increase trade promotion, or (5) fire the brand manager. These options do not fall along a continuum that is succinctly represented by smooth analytic functions and resolved by standard numerical methods. Or, consider the following 'response function' specifying how a retailer might react to a trade promotion [McCann & Gallagher, 1990, p. 168]:

> "This retailer always accepts a deal, but what is done with it is based on coop advertising dollars. If the deal includes coop money, the retailer will accept the deal and pass on all of the discount to the consumer. If the discount is greater than 30%, he will put up a big display. Otherwise, the retailer leaves the item at regular price and does not use an ad feature or a display."

Zoltners [1981] notes that decision-makers use both specified and unspecified criteria, but that existing decision models only focus on specified criteria. He also suggests that unspecified factors (qualitative factors) may even dominate specified factors. AI models can help reduce the number of 'unspecified' factors in the model by providing a method for representing and processing qualitative aspects of a decision situation. For example, the design of TV commercials is based on a consideration of the interactions between numerous aspects of the product, the target audience and the market environment. Marketing theory in this domain provides at best a partial ordering of the effects of the different variables on advertising effectiveness. A rule-based system such as ADCAD is able to represent and manipulate this knowledge in a useful manner for decision support. Logical inference extracts the appropriate advertising design components from the knowledge base suitable to a particular situation facing the user. Many AI systems in marketing such as INNOVATOR [Ram & Ram, 1988], NEGOTEX [Rangaswamy, Eliashberg, Burke & Wind, 1989], ADCAD [Burke, Rangaswamy, Wind & Eliashberg, 1990], and PROMOTION ADVISOR [McCann & Gallagher, 1990] rely exclusively on qualitative analysis. The Marketmetrics Knowledge System [McCann & Gallagher, 1990] and the INFER system [Rangaswamy, Harlam & Lodish, 1991], both designed for analysis of scanner data, use logic as a modeling language to enhance the managerial value of statistical analyses by providing qualitative insights.

A representation is not useful in itself but only in reference to the reality that it purports to capture and the purpose for which it is used. Ideally, the representation used should retain the topological characteristics of the underlying phenomenon. Kalagnanam, Simon & Iwasaki [1991] correctly argue that if the underlying phenomenon is known to be accurately represented by analytic functions, a reliance on qualitative reasoning may give inappropriate answers because it imposes a weaker ordering than is known to be the case. However, in marketing, analytic functions are mostly a convenience, not necessarily an accurate representation of a phenomenon. If the phenomenon of interest can at best be described using weaker ordering, such as ordinal relationships, then qualitative reasoning is not just a convenient approximation. It is an appropriate level of analysis for the phenomenon. If it is only possible to characterize consumer response to an ad as being positive, neutral, or negative, then a precise numerical model may be inappropriate for representing what is known. A numerical model would require that the managers provide an exact value rather than allowing them to express exactly what they know.

4.3. Representing uncertainty in decision models

Marketing decision-making takes place under situations of uncertainty. First, many relationships in marketing characterize conditions that are neither necessary nor sufficient for a phenomenon to occur. Decision models must incorporate this uncertainty in the relationships to accurately represent the known knowledge. Second, there is often uncertainty in the values of input parameters to the decision model as perceived by the model user.

In conventional decision models, uncertainty in the results is usually linked to the values of model parameters through sensitivity analyses. The parameters are varied in *some* fashion to reflect uncertainty in their values. At best, this approach provides an indication of the *range* of output values which might be expected under variations in input parameters. It cannot help estimate the *frequency distribution* of various output values unless the representation includes a probability model for the input parameters. This limitation may be addressed by employing Bayesian decision analysis which provides a formal method for handling uncertainty in decision-making. Although various tree-structured methods are available for implementing Bayesian analysis in conventional models, few marketing models have implemented these methods. AI models have also had to address issues regarding how best to incorporate uncertainty in their structures. Classical logic with its reliance on a representation of exact and unfailing relationships does not provide a favorable stratum for incorporating uncertainty. However, the obvious need for incorporating uncertainty in AI systems has led researchers to develop mechanisms for *representing* and *propagating* uncertainties in a knowledge base. An understanding of these mechanisms is useful for decision modeling, even in models that do not use AI techniques.

We first describe a well-known, non-Bayesian technique based on 'certainty factors' that has been developed for rule-based systems. We then summarize some key insights from promising new methods that incorporate Bayesian analysis in AI models. We make the following points: (1) Although the certainty-factor approach appears to be ad hoc, it is computationally attractive and relies on several intuitive assumptions that people implicitly use. However, it is consistent with the Bayesian approach in only a very restricted but precisely defined set of situations. (2) Although the Bayesian approach provides a consistent and coherent basis for making inferences under uncertainty, it is often computationally unattractive. However, there are ways to structure knowledge so that Bayesian methods become feasible even in large knowledge bases.

In many rule-based systems developed thus far, uncertainty representation is achieved by associating a degree of confidence, called certainty factor (CF), with each rule. Thus, for example, the logical relationship $A \Rightarrow B$ is modified as $A \Rightarrow B(\mathrm{CF})$, where CF is a number between -1 and 1 (equivalently, between -100 and 100). A positive number corresponds to an *increase* in belief regarding B when A is true while a negative number indicates a *decrease* in belief in B given A. With this representation, uncertainty propagation is accomplished by *local updating*. This means that, if A is determined to be true at any time during processing, it is then immediately asserted that B is true with a confidence of CF regardless of how A was arrived at and regardless of other conclusions that the system might have already made up to that point. This approach supports modularity in knowledge representation and monotonicity in the reasoning process (i.e. conclusions once made are not later 'withdrawn').

A 'certainty calculus' has been proposed for computing the confidence factor of a conclusion based on the confidence factors associated with (1) an uncertain premise, (2) a conjunction of premises, (3) a disjunction of premises, and (4) multiple sources of evidence [see, for example, Shortliffe, 1976]. Although many of the heuristics used in certainty calculus are intuitive, they have been criticized as being ad hoc in comparison to the Bayesian method of updating. It can be shown that in some situations (e.g. correlated sources of evidence) the certainty-calculus method leads to implausible conclusions whereas the Bayesian method continues to provide intuitively compelling updates. Heckerman [1986] and Heckerman & Horvitz [1988] identify the exact set of conditions under which the certainty-calculus approach will be consistent with Bayesian updating:

- The knowledge base consists of propositions (i.e. statements that can have one of two values: true or false) represented as nodes on a directed tree – i.e. a set of premises does not lead to more than one conclusion.
- Consider a rule $A \Rightarrow B(\mathrm{CF})$ where A is a set of propositions and let λ be the likelihood ratio:

$$\lambda = \frac{P(A \mid B)}{P(A \mid \neg B)}. \tag{4}$$

Then CF equal to the following monotonic increasing function of λ satisfies the heuristics associated with certainty calculus (incidentally, it may often be easier to ascertain λ rather than the CF value):

$$\mathrm{CF} = \frac{\lambda - 1}{\lambda + 1}. \tag{5}$$

These are severe restrictions that are unlikely to be fully satisfied in most marketing domains. This raises the question of whether Bayesian methods might be used instead. However, traditional approaches to implementing Bayesian updating impose a considerable computational burden even in reasonably sized knowledge bases, thereby reducing system response time. For example, a knowledge base consisting of 25 variables, each with three levels, would require the computation of nearly 3^{25} probabilities whenever a new inference is made during processing. Fortunately, there are many situations where local updating procedures (but not necessarily those used in conjunction with certainty calculus) are consistent with Bayesian methods as suggested by the following two important insights:

Representation: Suppose that the knowledge base is represented in the form of a directed acyclic graph (DAG) where the nodes are the variables and suppose that the joint probability distribution of the variables is P, then a necessary and sufficient condition for DAG to be a 'Bayesian network' of P is that each variable X be conditionally independent of all its non-descendants, given its parents Π_X, and that no proper subsets of Π_X satisfy this condition [Pearl, 1988, p. 120].

Propagation: Local updating is consistent with Bayesian updating only when the DAG is singly connected. That is, no more than one path exists between *any two nodes* of the graph [Pearl, 1988, pp. 175–184]. This requirement is more general than the 'directed tree' requirement for interpreting certainty factors in a Bayesian framework.

Consider, for example, the DAG shown in Figure 16.1 with nine variables x_1 to x_9. The arrows on the graph indicate the direction from *premises* to *conclusions* (or in a Bayesian interpretation, from *evidence* to *hypotheses*). The graph represents a part of the knowledge base of the ADCAD system which is organized hierarchically as: Consumer and market factors ⇒ marketing objectives ⇒ communication objectives ⇒ communication approaches ⇒ executional approaches. The graph is singly connected, but is not a directed tree. For the latter requirement to be satisfied, there should be no divergent arrows such as those emanating from the nodes 'purchase motivation' and 'communication objectives'.

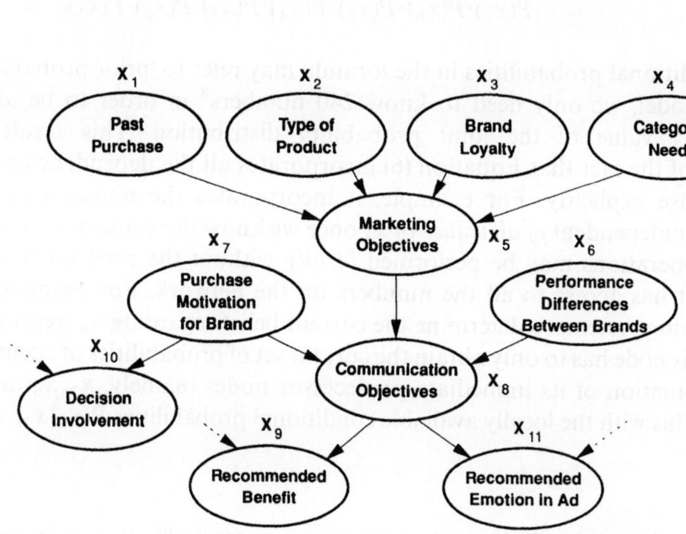

Fig. 16.1. An example of directed acyclic graph from the ADCAD knowledge base.

Bayesian networks are of particular interest to marketing model-builders. Decision-modeling sequences such as those in Table 16.2 can usually be designed to satisfy the requirements of singly connected DAGs because of the hierarchical nature of modeling procedures. Thus, it may well be feasible to combine logic modeling with Bayesian uncertainty propagation through local updating. There are also many domains where marketing knowledge may be organized as DAGs where variables form the nodes of the graph and the links establish the directional dependencies between the variables. The dependencies may be based on causal relationships between the variables, or they may be based on the principle of relevance of a variable to the other variables in the knowledge base (see Howard [1989] for an example of a network based on relevance relationships).

When a DAG does not initially satisfy the requirement of single-connectedness, it may sometimes be possible to modify the graph to satisfy this constraint by, for example, clustering the values of a variable into separate groups, each of which can then be labeled as a separate variable. Even if this modification is not possible, a DAG representation (without single-connectedness) provides a feasible approach to minimizing the number of computations required to implement Bayesian updating in knowledge-based systems.

Suppose that each of the nine variables (x_1 to x_9) in Figure 16.1 has three possible values that are mutually exclusive. Theoretically, a total of 19 682 numbers ($3^9 - 1$) are required to specify the joint probability distribution of the variables and their values represented in the graph. Suppose that we restate the links $A \Rightarrow B$ in the form of a conditional probability $P(B|A)$ (>0), then the joint probability corresponding to any particular state of this graph is given by

$$P(x_1, x_2, \dots, x_9) = P(x_9|x_8) \cdot P(x_8|x_7, x_6, x_5) \cdot P(x_5|x_4, x_3, x_2, x_1) \cdot P(x_7) \cdot P(x_6) \cdot P(x_5) \cdot P(x_4) \cdot P(x_3) \cdot P(x_2) \cdot P(x_1). \quad (6)$$

The unconditional probabilities in the formula may refer to 'prior probabilities'. Under this model, we only need to know 240 numbers[8] in order to be able to determine any value of the joint probability distribution. This result is a consequence of the fact that Equation (6) incorporates all the dependencies in the knowledge base explicitly. For example, it incorporates the notion that x_8 is conditionally independent *of all values* of x_3 once we know the value of x_5. Further, all required operations may be performed *locally* without the need for a central processor that has access to all the numbers on the network. For example, in a forward-chaining system, to determine the current belief regarding x_8 (represented as $\mathrm{CB}(x_8)$), this node has to only obtain the current set of probabilities of occurrence of each combination of its immediate predecessor nodes (namely, x_7, x_6 and x_5) and combine this with the locally available conditional probabilities $\mathrm{P}(x_8|x_7, x_6, x_5)$.

[8] This is obtained by noting that 6 numbers are required to specify $P(x_9|x_8)$, 54 for specifying $P(x_8|x_7, x_6, x_5)$, 162 for $P(x_5|x_4, x_3, x_2, x_1)$, and 3 each for $P(x_7), P(x_6), P(x_4), P(x_3), P(x_2)$ and $P(x_1)$.

In the example, this would amount to a local computation of

$$\mathrm{CB}(x_8) = \alpha \sum P(x_8 | x_7, x_6, x_5) \cdot P(x_7) \cdot P(x_6) \cdot P(x_5) \tag{7}$$

where α is a normalizing constant. The summation is taken over the domain of x_7, x_6 and x_5. In backward-chaining, each node has to obtain information from its immediate successor nodes. In systems where both forward- and backward-chaining are possible, two sets of information have to be simultaneously obtained in the updating process. Pearl [1988] contains a detailed discussion of these updating methods and their implementation details.

None of the AI systems developed in marketing is based on Bayesian networks. Instead, they have all relied on the built-in certainty-calculus methods provided by the software used for developing the system. It is not clear how many of the existing systems have attempted to design the knowledge base in a manner that enhances the compatibility between certainty calculus and Bayesian updating. Future research should explore ways to integrate Bayesian networks into AI models in marketing.

As an alternative to the use of Bayesian updating, several other schemes (both numerical and non-numerical) have also been proposed to modify classical logic to accommodate 'uncertain inferences'. Examples of such systems are fuzzy logic where $a \Rightarrow b$ is interpreted as 'the more one is a, the more one is b', and non-monotonic logic where $a \Rightarrow b$ is interpreted as 'if b is conceivable and if a, then b'. The interested reader is referred to Sombé [1990] for a comprehensive discussion of the relative merits of these approaches.

4.4. *Improving explanatory facilities of decision models*

As more managers begin to directly interact with decision models, the explanatory facilities provided by the system assumes greater importance. From a manager's viewpoint, explanations for the recommendations/conclusions may be as important as the recommendations themselves. In general, a good explanation should identify user inputs and model components that influence a particular result, distinguish between significant and insignificant influences, translate 'model syntax' into 'user semantics', as well as identify common factors that are responsible for a group of results (adapted from Kosy [1989]). Table 16.3 is an example of the type of explanation that the current version of the ADCAD system [Burke, Rangaswamy, Wind & Eliashberg, 1990] provides.

Likewise, the logic representation in Table 16.2 describing components of a model in verbal form allows generation of explanations using an English-like syntax. It must, however, be noted that explanations constructed from a logic representation need not necessarily be understandable. Consider, for example, the following logically equivalent representations each consisting of three statements:

– $\forall(x)(M(x) \wedge V(x) \Rightarrow \neg I(x))$
$M(\text{adbudg}) \wedge V(\text{adbudg})$
$\neg I(\text{adbudg})$

Table 16.3
An abbreviated example of an explanation from the ADCAD system

PRESENTER = NEED NOT BE SIMILAR TO TARGET AUDIENCE
When the creative strategy is transformational, the consumer is not highly involved in the brand-choice decision, and the brand is not highly visible in use, then the presenter need not be someone who is similar to the target audience. (Bearden & Etzel, 1982; Ogilvy, 1983; Young & Rubicam, personal communication).

When the advertising objective is to communicate brand image/mood/lifestyle, reinforce brand image/mood/lifestyle, communicate new brand image/mood/lifestyle, communicate category image/mood/lifestyle, or reinforce category, image/mood/lifestyle, then the appropriate creative strategy may be termed 'transformational' (Puto & Wells, 1984), 'feeling' (Foot, Cone & Belding, 1978), 'emotional' (Young & Rubicam, personal communication).

Consumer decision involvement is a function of the economic, psychosocial, and physical risks associated with purchasing and/or using the advertised brand. If all three risks are low, then the involvement associated with the purchase decision is likely to be low.

The psychological costs associated with making a wrong brand-choice decision are lower if one or more of the following conditions hold – (1) the social influence on the decision is low, (2) perceived differences in the performance of the brands are low, or (3) consumer knowledge of the product category is high.

If consumers are currently using the brand and therefore have considerable knowledge of the brand, then their decision to repeat the brand purchase is likely to have low economic risk (Ehrenberg, 1974; Smith & Swinyard, 1982). Likewise, economic risk will be low if the differences between brands are perceived to be small or the brand price is low.

The following information provided by you contributed to this recommendation:

advertising objective	communicate brand image/mood/lifestyle
brand-usage visibility	low
discretionary purchase	no
physical risk	low
price of brand	low

Note: The references in parentheses in the explanation are outputs from the ADCAD system [Burke, Rangaswamy, Wind & Eliashberg, 1990] and are not included in the list of references for this chapter.

– No model is included when it violates the constraints.
The adbudg model violates the constraints.
Therefore, adbudg is not now included.

It is clear that the latter set, which is rich in the language of market researchers, makes 'obvious' sense while the other does not. Thus, the use of logic does not guarantee expressive representations. It is simply a vehicle for developing such representations. Logic only provides form and not content to a representation. Further, as Birnbaum [1991, p. 67] notes, 'Logically equivalent ways of conceptualizing the world are not functionally equivalent'. Two examples will clarify this point:

– The following two statements are identical in formal logic because the connective AND is commutative:
We advertise AND sales go up.
Sales go up AND we advertise.
However, managers would interpret these two statements differently because they implicitly assign causal directions while formal logic does not. This is a

consequence of the fact that human reasoning is domain-dependent while formal logical inference is domain-independent.

– Suppose it is true that:

Some co-promotions are profitable *AND*

No successful brand is co-promoted.

Then, it is logically valid to conclude that some profitable co-promotions are for brands that are not successful. However, most managers are unlikely to make such a conclusion even if they accept the two premises. Thus, logical inferences could lead to valid conclusions that are functionally irrelevant for the problem domain. This is a 'nuisance' factor associated with traditional logical inference. (By creating explicit links between some of the knowledge elements using a frame-based approach, the modeler can minimize the occurrence of nuisance inferences.)

More such examples could be constructed. The ones here should be enough to suggest that explanations derived exclusively by relying on logic may appear to be contrived. The more complex and contrived an explanation, the less credible it is. This defeats the very purpose for which explanations are generated from decision models in the first place.

In addition to good explanations, the model's structure and operation should appear 'natural' to the users. The underlying model must not only be consistent with the world view of the managers, but must also use a representation that will make this transparent to users. Logic modeling, when carefully applied, enables modelers to design such models. For example, the structure of the decision process is transparent in the representations given in Table 16.2. The benefits from the user's point of view are clear. The model is no longer embedded in an illusion of precision that is formidable to managers.

4.5. *Modeling in data-intensive environments*

Until a few years ago, the elapsed time between marketing data collection and data use was often a few months. Today, the world is very different, especially in the packaged-goods industry. Weekly data are gathered electronically from many sources, including automated capture of transactions data through scanners and salesperson reports generated on PCs. Data from these multiple sources and locations are sent over satellite networks to central databases which are updated frequently. Users in diverse locations are able to log onto these databases, which may be maintained by outside vendors or within a company to access, merge and process many different types of data in a timely manner.

We live in an age of information overload. There is now a data deluge that is taxing our modeling capabilities with conventional approaches.[9] If they wish,

[9] This is a general problem that afflicts the post-industrial society. An interesting case in point is that in combat situations, pilots of the older F-4 jets are often able to perform better than pilots of the more advanced F-16 jets. Apparently, the amount of incoming information, coupled with the limited time available, exceeds the cognitive limits of the F-16 pilots.

brand managers can access data corresponding to each retail chain, in each of several markets, for each brand variety. In addition, they can get the same data for all competitive brands and product categories. Not only is there too much data, but the relative ease of access allows almost everyone in the industry to acquire the same data. As a result of these developments, there is a gradual shift in emphasis from model-based data collection towards data-based model development. Decision modeling has to adjust to these new rhythms. In this environment, AI techniques can enhance opportunistic model development as well as increase the strategic value of decision models. These are described next.

4.5.1. Opportunistic model-building

For the most part, marketing modeling occurs in a 'reactive' mode after the decision-maker has identified problems of interest. It is, however, limiting to think of decision models as simply augmenting decision-making after a problem has been identified. In the classical framework of Simon [1977], problem-solving is viewed as consisting of three phases, namely, intelligence, design and choice. Intelligence corresponds to identification of problems and conditions calling for decisions. The design phase generates many potential solutions to the problem, and choice involves the selection of a particular solution. Conventional modeling focuses on the design and choice phases. On the other hand, opportunistic modeling emphasizes the intelligence phase and views decision support as an 'active intervention' to improve decision-making by helping identify situations that require further evaluation and modeling.

A few attempts in this direction are being made in marketing. COVERSTORY [Schmitz, Armstrong & Little, 1990], INFER [Rangaswamy, Harlam & Lodish, 1991], SHANEX [Alpar, 1991], SCAN*EXPERT [Bayer & Harter, 1991], and several systems described in McCann & Gallagher [1990] are some of the early prototypes. COVERSTORY and INFER attempt to summarize volumes of data into actionable management summaries by interpreting statistical analyses of the data. Most of the other systems rely on heuristics to recognize managerially meaningful patterns from the data. An example of a heuristic is the following rule from McCann & Gallagher [1990, p. 153]:

IF: brand sales > 2*average brand sales and display > 0
THEN: week is a promotional one with some degree of certainty.

In addition to data summarization and interpretation in managerial terms, AI models may be used to recommend appropriate analytical approaches, identify exceptional situations, and suggest follow-up actions. More research needs to be directed towards developing modeling approaches for effectively identifying 'exceptions' in scanner data and suggesting management actions. Frame-based systems appear to be particularly well suited for this domain. Only when systems incorporate knowledge to identify fluctuations from expectations will marketing modeling be truly opportunistic.

4.5.2. Enhancing strategic value of decision models

In the packaged-goods industry, marketing data is a 'commodity' that is widely available. All those with access to the same data and information are unlikely to derive any differential advantage relative to each other. It might appear that some firms could obtain an edge by having superior ability to understand the available data. However, all major competitors also are likely to have equally talented analysts and managers to interpret and act upon the information. Even methods of analyses are being standardized (e.g. logit models, base-line sales, etc.). In such environments, information becomes a strategic necessity [Clemons, 1989], not necessarily a strategic advantage. To derive strategic benefits, the information has to be directed at influencing the deployment of *strategically advantaged resources of the company* [Rangaswamy & Wind, 1991]. Such decisions are less transparent to competitors and less likely to be replicated by others. The strategic resources are idiosyncratic to each company and, consequently, standardized analysis systems may not suffice to transform information into strategic insights. The models should also embed strategic knowledge relevant to the company. Again, AI modeling by providing more flexible and expressive representations is better suited for this purpose.

4.6. AI systems as front-ends and back-ends to conventional decision models

Many decision models are never used by decision-makers because of the difficulties in using them. Knowledge-based systems allow the underlying model to be described in terms familiar to those who have to understand and respond to system output. Features that support tasks such as choosing an existing model from a model base (e.g. selection of an appropriate forecasting model), determining the set of analyses appropriate for a decision situation, and interpreting model results in terms of the semantics of a domain are all improvements that increase the value of conventional decision models. For example, knowledge-based systems for linear programming and statistical packages [Gale, 1986] have been developed to simplify access for novice users. Although these aspects of model development may not interest modelers in academia, the value to decision-makers of simplified access and use should not be underestimated [Dos Santos & Bariff, 1988].

5. Conclusions

Decision modeling is a continuous dialogue between what we believe we know, how we represent what we know as a computer model, and how we enable users to tap into the model to deal with a particular decision situation. AI methods add to the repertoire of concepts and tools available to marketing scientists as they attempt to develop and implement more complex decision models. This chapter has provided a perspective on the current status of decision modeling in marketing and highlighted the potential contributions of AI techniques. The use of AI in marketing modeling is a relatively new field and there remain a number of issues that have to be examined by future research. We highlight some key areas of research for the near future.

Implementation issues. Perhaps the immediate concern is the paucity of reported implementations of AI models in marketing. In line with experiences in other domains, the development of AI systems in marketing has turned out to be a time-consuming affair. In the experience of this author, AI modeling with current tools takes about three times the effort of conventional modeling. It is not surprising that only successful prototypes of knowledge-based systems have so far been reported in the academic literature although some successful implementations have been reported in industry [see Feigenbaum, McCorduck & Nii, 1988]. Most industry applications are aimed at improving consistency of routine decisions involving marketing operations such as credit authorization, rather than for generating insights for managerial decisions.

The first generation of AI-based decision models is now reaching the stage where field testing can occur. There is an immediate need to understand the factors that affect success or failure of implementing these systems in real-world contexts. Careful evaluation of test implementations of systems such as COVERSTORY, SHANEX and ADCAD in managerial situations would be informative. Research aimed at identifying the major organizational factors and system features that contribute to both the short-term and long-term success or failure of implementation would be particularly useful. In evaluating an implementation, it is important to consider both the impact of AI models on decision-making (e.g. do they simply improve the speed and consistency of decision-making or do they also change the way managers make decisions?) and the potential value of the decision models (e.g. whether they are cost-effective and whether they improve the bottom line).

Validation issues. Along with research on implementation, there is a need for broader validation of AI models. Validation involves a comparison of model inputs, processes and outputs to appropriate reference points. The key problem in validating decision models has been the difficulty in identifying suitable reference points. Ideally, a decision model must be validated by comparing it to unambiguous and objective external criteria that are independent of the model (e.g. the presumed truth). This is all but impossible in many managerial situations. Instead, one has to settle for criteria such as correspondence of model outputs with expert judgements, or 'value-in-use' as compared to control groups, status quo time periods, or naive models. For example, if the ADCAD system recommends the use of a celebrity spokesperson, there is no obvious way to assess whether this is an accurate recommendation. One approach would be to use possibly equivocal 'expert judgements' to validate the model. The appropriateness of such criteria and the development of a methodology for carrying out such a validation exercise are worthwhile topics for future research.

There is also a need for evaluating the relative performance of AI models by comparing them to conventional models designed for the same domains. Such studies would help in characterizing the general value of knowledge-based systems in marketing. For example, resource allocation is an area that appears to be amenable to a comparative study. In one such study, Dhar & Ranganathan [1990] compare an integer-programming model for assigning faculty to courses with a knowledge-based system designed to do the same task. They report several advantages for the knowledge-based approach including the relative ease of dealing with multiple objectives, identifying partial solutions, and facilitating plan revisions by providing explanations for model outputs.

Another validation issue is the isolation of the specific components of knowledge systems that improve the decision process and outcomes. For example, it is not clear whether improved explanatory facilities actually lead to improved decisions. While such expressive facilities can certainly enhance the access and use of the system by novice users, do they also improve users' decision performance?

Modeling enhancements. The 'knowledge engineering' process has turned out to be much more complicated than anyone envisioned. The development of a coherent knowledge base of relationships in marketing (i.e. without discrepant elements) is time-consuming. Further, first-generation knowledge systems have encountered difficulties in handling dynamic situations and in faithfully capturing the uncertainties associated with a phenomenon. Similar issues have been encountered in other domains. As a result, there is now a trend towards the development of hybrid systems that combine the benefits of various approaches – the precision of mathematical analysis, the coherence of logical inferences, the structural economy of object-oriented modeling, and the learning abilities of neural networks. A comprehensive formal framework encompassing these diverse approaches is still lacking. Nevertheless, hybrid modeling approaches present a number of new challenges and opportunities for marketing model-builders addressing complex problems. In particular, research in this area enhances the prospects for developing comprehensive decision models that combine quantitative and qualitative relationships relevant to marketing phenomena.

Another research area that can help improve the knowledge-engineering process is the identification of the appropriate ways to partition decision tasks between the human user and the decision model. This requires a better understanding of the relative contributions of humans and computers in broad categories of decision problems such as resource allocation, diagnosis and synthesis. Perhaps, future decision models can be designed to minimize well-known cognitive biases in humans, while at the same time aiding users to exploit their own imagination, creativity and judgment.

Group-decision support. There are also several broader areas of research in decision modeling that arise from developments in computer technologies. Perhaps the most important is the ability to support multiple decision-makers, all of whom have varying types of influence on the decision process. Almost all marketing decision models have been designed to support a single user at a time. However, group-decision support systems [e.g. Nunamaker, Applegate & Konsynski, 1988] is an active area of research that is exploring modeling techniques for supporting group decisions. There are many decision situations in marketing that can capitalize on these developments. For example, group decisions involving marketing, production and design departments are common in new-product development. Negotiation between buyers and sellers is another area that could benefit from decision modeling.

There is now an emerging consensus that the 1990s will see the growth of highly connected computer networks [Malone & Rockart, 1991]. This provides opportunities for conceptualizing and developing decision models that support a number of decision-makers working on the same problem, but who may be geographically and temporally separated.

In conclusion, future research in decision modeling must continue to draw upon insights from a number of disciplines. Decision theory provides a framework to understand how should managers make decisions. OR/MS research provides methods for structuring complex problems to facilitate systematic evaluation. And, AI research is evolving innovative methods for computer representation and manipulation to solve problems that are rich in heuristic and contextual knowledge. Simultaneously, even as decision situations are becoming more complex, computer and information technologies are becoming ubiquitous in executive offices. A confluence of these research traditions, models and trends is imminent. This presents challenging opportunities to both researchers and practitioners interested in marketing decision models. We conclude on the same positive note as did Little [1979]. These are interesting and exciting times for model-builders.

References

Abraham, M., and L.M. Lodish (1987). PROMOTER: An automated promotion evaluation system. *Marketing Sci.* 6(2), 101–123.

Alpar, P. (1991). Knowledge-based modeling of marketing managers problem solving behavior. *Intern. J. Res. Marketing* 8(1), 5–16.

Amstutz, A.E. (1967). *Computer Simulation of Competitive Market Response*, The MIT Press, Cambridge, MA.

Bass, F.M. (1983). A discussion of different philosophies in the analysis of advertising–sales relationships. in F.S. Zufryden (ed.), *Proceedings of the 1983 ORSA/TIMS Marketing Science Conference*, University of Southern California, Los Angeles.

Basu, A.K., R. Lal, V. Srinivasan and R. Staelin (1985). Salesforce compensation plans: An agency theoretic perspective. *Marketing Sci.* 4 (Fall), 267–291.

Bayer, J., and R. Harter (1991). 'Miner', 'Manager', and 'Researcher': Three models of analysis of scanner data. *Intern. J. Res. Marketing*, 8(1) 17–28.

Bensoussan, A., A. Bultez and P. Naert (1978). Leader's dynamic marketing behavior in oligopoly. *TIMS Studies in the Management Sciences* 9, 123–145.

Birnbaum, L. (1991). Rigor mortis: A response to Nilsson's 'Logic and artificial intelligence'. *Artificial Intelligence* 47, 57–77.

Bonczek, R.H., C.W. Holsapple and A.B. Whinston (1981). *Foundations of Decision Support Systems*, Academic Press, New York.

Bultez, A., and P. Naert (1988). S.H.A.R.P.: Shelf Allocation for Retailers Profit. *Marketing Sci.* 7(3), 211–231.

Burke, R.R. (1991). Reasoning with empirical marketing knowledge. *Intern. J. Res. Marketing* 8(1), 75–90.
Burke, R.R., A. Rangaswamy, J. Wind and J. Eliashberg (1990). A knowledge-based system for advertising design. *Marketing Sci.* 9(3), 212–229.
Buzzell, R.D., and P.W. Farris (1976). Industrial marketing costs. Working Paper, Marketing Science Institute, Boston, MA.
Clemons, E.K. (1989). A resource based view of strategic information systems. Working Paper 89-09-14, Decision Sciences Department, The Wharton School, Philadelphia, PA.
Day, R.L. (1962). Linear programming in media selection. *J. Advertising Res.* 2 (June), 40–44.
Dhar, V., and N. Ranganathan (1990). Integer programming vs. expert systems: An experimental comparison. *Comm. ACM* 33(3), 323–336.
Dos Santos, B.L. and M.L. Bariff (1988). A study of user interface aids for model oriented decision support systems. *Management Sci.* 34(4), 461–468.
Eliashberg, J., S. Gauvin, G.L. Lilien and A. Rangaswamy (1992). An experimental study of alternative preparation aids for international negotiations. *J. Group Decision and Negotiation*, 1, 243–267.
Feigenbaum, E., P. McCorduck and H.P. Nii (1988). *The Rise of the Expert Company*, Vintage Books, New York.
Fudge, W.K., and L.M. Lodish (1977). Evaluation of the effectiveness of a model based salesman's planning system by field experimentation. *Interfaces* 8(1), Part 2 (November), 97–106.
Gale, W.A., ed. (1986). *Artificial Intelligence and Statistics*, Addison-Wesley, Reading, MA.
Gensch, D.H. (1973). *Advertising Planning*, Elsevier, New York.
Gensch, D.H. (1984). Targeting the Switchable Industrial Customer. *Marketing Sci.* 3(1), 41–54.
Geoffrion, A.M. (1975). A guide to computer-assisted methods for distribution systems planning. *Sloan Mamagement Rev.* (Winter), 17–41.
Geoffrion, A.M. (1987). An introduction to structured modeling. *Management Sci.* 33(5), 547–588.
Ghosh, A., and S.L. McLafferty (1982). Locating stores in uncertain environments: A scenario planning approach. *J. Retailing* 58(4), 5–22.
Green, P.E. (1963). Bayesian decision theory in pricing strategy. *J. Marketing* 27(1), 5–14.
Guadagni, P.M., and J.D.C. Little (1983). A logit model of brand choice calibrated on scanner data. *Marketing Sci.* 2(3), 203–238.
Hanssens, D., L. Parsons and R. Schultz (1990). *Market Response Models: Econometric and Time Series Analysis*, Kluwer, Dordrecht.
Heckerman, D. (1986). Probabilistic interpretations for MYCIN's certainty factors. In L.N. Kanal and J.F. Lemmer (eds.), *Uncertainty in Artificial Intelligence, Volume 1*, North-Holland, Amsterdam, 167–195.
Heckerman, D., and E.J. Horvitz (1988). The Myth of Modularity in Rule-Based Systems for Reasoning with Uncertainty. In J.F. Lemmer and L.N. Kanal (eds.), *Uncertainty in Artificial Intelligence, Volume 2*, North-Holland, Amsterdam, 23–34.
Horng, S. (1987). Sales response estimation: An analysis of the Delphi method and the integration of Delphi estimates and historical data, unpublished doctoral dissertation, Northwestern University, Evanston, IL.
Howard, R.A. (1989). Knowledge maps. *Management Sci.* 35(8), 903–922.
Huff, D.L. (1964). Defining and estimating a trading area. *J. Marketing* 28(7), 34–48.
Kalagnanam, J., H.A. Simon and Y. Iwasaki (1991). The mathematical bases for qualitative reasoning. *IEEE Expert* 6(2), 11–19.
Keen, P.G.W. (1987). Decision Support Systems: The Next Decade. *Decision Support Systems* 3 (September), 253–265.
Kimbrough, S.O., and R.M. Lee (1988). Logic modeling: A tool for management science. *Decision Support System* 4, 3–16.
Kosko, B. (1992). *Neural Networks and Fuzzy Systsms*. Prentice-Hall, Englewood Cliffs, NJ.
Kosy, D.W. (1989). Applications of explanation in financial modeling. In L.E. Widman, K.A. Loparo and N.R. Nielsen (eds.), *Artificial Intelligence, Simulation and Modeling*, Wiley, New York, 487–510.
Lilien, G.L. (1979). Advisor 2: Modeling the marketing mix for industrial products. *Management Sci.* 25(2), 191–204.

Lilien, G.L., and P. Kotler (1983). *Marketing Decision Making – A Model Building Approach*, Harper & Row, New York.
Lilien, G.L., P. Kotler and K.S. Moorthy (1992). *Marketing Decision Making – A Model Building Approach*, Prentice-Hall, Englewood Cliffs, NJ.
Little, J.D.C. (1970). Models and managers: The concept of a decision calculus. *Management Sci.* 16 (April), B466–B485.
Little, J.D.C. (1975). BRANDAID: Part I: Structure; Part II: Implementation. *Oper. Res.* 23, 628–673.
Little, J.D.C. (1979). Decision support systems for marketing managers. *J. Marketing* 43 (Summer), 9–26.
Little, J.D.C. (1983). Comments on Bass, 'A discussion of different philosophies in the analysis of advertising–sales relationships', In F.S. Zufryden (ed.), *Proceedings of the 1983 ORSA/TIMS Marketing Science Conference*, University of Southern California, Los Angeles.
Little, J.D.C., and L.M. Lodish (1969). A media planning calculus. *Oper. Res.* 17(1), 1–34.
Lodish, L.M. (1971). CALLPLAN: An interactive salesman's call planning system. *Management Sci.* 18(4) (Part II), 25–40.
Malone, T.W., and R.F. John (1991). Computers, networks and the corporation. *Sci. Amer.* 265(3), 128–136.
McCann, J.M., and J.P. Gallagher (1990). *Expert Systems for Scanner Data Environments*. North-Holland, Amsterdam.
McCann, J., A. Tadlaoui and J. Gallagher (1990). Knowledge systems in merchandising: Advertising design. *J. Retailing* 66(3), 257–277.
Montgomery, D.B., A.J. Silk, and C.E. Zaragoza (1971). A multiple product sales force allocation model. *Management Sci.* 18(4), Part II, 22–31.
Moorthy, K.S. (1993). Theoretical modeling in marketing. *J. Marketing* 57 (April), 92–106.
Naert, P.A., and P. Leeflang (1978). *Building Implementable Marketing Models*, Martinus Nijhoff, Leiden and Boston.
Naert, P.A., and M. Weverbergh (1981). Subjective versus empirical decision models. In R.L. Schultz and A.A. Zoltners (eds.), *Marketing Decision Models*, Elsevier, New York, 99-123.
Nilsson, N.J. (1991). Logic and artificial intelligence. *Artificial Intelligence*, 47, 31–56.
Nunamaker, J.F., L.M. Applegate and B.R. Konsynski (1988). Computer-aided deliberation: Model management and group decision support. *Oper. Res.* 36(6), 826–848.
Pearl, J. (1988). *Probabilistic Reasoning in Intelligent Systems: Networks of Plausible Inference*, Morgan Kaufmann, Palo Alto, CA.
Ram, S., and S. Ram (1988). INNOVATOR: An expert system for new product launch decisions. *Appl. Artificial Intelligence* 2, 129–148.
Rangan, V.K. (1987). The channel design decision: A model and an application. *Marketing Sci.* 6(2), 156–174.
Rangaswamy, A., J. Eliashberg, R. Burke and J. Wind (1989). Developing marketing expert systems: An application to international negotiations. *J. Marketing* 53(4), 24–49.
Rangaswamy, A., B. Harlam and L.M. Lodish (1991). INFER: An expert system for automatic analysis of scanner data. *Intern. J. Res. Marketing* 8(1), 29–40.
Rangaswamy, A., P. Sinha and A. Zoltners (1990). An integrated model-based approach for sales force structuring. *Marketing Sci.* 9(4), 279–298.
Rangaswamy, A., and Y. Wind (1991). Information technology in marketing. In Allen Kent and J.G. Williams (eds.), *Encyclopedia of Microcomputers* 9, Marcel Dekker, New York, 67–83.
Rao, A.G., and P.B. Miller (1975). Advertising/sales response functions. *J. Advertising Res.* 15, 7–15.
Robinson, J.A. (1965). A machine-oriented logic based on the resolution principle. *J. ACM* 12(1), 23–41.
Romaniuk, S.G., and L.O. Hall (1991). Injecting Symbol Processing into a Connectionist Model. In Branko Souček (ed.), *Neural and Intelligent Systems Integration*, Wiley, New York, 383–406
Schmitz, J.D., G.D. Armstrong and J.D.C. Little (1991). COVERSTORY – Automated news finding in marketing. *DSS-90 Trans.* 46–54.
Schultz, R.L., and A.A. Zoltners, eds. (1981). *Marketing Decision Models*. Elsevier, New York.
Scott Morton, M.S. (1971). *Management Decision Systems: Computer Based Support for Decision Making*, Harvard Business School Division of Research, Cambridge, MA.

Sharda, R., S.H. Barr and J.C. McDonnell (1988). Decision support system effectiveness: A review and an empirical test, *Management Sci.* 34(2), 139–159.

Shortliffe, E.H. (1976). *Computer-Based Medical Consultation: MYCIN*, Elsevier, New York.

Silk, A.J., and G.L. Urban (1978). Pre-test market evaluation of new packaged goods: A model and measurement methodology. *J. Marketing Res.* 15 (May), 221–234.

Simon, H.A. (1977). *The New Science of Management Decision.* Prentice-Hall, Englewood Cliffs, NJ.

Sombé, L. (1990). *Reasoning under Incomplete Information in Artificial Intelligence.* Wiley, New York.

Thuraisingham, B. (1989). From rules to frames and frames to rules; Knowledge-based system design. *AI Expert*, 4(10), 30–38.

Urban, G.L. (1969). A mathematical modeling approach to product line decisions. *J. Marketing Res.* 6 (February), 40–47.

Urban, G.L. (1970). SPRINTER MOD III: A model for the analysis of new frequently purchased consumer products. *Oper. Res.* 18, 805–854.

Urban, G.L., J.R. Hauser, and J.H. Roberts (1990). Prelaunch forecasting of new automobiles. *Management Sci.* 30(4), 401–421.

Urban, G.L., and G.M. Katz (1983). Pretest-market validation and managerial implications. *J. Marketing Res.* 20 (August), 221–234.

Wierenga, B. (1990). The first generation of marketing expert systems. Working Paper No. 90-009, Marketing Department, The Wharton School, Philadelphia, PA.

Winston, P.H. (1984). *Artificial Intelligence*, Addison-Wesley, Reading, MA.

Zoltners, A.A. (1981). Normative marketing models. In Randall L. Schultz and A.A. Zoltners (eds.), *Marketing Decision Models*, Elsevier, New York, 55–76.

Zoltners, A.A., and P. Sinha (1980). Integer programming models for sales resource allocation. *Management Sci.* 26(3), 242–260.

J. Eliashberg and G.L. Lilien, Eds., *Handbooks in OR & MS, Vol. 5*

Chapter 17

Marketing Strategy Models*

Yoram (Jerry) Wind
The Wharton School, University of Pennsylvania, Philadelphia, PA 19104, USA

Gary L. Lilien
Pennsylvania State University, University Park, PA 16802, USA

1. Introduction

Many of the models and approaches outlined in other chapters of this book address single marketing issues (promotional spending, pricing, salesforce deployment, etc.) within the context of any organization where other factors are assumed constant. For the most part, such approaches are 'bottom-up', and closely akin to the operational philosophy of traditional OR/MS.

Consider, in contrast, a large organization with several business divisions and several product lines within each division. Marketing plays a number of roles throughout that organization.

At the organizational level, marketing can provide both perspectives and information to help management decide on what the mission of the corporation should be, what the opportunities of the organization might be, what strategies for growth it might have, and how it might develop and manage its portfolio of businesses. The resulting corporate policies provide guidelines for development of strategy at each business division. And, at the lowest level, the managers of each product and/or market within each division develop their own marketing strategies within the context of the policies and constraints developed at divisional levels.

We use the term *strategic management process* to describe the steps taken at the corporate and divisional level to develop market-driven strategies for organizational survival and growth, while we use the term *strategic marketing process* to refer to the parallel steps taken at the product and/or market level to develop viable marketing plans and programs. Thus, the strategic marketing process takes place within the larger strategic management process of the organization.

Thus, in contrast with many of the approaches outlined in earlier chapters, marketing strategy models must reflect the overall corporate mission of the

*The authors would like to thank Josh Eliashberg for his extraordinary efforts in making this paper happen and Adam Fein for his assistance.

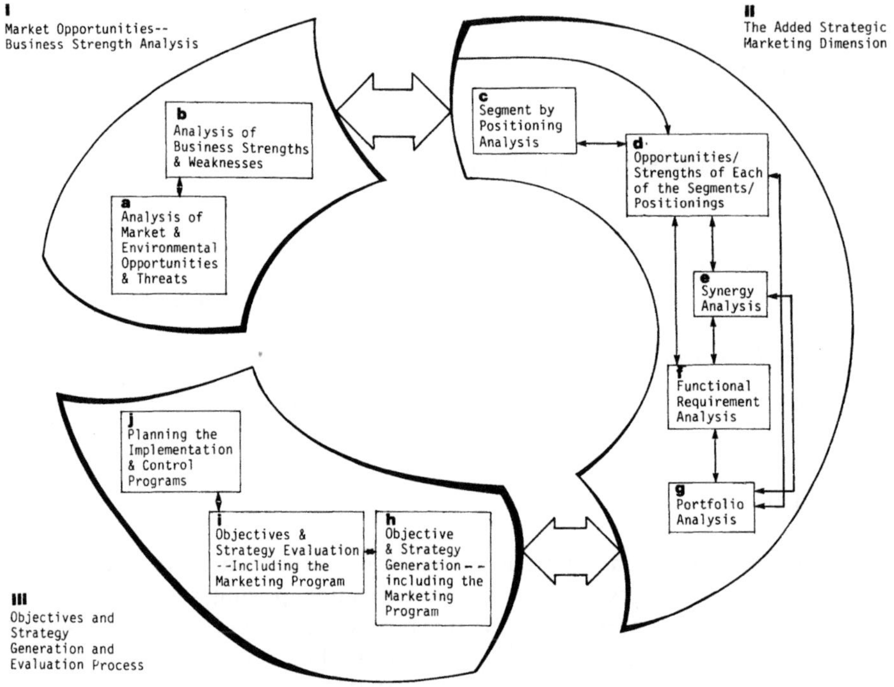

Fig. 17.1. A marketing-oriented approach to strategy formulation and evaluation (source: Wind & Robertson [1983, p. 16]).

organization. While the domain of marketing strategy models is murky, there are clearly a number of strategic marketing problems that have yet to be adequately addressed with existing models. One purpose of this chapter is to highlight those gaps and to propose and illustrate some solutions.

We take a broad view of the definition of strategy models in this chapter, including management-science models and less traditional process models which apply to the generation, evaluation and selection of strategic options at (1) the product/market level; (2) the strategic-business-unit level (which can include a number of product/market units); and (3) the corporate level (which can include a number of strategic business units).

The models and processes that are often employed in the development of marketing strategy and marketing-driven business (and corporate) strategy can be divided into three sets of models. These are highlighted in Figure 17.1 and include:

(1) A traditional assessment of market opportunities and business strengths, including:
    (a) analysis of opportunities and threats;
    (b) analysis of business strengths and weaknesses.
(2) Marketing-strategy analysis including:
    (c) segmentation and positioning analysis which provide the foundation for the selection of target segments and product-positioning;

(d) opportunity analysis linking the segments/positioning to market opportunities and business strengths/weaknesses;
(e) synergy analysis focusing on the positive and negative synergies in advertising, distribution, manufacturing, and so on, among products, segments and marketing-mix components;
(f) functional requirements analysis which include the specification of the key success factors in each segment/positioning and the company's competencies and abilities to satisfy those requirements;
(g) portfolio analysis, the analytical core of the process providing an integrated view of the product, market segments and businesses.

(3) Generation and evaluation of objectives and strategies, including:
(h) generation of objectives and strategies;
(i) evaluation of objectives and strategies;
(j) implementation, monitoring and control of the program.

The range of analytical approaches and models that underlie these ten phases highlight the broad scope of marketing strategy models. Lilien, Kotler & Moorthy [1992] use Figure 17.1 as a framework to discuss seven types of models that are designed to overcome the seven key limitations of current marketing strategy efforts. The seven model categories they discuss and the limitations they attempt to overcome are highlighted in Table 17.1. The types of models that Lilien, Kotler & Moorthy discuss include BRANDAID, ADVISOR, the PIMS ROI PAR Model, the Analytic Hierarchy Process, portfolio models, and others. Indeed, an informal survey we conducted of a number of leading marketing scholars aimed at identifying key marketing strategy models elicited these models and other models such as ASSESSOR [Silk & Urban, 1978; IRI, 1985], BASES [Burke Marketing Services, 1984], NEWPROD [Cooper, 1988], and POSSE [Green, Carroll & Goldberg, 1981].

Most of these models have been around for at least a decade. They include both models that focus on a specific element of the marketing mix and models that

Table 17.1
Seven limitations of typical marketing strategy and the type of marketing strategy models that can be used to address these limitations (source: Adapted from Lilien, Kotler & Moorthy [1992, pp. 508–509].)

Limitation of typical marketing strategy [Wind & Robertson, 1983]	The modeling solution
1. Improper analytic focus	Market definition and market structure
2. Functional isolation	Integration, especially models of cost dynamics (scale and experience effects)
3. Ignoring synergy	Marketing-mix/product-line methods
4. Short-run analysis	Dynamic models, especially product life-cycle analysis models
5. Ignoring competition	Competitive-analysis models
6. Ignoring interactions	Proper market-definition models
7. Lack of integrated view	Integrated models including shared-experience models such as PIMS, product-portfolio models and normative resource-allocation models

address business-strategy issues. The most serious problem with these and similar marketing strategy models is that most of them are *not* commonly used by management. Our work indicates that the reason for the lack of use includes the following:

- The models are *not* addressing the key strategic issues facing management.
- The models tend to focus on brand strategy and are not aimed at the higher-level business and corporate strategies of the firm.
- The most challenging parts of strategy are problem definition and generation of strategic options. Yet, most of the models are of little help in this area.
- Many of the models and especially those based on market data, may provide some useful input to the decision, but do not facilitate the process of making the strategic choice.
- Most of the models are *not* 'user-friendly'.
- Most of the models do not address the current key concerns of top management such as the introduction of quality, 'reengineering' key processes, becoming customer-driven, time-based competition, capitalizing on the enormous advances in information technology, globalization of customer and resource markets, and the shift from hierarchical to less hierarchical cross-functional team-empowered organizations.

These concerns have led to a growing gap between the supply of marketing-science-based strategy models and the demand for and use of these models.

The gap is especially striking given the advances in marketing science, as evident in the papers in *Marketing Science*, *Management Science* and similar publications. (See Chapter 1 for some empirical evidence.) In addition, the increasing receptivity and concern by management with the need to become more customer-oriented makes this gap even more difficult to accept.

The theme in this chapter is that there are many important OR/MS developments in marketing strategy models that are already available. Those developments, despite their low level of utilization, have the potential, once 'reengineered', to enhance the creativity, rigor and value of the marketing strategy process.

The chapter is organized as follows:

Following this section, we provide a taxonomy of strategy models and review what is currently available in Section 2. That section focuses mainly on what we refer to as 'traditional' OR/MS models. We include several examples of those traditional approaches in Section 3. In Section 4, we develop some non-traditional models, aimed at addressing some of the barriers to use, while Section 5 demonstrates the value of some of these non-traditional approaches. Section 6 provides a vision for strategy models in the 21st century and Section 7 draws conclusions.

2. Strategy models: Progress to date

Table 17.2 presents a taxonomy of marketing strategy models structured around six key attributes:

Table 17.2
A taxonomy of strategy models and assessment of current offerings

	No effort	Some effort		Significant effort	
		Limited utilization	Broad utilization	Limited utilization	Broad utilization
1. Focus					
1.1. Specific marketing-mix components					
1. Segmentation					*
2. Positioning					*
3. New products					*
4. Product line					*
5. Pricing					*
6. Promotion					*
7. Distribution					*
8. Advertising					*
9. Salesforce					
10. Public relations and public affairs		*			
1.2. Integrated marketing program		*			
1.3. Business strategy		*			
1. Overall business strategy		*			
2. Joint decision with other management functions		*			
a. Marketing–operations		*			
b. Marketing–R & D–operations–human resources	*				
c. Marketing–human resource	*				
d. Marketing–finances	*				
1.4. Corporate strategy		*			
1. Portfolio models					
2. Resource allocation models			*		
3. Simulations		*			
4. Screening models		*			
5. Process models		*			
2. Geographic and industry scope					
2.1. Geographic					
1. Global		*			
2. Regional		*			
3. Country		*			
4. Region within country		*			
2.2. Industry					
1. Consumer					
a. frequently purchased products					*
b. durables				*	
2. Industrial products and services		*			

Table 17.2. (cont'd)

	No effort	Some effort		Significant effort	
		Limited utilization	Broad utilization	Limited utilization	Broad utilization
3. Objectives of models					
A. Problem definition	*				
B. Generation of strategy options		*			
C. Evaluation of strategy options				*	
D. Optimal allocation of resources		*			
E. Selection of strategy		*			
F. Help implement the strategy					
4. Inputs					
4.1. 'Hard data'	*				
1. External					
a. Customers					
b. Competitors				*	
c. Other stakeholders					
d. Market performance type	*		*		
data (PIMS, etc)			*		
2. Internal					
a. Accounting, sales, profit					
4.2. Incorporate outcome of formal market analysis					
1. Conjoint analysis		*			
2. Brand-choice models		*			
3. Multidimensional scaling		*			
4. Diffusion models		*			
5. Econometric modeling		*			
6. Forecasting:		*			
a. Analogies		*			
b. Concept testing		*			
c. Pre-test-market models		*			
d. Test-market models		*			
e. Early sales models		*			
4.3. Integrate 'hard' data with management subjective judgments					
5. Type of model					
5.1. (1) Stand-alone vs. (2) part of a larger system				(1)	
5.2. (1) Descriptive vs. (2) predictive vs. (3) prescriptive				(1)	
5.3. (1) Static vs. (2) dynamic		(1)			
5.4. (1) Deterministic vs. (2) stochastic		(1)			
5.5. (1) Stand-alone models vs. (2) part of DSS		(1)			
5.6. Facilitate sensitivity analysis		*			
5.7. Process model		*			

Table 17.2. (cont'd)

	No effort	Some effort		Significant effort	
		Limited utilization	Broad utilization	Limited utilization	Broad utilization
6. The output–'benefits'					
6.1. 'Quality' of the selected strategy					
1. Short-term	*				
2. Long-term	*				
6.2. Speeding up decision-making	*				
6.3. Higher likelihood of successful implementation	*				
6.4. Enhance the unit/Create value		*			

– the focus of the model,
– the geographic and industry scope of the model,
– the objective of the model,
– the input to the model,
– the type of model,
– the output of the model.

The table also includes our subjective assessment of the current strategy models on two dimensions – the number of models in each category (none, little, or many) and the degree of utilization of these models (limited or broad).

The key models in each of the categories are identified below and discussed in the context of some general observations about the table.

2.1. The focus of marketing strategy models

2.1.1. Specific marketing-mix components

Market segmentation. The selection of target market segments is (together with the positioning decision) the foundation for most marketing programs. Yet there are few models for the selection of market segments. The segmentation decision is one of the major meeting grounds between marketing research and modeling, since models used for the selection of target segments require considerable information on the size of segments, their key characteristics, expected competitive activities, and expected market response of given segments to the offering of the firm and its competitors. Among the segmentation models used are normative models which try to offer prescriptive guidelines [Moorthy, 1984]. Also, models such as POSSE [Green, Carroll & Goldberg, 1981] and the Analytic Hierarchy Process (AHP) have been used effectively. POSSE is a decision support system for making product design decisions. The approach uses conjoint analysis to identify the relation between the attributes possessed by a product and the desirability of that product, for each of a set of potential customers. In a second step, the level of market demand for any potential product is estimated by aggregating the individual preference models across customers. An optimization routine then reveals the most desirable product (or products) in terms of some specific management objective (e.g. maximizing incremental market-share). This objective may take into account the presence of specific other products in the market and/or any cannibalization effect of the new product on specific existing products. The market segment most attracted to this optimal new product is identified [Green, Carroll & Goldberg, 1981]. For further discussion, see Green & Krieger [1989]. An AHP analysis is especially appropriate when one considers the portfolio of segments that product management, the SBU, or the firm wishes to reach. An example of the use of AHP to select a portfolio of segments is included in Section 5.

Positioning. Given the importance of positioning as the foundation of marketing strategy [Wind, 1990], it is not surprising that much attention has been given to the development of positioning models. Multidimensional scaling, clustering and conjoint analysis have been used primarily for positioning analysis [e.g. Wind, 1982]. Operational models for positioning strategy include multidimensional scaling and optimization models such as POSSE, which help to select a product's best position and then find the best market segment; or, alternatively, selects a target segment and then find the product's optimal position. Analytical models prescribing target positioning under various scenarios have also been developed [Eliashberg & Manrai, 1992]. AHP analysis has also been used to find the best positioning to reach selected target segments. A good review article on this topic is Green & Krieger [1989].

New product and product-line decisions. Marketing-science models have been applied to the entire range of product decisions from the generation of new product ideas to the evaluation of ideas, concepts and products, to new-product launch, to the management of the product life-cycle, and finally to product deletion [Urban & Hauser, 1980; Wind, 1982]. These models have encompassed all of the major modeling and research developments in marketing. They have been subject to some of the more creative modeling efforts which include simulated test markets and innovative models for new-product design optimization, product-line decisions and new-product forecasting models. For review articles of many of the models see Shocker & Hall [1986], Wilson & Smith [1989], Green & Krieger [1985] and Mahajan & Wind [1986].

Pricing. Most applied pricing models are aimed at assessing the price-sensitivity of the market. They include experimentation, econometric modeling, conjoint analysis, and a variety of consumer surveys focusing on customer attitudes toward price, price perceptions and expectations. Most conjoint-analysis models include price as a factor, leading to the determination of price-elasticity. More specialized models, such as the Mahajan, Green & Goldberg [1982]. Elasticon models, offer insights into the cross-elasticity of demand and the expected impact of price changes on brand shares. There is also increasing interest in bidding models, game-theoretic models for competitive pricing [Eliashberg & Jeuland, 1986], quantity discounts [Monahan, 1984], and identifying the best pricing strategy–not just the price itself but a number of associated 'services' such as terms of payment, premiums and life-cycle costing (Chapter 11).

Promotion. The proliferation of scanner data has resulted in a flood of models to measure the effects of sales promotional programs. The PROMOTER model by Abraham & Lodish [1987], for instance, uses artificial-intelligence technology. It offers on-line computer access to evaluate sales promotion programs using measures such as incremental sales and profit, consumer pull-through, and comparisons with other company sales promotions and those of competitors.

Distribution. Channels of distribution have also received attention by marketing scientists, focusing mainly on identifying the best distribution outlets [Rangan, 1987]. The tremendous growth of *direct-marketing* activities has led to significant modeling and research activities. This modeling is often linked to experimentation and is aimed at establishing the most effective direct-marketing program.

Advertising. Advertising models encompass copy-testing, media selection, advertising pulsing, campaign scheduling, and advertising budgeting [Burke, Rangaswamy, Wind & Eliashberg, 1990; Horsky & Simon, 1983]. Advertising is included in most market response models where it is used to assess the relative contribution of advertising to product sales, market share, or diffusion patterns [Eastlack & Rao, 1986]. Much of the recent development is associated with new research methods and the design of test markets where split-cable technology links with consumer-panels data collection and experimentally assesses the effect of different advertising strategies.

Salesforce. Significant modeling has been done in the salesforce area, focusing on allocations of salespeople to territories, territory realignment, frequency of sales calls, and scheduling of sales calls [Zoltners & Sinha, 1983]. Salesforce expenditures are often included as part of market response models. Analytical models have also examined the related issue of salesforce compensation [Basu, Lal, Srinivasan & Staelin, 1985].

Public relations and public affairs. Public relations focuses on communication with the desired target segments and other external stakeholders. Although this function is typically outside the responsibilities of marketing, public-relations and public-affairs programs should be consistent with the overall marketing strategy of the firm. Modeling activities from the advertising and communication areas could be applied here.

2.1.2. The integrated marketing program

An important modeling area which has had limited usage in practice is the modeling of the entire marketing program. Such models tend to focus on the interaction among the various marketing-mix variables. BRANDAID [Little 1975] is one of the few models that focuses on the entire marketing-mix program. This model, discussed in greater detail in Section 3.1, is a decision support system with modular components that are developed individually and then put together to form a customized marketing-mix program. Despite its early promise, BRANDAID is not commonly used by management.

Promising developments in the marketing-mix area include studies and models of synergy among the various marketing-program elements and approaches that allow for the development of an *integrated* program. These developments include the simultaneous selection of a target market segment, desired product-positioning, and the identification of a creative strategic thrust that links these with the rest of the marketing program. The AHP [Saaty, 1980; Wind & Saaty, 1980; Dyer & Forman, 1991] has been useful for this purpose.

2.1.3. Business strategy models

Overall business strategy models. Models that focus on business strategy can greatly benefit from a marketing-science perspective. Most notable in this regard are the PIMS-based models – PAR ROI and LOOK ALIKE ANALYSIS – and the portfolio models. They are discussed in more detail in the next section.

Portfolio by products, market segment and distribution outlets. One of the key decisions facing any business manager is the determination of the desired portfolio of products by market segment by distribution-outlet-type. This decision involves (1) an analysis of the current product, market and distribution portfolio and (2) the selection of the desired portfolio of products, market segments and distribution outlets. The analysis of the current product, market and distribution portfolio follows two major approaches: (1) factor listing and (2) determination of target portfolio.

Factor listing considers the factors used in making decisions on the width and depth of the portfolio. Product-portfolio models offer a more structured set of dimensions on which the current portfolio models can be analyzed. These dimensions include market share (as a measure of the business's strength) and market growth (as a measure of the business's attraction), as well as profitability, expected return, and risk. Most models focus on two dimensions – company (product) capabilities and market-attractiveness. Yet, the specific dimensions vary from one portfolio model to another. They include models with a normative set of dimensions (such as share and growth or risk and return) and the more flexible customized portfolio models which identify dimensions that management considers relevant.

Following an assessment of the existing (and any potential new) products of the firm on the chosen dimensions, the major managerial task is to decide on the desired target portfolio. The target portfolio should not be limited only to products. Ideally, it would also include target market segments and distribution outlets. Such a portfolio reflects management's objectives, desired direction of growth, and the interactions (synergy) among products, market segments and distribution outlets [Wind, 1982].

Joint decisions with other management functions. A relatively new area of investigation involves the development of joint-optimization-type models. Most notable among these efforts are some initial development of joint marketing-and-operations optimization models, focusing on new-product design [Cohen, Eliashberg & Ho, 1992] and pricing decisions [Eliashberg & Steinberg, 1987].

As the acceptance of marketing orientation increases, one would expect the other business functions to include marketing considerations in their functional plans, and, to the extent possible, utilize appropriate marketing-science research and models. Yet little progress in the direction has been seen to date.

2.1.4. Corporate strategy models

Corporate strategy models include portfolio models, resource-allocation models, simulations, some (venture) screening models and strategy process models.

Portfolio models. These include the standardized portfolio models introduced by consulting firms such as the BCG growth–share matrix and the GE/McKinsey market-attractiveness–business-strength matrix. Given the limitations of these models (as discussed in Wind, Mahajan & Swire [1983]), a number of customized portfolio models have been developed and employed. These include both modification of the customized portfolio models as well as specially designed conjoint-analysis-based and Analytic Hierarchy Process (AHP)-based portfolio models. Key characteristics of the customized models are their focus on management's criteria for evaluating strategic options and the focus on the allocation of resources among the portfolio elements while offering diagnostic guidance to corporate strategy involving the portfolio elements. (We develop some portfolio models in Section 3.)

Resource-allocation models. Given the importance of prioritization of objectives, strategies and businesses, management uses a variety of resource-allocation models. These range from the use of simple heuristics (such as matching a successful competitor), through models that help quantify management subjective judgments such as the AHP, to optimization-type models. The more powerful of these models tend to be based on market-response elasticities. The problem, however, is that the closer the model is associated with market response data, the less comprehensive it is in terms of the other key strategy determinants (such as likely competitor activities, technology, etc.). There are a number of elegant resource-allocation models such as STRATPORT [Larréché & Srinivasan, 1981, 1982]. Yet, their usage is quite limited. (We discuss STRATPORT in Section 3.2.)

Simulations. Business simulations are quite common. One of the first major business simulations was designed by Amstutz in the early 1960s [Amstutz, 1967]. Yet it has not been employed widely due to its complexity and unrealistic data requirements. Forrester [1961] represents another attempt to employ dynamic simulation models to aid strategic decision-making. Today, most simulations are designed and used for education purposes as business games. A significant number of firms do use business simulations as part of their business and/or corporate strategy. In recent years, some simulations have been developed as games adding an entertainment component to the business strategy and educational goals [Reality Technologies, 1990].

Screening models. The increased reliance on external sources of business expansion (i.e. licensing, forming strategic alliances, merging or acquiring products, businesses or even entire firms) has led to the development of screening models. Among the more popular of these models are discriminant analysis on the key discriminating characteristics of 'successful' vs. 'unsuccessful' entities.

Most of these models have been developed by firms that were able to put together a database on successful vs. unsuccessful products or businesses. At the product and SBU level, there have also been significant efforts to develop cross-industry databases. The most popular ones are the NEWPROD model for product screening [Cooper, 1988], and the PIMS database for business screening and evaluation [Buzzell & Gale, 1987].

A comparison of the NEWPROD cross-industry model with a customized industry-specific model developed by a pharmaceutical firm suggests that an industry-specific approach leads to better predictions. Yet, given the speed and cost at which one can get an answer from one of the cross-industry databases, both types of screening models have their role.

Process models. These are the most popular of the models used in the corporate strategy area. Most strategy books [Lorange, 1980; Day, 1986; Aaker, 1992], propose a process-flow model for strategy development. These are often used as blueprints for the design of strategy generation and evaluation processes.

2.2. Geographic and industry scope

2.2.1. Geography

Most of the marketing-science-based strategy models are domestic in nature. A number of the models have focused on segments and several have been applied to regions. The regional focus has received increased attention as a number of manufacturers of frequently purchased consumer goods, such as Campbell Soup, have restructured their operations along regional lines.

The few global models have focused on country selection [Wind, Douglas & LeMaire, 1972], global portfolio of countries and global portfolio of countries by segment by mode of entry [Wind & Douglas, 1981].

Despite the growing interest in regional blocks (i.e. European Community, NAFTA, etc.), none of the marketing-science models have focused on the development or evaluation of regional strategies.

2.2.2. Industry

Most of the brand-specific models have been developed for frequently purchased products, while a few (such as diffusion models–Chapter 6) focus primarily on consumer durables. With the exception of conjoint-analysis-based strategy models, which have been applied primarily to industrial and quasi-industrial products such as pharmaceuticals, little attention has been given to industrial goods and services. Services, including growth areas such as entertainment and leisure activities, have received less attention and, to date, have benefited very little from marketing-science-based strategy models.

2.3. Objectives of models

Current marketing strategy models focus on evaluation of strategic options and on optimal allocation of resources. Little attention has been given to models that help management define and formulate the problem, that help generate creative options, that help select a strategy, or that help implement the strategy. The latter category has been almost completely ignored in the marketing-strategy literature.

This lopsided focus on strategy evaluation overlooks the potential that marketing-science methods have in helping management in the process of:

- *Problem definition*: Scenario planning [e.g. Shoemaker, 1991], stakeholder analysis, SWOT analysis (strength–weakness, opportunities and threats), marketing audit, benchmarking, positioning analysis, and similar analyses can all help in defining the problems facing the firm.
- *Generation of strategic options*: The various approaches marketing scientists have been using for the generation of new-product ideas can all be used for the generation of strategic options. For a discussion of these approaches, and their application to the generation of strategic options, see Wind [1982, 1990]. The most powerful of these approaches are morphological analysis and stakeholder analysis.
- *Selection of a strategy*: The Analytic Hierarchy Process has been effective in helping management structure a problem hierarchically, evaluate the various options on a set of criteria, and make a choice following appropriate sensitivity analysis. For a review of AHP-based applications to marketing-strategy problems, see Wind & Saaty [1980], Dunn & Wind [1987] and Saaty [1990].
- *Help in implementing the selected strategy*: One of the major advantages of an AHP-like approach is that the participants in the process tend to 'buy in' and support the group decision, an important benefit considering the typical difficulty in implementation.

2.4. Inputs

2.4.1. 'Hard data'

One of the unique contributions of marketing science to business strategy is the nature of the inputs it provides to strategy models. Given the 'boundary' role of marketing, and its traditional focus on understanding consumer behavior, it is not surprising that marketing-science-based strategy models emphasize information about the consumers. More recently, the scope of marketing has been expanded to include all stakeholders. Figure 17.2 presents the '6C' model which emphasizes the need for expanding the scope of the inputs to the marketing strategy models,

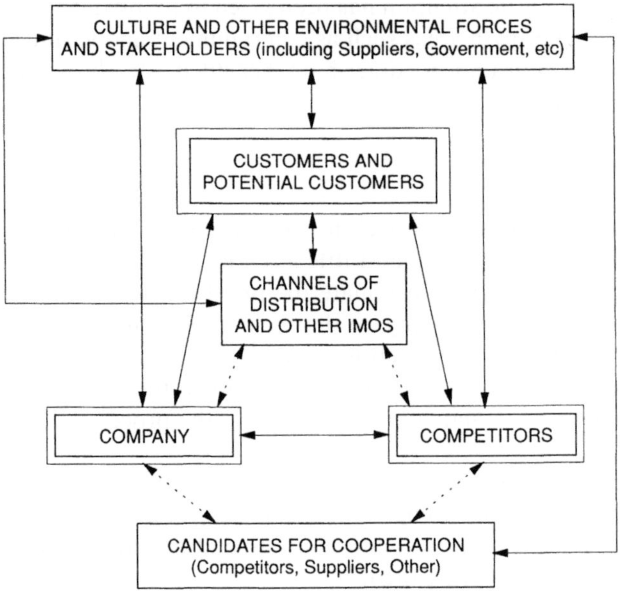

Fig. 17.2 The 6C model: an expanded view of the focus of marketing strategy models.

as well as the models themselves from the traditional 2C or 3C models – the 'company–customer' or the 'company–customer–competition' – to all the relevant stakeholders.

Many marketing-science models use data on consumer behavior generated from surveys, experiments, or secondary data services. These include scanner data and associated single-source data for frequently purchased consumer products, various forms of prescription data for the pharmaceutical industry, etc. Whereas most of the secondary data services include information on competitors as well, such data is typically at the product level and not the SBU or corporate level.

When surveys are used, they often collect data about perception preferences and reported behavior. Few syndicated data services are available to monitor the behavior of other stakeholders.

At the SBU level, important data services are the PIMS and Federal Trade Commission databases, as well as the databases of Dunn and Bradstreet and other information providers. Company-internal data are often important inputs to strategy models. These data often have significant problems concerning accuracy of profit figures, appropriateness of analytic unit (i.e. segments, distribution outlets), etc. Internal data should generally be supplemented with external data on relative competitive performance such as market-share, positioning and customer-satisfaction data.

2.4.2. Incorporate outcome of formal market analysis

A major advantage of marketing-science-based strategy models is that they can incorporate the outputs of formal market analyses including:

- the results of conjoint-analysis studies (see Chapter 10),
- brand-choice models (see Chapter 2),
- multidimensional scaling (see Chapter 5),
- diffusion models (see Chapter 8),
- econometric modeling (see Chapter 9).

2.4.3. *Management subjective judgment*

An important component of all strategy models is management subjective judgment. Strategy models vary with respect to the degree of formalism and qualification of management subjective judgment. AHP-based models, for instance, are based on management subjective judgment and incorporate 'hard' market data through management's assessment of the results of available studies. Most other strategy models do not explicitly incorporate management subjective judgment and thus leave management the task of deciding what to do.

2.5. *Type of model*

Marketing strategy models include a variety of models that can be classified on seven dimensions:

2.5.1. *Stand-alone vs. part of a larger system*

Most current models are developed on a stand-alone basis. Since most decisions require more than the output of a specific model, this may be one of the reasons for the relatively poor utilization of marketing strategy models. Consider, for example, the need to decide on a pricing strategy for a new product. Models for estimating the consumer price-elasticity, for example, are useful input to the decision, but must consider issues such as the likely trade reaction, likely competitive and government reaction, and the implication of the initial pricing on the firm's ability to change prices in the future.

2.5.2. *Descriptive vs. predictive vs. normative*

Models are often classified based on their primary objective. Most consumer-based marketing models have tended to be *descriptive* in nature. The interest in *predictive* models is evident from the many forecasting models in use. And MS/OR has always encouraged the development of *normative* models. The best strategy models should encompass all three objectives.

2.5.3. *Static vs. dynamic models*

Most models tend to be static in nature. Given the dynamic nature of business, there is a great interest in dynamic models, which consider factors such as competitors' reactions to the firm's strategy; entry of new competitors; changes in government regulations and technology; and changes in consumer demographics, needs and behavior. These and other dynamic factors are often dealt with via simulations, sensitivity analysis, and occasionally by complex analytical models.

2.5.4. Deterministic vs. stochastic models

Major developments in stochastic brand-choice models include the incorporation of marketing-mix variables and the use of these models as a basis for laws of market behavior. The Hendry system [Kalwani & Morrison, 1977], for example, partitions and defines a market in terms of current market-shares and a switching constant. Based on this, it calculates a par share for a new-brand entry and suggests implications for the new brand and its competitors.

Despite stochastic model developments and the obvious stochastic nature of marketing phenomena, most marketing models, especially those used at the SBU and corporate levels, are deterministic in nature. Even most new-product diffusion models have been mostly deterministic.

2.5.5. Stand-alone models vs. part of decision support systems

Many of the early marketing models had a single focus. A number of these models were linked to marketing decision support systems (MDSS) – a coordinated collection of data, models, analytical tools and computing power that help managers make better decisions. MDSSs generally replaced marketing information systems, which often failed because of lack of user-orientation. User-orientation and friendly marketing decision support systems are emerging, but are still quite limited in their diffusion. MDSSs utilize computer technology (including personal computers); artificial-intelligence approaches; management judgments; inputs on market, competitive and environmental conditions; and models of the market plan. Encouraging developments in this area include expert systems and their incorporation as part of a decision support system (Chapter 16).

2.5.6. Sensitivity analysis

Given the uncertainty surrounding most marketing strategy decisions, it is often beneficial to conduct sensitivity analysis to assess the sensitivity of the results to different assumptions. Simulation-based models and the AHP are especially conducive to sensitivity analysis.

2.5.7. Process models

Models of processes such as new-product development or a new-product launch, are common. They differ from traditional strategy models in their focus on the set of activities that should be considered to yield a set of actions. The most advanced strategy process models are those involving the various steps in the development of new products [Crawford, 1991]. More recently, with the increased attention to cross-functional processes, there has been an invigorated search for the design of processes for speeding up decisions and activities, incorporating customer/market input in the firm's decision, enhancing quality, etc. [Kleindorfer & Wind, 1992].

2.6. *The output-benefits of the models*

Aside from the obvious output of any model – has it answered the question that it has designed to answer? – little attention has been given to the four critical benefits of:

(1) The quality of the selected strategy. Did the model offer a solution that enhanced the short- and long-term quality of the selected strategy?
(2) The acceleration of decision-making and the resulting actions. The increased focus on time-based competition has not found its way to most of the strategy models, except for a few process models that are designed to speed up key processes.
(3) The enhancement of the likelihood of successful implementation. With the exception of the AHP, little attention has been given to this benefit in designing strategy models.
(4) The improvement of the unit's ability to create value. Given that a major objective of any business is value creation, it is important to assure that any major activity such as the design and implementation of strategy models will enhance the user's ability to create value.

3. Traditional strategy model examples

In this section, we discuss four types of strategy models: BRANDAID, STRATPORT, financial-portfolio models, and the PIMS shared-experience approach, in terms of their structure and applications.

3.1. BRANDAID

BRANDAID [Little, 1975] is a flexible marketing-mix model not linked to a specific database. The model is different from the other published efforts in that (1) its structure is generally inclusive (at the expense of leaving many parts of the model calibration to the manager), and (2) it is modular and flexible, providing specific, customized submodels that can be used or not used as desired.

Figure 17.3 shows the marketing system to be modeled. The elements are a manufacturer, competitive manufacturers, retailers, consumers and the general environment. The model is clearly addressed at consumer packaged goods.

Model structure. The model structure is based on the concepts of product-class and brand sales rates:

$$m_i(t) = \frac{s_i(t)}{S(t)}, \quad \text{market share of } i \text{ at } t, \tag{1}$$

where

$s_i(t)$ = sales of brand i at t,
$S(t)$ = product-class sales at t.

In addition, the model develops an annual profit rate, $z_i(t)$:

$$z_i(t) = g_i(t)s_i(t) - \text{marketing-cost rate} \tag{2}$$

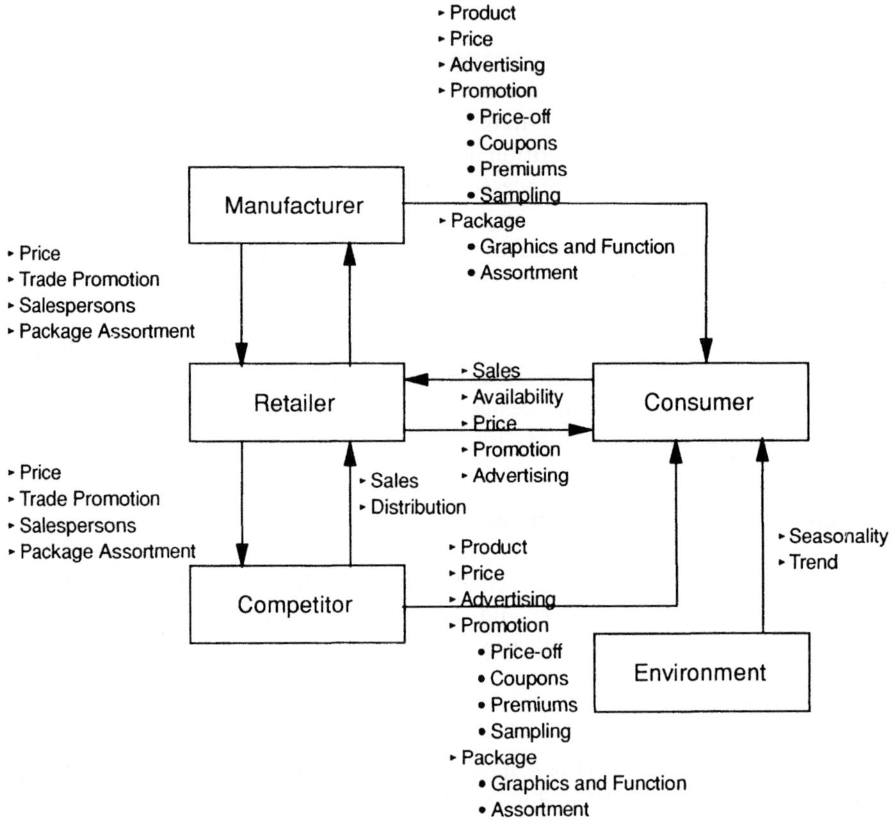

Fig. 17.3. The BRANDAID view of the marketing system to be modeled (source: Little [1975]).

where $g_i(t)$ is the contribution of brand i (in dollars per sales unit).

For a given brand (dropping the subscript i), the brand sales rate $s(t)$ is expressed as a reference value modified by the effect of marketing activities and other sales influence. The structure of the model is:

$$s(t) = S_0 \prod_{i=1}^{I} e_i(t) \tag{3}$$

where

S_0 = reference-brand sales rate, dollars per customer per year,
$e_i(t)$ = effect index in brand sales of the sales influence, $i = 1, \ldots, I$ (I = number of sales indices).

The specific submodels are described next, in turn. In each case, we drop the subscript i in $e_i(t)$ for t the particular promotional activity because it will be clear from the context.

Advertising submodel. The advertising submodel starts with the brand's sales at a reference value and assumes that there exist some advertising rate that will maintain sales at that level. This rate is called the maintenance or reference advertising rate. When advertising is above reference, sales are assumed to increase; below reference, they decrease.

The dynamics of the process are captured in the following equation:

$$e(t) = \alpha[e(t-1)] + (1-\alpha)r(a(t)) \tag{4}$$

where

$e(t)$ = advertising-effect index at time t,
$r(a)$ = long-run sales response to advertising (index),
α = carryover effect of advertising per period,
$a(t)$ = advertising rate at time t in dollars.

Operationally, the advertising rate is the rate of messages delivered to individuals by exposure in media paid for in dollars. Thus,

$$a(t) = \frac{h(t)k(t)X(t)}{h_0 k_0 X_0} \tag{5}$$

where

$X(t)$ = advertising spending rate,
$h(t)$ = media efficiency at t,
$k(t)$ = copy-effectiveness of t,
X_0, h_0, k_0 = reference values of the above quantities.

The model can also incorporate a memory effect:

$$\hat{a}(t) = \beta\hat{a}(t-1) + (1-\beta)a(t) \tag{6}$$

where

$\hat{a}(t)$ = effective advertising at t,
β = memory constant for advertising (fraction per period).

Price submodel. The price-index submodel has the form:

$$e(t) = r[a(t)]\,\Psi[X(t)] \tag{7}$$

where

$e(t)$ = effect of brand price on share at t,
$a(t) = x(t)/x_0$ = relative price,
$X(t)$ = manufacturer's brand price,
$r(a)$ = response function,
$\Psi(x)$ = price-ending effect.

Salesforce submodel. The salesforce submodel is also structured in the form of a response function. Salesperson effort is defined as

$$a(t)=\frac{h(t)k(t)X(t)}{h_0 k_0 X_0} \tag{8}$$

where

$X(t)$ = salesperson-effort rate, dollars per customer per year,
$h(t)$ = coverage efficiency, calls per dollar,
$k(t)$ = effectiveness in store, effectiveness per call,
$a(t)$ = index of normalized salesperson effort rate.

To account for memory and carryover effects, the following equation is employed:

$$\hat{a}(t)=\beta\hat{a}(t-1)+(1-\beta)a(t) \tag{9}$$

where

$\hat{a}(t)$ = effective effort at t,
β = carryover constant for memory effect (fraction per period).

Finally, the salesperson-effect index includes a carryover (loyalty) constant α, as well as a response function:

$$e(t)=\alpha e(t-1)+(1-\alpha)r(\hat{a}(t)). \tag{10}$$

Other influences. Other influences, such as seasonality, trends, package changes, and the like, can be handled by direct indices. For example, trend can be treated as a growth rate. In this case a trend would be modeled as

$$e(t)=e_0\prod_{i=1}^{t}[1+r(i)] \tag{11}$$

where $r(i)$ is growth rate in period i.

Competition. In BRANDAID, competition is handled in the same way as direct sales effects; each effect (competitive advertising, competitive pricing, etc.) goes into the model either as an index or as an additional submodel, depending on the level of detail available.

Application. The implementation of BRANDAID can be viewed as the development of a decision support system for aiding brand-management decisions. Little recommends a team approach to implementation; the ideal team involves an internal sponsor, a marketing manager, a models person on location, and a top-management umbrella.

Calibration of the model involves two types of data: state data (reference values of sales, share, product-class sales, etc.) and response information. The former are easy to obtain; the latter require a creative blending of judgment, historical analysis, tracking (running the model on past data and getting managers to review the results and, if necessary, refine parameters), field experimentation, and adaptive control (the formal processes of using marketing activities to refine parameter estimates through an ongoing measurement process).

Little describes a case, called GROOVY, for a well-established brand of packaged goods sold through grocery stores. The model tracked sales well over a five-year period and has proven useful for advertising, pricing and promotional planning. For example, by tracking months 72 to 78, analysis made it clear that year-to-date sales were good. However, since most of the year's advertising was spent, most of the promotional activity was over, and price had been increased, the prospects for the rest of year were bleak. The brand manager used this analysis to support a request for additional promotional funds, a proposal accepted by management. This action 'almost certainly would not have been taken without the tracking and forecasting of the model'.

In spite of this illustration the rich BRANDAID structure is apparently too complex for most managers to use and its operational impact has been slight.

3.2. *STRATPORT*

As theory and understanding about the factors underlying effective strategies are emerging, normative product-portfolio models that incorporate those ideas are also emerging. The STRATPORT model of Larréché & Srinivasan [1981, 1982] is an example of an integrative, normative approach.

STRATPORT focuses on the allocation of marketing resources across business units; it is not concerned with the allocation of resources within business units. The business units are assumed to be independent of one another – they share no experience-curve synergies or marketing synergies. The model is structured around two time-frames: the planning period and the post-planning period, common to all business units. Changes in market shares are assumed to be accomplished during the planning period, while the post-planning period captures the long-term profit impacts of the strategy implemented during the planning period, and the market shares are treated as if they had remained constant during this time. Marketing expenditures and changes in working capital follow the evolution of sales. In the model, the following notation is used. Time is at the end of period t. Flow variables (cost, revenue, production) have a start time and end time. Thus, ${}_{t1}C_{t2}$ is the cost from t_1 to t_2 and C_t is the cost from 0 to t. Also, T is the length of the planning period, and $S-T$ is the length of the post-planning period.

The driving force behind the model is the set of business-unit market shares $\{m_{Ti}\}$, $i=1,\dots,N$. The problem is then to find $m_{T1},\dots,m_{TN}$ to

$$\text{maximize} \quad \pi = \sum_{i=1}^{N} \pi_i(m_{Ti}) \tag{12}$$

$$\text{subject to} \quad Z_{1i} \leqslant m_{Ti} \leqslant Z_{2i}, \quad i=1,\dots,N, \tag{13}$$

$$F = \sum_{i=1}^{N} F_i(m_{Ti}) \leqslant \Delta \tag{14}$$

where

π = long-term profit,
Z_{1i}, Z_{2i} = limits imposed by management,
F = cash flow need during planning period,
Δ = net cash-flow limit.

Equation (12) represents total profit during the planning horizons (in constant dollars), Equation (13) represents the upper and lower limits on market share, and Equation (14) represents the cash-flow constraint. In effect, Equation (14) is not fixed since the value of Δ can be affected by borrowing. The constrained optimization problem (12)–(14) can be solved using the generalized Lagrange multiplier method [Everett, 1968].

We now consider the components of the model for a single business unit, dropping the i subscript (business-unit notation). The effect of marketing investment during the planning period is modeled by the market response function:

$$m_T = 1 + (U - L)\left(\frac{E^{\alpha}}{B + E^{\alpha}}\right) \tag{15}$$

where

L, U = lower and upper limits on m_t $(0 \leqslant L \leqslant U \leqslant 1)$,
α, B = parameters to be estimated,
E = marketing expenditures.

The evolution of market share from m_0 at 0 to m_T at T is modeled as

$$m_i = m_0 + (m_T - m_0)f(t) \tag{16}$$

where

$$f(t) = \left(\frac{t}{T}\right)^{\beta}, \quad \beta > 0. \tag{17}$$

Thus, values of β greater than 1 lead to a slow approach to m_T, while values of β near 0 lead to a rapid approach to ultimate shares.

The model assumes that industry demands are exogenous, given by $\{M_t\}$. Then the total production for the firm is given by

$$P_T = \sum_{t=1}^{T} \left(\frac{m_{t-1} + m_t}{2}\right) M_t \tag{18}$$

where the market share during a period is approximated by its average values.

Combining Equations (16), (17) and (18) yields:

$$P_t = k_1 + k_2 m_T \tag{19}$$

where k_1 and k_2 are constants that can be evaluated numerically following some algebra [Larréché & Srinivasan, 1982].

Total costs are driven by the experience curve and are modeled as:

$$C_T = \frac{C}{1-\lambda}[({}_{tF}P_T)^{1-\lambda} - ({}_{tF}P_0)^{1-\lambda}] \tag{20}$$

where

C_T = total cost of units sold,
λ = learning or experience constant,
${}_{tF}P_T$ = cumulative production from time of product introduction to end of planning horizon.

A similar expression is derived for costs during the post-planning period.

Industry unit price is assumed to fall with industry cumulative experience as:

$$p_I = pI^{-\eta} \tag{21}$$

where

p_I = average industry unit price,
I = industry cumulative value (in units),
p = constant,
η = industry learning constant, which potentially changes over time ($\eta > 0$).

Now following the reasoning in Equation (20), we get

$${}_{t1}Q_{t2} = \frac{p}{1-\eta}[({}_{t1}I_{t2})^{1-\eta} - ({}_{t1}I_{t1})^{1-\eta}] \tag{22}$$

where ${}_{t1}Q_{t2}$ is industry revenue from start time for industry (t_1) to present (t_2). The price set by the firm may be higher or lower than the industry price, so the firm's revenue during time period t is modeled as:

$${}_{t-1}R_t = \omega_{t-1}Q_t\left(\frac{m_t + m_{t-1}}{2}\right) \tag{23}$$

where ω is ratio of firm's price to industry average price. Revenue during the post-planning period is modeled similarly.

A market share of m_t at T requires production capacity of

$$X = m_T M_T. \tag{24}$$

If the current plant capacity is X_0 and $X_0 < X$, capacity-expansion expenditures will be incurred during the planning period; if $X < X_0$, then liquidation of excess capacity can generate a cash inflow. The capacity expenditures corresponding to X are modeled as

$$Y = \left(\frac{bX^{\gamma}}{a + X^{\delta}}\right) - q \tag{25}$$

where

Y = capacity-expansion expenditures,
q = cash value of divesting entire current capacity,
a, b, γ, δ = positive constants, with $0 < \gamma - \delta < 1$.

Expenditures above what is spent (through C_t and ${}_tC_s$ in the form of depreciation) during the planning period are expressed as a fraction (θ_1) of Y: $Z = \theta_1 Y$.

We also need to adjust C_t by an amount A, which represents the depreciation over the period 0 to T of assets acquired prior to $t = 0$.

In general, a change in market share calls for a change in working capital, modeled as a function of revenue in period t:

$$g_t = \alpha({}_{t-1}R_t)^{\beta} \quad (\alpha, \beta > 0) \tag{26}$$

The change in working capital corresponding to the change in market share is given by $g_t - g_0$. To avoid double-counting the working capital expenses included in C_t, we only take a fraction θ_2 of $g_t - g_0$:

$$G = \theta_2(g_T - g_0) \tag{27}$$

where G is the additional required working capital.

Let V denote the proportion of the firm's revenue spent to maintain market share at m_T; V is modeled as

$$V = d - e(m_T - L) \tag{28}$$

where d and e are constants to be determined. The cost of maintaining share from t to $t+1 (t \geqslant T)$ is

$${}_tH_{t+1} = V_t R_{t+1} \tag{29}$$

and from Equations (28) and (29), we get

$${}_tH_{t+1} = d_t R_{t+1} - e_t R_{t+1}(m_T - L). \tag{30}$$

The value of profit from the business unit can now be calculated as

$$\pi = (R_T + {}_TR_S) - (C_T + {}_TC_S) - (E + {}_TH_S) \tag{31}$$

where expressions for terms on the right-hand side of Equation (31) are developed above. Similarly, the cash flow need for the business unit during the planning period is

$$F = E + C_T - R_T + Z + G - A \tag{32}$$

where, again, the expressions are given above, and discounted dollars are used in all expressions. To account for taxes, we must multiply Equation (31) by (1 – tax rate), as we must also do for E, C_T and R_T in Equation (32).

Risk can be handled by discounting business units at different discount rates, reflecting their different risk profiles.

Application. Given a specific portfolio strategy, the model described above can evaluate its profit implications and cash-flow needs. In addition, STRATPORT has an optimization module to determine the best allocation of resources among business units with the maximum net present value over the time horizon, subject to market-share and cash-flow constraints. The cash-flow constraint can be evaluated over ranges of borrowing activity, if desired. One can utilize STRATPORT to update, via its optimization routine, $\{M_T\}$ which can be obtained initially by standard forecasting techniques. For more details of the solution algorithm and an illustrative run of the model, see Larréché & Srinivasan [1981, 1982].

However, as with BRANDAID, the model's richness and comprehensiveness has severely limited its use.

3.3. *Financial/product portfolio models*

STRATPORT incorporates risk in an implicit manner. Financial-portfolio-based models deal with risk explicitly. The financial approach to the portfolio-selection problem assumes that the profits from portfolio items (such as product lines, stocks, bonds, etc.) are random variables, and estimates concerning their distribution (subjective or objective) are known. Furthermore, the rates of profit for different items may be correlated and hence the need to examine the portfolio items collectively. The expected rate of return on a portfolio is simply the weighted average of the expected rates of return of the items contained in that portfolio, i.e.

$$\bar{R}_p = \sum_{i=1}^{m} w_i R_i, \qquad \sum_{i=1}^{m} w_1 = 1, \tag{33}$$

where w_i is the portion of funds invested in item i, R_i is the expected value of return for item i, m is the total number of items in the portfolio, and $\bar{R}_p$ is the expected rate of return for the portfolio. If variance is used as the measure of risk associated with a portfolio, it may be obtained by

$$V_p = \sum_{i=1}^{m} \sum_{j=1}^{m} w_i w_j \sigma_{ij} \tag{34}$$

where V_p is the portfolio variance, w_i and w_j are the portions of funds invested in items i and j, respectively, and σ_{ij} is the covariance between returns of items i and j.

The systematic steps that characterize the portfolio selection decision may be stated:

(1) *Determine all possible items to be considered in the portfolio and generate all feasible portfolios.* The major objective of this step is to specify a finite number (m) of items and generate a set of feasible portfolios. The number of feasible portfolios can be determined by generating combinational solutions to the equation $\sum_{i=1}^{m} w_i = 1$ within the constraints imposed on the values of w_i.

(2) *Generate the admissible (efficient or undominated) portfolios.* The objective here is to reduce the large number of feasible portfolios to a smaller number using certain 'efficient' rules. These rules are derived by making certain stated assumptions on the nature of the investor's underlying utility function. The reduced number of portfolios are termed efficient, admissible, or undominated portfolios. Although a number of efficient rules have been proposed in the financial literature, we concentrate on mean–variance (EV) and stochastic dominance (SD) rules for generating efficient product portfolios.

(3) *Determine the optimal portfolio from the admissible portfolios.* The efficient rules provide a mechanism to divide the feasible portfolios into two groups: those dominated by others and those not dominated by others. The undominated or admissible portfolios provide a smaller set of alternatives from which the optimal choice can be made by obtaining further information on the investor's utility function (risk/return trade-off).

The most widely used efficiency criterion for portfolio selection is the mean–variance (EV) rule suggested by Markowitz [1959]. Since the decisions about investment may be viewed as choices among alternative probability distributions of returns, the EV rule suggests that, for risk-averse individuals, the admissible set may be obtained by discarding those investments with a lower mean and a higher variance. That is, in a choice between the two investments, designated by return distributions F and G, respectively, a risk-averse investor is presumed to prefer F to G, or to be indifferent between the two if the mean of F is as large as the mean of G and the variance of F (reflecting the associated risk) is not greater than the variance of i.e., if $\mu_F \geqslant \mu_G$ and $\sigma_F^2 \leqslant \sigma_G^2$. Furthermore, if at least one of these inequalities is strict, then some investors prefer F to G in the strict sense, and F is said to dominate G in the sense of EV. In this case, G can be eliminated from the admissible set. If only one of the inequalities holds, the selection depends on the individual's personal mean–variance trade-off, and neither F nor G can be eliminated under the EV dominance rule. The rule can be applied easily to the portfolio-selection problem by ordering all portfolios by increasing means and excluding any portfolio i such that the variance of portfolio i is greater than or equal to the variance of portfolio j where $i < j$.

In spite of its popularity, the mean–variance approach has been subject to criticism as it requires specific information about the firm's utility function and ignores information about the complete distribution of the firm's returns.

To address these concerns, Hillier [1969] has proposed, for instance, the following approach. Let X_j be the random variable that takes on the value of the net cash-flow during the time period j, where $j = 0, 1, 2, \ldots, n$. Let i_j be the rate of interest, commonly referred to as the cost of capital, which properly reflects the investor's time-value and time-preference of money during the period j. The present value, P, of this investment or set of investments can then be defined as

$$P = \sum_{j=0}^{n} \left[\frac{X_j}{\prod_{k=1}^{j} (1 + i_k)} \right]. \tag{35}$$

Consider a set of m proposed investments. Define the decision variable δ_k as

$$\delta = \begin{cases} 1, & \text{if the } k\text{th proposed investment is approved,} \\ 0, & \text{if the } k\text{th proposed investment is rejected} \end{cases} \tag{36}$$

for $k = 1, 2, \ldots, m$.

Let $\delta = (\delta_1, \delta_2, \ldots, \delta_n)$. Assume that the investments can generate incoming (positive) or outgoing (negative) cash flows immediately and during some or all of the next n time periods, but not thereafter. Let the random variable $X_j(\delta)$ be the net cash-flow during time period j ($j = 1, 2, \ldots, n$). Let $U(p)$ be the utility if p is the realized present value of the approved set of investments. Let S be the set of feasible solutions, i.e. the subset of $[\delta \mid \delta_k = 0 \text{ or } 1;\ k = 1, 2, \ldots, m]$ whose elements are feasible decision vectors.

The problem that can be formulated to determine $\delta \in S$ so as to

$$\text{maximize} \quad \mathrm{E}[U(P(\delta))],$$

where

$$P(\delta) = \sum_{j=0}^{n} \frac{X_j(\delta)}{\prod_{k=1}^{j} (1 + i_k)\delta}. \tag{37}$$

This problem can be reformulated in a chance-constrained programming format. Hillier [1969] provides other solutions or approximate solutions under various conditions.

Another approach to the problem is the stochastic-dominance approach [Hadar & Russell, 1971]. Stochastic dominance is a relationship between pairs of probability distributions; in particular, it involves comparison of the relative positions of the cumulative distribution functions. Three types of stochastic-dominance rules have generally been presented for decision-making under uncertainty: first-order stochastic dominance (FSD), second-order stochastic dominance (SSD), and third-order stochastic dominance (TSD). These rules have been derived by considering certain stated assumptions on the form of the utility function U. If U', U'' and U''' stand for the first, second and third derivatives of the utility function, the FSD rule assumes that $U' \geqslant 0$; the SSD rule assumes that $U' \geqslant 0$ and $U'' \leqslant 0$, and the TSD rule assumes that $U' \geqslant 0$, $U'' \leqslant 0$ and $U''' \geqslant 0$. That is, the FSD rule requires only that the first derivative of the utility function be everywhere non-negative. These assumptions are clearly more reasonable than the assumptions of a quadratic utility function with increasing absolute risk-aversion implied by the EV rule. These stochastic-dominance rules result in the following:

(1) the FSD rule provides the efficient set of portfolios for all decision-makers with utility functions increasing in wealth;
(2) the SSD rule provides the efficient set of portfolios for the subset of decision-makers having increasing utility functions and risk-aversion;
(3) the TSD rule provides the efficient set of portfolios for the subset of risk-averse decision-makers with decreasing absolute risk.

The optimal portfolio for the investor can then be determined, based on his/her risk–return trade-off, from among the relevant smaller set of admissible choices.

Applications. Cardozo & Wind [1985] have suggested a modification of the risk–return portfolio model which overcomes some of the difficulty involved in applying the conventional model of the product-portfolio decisions. They report an application in one company whose disguised name is The Monitrol Company.

Discussion with executives revealed that Monitrol's performance was affected by three distinct sets of factors, corresponding to three distinct markets. On that basis, the company's product-market investments were divided into three separate business units which shared some support services, but were independent with respect to demand.

The business unit whose experience is described here contained four product lines, each of which had a different application in a technical market. These application markets were not related, and could be considered distinct and independent markets. The four lines shared some production and engineering facilities with each other and with the other two business units. Monitrol executives believed that resources relinquished by any one product line could be readily employed by other lines or units.

Using the portfolio approach required 10 managers within the business unit to: (a) forecast earnings for each product line; (b) identify the principal factors affecting those earnings, construct scenarios around these factors, and estimate the likelihood of occurrence of each of several scenarios or descriptions of future environments; (c) quantify these estimates and array them in table and chart form, then construct an efficient frontier, and (d) assess the trade-off between risk and return. Managers began by forecasting returns for the four product lines in the business unit during the coming three years (Monitrol's planning period), based on projections from historical experience and forecast changes in the environment. Managers' initial responses encompassed a wide range of estimates. They were then asked to specify the conditions under which the lowest and highest estimates would likely occur.

This procedure helped identify several factors on which one set of values would lead to high returns; another, to low returns. Managers next selected the major factors or 'driving forces' that were most critical in influencing returns. They identified two factors that were likely to account for most of the variation in future earnings: (1) whether a dominant competitor would attempt to limit the extent to which Monitrol and other small manufacturers could supply products compatible with a new product line it was introducing to replace existing products, and (2) the rate at which users accepted new technology pioneered by the dominant competitor and the new products associated with that technology.

After managers had described these factors, they were asked to specify ranges of values on each factor that would produce noticeable differences in returns. They divided the first factor into three ranges, 'favorable', 'neutral' and 'unfavorable'; the second into four, ranging from almost no adoption to prompt conversion of the entire industry. On that basis the authors constructed 12 scenarios (three values on the first factor times four values on the second).

Managers were also asked to estimate the likelihood that each of the 12 scenarios would in fact accurately describe the environment during the coming three years. Managers dismissed five scenarios as having less than one chance in 20 of occurring. After comparing and contrasting the remaining seven scenarios, managers decided that the ranges of values they had originally specified on each factor was unnecessarily detailed, and that two values on both the first factor ('favorable' or 'unfavorable' attitude) and the second ('rapid' or 'slow' adoption) would adequately describe what might happen. This redefinition allowed the authors to reduce the number of scenarios to four.

Finally, managers were asked to estimate the likelihood that each scenario would occur. Although individual managers' estimates differed somewhat, the group

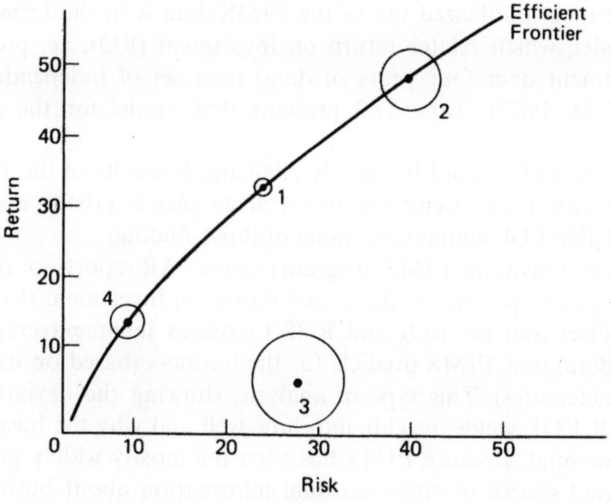

Fig. 17.4. Monitrol's current portfolio (source: Cardozo & Wind [1985]).

agreed that there was little reason to consider one scenario more or less likely to occur than any other. Managers also concluded that together the four scenarios represented a full range of foreseeable outcomes. (Subjective estimates like these could – and to the extent possible should – be supplemented with market research data in the form of conditional forecasts.)

This information was converted into forecast returns for a three-year planning period for each of four investments under four environmental scenarios and then converted into the return–risk chart in Figure 17.4, showing the efficient frontier for the business unit's current investments.

Monitrol managers recognized that investment 3 (control systems) appeared to offer lower returns than investments 1, 2 and 4 and higher variance than investments 1 and 4. This information prompted Monitrol executives to examine ways to reduce resources allocated to the control-systems line.

Mahajan & Wind [1985] describe the limitations of the financial-portfolio approach to product-portfolio problems and modifications needed to make the approach more easily applicable.

3.4. The shared-experience approach: PIMS

The PIMS (profit impact of marketing strategy) project began in 1960 at General Electric as an intra-firm analysis of the relative profitability of its businesses. It is based on the concept that the pooled experiences from a diversity of successful and unsuccessful businesses will provide useful insights and guidance about the determinants of business profitability. The term 'business' refers to a strategic business unit, which is an operating unit selling a distinct set of products to an identifiable group of customers in competition with a well-defined set of competitors. By the mid-1980s, the data base of about 100 data items per business included about 3000 businesses from about 450 participating firms.

Perhaps the most publicized use of the PIMS data is in the form of the PAR regression model, which relates return on investment (ROI, i.e. pretax income/average investment over four years of data) to a set of independent variables [Buzzell & Gale, 1987]. Table 17.3 presents that model for the entire PIMS database.

The most widely cited (and frequently challenged) results of the PIMS studies are associated with market selection and strategic characteristics associated with profitability: Table 17.4 summarizes some of those findings.

Firms participating in the PIMS program receive PAR reports for their business, which provides a comparison of the actual return on investment (ROI and ROS) of their businesses and the ROI and ROS (= pretax income/average sales over four years of data) that PIMS predicts for the business (based on its market and strategic characteristics). This type of analysis, showing the deviation of actual ROI from PAR ROI, yields insights into how well and why the business has met its strategic potential. Because PIMS has been the mostly widely publicized and widely supported source of cross-sectional information about business strategy, the results emerging from the program have undergone considerable scrutiny.

Table 17.3
The PIMS profitability equation; multiple regression equation for ROI and ROS (entire PIMS database) (source: Buzzell & Gale [1987, p. 274])

Profit influences	Impact on: ROI	ROS
Real market-growth rate	0.18	0.04
Rate of price inflation	0.22	0.08
Purchase concentration	0.02**	N.S.
Unionization, %	−0.07	−0.03
Low-purchase amount:		
Low importance	6.06	1.63
High importance	5.42	2.10
High-purchase amount:		
Low importance	−6.96	−2.58
High importance	−3.84	−1.11**
Exports–imports, %	0.06**	0.05
Customized products	−2.44	−1.77
Market share	0.34	0.14
Relative quality	0.11	0.05
New products, %	−0.12	−0.05
Marketing, % of sales	−0.52	−0.32
R & D, % of sales	−0.36	−0.22
Inventory, % of sales	−0.49	−2.09
Fixed capital intensity	−0.55	−2.10
Plant newness	0.07	0.05
Capacity utilization, %	0.31	0.10
Employee productivity	0.13	0.06
Vertical integration	0.26	0.18
FIFO inventory valuation	1.30*	0.62
R^2	0.39	0.31
F	58.3	45.1
Number of cases	2314	2314

Note: All coefficients, except those starred, are significant ($p < 0.01$).
*Significance level between 0.01 and 0.05.
**Significance level between 0.05 and 0.10.
ROI = return on investment
ROS = return on sakes

These criticisms fall into three main categories: specification problems, measurement error, and interpretation. Most of these criticisms are summarized in Anderson & Paine [1978], Lubatkin & Pitts [1983, 1985], Chussil [1984] and Ramanujam & Venkatraman [1984].

In terms of *specification*, questions have been raised about the structure of the regression model – whether additive effects, multiplicative effects, interactions, multicollinearity, or heteroscedasticity exist. Furthermore, the use of ROI forces a short-term focus on strategy questions, and there is misspecification resulting from the presence of an investment term (investment intensity) among the

Table 17.4
General PIMS principles relating marketing selection, strategic planning and profitability (source: Buzzell & Gale [1987])

Some market characteristics associated with higher profitability
- Market growth
- Early life-cycle
- Higher inflation
- Few suppliers
- Small purchase levels
- Low unionization
- Higher exports/low imports

Some strategic factors associated with higher profitability
- Higher market-share
- Low relative costs
- High perceived quality
- Low capital-intensity
- Intermediate level of vertical integration

independent variables, leading to a significant relationship with the dependent variable. In addition, the omission of business goals and the structure of the organization may be a problem, and the disguising of sales data and other units only allows the modeling of operating ratios. For some analyses this feature may lead to spurious relationships [see Lilien, 1979; Jacobson, 1990a, 1990b; Buzzell, 1990; Boulding, 1990].

In terms of *measurement error*, it is inevitable that different firms, with different accounting methods, interpretations, and levels of understanding of the data requirements, will provide noisy data. The potential significance of this problem was underscored by Rurnelt & Wensley [1980], who report little stability in the market-share estimates when different measures were correlated over different time periods. These types of problems are inherent in shared data; users of the results need to be made aware of the extent of the possible problem.

Potentially, the most serious problem is in the *interpretation*. The PIMS results are norms; therefore, the equations do not have a casual interpretation. High market-share and high profit occur together. Although it is tempting to predict the consequences on profitability of changes in the independent variables of the PAR model, it is not reasonable to do so. Lack of information about goals and the extent to which certain strategies, exercised over time, were able to achieve those goals make the problem more severe.

The PIMS models and database provide an important empirical base and structure for asking questions about strategy. The results, however, should be used cautiously.

4. Non-traditional models for marketing and business strategy

In this section, we highlight some of the models which offer valuable guidance to marketing strategy and marketing-driven business strategy although they do not follow the tradition of analytical models.

The 'non-traditional' models we discuss are of three types:

(1) Models for generating creative strategic options:
   – approaches borrowed from the new-product idea-generation area,
   – meta-analysis;
(2) Models addressing specific strategy needs such as:
   – creating a corporate and business vision,
   – scenario planning,
   – benchmarking,
   – portfolio analysis and strategy;
(3) Models that facilitate integration of 'hard' market data with management subjective judgments.

4.1. Models for generating creative strategic options

One of the most ignored areas of management-science models in general, and marketing strategy models in particular, is the generation of creative options. Yet, option generation may have the greatest strategic impact. Sophisticated evaluation models are not very useful if applied to a conventional set of 'me too' strategic options. Thus, greater attention should be given to the generation of innovative options.

4.1.1. Approaches borrowed from the new-product idea-generation area

In deciding how to generate creative strategic options, one can benefit from the approaches to the generation of new-product ideas.

Most of the approaches for generating new-product ideas can also be used to generate strategic options. Thus, the approaches listed in Table 17.5 (and discussed in Wind [1982, Chapter 9] should be considered.

Table 17.5
Approaches to the generation of new-product ideas (source: Wind [1982])

Source	Research approach	
	Unstructured	Structured
Consumers	Motivation research Focused group interviews Consumption system analysis Consumer complaints	Need/benefit segmentation Problem detection studies Market structure analysis/gap analysis Product deficiency analysis
'Experts'	Brainstorming 'Synectics' 'Suggestion box' Independent inventors	'Problem/opportunity' analysis Morphological analysis Growth opportunity analysis Environmental trends analysis Analysis of competitive products Search of patents and other sources of new ideas
	←—— The R & D process ——→	

Table 17.6
Morphological approaches for generating strategic options

A. The traditional use of morphological approaches for generating new-product ideas (source: Adams [1972, p. 83])

Example: Improved ball-point pen

Attributes			
Cylindrical	Plastic	Separate cap	Steel cartridge
Alternatives			
Faceted	Metal	Attached cap	No cartridge
Square	Glass	No cap	Permanent
Bladed	Wood	Retracts	Paper cartridge
Sculptured	Paper	Cleaning cap	Cartridge made of ink
.	.	.	.
.	.	.	.
.	.	.	.

B. Use of the morphological approach for generating strategic options

Market segment	Product-positioning	Product and service offerings	Distribution
· Top 20%	Price	A	Outlet 1
	Performance		
· Customers with potential for top 20%	Guaranteed performance	B	Outlet 2
		C	Outlet 3
· Prospects with potential for top 20%	Convenience	D	Outlet 4
	Service		
· Previous customers	Prestige	.	.
· Candidates for deletion		.	.
· Other customers	.	.	.
.	.	.	.
.	.	.	.

The lessons from using these approaches in generating new-product ideas are:

- generation of new ideas requires both structured and unstructured approaches;
- approaches to idea generation should include both internal (decision-makers) and external (consumer, competition, suppliers, etc.) sources;
- the more approaches one uses for generating new ideas, the higher the likelihood of success; and
- idea generation should be conducted on an ongoing basis.

One of the most valuable approaches for generation of creative new ideas is morphological analysis. Table 17.6 illustrates the morphological approach for the generation of new-product ideas and shows how the same approach can be used to generate strategic options.

In both of these cases, the key is (a) the structuring of the problem, (b) the identification of all possible options for each component, and (c) the evaluation of all possible combinations of options.

In Table 17.6B, marketing strategy consists of the following components: segments, positioning, product and service offering, distribution outlet, and others. For each of these components, a list of options is generated. For example, the positioning strategy includes the possibility of price, performance, guaranteed performance, convenience, service and prestige. Having identified the option under each of the strategy components, strategic options are identified consisting of a pattern of options from each of the components (one from each column).

4.1.2. Meta-analysis

A second approach to the generation of creative strategic options is reliance on hypotheses one can draw from existing theories, concepts and findings. In this context, any theory, concept or study that suggests a specific relationship between some strategic variables and performance can be used as a source of hypothesis for a similar strategic situation.

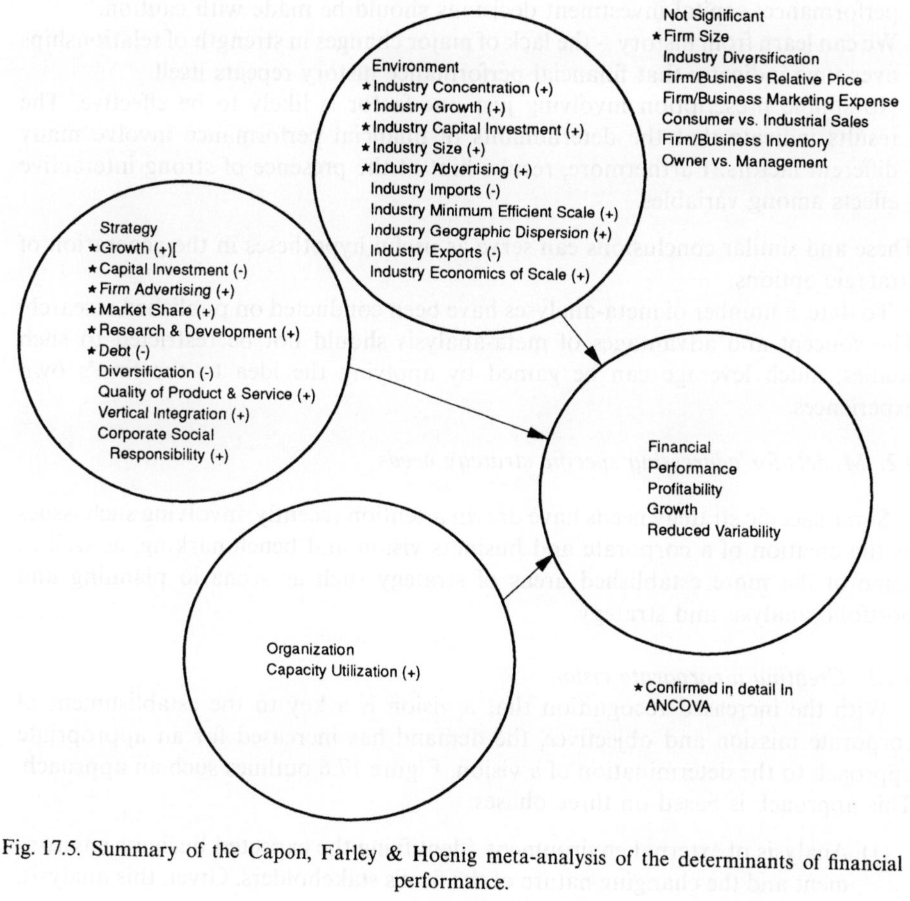

Fig. 17.5. Summary of the Capon, Farley & Hoenig meta-analysis of the determinants of financial performance.

A powerful source of strategic ideas is empirical generalization. These can be developed by either comparing and contrasting the findings of available empirical studies or by conducting a meta-analysis.

A recent meta-analysis of the determination of the financial performance of firms [Capon, Farley & Hoenig, 1990] resulted in the findings highlighted in Figure 17.5, and the following observations:

- High-growth situations are desirable; growth is consistently related to profits under a wide variety of circumstances.
- Having high market-share is helpful. Unfortunately, we do not have a clear picture of whether trying to gain market-share is a good idea, other things being equal.
- Bigness *per se* does not confer profitability.
- Dollars spent on R & D have an especially strong relationship to increased profitability. Investment in advertising is also worthwhile, especially in producer goods industries.
- High-quality products and services enhance performance; excessive debt can hurt performance; capital-investment decisions should be made with caution.
- We can learn from history – the lack of major changes in strength of relationships over time indicates that financial-performance history repeats itself.
- No simple prescription involving just one factor is likely to be effective. The results indicate that the determinants of financial performance involve many different factors. Furthermore, results hint at the presence of strong interactive effects among variables.

These and similar conclusions can serve as useful hypotheses in the generation of strategic options.

To date, a number of meta-analyses have been conducted on published research. The concept and advantages of meta-analysis should not be restricted to such studies; much leverage can be gained by applying the idea to the firm's own experiences.

4.2. Models for addressing specific strategy needs

Some specific strategy needs have drawn attention recently, involving such issues as the creation of a corporate and business vision and benchmarking, as well as some of the more established areas of strategy such as scenario planning and portfolio analysis and strategy.

4.2.1. Creating a corporate vision

With the increased recognition that a vision is a key to the establishment of corporate mission and objectives, the demand has increased for an appropriate approach to the determination of a vision. Figure 17.6 outlines such an approach. This approach is based on three phases:

(1) Analysis of external environment, identifying the expected business environment and the changing nature of the firm's stakeholders. Given this analysis,

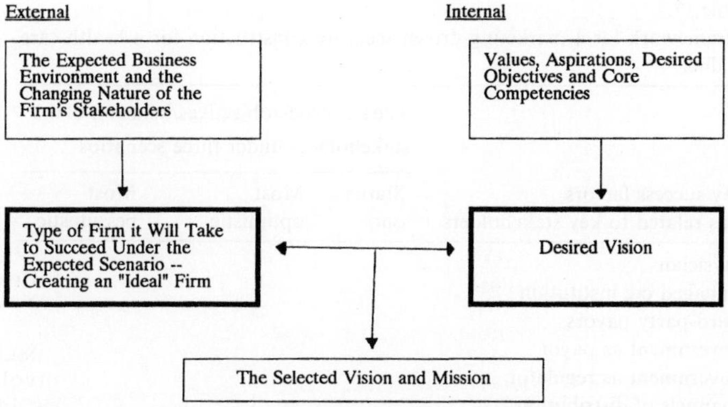

Fig. 17.6. A framework for selecting a vision and global business concept.

the focus is on the question, 'What type of firm could be successful under these expected conditions?' This would lead to the identification of characteristics of the 'ideal' firm.

(2) Internal analysis of the firm – its values, aspirations, desired objectives and core competencies. Based on this analysis, it is possible to identify an initial vision for the firm.

(3) A comparison and contrast of the 'ideal' firm resulting from the external analysis and the initial vision resulting from the internal analysis. The result of this comparison is a vision which satisfies the requirements of both the external and internal analyses.

A useful methodology for this problem, described in detail at the end of this section is the Analytic Hierarchy Process. As in most of the strategy applications of the AHP, this approach requires input from a group of executives in a structured brainstorming session. In this case, the group is typically the CEO and his or her executive committee. This procedure stimulates a broad discussion and evaluation of alternative visions. The evaluation should include both fit with internal competencies and aspirations, and appropriateness under the expected business environment.

Another major advantage, which is common to most AHP applications, is the building of consensus and 'buy-in' for the selected vision by the participants.

The weaknesses of this and most AHP applications is that the quality of the process and output depends on the composition of the group and the willingness of the top executives to engage in an open discussion. The analytical weakness of this approach is that the evaluations are typically made informally and at best either as a matrix of options by criteria or as an AHP hierarchy [Saaty, 1980].

4.2.2. Scenario planning

Scenario planning is a commonly used process in strategic planning, and it is increasingly employed in marketing planning as well.

Table 17.7
A framework for a marketing-driven scenario construction for a health-care product

Key success factors as related to key stakeholders	The key needs/objectives/behavior of the stakeholders under three scenarios		
	Status quo	Most optimistic	Most pessimistic
Physicians			
Managed cre institution			
Third-party payors			
Government as payor			
Government as regulator			
Channels of distribution			
Media			
Patients			
Competitors			
Our firm			
Employees			
⋮			
Financial analysts			
⋮			

The critical component of scenario planning is the development of a number of expected scenarios – typically status quo, optimistic and pessimistic scenarios. An important marketing perspective in the development of the scenarios is the focus on the various stakeholders of the firm and their needs. Table 17.7 provides a framework for such an analysis in a strategic analysis in the health-care industry.

Scenario planning is based on two key steps: (a) identification of the relevant stakeholders that affect the firm, and (b) identification of their expected needs/objectives.

This analysis results in a profile of each of the expected scenarios. More formal analysis of the scenario can involve a forecast of each of the expected trends as they relate to the various stakeholders and key environmental forces (such as the economy, socio-political trends, etc.). This trend analysis can also be supplemented with a cross-impact analysis which focuses on the interdependencies among the trends.

Once the scenarios have been established, it is typically helpful to assess the likely occurrence of each scenario given such information.

The major advantage of this process is the focus on the stakeholders that can affect the business and their needs. This is an extension of the marketing concept from a narrow focus on consumers to a more appropriate emphasis on all relevant stakeholders (see Figure 17.2). The rest of the planning process can be directed at the development of either the best strategy for each of the scenarios, or the strategy that would be best assuming that any of the scenarios may occur. In the former case, the analysis is typically presented as a strategic plan under the most likely scenario and a series of contingency plans for each of the other likely scenarios.

The difficulty in implementing this approach is its dependency on information about the stakeholders' needs/objectives and their likely evolution under a pessimistic or optimistic scenario. Stakeholder surveys are helpful here and can be effectively supplemented by available secondary information and insights of various members of the firm who have regular contact with the various stakeholders.

For further discussion and illustration of this approach, see Shoemaker [1991].

4.2.3. Benchmarking

The increased interest in quality programs and the widely publicized success of the Xerox benchmarking initiatives [Kamp, 1989] have drawn attention to benchmarking as a strategic tool.

Figure 17.7 outlines design guidelines for a benchmarking system. The basic benchmarking process involves:

(1) The selection of the factors for benchmarking. These should reflect the firm's key success factors.
(2) The selection of a benchmarking target. Who do we want to compare ourselves to – best in industry vs. best in any industry and best in our country vs. best in the world?
(3) The development of a measurement process and collection of data on the benchmark target and the firm's own operations and position.

Once the gap, if any, between the benchmark target and the firm has been established, there are three additional steps that have to be undertaken:

(4) Analysis of the results and the development of a strategy that could lead to moving the firm's position closer to the position of the best in the class.
(5) A link of the results to the reward and compensation system of the firm.
(6) A link of the process to the ongoing data-collection and monitoring activities of the firm and incorporation as part of the DSS of the firm.

Many of the benchmarking applications undertake the first three steps without any rigorous process for the determination of the key success factors, the selection of target benchmark, and the development of the measurement instrument. Marketing-science models and processes could be used in all six phases.

The following marketing-science approaches could be used for each of the six steps:

Step 1. Selection of benchmarking factors. Key success factors can be identified using discriminant, regression, or logit analysis on the characteristics of successful vs. unsuccessful firms. This can be done using available cross-sectional databases such as PIMS or any other available data.

Step 2. Selection of benchmarking target. The firm should sample a broad universe of successful firms or develop models to identify firms similar to a target model ('ideal' firm).

Step 3. Development of a measurement process and data collection. Multidimensional scaling, clustering and related approaches used in positioning analysis can be employed in a benchmarking study.

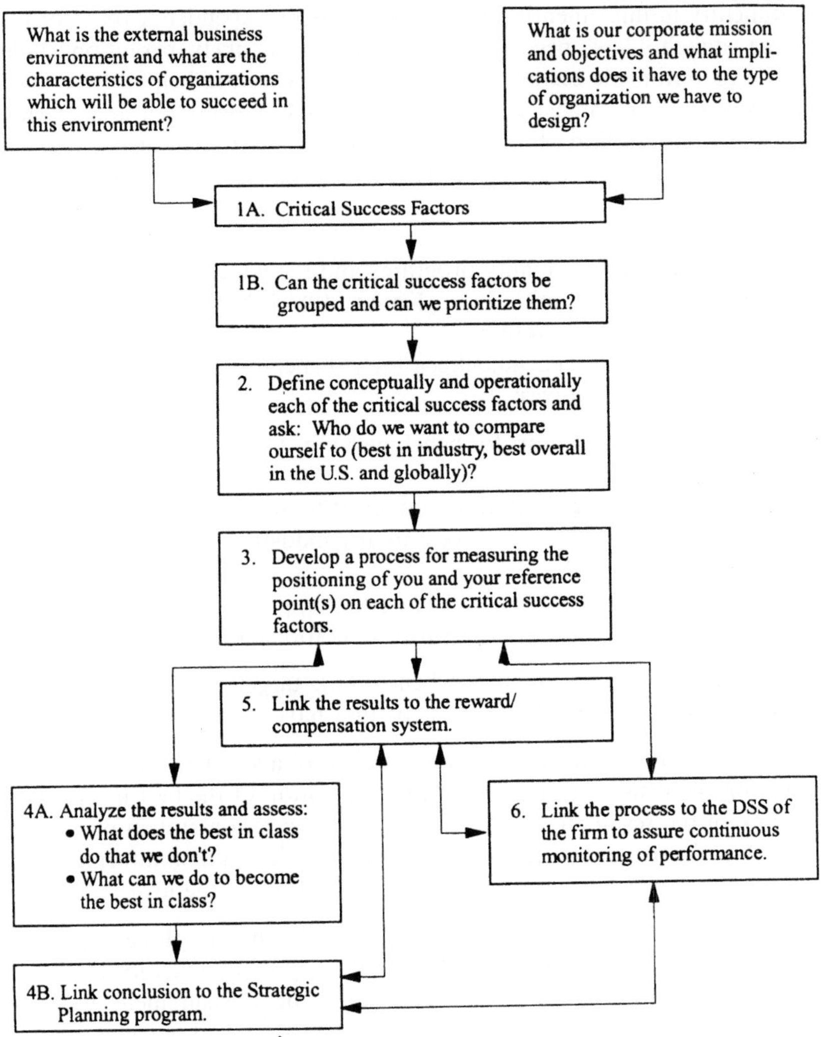

Fig. 17.7. Design guidelines for a benchmarking system.

Step 4. Generation and evaluation of strategies to close the gap between the firm and the benchmarking target. The approaches used for generating options and evaluating options can be employed in the benchmarking area as well.

Step 5. Link to the reward and compensation. Marketing-science models of compensation (see Chapter 13) can be extended to include activities leading to the accomplishment of the benchmarking targets.

Step 6. Link to the monitoring and data-collection activities and the DSS of the firm. This area can benefit from advances in marketing research, modeling and DSS development in general.

To date, only partial application of these models and approaches to the benchmarking area have been conducted. Resistance to employing the approaches has stemmed from the added cost and time these approaches require. Yet, the few (and unpublished) partial applications suggest that the benefit of a more rigorous process may be worth the added cost and effort.

4.2.4. Portfolio analysis and strategy

As illustrated in Figure 17.8, product portfolio models can be divided into four sets – standardized models, customized models, financial models and hybrid approaches. (For a detailed discussion of the models, see Wind, Mahajan & Swire [1983] and for a review see Lilien, Kotler & Moorthy [1992].)

Standardized models. These are useful ways of classifying a firm's products and businesses. The products and businesses are classified as in the GE/McKinsey matrix on their market-attractiveness and business strength. The two dimensions employed in these models are often a composite of a number of key attributes (attractiveness, for example, reflects size of market, growth rate, intensity of competition, etc.).

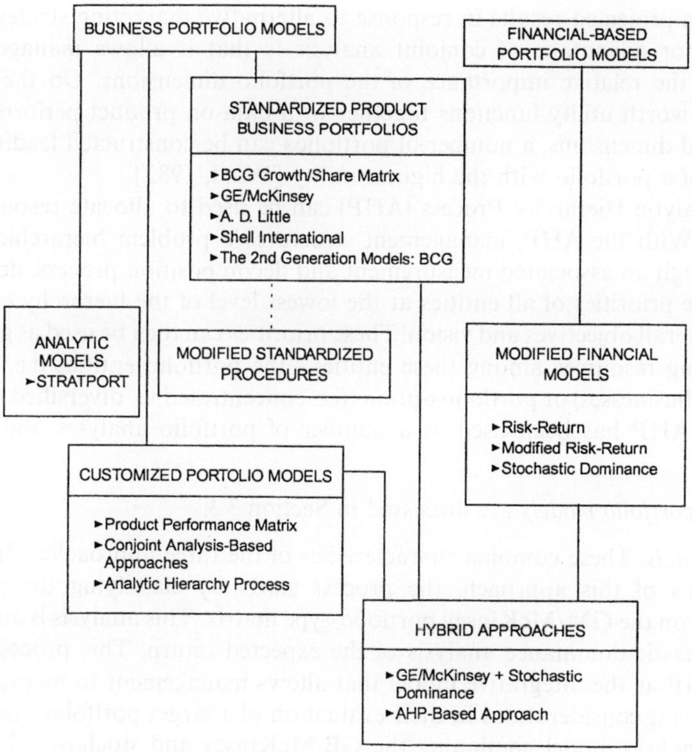

Fig. 17.8. A classification of product/business portfolio models.

Standardized portfolio models are the most commonly used portfolio models. Yet, these models, and especially the Boston Consulting Group's growth-share matrix, have a number of severe limitations. These include a focus on only two dimensions, lack of explicit consideration of risk factors, lack of dimensions weighting, neglect of any interdependency among the portfolio units, lack of rules for portfolio formation, questionable guidelines for resource allocation and, most critically, dependency of the results on the specific operational definitions used to measure the portfolio dimension.

Despite these limitations, the concept of a standardized model as a way of classifying a set of products and businesses on some relevant dimensions has value in making management think about business as a portfolio of businesses, product markets and segments.

Customized models. In contrast to the standardized-portfolio approaches, these do not prespecify dimensions or objectives. In customized approaches, including the product–performance matrix approach [Wind & Claycamp, 1976], conjoint analysis [Wind, 1982] and the analytic hierarchy process [Wind & Saaty, 1980], management chooses the specific dimensions.

The product–performance matrix is similar to the standardized models in its classification of products/businesses. However, in allocating resources, this approach is based on projected results in response to alternative marketing strategies.

The major advantage of conjoint analysis is that it allows management to determine the relative importance of the portfolio dimensions. On the basis of these part-worth utility functions together with data on product performance on the selected dimensions, a number of portfolios can be constructed leading to the selection of a portfolio with the highest utility [Wind, 1982].

The Analytic Hierarchy Process (AHP) can be used to allocate resources in a portfolio. With the AHP, management structures a problem hierarchically and then, through an associated measurement and decomposition process, determines the relative priorities of all entities at the lowest level of the hierarchy consistent with the overall objectives and vision. These priorities can then be used as guidelines in allocating resources among these entities – the portfolio entities (i.e. product/models or businesses) or portfolio options (i.e. concentrated vs. diversified portfolio, etc.). The AHP has been used in a number of portfolio analyses and strategy projects.

Financial portfolio models are discussed in Section 3.3.

Hybrid models. These combine characteristics of the three approaches. In the few applications of this approach, the process starts by classifying the products/businesses on the GM/McKinsey portfolio-type matrix. This analysis is augmented by a stochastic-dominance analysis of the expected return. This process centers on the AHP as the integrative model that allows management to incorporate all other relevant considerations in their evaluation of a target portfolio. An application of a hybrid model combining the GE/McKinsey and stochastic-dominance analysis is described in Mahajan & Wind [1985]. Most of the applications which incorporate these two approaches with the AHP have not been published. Yet, the experience with these applications suggest that they offer better guidelines than any of the approaches by themselves.

4.3. Models that facilitate integration of 'hard' market data with management subjective judgments

The Analytic Hierarchy Process, mentioned earlier as a key approach to customized and hybrid portfolio analysis, is also a useful methodology for integrating hard data with management subjective judgment.

The AHP is an interactive structured process that brings together the key decision-makers who represent diverse functions and experiences. This group process allows the integration of 'objective' market data with subjective management judgment. The process is based on three steps:

(a) Structuring the problem hierarchically – an illustrative 'generic' hierarchy is included in Figure 17.9. The construction of the hierarchy encourages the generation of creative options and the identification of the criteria for their evaluation.

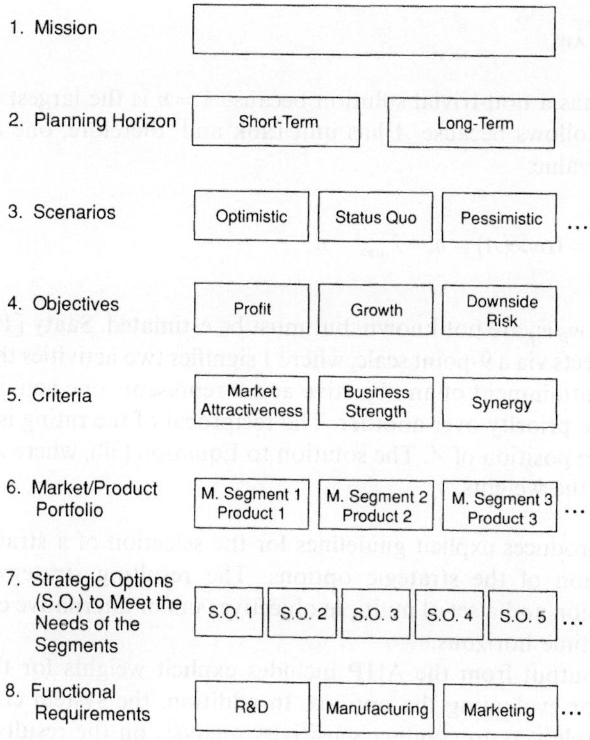

Fig. 17.9. Illustrative planning hierarchy.

(b) Evaluating the elements in each level against each of the elements in the next higher level of the hierarchy. The evaluation is made using a nine-point scale and is based on a series of paired comparisons.

(c) A weighting algorithm that determines the importance of any set of options on a set of multiple criteria/objectives. It is based on the idea that pairwise comparisons can be used to recover the relative weights (importance) of items or objects at any level of a hierarchy. Given, for example, n objects, $A_1,\ldots, A_n$ and a known vector of corresponding weights, $w = (w_1,\ldots, w_n)$, we can then form a matrix of pairwise comparisons of weights:

$$A = \begin{array}{c} \\ A_1 \\ \vdots \\ A_n \end{array} \begin{array}{c} \begin{array}{ccc} A_1 & \cdots & A_n \end{array} \\ \begin{bmatrix} \dfrac{w_1}{w_1} & \cdots & \dfrac{w_1}{w_n} \\ & & \\ \dfrac{w_n}{w_1} & \cdots & \dfrac{w_n}{w_n} \end{bmatrix} \end{array}$$

We can recover the scale of weights, $w_1,\ldots, w_n$ by multiplying A on the right by w and solving the eigenvalue problem:

$$Aw = \lambda w. \tag{38}$$

Equation (38) has a non-trivial solution because $1 = n$ is the largest eigenvalue of A. This result follows because A has unit rank and, therefore, one and only one non-zero eigenvalue:

$$\sum_{i=1}^{n} \lambda_i = \text{trace}(A) = n, \quad \lambda_{\max} = n. \tag{39}$$

In application, w_i/w_j are not known, but must be estimated. Saaty [1990] suggests comparing objects via a 9-point scale, where 1 signifies two activities that contribute equally to the attainment of an objective and 9 represents one activity having the highest possible priority over another. The reciprocal of the rating is then entered in the transpose position of A. The solution to Equation (38), where $\lambda = \lambda_{\max}$, gives an estimate of the weights.

This process produces explicit guidelines for the selection of a strategy based on the prioritization of the strategic options. The resulting strategy satisfies the corporate mission and a set of multiple objectives under alternative environmental scenarios and time horizons.

Secondary output from the AHP includes explicit weights for the objectives/criteria used for evaluating the options. In addition, the system encourages and provides a simple way to conduct sensitivity analysis on the results. Through its computer software (Expert Choice), the process also helps identify areas requiring the collection of additional information – those relationship on which no consensus can be reached and where the results can vary significantly depending on which of the conflicting points is accepted.

For more details on the development and use of the AHP, see (Saaty [1980, 1990]).

5. Examples of effective use of non-traditional marketing strategy models

In this section, we discuss two examples that illustrate the value of marketing models in enhancing specific marketing and business strategies. The examples include: (a) the application of the Analytic Hierarchy Process to the selection of a portfolio of market segments; and (b) the application of analogies, morphological approaches, and studies of success and failure to the design of a preemptive strategy.

5.1. *Selection of a target portfolio of segments using the AHP*

The problem. A leading pharmaceutical firm was concerned about the allocation of resources among its various segments. Discussions with management focused the problem on the need to select a target portfolio of segments.

The approach. The AHP was selected as the approach to solve the problem. The president of the division and all his direct reports comprised the decision-making group.

The modeling framework. The group reviewed the various studies they had on the attractiveness of the various market segments and their position in them, and structured the problem as a hierarchy which is illustrated in Figure 17.10. Following the structuring of the problem, the group started the evaluation of the components at each level against each of the items in the level above. The evaluation resulted in the priorities that are included in Figure 17.10. The most valuable part of the process was the discussion among the participants, which led to the identification of 'hidden' assumptions and beliefs, and to the resolution of a number of fundamental conflicts among the group members.

The results. The results summarized in Figure 17.10 indicate the following:

- The time horizon focuses primarily on the short term.
- The objectives are driven by: profit (39%), profit growth (34%), and sales growth (20%). Reducing downside risk is not considered very important (7%).
- Criteria: The three criteria for evaluating the segments were strength in segment, segment attractiveness and the synergy among the segments. Each of these was defined operationally as reflecting a number of measurable factors. Effectiveness, for example, included size of segment, growth of segment, and willingness to pay a premium price. The relative importance of these criteria in terms of the importance of the criteria to the achievement of the objective is strength (51%), attractiveness (28%), and synergy (21%).

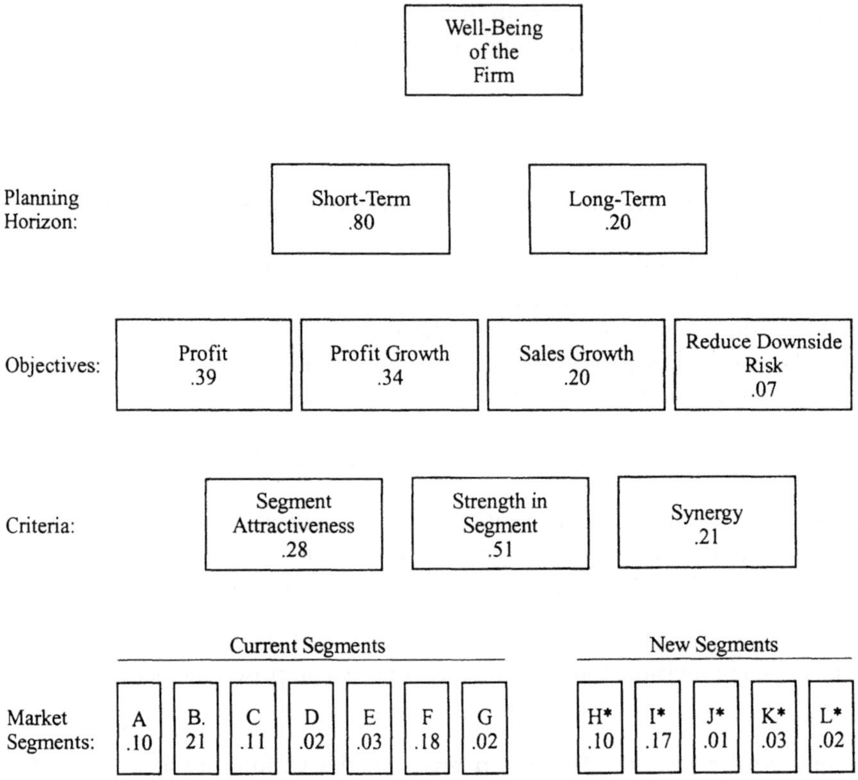

Fig. 17.10. Output of an analytic hierarchy process designed to select a portfolio of market segments for a pharmaceutical firm (note: the numbers are the composite priorities of each item).

- The segments: The initial portfolio of segments included the seven segments that the firm served. As part of the discussion, five new segments were identified. The evaluation of the segments on the criteria, reflecting the relative importance of the criteria in meeting the objective and, in turn, reflecting the importance of the objectives in achieving the mission of the firm in the short and long term, led to the selection of a new portfolio of segments including three of the original segments (A, B and F) and two new segments (H and I).

The process also led to the designation of a task force to explore how to increase the value of some of the less important segments, and to a major reallocation of resources: the original resource allocation was about 40% to segment and about 10% to each of the other six segments.

5.2. Generating a preemptive strategy using analogies, morphological approaches and studies of success vs. failures

The problem. A leading industrial firm was concerned about the likely impact of a competitors' entry into one of their major product markets, and wanted to develop a preemptive strategy.

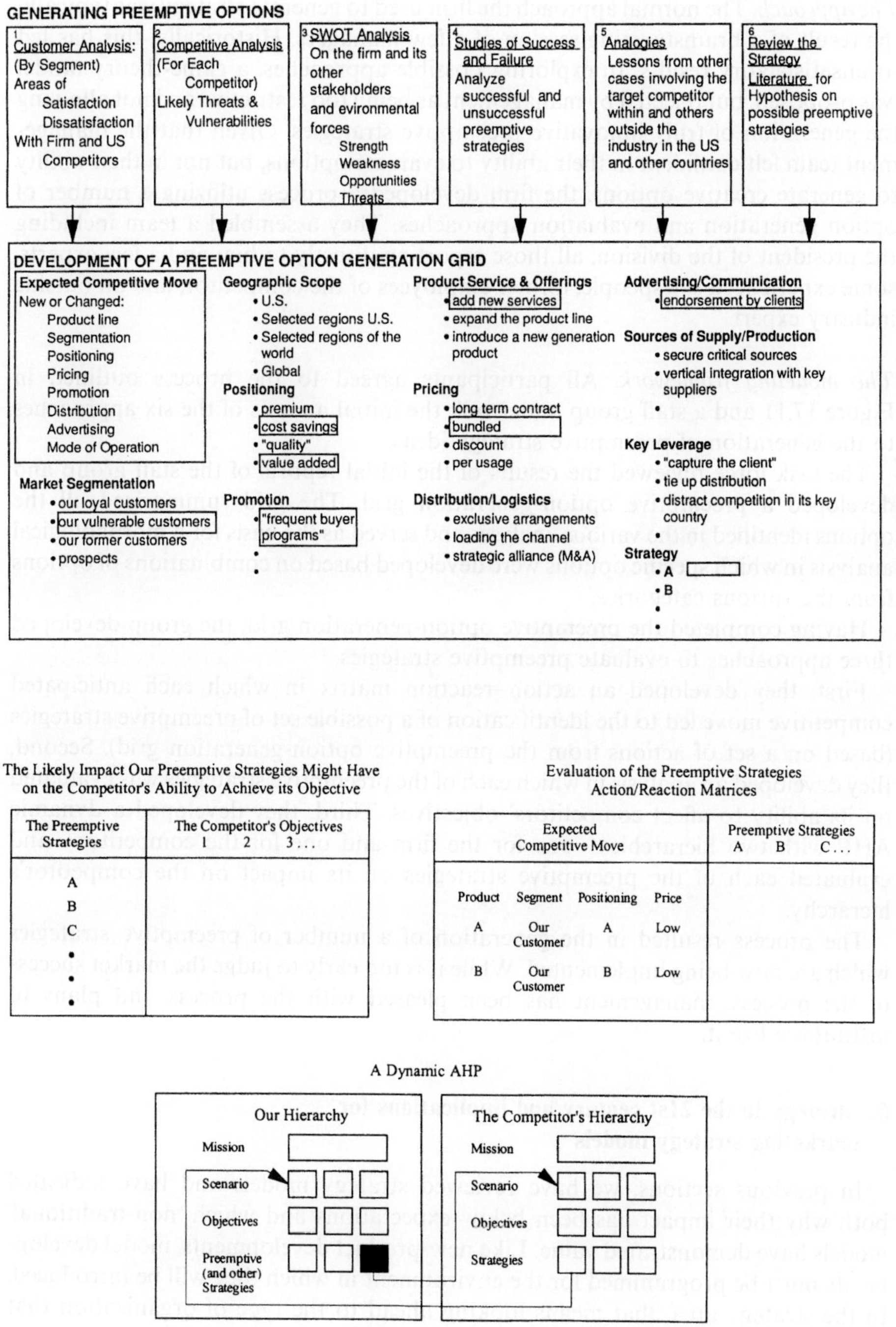

Fig. 17.11. Developing a preemptive strategy for a large industrial firm: the process and illustrative results.

The approach. The normal approach the firm used to generate strategy was typically the result of a brainstorming session of a few managers. Historically, this has led to unsatisfactory results. In exploring possible approaches, a game-theory model was proposed, but rejected by management as being too restrictive and not allowing the generation of truly innovative preemptive strategies. Given that the management team felt confident in their ability to evaluate options, but not in their ability to generate creative options, the firm developed a process utilizing a number of option generation and evaluation approaches. They assembled a team including the president of the division, all those reporting directly to him and a few experts, some experienced salespeople, former employees of the competitor, and an outside industry expert.

The modeling framework. All participants agreed to the process outlined in Figure 17.11 and a staff group undertook the initial anaysis of the six approaches to the generation of preemptive strategy ideas.

The task force reviewed the results of the initial reports of the staff group and developed a preemptive option-generation grid. The grid summarized all the options identified in the various analyses and served as the basis for a morphological analysis in which specific options were developed based on combinations of options from the various categories.

Having completed the preemptive option-generation grid, the group developed three approaches to evaluate preemptive strategies.

First, they developed an action–reaction matrix in which each anticipated competitive move led to the identification of a possible set of preemptive strategies (based on a set of actions from the preemptive option-generation grid). Second, they developed an analysis in which each of the preemptive strategies was evaluated on its ability to affect competitors' objectives. Third, they developed a dynamic AHP with two hierarchies – one for the firm and one for the competitor – and evaluated each of the preemptive strategies on its impact on the competitor's hierarchy.

The process resulted in the generation of a number of preemptive strategies which are now being implemented. While it is too early to judge the market success of the process, management has been pleased with the process and plans to institutionalize it.

6. Strategy in the 21st century and implications for marketing strategy models

In previous sections, we have reviewed strategy models and have indicated both why their impact has been below expectations and which 'non-traditional' models have demonstrated value. Like new-product developments, model developments must be programmed for the environment in which they will be introduced. In the strategy area, that means looking ahead to the type of organization that will be successful in the next several decades, an organization we call the successful '21st century enterprise'.

Table 17.8
Toward a new marketing paradigm

From	To
1. Function	1. Philosophy
2. Separate function	2. Integrated with others
3. Product management	3. Market management
4. Mass market	4. Segmented market
5. Domestic focus	5. Global focus
6. Consumers	6. Stakeholders
7. Limited use of information technology	7. Expanded use of information-technology strategies
8. Limited scope of research and modeling and limited utilization	8. Expanded view of research and modeling and broader utilization
9. Limited learning	9. Focus on organizational learning
10. Traditional institutions	10. Innovative marketing institutions
11. Focus on transaction	11. Long-term relationship
12. Self-sufficiency bias	12. Co-marketing and other strategic alliances

We have been involved [Wind & West, 1991], with a continuous study among hundreds of top executives (mostly of US firms), trying to identify key characteristics of the successful '21st century enterprise'. The types of characteristics that emerge that are of most concern to us here are that those organizations will be (a) flatter, less hierarchical and cross-functional, (b) based on information and information technology as competitive advantage, (c) networked with a global perspective, (d) customer-driven with a focus on customer value and total quality, and (e) organized to incorporate all stakeholders in the strategic focus.

As a result of the emergence of these critical characteristics, we envision a new marketing paradigm. The characteristics of that paradigm are outlined in Table 17.8. That paradigm has critical implications for the development of marketing strategy models.

The paradigm broadens the scope of marketing from that of a function to a philosophy that drives all business decisions. It also establishes the strong cross-functional integration between marketing and the other management disciplines.

It further suggests that the focus of marketing should be on market management and not on the traditional brand/product management. This focus can be captured as a market-driven matrix organization of product by markets.

The domestic mass-market perspective is being replaced by a focus on market segments in a global-strategy context, and the traditional focus on the consumer is being augmented by considering the needs of all stakeholders (including employees, security analysts, regulators and the like).

The current emerging use of information-technology strategies will take a broader reliance on appropriate, shared IT as input to all decisions, as well as on IT-based marketing strategies drawing on deep knowledge of the customer and customer needs.

Table 17.9
The desired characteristics of marketing strategy models for the 21st-century enterprise

1. *Scope*
   - Permit *any* strategy issues to be addressed (at any level) while linking the strategy to higher-level strategies, objectives and mission, and assuring integration with other business functions.
2. *Geographic scope*
   - All relevant levels from the target segment to global considerations.
3. *Objective*
   - Multiple objectives ranging from problem definition, through the generation of creative options, evaluation of the options, and selection of a strategy, to help in implementing it.
4. *Input*
   - Incorporate 'hard' data on all relevant stakeholders (customer, prospects, competitors, distributors, suppliers, etc.), the outcome of formal market analysis, *and* management subjective judgments.
5. *Type of model*
   - Linked to the strategy process and as part of a DSS that includes an expert system, the model should have relevant dynamic and stochastic components and facilitate sensitivity analysis.
6. *Output*
   - Adds value to the strategy process by improving the quality and speeding up the strategy process and helping the unit create value.

Changes in the needs of the various stakeholders, the globalization of the consumer and resource markets, and the dramatic advances in technology are likely to result in the creation of innovative marketing institutions and especially new media and distribution vehicles.

Finally, the traditional transaction focus is being replaced by an emphasis on long-term relationships and the realization that increasingly marketing and business services require the reliance on strategic alliances and other forms of co-marketing activities.

As a result of the expected changes in the characteristics of the 21st-century enterprise and the marketing paradigm, the desired characteristics of marketing strategy models must change quite dramatically from the characteristics of the models used most frequently today.

Table 17.9 outlines our view of desired characteristics of marketing strategy models. A comparison of this table against the characteristics of current models offered in Table 17.2 suggest that few of the marketing strategy models employed today measure up well. (The AHP appears to be an exception here.)

These desired models are broader, more flexible and more adaptive than most models in place today, mirroring the flexibility and adaptive nature of the 21st-century organization.

7. Conclusions

Despite the advances in the sophistication and proliferation of marketing-science models, relatively few true marketing strategy models have been developed, and those that have been developed generally had limited impact on management. The gap between management needs (for models that help them generate, evaluate and implement better marketing strategies) and the available models (especially non-traditional) is narrowing. As the environment and the characteristics of successful businesses are changing, the nature of the marketing paradigm, and the nature of desired marketing strategy models (as outlined in Table 17.9) is changing as well.

Closing the gap between marketing strategy models (as developed by marketing scholars) and management needs, requires a research program that will affect both supply and demand.

On the *demand side*, our suggested research agenda includes:

(1) Confirming management needs for strategy models. Are the desired model characteristics outlined in Table 17.9 consistent with the expectations of management? How should the 'market for strategy models' be segmented and what 'model' product best meets the needs of those segments?
(2) Conducting empirical work on the determinants of 'successful' marketing strategy models vs. unsuccessful ones and on the determinants of successful implementation of marketing strategy models. The new-product-success literature [see, Lilien and Yoon, 1989, for a review] provides some guidelines.
(3) Studying the adoption of marketing strategy models and their diffusion within the adopting firms. (The studies on the adoption and diffusion of conjoint analysis by Cattin & Wittink [1982] and Wittink & Cattin [1989] provide examples here.)

On the *supply side*, our suggested research agenda includes:

(1) Development of models that both meet the criteria outlined in Table 17.9 and that can be used. These models should consider:
   – market response to the complete set of marketing-mix variables of the firm and their interactions;
   – interaction of marketing and other strategy variables (i.e. manufacturing, R & D, etc.);
   – incorporation, as needed, of analysis based on multiple products, segments, (geographical) markets, time periods, and objectives;
   – competitors' actions and reactions.
(2) Studies among potential developers of marketing strategy models, on what can be done to stimulate the development of valid and applicable models.
(3) Experiments with different approaches to stimulate the development of strategy models that meet the criteria outlined in Figure 17.11 including support for joint projects with industry, promotion of such models as research priorities of key research institutes and the like.

Undertaking such research could help capitalize on the potential that MS/OR can offer the marketing strategy modeling area. Such effort is likely to lead to the development and implementation of higher-quality and more relevant marketing strategy models. It will also require that MS/OR broaden its scope and its toolkit if it is to truly address real management problems.

To conclude, we have seen that there are many OR/MS models and tools that have been developed whose impact has been less significant than they might have been. Part of the reason for that lack of success has been the rather inflexible and limited scope of the models to date. As we better learn how to make our models broader, more flexible and adaptive, we will have models that more closely mirror the marketing strategy environment of current and future organizations.

There are many fine ideas and developments in the literature of OR/MS in marketing at the moment that can and should be modified and adapted to address the needs of marketing strategists. Our hope is that adoption of those developments and execution of portions of the research agenda we have outlined above will lead to both more realistic and more widely used marketing strategy models.

References

Aaker, D.A. (1992). *Strategic Market Management, 3rd edition.* Wiley, New York.

Abraham, M.M., and L.M. Lodish (1987). PROMOTER: An automated promotion evaluation system. *Marketing Sci.* 6(2), 101–123.

Adams, L. (1972). *Conceptual Blockbusting.* The Portable Stanford, Stanford, CA.

Amstutz, A.E. (1967). *Computer Simulation of Competitive Market Response*, MIT Press, Cambridge, MA.

Anderson, C.R., and F.T. Paine (1978). PIMS: A reexamination. *Acad. Management Rev.* 3 (July), 602–612.

Basu, A.K., R. Lal, V. Srinivasan and R. Staelin (1985). Salesforce compensation plans: An agency theoretic perspective. *Marketing Sci.* 4 (Fall), 267–291.

Boulding, W. (1990). Commentary on 'unobservable effects and business performance: Do fixed effects matter?, *Marketing Sci.* 9(1), 88–91.

Burke Marketing Services (1984). Bases: Introduction, services, validation, history. Descriptive brochure, Burke Marketing Services, Cincinnati, OH.

Burke, R., A. Rangaswamy, Y. Wind, and J. Eliashberg (1990). A knowledge-based system for advertising design. *Marketing Sci.* 9(3), 212–229.

Buzzell, R.D. and B.T. Gale (1987). *The PIMS Principles*, The Free Press, New York.

Buzzell, R.D. (1990). Commentary on 'unobservable effects and business performance'. *Marketing Sci.* 9(1), 86–87.

Capon, N.J., J.U. Farely, and S. Hoenig (1990). Determinants of financial performance: A meta-analysis. *Management Sci.* 36(19), 1143–1159.

Cardozo, R., and Y. Wind (1985). A risk return approach to product portfolio strategy. *Long Range Planning* 18(2), 77–85.

Cattin, P., and D.R. Wittink (1982). Commercial use of conjoint analysis: A survey. *J. Marketing* 46, (Summer), 44–53.

Chussil, J. (1984). PIMS: Fact or folklore – Our readers reply. *J. Business Strategy* (Spring), 90–96.

Cohen, M., J. Eliashberg and T.H. Ho (1992). New product development: Performance, timing, and the marketing–manufacture interface, Working Paper, Wharton School, University of Pennsylvania, Philadelphia, PA.

Cooper, R.G. (1988). *Winning at New Products*, Addison-Wesley, Reading, MA.

Crawford, C.M. (1991). *New Products Management*, Irwin, Homewood, IL.

Day, G.S. (1986). *Analysis for Strategic Market Decisions*, West Publishing Co., New York.

Dunn, E., and Y. Wind (1987). Analytic hierarchy process for generation and evaluation of marketing mix strategies, in: G. Frazier and J. Sheth (eds.), *Contemporary Views on Marketing Practices*, Lexington Books, Lexington, MA, 111–131.

Dyer, R.F. and E.H. Forman (1991). *An Analytic Approach to Marketing Decisions*, Prentice-Hall, Englewood Cliffs, NJ.

Eastlack, J.O. and A.G. Rao (1986). Modelling response to advertising and price changes for 'V-8' Cocktail vegetable juice, *Marketing Sci.* 5(3), 245–259.
Eliashberg, J. and A.P. Jeuland (1986). The impact of competitive entry in a developing market upon dynamic pricing strategies, *Marketing Sci.* 5 (Winter), 20–36.
Eliashberg, J., and A. Manrai (1992). Optimal positioning of new product concepts: Some analytical implications and empirical results. *Eur. J. Oper. Res.* 63(3), 376–397.
Eliashberg, J. and R. Steinberg (1987). Marketing–production decisions for an industrial channel of distribution, *Management Sci.* 33(8), 981–1000.
Everett, (1968). Generalized Lagrange multiplier method for solving problems of optimum allocation of resources, *Oper. Res.* 11(3), 399–417.
Forrester, J.W. (1961). *Industrial Dynamics*, MIT Press, Cambridge, MA.
Green, P.E., J.D. Carroll, and S.M. Goldberg (1981). A general approach to product design optimization via conjoint analysis. *J. Marketing*, 45 (Summer), 17–37.
Green, P.E., and A.M. Krieger (1985). Models and heuristics for product line selection. *Marketing Sci.* 4, 1–19.
Green, P.E., and A.M. Krieger (1989). Recent contributions to optimal product positioning and buyer segmentation. *Eur. J. Oper. Res.* 41, 127–141.
Hadar, J., and W.R. Russell (1971). Stochastic dominance and diversification. *J. Econom. Theory* 3(3), 288–305.
Hillier, F.N. (1969). *The Evaluation of Risky Interrelated Investments*, North-Holland, Amsterdam.
Horsky, D., and L.S. Simon (1983). Advertising and the diffusion of new products, *Marketing Sci.* 2(1), 1–17.
Information Resources, Inc. (1985). Assessor-FT: The next generation, Descriptive Brochure, Information Resources, Chicago.
Jacobson, R. (1990a). Unobservable effects and business performance, *Marketing Sci.* 9(1), 74–85.
Jacobson, R. (1990b). Unobservable effects and business performance, Reply to the comments of Boulding and Buzzell. *Marketing Sci.* 9(1), 92–95.
Kalwani, M.U., and D.G. Morrison (1977). A parsimonious description of the Hendry system. *Management Sci.* 23, 467–477.
Kamp, R.C. (1989). *Benchmarking*, Quality Press. Milwaukee, WI.
Kleindorfer, P., and J. Wind (1992). The strategic impact of marketing driven quality, ORSA/TIMS San Francisco Conference, November.
Larréché, J.C., and V. Srinivasan (1981). STRATPORT: A decision support system for strategic planning. *J. Marketing* 45(4), 39–52.
Larréché, J.C., and V. Srinivasan (1982). STRATPORT: A model for the evaluation and formulation of business portfolio strategies, *Management Sci.* 28, 979–1001.
Lilien, G.L. (1979). Advisor 2: Modeling the marketing mix for industrial products, *Management Sci.* 25(2), 191–204.
Lilien, G.L., P. Kotler, and K.S. Moorthy (1992). *Marketing Models.* Prentice-Hall, Englewood Cliffs, NJ.
Lilien, G.L., and E. Yoon (1989). Determinants of new industrial product performance: A strategic re-examination of the empirical literature. *IEEE Trans. Engrg. Management* 36 (February), 3–10.
Little, J.D.C. (1975). BRANDAID: A marketing mix model. Part I: Structure; Part II: Implementation. *Oper. Res.* 23, 628–673.
Lorange, P. (1980). *Corporate Planning: An Executive Viewpoint*, Prentice-Hall, Englewood Cliffs, NJ.
Lubatkin, M., and M. Pitts (1983). PIMS: Fact or folklore, *J. Business Strategy* (Winter), 38–44.
Lubtakin, M., and M. Pitts (1985). PIMS: and the policy perspective. *J. Business Strategy* (Summer), 88–92.
Mahajan, V., P.E. Green, and S.M. Goldberg (1982). A conjoint model for measuring self- and cross-price/demand relationships. *J. Marketing Res.* 19, 334–342.
Mahajan, V., and Y. Wind (1985). Integrating financial portfolio analyses with product portfolio models. In H. Thomas and D. Garner (eds.). *Strategic Marketing and Management*, Wiley, New York, 193–212.
Mahajan, V., and Y. Wind (1986). *Innovation Diffusion Models of New Product Acceptance*, Ballinger, Cambridge, MA.
Markowitz, H. (1959). *Portfolio Selection.* Yale University Press, New Haven, CT.

Monahan, G.E. (1984). A pure birth model of optimal advertising with word-of-mouth. *Marketing Sci.* 3(2), 169–178.

Moorthy, K.S. (1984). Market segmentation, self-selection, and product line design. *Marketing Sci.* 3 (Fall), 288–305.

Ramanujam, V., and N. Venkatraman (1984). An inventory and critique of strategy research using the PIMS data base, *Acad. Management Rev.* 9, 138–151.

Rangan, V.K. (1987). The channel design decision: A model and an application. *Marketing Sci.* 6 (Spring), 156–174.

Rangan, V.K., A.A. Zoltners and R.J. Becker (1986). The channel intermediary selection decision: A model and an application. *Management Sci.* 32(9), 1114–1122.

Reality Technologies (1990). *Business Week's Business Advantage*, Business simulation software, Reality Technologies Philadelphia, PA.

Rurnelt, R.P., and R. Wensley (1980). In search of the market share effect. Working Paper, University of California at Los Angeles.

Saaty, T.L. (1980). *The Analytic Hierarchy Process*, McGraw-Hill, New York.

Saaty, T.L. (1990). *The Analytic Hierarchy Process: Planning, Priority Setting Resource Allocation, 2nd edition.* RWS Publications, Pittsburg, PA.

Shocker, A.D., and W.G. Hall (1986). Pre-test market models: A critical evaluation. *J. Product Innovation Management.*

Shoemaker, P.J. (1991). When and how to use scenario planning. *J. Forecasting*, to appear.

Silk, A.J., and G.L. Urban (1978). Pre-test market evaluation of new packaged goods: A model and measurement methodology. *J. Marketing Res.* 15, 171–191.

Thurstone, L.L. (1927). A law of comparative judgment. *Psychol. Rev.* 34, 273–286.

Urban, G.L., and J.R. Hauser (1980). *Design and Marketing of New Products.* Prentice-Hall, Englewood Cliffs, NJ.

Wilson, D.R., and D.K. Smith, Jr. (1989). Advances and issues in new product introduction models, in W. Henry, M. Marasco and H. Takada (eds.), *New Product Development and Testing.* Lexington Books, Lexington, MA.

Wind, Y. (1982). *Product Policy: Concepts, Methods and Applications.* Addison-Wesley, Reading, MA.

Wind, Y. (1987). An AHP based approach to the design and evaluation of a marketing-driven business and corporate strategy, *Math. Modelling* 9(3–5), 285–291.

Wind, Y. (1990). Positioning analysis and strategy, in G. Day, B. Weitz and R. Wensley (eds.), *The Interface of Marketing and Strategy*, JAI Press, Greenwich, CT.

Wind, Y., and H. Claycamp (1976). Planning product line strategy: A matrix approach, *J. Marketing* 40 (January), 2–9.

Wind, Y., and S.P. Douglas (1981). International portfolio analysis and strategy: The challenge of the 80's, *J. Intern. Business Studies* (Fall), 69–82.

Wind, Y., S.P. Douglas, and P. LeMaire (1972). Selection of global target markets: A decision theoretic approach, in *Marketing in a Changing World: Their Role of Market Research*, Proceedings of the 24th ESOMAR Congress, Cannes, France.

Wind, Y., and V. Mahajan (1981). Designing product business portfolios, *Harvard Business Rev.* 59(1), 155–165.

Wind, Y., V. Mahajan and D.J. Swire (1983). An empirical comparison of standardized portfolio models, *J. Marketing* 47 (Spring), 89–99.

Wind, Y., and T.S. Robertson (1983). Marketing strategy: New directions for theory and research, *J. Marketing* 47 (Spring), 12–25.

Wind, Y., and T.L. Saaty (1980). Marketing applications of the analytic hierarchy process, *Management Sci.* 26, 641–658.

Wind, Y., and A. West (1991). Reinventing the corporation, *Chief Executive* 71 (October), 72–75.

Wittink, D.R., and P. Cattin (1989). Commercial use of conjoint analysis: An update, *J. Marketing* 53 (July), 91–96.

Yellott, J.I., Jr. (1977). The relationship between Luce's choice axiom, Thurstone's theory of comparative judgment, and the double exponential distribution *J. Math. Psychol.* 15, 109–144.

Zoltners, A.A., and P. Sinha (1983). Sales territory alignment: A review and model, *Management Sci.* 29(11), 1237–1256.

J. Eliashberg and G.L. Lilien, Eds., *Handbooks in OR & MS, Vol. 5*

Chapter 18

Marketing–Production Joint Decision-Making

Jehoshua Eliashberg

Marketing Department, The Wharton School, University of Pennsylvania, Philadelphia, PA 19104, USA

Richard Steinberg

AT&T Bell Laboratories, MH 7E-510, 600 Mountain Avenue, Murray Hill, NJ 07974, USA

1. Introduction

1.1. The interface between marketing and production

The last decade was characterized by an increased emphasis on the integration of the separate functional areas of the firm. This can be traced to some extent to the successful performance of Japanese businesses that typically have a highly integrated organizational structure. This phenomenon has been reflected in a number of recent textbooks addressing the integration issues between marketing and production management. Marketing textbooks have recognized the importance of harmonious interactions among business functions. Kotler [1991, p. 701] puts it this way: "Companies need to develop a balanced manufacturing/marketing orientation, in which both sides codetermine what is in the best interests of the company". Such a viewpoint has the potential to alleviate inherent interdepartmental conflicts. In the production literature, Aquilano & Chase [1991, p. 17] mention that marketing specialists "need an understanding of what the factory can do relative to meeting customer due dates, product customization, and new product innovation. In service industries, marketing and production often take place simultaneously, so a natural mutuality of interest should arise between marketing and OM [operations management]". Similarly, McClain & Thomas [1985, p. 88] discuss marketing considerations such as price, quality and availability in the design of operations.

In this chapter, we will adopt the definition of Kotler [1991, p. 11]: "Marketing (management) is the process of planning and executing the conception, pricing, promotion, and distribution of ideas, goods, and services to create exchanges that satisfy individual and organizational objectives". In parallel, we will adopt the definition of Aquilano & Chase [1991, p. 6]: "*Operations management* (or *production management*, as it is often called) may be defined as the management of the direct resources required to produce the goods and services provided by an organization". Obviously, both sides recognize the importance of the interface from a managerial standpoint.

The interface between marketing and production is also beginning to be recognized as a legitimate research domain. For instance, Karmarkar & Lele [1989] point out that in most manufacturing firms the marketing and production functions are organizationally separate. One explanation they provide is that production is typically concerned with cost minimization, while marketing is concerned with revenue maximization. Typically, production is required to produce the required output at minimum cost, while marketing might be required to maximize revenue net of marketing and sales expenses. In this way, marketing sets prices and advertising policy, the market determines the quantities demanded, and production produces the quantities demanded at minimum unit cost. However, this decomposition results in conflicts due to inconsistent objectives or externalities imposed by one function on the other. As we shall see in the sequel, such decomposition may also yield suboptimal overall performance.

As a specific example, Karmarkar & Lele [1989] discuss the effect of annual promotional cycles on production policy. Price promotions in many companies are driven by the fact that sales quotas are reviewed, or internal reports are generated, on a quarterly basis, leading to an 'end-of-quarter push'. Due to the way in which profits are computed, the cost-of-goods-sold calculation may look more favorable if inventories are high. Although marketing may have other arguments for promotions, the authors suggest that those who set these promotion and price policies may not be aware of the costs imposed by these policies on manufacturing and on inventory levels.

By way of illustration, Karmarkar & Lele present an actual demand pattern for an industrial-equipment manufacturer's product line. The data clearly exhibits a quarterly pattern of demand. The authors convincingly argue that the seasonality is artificially induced by promotional activity, since the end-demand at the distribution level exhibits no intrinsic seasonality, and the peaks in production demand are highly correlated to the timing of promotions and price discounts. The authors present graphically the production and inventory policies determined by a standard linear-programming model. The production level remains essentially flat over time, except during shut-down and vacation periods, and the quarterly inventory accumulation pattern is roughly counter-cyclical to the demand pattern.

For comparison, Karmarkar & Lele present graphically the inventory pattern where stock is held only to cover the shut-down and vacation periods. The reductions in inventories and in holding costs from the earlier case are significant. The authors assert that, if it is recognized that increased inventory levels are not an asset, and if the effect on the inventory-holding costs is assessed correctly in implementing the marketing strategy, then the incentive for the sales push would essentially disappear.

1.2. A marketing–production game

In the journal *Interfaces*, Davis [1977] describes an ingenious game designed to model the conflict between marketing and production. Although the objective was to develop a procedure by which these two functional areas could identify problems, no attempt was made in the study to resolve the problems themselves. The project was in response to a call to readers in an earlier *Interfaces* article requesting descriptions of the process of problem identification in management science [Graham, 1976].

Davis enlisted the aid of a group of managers from both the marketing and production areas – presumably from the same division – in a large industrial firm. (Davis's research was conducted while he was a staff member with Texas Instruments.) The managers from the two areas worked separately to develop 'subset models' of their respective functional areas. These two models were later integrated by an analyst working with the division manager to obtain an interactive dynamic model to simulate the two areas. This grand model, consisting of a portion representing the firm developed from the marketing and production submodels, together with a portion representing the industry in which the firm competed, reflected the dynamic characteristics of the business in a competitive environment. The 'firm' portion included six sectors: market share, price, orders, production, labor and process yield, as well as a financial and accounting sector which reported revenues, costs and cash flows. The 'industry' portion consisted of four sectors: market share, production, orders and capacity, where price and capacity factors could be chosen to simulate various levels of industry competition.

First, the marketing submodel was developed with the marketing managers; it allowed for the study of different pricing strategies under the assumption that production capabilities existed that would support any marketing strategy. The marketing managers confirmed that the resulting submodel was representative of the market environment, with the exception of production capabilities. Next, the production submodel was developed with the production managers. It included a forecast algorithm that generated orders based on prior demand. Each submodel was validated using test runs.

The grand model identified two problems. One was that an aggressive price-leader strategy sought by the marketing group was not possible due to the firm's labor practices. Marketing's intended strategy of increasing market share through price reduction did not account for the lead time needed to increase the size of the work force.

The other problem consisted of a mismatch between sales and production. When sales were rising and inventory was falling, production was increased to slightly more than the demand rate so as to meet demand and replenish inventory. Due to the production lead time, an increase in production did not result in an immediate increase in finished-good inventory. Consequently, production was increased further until the output of finished goods exceeded sales, and inventory began once again to build. Although this resulted in greatly reduced delivery-response time, sales began to fall off as customers began holding orders due to the short response time. Thus, despite a reduction in the production rate, inventory increased to greater than target levels as the goods in the production pipeline were completed. As we shall see throughout this chapter, the relationship between marketing and inventory policies plays a key role in many marketing–production models.

More generally, Shapiro [1977] discusses the need for cooperation between marketing and production, especially in those companies manufacturing industrial goods. He lists eight problem areas of 'necessary cooperation but potential conflict' between marketing and manufacturing.

Montgomery & Hausman [1986; Hausman & Montgomery, 1990] also consider marketing/production interactions and cite six important interfaces between the two functions. The Hausman–Montgomery list coincides closely with that of Shapiro. The issues raised by Shapiro and by Hausman & Montgomery are outlined in detail in Section 5, including references and suggestions for further research.

The need for enhancing the interface between marketing and production has been expressed by others as well. Crittenden [1992], for example, believes that capacity allocation is the most critical issue the two functions need to address. She has identified eighteen rules for making capacity-allocation decisions (e.g. produce and fill orders by customer priority), arguing that these rules allow for both objective and subjective allocations of capacity. She then refers to the contention of Shapiro [1977] that the main conflict over marketing and manufacturing strategies lies with customer and product-mix decisions which constrain demand and supply decisions. Hence, she suggests, "a truly integrative model of marketing and manufacturing allows for both supply and demand concerns".

In a somewhat similar spirit, Crowe & Nuno [1991] suggest that, traditionally, manufacturing planning has focused on two dimensions: (1) product life-cycle which varies from low to high volume, and (2) process life-cycle varying from job shop to batch to assembly line to continuous production. They argue for a 'cubic' approach (i.e. making strategic decisions based on three dimensions), where the third dimension could be flexibility or cost or quality or service. The latter two dimensions clearly represent the marketing department's immediate concerns.

1.3 The marketing–production domain

In this chapter, we consider the interface between marketing and production, focusing specifically on decision-making from the viewpoint of management science and operations research. Before outlining the material covered, we would like to discuss what, in our opinion, constitutes the domain of marketing–production decision-making from the research standpoint, and explain why some topics that could easily be considered as falling within the purview of this chapter were *not* included. In most of these cases, there exists a considerable literature on the topic, but we feel that there is no true balance between the marketing and production aspects; sometimes, it is the marketing component that has the secondary role (e.g. forecasting issues in planning-horizon problems); other times it is the production side that receives little attention (e.g. manufacturing issues in new-product introduction problems). Other topics not included in this chapter are those for which substantive management-science techniques have yet to be developed (e.g. technology, design, and time-based competition).

In our assessment, some of the excluded topics that still offer research opportunities in the marketing–production interface include planning horizons, the economic lot-scheduling problem (ELSP) and product mix, the learning curve, just-in-time manufacturing (JIT), and time-based competition (TBC). For other topics usually considered part of traditional stochastic inventory theory (e.g. shortages, backorders, lost sales), but that could be considered to fall within the marketing–production domain, see Porteus [1990].

Planning horizons is a substantial research area in production. The basic idea is that in a production-scheduling problem the optimal decisions for an initial portion of the schedule (the 'planning horizon') may be partially or wholly independent of the data from some future period onwards. Later in the chapter we will introduce this topic in more detail and discuss planning-horizon results involving pricing. However, even without the pricing decision, planning horizons can be considered to be an active area of marketing–production joint decision-making, with forecasting as the major marketing component. For more on planning horizons, see the survey of Bhaskaran & Sethi [1987]. For a concise treatment of forecasting itself, see Johnson & Montgomery [1974, Chapter 6] and Wind, Mahajan & Cardozo [1981].

The economic lot-scheduling problem (ELSP) considers the sequencing and timing of several different products on a single production facility on a repetitive basis. The key restriction is that, at any point in time, the facility is either idle or is processing only one product. During each production run, sufficient inventory for the product being processed must be accumulated so as to satisfy demand during the intervening runs until that product is again manufactured. Associated with each product are a setup cost and a setup time, an inventory-holding cost, and a demand rate and a production rate. The naive approach is to independently calculate for each product the economic production quantity (the EOQ where the production rate is finite), although this will invariably lead to an infeasible schedule. The problem, which is inherently dynamic, has been addressed through the construction of a feasible cyclical production schedule so as to minimize average costs over time. (See, for example, the classic paper of Elmaghraby [1978].) The corresponding marketing modeling perspectives on this issue are given in the literature addressing the product-mix design. The problem has been typically formulated as a static mathematical-programming problem [Green & Krieger, 1985], where production considerations are taken into account merely through variable and fixed costs associated with each product [e.g. Dobson & Kalish, 1993]. See Lancaster [1990] and Ratchford [1990] for further references. A recent paper which begins to address the simultaneous problem is that of Hum & Sarin [1991]. This area clearly offers research opportunities for further modeling.

The learning curve (or experience curve) concept is based on the principle that, when the cumulative experience of producing a complex product or service doubles, the average cost of that production activity typically declines by a fixed percentage – on the order, say, of 20% – reflecting the learning achieved. This reduction in costs with accumulated experience can be traced to increased worker and management efficiency due to learning, the availability of new materials and technologies, and other factors. Initial observation of this phenomenon is usually traced to the manufacture of aircraft in the U.S. in the mid-1920s. A good presentation of this topic from the production perspective is provided in Hayes & Wheelwright [1984, Chapter 8]. The concept has been applied in marketing to determine new-product pricing strategies [Dolan & Jeuland, 1981]. The papers of Teng & Thompson [1983] and of Smunt [1986] would be good starting points for further information on applications.

During the 1980s there was much interest in just-in-time production systems from Japan. Developed originally by Toyota, JIT can perhaps be best summarized as a collection of principles, a representative list of which would include: minimal inventory; short setup times; small batch sizes; smoothed, rapid production; high quality standards; and constant process improvement. Key references include Sugimori, Kusunoki, Cho & Uchikawa [1977], Monden [1981] and Ohno [1982]. However, the subject has received scant modeling attention.

A related area which has recently garnered considerable attention in the management literature and popular press goes by the name of 'time-based competition' (TBC). The term was coined by George Stalk and his colleagues at the Boston Consulting Group in the early 1980s while studying the evolution of JIT production systems [Blackburn, 1991]. Like JIT, TBC aims to eliminate time waste in the production process. TBC presumably goes further beyond manufacturing than JIT to include not only marketing, but research and development, distribution, and other functional areas as well. Stalk & Hout [1990] describe TBC in terms of two new dimensions of competitive advantage: low-cost variety and fast response time. This includes compressing the manufacturing and distribution lead time as well as the time to develop and introduce new products. However, as Blackburn explains in his recent book on the subject [Blackburn, 1991, p. vi]: "The study of the strategic consequences of time does not yet lend itself to mathematical models. Most of the research to date has been empirical and has relied heavily on anecdotal evidence. This should change, however, as we learn to build better models...." From the marketing perspective, this is closely related to the research area addressing the advantage of being a brand pioneer [Urban, Carter, Gaskin & Mucha, 1986; Lieberman & Montgomery, 1991]. For the specific issue of lead times, see Karmarkar [1987], which includes an extensive bibliography.

1.4. Overview of the Chapter

We finally arrive at the topics that we *do* cover in this chapter. In Section 2, we discuss the benefits of coordinating marketing and production strategies. Specifically, we employ an early inventory-problem formulation of Whitin [1955] as a paradigm to compare two modes of operation: one in which the marketing and production decisions are decentralized, and the other in which the decisions are coordinated. Then we review a number of papers that model joint marketing and production policies and attempt to ascertain the advantages of coordinated decision-making.

In Section 3, we discuss marketing–production mechanisms for smoothing unstable demand. The essence of such problems is the classic economic argument of increasing marginal production costs. This paradigm thus leads naturally to models in which production costs are convex. The section first covers some 'pure' production approaches; then it shows how one or more marketing decision variables – usually price – bring us into the marketing–production domain.

In Section 4, we discuss order quantities and pricing decisions. Due to the usual existence of a setup cost and nonincreasing unit costs, this paradigm leads to models in which production (ordering) costs are concave. We first consider in this section static deterministic models, then dynamic deterministic models, and finally stochastic models.

In Section 5, we provide managerial perspectives on the problem. These highlight the gaps that still exist and thus offer opportunities for further research. The list of references contains all work viewed by us as making a contribution to the domain of marketing–production joint decision-making. However, space limitations necessitated that we be selective.

2. Decentralized vs. coordinated marketing–production decision-making

2.1. *An example of decentralized vs. coordinated decision-making*

One of the first attempts to address marketing–production joint decision-making was presented by Whitin [1955], who provides extensions of two very basic inventory models which model staple merchandise and style goods, respectively. The models Whitin proposed incorporate both lot-size analysis and demand functions which are controlled via price by the decision-maker. Of more interest to us is his first model for staple goods; it is perhaps the earliest in the literature to include the pricing decision in the standard EOQ model. The stationary demand model considered by Whitin is of the form:

$$D(P) = a - bP \tag{2.1}$$

where D and P are demand and price, respectively, and where a and b are given constants. For any amount demanded annually, the total variable costs (TVC) involved in carrying, ordering, and operating costs are:

$$\mathrm{TVC}(P, Q) = \frac{Q}{2}h + \frac{D(P)}{Q}K + \bar{c}D(P) \tag{2.2}$$

where Q is the amount ordered in each lot, h is the per-unit inventory carrying cost, K is the setup cost, and $\bar{c}$ is the cost associated with each unit demanded. By simple differentiation of (2.2) with respect to Q, and substitution of the result back into the objective function, one obtains the minimal total variable costs (TVC) as a function of the demand, D, and consequently price:

$$\mathrm{TVC}^*(P) = \sqrt{2KhD(P)} + \bar{c}D(P). \tag{2.3}$$

Consider now the marketing department with an objective function, Π_{M}, identical to the total firm's profits, Π_0. It may be stated as total revenues minus total costs:

$$\begin{aligned}\Pi_{\mathrm{M}}(P) = \Pi_0(P) &= D(P)\cdot P - \mathrm{TVC}^*(P) - f \\ &= (P - \bar{c})D(P) - \sqrt{2KhD(P)} - f\end{aligned} \tag{2.4}$$

where f is some fixed cost. By substituting the demand function from (2.1), and differentiating with respect to the marketing variable price, P, Whitin obtains the following cubic equation that may be solved by radicals for the maximizing value of P:

$$\begin{aligned}&-8b^3P^3 + (16ab^2 + 8\bar{c}b^3)P^2 - (10ab^2 + 12\bar{c}ab^2 + 2\bar{c}^2b^3)P \\ &\quad + 2a^3 + 4\bar{c}a^2b + 2\bar{c}^2ab^2 - Khb^2 = 0.\end{aligned} \tag{2.5}$$

Whitin then argues that: "From the standpoint of business practice, a method is provided for obtaining the optimum price at the same time the lot size is determined". (We discuss the assumptions of Whitin's model in Section 4.)

Three observations are in order. First, Whitin's model can be construed as a decentralized decision-making problem, where the production department moves first and the marketing department moves next. Second, note that Whitin does not address *explicitly* the following question: "*What is the economic benefit of coordinating the marketing and production policies*?" This issue is variously referred to as *decentralized vs. coordinated* or *sequential vs. simultaneous* decision-making [e.g. Freeland, 1980; Abad, 1987]. Third, suppose that the problem has been formulated as a coordinated rather than decentralized decision-making problem. That is, if the two departments were to adopt Π_0, the firm's total profits, as the system objective to be maximized, then the problem would be formulated as:

$$\underset{P,Q}{\text{maximize}}\ \Pi_0(P,Q) = D(P)\cdot P - \frac{Q}{2}h - \frac{D(P)}{Q}K - \bar{c}D(P) - f. \tag{2.6}$$

Differentiating with respect to Q and P separately yields the following two necessary conditions:

$$Q^* = \sqrt{\frac{2KD^*(P^*)}{h}} = \sqrt{\frac{2K(a - bP^*)}{h}}, \tag{2.7}$$

$$P^* = \frac{1}{2}\left(\frac{a}{b} + \frac{K}{Q^*} + \bar{c}\right). \tag{2.8}$$

Solving simultaneously the two necessary conditions (2.7) and (2.8) for P^* yields the same cubic Equation (2.5) necessary to solve for P^* as in the sequential formulation. Hence, the conclusion is that, for Whitin's model, coordinating the marketing–production policies (i.e. simultaneous maximization of Equation (2.6)) yields the same decisions and profits as the case in which the production department decides first on the lot size, Q, with the objective of minimizing total variable costs (carrying, ordering and operating), and the marketing department chooses next the price, P, that maximizes the firm's total profits (revenues net of the minimized production cost and the fixed costs). That is, under these circumstances there is no *tangible* (i.e. strictly positive) benefit in coordination. This result relies on how the objective functions have been formulated for the individual functional areas.

The issue of comparing decentralized (sequential) vs. coordinated (simultaneous) optimization problems between two or more systems once the objective functions have been defined is the essence of investigating the nature of coordination between the systems. Damon & Schramm [1972], for instance, have noted in this regard: "In investigating the relative merits of the simultaneous vs. sequential models, it is necessary to compare models with similar objective criteria". Welam [1977b] points out: "In using the strategy of comparing the sum of two optima against a joint optimum... [s]ymbolically, one has optimum(system1 + system2) ≥ optimum(system1) + optimum(system2)". Special attention must be given, however, to the definition of optimum(·). The following example illustrates this point.

Consider the following ad-hoc – but not unrealistic – mode of operation in which the marketing decision is made first, and the firm's total profits, given by objective function (2.6) is decomposed such that marketing seeks to maximize the following subobjective:

$$\underset{P}{\text{maximize}} \quad \Pi_M = (P - \bar{c})D(P) - f = (P - \bar{c})(a - bP) - f. \tag{2.9}$$

(Note that subobjective function (2.9) ignores the term $[D(P)/Q]K$ in (2.6) which, one may argue, could still be under marketing responsibility.) This yields the following optimal price (which is different from the coordinated optimal price (2.8)):

$$P^{**} = \frac{1}{2}\left(\frac{a}{b} + \bar{c}\right). \tag{2.10}$$

The corresponding demand is

$$D^{**} = D(P^{**}) = \frac{a - b\bar{c}}{2} \tag{2.11}$$

and the maximized subobjective function, Π_M^{**}, is obtained by substituting into (2.9):

$$\Pi_M^{**} = \frac{(D^{**})^2}{b} - f. \tag{2.12}$$

Next, let the production department make its decision. Suppose it minimizes its variable costs (VC) (taking the responsibility for the term $[D(P^{**})/Q]K$):

$$\underset{Q}{\text{minimize}} \quad \text{VC} = \frac{Q}{2}h + \frac{D^{**}}{Q}K. \tag{2.13}$$

This yields the following results:

$$Q^{**} = \sqrt{\frac{2KD^{**}}{h}} = \sqrt{\frac{2K(a - bP^{**})}{h}} \tag{2.14}$$

and

$$\text{VC}^{**} = \text{VC}(Q^{**}) = \sqrt{2KhD^{**}}. \tag{2.15}$$

The system's total profit under this sequential decision-making approach is given by:

$$\Pi_0^{**} = \Pi_M^{**} - \text{VC}^{**} = \frac{(D^{**})^2}{b} - \sqrt{2KhD^{**}} - f. \tag{2.16}$$

Recall that the simultaneous (coordinated) optimization problem (2.6) yields solutions given by (2.7) and (2.8) for (P^*, Q^*). These give the following total maximized profits:

$$\Pi_0^* = (P^* - \bar{c})D^* - \frac{Q^*}{2}h - \frac{D^*}{Q^*}K - f \tag{2.17}$$

where

$$D^* = D^*(P^*) = a - bP^*. \tag{2.18}$$

A number of comparisons are of interest. First, comparing P^* and P^{**} from (2.8) and (2.10) indicates readily that $P^* > P^{**}$. The coordinated system yields a higher price. A comparison of Q^* with Q^{**} from (2.7) and (2.14) shows that, since $P^* > P^{**}$, $Q^* < Q^{**}$. That is, the optimal lot size is smaller under the coordinated system vis-à-vis a system in which the marketing decision is made first and the production decision is made second. Thus, in this example (unlike the previous), the two modes of operation lead to two different decision outcomes.

To gain some insight into the possible advantages of coordination (i.e. the simultaneous optimization), we employ the following numerical example. Let:

$f = 0$, $\bar{c} = 10$, $h = 0.2$, $K = 1000$, $a = 100$, $b = 5$. Substituting into the appropriate equations, we obtain:

From (2.10): $P^{**} = 15$.
From (2.11): $D^{**} = 25$.
From (2.12): $\Pi_{\mathrm{M}}^{**} = 125$.
From (2.14): $Q^{**} = 500$.
From (2.15): $\mathrm{VC}^{**} = 100$.
From (2.16): $\Pi_0^{**} = 25$.

For the coordinated system, we get:

From (2.7) and (2.8): $Q^* = 439.44$ and $P^* = 16.14$.
From (2.18): $D^* = 19.31$.
From (2.17): $\Pi_0^* = 30.64$.

Hence, there exists *potential* for improvement (strictly positive now, in contrast to Whitin's model) when marketing and production act coordinately vis-à-vis the ad-hoc sequential procedure where the marketing decision is made first and the production decision next.

The reason for the suboptimality of the decentralized problem, (2.9) and (2.13), is because the nonseparable term $[D(P)/Q]K$ is optimized by only one party. By contrast, in Whitin's decentralized problem, (2.2) and (2.4), both parties have the nonseparable term $[D(P)/Q]K$ in their individual objective functions. Hence, the solution is identical to the coordinated problem. (We thank Teck H. Ho for this observation.)

Papers that have explicitly considered the coordinational aspects of joint marketing–production policies include Damon & Schramm [1972], Welam [1977a], Freeland [1980], Abad [1987] and Sogomonian & Tang [1990]. Modified approaches include those of Porteus & Whang [1991] and De Groote [1991], who incorporate ideas from economics (agency theory, utility theory), and of Cohen, Eliashberg & Ho [1992], who focus on the new-product development process. We review each of these models in more detail below.

2.2. *Benefits of coordination*

Damon & Schramm [1972] formulate a rather complicated model that incorporates the finance function together with production and marketing. In their model, production makes decisions along the lines of the 'HMMS' model given by Holt, Modigliani, Muth & Simon [1960]. (This model will be discussed in more detail in Section 3.) Damon & Schramm's modifications to the HMMS model are as follows. To begin with, they transform the cost relationships of the HMMS model to cash-flow relationships. This necessitates a change of variables. In the HMMS model, Q_t, the per-period level of production, is a direct decision variable, but here it is a function of the size of the work force and the average number of hours worked per period:

$$Q_t(W_t, H_t) = \alpha_0 W_t H_t - \alpha_1 (W_t - W_{t-1})^2 - \alpha_2 (H_t - H_{t-1})^2 \tag{2.19}$$

where in each period t:

Q_t = per-period production level,
W_t = size of the work force,
H_t = average number of hours worked by the work force,
$\alpha_0, \alpha_1, \alpha_2$ = parameters.

The formulation also includes a new decision variable, M_t, the amount of material ordered in period t. The role of marketing is defined rather narrowly to consist of estimating final-product demand for any given level of advertising and price. The demand is assumed to have the following form:

$$D_t = a_{0t} + a_{1t}D_{t-1} + a_{2t}A_t + a_{3t}/P_t \tag{2.20}$$

where

A_t = advertising efficiency in period t,
P_t = price in period t,
a_{it} = coefficients estimated across decision periods.

The finance sector of the model guarantees that the benefits from the cash flow are realized. It includes variables representing per-period investment/disinvestment in marketable securities and additional short-term debt incurred or retired.

The problem is formulated as an enormously complicated nonlinear-programming problem in which the objective function to be maximized represents the terminal cash position of the firm. The authors employ an algorithm of Fiacco & McCormick [1968] called the 'sequential unconstrained minimization technique' (SUMT). However, as Damon & Schramm admit, their model does not meet the convexity requirements required by the SUMT algorithm, and thus they can obtain only a local optimum.

Nonetheless, Damon & Schramm are able to make comparisons between coordinated and decentralized decisions. They demonstrate that, for certain hypothetical parameter values, the solution to the coordinated-decisions case, even though not optimal, is better than the result obtained under the decentralized-decisions case for which the best solution is obtained. The decentralized case is analyzed by optimizing the marketing system first and using the resulting demand as an input when optimizing the production and finance sectors.

Welam [1977b] commends Damon & Schramm's paper for combining marketing, production and financial decision-making, and for their idea of 'assessing experimentally' the advantages of coordination of such decisions. However, Welam points out what he sees as a few shortcomings of the Damon & Schramm model. These objections center mainly on Damon & Schramm's assumed demand function. Welam argues that empirical evidence supports a demand function of the following form that does *not* incorporate price (compare with (2.20)):

$$D_t = a_0 + a_1 D_{t-1} + a_2 f(A_t). \tag{2.21}$$

Welam also claims that the inclusion of price variables in lag equations poses potentially troublesome questions. The problem is that "under certain conditions demands can remain positive no matter how high prices are, so arbitrarily large profits can be earned by posting exorbitant prices". This observation, in Welam's opinion, renders the interpretation of the numerical results reported by Damon & Schramm rather difficult. As a concrete illustration, Welam shows that it is possible to obtain an arbitrarily high profit for only the marketing sector, using the parameter values employed by Damon & Schramm, thus contradicting the superiority of the simultaneous (i.e. coordinated) decision-making case. (Later, Damon & Schramm [1977] published a rejoinder to Welam's note.)

That same year, Welam [1977a] provided his own formulation for evaluating the benefits of coordination of short-run production and marketing decisions by constructing two models. The first is a coordinated production–marketing model, denoted PD (for production smoothing and demand). The second is a sequential model composed of a marketing submodel, denoted D, which determines the optimal marketing mix and yields a demand forecast, and a production submodel, denoted P, which takes the demand forecast of the D-submodel as input and seeks to minimize the total cost of smoothing production. (This sequential procedure is in line with the one discussed earlier and represented through Equations (2.9)–(2.16).)

Welam's D-model considers short-run marketing decisions. The decision variables are as follows. In period t:

P_t = price,
S_t = amount of sales promotion,
M_t = vector of all other marketing variables in period t.

Let $\boldsymbol{P}$, $\boldsymbol{S}$, $\boldsymbol{M}$ denote, respectively, the vectors of price, sales promotion, and all other marketing variables in periods 0, 1, 2,…, T, where P_0, S_0 and M_0 are initial values. Then demand in period t is given by $D_t = f(P_t, S_t, M_t)$.

The objective for the marketing submodel (D) is:

$$\underset{\boldsymbol{P},\boldsymbol{S},\boldsymbol{M}}{\text{maximize}} \sum_{t=1}^{T} R_t = \sum_{t=1}^{T} \{(P_t - \bar{c}_t)D_t - S_t - c(M_t)\} \tag{2.22}$$

where, in each period t:

R_t = revenue net of the marketing-related costs,
$\bar{c}_t$ = production cost,
$c(M_t)$ = total cost of all marketing instruments other than price and promotion.

Welam's P-model is precisely the formulation of Holt, Modigliani, Muth & Simon [1960] which, unlike Damon & Schramm, he does not modify. Here, the decision variables consist of production rate and work-force level in each of T periods, where the objective function to be minimized contains the following cost terms: regular payroll, hiring and layoff, overtime, and inventory-connected costs. The HMMS total cost function is quadratic, which leads to linear decision rules. The formulation is:

$$\underset{W,Q}{\text{minimize}} \quad \sum_{t=1}^{T} C_t \tag{2.23}$$

$$\text{subject to} \quad I_t = I_{t-1} + Q_t - D_t \quad t = 1, 2, \ldots, T, \tag{2.24}$$

$$W_t, Q_t \geqslant 0 \quad t = 1, 2, \ldots, T, \tag{2.25}$$

where

C_t = total cost per period t, which includes regular payroll costs, hiring and layoff costs, overtime costs, and inventory-connected costs.

In each period t:

W_t = size of the work force,
Q_t = aggregate production rate

where

I_t = inventory level,
D_t = forecasted demand.

Under the simultaneous (coordinated) decision problem (PD) the formulation is given as:

$$\underset{Q,W,x,y}{\text{minimize}} \quad \sum_{t=1}^{T} [C_t - \Delta R_t] \tag{2.26}$$

$$\text{subject to} \quad I_t = I_{t-1} + Q_t - (D_t^* + \Delta D_t) \tag{2.27}$$

where

$$x_t = P_t - P_t^*,$$
$$y_t = S_t - S_t^*,$$
$$\Delta D_t = D_t - D_t^*,$$
$$\Delta R_t = R_t - R_t^*$$

represent deviations of the variables P_t, S_t, D_t, R_t in the marketing system from their optimal values, $P_t^*, S_t^*, D_t^*, R_t^*$. (Welam makes the assumption that all marketing instruments other than price and promotion do not change. Hence, no deviations with respect to $\boldsymbol{M}$ are considered.)

The model is solved via nonlinear programming. Simulation analyses suggest, numerically, that coordinating the marketing and production decisions yields some (albeit not dramatic) total cost savings vis-à-vis the case where the two systems operate in a decentralized manner. Additionally, in two out of the three simulation runs the marketing unit underpriced and overpromoted in the sequential (decentralized) model as compared with the simultaneous (coordinated) model.

Another investigation of the nature of coordination between marketing and production strategies has been undertaken by Freeland [1980]. His paper analyzes a single-period model which allows marketing to choose prices and promotion strategies in a decentralized manner. The focus is on the type and manner of information which must be known in order to find the joint optimum.

The simultaneous case is modeled by Freeland as:

$$\underset{P,S,U}{\text{maximize}}\ P\cdot D(P,S) - c(U, D(P,S)) - S \tag{2.28}$$

where the decision variables are

P = price,
S = amount of sales promotion,
U = variable representing production technology.

(Freeland is not very specific about how U is measured, but in an example he allows it to take on the discrete values 1 and 2 corresponding to two different production cost functions.)

$$D(P,S) = aP^{-\alpha_1}S^{\alpha_2} = \text{demand}, \tag{2.29}$$

$$c(U, D(P,S)) = \text{total production cost, assumed to be convex.}$$

The parameters α_1, α_2 are the price and promotion elasticity, respectively, and a is a normalization factor. For the decentralized mode, marketing determines P and S by maximizing revenue minus production cost minus production expenses where it is assumed that marginal unit cost, $\bar{c}$, is constant. That is, the marketing objective is:

$$\underset{(P,S)}{\text{maximize}}\ P\cdot D(P,S) - \bar{c}\cdot D(P,S) - S. \tag{2.30}$$

The above problem could generate an optimal demand D^{**}, and production could then find the profit-maximizing value of U by minimizing $c(U, D^{**})$. The difficulty, notes Freeland, is that in order for marketing to find the optimal price and promotion they need to know the marginal cost, $\bar{c}$. This figure can be supplied by production only if it knows what the demand is. This provides another motivation for coordinating the decision-making. Freeland shows, however, that if marketing solves its problem (2.30) using an *estimate* of marginal cost based on historical information or on information supplied by production, then an error in this approximation will have the following consequences: If the estimate of marginal cost used by marketing underestimates the actual marginal cost, then marketing will set prices lower and promotion higher than is optimal. As a result, demand will be higher than is optimal, and profit will be lower than optimal. Similarly, if the estimate of marginal cost overestimates the actual marginal cost, then demand will be lower than is optimal, and profit will again be lower than optimal. In a multi-period setting, Freeland proposes the use of a computer model to determine the interaction effects between marketing and production systems with information autonomy and decentralization.

Abad [1987] formulates a continuous-time dynamic optimal control model of joint finance–marketing–production systems. The marketing subsystem is represented by the Nerlove–Arrow [1962] model:

$$\dot{G} = u - \delta G, \tag{2.31}$$

$$D = f(P, G, Z), \tag{2.32}$$

where

$G(t)$ = level of goodwill at time t,
$u(t)$ = advertising expenditure at time t,
$P(t)$ = price at time t,
$D(t)$ = sales (demand) rate at time t,
$Z(t)$ = exogenous variables at time t representing factors affecting the sales rate,
δ = (constant) rate of depreciation.

The production function is represented by a continuous-time version of the Holt, Modigliani, Muth & Simon [1960] model:

$$\dot{I} = Q - D, \tag{2.33}$$

$$\dot{W} = m, \tag{2.34}$$

where

$I(t)$ = level of inventory at time t,
$W(t)$ = size of the work force at time t,
$Q(t)$ = rate of production at time t,
$m(t)$ = rate of change of work-force level (hire-and-fire rate) at time t.

Total production–marketing costs include the following components: regular payroll costs, overtime–undertime costs, inventory costs, raw materials cost, and hiring-and-firing costs.

The finance subsystem is modeled as:

$$\dot{X} = r_1 X - r_2 Y + B - E, \tag{2.35}$$

$$\dot{Y} = B, \tag{2.36}$$

where

$X(t)$ = cash reserves at time t,
$Y(t)$ = short-term debt at time t,
r_1 = rate of interest associated with cash reserves (which may be a function of time),

r_2 = rate of interest associated with short-term debt (which may be a function of time),
$B(t)$ = rate of borrowing at time t,
$E(t)$ = rate of overall cash outflow at time t.

The objective function of the coordinated (centralized) system is to maximize the cash reserves minus the short-term debt plus the value of goodwill, inventory and work-force level at the end of the time horizon:

$$\text{maximize } X(T) - Y(T) + b_1 G(T) + b_2 I(T) + b_3 W(T) \tag{2.37}$$

where b_1, b_2 and b_3 represent the unit value at time T, respectively, of goodwill, inventory and work-force level.

The model thus has five state variables, (X, Y, G, I, W) and five control variables, (B, u, P, Q, m). Abad proposes a solution procedure for the coordinated problem based on decomposing the overall system. The case where the marketing–production and financial policies are made sequentially is also analyzed. Abad concludes that: "The decentralized procedure presented... highlights the role the discount interest rate and the transfer price play in the coordination of functional decisions in a firm.... sequential planning becomes feasible when the discount interest rate is pre-set to some appropriate level".

Sogomonian & Tang [1993] have also presented a modeling framework for evaluating the benefits of coordinating promotion and production decisions. Their promotion decision includes the timing and the level of promotion. The modeling framework consists of the development of a baseline (decentralized) model and an integrated (coordinated) model. For each model the problem is formulated as a mixed integer program. The decentralized problem is formulated such that the marketing subsystem has to decide whether to promote or not promote (and, if to promote, at what level):

$$\underset{S \subseteq \{1,2,\ldots,T\}}{\text{maximize}} \quad \sum_t P_t D[t - L(t), s(L(t))] - \sum_{\tau \in S} A[\tau, s(\tau)] \tag{2.38}$$

$$\text{subject to} \quad L(t) = \max\{\tau : \tau \in S, \tau \leqslant t\} \quad \text{for each } t, \tag{2.39}$$

$$s(\tau) \in \{1, 2, \ldots, N\} \quad \text{for each } \tau \in S \tag{2.40}$$

where

P_t = retail price per unit in period t,
$D[\cdot,\cdot]$ = demand in period t,
$L(t)$ = period in which the last promotion takes place at or before period t,
$t - L(t)$ = time elapsed since the last promotion,
$A[\cdot,\cdot]$ = cost of promoting in period τ at level $s(\tau)$.
S = set of promotion periods.

The decision variables are τ and $s(\tau)$, where

τ = any promotion period,
$s(\tau) \in \{1, 2, \ldots, N\}$ = promotion level incurred in period τ.

That is, the objective of the marketing subsystem is to maximize total net revenue, which equals total revenue minus total promotion cost. Constraint (2.39) guarantees that $L(t)$ is the period at which the last promotion before t is held, and constraint (2.40) specifies that the promotion effort $s(\tau)$ is discrete. This problem, above, can be reformulated as a longest-path problem over a directed network and then solved in polynomial time.

The decentralized production problem is formulated in a similar manner:

$$\underset{Q_t}{\text{minimize}} \quad \sum_t \{K_t\delta(Q_t) + c_tQ_t + h_tI_t\} \tag{2.41}$$

$$\text{subject to} \quad I_{t+1} = I_t + Q_t - D[t - L(t), s(L(t))] \quad \text{for each } t, \tag{2.42}$$

$$I_t \geqslant 0, \; Q_t \geqslant 0, \tag{2.43}$$

where

K_t = setup cost in period t,
$\delta(Q) = 1$ if $Q > 0$ and 0 otherwise,
Q_t = production quantity in period t (a decision variable),
c_t = production cost per unit in period t,
h_t = unit inventory holding cost in period t.

The production problem is recognized here as a dynamic lot-sizing problem which can be solved by applying the Wagner–Whitin [1958b] algorithm once the demand is determined from the previous problem. (We discuss the Wagner–Whitin algorithm in more detail in Section 4.)

The coordinated decision-making problem is formulated as the following program:

$$\underset{\substack{Q_t \\ S \subseteq \{1,2,\ldots,T\} \\ s(\tau)}}{\text{maximize}} \quad \left\{ \sum_t P_t D[t - L(t), s(L(t))] - \sum_{\tau \in S} A[\tau, s(\tau)] - \sum_t \{K_t\delta(Q_t) + c_tQ_t + h_tI_t\} \right\}, \tag{2.44}$$

$$\text{subject to} \quad L(t) = \max\{\tau : \tau \in S, \tau \leqslant t\} \quad \text{for each } t, \tag{2.45}$$

$$s(\tau) = \{1, 2, \ldots, N\} \quad \text{for each } \tau \in L, \tag{2.46}$$

$$I_{t+1} = I_t + Q_t - D[t - L(t), s(L(t))] \quad \text{for each } t, \tag{2.47}$$

$$I_t \geqslant 0, Q_t \geqslant 0 \quad \text{for each } t. \tag{2.48}$$

That is, the objective function is the total net profits which is equal to the total revenue minus the total promotion, setup, production, and inventory-holding costs. The authors note that the solution generated from the decentralized decision-making problems is feasible, but not necessarily optimal, for the coordinated problem. Recall: optimum(system1 + system2) $\geqslant$ optimum(system1) + optimum(system2). The coordinated problem is a mixed-integer-programming problem which in general is difficult to solve. However, by exploiting a network structure similar to that associated with the two decentralized problems, the authors are able to reformulate the problem as a 'nested' longest-path problem which is solvable. The approach calls for a decomposition of the large problem into two subproblems. A numerical example provided by the authors suggest that, for certain parameter values, the total net profit generated by the coordinated mechanism leads to a 13% increase relative to making the marketing and production decisions in a decentralized fashion.

2.3. Other approaches

Using agency theory, which is based on the assumption that managers of a firm will each act in their own self-interest, Porteus & Whang [1991] consider incentive plans that will induce manufacturing and product managers to act so that the owner of the firm can maximize as much as possible of the residual returns.

The formulation centers around a capacity-allocation subproblem modeled as a newsboy problem [Hax & Candea, 1984]. The firm is assumed to produce N products in a single period manufactured by a single facility. Each unit of product i requires a_i units of production capacity, costs c_i to produce, and sells at market price P_i. By assumption, $0 < c_i < P_i$. Unsatisfied demand is lost, and each unit of inventory unsold at the end of the period has a salvage value of $r_i < c_i$. The available capacity b of the manufacturing facility is a random variable which is the sum of the fixed capacity, b_0, a component e_0 consisting of the effort exerted by the manufacturing manager, each unit of which results in an additional unit of capacity, and an additive stochastic shock ε having mean zero whose realization is observed only by the manufacturing manager. Thus, the available capacity b is simply expressed as

$$b = b_0 + e_0 + \varepsilon. \tag{2.49}$$

Each of the N products has its own product manager who can exert effort e_i to increase the demand $D_i(e_i)$ for his product. Further, each of the $N+1$ players maximizes his respective utility given by

$$U_i(s_i, e_i) = s_i - g_i(e_i) \tag{2.50}$$

for $i = 0, 1, 2, \ldots, N$ (where $i = 0$ denotes the manufacturing manager), where s_i is the realized monetary payment to the manager from the owner, and g_i is an effort-cost function. In addition, Porteus & Whang make the assumption that each manager, including the manufacturing manager, is risk-neutral. The owner's problem is to find an incentive plan for the managers which will maximize net expected return of the firm.

Porteus & Whang [1991] present two alternatives. In the first plan, the owner seeks a scheduled $N+1$-vector e^S of effort levels, and a scheduled contingent N-vector $I^S(b)$ of inventory levels for every possible realization b of capacity, so as to maximize the net expected return of the firm. There are three constraints that need to be taken into account: each contingent inventory vector must be feasible for each realized capacity level, each manager must receive at least zero expected utility, and the scheduled effort vector must be a Nash equilibrium. (An effort vector is a Nash equilibrium if no manager can obtain a higher utility for himself while all the other managers maintain their own effort vectors.) Once the incentive plan is announced, the $N+1$ managers simultaneously face their respective optimization problem of selecting an effort level e_i and maximize their respective expected utility. Here, each manager's effort level e_i is unobservable by all others and the capacity shock ε is observable only by the manufacturing manager. Next, the resulting available capacity b is observed by all, and the scheduled inventory level $I^S(b)$ is implemented. Finally, demand, sales and contribution are realized, and the owner pays the managers in accordance with the incentive plan.

Porteus & Whang interpret this first plan as the owner setting up a subcontracting/franchising arrangement by subcontracting to pay the manufacturing manager a fixed rate for all capacity he delivers, and franchising out a product line for a fixed fee to each product manager who receives all returns realized from sale of his respective product. The authors show that this plan induces the same effort levels and achieves the same expected returns as the case in which managerial effort is observable. However, this incentive plan may result in insufficient capacity, and the marketing managers will likely complain about the inventory-level decisions despite these levels being announced in advance.

The second incentive plan is a revised version of the first; now the owner can eliminate marketing's complaints by delegating the inventory decisions to the respective product managers. Under the revised plan, each product manager pays not only an (adjusted) fixed franchise fee, but also a levy for each unit of capacity used that is contingent on the total capacity realized. Under this plan, the owner no longer announces a scheduled vector of inventory levels for each possible realization of capacity. Rather, the inventory level for product i is selected by product manager i. Thus, each product manager is required to obtain from the owner's firm the capacity needed to make his product at the scheduled unit marginal value. With this incentive structure in place, the product managers will now agree with the owner on the inventory levels being chosen.

Porteus & Whang interpret this revised incentive plan as the owner making a futures market for manufacturing capacity by paying the manufacturing manager the expected value for each unit of capacity delivered and reselling this capacity to the product managers at the realized marginal value. By paying on the basis of expected rather than realized marginal value, the owner avoids encouraging the managers to exert less than optimal effort, to increase the marginal value on average and obtain additional returns for themselves. While the owner must be prepared to accept a loss in the process of making this market, the same returns are achieved as in the observable case, as the fixed fees are adjusted to compensate for this loss.

Flexibility of manufacturing is the topic of De Groote [1991], who is motivated in part by issues on this topic raised by Shapiro [1977] and by Montgomery &

Hausman [1986]. First, De Groote considers the marketing problem of choosing the optimal mix of product variety as a function of the flexibility of the production process. Second, he considers the production problem of optimal investment in process flexibility as a function of the variety of the product line. Finally, he considers the joint decision problem.

The scenario De Groote considers involves a monopolist facing a market with consumer preferences distributed uniformly over the real line $[0, \bar{a}]$ where the total market potential is given by $a = \bar{a}\theta$, for some market parameters $\bar{a}$ and θ. The firm chooses how many products n to produce as well as the characteristic x_i and price P_i for each product, $i = 1, 2, \ldots, n$. Every consumer $\alpha \in [0, \bar{a}]$ is assumed to have the same reservation price $\bar{P}$, and each a single product i, where

$$\arg\min_{i \in n} \{P_i + \delta|\alpha - x_i|\}, \tag{2.51}$$

assuming that the minimum is smaller than the reservation price $\bar{P}$; otherwise, the consumer does not patronize the firm. Here δ is a parameter representing *intensity of consumer preference*. The production sector of the firm is modeled as a multi-product EOQ problem [Hax & Candea, 1984, Section 4.2] under the simplifying assumption that the cost parameters – i.e. change-over/setup cost K, unit production cost c, and unit inventory-holding cost h – are identical for the n products.

The decentralized marketing problem is as follows. Given a technology specified by a cost triple (c, h, K), the marketing department chooses the number of different products n to produce; their characteristics, x_i $(i = 1, 2, \ldots, n)$; and their selling prices, P_i $(i = 1, 2, \ldots, n)$. The market then determines the quantity sold. Here, De Groote acknowledges the parallel between his model and the classic model of Hotelling [1929].

Under his assumptions, De Groote finds the following: the segments of the market that are served should be of equal lengths and the characteristics of the products should correspond to the favorite characteristics of the customer located in the middle of the market segment. Further, the profit associated with a segment of size μ in the space of consumers' characteristics $[0, a]$ is

$$\Pi(\mu) = \left(\bar{P} - \frac{\delta\mu}{2}\right). \tag{2.52}$$

Further, De Groote finds that it is always optimal to serve the whole market and that the optimal number of products associated with a given technology c, h, K is

$$n^*(K) = \bar{a} \cdot \sqrt[3]{\frac{\delta^2\theta}{2Kh}}. \tag{2.53}$$

Next, based on his findings that the optimal product-line has a very simple structure, De Groote proceeds to consider the decentralized production problem under the assumption that each of the n products equally split the market demand, together with his earlier assumption that the cost structure for all products are identical. He uses this in his third proposition in which he considers the problem of the comparison of two technologies which differ in setup and investment costs. He points out that the same problem for the case of one product is analyzed by Porteus [1985], which we will discuss in Section 4.1.

Let $\boldsymbol{K}$ denote the set of available technologies identified by a setup cost K. An investment cost $s(K)$ is associated with a technology of setup cost $K \in \boldsymbol{K}$. His production problem of optimal technology choice is

$$\min_{K \in \boldsymbol{K}} \{s(K) + \sqrt{2Kh} + ca\}. \tag{2.54}$$

He then proceeds to compare two technologies (differing only in setup cost and investment cost).

The coordinated marketing–production problem considers how the optimal design of the product line and of the production process can be combined for a globally optimal strategy. Here, De Groote provides a sufficient condition for the decentralized solution to be globally optimal. He points out that the logarithmic form of the setup cost employed by Porteus [1985] is easily seen to satisfy his condition (see Section 4.1). His condition is: If $\bar{s}(K) \equiv s(K^3)$ is a convex function of K, then the Nash equilibrium solution for the two-player game is sufficient for profit maximization.

Further, De Groote points out that "inefficient decisions may obtain even when both departments are basing their decision on the overall long-term profit of the firm". Such inefficiencies stem from the coordination problem created by the presence of local optima (nonconvexities). He further suggests consideration of an iterative process by which the firm could coordinate its marketing and production decisions. As he explains it:

> "Conventionally, different departments are specialized in making different decisions, taking the decisions of the other departments as given. The following decision process seems natural in that context: Marketing (say) first announces a candidate for its part of the strategy. Production then computes the best technology given that strategy, and announces that technology to marketing. At that point, given that technology, marketing revises its part of the strategy. Production then recomputes the optimal technology".

The procedure continues until a stopping condition is met, although the solution obtained is not necessarily optimal. In Section 4.2, we discuss a pricing/ordering algorithm due to Kunreuther & Schrage [1973] that works along these lines.

Here, De Groote has two main conclusions about the managerial implications relating to the coordination of marketing and production decisions. The first is that "marketing strategy should be evaluated not only on the basis of revenues (or market share) and direct costs, but also on the basis of its effect on indirect operations criteria (such as inventory and changeover costs)". The second managerial conclusion is that "changes in marketing and manufacturing strategy should be planned and evaluated jointly. In particular, the justification of investment in flexibility should not be based on the current marketing strategy. It should be based on a new marketing strategy that takes advantage of the increased flexibility". (See also the related work of Caulkins & Fine [1990], Fine & Freund [1990] and Milgrom & Roberts [1990].)

Cohen, Eliashberg & Ho [1992] address the coordination aspect from a somewhat different perspective. Their analysis focuses on the new-product development process and includes the following issues:

- What is the point at which investment in the new-product performance-enhancement becomes counter-productive because of resulting delay in the new-product introduction?
- What is the optimal launching time?
- What is the potential impact of the sales of an existing product on the time to market the new product (i.e. cannibalization)?
- Is a new-product development metric such as break-even time [House & Price, 1991] consistent with a profit-maximization objective?

This process is divided conceptually into three major stages of activity: development, process (production), and marketing. The output of each stage is the performance of the product. The rate at which performance is being enhanced at each stage is given by:

$$\dot{Q}_i(t) = W_i(t)^{\alpha_i(t)} V_i^{\beta_i}, \quad T_{i-1} \leqslant t < T_i, \tag{2.55}$$

and the overall new-product performance-level at time t is

$$Q(t) = Q(T_{i-1}) + Q_i(t), \quad T_{i-1} \leqslant t < T_i, \tag{2.56}$$

where $i = 1, 2, 3$ correspond respectively to the development, process and marketing phases, and

$W_i(t)$ = labor input rate for stage i,
V_i = capital input for stage i,
$\alpha_i(t)$ = labor-production-productivity parameter at time t for stage i,
β_i = capital-production-productivity parameter at time t for stage i,
T_i = completion time for stage i, where $T_i = T_{i-1} + \tau_i$ $(T_0 = 0)$,
τ_i = elapsed development time for stage i,
$Q_i(t)$ = performance level at time t in stage i, where $Q(0) = Q_0$.

Equation (2.55) captures the notion of a Cobb–Douglas production function that transfers inputs into outputs in a dynamic context.

It is further assumed that each stage i invests resources over the half-open interval (T_{i-1}, T_i). The single-stage total cost functions are defined as

$$\mathrm{TC}_i(t) = \int_{T_{i-1}}^{t} L_i(s) W_i(s) \mathrm{d}s + C_i V_i, \quad T_{i-1} \leqslant t < T_i, \tag{2.57}$$

and the total costs invested in the new product by time t is

$$\mathrm{TC}(t) = \mathrm{TC}(T_{i-1}) + \mathrm{TC}_i(t), \quad T_{i-1} \leqslant t < T_i, \tag{2.58}$$

where

$L_i(t)$ = labor wage rate for stage i at t,
C_i = lumpy unit cost of capital charged at the beginning of stage i.

The auhtors formulate a total profit function, based on the previous components and the fact that the demand for the product is influenced by its performance relative to that of competing products. Insights that can be gained from the Cohen, Eliashberg & Ho [1992] analyses include:

- Under certain conditions $(W_1^{\alpha_1} V_1^{\beta_1} \neq W_2^{\alpha_2} V_2^{\beta_2})$ it is optimal to spend efforts *either* in the development stage only *or* the process stage only. That is, resources should be allocated to the most productive phase, thereby minimizing the time spent on the less productive phases.
- Based on the above insight, a closed-form solution is derived for the optimal launching time. Comparative statics indicate that the optimal time to market a new product increases with (1) the existing product margin, (2) the new-product profit margin, (3) the product-category demand rate, and (4) the length of the window of opportunity.
- Cannibalization always delays the new-product launching time.
- Minimizing break-even time tends to induce premature introductions of new products from a profit-maximization standpoint.

2.4. Summary

This section has discussed various possible formulations of decentralized vs. coordinated problems of marketing–production joint decision-making. The material of this section shows that typically the coordinated decision-making problem results in better performance for the system. The magnitude of the improvement depends on how the objective functions are defined for the two separate departments and which department is assumed to act first. Various models have been reviewed and it has been characteristically assumed that, under the decentralized decision-making approach, the marketing decisions are made first, determining the demand and hence the total production quantity, which the production function needs to consider in its (normally specified) subsequent minimization-of-total-costs problem. Other approaches have shed light on the role of asymmetric information, risk-aversion, flexibility, and the new-product development process. They too indicate the benefits that emerge from a harmonious relationship between the marketing and production functions.

3. Smoothing unstable demand: Convex-cost models

Production researchers have identified several ways that management can use to absorb changing (unstable) demand patterns. These include:

(1) Changing the size of the work force by hiring and laying off workers, thus allowing for changes in the production rate.
(2) Accumulating *seasonal* inventory while maintaining a uniform production rate, thus anticipating future demand [Hax & Candea, 1984, p. 70].

This stream of research is often referred to in the production literature as 'aggregate production planning'. As Hax & Candea [1984, p. 69] explain: "This aggregation can take place by consolidating similar items into product groups, different machines into machine centers, different labor skills into labor centers, and individual customers into market regions [i.e. segments]". The essence of the problem is the production-cost structure faced by management. When the objective (cost) function to be optimized (minimized) has a *convex* cost component, the various models developed in this area are known as convex-cost models. Johnson & Montgomery [1974, p. 208] have lucidly described how such a cost structure can arise:

> "The convex model often results from situations where there are multiple production (or procurement) sources in a period and it is assumed that production costs are proportional to the quantity produced by a source. By assigning production first to the source with the lowest unit cost until its capacity is reached, then proceeding to use the next cheapest source to capacity, etc., one develops a total production cost that is convex in the total amount scheduled for the period".

Abel [1985] makes a similar observation in the opening paragraph of his paper:

> "It is a well-known proposition that a firm producing a storable good under conditions of increasing marginal cost will tend to smooth the time profile of its production relative to the time profile of its sales. The incentive to smooth production arises from the fact that the cost function is a convex function of the level of production. For a given average level of production, average costs can be reduced by reducing the variation in production. Of course, if the cost function is linear in the level of production, then this incentive to smooth production disappears".

Empirically, the convexity-of-the-cost-function assumption has received some support via an approach called 'process analysis' which was taken up by Griffin [1972]. Griffin has demonstrated that a process-analysis approach [Manne, 1958] to estimating production-cost functions, rather than a statistical cost-function approach, indeed yields the property of increasing marginal costs (i.e. convexity). The statistical cost function makes use of accounting data and uses sample observations of costs and outputs. The process-analysis approach, on the other hand, estimates the cost function from engineering data.

3.1. The pure production approach

Production-based problems considering convex cost of production per unit time (usually taken to be a year) in the objective function have been formulated as both discrete-time and continuous-time models. We will begin our survey by first focusing, rather selectivity, on a number of purely production-based models, which we will discuss in chronological order. These models have typically been constructed to minimize costs. We will then proceed to discuss a more recent subset of models that incorporate both production and marketing variables, in particular, pricing; these models have typically been formulated to maximize profits.

Under the assumption of convex production costs and linear inventory-holding costs, Modigliani & Hohn [1955] consider how production should be scheduled over T time periods in order to satisfy known demand in each period at lowest total cost. Their model can be solved via an algorithm that can be implemented graphically. Hax & Candea [1984, p. 105] point out that what is most important in the work of Modigliani & Hohn is the *qualitative* properties associated with the *planning horizon.*

The planning horizon concept can be easily summarized. Consider a production-scheduling problem in which optimal decisions are to be made over a time period from time zero to time T. It is possible that the optimal decisions made during an initial time interval $[0, t^*]$ $(0 < t^* < T)$ are either partially or wholly independent of the data from some point t^{**} $(t^* < t^{**} < T)$ onwards, i.e. over the interval $[t^{**}, T]$. In such a case, t^* is called the *planning horizon*, and t^{**} is called the *forecast horizon.* If the optimal decisions during the interval up until the planning horizon t^* are completely independent of the data beyond the forecast horizon t^{**}, then the planning horizon is called a *strong planning horizon* and the forecast horizon is a *strong forecast horizon.* If, however, there exist mild restrictions on the data after the forecast horizon, i.e. on $[t^{**}, T]$, then the forecast and planning horizons are said to be *weak.*

Modigliani & Hohn [1955] show that for their convex-cost model there is no strong planning horizon $(0 < t^* < T)$, but there may be a weak planning horizon which coincides with the weak forecast horizon, in which case only the *cumulative* demand over the interval $[t^*, T]$ is required to make optimal decisions over $[0, t^*]$. In general, the interval $[0, T]$ can be partitioned into subintervals defined by a series of planning horizons, where the optimal plan within each subinterval is independent of the requirements and the costs outside the subinterval. (As we discuss in more detail in Section 4.2, Wagner & Whitin [1958b] and Eppen, Gould & Pashigian [1969] show that a strong planning horizon may exist under the assumption of concave costs and that the planning horizon and the forecast horizon are identical.) Modigliani & Hohn explain that in their problem the inventory variable provides the link between current and future production decisions, and that there are two major factors that tend toward breaking this link, viz., the cost of carrying inventories and the non-negativity constraint on inventories. Without the non-negativity constraint on inventory, the optimal production and inventory levels depend on all T periods. With the non-negativity constraint, the link to future production is broken whenever the optimal schedule calls for zero inventory, since future demands cannot reduce the inventory level below zero. Further, as the cost of inventory rises, it becomes increasingly less attractive to produce for future demand; the further out the time period the less relevant the demand in that period, and past a certain point forward the demand requirements are irrelevant to current-period decisions.

Arrow & Karlin [1958] present one of the pioneering continuous-time convex-production-cost models. In their model,

$Q(t)$ = rate of production at time t,
$c(Q)$ = cost of production per unit of time when the rate of production is Q,
$D(t)$ = demand rate at time t,
$I(t)$ = number of units in inventory at time t,
h = per-unit inventory-holding cost per unit time.

The problem of interest is to choose $Q(t)$, the production rate at time t $(0 \leqslant t \leqslant T)$, so as to minimize the production and inventory costs incurred during time period $[0, T]$.

Mathematically, the problem is formulated as:

$$\underset{Q(t)}{\text{minimize}} \quad J(Q) = \int_0^T \left\{ c[Q(t)] + h\left[I(0) + \int_0^t Q(\tau)\mathrm{d}\tau - \int_0^t D(\tau)\mathrm{d}\tau \right] \right\} \mathrm{d}t \tag{3.1}$$

$$\text{subject to} \quad I(0) + \int_0^t Q(\tau)\mathrm{d}\tau \geqslant \int_0^t D(\tau)\mathrm{d}\tau, \tag{3.2}$$

$$Q(t) \geqslant 0. \tag{3.3}$$

The objective function (3.1) represents the totality of the production and inventory-holding costs, whereas constraints (3.2) and (3.3) capture the fact that both the inventory level and the production rate are non-negative. Arrow & Karlin note that their model represents a continuous-time analogue of the Modigliani & Hohn [1955] discrete-time model.

Noting that it is obvious that for any optimal production policy no inventory will remain at time T, Arrow & Karlin provide, by construction, a solution to problem (3.1)–(3.3) through characterization of the optimal cumulative production through time t, $\int_0^t Q^*(\tau)\mathrm{d}\tau$. A special case provided by the authors involving a quadratic cost function, $C(Q) = Q^2/2$, and a linear demand rate, $D(t) = D \cdot t$, illustrates the dependency of the optimal production policy, $Q^*(t)$, upon the relationship that exists between the inventory unit holding cost, h, and the demand-slope parameter, D. When $h < D$, the optimal production policy is one of the following two forms, depending on the parameters of the problem:

$$Q^*(t) = \frac{1}{2}(D - h)T - \frac{1}{T}I(0) + ht, \tag{3.4a}$$

$$Q^*(t)=\begin{cases}0 & \text{for } 0<t<v_0\\ h(t-v_0) & \text{for } v_0\leqslant t\leqslant T,\end{cases} \tag{3.4b}$$

where v_0 in (3.4b) is a function of the basic parameters of the problem. The authors show that v_0 will be positive if and only if the cumulative demand over the time horizon exceeds the starting inventory. However when $h\geqslant D$, a different solution obtains:

$$Q^*(t)=\begin{cases}0 & \text{for } 0<t<v^0,\\ D\cdot t & \text{for } v^0\leqslant t\leqslant T,\end{cases} \tag{3.5}$$

where v^0 is a function of the basic parameters of the model.

Qualitatively, if the holding cost is strictly less than the rate of increase in the demand rate, the optimal policy is either to produce at a constantly increasing rate (3.4a), *or* to first withhold production and draw down the initial inventory, and then to produce at a constantly increasing rate (3.4b). If, however, the holding cost is at least as great as the rate of increase in demand, production should be withheld until inventory is drawn down to zero, after which production should precisely meet demand (3.5).

Holt, Modigliani, Muth & Simon [1960, Section 2-2] present a discrete-time formulation for responding to demand fluctuations by setting the aggregate production rate and the work-force size. Their model grew out of a study of factory decisions for one of the divisions of a large company which manufactured paint. The authors' objective was to obtain simple mathematical decision rules to achieve optimal or near-optimal solutions to the management's objectives. The resulting quadratic cost objective function incorporates inventory, overtime and employment costs for any set of cost parameters:

$$\underset{W,Q}{\text{minimize}} \quad C_T=\sum_{t=1}^{T} C_t \tag{3.6}$$

$$\text{subject to} \quad I_t=I_{t-1}+Q_t-D_t, \quad t=1,2,\ldots,T, \tag{3.7}$$

$$Q_t,\, W_t\geqslant 0, \qquad t=1,2,\ldots,T, \tag{3.8}$$

where $\boldsymbol{W}$ and $\boldsymbol{Q}$ are two vectors of decision variables, corresponding to the period-by-period size of the work force and the aggregate production rate, respectively. The total cost per period, C_t, is the sum of the following components:

$$c_1W_t+c_{13} \qquad \text{regular payroll costs,} \tag{3.9}$$

$$c_2(W_t-W_{t-1}-c_{11})^2 \qquad \text{hiring and layoff costs,} \tag{3.10}$$

$$c_3(Q_t-c_4W_t)^2+c_5Q_t-c_6W_t+c_{12}Q_tW_t \qquad \text{overtime costs,} \tag{3.11}$$

$c_7(I_t - c_8 - c_9 D_t)^2$ inventory-connected costs, (3.12)

where the c_i are constants.

By differentiating the quadratic objective function with respect to each decision variable, a system of linear equations is obtained. The solution of this system yields an algorithm based on two decision rules to be applied at the beginning of each period. The two rules determine the aggregate production rate and the work-force level. The rule for the production rate incorporates a weighted average of the forecasts of future demands, resulting in smoothed production. Due to the cost of holding inventory, the weight given to future orders decreases rapidly as the forecast extends forward in time; hence it does not make economic sense to produce for shipment too far into the future. Neither does it make sense to forecast order too far forward: for the actual cost estimates from the paint factory, forecasts of three periods were found to be the major determinants of production orders.

A somewhat more general production-cost function has been adopted by Johnson & Montgomery [1974, Section 4-3.3]. They assume that the cost of production and inventory in period t is given by

$$C_t(Q_t, I_t) = c_t(Q_t) + h_t(I_t) \tag{3.13}$$

where $c_t(Q_t)$ is *convex* for $Q_t \geqslant 0$, and $h_t(I_t)$ is also *convex* where I_t is unconstrained in sign. The only decision variable considered by the authors, however, is Q_t^*, the optimal production program. A general solution approach – called simply the Convex Cost Algorithm – is suggested. It considers demand period-by-period, where production in each period is chosen in order of increasing marginal cost among three alternatives: production in the current period, production in a prior period with storage, and production in a future period with backlogging.

When the production functions $c_t(Q_t)$ are piecewise-linear and the holding and backlogging functions $h_t(I_t)$ are linear, the problem can be solved more efficiently by a transportation algorithm, as the authors demonstrate with an example. They also show that in the convex-cost case the production and inventory levels can be bounded without creating difficulties. (Details are provided by Johnson & Montgomery based on the original article of Veinott [1966].)

Pekelman [1975] gives a characterization of a strong planning horizon for a case with convex production cost. Specifically, Pekelman considers the case of a firm in a perfectly competitive industry facing a dynamic price provided exogenously to the firm. The firm can choose the amount it sells at the given price, but faces an increasing marginal production-cost function and an asymmetric production smoothing cost function, and seeks to maximize profit over the horizon by choosing a dynamic production rate over the horizon. Thus, while Pekelman's 1975 paper cannot be truly classified as falling within production–marketing joint decision-making, since there is no marketing decision (e.g. pricing), it shows that strong planning horizons may exist for the convex-production-cost case. However, as we shall see in Section 3.2, Pekelman considers in a second paper (which appeared in print a year earlier) the joint pricing–production decision.

3.2. The marketing–production joint decision-making approach

The second paper of Pekelman [1974] addresses a continuous-time convex-production-cost problem with controllable price and time-dependent demand curve. He presents an algorithm that assures an optimal and unique solution. The scenario captured by this model is that of a profit maximizing monopolist who, with the aid of pricing and production rate, smooths his fluctuating demand, and therefore his production. The major trade-off the monopolist faces is operating at a *high* production rate and *low* inventory levels close to the demand peaks vis-à-vis a *lower* production rate having previously accumulated a *higher* level of inventory. The mathematical problem is formulated as:

$$\underset{p(t),Q(t)}{\text{maximize}} \quad \int_0^T \{P(t)[a(t)-b(t)P(t)] - hI(t) - c(Q(t))\}\mathrm{d}t \tag{3.14}$$

$$\text{subject to} \quad \dot{I}(t) = Q(t) - [a(t) - b(t)P(t)], \tag{3.15}$$

$$Q(t), I(t) \geqslant 0, \tag{3.16}$$

$$0 \leqslant P(t) \leqslant a(t)/b(t), \tag{3.17}$$

where $P(t)$ is price at time t, and $a(t)$, $b(t)$ are time-varying demand parameters that can be interpreted as market size and price-sensitivity, respectively. In problem (3.14)–(3.17), constraint (3.16) ensures that production rate and inventory never drop below zero. Constraint (3.17) guarantees that the price charged for the product will never be so high as to drive the demand to a negative value; hence, the ratio $a(t)/b(t)$ – which depends, of course, on the time-varying demand parameters – provides an upper bound for the level of price that the monopolist can charge at any given point in time. Pekelman constructs the solution to the problem under low, medium and high initial inventory levels, $I(0)$, where these levels are taken relative to $\bar{I}$, where

$$\bar{I} = -\int_0^T \dot{I}^*(t)\mathrm{d}t. \tag{3.18}$$

Thus, $\bar{I}$ is the difference between the initial and terminal levels under optimality.

In structuring his solution, Pekelman introduces a function $\psi(t)$, which is defined in terms of the parameters of the demand function and plays a role analogous to demand in the 'pure' production model of Modigliani & Hohn [1955]. This allows him to obtain planning-horizon results analogous to those given by Modigliani & Hohn. (Pekelman does not go into details, but provides references and a numerical example.)

Thompson, Sethi & Teng [1984] obtain strong planning and forecast horizons for a price and production problem for a firm over a finite horizon T. Their model is along the lines of Pekelman [1974], with a linear demand function, but where the production cost is either linear or strictly convex, and where upper bounds have been imposed on the production rate and inventory. The strong planning and forecast horizons are obtained when the state variable (inventory) reaches its upper or lower bound. The problem is solved via branch and bound.

Feichtinger & Hartl [1985] considered demand functions different than that of Pekelman, viz., nonlinear demand functions. Also, rather than constraining inventory to be non-negative, they consider a penalty cost $h(I)$ which is the inventory cost (for $I \geqslant 0$) and shortage cost (for $I < 0$). They consider two types of cost functions, where: (i) $h(x)$ is continuously differentiable and strictly convex, and (ii) $h(x)$ is nonsmooth and piecewise-linear (the more interesting case). In this second case, since the function $h(x)$ is nondifferentiable, standard optimal control does not apply. Their conclusions include that it is not optimal to compensate an increase in production rate by a decrease in price in order to increase the demand. They also show the existence of a unique equilibrium point. In the more interesting case of (ii), it is optimal to have no shortage and no inventory in the long run; otherwise, there is no equilibrium and the level of shortage will increase at a constant rate.

Jorgensen [1986a] considers a distribution channel consisting of a vertical structure comprised of a manufacturer and a retailer, where the manufacturer controls his production rate and the selling price (i.e. the transfer price) towards the retailer, who in turn controls his purchasing rate and the price to the outside market. Although – as in Pekelman [1974] – the retailer's production cost is taken to be quadratic, Jorgensen assumes the manufacturer's production cost to be linear. Further, rather than constraining each player's inventory to be non-negative, he models a quadratic holding/shortage cost for each player, akin to the 'inventory-connected costs' (3.12) of Holt, Modigliani, Muth & Simon [1960] and the first penalty cost of Feichtinger & Hartl [1985]. He seeks a Nash equilibrium under the assumption of a stationary linear demand function. Due to the model's cost structure, the manufacturer always charges his maximal price to the retailer. The retailer's price to the market is either monotonically increasing or is increasing-then-decreasing. The manufacturer's pricing policy is 'bang-bang' and the retailer always begins and ends the time horizon with a zero purchase policy, with possibly a positive purchasing rate on an intermediate interval. Jorgensen makes several suggestions for extensions of his model. He suggests that "the game could be played with other solution concepts than the Nash solution". One of his suggestions is the use of the Stackelberg solution [Kreps, 1990]:

> "In a Stackelberg game one could visualize the manufacturer as the leader, knowing both payoffs and announcing his strategy first. With respect to the manufacturer's pricing policy this is, in particular, realistic. Facing the manufacturer's strategies, the retailer reacts rationally and determines his ordering and pricing policies".

Working independently of Jorgensen, Eliashberg & Steinberg [1984, 1987] did exactly this. They consider an industrial channel of distribution comprised of a manufacturer and a distributor. The manufacturer, acting as the leader in this relationship, controls his production rate as well as the static transfer price at which he sells the product to the distributor. The latter controls his rate of processing the inputs provided by the manufacturer as well as the market price that he (the distributor) sets in his market. The model differs from that of Jorgensen in several respects. In Eliashberg & Steinberg [1987], both the distributor *and* the manufacturer face quadratic cost functions, the distributor faces a seasonal (i.e. increasing-then-decreasing) demand condition, and both the manufacturer and distributor are constrained – as in Pekelman [1974] – so that inventory never drops below zero. Although both Jorgensen's model and Eliashberg & Steinberg's model are formulated as dynamic optimal control problems, they differ with respect to their solution approaches. See Jorgensen [1986b] for further details concerning the comparison between the two approaches.

The focus of the Eliashberg & Steinberg's analysis includes the following issues:

- Under what conditions should the distributor operate under a stockless [zero-inventory] policy throughout the seasonal period? Under what conditions should the manufacturer operate under a stockless policy?
- Which of the two parties should reach zero inventory earlier as the end of the season approaches?
- What can be said about the transfer price between manufacturer and distributor?

The problem is modeled as a Stackelberg leader–follower game where the distributor's problem is first formulated as:

$$\underset{P_D(t),Q_D(t)}{\text{maximize}} \int_0^T \{(P_D(t)-P_M)(a_D(t)-b_D P_D(t))-(1/K_D)Q_D^2(t)-h_D I_D(t)\}\mathrm{d}t \tag{3.19}$$

$$\text{subject to} \quad \dot{I}_D(t)=Q_D(t)-a_D(t)+b_D P_D(t), \tag{3.20}$$

$$I_D(t)\geqslant 0, \tag{3.21}$$

$$Q_D(t)\geqslant 0, \tag{3.22}$$

$$P_M\leqslant P_D(t)\leqslant a_0(t)/b_D, \tag{3.23}$$

$$I_D(0)=I_D(T)=0, \tag{3.24}$$

where $a_D(t)=-\alpha_1 t^2+\alpha_2 t+\alpha_3$.

Here

$P_D(t)$ = distributor's market price at time t,
$Q_D(t)$ = distributor's production rate at time t,
P_M = transfer price over the season,
$a_D(t)-b_D P_D(t)$ = market demand faced by the distributor,
h_D = distributor's unit inventory-holding cost per unit time,

K_D = distributor's processing efficiency,
α_1, α_2 = parameters determining timing and magnitude of the peak sales ($\alpha_1, \alpha_2 > 0$),
α_3 = 'nominal' size of market potential before beginning of season ($\alpha_3 > 0$),
T = time horizon = α_2/α_1.

Once the distributor's policies are determined as functions of the transfer price, P_M, the problem faced by the manufacturer can be formulated in a similar fashion recognizing that he is facing a *derived* demand function of $Q_D^*(P_M, t)$:

$$\underset{Q_M(t), P_M}{\text{maximize}} \quad \int_0^T \{(P_M - C_M)Q_D^*(t) - (1/K_M)Q_M^2(t) - h_M I_M(t)\}\,\mathrm{d}t \tag{3.25}$$

$$\text{subject to} \quad \dot{I}_M(t) = Q_M(t) - Q_D^*(t), \tag{3.26}$$

$$I_M(t) \geqslant 0, \tag{3.27}$$

$$Q_M(t) \geqslant 0, \tag{3.28}$$

$$P_M \leqslant P_D(t), \tag{3.29}$$

$$I_M(0) = I_M(T) = 0, \tag{3.30}$$

where

$Q_M(t)$ = manufacturer's production rate at time t,
C_M = manufacturer's unit raw-material price,
h_M = manufacturer's unit inventory-holding cost per unit time,
K_M = manufacturer's processing efficiency.

Insights that can be obtained from the Eliashberg & Steinberg [1987] analysis include:

- Only under certain conditions, e.g. low inventory-holding cost, low distributor-processing efficiency and volatile demand, is it worthwhile for the distributor and the manufacturer to smooth out their operations. Otherwise, either may find it optimal to act according to a stockless policy throughout the season.
- If it is optimal for both parties to smooth out their operations, each will nevertheless reach zero inventory before the end of the season and remain there for the remainder of the season. The time at which the distributor reaches zero inventory is earlier than that for the manufacturer.
- If the manufacturer finds it worthwhile to smooth out his operations, the transfer price becomes a weighted average of his minimum and average (over the season) maximum prices.

Mathematically, the contractual transfer price takes the following convex combination form:

$$P_{\mathrm{M}}^{*} = (1 - w)\left[(1/T)\int_0^T (a_{\mathrm{D}}(t)/b_{\mathrm{D}})\mathrm{d}t\right] + wC_{\mathrm{M}} \tag{3.31}$$

where

$$w = \frac{1}{b_{\mathrm{D}}K_{\mathrm{D}}/[(b_{\mathrm{D}} + K_{\mathrm{D}})K_{\mathrm{M}}] + 2}. \tag{3.32}$$

Eliashberg & Steinberg [1988] have shown a further result. Suppose that, in the distribution channel model of Eliashberg & Steinberg [1987], each firm is unable to (or *ex ante* decides not to) hold inventory. Then the transfer price chosen by the manufacturer that arises from this special scenario will be identical to the transfer price that would have been chosen by the manufacturer had the two firms been holding inventory and acting optimally. That is, the transfer price presented in (3.31) and (3.32), which represents some sort of compromise between maximum and minimum possible prices, remains robust with respect to the intra-channel inventory policies.

The robustness of the marketing–production interface in light of unstable demand has been investigated further in Eliashberg & Steinberg [1991]. There, the scenario modeled is that of two competing firms with asymmetric production-cost structures. The first firm, called the 'production-smoother', faces a convex production cost and linear inventory-holding cost. The second firm, called the 'order-taker', faces a linear production cost and holds no inventory. Equilibrium strategies for the two competing firms are derived and compared. In addition, the competitive production-smoother's prices are derived and compared with its monopolistic counterpart.

Mathematically, the two objective functions can be written as:

$$\underset{P_X(t),Q_X(t)}{\text{maximize}} \int_0^T \{P_X(t)\cdot D_X[P_X(t), P_{\bar{X}}(t), t] - v_X Q_X(t) - c_X(Q_X(t)) - h_X I_X(t)\}\mathrm{d}t \tag{3.33}$$

where

$X \in \{1, 2 | 1 = \text{production-smoother}, 2 = \text{order-taker}\}$, $\bar{X} = \{1, 2\} \backslash \{X\}$,

$P_X(t)$ = price charged at time t by firm X,

$Q_X(t)$ = firm X's production rate at time t,

$D_X[P_X(t), P_{\bar{X}}(t), t]$ = demand rate at time t for firm X's product given that firm X charges $P_X(t)$ and firm $\bar{X}$ charges $P_{\bar{X}}(t)$,

v_X = firm X's per-unit (variable) cost,

$c_X(Q_X(t))$ = firm X's production-cost function exclusive of raw-materials cost,

h_X = firm X's per-unit inventory-holding cost,
$I_X(t)$ = firm X's inventory level at time t,
Π_X = firm X's profit.

In addition, the production-smoother's problem considers explicitly the following state equation:

$$\dot{I}_1 = Q_1 - D_1. \tag{3.34}$$

In contrast, in the order-taker's problem, $I_2(t) = 0$ for $t \in [0, T]$. Hence, $Q_2^*(t) = D_2^*(t)$, and the order-taker's problem reduces to maximizing the integrand of Equation (3.33) with $I_2(t) = 0$ for $t \in [0, T)$.

The analysis reveals that the general structure of the production-smoother's inventory policy – that is, building up inventory, continuing by drawing down inventory until it reaches zero at time t^* ($t^* < T$), and concluding by following a 'zero-inventory' policy from t^* until the end of the seasonal period, T – is robust with respect to the market structure he is facing. Pekelman [1974] demonstrates this for a pure monopolist, and Eliashberg & Steinberg [1987] show it for a channel of distribution facing no competition. It is to be expected that this result will be obtained in differing settings, because it captures the essence of production-smoothing. However, Eliashberg & Steinberg [1991] also show that the competitive pressure faced by the production-smoother pushes him to begin his 'zero-inventory' policy *earlier* than had he acted as a monopolist. Another interesting comparison reveals that the 'production-smoother', acting under competition, decreases his production rate as he approaches the end of the season at a rate that is *lower* than that of the monopolistic production-smoother. Finally, in comparing directly the two competing firms, it is found that the order-taker's price is strictly less than the production-smoother's price over the entire period whenever the sum of the order-taker's variable and unit production costs does not exceed the production-smoother's variable cost.

3.3. Summary

Various production processes may give rise to convexity in the firm's production-cost structure. Such situations provide management with an incentive to smooth unstable demand by carrying seasonal inventory. Managerial questions of interest become: Do planning horizons exist? What should be the nature of the production, inventory and marketing policies that maximize the profitability of the entire system? This section has addressed these issues. We have reviewed work indicating that planning horizons can be determined for convex-cost models which explicitly incorporate marketing strategies. Incentives to smooth out unstable demand patterns do not vanish when one moves from monopolistic, to duopolistic, to vertical-distribution market structures. The necessary parametric conditions do change, of course, depending on the specific market-structure context.

4. Choosing production-run quantities and order quantities: Concave-cost models

Clearly, a firm does not invariably face convexity in its production-cost structure. Hax and Candea [1984] offer that concave costs become an issue in problems involving setup (change-over) charges, discounting, and economies of scale in the production process. Most of the modeling in marketing–production involving concave costs has focused on situations where these costs have arisen from production-run setup charges associated with batch production, or from fixed charges associated with order quantities. (Hax & Candea [1984] provide a good overview of ncave-cost production models. See also the recent monograph by Salomon [1991].)

Hax & Candea [1984] point out three difficulties that arise from including the production-run setup cost in the problem formulation: (i) every item that generates a setup must be identified and treated independently, and this expands the number of variables and constraints; (ii) since a setup is associated with each batch, this requires the use of integer variables; (iii) fixed-cost components are introduced in the objective function, and the corresponding downtime introduces nonlinearities in the constraint set. Thus, they point out, these three difficulties can result in large-scale, integer, nonlinear-programming models that are computationally difficult.

On the other hand, there are cases where these problems are very tractable. Formulations involving production-run setup costs tend to have concave objective functions. (An interesting exception is the model of Porteus [1985], discussed below.) If the constraints are linear, an optimization procedure can make use of the well-known result that the minimum of a concave function subject to linear constraints occurs at an extreme point of the convex set formed by the constraint set. Although exhaustive enumeration of the extreme points is rarely practical and often impossible, Wagner & Whitin [1958b] introduced a highly effective approach to utilize the structure inherent in these formulations which has been employed by several of the models we will discuss.

4.1. *Static-price models*

One of the earliest papers to incorporate pricing decisions in classical production–inventory theory is that of Whitin [1955] (discussed in Section 2). He writes: "In spite of the high level of interest in inventory control that has sprung up recently among statisticians, economists, and businessmen, very little has been written that indicates the fundamental connection between price theory and inventory control".

The basic and very well-known Wilson–Harris economic order quantity (EOQ) model seeks the optimal order quantity for a single product, where the total ordering cost consists of a fixed cost per order K plus a cost per unit c, inventory-holding cost is h per unit, demand D is known and continuous at a constant rate, the time horizon is infinite, replenishment is instantaneous, and all demand must be met without backlogging.

Whitin considers the EOQ model in the context of a retailer whose unit holding cost is given by $h = rc$, where r is some fraction of the unit cost. Although not explicitly discussed, the rate r presumably incorporates the fractional opportunity cost of capital along with other, i.e. nonfinancial, carrying costs. Further, Whitin assumes a linear price–demand curve which is known to the retailer. Whitin also assumes that the retailer incurs an *operating cost* consisting of a fixed yearly component f plus a unit operating cost $\bar{c}$. (Although Whitin is not clear on this point, presumably $\bar{c}$ incorporates, but is not necessarily equal to, the unit purchase cost c.) The problem is to determine the price P the retailer should charge in order to maximize profits. Whitin's contribution here is to consider the firm's total profit Π_0, which is given by total revenues minus total costs. Whitin does not explicitly provide the closed-form solution, although of course it is easily calculated. We have already seen a numerical example in Section 2.

Kunreuther & Richard [1969, 1971] later considered a model similar to that of Whitin [1955]. Their motivation, which opens their 1969 working paper, is essentially the same as Whitin's: "A survey of economics and operations research literature on the theory of the firm provides an interesting contrast". They point out that economists – and, in our view, marketing modelers – have been concerned for the most part with the effect of price changes on demand without much regard to internal inventory and production problems, while operations-research practitioners have started from the assumption that price is fixed at some level and then attempted to minimize inventory or production costs subject to some given demand pattern. Kunreuther & Richard add that: "Even though pricing and output decisions are frequently made sequentially or independently in firms, they are, in fact, interrelated".

The assumption of a linear demand function in their model leads to a cubic equation for the optimal order quantity which is analogous to the optimal price equation obtained by Whitin. They also provide a numerical example for which the profit is 12.5% higher if the pricing and ordering decisions are made simultaneously rather than sequentially. Finally, they indicate how the model would change if, rather than purchasing from an outside distributor, the firm produces its product at a finite rate.

Porteus authored and coauthored a series of articles based on extending the standard EOQ model. Of particular interest to us is Porteus [1985], which considers the advantages of reducing setup cost on inventory-related operating costs. The author is motivated by the then widely reported Japanese effort to decrease setup costs in their manufacturing processes. Although a considerable literature developed on this topic during the 1980s, Porteus's 1985 paper is notable in that it begins to deal with the marketing implications as well. Porteus further suggests that his paper begins to provide a framework for evaluating flexible manufacturing systems, on the assumption that the introduction of such systems can result in lowered setup costs.

Porteus approaches in three stages the problem of simultaneously determining the optimal sales rate and setup cost. Let i denote the fractional opportunity cost of capital per year. Porteus defines the *effective unit holding cost* per year, $h = ic + \bar{h}$, where $\bar{h}$ is the nonfinancial unit holding cost per year. He next writes the expression for total variable costs as a function of K, the setup cost, where the demand rate D is assumed constant (compare with (2.15)):

$$\mathrm{TVC}(K) = \sqrt{2KhD}. \tag{4.1}$$

Letting $s(K)$ denote the cost of changing the setup cost to the level K, the expression $i \cdot s(K)$ will then represent the discounted cost of changing the setup cost to the level K.

In the first state, Porteus considers the problem of minimizing, with respect to K, what might be termed the 'extended' total variable costs. $\overline{\mathrm{TVC}}(K)$, which here consists of the total variable costs as a function of K plus the discounted cost of changing the setup cost to K:

$$\overline{\mathrm{TVC}}(K) = \mathrm{TVC}(K) + i \cdot s(K). \tag{4.2}$$

The first expression on the right-hand side is strictly concave and increasing in K; the second expression is assumed to be convex and strictly decreasing on some given interval on which it is defined. Porteus remarks that this "unorthodox optimization problem actually has a great deal of structure and generality".

In the second stage, Porteus considers the Whitin [1955] problem where the objective function now also includes the cost per unit time required to change to a given sales rate (as a function of price). Porteus seeks to maximize profit as a function of the sales rate D, where he momentarily sets aside the issue of the cost of changing the setup. Using the linear demand function as in (2.1), as well as the expression $(a - D)/b$ in place of P, his objective function becomes

$$\Pi(D) = \frac{(a - D)D}{b} - \sqrt{2KhD} - cD. \tag{4.3}$$

In the case of a linear demand function, he finds that the optimal sales rate D^* is given by

$$D^* = \begin{cases} D_0 & \text{if } \Pi(D_0) > 0, \\ 0 & \text{otherwise,} \end{cases} \tag{4.4}$$

where

$$D_0 = \frac{2(a - bc)}{3} \cos^2(\phi/3), \tag{4.5}$$

$$\phi = \arccos\left[\frac{-b\sqrt{Kh/2}}{4[(a - bc)/6]^{3/2}}\right]. \tag{4.6}$$

In the third and final stage, Porteus examines the simultaneous selection of the optimal sales rate and setup cost. For tractability, he assumes that the setup cost function is given by

$$s(K) = \bar{a} - \bar{b}\ln(K) \quad \text{for } 0 < K \leqslant K_0 \tag{4.7}$$

where $K_0 = e^{\bar{a}/\bar{b}}$ is the original setup cost and $\bar{a}$ and $\bar{b}$ are given positive constants. His objective function is

$$\Pi(D, K) = \frac{(a - D)D}{b} - \sqrt{2KhD} - cD - i(\bar{a} - \bar{b}\ln(K)). \tag{4.8}$$

Due to the complexity of the problem, closed-form expressions for the optimal solution are not provided. However, he is able to conclude that there will be a critical sales level above which setup reduction is appropriate.

Porteus also obtains qualitative insights for the multiple-products case. For a firm with many products distinguished by their demand rates, the optimal order quantity for the low-volume products is the standard EOQ; for high-volume products the optimal order quantity is independent of demand rate, and thus the lot size for all such products will be identical.

Costs associated with changing the setup is just one of many factors that can be incorporated in such models in order to make them more realistic. A completely different factor is the perishability of the good offered for sale. A review of perishable-inventory theory is provided in Nahmias [1982]; however, most of these models do not incorporate pricing or any other marketing-related decision.

One of the first ordering/pricing models to account for perishability is that of Cohen [1977], who considered the problem of simultaneously setting price and production levels for a product whose inventory exponentially decays. In the first half of his paper, Cohen formulates a continuous review model in which shortages are not permitted and an optimal constant price is sought. Inventory is assumed to decay at a rate δ. By minimizing the total costs per unit with respect to cycle length, this leads to an expression which implicitly gives the optimal cycle length, T^*:

$$e^{\delta T^*(\delta T^* - 1)} = \frac{K\delta^2}{D(P)[c\delta + h]} - 1. \tag{4.9}$$

By employing a Taylor series approximation for $e^{\delta T}$, Cohen obtains

$$T^* = \sqrt{\frac{2K}{D(P)[c\delta + h]}}. \tag{4.10}$$

This reduces to the standard EOQ formula with price-dependent demand when there is no perishability, i.e. when $\delta = 0$. Cohen shows that, under some mild and realistic assumptions on the demand function, it is possible to solve for the optimal (i.e. profit-maximizing) price by numerical methods. In the second half of his paper, he extends his model to allow for backlogging of excess demand and obtains results similar to the non-backlogging case.

4.2. Dynamic-price models

Monroe & Della Bitta [1978] reviewed pricing models in marketing and cited the need for pricing strategies to allow for market dynamics. Rao [1984] reviewed pricing models between 1978 and 1984 and remarked on the intense amount of activity on models that had been developed in that period. Most of those models examined in these two surveys deal with medium-to-long-term dynamic pricing policies, and account for such factors as life-cycle, experience-curve, and adoption-and-diffusion effects. Rajan, Rakesh & Steinberg [1992] reviewed the relatively small amount of research on short-term price changes. Since many production–pricing decisions are of a short-term nature, these models are of special interest to us. Examples of short-term price changes occur due to markups and markdowns in the clothing industry [Pashigian, 1988], and in catalogue goods and food retailing [Kunreuther & Schrage, 1973].

An early dynamic production–price model is 'Dynamic problems in the theory of the firm', in which Wagner & Whitin [1958a] use the theory of the firm to analyze the problem of maximizing profit when demand and cost functions vary in different time periods and when inventory costs and setup costs exist. In their scenario, the firm can be interpreted as either a producer who sells his goods or a jobber whose costs are those of buying and storing and whose revenue is derived from sales.

They demonstrate that inventory charges can be handled in a manner analogous to transportation-cost problems between spatial markets, or to price discrimination with the added complication that the time sequence of the periods may lead to infeasible situations if the standard price-discrimination model is used. They also show that setup costs indicate that some type of enumeration is needed to determine the true optimum, although they realize that attempting to enumerate all of the possible configurations of setups leads to a procedure which is exponential in the number of periods.

Wagner & Whitin [1958a] propose that a more efficient algorithm can be developed along the following lines. For any given inventory position the optimal values for sales and production are obtained. Profit in each period is then determined for each possible amount of entering inventory. The method they suggest involves developing a forward dynamic-programming solution as an analogue to the EOQ model, although they do not explicitly provide such a formulation.

In another paper, Wagner & Whitin [1958b] provide the promised algorithm. However, unlike the model sketched in their previous paper, the formulation does not allow demand in each period to be a function of price. Rather, they assume that the selling price of the item is constant from period to period (and thus it is not explicitly incorporated in the model) as is the item's unit purchase or production cost. An additional assumption of their model is that initial inventory is zero. For period t, where $t = 1, 2, \ldots, T$, define:

D_t = demand in period t,
h_t = holding cost per unit of inventory carried forward from period t to period $t+1$,
K_t = ordering or setup cost in period t,

where the decision variables are

Q_t = quantity ordered or manufactured in period t.

Assuming that all period demands and costs are non-negative, the problem is to find a program $Q_t \geqslant 0$, $t = 1, 2, \ldots, T$, such that all demand in each period is met at minimum total cost.

The Wagner–Whitin dynamic-programming algorithm is based on the result that there exists an optimal solution with the following four properties: (i) in no period is both inventory carried in and production occurrring; (ii) in each period, t, production is either zero or equal to the sum of the demands in periods $t, t+1, \ldots, t+k$, for some $k \geqslant t$; (iii) if demand in some period is satisfied by production in an earlier period, then all of the intermediate period demands must also be satisfied by production in that earlier period; (iv) given that entering inventory in some period t is 0, it is optimal to solve the subproblem for periods $1, 2, \ldots, t-1$ independently of the later periods.

Using these four properties, a minimal-cost policy can be given by the following functional equation, where $C(t)$ denotes the minimum-cost program for periods 1 through t, and $C(0) = 0$ and $C(1) = K_1$:

$$C(t) = \mathrm{Min} \begin{cases} \displaystyle \mathop{\mathrm{Min}}_{1 \leqslant j < t} \left[K_j + \sum_{u=j}^{t-1} \sum_{v=u+1}^{t} h_u D_v + C(j-1) \right], \\ K_t + C(t-1). \end{cases} \tag{4.11}$$

Thus, the first term in the outside minimum operator is the minima cost which comprises a setup cost K_j in period j, plus charges for filling demand in periods $j+1, j+2, \ldots, t$, by carrying inventory from period j, plus the cost of adopting an optimal policy in the subproblem of satisfying demand in periods 1 through $j-1$. For any period t, only t choices for j need to be considered. (Wagner & Whitin point out that the minimum in (4.11) need not be unique, and thus there may be alternative optimal solutions.) By solving (4.11) successively for $C(1), C(2), \ldots, C(T)$, an optimal solution is obtained. (It is easily shown that the algorithm runs in $O(T^2)$ time. An excellent analysis of the computational complexity of deterministic production-planning problems is given in Florian, Lenstra & Rinnooy Kan [1980].)

As a bonus, Wagner & Whitin obtain what they aptly describe as perhaps the most interesting property of their model:

The planning horizon theorem. *If at period t^* the minimum-cost program in (4.11) occurs for $j = t^{**} \leqslant t^*$, then in periods $t > t^*$ it is sufficient to consider only $t^{**} \leqslant j \leqslant t$.* □

Corollary. *In particular, if $t^* = t^{**}$, then it is sufficient to consider policies such that $Q_t^* > 0$.* □

The planning horizon theorem states that if the problem is extended to a larger number of time periods, then in an optimal solution the final production will not occur any earlier. As discussed in Section 3, here t^{**} is called the *planning horizon.* (More precisely, it is a strong planning horizon.)

In a postscript to "Dynamic problems in the theory of the firm", Wagner [1960] shows that the algorithm in Wagner & Whitin [1958b] holds not only when production costs are of the form fixed-plus-linear, but in the general case of concave-cost functions which may differ from period to period. However, Wagner shows by means of an example that the planning horizon theorem does not hold in this more general case. Following a marginal-cost-analysis approach from economics which parallels that of their earlier paper [Wagner & Whitin, 1958a], Wagner also discusses the question of obtaining optimal prices under the general concave-cost structure, without explicitly presenting an algorithm.

Following the early work of Wagner & Whitin, a substantial literature developed to investigate planning-horizon issues based on concave-cost models. Zabel [1964] shows how to handle the case of positive initial inventory in the Wagner–Whitin formulation [1958a]. More importantly, he provides a dynamic-programming algorithm for the situations in which the unit holding cost can vary from period to period. The significance of this extension is that it allows for the discounting of future costs; unfortunately, the algorithm works backward rather than forward and thus does not provide planning-horizon results. For the same model, however, Eppen, Gould & Pashigian [1969] do provide a forward dynamic-programming algorithm and a corresponding planning-horizon theorem. Zangwill [1968] elegantly shows how the Wagner–Whitin algorithm can be formulated in terms of extreme flows in networks. Recently, Federgruen & Tzur [1991] have presented a forward dynamic-programming algorithm which solves the Wagner–Whitin problem in $O(T \log T)$ time. However, none of this work explicitly incorporates pricing.

Thomas's first paper [1970] extends the famous Wagner–Whitin [1958b] algorithm to the marketing–production domain where price is included as a decision variable, and where demand in period t is of the form $D_t(P_t)$ and P_t is the price charged in period t. Thomas [1970] shows that the four Wagner–Whitin-algorithm properties carry over to the case where the pricing decision is included. Based on this, he presents a forward dynamic-programming algorithm along the lines of Wagner & Whitin [1958b] and Eppen, Gould & Pashigian [1969] which optimally selects prices, in addition to the optimal production schedule. He also obtains planning-horizon results.

His major pricing result is that the prices between setups may be optimized one at a time. More formally:

Theorem. *If a setup occurs in a period t^0 and next in period t', then for periods $t = t^0, t^0 + 1, \ldots, t' - 1$, the price P_t can be chosen so as to maximize*

$$\left(P_t - c_{t^0} - \sum_{u=t^0}^{t-1} h_u\right) \cdot D_t(P_t), \tag{4.12}$$

where c_{t^0} is the variable cost per unit in period t^0.

Thomas also includes two lemmas which provide upper and lower bounds on the period-t optimal price, P_t^*. In a subsequent paper Thomas considers a stochastic version of his model, which we will discuss later in this section.

Kunreuther & Schrage [1973], working in discrete time over T periods, consider the case of a deterministic demand function that differs from period to period, but where the price remains fixed. Their problem is to determine the optimal static price, P^*, and the periods in which to place orders. They suggest three situations for which their model may be appropriate: catalogue goods, price planning by retail stores, and new products when economic conditions dictate that future price changes are undesirable.

If the optimal price were to be known, then the determination of the ordering schedule could be accomplished via the Eppen–Gould–Pashigian algorithm. If, on the other hand, the ordering periods were known, the calculation of the optimal price would be a straightforward calculus problem. Based on this pair of observations, Kunreuther & Schrage obtain an algorithmic solution for determining the optimal constant price as well as the periods in which it is optimal to place an order. We require some notation for exposition:

P = selling price, a decision variable,
$D_t(P) = a_t + b_t\gamma(P)$ = demand function, where a_t, b_t ($b_t > 0$) are parameters, and where $\gamma(P)$ is not a function of t and is differentiable, with $\mathrm{d}\gamma(P)/\mathrm{d}P \leqslant 0$ for all feasible P,
$R(P) = \sum_{t=1}^{T} PD_t(P)$ = total revenue over all T periods,
$C(P', P)$ = cost of satisfying demand for all T periods when the price is P, under the ordering policy which is optimal for price P'.

The Kunreuther & Schrage algorithm is:

(0) Set $i = 0$ and select an initial price P_i.
(1) Calculate the demands $D(P_i) = a_t + b_t\gamma(P_i)$ for $t = 1, 2, \ldots, T$, and use the Eppen–Gould–Pashigian algorithm to determine an optimal ordering policy and corresponding profit, Π_i.
(2) Set $i = i + 1$.
(3) For the ordering policy derived in Step (1), find a price P_i which maximizes $R(P_i) - C(P_{i-1}, P_i)$.
(4) If $R(P_i) - C(P_{i-1}, P_i) > \Pi_i$ then return to Step (1).
(5) Let $P = P_i$. Stop.

Although the algorithm will terminate in a finite number of steps, the solution obtained is not necessarily optimal. The authors suggest running the algorithm twice, with $P_0 = 0$, and with $P_0 = M$ where M is a feasible upper bound on the optimal price, obtaining values $P = P_L$ and $P = P_U$, respectively. The authors show that P_L and P_U bound the optimal price P^*.

The paper is significant also for the empirical study associated with the theoretical results. The authors report on an interesting application of their algorithm to determine the optimal price and ordering policy for six speciality food items sold by a store in the Chicago area. They also consider the effect of a variable-pricing policy on the firm's profits and found that, for two of the items, a variable-pricing policy such that suggested by Thomas [1970] would have increased profits significantly. However, they warn that this would have required "an unusually wide range of prices between slack and peak demand periods so as to make the results somewhat unrealistic in practice".

Rajan, Rakesh & Steinberg [1992] derive simultaneous pricing and ordering policies for a retailer under the standard EOQ cost assumptions. The retailer is assumed to be able to vary continuously the selling price of the product over the inventory cycle. Like Cohen [1977], they allow the product to exhibit physical decay over time which they refer to as *wastage*; in addition they allow for the product to exhibit a decrease in market value over time called *value drop* associated with each unit of inventory on hand.

The retailer's objective is to maximize average profit per unit time by choosing both an optimal cycle length θ^*, and an optimal dynamic price $P^*(t)$ for all t in the interval $[0, \theta)$. In their formulation, $c(t)$ is the *total unit cost* which includes the purchase cost, the holding cost and a *wastage cost* which incorporates a factor which accounts for the possible physical deterioration of the inventory. The average profit $\Pi(\theta, P(\cdot))$ is given by the revenue over a cycle, minus the purchase cost, the wastage cost and the inventory-holding cost over the cycle, minus the fixed cost per cycle, all divided by the cycle length:

$$\Pi(\theta, P(\cdot)) = \frac{1}{\theta}\left[\int_0^\theta \{(P(t) - c(t))D(P(t), t)\}\mathrm{d}t - K\right]. \tag{4.13}$$

The demand function $D(P(t), t)$ is the form

$$D(P(t), t) = D(\lambda(t) \cdot P(t)) \tag{4.14}$$

where the function $D(\cdot)$ is a standard demand function such as the linear demand function (2.1), and $\lambda(t)$ is a nondecreasing function of t such that $\lambda(0) = 1$. Here, $\lambda(t)$ is the value-drop rate and $1/\lambda(t)$ is the price discount required to maintain demand level over time. The integrand in (4.13) is the *instantaneous margin*:

$$v(P, t) = (P(t) - c(t)) \cdot D(P(t), t) \tag{4.15}$$

which is the rate of contribution to profit at time t exclusive of fixed cost. The average profit corresponding to an optimal policy $(\theta^*, P^*(\cdot))$ is given by:

$$\Pi(\theta^*, P^*(\cdot)) = \max_{\theta, P(\cdot)} \frac{1}{\theta}\left[\int_0^\theta v(P(t), t)\mathrm{d}t - K\right]. \tag{4.16}$$

One of the key observations they make about their formulation is that problem (4.16) can be solved in two stages. The first stage consists of obtaining the optimal price as a function of t:

$$P^*(t) = \arg\max_{P} v(P, t). \tag{4.17}$$

The second stage consists of substituting in the optimal dynamic price $P^*(t)$ from (4.17) into the expression for the optimal average profit (4.13) and solving for the optimal cycle length θ^*:

$$\theta^* = \arg\max_{\theta} \frac{1}{\theta}\left[\int_0^{\theta} v(P^*(t), t)\mathrm{d}t - K\right]. \tag{4.18}$$

Thus, the optimal dynamic price is independent of the choice of cycle length, which is not the case when a fixed price is sought, as in Cohen [1977].

Rajan, Rakesh & Steinberg make several assumptions on the demand function which are similar to those employed by Cohen [1977]. They find that the optimal price increases directly with the unit cost and the inventory-carrying cost. Under the assumption of linear demand, they obtain a closed-form solution of the optimal price path as well as provide simple parametric conditions for the optimal price to be strictly increasing or strictly decreasing over the cycle.

4.3. *Stochastic-demand models*

Karlin & Carr [1962] consider two classes of the standard stochastic inventory model [see Porteus, 1990] with the incorporation of price as a decision variable. In each model, the demand is assumed to be a random variable with a known probability distribution which depends on the price as a parameter, and where uncertainty in demand is introduced either multiplicatively or additively.

A static model is first discussed under the assumption that demand is defined multiplicatively:

$$D(P) = g(P) \cdot W \tag{4.19}$$

where W is a non-negative random variable having expected value $\mathrm{E}(W) = 1$, and $g(P)$ is a non-negative, decreasing deterministic demand function of price (such as the linear demand function). Another model considered is the additive stochastic demand:

$$D(P) = g(P) + U \tag{4.20}$$

where U is a random variable having expected value $\mathrm{E}(U) = 0$. The primary result derived from these models is the following: compared with the optimal price in the corresponding deterministic model, the optimal price in the presence of multiplicative uncertainty is always greater and in the presence of additive uncertainty is always less.

Dynamic models for both types of uncertainty are also considered where a single price is set at the beginning of the process. The primary results for these models are: for the additive model the optimal dynamic price is closer than the optimal static price to the optimal certainty price. The same result holds for the dynamic multiplicative model if the random variable W is represented by a uniform distribution. (See also the related work of Mills [1959].)

Thomas [1974] considers the rather difficult problem of jointly setting price and production levels in a series of T periods, where price is modeled as a parameter in the probability distribution of demand, where this distribution in general varies from period to period, and where the demand function in each period is stochastically decreasing in price. No further assumptions are made about the demand function. Thomas first formulates the problem as a dynamic program from which an optimal policy can be derived, although the computations involved are rather complex. He thus seeks a characterization of the optimal policy that will facilitate the computations. The approach he takes is to modify the standard (s, S) inventory control system. (This system, also called an 'order-point, order-up-to-level' system, involves continuous review and the determination of two inventory levels s and S, where replenishment is made to bring the inventory up to level S whenever the inventory level drops to the order point s or lower.) Thomas proposes what he calls an (s, S, P) inventory control system which involves determining in each period t two inventory levels s_t and S_t as well as an optimal price function $P_t(I)$, where I is the stock level. Here, whenever the inventory level drops below s_t, replenishment is made to bring inventory up to level S_t and a price $P_t(S_t)$ is charged; otherwise, no production order is placed and the price is set equal to $P_t(I)$ for that stock level.

Although he provides a counter-example to the optimality of this policy, Thomas obtains several results that suggest (s, S, P) is optimal in most cases. Further, although he finds it difficult to obtain conditions for optimality that can be verified *a priori*, he is able to introduce an algorithm that checks for optimality after s_t and S_t are determined. He also discusses some technical points that shed light on the difficulty in analyzing joint pricing–production decisions with random demand.

Thowsen [1975] considers an additive model along the lines of Karlin & Carr [1962], but where unsatisfied demand is handled through backlogging or lost sales, or a combination of both. He assumes that selling price of the backordered demand is the price which was in effect at the time that the backlogging occurred. He also allows for deterioration of inventory. Thus, his paper is in some sense a stochastic version of Cohen's model [1977], although the two authors worked independently of each other. He assumes that there are no setup costs and that ordering (or production) costs are linear. He finds that the optimal policy for the T-period case is given by a sequence of T order-up-to points, $\{S_t\}$, and two sequences of T prices, $\{P_t^*\}$ and $\{P_t^*(I_t)\}$, where the second sequence is dependent on the inventory levels. If the inventory level at the beginning of period t, I_t, is below the period-t order-up-to level, S_t, then an order is placed for $S_t - I_t$ and the price P_t is charged. If $I_t > S_t$, then it is optimal to not order and to charge the price $P_t(I_t)$. The optimality of Thowsen's policies depend on a series of assumptions, some of which he admits "do not have any straightforward economic interpretation" and "will in some cases be difficult to verify". However, he does provide a special case for which all his assumptions are always satisfied.

Surprisingly little has been done since the mid-1970s on stochastic concave-cost models. This may be due to the inherent complexity of this class of problems.

4.4. Summary

We have found that concave-cost models, usually arising from the existence of production-run setup charges associated with batch production (orders), fall naturally into three categories: static-price, deterministic-demand models; dynamic-price, deterministic-demand models; and stochastic-demand models. The comparison of decentralized vs. coordinated marketing–production decision-making has been included in this research domain. Although the static-price models tend to be easier to solve, it is not necessarily true that they are less valid than dynamic-price models; the former may be more valid when considering short-term price changes. We reviewed the contributions on the topic of planning horizons for concave-cost models. Here, we saw that price has been successfully incorporated as a dynamic decision variable in the classic Wagner–Whitin result. Stochastic-demand models were first looked at over thirty years ago, but research in this area has been sparse. Nonetheless, such models are undoubtedly more realistic in many circumstances; clearly this would be a worthwhile area for future modeling research.

5. Conclusions

"Can marketing and manufacturing coexist?", asked Benson P. Shapiro fifteen years ago in the *Harvard Business Review* [Shapiro, 1977]. Of course, the question is not whether marketing and production *can* coexist – they can and must – but rather, *how can marketing and production best work together to achieve the goals of the firm?* In this chapter we have demonstrated some tangible benefits that emerge from coexistence and have outlined some techniques in management science which have been developed to address this issue. At this point, it seems worthwhile to consider some additional perspectives in order to identify existing gaps which may offer further research opportunities.

Shapiro [1977] discusses the need for cooperation between marketing and production, especially in those companies producing industrial goods. He adds that some consumer-goods companies – particularly fashion industries with broad product lines such as apparel and furniture – also experience antagonism between these two key functional areas. Shapiro lists eight problem areas of "necessary cooperation but potential conflict" between marketing and production: (i) capacity planning and long-range sales forecasting, (ii) production scheduling and short-range sales forecasting, (iii) delivery and physical distribution, (iv) quality assurance, (v) breadth of product line, (vi) cost control, (vii) new-product introduction, and (viii) adjunct services, e.g. spare-parts inventory support, installation and repair.

Shapiro also lists the marketing/production complaints in each case: (i) insufficient capacity/lack of accurate long-range sales forecasts; (ii) excessive lead times/unrealistic customer commitments and mercurial short-range sales forecasts; (iii) insufficient inventory/excessive inventory requirements; (iv) insufficient quality at excessive cost/too many options offered with insufficient customer interest; (v) insufficient product variety to satisfy customer demand/excessive product variety necessitating short, uneconomical production runs; (vi) excessive costs which hamper competitiveness/unrealistic requirements on quality, delivery time, product variety and response to change; (vii) new products are important/unnecessary design changes are expensive; (viii) field service costs are excessive/products should not be used in ways for which they were not designed.

Shapiro in addition outlines some basic causes underlying these areas of conflict. One is the inherent complexity of these areas. Other causes include the differing experiences of managers in marketing and production, the differing criteria for evaluation and reward, and the differing 'cultures' of these two areas.

In a similar vain, Montgomery & Hausman [1986] explain that marketing and production "may either assist and reinforce one another or work at cross purposes, to the competitive detriment of the firm". They claim that marketing and production must each have both an appropriate, shared understanding of the firm's competitive strategy in order to make trade-offs, and that each must communicate with, understand and cooperate with each other. In particular, production should understand the opportunity costs of particular production decisions, while marketing should avoid costly over-segmentation of the market and provide guidance as to what product and service features are valued by customers.

In a later paper, Hausman & Montgomery [1990] identify the following production priorities: (i) cost, (ii) quality, (iii) dependability, (iv) short-term flexibility, and (v) innovation. At the same time, they argue that a linkage should be established between these priorities and the dimensions on which customers evaluate products and services relative to competition: (i) price, (ii) quality, (iii) availability, (iv) variety, (v) features, and (vi) post-sales service. Conjoint analysis is proposed as a methodology to facilitate the establishment of such linkage and thus move the firm in the direction of making production market-driven.

Montgomery & Hausman [1986] cite the following as being the most important interfaces between the two functions: (i) strategy, (ii) forecasting, (iii) the order-delivery cycle, (iv) product line, (v) quality, and (vi) customer service. It is interesting to note that all these issues were also listed by Shapiro, with the exception of strategy. Hence, we will invoke Shapiro's list as a framework for outlining achievements and challenges.

Shapiro's first two problem areas are comprised of three research topics: capacity planning, production scheduling and sales forecasting. These all fall under the general heading of aggregate production planning; see Chapter 3 of Hax & Candea [1984] for a good discussion of this area. The discussion provided in Section 3 of this chapter suggests that at least the production scheduling area has received some attention by MS/OR modelers. A related topic here is flexible manufacturing systems (FMS) [Buzacott & Yao, 1986].

Shapiro's third problem area – delivery and physical distribution – is usually classified in the modeling literature within two topics: distribution management and facility location. For distribution management from the production viewpoint, see the book by Eilon, Watson-Gandy & Christofides [1982]; for marketing perspectives on distribution, see the book by Stern & El-Ansary [1988]; for facility location, see the book edited by Mirchandani & Francis [1990]. It appears that these problem areas are still approached disjointly by marketing and production modelers.

Shapiro's fourth problem area is quality assurance. Quality issues are in vogue at present, and there exists a considerable literature [e.g. Farsad & Elshennawy, 1989; Godfrey, 1986; Hauser & Clausing, 1988]; however, there is little OR/MS modeling of the extant marketing/production issues.

Shapiro's fifth problem area, breadth of product line (product variety), has been addressed distinctly by production modelers [Johnson & Montgomery, 1974; Elmaghraby, 1978] and by marketing modelers [Green & Krieger, 1985; Lancaster, 1990]. More joint work is badly needed here.

The sixth problem area, cost control, is an important one which also deserves further modeling attention. For the related area of quantity discounts, see Monroe [1990] and Silver & Peterson [1985] for marketing/production perspectives.

Shapiro's seventh problem area, new-product introduction, certainly deserves further joint work. In particular, little has been done from the production viewpoint; see, for instance, Urban & Hauser [1980] for marketing perspectives.

For the most part, there does exist modeling literature (albeit, not cross-functional) in Shapiro's eighth problem area, adjunct services. Concerning the three sub-areas he specifically cites: for spare-parts inventory support, see for example Keilson & Kubat [1984]; for installation, apparently not much modeling work has been done and this area may be worthy of further modeling attention; for repair and maintenance there exists a considerable amount of work [see, for example, Assaf & Shanthikumar, 1987; Li, 1987], and in fact this sub-area may merit another review article. For the related production-warranty problem, see Murthy [1990] and Menezes & Currim [1992].

As to the one issue cited by Montgomery & Hausman [1986] which was not included as a problem area of Shapiro, the strategic interface between marketing and production is considered by many of the papers we have discussed in this chapter and in some sense has served as an underlying theme for us.

Hayes & Wheelwright [1984, Chapter 7] remark that in general dealing with Shapiro's eight problem areas is not likely in itself to lead to a substantial increase in cooperation between marketing and production. Rather, they argue, one needs to understand in managerial terms why that interface can so easily become a source of conflict. (See Shapiro's list of eight conflict issues.) They suggest that one approach to developing that kind of understanding could be based on an analysis of how product and process life-cycles intersect; their book goes into this topic in some detail. Clearly, this is an interesting perspective for future modeling efforts.

Our review of the existing models in MS/OR suggests that there still exists a wide gap between the critical issues outlined by Shapiro and by Montgomery & Hausman on the one hand, and the kind of issues that modelers have thus far addressed on the other. In addition, very few real-world implementations have been reported. These observations obviously suggest possibilities for further analytical as well as empirical research.

We have found that many of the papers in management science dealing with marketing–production joint decision-making fall naturally into two categories of managerial problems, depending on whether the production/ordering costs are convex or concave. This dichotomy is not surprising, since convex production costs are often associated with production arising from short-term diseconomies of scale, and concave production costs are often associated with production runs and order quantities arising from the existence of fixed costs. These models can also be classified as to whether they are continuous- or discrete-time and whether they are deterministic or stochastic. A further dichotomy is the classification into finite and infinite time-horizon models. The continuous-time concave-cost models tend to be formulated over an infinite horizon; otherwise, the modeling is usually taken over a finite horizon.

Looking over the diversity of marketing–production models available in the literature, we observe that the most common decision variable from the marketing side has been price (static or dynamic), and the most common decision variable from the production side has been order quantity or production rate. Future research should consider other marketing decision variables such as sales promotion and advertising expenditure, as well as decision variables corresponding to timing of introduction of new products and their level of quality. From the production side, decision variables not associated with the production quantity have included the amount or type of production technology. The area of flexible manufacturing systems (FMS) seems to offer interesting opportunities for investigating issues related to the level of technology needed by the firm to consistently satisfy changing consumer preferences.

Few of the models incorporate competition, undoubtedly due to the fact that the existence of both production and marketing decisions creates models which are already considerably complex. Despite the daunting nature of competitive formulations, these would be well worth investigating. Another dimension which should be looked into is the case of multiple products. Such models may be quite difficult to analyze, however, with our existing tools. As Hum & Sarin [1991] explain: “The integrated product-mix planning, lot sizing, and scheduling problem yields a nonconvex, mixed-integer nonlinear program which is difficult to solve for global optimality”. The explicit incorporation of financial decision-making has been attempted on a few occasions; however, these models have provided only limited insight. Clearly, more can be done in this direction and in the direction of other functional areas.

We close expressing the hope that the material reviewed and discussion provided in this chapter will help narrow the gap between marketing and production models and foster further interdisciplinary collaboration.

References

Abad, P.A. (1987). A hierarchical optimal control model for co-ordination of functional decisions in a firm. *Eur. J. Oper. Res.* 32, 62–75.

Abel, A.B. (1985). Inventories, stock-outs and production smoothing. *Rev. Econom. Studies* 52, 283–293.

Aquilano, N.J., and R.B. Chase (1991). *Fundamentals of Operations Management*, Irwin, Homewood, IL.

Arrow, K.J., and S. Karlin (1958). Production over time with increasing marginal costs, in: K.J. Arrow, S. Karlin and H. Scarf (eds.), *Studies in the Mathematical Theory of Inventory and Production*, Stanford University Press, Stanford, CA, pp. 61–69.

Assaf, D., and J.G. Shanthikumar (1987). Optimal group maintenance policies with continuous and periodic inspections. *Management Sci.* 33, 1440–1452.

Bhaskaran, S., and S.P. Sethi (1987). Decision and forecast horizons in a stochastic environment: A survey. *Optimal Control Appl. and Methods* 8, 201–217.

Blackburn, J.D., ed. (1991). *Time-Based Competition: The Next Battleground in American Manufacturing*, Business One Irwin, Homewood, IL.

Buzacott, J.A., and D.D. Yao (1986). Flexible manufacturing systems: A review of analytical models. *Management Sci.* 32, 890–905.

Caulkins, J.P., and C.H. Fine (1990). Seasonal inventories and the use of product-flexible manufacturing technology. *Annals Oper. Res.* 26, 351–375.

Cohen, M.A. (1977). Joint pricing and ordering policy for exponentially decaying inventory with known demand. *Naval Res. Logist. Quart.* 24, 257–268.

Cohen, M.A., J. Eliashberg and T.H. Ho (1992). New product development: Performance, timing and the marketing-manufacturnig interface. Working Paper, University of Pennsylvania, Philadelphia, PA, April.

Crittenden, V.L. (1992). Close the marketing/production gap. *Sloan Management Rev.* 33 (Spring), 41–52.

Crowe, T.J., and J.P. Nuno (1991). Deciding manufacturing priorities: Flexibility, cost, quality and service. *Long Range Planning* 24 (December), 88–95.

Damon, W.W., and R. Schramm (1972). A simultaneous decision model for production, marketing and finance. *Management Sci.* 19, 161–172.

Damon, W.W., and R. Schramm (1977). On a simultaneous decision model for marketing, production and finance: A rejoinder. *Management Sci.* 23, 1010–1011.

Davis, K.R. (1977). The process of problem finding: A production–marketing example. *Interfaces* 8(1), 82–86.

De Groote, X. (1991). Flexibility and marketing/manufacturing coordination, Working Paper 91/60/TM, INSEAD, November.

Dobson, G., and S. Kalish (1993). Heuristics for pricing and positioning a product-line using conjoint and cost data. *Management Sci.* 39, 160–175.

Dolan, R.J., and A. Jeuland (1981). Experience curves and dynamic demand models: Implications for optimal pricing strategies. *J. Marketing* 45, 52–62.

Eilon, S., C.D.T. Watson-Gandy and N. Christofides (1982). *Distribution Management: Mathematical Modeling and Practical Analysis*, Lubrecht and Cramer.

Eliashberg, J., and R. Steinberg (1984). Marketing–production decisions in industrial channels of distribution. Working Paper, No. 84–009R, University of Pennsylvania, Philadelphia, PA, August.

Eliashberg, J., and R. Steinberg (1987). Marketing–production decisions in an industrial channel of distribution. *Management Science* 33, 981–1000.

Eliashberg, J., and R. Steinberg (1988). On transfer pricing in an industrial channel of distribution. Working Paper, University of Pennsylvania and AT&T Bell Laboratories, July.

Eliashberg, J., and R. Steinberg (1991). Competitive strategies for two firms with asymmetric production cost structures. *Management Sci.* 37, 1452–1473.

Elmaghraby, S.E. (1978). The economic lot scheduling problem (ELSP): Review and extensions. *Management Sci.* 24, 587–598.

Eppen, G.D., F.J. Gould, and B.P. Pashigian (1969). Extensions of the planning horizon theorem in the dynamic lot size model. *Management Sci.* 15, 268–277.

Farsad, B., and A.K. Elshennawy (1989). Defining service quality is difficult for service and manufacturing firms. *Indust. Engrg.* 21 (March), 17–19.

Federgruen, A., and M. Tzur (1991). A simple forward algorithm to solve general dynamic lot sizing models with n periods in $O(n \log n)$ or $O(n)$ time. *Management Sci.* 37, 909–925.

Feichtinger, G., and R. Hartl (1985). Optimal pricing and production in an inventory model. *Eur. J. Oper. Res.* 19, 45–56.

Fiacco, A.V., and G.P. McCormick (1968). *Nonlinear Programming: Sequential Unconstrained Minimization Techniques*, Wiley, New York.

Fine, C.H., and R.M. Freund (1990). Optimal investment in product-flexible manufacturing capacity, *Management Sci.* 36, 449–466.

Florian, M., J.K. Lenstra and A.H.G. Rinnooy Kan (1980). Deterministic production planning: Algorithms and complexity. *Management Sci.* 26, 669–679.

Freeland, J.R. (1980). Coordination strategies for production and marketing in a functionally decentralized firm, *AIIE Trans.* 12, 126–132

Godfrey, B.A. (1986). The history and evolution of quality in AT&T, *AT&T Tech. J.* 65, 9–20.

Graham, R.J. (1976). Problem and opportunity identification in management science, *Interfaces* 6(4), 79–82.

Green, P.E., and A.M. Krieger (1985). Models and heuristics for product line selection. *Marketing Sci.* 4, 1–19.

Griffin, J.M. (1972). The process analysis alternative to statistical cost functions: An application to petroleum refining. *Amer. Econom. Rev.* (March), 46–56.

Hauser, J., and D. Clausing (1988). The house of quality. *Harvard Business Rev.* 66 (May–June), 63–73.

Hausman, W.H., and D.B. Montgomery (1990). Making manufacturing market driven. Research Working Paper #1103, Stanford University, Stanford, CA, October.

Hax, A.C., and D. Candea (1984). *Production and Inventory Management*, Prentice-Hall, Englewood Cliffs, NJ.

Hayes, R.H., and S.C. Wheelwright (1984). *Restoring our Competitive Edge: Competing through Manufacturing*, Wiley, New York.

Holt, C., F. Modigliani, J. Muth and H. Simon (1960). *Planning Production, Inventories, and Work Force.* Prentice-Hall, Englewood Cliffs, NJ.

Hotelling, H. (1929). Stability in competition, *Econom. J.* 39, 41–57.

House, C.H., and R.L. Price (1991). The return map: Tracking product teams. *Harvard Business Rev.* 69 (January–February), 92–100.

Hum, S.H., and R.K. Sarin (1991). Simultaneous product-mix planning, lot sizing and scheduling at bottleneck facilities. *Oper Res.* 39, 296–307.

Johnson, L. A., and D.C. Montgomery (1974). *Operations Research in Production Planning. Scheduling and Inventory Control*, Wiley, New York.

Jorgensen, S. (1986a). Optimal production, purchasing and pricing: A differential game approach. *Eur. J. Oper. Res.* 24, 64–76.

Jorgensen, S. (1986b). Optimal dynamic pricing in an oligopolistic market: A survey, in T. Bascar (ed.), *Dynamic Games and Applications in Economics*, Lecture Notes in Economics and Mathematical Systems, Vol. 265, Springer, Berlin, 179–237.

Karlin, S., and C.R. Carr (1962). Prices and optimal inventory policy, in K.J. Arrow, S. Karlin and H. Scarf (eds.), *Studies in Applied Probability and Management Science*, Stanford University Press, Stanford, CA, 159–172.

Karmarkar, U.S. (1987). Lot sizes, lead times and in-process inventories. *Management Sci.* 33, 409–418.

Karmarkar, U.S., and M.M. Lele (1989). The marketing/manufacturing interface: Strategic issues, Working Paper CMOM 89-10, Center for Manufacturing and Operations Management, William E. Simon Graduate School of Business Administration, University of Rochester, Rochester, NY, December.

Keilson, J., and P. Kubat (1984). Parts and service demand distribution generated by primary production growth. *Eur. J. Oper. Res.* 17, 257–265.

Kotler, P. (1991). *Marketing Management, 7th-Edition*, Prentice-Hall, Englewood Cliffs, NJ.

Kreps, D.M. (1990). *A Course on Microeconomic Theory*, Princeton University Press, Princeton, NJ.

Kunreuther, H., and J.F. Richard (1969). Optimal pricing and inventory decisions for retail stores, Report 6934 (Working Paper), August.

Kunreuther, H., and J.F. Richard (1971). Optimal pricing and inventory decisions for non-seasonal items. *Econometrica* 39, 173–175.

Kunreuther, H., and L. Schrage (1973). Joint pricing and inventory decisions for constant priced items. *Management Sci.* 19, 732–738.

Lancaster, K. (1990). The economics of product variety: A survey. *Marketing Sci.* 9, 189–206.

Li, K.F. (1987). Serial production lines with unreliable machines and limited repairs. *Naval Res. Logist. Quart.* 34, 101–108.

Lieberman, M.B., and D.B. Mongomery (1991). To pioneer or follow? Strategy of entry orders, in H. Glass (ed.), *Handbook of Business Strategy, 2nd edition*, Warren, Gorham, and Lamont, New York.

Manne, A. (1958). A linear programming model of the U.S. petroleum refining industry. *Econometrica* 26, 67–106.

McClain, J.O., and L.J. Thomas (1985). *Operations Management: Production of Goods and Services, 2nd edition*, Prentice-Hall, Englewood Cliffs, NJ.

Menezes, M.A.J., and I.S. Currim (1992). An approach for determination of warranty length. *Intern. J. Res. Marketing* 9, 177–195.

Milgrom, P., and J. Roberts (1990). The economics of modern manufacturing: Technology, strategy, and organization. *Amer. Econom. Rev.* 80, 511–528.

Mills, E.S. (1959). Uncertainty and price theory. *Quart. J. Econom.* 73, 116–130.

Mirchandani, P.B., and R.L. Francis, eds. (1990). *Discrete Location Theory*, Wiley, New York.

Modigliani, F., and F.E. Hohn (1955). Production planning over time and the nature of the expectation and planning horizon. *Econometrica* 23, 46–66.

Monden, Y. (1981). What makes the Toyota production system really tick?. *Indust. Engrg.* 13 (January), 36–46.

Monroe, K.B. (1990). *Pricing: Making Profitable Decisions, 2nd edition*, McGraw-Hill, New York.

Monroe, K.B., and A.J. Della Bitta (1978). Models for pricing decisions. *J. Marketing Res.* 15, 413–428.

Montgomery, D.B., and W.H. Hausman (1986). Managing the marketing/manufacturing interface. *Gestion 2000: Management and Perspective* 5, 69–85.

Murthy, D.N.P. (1990). Product warranty: A review and technology management implications, in T.M. Khalil et al. (eds.), *Management of Technology II: The Key to Global Competitiveness*, Industrial Engineering and Management Press, Miami, FL.

Nahmias, S. (1982). Perishable inventory theory: A review. *Oper. Res.* 30, 680–708.

Nerlove, M., and K.J. Arrow (1962). Optimal advertising policy under dynamic conditions. *Economica* 39, 129–142.

Ohno, T. (1982). The origin of Toyota production system and kanban system. *Proceedings of the International Conference on Productivity and Quality Improvement*, Tokyo.

Pashigian, B.P. (1988). Demand uncertainty and sales: A study of fashion and markdown pricing. *Amer. Econom. Rev.* 78, 936–953.

Pekelman, D. (1974). Simultaneous price–production decisions. *Oper. Res.* 22, 788–794.

Pekelman, D. (1975). Production smoothing with fluctuating price. *Management Sci.* 21, 576–590.

Porteus, E.L. (1985). Investing in reduced setups in the EOQ model. *Management Sci.* 31, 998–1010.

Porteus, E.L. (1990). Stochastic inventory theory, in D. Heyman and M. Sobel (eds.), *Handbook in Operations Research and Management Science, 2: Stochastic Models*, Elsevier, Amsterdam.

Porteus, E.L., and S. Whang (1991). On manufacturing/marketing incentives. *Management Sci.* 37, 1166–1181.

Rajan, A., Rakesh, and R. Steinberg (1992). Dynamic pricing and ordering decisions by a monopolist. *Management Sci.* 38, 240–262.

Rao, V.R. (1984). Pricing research in marketing: The state of the art. *J. Business* 57, S-39–S-60.

Ratchford, B.T. (1990). Commentary: Marketing applications of the economics of product variety. *Marketing Sci.* 9, 207–211.

Salomon, M. (1991). *Deterministic Lotsizing Models for Production Planning*, Lecture Notes in Economics and Mathematical Systems, 355, Springer, Berlin.

Shapiro, B.P. (1977). Can marketing and manufacturing coexist?. *Harvard Business Rev.* 55, 104–114.

Silver, E.A., and R. Peterson (1985). *Decision Systems for Inventory Management and Production Planning, 2nd edition*, Wiley, New York.
Smunt, T.L. (1986). Incorporating learning curve analysis into medium-term capacity planning procedures: A simulation experiment. *Management Sci.* 32, 1164–1176.
Sogomonian, A.G., and C.S. Tang (1990). A modeling framework for coordinating promotion and production decisions within a firm, Working Paper, Anderson Graduate School of Management, *Management Sci.* 39, 191–203.
Stalk, Jr., G.S., and T.M. Hout (1990). *Competing against Time: How Timebased Competition is Reshaping Global Markets*, The Free Press, New York.
Stern, L.W., and A.I. El-Ansary (1988). *Marketing Channels, 3rd edition*, Prentice-Hall, Englewood Cliffs, NJ.
Sugimori, Y., K. Kusunoki, F. Cho and S. Uchikawa (1977). Toyota production system and kanban system. Materialization of just-in-time and respect-for-human system. *Intern. J. Production Res.* 15, 553–564.
Teng, J.-T., and G.L. Thompson (1983). Oligopoly models for optimal advertising when production costs obey a learning curve. *Management Sci.* 29, 1087–1101.
Thomas, J. (1970). Price-production decisions with deterministic demand. *Management Sci.* 16, 747–750.
Thomas, L.J. (1974). Price and production decisions with random demand. *Oper. Res.* 22, 513–518.
Thompson, G.L., S.P. Sethi and J.-T. Teng (1984). Strong planning and forecast horizons for a model with simultaneous price and production decisions. *Eur. J. Oper. Res.* 16, 378–388.
Thowsen, G.T. (1975). A dynamic, nonstationary inventory problem for a price/quantity setting firm. *Naval Res. Logist. Quart.* 22, 461–476,
Urban, G.L., T. Carter, S. Gaskin and Z. Mucha (1986). Market share rewards to pioneering brands: An empirical analysis and strategic implications, *Management Sci.* 32, 645–659.
Urban, G.L., and J.R. Hauser (1980). *Design and Marketing of New Products*, Prentice-Hall, Englewood Cliffs, NJ.
Veinott, A.F. (1966). The status of mathematical inventory theory. *Management Sci.* 12, 745–777.
Wagner, H.M. (1960). A postscript to 'dynamic problems in the theory of the firm'. *Naval Res. Logist. Quart.* 7, 7–12.
Wagner, H.M., and T.M. Whitin (1958a). Dynamic problems in the theory of the firm. *Naval Res. Logist. Quart.* 5, 53–74. Also contained in: T.M. Whitin, *The Theory of Inventory Management, 2nd Edition*, Princeton University Press Princeton, NJ, 1957, Appendix 6.
Wagner, H.M., and T.M. Whitin (1958b). Dynamic version of the economic lot size model. *Management Sci.* 5, 89–96.
Welam, U.P. (1977a) Synthesizing short run production and marketing decisions, *AIIE Trans.* 9, 53–62.
Welam, U.P. (1977b). On a simultaneous decision model for marketing, production and finance. *Management Sci.* 23, 1005–1009.
Whitin, T. M. (1955). Inventory control and price theory. *Management Sci.* 2, 61–68.
Wind, Y., V. Mahajan and R.N. Cardozo, eds. (1981). *New-Product Forecasting: Models and Applications*, Lexington Books, Lexington, MA.
Zabel, E. (1964). Some generalizations of an inventory planning horizon theorem. *Management Sci.* 10, 465–471.
Zangwill, W.I. (1968). Minimum concave cost flows in certain networks. *Management Sci.* 14, 429–450.

Subject Index

A
Accelerated purchases. *See* Purchases, accelerated
Acceleration effects of promotion. *See* Promotion, acceleration effects of
ACE. *See* Autoregressive current effects model
Acquisition utility. *See* Utility, acquisition
Actionable variables. *See* Variables, actionable
Adaptation-level theory, 297
Adaptive conjoint analysis. *See* Conjoint analysis, adaptive
ADBUDG model. *See* Models
ADCAD model. *See* Models
Additive Models. *See* Models
Additive tree-fitting. *See* Tree-fitting, additive
ADDTREE model. *See* Models
ADDUCE model. *See* Models
Adjunct services. *See* Services, adjunct
Adverse selection, 624
Advertising, 414, 420
– carryover, 452
– competition, 176
– cumulative effects, 425
– decision rules, 429
– dynamics, 425
– effects, 310
– elasticity, 436
– expenditure, 876
– primary, 443
– threshold, 415
– wearout, 427
Advertising models. *See* Models
ADVISOR model. *See* Models
Agency theory, 623, 638, 837, 845
Aggregate demand models. *See* Models
Aggregate marketing-mix model. *See* Models
Aggregate production planning, 851
AHP. *See* Analytic Hierarchy Process
AI. *See* Artificial intelligence
AID model. *See* Models
Allocation of resources. *See* Resources, allocation of
Allocation, optimal, 309
ALPH model. *See* Models
Alternating least-squares. *See* Least-squares, alternating
Analysis, qualitative, 755
Analytic Hierarchy Process, 467, 815
Arctan, 37
Artificial intelligence, 733, 749
ASSESSOR model. *See* Models
Asymmetric competition. *See* Competition, asymmetric
Asymmetric Nash equilibrium, 98
Asymmetric production-cost structures. *See* Production-cost structures
Asymmetries in markets and competition, 261, 282
Asymmetry in response, 433
Asymmetry of deviations from expected price, 541
Asymmetry of effects of price, 539
Attitude models. *See* Models
Attitude-change models. *See* Models
Attraction model. *See* Models
Attribute-based screening model. *See* Models
Autocracy model. *See* Models
Autoregressive current effects model. *See* Models
Average baseline utility. *See* Utility, average baseline
Awareness (aided/unaided), 30
Awareness creation, 42

B
Bait-and-switch, 156
Balance model for bundling. *See* Models
Bargaining, 85, 91, 133
Barrier penalty functions, 223
Baseline, 553, 564, 565, 568, 579
Bass model. *See* Models
Bayes's rule, 40
Bayesian decision analysis, 757
Bayesian estimation, 445
Bayesian network, 759
Behavioral intention model. *See* Models
Behavioral pricing model. *See* Models

Behavioral theories, 518
Belief dynamics, 30
Benefit segmentation, 291
Bertrand equilibrium. *See* Equilibrium, Bertrand
Biases, 73
Binary choice models. *See* Models
Binary logit model. *See* Models
Binary probit model. *See* Models
Bradley-Terry-Luce model. *See* Models
Brand choice model. *See* Models
Brand image, 31
Brand loyalty and promotions, 592
Brand plans, 308
Brand satisfaction/satiation, 30
Brand share, 10
Brand-loyalty variables, 576
Brand-switching and category sales, 573
Brand-switching data, 196, 225, 297
BRANDAID model. *See* Models
Bundling, 536
Business strategy models. *See* Models
Business strengths/weaknesses model. *See* Models
Buyer-choice simulators, 482
Buyer-seller negotiations, 115

C

Calibration, 5, 741
CALLPLAN model. *See* Models
Cannibalization, 326, 849
Capacity planning, 874
Capacity-allocation, 845
Carryover in loyalty. *See* Loyalty, carryover in
CART model. *See* Models
Case allowance discount. *See* Discount, case allowance
CASEMAP procedure, 474
Categorization, 74, 344
Category-volume models. *See* Models
Causal models. *See* Models
CHAID model. *See* Models
Channel of distribution, 16, 412
Choffray & Lilien model. *See* Models
Choice map, 247
Choice probabilities, 273
Choice set, 30, 31
Choice, low-involvement, 29
CLS model. *See* Models
Clustering, hierarchical, 201
Cobb-Douglas production function. *See* production function
Cohesiveness, 127
Collusion, implicit, 157
Common-factor analysis, 45
Communality, 48
Communications/network models. *See* Models
Compensation scheme, 14, 15
Compensatory models. *See* Models
Competition, 17, 678, 689, 876
– asymmetric, 578
– Condorcet, 109
– in advertising, 385
– in distribution channels, 182
– in media scheduling, 180
– quantity, 149
– time-based, 832
Competitive effect, indirect, 287
Competitive map. *See* Map, competitive
Competitive market structure. *See* Market structure, competitive
Competitive price paths. *See* Price paths, competitive
Competitive reaction. *See* Reaction, competitive
Competitive strategy. *See* Strategy, competitive
Compositional models. *See* Models
Compromise model. *See* Models
Computational complexity, 867
Concave sales response, 437
Concave-cost models. *See* Models
Condition index, 307
Condorcet competition. *See* Competition, Condorcet
Configural models. *See* Models
Confirmatory factor analysis. *See* Factor analysis, confirmatory
Conflict-resolution, 132
Conjoint analysis, adaptive, 474, 481
Conjoint analysis, 468, 472, 535, 544
Conjunctive model. *See* Models
Consideration models. *See* Models
Consideration-set formation, 30, 31, 41
Constant-sum judgments, 478
Constant-utility model. *See* Models
Consumer behavior models. *See* Models
Consumer expectations, 387
Consumer heterogeneity, 518, 524
Consumer preferences, 847
Consumer promotions, 555
Consumer response, 337
Consumer satisfaction, 61
Consumer search costs, 539
Consumer stockpiling, 581
Contextual effects, 73
Control theory, optimal, 17
Convex-cost models. *See* Models
Cooperative game theory. *See* Game theory, cooperative
Corporate strategy models. *See* Models

Correspondence analysis, 47, 50
Cost control, 873, 875
Cost-declines, 518
Coupon distribution, lagged effects of, 563
Coupon drop, 556
Coupon promotions, design of, 593
Coupon-redemption timing models. *See* Models
Couponing, 556, 594
Cournot equilibrium. *See* Equilibrium, Cournot
COVERSTORY model. *See* Models
Cross calibration, 306
Cross validation. *See* Validation, cross
Cross-competitive effects. *See* Effects, cross-competitive
Cross-elasticities, 284, 442
Cross-price-demand relationships, estimating, 535
Cross-sectional varying-parameter models. *See* Models
Cumulative demand. *See* Demand, cumulative
Customized models. *See* Models

D

Data sources, 16
Data, panel, 10, 300
Data-interval-bias, 427
Deadline effect, 101
Deal decay, 578
Deal versus regular price effects, 579
Deal-to-deal buying, 571
Dealing, 591
DEALMAKER model. *See* Models
Decision history, 112, 115
Decision models. *See* Models
Decision rule, 127
Decision support systems, 641, 734
Decision theory, 114
Decision-calculus, 714
Decision-making, 85, 135
Decompositional models. *See* Models
DEFENDER model. *See* Models
Defensive strategy. *See* Strategy, defensive
Demand curves, kinked, 430
Demand, cumulative, 852
Demand, time-dependent, 856
Derived demand function. *See* Function, derived demand
Descriptive models. *See* Models
Desired target portfolio, 782, 817
DETAILER model. *See* Models
Deterministic models. *See* Models
Diffusion models. *See* Models
Diffusion of innovations. *See* Models
Diminishing returns, 437
Direct competitive effect, 287
Dirichlet distribution, 276
Disaggregate choice models. *See* Models
Discount, case allowance, 556
Discount, quantity, 133
Discrete choice models. *See* Models
Discriminant analysis, multiple, 47, 50
Disjunctive model. *See* Models
Distributed lag model. *See* Models
Distribution, 33, 421, 445, 857, 875
Distribution models. *See* Models
Distribution, double-exponential, 33
Distribution, purchase frequency, 273
DSS, *See* Decision support systems
Dynamic models. *See* Models
Dynamic pricing models. *See* Models
Dynamic pricing, 373, 519, 527, 531–533, 866

E

EBA model. *See* Models
EBF model. *See* Models
EBT model. *See* Models
Econometric models. *See* Models
Economic lot-scheduling problem, 831
Economic order quantity, 862
Economics of search, 539
Effect of consumer expectations. *See* Consumer expectations
Effects, cross-competitive, 286, 305
Effects, temporary, 449
Eigenvalue, 48
Elasticity of price. *See* Price elasticity
Elasticity of selective advertising. *See* Selective advertising
Elasticity, point, 270
Elasticity, promotion, 567, 841
Elasticity, segment, 292
ELSP. *See* Economic lot-scheduling problem
End-9 and n-for pricing, 603
Entry, sequential, 171
EOQ. *See* Economic order quantity
Equilibria, sequential, 101, 147
Equilibrium analysis, 526
Equilibrium, Bertrand, 149
Equilibrium, Cournot, 149
Equiprobability model. *See* Models
Estimating cross-price-demand relationships. *See* Cross-price-demand relationships
Estimating self-price-demand relationships. *See* Self-price-demand relationships
Estimation, nonlinear, 422
Estimation, parameter, 656
Evoked set, 31, 329
EVSI. *See* Expected value of sample information

Existing stock model. *See* Models
Expected prices. *See* Prices, expected
Expected utility. *See* Utility, expected
Expected value of sample information, 40
Experimental choice analysis, 479
Expert systems, 9, 749
Expertise, 115
Exponential models. *See* Models
Extended Fishbein model. *See* Models
EXTREE model. *See* Models
Extreme-value distribution of type I, 280
Extreme-value distribution of type II, 281

F

FA. *See* Factor analysis
Facility location, 875
Factor analysis, 44–46, 49
Factor analysis, confirmatory, 46, 48, 49
Factor listing, 782
Finance-marketing-production systems, 842
Financial/Product portfolio models. *See* Models
Finite time-horizon models. *See* Models
First repeat, 321
First-mover advantages, 171
Flexible logistic growth, 364
Flexible manufacturing systems, 876
FLOG. *See* Flexible logistic growth
Flow measure, 205
Flow models. *See* Models
Flow variable, 447
FMS. *See* Flexible manufacturing system
Folk theorems, 158
Forcing contract, 624
Forecast accuracy, 309
Forecast horizon, 852
Forecasting, 315, 423
Formation, preference, 31
Forward-buy by retailers, 566, 589
Forward-buy equation, 590
Forward-buying by consumers, 581
Fraction factorial designs, 472
Frame-based systems, 751
Free-standing insert, 557, 562
Friction pricing model. *See* Models
Fully extended attraction models. *See* Models
Function, derived demand, 859
Functions, reaction, 411, 429
Fundamental theorem of market share. *See* Market share

G

Game theoretic models. *See* Models
Game theory, cooperative, 92
Game theory, noncooperative, 99, 104, 105
Gamma function, 276
Generalized attraction model. *See* Models
Generalized extreme-value model. *See* Models
Generalized logit, 59
Generalized network structures, 230
Geography model. *See* Models
GEOLINE model. *See* Models
Globalization, 691
GO/NO GO, 316
Gross rating point, 438
Group processes, 84, 88, 90, 116, 118, 126, 128, 136
Group-decision support, 767
GRP. *See* Gross rating point
GSTUN model. *See* Models
Guerilla price wars. *See* Price-wars, guerilla
Gupta & Livne model. *See* Models

H

Hazard function, 583
Hazard rate models. *See* Models
Heavy users, 275, 303
HEM model. *See* Models
Hendry model. *See* Models
Heuristics, simplifying, 73
Hierarchical clustering. *See* Clustering, hierarchical
Hierarchical market-share model. *See* Models
Hierarchical models of choice. *See* Models
Hierarchical models. *See* Models
Hierarchies of market segments. *See* Market segments
High-involvement buying, 29
High-technology products, 365
HIRACH model. *See* Models
HMMS model. *See* Models
Home-delivery measures, 322
Homogeneous purchase frequencies, 274
Hotelling's model. *See* Models
Household heterogeneity, 577
Hybrid models. *See* Models

I

Ideal-point model. *See* Models
IIA. *See* Independence of irrelevant alternatives
Imitators, 355
Implementation, 523, 664, 665, 667, 671, 676, 677, 775
Implicit collusion. *See* Collusion, implicit
Incentive alignment, 613, 618
Inclusive value, 58, 67
Incomplete-information, 101
Incremental sales. *See* Sales, incremental

Incremental store profits. *See* Store profits, incremental
Independence of irrelevant alternatives, 56, 278
Index of distinctiveness, 294
Indirect competitive effect. *See* Competitive effect, indirect
Individual awareness models. *See* Models
Individual choice axiom, 277
Individual-level diffusion models. *See* Models
INDTREES model. *See* Models
INDUCE model. *See* Models
Industry models. *See* Models
Inequality, ultrametric, 208
INFER model. *See* Models
Infinite time-horizon models. *See* Models
Information integration models. *See* Models
Information overload and inferencing, 74
Information search, 30, 37, 43
Information set, 410
Information technology, 454
Information-acceleration, use of, 345
INNOVATOR model. *See* Models
Innovators, 355
Integer-programming, 668
Integrated marketing program, 781
Intensity of consumer preference. *See* Consumer preference, intensity of
Interaction model. *See* Models
Interaction, between marketing-mix variables, 726
Interaction, on the allocation decision, 726
Interaction, strategy and synergy, 21
Interaction, 17, 416, 440, 697, 727
Interbrand competition, 182
Intrabrand retail competition, 182
Intrinsically nonlinear models. *See* Models
Inventory models. *See* Models
Inverse log-centering transformation, 268

J

JIT. *See* Just-in-time production
Joint pricing-production decision, 855
Judgment, 121, 317
Just-in-time production systems, 832

K

Kalai & Smordinsky model. *See* Models
Kinked demand curves. *See* Demand curves, kinked
Knowledge processing, 750
Knowledge representation, 735, 750
Knowledge-based systems, 733, 750
Kohli & Park model. *See* Models
Krumhansi distance-density model. *See* Models

L

Lagged effects of coupon distribution. *See* Coupon distribution, lagged effects
Launch time, optimal, 849
Learning, 434, 831
Least-squares, alternating, 218
Levels of aggregation for sales-promotion models. *See* Models, sales promotion
Lexical maximin, 97
Lexicographic model. *See* Models
Life-cycle, 3
Light-users segment, 275, 304
Line extension, 505
Linear model. *See* Models
Linear probability model. *See* Models
Linear program, 34
Loadings, 45
Log-centering transformation, 267
Log-linear models. *See* Models
Logit model. *See* Models
Logrolling, 99
Long-term attraction, 292
Loss-leader promotions, 586
Low-involvement choice. *See* Choice, low-involvement
Loyalty, carryover in, 576
Luce model. *See* Models
Luce's axiom, 56

M

Management subjective judgment, 787
Map, competitive, 289
MAPNET model. *See* Models
Marginal cost, 841
Market intervention, 389
Market phenomena, 20
Market response model. *See* Models
Market segmentation, 779
Market segments, hierarchies of, 290
Market share, 10, 829
Market share, elasticities, 269, 271
Market share, fundamental theorem, 262
Market share/response models. *See* Models
Market structure, 193, 259, 452, 530
Market size, 856
Marketing and production, 830
Marketing channels, 133
Marketing decision making system, 5
Marketing decision support system, 8, 715
Marketing decision variables, 697
Marketing effectiveness, 703
Marketing effort, 261
Marketing generalizations, 18, 437

Marketing mix, 21, 697
– allocation rules, 713
– effects, 529
– interactions, 698, 706
– variables, 4, 728
Marketing plans, 326
Marketing practice, 16
Marketing production game, 829
Marketing production interactions, 830
Marketing production/financial decision-making, 838
Marketing strategy models. *See* Strategy models
Marketing systems, 19
Marketing variables, 701
Marketing-mix models. *See* Models
MAUT. *See* Multiattribute utility theory
MCI model. *See* Models
MDA. *See* Multiple discriminant analysis
MDS. *See* Multidimensional scaling
MDSS. *See* Marketing decision support system
Means-ends model. *See* Models
Measurement models. *See* Models
Measurement, cross-price relationships, 544
– price effects, 519, 543
– self-price relationships, 544
– technologies, 18
– willingness-to-pay, 544
MEDIAC model. *See* Models
Meta-analysis, 445, 543
Microeconomics, use of, 518
Minimum endorsement model. *See* Models
Mixed bundling, 536
Mixed-integer-programming, 844
Mixed-strategy Nash equilibrium. *See* Nash equilibrium, mixed-strategy
MLH model. *See* Models
MNL model. *See* Models
Models
– ADBUDG, 737
– ADCAD, 756, 762
– additive, 471
– ADDTREE, 214
– ADDUCE, 752
– advertising, 781
– ADVISOR, 720, 721, 738
– aggregate demand, 535
– aggregate marketing-mix, 711
– AID, 247
– ALPH, 508
– ASSESSOR, 323, 738, 743
– attitude, 30, 324
– attraction, 418
– attribute-based screening, 68
– autocracy, 114
– autoregressive current effects, 425
– awareness, 38
– balance, for bundling, 548
– Bass, 435
– behavioral intention, 52
– behavioral pricing, 538
– binary choice, 30, 32
– binary logit, 35, 67
– binary probit, 35, 37
– Bradley-Terry-Luce, 494
– brand choice, 30
– BRANDAID, 595, 738, 740, 789
– business strengths/weaknesses, 774
– CALLPLAN, 660–664, 666, 667, 672, 737
– CART, 247
– category-volume, 260
– causal, 16
– CHAID, 247
– Choffray & Lilien, 113
– CLS, 247
– communications/networks, 30
– compensatory, 30, 39, 50–52
– competition and coordination, 18
– competitive reactions, 548
– compositional, 469
– compromise, 108, 111, 114
– concave-cost, 862
– configural, 471
– conjunctive, 50–52
– consideration, 30, 38, 43
– constant-utility, 277
– consumer behavior, 9, 16, 27
– convex-cost, 851
– coupon-redemption timing, 562
– COVERSTORY, 764
– cross-sectional varying-parameter, 705
– customized, 814
– DEALMAKER, 752
– decision, 4, 733, 734
– decompositional, 469
– DEFENDER, 167, 173
– descriptive, 8, 743
– DETAILER, 664–666, 736
– deterministic, 200, 871
– diffusion, 349, 350, 356, 366, 726
– – estimation procedures, 391
– – flexibility in, 361
– – individual-level, 360
– – use of, 369
– disaggregate choice, 60
– discrete choice, 30
– disjunctive, 54
– distributed lag, 310, 426
– distribution, 781

Models (*cont'd*)
- dynamic pricing, 519, 527
- dynamic, 422, 872
- EBA, 234
- EBF, 238
- EBT, 234
- econometric, 409, 697, 698, 714
- equiprobability, 107, 108
- existing stock, 35
- exponential, 266
- extended Fishbein, 52
- EXTREE, 231
- financial/product portfolio, 797
- finite time-horizon, 876
- flow, 340
- fricition-pricing, 297
- fully extended attraction, 286
- game theoretic, 17, 91, 143
- generalized attraction, 272, 299
- generalized extreme-value, 60
- geography, 784
- GEOLINE, 670–672
- GSTUN, 242
- Gupta & Livne, 98, 116, 136
- Hazard rate, 35
- HEM, 234
- Hendry, 200
- hierarchical, 30
- hierarchical, choice, 56
- HIRACH, 237
- HMMS, 837
- Hotelling, 162
- hybrid, 814
- ideal-point, 52, 53, 475
- implementation, 766
- individual awareness, 30
- INDTREES, 219
- INDUCE, 251
- industry, 784
- INFER, 764
- infinite time-horizon, 876
- information integration, 30, 39, 42
- INNOVATOR, 756
- intrinsically nonlinear, 267
- inventory, 828, 842, 846, 872
- Kalai & Smorodinsky, 95
- Kohli & Park, 133
- Krumhansi distance-density, 222
- lexicographic, 52, 55
- linear probability, 37
- linear, 266
- log-linear, 268
- logit, 33, 39, 58, 59, 66, 69, 328, 479, 745
- logit, multinomial, 263
- logit, nested, 57, 59, 60, 68
- Luce, 59, 64, 235
- MAPNET, 232
- market response, 409
- market share, hierarchical, 419
- market share/response, 17, 259, 411, 418
- marketing-mix, 259, 697, 699, 714, 716, 728
- mathematical programming, bundling, 537
- MCI, 263
- means-end, 542
- measurement, 4
- MEDIAC, 736
- minimum endorsement, 113
- MLH, 237
- MNL, 263
- MONANOVA, 478
- multiplicative, 266
- multiplicative, competitive-interaction, 263
- NEGOTEX, 739
- NEPALS, 219
- NETSCAL, 231
- NILES, 219
- non-compensatory, 30, 39, 50
- non-traditional, 804
- non-uniform-influence, 361
- normative, 85, 742
- objectives and strategies, 775
- opportunities and threats analysis, 774, 775
- organizational buying, 28
- PAIRS, 666
- paramorphic, 469
- part-worth, 475
- partial adjustment, 426
- perceptual mapping, 30, 43
- plurality, 107, 108
- portfolio analysis, 775
- positioning, 780
- POSSE, 492
- preference perturbation, 113
- prescriptive, 743
- pretest-market, 315, 346
- PRETREE, 234
- pricing, 520, 521, 535, 780
- pricing, factors for describing, 520, 521
- pricing, multiple product, 534
- probit, 59, 479
- probit, multinomial, 60
- probit, multivariate, 279
- process, 9, 17, 784
- projection, 12, 44
- PROMOTER, 568, 579, 739
- PROMOTION ADVISOR, 756
- promotion, 601, 781

Models (*cont'd*)
- promotional decision calculus, 601
- proportionality, 107
- random-utility, 279
- ratchet, 433
- Rawls, 98
- redemption at retail, 562
- redemption timing, 563
- reference price, with, 540
- response, 478, 697, 702, 740
- Rubinstein, 100
- Sales force, 658, 659, 781
- sales promotion, levels of aggregation, 605
- satisfaction, 30
- SCAN*EXPERT, 764
- screening, 784
- SCULPTRE, 244
- segment-level, 307
- segmentation, 59, 300, 774, 779
- SHANEX, 764
- SIMOPT, 494
- simple-effects attraction, 284
- social communication networks, 65
- SPRINTER, 737
- SSTUN, 242
- STAR, 251
- static, 519, 871
- stochastic, 29, 234, 320
- stochastic-demand, 871
- strategy, 774, 782, 787
- strategy, objectives of, 785
- strategy, simulations, 783
- STRATPORT, 793
- structural equation, 52, 53
- stylized theoretical, 4, 9
- survival, 562
- switching, 435
- symmetric market-share, 305
- synergy analysis, 775
- time-series, 260
- time-varying-parameter, 704
- VAF, 306
- validity, 747, 766
- variety-seeking, 30
- varying-parameter, 702, 727
- vector, 475
- voting, 113
- weighted linear, 110, 111
- weighted probability, 112, 113, 115

MONANOVA model. *See* Models
Monotone transformations. *See* Transformations, monotone
Monotonicity, 95
Moral hazard, 624, 625
Most-favored-customer pricing. *See* Pricing, most-favored-customer
Moving-window regressions. *See* Regressions, moving-window
Multi-media computer system, 344
Multiattribute utility theory. *See* Utility theory, multiattribute
Multidimensional scaling, 44, 46, 49, 493
Multinomial logit model. *See* Models
Multinomial probit model. *See* Models
Multiple discriminant analysis. *See* Discriminant analysis, multiple
Multiple-product pricing models. *See* Models
Multiple-tree-structures, 218
Multiplicative model. *See* Models
Multiplicative, competitive-interaction model. *See* Models
Multivariate-probit model. *See* Models

N

N items for pricing, 578
Nash equilibrium, 91, 93, 136, 147, 857
- mixed-strategy, 147
- open-loop, 530
- pure-strategy, 147

Need arousal, 30, 32
NEGOTEX model. *See* Models
Negotiations, 9, 136
NEPALS model. *See* Models
Nested logit model. *See* Models, logit
NETSCAL model. *See* Models
Neural networks, 752
New product
- decisions, 780
- development process, 850
- growth, 350
- introduction, 873, 875
- performance, 849

NILES model. *See* Models
Non-compensatory models. *See* Models
Non-spatial methods, 195
Non-traditional models. *See* Models
Non-uniform-influence model. *See* Models
Noncentral moment of inertia, 296
Noncooperative game theory. *See* Game theory, noncooperative
Nonlinear estimation. *See* Estimation, nonlinear
Nonlinear programming. *See* Programming, nonlinear
Normative decision models. *See* Models
Normative models. *See* Models
NUI. *See* Non-uniform-influence model

O
Objective function, quadratic, 855
Objectives and strategies model. *See* Models
Open-loop Nash equilibrium. *See* Nash equilibrium, open-loop
Opportunites and threats analysis model. *See* Models
Optimal allocation. *See* allocation, optimal
Optimal control theory. *See* Control theory, optimal
Optimal launching time. *See* launching time, optimal
Optimal prices for a product line. *See* Product line, optimal prices
Optimal pricing. *See* Pricing, optimal
Optimal product line. *See* Product line, optimal
Optimal product positioning. *See* product positioning, optimal
Optimal sales rate. *See* Sales rate, optimal
Optimal static price. *See* Static price, optimal
Optimal stopping rules. *See* Stopping rules, optimal
Optimal-pricing rule. *See* Pricing rule, optimal
Organizational buying models. *See* Models
Overall business strategy models. *See* Models

P
PAIRS model. *See* Models
PAM. *See* Partial adjustment model
Panel data. *See* Data, panel
Parameter estimation. *See* estimation, parameter
Paramorphic model. *See* Models
Pareto frontier, 92, 504
Part-worth model. *See* Models
Partial adjustment model. *See* Models
Pass through, 556, 568
Penalty function, 209
Penetration, 10, 321
Perceived risk. *See* Risk, perceived
Perception formation, 31
Perceptual mapping/multidimensional scaling models. *See* Models
Personal selling, 337, 442
Phased decision rules, 52
PIMS. *See* Profit impact of market stategies
Planning horizon, 831, 852, 868
Plurality model. *See* Models
Point elasticity. *See* Elasticity, point
Poisson regression. *See* Regression, Poisson
Portfolio analysis models. *See* Models
Positioning models. *See* Models
POSSE model. *See* Models
Post-purchase attitudes and behavior, 30, 32, 61
Prediction, 10, 330
Preference formation. *See* Formation, preference
Preference intensity, 111, 112, 115
Preference perturbation models. *See* Models
Preference-formation, 50
Preference/choice trees, 234
Premium bundling, 536
Prescriptive models. *See* Models
Pretest market models. *See* Models
PRETREE model. *See* Models
Price asymmetry, tier form of, 578
Price changes, short-term, 866
Price competition, 149
Price discrimination, 866
Price dynamics, 428
Price elasticity, 434, 441, 841
Price expectations, 528
Price forecasting problem, 338
Price leadership, 383, 829
Price paths, competitive, 384
Price perceived quality, 542
Price promotional effects, 577
Price quality relationships, 542
Price reaction, 517
Price, reference, 541, 576
Price sensitivity, 856
Price-setting, two-stage theory, 536
Price, transfer, 858
Price wars, 157
Price-wars, guerilla, 288
Prices, expected, 541
Pricing, 16, 833
– differentiated, 524
– most-favored-customer, 158
– multiple products or bundling, 519
– optimal, 523, 525
– psychological, 603
– quality sensitive markets, 525
Pricing decision, 517
Pricing models. *See* Models
Pricing under demand uncertainty, 548
Pricing under patent expiration, 531
Primary advertising. *See* Advertising, primary
Principle components analysis, 46, 48
Probit model. *See* Models
Process models. *See* Models
Product competition, 162
Product design-decision, 518
Product life cycle, 433, 436
Product line, 873
– optimal, 847
– optimal prices, 534
Product line competition, 169
Product perceptions, 30, 43
Product policy, 16

Product positioning, optimal, 468
Product preferences, 30
Production, 829
Production constraints, 338
Production cost function, 855
Production function, Cobb-Douglas, 849
Production management, 827
Production quantity, 850, 876
Production scheduling, 873, 874
Production smoothing, 860
Production submodel, 829
Production-cost structures, asymmetric, 860
Profit impact of market strategies, 420, 421, 717, 721, 802
Programming, nonlinear, 840
Projection model. *See* Models
PROMOTER. *See* Models
Promotion, 16, 412, 414, 420
PROMOTION ADVISOR. *See* Models
Promotion models. *See* Models
Promotion planning, 309
Promotion wearout, 567
Promotion, acceleration effects of, 603
Promotional competition, 151
Promotional cycles, 828
Promotional decision calculus model. *See* Models
Promotional effects on brand franchise, 604
Promotional effects on brand image, 604
Promotional effects on time and quantity purchased, 583
Promotional price ends in 9, 578
Proportionality model. *See* Models
Proportionate cooperation, 94
Prospect theory, 518
Psychological pricing. *See* Pricing, psychological
Pulsing, 438
Purchase, 30, 55
Purchase acceleration, 581, 584
Purchase deceleration, 603
Purchase decision, 31
Purchase incidence, 446
Purchase probability, 329
Purchase reinforcement, 452
Purchase timing, 30
Purchase, category choice, 30
Purchase-frequency distribution. *See* Distribution, purchase frequency
Pure bundling. *See* Bundling, pure
Pure-strategy Nash equilibrium. *See* Nash equilibrium, pure-strategy

Q

Quadratic objective function. *See* Objective function, quadratic
Qualitative analysis. *See* Analysis, qualitative
Quantity competition. *See* competition, quantity
Quantity discounts. *See* Discounts, quantity
Quota-bonus plan, 646
Quota-setting, 619, 621

R

Random-utility models. *See* Models
Ratchet models. *See* Models
Rawls model. *See* Models
Reaction functions. *See* Function, reaction
Reaction, competitive, 430
Redemption rates, 557, 558
Redemption-at-retail models. *See* Models
Redemption-timing model. *See* Models
Reference price. *See* Price, reference
Regression
– moving-window, 436
– Poisson, 446
– robust, 580
Repeat buying, 10, 129
Resources, allocation of, 712, 718, 726, 727
Response model. *See* Models
Retail outlets, 440
Returns to scale, 413, 414
Reward structure, 127
Risk, 122
– perceived, 114, 123
Risk adjusted preference, 70
Risk attitude, 624, 625
Risk aversion, 15
Risk neutral, 15, 845
Risk supported, 108, 109
Risky choice, 108, 109
Robust regression. *See* Regression, robust
Rubinstein model. *See* Models
Rule-based systems, 751

S

S-shaped sales response, 438
Sales, incremental, 556, 557
Sales, response, 411, 412, 613, 614, 624
Sales force compensation, 13, 638
Sales force heterogeneity, 622
Sales force implementation, 654
Sales force models. *See* Models
Sales forecasting, 873, 874
Sales management, decision areas, 654
Sales models. *See* Models
Sales promotions, 442, 876
Sales rate, optimal, 865
Sales response, territory, 675, 681
Sales territory design, 670–673

Salesperson evaluation, 681
Satisfaction models. *See* Models
Satisfaction, 61–63
Saturation, 415, 439
SCAN*EXPERT model. *See* Models
Scanner data, 16, 299
Screening models. *See* Models
SCULPTRE model. *See* Models
Seasonality, 828
Segment elasticity. *See* Elasticity, segment
Segment-level models. *See* Models
Segmentation analysis, 277
Segmentation models. *See* Models
Selective advertising, elasticity of, 441
Self-price-demand relationships, estimating, 535
Sequential entry. *See* Entry, sequential
Sequential equilibria. *See* Equilibria, sequential
Services, adjunct, 875
SHANEX Model. *See* Models
Short-term price changes. *See* Price changes, short-term
SIMOPT model. *See* Models
Simple-effects attraction models. *See* Models
Simplifying heuristics. *See* Heuristics, simplifying
Simulation, 744, 840
Size-loyalty variables, 576
Spatial methods, 194
SPRINTER model. *See* Models
SSTUN model. *See* Models
Stackelberg solution, 429, 857
STAR model. *See* Models
Static models. *See* Models
Static price, optimal, 872
Stochastic models. *See* Models
Stochastic ultrametric tree-unfolding. *See* Tree-unfolding, stochastic
Stochastic-demand models. *See* Models
Stopping rules, optimal, 40
Store choice, 30
Store profits, incremental, 572, 573
Store-tracking data, 299
Strategic marketing process, definition, 773
Strategic allocation of resources. *See* Resources, allocation of
Strategic decision-making. *See* Decision-making, strategic
Strategy, competitive, 721, 874
Strategy, defensive, 145, 171, 723
STRATPORT model. *See* Models
Structural equation models. *See* Models
Stylized theoretical models. *See* Models
Subgame perfection, 100, 147
Subjective estimates, 12, 741
Supersaturation, 416, 440
Supply-side feedback, 75
Survival models. *See* Models
Switching costs, 154
Switching models. *See* Models
Symmetric market-share models. *See* Models
Synergy analysis models. *See* Models

T

TBC. *See* Time-based competition
Technological substitution, 366
Temporal distinctiveness, 279, 298
Temporary effects. *See* Effects, temporary
Territory sales response. *See* Sales response, territory
Test-market, 319
Testing of competitive market structures, 249
Theoretical model. *See* Models
Threshold effect, 439
Time pressure, 124
Time-series analysis, 410
Time-series models. *See* Models
Time-varying coefficients, 435
Time-varying-parameter models. *See* Models
Trade promotions, 555
Transaction utility, 560
Transfer price. *See* Price, transfer
Transformations, monotone, 294
Tree-fitting, additive, 213
Tree-fitting, ultrametric, 208
Tree-unfolding, stochastic ultrametric, 239
Trial and repeat, 11, 319
Two-mode trees, 227

U

Unfolding, 44
Utility, 54, 90, 837
– acquisition, 560
– average baseline, 575
– expected, 14
Utility theory, multiattribute, 467

V

VAF model. *See* Models
Validation, 332, 342, 547, 747
– cross, 305
Value priority algorithm, 34, 35
Variables, actionable, 301
Variety seeking, 62, 63, 129
Variety-seeking models. *See* Models
Varying-parameter model. *See* Models
Vector model. *See* Models
Voting model. *See* Models

W
Wagner-Whitin dynamic-programming algorithm, 867
Weighted linear model. *See* Models
Weighted probability model. *See* Models
Word-of-mouth, 30, 336, 351, 355

Z
Zero-order process, 130
Zeta-score, 295

Handbooks in Operations Research and Management Science
Contents of Previous Volumes

Volume 1. Optimization
Edited by G.L. Nemhauser, A.H.G. Rinnooy Kan and M.J. Todd
1989. xiv + 709 pp. ISBN 0-444-87284-1

1. A View of Unconstrained Optimization, *by* J.E. Dennis Jr. and R.B. Schnabel
2. Linear Programming, *by* D. Goldfarb and M.J. Todd
3. Constrained Nonlinear Programming, *by* P.E. Gill, W. Murray, M.A. Saunders and M.H. Wright
4. Network Flows, *by* R.K. Ahuja, T.L. Magnanti and J.B. Orlin
5. Polyhedral Combinatorics, *by* W.R. Pulleyblank
6. Integer Programming, *by* G.L. Nemhauser and L.A. Wolsey
7. Nondifferentiable Optimization, *by* C. Lemaréchal
8. Stochastic Programming, *by* R.J.-B. Wets
9. Global Optimization, *by* A.H.G. Rinnooy Kan and G.T. Timmer
10. Multiple Criteria Decision Making: Five Basic Concepts, *by* P.L. Yu

Volume 2. Stochastic Models
Edited by D.P. Heyman and M.J. Sobel
1990. xv + 725 pp. ISBN 0-444-87473-9

1. Point Processes, *by* R.F. Serfozo
2. Markov Processes, *by* A.F. Karr
3. Martingales and Random Walks, *by* H.M. Taylor
4. Diffusion Approximations, *by* P.W. Glynn
5. Computational Methods in Probability Theory, *by* W.K. Grassmann
6. Statistical Methods, *by* J. Lehoczky
7. Simulation Experiments, *by* B. Schmeiser
8. Markov Decision Processes, *by* M.L. Puterman
9. Controlled Continuous Time Markov Processes, *by* R. Rishel

10. Queueing Theory, *by* R.B. Cooper
11. Queueing Networks, *by* J. Walrand
12. Stochastic Inventory Theory, *by* E.L. Porteus
13. Reliability and Maintainability, *by* M. Shaked and J.G. Shanthikumar

Volume 3. Computing
Edited by E.G. Coffman, Jr., J.K. Lenstra and A.H.G. Rinnooy Kan

1992. x + 682 pp. ISBN 0-444-88097-6

1. Computer Systems – Past, Present & Future, *by* H.J. Sips
2. Programming Languages, *by* H.E. Bal and D. Grune
3. Operating Systems – The State of the Art, *by* A.S. Tanenbaum
4. Databases and Database Management, *by* G. Vossen
5. Software Engineering, *by* R.T. Yeh, M.M. Tanik, W. Rossak, F. Cheng and P.A. Ng
6. A Survey of Matrix Computations, *by* C. Van Loan
7. Fundamental Algorithms and Data Structures, *by* J. Van Leeuwen and P. Widmayer
8. Design (with Analysis) of Efficient Algorithms, *by* D. Gusfield
9. Computational Complexity, *by* L.J. Stockmeyer
10. Computer System Models, *by* I. Mitrani
11. Mathematical Programming Systems, *by* J.A. Tomlin and J.S. Welch
12. User Interfaces, *by* C.V. Jones

Volume 4. Logistics of Production and Inventory
Edited by S.C. Graves, A.H.G. Rinnooy Kan and P.H. Zipkin

1993. xiv + 760 pp. ISBN 0-444-87472-0

Part I. Fundamentals

1. Single-Product, Single-Location Models, *by* H.L. Lee and S. Nahmias

Part II. Multiple Products and Locations

2. Analysis of Multistage Production Systems, *by* J.A. Muckstadt and R.O. Roundy
3. Centralized Planning Models for Multi-Echelon Inventory Systems under Uncertainty, *by* A. Federgruen
4. Continuous Review Policies for Multi-Level Inventory Systems with Stochastic Demand, *by* S. Axsäter

5. Performance Evaluation of Production Networks, *by* R. Suri, J.L. Sanders and M. Kamath
6. Manufacturing Lead Times, Order Release and Capacity Loading, *by* U.S. Karmarkar

Part III. Production Planning and Scheduling
7. An Overview of Production Planning, *by* L.J. Thomas and J.O. McClain
8. Mathematical Programming Models and Methods for Production Planning and Scheduling, *by* J.F. Shapiro
9. Sequencing and Scheduling: Algorithms and Complexity, *by* E.L. Lawler, J.K. Lenstra, A.H.G. Rinnooy Kan and D.B. Shmoys
10. Hierarchical Production Planning, *by* G.R. Bitran and D. Tirupati

Part IV. Additional Topics
11. Requirements Planning, *by* K.R. Baker
12. The Just-in-Time System, *by* H. Groenevelt
13. Scientific Quality Management and Management Science, *by* P.J. Kolesar
14. Developments in Manufacturing Technology and Economic Evaluation Models, *by* C.H. Fine

Printed and bound by CPI Group (UK) Ltd, Croydon, CR0 4YY
08/05/2025
01865023-0004